D0086677

Disposable Income and Personal Saving 1929–1987

Year	Disposable income (billions of dollars)	Personal saving	Personal saving as a percentage of disposable income
1929	81.7	2.6	3.2
1933	44.9	− 1.6	− 3.6
1939	69.7	1.8	2.6
1940	75.0	3.0	4.0
1941	91.9	10.0	10.9
1942	116.4	27.0	23.2
1943	132.9	32.7	24.6
1944	145.6	36.5	25.1
1945	149.2	28.7	19.2
1946	158.9	13.6	8.6
1947	168.8	5.2	3.1
1948	188.1	11.1	5.9
1949	187.9	7.4	3.9
1950	207.5	12.6	6.1
1951	227.6	16.6	7.3
1952	239.8	17.4	7.3
1953	255.1	18.4	7.2
1954	260.5	16.4	6.3
1955	278.8	16.0	5.8
1956	297.5	21.3	7.2
1957	313.9	22.7	7.2
1958	324.9	24.3	7.5
1959	344.6	21.8	6.3
1960	358.9	20.8	5.8
1961	373.8	24.9	6.6
1962	396.2	25.9	6.5
1963	415.8	24.6	5.9
1964	451.4	31.5	7.0
1965	486.8	34.3	7.0
1966	525.9	36.0	6.8
1967	562.1	45.1	8.0
1968	609.6	42.5	7.0
1969	656.7	42.2	6.4
1970	715.6	57.7	8.1
1971	776.8	66.3	8.5
1972	839.6	61.4	7.3
1973	949.8	89.0	9.4
1974	1,038.4	96.7	9.3
1975	1,142.8	104.6	9.2
1976	1,252.6	95.8	7.6
1977	1,379.3	90.7	6.6
1978	1,551.2	110.2	7.1
1979	1,729.3	118.1	6.8
1980	1,918.0	136.9	7.1
1981	2,127.6	159.4	7.5
1982	2,261.4	153.9	6.8
1983	2,428.1	130.6	5.4
1984	2,668.6	164.1	6.1
1985	2,841.1	127.1	4.5
1986	3,022.1	130.6	4.3
1987	3,181.1	120.2	3.8

Source: *Economic Report of the President*, 1988.

Inflation 1929–1987 (Percent change in CPI)

Year	Percent change in CPI (all items)
1929	0
1933	− 5.1
1939	− 1.4
1940	1.0
1941	5.0
1942	10.7
1943	6.1
1944	1.7
1945	2.3
1946	8.5
1947	14.4
1948	7.8
1949	− 1.0
1950	1.0
1951	7.9
1952	2.2
1953	.8
1954	.5
1955	− .4
1956	1.5
1957	3.6
1958	2.7
1959	.8
1960	1.6
1961	1.0
1962	1.1
1963	1.2
1964	1.3
1965	1.7
1966	2.9
1967	2.9
1968	4.2
1969	5.4
1970	5.9
1971	4.3
1972	3.3
1973	6.2
1974	11.0
1975	9.1
1976	5.8
1977	6.5
1978	7.7
1979	11.3
1980	13.5
1981	10.4
1982	6.1
1983	3.2
1984	4.3
1985	3.6
1986	1.9
1987	3.7

Source: *Economic Report of the President*, 1988.

Year	Percent change in real GNP
1933	− 2.1
1939	7.9
1940	7.8
1941	17.7
1942	18.8
1943	18.1
1944	8.2
1945	− 1.9
1946	− 19.0
1947	− 2.8
1948	3.9
1949	.0
1950	8.5
1951	10.3
1952	3.9
1953	4.0
1954	− 1.3
1955	5.6
1956	2.1
1957	1.7
1958	− .8
1959	5.8
1960	2.2
1961	2.6
1962	5.3
1963	4.1
1964	5.3
1965	5.8
1966	5.8
1967	2.9
1968	4.1
1969	2.4
1970	− .3
1971	2.8
1972	5.0
1973	5.2
1974	− .5
1975	− 1.3
1976	4.9
1977	4.7
1978	5.3
1979	2.5
1980	− .2
1981	1.9
1982	− 2.5
1983	3.6
1984	6.8
1985	3.0
1986	2.9
1987	2.9

Source: *Economic Report of the President*, 1988.

Source: *Economic Report of the President*, 1988.

Medical care	Entertainment	Other goods and services	Energy	Year	All items	Food	Housing	Apparel & upkeep	Transportation	Medical care	Entertainment	Other goods and services	Energy
150.5	139.8	142.0	159.7	1981	272.4	267.3	293.5	186.9	280.0	294.5	221.4	235.7	410.0
168.6	152.2	153.9	176.6	1982	289.1	278.2	314.7	191.8	291.5	328.7	235.8	259.9	416.1
184.7	159.8	162.7	189.3	1983	298.4	284.4	323.1	196.5	298.4	357.3	246.0	288.3	419.3
202.4	167.7	172.2	207.3	1984	311.1	295.1	336.5	200.2	311.7	379.5	255.1	307.7	423.6
219.4	176.6	183.3	220.4	1985	322.2	302.0	349.9	206.0	319.9	403.1	265.0	326.6	426.5
239.7	188.5	196.7	275.9	1986	328.4	311.8	360.2	207.8	307.5	433.5	274.1	346.4	370.3
265.9	205.3	214.5	361.1	1987	340.4	324.5	371.0	216.9	316.8	462.2	283.2	366.5	371.7

ECONOMICS

ECONOMICS

DAVID N. HYMAN

North Carolina State University

with 427 illustrations

1989

Homewood, IL 60430
Boston, MA 02116

Cover photograph by Aaron Jones Photography. © 1988.

© RICHARD D. IRWIN, INC., 1989

All rights reserved. No part of this publication may be reproduced,
stored in a retrieval system, or transmitted in any form by any means,
electronic, mechanical, photocopying, recording, or otherwise,
without prior written permission from the publisher.

Acquisitions Editor: *Denise Clinton*
Developmental Editor: *Terry Eynon*
Developmental Editor for Supplements: *Jean Babrick*
Copy Editor: *Elisabeth Heitzeberg*
Project Manager: *Patricia Tannian*
Production Editor: *Kathy Lumpkin*
Designer: *John Rokusek*
Compositor: *The Clarinda Company*
Typeface: *ITC Garamond*
Printer: *Von Hoffman Press*

Library of Congress Cataloging-in-Publication Data

Hyman, David N.
    Economics / David N. Hyman.
        p.   cm.
    Includes index.
    ISBN 0-256-07504-2
    1. Economics. I. Title.
  HB171.5.H96 1989
  330—dc19

                                                   88–7585
                                                   CIP

Printed in the United States of America
1234567890 VHP 54321098

About the Author

David N. Hyman is presently Professor of Economics and Business at North Carolina State University. He received the Ph.D. degree in economics from Princeton University in 1969. The recipient of numerous academic honors and teaching awards, Professor Hyman is the author of *The Economics of Governmental Activity, Public Finance: A Contemporary Application of Theory to Policy,* and *Modern Microeconomics: Analysis and Applications.* He also is the author of a number of monographs, study guides, and articles published in economics journals and anthologies.

Preface

Today more than ever, the study of economics is a vital component of any student's education. Knowledge of economic principles is essential for success in dealing with day-to-day affairs in the modern world. The purpose of this text is to explain how the U.S. and world economies function and how their daily operation affects the reader. As newly elected President Bush assumes the leadership of the United States, I want to help students learn to fit together all the pieces of the puzzle we know as the economy.

In the 1990s we no longer can afford to neglect the way our own lives are affected by changes in the world economy. In fact, the rapid evolution of a global interdependence among both highly developed and less developed economies demands a fundamental change in the manner in which we teach this course. To reflect this and to demonstrate the ever-increasing importance of international trade in the U.S. economy, I have attempted to clearly integrate international issues throughout the text.

My goal in writing this book is to communicate the relevance of economics to everyday life by blending examples and applications with economic theory in each chapter. I have sought to show students the power, usefulness, and excitement of economics as a discipline. The text comprises a comprehensive learning resource that I hope students will enjoy reading and using.

Style and Level

This book is intended for use in introductory courses in economics at colleges and universities. Students need not have had any previous training in economics. I have written in a lively style and on a level that is easily understandable to undergraduates.

Appendix on Graphs

Graphs are used extensively throughout the book, and students who need to sharpen their skills in using graphs can benefit from studying the Appendix to Chapter 1. This appendix develops the basic tools for constructing graphs and defines important analytical concepts that students will find helpful even if they are already accustomed to working with graphs.

Flexible Teaching and Learning Resource

This book is designed to serve as a flexible teaching and learning resource that can accommodate a wide number of approaches to teaching economics. The prologue and first seven chapters comprise Parts I and II of the book's 10 parts and are fundamental to understanding both microeconomic and macroeconomic principles. This is a micro-first text, and Parts II through V cover microeconomic theory and issues. Of course, instructors who wish to cover macroeconomics before microeconomics can easily do so by moving directly to Chapter 25, which begins macroeconomic analysis. Macroeconomic theory and issues are covered in Parts VI through IX. Part X deals with international and world economic issues, and in view of the growing importance of these issues some instructors may wish to cover these chapters earlier.

Balance of Applications

Throughout the text I have developed a careful balance of business, policy, social, and international applications. The coverage of both microeconomics and macroeconomics is interspersed with examples, information, and applications that help bring economics to life for students.

Teaching and Learning Economics from This Book: What's Different?

1. *More Extensive Development of Marginal Analysis and Supply and Demand Analysis*

   Too often introductory economics textbooks gloss over basic concepts without showing students how they are used. I believe it is important to give students a thorough grounding in the use of such concepts as opportunity cost, the production possibilities curve, and supply and demand analysis. For this reason I have devoted seven chapters to developing and using these basic tools. Chapter 1 details the concepts of scarcity and opportunity cost. Chapter 2 introduces students to model building and the concept of rational behavior by showing how marginal analysis is used to understand and forecast behavior. In Chapter 3 the concept of opportunity cost is further applied in explaining production possibilities and personal budgeting.

In Chapter 4 basic supply and demand analysis is painstakingly developed. Chapters 5 and 6 give students ample opportunity to see how supply and demand analysis can be applied. The applications not only allow students to gain knowledge through practice but also set the stage for the development of microfoundations of macroeconomics by analyzing markets for credit, labor, and foreign exchange. Chapter 7 is devoted entirely to the concept of elasticity and its uses and contains numerous practical applications. A major advantage of this text compared with others on the market is that an instructor who wishes to emphasize the microfoundations of macroeconomics can do so by using the material in the first seven chapters without covering the microeconomic theory portions of the text. I believe this flexibility will prove to be highly beneficial to both students and instructors.

In the introductory chapters you will find applications dealing with economic policies designed to reduce drunken driving, management techniques in Japan, the operation of the stock market, marketing of new products, labor market adjustment, rent controls, and entrepreneurship, to mention just a few.

2. *Coverage of Microeconomics Provides Extensions and Applications that Use the Theory*

Basic microeconomic theory is used in the book to help students understand business, social, and policy issues. The themes developed in the early chapters are continued. For example, Chapter 8 shows how marginal analysis is used to analyze consumer choices and presents a wide range of examples from selecting items on a menu to deciding whether to have children. You will find a modern approach to the theory of the firm in Chapter 9 where the firm's functions and degree of vertical integration are explained using many examples and where the idea of profit maximization is applied to the timely issue of corporate takeovers. The basic theories of production, cost, and supply are developed in Chapters 10

through 12 with applications on how advances in technology improve productivity and how productivity and cost are related. Students will see how changes in input prices and technology can affect profitability, supply, and price in competitive industries and how limits to entry in the New York City taxi industry have created a valuable asset known as the taxi medallion that currently sells for over $100,000. They also will see how taxes, license fees, and other government-imposed restrictions affect supply and prices.

Chapters 13 through 15 discuss imperfectly competitive product markets, and the theory is enlivened with applications showing how a syndicate acts to control the price of diamonds and how the theory can be extended to reach some surprising conclusions regarding the behavior of monopoly firms. Chapters 16 through 19 are policy-oriented chapters that develop the concepts of market failure and externalities and discuss social regulation, environmental policy, the economics of special-interest groups, the impact of subsidies and tax breaks to agriculture and industry, and the basics of government expenditure and taxation. These chapters draw on modern developments in the theories of externalities, public goods, and public choice.

The last part of the microeconomics section examines input markets with applications to the issues of wage differentials, comparable worth, signaling, screening, personnel management, and the principal-agent problem. In discussing imperfectly competitive input markets, I present a balanced analysis of labor unions and enliven the theory of monopsony with applications to professional sports. Marginal analysis is used to explain investment decisions, and the concept of present value is carefully developed in a chapter on capital.

Appropriately, I end the microeconomics portion of the text with a discussion of income distribution issues and programs of assistance to the poor in the United States.

You will find the approach to both theoretical and policy issues up-to-date and modern in orientation.

3. *Macroeconomic Analysis Is Firmly Based in an Aggregate Demand/Aggregate Supply Framework that Considers International Linkages*

In covering macroeconomics I emphasize basic principles using an aggregate demand/aggregate supply framework. To set the stage, the early macroeconomics chapters define such fundamental concepts as real GNP, the price level, inflation, and cyclical unemployment. The basic identity between production and real income is emphasized in the introductory chapter, and the circular flow analysis of expenditure and income shows students how the financial and international sectors of the economy fit into the picture. Two separate chapters explain why cyclical unemployment and inflation are problems that merit serious concern. These chapters contain a wealth of data and information on prices, inflation, and unemployment.

After the stage is set by defining the problems and their consequences, students are taught how to use aggregate demand and aggregate supply analysis to understand the causes of cyclical unemployment and inflation and the process of economic growth. The general concept of macroeconomic equilibrium is developed early in the macroeconomic analysis. Shifts in various components of aggregate demand, including those affecting net export demand, are analyzed and their possible effects on the economy examined. The impact of shifts in aggregate supply on macroeconomic equilibrium also is explained.

Macroeconomic policy is covered in an even-handed way. First students are shown how the economy can either contract or expand in response to shifts in both aggregate demand and aggregate supply. The consequences of an economy operating below potential or overheating are then explored. Early in the development of the theory the classical model of macroeconomic equilibrium is introduced so students can understand the concept of a self-regulating economy. Then the Keynesian model is developed to show students how economic policy can adjust for the sluggishness of the economy's stabilization mechanism. The importance and sources of economic growth are covered before economic policy is considered.

Students are shown how both monetary policy and fiscal policy can stabilize the economy. Problems in effective use of stabilization policy are also highlighted. The issues of the federal budget deficit and the national debt are discussed in a separate chapter. Throughout the macroeconomics chapters, consideration is given to the impact of shifts in the demand for U.S. exports and in U.S. demand for imports.

The chapters on international trade carefully develop the concepts of absolute and comparative advantage and show how exchange rates are determined. The impact of changes in real exchange rates on macroeconomic equilibrium is covered using the tools of aggregate demand and aggregate supply analysis. The book closes appropriately with a discussion of socialism vs. capitalism and a view of the rapidly changing Soviet economy under *perestroika*.

How to Make the Best Use of This Book

There are a wide variety of approaches to teaching economics. This book is designed for flexible use. Most instructors will want to have their students read the prologue and the first seven chapters even if they do not cover all of the material in class. A significant advantage of this book is that much of the material is clear enough for students to learn by themselves. Instructors can skip some material or highlight in class the examples and applications that most interest them and rely on the book to provide students with the necessary background. You can use the Principles in Practice features as applications in class or use your own favorite current examples to show students the relevance of economics.

Some instructors will prefer to cover macroeconomics immediately after covering the first six chapters. If you choose this approach, you can move directly to Chapter 25 or first cover the chapter on elasticity. Elasticity is an important topic, but it is also one that students find quite difficult to master. If instructors wish to emphasize macroeconomics, they might prefer to avoid the loss in continuity that would result from taking a week or so to cover elasticity and its applications. The transition from Chapter 6 to Chapter 25 will be quite smooth.

The introductory macro section of the book (Part VI) sets the stage by defining the relevant variables and policy issues. Part VII develops aggregate demand/aggregate supply analysis. Part VIII discusses monetary issues and the banking system, while Part IX brings the various parts of the puzzle together and examines stabilization issues. Note that my monetary policy chapter precedes the chapter on fiscal policy. I believe it is important for students to understand the forces influencing interest rates and the role of money in the economy before coping with issues such as crowding out and the impact of the federal deficit on the economy. However, some instructors may wish to cover fiscal policy first, and this can be done easily. If you want to cover international aspects of stabilization problems, you will find it useful to assign Chapter 40 immediately after your coverage of the stabilization chapters.

Instructors pursuing a micro-first approach will not want to skip Chapter 7. They can, however, choose among the many theoretical and policy chapters included in the microeconomics part of the book to suit their preferences.

One innovative way to teach the course if you wish to emphasize international issues is to cover the last part of the book (Part X) immediately after covering the core material (Chapters 1-6), the basic macroeconomic material (Chapters 25-31), and the chapters on money and financial markets (Chapters 32-35). You can pick and choose among the topics in these chapters and intersperse your lectures with policy issues from Chapters 36 through 38 as you move along.

As you can see, the way an instructor will use this book depends on his or her interests and desired emphasis. This book is a flexible teaching tool, and I encourage instructors to be creative in the way they use it.

Distinctive Features of the Book and How They Assist Students in Learning

Above all, this text and its supplements have been designed to develop complex ideas in a way students can easily understand. An outstanding feature of this student-oriented approach is its user-friendly writing style that helps students see readily how economic problems and issues affect them. I have long maintained that economics is a favorite subject of students and that with the right approach they will enjoy learning and applying economic concepts. A lively prologue points out the benefits of studying economics from the student's point of view and provides information on careers in economics. The prologue also offers students hints about how to succeed in the course through use of the book's pedagogy.

To aid students in learning, I have incorporated the following features in each chapter:

1. **Concept Preview:** The learning objectives of each chapter are listed to aid students in organizing their study sessions.

2. **Concept Checks:** A series of three review questions at the end of each major section is designed to help students test their comprehension and mastery of the main points in that section.

3. **Key Terms and Concepts:** Key terms and concepts are boldfaced and carefully defined as they are introduced. Each definition is highlighted in the margin of the book at the place where it is introduced. This feature helps students learn and

helps them review important concepts when studying for examinations. All key terms appear in an alphabetized glossary at the end of the book.

4. **Principles in Practice:** Each chapter contains one or more real-world applications or perspectives using economic principles that show students how the topics they are studying are relevant to business, financial, personal, social, policy, or international issues. These features bring economics to life by providing up-to-date information and insights on a wide array of topics.

5. **Economic Thinkers:** From Adam Smith to Karl Marx, economists over the years have shaped our thinking and our policies. In selected chapters you will find short sketches that highlight the ideas, times, and lives of important economists and other key figures in economic history.

6. **Career Profiles:** Each of the book's 10 parts opens with a profile of an American who earned a college degree in economics. Students can see how these successful people benefited from studying economics and can gain insights from the experiences of these productive individuals. The subjects of the profiles include people who have continued to pursue economics in their careers, and also people who have chosen to enter other fields. The Career Profiles offer students clear evidence of the many reasons why economics is a valuable course of study.

7. **Boxed Graphs and Tables:** Each graph and related table appear in a self-contained boxed exhibit. Having all the relevant material within a single box aids learning and makes it easier for students to review material while studying for examinations. Each graph has a carefully written legend that appears within the box.

8. **Problems and Applications:** These end-of-chapter questions are more challenging than those appearing in the Concept Checks. Students will find working through the problems a useful way to study and review and to practice and apply what was learned in the chapter.

9. **Suggested Readings:** This feature presents a number of supplementary sources that students can use to extend their knowledge or write term papers. The listings are annotated to show students what they can gain by reading them.

Supplementary Resources

The book has a number of ancillary materials that have been carefully designed to assist the instructor in teaching the material and the student in learning.

1. **Instructor's Manual:** I have written a comprehensive manual to help instructors organize their lectures. The manual contains conversion notes, instructional objectives, a list of key terms, a point-by-point discussion of chapter contents that includes hints for clarifying difficult material as well as indications of where transparencies will be most helpful, and answers to text problems. The manual includes 160 transparency masters.

2. **Study Guide:** Each chapter of the guide contains chapter objectives, a fill-in chapter summary, vocabulary exercises using the key words in the chapter, and a series of topic-centered modules that include activities designed to reinforce key concepts. Among these activities are additional work with graphs, fill-in charts and tables, completion exercises, and other interactive tasks. The modules are followed by a self-test for understanding, consisting of multiple-choice questions plus one or two short essay questions. To encourage understanding answers are provided for all answers.

3. **Test Bank:** The test bank contains over 4,000 questions, with a significant percentage of items requiring graphical analysis. One hundred items are essay questions; the balance are four- and five-item multiple-choice questions. The test bank also contains a math pretest that allows instructors to assess their students' math skills before getting into the course and provides students with feedback on their readiness to handle the math in the course.

4. **Computerized Test Bank:** The EXAMgen test generation software includes all the questions in the test bank and prints out the graphs required for graphical analysis as the test itself is printed. Items may be edited, added, or deleted; test items may be selected manually or by computer for varying question types, topics, and levels. Choices in multiple-choice questions may be scrambled and up to nine versions of a test produced.

5. **Transparency Acetates:** There are 200 acetates, including many two-color reproductions of key tables and graphs from the text, and additional overlays illustrating how curves change in response to changes in conditions.

6. **Software:** A set of menu-driven tutorials and simulations was developed by a team of experienced economics instructors who are also experts in the programming and educational use of computer software. This user-friendly software was created on the basis of an extensive review of the strengths and weaknesses of other currently available economics software packages. There are eight MicroVision and MacroVision tutorials. One presents key concepts in graphical analysis, and seven are linked to the text content. Each tutorial includes questions, an "Exploring Possibilities" feature, and a quiz.

Extensive Development

An unprecedented number of research and development steps were taken to make this the most contemporary and pedagogically effective economics text you will ever use.

A detailed questionnaire was mailed to 4,000 principles of economics instructors to ask their preferences in terms of coverage, organization, pedagogy, and supplements. Additionally, the instructors were asked to comment on the utility and effectiveness of their current text and its supplements.

A panel of 20 reviewers critiqued the first draft. These comments helped identify consensus points and controversial areas that were discussed at a two-day focus group attended by six key reviewers. A second panel of reviewers, two of whom had critiqued the first draft, examined the revised draft.

To enhance the text's student orientation, selected members of the reviewer panel taught from the manuscript for a semester. They and their students provided input on content and pedagogy.

Seven instructors selected from the panel of second-draft reviewers met for another two-day focus group, which covered comments on the first two drafts, results of the class testing, and preferences for supplements.

Three professional, technical experts critiqued the third draft for accuracy, writing style, organization, and clarity of presentation. To further ensure the material's clarity and accuracy, the third draft also was reviewed by 11 instructors with different specialties in the field of economics. During each stage of production, the text was reviewed by experienced instructors as additional confirmation of technical accuracy.

Finally, each component of the supplements package was created to enhance the text and make teaching and learning more rewarding. The test bank, study guide, and software were thoroughly reviewed by qualified individuals.

Acknowledgments

An undertaking of this magnitude requires the skills and efforts of many people. Special credit goes to Glenn Turner, Senior Vice President; Denise Clinton, Acquisitions Editor; Terry Eynon, Developmental Editor; Elisabeth Heitzeberg, Copy Editor; Jean Babrick, Supplements Developmental Editor; Patricia Tannian, Project Manager; and Kathy Lumpkin, Production Editor.

These publishing professionals and their colleagues put in many hours of effort to help the author produce a polished text. They also helped guide the project to completion by overseeing the many complicated steps necessary to convert a raw manuscript into a finely produced book. John Rokusek provided a practical and pleasing design for the book that facilitates its use.

Reviewers

The reviewers of the manuscript and supplements provided numerous excellent suggestions. I am indebted to them for their many contributions and insights.

Curt L. Anderson
University of Minnesota at Duluth

Lloyd Dwayne Barney
Boise State University

Philip F. Bartholomew
University of Michigan at Dearborn

Gil Becker
Indiana University/Purdue University

Charles R. Britton
University of Arkansas

Rick L. Chaney
St. Louis University

Howard Chernick
Hunter College

Mary E. Cookingham
Michigan State University

David Denslow
University of Florida at Gainesville

Loraine Donaldson
Georgia State University

Frances Durbin
University of Delaware

Gary A. Dymski
University of Southern California

Patricia J. Euzent
University of Central Florida

Donald H. Farness
Oregon State University

Irwin Feller
Pennsylvania State University

James Gerber
San Diego State University

Anthony O. Gyapong
Wayne State University

Charles M. Hill
Prairie State College

Arnold Hite
The Citadel

Dennis L. Hoffman
Arizona State University

Janet Hunt
University of Georgia

Walter L. Johnson
University of Missouri at Columbia

Michael Klein
Clark University

Leonard P. Lardaro
University of Rhode Island

Robert L. Lawson
Ball State University

Charles Leathers
University of Alabama

Jane H. Lillydahl
University of Colorado at Boulder

Don Maxwell
Central State University

Herbert C. Milikien
American River College

David Molina
North Texas State University

Margaret D. Moore
Franklin University

Michael Nieswiadomy
North Texas State University

James Price
Syracuse University

Victor H. Rieck
Miami-Dade Community College

Teresa Riley
Youngstown State University

Jaime M. Rodriguez
Edmonds Community College

Raymond Sauer
University of New Mexico

Davinder Singh
California State University at Long Beach

Richard N. Spivack
Bryant College

Frederick E. Tank
University of Toledo

Abigail Taubin
University of Maryland—West Germany

Robert W. Thomas
Iowa State University

John Trapani
University of Texas at Arlington

Abdul M. Turay
Mississippi State University

John Vahaly
University of Louisville

Mark Vaughan
Washington University

Percy O. Vera
Sinclair Community College

William V. Weber
Illinois State University

James N. Wetzel
Virginia Commonwealth University

Arthur Wright
University of Connecticut

Darrel Young
University of Texas at Austin

I regard these reviewers as partners in the development of this text. Their detailed reviews forced me to think carefully about basic issues in economics and guided me to produce a text that I believe is both technically sound and easy to read. I have learned a great deal from the comments of the reviewers listed above, and I thank them for the time and effort they put in.

My colleagues at North Carolina State University were always available to help me sound out my ideas and supply information on their areas of specialization. My students, who participated in a classroom test of the manuscript in the spring of 1988, offered me encouragement and criticism, and I thank them heartily. Joan Livingood and Carolyn Smith provided expert secretarial assistance at various stages of the project, and I am indebted to them for their highly competent service.

Finally, I must thank my wife Linda for her support during the period I have worked on this project. She certainly deserves a medal for her patience with a writer who had little time to do anything other than write for a period of two and a half years.

David N. Hyman

Contents in Brief

Contents

PART VIII   Money, Financial Markets, and Macroeconomic Equilibrium

Career Profile: *Saul Steinberg*

32   The Functions of Money, 704

33   The Banking System, 724

34   The Federal Reserve System and Its Influence on Money and Credit, 747

Contents   **xxix**

Career Profile

JOHN WHITAKER

John Whitaker ended up in economics mostly by accident, but he's happy he did. He began his studies at the University of Missouri-Columbia as an engineering major, only to find he hated the courses. He changed his major to business and in his sophomore year took a required economics course. Three years later he was a teaching assistant for that same course.

Born in Denver, Colorado, in 1963, Whitaker earned his undergraduate degree in business administration. After receiving his master's degree in economics in December 1986, Whitaker went to the state capital, where he served as a budget research analyst for the Missouri State Senate. He now works for Hallmark as a market research analyst doing strategic market analysis, forecasting sales, and tracking trends. He gathers information and analyzes data, developing and using econometric models. Both jobs have required a lot of time at the computer terminal. The Missouri senate had not previously used formal models to support forecasts. Whitaker says designing and implementing them was a great experience. However, the environment was obviously political, and much of the information he provided senators was not used or was misused, which Whitaker found frustrating.

For Whitaker, graduate school was the right choice. A master's degree was a requirement for both jobs he's held so far, and he says it's made a big difference in salary and career possibilities. Since he's not interested in an academic career, he doesn't plan to pursue a Ph.D.

For those considering the possibility of graduate economic study, Whitaker says a knowledge of calculus is essential. He found course work at the graduate level to be more detailed and rigorous than undergraduate classes, but also more challenging. He says graduate study allowed him more academic freedom, more personal attention from professors, and more control over the topics he studied.

Whitaker advises prospective economics majors to take speech courses and as many English, mathematics, and statistics courses as they can. He has found that the courses he took in business communication and technical writing are as useful as his statistics courses, even though he spends much of his time in front of a computer. Studying economics has affected his daily life in the sense that he's always trying to maximize utility, particularly when it comes to managing his finances.

Introduction to Economics

Prologue

Economics: What's in It for You?

Do you really understand what happened in the stock market crash of '87?

On "Black Monday"—October 19, 1987—Wall Street watched in frozen disbelief as the numbers on its monitors dipped, slid, then plummeted downward. As the sun rose in Europe, Japan, and Australia, their financial communities awakened to the same towering wave of panic selling that had stunned the United States the day before.

In the tense, uncertain days and weeks that followed, questions about what caused the crash by far outnumbered answers—and the answers varied markedly depending on who was asked. Coming in for large chunks of blame were the burgeoning U.S. federal budget and trade deficits, the unchecked fall of the American dollar against foreign currencies, and the relatively new and in some circles suspect phenomenon known as portfolio insurance.

What economists know, and what you as a student of economics have the opportunity to discover, is that there is never a single, clear-cut reason for an event like the stock market crash of '87. The study of economics can help you comprehend the myriad causes of such events and view them in perspective. As you will see, economics is influenced by developments in the diverse arenas of business, politics, sociology, science, nature, religion, and history. Economic trends make headline news almost daily; and whether or not you are aware of it, economics is a vital and pervasive part of your everyday life.

This is one reason why, even if you don't choose it as your major subject, a course in the principles of economics is an essential element of your undergraduate education. In fact, many educators would suggest that this course is among the two or three most important ones a college student will ever take. An understanding of the financial, social, and political context in which the economy operates will help you develop informed opinions on a wide range of business and public issues. You'll also discover numerous ways in which the U.S. economy is linked to the economies of other nations: Japan, the countries of Western Europe, and a host of Third World states in various stages of development. Not only our well-being but our very survival may depend on our relationships with these trading partners.

From a practical standpoint, your study of economics will help you sharpen your decision-making skills by showing you a logical way to evaluate alternative courses

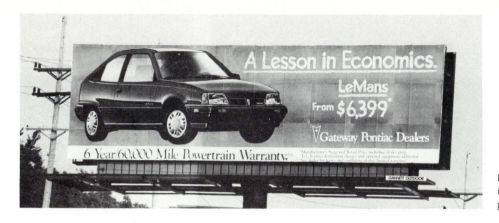

Economics helps you make informed choices in your personal and business life.

of action. As you explore the concept of *opportunity cost,* you'll discover that every choice you make has both a benefit and a cost. For example, suppose you decide to get a part-time job so you can earn money to buy a car. You'll have the benefit of owning the car, but you'll pay a cost in terms of the study and leisure hours you now must devote to working so as to pay for and maintain the car. After weighing your choices in cost-benefit terms, you may decide you don't need a car now after all!

This course in economics also will enhance your analytical abilities in the important area of personal finance. You'll become familiar with the concepts of *rational behavior* and *marginal cost and benefit* as they affect your budgeting decisions. Economic analysis explains why even at bargain prices there's a limit to the quantity of an item you'll choose to buy, be it Taco Supremes or compact discs!

What's more, you'll learn the meanings of some terms you probably hear every day but may not fully comprehend. For example, what exactly is *inflation?* How does it happen, and what causes it to accelerate or diminish? What is a *recession* and what are its warning signs? Why does the government say the economy is operating at *full employment* when the unemployment rate is actually 5.5%? What is the U.S. *trade deficit,* and why is it both good and bad for our economy as a whole or for you personally?

You've seen all of these terms in newspaper headlines and on the nightly TV news, but you may not realize the ways in which you personally are affected by each of these economic trends. This course is your opportunity to find out. You'll gain a thorough understanding of the interplay of economic forces and of your role in our dynamic economy. Although you may not plan to major in economics, this course might cause you to become so intrigued with the subject that you change your mind!

Career Opportunities

If you should decide to major in economics, what career possibilities will be open to you?

Armed with a degree in economics, you can seek a career in literally dozens of fields. Economics majors are succeeding as entrepreneurs, diplomats, bankers, journalists, Cabinet heads, corporate leaders, consultants, judges, and politicians.

Because economics is such a wide-ranging discipline, it's an excellent adjunct to many programs of study. If your major is business administration, political science, or international relations, a minor in economics will provide valuable insights into the contemporary social environment. If you elect to concentrate in marketing or finance, you can profitably pursue economics as a second major or a minor. A pairing of economics and journalism can help you lay the groundwork for a successful career in business communications.

While an undergraduate degree in economics is a prerequisite for advanced studies in the discipline, it also serves as an excellent foundation for graduate work in a variety of other fields: business, law, public administration, and health, to name a few.

Then, of course, you may decide to become a professional economist. In this case you almost certainly will need a graduate degree and will be pursuing career opportunities in business, teaching, research, or government. The National Association of Business Economists publishes a helpful booklet, *Careers in Business Economics,*[1] that describes the responsibilities of economists in government, insurance, banking, consulting, investments, industry, and communications. The booklet also outlines the education requirements for business economists and provides information on salaries.

Career Profiles

To give you an idea of the diversity of careers available to students who choose to major in economics, we present in this text a series of Career Profiles. Each of the book's 10 sections opens with a profile of an American whose name or face you may readily recognize. Although there is as much as a 45-year age span among our subjects, and although they are enjoying success in widely different fields, they all have one important thing in common: a degree in economics.

As you study these profiles, don't focus only on the subject's credentials and accomplishments. Take the opportunity to do a little brainstorming about your own future. Ask yourself which of these fields is most appealing to you. Why? Do you want to get on the fast track in a major corporation, with the attendant perquisites and power struggles? Or would you thrive as an entrepreneur, with all the risks and rewards of being your own boss? Do you see yourself as a Wall Street guru, crunching numbers to forecast stock market trends with billions of dollars at stake? How about a position on the trading desk of the Federal Reserve Board's Open Market Committee, executing large-volume sales and purchases of government securities?

The purpose of this exercise isn't to fantasize about a future of wealth and power (although these certainly are valid ambitions). Rather you'll want to consider possible careers in light of your interests, abilities, and temperament, and your willingness to invest time and effort in acquiring the necessary background.

Whether you choose the career path of one of our profile subjects is less important than that you become aware of the exciting and extensive array of options open to you as an economics major. And if you select another field of concentration, you'll find that in all your endeavors you'll be well served by the discipline of the eco-

---

[1]Copies of this booklet may be obtained from the National Association of Business Economists, 28349 Chagrin Blvd., Suite 201, Cleveland, OH 44122. Single copies are free of charge; quantity discounts are available.

The study of economics can lead to success in a diversity of careers.

nomic way of reasoning. It's hard to think of a situation in which you wouldn't benefit from thinking logically and weighing alternatives. You'll acquire these facilities in your study of economics.

Salaries for Economists

Whatever your career objectives, it's probably safe to assume that they include earning a living for yourself, and perhaps eventually helping to support a family. What can economics majors expect to earn in the various career paths open to them?

Table 1 on p. 6 shows 1987 salaries for five occupational titles. The data in Tables 2, 3, and 4 (see p. 6) are based on information contained in *Salary Characteristics 1986,* a report of a survey conducted by the National Association of Business Economists. Table 2 gives base salary data for 17 employment classifications. Table 3 shows economists' compensation by area of responsibility, and Table 4 breaks down economists' income by level of education.

You'll notice that the highest-paid economists in the NABE survey worked in securities and investments, retail and wholesale trade, insurance, banking, and nondurable manufacturing. At the lower end, the survey shows, were economists in the fields of real estate, nonprofit research, and academics.

Table 1   Occupational Titles and Salaries

Occupational titles or job functions	1987 salary
Financial analyst (finance and economics)	$26,580
Accounting, auditing	21,780
Retail, wholesale sales	20,388
Business administration	19,824
Communications	18,144

Source: College Placement Council, 1987.

Table 2   Median Base Salary of Business Economists by Industry of Employment

Securities and investments	$75,000
Retail and wholesale trade	62,700
Insurance	62,000
Banking, all types	60,000
Nondurable manufacturing	60,000
Mining	59,300
Consulting	58,100
Durable manufacturing	56,000
Trade association	55,000
Publishing	49,000
Transportation	46,500
Government	46,000
Communications and utilities	45,000
Real estate	42,500
Nonprofit research organization	40,900
Academic	37,800
Other	52,100

Source: National Association of Business Economists: *Salary Characteristics 1986.*

Table 3   Median Base Salary of Business Economists by Area of Responsibility

Corporate planning	$55,000
Econometrician	40,000
Energy economist	50,000
Financial economist	52,000
General administration	59,000
General administration/economist	64,500
Industrial economist	51,450
Consulting economist	56,100
International economist	62,250
Macro forecaster	57,000
Marketing research	45,500
Statistician	33,600
Teaching	36,186
Micro/regional	45,911
Other	63,000

Source: National Association of Business Economists: *Salary Characteristics 1986.*

Table 4   Compensation of Business Economists by Level of Education

Highest degree obtained	Median base salary
Bachelor's	$45,000
Master's	47,500
PhD	61,000
All but dissertation	55,000

Source: National Association of Business Economists: *Salary Characteristics 1986.*

In this connection, three points should be emphasized. First, while remuneration unquestionably is a key factor in the choice of a career path, equally serious consideration should be given to the issues of job satisfaction, working environment, and opportunity for personal growth and professional advancement. Second, many economists wear more than one hat. For example, university professors may augment their income by serving as consultants to business, industry, or government, or by publishing textbooks. Finally, the forces of economic, social, political, and technological change are constantly at work, creating new disciplines and career paths and causing some established ones to decline in importance. Thus the menu of career choices open to you upon graduation may differ in some key respects from the opportunities available to economics majors today.

Resources: How to Get the Most Out of This Course

If this course is as important to you as previously suggested, then how should you go about maximizing the return on the time you will invest? Several resources exist, of which you can and should take full advantage. The more thorough you are in your commitment and utilization of each, the greater will be your payoff in years to come.

In addition to this course in economics, you've probably signed up for (or already taken) a course in one of the physical sciences: biology, chemistry, physics. In these courses you can expect to spend a good amount of time in the laboratory, conducting experiments, performing dissections, and participating in other types of "hands-on" learning experiences.

In economics you won't be peering at tissue sections under a microscope or cooking up exotic mixtures over a Bunsen burner. In economics, your laboratory is no less than the world you live in, and the world in which you'll eventually pursue a career. It's in this wider environment that you'll find valuable resources that will both reinforce the economic concepts you'll be learning and suggest some helpful career directions.

Your first resource, of course, is this **textbook** and the accompanying **study guide.** You'll find it beneficial to use the text as a blueprint that details the relationships among various economic principles. To enhance your comprehension of the material, the book contains a number of useful learning aids.

The introduction to each chapter is followed by a **Concept Preview** that outlines the key points you'll be exploring and that you should understand when you've finished the chapter. At the end of each major chapter section is a **Concept Check:** a series of questions that will help you test your grasp of what you've just read. Stop and respond to these questions to make sure you've acquired the background you'll need to go on to the next section. The Concept Checks also will be useful when you're reviewing material for a test.

Throughout each chapter, **Key Terms and Concepts** are highlighted in boldface type and defined when introduced. These terms also are defined in the margins and are listed at the end of the chapter. The marginal definitions will be a valuable aid in building your economic vocabulary. In the back of the book you'll find all of the text's key terms in a comprehensive **Glossary.**

Learning economic theory is first-rate mental exercise—but how do we translate theory into application? In addition to the many relevant real-world examples provided throughout the text, each chapter also contains one or more boxed analyses that enlarge on and illustrate an important concept discussed in the text. Entitled **Principles in Practice,** each of these commentaries offers you a close-up view of an economic theory in action, from supply and demand to the pros and cons of trade protectionism.

In addition to the **Career Profile** that appears at the beginning of each of the book's 10 parts, you'll encounter throughout the text a series of profiles of leading economists entitled **Economic Thinkers.** From Adam Smith through Karl Marx, these profiles provide information about the subjects' major contributions to economic thought and also offer some intriguing personal sidelights.

The **Summary** at the end of each chapter enumerates the important concepts you've just learned, and the **Problems and Applications** give you the opportunity to demonstrate your understanding of these concepts in both expository and graphic form. Like the Concept Checks, these end-of-chapter features are helpful review aids.

At the end of each chapter is a list of **Suggested Readings:** magazine articles or selected chapters in textbooks and other reference works that will enhance your comprehension of key material you've just studied. Go to the **library** and find these readings. You may be surprised to discover how much they can add to your growing store of knowledge about economics.

Talk to your **instructor.** He or she is an experienced, knowledgeable professional who wants to serve as a resource for you and your classmates. As was suggested earlier, this text is your blueprint for the study of the relationships among

Business literature is a major resource for understanding economic principles in action.

economic principles. Your instructor can provide the guidance you need to comprehend and connect the details of the blueprint, and can serve as your interpreter as you learn the language of economics. In class and after class, ask your instructor questions. Challenge points you disagree with; request clarification of those you don't fully understand. Ask your instructor to recommend additional readings; seek his or her advice about career paths.

If any of your family members are business people, chances are you've seen them reading *The Wall Street Journal,* the business section of *The New York Times, U.S. News & World Report, Business Week,* and *Fortune.* Alone and in combination, these resources contain a wealth of information you'll find pertinent to your study of economics. All of these publications are available free at your library, and you should plan to become a regular reader. Their analyses, editorials, and features will bring into sharp focus the material you'll be studying, from monetary policy to international trade, from the consumer price index to the rate of inflation. In the pages of these publications you'll be introduced to new industries and growing companies (your future job market!); to talented young entrepreneurs and corporate leaders with decades of experience; to high government officials and foreign heads of state. Reading these publications regularly gives you the chance to expand your horizons beyond the classroom and to see how the economic principles you're learning work in the real world.

Talk to your classmates outside of class. Discuss what you're learning and how it fits in with your curriculum and your ambitions. Their interests, family backgrounds, job experience, and career plans can be a productive resource for you. Classmates may be related to or acquainted with someone who's succeeding in a career to which you're attracted—and you may be helpful to them in the same way. Consider forming a study group for review and discussion of the material you're covering, or enhance your personal interaction skills by organizing a team to prepare a class project. Whatever career path you decide to follow, you'll need to work productively and harmoniously with others. Now is the time to begin developing this facility.

Earlier we suggested that you do some brainstorming as you read the Career Profiles in this book. In addition to "trying on" these careers to see how they fit with your skills and interests, do the same exercise as part of your daily routine. Start by asking your friends and relatives how they like their jobs; how they chose these careers; what was their major field of study; what they'd do differently if they could plan their college curriculum over again. Strike up conversations with employees you meet in the stores and offices you patronize and in the places of entertainment you visit. If one of these careers seems like a good "fit" for you, find out more about it; possibly arrange a part-time or summer job in the field. By starting this process now, you'll be laying the groundwork for a serious career development program that will make your experience in college and in this course both meaningful and productive.

Good luck!

Economics: What It's All About

When you graduate from college, will it be difficult or easy for you to find a job? How will changes in the prices of things you want to buy affect your standard of living? Will you be able to qualify for a car loan or a mortgage? What impact will federal budget deficits have on your future well-being as your tax funds are used to pay interest on the national debt?

As these questions make clear, economics is about you: student, consumer, employee, and voter. Economics is about the constraints you face, the choices you make, and your interdependence with others for survival.

In economics we study the opportunities and obstacles all of us confront as we seek to make a living and to satisfy our desires for both the necessities and luxuries of life. As you learn economic principles you'll develop a systematic way of thinking about the consequences of human behavior. You'll also gain insights into social problems and various approaches to resolving or alleviating them. The emphasis in this book is on how you can *use* economics as a practical tool to comprehend and deal responsibly with personal, business, and social issues.

After reading this chapter, you should be able to: *Concept Preview*

1   Describe the mechanism of the economy and the discipline of economics.
2   Understand the concepts of scarcity and opportunity cost.
3   Discuss major branches of economic inquiry: microeconomics, macroeconomics, positive analysis, and normative analysis.

Some Basic Definitions

Economy:
The mechanism through which the use of labor, land, structures, vehicles, equipment, and natural resources is organized to satisfy the desires of those who live in a society.

Economics:
The study of the use of limited productive resources in a society to satisfy the unlimited desires of its members.

Before we define economics, we need to know what constitutes the economy.

The **economy** is the mechanism through which the use of labor, land, structures, vehicles, equipment, and natural resources is organized to satisfy the desires of those who live in a society. The rules, institutions, and traditions used to coordinate economic activity differ considerably among nations, but all societies must deal with similar economic issues.

The discipline of **economics** is concerned with the use of available productive resources in a society to satisfy what often are conflicting desires and demands. In economics we're concerned with *choices*: with evaluating and selecting among alternatives, realizing that each time we make a choice we also forgo an opportunity. One goal of this book is to help you to develop an understanding of the issues of scarcity and choice within the context of the way modern economies function.

The Basic Task of an Economy: Grappling with Scarcity

The economy is a dynamic, constantly changing mechanism. Natural resources, the supply of workers, managers, innovators, equipment, structures, and the amount of technical know-how available to produce useful goods and services are all in some way limited. The wants we seek to satisfy, however, are seemingly unlimited. We all have biological needs for minimum amounts of food, clothing, and other basic goods—but few of us are content with minimum amounts of these items. We want amenities, comfort, and luxuries.

Scarcity:
The imbalance between the desires of those in a society and the means of satisfying those desires.

Scarcity is the imbalance between our desires and the means of satisfying those desires. The problem of scarcity is faced by rich as well as poor societies. We can probably agree that even the vast wealth of the United States is inadequate to satisfy all of our desires. Scarcity is the fundamental economic problem. The importance of scarcity as a unifying topic in economics is highlighted by the fact that many economists would define their discipline in the following way:

Economics is the study of how human beings make choices to use scarce resources as they seek to satisfy their seemingly unlimited wants.

Opportunity Cost

When scarcity exists, we know we must sacrifice something of value to obtain more of any scarce good or service. The limited availability of resources such as land, skilled labor, structures, and equipment within a nation over a year means that the more resources are used for one purpose, the less will be available for other purposes. The **opportunity cost** of choosing to use resources for one purpose is the sacrifice of the next best alternative for the use of those resources. For example, if your next best alternative to studying for an hour is an hour of swimming, then the opportunity cost of studying is the hour of swimming you sacrifice when you choose to study. If you're considering the choice between a bicycle and new speakers for your stereo and each costs $200, then the opportunity cost of choosing to buy the bike is the speakers, and vice versa.

Opportunity cost:
The cost of choosing to use resources for one purpose measured by the sacrifice of the next best alternative for using those resources.

The concept of opportunity cost is vitally important because it's a measure of everything you sacrifice to attain a given objective. When you make a decision, you'll want to consider carefully its opportunity cost before deciding if the gain is worth the sacrifice you must make.

For example, the actual opportunity cost of attending college is more than the sacrifice of the goods and services you could buy with the sum of money, say $5,000 per year, you must give up to pay for tuition, books, and equipment. Suppose attending college requires that you devote full time to your studies so that you forgo the opportunity of working at a paying job. If the next best use of your time is a job that would pay $10,000 over the college year, you must add the value of this forgone opportunity to your other annual money costs of attending college.

Your actual opportunity cost of attending college is the goods and services you could have bought with the $15,000 per year you sacrifice to go to college. You now can weigh the full opportunity cost of attending college with the gains you expect from doing so. The gains include possible higher future income and improvement of the quality of your life, as well as the chance to socialize with fellow students and participate in sports and other activities.

Note: Be sure you don't confuse opportunity cost with dollar cost. While our choices often involve financial considerations, the alternatives we select and forgo aren't measured solely in dollars.

The concepts of scarcity and opportunity cost are vital to understanding how the economy works. In the face of the inevitable imbalance between limited productive capability and limitless wants, decisions are made that guide the operation of the economy with respect to the following questions:

1. *What will be produced?* The productive potential of an economy can't be used to do everything for everybody. Decisions must be made about what to produce and how much of each item to produce with the limited resources available. These decisions are political in nature, and they involve balancing needs and wants of various groups. For example, an increase in the use of productive capacity to provide military equipment inevitably reduces the availability of consumer goods such as VCRs, microwaves, and automobiles. Choices must be made about which goods and services to make available and which to forgo each day and over a year and longer periods.

2. *How will goods and services be produced?* There's more than one way to accomplish any given objective. For example, a certain quantity of iceberg lettuce could be produced on a large tract of land without the use of pesticides or fertilizers. Alternatively, the same amount of lettuce could be grown on less land with chemical agents. Food and other goods can be imported from foreign suppliers. Goods and services can be produced for profit by business firms or can be produced by government or nonprofit enterprises. Crops can be harvested by many workers using hand tools or with specialized machines and fewer workers. Textiles can be loomed and finished by hand or can be made in automated plants where machines perform many of the tasks in place of workers. Machines or other products (such as chemicals) can be substituted for labor or land when producing any mix of goods. Productive methods that squeeze the most out of available means allow the greatest possible material well-being from limited resources.

3. *To whom will goods and services be distributed?* Are they to be distributed equally to everyone so each of us lives in the same type of house, eats the same amount and kinds of food, and wears the same clothes? Or, are goods to be sold to those willing and able to pay? Under this latter method, it's clear that those with higher incomes would enjoy more and better products and services than

those with lower incomes. Will some of us be given special privileges to enjoy goods and services independent of our ability to pay for those items? What rules will be used to decide who gets what is produced during the year? Should free exchange of goods and services be permitted among everyone in a society?

The distribution of material well-being is never perfectly equal. Some people have the financial resources to enjoy great quantities of goods and services of the highest quality. Others, even in a nation with the vast productive potential of the United States, live in poverty. No society has yet discovered how to provide equally for the needs and wants of everyone while still offering the incentives that encourage high-quality production and technological innovation.

Concept Check

1 What constitutes the economy?

2 What is the discipline of economics?

3 Define scarcity and opportunity cost, and explain the opportunity cost of your decision to attend college.

Microeconomics vs. Macroeconomics

Economic analysis is divided into two main branches: microeconomics and macroeconomics.

In **microeconomics** we take a close-up view of the economy by concentrating on the choices made by individual participants in the economy such as consumers, workers, business managers, and investors. We'll study microeconomics in the first segment of this book.

In **macroeconomics** we look at the economy from a broader perspective by considering its overall performance and the way various sectors of the economy relate to one another. We gauge the performance of the economy by the total value of annual production, the capacity of the economy to provide jobs, the changes in the purchasing power of money, and the growth of employment and output. Macroeconomics is the subject of the second segment of this book.

Microeconomics:
A branch of economic analysis that concentrates on the choices made by individual participants in an economy. Also called *price theory*.

Macroeconomics:
A branch of economic analysis that considers the overall performance of the economy with respect to total national production, consumption, average prices, and employment levels.

Microeconomics

In microeconomics we analyze how individuals choose among various courses of action by weighing the benefits and costs of alternatives available to them. In microeconomic analysis we place special emphasis on the role of prices in business and personal decisions. A major goal is to understand how the prices of particular goods and services are determined and how prices influence decisions. Because of its preoccupation with prices and trading of goods and services, microeconomics is sometimes called *price theory*.

In microeconomics we study the actions of individuals as they buy and sell in market transactions. As you know, some services, such as education and police protection, are provided by government agencies rather than being sold in markets. What are the advantages and disadvantages of alternatives to markets as a means of accomplishing the basic tasks of the economy? What role does government play in the economy? How do political choices influence the functions and performance of the economy? We'll examine each of these important questions as we learn to look at the economy from the micro perspective. You'll find that microeconomic analysis provides a useful point of view about human behavior that will give you insights into important social and political issues.

Macroeconomics

In macroeconomics we study changes in total national production and consumption, averages of the prices of broad groups of goods and services, and employment of workers in the economy. Macroeconomists seek to explain the causes of economic fluctuations and to suggest policies that will make the fluctuations less abrupt, with the aim of preventing excessive unemployment and rapid price increases.

In macroeconomics we place special emphasis on understanding the causes of unemployment and inflation. The *unemployment rate* is the number of jobless workers who are actively looking for work or who have been laid off from a job, expressed as a percentage of the total labor force. Unemployment is often a major issue in congressional and presidential elections. In fact, the federal government is required by law to pursue policies that seek to keep unemployment from becoming excessively high. If such policies are to succeed, the individuals who develop them must have a keen understanding of how the economy works.

Inflation is another highly charged political issue. *Inflation* is a general yearly increase in the average level of prices for a broad spectrum of goods and services. Inflation erodes the purchasing power of money. It can create economic instability in a nation by harming the competitiveness of firms seeking to sell products in foreign markets and by distorting economic choices as people try to unload money today that they think will be worth less tomorrow. During the late 1970s inflation was a severely disrupting influence in the U.S. economy, rising to double-digit levels along with escalating interest rates. Macroeconomics seeks to understand the causes of inflation and to help government authorities pursue policies aimed at keeping the inflation rate low and within fairly predictable bounds. Stable and predictable prices facilitate planning for the future and reduce the uncertainty associated with market transactions.

In studying aggregate production in the economy and its fluctuations, macroeconomists seek to uncover the basic influences that cause national production to increase. The key to prosperity in an economy is steady growth in national output. When growth in a nation's output exceeds its growth in population, the output per person in the economy will grow, thus improving the well-being of the population on average.

Concept Check

1 Describe the focus of microeconomic analysis.

2 What economic issues are the focus of macroeconomics?

Positive Analysis vs. Normative Analysis

In the field of economics we're concerned with more than understanding *how* the economy functions. We also look at ways of improving the outcomes that emerge as the economy accomplishes its tasks of producing and distributing goods and ser-

---

vices. The operation of the economy isn't flawless, nor does it please all of us. As individuals we differ in our opinions about the goals for which resources in the economy should be used. We also disagree about the appropriate nature and extent of government involvement in the economy, and through political channels we express our views about which groups government should help. Because we understand the concept of opportunity cost, we know that a government action that benefits one group inevitably imposes a cost on another group.

Positive Analysis

Positive analysis:
Seeks to forecast the impact of changes in economic policies or conditions on observable items like production, sales, prices, and personal incomes, then tries to determine who gains and who loses as a result of the changes.

In evaluating economic policies, we must understand the basic functioning of the economy before we can predict the impact of such policies on the economy. **Positive analysis** of changes in economic policy or conditions seeks to forecast the impact of the changes on observable items like production, sales, prices, and personal incomes. It then tries to determine who gains and who loses as a result of the changes. Positive analysis makes statements of the "if . . . then" type that can be supported or rejected by empirical evidence. An example of a positive statement is: "If electronics import quotas are imposed, then the price of VCRs for U.S. consumers will increase." Another positive statement is: "If the federal government deficit is reduced, then interest rates will fall." We can support or reject these statements by observing whether evidence exists that changes in prices, incomes, or interest rates actually do occur directly as a result of the policy changes.

Principles in Practice

The Economics of Drinking, Driving, and Highway Deaths: An Example of Positive Analysis

What does drunken driving have to do with economics? The answer is "a whole lot," according to recent positive analysis of the impact on fatal motor vehicle accidents of raising the drinking age and taxing beer.

For people between the ages of 16 and 24 in the United States, automobile accidents are a leading cause of death. Evidence suggests that policies that increase the cost of obtaining alcoholic beverages also reduce highway deaths. For example, taxes on beer increase the price of beer and tend to decrease its consumption. Similarly, raising the drinking age to 21 makes it more difficult for persons under that age to obtain alcoholic beverages.

Since 1984 all 50 states have raised their minimum drinking age to 21. Positive analysis by economists of the impact of the increased drinking age has concluded that it would reduce nighttime fatal crash involvements by 13%.*

Recent research also suggests that increased taxes on beer can be very effective in reducing drinking by young people. Most young drinkers haven't been drinking long enough to become habitual alcohol users, and they typically have low incomes. Because a tax on beer will cause its price to increase, it's likely to induce young drinkers with low incomes to cut back their consumption of beer. Positive analysis of the impact of taxes on beer suggests that this too can save lives. Economists in a recent study estimated that if beer taxes in the United States had increased faster than they actually did between 1975 and 1982, over 1,000 lives of youths between the ages of 18 and 20 could have been saved annually!†

You might have your own views on what the legal drinking age should be or whether taxes on beer should be increased. You might very well change your views in response to positive analysis of the economics of drinking and driving!

*William Du Mouchel, Allan F. Williams, and Paul Zador, "Raising the Alcohol Purchase Age: Its Effects on Fatal Motor Vehicle Crashes in Twenty Six States," *Journal of Legal Studies*, 16, 1, January 1987, pp. 249-266.
†Michael Grossman and Henry Saffer, "Beer Taxes, the Legal Drinking Age, and Youth Motor Vehicle Fatalities," National Bureau of Economic Research, Working Paper No. 1914, May 1986.

Because no one completely understands how the economy works, economists often disagree about actual cause-and-effect relationships. These disagreements must be resolved by examining the facts, using statistical methods to test the relationships.

Normative Analysis

Positive analysis cannot be used to evaluate an outcome. For example, positive analysis of government welfare programs might look at the impact of such programs on the incentives of recipients to work and on national production without trying to determine whether the programs are good or bad. To evaluate the performance of an economy we must establish criteria or norms against which we'll compare actual outcomes.

We use **normative analysis** to evaluate the desirability of alternative outcomes according to underlying *value judgments* about what is good or bad. An example of a normative statement is: "Families of four with incomes below $15,000 per year should be exempted from federal income taxes." This statement presents a point of view about what a policy *should* accomplish. Another normative statement is: "Tariffs and other restrictions that impede free international trade should be eliminated."

Normative analysis: Evaluates the desirability of alternative outcomes according to underlying value judgments about what is good or bad.

The normative approach used by many economists is based on an underlying value judgment that evaluates well-being in a nation only in terms of well-being of individuals. The normative approach makes recommendations regarding *what ought to be*. It's used to *prescribe* changes in policy and the use of productive capacity in an economy as well as to evaluate performance.

Gains and Losses from Economic Policies

Economic policies and other changes affecting the way the economy functions usually result in gains to some groups and losses to others. In making judgments about whether an outcome is good or bad, we must weigh the gains against the losses. For example, a proposal to protect the U.S. automobile industry from foreign competition can benefit you as an auto company owner or employee. However, as a consumer of domestic autos you could lose, because prices of cars produced by this protected industry are likely to be higher than they would be if foreign competition were unrestricted.

Economists don't always share the same values. In particular, there are many different opinions about how the economy should be evaluated in terms of its success in distributing material well-being. Opinions about the fairness of outcomes influence the recommendations economists make about alternative policies. For example, economists often support policies recommending that tax revenues be used to provide income to the poor. However, using tax revenues in this way could have unfavorable effects on the economy by reducing productive capacity. We use positive analysis to show the effects on production and on the incomes of the poor, while we use normative analysis to make judgments about whether the results are good or bad.

Normative analysis differs from positive analysis in that it's used to derive prescriptions based on a point of view about what *should* be done rather than seeking to establish relationships between cause and effect. In short, normative analysis is used to evaluate policies and outcomes in terms of specific goals. Normative analysis does, however, benefit from positive analysis. For example, even if we agree that it's good to support policies that reduce poverty, we still need to know whether or not a particular program designed to aid the poor *can* achieve its objective. Positive analysis can help us choose intelligently among proposed policies whose predicted outcomes are in accord with our value judgments.

Disagreements about what the resources of the economy ought to be used for cannot be settled by looking at evidence. Instead these disagreements must be settled through political means. In a democratic nation, normative issues are settled through voting.

Concept Check

1 Explain what is meant by positive analysis and give two examples of positive statements.

2 Explain what is meant by normative analysis. Describe how it differs from positive analysis, and give two examples of normative statements.

Graphs: An Aid to Understanding Economics

If you were offered a guaranteed way to enhance your grasp of economic concepts, you'd leap at it, wouldn't you?

The Appendix to Chapter 1, *Basic Tools for Analyzing Economic Relationships*, provides exactly that. It's a step-by-step guide to constructing, reading, and understanding graphs, which are a key component in the study of economics. When you've mastered the material in this appendix, you'll realize how graphs can simplify key economic relationships that might take paragraphs to explain. You'll be able to draw and label your own graphs and to interpret the graphs you'll find later in almost every chapter of the book. If you take some time now to become comfortable with graphs, you can be sure they'll serve you well throughout the course.

Summary

1. Economics is concerned with the use of available productive resources to satisfy the desires and demands of those in a society.
2. Scarcity is the imbalance between the desires of members of a society and the means of satisfying those desires. Scarcity is the fundamental economic problem.
3. The opportunity cost of choosing to use resources for one purpose is the sacrifice of the next best alternative for the use of those resources.
4. There are two main branches of economics. Microeconomics views the economy from the perspective of its individual participants. Because of its emphasis on the role of prices in business and personal decisions, microeconomics is sometimes called *price theory*. Macroeconomics considers the overall performance of the economy and the way its various sectors relate to one another. Macroeconomics places special emphasis on understanding the causes of unemployment and inflation.
5. Positive analysis seeks to predict the impact of changes in economic policy on observable items like production and income, then tries to determine who gains and who loses as a result of the changes. Positive analysis makes statements of the "if . . . then" type. Normative analysis evaluates the desirability of alternative outcomes according to underlying value judgments about what is good or bad. Normative statements present a point of view about what an economic policy *should* accomplish.

Key Terms and Concepts

Economy
Economics
Scarcity
Opportunity cost

Microeconomics
Macroeconomics
Positive analysis
Normative analysis

Suggested Readings

Knight, F.H.: "Social Economic Organization," in *Readings in Microeconomics*, St. Louis, 1986, Times Mirror/Mosby. This essay is a classic analysis of the functions that must be performed by an economy and the ways of organizing production.

The Margin. This is an excellent periodical designed to show students how economic analysis is applied and to discuss social and business issues in light of economic principles. It is published eight times a year by the University of Colorado, Colorado Springs, Colo.

A Forward Look

In the next chapter we examine the methods economists use to analyze the choices individuals make under the constraints they face. We introduce the concept of marginal analysis to show how gains are sought as individuals make business and personal decisions. We discuss in detail the development of economic models, also known as economic theories.

Basic Tools for Analyzing Economic Relationships

Does the idea of graphs make you nervous? If so, relax—you're about to discover how helpful they'll be as you study economics.

Economists use graphs often to express relationships, such as the way the maximum possible production of one item is affected by the production of another item. Graphic analysis is a tool to aid you in learning economics and using it to reach important conclusions. Graphs show how the value of one variable changes as the value of some other variable is increased or decreased. The graphs used in this book are two dimensional. This means that they plot values for two variables. In many cases, however, a third variable can be introduced in a two-dimensional graph by showing how changes in its value affect the values of the two initial variables.

Plotting Points on a Set of Axes

A two-dimensional graph has a vertical axis along which one variable, designated in general by the symbol Y, whose value as related to that of another variable, X, is measured. The X variable is measured on the horizontal axis. As the value of X changes, so will the value of Y.

The table in Box 1 shows a relationship between X and Y. The second column gives the value of Y for each value of X in the first column. The pairs of numbers on each line of the table denote a *functional relationship* between X and Y. The functional relationship implies that the value of the Y variable changes as the value of the X variable increases or decreases. In this sense the value of Y *depends on* or is a *function of* the value of X. You can use the table to find the value of Y for each value of X or vice versa.

The graph in Box 1 plots the data from the table on a set of axes. The **origin** of the axes is the point, designated by 0, at which both X and Y take on values of zero. The axes drawn for most economic data are at a right angle, with measurement scales drawn horizontally and vertically from the origin. This reflects the fact that

Origin:
On a set of axes, the point designated by 0, at which variables X and Y both take on values of zero.

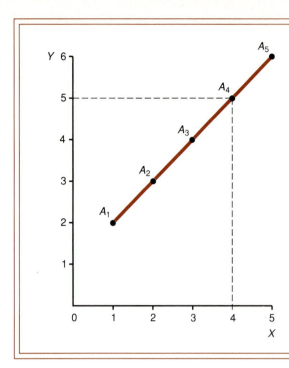

Box 1   A Curve Showing a Positive Relationship Between X and Y

The curve drawn at left is based on the data in the table below. The value of Y increases as the value of X increases, indicating a positive relationship between the two variables.

A Positive Relationship Between X and Y

Value of X	Corresponding value of Y	Point on graph
1	2	A_1
2	3	A_2
3	4	A_3
4	5	A_4
5	6	A_5

most data used in economics are positive rather than negative. If, however, Y were to take on negative values in the table, the vertical axis would have to be extended downward below the origin to accommodate negative values of Y. Similarly, if X were to take on negative values, the horizontal axis would have to be extended to the left of the origin to accommodate the points.

The data from the table in Box 1 are plotted on the set of axes shown in the graph next to the table. Each line of the table has been designated a letter A followed by a number to identify the points on the graph. The point A_1 corresponds to the pair of values $X = 1$, $Y = 2$. When plotted, this pair of numbers is called the **coordinates** of point A_1. Similarly, when X is equal to 2, Y is equal to 3. These coordinates correspond to point A_2 on the graph. Point A_3 on the graph is the point for which X is equal to 3 and Y is equal to 4. Similarly, points A_4 and A_5 from the table are plotted on the axes and a line is drawn connecting each point. This line connecting the points corresponding to the coordinates of X and Y from the table depicts the relationship between X and Y. This line is called a **curve** even when its shape is not actually curvy. Many of the curves depicting economic relationships in this book will be straight lines.

Along the curve drawn in the graph in Box 1, there is a **positive** or **direct relationship** between X and Y, meaning that Y *increases* whenever X *increases*. For example, the Y variable might indicate the cost of producing each microcomputer in a factory. The X variable could be the number of computers produced per month in the factory. Assume that the numbers for both these variables could be estimated and the functional relationship established to draw up a table like the one in Box 1. An upward-sloping curve, like in the graph in the box (with different numbers, of course), would mean that there was a positive relationship between the unit cost of the computers and the number produced each month in the factory.

Coordinates:
A pair of numbers that corresponds to values for variables X and Y when plotted on a set of axes.

Curve:
A straight or curved line drawn to connect points plotted on a set of axes.

Positive (direct) relationship:
Depicted by an upward-sloping curve on a set of axes; indicates that variable Y increases whenever variable X increases.

The curve drawn in any graph is used to find the value of Y for any possible value of X. To do this, for example, for the value of X equal to 4, follow the dashed line for the point on the horizontal axis corresponding to 4 *just up to the curve* in the graph in Box 1. From that point follow the dashed horizontal line from the curve to the vertical axis to find the corresponding value of Y, which is 5 in this case.

The table in Box 2 shows a relationship between X and Y of the type assumed for the data on the budget line drawn in Box 7 in Chapter 3. The data in the table depict a **negative** or **inverse relationship** between X and Y because when the value of X increases, the corresponding value of Y, indicated in the second column, *decreases*. The graph in Box 2 plots the points that show the value of Y corresponding to each value of X. The points are labeled to correspond to the B letters followed by numbers in the last column of the table. The curve shows that whenever the value of X increases, the corresponding value of Y declines.

Negative relationships between economic variables are quite common. For example, the Y variable might be the price of a VCR. The X variable could be the number of VCRs that buyers in a market are willing and able to purchase during a certain period. A curve like the one drawn in the graph in Box 2, with appropriate numbers, would indicate that the lower the price of the VCR, the greater the number of units buyers are willing and able to buy over the given period. In other words, the graph would indicate a negative relationship between the price of the VCR and the quantity buyers will purchase over a period.

Negative (inverse) relationship: Depicted by a downward-sloping curve on a set of axes; indicates that variable Y decreases whenever variable X increases.

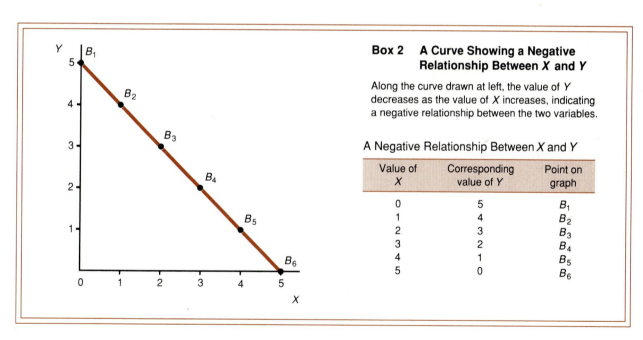

Box 2   A Curve Showing a Negative Relationship Between X and Y

Along the curve drawn at left, the value of Y decreases as the value of X increases, indicating a negative relationship between the two variables.

A Negative Relationship Between X and Y

Value of X	Corresponding value of Y	Point on graph
0	5	B_1
1	4	B_2
2	3	B_3
3	2	B_4
4	1	B_5
5	0	B_6

The Concept of Slope and Its Uses in Economic Analysis

The **slope** of a curve measures the rate at which the Y variable, on the vertical axis, rises or falls as the X variable, on the horizontal axis, increases in magnitude. The slope of a line or curve is $\Delta Y/\Delta X$ where the Greek symbol Δ (delta) represents the amount of an increase (or decrease) in the value of each variable along the line or curve.

Slope: On a curve, measures the rate at which the Y variable, on the vertical axis, rises or falls as the X variable, on the horizontal axis, increases in magnitude.

A curve or line that is upward sloping has positive slope. For example, along the upward-sloping line drawn in the graph labeled **A** in Box 3, *Y increases* as *X* increases. For each one-unit increase in *X* along the line, the value of *Y* increases by two units. The slope of the line at any point is therefore $2/1 = 2$.

A curve or line that is downward sloping has negative slope. Along the downward-sloping line drawn in the graph labeled **B** in Box 3, *Y decreases* as *X* increases. For each one-unit increase in *X* along the line drawn in the graph, *Y* decreases by one unit. The slope of this line at any point is therefore $-1/1 = -1$. A downward-sloping curve has negative slope because ΔY will always be negative when ΔX is positive.

Box 3   Curves with Positive Slope, Negative Slope, or Zero Slope

A, *A curve with positive slope.* An upward-sloping curve has positive slope. Along the line below, each one-unit increase in *X* always results in a two-unit increase in *Y*.

B, *A curve with negative slope.* For each one-unit increase in *X* along the line below, the value of *Y* decreases by one unit.

C, *A curve with zero slope.* No matter how much *X* changes along the flat line drawn below, the corresponding change in *Y* is zero, indicating a zero slope. The value of *Y* is always 3 no matter what the value of *X.*

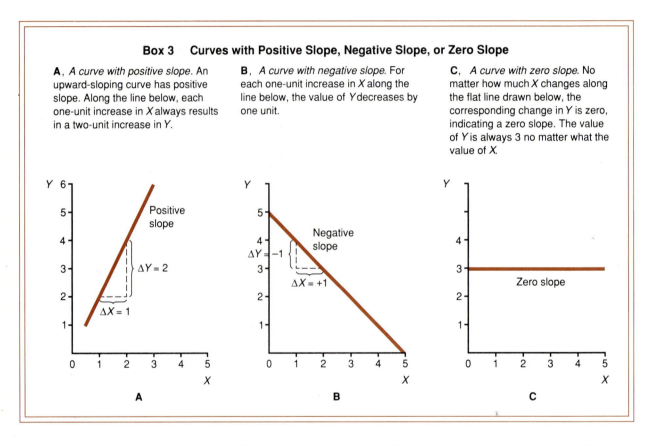

A line with zero slope is, as you might expect, flat. Along the flat line illustrated in the graph labeled **C** in Box 3, there is no increase in *Y* as *X* increases. It follows that $\Delta Y = 0$ for any ΔX so that $\Delta Y/\Delta X = 0$.

Changes in Slope Along a Curve

Nonlinear curves are those for which the slope changes from point to point. For example, the slope of the production possibilities curve drawn in Box 1 of Chapter 3 becomes increasingly more negative as annual food production is increased along the curve. In Box 4, graph **A** shows a curve that has negative slope throughout but becomes steeper as *X* increases. Graph **B** shows a curve that also has negative slope throughout but whose slope becomes less negative, and therefore closer to zero, as

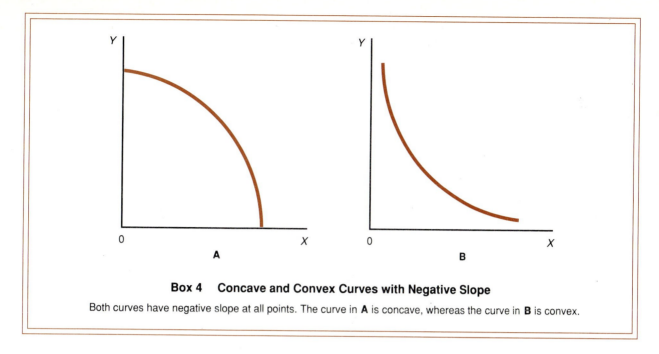

Box 4   Concave and Convex Curves with Negative Slope

Both curves have negative slope at all points. The curve in **A** is concave, whereas the curve in **B** is convex.

X increases. The curve in **A** has a *concave* shape, while the one in **B** has a shape that is called *convex*.

Box 5 shows two curves, each with positive slope throughout for which the slope changes as *X* increases. In **A** the slope of the curve increases as *X* increases. In **B** the slope of the curve decreases as *X* increases. The curve in **A** is convex, and the curve in **B** is concave.

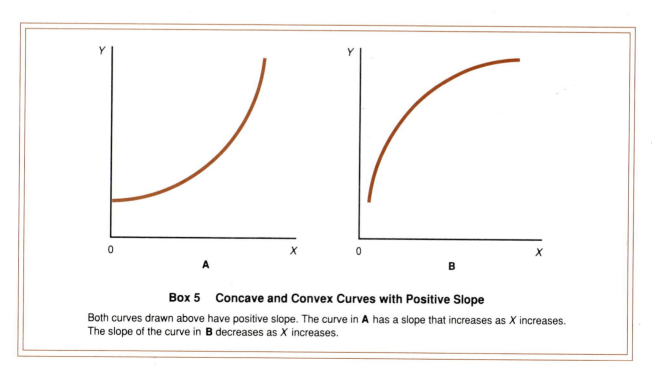

Box 5   Concave and Convex Curves with Positive Slope

Both curves drawn above have positive slope. The curve in **A** has a slope that increases as *X* increases. The slope of the curve in **B** decreases as *X* increases.

Slope and Extreme Values of Variables

Many of the most important curves drawn in economic analysis have negative, zero, and positive slope depending on the value of the X variable. For example, graph **A** in Box 6 shows a curve that has positive slope at first and then, for just the value at which X equals 5, has zero slope. Thereafter the slope of the curve is negative because Y decreases as X increases beyond the value of 5. The point labeled M, at which the slope of the curve in **A** is just equal to zero as slope shifts from being positive to being negative, is of great significance. The coordinates of that point give the value of X for which the corresponding value of Y is at its *maximum* value. The distinguishing feature of that point is that the slope is *zero*.

Box 6   Maximum and Minimum Values for Y

A, *Maximum values for Y*. The value of Y is at a maximum when the value of X is 5 in the graph below. At point M, the slope of the curve is equal to zero.

B, *Minimum values for Y*. The slope of the curve below is zero at point E, at which the value of Y is at a minimum.

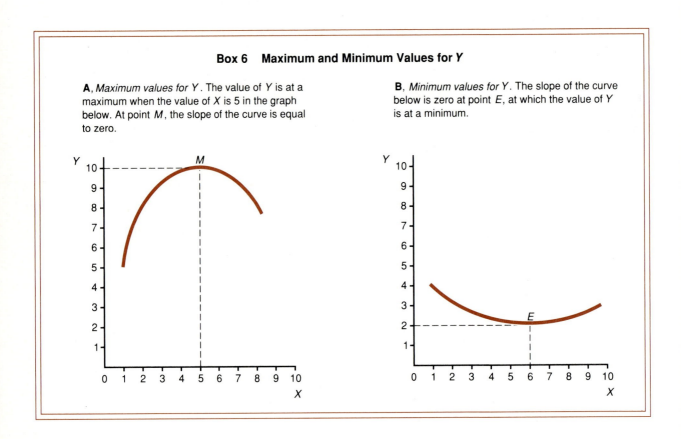

A zero slope can also indicate a minimum value of a variable. For example, in graph **B** in Box 6, the coordinates of point E give the value of X for which the value of Y is at a *minimum*. For values greater than 6, the slope is positive. At the value of X equal to 6, the slope just equals zero.

Be sure you understand the meaning of the concept of slope, because you'll find it very useful in economic analysis. Throughout the book we'll make assumptions about the way the slope of a curve varies as one variable is increased in value and a related variable responds. We'll use these assumptions to reach important conclusions about economic behavior and relationships.

Units of Measurement

When discussing economic relationships, we need to specify units of measurement. Suppose the *Y* variable for graph **A** in Box 6 were profits. Its units would be measured in dollars. The *X* variable could be number of cars sold per day for an auto dealer. The curve would therefore represent the relationship between profits and daily sales. The curve then shows that the firm would maximize profits by selling five cars per day.

The smoothness of a curve depends on how compact the units of measurement are along an axis and whether it makes sense to talk about fractions of units. For example, a car dealer can't sell half or one-quarter of a car. Therefore points on a graph between 1 and 2 or any other two integers really don't exist. In actuality, profits are likely to change substantially rather than only minutely when each car is sold. The actual graph would look like the one drawn in Box 7. This is a **bar graph.** The height of each bar shows profits for each number of cars sold. The first bar shows profit when only one car per day is sold. The second bar shows how profit jumps when two cars per day are sold. Variables that cannot vary by fractions of units are called **discrete variables**. Variables that can realistically and meaningfully take on minute fractions of values are called **continuous variables**. For example, any variable measured in dollars can be regarded, more or less, as a continuous variable because each dollar can be broken down into hundredths.

Bar graph:
A graph that shows the value of a *Y* variable as the height of a bar for each corresponding value of the *X* variable.

Discrete variable:
A variable that cannot vary by fractions of units.

Continuous variable:
A variable that can realistically and meaningfully take on minute fractions of values.

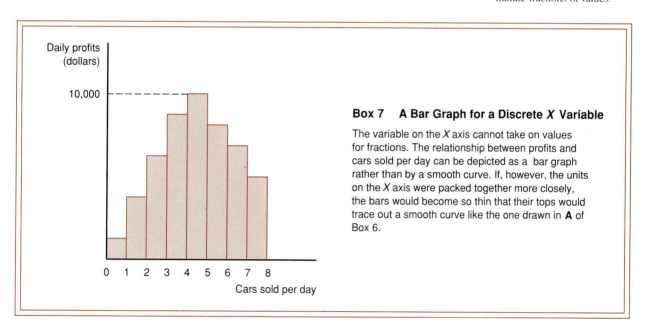

Box 7   A Bar Graph for a Discrete *X* Variable

The variable on the *X* axis cannot take on values for fractions. The relationship between profits and cars sold per day can be depicted as a bar graph rather than by a smooth curve. If, however, the units on the *X* axis were packed together more closely, the bars would become so thin that their tops would trace out a smooth curve like the one drawn in **A** of Box 6.

Economists often draw graphs of economic relationships assuming that variables that are actually discrete can be regarded as continuous. Little is lost by doing so, because the main point of drawing curves is to analyze the way one variable depends on another. The curves drawn are meant to show positive or negative relationships rather than be realistic depictions of actual variation of the discrete units. You should also note that graphs of relationships between discrete variables can have smooth curves if the scale of measurement along the axes is very compact. For example, suppose a graph shows the relationship between profits of all automakers and number of cars sold per day. If the *X* axis depicts the variation in cars sold from 0 to 8 million per year, the distance between any number of cars sold and *one more car* sold on the *X* axis will be microscopic for a graph drawn on the page of a book. Similarly, the change in profits when one more car is sold will be quite small on the vertical axis when the scale of measurement is designed to accommodate millions of dollars for the millions of cars sold each year. The resulting graph of the economic relationship is therefore likely to be like the smooth curve in Box 6 rather than the bar graph in Box 7.

In most cases in this book, smooth curves will be drawn to depict economic relationships. However, on occasion, when the variables are clearly discrete or the scale of measurement is not very compact between integers, bar graphs like the one in Box 7 will be drawn.

Intersections and Tangencies

Intersections

Intersection:

The point at which two curves drawn on the same set of axes cross.

In many graphs drawn to facilitate economic analysis, *two* curves will be drawn on the same set of axes. The **intersection** of two curves is the point at which they cross. An intersection usually reveals some important economic information. The graph in Box 8 shows the intersection of two curves at point *E*. At point *E*, the value of *X* is such that the corresponding value of *Y* is the same for the relationship indicated by curve 1 and that indicated by curve 2. In Chapters 4 and 5 you'll have lots of practice in interpreting the intersections of two curves.

When graphs are drawn in this way, the effect of a third variable other than *X* or *Y* can be investigated. To do this we can hypothesize the impact of the third variable, *Z*, on the relationship represented by curve 1. If the change in this variable has no effect on the relationship between *X* and *Y* depicted by the upward-sloping curve

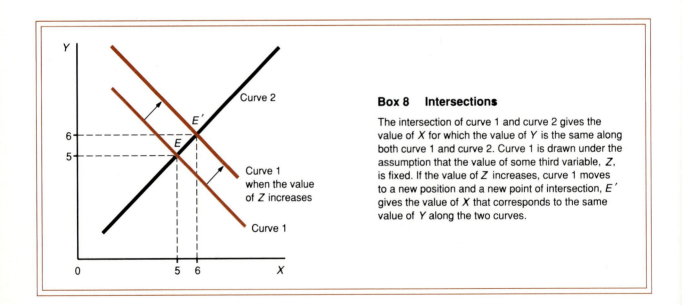

Box 8   Intersections

The intersection of curve 1 and curve 2 gives the value of *X* for which the value of *Y* is the same along both curve 1 and curve 2. Curve 1 is drawn under the assumption that the value of some third variable, *Z*, is fixed. If the value of *Z* increases, curve 1 moves to a new position and a new point of intersection, *E′*, gives the value of *X* that corresponds to the same value of *Y* along the two curves.

labeled curve 2, then only the downward-sloping curve will move as the value of Z changes. If, for example, curve 1 shifts outward as Z increases, there will be a new point of intersection, at E', as shown in Box 8. The role of economic analysis would then be to interpret the new point of intersection.

Tangencies

A **tangency** between two curves is a point at which the two curves just touch each other *but do not intersect. At a point of tangency, the slopes of the two curves are equal.* Box 9 shows the tangency between a straight line and a convex curve. The slope of the convex curve varies from point to point. At the point of tangency, T, the slope of the convex curve is precisely equal to the slope of the straight line. The straight line has slope equal to -1 at all points. It follows that the slope of the convex curve is equal to -1 at point T. The corresponding value of X is 4. For all values of X less than 4, the slope of the convex curve is more negative than -1. For values of X greater than 4, the slope of the convex curve is less negative, that is, closer to zero, than -1.

Tangency:
A point at which two curves just touch each other but do not intersect.

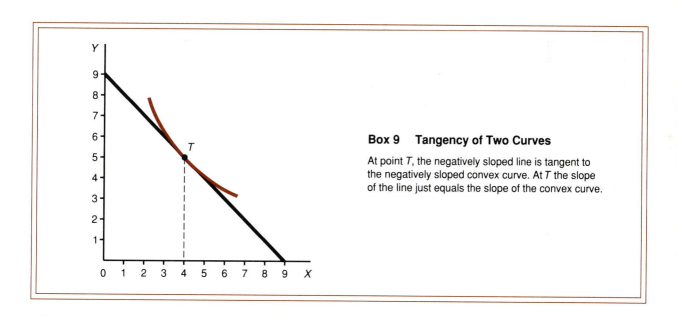

Box 9   Tangency of Two Curves

At point T, the negatively sloped line is tangent to the negatively sloped convex curve. At T the slope of the line just equals the slope of the convex curve.

Descriptive Graphs

Most graphs drawn in this book are designed to illustrate functional relationships. In many cases these graphs will not be based on actual data. Instead their purpose might be simply to show the consequences of a positive or negative relationship and to aid in predicting the values of certain key economic variables.

In other cases graphs are drawn simply to describe how actual variables vary over time without trying to interpret the trend depicted. Most *descriptive graphs* are plots of **time series data**. For example, a graph might show how unemployment in a nation fluctuates over time. Such a graph is drawn in Box 10 for the years 1965-1985. This graph shows trends but does not necessarily illustrate a functional relationship. Graphs like this will be drawn in the book to describe what actually hap-

Time series data:
Data that show the fluctuations in a variable over time.

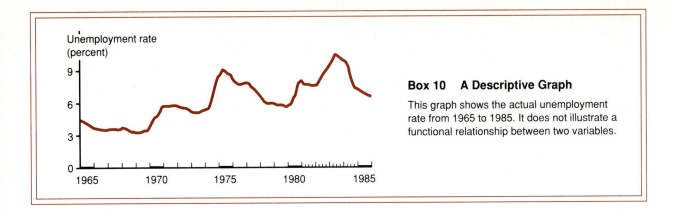

Box 10   A Descriptive Graph

This graph shows the actual unemployment rate from 1965 to 1985. It does not illustrate a functional relationship between two variables.

pened to a variable. However, to *understand* what causes fluctuations of the sort illustrated in the graph requires economic analysis of the type that allows functional relationships to be established. The purpose of Chapter 2 is to show how economists seek to establish the functional relationships that are used to obtain such insights.

Summary

Many students have difficulty using graphs and interpreting the relationships that curves are designed to explain. The way to avoid this difficulty yourself is to practice using the graphs. You'll find it helpful to refer to this appendix whenever you have a problem with a graph. Also, a few basic points should make it easier for you to deal with the graphs you'll encounter in this book:

1. *Make sure you know the economic variables that are being graphed on the set of axes.* You'll have a great deal of difficulty understanding a graph if you simply memorize the shape of the curve but forget the names or units of measurement of the economic variables!
2. *Remember that the main point of drawing a curve on a set of axes is to depict an economic relationship. Make sure that the purpose of trying to understand that relationship is clear to you.* For example, is the purpose of the graph to find the minimum value or the maximum value of an economic variable? Is the graph supposed to show how quantities purchased vary with the price of a good? Is it designed to show how unemployment fluctuates with interest rates? Is the purpose of the graph to show how the average level of prices in the economy varies with the amount of money in circulation?
3. *Always try to understand the significance of the positive or negative relationships depicted by graphs.* Practice drawing the graphs yourself from the information given in the text. Make sure you label your axes and follow the common sense of the relationship the graph is designed to illuminate.
4. *Make sure you understand how economic relationships depicted by curves change when other variables change that are not explicitly drawn on the set of axes.* For example, suppose a curve shows how consumer spending varies with income. This curve might shift if interest rates or tax rates change.
5. *Make sure you can interpret points of intersection or tangency between two curves.* These points almost always have great significance in economic analysis.

Remember that graphs represent a shortcut to reasoning. Use them as a tool. If you practice with them, you'll find they'll save you a great deal of time and enable you to reach conclusions that would be much more difficult to arrive at with purely verbal reasoning.

Key Terms and Concepts

Origin	Bar graph
Coordinates	Discrete variable
Curve	Continuous variable
Positive (direct) relationship	Intersection
Negative (inverse) relationship	Tangency
Slope	Time series data

Problems and Applications

1. The following table gives a relationship between X and Y:

Value of X	Corresponding Value of Y
1	4
2	6
3	8
4	10
5	12

   Plot the coordinates of X and Y on a graph and draw a line through the points to show the relationship between the two variables.

2. Indicate whether the graph you have drawn in answer to question 1 shows a positive or negative relationship between X and Y. Calculate the slope of the line you have drawn.

3. Draw up a table like the one shown in question 1 that shows a negative relationship between X and Y. Choose your numbers so that a curve with constant slope can be drawn through the coordinates. Calculate the slope of your line.

4. Weekly sales of personal computers are unaffected by the temperature of the outside air. Draw a curve that shows the absence of a relationship between temperature and sales of PCs. Let Y be PC sales and X be the temperature. What is the slope of the curve?

5. The owner of a factory producing rugby shirts can sell as many shirts as he wishes at a price of $20. The total revenue he receives is equal to the price of shirts multiplied by the number of shirts shipped. Draw a graph that shows how his monthly revenue will vary with monthly shipments of shirts. Calculate the slope of the curve you have drawn and interpret its meaning from an economic point of view.

6. Suppose the owner of the rugby shirt factory notices that his total costs of producing and shipping shirts form a concave curve similar to the one drawn as graph **A** in Box 5. His monthly profit is the difference between monthly revenue and monthly cost. Draw the cost curve on the same set of axes you used to draw the revenue curve and then draw another curve that shows how monthly profit will vary with shirt production. Locate the point of maximum profits.

7. The following table shows how the unit cost of producing denim jackets varies with monthly output in a certain factory:

Monthly Number of Jackets Produced	Cost per Jacket
1,000	$80
2,000	70
3,000	60
4,000	70
5,000	80

Plot the points from the table and trace a curve through them. Describe the relationship between cost per denim jacket and number of jackets produced per month. What is the slope of the curve at the point at which the cost per jacket is at a minimum?

8. Draw a bar graph that shows the relationship between X and Y using the data from question 1.

9. An equation is a way of using algebra to express a relationship between variables. The following equation describes a relationship between the price of running shoes and the quantity buyers will purchase per month:

Quantity buyers will buy $= 300 - 3P$

The quantity sellers will sell is related to the price of running shoes in the following way:

Quantity sellers will sell $= 2P$

where P is the price per pair of running shoes.

Plot the graphs for the above two equations using the following values for P: $30, $40, $50, $60, $70, $80. Identify the value of P at which the two curves intersect and indicate the corresponding number of pairs of running shoes that will be bought and sold.

10. A curve showing the relationship between X and Y has a slope equal to -2 at all points. Draw this line and then draw a convex curve that is tangent to this line. What is the slope of the convex curve at the point of tangency?

The Economic Way of Reasoning: Models and Marginal Analysis

What makes us behave the way we do? Given a number of alternatives from which to choose, why do you take one course of action while your roommate or your best friend pursues a completely different direction?

In the discipline of economics we seek to isolate relationships of cause and effect in the economy as we study the behavior of human beings. To accomplish this objective we gather information to help us make generalizations about production, technology, and human behavior.

A chief goal of economic analysis is to help us understand how the economy functions and the forces influencing the choices people make under the constraints they face. In this chapter we examine the methods economists use to develop theories that explain how the economy functions. Because much of economic analysis is concerned with human behavior, we devote a good part of the chapter to discussing methods used to analyze the choices made by individuals.

Much of economic theory is based on the premise that our behavior is quite predictable. Economists often assume that we systematically pursue certain objectives, such as seeking the greatest satisfaction from our purchases or the highest profit from the sale of a product.

In economics, the method we use to study decision making is called **marginal analysis**. This method is based on the idea that it's possible for you to gain from engaging in more of an activity if the extra benefits exceed the extra costs of doing so. You'll discover that marginal analysis is more than a technique for studying decisions—it can actually guide you in decision making. In fact, we can regard marginal analysis as applied common sense in that it involves a systematic comparison of benefits and costs of actions. By studying marginal analysis you can understand

Marginal analysis:
A method economists use to study decision making; involves a systematic comparison of benefits and costs of actions.

how gains are sought as you and others make business and personal choices. For example, you decide whether or not to take additional courses in a semester based on whether the additional benefits of doing so outweigh the additional costs. Among the benefits are the possibility of graduating earlier or having a lighter course load next semester. The costs include the dollar expense of adding courses and the extra time you'll have to spend studying instead of socializing and participating in sports or other leisure-time activities. If you have a job, your employer decided to hire you by comparing the expected benefits of doing so—the value of your services—with the cost of having you on the payroll and the time needed to train and supervise you. As you read this chapter you'll discover how often you already use marginal analysis in your personal affairs.

Concept Preview   *After reading this chapter, you should be able to:*

1   Understand the concept of an economic model and its uses.
2   Explain the notion of rational behavior and a method of analyzing the way we make decisions, which is called marginal analysis.

Economic Theory and Models

Economic theories simplify reality to allow us to understand basic economic forces and how individuals cope with the problem of scarcity. We can observe actions and their consequences. Observation and description, however, are not sufficient for understanding and ultimately predicting actions. **Theory** establishes relationships between cause and effect. We use it to interpret actions and outcomes so we can explain the process by which the actions were undertaken and the outcomes achieved. The purpose of theory in all scientific analysis is to *explain* the causes of phenomena we observe. To conduct economic analysis, we frequently need to engage in abstraction. This involves making assumptions about the economic environment and human motivation that simplify the real world enough to allow us to isolate forces of cause and effect. Any theory is a simplification of actual relationships.

Theory:
Establishes relationships between cause and effect; a simplification of actual relationships.

A successful theory provides insights into the physical or social relationships it studies. We develop economic theories to explain such important observable quantities as the production, prices, and consumption of goods and services, the employment of workers, and levels of saving and investment.

Economic **variables** are quantities or dollar amounts that can have more than one value. For example, the price of an item is an economic variable representing what we must give up in exchange for each unit of that item. Price is an economic variable because it can go up or down as changes occur in the economy. An economic theory of price seeks to determine the *causes* for changes in the price of an item. The number of unemployed workers is another economic variable that fluctuates. An economic theory to explain unemployment isolates the *causes* of unemployment.

Variable:
A quantity or dollar amount that can have more than one value.

Just as you can't cure a disease if you don't know its cause, it's essential to understand *how* the economy works if you're interested in changing economic outcomes you consider undesirable. For example, if a goal of your economic policy is to reduce unemployment, the methods you propose will be more effective if you understand the causes of unemployment. A policy can fail miserably in achieving its objectives or can have unanticipated adverse effects if policy makers don't understand the impact of their policy on the economy. For example, economic theory can show that government policies designed to benefit consumers by controlling prices of basic goods inevitably result in shortages of those goods. If the objective of such policies is to increase the incomes of certain persons, economic theory can help policy makers consider other methods of accomplishing the same objective that don't result in shortages.

Economic Models

An **economic model** is a simplified way of expressing how some sector of the economy functions. An economic model contains assumptions that establish relationships among economic variables. We use logic, graphs, or mathematics to determine the consequences of the assumptions. In this way we can use the model to make predictions about how a change in economic conditions results in changes in decisions affecting economic variables. Economists often use the term *model* as a synonym for *theory*.

Economic model:
A simplified way of expressing how some sector of the economy functions. Consists of assumptions that establish relationships among economic variables.

Many economic models are developed using the *deductive method,* through which observations or insights are used to make assumptions about economic behavior or productive and technological relationships. Logic is then used to trace out the implications of the assumptions using a model. For example, a model of the supply of compact disc players might assume that suppliers seek to maximize profits from selling that item. The economic variables affecting the profitability of selling CD players are isolated. Logic can then be used to show how a change in one of the economic variables affects the profitability of selling more CD players. For example, if it can be shown that an increase in the price of CD players makes it profitable to sell more, the model would imply that whenever the price increases, the quantity supplied will also go up. The conclusions of the model can be tested by examining factual data to see if actual relationships are consistent with those of the underlying theory. Conclusions that are consistently supported by evidence are called *economic laws* or *economic principles*.

Another model might seek to explain how changes in the rate of increase or decrease of the prices of goods and services affect interest rates in the economy by assuming that lenders seek to maximize the profit they make from loans. Still another model might examine the way an improvement in technology that lowers the cost of producing computers affects the price of computers, assuming that businesses seek to maximize profit.

A good economic model is comparable to a schematic drawing that shows that when you jiggle a certain lever, a series of reactions takes place that results in the movement of certain gears. Just as the drawing doesn't capture the texture and intricacy of the actual machine, neither does an economic model mirror the complexity of the real-life sector of the economy it seeks to explain. A model is a *tool* we can use to understand the consequences of a theory. A good model also can accurately predict changes in the economic variables it is set up to explain.

Economic models are abstract because they don't attempt to capture all the relevant influences on behavior. For example, an economic model set up to explain the rate of marriage and divorce might assume that the earnings differences between males and females have an effect on marriage and divorce. The model might assume that, as the gap between earnings by males and females is reduced, the gains from marriage decline. This would imply that as more women pursue careers and their earning potential reaches that of men, the rate of marriage would decline and the rate of divorce would go up. This model concentrates only on economic reasons for marriage and divorce and ignores other reasons.

Similarly, an assumption that sellers seek to maximize profit from the sale of their product might not capture the full complexity of business motivation. Business owners might have other goals in addition to earning profit. The owners might also be concerned with their public image, their sales revenue, or the dividends they pay their stockholders. However, by concentrating on only one goal, even though this is not realistic, a model can more clearly unveil basic forces of cause and effect.

Other Things Being Equal: An Important Qualifier

Hypothesis:
Statement of a relationship between two or more variables.

Hypotheses represent the untested implications of a model. A **hypothesis** is a statement of a relationship between two or more variables. An example of a testable hypothesis is: "The number of compact discs sold per year will increase if their price falls while all other influences on willingness and ability of consumers to buy compact discs are unchanged." Testing this hypothesis involves finding out whether buyers *actually do* purchase more CDs when their price falls while nothing else changes. Unfortunately, it's common for more than one influence on an economic variable to change at a time. To test our hypothesis we therefore need a method of accounting for the effects of changes in all economic conditions on the value of the economic variables our model seeks to explain.

Ceteris paribus:
A Latin phrase meaning "other things being equal." Used to acknowledge that other influences aside from the one whose effect is being analyzed must be controlled for in testing a hypothesis.

Suppose we hypothesize that an increase in the availability of compact discs over a year will lower the price of CDs. The phrase *other things being equal* or its Latin equivalent, **ceteris paribus,** is used to acknowledge that other influences aside from the one whose effect is being analyzed must be controlled in testing a hypothesis.

The hypothesis and the theory aren't necessarily refuted by the facts if other things *are not* equal. For example, in 1987 a number of new factories began producing compact discs. CDs became much more plentiful that year and even began to outsell long-playing records. However, despite the increased abundance of the discs, their price didn't decline. Does this mean that the theory is incorrect? Before we scrap the theory, we need to determine if *other influences* on the price of compact discs changed at the same time the available supply increased. In fact, as a result of increased sales of compact disc players in 1987 it's likely that the number of buyers of CDs increased. In addition, growth in consumer income during the year could have increased the willingness to pay for compact discs. Both of these influences could have put upward pressure on the price of compact discs that offset the downward pressure on price resulting from increased availability of CDs.

When constructing economic models to explain the values of economic variables, economists seek to understand all the important determinants of the values of these variables. However, in concentrating on cause-and-effect relationships among particular variables, economists ignore the influence of other determinants on the values of variables by making the "other things being equal" assumption. Unlike physical scientists, who can conduct controlled laboratory experiments, economists are concerned with social relationships. In testing hypotheses economists must therefore attempt to account for the influence of many simultaneous changes in economic conditions on data by adjusting for the effects in other ways using statistical methods.

Support for hypotheses and theories from actual data is often elusive and subject to debate because in the real world other things are seldom equal. Economics is not an exact science, and for that reason there is often considerable disagreement among economists on how to interpret data.

In Box 1 there's a convenient diagram to help you review and understand the steps necessary to construct an economic model.

Box 1   Constructing and Using an Economic Model

Step 1: ECONOMIC VARIABLES
Selected quantities or dollar sums among which cause-and-effect relationships are to be explained.

Examples of economic variables: Prices, quantities of goods and services sold over a period, number of workers employed, total value of annual production of a nation.

Step 2: ASSUMPTIONS
To establish cause-and-effect relationships among economic variables of a model, insights and observations are used to make assumptions about technology, constraints, and human behavior.

Examples of assumptions: Businesses maximize profits; resources are specialized; only a fixed amount of labor is available over a month; consumers seek to maximize satisfaction from their purchases.

Step 3: IMPLICATIONS
Logic is used to analyze the implications of the assumptions of the model for the relationships among the economic variables it seeks to explain.

Examples of implications: An increase in price increases the quantity of a good sellers are willing to sell over a year; an increase in interest rates will decrease annual business investment; a decrease in the federal government's deficit will put downward pressure on interest rates.

Step 4: TESTABLE HYPOTHESES
Other things being equal, the implications of the model must be supported by empirical evidence. An economic model whose hypotheses are consistently supported by empirical evidence has implications that are generalized and are called economic laws. A model whose implications are contradicted by empirical evidence is abandoned.

Concept Check

1 What is the purpose of economic theory?

2 Give some examples of economic variables and describe how an economic model might make assumptions that imply relationships between economic variables.

3 Give an example of a hypothesis about the cause-and-effect relationship between two economic variables that can be tested. What are some of the problems involved in testing hypotheses derived from economic models?

Rational Behavior: A Key Behavioral Assumption in Economic Models

Behavioral assumption:
Establishes the motivation of persons for the purpose of understanding cause-and-effect relationships among economic variables.

A key component of any economic model is the assumption it makes about the way people behave. We use **behavioral assumptions** to establish the motivation of individuals so we can understand cause-and-effect relationships among economic variables. For example, it's typically assumed that the owners of business firms seek to maximize their annual profits from the sale of a product. Once we make this assumption, we can use a model to trace out the impact of a change in an economic variable, such as the wages paid to the firm's employees, on the quantity of a product the seller is willing to sell. It's also commonly assumed that consumers act to obtain the most satisfaction possible from purchasing goods and services. We can use the assumption of maximization of satisfaction to examine how changes in such economic variables as the price of an item affect the quantity buyers are willing and able to purchase.

Rational behavior:
Seeking to gain by choosing to undertake actions for which the extra benefit exceeds the associated extra cost.

When you seek to gain by choosing to undertake actions for which the extra benefit exceeds the associated extra cost, you're engaging in **rational behavior**. For example, you'll be considered rational if you choose to take additional courses each semester as long as the extra benefit you associate with those courses exceeds the extra cost you incur when you take them. If you took courses to the point at which the last course cost you more than the benefit it provided you, you'd be considered irrational. You evaluate the benefits of actions subjectively in relation to your personal objectives. The cost of an action you take is the value you place on the sacrifice you must make to enjoy the benefits of the action. Scarcity implies that you can obtain a benefit only at the cost of forgoing an alternative opportunity. Thus, if you want to act in the dramatic society's new play and begin training for the cross-country squad and the two activities are scheduled at the same time, you decide to bask in the glow of the footlights at the cost of the chance to win glory on foot. You behave rationally when you actively pursue your self-interest, as you evaluate it, by trying to get the greatest possible well-being from the resources you have. In this case you've decided that you'll make the best (and perhaps most enjoyable) use of your resource, time, by acting instead of sprinting.

The assumption of rational behavior is a key component in many economic models. The term *rational* as used in economics implies nothing about a person's sanity. It merely supposes that each of us has certain objectives. You're regarded as rational in the economic sense if you systematically undertake actions to achieve your desired objectives. Those objectives might be good or bad from another person's point of view. For example, the objective of a burglar might be to support himself by breaking into homes and stores each month. We can regard the burglar as rational if he chooses the monthly number of burglaries in a way that considers both his personal benefits (such as the value of goods stolen) and his personal costs (such as tools, the value of his time in its next best use, and the possibility of being caught and having to pay a penalty). Likewise, altruistic motives are entirely consistent with rational behavior. A person who is altruistic receives benefit when she uses some of her resources to provide material gains to others. There's nothing irrational about parents feeding and caring for their children! Parents receive benefits from these activities and consider those benefits as well as the costs when choosing to have children and to support and guide them. When economists say we are rational, they neither deny the fact that we differ in our objectives, nor do they make any judgments that applaud or condemn those objectives.

Economic Thinkers

ADAM SMITH

You don't have to have a photographic memory for dates to know that 1776 was a significant year in history. In that year, as we all know, the Declaration of Independence was signed in Philadelphia. Fewer people probably know that also in that year, a Scottish professor of philosophy published a book entitled *An Inquiry into the Nature and Causes of the Wealth of Nations.* (This work is known universally as *The Wealth of Nations.*) This event represented a watershed in the development of intellectual thought on economic issues and problems. Although many of the ideas in the book weren't entirely new at the time, the philosophy professor, whose name was Adam Smith, is generally credited with being the father of the discipline of economics.

Professor Smith taught moral philosophy at the University of Glasgow. His specialty was "natural theology," which sought to understand and formulate the natural laws that governed physical and social phenomena. At that time the field of economics was a branch of the discipline of philosophy, which also encompassed, as it still does today, ethics and theology. The branch of philosophy that included economics in the eighteenth century was called "political economy."

At the time Smith wrote his monumental work, the affluence of a nation was measured by many politicians in terms of the gold and silver accumulated in national treasuries. Smith pointed out that the wealth of nations was chiefly determined by people conducting their daily business rather than by the amount of gold and silver in a government treasury. He believed that the accumulation of capital equipment, such as machines and structures used by factories, was a vital determinant of wealth because it enhanced the division of labor. The thrifty Scot argued that saving was critically important as a means of providing the funds to finance the accumulation of capital.

Smith's main task in the book was to develop a framework for understanding the mechanism through which the seemingly chaotic hubbub of daily trading actually resulted in a natural order. His background in natural theology led him to conclude that trade in unregulated markets would maximize the wealth of nations. The foundation for this belief was the notion of rational behavior. The main and lasting contribution of Adam Smith was therefore the formulation of a theory of economic interaction based on a view of humans who carefully pursue net gains.

Smith believed that rational behavior is biologically determined and that people have an innate tendency to pursue their self-interest. Yet Smith concluded that in pursuing personal gains, individuals are impelled by the requirements of survival to act in the interests of society. In his eloquent statement of this principle of "enlightened self-interest," Smith was careful to emphasize that individuals are motivated not by altruism but by need for the cooperation of others.

The following quotes from *The Wealth of Nations* speak for themselves*:

". . . man has almost constant occasion for the help of his brethren, and it is in vain for him to expect it from* their benevolence only. He will be more likely to prevail if he can interest their self-love in his favor, and show them that it is for their own advantage to do for him what he requires of them. . ."* (Book 1, Chapter 2, p. 14)

". . .As every individual, therefore, endeavors as much as he can to employ his capital in support of domestic industry, so as to direct that industry that its product may be of the greatest value; every individual necessarily labors to render the annual revenue of the society as great as he can. . .by directing that industry in such a manner as its produce may be of the greatest value, he intends only his own gain, and he is in this, as in many other cases, led by an invisible hand to promote an end which was no part of his intention. By pursuing his own interest he frequently promotes that of the society more effectually than when he really intends to promote it."* (Book 4, Chapter 2, pp. 421-423)

Smith believed that rational human beings have an inherent tendency to "truck and barter," thereby seeking out means for mutually advantageous exchanges. The belief in the effectiveness of a system of unregulated markets in maximizing well-being is another hallmark of Smith's views. Smith is often credited with supporting *laissez-faire*, a French term used to mean lack of government intervention in business affairs. His views on the role of government were quite complex. In general, he believed that much government intervention in markets did more harm than good.†

Smith can justly be credited with establishing economics as a separate social science. He firmly established the individual as the main object of study and provided the first attempt to systematically analyze how the economy functions.

*Page references are from Adam Smith, *An Inquiry into the Nature and Causes of the Wealth of Nations,* New York: The Modern Library, 1937. This edition was edited by Edwin Cannan. The book was first published in 1776.
†For a discussion of Adam Smith's views on government, see "Adam Smith on Laissez Faire" in Joseph J. Spengler and William R. Allen, eds., *Essays in Economic Thought,* Chicago: Rand McNally, 1960.

The concept of all of us as rational decision makers relentlessly pursuing goals intended to improve our well-being has proved to be particularly fruitful in building economic models whose hypotheses are supported by facts. You may not agree with this assumption. In fact, some of us don't consistently do what is in our best interest. However, the underlying assumptions of a model needn't be either realistic or without exception to be useful. Remember, the test of the usefulness of an economic model is the validity of the principles we can derive from it.

Illustrating Rational Behavior: A Model to Explain Consumer Purchases

We now can use the assumption of rational behavior to set up a very simple economic model that explains the quantity of a particular item that a consumer chooses to buy in a given month. A main goal of the model is to examine the causal relationship between the price of an item and the monthly quantity that is purchased, *other things being equal*. Our key assumption is that of rational behavior. We'll make additional assumptions as we develop the model.

Think about your own behavior as a buyer. When you go to the store to purchase something, like a compact disc, you probably have an idea about how much better off you'd be if you had the CD. There's a certain maximum dollar sum you'd be willing to give up to obtain more CDs after you've already bought a certain number. This maximum sum probably depends on your preference for CDs and your income. For example, if you don't have a compact disc player, you're unlikely to be willing to give up any of your income for compact discs. Because the model we'll construct here is designed to investigate the relationship between price and quantities purchased, we'll assume that your monthly income is constant and your preferences are well established and don't change.

When deciding on a purchase you also must consider the fact that to obtain the CD you must pay a price. You must give up a certain sum of dollars to enjoy each recording and add it to your collection. The price of the disc measures the number of dollars you sacrifice to buy each unit. *By sacrificing those dollars you sacrifice the opportunity to buy other items that can also be purchased for the same number of dollars.* For example, suppose the price of the compact disc is $11.99 and admission to a concert also costs $11.99. If the concert ticket is the next best use of the portion of your income you give up to buy the disc, then forgoing the concert is the opportunity cost of choosing to buy the disc. Assume that, whenever the price of compact discs changes, other prices don't change. A change in the prices of other goods can affect the opportunity cost of the disc. If the price of concerts fell to $5.99, you'd give up the opportunity of attending two concerts instead of one every time you bought a disc. This would increase the opportunity cost of buying a disc, assuming that going to concerts remains the next best alternative use of your income.

You'll buy a compact disc only if you believe the benefit you'll receive from it exceeds the opportunity cost of $11.99 worth of other goods and services you must give up to get it. In other words, which do you like better: the compact disc or what you have to give up to get it? If you're rational, you buy more compact discs only if you think the benefit you'll obtain from each additional CD exceeds the opportunity cost of obtaining it.

By assuming that all other variables affecting your choice are constant, we can isolate the cause-and-effect relationship between the price of an item and the quantity you'll purchase.

Marginal Analysis of Rational Behavior

Marginal analysis is a step-by-step way of analyzing how people engaging in rational behavior make choices. Marginal analysis of your decision to buy compact discs would look at the benefits and costs associated with your purchase of each *extra* compact disc starting from zero.

If the additional benefit you obtain from another unit of an item exceeds its price, you'll be better off buying the item rather than keeping your money to spend on something else. The dollar value you place on the satisfaction you obtain from another unit of an item is its **marginal benefit** to you. The marginal benefit of an item in dollars represents the maximum sum of money you're willing and able to give up to obtain one more unit of the item without becoming worse off or better off by doing so. The **marginal cost** of an item is the sacrifice you must make to obtain each extra unit. The marginal cost of buying another unit of an item is what you forgo to obtain one more unit. If you choose to buy a compact disc that costs $11.99, you forgo the opportunity to use that sum to purchase another item.

You're no worse off by buying one more compact disc, if the marginal cost of the disc doesn't exceed its marginal benefit. Examine your own behavior. Do you ever buy an item that would provide less benefit than the cost you must incur to acquire it? As a rational person, you'll always decide to purchase an additional unit of any good or service if its marginal benefit exceeds its marginal cost. By doing so you can obtain *net gains* from buying extra units of the good or service. A net gain is possible when the marginal benefit of a good exceeds its marginal cost. For example, if the marginal benefit to you of a compact disc is $20 and the price of a CD is only $11.99, then your net gain from buying it will be $20 − $11.99 = $8.01. As a

Marginal benefit:
The dollar value placed on the satisfaction obtained from another unit of an item.

Marginal cost:
The sacrifice made to obtain an additional unit of an item.

"I want you to know that emotion overrode reason."

rational person you'll never purchase another unit of a good if its marginal benefit is less than its marginal cost. For example, if the value you place on one more compact disc is only $10 and the price is still $11.99, then buying that extra disc will result in a negative net gain of $10 − $11.99 = −$1.99. Obviously, a negative net gain means that the purchase of the extra disc makes you *worse off*.

Rational behavior means that in deciding on any course of action, such as buying another unit of a good in a market, you compare the marginal benefit of that action with its marginal cost. As a rational person you undertake actions as long as the marginal cost doesn't exceed the marginal benefit. By behaving in this way you undertake all those activities that provide you with additional net gains in well-being but avoid all those activities for which additional net gain would be negative.

Using Marginal Analysis

To understand the decisions made by rational persons, we need to take the following steps:

1. Determine how a person evaluates the benefit and cost of the activity and how marginal benefit and marginal cost are likely to change as more or less of an activity is undertaken over a given period.
2. Figure out how changes in the economy or other factors (such as changes in prices) change the marginal benefit and marginal cost associated with various quantities. Analyzing the impact of changes in economic conditions on marginal benefits and marginal costs of transactions allows a model based on rational behavior to develop hypotheses about how changes in economic conditions affect choices and the magnitudes of economic variables.

The illustration in Box 2 summarizes the steps necessary to set up a model based on rational behavior.

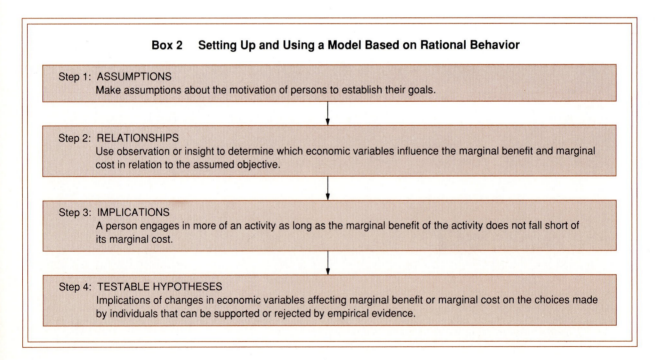

Box 2   Setting Up and Using a Model Based on Rational Behavior

Step 1: ASSUMPTIONS
Make assumptions about the motivation of persons to establish their goals.

Step 2: RELATIONSHIPS
Use observation or insight to determine which economic variables influence the marginal benefit and marginal cost in relation to the assumed objective.

Step 3: IMPLICATIONS
A person engages in more of an activity as long as the marginal benefit of the activity does not fall short of its marginal cost.

Step 4: TESTABLE HYPOTHESES
Implications of changes in economic variables affecting marginal benefit or marginal cost on the choices made by individuals that can be supported or rejected by empirical evidence.

Principles in Practice

Using a Graph to Analyze Rational Behavior

A bar graph can be used to show how the marginal benefit of an item is likely to vary as you buy more of it over a period. As you buy more of an item over a month, the extra satisfaction you get from each extra unit tends to decline because you tend to tire of the item.

The graph shows how the marginal benefit of compact discs might decline as you buy more CDs in a month. The top of each bar indicates the marginal benefit of a compact disc after you've already bought a certain number of CDs that month. For example, the marginal benefit of the first compact disc you buy in a month is $20. This is the maximum amount of expenditure on other goods you'd give up to acquire the first disc that month when you haven't purchased any previously that month.

Suppose the price of compact discs is currently $11.99. In the graph this is represented by a horizontal line drawn from $11.99 on the vertical axis. This line shows that each additional

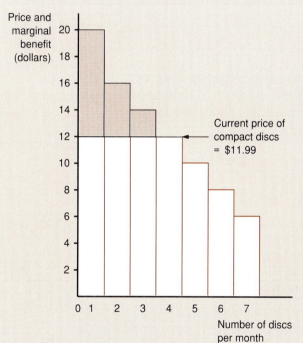

analysis therefore concludes that you'll purchase the first disc because its marginal benefit to you exceeds its marginal cost. The shaded portion of the bar *above* the price line represents the net gain of $8.01 from the first disc you buy each month.

The second bar indicates that the marginal benefit of a second disc is $16 when you've already bought one CD that month. Similarly, the marginal benefit of a third disc is $14 when you've already bought two that month. The marginal benefit of a fourth disc is $12 when you've already bought three that month. The graph indicates that the marginal benefit of a fifth disc that month is only $10 when you've already purchased four that month. Similarly, the marginal benefit of the sixth and seventh discs also declines.

How many discs will you buy this month? *A rational person continues purchasing an item up to the point at which there is no additional net gain.* It's easy to see that this condition isn't met until you've bought four discs that month. This is because the marginal benefit of the second disc exceeds its marginal cost, as do the marginal benefits of the third and fourth discs. As shown in the table, the net gain from purchasing a second disc would be $4.01 ($16 − $11.99 = $4.01). The net gain from purchasing a third disc would be $2.01. However, the marginal benefit of the fourth disc is just barely above the price. You do buy the fourth disc that month because you enjoy an additional net gain of 1¢ by doing so, as shown.

Monthly Purchases, Marginal Benefit, Marginal Cost, and Net Gain

Number of compact discs purchased	Marginal benefit of discs (dollars)	Price = marginal cost of discs (dollars)	Net gain from the additional disc (Marginal benefit minus marginal cost)
1	20	11.99	8.01
2	16	11.99	4.01
3	14	11.99	2.01
4	12	11.99	.01
5	10	11.99	− 1.99
6	8	11.99	− 3.99
7	6	11.99	− 5.99

disc will cost you $11.99 of expenditure on other items. The line therefore represents the marginal cost of each disc to you. Will you buy that first disc? To answer the question you must begin using the economic way of reasoning through marginal analysis. What is the marginal benefit of the first disc? The graph indicates that it is $20. As long as the marginal benefit exceeds the marginal cost, you'll enjoy a net gain by making the purchase. In the graph, the marginal benefit of $20 exceeds the marginal cost of $11.99. The net gain from exchanging your cash for the first disc will be $20 − $11.99 = $8.01. Marginal

Why will you not buy five discs that month? Look at the graph and notice that the marginal benefit of the fifth disc is only $10. This falls short of the marginal cost of $11.99. As shown in the table, the net gain from a fifth disc per month would be − $1.99. This is negative because the marginal benefit of the disc falls short of its marginal cost. The negative net gain for that disc implies that purchasing it would make you worse off. If you're rational, you therefore buy no more than four discs per month. As shown in the table, no positive net gain is possible from purchasing more than four discs per month.

1   What is rational behavior?

2   Explain why you can realize a net gain from undertaking more of an activity if the marginal benefit of that activity exceeds its marginal cost.

3   What can cause the marginal cost of purchasing an item to increase?

Summary

1. Economic theories are designed to establish cause-and-effect relationships to help explain how economies function.
2. An economic model is a simplified way of expressing how a sector of the economy functions. Models are based on assumptions about human behavior or the economic environment and are used to investigate relationships among economic variables using logic, graphs, or mathematics.
3. Economic models can be used to develop hypotheses about the relationships among economic variables. These hypotheses represent implications of economic models that can be supported or rejected by examining facts.
4. Economic theories based on rational behavior assume that persons consider the marginal benefits and marginal costs of their actions. Net gains are possible when the marginal benefit of additional activity exceeds the associated marginal cost. Rational persons seek out net gains by choosing to undertake more of an activity when its marginal benefit exceeds its marginal cost.
5. Rational persons compare the marginal benefit of additional purchases with the marginal cost. Consumers buy a good just up to the point at which the marginal benefit of doing so is equal to the marginal cost.
6. Any change that affects the marginal benefit or marginal cost curves for a rational person generally will result in a change in choices.

Key Terms and Concepts

Marginal analysis	*Ceteris paribus* (other things being equal)
Theory	Behavioral assumption
Variable	Rational behavior
Economic model	Marginal benefit
Hypothesis	Marginal cost

Problems and Applications

1. Suppose an economic theory sets up a model that implies that, *other things being equal,* an increase in interest rates will reduce the growth of national production. How can you test the validity of the theory?
2. An economic model to explain sales of automobiles establishes a relationship between the price of cars and the quantity buyers are willing to purchase. A hypothesis developed from the model is that whenever the price of cars goes up, the quantity buyers will buy will go down. During the year consumer income increases as the price of cars goes up. However, the quantity of cars sold also increases. Does this mean that the theory establishing the relationship between

the price of cars and the quantity consumers are willing and able to purchase is invalid?

3. In what ways do economic theories and models abstract from reality? Why are unrealistic models useful nonetheless?
4. Give an example of a behavioral assumption in an economic model. What is the purpose of using behavioral assumptions in economic models?
5. In what sense can an insane person or a criminal be regarded as engaging in rational behavior?
6. A person makes all his decisions by habit. This person considers neither the benefits nor the costs of his actions. Can this person be considered rational?
7. Suppose the marginal benefit to you of acquiring another suit this year is $200. If the price of suits is $250 and you are rational, will you buy another suit this year?
8. You currently choose to buy two compact discs per month with your income. The current price of CDs is $14.99. Other things being equal, explain why a drop in the price of discs to $12.99 next month is likely to increase the quantity you'll buy.

Suggested Readings

Milton Friedman, *Essays in Positive Economics,* Chicago: University of Chicago Press, 1953. This book contains many essays on the nature and functions of economic theory. The essay entitled "The Methodology of Positive Economics," pp. 2-43, is particularly enlightening.

Jack Hirschleifer, "The Expanding Domain of Economics," *American Economic Review,* 75, 6, December 1985, pp. 17-22. This is a lively discussion of the methods used by economists and the relevance of the concept of rationality to a wide variety of activities.

Donald N. McCloskey, *The Rhetoric of Economics,* Madison, Wis.: University of Wisconsin Press, 1985. This book provides a critical discussion of the methodology of modern economics that compares economics with other sciences.

A Forward Look

In the following chapter we examine production possibilities in an economy and the opportunity cost of choices. The analysis is designed to illuminate the concept of scarcity by examining the relationship between the quantity of a good made available over a year and its opportunity cost. In this way we can set forth the realities of the economic environment in which choices must be made to use resources.

Production Possibilities and Opportunity Cost

Scarcity, the ever-present imbalance between desires and the capability of satis-fying those desires, is the fundamental economic problem we all must grapple with: households, business firms, governments, and society at large. In this chapter we examine the influences on production possibilities for a society using the concept of opportunity cost to show how choices involve sacrifices. In this way we can paint a picture of the economic environment and the constraints we and other decision makers in the economy face each day in our personal and business lives.

As a student you deal with the problem of scarcity and the reality of opportunity cost every time you make choices about how to spend your income. The greater your income, the wider the range of goods and services you can choose from. Yet no matter how much income you have, the more of it you use to buy any one item, the less you can use to buy other items in any given period. Rich or poor, each of us must face the problem of scarcity and consider the opportunity cost of our choices.

Similarly, the better endowed a nation is with productive resources, the more opportunities its citizens have to choose among. However, no matter how rich in resources a nation might be, the basic economic problem of scarcity remains. This is because all resources are in some way limited, and in choosing to use resources for one purpose we sacrifice the opportunity to use them for alternative purposes.

1   Show how limited available technology and scarce resources imply limited production possibilities over a period.
2   Demonstrate that the use of productive capacity to make more of any one good or service available involves sacrificing the opportunity to make more of other items available.
3   Discuss the basic determinants of a nation's production possibilities and how these can expand over time.
4   Understand the concept of productive efficiency and discuss its significance.
5   Demonstrate that when you use income over a period to buy more of one item, you sacrifice the opportunity to buy more of some other item over the period.

Resources, Technology, and Production Possibilities

Production is the process of using the services of labor and other resources to make goods and services available. **Economic resources** are the *inputs* used in the process of production. The *outputs* are the goods and services made available for our use. Economic resources are divided into four broad categories:

Economic resources:
The inputs used in the process of production.

1. **Labor** represents the services of human beings in the production of goods and services. Both physical and mental effort are included in this category. The number of workers, their general education, training, and skills, and their motivation to work are prime determinants of a nation's productive capability. The services of factory workers, truck drivers, salespeople, college professors, police officers, and physicians are all part of a nation's labor resources.

Labor:
The physical and mental efforts of human beings in the production of goods and services.

2. **Capital** is the equipment, tools, structures, machinery, vehicles, materials, and skills created to help produce goods and services.[1] Don't confuse capital resources with financial resources. As you'll see later, firms often raise funds to acquire new capital by borrowing money or issuing new corporate stock. However, the funds acquired in this way are not an input into production. They merely represent the purchasing power needed to build or purchase new capital.

Capital:
The equipment, tools, structures, machinery, vehicles, materials, and skills created to help produce goods and services.

3. **Natural resources** include land used as sites for structures, ports, and other facilities, as well as natural materials that are used in crude form in production. Examples of land and other natural resources are farmland, industrial sites, deposits of minerals and petroleum, harbors, navigable rivers, sources of hydroelectric power, timber, and the advantages of a regional climate.

Natural resources:
Acreage and the physical terrain used to locate structures, ports, and other facilities; also, natural materials that are used in crude form in production.

4. **Entrepreneurship** is the talent to develop products and processes and to organize production to make goods and services available. Entrepreneurs are innovators and risk-takers. Entrepreneurs in business seek to earn profits by satisfying the desires of consumers and developing better and less costly ways of satisfying those desires. They undertake the tasks necessary to get the process of production started and make many of the decisions relating to the use of inputs.

Entrepreneurship:
The talent to develop products and processes and to organize production of goods and services.

[1]Capital inputs can be physical or human. A portion of the labor used in production includes human capital, which represents skills acquired for the purpose of producing medical, engineering, legal, and other services.

Nations differ in their endowments of economic resources. The United States is a very rich country in the sense that it has many natural resources, a highly skilled labor force, and a great deal of capital. Many nations lack the skilled labor force, entrepreneurial ability, and capital equipment necessary to enjoy even a fraction of the goods and services per person that we take for granted in the United States. Scarcity is therefore a matter of degree. It is, however, ever present in rich and poor nations alike given our tendency as human beings to want more than we have.

Technology

Technology:
The knowledge of how to produce goods and services.

Technology is the knowledge of how to produce goods and services. Improved technology can streamline production or allow more goods and services to be produced from a given quantity of economic resources. Advances in technology help us cope with the problems of scarcity by making workers, capital, and land more productive. For example, as a result of improvements in the technology of agriculture, the output of farms in the United States rose by 150% between 1930 and 1980 while the quantity of inputs in agriculture increased by only 7%. In the near future the introduction of superconducting materials will allow transmission of electricity over long distances without loss of energy. This means that a given amount of capital, fuel, and workers will be able to generate significantly more electricity than they can now. Development of materials that can withstand high temperatures and pressures will enable new jet engines to build more thrust using less fuel. This will make it possible for commercial aircraft to travel faster without using more fuel per mile and without sacrificing safety.

Closer to home, advances in electronics and software have permitted the development of something you may own yourself: a personal computer and printer. It's amazing how much more quickly you can write a term paper on your PC than students of a generation ago could with the cumbersome manual electric typewriters they used in college!

The Production Possibilities Curve

You'll see the problem of scarcity more clearly with the aid of a simple model whose purpose is to examine the relationship between the production of goods and services and the availability and use of resources. In the analysis we make the following assumptions:

1. *The quantity and quality of economic resources available for use during the year are fixed.* There is a given amount of labor, capital, natural resources, and entrepreneurial ability available for use during the year. This limits the extent to which our desires for goods and services can be satisfied during the year.

2. *There are two broad classes of outputs we can produce with available economic resources over the year: food and clothing.* We make the assumption of only two products to simplify the analysis while showing the basic tradeoffs we must consider while coping with the problem of scarcity.

3. *Some inputs are better adapted to the production of one good than to the production of the other.* A pickup truck can as easily be used to transport materials needed to produce clothing as to transport materials needed to produce food. However, a loom that's used to weave cloth is virtually useless in the production of food. The loom might be dismantled and its parts used in agricultural machinery, but it's

much more productive when used intact to manufacture clothing. Similarly, some workers have skills that are better adapted to one use than the other. Transferring a skilled tailor from clothing to food production will cause a greater loss in output of clothing than when a truck driver's labor is transferred from delivering clothing to delivering food. Transferring the labor of an experienced farmer from agricultural to clothing production results in a greater loss in food output than does transferring the labor of a crop picker. The more specialized a worker, the higher the opportunity cost of transferring him or her to an area out of that specialty.

4. *Technology is fixed and does not advance during the year.* In general, advances in technology take more than 1 year to develop. In assuming fixed technology, we're implying that the productiveness of inputs doesn't change during the year as a result of improved knowledge or technical advances.

Given available resources, their quality, and current technology, there is a limited amount of any one good that can be produced in an economy given the output of other goods. A **production possibilities curve** shows this graphically. The curve shows the maximum possible output of one good that can be produced with available resources given the output of the alternative good over a period. A production possibilities curve for food and clothing shows the maximum number of garments that can be produced each year given each possible level of food production. The curve shows the *options* available to produce various combinations of goods and services under current technology during a year, assuming the resources are fully utilitized.

Given the assumptions made above, we can derive a production possibilities curve using hypothetical data. Suppose we're considering whether to devote all resources to the production of food or to the manufacture of clothing. If we devote all resources to food production in a year, no clothing can be produced that year.

The table in Box 1 shows that if all resources were used to produce food during the year, the maximum possible output would be 55,000 tons that year. This corresponds to production possibility I in the table, for which clothing output is zero and food output is 55,000 tons. Alternatively, we might interpret production possibility I as implying that if food output were 55,000 tons, the maximum possible clothing output during the year would be zero. The graph in Box 1 plots this production possibility, labeled *I,* on a set of axes on which food output is measured on the vertical axis and clothing output is measured on the horizontal axis.

Now let's consider the option of producing less food and more clothing for the year. Because resources are scarce, increasing the annual output of clothing means we must sacrifice some of the annual output of food. Production possibility II consists of 10,000 garments and 50,000 tons of food per year. The opportunity cost of producing 10,000 garments per year is the 5,000 tons of food we must sacrifice to make that number of garments available. Production possibility II is also graphed in Box 1 and is labeled as point *II.*

Production possibility III shows the option available to us if 20,000 garments are produced per year. This option would require us to allocate still more resources away from food production to use in clothing production. If we chose this option, maximum possible food output would only be 40,000 tons per year. Notice that increasing clothing production by an additional 10,000 garments per year results in a 10,000-ton reduction in food output; this exceeds the 5,000-ton reduction that was required to produce the first 10,000 garments. The opportunity cost of the second 10,000 garments exceeds the opportunity cost of the first 10,000 garments.

Production possibilities curve: Shows the maximum possible output of one good that can be produced with available resources given the output of an alternative good over a period.

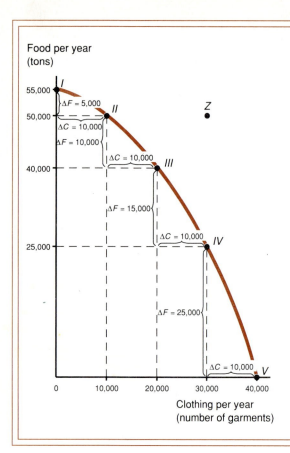

Food per year
(tons)

Box 1   A Production Possibilities Curve

Points on this production possibilities curve show alternative combinations of clothing and food that can be produced in an economy assuming that no other products are made. Each point on the curve gives the maximum amount of one good that can be produced given the output of the other good. To reach a point on the curve, resources must be fully utilized and there must be no waste or mismanagement in production.

Annual Production Possibilities for Food and Clothing*

Type of good	Production possibilities				
	I	II	III	IV	V
Food per year (tons)	55,000	50,000	40,000	25,000	0
Clothing per year (number of garments)	0	10,000	20,000	30,000	40,000

* Hypothetical data assuming full utilization of economic resources and no waste or mismanagement in production.

Clothing per year
(number of garments)

This pattern of increasing opportunity cost continues as we allocate more resources away from food production and toward clothing production, as you can see in the table in Box 1. At production possibility IV, increasing the output of clothing from 20,000 to 30,000 garments per year means we sacrifice an additional 15,000 tons of food per year. Finally, production possibility V shows that the output of food would fall to zero if we used our resources to produce 40,000 garments per year. The opportunity cost of increasing the production of clothing from 30,000 to 40,000 garments per year is the 25,000 tons of food we must sacrifice.

The points corresponding to production possibilities III, IV, and V are also plotted as points in the graph in Box 1. A smooth line has been drawn through the points corresponding to production possibilities I to V. The result is a production possibilities curve showing the maximum possible output of food for each possible output of clothing during the year given available resources and technology. Points lying outside the area enclosed by the production possibilities curve and the two axes, such as Z, represent unattainable combinations of food and clothing per year. Point Z corresponds to 50,000 tons of food and 30,000 garments per year. The economy lacks the resources or technology to produce the annual combinations of food and clothing represented by points like Z. When resources are used to produce 50,000 tons of food, the maximum amount of clothing that can be produced during the year is 10,000 garments.

All points on or within the production possibilities curve represent annual combinations of goods that can be produced. However, points *within* the area bounded by the curve and the two axes represent combinations of the two goods that correspond to *less than* the maximum possible annual production of one of the goods given the annual production of the other. Our economy might end up at a point within the area bounded by the curve and the axes if it did not utilize all the productive resources available or if resources were wasted or mismanaged.

The production possibilities curve therefore illustrates the idea of scarcity in two important ways. First, it shows that only a limited number of production possibilities exist over a year given available resources and technology. The possibilities are represented by points within and on the curve. Second, it shows that once the maximum amount of any one good is produced per year, given the output of the other good per year, additional annual production of the first good requires an annual reduction in the output of the other.

The Law of Increasing Costs

The table in Box 2 shows the opportunity cost of each 10,000-garment batch of clothing production for the economy. The first column of the table shows the annual output of clothing. The second column shows the increase in clothing output. The little triangle Δ is the Greek letter delta that is used to mean *change in* the variable *C*. In this case *C* stands for clothing. When output increases from zero to 10,000 garments per year, the change in clothing production is $\Delta C = 10,000$. To obtain

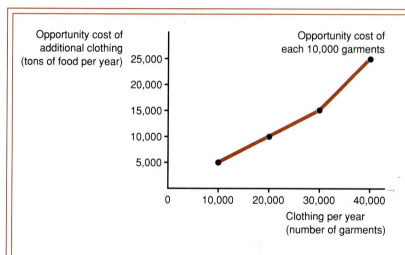

Box 2   Increasing Opportunity Cost of Additional Clothing

The opportunity cost of each 10,000-garment batch of clothing increases as more clothing is produced per year.

Opportunity Cost of Successive 10,000-Garment Batches of Clothing

Annual output of clothing (number of garments)	Increase in clothing output (number of garments) = ΔC	Opportunity cost of each successive 10,000 garments = ΔF
0		
10,000	10,000	5,000 tons of food per year
20,000	10,000	10,000 tons of food per year
30,000	10,000	15,000 tons of food per year
40,000	10,000	25,000 tons of food per year

that increase in the output of clothing, the opportunity cost is 5,000 tons of food per year. The change in food output as the economy moves from point *I* to point *II* on the production possibilities curve in Box 1 is $\Delta F = 5,000$ tons, as shown in the last column of the table in Box 2. By sacrificing 5,000 tons of food per year the economy moves from point *I* to point *II* on its production possibilities curve in Box 1.

The last column of the table in Box 2 shows how the opportunity cost of each successive batch of 10,000 garments per year increases as we allocate more resources from food to clothing production during the year. The graph in Box 2 plots the opportunity cost of each 10,000-garment batch of clothing per year in terms of food sacrificed for each level of annual clothing production.[2] An upward-sloping curve has been fitted through the points to show how opportunity costs of additional clothing production increase.

A basic reason that costs increase with successive units of output is the existence of specialized inputs that are more productive in a particular use. As we increase clothing production during the year, we have to sacrifice more and more food for each successive increment in the number of garments produced per year. You can see this by concentrating on the land that would have to be reallocated to building clothing factories and growing the fibers used to make cloth. At first the land least specialized to growing food could be reallocated to clothing production. As more fertile food land is transferred for successive increments in the annual production of clothing, the loss per acre transferred increases simply because the land more adapted to food production produces more food per acre than the less specialized land.

Similarly, at first the vehicles and equipment least specialized in the production of food, such as trucks and tractors, can be transferred at low opportunity cost to clothing production. However, as we produce more clothing, we must adapt more specialized agricultural machinery, such as combines, for use in clothing production. Because this type of machinery is more productive in food than in clothing production, the opportunity cost of additional clothing increases in terms of food sacrificed. Likewise, as clothing output increases, at first the workers least specialized in agricultural production are transferred to clothing production. As more and more workers are required to produce additional clothing, the more skilled and therefore more productive workers must be transferred out of food production. This increases the amount of food we must sacrifice to produce extra units of clothing.

Law of increasing costs:
States that the opportunity cost of each additional unit of output of a good over a period increases as more of that good is produced.

The **law of increasing costs** states that the opportunity cost of each additional unit of output of a good over a period increases as more of that good is produced. This law is an implication of the assumption that some economic resources are more suited than others to the production of particular goods. Because this implication has been widely supported by empirical evidence, it is called a "law."

The concave shape of the production possibilities curve in Box 2 reflects the law of increasing costs. The slope of the curve at any point is $\Delta F/\Delta C$ where ΔF is the annual reduction in food output necessary for each extra garment per year. As you move from point *I* toward point *V*, the curve becomes steeper, reflecting the increase in the sacrifice of food, ΔF, required for each additional one-unit increase in clothing output.

The law of increasing costs is relevant to the world we live in. For example, if the United States were to engage in a military buildup, the opportunity cost of de-

---

[2] The opportunity cost of each 10,000-garment batch of clothing is the marginal cost of clothing when the units of clothing are 10,000-garment packages.

CHAPTER 3 Production Possibilities and Opportunity Cost

voting more and more resources to the military would increase. During wartime the cost of additional military goods increases rapidly as more resources specialized in the production of nonmilitary goods are reallocated to military use.

Concept Check

1 **What do points on a production possibilities curve show?**

2 **Use a production possibilities curve to show how an increase in resources devoted to producing military goods implies that annual availability of such nonmilitary goods as housing, private automobiles, and clothing is reduced.**

3 **What is the law of increasing costs, and how is it illustrated by the shape of a nation's production possibilities curve?**

Productive Efficiency

We can use the production possibilities curve to show the consequences of not fully utilizing or of mismanaging economic resources in a nation. For example, suppose a nation's labor force isn't fully utilized in production. This generally occurs when the unemployment rate is excessively high. While some unemployment is normal because people who have just entered the labor force or have lost their previous job take time to search for a new job, excessive unemployment affects everyone in the economy. We can use the production possibilities curve to show why excessive unemployment of labor is a matter of concern to all of us and not just those who are unfortunate enough to be out of work.

Suppose it's possible to employ more workers in the production of clothing without withdrawing workers from food production. This implies that we have enough resources to increase the annual output of garments without any corresponding reduction in annual food output. Alternatively, we can use idle resources to produce more food without reducing clothing production. When resources are idle, we're not achieving our full productive potential: we could increase the output of all or some goods without decreasing the production of others. The basic reason for concern about excessive unemployment and idle factories is that it harms everyone by preventing the economy from achieving production possibilities for which it has the capacity.

Excessive unemployment of labor or failure to fully utilize capital and natural resources implies that an economy is operating at a point *within* rather than on its production possibilities curve. You can see this in the graph in Box 3. If the economy were not fully utilizing its economic resources, actual annual production of food and clothing might correspond to a point like *R* in the graph. At that point we could produce more food by moving to point *II* without sacrificing any clothing each year. Alternatively, we could produce more clothing without sacrificing any food each year by moving to point *III*. If resources were not fully utilized, we could attain all combinations of the two goods within the shaded triangular area enclosed by the points *R, II,* and *III* without acquiring more resources or without an advance in technology.

Mismanagement of economic resources also causes the economy to operate within its production possibilities curve. Suppose all economic resources are being utilized in production but aren't managed so that we obtain the maximum amount of any one good given the output of other goods under existing technology. In the graph in Box 3, mismanaging resources would result in a point like *R*. As was the case for excessive unemployment, all the combinations of clothing and food represented by points within the shaded triangular area are possible without additional resources or improvement in technical know-how. Sloppy management therefore also prevents an economy from attaining production possibilities for which it has the capability.

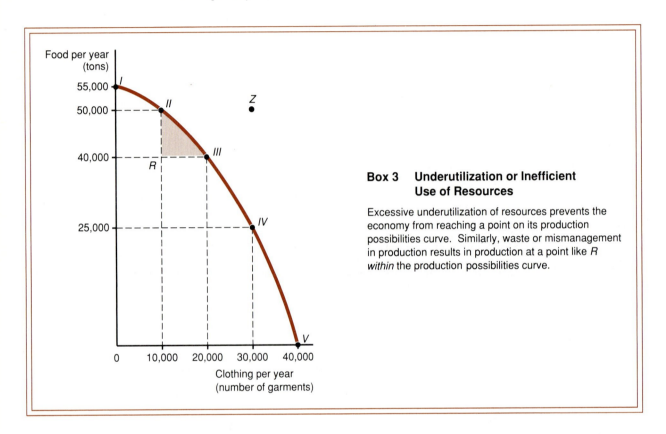

Box 3   Underutilization or Inefficient Use of Resources

Excessive underutilization of resources prevents the economy from reaching a point on its production possibilities curve. Similarly, waste or mismanagement in production results in production at a point like *R* *within* the production possibilities curve.

Productive efficiency:
Attained when the maximum possible output of any one good is produced given the output of other goods. At this point it is not possible to reallocate economic resources to increase the output of any single good or service without decreasing the output of some other good or service.

Productive efficiency is attained when the maximum possible output of any one good is produced given the output of other goods. Attainment of productive efficiency means we can't reallocate economic resources so as to increase the output of any single good or service without decreasing the output of some other good or service. Points on a production possibilities curve represent efficient use of productive resources, because once on the curve it's impossible to increase the output of one good without reducing the output of the other.

The Division of Labor and Productive Efficiency

Division of labor:
The specialization of workers in particular tasks that are part of a larger undertaking to accomplish a given objective.

One factor that contributes to productive efficiency is the **division of labor,** which is the specialization of workers in particular tasks that are part of a larger undertaking to accomplish a given objective. By specializing, workers become more proficient at their jobs. The division of labor lets factories use mass production techniques that allow workers to produce more.

CHAPTER 3 Production Possibilities and Opportunity Cost

Principles in Practice

Avoiding Waste and Mismanagement in Production: The Toyota *Kan-ban* System

Whether they're making linguini or nuclear weapons, managers of business firms continually grapple with the problem of waste and mismanagement in production. By eliminating waste, firms can keep costs down by ensuring that the maximum output of goods is obtained from any combination of resources employed over a given period.

In recent years the production management techniques used by Japanese industrial firms have been highly successful in avoiding the waste of resources in production. For example, the Toyota Motor Corporation of Japan has developed a management system designed to *eliminate surplus workers from assembly line operations.* Workers on assembly lines for various products are assigned daily standardized tasks. They are instructed to leave the assembly line and report to a specific area in the factory after their daily tasks are completed. Company managers keep records of the various assembly lines to see where there's a surplus of labor. Workers on assembly lines with surpluses are permanently reassigned to other tasks to make sure they're adequately utilized.*

Another key to the Toyota production management system is the *Kan-ban,* which is a work order sheet accompanying materials used in production. The *Kan-ban* is issued by managers to foremen at various stages of the production process to ensure that at all times there's an adequate supply of materials and parts to produce the final product. The *Kan-ban* is also used to make sure there's no surplus of materials at any time. The goal is to produce various items at any given time with the minimum required amount of materials on hand (called an *inventory*).

The Toyota system also seeks to motivate workers to suggest improvements in work procedures that will further eliminate waste in production. The low parts inventory is supplemented with techniques to increase flexibility in production by modifying supplies of materials on short notice. Workers are trained to be proficient in a variety of tasks.

You can understand the goals of the Toyota system with the aid of the production possibilities curve shown in the graph. The system has three major goals:

1. *The system seeks to use resources in ways that result in the attainment of points on the production possibilities curve for each factory.* This is accomplished by making sure that available materials and labor services are utilized in ways to allow the greatest output of any one item, say a Camry sedan, given the output of any other product, say a 4 × 4 four-wheel-drive vehicle. In the graph this means avoiding points like *W* and aiming for points on the curve like *A.* This is accomplished by eliminating surplus labor and material over any given production period. The *Kan-ban* system saves resources by preventing idle inventories, which waste material

inputs, and by economizing on scarce storage space within factories. Space that would have been allocated to inventory storage can be used for machines and equipment that can turn out more cars per year. Lower inventories contribute to higher profits by allowing the firm to invest idle funds that would otherwise be used to purchase and store inventories of materials, parts, and components. This decreases the opportunity cost of production.

2. *The system seeks to attain maximum flexibility in moving from one point on the production possibilities curve like* A *to another point like* B. For example, if the firm suddenly receives an increase in orders for 4 × 4s and a decrease in orders for Camrys, its small-lot production techniques enable it to quickly turn out the parts to produce the 4 × 4s instead of the Camrys. Its flexible work force can easily adapt to the new production requirements because they're trained to be skilled in a variety of tasks.

3. *The system seeks worker input to change production techniques in ways that move the production possibilities curve outward.* Improvements in technical know-how or changes in organization suggested by workers can allow the firm to attain points like *Z* that wouldn't otherwise be possible. Workers often form their own groups to suggest ways to prevent product defects and slowdowns in production. The small-lot production system contributes to rapid feedback of mistakes in production. In a small lot, in which parts are used almost immediately, worker mistakes are quickly noticed. This provides incentives to workers to work more effectively and allows improvements to be noticed almost immediately.

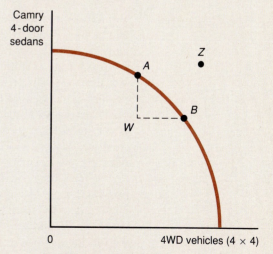

*For an in-depth discussion of Japanese management techniques, see Eiji Ogawa, *Modern Production Management: A Japanese Experience,* Tokyo: Asian Productivity Organization, 1984.

By dividing tasks, a factory obtains much more output per worker than if each worker had to build each unit of an entire finished product alone. For example, suppose you were given all the responsibility for constructing an automobile. You'd have to mold the steel, assemble the body, chassis, and motor, and do all interior assembly. You'd have to be an expert in welding, electrical wiring, painting, upholstering, and other tasks. Even if you were skilled in all these operations, it might take you as long as a year to produce a finished automobile.

With a division of labor, the numerous tasks involved in producing a car are assigned to many workers, each specializing in one task. By dividing tasks, managers can use sophisticated machinery and equipment and produce many more cars than would be possible if each worker in the factory tried to do all the tasks. The division of labor exists in a broader sense throughout the economy. People with specialized skills function as physicians, police officers, architects, musicians, farmers, and so on.

Economic Growth: Expanding Production Possibilities

Economic growth:
The expansion in production possibilities that results from increased availability and increased productivity of economic resources.

From year to year, growth in available supplies of economic resources, improvements in resource quality, and advances in technology can expand production possibilities in a society. **Economic growth** is the expansion in production possibilities that results from increased availability and increased productivity of economic resources. When economic growth occurs over time, the production possibilities curve will shift outward. This means that the economy will be able to produce more of all goods. In this section we'll consider three sources of economic growth:

1. Increased quantities of economic resources
2. Improved quality of economic resources
3. Advances in technology

Annual Growth in Available Resources

An increase in available economic resources allows us to produce more in an economy. Other things being equal, the more workers willing and able to work, the more capital, and the more land, the greater the production possibilities. This means the production possibilities curve will shift outward in response to an increase in available economic resources, as you can see in the graph in Box 4. Production possibilities that were previously unattainable are now feasible. Increases in economic resources available for production will therefore result in a new production possibilities curve. The shaded area in the graph represents previously unattainable combinations of food and clothing that become feasible when resources become more plentiful or their quality improves.

The availability of new capital is especially effective in pushing the production possibilities curve outward. This is because new capital often complements labor, land, and other natural resources. This means that additional capital tends to increase the *productivity* of available labor and land. For example, supplying workers with more and better equipment increases the *output per worker*. Similarly, using more capital per acre of farmland can be very effective in increasing the production of *food per acre*. Growth in capital is an especially important determinant of our well-being as individuals. This is because increases in capital per worker re-

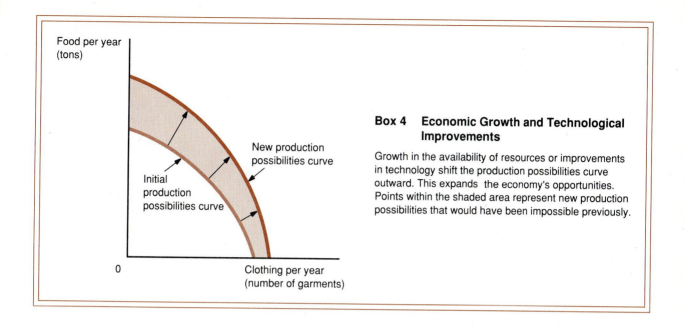

Box 4   Economic Growth and Technological Improvements

Growth in the availability of resources or improvements in technology shift the production possibilities curve outward. This expands the economy's opportunities. Points within the shaded area represent new production possibilities that would have been impossible previously.

sult in more goods per person, thereby increasing the material well-being of each of us.

By the same token, the destruction of economic resources in a nation will move the production possibilities curve inward. For example, a war destroys both human and physical resources, causing the production possibilities curve to shrink inward. A sudden decrease in the availability of a key input into production could also cause the production possibilities curve to shift inward. For example, if the United States found its fuel supplies cut in half because of difficulty in obtaining crude oil, our production possibilities curve would shift inward, making some previously attainable production possibilities no longer feasible.

Improved Quality of Inputs

Improvement in skills, education, or training of the labor force can also increase the output obtainable from any given combination of inputs. Devoting more economic resources to education and job training in the current year pays off in the future in terms of greater production possibilities. However, those of us who pursue more education must forgo current opportunities to work full time. Recall the analysis of the opportunity cost of going to college in Chapter 1. The opportunity cost to the economy of more education is the production lost when you and others attend college rather than immediately entering the work force after graduating from high school. The loss in current output from more education is often more than made up by an increase in future output, assuming that college graduates are more productive than high school graduates.

Similarly, the quality of capital also improves as new machines are introduced that can accomplish more tasks or accomplish tasks more quickly or more accurately. Improvements in the quality of capital require advances in technology, which is the next source of economic growth we'll consider.

Improvements in Technology

Increased productive potential resulting from the development of new technologies is a very important source of economic growth. For example, technological improvements that increase the speed of computers mean that a given quantity of computers can process more information. One worker operating a more advanced computer can do the job that two or more workers were required for previously. Similarly, improvements in agricultural technology mean that a given quantity of land, labor, and capital can produce more food and fiber.

As in the case of improvements in worker skills, there is a cost associated with development of new technologies. To conduct research and development to advance technology, we must withdraw resources from current production of goods for immediate consumption. By sacrificing current consumption opportunities, however, we gain future production possibilities that we otherwise wouldn't attain.

Surprisingly, technological advances in one sector of the economy cause gains in production possibilities in other sectors as well. For example, suppose there's a technological advance in the food sector of the economy but not in the clothing sector. Improved technology in food production means that for any given quantity of food output *more* economic resources will now be available for clothing production, other things being equal. For any given positive quantity of food output, we can produce more clothing output than before. You can see this effect in the graph in Box 5, where the production possibilities curve moves upward but its intercept on the clothing axis doesn't change. In other words, if we were to devote all our resources to clothing production after the advance in technology in food production, we wouldn't be able to produce more clothing than before. However, the advance in food technology means we can devote more of our available resources to clothing production for any given amount of food produced. As a result, the maximum amount of clothing corresponding to any given amount of food output is now greater. The shaded area in the graph represents the production possibilities of both food *and* clothing gained from a technological advance in food production. In fact, improvements in agricultural technology in the United States and other nations have freed labor so it can be employed in the production of other goods and services.

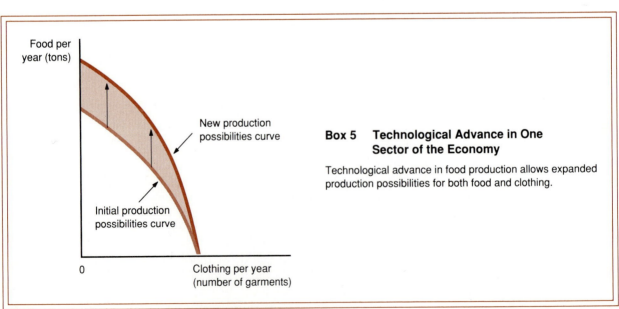

Box 5 Technological Advance in One Sector of the Economy

Technological advance in food production allows expanded production possibilities for both food and clothing.

Production for the Present vs. Production for the Future: A Basic Economic Choice

In each economy decisions must be made about how to allocate currently available resources between uses that provide goods for current consumption and uses that provide goods for future consumption. Education, new structures and equipment to be used in production, and research for and development of new technologies are *investments* in future production possibilities. The gain from these investments is the expansion in production possibilities they allow in the future.

The graphs in Box 6 show how the choice to allocate available economic resources to production of current consumption goods as opposed to investments during a year affects future production possibilities. Suppose the current production possibilities for these two alternative uses of currently available resources are identical in the two nations. However, decisions in nation A result in a choice of point A on its initial production possibilities curve, which involves the sacrifice of ΔC_A units of consumption goods to produce I_A units of investment goods. The citizens in nation B end up choosing point B on their production possibilities curve in the current year. They sacrifice a smaller amount of consumption goods, ΔC_B, which is less than ΔC_A, but produce only I_B units of investment goods, which is less than I_A. In the future, citizens of nation A are rewarded for their sacrifice of current consumption possibilities with a greater outward shift of their production possibilities curve than that enjoyed by citizens of nation B.

In addition to deciding what to produce, how to produce it, and who will receive it, each economy also must decide what and how much it will sacrifice today to make investments that expand future production possibilities.

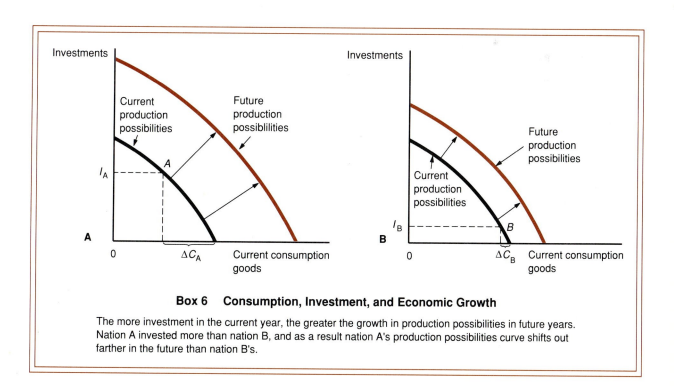

Box 6   Consumption, Investment, and Economic Growth

The more investment in the current year, the greater the growth in production possibilities in future years. Nation A invested more than nation B, and as a result nation A's production possibilities curve shifts out farther in the future than nation B's.

1   How must resources be used to achieve productive efficiency in a nation?

2   A nation is currently producing a combination of goods and services corresponding to a point inside its production possibilities curve. What does this imply about its use of resources?

3   What can cause the production possibilities curve to shift outward? What does an outward shift of the curve imply about a nation's production possibilities?

Personal Budgeting and the Opportunity Cost of Choices

Now that you understand the basic constraints the economy faces each year, let's focus on the constraints we as individuals face in satisfying our desires. Few of us have enough income to buy everything we want each month. Scarcity of both resources and time to satisfy all wants is a common personal problem. Most students have pretty tight budgets that allow them to buy only a small portion of what they want. For example, suppose you receive a monthly allowance from your parents of $100 that you spend entirely on gasoline and records. The rest of your living expenses, such as room and board at the university, are paid directly by your parents. In this simple example, you therefore have only two alternatives on which you're interested in spending your available income: gasoline and records.

Suppose the price of gasoline is $1 per gallon and the price of records is $5 each. It's now possible to derive the combinations of these two goods that you can afford with your $100 monthly income. The table in Box 7 shows five possible combinations of gasoline and records per month you can buy if you spend all of your $100 monthly income on these two items. For example, it's feasible to consume 100 gal-

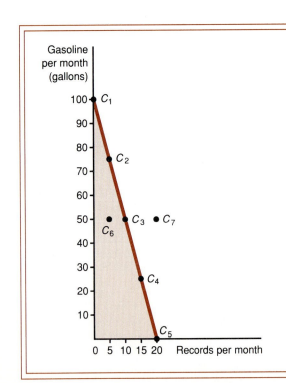

Box 7   A Budget Line

Points on the budget line give all the combinations of two goods that can be purchased given income and the prices of the two goods assuming that all income is spent.

Consumption*

Good	C_1	C_2	C_3	C_4	C_5
Gasoline (gallons)	100	75	50	25	0
Records (number)	0	5	10	15	20
Total monthly expenditure	$100	$100	$100	$100	$100

*Monthly possible consumption of gasoline and records when monthly income is $100, the price of gasoline is $1 per gallon, and the price of each record is $5.

lons of gasoline per month. However, because gasoline costs $1 per gallon, you'd spend all your monthly income on gasoline and forgo the opportunity to buy records that month. This option is labeled C_1. It's plotted in the graph in Box 7 on a set of axes for which the monthly quantity of gasoline purchased is measured on the vertical axis while the monthly quantity of records purchased is measured on the horizontal axis. You also have the opportunity to choose a point like C_5. At that point you'd be consuming 20 records per month but would have no income left to buy gasoline.

The options for spending your income corresponding to points C_2, C_3, and C_4 have also been plotted on the graph in Box 7. The monthly **budget line** shows your opportunities to purchase two items, such as gasoline and records, if you spend all your monthly income on these two items at their current prices. With your current income and at current prices it's possible to buy all combinations of records and gasoline on or below the budget line. Of course, if you choose a point below the line, you'll have some of your monthly income left over to save or spend on other items. If you choose a point like C_6, corresponding to 50 gallons of gasoline and five records per month, you'll be spending $50 on gasoline and $25 on records for a total monthly outlay of $75, leaving $25 to save or spend on other items.

Budget line:
Shows an individual's opportunities to purchase two goods if he spends all of his monthly income on these two goods at their current prices.

On the other hand, a point like C_7 is unattainable with your current monthly income given the current prices of gasoline and records. Point C_7 corresponds to 20 records, which would cost $100, and 50 gallons of gasoline, which would cost $50. This combination is infeasible because it would require a monthly expenditure of $150, which exceeds your available $100 income.

The budget line therefore shows certain combinations of items are unattainable given your limited income and the prices of the items. The shaded area represents your monthly opportunities to purchase gasoline and records. Of course, an increase in your income shifts the budget line outward given the prices of the two items. To see this, recalculate your possible consumption options in the table in Box 7 when your income increases to $200 per month. An equal percentage decrease in the prices of both items would also shift the curve outward by increasing the quantities of the items you could buy with your $100 monthly income. To see this, recalculate the points on your budget line when the price of gasoline is only 50¢ per gallon and the price of records is $2.50. Conversely, a decrease in income or an equal percentage increase in the prices of both items shifts the budget line inward. Inflation in the prices of goods consumed decreases the opportunities available to consumers with fixed money income. This is one of the harmful effects of inflation.

The Opportunity Cost of Purchasing Goods

If you move along the budget line from C_1 to C_5, each extra record you buy will absorb $5 of your monthly income. Because the price of gasoline is $1 per gallon, each extra record you buy per month involves the sacrifice of 5 gallons of gasoline. *The opportunity cost of each extra record is therefore always 5 gallons of gasoline at the current prices of these two items.*

In general, the opportunity cost of a record or any other item depends on its price relative to the price of the item you give up to purchase more of the item you choose. For example, if the price of records were $5 each and the price of gasoline were $1 per gallon, the opportunity cost of each record would be 5 gallons of gasoline. If instead the price of records were $10 each and the price of gasoline were $2 per gallon, the opportunity cost of records would *still* be 5 gallons of gasoline. This might surprise you, because the money cost^of units of both items goes up in each case. However, the opportunity cost of an item depends on the *quantity* of the alternative item you forgo when you purchase more of the item you choose. When the price of gasoline is $2 and the price of a record is $10, each record you buy results in the sacrifice of 5 gallons of gasoline, because you could have used the $10 to buy that amount of gasoline.

Similarly, the opportunity cost of each gallon of gasoline is one fifth of a record when the price of gasoline is $1 per gallon and the price of records is $5. For each 5 gallons of gasoline you buy each month, you sacrifice the opportunity to buy one record.

Scarcity and Tradeoffs

We deal every day with the tradeoffs implied by scarcity. Both production possibilities for a society and options for us as individuals to spend our available income are limited over any given period. In Chapter 1 we discussed the questions of what to produce, how to produce it, and to whom goods and services will be distributed. Now you can understand these questions better within the context of the constraints a nation faces. The problem of *what to produce* involves making decisions that eventually result in achievement of a particular production possibility. The problem of *how to produce it* affects the ability of participants in an economy to get to a point on their production possibilities curve instead of below the curve. If efficient methods are employed to produce any given output and economic resources are fully utilized, then the maximum possible output of any one good will be attained given the output of other goods. Given current prices for goods and services, *who gets what is produced* depends on the way income is distributed among those of us in an economy. Naturally, the greater our income, the greater our options for consumption.

Summary

1. Production is the process of using economic resources to make goods and services available.
2. A production possibilities curve shows the maximum possible output of any one good that can be produced over a period of time with available economic resources and existing technology, given the output of other goods.
3. The law of increasing costs implies that the opportunity costs of extra production of any one good in an economy will increase as more and more specialized resources best suited for the production of other goods are reallocated away from their best use.
4. Not fully utilizing or mismanaging economic resources prevents the economy from achieving its full output potential and results in attainment of a point below the production possibilities curve.
5. Increased availability of labor, capital, and natural resources, and improvements in technology or in worker skills, can shift a nation's production possibilities curve outward.
6. A budget line shows the combinations of goods and services a consumer with limited income can purchase over a period given the prices of goods desired. The opportunity cost of consuming more of any one good is the quantity of the next best alternative good that is sacrificed.

Key Terms and Concepts

Economic resources   Production possibilities curve
Labor   Law of increasing costs
Capital   Productive efficiency
Natural resources   Division of labor
Entrepreneurship   Economic growth
Technology   Budget line

Problems and Applications

1. The United States is a rich and powerful nation with a skilled and productive labor force and a great deal of capital. Some less developed nations have few skilled workers and little capital available. Why is scarcity an economic problem in rich and poor nations alike?

2. Make a list of the economic resources that are required to operate a restaurant. How is the number of meals per day that can be served in a restaurant limited by available economic resources and current technology for meal preparation and service?

3. Suppose you can divide the goods and services produced in the United States into two broad categories: military goods and civilian goods. Draw a production possibilities curve between these two goods and show how an increase in the annual production of military goods will imply a decrease in the annual production of civilian goods if the economy operates along points on its production possibilities curve.

4. The small nation whose annual production possibilities for food and clothing are illustrated in the table and graph in Box 1 receives a gift of new machines for use in clothing production and agriculture. The new machines allow the nation to produce twice as much food and clothing with the same number of workers and natural resources. Draw the new production possibilities curve for the nation and show how the gift of capital expands its production possibilities.

5. Referring again to Box 1, suppose the nation receives a gift of new agricultural machinery that would double the maximum quantity of food that could be produced for any given quantity of clothing produced. Draw the new production possibilities curve and show why the gift expands the production possibilities of the nation to allow it to consume more food *and* clothing. Shade in the new combinations of food and clothing made possible by the gift.

6. A civil war erupts in the small nation whose production possibilities curve is shown in Box 1. The war results in the destruction of capital and natural resources, and causes casualties that reduce the supply of labor available for production of food and clothing. Show the impact of the war on the nation's production possibilities curve for food and clothing.

7. Suppose the production possibilities curve for the production of trucks and cars in a two-product factory has a constant slope equal to -2 when weekly car production is plotted on the vertical axis and weekly truck production is plotted on the horizontal axis. Draw the production possibilities curve and explain why the law of increasing costs doesn't hold for the production of cars and trucks in the factory.

8. Suppose you own and run a small business. You spend 40 hours per week managing the operation. By operating the business you forgo your next best alternative, which is working at a job for someone else that pays $10 per hour. An accountant calculates all the money costs and revenues from the business

and tells you you're making a $300 profit per week. However, the accountant doesn't include the opportunity cost of your time as part of the money costs because you don't incur any cash outlay to pay for your time. Does it make sense for you to continue in business? Explain your answer.

9. Imagine you're the manager of a small textile factory that has two product lines: flannel fabric and corduroy fabric. Some workers and some machines are specialized in the production of only one of these goods. The maximum amount of flannel that can be produced when 1,000 yards of corduroy are also produced is 1,500 yards per month with 10,000 labor hours per month. You can't vary the number of machines or floor space in the factory. Suppose you are currently producing at an efficient level. If monthly orders drop to 1,000 yards of corduroy and 1,000 yards of flannel, what could you do to reduce costs during the month? Explain your answer using a production possibilities curve.

10. Your younger sister receives a weekly allowance of $20, which she spends entirely on movie admissions and ice cream cones. Movie admission is $4 per show and ice cream cones are $1. Draw your sister's budget line. What is the opportunity cost of a movie show for her? Would the opportunity cost of a movie show change if the prices of movies and ice cream cones doubled?

Show how the budget line will shift for each of the following changes. Calculate the opportunity cost of each item for each of the changes.

    a. An increase in the weekly allowance to $24
    b. A decrease in the weekly allowance to $12
    c. A reduction in the price of movie admission to $2
    d. An increase in the price of ice cream cones to $2

Suggested Readings

Economic Report of the President, Washington, D.C.: U.S. Government Printing Office, annual. Are you interested in finding out how well the U.S. economy is using its resources? The federal government publishes reams of information on the economy each year. The *Economic Report of the President* is published at the beginning of each year and provides information about economic issues, resource utilization, and statistical data on the extent to which the economy is achieving its potential.

Andrew S. Grove, *High Output Management,* New York: Random House, 1983. In this book one of the founders of the Intel Corporation discusses some of the problems and opportunities involved in squeezing the most out of economic resources in business.

Richard J. Schonberger, *Japanese Manufacturing Techniques,* New York: The Free Press, 1982. This is a description and analysis of how Japanese manufacturing firms cope with the problem of scarcity. The technique of "just-in-time" production is extensively discussed.

A Forward Look

In the following chapter we introduce the concept of a market and show how prices are determined in a market in which many rival buyers and sellers compete. We examine the impersonal forces of supply and demand and their influence on the prices of goods and services sold in markets.

Career Profile

ELAINE GARZARELLI

Since accurately predicting a 600- to 700-point drop in the stock market just a week before the October 1987 crash, Elaine Garzarelli has become one of the most respected mutual fund managers on Wall Street. Not a bad way to start for a talented and savvy analyst who's still well under age 40.

Garzarelli had begun managing a brand-new $430 million mutual fund for Shearson Lehman Hutton, Inc., in August 1987, which as it turned out was 2 days after 1987 stock prices peaked. Only half of the market indicators she studied said stock prices would rise, so she invested only half of the fund's assets in stocks. As more and more indicators predicted falling stock prices, she eliminated stocks from her fund altogether, much to the surprise of her colleagues. Her fund was completely out of the market at the time of the stock crash, and she received much attention for her cautious stance.

Garzarelli began working as a market analyst under the direction of Roy Moore, chief economist for the Philadelphia investment firm of Drexel Harriman Ripley, while studying economics at Drexel University. She attempted to isolate the economic factors that most strongly influence the direction of stock prices. In a mathematical effort to link microeconomics to macroeconomics, she began to recognize how a variety of industry and economic factors affect stock prices. Garzarelli became the first female managing director at A. G. Becker in 1982. When that firm merged with Merrill Lynch, she joined Shearson. Her reputation in the field is built around a computer model she created of 13 indicators, including monetary growth rates, economic growth rates, and stock value measurements. For nearly two decades she has struggled to quantify market relationships, and for the past 4 years she has been declared the champion quantitative analyst by *Institutional Investor* magazine.

At Shearson Garzarelli initially served as a market strategist, analyzing stock prices and advising the company's clients on how to invest their money. Today, as a fund manager, it is she who makes the investments, which she says is much harder than telling other people how to spend their money.

Supply and Demand:
Markets and the Price System

4

Market Transactions: Basic Supply and Demand Analysis

No matter how independent we may be in spirit, virtually none of us is self-sufficient. Our mutual interdependence for goods and services is a fact of life. Just think how you rely on others to satisfy your most basic needs. You go to the supermarket to buy your food. The local power company provides you with electricity. The car you drive and the fuel you put in the tank are provided by people who specialize in making those items available. The road you drive on is most likely provided and maintained by a government and financed with taxes. Few people, even those who live on farms, produce all the food and fiber they need to feed and clothe themselves.

Even those of us who do have the skills to grow our own food, make our own clothes, build our own housing, and repair our own cars will rarely, if ever, find it in our interest to be self-sufficient. Instead, there's an incredibly complex division of labor and specialization in economic activities. Specialized firms and agencies make particular goods and services available to consumers, investors, and governments. Workers specialize in particular trades and occupations, and this makes economic interdependence inevitable. If all of us spend our working days making particular goods or services available, we simply don't have the time to produce the variety of items we need and want.

The most common way we obtain goods and services we don't produce ourselves is to buy them from others who specialize in producing them. To make such purchases, buyers seek out sellers in markets. The purpose of a market is to make information available on the goods and services sellers are willing to sell and buyers want to purchase. This exchange of information is the basis for determining prices, which in turn influence the actual amounts of goods and services exchanged. Prices are a major determinant of the choices we make as both buyers and sellers.

This chapter introduces you to supply and demand analysis of market transactions, which shows how prices are established by the competition among buyers for goods offered by competing sellers. Market prices play a vital role in coping with the problem of scarcity because they ration available amounts of goods and services.

The techniques developed in this chapter are ones we'll use throughout the book. As you learn how markets operate without any government intervention, you'll have a basis for understanding both the reasons for and the consequences of government policies that affect market prices and trading.

After reading this chapter, you should be able to:

1 Discuss the purposes and functions of markets.
2 Explain how a demand curve illustrates the law of demand and distinguish between a change in demand and a change in quantity demanded.
3 Show how a supply curve illustrates the law of supply and distinguish between a change in supply and a change in quantity supplied.
4 Describe the conditions required for market equilibrium and locate the equilibrium point on a supply and demand diagram.
5 Explain the consequences of shortages and surpluses in markets and how prices adjust in a free and unregulated competitive market to eliminate shortages or surpluses.
6 Show how changes in demand and supply affect market equilibrium.

Markets: Purposes and Functions

A **market** is an arrangement through which buyers and sellers meet or communicate for the purpose of trading goods or services. Markets are a way in which buyers and sellers can conduct transactions resulting in mutual net gains that otherwise wouldn't be possible. For example, your local electronics store is a place where you can see the range of stereos, VCRs, TVs, and compact disc players that various manufacturers are offering. At a flea market you can be both a buyer and a seller: you can offer to sell your used bicycle or car stereo and at the same time build up your collection of old records or find a couch for your apartment.

Many market transactions are conducted without buyers and sellers actually meeting at a particular location. For example, you can browse through catalogues or magazine advertisements to see what various merchants are offering. If you find something you like, you can order it by mail or telephone, without face-to-face contact with the seller. You also can hire an intermediary to carry out a transaction for you. For example, if you want to fly home for Christmas vacation, you can call a travel agent, who will check the fares of all airlines and make the best deal for you.

Supply and demand analysis explains how prices are established in markets through competition among buyers and sellers, and how those prices affect quantities traded. In a *competitive* or *free* market, many sellers compete for sales to many buyers who compete for available goods and services. In such a market all those who wish to sell and all those who wish to buy can do so.

Market:
An arrangement through which buyers and sellers meet or communicate for the purpose of trading goods or services.

Supply and demand analysis:
Explains how prices are established in markets through competition among buyers and sellers, and how those prices affect quantities traded.

Economic Thinkers

ALFRED MARSHALL

The decision to study mathematics instead of theology may have given the world one of its most brilliant and influential economists. Alfred Marshall, who is credited with founding the neoclassical school of economics, was born in London in 1842. Despite intense pressure from his ambitious father, Marshall declined a theological scholarship to Oxford and instead worked toward a master's degree in mathematics at Cambridge. After receiving his degree in 1865, he remained at Cambridge to teach mathematics, and it was then that he began seriously to study economics.

Holding in high esteem the classical writers in economics, such as Adam Smith and David Ricardo, Marshall initially concentrated on using his knowledge of mathematical principles to reinforce the tenets of the classical school. His first effort was to translate into mathematical equations the text of John Stuart Mill's *Principles*. As his ideas gained acceptance, Marshall's influence grew, and in 1885 he was appointed to the Chair of Political Economy at Cambridge. He retained this position for nearly 25 years.

In his ground-breaking *Principles of Economics,* published in 1890, Marshall established the foundation for the now-dominant neoclassical school of economics, and in so doing set forth many of the principles that underlie contemporary microeconomic theory. Through his teachings and writings Marshall influenced many of the leading economists of succeeding generations, and 100 years later his *Principles* text still has much to offer the student of economics. As you study supply and demand, elasticity, equilibrium, the short run, and the long run, reflect on the astonishing fact that each of these concepts originally was articulated by one man: Alfred Marshall.

To analyze the way markets operate, you first must understand the concept of supply and demand. This concept was introduced in 1890 by British economist Alfred Marshall, who first articulated many of the principles that underlie modern microeconomic theory (see Economic Thinkers box).

Demand

The quantity of an item buyers actually purchase in a market over a given period is influenced by a number of important determinants:

1. The price of the item
2. Income available to spend
3. Accumulated savings in the form of bank deposits, stocks, bonds, and ownership of homes, other structures, and equipment. Such savings are called *wealth.*
4. Expectations of future price changes
5. The prices of alternative items
6. Tastes or current fashions
7. The population served by the market

In analyzing the behavior of buyers in markets, we concentrate on the effect of each of these determinants one at a time. We pay special attention to the relationship between the price of an item and the quantities buyers will purchase. The **quantity demanded** of an item is the amount that buyers are willing and able to purchase over a period at a certain price, *given all other influences on their decision to buy.*

Demand is a relationship between the price of an item and the quantity demanded. The term "demand" as used in economics is not a fixed number. When analyzing a given demand for a product, we assume that *demand determinants other than the price of the item* are held fixed. For example, the demand for cars over a year indicates how the annual quantity demanded would vary as the price of cars changes, *other things being equal.* The other things held constant are all demand determinants *other than* the price of cars, such as income available for spending. Similarly, the demand for subway rides in a city would isolate the relationship between the price of a ride and the number of rides demanded over a given period.

Quantity demanded:
The amount of an item that buyers are willing and able to purchase over a period at a certain price, given all other influences on their decision to buy.

Demand:
A relationship between the price of an item and the quantity demanded.

The Market Demand Curve and the Law of Demand

A **demand schedule** is a table that shows how the quantity demanded of an item actually would vary with price given all other demand determinants. The table in Box 1 shows a hypothetical demand schedule for eggs sold per week in a local farmers' market where egg buyers meet with egg sellers. The first column of the table shows possible prices per dozen grade A eggs. The quantity demanded, shown in the second column, represents the weekly number of eggs that buyers are willing and able to purchase at each price. The schedule is based on the assumption that there's no change in any other demand influence as the price of eggs changes. The schedule shows a number of possible outcomes in the market. The actual quantity purchased over the period depends on the price of eggs given all other demand determinants.

Demand schedule:
A table that shows how the quantity demanded of a good would vary with price, given all other demand determinants.

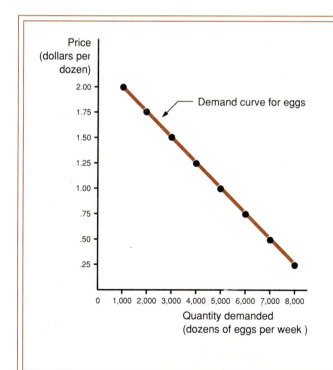

Box 1   A Demand Curve

The downward-sloping demand curve shows the quantity of eggs demanded per week at various prices. This curve is based on the demand schedule shown in the table below. A change in quantity demanded is a movement along a demand curve caused by a change in the price of the good. For example, a decrease in the price of eggs from $1.25 to $1 per dozen would increase quantity demanded from 4,000 to 5,000 dozen per week.

A Demand Schedule for Grade A Eggs

Price (dollars per dozen)	Quantity demanded (dozens per week)
2.00	1,000
1.75	2,000
1.50	3,000
1.25	4,000
1.00	5,000
.75	6,000
.50	7,000
.25	8,000

The data in the hypothetical demand schedule indicate an inverse relationship between price and quantity demanded that is likely to be observed in general for all goods and services. When price goes down, the quantity that is demanded per week (or over any other period) goes up. For example, at a price of $2 per dozen the schedule shows that the quantity of eggs demanded per week is only 1,000 dozen. At a price of $1.50 per dozen, buyers would demand 3,000 dozen eggs per week.

Law of demand:
States that in general, other things being equal, the lower the price of a good, the greater the quantity of that good buyers are willing and able to purchase over a given period.

The **law of demand** states that in general, other things being equal, the lower the price of a good, the greater the quantity of that good buyers are willing and able to purchase over a given period. Conversely, the law implies that buyers will buy less of a good over any given period if the price of the good increases while nothing else changes. The data in the table in Box 1 reflect the law of demand because they indicate an inverse relationship between the price of eggs and the quantity demanded. The law is relevant to all goods and services. For example, the lower the price of subway rides, other things being equal, the greater the quantity demanded. Similarly, the lower the price of stereo speakers, the greater the quantity demanded. Lower prices make goods more attractive to us as consumers and increase our willingness to buy. To see this, just visit a store that's running a sale and watch how much more quickly goods leave the shelf when prices are lowered!

The law of demand can be derived as an implication of an economic model based on rational behavior (which we examined in Chapter 2), and the law is generally supported by empirical evidence. Other things being equal, lower prices induce us to buy more of an item over a period because we enjoy additional net gains that weren't possible at the higher price.

Examine your own behavior as a buyer to convince yourself that the law of demand is quite reasonable. You might not buy any eggs at all if they were priced at $2 per dozen, but you'd probably be willing to purchase a few dozen if they were priced at only 25¢. If you're like most people, you buy more records, more clothing, and more of most items over any given period when their prices decline and nothing else changes. When the price of an item rises, you tend to buy less of it. If the price of going to a movie increased from $4 to $8, you'd probably attend movies less often and look for other forms of entertainment. Other consumers like you will behave the same way.

Demand curve:
A graph that shows how quantity demanded varies with the price of a good.

A **demand curve** is a graph of the data that comprise a demand schedule that shows how quantity demanded varies with the price of a good. The graph in Box 1 shows the weekly demand curve for eggs by plotting the data from the table in the box. Price is represented by points on the vertical axis, while quantity demanded is represented by points on the horizontal axis. To see how the curve is plotted, go to the demand schedule and note that if the price of grade A eggs were $1 per dozen, the quantity demanded would be 5,000 dozen per week. A horizontal line drawn from the point corresponding to $1 on the price axis intersects the demand curve at the point that corresponds to 5,000 dozen eggs per week on the horizontal axis.

The downward slope of the demand curve reflects the law of demand. It's also useful to interpret points on a demand curve as indicating how the willingness of buyers to pay will vary with the quantity of an item actually available in a market over a period. The demand curve indicates that the fewer eggs offered for sale each month, the higher the price buyers will pay. Conversely, the more eggs available, the less buyers are willing to pay.

You can see the relationship between quantity available and price by examining your own experience in markets. If you've ever bought a car, you know that in periods during which car dealers have few cars in stock, buyers are willing to pay higher prices for available cars. This is because buyers who are willing and able to pay the price for cars compete with each other for those available. When there's a reduction in the number of cars available, some buyers are willing to pay more for a car rather than lose the opportunity to buy one to a competing buyer. For more proof, consider the oil embargoes of the 1970s and what these did to people's willingness to pay for gasoline. In some parts of the country the price of a gallon of gas tripled, and drivers sat in lines for hours, willing to buy the scarce fuel at that price.

Changes in Relative Price

The price of an item is usually measured as a sum of money. However, the money price of an item isn't always the best indication of what we must give up to obtain a unit of the item. One reason for this is that the purchasing power of money can change over time. For example, when an average of the prices of all goods available in an economy increases by 5% over a year, the *quantity* of goods that each dollar will buy on average will fall. This means that the purchasing power of the dollar is less.

A **change in the relative price** of a good is an increase or decrease in the price of that good relative to the average change in the prices of all goods. The relative price of a good might not always change when its money price changes. For example, suppose an average of the money prices of all goods goes up by 7% over a year. If the money price of cars also goes up by that amount, the relative price of cars would be unchanged. If college tuition were to increase by 10% over the same year, its relative price would have risen because its money price has increased by a percentage that exceeds the average. Similarly, if the money price of VCRs increased by only 3%, the relative price of VCRs would have fallen over the year even though the money price had gone up. This is because the money price of VCRs increased by less than the average over the year.

When the purchasing power of money is not constant, changes in relative prices of goods measure changes in the opportunity cost of a purchase better than changes in money prices. Strictly speaking, the law of demand expresses a relationship between changes in the *relative price* of a good and resulting changes in the quantities demanded.

Change in relative price:
An increase or decrease in the price of a good relative to the average change in the prices of all goods.

Changes in Quantity Demanded

In general, the demand curve is *downward sloping*. The negative slope reflects the inverse relationship between price and quantity demanded according to the law of demand. Although the demand curve in Box 1 has been drawn as a straight line, it could also be curvilinear. Along the demand curve, quantity demanded increases as the price of the good decreases. A **change in quantity demanded** is a change in the amount of a good buyers are willing and able to buy in response to a change in the price of the good. *A change in quantity demanded is a movement along a given demand curve caused by an increase or decrease in the price of the good.*

For example, for the demand curve depicted in Box 1, an increase in the price of eggs from $1 to $1.25 per dozen would result in a decrease in weekly quantity demanded from 5,000 dozen to 4,000 dozen. The 1,000-dozen decline in the quantity buyers are willing to purchase as the price of eggs increases is called a *decrease in*

Change in quantity demanded:
A change in the amount of a good buyers are willing and able to buy in response to a change in the price of the good.

quantity demanded. Similarly, if the price of eggs declined from $1 to 75¢ per dozen, there would be an *increase in quantity demanded* from 5,000 dozen to 6,000 dozen per week.

Changes in Demand

As we observed earlier, the relationship between the price of a good and the quantity of the good demanded over a given period also depends on such demand determinants as income available for spending, wealth, prices of related goods, expectations of future prices, consumer preferences, and the number of buyers in the market. The quantity of a good that consumers are willing and able to buy at any given price will change if any one of these demand determinants changes. A **change in demand** is a change in the relationship between the price of a good and the quantity demanded caused by a change in a demand determinant other than the price of the good.

A change in demand implies a movement of an entire demand curve for a good. A new demand schedule must be drawn up, because the quantity demanded by consumers *at each price* will change. *Be careful not to confuse a change in demand with a change in quantity demanded. A change in demand is a response to a change in a demand influence other than the price of the good, while a change in quantity demanded is a response to a change in a good's own price.*

The table in Box 2 shows a new demand schedule resulting from an increase in demand and also displays the old demand schedule. You'll notice that the quantity demanded in the new schedule is greater than the quantity demanded in the old schedule at *each possible price*. The graph in Box 2 plots the new demand curve corresponding to the data in the adjacent table on the same set of axes as the old demand curve. The increase in demand is represented by a shift *outward* of the demand curve.

Similarly, a decrease in demand for eggs would imply an inward shift of the weekly demand curve. At each possible price, the quantity of eggs demanded by consumers would decline. The graph in Box 3 illustrates a decrease in demand as an inward shift of the entire demand curve. Note that the new demand curve need not be parallel to the old demand curve.

Using logic and observation, it's possible to make hypotheses about the possible impact of changes in various determinants on the demand for a good:

1. *Changes in consumer income.* An increase in income available for spending increases the *ability* of consumers to buy an item. Increases in income usually increase the demand for most goods, while decreases in income tend to decrease the demand for most goods.

Although the demand for most goods increases as income goes up, there are some exceptions. The demand for products like poor cuts of meat, low-quality clothing, and second-hand furniture might decline for many people as their income goes up. Goods whose demand will decline as income increases are called *inferior* goods. *Normal* goods are those whose demand increases when income goes up.

2. *Changes in wealth.* Wealth is the net accumulated savings in a nation. The demand for some goods is particularly sensitive to changes in wealth. For example, the demand for luxury goods is likely to decline if there's a sharp decline in wealth. This is because much of the wealth is in the hands of a few people who constitute the market for luxury items. On "Black Monday"—October 19, 1987—some $500

Change in demand:
A change in the relationship between the price of a good and the quantity demanded caused by a change in a demand determinant other than the price of the good.

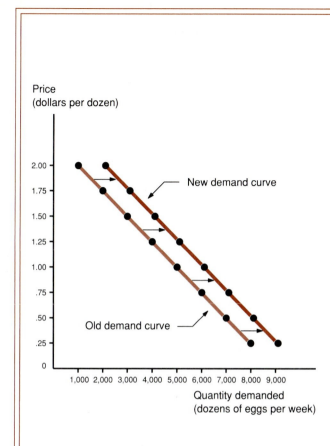

Price
(dollars per dozen)

New demand curve

Old demand curve

Quantity demanded
(dozens of eggs per week)

Box 2   An Increase in Demand

An increase in demand is represented by an outward shift of the entire demand curve. An increase in demand for an item can be caused by:

- an increase in income or in wealth if the item is a normal good (if it is an inferior good, an increase in income would decrease demand)
- an increase in the price of a substitute
- a decrease in the price of a complement
- expectations of a future increase in the relative price of the item
- a change in tastes or fashion that makes the item more popular
- an increase in the number of buyers served by the market

A New Demand Schedule After an Increase in Demand

Price (dollars)	Quantity demanded of eggs (dozens per week)	
	Old demand schedule	New demand schedule
2.00	1,000	2,000
1.75	2,000	3,000
1.50	3,000	4,000
1.25	4,000	5,000
1.00	5,000	6,000
.75	6,000	7,000
.50	7,000	8,000
.25	8,000	9,000

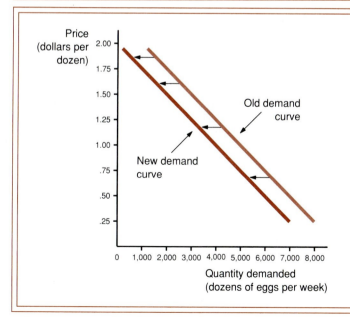

Price
(dollars per dozen)

Old demand curve

New demand curve

Quantity demanded
(dozens of eggs per week)

Box 3   A Decrease in Demand

A decrease in demand is an inward shift of a demand curve. After a decrease in demand, the quantities that consumers will be willing to buy at each price will be smaller than previously. A decrease in demand for an item can be caused by:

- a decrease in income or in wealth if the item is a normal good (if it is an inferior good, a decrease in income would increase demand)
- a decrease in the price of a substitute
- an increase in the price of a complement
- expectations of a future decrease in the relative price of the item
- a change in tastes or fashion that makes the item less popular
- a decrease in the number of buyers served by the market

billion of wealth evaporated as the market value of stocks held by individuals and organizations plummeted. The stock market plunge sent shock waves through the markets for luxury cars, penthouses, vacation homes, fine jewelry, yachts, and other costly items.

Some goods are relatively insensitive to wealth changes. The demand for bathroom tissue, for example, is unlikely to be affected by changes in wealth. The demand for other goods might actually increase in response to a decline in wealth. For example, those whose wealth declines might increase their demand for automobiles in the mid-price range because they can no longer afford luxury cars.

3. *Changes in the prices of other goods.* Our willingness to buy a particular item also depends on the prices of related items. Alternatives are available for most items. Items that serve a purpose similar to that of a given item are **substitutes** for that item. If the price of a substitute for English muffins changes, the demand for English muffins will change as well. An increase in the price of bagels at your local diner is likely to increase the demand for English muffins because you can substitute English muffins for bagels when you have breakfast. Conversely, a decrease in the price of substitutes for English muffins will tend to decrease the demand for English muffins. Similarly, Reebok and Adidas athletic shoes are substitutes. An increase in the price of Reeboks will be likely to increase the demand for Adidas. An increase in the price of off-campus housing near your school might increase the demand for dormitory rooms.

The demand for a good also can be influenced by a change in the price of its complements. **Complements** are goods whose use together enhances the satisfaction a consumer obtains from each. For example, a decrease in the price of compact disc recordings is likely to increase the demand for compact disc players because these two goods complement each other. Similarly, coffee and nondairy creamers are complements. An increase in the price of coffee is likely to decrease the demand for nondairy creamers. If the price of gasoline goes up significantly, the demand for cars could go down because cars and gasoline are complements.

4. *Changes in expectations of future prices.* The demand for an item also depends on expectations buyers have about future events. In particular, if you as a buyer expect that the price of an item will increase next week, you're likely to buy more of the item this week. If the item can be stored, like shampoo or socks, you'll increase your demand for the item and stock up. Expectations of future price increases therefore tend to shift current demand curves outward. By the same token, expectations of price declines in the future for an item tend to decrease current demand for that item. If you expect the price of personal computers to decline next month, you'll be less willing to buy a PC this month. The expectation of a price decline therefore tends to decrease current demand and shift the demand curve for the product inward.

5. *Changes in tastes or fashion.* The general appeal of an item to buyers can change from time to time. If your taste for an item changes, the demand for it may decrease because you're less willing to buy the item at any given price. For example, the demand for long-playing records has decreased in recent years as you and other buyers have been attracted by the superior sound quality of compact discs. A change in tastes can also increase the demand for an item. For example, if you and your friends decide that Padre Island, not Fort Lauderdale, is the place to head for over spring break, the demand for plane tickets to that island paradise is sure to increase. You're well aware of the influence of fashion on the demand for clothing. As styles change, you become more reluctant to buy certain items no matter how low the

Substitutes:
Goods that serve a purpose similar to that of a given item.

Complements:
Goods whose use together enhances the satisfaction a consumer obtains from each.

price. Even if they cost only 25¢, you're not likely to buy a pair of plaid polyester bell-bottom pants, unless you're planning to attend a costume party. Twenty years ago these items were the height of fashion, and only the hopelessly unstylish would have been seen in the straight-leg jeans we're now cheerfully paying $50 a pair for.

6. *Changes in the number of buyers served by the market.* The total quantity of any item demanded at any price also depends on the *number* of buyers in the market interested in buying the item at that price. Higher population tends to be associated with increases in demand for goods. The number of buyers also can change when buyers in foreign countries become willing and able to purchase an item. For example, if Europeans become more willing and able to buy U.S. cars, the demand for U.S. cars will increase, other things being equal. A breakdown of trade barriers allowing U.S. firms to sell more beef in Japan will increase the demand for U.S. beef. An increase in the number of buyers in a market tends to increase demand, shifting the demand curve outward. A decrease in the number of buyers in the market tends to decrease the demand for a good, shifting the demand curve inward.

In addition to the influences we've just examined, the demand for particular goods can be influenced by weather, demographic trends, government subsidies or taxes, and other factors. For example, a cold winter can increase the demand for sleds and warm clothing. An increase in the proportion of the U.S. population over the age of 65 is increasing the demand for retirement residences and nursing homes.

Concept Check

1 **What is the purpose of a market?**

2 **Explain how a demand curve illustrates the law of demand. What influences the demand for a good?**

3 **What is the distinction between changes in quantity demanded and changes in demand for a good? Indicate what can cause changes in demand and what can cause changes in quantity demanded of a good.**

Supply

The quantity of a good or service sellers are willing to sell in a market is affected by a number of important influences:

1. The price of the good
2. The current prices of inputs needed to produce and market the good
3. Current technology available to produce and market the good
4. The prices of other goods that can be produced with inputs used or owned by the seller
5. Expectations about future prices
6. The number of sellers serving the market

In analyzing the quantity of a good made available for sale in a given period, we must sort out the separate influences of each of the determinants just listed. We'll

Quantity supplied:
The quantity of a good sellers are willing and able to make available in the market over a given period at a certain price, other things being equal.

Supply:
A relationship between the price of an item and the quantity supplied by sellers.

single out for special attention the influence of price on the quantity sellers are willing to sell. The **quantity supplied** of a good is the quantity sellers are willing and able to make available in the market over a given period at a certain price, *other things being equal*. In this case the *other things* being held equal are all the previously listed *supply determinants* other than the price of the good itself.

The concept of **supply** as used in economics is a relationship between the price of an item and the quantity supplied. Like demand, supply is not a fixed quantity. Instead it signifies how the quantity sellers will offer varies with price. The amount sellers bring to the market over any given period depends on the price of the product and the other supply determinants listed earlier.

The Market Supply Curve and the Law of Supply

The price is the payment a seller receives for each unit of a good sold. Just as changes in relative price influence incentives to buy a good, so do changes in relative price influence incentives to sell a good. The table in Box 4 provides hypothetical data for the price and quantity of eggs supplied in a local farmers' market each week. Other supply determinants are assumed not to change as price changes. The data in the table comprise the **supply schedule**, which shows how the quantity supplied per week is related to the price. The first column of the table shows possible prices per dozen grade A eggs. The second column shows the quantities supplied per week at each possible price. The data in the table indicate a direct relationship between price and quantity supplied: the higher the price, the greater the quantity supplied. For example, as the price of eggs increases from $1 to $1.25 per dozen, the weekly quantity supplied increases from 5,000 dozen to 6,000 dozen.

Naturally, the higher the price per unit of a good, other things being equal, the

Supply schedule:
A table that shows how the quantity supplied of a good is related to the price.

Box 4 A Supply Curve

A supply curve describes the relationship between price and quantity supplied. An upward-sloping supply curve reflects the law of supply. This supply curve is based on the supply schedule in the table below.

A Supply Schedule for Eggs

Price (dollars per dozen)	Quantity supplied (dozens per week)
2.00	9,000
1.75	8,000
1.50	7,000
1.25	6,000
1.00	5,000
.75	4,000
.50	3,000
.25	2,000

greater the potential gain from supplying it. The **law of supply** states that in general, other things being equal, the higher the price of a good, the greater the quantity of that good sellers are willing and able to make available over a given period.

The law of supply is an implication of a model that is based on the assumption that sellers seek to maximize net gains from their activities. The law represents a hypothesis that is widely supported by empirical evidence. Let's sketch out the idea underlying the law of supply by using an example. Over any given period, say a week, there's a given number of suppliers of stone-washed denims in the United States. Each supplier can make only a certain number of pairs of jeans available over a week. Some inputs, such as factory space and machinery, can't easily be increased over such a short period of time. As sellers try to make more pairs of jeans available over a week by hiring more labor and other inputs that can be more easily obtained, their operations become less efficient. Workers overutilize machines, which tends to make them break down more often. As the limit of productive capacity is approached, the costs per pair of jeans tend to rise, as does the marginal cost of making the jeans available to you and other prospective buyers. These increasing marginal costs imply that sellers are unwilling to make more stone-washed denims available unless higher prices prevail to cover their increasing costs for additional pairs. Unless prices rise, sellers can't enjoy a net gain (profit) from producing more jeans. At higher prices, each existing seller is likely to want to make more pairs of jeans available over a given period.

A **supply curve** is a graph of the data from a supply schedule that shows how quantity supplied varies with price. The graph in Box 4 plots the weekly supply curve for eggs based on the data in the table in the box. Price is plotted on the vertical axis, while quantity supplied corresponds to points on the horizontal axis. For example, if the price were $2 per dozen, suppliers would be willing to make 9,000 dozen eggs available to the market. To see this, draw a horizontal line from the point on the price axis corresponding to $2 across to the supply curve and then draw a vertical line to the quantity axis that will intersect that axis at a quantity supplied of 9,000 dozen eggs per week. Assume that if the price fell below 25¢ per dozen, no one would be willing to sell eggs, so the quantity supplied would fall to zero. Understandably, sellers require a minimum price to cover their costs before they'll make goods available to buyers.

The upward slope of the supply curve reflects the law of supply. Note that you could also interpret points on a supply curve as indicating the price sellers will accept to make each possible quantity available to buyers in the market over the period. The greater the quantity buyers want to purchase, the higher the price necessary to induce suppliers to make the desired quantity available.

Changes in Quantity Supplied

The positive slope of the supply curve reflects the law of supply. As the price increases, the quantity supplied over the period goes up. A **change in quantity supplied** is a change in the amount sellers are willing to sell over a period in response to a change in the price of the good. Changes in quantity supplied represent movements along a given supply curve in response to price changes while all other factors affecting the willingness of sellers to sell are unchanged. For example, if the price of eggs declined from $2 to $1.75 per dozen, there would be a *decrease in quantity supplied* and the quantity sellers would make available to the market would decline from 9,000 dozen to 8,000 dozen per week. Similarly, if the price

Law of supply:
States that in general, other things being equal, the higher the price of a good, the greater the quantity of that good sellers are willing and able to make available over a given period.

Supply curve:
A graph that shows how quantity supplied varies with the price of a good.

Change in quantity supplied:
A change in the amount of a good sellers are willing to sell in response to a change in the price of the good.

increased from \$1 to \$1.25 per dozen, there would be an *increase in quantity supplied* as sellers would be willing to increase the quantity available for sale from 5,000 dozen to 6,000 dozen per week.

Changes in Supply

Change in supply:
A change in the relationship between the price of a good and the quantity supplied in response to a change in a supply determinant other than the price of the good.

A **change in supply** is a change in the relationship between the price of a good and the quantity supplied in response to a change in a supply determinant other than the price of the good. A change in supply implies a shift of the entire supply curve. A new supply schedule must be drawn up, because the quantity supplied by sellers *at each price* will change. For example, in the table in Box 4, a change in supply would mean that the data in the second column would change.

Among the important changes in economic conditions that can cause changes in supply are:

1. *Changes in the prices of the inputs necessary to produce and sell a good.* The profit possible at any given price depends on the prices a seller must pay for the economic resources to produce the good. Increases in input prices and transaction

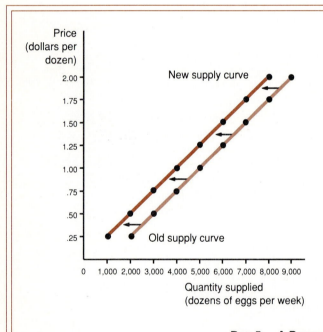

A New Supply Schedule After a Decrease in Supply

Price (dollars per dozen)	Quantity supplied of eggs (dozens per week)	
	Old supply schedule	New supply schedule
2.00	9,000	8,000
1.75	8,000	7,000
1.50	7,000	6,000
1.25	6,000	5,000
1.00	5,000	4,000
.75	4,000	3,000
.50	3,000	2,000
.25	2,000	1,000

Box 5   A Decrease in Supply

A decrease in supply is an inward shift of the supply curve. A change in supply of an item can be caused by:

• a change in the prices of inputs used to produce it: an increase in input prices decreases supply, while a decrease in input prices increases supply.

• a change in technology: an improvement in technology increases supply, while the unlikely event of a deterioration in technology (caused by some catastrophe) would decrease supply.

• a change in the prices of other items: an increase in the relative price of an alternative item that can be produced with the same resources decreases the supply of the first item, while a decrease in the relative price of the alternative item would increase the supply of the first item.

• a change in the number of sellers serving the market: a decrease in the number of sellers decreases supply, while an increase in the number of sellers increases supply.

costs associated with selling the good result in less profit for selling any given quantity. This decreases the supply of the good. Conversely, a decrease in input prices would increase the profitability of selling the good and result in an increase in supply. Suppose, for example, that there's an increase in the price of chicken feed. This is likely to decrease the willingness of egg producers to make eggs available at any given price because it will now be more costly to produce any given quantity of eggs. The table in Box 5 shows that the quantity supplied *at each price* is now less than was the case when the old supply schedule prevailed.

The graph in Box 5 plots the new supply curve alongside the old supply curve. The new supply curve, corresponding to the data in the table in Box 5, is closer to the vertical axis at each possible price than the old curve. A *decrease in supply* therefore is represented by an *inward* shift of the entire supply curve. Similarly, an *increase in supply* would be represented by an *outward* shift of the entire supply curve. The graph in Box 6 illustrates an increase in supply. Note that the new supply curves do not have to be parallel to the old ones.

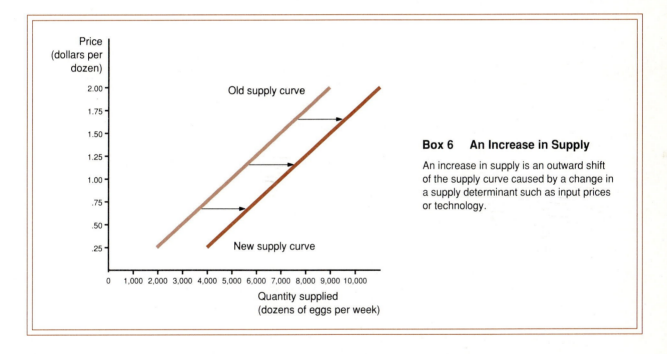

Box 6   An Increase in Supply

An increase in supply is an outward shift of the supply curve caused by a change in a supply determinant such as input prices or technology.

2. *Changes in the technology available to produce the good.* Improvements in technology tend to increase the output from economic resources used to produce a good. Assuming that input prices are unchanged, advances in technology lower the cost per unit of output and tend to increase the profit possible from selling the product at various prices. For example, an improvement in the technology of producing VCRs will lower the unit and marginal costs of making VCRs available. The lower costs will increase the potential profit from selling VCRs and will encourage existing sellers to supply more while attracting new sellers to enter the market as well. Improvements in technology will shift the supply curve to the right, as you can see in the graph in Box 6.

3. *Changes in the prices of other goods that can be produced with the seller's resources.* The opportunity cost of producing and selling any one good is the sacri-

fice of the opportunity to sell some other good. Changes in the prices of alternative goods change the opportunity cost of producing a given good, resulting in changes in its supply. For example, given the price of T-shirts, an increase in the price of sweatshirts could decrease the supply of T-shirts as manufacturers use their facilities to produce more sweatshirts and fewer T-shirts. This would shift the supply curve for T-shirts to the left. Similarly, a decrease in the price of sweatshirts could increase the supply of T-shirts, shifting the supply curve for this item to the right.

4. *Changes in the number of sellers serving the market.* Other things being equal, an increase in the number of sellers increases the supply of a good. For example, an increase in the number of firms producing compact discs increases the number of CDs available at any given price. Over long periods of time, changes in the number of sellers in a market are a very important determinant of supply. The number of sellers in a market changes with the profitability of producing the good.

There are other important determinants that can affect the supplies of particular goods. For example, the weather can affect the supply of agricultural commodities. A frost in Florida that ruins the citrus crop could decrease the supply of oranges in the market over a year. Expectations about future prices of goods and services and inputs can also affect current supply, as can taxes and subsidies.

Concept Check

1 Explain how a supply curve illustrates the law of supply. List the supply determinants that must be held constant to draw a supply curve.

2 What can cause a change in quantity supplied? What can cause a change in supply?

3 An improvement in technology allows a given amount of inputs to produce more pocket TVs per week. Use a graph to show the impact of the improvement on the weekly supply of pocket TVs.

Market Equilibrium Price and Quantity

Equilibrium:
Prevails when economic forces balance so that economic variables neither increase nor decrease.

Market equilibrium:
Attained when the price of a good adjusts so that the quantity buyers are willing and able to buy at that price is just equal to the quantity sellers are willing and able to supply.

Shortage:
Exists if the quantity demanded exceeds the quantity supplied of a good over a given period.

An **equilibrium** prevails when economic forces balance so that economic variables neither increase nor decrease. A **market equilibrium** is attained when the price of a good adjusts so that the quantity buyers are willing and able to buy at that price is just equal to the quantity sellers are willing and able to supply. When a market equilibrium is attained, forces of supply and demand balance so that there's no tendency for the market price or quantity to change over a given period. The equilibrium price acts to ration the good so that everyone who is willing and able to buy the good will find it available. Similarly, at the equilibrium price, everyone who wants to sell the good will be able to do so successfully. For example, equilibrium in the personal stereo market requires that the price of personal stereos be such that the quantity demanded equals the quantity supplied over a period. When quantity demanded equals quantity supplied in a market, the market is said to *clear*.

A **shortage** exists in a market if the quantity demanded exceeds the quantity supplied of a good over a given period. For example, there will be a monthly shortage of compact disc players if at the current market price the monthly number of players that sellers are willing and able to make available falls short of the monthly number that buyers are willing and able to purchase.

A **surplus** exists in a market if the quantity supplied exceeds the quantity demanded of a good over a given period. There would be a monthly surplus of gasoline if the monthly quantity supplied by sellers exceeded the monthly quantity demanded by buyers at a certain price. At the market equilibrium price of the good, there can be neither surpluses nor shortages in the market over any given period. When a market clears, the good is rationed in the sense that there are neither surpluses nor shortages over a period.

Surplus:
Exists if the quantity supplied exceeds the quantity demanded of a good over a given period.

Graphic Depiction of Market Equilibrium

The graph in Box 7 plots the demand curve corresponding to the data in the table in Box 1 on the same set of axes as the supply curve corresponding to the data in the table in Box 4. Suppose the price of eggs is $2 per dozen. At that price the quantity supplied by sellers would be 9,000 dozen per week, and the weekly quantity demanded by buyers would be 1,000 dozen. There would be a surplus of 8,000 dozen eggs at this price. *It follows that the price of $2 per dozen cannot result in a market equilibrium because quantity supplied would exceed quantity demanded at that price.*

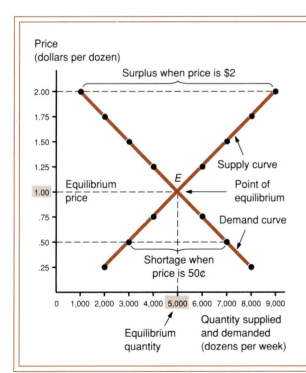

Box 7   Market Equilibrium

The market equilibrium price is $1 per dozen. The corresponding market equilibrium quantity is 5,000 dozen per week. Any price higher than $1 will result in a weekly surplus of eggs. Similarly, any price lower than $1 will result in a weekly shortage of eggs.

Market Equilibrium

Price (dollars per dozen)	Quantity demanded	Quantity supplied	Shortage or surplus	Pressure on price
	(dozens of eggs per week)			
2.00	1,000	9,000	Surplus	Down
1.75	2,000	8,000	Surplus	Down
1.50	3,000	7,000	Surplus	Down
1.25	4,000	6,000	Surplus	Down
1.00	5,000	5,000	Equilibrium	None
.75	6,000	4,000	Shortage	Up
.50	7,000	3,000	Shortage	Up
.25	8,000	2,000	Shortage	Up

Now suppose instead that the price of eggs is 50¢ per dozen. Would this price result in a market equilibrium? To find out, just draw a horizontal line from that price to the demand and supply curves. The quantity demanded at a price of 50¢ per dozen would be 7,000 dozen. However, the weekly quantity supplied at that price would be 3,000 dozen. Because the quantity demanded exceeds the quantity supplied by 4,000 dozen, it's clear that there would be a weekly shortage of eggs in the market at that price, as you can see in the graph. *It follows that the price of 50¢ per dozen cannot result in a market equilibrium because the weekly quantity of eggs demanded would exceed the weekly quantity supplied at that price.*

Finally, let's look at the price of $1 per dozen. Draw a horizontal line from that price to both curves. Note that this line will just touch the demand curve and the supply curve at point *E* where the two curves intersect. At the price of $1 per dozen the weekly quantity supplied will be 5,000 dozen. The weekly quantity demanded will also be 5,000 dozen. *Because the weekly quantity demanded equals the weekly quantity supplied, it follows that the $1 price would result in a market equilibrium. At that price there is neither a weekly surplus nor a weekly shortage of eggs on the market.* Note that, given all other influences on demand and supply, the $1 per dozen price is the *only* price that will result in market equilibrium. To check your understanding of this, examine the relationship between quantity demanded and quantity supplied at any other price. You'll see that any price other than $1 per dozen would result in either a weekly shortage or a weekly surplus of eggs.

Self-Equilibrating Markets

If the equilibrium price is not initially established in a market, competition among buyers for goods, and sellers for sales, will set up forces that cause the price to change. Whenever price exceeds its equilibrium level, there will be a surplus of goods on the market. Goods brought to market will go unsold. Sellers of eggs will be willing to accept lower prices rather than allow their weekly supply of eggs to spoil. In the case of goods whose quality doesn't deteriorate over time, sellers will be willing to accept lower prices to avoid the costs of maintaining inventory or transporting goods back to the point of production. *A surplus results in downward pressure on price.* As price falls, weekly quantity supplied will decline while weekly quantity demanded increases, serving to eliminate the surplus. The weekly surplus in the egg market will be completely eliminated when the price reaches the equilibrium level where quantity demanded equals quantity supplied each week.

A shortage implies that some buyers willing and able to pay the price will find the good unavailable in the market. Although eggs seem to be a bargain when their price is below the market equilibrium level, there aren't enough of them to go around! Competition among consumers for the available weekly quantity of eggs supplied will inevitably increase the price. Some consumers would be willing to pay more than the prevailing price rather than go without eggs that week. *A shortage therefore results in upward pressure on market price.* As market price increases, weekly quantity supplied will also increase while weekly quantity demanded will decline. This will continue until quantity demanded once again equals quantity supplied at the market equilibrium price and the shortage is eliminated.

As you can see, a competitive market tends to be self-equilibrating as a result of the competition between many buyers and sellers. The competition among buyers for available goods and among sellers for sales ensures that prices will adjust to achieve an equilibrium.

The table in Box 7 summarizes the relationship between quantities demanded and supplied at various prices using the hypothetical data in this example. The table shows that only at the equilibrium price of $1 per dozen is there neither upward nor downward pressure on price. The $1 price is the only price at which quantity demanded equals quantity supplied given the current demand and supply curves.

Principles in Practice

The Dollar Has Its Price Too! Demand for and Supply of the Dollar in Foreign Exchange Markets

How can the dollar *have* a price? Like most goods and services produced in the United States, the dollar itself is traded—for currencies of other nations. Just like cars, wheat, and running shoes, the value of the dollar is subject to the forces of supply and demand in international markets. Here's how it works.

On February 26, 1985, it took 261.5 Japanese yen to buy one U.S. dollar in the international currency markets. By early 1988 a dollar could be purchased at a bargain rate of only about 125 Japanese yen! The dollar has its price too in terms of foreign currencies, and that price can and does fluctuate with changes in supply and demand.

The graph shows the supply and demand curves for the dollar in international markets. The vertical axis shows the price of a dollar in terms of Japanese yen. The horizontal axis shows the number of dollars exchanged for yen per day. Like the demand curve for almost any commodity, that for dollars is downward sloping. Similarly, the higher the price of dollars in terms of yen, the greater the quantity of dollars supplied in exchange for yen, indicating an upward-sloping supply curve.

You can understand why the laws of supply and demand hold for dollars if you examine the consequences of changes in the exchange rate. Suppose the cost of production and the minimum acceptable profit for both Japanese and American goods are given. The price U.S. farmers will accept for each bushel of wheat is $2. The price Japanese electronics firms will accept for each compact disc player is 50,000 yen. Suppose the current equilibrium price of the dollar is 250 yen. You can now use the equilibrium exchange rate to convert the price of wheat into yen and the price of compact disc players into dollars.

Case 1: $1 = 250 yen

Price of wheat in yen = $2(250 yen/$1) = 500 yen

Price of compact disc
   players in dollars = 50,000 yen ($1/250 yen) = $200

Now suppose the price of the dollar falls to 125 yen. *Assuming there is no change in the prices sellers of these goods will accept in terms of their own currencies:*

Case 2: $1 = 125 yen

Price of wheat in yen = $2(125 yen/$1) = 250 yen

Price of compact disc
   players in dollars = 50,000 yen ($1/125 yen) = $400

The *decrease* in the price of the dollar makes Japanese goods more expensive in dollars and makes U.S. goods less expensive in yen. This means that, other things being equal, the Japanese will be more eager to buy U.S. wheat and other U.S. goods when the price of the dollar falls. The increase in the demand for U.S. goods caused by the decrease in the price of the dollar induces holders of yen to increase the number of dollars demanded.

Similarly, because a decrease in the price of dollars makes Japanese goods more expensive in terms of dollars, the number of dollars supplied in exchange for yen will decrease as the price of the dollar falls.

The next obvious question is: What causes the demand for and supply of dollars offered for yen to change over time?

1. *Interest rates in the U.S. and Japan affect Japanese demand for dollars.* The higher interest rates are in the U.S. relative to Japan, the greater the demand for dollars by the Japanese. This is because when interest rates are high on assets denominated in U.S. dollars, Japanese holders of yen can earn more by acquiring dollars to buy U.S. assets than by using yen to invest in Japanese assets. Relatively high interest rates in the U.S. therefore raise the price of the dollar by increasing Japanese demand for dollars. On the other hand, a decline in U.S. interest rates relative to those in Japan (as occurred in 1987) decreases the Japanese demand for dollars and puts downward pressure on the price of the dollar in terms of yen.

2. *The prices in domestic currencies that sellers in Japan and the United States will accept for products offered in international trade affect the supply of and demand for dollars.* An increase in the prices (in yen) Japanese automobile producers will accept for cars they want to export to the U.S. will, other things being equal, make those cars less attractive to U.S. citizens. An increase in Japanese prices in yen relative to those of competing U.S. products therefore decreases the supply of dollars offered in exchange for yen. The decrease in the supply of dollars tends to increase the price of the dollar in terms of yen.

Sometimes a government steps in and buys and sells its own currency. The purpose is to adjust the price of the currency in terms of foreign exchange so as to improve the balance of exports and imports.

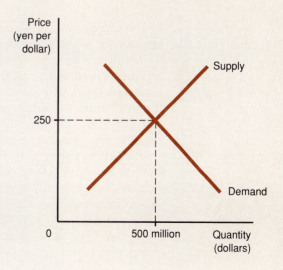

The Impact of Changes in Demand on Market Equilibrium

Changes in either demand or supply can change market equilibrium prices and quantities. You can now begin to use supply and demand analysis to make forecasts about what will happen to prices and quantities sold in response to these shifts in demand and supply.

Changes in demand affect market equilibrium. For example, suppose there's a decrease in demand for eggs because of concern about the high cholesterol content of eggs and its effect on health. In fact, in recent years this concern is likely to have contributed to a decrease in the demand for eggs. Recall that a decrease in the demand for eggs means an inward shift of the entire demand curve.

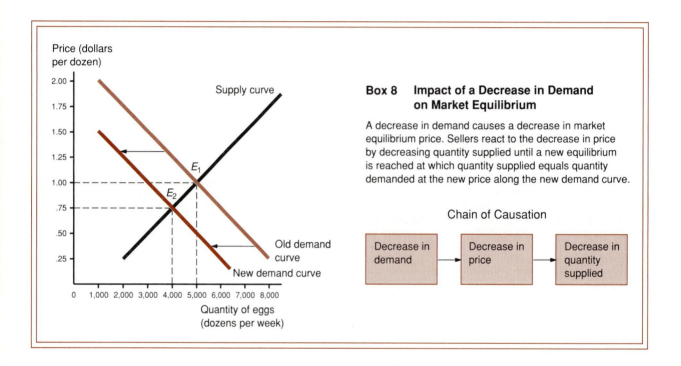

Box 8   Impact of a Decrease in Demand on Market Equilibrium

A decrease in demand causes a decrease in market equilibrium price. Sellers react to the decrease in price by decreasing quantity supplied until a new equilibrium is reached at which quantity supplied equals quantity demanded at the new price along the new demand curve.

Chain of Causation

The graph in Box 8 shows the impact of a decrease in demand for eggs on the egg market. As the demand curve shifts inward, the old price of $1 and quantity of 5,000 dozen eggs per week, corresponding to point E_1 in the graph, no longer represent the market equilibrium. To see why this is so, move along the dotted horizontal line drawn from the point corresponding to $1 on the vertical axis. The quantity demanded at that price along the *new* demand curve is now 3,000 dozen eggs per week. The quantity supplied at that price would still be 5,000 dozen eggs because there has been no change in supply. If the price remained at $1, there would be a weekly surplus of 2,000 dozen eggs. The market attains a *new* equilibrium in response to the decrease in demand as price declines to eliminate the surplus. The new market equilibrium corresponds to point E_2, at which the *new* demand curve intersects the supply curve. The price corresponding to that point is 75¢ per dozen. At the lower price, the quantity supplied by sellers declines to 4,000 dozen per week, which exactly equals the quantity demanded by buyers along the new demand curve at that price.

Principles in Practice

Just Like Humpty Dumpty: Egg Prices Fall in the 1980s

Humpty Dumpty sat on a wall, Humpty Dumpty had a great fall. Since 1984, egg prices in the United States might just as well have been on the same wall, because their fall has been precipitous! The cause, as you might guess, has been changes in supply and demand.

In 1984 the average retail price in the U.S. for a dozen large eggs was $1.02. At that price egg producers found egg production a profitable business. By March 1988 the average price for a dozen large eggs had fallen to 74¢, and between 1984 and 1988 thousands of egg producers were driven out of business because they could no longer profitably sell eggs.

A major cause of the price drop has been a massive decline in the demand for eggs because of health concerns. Many Americans now carefully watch their intake of cholesterol and as a result have cut back egg consumption. Egg consumption in the U.S. fell 5% to 249 eggs per person in 1988. As demand has decreased, the number of firms producing eggs has dropped as well. The total number of U.S. egg producers fell from 6,000 in 1979 to only 1,600 in 1987. However, remaining egg producers tend to be very large firms with more than 100,000 hens. As a result, despite the decline in the number of firms, there has been no significant decrease in the supply of eggs since 1970. The large operations also have adopted new technology that results in more eggs per hen. The double whammy for egg producers therefore stems from the fact that supply has not de-

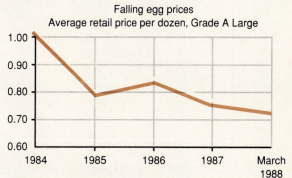

Falling egg prices
Average retail price per dozen, Grade A Large

Source: U.S. Department of Agriculture.

creased—it has actually increased because changes in technology and movement to large-scale production have offset the impact of the reduction in the number of firms.

At 1988 prices, egg producers estimate they have been incurring losses amounting to 5¢ per dozen. In early 1988 many producers were therefore contemplating going out of business or reducing the number of hens they have in production. As soon as the slaughterhouses can accommodate the hens, the supply of eggs is likely to decrease, thus putting upward pressure on egg prices.

The decrease in demand, other things remaining unchanged, sets up the following chain of events in the market: First, the price declines as a surplus develops at the original price. Second, sellers *respond* to the decrease in price by decreasing the quantity supplied. Finally, as the quantity supplied declines, a new equilibrium is attained at a price for which quantity demanded on the *new* demand curve equals quantity supplied on the existing supply curve. *Notice that sellers do not respond directly to the decrease in demand. Instead they respond to the decline in price caused by the decrease in demand.* This illustrates the role of price as a *signal* through which buyers communicate a change in their desires to sellers.

The chain of reasoning for an increase in demand is exactly the reverse. Suppose an increase in income causes an increase in the demand for stereo speakers. An increase in demand is a shift of the entire demand curve outward. The graph in Box 9 shows that an increase in demand for speakers will increase the market equilibrium price. As the price increases, there's a corresponding increase in quantity supplied until quantity demanded, on the new demand curve, once again equals quantity supplied. In the graph the initial equilibrium corresponds to point E_1, at which the price of a standard-quality speaker is $100, and 10,000 speakers are sold per month at that price. After the increase in demand the new equilibrium corresponds to point E_2, at which the price is $125 per speaker and the quantity supplied is 12,000 per month. The increase in price is a signal that induces sellers to increase the quantity supplied.

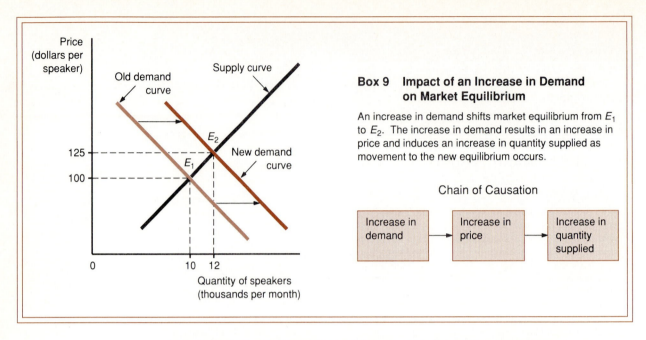

Price
(dollars per
speaker)

Old demand
curve

Supply curve

E_2

125

New demand
curve

100

E_1

0   10   12

Quantity of speakers
(thousands per month)

**Box 9   Impact of an Increase in Demand
on Market Equilibrium**

An increase in demand shifts market equilibrium from E_1
to E_2. The increase in demand results in an increase in
price and induces an increase in quantity supplied as
movement to the new equilibrium occurs.

Chain of Causation

| Increase in demand | → | Increase in price | → | Increase in quantity supplied |

The Impact of Changes in Supply on Market Equilibrium

Remember that a change in supply is a shift of the entire supply curve for a good
caused by a change in some influence other than the price of the good. For example,
an increase in the price of chicken feed is likely to decrease the supply of eggs. The
graph in Box 10 shows how a decrease in supply will affect market equilibrium.
Assume that the initial market equilibrium, corresponding to point E_1 on the graph,

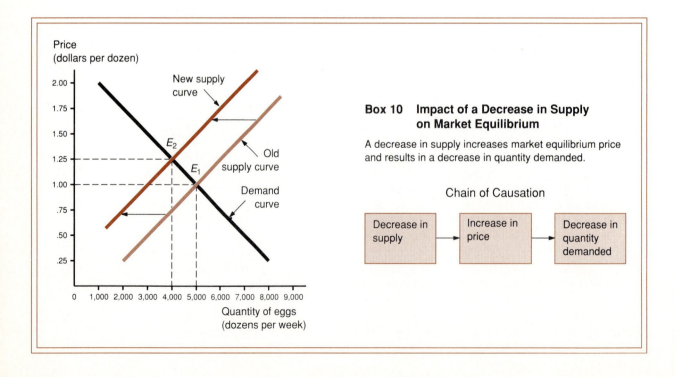

Price
(dollars per dozen)

New supply
curve

2.00

1.75

1.50

E_2

1.25

Old
supply curve

E_1

1.00

Demand
curve

.75

.50

.25

0 1,000 2,000 3,000 4,000 5,000 6,000 7,000 8,000 9,000

Quantity of eggs
(dozens per week)

**Box 10   Impact of a Decrease in Supply
on Market Equilibrium**

A decrease in supply increases market equilibrium price
and results in a decrease in quantity demanded.

Chain of Causation

| Decrease in supply | → | Increase in price | → | Decrease in quantity demanded |

is once again a price of $1 per dozen and that 5,000 dozen eggs are sold per week at that price. As the supply curve shifts inward, the initial price can no longer result in an equilibrium. This is because the quantity supplied at that price along the *new* supply curve is now only 3,000 dozen per week. Because there's been no change in demand, the quantity demanded at that price would still be 5,000 dozen per week. There would therefore be a weekly shortage of eggs on the market if the price remained at $1 per dozen. Competition among buyers eliminates the shortage and raises the price. As price increases, quantity demanded declines until it equals quantity supplied. The new market equilibrium corresponds to point E_2, at which market price is $1.25 per dozen and quantity sold is 4,000 dozen per week. This is the point at which the *new* supply curve intersects the original demand curve. Note that *buyers do not respond directly to the decrease in supply. Instead they respond to the increase in market price caused by the decrease in supply.* Once again you can see how price serves as a device for communication between buyers and sellers. Buyers are motivated to reduce the quantity demanded in response to the higher price caused by the decrease in supply.

The reasoning is similar for an increase in supply. For example, in recent years improvements in technology have served to increase the supply of television sets. A number of years ago the equilibrium price for a standard 13-inch color TV was about $300. As advances in technology increased supply, there was downward pressure on the price of TVs. The graph in Box 11 shows the impact of the increase in supply on market equilibrium. Start out once again at point E_1, at which the original demand curve intersects the original supply curve. At that point the market price of TVs is $300 and the quantity sold per year is 4 million. The increase in supply means that the original supply curve shifts outward. The new market equilibrium now corresponds to point E_2, at which the *new* supply curve intersects the original demand curve. If market price remained at $300 per set, there would be an annual surplus of TVs on the shelves of retailers. The price must fall to clear the market. The new equilibrium price is now $200 per TV. Quantity demanded at that price is 5 million

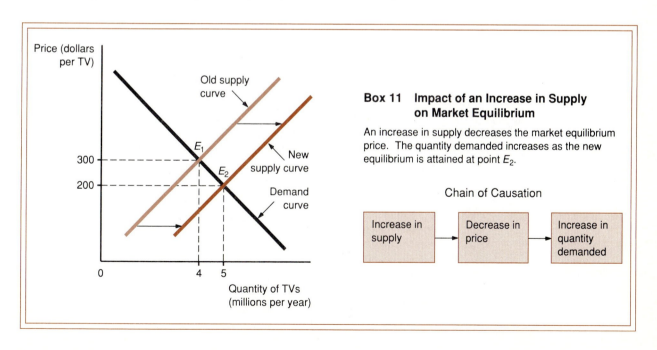

Box 11 Impact of an Increase in Supply on Market Equilibrium

An increase in supply decreases the market equilibrium price. The quantity demanded increases as the new equilibrium is attained at point E_2.

Chain of Causation

| Increase in supply | → | Decrease in price | → | Increase in quantity demanded |

TVs per year, which exactly equals the quantity sellers are willing to supply at that price along the *new* supply curve. An improvement in technology therefore tends to lower the market price of a good and increase the quantity demanded.

Concept Check

1 Explain why shortages and surpluses of goods in a market imply that it is not in equilibrium.

2 What opposing forces balance when a market equilibrium is attained? How do markets self-equilibrate?

3 An increase in the popularity of skiing as a sport increases the demand for skis. Use supply and demand analysis to forecast the impact of the increase in demand on the price and quantity of skis supplied by sellers.

Mastering the Art of Supply and Demand Analysis

The forces of supply and demand determine prices in competitive markets. If you thoroughly understand how buyers and sellers respond to changes in opportunities for gains in markets and how market equilibrium prices serve to equate quantity demanded with quantity supplied in a market, you're on your way to understanding the most basic of economic relationships.

Supply and demand analysis is relevant to all goods and services exchanged in markets: labor, machines, land, and structures. You must understand how to manipulate supply and demand curves so that you'll be able to explain changes in interest rates, wages, and rents as we move through the book.

You'll also want to keep in mind that supply and demand influences are constantly changing. We usually base our analysis of markets on a "snapshot" of the market at a single point in time. We then make hypotheses about how market equilibrium would change if a certain demand or supply determinant were to change. In actuality, many changes occur simultaneously in a market. Supply and demand curves are constantly shifting. Perhaps the best example of this is the stock market, where prices can move quickly and often erratically over a short period of time as market conditions change (see the Principles in Practice box). However, you'll gain little understanding of the relationship between price and other variables by trying to analyze all variables at the same time. You'll find that the best way to understand the process of price determination in markets is to study one variable at a time. This will help you isolate the impact of important influences on price and quantities traded.

Part of the art of supply and demand analysis is knowing the relevant influences affecting the decisions of buyers and sellers in a market and their ability to purchase or sell goods. You need to understand the causes of changes in supply or demand so you can forecast market prices and trading. For example, weather is likely to be an important supply influence on an agricultural market but has little effect on the market for computers. Interest rates are likely to be an important influence on the net gains we can enjoy from buying homes and cars, and thus interest rates affect demand for these items. Improvements in technology are a major influence on the supply of electronic goods like VCRs, microwave ovens, and personal computers.

Principles in Practice

The Stock Market: How It Works and What Happened on "Black Monday"

Do you understand what happened to the stock market on "Black Monday"? If you don't, you're not alone—distinguished economists, respected stock market analysts, and U.S. Treasury officials are still arguing about it! Let's take a closer look at the stock market and its 1987 crash.

On Monday, October 19, 1987, a wave of selling triggered widespread price declines in stock markets from New York to Australia. On that day, now infamous as "Black Monday," over 600 million shares were traded on the New York Stock Exchange—more than twice the NYSE's average sales volume. The Dow Jones Industrial Average of the prices of 30 stocks of major U.S. companies lost 22.6% of its value on that memorable day, plunging 508 points in the panicked rush to sell.

What is the stock market, and how is it affected by the forces of supply and demand?

The stock market is the means through which previously issued corporate stocks are traded. A stock is a share of ownership in a corporation. Stock exchanges are organizations whose members act as intermediaries to buy and sell stocks for their clients. About 80% of all stock trading in the United States takes place at the New York Stock Exchange. Stocks of smaller companies are traded on the over-the-counter market, a network of independent brokers who communicate by telephone and telex rather than meeting at a specific location. There are other stock exchanges in the United States, and major stock exchanges in foreign countries are located in Paris, London, Sydney, Tokyo, and other large cities.

How are stock prices determined? The answer, as you might expect, is by supply and demand. However, the forces influencing the prices of corporate stocks are quite different from those influencing the prices of goods and services. People and organizations who buy and hold stock do so for the incomes they hope to earn. The income depends on dividends paid to stockholders, changes in the price of a stock over time, and the expected return on a stock compared to the return on alternative investments.

On any given day in the stock market, there are orders to buy and orders to sell. The orders to buy constitute the quantity of a stock demanded at the current (or anticipated) price per share, while the orders to sell constitute the quantity supplied at that price. The chief influence on both the supply of and demand for stocks is the income potential of holding the stock compared to the income potential of holding alternative assets such as bonds and other types of securities and real property like buildings and land.

The way in which the forces of supply and demand actually influence stock prices depends on the rules of trading of the particular stock exchange. For example, the Paris stock exchange uses a "call market" method. Under this technique brokers have time to accumulate their orders to buy and sell specific stocks. When there's a call for the stock, a clerk acts like an auctioneer to establish an equilibrium price at the time of the call. The clerk might begin by calling out the most recent trading price of the stock, say 1,000 francs. If after the call all the selling orders are filled and brokers still have orders to buy, the clerk will call out a higher price. Similarly, if at the initial price of 1,000 francs all the orders to sell aren't matched by orders to buy, the clerk will call out a lower price. In this way the clerk acts to adjust price until quantity demanded equals quantity supplied at the call session. Naturally, if there are more sell orders than buy orders at the current price, stock prices will tumble during the call.

On the New York Stock Exchange, trading in all stocks is continuous rather than at specific call sessions. A specialist is assigned to oversee trading in each stock. This specialist is a "broker's broker" who tries to adjust the price of the stock so that quantity demanded equals quantity supplied. However, the specialist is also allowed to purchase the stock to hold as a personal investment if no buyer can be found. In this way the specialist can exert some influence on the supply of and demand for stocks, and will do so if it's profitable.

When the orders to sell far outnumber the orders to buy, specialists and call clerks in the market must lower prices to equate quantity demanded with quantity supplied. On October 19, 1987, there were hardly any buy orders, and the markets were flooded with sell orders. Because of the tremendous surplus of stocks at the prevailing prices, specialists and call clerks lowered prices until quantity demanded equaled quantity supplied. When Black Monday finally reeled to a close, many a portfolio had lost over a fifth of the value it had the day before. The dollar value of outstanding stocks in the United States declined by a whopping $500 billion on that single day!

In terms of supply and demand, the graph shows that the Crash of '87 resulted from a sharp increase in the supply of stocks coupled with a decrease in demand.

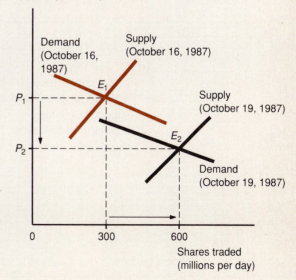

Average price (dollars per share)

Demand (October 16, 1987)
Supply (October 16, 1987)
Supply (October 19, 1987)
Demand (October 19, 1987)

E_1 P_1 E_2 P_2

0 300 600

Shares traded (millions per day)

Summary

1. Markets are arrangements through which buyers and sellers can communicate and conduct transactions to enjoy mutual gains. In a free and competitive market there are large numbers of rival buyers and sellers, no one of which can influence the price of the product traded. There are no restrictions on who can buy and sell. Supply and demand analysis explains how prices are established in competitive markets and how those prices affect the quantities traded.

2. The law of demand states that, in general, other things being equal, there is a negative relationship between the price of a good and the willingness and ability of buyers to purchase the good.

3. A demand curve illustrates the relationship between price and quantity demanded.

4. A change in quantity demanded is a movement along a demand curve in response to a change in the price of a good. A change in demand is a response to a change in a determinant other than the price of a good that shifts an entire demand curve. Changes in demand can be caused by changes in such factors as consumer income, prices of other goods, expectations, tastes, or population.

5. The law of supply states that, in general, other things being equal, there is a positive relationship between price and the amount of a good sellers are willing and able to make available.

6. A supply curve shows how quantity supplied varies with the price of a good.

7. A change in quantity supplied is a movement along a given supply curve caused by a change in the price of a good. A change in supply is a shift of an entire supply curve caused by a change in a determinant other than the price of a good that affects the willingness and ability of sellers to make the good available. Changes in supply can be caused by changes in input prices, improvements in technology, changes in the prices of other goods that can be produced with the seller's resources, and changes in sellers' expectations about the future.

8. A market equilibrium is attained when the price of a good adjusts so that the quantity demanded equals the quantity supplied. If price exceeds the market equilibrium level, a surplus will prevail. If price is below the market equilibrium, a shortage will prevail. Surpluses put downward pressure on prices, while shortages put upward pressure on prices.

9. Market equilibrium prices ration goods by ensuring that everyone who is willing and able to buy a good will find it available, while everyone who is willing and able to sell the good will do so successfully. Prices accomplish this objective because they influence the personal gains possible from buying and selling the good.

10. Changes in demand or supply result in new market equilibrium prices. A change in demand affects market price. A change in market price affects the gains from selling the good and causes sellers to respond by adjusting the quantity they supply. A change in supply also affects market equilibrium price. The resulting change in price affects the personal gain possible from purchasing the good and therefore causes buyers to respond by adjusting quantity demanded.

Key Terms and Concepts

Market
Supply and demand analysis
Quantity demanded
Demand
Demand schedule
Law of demand
Demand curve
Change in relative price
Change in quantity demanded
Change in demand
Substitutes
Complements

Quantity supplied
Supply
Supply schedule
Law of supply
Supply curve
Change in quantity supplied
Change in supply
Equilibrium
Market equilibrium
Shortage
Surplus

Problems and Applications

1. A new report by the surgeon general on the harmful effects of cholesterol on health decreases the demand for eggs. Suppose the resulting decrease in demand reduces by 50% the quantities buyers are willing to buy each week at each possible price for the demand schedule in Box 1. Draw up the new demand schedule and show the decrease in demand on a graph by drawing both the old and new demand curves.

2. An improvement in the technology of egg laying doubles the number of eggs each chicken can lay per week. Assuming that the improvement in technology doubles the weekly quantity supplied at each price in the table in Box 4, draw up the new supply schedule. Graph both the old and new supply curves to illustrate the change in supply.

3. Assuming that both the decrease in demand and the increase in supply of eggs described in problems 1 and 2 occur simultaneously, use a graph to show the impact on the market equilibrium price of eggs and the quantity sold per week.

4. Suppose the market for coffee is currently in equilibrium at a price of $3 per pound. An early frost in coffee-growing nations decreases the supply of coffee. Use supply and demand analysis to forecast the impact of the freeze on the market equilibrium price and quantity of coffee.

5. Suppose the market rate of interest on car loans declines substantially. Use supply and demand analysis to predict the impact of the interest rate decline on the prices of cars and the quantity sold.

6. Suppose you want to buy a particular brand of compact disc player that's very popular. You go to every store in town, and all of them are out of stock. You and many others like you are willing and able to pay the market price of $300 for the players, but you can't find any available. Is the market for this compact disc player in equilibrium? Use supply and demand analysis to explain your answer.

7. The federal government announces that it will buy for $3 a loaf all the bread that can't be sold in a competitive market at that price. At the end of each week the government purchases 1 million loaves of bread. Use supply and demand analysis to show that the market equilibrium price is less than $3 per loaf. Why doesn't the market price fall in this case?

8. Show how a decrease in the supply of bread in the graph that you drew for

problem 7 can raise its market equilibrium price above $3 a loaf. How much bread would the government buy each week under these circumstances?

9. Assume the market price of Mustang convertibles is $15,000. At that price the quantity demanded is 1 million per year, while the quantity supplied is only 500,000 per year. Is the market in equilibrium? Explain your answer.

10. A decrease in demand for personal computers results in a surplus of PCs on the market. Explain how market forces will be set up to eliminate the surplus.

Suggested Readings

Fortune magazine: *Fortune* and other business magazines, such as *Business Week,* often have timely articles on supply and demand trends for various goods and services. Try reading some of these articles and then draw supply and demand curves to help you understand the implications of changes in economic trends.

Karl Polanyi, *The Great Transformation,* Boston: Beacon Press, 1963. This book, which was first published in 1944, traces the historical development of markets. The book is easy to read and requires no extensive background in economics.

The Wall Street Journal: Do you want to know how supply and demand influence the prices of stocks, bonds, economic resources, and goods and services? This newspaper concentrates on economic affairs and often has articles on events in particular markets that show how changes in demand and supply affect prices and quantities sold. For that matter, you can just open your local newspaper and find articles about supply and demand almost every day.

A Forward Look

The best way for you to understand supply and demand analysis is to use it. In the following chapter we'll concentrate on applications that show you the relevance of supply and demand analysis in understanding business and social policies. As you'll see, the basic analysis is important in grasping both microeconomic and macroeconomic issues.

Using Supply and Demand Analysis

What are the prospects for profitably marketing a new product? Will an increase in interest rates bring on an economic recession? Should the federal government continue to subsidize farmers by guaranteeing them minimum prices for their crops? Should the federal minimum wage be increased, held constant, or repealed? Should landlords be bound by laws that place a ceiling on the rents they can charge?

Each of these actions or policies has predictable consequences that we can forecast using supply and demand analysis. In this chapter you'll have more opportunities to master and use supply and demand analysis, and to understand its relevance to a wide range of business, political, and social issues.

As you'll see after reading the chapter, the laws of supply and demand cannot be repealed. Because so many goods and services are bought and sold in markets, market outcomes influence the daily lives of all of us. Changes in supply and demand conditions change market prices. Changes in prices inevitably affect the gains possible from buying and selling goods and thereby change the choices we make.

After reading this chapter, you should be able to: *Concept Preview*

1 Demonstrate how market equilibrium prices deal with the problem of scarcity by rationing goods and services, and explain why prices would be zero for nonscarce goods.
2 Explain how supply and demand conditions affect the price and sales potential for new products.
3 Show how wages and interest rates are determined in competitive markets.
4 Use supply and demand analysis to show how government control of prices in competitive markets can result in shortages or surpluses.
5 Discuss nonprice rationing systems and show how these alternatives work when the rationing function of prices in markets is impaired.

Prices, Scarcity, and Marketing Prospects

Why Are Prices Necessary?

Imagine you were able to go shopping at all your favorite stores, pick out every item your heart desired, and sail right by the checkout counter without paying a dime. In this consumer's dream, you could enter any market for any good or service and have the pleasure of acquiring as much as you choose at zero price: designer fashions, a high-end audio/video system, a home gym, a chauffeur-driven limousine. Surely you'd obtain more and better goods and services in such a fantasy world than you do when confronted with the reality of market prices and your limited income.

Suppose *everyone* were given the privilege of bypassing the checkout counter for all goods and services. Try to picture such a giveaway at your local imported car dealer. How would the available Porsches, BMWs, and Audis be allocated among the hordes of eager consumers clamoring to obtain them? Would customers obediently line up for their turn to obtain luxury cars for free? Or would they be more likely to turn into an unruly and perhaps violent mob, fighting over 735i's and 944's? And who would make the cars available? After all, business firms seek to make profits. How can they cover their production and distribution costs and make a profit for their owners if they give their products away for free?

If business firms couldn't charge for their goods, they wouldn't make them available to consumers. If you're looking for a sleek Corvette at zero price, you probably know you're out of luck! This fantasy of a giveaway world should make it clear to you how prices are necessary to cope with scarcity.

Nonscarce Goods

There's only one case in which zero prices for goods we want would not create hopeless shortages. This is the rather improbable case of a good that's not actually scarce. A **nonscarce (or free) good** is one for which the quantity demanded does not exceed the quantity supplied at zero price. In other words, a nonscarce good is available in amounts that result in no shortage even if the price of the good is zero.

Nonscarce (or free) good: A good for which the quantity demanded does not exceed the quantity supplied at zero price.

Of course, few if any goods can be described as nonscarce. However, we can fantasize about situations in which nonscarcity might prevail. For example, coconuts might be so plentiful in an island nation with a small population that people on the island can enjoy all they wish at zero price. Assume that no one in this isolated island paradise thinks about exporting the coconuts to other areas of the world where the fruit is scarce in relation to desires to use it. The graph in Box 1 shows you the demand and supply curves for coconuts in such a paradise. You'll notice that the demand curve intersects the horizontal axis without intersecting the supply curve first. At zero price 10 tons of coconuts per season are demanded. At zero price the quantity of coconuts available is 20 tons per season. Because the quantity supplied exceeds the quantity demanded at zero price, there's a surplus of coconuts even when they're available free. Anyone who tried to sell coconuts on the island would be unable to find any buyers, because the availability of the fruit exceeds the amount desired at zero price.

However, the laws of supply and demand are still relevant. The higher the price of coconuts, the lower the quantity demanded, as you can see by the downward-sloping demand curve. For example, if the price were $5 per ton, as shown in the graph, the quantity demanded would fall below 10 tons per year. Similarly, the

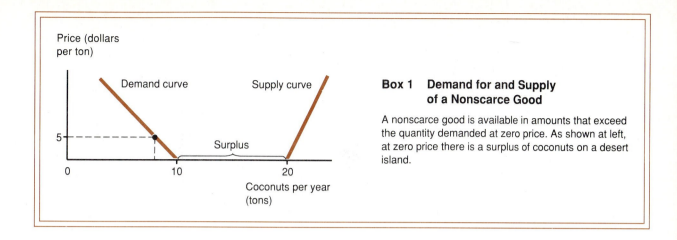

Box 1 Demand for and Supply of a Nonscarce Good

A nonscarce good is available in amounts that exceed the quantity demanded at zero price. As shown at left, at zero price there is a surplus of coconuts on a desert island.

higher the price of coconuts on the island, the greater the quantity supplied as residents of other coconut-rich islands make their coconuts available. However, the quantity available at zero price exceeds the quantity demanded at that price, making it impossible for people with coconuts to sell them at a positive price.

We can make a similar analysis for air. The amounts of air available for breathing at zero price exceed the quantity demanded at that price. Therefore you wouldn't succeed in packaging air for sale at a positive price.

Garbage is a negatively valued item that we pay someone to take away. However, items we currently toss away as garbage can become scarce goods with changes in either demand or supply. For example, the current quantity of plastic soft drink bottles exceeds the quantity demanded by people who don't regard this item as garbage at zero price. However, in the future the supply curve for today's empty bottles of a given soft drink will move to the left. The demand curve for such bottles by collectors will move to the right. If the supply and demand curves continue to shift in this way, they'll intersect at a positive price. Today's trash can end up being tomorrow's treasures—something you already know if your mother threw out your shoebox of baseball cards!

How Demand and Supply Conditions Affect the Success of New Products

We can use supply and demand analysis to evaluate the prospects for marketing new products profitably. The price of a new product influences the quantity demanded. Firms must be able to sell new products at prices that exceed costs sufficiently to allow a profit.

Suppose you're considering investing in a firm that plans to market a new and improved method of reproducing recorded sound. The company estimates that when it first puts the product on the market, the minimum price it can accept is $1,000 per unit. For example, the Sony Corporation marketed its newly developed compact disc player at that price when it was introduced in the Japanese market in 1982.

Will the new product sell at that price? To find out, we need to guess how the supply and demand curves for the product look. Suppose the demand curve for the product is like the one illustrated in the graph in Box 2. A number of supply curves

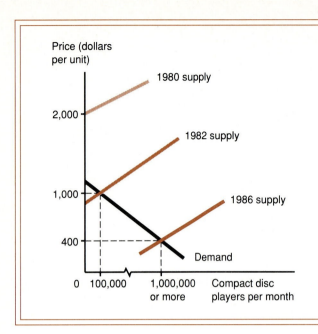

Box 2   The Market for New Products

If the supply curve of a new product intersects the price axis before intersecting the demand curve, sellers will be unable to sell any of the new product at the minimum price they require to cover their opportunity costs.

are also drawn in the graph. The first supply curve shows the supply of the compact disc player in 1980. At that time the technology for the product wasn't fully developed. However, let's assume that a prototype of the product could have been marketed at that time along with a reasonable number of selections on compact disc. The supply curve for 1980 hits the price axis at $2,000. The demand curve for that year hits the price axis at about $1,100. This implies that the minimum price sellers will accept to make only one compact disc player per year available exceeds the maximum price that any buyer would pay to purchase the player. *Using business jargon, this means that there is no market for the product.* The supply and demand curves don't intersect at a positive quantity.

This analysis illustrates an important business-related lesson: *The price of a new product is a crucial determinant of its success in a market.* You might develop an idea for a fantastic new electronic product, like a computerized household robot that cleans and cooks. However, unless you can price the product at a level that allows you to make sufficient sales while at the same time at least covering your opportunity costs, your product will have no market.

It's worthwhile to continue this analysis because it illustrates how changing supply and demand conditions can expand the market for new products. As we noted earlier, Sony introduced its compact disc player in Japan in 1982 at a price of $1,000. At that price the company quickly sold 100,000 units in the first month! Apparently the demand and supply curves did intersect at a positive quantity. It's reasonable to assume that in 1982 the technology for mass producing the new product had improved, resulting in an outward shift of the market supply curve as illustrated in the graph in Box 2. In that graph it's assumed that there was no change in demand for compact disc players between 1980 and 1982. However, the lower price made possible by the increase in supply caused an increase in the quantity demanded.

By the mid-1980s improvements in technology, coupled with an increase in the number of firms producing compact disc players, caused the supply to grow, and a worldwide market opened up as the price fell. Assuming no change in demand and no change in the quality of the product, the graph in Box 2 shows the supply curve existing in 1986. At that time the market price of CD players was in the range of $150 to $1,000 depending on the features of the particular model. The average price at that time was about $400. At that price over a million units were sold per year, showing that the quantity demanded had increased. The graph in Box 2 doesn't consider possible increases in demand (outward shifts of the demand curve) caused by increased availability of musical selections on compact discs and aggressive advertising campaigns by Sony and other manufacturers of CDs and players. Increases in demand would have offset some of the price-depressing effects of the increases in supply by putting upward pressure on prices.

The expansion of markets as a result of improved technology and other factors contributing to lower production costs has been common for electronic products in recent years. The hand-held calculator, the personal computer, and the home video cassette recorder all were unheard of 30 years ago. Thanks to improved technology, these products are now available at affordable prices and are owned by millions.

Markets for Labor and Credit

Labor Markets

We also can apply supply and demand analysis to markets for *economic resources*, such as the services of labor. Many macroeconomic issues we'll examine in the second half of the book deal with analysis of prices and employment of productive resources. To understand these issues, you need to understand how the laws of supply and demand operate in these markets. In this section you'll learn how a typical resource market operates: in this case the market for labor services.

In modern economies, workers sell their services to employers in labor markets. In a competitive labor market there are many workers independently offering skills of a given quality to many employers who compete for the workers' services. As is the case in product markets, the prices paid for labor services, hourly **wages** or yearly salaries, are important determinants of the amount of labor demanded and supplied over a given period, say per week.

Wages:
The prices paid for labor services.

It's reasonable to expect the laws of demand and supply to prevail in labor markets as they do in product markets. The lower the wage, the greater the quantity of labor services demanded by employers. The demand curve for labor services is therefore downward sloping. This is because employers substitute other inputs, such as machines, for labor services as wages go up while substituting labor services for other inputs as wages decline.

The higher the wage, the greater the quantity of labor services supplied. At higher wages individual workers are willing to work more hours per week. In addition, higher wages are likely to induce workers not currently seeking employment, such as students, retirees, and homemakers, to enter the market and seek work. Also, an increase in wages in one part of the country is likely to attract workers from other parts of the country looking for jobs at the higher wages.

The graph in Box 3 shows the demand and supply curves for labor services in a market for unskilled labor. Employers have no reason to prefer the services of one worker over another in such a market because labor services are standardized. In the graph the equilibrium wage is $4 per hour. At that wage 3 million labor hours per week are employed.

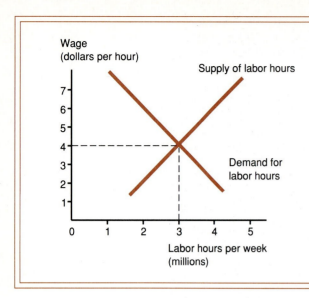

Wage
(dollars per hour)

Supply of labor hours

7
6
5
4
3
2
1

0   1   2   3   4   5

Demand for
labor hours

Labor hours per week
(millions)

**Box 3   Demand for and Supply
of Labor Hours**

The equilibrium wage is $4 per hour. At that wage the
quantity demanded and quantity supplied is 3 million
labor hours per week.

There are a multitude of labor markets in the economy for services that require
many different kinds of skills. There are, for example, markets for economics professors, heart surgeons, plumbers, musicians, grape pickers, cruise directors, and
various other specialists. In each market, workers have similar skills. Wages, of
course, differ widely in these markets depending on the value employers place on
the skills of workers and on the factors influencing the supply of each type of labor.
Later in the book we'll investigate in greater depth the factors influencing the demand for and supply of labor.

Notice how the market equilibrium wage rations the available number of labor
hours per month. At the equilibrium wage of $4 per hour, the quantity of labor
hours demanded just equals the quantity supplied. This means that all workers willing and able to work will find jobs, while all employers willing and able to hire
workers at that wage will find them available. There's neither a shortage of labor
services nor a surplus.

The demand for labor is derived from the demand for the products that labor is
used to produce. When a business using a particular type of labor enjoys an increase
in orders for its products, it will have to hire more labor to fill those orders. Consider the workers whose labor market is illustrated in Box 3. An increase in demand
for labor caused by increased orders for the products these workers produce will
increase wages. An increase in wages will make work more attractive to workers and
cause an increase in the number of labor hours supplied per month.

You can see the effect of an increase in demand for labor services by looking at
the graph in Box 4. The increase in demand for workers increases the wage from
$4 to $5 per hour. If the wage were to remain at $4 after the increase in demand,
the quantity demanded would be 4 million hours per month while the quantity
supplied would remain at 3 million hours per month. There would therefore be a
shortage of workers. Competition among employers would put upward pressure on
wages. As the wage increases from $4 to $5, the quantity of labor hours supplied
increases. A new labor market equilibrium is achieved and 3.5 million labor hours
per month are employed. As in product markets, the price of labor services, in this
case wages, acts as a signal to workers by increasing the gains possible from addi-

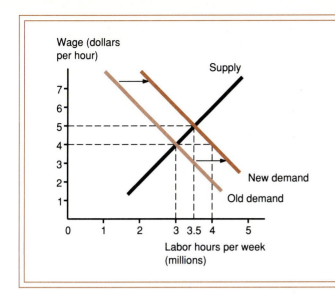

Box 4   Impact of an Increase in Demand for Labor Hours

An increase in the demand for weekly labor hours increases the market wage and increases the quantity of labor hours supplied. If the market wage did not increase to $5 per hour, there would be a weekly shortage of labor hours.

tional work. Workers respond to higher wages by increasing the quantity of labor supplied.

Conversely, a decrease in orders for products will cause a decrease in the demand for labor. Suppose the bicycle industry in the United States experiences a decline in orders because of increased popularity of inexpensive foreign-produced bikes that are substitutes for the U.S. products. The decrease in demand for U.S.-made bikes will decrease the demand for bicycle workers. This will put downward pressure on the wages earned by such workers and will decrease the quantity of labor supplied.

An increase in the supply of labor hours caused by, say, an increase in the working-age population also will affect labor market equilibrium. An increase in the supply of workers, other things unchanged, puts downward pressure on wages. As shown in the graph in Box 5, if market wages remained at $4 per hour after an

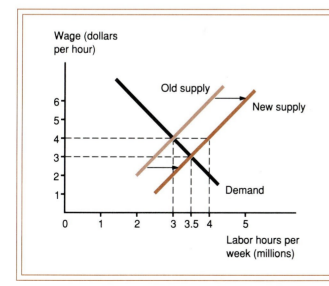

Box 5   Impact of an Increase in Supply of Labor Hours

An increase in the supply of labor hours decreases the equilibrium wage and increases the quantity of labor demanded. If the wage did not fall, there would be a weekly surplus of labor hours.

Principles in Practice

Operation of Labor Markets in the United States: How Lags in Wage Adjustment Result in Surpluses and Shortages of Labor

ın practice, labor markets don't always move to instantaneously adjust wages and thus eliminate surpluses and shortages of labor. For example, during a recession the demand for factory workers typically declines as the demand for factory output decreases. If wages were to adjust immediately after the decline in demand, the quantity of labor demanded would equal the quantity supplied at a lower wage, as shown in the graph.

Hourly labor
compensation
(dollars per hour)

Labor supply

Initial equilibrium
point

W_1

W_2

Hourly labor
compensation
that would
prevail if
market quickly
reequilibrated

Initial
demand

Demand after a
recession hits

0   Q_3 Q_2 Q_1 Labor employment
                            (factory labor hours
                            per month)

Surplus of labor hours
when compensation
per hour does not fall
after demand decreases

However, the data on wage adjustment in the United States during recessions that have occurred since the end of World War II indicate that wages adjusted for the effects of inflation actually *rise* slightly during recessions! This suggests that labor markets don't adjust quickly to temporary declines in labor demand. During a typical recession in the United States, the unemployment rate rises about 2 to 4 percentage points.*

As a result of downward rigidity in wages during recessions, employment declines by more than would otherwise be the case. In the graph, employment would fall from Q_1 to Q_2 during a recession if wages fell in response to the decrease in labor demand. However, when wages don't fall quickly in response to the decline in demand, employment falls to Q_3. Rigid wages therefore result in a surplus of labor and excessive unemployment during a recession. However, workers who keep their jobs during recessions don't suffer a decline in income. The way U.S. labor markets operate, the workers with the greatest seniority are laid off last during a recession. This implies that much of the loss of income caused by layoffs in a recession is borne by younger workers.

In some cases wages in labor markets aren't quick to adjust upward in response to changes in demand and supply. A prime example is the market for the services of nurses. In 1986 there was a serious shortage of nurses. A survey by the American Hospital Association in 1986 indicated that 14% of the budgeted nursing positions that year were unfilled. Many hospitals had particular difficulty that year in filling positions for specialized nursing services, and it often took 3 months to fill such vacancies.†

increase in labor supply, there would be a surplus of labor hours at that wage. The surplus causes market wages to decline to $3 per hour, and the number of labor hours demanded by employers per month increases.

Credit Markets: The Demand for and Supply of Loanable Funds

We also can use supply and demand analysis to analyze markets for credit. **Credit** is the use of loanable funds supplied by lenders to borrowers who agree to pay back the funds borrowed according to an agreed-upon schedule. The price for the use of loanable funds is called **interest.** Interest is usually expressed as a percentage per dollar of funds borrowed, which is referred to as the interest *rate*. When you borrow funds, you must pay interest to your creditor. If you lend funds, you'll re-

Credit:
The use of loanable funds supplied by lenders to borrowers who agree to pay back the borrowed funds according to an agreed-upon schedule.

Interest:
The price for the use of funds, expressed as a percentage per dollar of funds borrowed.

During the mid-1980s there was a sharp increase in demand for nurses coupled with a decrease in supply. This should have increased wages substantially, as shown in the graph. If the market were to quickly equilibrate, wages would increase from W_1 to W_2. However, when wages only go up to w' after the shifts in demand and supply, there's an enormous shortage of nursing services.

The increase in demand for nurses came from clinics and from elderly patients who were being treated at home. There was a decrease in the supply of nurses because fewer women, who have traditionally filled nursing jobs, were interested in enrolling in nursing curriculums. Women with more education now found other options open to them, such as studying medicine and pursuing a career as a physician. Greater employment opportunities for women in general during the 1980s decreased the attractiveness of nursing as an occupation.

A nursing shortage in the 1970s eventually resulted in sharp increases in wages paid to nurses. The same trend is likely to result from the shortage of the 1980s. As wages rise, more people, men as well as women, will be attracted into nursing occupations. However, it takes time for the supply of nurses to increase. The slow pace at which wages rise in the nursing market contributes to shortages of nurses. If wages were to rise more rapidly, more people with nursing skills could be induced to work overtime, retired nurses could be induced to start practicing again, and nurses from foreign nations could be induced to take jobs in the United States.

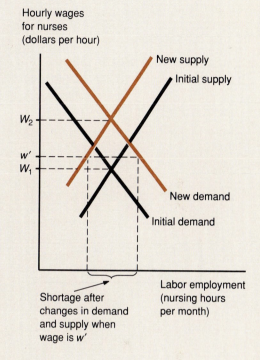

Hourly wages for nurses (dollars per hour)

New supply
Initial supply
W_2
w'
W_1
New demand
Initial demand

Labor employment (nursing hours per month)

Shortage after changes in demand and supply when wage is w'

*See Thomas J. Kniesner and Arthur H. Goldsmith, "A Survey of Alternative Models of the Aggregate U.S. Labor Market," *Journal of Economic Literature,* 25, 3, September 1987, pp. 1241-1280.
†See Timothy Tregarthen, "Critical Condition: Supply of Nurses Wearing Thin," *The Margin,* 3,2, October 1987, pp. 12-13.

ceive interest payments. For example, if you borrow money from a bank to buy a car, the bank is the creditor and you, as the debtor, will make monthly payments that include an interest charge. If you deposit money in an interest-bearing account, you are in effect lending money to the bank and the bank will pay interest to you. Most of us conduct transactions as both lenders and borrowers and therefore both earn and pay interest.

Interest is a price, and its level depends on the demand for and supply of loanable funds in financial markets where credit is available. The demand for loanable funds depends on the willingness and ability of consumers, business firms, and governments to borrow funds. Among the factors these potential borrowers consider are the general business outlook, the expected profitability of business investment, and the level of consumer income. As you'd expect, the total quantity of loanable funds demanded in any year depends on the interest rate. You can see the demand curve in the graph in Box 6. The lower the interest rate, other things being equal, the greater the quantity of loanable funds demanded.

The supply of loanable funds depends on the willingness and ability of lenders to make funds available to borrowers. In general, the gains possible from lending funds depend on the interest rate paid for the use of funds. The higher the interest rate, the greater the gains. The supply curve of loanable funds as shown in Box 6 is therefore assumed to be upward sloping. In general, the supply of loanable funds depends on the willingness and ability of individuals, businesses, and governments to save rather than spend all their current income in the current year. Such factors as consumer income, expectations of future price levels, population, and average age of people in the population affect the supply of loanable funds. As you'll see later in the book, the supply of loanable funds also depends on policies pursued by authorities that regulate banks and other financial institutions.

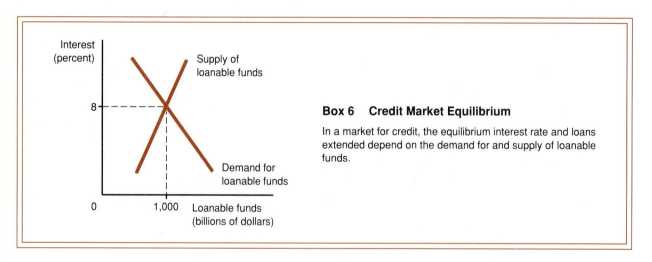

Box 6   Credit Market Equilibrium

In a market for credit, the equilibrium interest rate and loans extended depend on the demand for and supply of loanable funds.

The graph in Box 6 shows the equilibrium in the market for loanable funds. The equilibrium market rate of interest is 8%, and at that interest rate $1,000 billion of funds are loaned out. The equilibrium interest rate rations available credit by adjusting to equate the quantity of loanable funds demanded with the quantity supplied.

Changes in conditions affecting the demand for or supply of loanable funds will result in shifts of either the demand curve or the supply curve. This will cause changes in the market rate of interest. For example, an increase in the demand for credit by consumers caused, say, by increased confidence that future income will increase will move the demand curve outward. As shown in the graph in Box 7, this will, other things unchanged, result in an increase in the market equilibrium interest rate, and lenders will respond by increasing the quantity of loanable funds supplied.

Upward pressure on interest rates also can result from increased business demand for credit and from government borrowing. Many economists argue that the enormous federal budget deficits of the 1980s were a significant factor in pushing interest rates up at that time. When federal tax revenues fell short of expenditures by more than $200 billion annually for some years in the mid-1980s, the U.S. Treasury borrowed heavily in financial markets, which increased the demand for credit.

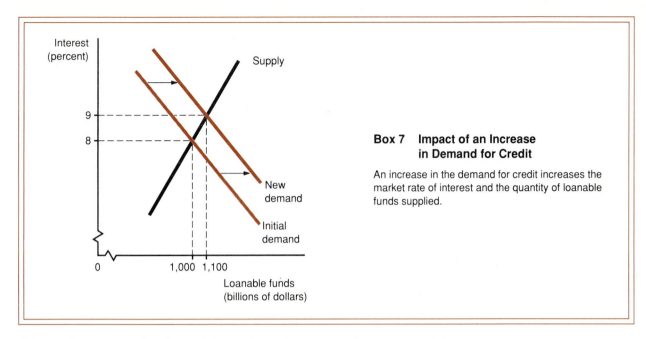

Interest (percent)

Supply

9

8

New demand

Initial demand

0   1,000   1,100

Loanable funds (billions of dollars)

Box 7   Impact of an Increase in Demand for Credit

An increase in the demand for credit increases the market rate of interest and the quantity of loanable funds supplied.

Other influences on the demand for and supply of loanable funds remaining unchanged, this tended to push equilibrium interest rates up. Does this help you understand better the widespread concern about government budget deficits? As you can see, borrowing to cover deficits has the potential to raise interest rates. This tends to choke off consumer spending and business borrowing for new equipment. Later on, in the macroeconomic sections, we'll discuss in greater detail the controversy surrounding government budget deficits. At this point you need to know how you can use the laws of supply and demand to understand the issues surrounding an important current controversy, such as deficit spending by government.

Using similar reasoning, you should be able to use supply and demand analysis to show that a decrease in the demand for credit will decrease the market interest rate and cause a decrease in the quantity of loanable funds supplied. An increase in the supply of loanable funds will put downward pressure on interest rates by shifting the supply curve outward. Finally, a decrease in the supply of loanable funds will shift the supply curve inward and put upward pressure on interest rates. As you can see, forecasting movements in interest rates in competitive markets requires a solid understanding of the forces influencing both the supply of and demand for loanable funds.

Concept Check

1   Under what circumstances will zero price not result in a shortage of a good?

2   How would you determine whether a market exists for a new product you plan to develop?

3   The federal government borrows a substantial sum of money at the end of the year to cover a budget deficit when taxes don't cover expenditures. Use supply and demand analysis to show how, other things being equal, increased government borrowing could increase interest rates.

Price Ceilings: Using Supply and Demand Analysis to Forecast Their Effects in Markets

Not all of us are satisfied with market outcomes. Undoubtedly you'd like prices to be lower than actual equilibrium prices. You probably wouldn't complain if a law were enacted that would cut your monthly rent in half, provided you weren't adversely affected in any other way by the law.

People who are dissatisfied with outcomes in unregulated markets often organize politically and seek legislation that allows government authorities to control or set prices in markets. A **price ceiling** establishes a maximum price that can legally be charged for a good or service. When price ceilings are lower than market equilibrium prices, the government, rather than the forces of supply and demand, would set the price or prevent it from increasing in response to changes in demand or supply. Government control of prices inevitably prevents the market system from performing its function of rationing goods and services. To help you see why this is so, in this section we'll look at the consequences of two common price control policies. As you'll see, the laws of supply and demand can't be repealed even by government action!

Rent Control

Rent control is an example of a price ceiling that government authorities sometimes use to set the price for rental housing. Rent control can prevent housing markets from reaching equilibrium only when rents are set *below* market equilibrium rents. After the end of World War II there was a sharp increase in the demand for housing. Many cities instituted rent controls to prevent spectacular increases in rents that were anticipated in response to the housing shortage. Rent control was abandoned by most cities in the 1950s but has regained popularity, particularly in cities on the West Coast where rents rose rapidly during the 1970s.

Rent controls typically limit increases in monthly rent, or they establish rules that are used to determine "fair" monthly rental rates for housing of varying kinds and quality. Rent controls seek to keep rents lower than those that would prevail in equilibrium in a competitive market for rental housing. Many supporters of rent controls believe they benefit lower-income people who would otherwise have to pay higher percentages of their income in rent. There's no doubt that those fortunate enough to snare rent-controlled apartments do benefit from rent controls. However, the beneficiaries aren't always in the low-income bracket!

Rent controls cause shortages. The graph in Box 8 uses supply and demand analysis to show how rent controls cause housing shortages when the rents set by law are below the market equilibrium rents. A price ceiling is said to be *effective* if it is set below the price that would otherwise emerge as the market equilibrium price. Suppose the market equilibrium rent per room in a certain city would normally be $100. This would mean, for example, that a standard four-room apartment would rent for $400. At the market equilibrium rent of $100 per room, 8,000 rooms per year are rented.

Suppose a local rent control ordinance establishes a ceiling of $50 per room on rents landlords can charge. Because the controlled rent is below the market equilibrium rent, the result is a shortage of housing. At the $50 per room rent, the quantity of rooms demanded per year is 10,000, while the quantity supplied is only 6,000, resulting in an annual shortage of 4,000 rooms. The shortage arises from an increase

Price ceiling:
Establishes a maximum price that can legally be charged for a good or service.

How Landlords Respond to Rent Control: The Case of New York City

It's common to think of landlords as greedy villains and tenants as their innocent, overcharged victims. Under New York City's rent control laws, although tenants may not be villains, it looks as though many landlords really are victims.

Rent control has been used in New York City since 1943. Nearly two thirds of the city's population lives in rental units, and 1.2 million of these units are subject to some form of rent control. Because rent control applies to units of housing and isn't based on the income or needs of individuals, the benefits of the program extend to rich and poor alike. However, some apartments are not subject to the controls. The rents for these apartments average nearly 70% higher than those for similar apartments for which rents have been controlled. The median rent for rent-regulated apartments in New York City was about $330 in 1986. Ironically, many of the beneficiaries of rent control are middle-income and upper-middle-income families.

Rent controls in New York City prevented rents from rising during a period of increasing housing maintenance costs from 1965 to 1975. This contributed to the loss of nearly 200,000 housing units through abandonment during that period. Although tenants in rent-controlled apartments pay lower rents, the quality of their housing is often lower than that enjoyed by people whose units aren't under rent control. Vacancy rates in New York City for rental housing have consistently been below those of other cities without rent controls, suggesting that the controls have in fact contributed to housing shortages.*

Rent control is a government-mandated subsidy from landlords to tenants. One study estimates the value of this subsidy in New York City at $20 billion between 1943 and 1976. Many of the landlords whose income is reduced as a result of the program are small investors of modest means.†

One way a landlord in New York City can avoid the unfavorable effects of rent control on his income is to convert rental apartments to condominiums that he can sell at the market price for owner-occupied housing. Landlords can also convert rental housing to industrial and commercial property, for which rents are not controlled.

Converting rental housing to condominiums has been a common response of landlords in New York City to rent regulations during the 1980s. When a rent-controlled apartment becomes vacant, the landlord often chooses not to re-rent the unit. In 1987 it was estimated that as many as 90,000 of the city's 1.2 million rent-regulated apartments were being held off the market. Landlords not renting rent-regulated apartments "warehouse" the units to avoid legal difficulties in converting the units to condominiums. The warehousing aggravates the shortage of rental units caused by controls in the first place. The landlords argue that it's their right to choose not to rent apartments they own. Critics of warehousing argue that it should be outlawed.

You can easily understand the motivation for warehousing if you look at some of the costs landlords incur in converting rental units to salable owner-occupied condominium units. When a building in New York City is converted to condominiums, the tenants in rent-regulated apartments are protected by law against eviction. Tenants have three options: retain the right to rent (and to renew the lease at a modest increase in rent); buy their apartment at a discounted "insider" price, or accept a payment from the landlord in return for giving up their tenant rights. Before a condominium conversion can begin in New York City, a certain minimum number of apartments must be vacant or tenants must agree to vacate or purchase their unit. Landlords gladly offer tenants discounts and payments to induce them to give up their legal rights to the rent-controlled units.

One Manhattan tenant was given the option to purchase the apartment he currently leased at a price of $72,000, which represented a 28% discount from the outsider price. Alternatively, the landlord would have happily paid the tenant $36,000 to give up his tenant rights. This tenant chose to keep renting the apartment at the current regulated rent of about $400 a month. The tenant wasn't acting irrationally. The controlled rent was a good deal compared to the other alternatives. Had the tenant accepted the payment and bought the apartment, his monthly housing costs would likely have tripled! About two thirds of the tenants in condominium conversions in New York City find keeping their rent-controlled apartments the best alternative when compared to accepting payments to vacate or buying their apartment at the insider price.

Other tenants make different choices. For example, many tenants believe the price of their units will rise in the future and choose to give up their tenant rights in exchange for ownership. Some tenants buy their apartments and immediately resell them at a handsome profit. One tenant in a recent condominium conversion of a building in New York City purchased his 1,600-square-foot rent-regulated apartment for the insider price of $178,000. He turned around and sold the unit for $400,000. This lucky beneficiary of rent control in New York City enjoyed a $222,000 net gain on the deal!§ Finally, some tenants find it in their interest to accept hefty "bribes" offered by landlords to vacate. As you can see, there's no way for tenants of rent-controlled apartments to lose—and no way landlords can win.

*See Frank S. Kristof, "The Effects of Rent Control and Rent Stabilization in New York City," in Walter Block and Edgar Olsen, eds., *Rent Control: Myths and Realities,* Vancouver: The Fraser Institute, 1981.

†See Kristof.

‡See Michael de Courcy Hinds, "For New Yorkers, Is There Life After Rent Regulation?" *The New York Times,* Real Estate, Sunday, October 26, 1986, p. 2.

§See Michael de Courcy Hinds, "The Windfall Profits in Insider Flips," *The New York Times,* Real Estate, Sunday, August 30, 1987, Section 8, p.1.

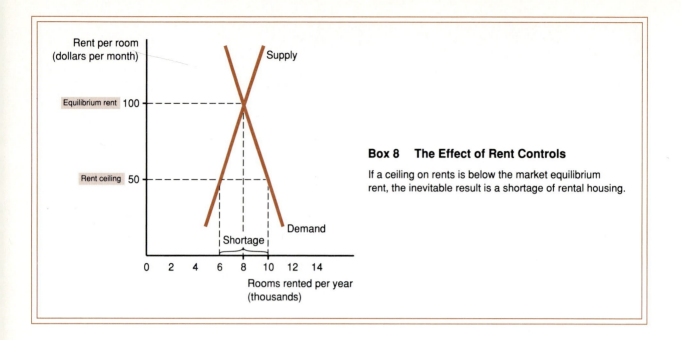

Box 8   The Effect of Rent Controls

If a ceiling on rents is below the market equilibrium rent, the inevitable result is a shortage of rental housing.

in the quantity of housing demanded over that which would prevail at the equilibrium rent, and a decrease in the quantity of housing space supplied below that which would prevail at the equilibrium rent.

Rent controls do make rental housing less expensive to tenants than it would otherwise be. Unfortunately, not everyone who wants to rent housing at the legal rent will find it available. Rent controls also make landlords worse off by reducing the gain possible from renting housing. Landlords respond by decreasing the quantity and often the quality of rental housing supplied. The inevitable result of rent control is therefore a shortage of rental housing. The gainers under rent control are those fortunate enough to have found rent-controlled apartments. Many of these people are in the middle- and upper-middle-income brackets. The losers under rent control are often young people just starting out who seek a rent-controlled apartment but fail to find one because the established tenants with rent-controlled apartments don't easily give up their leases!

Interest Rate Ceilings

Another common price ceiling is imposed by law in credit markets to place a lid on interest rates lenders can charge. When interest rate ceilings (called *usury laws*) prevent interest rates from rising to their market equilibrium level, the result is a shortage of funds available for credit.

Once again, we can use supply and demand analysis to show the impact of these laws on the behavior of market participants and predict their consequences. For example, in the late 1970s, a period of rapid inflation of prices and interest rates, the market rates of interest on many loans rose to astronomical levels: higher than 20% in many cases. Federal and state laws placed ceilings on the interest that banks and savings and loan associations could pay on deposits and the interest they could charge on some types of loans. Prior to the period of rising interest rates, the laws weren't much of a problem because the legal ceilings in many cases were *above* the market equilibrium interest rates. However, when interest rates rose rapidly in the late 1970s, the interest rate ceilings became effective and prevented credit markets from achieving equilibrium. The resulting chaos in credit markets spurred political action to repeal many interest rate ceilings and Congress passed the Depository Institutions Deregulation and Monetary Control Act of 1980.

The graph in Box 9 uses supply and demand analysis to show the impact of interest rate ceilings on the market for credit. Suppose there is a ceiling of 9% on the interest that can be charged on a certain type of loan, such as a mortgage. If 9% is also the equilibrium interest rate, there will be no problem because the quantity demanded will equal the quantity supplied of loanable funds, as shown at point E in the graph. Now suppose the demand for loanable funds increases sharply. The resulting outward shift in the demand curve would raise the market equilibrium rate of interest to 15%. This would normally increase the quantity of loanable funds supplied from Q_1 to Q_2 as the market equilibrium would move to point E'. However, the ceiling prevents interest rates from rising above 9%. As a result, the gain from making this type of loan doesn't increase and lenders don't make more loanable funds available. The quantity of loanable funds demanded at 9% along the *new* demand curve at point B is Q_3, which exceeds the Q_1 that will be supplied at the 9% interest rate. As a result, there is a shortage of loanable funds for mortgages. The shortage means that some borrowers who are willing and able to pay the 9% interest rate won't be able to find funds to borrow.

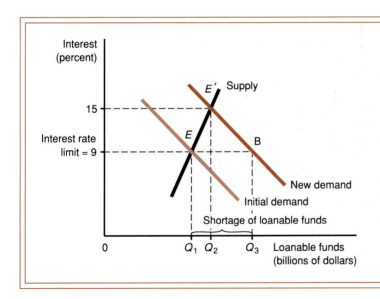

Box 9   Impact of an Interest Rate Ceiling

A law establishes a ceiling on interest rates in credit markets. At the initial demand the interest rate limit of 9% equals the equilibrium interest rate. There is no shortage in this case. An increase in demand normally would increase the market rate of interest. Here, however, the interest rate ceiling prevents the market interest rate from increasing to15%; consequently, there is a shortage of loanable funds.

As with most price ceilings, there are gainers and losers when interest rate ceilings are in effect. The gainers, of course, are those fortunate enough to obtain credit at the interest rate ceiling. These people tend to be the most creditworthy borrowers who lenders believe are least likely to default on their loans. Naturally, these borrowers also tend to be people with high incomes. This is really ironic if the purpose of an interest rate ceiling is to allow people of more modest means to obtain loans. Instead the law benefits upper-income people, who get credit at a lower interest rate than they would otherwise have had to pay!

The losers are likely to be the borrowers with the lowest incomes or younger people who haven't yet established a credit rating and whom banks regard as less creditworthy. These people probably will be forced to go to lenders who aren't subject to the interest rate regulations, like finance companies and loan sharks who operate illegally. Because of the shortage caused by the ceiling, such lenders may be able to obtain even higher interest rates than usual. This is because, in addition to meeting demands of their usual clients, they'll have to meet the increased demand from new clients who would be served by regulated lenders if not for the interest rate ceiling.

Nonprice Rationing of Shortages Resulting from Price Ceilings

Nonprice rationing:
A device that distributes available amounts of goods and services on a basis other than willingness to pay.

Price ceilings inevitably result in shortages when they are set below market equilibrium prices. Because prices can't increase to ration the shortage when the ceiling is enforced, other means must be developed to distribute available supplies to those willing and able to pay. These means often reflect a high degree of human ingenuity. **Nonprice rationing** devices distribute available goods and services on a basis other than willingness to pay. Many people argue that nonprice rationing is favorable to lower-income people who get the opportunity to consume a good they otherwise wouldn't be able to afford. Although this is true in some cases, the poor aren't always the ones fortunate enough to obtain available supplies when there's a shortage.

The simplest form of nonprice rationing is the use of a "first come, first served" rule. Available supplies are rationed by time spent waiting in line. There's no way of knowing whether low-income people will be first in line or last. The waiting rations the good by doling out supplies to the next person in line only as they become available. Of course, waiting in line is time consuming and annoying to many people. These people often choose to do without the good if the gain they expect from it is less than the price they must pay plus the value of their time and the annoyance of waiting.

Another method of rationing scarce goods is the use of eligibility criteria to select from the pool of people who are willing and able to pay the controlled price. This requires people to fill out forms to establish their eligibility for the goods. Government officials then decide who gets served first on the basis of predetermined criteria. For example, if price controls resulted in a shortage of milk, authorities might decide that families with children would get first priority to purchase available supplies. Similarly, if there were a shortage of housing, families might get priority over single people.

Prices typically are controlled in wartime, and the price ceilings result in shortages. A common method of rationing scarce goods is the use of special stamps with a certain number issued to consumers each week. The stamps are usually valid for only a week to prevent people from hoarding them. Prices for goods are stated both in money and in terms of the stamps. Under this system of nonprice rationing, it isn't enough to be willing and able to pay the money price to obtain the good. You must also have the stamps. For example, during World War II, stamps issued to civilians limited gasoline consumption to 3 gallons or so per week. Other stamps were issued for food, and a system of "points" was used to limit purchases of scarce items like meat.

With price ceilings and nonprice rationing there are always dissatisfied potential buyers who would be willing to pay more than the legal price to get the goods or services they want. Selling goods at prices higher than those legally set is punishable by fines or even imprisonment. Nonetheless, there are always sellers willing to take the risk of charging more than the ceiling prices. A market in which sellers sell goods to buyers for more than the legal prices is referred to as a **black market.** In a black market, prices invariably are higher than those that would prevail if the controlled market were allowed to reach equilibrium. For example, it's not uncommon for eager people searching for housing in rent-controlled markets to agree to make illegal payments to landlords to obtain choice apartments. Sometimes these payments are outright bribes to get names placed at the top of waiting lists for apartments. In other cases they take the form of exorbitant security deposits and purchase of improvements to the apartment at greatly inflated prices.

Black market:
A market in which sellers sell goods to buyers for more than the legal prices.

Price Floors: Supply and Demand Analysis of Their Effects

A **price floor** is a minimum price established by law. Two commonly used price floors are minimum wages and agricultural price supports. Minimum wages prohibit employers from paying less than a certain stipulated wage. Agricultural price supports guarantee farmers a minimum price per unit for their crops. As with price ceilings, providing benefits in this way can impair the rationing function of prices. When price floors are set *above* market equilibrium prices, the inevitable result is a surplus on the market. Again we can use supply and demand analysis to see how these surpluses arise and to identify who gains and who loses as a result of the price floor.

Price floor:
A minimum price established by law.

Minimum Wages

Minimum wages are an example of a price floor that government establishes on the price for labor services. The government enforces minimum-wage laws by imposing penalties on employers who pay less than the stipulated hourly wage.

In modern industrial nations, skilled workers and those who work in factories typically earn equilibrium wages that exceed the minimum wage. However, equilibrium wages for unskilled workers are usually lower than the minimum wage. The graph in Box 10 shows you the effect of a minimum wage in a market for unskilled labor.

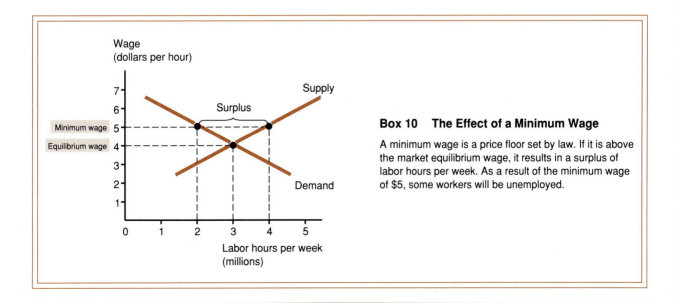

Box 10   The Effect of a Minimum Wage

A minimum wage is a price floor set by law. If it is above the market equilibrium wage, it results in a surplus of labor hours per week. As a result of the minimum wage of $5, some workers will be unemployed.

The market equilibrium wage for the services of unskilled workers is $4 per hour. At that wage the quantity of labor services demanded per week just equals the quantity supplied of 3 million hours. The minimum wage is set at $5 per hour. At that floor, the quantity of labor supplied is 4 million hours per week, while the quantity demanded is only 2 million hours per week. There is therefore a weekly surplus of 2 million labor hours. This means that some workers seeking employment at the minimum wage will be unable to find jobs. This is inevitable when minimum wages are set above market equilibrium wages. Of course, if the wage floor were set below or equal to the market wage, it would have no effect on the market equilibrium, because employers would pay more than the minimum wage to avoid labor shortages (see Principles in Practice box).

Minimum wages benefit workers who are fortunate enough to find work at wage levels that exceed the equilibrium wage. However, they harm workers who seek employment at the higher wage but are unsuccessful in finding jobs. Evidence has linked minimum-wage laws with teenage unemployment. Each 10% increase in the minimum wage appears to be associated with about a 1% to 3% reduction in total teenage employment. Minimum wages also appear to reduce employment of young adults aged 20 to 24 and of the elderly. Some studies, however, have found that the minimum wage does increase employment of some adults, particularly women, between the ages of 25 and 55.[1]

As you might expect, minimum wages have the most adverse effects on employment in low-wage industries like retail sales. Employers often react to increases in minimum wages by decreasing the quality of working conditions and reducing fringe benefits. As minimum wages rise, the pace of work is increased and the number of vacation days tends to decline.[2]

Despite the adverse effects of minimum wages on employment opportunities for teenagers and on working conditions for workers in low-wage industries, many politicians and economists argue that minimum wages are an effective way of benefiting the working poor. A person working full time at the $3.35 minimum wage prevailing in 1987 would earn $6,968 annually. If this person were a single parent with two dependent children, that level of annual earnings would put those people well below the 1987 official poverty line of slightly more than $9,000 for a family of three. For this reason some economists argue that increasing the minimum wage is an effective way of aiding the *working* poor without increasing taxes. Of course, the aid to the poor will be financed by employers. These employers, whose marginal costs increase because of an increase in the minimum wage, are likely to respond by decreasing the supply of their products in markets. Consequently, the prices of goods and services produced with unskilled labor will rise. This also means that consumers will pay part of the cost of increasing assistance to the working poor through an increase in the minimum wage.

In 1988 some politicians were pushing legislation to increase the minimum wage to nearly $5 per hour from the $3.35 per hour that prevailed since 1980. Because the purchasing power of the dollar declined markedly from 1980 to 1988, the $3.35 minimum wage bought much less in 1988 than it did in 1980. Increasing the minimum wage will undoubtedly aid the working poor who are fortunate enough to

[1]For a summary of these studies, see Charles Brown, Curtis Gilroy, and Andrew Kohen, "The Effect of the Minimum Wage on Employment and Unemployment," *Journal of Economic Literature,* 20, 2, June 1982, pp. 487-528.
[2]Walter J. Wessels, *Minimum Wages, Fringe Benefits, and Working Conditions,* Washington, D.C.: The American Enterprise Institute for Public Policy Research, 1980.

Principles in Practice

The Minimum Wage Isn't Always Above the Equilibrium Wage

"It was a very good year." That old Frank Sinatra lyric is a good description of what 1986 was like for New England. Economic growth was strong, and an influx of new businesses into states like New Hampshire greatly increased employment opportunities. In the summer of 1986, everyone willing and able to work in and around such urban areas as Manchester in New Hampshire had a job. The demand for unskilled workers was particularly strong. Chambermaid jobs, for example, which usually pay no more than the minimum wage of $3.35 per hour, were paying $5 to $6 per hour. Part-time retail sales workers were able to bargain for wages and fringe benefits. For example, stores in Pheasant Lane Mall in Nashua, which opened in 1986, had to pay $4.50 to $6 per hour to find workers. Many stores offered generous employee discounts. The situation was particularly tight in operations like fast-food restaurants, which typically pay no more than the minimum wage.*

The situation in New Hampshire in 1986 demonstrates how changes in demand or supply affect wages. Many observers pointed out that the supply of unskilled workers was low because the decline in the birth rate in the late 1960s and early 1970s decreased the state's population of teenagers. Remember that minimum wages are a floor on wages only when the minimum wage is set above the market equilibrium wage for unskilled labor. In New Hampshire in 1986, the equilibrium wage was apparently well above the legal minimum wage of $3.35 per hour!

*"Employers scramble for workers in N.H.," *The News and Observer,* Raleigh, N.C., Sunday, June 8, 1986.

---

keep their jobs. On the other hand, an increase in the minimum wage is likely to decrease employment opportunities for teenagers, reduce the quality of working conditions for the working poor, and decrease job training for workers with minimum-wage jobs.

Agricultural Price Supports

Agricultural price support programs are another example of a price floor. These supports, which are common in the United States, are a direct benefit to farmers. However, when price supports are established above equilibrium prices, the inevitable result is a surplus of agricultural commodities. Usually the federal government acquires these surpluses (at taxpayer cost) and holds them in storage. Limited amounts are given away as foreign aid. You may wonder why the government doesn't simply give all the surplus commodities away, in light of the great need for food in famine-stricken Third World countries. The reason is that this would increase world food supplies tremendously and sharply reduce prices. This would create political problems, as farmers in other nations would find the prices they receive for their products plummeting.

Later in the book we'll examine in detail the agricultural price support programs used in the United States. At this point we can easily use supply and demand analysis to outline the basic method that has been used to provide price supports to farmers and the effects of such supports.

Let's briefly sketch how the price floor works for one farm commodity: milk. For many years dairy farmers have benefited from price supports for milk set by the U.S. Department of Agriculture. Farmers decide how much milk to supply on the basis of the price floor. The graph in Box 11 shows how a surplus of milk results when the actual market price turns out to be less than the price floor. Suppose that the

---

price floor is $2 per gallon while the market equilibrium price would be $1.50 per gallon. Dairy farmers produce 11 billion gallons of milk per year, which corresponds to point L on the supply curve. At a price of $2 per gallon the quantity demanded is only 10 billion gallons per year, corresponding to point M on the demand curve. As a result there's a surplus of 1 billion gallons per year. To prevent this surplus from putting downward pressure on price, the government buys the 1-billion-gallon surplus at the official price floor each year and stores it. The shaded rectangle shows you the total cost of the program to taxpayers, which in this case is $2 billion. In addition, consumers pay $2 per gallon of milk rather than the $1.50 per gallon market equilibrium price. At the higher price, the quantity demanded by consumers is 10 billion gallons per year instead of the 10.5 billion gallons per year that would be demanded if there were no government-established price floor.

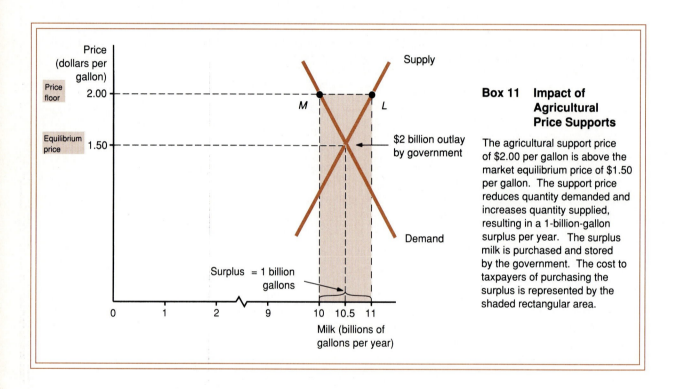

Box 11   Impact of Agricultural Price Supports

The agricultural support price of $2.00 per gallon is above the market equilibrium price of $1.50 per gallon. The support price reduces quantity demanded and increases quantity supplied, resulting in a 1-billion-gallon surplus per year. The surplus milk is purchased and stored by the government. The cost to taxpayers of purchasing the surplus is represented by the shaded rectangular area.

You can note these important results of the price support policy:

1. Prices paid by consumers of milk (and other agricultural commodities whose prices are supported by government programs) increase when the price floor is higher than the market equilibrium price.
2. Taxpayers foot the bill for purchase and storage of surplus commodities that result from the price floor. However, the government acquires the commodities as assets that it can sell later to generate revenue.
3. Incomes of farmers are higher when the government-established price floor exceeds the equilibrium price of the commodities they sell. As a result of the price supports they can sell more output than they could otherwise, and they also receive a higher price than that which would prevail in the free market.

1 What are price ceilings? Under what circumstances do price ceilings cause shortages in competitive markets?

2 What is nonprice rationing?

3 A price floor is established for eggs. Under what circumstances will the price floor result in a surplus of eggs?

Price Controls: The Cost of Government Intervention

Price ceilings and price floors prevent the price system from rationing goods and services. Seeking to provide benefits to certain groups through regulation of the market mechanism therefore always impairs the function of prices in allocating goods and services. Government intervention in otherwise competitive markets often carries unfortunate consequences. In the case of price ceilings, otherwise honest people are often tempted to enter into illegal transactions to obtain scarce goods or services. When price controls cause severe shortages, the costs of preventing illegal transactions are often very high. Extra police officers must be hired, and many people may be subjected to what they regard as undue interference in their private affairs. Price ceilings also can cause the quality of goods to deteriorate as sellers who can't cover their opportunity costs at the controlled prices provide shoddier products.

In the case of price floors, inefficient, high-cost producers can still make profits as a result of government support of prices in their industry. The costs of dealing with stored surplus commodities purchased by the government can be quite high. Taxpayers end up subsidizing farmers as tax money is used to purchase and store surplus crops. Finally, consumers of products or services protected by price floors are made worse off because they must pay higher prices than would prevail without the floors.

As you can see, interference with the functioning of free and competitive markets is likely to result in resource allocation problems and reduced efficiency. However, you shouldn't conclude that government intervention in markets is never justified. Making a judgment on the desirability of government intervention clearly depends on your point of view and goals. In all the cases we've discussed, there were gainers as well as losers. Elimination of price controls always causes some business firms to fail as prices move to equilibrium levels. Obviously, you might rationally support rent control, minimum wages, interest rate ceilings, and agricultural price supports if you and people you care about gained as a result. *However, the important question is whether the gainers could have been made just as well off in other ways that didn't impair the rationing function of market prices.*

Finally, remember that the analysis in this chapter assumed that markets were in fact freely competitive. In many cases markets are not competitive, nor are buyers and sellers the only people who gain or lose when they transact their business. In such cases we must reassess the role of government in modifying market outcomes, and we'll do this later in the book.

Summary

1. Prices serve to ration scarce goods sold in competitive markets by preventing shortages and surpluses.
2. A nonscarce good is one for which quantity demanded would not exceed quantity supplied at zero price.
3. Successful marketing of a new product depends on conditions of supply and demand for the item. If the minimum price sellers will accept exceeds the maximum price buyers will pay for the first unit made available, the item is not marketable. Changes in technology lower the minimum prices sellers can accept for items and expand markets for these goods.
4. Wages and hours worked in competitive labor markets depend on the demand for and supply of labor. Similarly, interest rates and credit extended in competitive financial markets depend on the demand for and supply of loanable funds.
5. Price ceilings establish maximum prices that can legally be charged in competitive markets and result in shortages when they are below market equilibrium prices. Rent control and usury laws are examples of price ceilings.
6. Nonprice rationing distributes available amounts of goods and services on a basis other than willingness to pay when shortages caused by price ceilings exist in competitive markets. The most common nonprice rationing device is "first come, first served."
7. Price ceilings usually result in illegal transactions in a black market at prices that exceed the legal limits.
8. Price floors establish minimum prices, which can result in surpluses when they exceed equilibrium prices in competitive markets. Minimum wages and agricultural price supports are common examples of price floor programs.
9. Price ceilings and price floors benefit certain groups but impair the rationing of goods and services by the price system in competitive markets. Government interference in the functioning of competitive markets is therefore likely to result in resource allocation problems and reduced efficiency. In evaluating price control programs, the gains to the beneficiaries of price ceilings and floors must be weighed against the resulting resource allocation problems. Alternative means that will make the gainers just as well off without impairing the rationing function of prices can be considered as ways to improve efficiency in the economy.

Key Terms and Concepts

Nonscarce good	Price ceiling
Wages	Nonprice rationing
Credit	Black market
Interest	Price floor

Problems and Applications

1. A local record store advertises that it will give away free Bruce Springsteen albums from 8 a.m. to 5 p.m. on Saturday. Explain what is likely to happen and why you might be better off waiting until Monday to buy your album at the market price.
2. Residents on an island for which coconuts are a nonscarce good discover that

people in the rest of the world don't consider coconuts nonscarce and will pay high prices to obtain them. Explain what is likely to happen to the demand for coconuts as island residents discover they can export the fruit to foreign markets.

3. The price of personal computers was well over $5,000 when they were introduced in the early 1980s. Since then the price has fallen drastically. Use supply and demand analysis to explain the likely cause of the fall in prices. What was the effect of decreasing prices on the quantity demanded of this good?

4. Rising enrollment in college accounting curriculums causes a sharp increase in the supply of accountants four years later. Other things being equal, use supply and demand analysis to forecast the impact of the increase in the supply of accountants on annual salaries of accounting graduates.

5. A drop in profits for oil companies results in a sharp decrease in the demand for chemical engineers. Use supply and demand analysis to predict the effect on salaries paid to chemical engineers and on the quantity of their labor supplied.

6. Suppose the federal government finally balances the budget. The decrease in demand for loanable funds to cover the deficit is likely to have a significant effect on credit markets. Use supply and demand analysis to forecast, other things being equal, the impact of a decrease in government demand for loanable funds on interest rates and on borrowing by business firms and consumers.

7. The market equilibrium rent per room in a small city is $50. A rent control law is passed that establishes a price ceiling of exactly $50 per room. What will be the impact of the law on the market for rental housing? How would your answer change if immediately after the rent controls are passed, a major corporation announces it will build a new factory in the city that will employ 10,000 workers? The new plant is expected to sharply increase the demand for housing.

8. A 50¢-per-gallon price ceiling is established for gasoline. As a result of the ceiling, a weekly shortage of 10,000 gallons develops. How can the shortage be rationed?

9. Although minimum wages prevent labor markets from rationing unskilled labor services, they are widely praised by labor leaders and generally regarded as good by most people. How can you explain the political support for minimum wages?

10. How could agricultural surpluses be eliminated in the United States? Use supply and demand analysis to show how agricultural price floors cause surpluses and how taxpayers pay the cost of the surpluses. Who would gain and who would lose if agricultural price support programs were phased out?

Suggested Readings

Eric N. Berkowitz, Roger A. Kerin, and William Rudelius, *Marketing,* 2nd ed., Homewood, Ill.: Richard D. Irwin, Inc., 1989. Chapter 9 of this book examines some of the issues involved in marketing new products and discusses why new products might fail.

Walter Block and Edgar Olsen, eds., *Rent Control: Myths and Realities,* Vancouver: The Fraser Institute, 1981. This book contains essays that discuss the pros and cons of rent control and the actual consequences of such laws.

Charles Brown, Curtis Gilroy, and Andrew Kohen, "The Effect of the Minimum Wage on Employment and Unemployment," *Journal of Economic Literature,* 20,2 June 1982, pp. 487-528. This is a comprehensive review of research by economists on the impact of minimum-wage laws on employment opportunities and their impact on particular groups.

A Forward Look

Now that you understand the basics of supply and demand analysis, you're ready for an overview of an economy in which markets are used primarily to allocate resources. In the following chapter we look at the basic features of a capitalistic economy. As you'll see, no nation has an economy that can be regarded as purely capitalistic. Because of common shortcomings of a system in which prices and the pursuit of profit are relied on to allocate resources, most modern economies are characterized by significant government use of resources.

The Price System: How It Functions and When It Fails

Free and competitive markets are often identified as the cornerstone of a capitalistic economy. **Capitalism** is characterized by private ownership of economic resources and freedom of enterprise in which owners of factories and other capital hire workers to produce goods and services. Freedom of enterprise means that anyone is free to use economic resources to start a business and sell a product in a market. In a purely capitalistic economy the role of government is quite limited, and the economy relies exclusively on the pursuit of profit through market sales of goods and services.

Capitalism:
Characterized by private ownership of economic resources and freedom of enterprise in which owners of factories and other capital hire workers to produce goods and services.

In most modern nations, however, governments control substantial amounts of resources, and criteria other than personal gain and business profit are used to decide how resources will be employed. Most modern noncommunist nations have a **mixed economy** in which governments as well as business firms provide goods and services. In such economies governments supply roads, defense, pensions, and schooling directly to citizens. In modern economies governments also commonly intervene in markets to control prices and correct for the shortcomings of a system in which prices and the pursuit of personal gain influence resource use and incomes.

Mixed economy:
An economy in which governments as well as business firms provide goods and services.

Now that you understand how competitive markets operate, you can begin to appreciate how a *system* of markets can allocate resources. In this chapter we'll first look at how resources would be allocated in an economy in which all useful goods and services were traded in free and competitive markets. In such an economy, prices would act as signals that influence the possibilities for gain. The **price system** is a mechanism by which resource use in a free market economy is guided by prices. In such a system, changes in prices caused by changes in demand and supply affect opportunities for profit and personal gain and cause changes in resource use.

Price system:
A mechanism by which resource use in an economy is guided by prices.

A pure market economy would leave much to be desired, because it might be impossible for many useful goods and services to be sold profitably. In addition, some resources, particularly environmental resources, would be overused because of difficulties in pricing the right to their use. We therefore must address the short-comings of capitalistic economies in which prices guide resource use. In this chapter we not only look at *how* the price system functions, but also consider *when it fails*.

Concept Preview

After reading this chapter, you should be able to:

1 Examine the framework of a pure market economy and show how the circular flow of income and expenditure in a capitalistic economy keeps it functioning.
2 Provide an overview of the price system as a mechanism for coordinating decisions and allocating resources to influence what is produced, how it is produced, and how output is distributed.
3 Point out the defects of a pure market system by showing how in reality the price system doesn't work to easily attain all possible gains from resource use and how it sometimes results in low living standards for large numbers of people.
4 Briefly outline the functioning of the modern mixed economy.

An Overview of a Pure Market Economy: Circular Flow of Income and Expenditure in Resource and Product Markets

The Essential Features of Capitalism

In a capitalistic economy people are free to organize business firms for the purpose of selling goods and services at a profit. There are few restrictions on what can be bought or sold. The people who manage and assume the risks of business enterprises are called *entrepreneurs*. Entrepreneurs are innovators who develop new products and processes or reorganize production in ways that reduce costs or better satisfy consumers. Profit is both the reward and the incentive that motivates the organization of business firms. The driving force behind the capitalistic economy is the pursuit of personal gain by both entrepreneurs and consumers who seek to get the most satisfaction from their income.

The owners and managers of business firms acquire capital equipment and inventories of materials, and negotiate contracts to hire workers to produce goods and services for sale in markets. The private ownership of capital and other resources is a dominant feature of capitalism. In the capitalistic system *freedom of enterprise* is the right of business firm owners to employ private economic resources for whatever purpose they wish. In a pure market economy government would have only a limited role because all useful goods and services would be available for purchase in markets.

Capitalism is also characterized by *economic rivalry*. This means that in each market there are large numbers of buyers competing for available supplies of goods

The Entrepreneurial Spirit in American Capitalism: Thomas Edison and Electric Power, Fred Smith and Federal Express

In the United States, entrepreneurs often attain the status of folk heroes. When successful, these innovators are rewarded with spectacular profits that enable them to accumulate vast fortunes. Entrepreneurs are opportunists. They seek to exploit the moment when it's right for an innovation in products or processes. Entrepreneurs are dynamic and driving spirits in the capitalistic economy who start businesses, satisfy demands for resources or products, and prosper from doing so.

Who are the great entrepreneurs of American history? An outstanding example is Thomas Edison. Edison was, of course, an inventor whose research was responsible for electric lighting and the phonograph. But Edison was foremost an entrepreneur who was interested in marketing his inventions and profiting from doing so. He engineered a profitable way to deliver electrical power to homes and businesses. The delivery system was the key, because electricity had to be priceable for it to be profitable. The Edison Electric Illuminating Company of New York was organized in 1880 to provide street lighting. By 1883 it was supplying electricity to over 700 private customers. To make his inventions profitable, Edison had to acquire funds to purchase the necessary capital. He acted as an entrepreneur in doing so and capped his skill as an inventor with equal skill as an entrepreneur to translate his ideas into revenue and profit.*

Fred Smith is a modern-day entrepreneur who had the idea for a new express service guaranteeing overnight delivery of small packages. Smith can't be considered an inventor like Edison, but he had the gift of seeing the demand for a new service and organized the resources to satisfy that demand. The vision Smith saw was an economy with dispersed production and service facilities. Dispersal created a demand for a quick and reliable means of shipping throughout the country documents, drugs, disks and tapes, and small electronic components.

In 1970 no one was providing such a service. The United States Postal Service has a monopoly on the shipment of first-class mail. The performance of the Postal Service wasn't reliable enough for most business firms that needed guaranteed 24-hour delivery. Private freight services likewise were incapable of providing guaranteed overnight delivery. Air mail and air freight were carried by a number of airlines, and the inevitable delays involved in loading and unloading made overnight delivery infeasible. Smith envisioned a profitable opportunity for a firm specializing in overnight delivery of small parcels. In a term paper he wrote when he was a junior at Yale, he outlined his idea. The professor gave the paper a grade of "C."

In 1971 Smith began to put his idea into action. He succeeded in raising the enormous sum of $90 million to start up his company, which he called Federal Express. He purchased 33 small Dassault Falcon jets and developed a hub at Memphis, Tennessee, for sorting packages. Packages accepted for delivery were restricted in size and weight. All packages picked up during the day were sent to the Memphis hub for sorting. They were shipped out the same night to their ultimate destination for delivery the next morning. The company invested considerable resources in developing its distinctive logo and its reputation for reliability. When Federal Express began in 1973, it served 22 cities. The company wasn't immediately profitable. In fact, it didn't turn a profit until 1976. After that time, changes in government regulations enabled the company to expand more easily and to operate larger aircraft. In 1977 Federal Express earned $20 million. In 1980 it took in nearly $600 million in revenues and earned profits totaling $60 million.

As happens with most successful enterprises, competition stiffened. By the 1980s many other firms, such as Purolator, United Parcel Service, Airborne, and even the U.S. Postal Service, were offering overnight delivery service for small parcels. As you can see, the price system works in the long run both to create entrepreneurs and to encourage other firms to emulate the innovations of successful entrepreneurs.

*For a more detailed account of Edison's achievements, see Robert Sobel and David B. Sicilia, *The Entrepreneurs: An American Adventure*, Boston: Houghton Mifflin Co., 1986, pp. 7-16.

and services offered by large numbers of sellers. Economic rivalry means that there is a diffusion of economic power so that no single buyer or seller can make a good significantly more abundant or scarce. Markets are free when there are no restrictions that prevent either buyers or sellers from entering or exiting a market. No one is compelled to enter into market transactions. In this way only those transactions that provide mutual gains to buyers and sellers will be pursued.

Specialization, Exchange, and the Use of Money for Allocative Efficiency

Specialization and division of labor means that workers and entrepreneurs devote most of their time to producing one or a few goods and services. These specialists use their income to buy goods and services they want that are offered for sale by other specialists. Specialization and voluntary exchange improve efficiency by allowing people to enjoy additional gains from existing production. Such exchange involves *mutual gains* to the traders. If no one else is harmed when people specialize and trade in goods and services and there is no deception, then more benefit can be obtained from an existing amount of production.

Allocative efficiency is attained when all possible mutual gains from exchange are enjoyed. Mutual gains are always possible when the seller is willing to accept less than the buyer is willing to offer for a good or service. When mutual gains from exchange are possible, both parties to the exchange are made better off and no one is made worse off. All voluntary exchanges that allow the traders to gain without harming anyone else help the economy move toward the goal of allocative efficiency.

Allocative efficiency permits additional gains even after the economy attains a point on its production possibilities curve. After the maximum production is squeezed from available resources and current technology, mutually gainful exchanges allow traders to obtain even more satisfaction from those resources. In other words, *allocative efficiency implies that people specialize so as to squeeze the most output from available resources. They then seek additional gains by trading some of their resulting income for other items.*

For example, suppose a farmer produces more food than she can use for her own consumption. This farmer can gain if she's allowed to exchange the food that results from her specialization for another item she values more, like clothing. Similarly, a tailor is likely to produce more clothing than he wants to use himself. The tailor can gain by exchanging some of his clothing for food that he values more highly than the clothing he gives up in trade. Even if both the tailor and the farmer produce their products without waste, they can both enjoy further mutual gains by exchanging their food and clothing in a market trade.

Actual Exchange: Barter vs. Money

The mutual gains possible from exchange explain the innate tendency rational people have, as pointed out by Adam Smith (see the Principles in Practice box in Chapter 2), to "truck and barter." **Barter** is the process of exchanging goods (or services) for goods (or services). For example, a farmer might truck his produce into a market and barter it for clothing offered by a tailor. Barter is an inconvenient means of exchange because it requires *double coincidence of wants*. This means that to exchange an item a trader must truck his goods around to find someone else who both wants what he offers and has what he desires.

For example, suppose you have the skills to work as an accountant. This week you want to buy a new stereo system. To exchange your accounting services for a stereo system, you'll need to find someone willing to exchange exactly the stereo system you want for a certain number of hours of your accounting services. Making this exchange could require a time-consuming search for such a person. You might find someone who has exactly the kind of stereo system you want but who has

Allocative efficiency:
Attained when all possible mutual gains from exchange are enjoyed.

Barter:
The process of exchanging goods (or services) for goods (or services).

absolutely no desire for your accounting services. You might also find that people who are willing to accept your accounting services don't have anything you want. With a barter system of exchange, each trader must seek out people who simultaneously have the goods that are desired and want the goods that are offered in exchange.

Money exchange doesn't require double coincidence of wants. All you have to do is sell your accounting services to anyone willing to pay for them. When you've earned enough money income from selling your services to others, you go to the store and exchange your money for a stereo system. The seller gladly accepts the cash because he can use it to buy anything he wants. *Money* is what sellers generally accept as payment for goods and services. Governments usually are the sole issuers of money. However, items other than currency issued by governments have been used as money, including cigarettes, furs, and trinkets. The characteristics of money are so important that we'll devote an entire chapter to its functions later in the book. At this point you should realize that a generally accepted medium of exchange serving as money greatly facilitates specialization and market exchange of goods and services.

Circular Flow of Income and Expenditure in the Pure Market Economy

In a purely capitalistic economy all goods and services would be made available through markets. Business firms would acquire resources from households, whose members would provide labor services, entrepreneurial talent, and funds to acquire new capital, and also would provide natural resources if they owned land. The illustration in Box 1 gives you a simplified overview of a pure market economy.

In such an economy, business firms are buyers of resources offered for sale in input markets. Households supply economic resources as sellers in these input markets. The competition among the many buyers and sellers of inputs then results in market prices for labor, the use of funds, capital, and natural resources. The prices depend on conditions of supply and demand in each input market.

The sale of input services provides a flow of income in the form of wages, rent, interest, and profit to the members of each household who supply resources and own businesses. For example, people in a given household might earn wages as employees of a department store. They might also own some land and buildings that they allow a business to use in exchange for rent. They might deposit money in a bank that provides them with interest income. They might own stock in a corporation that pays dividends or run a small business that generates profits. The flow of payments for resource use and distribution of profit to the members of households who own businesses equals the income earned in the economy.

Household members use the money income they earn to express their demand for goods and services. Business firms respond to that demand by producing a variety of goods and services. The price of each good and service is determined by its supply and demand in product markets. The expenditures of consumers constitute revenue for business firms that they use to finance the outlays for inputs and profit payments.

The picture of the economy as a set of interrelated markets in which income and expenditure move in a circular flow between business firms and households is a simplified but enlightening view of a pure market economy. It points out that both

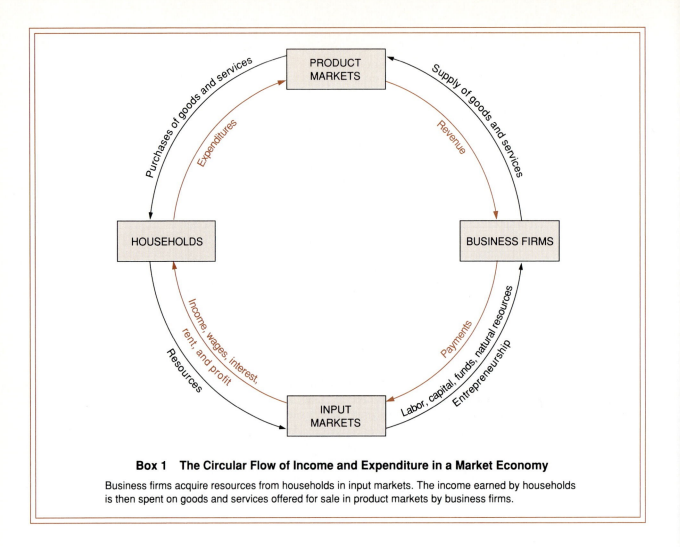

Box 1   The Circular Flow of Income and Expenditure in a Market Economy

Business firms acquire resources from households in input markets. The income earned by households is then spent on goods and services offered for sale in product markets by business firms.

households and business firms meet in two sets of markets. Households are sellers in input markets but are buyers in product markets. Business firms are buyers in input markets and sellers in output markets. Money lubricates the wheels of exchange in markets. The money changes hands many times each year and provides income to households that they in turn spend on products. The money then becomes revenue to business firms and is used to cover costs and other payments necessary to make goods available. These payments provide income as the cycle goes on and on. There is also a steady flow of resources employed by business firms that are used to supply goods and services each day to households. The clockwise flow of expenditures, revenue, payments, and income fuels the counterclockwise flow of goods and services and resources in the circular flow diagram in Box 1.

The diagram ignores the role of government in the economy. This is because in a pure market economy government would have a minor role to play.

1   What are the basic features of a capitalistic economy?

2   How does the concept of allocative efficiency differ from that of productive efficiency?

3   Explain how the use of money facilitates exchange in a market economy and describe the circular flow of money in a pure market economy. Why are total expenditures each year in a market economy likely to exceed the number of dollars available for use as money in the economy?

The Price System: How It Works to Influence What Is Produced, How It Is Produced, and Who Gets It

A lot goes on in the boxes illustrated in the circular flow diagram in Box 1. We need to elaborate on this to show you how the price system works and then to help you understand when it fails. Within the box labeled "households," you and other individuals constantly weigh the costs and benefits of working vs. enjoying leisure, of using land for personal purposes or renting it out to business firms, and of providing funds for business firms to expand or spending those funds on consumer goods. Within the box labeled "business firms," managers decide how to employ resources and what to produce. *The unifying feature of all these decisions is that they are influenced by prices determined by free play of the forces of supply and demand in competitive markets.*

How the Price System Influences What Is Produced

No one directs a pure market economy. Instead the prices established in markets act as signals for personal gain and profit to which households and business managers respond. *What* gets produced in a market economy is determined chiefly by profitability. When demand for a particular good increases, so does its price. For example, other things being equal, an increase in demand for exercise bikes increases the price of this item. The higher price increases the profitability of producing exercise bikes. Entrepreneurs seek out profits and avoid losses. When more profits are possible from making exercise bikes than from making automobiles, there will be a reallocation of resources and entrepreneurship from automobiles to exercise bikes. In this way, through the price system, suppliers respond to demand by producing the products that consumers are most willing and able to purchase.

The graphs in Box 2 show how the price system works to respond to an increase in demand for a product. The graph labeled **A** shows that, given the initial demand and supply, the market price of exercise bikes is $300 and 1 million per year are sold. An increase in demand increases the market price of exercise bikes to $350 and results in an increase in quantity supplied over the year to 1.2 million. This increase occurs as existing firms hire more workers and use material in existing factories in response to the profit opportunities that arise when the price increases.

Over a longer period of time, the higher price makes it profitable for entrepreneurs to start new factories specializing in the production of exercise bikes. More

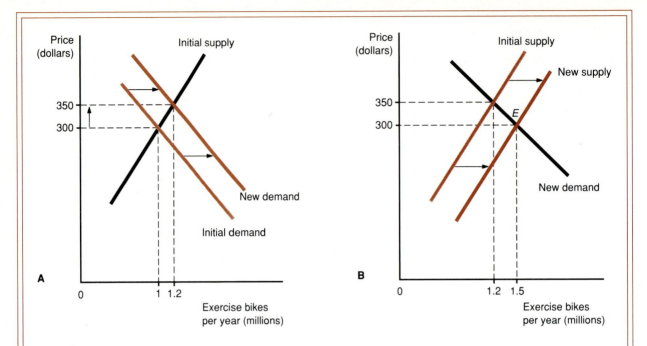

Box 2   The Price System in Action: The Response to an Increase in the Demand for a Product

Over a short period of time, as shown in **A**, an increase in demand for exercise bikes increases the price and the quantity supplied. Over a longer period, the increased profit made possible by the higher price attracts new firms to produce exercise bikes. As shown in **B**, the resulting shift in the supply curve makes more bikes available and reduces their price until additional profit is no longer possible.

resources are devoted to the production of exercise bikes over time. As shown in graph **B,** this increases the supply of exercise bikes. The final equilibrium is at point *E* in graph **B,** at which the new supply curve intersects the new demand curve. The quantity of exercise bikes sold increases to 1.5 million per year, and the price falls from $350 to $300. No single person planned the increase in availability of exercise bikes. Instead competition among entrepreneurs for profit opportunities caused the increase in supply that ultimately lowered prices and made more exercise bikes available.

Adjustments like this occur all the time in markets. For example, in 1986 the market price of compact disc recordings remained fairly high and many popular titles were in short supply. Throughout the world, the factories capable of producing the discs were working around the clock to keep up with the demand. However, in 1986, 15 *new* compact disc production facilities were being completed in the United States. Business firms, seeing the opportunity to increase profits by producing CDs, were expanding their productive capacity to do so. The supply of compact discs increased substantially in 1987 and 1988, putting downward pressure on prices. Meanwhile, the markets for long-playing records and cassette tape recordings were also affected. Demand for these items declined, and fewer resources were devoted to their production.

We can conduct a similar analysis for a decrease in demand for a product. A decrease in the demand for petroleum products like gasoline would lower their price. This would decrease the profitability of producing oil and cause the quantity to decrease over a short period of time. Over a longer period of time the decrease in profitability would cause oil production facilities to close down. As less labor, capital, and natural resources were devoted to drilling for oil, the supply of oil would decrease, placing upward pressure on prices. Once again, no single person makes the decision to produce less oil. Instead the change in the price of oil sets up a chain of events that leads to fewer resources being allocated to oil production. In fact, such a scenario was played out in 1986 and 1987. The long-term decline in the demand for oil caused the price to fall in 1986. Oil drilling operations in the American Southwest and other parts of the world were abandoned. As fewer resources were devoted to oil production, supplies gradually decreased. In 1987 upward pressure on oil prices resulted from the withdrawal of resources from oil production.

Similarly, changes in resource prices can affect the profitability of producing certain items. For example, a decrease in the cost of fuel can make supplying air travel more profitable, causing a reallocation of resources toward air travel services. As shown in Box 3, a decrease in fuel prices increases the supply of air travel offered between two points: New York and San Francisco. The increase in supply lowers the price of air travel between these two points. The decrease in input prices allows more profits to be made on this route. As firms compete for the extra profit, supply increases. In Box 3, you can see that the increase in supply lowers the air fare from $300 to $200. As a result of the lower price, the number of passenger miles of travel demanded increases from 3 million to 4 million per year on this route.

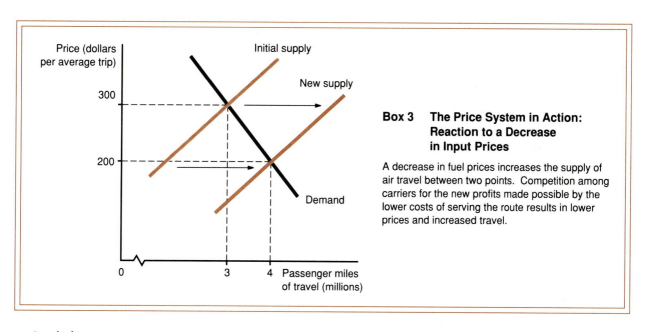

Box 3   The Price System in Action: Reaction to a Decrease in Input Prices

A decrease in fuel prices increases the supply of air travel between two points. Competition among carriers for the new profits made possible by the lower costs of serving the route results in lower prices and increased travel.

Similarly, an improvement in technology would increase the supply of a good by lowering costs and increasing profit opportunities. Rapid-fire improvements in technology in recent years created opportunities for increased profit in producing personal computers, VCRs, and other home electronic items. As the supply of these goods increased in response to the profit opportunities, the price fell and the quantity demanded increased.

Changes in price signal changes in scarcity, and both business firms and households respond by altering their choices. Later in the book we'll study in greater detail the decisions made by business managers selling in competitive markets. This will help you gain further insight into the workings of a price system.

How the Price System Influences Production Methods

The pursuit of profit also influences *how* goods and services are produced. Business firms can earn more profit by producing any given quantity of goods and services at lower cost. Managers therefore try to use the *least costly* productive techniques to supply a given quantity of goods. If they don't adopt such new techniques, their competitors are likely to do so. The lower costs will enable rival firms to profitably increase supply. This will put downward pressure on prices and make it more difficult for a firm using older techniques to enjoy a profit.

Entrepreneurs seek opportunities for profit by developing new techniques that lower costs in much the same way that they seize the opportunity to earn additional profit by responding to changes in consumer demands. Once again prices, in this case those of inputs, play an important role in entrepreneurial and managerial decisions.

For example, an increase in the price of labor services is likely to induce firms to look for ways to reduce labor use. If wages paid to farm workers increase, farm operators will find it more attractive to switch to mechanized harvesting and cultivation techniques. During the 1970s wages paid to agricultural workers increased substantially in states producing tobacco. As a result, tobacco growers shifted to a new mechanized method of harvesting the golden leaf. Similarly, an increase in the price of pesticides is likely to cause farmers to seek new methods of dealing with crop pests.

Entrepreneurs can also make more profit by devising new and less costly methods of production. For example, Henry Ford developed mass production techniques in the early twentieth century that enabled him to sell automobiles at much lower prices than his competitors. This innovation expanded the market for automobiles, and soon competing sellers adopted similar techniques. In this way an innovation in the method of production resulted in more resources being allocated to the production of automobiles. Similarly, in the 1980s some steelmakers in the United States began using scrap steel instead of blast furnaces to produce steel directly from iron ore and coal. This method, used in small mills, allowed cost reductions in steel production. As a result, there was more investment in the so-called mini-mills and less investment in the larger "integrated" steel mills as profit opportunities in mini-mills expanded.

Who Gets the Goods and Services Under the Price System?

Who gets what in the capitalistic system? Remember that in such a system your income is determined by your labor skills and other economic resources you possess and choose to sell at market prices. Your ability to buy goods and services in product markets therefore depends on your ability to register a demand for products. Remember that demand is much more than the desire for an item. Demand is desire that can be *backed up* with the willingness and ability to pay, and this is the basis on which the price system allocates goods and services among consumers. Your ability to pay in turn depends chiefly on your money income.

People who are poorly skilled, lack funds, and own no land or capital will have low incomes in a pure market economy. The poor will receive low wages for their labor and will have no other economic resources to provide them with income to buy goods and services. People whose skills are highly valued will earn high wages. People who have accumulated funds through saving or inheritance and are fortunate enough to own land and capital will enjoy nonlabor income. Entrepreneurs often earn spectacular incomes if their profitable innovations allow them to accumulate a great deal of capital. The market system can't guarantee support and sustenance to people who don't (or can't) work and who have no other economic resources aside from their own labor. As you can see, income inequality is a likely occurrence in a market economy.

A Recap: The Price System in Motion

Given the ownership of economic resources, the market system is driven by prices. Changes in prices or technology signal changes in opportunities for private gain. The system is dynamic in the sense that the pursuit of gain results in changes in resource use as economic conditions change. Profits and personal gain fuel the system while competition keeps it on course. Profitable innovations are inevitably copied. As long as profit is possible from making more of a good available in a market, supply will increase and prices will fall. The competition for profit eventually lowers prices and results in the elimination of profits. Competition eliminates profits after they have served the purpose of allocating resources to uses that are in the greatest demand.

Concept Check

1 Explain how resource use will be affected when the demand for gasoline decreases. Who makes the decisions to reallocate resources in a market system?

2 An advance in technology lowers the cost of producing personal computers. How is this change communicated to consumers by the price system?

3 How does the price system influence personal incomes?

The Price System: When It Fails

Market failure occurs when the price system fails to allocate resources so as to achieve allocative efficiency. When market failure exists, additional net gains from resource use are possible either by changing productive methods or by allowing people to negotiate with one another to adjust resource use. When market failure exists, people often use political means to induce governments to step in and compensate for the shortcomings of the market. In this section we look at some common causes of market failure.

Market failure:
Occurs when the price system fails to allocate resources so as to achieve allocative efficiency.

Public Goods and Externalities

The picture of the pure market economy painted earlier assumes that all useful goods and services can be sold in markets for a profit. However, services like environmental protection, national defense, and police and fire protection are hard to sell by the unit in a market. You can't buy cleaner air and national security the way you can buy bread by the loaf! If we relied on competing sellers to produce these useful goods for profit in a competitive market, it's possible that none of them would be made available. For this reason people often find it convenient to have goods like national defense made available through government. The quantity and means of financing these goods are then determined politically by voters.

Public goods:
Goods that are consumed equally by everyone whether they pay or not.

Public goods are those that are consumed equally by everyone whether they pay or not. Environmental protection and national security are good examples of public goods because they benefit all of us, regardless of whether or not we pay. Because we can't rely on competing sellers to provide public goods, revenue to make them available can be obtained only through a sharing arrangement such as taxation. In the modern mixed economy, we rely on government to provide roads, military defense, air traffic control, and many other public goods. In fact, purchases of economic resources by governments to provide various services amount to 20% of the value of all goods and services produced in the United States.

In a nutshell, one common problem in a pure market economy is that not all goods we want and are willing to pay for can easily be sold in neat packages that can be priced. The market often fails to provide public goods even though net gains are possible from doing so.

A related problem with the price system is that market transactions often result in costs or benefits to third parties other than the buyers and sellers. For example, if a firm disposes of wastes in a stream, it imposes costs on people who want to use the stream for swimming, fishing, and drinking water. It's not easy to put a price on economic resources like streams, the ocean, and the atmosphere when these are used as convenient receptacles for industrial wastes. When natural resources that no single person owns are used for the purpose of disposing of harmful waste products, the result is pollution. These damaging side effects of market transactions represent another failure of the price system to use resources efficiently.

Externalities:
Costs or benefits of market transactions that are not reflected in the prices buyers and sellers use to make their decisions.

Externalities are costs or benefits of market transactions that are not reflected in the prices buyers and sellers use to make their decisions. For example, aircraft noise in a neighborhood is a *negative* externality (or external cost) of the transaction between airlines and their passengers that imposes an annoying cost on residents who live near airports.

Insofar as you and other college students make all members of society better off by improving the quality of life, transactions between college students and the university result in *positive* externalities (external benefits) to third parties. Externalities prevail because the use of resources like streams and the air, or the external benefits resulting from education, can't easily be priced. To understand the failure of the price system to allocate resources efficiently when externalities exist, we first need to examine the prerequisites for market exchange.

Why Some Goods and Resource Services Cannot Be Easily Priced: Property Rights, Transaction Costs, and the Prerequisites for Market Exchange

The existence of a market for a particular item requires that certain conditions prevail to induce buyers and sellers to engage in transactions. As a buyer, you have an incentive to buy something only if you're assured that you'll obtain certain benefits when you actually pay the price to purchase the item. When you buy something you usually obtain the right of ownership and use of your purchase. **Property rights** are privileges to use or own goods, services, and economic resources. As a con-

Property rights:
Privileges to use or own goods, services, and economic resources.

sumer, you acquire property rights when you make market purchases. Similarly, sellers are induced to offer items for sale because they know they have the right to transfer the goods for a payment from buyers. *Markets can be established only for items for which property rights can be guaranteed and easily exchanged.* If you know you can enjoy the right to cleaner air and other public goods without purchasing that right from someone else, you have little incentive to pay a price for these goods.

For example, you'd scoff at an opportunity to buy the Brooklyn Bridge or an acre of the ocean because you know those are items that individuals can't own. You're motivated to engage in market transactions only when you can gain by obtaining something of value. Similarly, you'd be unwilling to invest in the production of a good for which property rights of use or ownership couldn't easily be withheld from those who refuse to pay. The incentives to produce cable television programming for sale to viewers therefore are affected by the ease with which those who don't pay the price can be prevented from benefiting from its availability. If all viewers can receive the programs even if they don't pay, sellers will have no incentive to make cable TV available. Similarly, you wouldn't offer to sell your used car stereo to someone you know couldn't or wouldn't pay you for it or give you something you'd value in exchange.

If people are to be motivated to engage in market transactions, resources must be devoted to establishing and enforcing property rights. **Transaction costs** are costs incurred in enforcing property rights to traded goods, locating trading partners, and actually carrying out the transaction. Transaction costs are associated with exchanging rather than producing goods and services. Examples of transaction costs to enforce property rights are the costs of burglar alarms and locks for vehicles and homes, the costs of scrambling satellite transmissions of television programs by firms like HBO, and the costs of monitoring workers to ensure that they're providing the services for which they're being paid. Examples of transaction costs to locate trading partners and carry out transactions are advertising and brokerage fees, the salaries of sales personnel, and the costs of transporting goods to and from the point of sale.

High transaction costs can prevent markets from being organized for the exchange of items. For example, the right to use the ocean for fishing is rarely sold in a market. The reason is that exclusive ownership rights for the use of the ocean can't be easily established and granted to a particular seller in ways that allow the ocean to be rented out to others for payment. Even if such a right were granted, the ocean is so vast that the seller would have to invest in a fleet of sophisticated vessels to monitor use of ocean regions. The cost of actually enforcing these rights would be so high as to render it infeasible to actually sell the rights to ocean use in a market. Similarly, you're unlikely to be able to sell the right of aircraft to use the air space over land you own because of the high transaction costs of actually making users of the air space pay. Neither can you make people pay for the right to emit exhaust fumes into the air you breathe. The transaction costs of pricing the right to use each mile of city streets or sidewalks are also likely to be high, because this would involve setting up many toll booths. The costs of maintaining the booths might not be worth the revenue that could be collected from users of the streets.

The concepts of property rights and transaction costs are intertwined. The establishment of property rights to own or use goods or services depends on the transaction costs of guaranteeing those rights. Government plays an important role in markets by using its power to guarantee property rights and enforce agreements to

Transaction costs:
Costs incurred in enforcing property rights to traded goods, locating trading partners, and actually carrying out the transaction.

Principles in Practice

Property Rights, Transaction Costs, and Pricing: Two Examples

Example 1: Scrambling Satellite TV Signals

Who owns the airwaves? These days, the answer depends on whom you ask.

Over 1.5 million Americans use satellite dish antennas to pick up television programming. The dishes cost as much as $10,000 when they were introduced in 1970. However, improvements in technology have reduced their price to as low as $1,000, making them affordable to many avid TV viewers. Many of these viewers have no access to cable television. With satellite dishes they can pick up cable TV programming transmitted by satellite free of charge.

Up until January of 1986, satellite dish owners could receive Home Box Office and Cinemax programming without paying the usual monthly fee. Since that time, these two popular cable TV services have been scrambling their satellite transmissions so they can't be readily picked up by satellite dishes. Other premium programming services have also announced the intention to scramble their signals. Special decoders are now required to unscramble the signals. The decoders cost $395 in 1986. But it's not enough to buy a decoder to receive the scrambled programming. Dish owners must also pay a monthly fee to receive HBO. If they don't pay the fee, the decoder can be turned off by remote control!

Sellers of cable programming argue that they have the right to charge for their services. They consider the receipt of such programming without payment of fees to be theft! Now that the technology is available to prevent such theft of service, the companies have no reluctance to use it.

This issue of property rights and pricing has become a political controversy. Opponents say the airwaves are public property and no firm can restrict their use or use pricing to prevent dish owners from receiving signals. There have even been demonstrations and other protests against the scrambling. In March of 1986, satellite dish dealers and owners massed in Nashville, Tennessee, to demonstrate and lobby for legislation to make scrambling satellite programming illegal. There have also been demonstrations for "viewer rights" in the states of Oregon and Washington. The most dramatic protest was made by the notorious "Captain Midnight." On April 27, 1986, this ingenious protestor managed to use a powerful electronic signal to invade the airwaves used by HBO to transmit its programs. The intrepid Captain used the signal to indicate his distaste for HBO's scrambling!

Example 2: Paying for the Right to Park

Almost universally despised, the parking meter is a familiar fixture in the American urban landscape. Its purpose is simple: to charge people for the right to park on city streets. As of 1986, New York City had 62,778 parking meters in operation. However, collection costs have been rising substantially. It takes a lot of labor to empty each meter of its daily load of quarters. In 1986 the price to park in metered spaces in midtown Manhattan was 25 cents per 10 minutes. This means that an hour's worth of parking time at choice locations on city streets cost $1.50. If the meters are kept busy with customers pumping in quarters, they have to be emptied four times a week. In 1985 the Transportation Department of the City of New York collected a whopping $32 million in coins from parking meters. However, they incurred transaction costs of $1.6 million for collecting the coins and $8 million for meter maintenance. The city is now looking to new technology to reduce the transaction costs of pricing the right to park on city streets. City officials predict that the parking meter, in its current coin-operated incarnation, will be extinct by the mid-1990s.

The City of New York is currently considering replacing its meters with a new electronic meter that will be operated by a card similar to those used to operate gates at parking lots.* The card could be purchased at newsstands and convenience stores. Instead of putting coins in the meter, parkers would simply insert their electronically coded card. At the end of the month each motorist would receive a bill in the mail for parking fees.

Another approach the city is considering is simply to abolish the meters completely. Instead of putting coins in meters, motorists would be required to buy paper vouchers or disposable cards that they would display in their windshields. The vouchers would be valid for a certain period of time. After parking, the driver would display a certain number of cards in the window of the car and mark the time and date on the cards. The city is even considering the use of a disposable electronic timer to be displayed in the windshield. Drivers would be required to buy the timer, which would give them the right to use up to 10 hours of parking time.

*See James Brooke, "Time is Running Out for the Coin-Operated Parking Meter," *The New York Times,* Sunday, September 7, 1986.

exchange property rights. In effect, the government is the silent partner in all market transactions because its system of courts and police power is used to guarantee property rights acquired in market exchanges and to settle disputes concerning such exchanges. The effectiveness of government in establishing and facilitating the exchange of property rights is crucial to the smooth functioning of markets.

In addition, changes in technology often reduce transaction costs, thereby providing the opportunity for gains from market exchanges of new goods and services. For example, the right to park on city streets (see Principles in Practice box) wasn't priced until the development of the parking meter. It wasn't possible to prevent satellite dish antenna owners from receiving satellite TV transmissions until a change in technology enabled the cable companies to scramble those transmissions.

Property Rights of Third Parties to Market Transactions

Buyers and sellers in competitive markets seek personal gains. If no one other than buyers and sellers is harmed or benefited by the sale of the good, then those personal gains will be the only gains in the society at large. However, when externalities prevail, there are *third parties* in addition to the buyers or sellers who are affected by market transactions. For example, suppose pollution from the purchase and use of gasoline makes people other than the buyers or sellers worse off by impairing their health. The property rights of these third parties aren't considered during market transactions. The transaction costs of establishing the property rights of these third parties to use of the air for breathing are likely to be high. Part of the cost of making gasoline available is the impaired health of those harmed by pollution. Because of the difficulty of establishing the property right to clean air, the market price of gasoline is *too low* because it's not based on *all* the costs of making gasoline available. In this case the price system fails to price a valuable environmental resource, and consequently a negative externality prevails.

Similarly, you might not consider the fact that when you buy a particular item you benefit some third party other than the seller. For example, if you buy a smoke detector, you benefit your neighbors by reducing the risk of fire that can spread to their homes. The third parties in this case benefit from your purchase of the good but aren't charged for the benefit they receive. In this case the price system fails to price a benefit to third parties to a market transaction.

When a negative externality prevails, the unit and marginal costs that sellers consider in deciding how much to supply are lower than the actual marginal costs to make the product available. This is because the sellers aren't charged for the damage they cause to third parties. As a result, the firms produce more than they would if they were charged for the external cost they impose. If it were possible to price the use of the resources, such as the air or water that are used free of charge, the marginal cost of any given output of sellers would increase. This increase in cost would cause them to decrease the supply of the product, and as a result price would increase. As a consequence of the higher price, the quantity of the good demanded would decline. For example, if the emissions of harmful pollutants resulting from the production of gasoline could be measured, sellers could be charged according to the damage these emissions cause. This charge would increase the sellers' marginal cost by charging for the right to emit and would therefore decrease supply and result in an increase in price. The charges would also induce firms to change their productive methods to reduce the harmful emissions.

In the graph in Box 4 you can see how charges for emitting damaging wastes affect the market for goods whose production or use causes such damage. Suppose that the market equilibrium for gasoline when the externality prevails corresponds to point E_1. At that equilibrium the price is $1 per gallon and 5 million gallons are sold at that price per year. When sellers are charged for the damage they cause to third parties, the sellers now have to include a previously unpriced input (the air) as part of the cost of producing and using gasoline. This results in a decrease in supply. The new market equilibrium is now at E_2, and the price of gasoline rises to $1.40 per gallon. As a consequence, quantity demanded declines to 4 million gallons per year. Reducing the emissions provides benefits to third parties and results in more efficient resource use, as sellers must consider the marginal cost of emissions as well as other costs when choosing output. However, because they're now charged for the emissions, the price of gasoline goes up. Without such charges, the price of the product doesn't reflect the entire cost of producing it or using it, and too much is sold relative to the allocatively efficient amount.

Similarly, when a positive externality prevails, the sale of a good benefits someone other than the buyer or seller. If it were possible to charge these third parties for the benefit they receive, the seller could use the funds obtained to reduce the cost of making the good available. Such a subsidy to output would increase the gain from selling it and result in an increase in supply. The increase in supply would lower the price to buyers and increase the quantity demanded. For example, if colleges could induce the third parties who enjoy external benefits from college education to contribute to the costs of providing each qualified student with instruction, then the marginal cost of educating a student would decline. This would increase the supply of higher education services and cause a decline in tuition.

In the graph in Box 5 you can see the impact of subsidies to encourage consumption of a good whose use results in a positive externality. When there are no

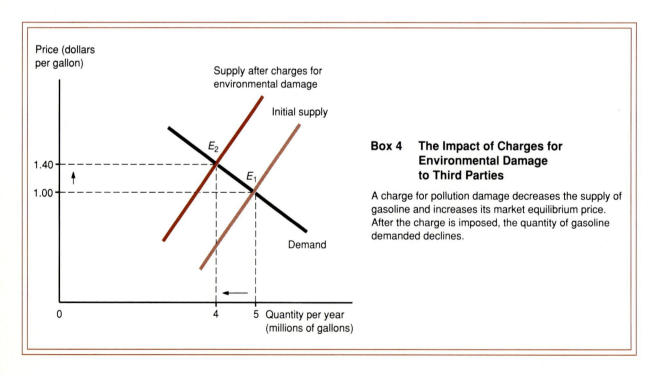

Box 4   The Impact of Charges for Environmental Damage to Third Parties

A charge for pollution damage decreases the supply of gasoline and increases its market equilibrium price. After the charge is imposed, the quantity of gasoline demanded declines.

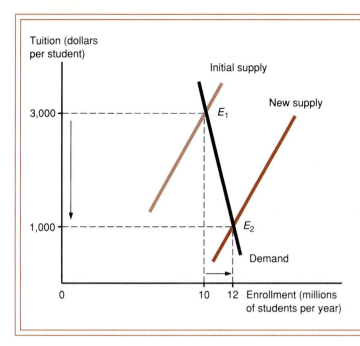

Tuition (dollars
per student)

Initial supply

New supply

3,000

E_1

1,000

E_2

Demand

0   10   12   Enrollment (millions
of students per year)

**Box 5   Impact of Subsidies to
Higher Education**

When third parties who benefit from positive externalities associated with higher education contribute to colleges and universities according to enrollment, the resulting subsidies increase the supply of education available on the market. This lowers the market tuition and results in an increase in enrollment.

means for third parties to contribute to the cost of higher education, the market equilibrium corresponds to point E_1. The corresponding tuition per year is $3,000, and the number of students enrolling in colleges and universities is 10 million. After subsidies by third parties to higher education, the supply of higher education services increases and the new market equilibrium corresponds to E_2. At that point the tuition per student declines to $1,000 per year and the number of students enrolled increases to 12 million per year. In the absence of any means for third parties to contribute toward the cost of higher education from which they benefit, the market devotes less than the efficient amount of resources to higher education.

In a later chapter we'll discuss in detail the policies government employs to deal with externalities. We'll analyze in depth the consequences of current government regulations designed to cope with market failure resulting from externalities.

Other Common Problems in a Market System

1. *Lack of competition.* Markets are not always competitive. In noncompetitive markets there are barriers that prevent all gains from trade from being achieved. For example, suppose there's only a single seller of eggs in the market and that it's impossible for additional sellers to enter the market. Buyers now have only one source of supply if they want eggs. Additional sellers, who might be able to gain by using their resources to make more eggs available at the very profitable price set by the single seller, are prevented from doing so. Under these conditions the seller who monopolizes the supply could control the price to buyers who have no other source of supply.

Lack of adequate competition impairs the ability of the price system to respond to changes in demand. This is because monopolization of supply prevents profits from serving as a signal for more output in markets in which additional output would be profitable.

2. *Income inequality and poverty.* In a pure market economy your income would depend entirely on the quantity, quality, and types of resources you're willing and able to sell. Your income would influence your willingness and ability to pay for goods. People with very low incomes might be unable to buy the minimal amounts of goods and services required for their survival. If a large number of people in the economy lack skills that enable them to earn labor income, and the ownership of capital and land is concentrated in the hands of a few wealthy individuals, the masses will be poor while an elite class will earn most of the income each year.

In the United States, for example, families that rank in the top 20% according to their income account for nearly half of all the income earned each year. On the other hand, the poorest 20% of families make less than 4% of the annual income earned in the nation each year. As you can see, the gap between the rich and the poor is vast.

Many critics of the pure market economy argue that its outcomes can't be given high marks using normative criteria for evaluating income distribution, even when the results of market exchange rank high in terms of efficiency criteria. The paradox of poverty in the midst of wealth is a common criticism of the performance of the capitalistic economy. In the mid-1980s an astounding 15% of the U.S. population was estimated to have inadequate money income to attain minimum acceptable living standards in the country. In a later chapter we'll discuss income distribution in the United States and government policies to influence it.

3. *Instability.* When markets react to changes in demand or supply, it often takes a considerable amount of time for them to achieve equilibrium again. For example, fluctuations in the demand for products result in fluctuations in the demand for labor. A decrease in demand for labor is likely during a recession. Market wages don't always decline quickly enough to eliminate the surplus of labor that occurs at the initial wage after the decrease in demand. As a result, during recessions there is excessive unemployment.

Similarly, prices sometimes are quite unstable and subject to sharp and unpredictable increases. Unpredictable inflation of the price level can make planning for the future difficult and can result in price changes that distort the way we conduct our daily affairs. For example, fear of future price increases can cause us to stock up on goods. When we do this, we further increase the demand for those items, thereby putting more upward pressure on prices.

The fluctuations in demand and supply and consequent periods of market disequilibrium are an inherent problem that results from lack of coordination of decision making in the price system. Governments often regulate markets and seek to influence the demand for products and loanable funds in an attempt to correct market instability.

Evaluating Market Performance

To evaluate economic outcomes such as prices or quantities sold in any market, we must take the following steps:

1. Set up normative criteria against which to compare the market performance. Later in the book we'll use the criterion of allocative efficiency to evaluate market performance. We also can evaluate markets in terms of objectives re-

lating to the distribution of well-being among people in a nation.

2. Use positive analysis to forecast actual market outcomes so we can assess the performance of the market against the normative goals.

3. When a market performs poorly in relation to the normative goals, look for means to modify the way the market works to provide incentives for gain that will help achieve the desired goals. If this isn't possible, look for an alternative to the market to accomplish the tasks the market is judged to do poorly.

4. Use positive analysis to evaluate alternatives to markets to see how resource allocation is affected, who gains, and who loses as a result of government or other types of nonmarket mechanisms for allocating resources.

Concept Check

1 Why is it difficult to establish a price for certain useful goods and services?

2 In what way are externalities indicative of a market failure?

3 Make a list of problems that are likely to prevail in an economy that relies exclusively on markets to allocate economic resources.

The Modern Mixed Economy

The shortcomings of a pure market economy have led to the evolution of the modern mixed economy. When markets do a poor job of allocating resources, we look to government to improve matters. The impact of government on allocative efficiency and income distribution is a controversial question we'll address in many parts of the book. However, the fact is that neither the United States nor any other noncommunist nation can be regarded as having a purely capitalistic economy.

In the United States the federal, state, and local governments levy taxes on both businesses and households to finance the provision of public goods and services. Governments also borrow funds to help meet their expenses. Finally, governments intervene in decisions made by households and business managers to protect environmental resources, prevent restraints on competition in markets, and correct for failure of the price system to account for the property rights of third parties to market transactions.

Governments in the United States acquire resources to provide hospital and health services, provide free and compulsory elementary and secondary education, assist the poor in maintaining minimum standards of living, provide for the national defense, and make pensions and insurance services available to the elderly and other groups. About 20% of all workers in the United States are employed by governments.

The U.S. government supports the prices of some agricultural products. Government regulations influence the quality of products like automobiles and new drugs, and through various taxes government affects the prices of gasoline, cigarettes, and alcoholic beverages. Governments provide the legal structure that facilitates market transactions. Finally, governments seek to stabilize the general level of economic activity to correct for the difficulty the price system often encounters in maintaining stable prices and full employment of labor and other economic resources.

Compared to the United States, the extent of government activity is much greater in the Soviet Union and other communist countries in which governments run the enterprises that use economic resources to produce products. In such nations government boards often plan and direct production and set prices to achieve certain goals. However, even in communist nations there's a market sector of the economy in which prices and pursuit of gain guide decisions. This sector is quite small in the Soviet Union but much larger in other socialist nations like Hungary and Yugoslavia. In many Western European nations, such as France and the United Kingdom, large enterprises, including many heavy industries and railroads, are owned and operated by the government. The scope of government activity varies from nation to nation but all nations, including those under communist regimes, can more often than not be regarded as mixed economies.

Summary

1. Capitalism is characterized by private ownership of economic resources and freedom of enterprise in competitive markets. The people who manage and assume the risks of business enterprises in a capitalistic economy are its entrepreneurs.
2. In modern economies people tend to specialize in specific productive endeavors. The resulting division of labor makes people dependent on each other to obtain items that they choose not to produce for themselves.
3. Allocative efficiency is attained when all possible mutual gains from the production of a certain mix of goods are exhausted. Mutual gains from exchange are possible when the minimum amount of goods or sum of money a person will accept in trade for an item is less than the maximum amount a trading partner would surrender in exchange for that item.
4. In modern economies most exchange involves trades of money for goods (or services) rather than barter of goods for goods (or services). Barter is inconvenient because it requires double coincidence of wants.
5. In a market economy there is a circular flow of income and expenditure. Business firms employ economic resources offered for sale in input markets. The payments they make for the resources they use constitute income to members of the economy's households. Households use their income to buy goods and services offered for sale in markets by business firms.
6. The price system is the mechanism by which resource use is guided by prices in a market economy. Price changes occur in response to shifts in demand and supply. These price changes affect the opportunities for personal gain in market transactions and result in resource reallocation until no further gain is possible. In this way prices guide what is produced and influence business managers' choice of production methods.
7. The amounts of goods and services you can enjoy depend on your money income, which you use to back up your desire for goods and services insofar as your income influences your ability to pay. Your money income is determined by the prices of the services or economic resources you have and are willing to sell.
8. Public goods are those that are consumed equally by everyone whether they pay or not.
9. The price system fails when some goods people want and are willing to pay for can't be easily packaged into units that can be priced. Market exchange is feasible only for items for which property rights can be guaranteed and easily exchanged. Transaction costs of exchange include those incurred in enforcing property rights, locating trading partners, and actually carrying out transactions.

High transaction costs that make it difficult to assign or transfer property rights can make market exchange infeasible.

10. Externalities are costs or benefits of market transactions not reflected in market prices. Externalities are indicative of market failure to price the use of a valuable resource.

11. Markets are not always competitive. For example, one or several buyers or sellers can control price if entry into the market is limited. This can prevent the market from achieving allocative efficiency.

12. In the modern mixed economy, governments supply goods and services and can use their power to attempt to correct for the shortcomings of the price system.

Key Terms and Concepts

Capitalism
Mixed economy
Price system
Allocative efficiency
Barter

Market failure
Public goods
Externalities
Property rights
Transaction costs

Problems and Applications

1. Suppose you start a new business distributing software for personal computers. The business proves to be extremely profitable. Explain how freedom of enterprise and economic rivalry are likely to come into play in a market economy in a way that will eventually reduce your profits.

2. The marginal benefit of a good represents the sum of money a consumer is willing and able to pay for one more unit of the good. The marginal cost of the good represents the minimum sum of money a seller is willing to accept to make more of the good available. Suppose the marginal benefit of color televisions is $200 while the marginal cost is only $100. Assuming that the marginal benefit of color TVs declines and the marginal cost increases as more are made available, show that more color TVs must be sold to achieve allocative efficiency.

3. An economy is producing a mix of food and clothing that corresponds to a point on, instead of within, its production possibilities curve. Explain how it's possible for this economy not to have attained allocative efficiency even though it's on its production possibilities curve.

4. Use supply and demand analysis to show how an increase in the demand for four-wheel-drive recreational vehicles accompanied by a decrease in the demand for standard full-size passenger cars will affect resource allocation in the automobile industry.

5. During the energy crisis of the early 1970s, the price of smaller cars actually increased above the price of gas-guzzling full-size models. How did the U.S. automobile industry react to the change in prices? What do you expect will happen to the kinds of cars made available if the supply of gasoline increases substantially in the 1990s to push the price down permanently to an average of 75 cents per gallon?

6. Use supply and demand analysis to trace out the impact of a sharp reduction in the price of electronic components on the price, use, and profitability of pro-

ducing goods that use electronic components as inputs. What effect is the change in price likely to have on production techniques?

7. Your parents own 1,000 acres of land. The land is in the flight path to an airport, and planes regularly fly over it as they make their approach to the airport. Why can't your parents charge the airlines for using their air space?

8. You have a bicycle that you plan to sell at the end of the year when you graduate. You'd like to get $100 for the bike, for which you originally paid $300. List the transaction costs you must incur to find a buyer for your bike. Under what circumstances might you be better off to give the bike away instead of trying to sell it?

9. A firm that manufactures paper products dumps its wastes into a stream and doesn't pay for the right to do so. The stream is used by fishermen and boaters as a source of recreational enjoyment. The waste products dumped into the stream make it less useful for recreation. Explain why an externality exists and identify the groups involved in the externality. In what sense is there a failure of the price system in this case?

10. Make a list of the goods and services provided to you by governments. List the shortcomings of the pure market economy that each of these government services is designed to correct.

Suggested Readings

Milton Friedman, *Capitalism and Freedom,* Chicago: The University of Chicago Press, 1962. Milton Friedman is one of the foremost advocates of the advantages of free market exchange. In this classic book Friedman analyzes the way the price system works and the virtues of freedom of enterprise and exchange.

Robert Sobel and David B. Sicilia, *The Entrepreneurs: An American Adventure,* Boston: Houghton Mifflin Co., 1986. This is a delightful collection of essays on the entrepreneur in America. The authors show how successful entrepreneurs have seized opportunities to introduce new products, new productive processes, and new methods of marketing products, and how they have profited from doing so.

Oliver E. Williamson, *The Economic Institutions of Capitalism,* New York: The Free Press, 1985. This is a provocative work that uses the concept of transaction costs to explain various aspects of the economy, including markets and the incentives to enter into contracts. Some of the analysis in the book is quite technical.

A Forward Look

The laws of supply and demand indicate the direction of change in quantities demanded and supplied when prices change. It's useful, in many practical applications of supply and demand analysis, to have measures of the *sensitivity* of reactions of buyers and sellers to changes in price and other economic conditions. In the following chapter we develop such measures and show you how to use them.

Elasticity of Supply and Demand

Suppose you're the owner of a popular pizzeria near your school's campus. You're considering raising the price of your double-cheese deluxe by $1—but how will your customers react?

You already know that, according to the law of demand, whenever the price of a good goes up, the quantity demanded generally goes down. But what you really need to know is the *extent* to which the quantity demanded of your deluxe pizzas will fall off if you boost the price by $1.

To forecast the effect of price changes on their revenues, businesses require a measure of buyer sensitivity to changes in price called the *elasticity of demand*. In this chapter we'll look at the conceptual problems involved in measuring elasticity of demand along points on the demand curve for a good. This will allow us to sketch out methods of estimating demand elasticities. We'll also develop measures of demand sensitivity to changes in such important demand determinants as consumer income and prices of substitutes and complements. Knowledge of demand sensitivity to income and the prices of related goods helps businesses market their products and manage resource use. For example, a retailer of casual clothing who knows the sensitivity of demand for jackets to fluctuations in consumer income can manage her inventory to avoid running short of jackets or incurring high costs for storing and financing stocks of the jackets.

Elasticity of supply is a measure of the sensitivity of *supply* to changes in prices. We'll develop the concept of elasticity of supply to help us gauge *how much* the quantity supplied changes in response to price changes. As you'll see, knowledge of the elasticity of supply of products is very useful in forecasting the impact of policies designed to influence the quantities supplied by sellers in markets. You'll also learn how knowledge of elasticity of both supply and demand is crucial in forecasting the impact of taxes and changes in tax rates on prices and government tax collections.

1   Explain the purpose and uses of the concept of price elasticity of demand.
2   Show how price elasticity of demand can be calculated for points on a given demand curve.
3   Explain how to use other elasticity measures, including the income elasticity of demand, the cross-elasticity of demand, and the price elasticity of supply.
4   Show how the price elasticities of supply and demand are relevant for explaining the impact of taxes on market prices of goods and services.

Price Elasticity of Demand

Price elasticity of demand:
A number representing the percentage change in quantity demanded of a good resulting from each 1% change in the price of the good.

Price elasticity of demand is a number representing the percentage change in quantity demanded resulting from each 1% change in the price of a good. This number is used to gauge the sensitivity of quantity demanded of a good to percentage changes in the price of that good. Price elasticity of demand is a *measure* of the responsiveness of quantity demanded to price changes along a given demand curve. We can estimate the measure from actual data on changes in quantity demanded in response to changes in price.

Price elasticity is calculated by dividing the percentage change in quantity demanded of a good by the percentage change in price that caused it, other things being equal:

Price elasticity of demand = % change in quantity demanded/% change in price

For example, suppose the price of cars went up by 1% this year and the resulting decline in cars purchased was 2%. The price elasticity of demand would be

$$\frac{-2\%}{1\%} = -2$$

Notice that price elasticity of demand is a number without units of measurement because it's obtained by dividing two percentage changes. Also note that price elasticity of demand is a negative number. This is because an increase in price will generally result in a decrease in quantity demanded, other things being equal. Therefore, if the percentage change in price is positive, the percentage change in quantity demanded will be negative, as shown in the calculation just presented. Similarly, if price were to decline, the percentage change in price would be negative but the percentage change in quantity demanded would be positive. For example, suppose the price of gasoline declines by 2% and the annual increase in gasoline sales attributable to this price decline is also 2%. The price elasticity of demand for that price decline would therefore be:

$$\frac{2\%}{-2\%} = -1$$

How to Use Price Elasticity of Demand to Make Market Forecasts

You've just learned how to calculate price elasticity of demand from percentage changes in quantities demanded that result from certain percentage changes in price. Suppose instead you have a good estimate of the price elasticity of demand for the product you sell. Now you can work backwards and use the concept of elasticity to make predictions of changes in quantity demanded in response to price changes.

For example, imagine you run a car dealership. Last year you sold 10,000 cars. This year you know that the price of each car you sell will go up by 10%. You know the law of demand implies that, other things unchanged, you'll sell fewer cars this year; but the law gives no hint of *how many* fewer you'll sell. You can now see the relevance of the concept of price elasticity of demand. You know from past experience that the price elasticity of demand for cars you sell is -2. Because you know the percentage change in price and the price elasticity of demand for your product, you can easily calculate the percentage change in quantity demanded:

$$\% \text{ change in quantity demanded}/10\% = -2$$

Therefore

$$\% \text{ change in quantity demanded} = -20\%$$

You therefore expect a 20% reduction in sales as a result of the price increase. This means you can expect to sell only 8,000 cars instead of 10,000 this year, assuming your estimate of price elasticity of demand is accurate and nothing else changes that might affect car sales. You can use this estimate of reduced sales volume to cut back on your orders for cars from the manufacturer and avoid tying up your funds in a large inventory of unsold cars.

You also can use price elasticity of demand to formulate pricing strategies if you own a firm that can control its prices. For example, suppose you manage a stereo store and you want to increase your annual quantity of rack systems sold by 20%. You estimate that the price elasticity of demand for your rack systems is -4. One obvious way to increase the quantities you sell is to lower prices. Other things being equal, how much must you cut prices to increase sales by 20%? The answer is easy because you know the price elasticity of demand for your rack systems and you know the percentage increase in quantity demanded. To calculate the necessary percentage price reduction, simply use the formula for price elasticity of demand:

$$\frac{20\%}{\% \text{ change in price}} = -4$$

Therefore

$$\% \text{ change in price} = -5\%$$

In this case you'd need to reduce prices by 5% to achieve your desired increase in rack system sales volume.

Categorizing Price Elasticity of Demand as Elastic or Inelastic

In categorizing demand as more or less elastic, it's convenient to *ignore the minus sign* in front of the number measuring the elasticity of demand. The larger the number after the minus sign, the more elastic the demand. In other words, the larger the *absolute value* of the price elasticity of demand, the more elastic the demand. For example, if the elasticity of demand for cars is -2 while the elasticity of demand for bread is -0.5, the demand for cars is more elastic than the demand for bread.

An **elastic demand** prevails if the price elasticity of demand for a good turns out to be a number that exceeds 1, ignoring the minus sign. For example, if the number that measures the price elasticity of demand for fur coats is -5, the demand for fur coats would be elastic. If the price elasticity of demand for sweatshirts is -2, their demand would also be elastic. However, note that the demand for fur coats would be more elastic than the corresponding demand for sweatshirts. If demand is elastic, the percentage change in quantity demanded caused by a price increase will exceed the percentage change in the price (ignoring the direction of change).

A good has an **inelastic demand** if its price elasticity of demand is a number equal to or greater than zero but less than 1, ignoring the minus sign. The smaller the number after the minus sign, the more inelastic the demand for the good. For example, the demand for milk would be categorized as inelastic if its price elasticity of demand were -0.8 because 0.8 is less than 1. If the price elasticity of demand for aspirin were -0.5, its demand would be considered more inelastic than the demand for milk because 0.5 is less than 0.8. Ignoring the direction of change, the percentage change in quantity demanded will be less than the percentage change in price that caused it when demand is inelastic. If the price elasticity of demand for a good were zero, it would imply that consumers wouldn't respond at all to price changes and demand would be considered *perfectly* inelastic.

Finally, a good has a **unit elastic demand** if the number that measures its price elasticity of demand is exactly equal to 1 when the minus sign is ignored. If the demand for a good is unit elastic, the percentage change in its quantity demanded caused by a price change will equal the percentage change in price, again ignoring the direction of change. For example, if each 1% increase in the price of milk resulted in a 1% decline in the quantity demanded, the demand for milk would be unit elastic.

The table in Box 1 summarizes the range of variation for price elasticity of demand and the various ways of categorizing the demand for a product according to its price elasticity. Remember, the larger the number after the minus sign, the more elastic the demand.

Elastic demand:
Prevails if the price elasticity of demand for a good is a number that exceeds 1, ignoring the minus sign.

Inelastic demand:
Prevails if the price elasticity of demand for a good is a number equal to or greater than zero but less than 1, ignoring the minus sign.

Unit elastic demand:
Prevails if the number that measures the price elasticity of demand for a good is exactly equal to 1 when the minus sign is ignored.

Box 1 Price Elasticity of Demand as a Gauge of Demand Responsiveness

Demand response	% change in quantity demanded relative to % change in price (ignoring direction of change)	Value of elasticity of demand (ignoring minus sign)
Inelastic	% change in quantity demanded is *less than* % change in price	Equal to or greater than 0 but less than 1
Unit elastic	% change in quantity demanded *equals* % change in price	1
Elastic	% change in quantity demanded is *greater than* % change in price	Greater than 1

Determinants of Price Elasticity of Demand

There are a number of factors that can influence the price elasticity of demand for an item. These factors include:

1. *The availability of substitutes.* Remember that a substitute for a good is one that serves the same general purpose. In general, the more and better substitutes that exist for an item, the more elastic its demand. For example, it's quite likely that the demand for insulin by diabetics is extremely inelastic because insulin has few if any substitutes. However, the demand for a particular brand of automobile is likely to be very elastic because there are many substitute brands available in the market.

2. *Time.* In general, demand tends to become more elastic with *time* because we find more substitutes for goods over longer periods. Over longer periods we also have more time to adjust our consumption patterns in response to price changes, which also contributes to a more elastic demand over longer periods. For example, there might be little that we as drivers can do within a period of a month or two to react to an increase in the price of gasoline. However, over several years we can seek out more fuel-efficient cars and buy them to replace our older gas guzzlers. We can also move closer to work. Also over a period of several years more substitutes are developed for goods whose prices go up. For example, a sharp permanent increase in the price of gasoline might lead to development of substitute fuels.

3. *The proportion of income consumers spend on the good.* As consumers we tend to spend high proportions of our income on housing and cars. A 10% increase in the prices of these goods is likely to reduce substantially our ability to buy these items and result in sharp percentage declines in quantities demanded. The demand for goods on which we spend large percentages of our income is likely to be quite elastic. On the other hand, a 10% increase in the price of pencils will have little effect on the purchasing power of our income and is unlikely to result in sharp percentage declines in quantities demanded. Of course, there are exceptions to this rule. We might spend only a small portion of our income on oysters, but the demand for oysters might be elastic because oysters are considered dispensable luxuries. In general, other things being equal, the smaller the percentage of income spent on a good, the less elastic the demand unless the good is considered a dispensable luxury.

Calculating Price Elasticity of Demand from Two Points on a Demand Curve

We can use the concept of price elasticity of demand together with the demand curve to reach some interesting conclusions. The graph in Box 2 shows a downward-sloping linear demand curve for granola bars. Suppose the equilibrium price of granola bars is currently $1 and 20,000 bars are sold at that price each week. This corresponds to point A on the demand curve. Now suppose, as a result of a decrease in the supply, the price of granola bars increases to $1.10 and the quantity demanded falls to 15,000 per week as the equilibrium moves from point A to point B on the demand curve. To calculate the price elasticity of demand from the data, we follow these steps:

1. Calculate the change in price (ΔP) and the change in quantity demanded (ΔQ). In this case the change in price is $\Delta P = 10¢$ and the resulting change in quantity demanded is $\Delta Q = -5,000$.

2. Calculate the *percentage change* in price caused by the decrease in supply. Here a slight problem occurs when the change in price or quantity demanded is

substantial. The 10¢ increase in price is 10% of the initial price (P_1) of $1 but is only 9.1% of the *new* price (P_2) of $1.10. To see this, divide the 10¢ change in price by the new price. This will give you the following result: $0.10/$1.10 = 0.091. To convert this to a percentage, multiply the result by 100%, which gives you 9.1%.

Because you'll get a different percentage change depending on whether you use the initial or new market price to make your calculation, economists often use the *average* of the initial and new prices to calculate a compromise percentage change. In this case the average price will be ($1.00 + $1.10)/2, which equals $1.05. The percentage change in price can therefore be calculated as ($0.10/$1.05) (100%) = 9.5%.

In symbolic terms the percentage change in price can be written as

$$\left[\frac{\Delta P}{\frac{1}{2}(P_1 + P_2)} \right] 100\%$$

where P_1 is the initial price and P_2 is the new price.

3. Calculate the percentage change in quantity demanded caused by the price increase. Here the change in quantity demanded is −5,000 granola bars per week. This is equal to 25% of the initial quantity demanded (Q_1) of 20,000 bars and 33% of the *new* quantity demanded (Q_2) of 15,000 bars after the price increase. To resolve the ambiguity, once again calculate the percentage change on the basis of the average of the initial and new quantities demanded. The average quantity demanded is (20,000 + 15,000)/2 = 17,500 granola bars per week. The percentage change in quantity demanded will therefore be (−5,000/17,500) (100%) = −28.6%.

In symbols, the percentage change in quantity demanded is:

$$\left[\frac{\Delta Q}{\frac{1}{2}(Q_1 + Q_2)} \right] 100\%$$

where Q_1 is the initial quantity demanded and Q_2 is the new quantity demanded.

4. Divide the percentage change in quantity demanded by the percentage change in price to get the price elasticity of demand:

$$\text{Price elasticity of demand} = \frac{-28.6\%}{9.5\%} = -3.01$$

Because the number after the minus sign exceeds 1, the demand for granola bars can be categorized as *elastic*.

The formula for calculating the price elasticity of demand between two points on a demand curve can be written as:

$$\text{Price elasticity of demand} = \frac{\Delta Q/(Q_1 + Q_2)}{\Delta P/(P_1 + P_2)}$$

which is obtained simply by dividing the expression for the percentage change in quantity demanded just shown by the expression for the percentage change in price.

How Price Elasticity Can Vary Along a Demand Curve

Can you conclude from the calculation you just made that the price elasticity of demand for granola bars will *always* be −3.01 no matter what the price? The answer is *no*. In fact, we can easily show that the price elasticity of demand varies continuously at different points on a downward-sloping linear demand curve. To see why this is so, suppose the initial price of granola bars was 20¢ instead of $1. Of course, at a price that much lower, the quantity of granola bars demanded would be substantially higher. The graph in Box 2 shows that the quantity demanded is 60,000 bars per week when the price is 20¢. This corresponds to point E on the demand curve drawn in the graph in Box 2. Now suppose the price of granola bars goes up by 10¢ as before. The percentage increase in this case, based on the average of the initial price of 20¢ and the new price of 30¢, would be 40%. Because the downward-sloping demand curve is *linear,* the reduction in quantity demanded for each 10¢ increase in price will be the same as before: 5,000 bars. A linear demand curve is one with constant slope: each 10¢ increase in price results in a 5,000-bar reduction in weekly quantity demanded, no matter what the initial price and quantity demanded (see the Appendix to Chapter 1). After the price increases from 20¢ to 30¢, we find that the change in quantity demanded expressed as a percentage of the average of initial quantity demanded (60,000) and new quantity demanded (55,000) equals −9%. The price elasticity of demand is therefore

$$\frac{-9\%}{40\%} = -0.23$$

Because the number after the minus sign is less than 1, we'd now categorize the demand for granola bars as *inelastic.*

If you use elasticity estimates to make forecasts, heed this warning: If the demand curve for your product is linear, like the one drawn in the graph in Box 2, then price elasticity of demand will change as price changes. When using past data based

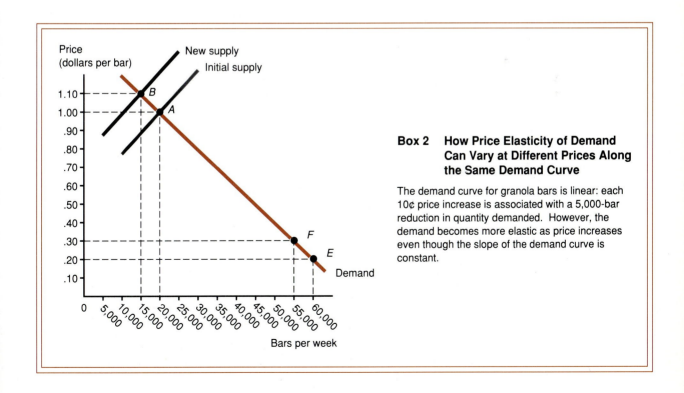

Box 2   How Price Elasticity of Demand Can Vary at Different Prices Along the Same Demand Curve

The demand curve for granola bars is linear: each 10¢ price increase is associated with a 5,000-bar reduction in quantity demanded. However, the demand becomes more elastic as price increases even though the slope of the demand curve is constant.

on previous price changes, be very careful to calculate the *current* price elasticity of demand for your product. *Assuming that the demand curve for your product is linear (or almost linear) like the one in Box 2, the demand for your product will tend to be more elastic at higher prices than at lower prices.* We can also state this proposition in a slightly different way: The greater the quantity demanded along a given linear demand curve, the more inelastic the demand in response to further price declines.

We can apply this proposition directly to the marketing of products. When a new product is introduced at a relatively high price, demand is likely to be quite elastic. This means sellers can expect consumers to be quite responsive to price declines for a new product. For example, when the personal computer was introduced in the early 1980s, increases in supply resulted in small percentage price declines but much larger percentage increases in quantity demanded. By the late 1980s the market became saturated with computers, meaning that the quantity sold per year was quite large as prices fell drastically in response to increased supply. In 1987 sellers found that further price declines resulted in only modest percentage increases in quantity demanded and that demand had become much more inelastic than it had been.

Here's a simple way to understand why price elasticity along a linear demand curve changes as price changes: When the initial price is low instead of high, a 10¢ change in price is a higher percentage of the average of the initial and final prices. Also, when the initial price is low, the quantity demanded will be high. Along a linear demand curve, each given change in price will result in the same change in quantity demanded. So, even though the quantity demanded is high at low prices, each 10¢ increase in price will still result in a 5,000-bar reduction in weekly quantity of granola bars demanded. Naturally, the 5,000-bar change in quantity demanded is a smaller percentage of the average of the initial and final quantities demanded at low prices when quantity demanded is high than at high prices when quantity demanded is lower. For given price increases along a linear demand curve, therefore, the percentage change in price decreases while the percentage change in quantity demanded tends to increase as price rises. Price elasticity of demand will move further away from zero as price increases along a linear demand curve, meaning that demand becomes more elastic (see graph in Box 2).

In summary:

1. Even though a linear demand curve has constant slope, its elasticity varies from point to point. The slope of the demand curve in Box 2 can be expressed as − $0.10/5,000 granola bars because each 10¢ change in price is always associated with a 5,000-bar change (in the opposite direction) in quantity demanded. This number can be expressed only as a ratio of dollars to granola bars and is therefore a cumbersome measure of responsiveness that varies with units of measurement. The price elasticity of demand is, however, a negative number with no units of measurement.

2. Along a downward-sloping linear demand curve, demand is very elastic at high prices but becomes less elastic as price declines. At relatively low prices demand becomes inelastic and approaches zero as prices get lower and lower.

3. Don't try to judge the price elasticity of demand at points on different demand curves by looking at their slopes. To calculate price elasticity of demand for points on each demand curve, you need to calculate percentage changes in prices

and quantities demanded. These percentage changes will vary with the actual price and quantity demanded.[1]

Perfectly Inelastic and Perfectly Elastic Demand Curves

Suppose the price elasticity of demand for a product were *always* zero, no matter what the price. What would its demand curve look like? If the price elasticity of demand is zero, the percentage change in quantity of the good demanded will always be zero no matter what the price or how much the price changes. For this to be the case, the quantity demanded of the good would have to be completely insensitive to changes in price. A demand curve that corresponds to such a situation is drawn in the graph labeled **A** in Box 3. This demand curve is a vertical line, indicating that if the price changes, there's no change in quantity demanded. The percentage change in quantity demanded along this demand curve is therefore zero, and its price elasticity at all points is 0/percentage change in price = 0.

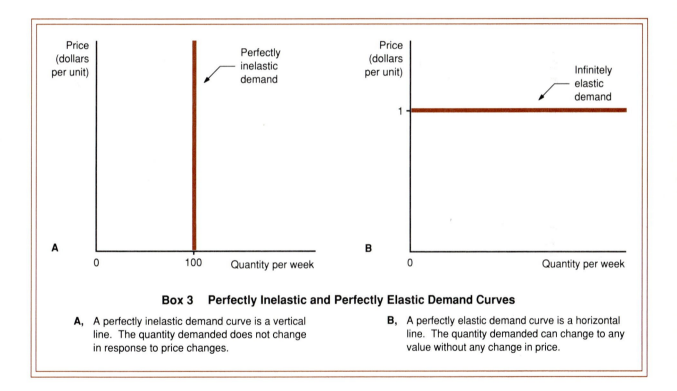

Box 3   Perfectly Inelastic and Perfectly Elastic Demand Curves

A, A perfectly inelastic demand curve is a vertical line. The quantity demanded does not change in response to price changes.

B, A perfectly elastic demand curve is a horizontal line. The quantity demanded can change to any value without any change in price.

[1]When the price change is very small, there will be little difference between the initial and final prices and quantities. For points on a demand curve, the formula for price elasticity of demand can be written as

$$\frac{(\Delta Q/Q)\ 100\%}{(\Delta P/P)\ 100\%} = \frac{(\Delta Q/Q)}{(\Delta P/P)} = \frac{P}{Q}\frac{\Delta Q}{\Delta P}$$

for any given P or Q. As Q approaches zero, price elasticity of demand approaches an infinitely large negative number. As P approaches zero, price elasticity of demand also approaches zero.

It's doubtful that any good has a perfectly inelastic demand curve. For this to be the case, the good would have to have virtually no substitutes or be a good on which consumers spend only minute fractions of their income. In most cases, we'd expect the demand curve for a good to have at least some downward slope. The demand curve for insulin by diabetics might be close to a vertical line because insulin has few if any substitutes. However, higher prices for insulin could induce diabetics to watch their diet more carefully and pursue other measures that might affect the frequency with which they take insulin.

In Box 3, the graph labeled **B** illustrates a demand curve that can be regarded as infinitely elastic at all prices. This demand curve is flat. You can think of such a demand curve as one that is approached when a downward-sloping demand curve becomes so flat that it can't be distinguished from a horizontal line. An almost flat downward-sloping demand curve implies that the most minute change in the price of a good will result in an infinite change in the quantity demanded. You can also understand why the demand curve shown in **B** is considered perfectly elastic by reasoning that along the curve, no change in price is necessary to change quantity demanded.

An infinitely elastic demand curve would prevail for a product that had a great many perfect substitutes. In fact, such a demand curve can be regarded as existing for a particular seller in a competitive market. For example, suppose you're one of a million sellers of eggs in the egg market. Because eggs are a standardized product, buyers will view your eggs as a perfect substitute for those of any other seller. You could sell all the eggs you wanted at the market price of $1 per dozen, and the demand curve for *your* eggs would be infinitely elastic like the one shown in **B** in Box 3.

Concept Check

1 How is price elasticity of demand calculated? If the price elasticity of demand for ice cream is equal to -0.8, calculate the effect of a 10% decrease in the price of ice cream on the quantity demanded.

2 Under what conditions is demand for a good categorized as elastic? When would it be inelastic? Relate your answer to percentage changes in price and quantities demanded.

3 The slope of the demand curve for cassette tapes is -2 at all points. Will its price elasticity also be constant at all points?

Using Price Elasticity of Demand to Forecast Changes in Total Expenditure and Total Revenue When Prices Change

Total Expenditure and Total Revenue

Total revenue:
The dollars earned by sellers of a product; the amount sold over a period multiplied by the price *(PQ)*.

As the manager of a pizzeria, you know that the more pizzas you sell, the more money you'll make. All sellers are interested in the amounts consumers will spend on an item because consumer expenditure is an important determinant of their profits. Expenditures by consumers represent the **total revenue** sellers take in from selling their products.

Total expenditure over any given period is the number of units of a product sold over that period, *Q*, multiplied by the price of the product, *P*:

$$\text{Total expenditure} = PQ = \text{Total revenue}$$

This equation shows that *PQ*, price times quantity, over any period equals *both* the total expenditure on that product by consumers *and* the total revenue sellers receive from selling the product.

For example, if the price of ground beef, on average, is $1.50 per pound and 20 million pounds were sold last month, total expenditure on ground beef was $30 million. This sum also equals the total revenue received that month by sellers in the market.

The graph in Box 4 shows the demand for and supply of ground beef assuming a $1.50 per pound equilibrium price and an equilibrium quantity of 20 million pounds per month. The total expenditure by consumers can be represented as the rectangular area 0*AEQ* on the graph. The width of this rectangle is the $1.50 price per pound represented by the distance 0*A* on the vertical axis. The length of the rectangle is the 20 million pounds sold per month represented by the distance 0*Q* on the horizontal axis. Multiplying the length by the width gives the rectangle 0*AEQ*, which represents $30 million per month. This area represents both the total expenditure by consumers and the total revenue received by sellers.

Total expenditure:
Over any given period, the number of units of a product purchased over that period multiplied by the price of the product *(PQ)*; equals the total revenue of sellers.

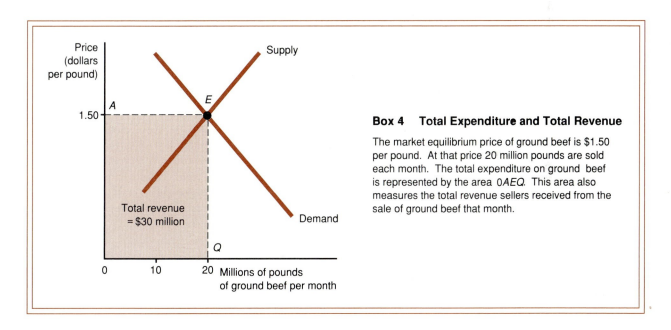

Box 4   Total Expenditure and Total Revenue

The market equilibrium price of ground beef is $1.50 per pound. At that price 20 million pounds are sold each month. The total expenditure on ground beef is represented by the area 0*AEQ*. This area also measures the total revenue sellers received from the sale of ground beef that month.

Predicting Changes in Total Expenditure and Revenue in Response to Price Increases

Suppose there's a decrease in the supply of ground beef. The graph in Box 5 shows how the decrease in supply affects the price of ground beef and the quantity demanded. As a result of the decrease in supply, the market equilibrium price of ground beef increases from $1.50 per pound to a new price, P_2. The increase in price causes the quantity demanded per month to decline to Q_2. What effect will the

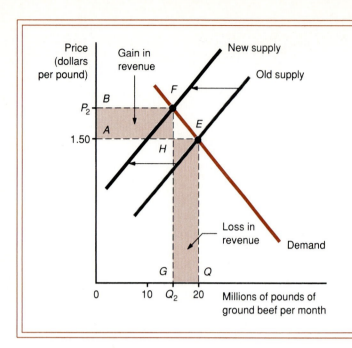

Box 5   Impact of an Increase in Price on Expenditure and Revenue

An increase in price caused by a decrease in supply tends to increase revenue. However, the decrease in quantity demanded caused by the increase in price tends to decrease revenue and expenditure on the good.

increase in price have on consumer expenditure on ground beef and on the total revenue received by sellers?

There's no clear-cut answer to this question. The increase in the price of ground beef acts to increase total consumer expenditure by increasing the P component of PQ. However, the law of demand indicates that as price goes up, the quantity of ground beef demanded per month will go down. The Q component of PQ thus will decrease whenever price goes up. There are therefore two forces that influence PQ when price goes up, and they act in opposite directions. If we know the price elasticity of demand for ground beef, however, we can forecast the change in PQ. This is because we can use price elasticity of demand to predict the relative magnitudes of the upward and downward forces influencing expenditure and revenue. Thus sellers can use price elasticity of demand to predict changes in their total revenue when prices change.

Suppose the demand for ground beef is *inelastic*. This means the percentage reduction in quantity demanded caused by the price increase would be *smaller* (ignoring the direction of change) than the percentage increase in price that caused it. Under such circumstances, the *upward* influence of the price increase on revenues is stronger than the *depressing* effect of the reduction in quantity demanded on revenues. For example, if a 10% price increase results in only a 5% decline in quantity demanded, as would be the case if the elasticity of demand for ground beef were −0.5, total revenue will *increase* as a result of the price increase. *An inelastic demand therefore implies that total revenue and total expenditure on a good will increase when price rises.*

In the graph in Box 5, the gain in revenue as a result of the price increase is represented by the area *ABFH*. This represents the increase in revenue from the Q_2 pounds of ground beef sold at the higher price. The loss of revenue from the reduction in quantity demanded is represented by the area *GHEQ*. This represents revenue that sellers would have enjoyed by selling more units had the price re-

Principles in Practice

How to Maximize Revenue: Pricing Theatre Tickets During Off-Peak Hours

Suppose you manage a movie theatre and want to maximize profits for midweek screenings. Demand is slack during midweek, and it's likely to take a very low price to fill the theatre. You know that once you open the theatre and screen a movie, your costs are independent of the number of admissions you sell. Under these circumstances, you can maximize your profit from the sale of tickets when you maximize revenue from admissions.

Assuming the demand curve for admissions to your midweek screenings is linear, it's easy to apply the analysis in this chapter to choose the price that maximizes revenue. Graph **A** shows the demand curve for midweek screenings. Along the linear demand curve, each 1¢ reduction in ticket prices results in two more tickets being sold for the evening. The theatre's capacity is 600 persons.

The demand curve indicates that if you choose a price of $3 for your tickets, the number of admissions demanded would be 200. Total revenue would be $600 for the evening (the $3 admission multiplied by the 200 admissions). Because $3 is a relatively high price, demand for theatre admissions is elastic at that price. This means that if you were to lower the price, your total revenue would increase. You can verify this by choosing a lower price, such as $2.50, and remembering that each 1¢ reduction in price results in the sale of two more admissions. It follows that if price were $2.50, the number of admissions demanded would increase by 100 to 300 and your total revenue would be $750 per screening.

Total revenue will continue to increase as long as demand remains elastic and will begin to decline just at the point at which price is reduced to make demand inelastic. For example, if you reduced the price to $2 per admission, the number of admissions demanded would be 400 and your total revenue would be $800 for the evening. At a price of $2, demand is unit elastic, because if price were reduced an additional 1¢ to $1.99, admissions would increase to 402 and total revenue would decline to $799.98. If the price were reduced to $1.50, the quantity demanded would go up to 500 but total revenue would decline still further to $750 because demand would be inelastic. Graph **B** shows how total revenue varies with the number of admissions when the demand curve shown in graph **A** prevails.

Also note from the table and graph **A** showing the demand curve that you could fill up the theatre if you charged $1 for admission. At that price you'd fill all of your 600 seats for each screening, but your total revenue would only be $600! To maximize revenue, you'd therefore choose to price your tickets at $2 and be content with filling only two thirds of your seating capacity but enjoying $800 revenue for the evening.

The point of this example is that if a business wants to maximize revenue, it must choose the price at which demand just becomes inelastic. This is the price for which demand is unit elastic.

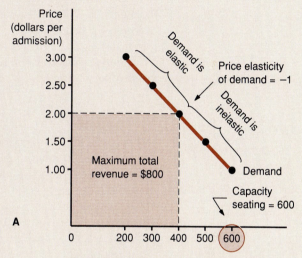

A

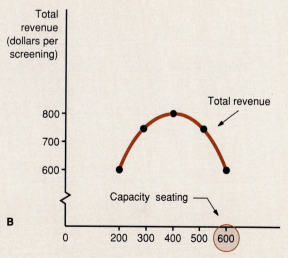

B

Demand and Total Revenue per Midweek Screening

Price (dollars)	Number of admissions demanded	Total revenue	Price elasticity of demand
3.00	200	600	Elastic
2.50	300	750	Elastic
2.00	400	800	Unit elastic
1.50	500	750	Inelastic
1.00	600	600	Inelastic

mained at $1.50 per pound. *When demand is inelastic, the gain in revenue from the price increase will exceed the loss in revenue from the decline in sales volume.* At the extreme, suppose the price elasticity of demand for a good were zero. This implies that an increase in price would have no effect on the quantity demanded. If this were the case, the total revenue taken in by sellers would increase by the percentage increase in price.

Now suppose demand were *elastic*. This implies that the percentage reduction in quantity demanded (ignoring the direction of change) would exceed the percentage increase in price that caused it. In this case the upward pressure on revenue caused by the price increase would be offset by the downward pressure on revenue resulting from the reduction in quantity demanded. As a consequence total revenue, and therefore total expenditure, would decline. For example, if the demand for ground beef were equal to −1.50, indicating an elastic demand, sellers could expect the price increase to adversely affect their revenues.

Finally, if the demand for a product is unit elastic, any given percentage change in price will result in an equal but opposite percentage change in quantity demanded. The net effect would be no change in total revenue, because the upward force on revenues would be exactly offset by the downward force. For example, estimates of the demand for housing indicate that its price elasticity is about −1. This implies that consumers tend to spend constant amounts on housing irrespective of its price.

Price Decreases, Total Expenditure, and Total Revenue

When price falls, it exerts downward pressure on total expenditure that can be offset by increases in quantity demanded. The net effect on revenue or expenditure of a price decrease depends on the relationship between the percentage decrease in price and the percentage increase in quantity demanded. Why would a decrease in price have a favorable effect on the total revenue from sale of a good for which demand is elastic, but an unfavorable effect on the total revenue from sale of a good whose demand is inelastic? An elastic demand implies that the percentage increase in quantity demanded would be greater than the percentage decrease in price that caused it. The downward pressure on total revenue caused by the price decline would therefore be more than offset by the upward pressure on total revenue resulting from increases in quantity demanded.

Box 6   Price Elasticity of Demand and Total Revenue or Expenditure

Price elasticity	Implication (ignoring direction of change)	Change in $P \cdot Q$ for price decrease	Change in $P \cdot Q$ for price increase
Elastic	% change in quantity demanded exceeds % change in price	+	−
Unitary	% change in quantity demanded equals % change in price	0	0
Inelastic	% change in quantity demanded is less than % change in price	−	+

Similarly, a decrease in the price of ground beef would decrease total revenue of sellers if the demand for ground beef were inelastic. For example, assuming the price elasticity of demand for ground beef is -0.5, a 10% decline in the price of ground beef would result in only a 5% increase in quantity demanded by consumers. The 5% increase in purchases wouldn't offset the 10% decline in price, and PQ would decline.

Of course, if demand is unit elastic, a decrease in price will have no effect on either total revenue or total expenditure. This is because the downward pressure of the price decline would be exactly offset by the upward pressure of the increase in quantity demanded as price fell.

The table in Box 6 summarizes the relationship between price elasticity of demand and total revenue or expenditure.

Other Demand Elasticity Measures

In addition to price elasticity of demand, the income elasticity of demand and the cross-elasticity of demand provide useful information. **Income elasticity of demand** is a number that measures the sensitivity of consumer purchases to given percentage changes in income. The **cross-elasticity of demand** is a number used to measure the sensitivity of consumer purchases of one good to percentage changes in the prices of substitute or complementary goods.

> **Income elasticity of demand:**
> A number that measures the sensitivity of consumer purchases to each 1% change in income.

> **Cross-elasticity of demand:**
> A number used to measure the sensitivity of consumer purchases of one good to each 1% change in the prices of related goods.

Income Elasticity of Demand

Income elasticity of demand measures the percentage change in the number of units of a good consumers demand, other things being equal, resulting from each 1% change in income. We can calculate income elasticity by dividing the percentage change in the quantity of a good purchased by a corresponding percentage change in income, assuming that only income and no other demand determinant changes[2]:

$$\text{Income elasticity of demand} = \frac{\text{Percentage change in number of units consumers demand}}{\text{Percentage change in income}}$$

For example, an income elasticity of 3 for foreign travel means that a 1% increase in income will result in a 3% increase in consumer trips overseas.

Income elasticity of demand for a good may be positive or negative. A positive income elasticity implies that increases in income (other things being equal) are associated with increases in the quantity of a good purchased. Goods that have positive income elasticity of demand are called **normal goods.** The quantity of such goods that consumers demand is positively associated with consumer income. A good whose income elasticity is greater than 1 is sometimes called a luxury good. Foreign travel in fact has an estimated elasticity of about 3, indicating that it can be considered a luxury good. Goods with income elasticities between zero and 1 are considered necessities.

> **Normal goods:**
> Goods that have positive income elasticity of demand.

A negative income elasticity of demand implies an inverse relationship between income and the amounts of a good purchased. Goods with negative income elasticities are those that consumers will eventually stop buying as their incomes increase. For example, if the income elasticity of demand for bus travel is negative, bus travel can be expected to decline as income in a nation increases. Goods that have negative

[2]For small changes in income, the income elasticity of demand is $\frac{\Delta Q/Q}{\Delta I/I}$ where Q is the initial quantity consumers demand and I is the initial income.

Principles in Practice

Empirical Estimates of Demand Elasticities

The key to understanding market demand for products often lies in estimating the relevant elasticities of demand. Business firms and governments are well aware of this and spend large sums of money each year to estimate these elasticities for products. Economists regularly estimate demand elasticities as part of their research. The three tables in the box show estimated demand elasticities for various goods and services. **A** shows both short-run and long-run estimated price elasticities. For most goods, demand is more elastic with respect to price over longer periods of time. Over longer periods consumers have more time to find substitutes for goods whose prices increase. In addition, more substitutes are developed and made available by sellers in the long run. Thus increased pursuit and availability of substitutes over longer periods of time are likely to make demand more elastic in the long run than in the short run.

For the items in table **A**, all the estimated short-run elasticities (except for china, glassware, and tableware, intercity rail travel, household natural gas use, and automobiles and parts) indicate inelastic demand because the values of the estimated elasticities are between zero and −1. The short-run price elasticity of demand for household electricity use is nearly zero. Demand is quite elastic for most products in the long run.

Table **B** presents some empirical estimates of income elasticities for various goods and services. Estimated income elasticities for automobiles, foreign travel by U.S. citizens, and household appliances are quite high (greater than 1) and positive. These are goods whose demands are quite responsive to changes in income and whose demands increase when income goes up.

Both short-run and long-run estimates of income elasticities are presented in table **B**. In most cases, as we'd expect, long-

A, Estimated Price Elasticities of Demand

Item	Short run	Long run
Stationery	−0.47	−0.56
Jewelry and watches	−0.41	−0.67
Tires and tubes	−0.86	−1.19
Gasoline	−0.4*	−1.5†
Foreign travel by U.S. residents	−0.14	−1.77
Housing	−0.3	−1.88
Household electricity use	−0.13	−1.89
Tobacco products	−0.46	−1.89
Household natural gas use‡	−1.4	−2.1
Automobiles and parts	−1.87	−2.24
China, glassware, tableware	−1.54	−2.55
Toilet articles and preparations	−0.20	−3.04
Intercity rail travel	−1.4	−3.19
Movies	−0.87	−3.67
Radio and TV repair	−0.47	−3.84

Except where otherwise indicated, data are from Hendrik S. Houthakker and Lester D. Taylor, *Consumer Demand in the United States: Analyses and Projections,* Cambridge: Harvard University Press, 1970.

*Robert Archibald and Robert Gillingham, "An Analysis of the Short-Run Consumer Demand for Gasoline Using Household Survey Data," *The Review of Economics and Statistics,* 62, November 1980, pp. 622-628.

†J.M. Griffin, *Energy Conservation in the OECD, 1980-2000,* Cambridge: Ballinger, 1979.

‡G.R. Lakshmanan and William Anderson, "Residential Energy Demand in the United States," *Regional Science and Urban Economics,* 10, August 1980, pp. 371-386.

Inferior goods: Goods that have negative income elasticity of demand.

income elasticity of demand are called **inferior goods.** These are goods we tend to consume less of as our income increases. You'd expect such goods as poor cuts of meat, turnips, second-hand clothing, and used furniture to have negative income elasticity of demand.

Estimates of income elasticity of demand from market data provide an indication of the sensitivity of consumer purchases of an item to fluctuations in consumer income. For current and potential sellers, income elasticity of demand for a product is an extremely important number. For example, if you believe Americans will become more affluent in the future, you'll probably want to market products that have income elasticities greater than 1—luxury items like yachts, Rolls-Royces, and world tours.

The income elasticity of food, on the other hand, is usually estimated to be less than 1. This means that the percentage increase in the demand for food is likely to be less than the percentage increase in income over time. Thus if you're a dairy farmer, you can expect the demand for your milk to grow less quickly than income grows in a nation.

B, Estimated Income Elasticities of Demand

Item	Short run	Long run
Potatoes*	N.A.	−.81
Pork†	0.27	0.18
Beef†	0.51	0.45
Furniture	2.6	0.53
China, glassware, tableware	0.47	0.77
Dental services	0.38	1.00
Chicken†	0.49	1.06
Automobiles	5.5	1.07
Spectator sports	0.46	1.07
Physician services	0.28	1.15
Clothing	0.95	1.17
Gasoline and oil	0.55	1.36
Household appliances	2.72	1.40
Shoes	0.9	1.5
Jewelry and watches	1.0	1.6
Owner-occupied housing	0.07	2.45
Foreign travel by U.S. citizens	0.24	3.09
Toilet articles and preparations	0.25	3.74

Unless otherwise indicated, data are from Hendrik S. Houthakker and Lester D. Taylor, *Consumer Demand in the United States: Analyses and Projections,* Cambridge: Harvard University Press, 1970.
*Dale M. Heien, "The Structure of Food Demand: Interrelatedness and Duality," *American Journal of Agricultural Economics,* 64, 2, May 1982, pp. 213-221.
†M.K. Wohlgenant and W.F. Hahn, "Dynamic Adjustment in Monthly Consumer Demand for Meats," *American Journal of Agricultural Economics,* 64, 3, August 1982, pp. 553-557.

run elasticity exceeds short-run elasticity. Notable exceptions are household appliances, furniture, and automobiles. These are durable goods. Consumers don't always replace them as their incomes increase. Note that the income elasticity of demand for potatoes is negative, indicating that on average, consumers tend to reduce purchases of potatoes as their incomes increase.

Table **C** presents some estimated cross-elasticities. The estimates indicate that goods like margarine and butter, pork and beef, and natural gas and electricity are regarded as substitutes by consumers. The estimated cross-elasticities for these goods are positive.

C, Estimated Cross-Elasticities of Demand*

Item	Estimate
Natural gas with respect to price of electricity	0.8†
Full-size Impala with respect to price of mid-size Chevrolet Chevelle's (1968-1975)	11.0‡
Margarine with respect to price of butter	1.53§
Pork with respect to price of beef	0.40§
Chicken with respect to price of pork	0.29§

*These are long-run elasticities.
†G.R. Lakshmanan and William Anderson, "Residential Energy Demand in the United States," *Regional Science and Urban Economics,* 10, August 1980, pp. 371-386.
‡F.O. Irvine, Jr., "Demand Equations for Individual New Car Models Estimated Using Transaction Prices with Implications for Regulatory Issues," *Southern Economic Journal,* 49, 3, January 1983, pp. 764-782.
§Dale M. Heien, "The Structure of Food Demand: Interrelatedness and Duality," *American Journal of Agricultural Economics,* 64, 2, May 1982, pp. 213-221.

Cross-Elasticity of Demand

Another useful price elasticity concept is the cross-elasticity of demand, which measures the sensitivity of purchases of one good to changes in the price of *another good*. For example, the cross-elasticity of demand for beef with respect to the price of pork would measure the percentage change in purchases of beef resulting from a 1% change in the *price of pork,* other things being equal. Cross-elasticity of demand between the demand for good X and the price of some other good, Y, is[3]:

$$\text{Cross-elasticity of demand} = \frac{\% \text{ change in the number of units of } X \text{ consumers demand}}{\% \text{ change in the price of } Y}$$

Cross-elasticity of demand may be positive or negative. A positive cross-elasticity of demand implies that the two goods are substitutes. Whenever the price of one

[3]The cross-elasticity of demand for small changes in the price of good Y is $\dfrac{\Delta Q_X / Q_X}{\Delta P_Y / P_Y}$ where Q_X is the number of units of X consumers demand and P_Y is the price of good Y.

good changes, other things being equal, the demand for the other moves in the same direction. This means that a price increase for one of the goods leads to an increase in the amounts purchased of the other. For example, one estimate of the cross-elasticity of demand between chicken and the price of pork is 0.299.[4] Since this is a positive cross-elasticity, it indicates that consumers treat these two meats as substitutes. In general, the greater the substitutability between two goods, the higher the value of their cross-elasticities of demand. A zero cross-elasticity of demand would mean that the consumption of one good was independent of the price of the other.

The cross-elasticity of demand between two competing brands like Coke and Pepsi is likely to be quite high. The same is probably true for any two brands of 19-inch televisions. However, the cross-elasticity of demand for unrelated goods like ice cream and typewriters is likely to be zero.

Goods that are complements have negative cross-elasticity of demand. Coffee and nondairy creamer are complements. An increase in the price of coffee is likely to decrease the demand for nondairy creamer. We'd therefore expect the cross-elasticity of demand between nondairy creamer and the price of coffee to be negative.

Estimates of the cross-elasticity of demand for a product are important for business planning. For example, suppose a sharp increase in the price of natural gas is expected. This is likely to increase the demand for electricity because the two are regarded as substitutes for heating, cooking, and other uses. Electric companies can plan to meet the increased demand for their product if they know its cross-elasticity with respect to the price of natural gas. For example, if the cross-elasticity of demand for electricity with respect to the price of gas is 0.8, then a 20% increase in the price of natural gas can be expected to result in a 16% increase in the number of kilowatt hours that consumers demand per year.

Concept Check

1 If the price elasticity of demand for shirts is -2, what will happen to expenditure on shirts and total revenue of shirt sellers if the market price rises? What will happen if the market price falls?

2 Explain how furniture sales would fluctuate with income if the income elasticity of demand for furniture were 5. How would sales of potatoes fluctuate with income if the income elasticity of demand for potatoes were -0.5?

3 The cross-elasticity of demand for wine with respect to beer is 2. What conclusions would you draw from this?

Price Elasticity of Supply

Price elasticity of supply:
A number that indicates the percentage change in quantity supplied resulting from each 1% change in the price of a good, other things being equal.

The **price elasticity of supply** is a number used to measure the sensitivity of changes in quantity supplied to given percentage changes in the price of a good, other things being equal. Price elasticity of supply indicates the percentage change in quantity supplied resulting from each 1% change in price. It can be calculated by

[4]See Dale M. Heien, "The Structure of Food Demand: Interrelatedness and Duality," *American Journal of Agricultural Economics,* 64, 2, May 1982, pp. 213-221.

dividing the percentage change in quantity supplied by the percentage change in price that caused it, given all other supply determinants:[5]

$$\text{Price elasticity of supply} = \frac{\%\ \text{change in quantity supplied}}{\%\ \text{change in price}}$$

For example, if a 10% increase in price results in a 20% increase in quantity supplied, the price elasticity of supply would be:

$$\frac{20\%}{10\%} = 2$$

Since supply curves generally slope upward, the elasticity of supply tends to be positive. An increase in price tends to generate an increase in quantity supplied, while a decrease in price generates a decrease in quantity supplied. In the equation for price elasticity of supply, the signs of the numerator and the denominator will be the same. The ratio will therefore have a positive sign.

As is the case for demand, be sure you remember that the slope of a supply curve is an unreliable measure of its elasticity. The price elasticity of supply is related to the slope of the supply curve but isn't the same as slope.[6]

Price elasticity of supply ranges from zero to infinity. An **elastic supply** prevails when the price elasticity of supply is greater than 1. If the price elasticity of supply is equal to or greater than zero but less than 1, an **inelastic supply** prevails. Finally, when elasticity of supply is just equal to 1, a **unit elastic supply** prevails. The table in Box 7 summarizes the relationship between percentage changes in price and quantity supplied for various cases. The greater the price elasticity of supply of an item, the more responsive, or elastic, is the quantity supplied to given percentage price changes.

Elastic supply:
Prevails when the price elasticity of supply is greater than 1.

Inelastic supply:
Prevails when the price elasticity of supply is equal to or greater than zero but less than 1.

Unit elastic supply:
Prevails when elasticity of supply is just equal to 1.

Box 7   Price Elasticity of Supply as a Gauge of Supply Responsiveness

Supply response	% change in quantity supplied relative to % change in quantity demanded	Value of elasticity of supply
Inelastic	% change in quantity supplied is *less than* % change in price	Equal to or greater than 0 but less than 1
Unit elastic	% change in quantity supplied *equals* % change in price	1
Elastic	% change in quantity supplied is *greater than* % change in price	Greater than 1

---

[5]For small changes in price, the price elasticity of supply can be expressed as

$$\frac{\Delta Q_S / Q_S}{\Delta P / P} = \frac{P \Delta Q_S}{Q_S \Delta P}$$

where Q_S is quantity supplied.

[6]For an analysis of the relationship between price elasticity of supply and the slope of the supply curve, see David N. Hyman, *Modern Microeconomics: Analysis and Applications,* 2nd ed., Homewood, Ill.: Richard D. Irwin, 1989, Chapter 8.

Determinants of Price Elasticity of Supply

In general, the price elasticity of supply of a good depends on the extent to which costs per unit rise as sellers increase output. If unit costs of production don't rise rapidly as output expands, small percentage increases in price will result in large percentage increases in quantity supplied. Under such circumstances, supply will be very elastic because small increases in price will allow sellers the possibility of additional gain without substantial price increases.

When the price of an item increases, not only do existing firms tend to produce more, but additional firms are attracted to make the item available. However, it often takes a considerable amount of time for new enterprises to start producing an item. For this reason, supply tends to become more elastic over time, as the lure of profits attracts more sellers.

For example, when petroleum prices rose in the 1970s, new exploration and the development of previously unprofitable sources of oil proceeded. Over time the quantity of petroleum products supplied increased substantially. After the sharp increase in the price of crude oil in 1973, oil reserves from the North Sea, Alaska, and Mexico were slowly developed. High oil prices slowly, but surely and massively, resulted in a response by suppliers.[7] However, an immediate response was impossible because of the length of time required to develop new petroleum resources. The time necessary to gear up and make new supplies available varies from industry to industry. This variation in response time is an important determinant of variations in price elasticity of supply among industries.

The supply of housing also tends to become more elastic over time. For example, suppose rent controls, like those described in Chapter 5, reduce market rents to 20% lower than would be the case without the regulation. Over a short period of time the supply of housing is likely to be quite inelastic, say equal to 0.7. We can easily calculate the reduction in rental housing in the short run caused by the 20% reduction in market rents:

$$0.7 = \frac{\% \text{ change in quantity supplied}}{-20\%}$$

$$\% \text{ change in quantity supplied} = -14\%$$

Let's assume that over 10 years the price elasticity of supply of rental housing is higher, say equal to 2. In this case the percentage reduction in the quantity of housing supplied ultimately resulting from the 20% decline in rents will be:

$$2 = \frac{\% \text{ change in quantity supplied}}{-20\%}$$

$$\% \text{ change in quantity supplied} = -40\%$$

The reaction of landlords to the rent controls will therefore intensify as time goes by. This implies that the shortage resulting from the rent controls would become more acute over time.

Perfectly Inelastic and Perfectly Elastic Supply

When supply is fixed, sellers have no opportunity to vary the quantity they can offer. A perfectly inelastic supply curve is a vertical line above a certain minimum price necessary to induce sellers to make the good available for sale. No matter what the

[7]See Arlon R. Tussing, "An OPEC Obituary," *The Public Interest,* 70, Winter 1983, p. 12.

percentage change in price above this minimum price, the percentage change in quantity supplied is always zero. Price elasticity of supply is always zero along such a curve. Note that the supply curve doesn't hit the horizontal axis. This is because the sellers require a minimum price before they'll make the item available for sale in a market. The supply of land in the United States is close to perfectly inelastic. No matter how much the price of land changes, there's unlikely to be any appreciable change in the total amount of usable land in the country.

The elasticities of supply of many goods are likely to be close to zero for very short periods of time. For example, the supply of fresh fish available in markets on a given day after the fishing fleet has brought in its catch will be perfectly inelastic. It takes time to catch more. Over time the supply of fish will be more elastic as higher prices induce fishermen to catch more. As you can see in graph **A** in Box 8, when supply is perfectly inelastic, an increase in demand results in an increase in market price but has no effect on quantity supplied. However, if the price were below P_0, fishermen wouldn't go out fishing and quantity supplied would be zero.

A perfectly elastic supply curve is a horizontal line such as that illustrated in graph **B** in Box 8. The price elasticity of supply is infinite on this line. You can think of such a supply curve as meaning that the slightest change in price would result in an infinite change in quantity supplied. The horizontal line also means that any change in demand results in a change in quantity supplied, but no change in price is necessary to induce sellers to supply more.

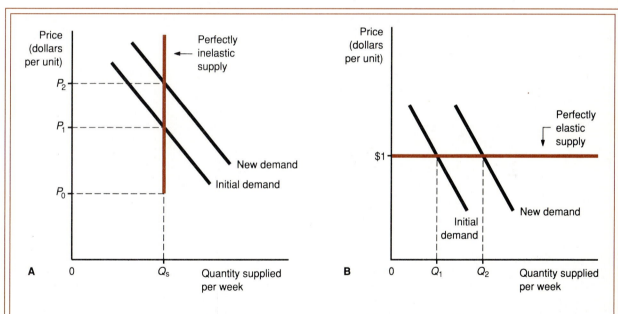

Box 8   Perfectly Inelastic and Perfectly Elastic Supply Curves

A, Above a minimum price acceptable to sellers, the quantity supplied does not change from Q_s units per week in response to price changes. An increase in demand increases price from P_1 to P_2 but results in no change in quantity supplied.

B, At a price of $1, any quantity can be made available to buyers without the need for a price increase. The horizontal supply curve is perfectly elastic because the percentage change in price necessary for a percentage change in quantity is always zero. An increase in demand results in an increase in quantity supplied but no change in price.

In effect, the supply curve of cheeseburgers to you in a McDonald's is probably shaped like the one drawn in graph **B.** You can buy all the cheeseburgers you want at the established price without causing the price to go up. In effect, to any particular buyer in a competitive market, the supply curve of a good will be infinitely elastic.

Another example of perfectly elastic supply would be an industry where over a long period of time the prices of inputs necessary to produce output don't increase as output increases. This means that no price increases would be required to increase quantities supplied because costs per unit of the good wouldn't increase as more was made available. There's evidence that the supply of new residential construction is nearly infinitely elastic over the long run.[8] Other things being equal, this implies that any temporary increases in the price of new construction per square foot over short periods will eventually be balanced by future price declines. Over a long period an increase in demand results in an increase in quantity supplied but no increase in market price. Temporary price increases tend to attract new firms into the construction industry. The resulting increase in supply of the service acts to decrease price over a longer period of time.

Concept Check

1 What is measured by the price elasticity of supply? List some of the influences on price elasticity of supply.

2 Other things being unchanged, an increase in demand for a good increases its market price but has no effect on quantity supplied. What is the price elasticity of supply?

3 Under what circumstances is the price elasticity of supply infinite?

The Relevance of Elasticity of Supply and Elasticity of Demand in Analyzing the Impact of Taxation in Competitive Markets

Tax shifting:
Occurs when a tax levied on sellers of a good causes the market price of the good to increase.

The concepts of price elasticity of demand and supply are relevant to the analysis of taxes levied on sellers of such goods as gasoline, cigarettes, and alcoholic beverages. However, even though these taxes are collected from sellers, buyers often are made worse off because the tax can result in shifts in supply that cause prices to rise. **Tax shifting** occurs when a tax levied on sellers of a good causes the market price of the good to increase. Under certain circumstances the price of the good can rise by exactly enough to cover the tax levied on each unit of the item. If we know the price elasticities of demand and supply of a taxed good, we can forecast the impact of the tax on the good's market price.

To find out how a tax affects market price, we need to analyze its impact on supply and demand conditions. Assume the government collects from sellers a 10¢ tax per gallon of gasoline. *From the sellers' standpoint, this means that the cost of each gallon of gasoline sold will go up by exactly 10¢.* This is because sellers must pay the government 10¢ for each gallon sold. The effect is exactly the same as if the price of one of the inputs used to produce gasoline were to go up by 10¢. This will

---

[8]James R. Follain, Jr., "The Price Elasticity of the Long-Run Supply of New Housing Construction," *Land Economics*, May 1979, pp. 190-199.

increase the minimum price sellers will accept for each gallon of gasoline by the amount of the tax. The supply curve for gasoline will therefore shift upward by 10¢ for each quantity of gasoline sold. In effect, the tax causes a decrease in the supply of gasoline by reducing the gain from selling each gallon.

The graphs in Box 9 show two cases in which the decrease in supply caused by the tax will cause the market price to increase by the *full amount* of the tax per gallon. In **A,** the demand for gasoline is perfectly inelastic. Here, as the supply decreases, buyers don't respond by decreasing the quantity demanded. The quantity demanded is 1 million gallons per month before and after the tax. The initial price is $1 per gallon. After the tax shifts the supply curve upward by 10¢ for any quantity, the price increases by exactly the amount of the tax per unit. The tax will collect $100,000 per month in this case, which equals the 10¢ per gallon tax multiplied by the 1 million gallons sold each month. The tax revenue is represented by the shaded area in **A.** *In effect, consumers pay this entire tax in the form of a 10¢ increase in the price of gasoline.* After the tax is imposed, the market price paid by buyers increases to $1.10. After paying the tax of 10¢ per gallon, sellers receive a net price of $1 per gallon, which is exactly the price they received before the tax was imposed. *When the demand for gasoline is perfectly inelastic, a tax collected from sellers of gasoline is fully shifted to buyers of gasoline as the price of gasoline rises to cover the tax per unit.*

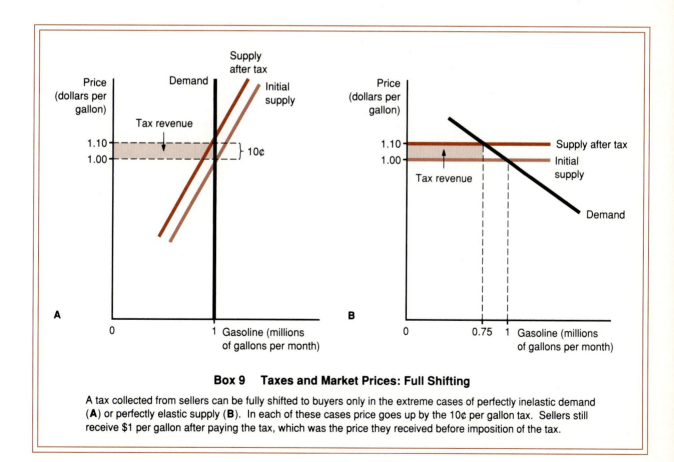

Box 9   Taxes and Market Prices: Full Shifting

A tax collected from sellers can be fully shifted to buyers only in the extreme cases of perfectly inelastic demand (**A**) or perfectly elastic supply (**B**). In each of these cases price goes up by the 10¢ per gallon tax. Sellers still receive $1 per gallon after paying the tax, which was the price they received before imposition of the tax.

Principles in Practice

The Price of the Dollar and the Price Elasticity of Demand for Imported Goods: Why Expenditure on Imports Might Not Decline When the Price of the Dollar Decreases

As you discovered in Chapter 4, the dollar has a price in terms of foreign currency. The price of the dollar in terms of Japanese yen or West German marks affects the dollar price at which Japanese and German producers can profitably sell their merchandise in the United States. Other things being equal, a decrease in the price of the dollar makes imported goods priced in dollars more expensive to U.S. consumers. (At the same time it makes U.S. goods cheaper to foreigners in terms of their own currencies.) But does a decline in the price of the dollar imply that U.S. consumers will spend fewer dollars on foreign goods?

For example, between 1985 and early 1988 there was a 50% decline in the price of the dollar in terms of Japanese yen and German marks. The value of the dollar also fell against other key currencies over the same period. Yet despite these declines, there was little change in the balance between U.S. expenditures on imported goods and the value of U.S. exports sold abroad. In 1987 Americans spent over $150 billion more on imports than they did on exports.

There are a number of possible explanations for insensitivity of the dollar value of exports and imports to changes in the price of the dollar. Other things being equal, a substantial drop in the price of the dollar in terms of the yen and the mark would be expected to increase the prices of Japanese and German goods sold in the United States. However, other things might not be equal. Japanese and German sellers might be willing to accept lower profit margins to maintain their U.S. markets. In addition, declines in production costs in those countries might exert downward pressure on the prices of those goods, offsetting some of the upward pressure from the decline in the price of the dollar. There's yet another explanation—rooted in the concept of price elasticity of demand—for the fact that U.S. consumer spending on imports is unresponsive to declines in the price of the dollar.

Suppose that on average the U.S. demand for Japanese and German goods is actually quite inelastic. This means that increases in the dollar prices of these goods would actually *increase* U.S. consumer expenditure on them. Such a scenario is likely if American consumers are reluctant to give up their acquisition of Toyotas, Nikons, Sonys, BMWs, Mercedes Benzes, and other such goods, despite increases in their dollar prices.

By the same token, suppose the demand for U.S. goods abroad is also quite inelastic. This means that the reduction in the prices of these goods resulting from the decrease in the price of the dollar won't generate a substantial increase in the quantity demanded. As a result, a decrease in the price of the dollar can actually cause a *decrease* in foreign expenditure on U.S. goods.

The worst of all possible worlds for a battered dollar would be the case just outlined, in which the demand for imported goods by U.S. consumers and for U.S. exports by foreigners is inelastic. If this were the case, the decline in the dollar would actually increase U.S. expenditure on imported goods while decreasing foreign expenditure on U.S. imports.

You can reach two important conclusions from this analysis:

1. Other influences on imports being unchanged, a decline in the price of the dollar in terms of a foreign currency results in a decrease in expenditure on imports from that country only if the domestic demand for those imports is elastic.
2. Other influences on exports being unchanged, a decline in the price of the dollar in terms of a foreign currency results in an increase in revenue from exports to that country only if the foreign demand for U.S. exports is elastic.

Sellers would also succeed in shifting the entire tax per unit to buyers if the *supply* of gasoline were perfectly elastic. In **B** in Box 9 the supply of gasoline is assumed to be a horizontal line, implying a perfectly elastic supply. As before, the tax would shift the supply curve upward by 10¢ per gallon. However, in this case the demand curve is assumed to be downward sloping as is normally the case. As a result, the quantity demanded declines from 1 million gallons to 750,000 gallons per month. However, the new supply curve intersects the demand curve at a price that is exactly 10¢ higher than the initial price of $1.00. At any price lower than that, sellers wouldn't be able to cover their costs and would reduce production until price increased.

When the supply of gasoline is perfectly elastic at the $1 per gallon price before the tax is imposed, sellers will be unwilling to make gasoline available at any price below $1 per gallon. The market price must rise to $1.10 per gallon for sellers to receive a net price of $1 per gallon after paying the 10¢ per gallon tax. Here, as in the first case, the price of gasoline goes up by the full amount of the tax per gallon. However, in this case the quantity demanded does decline; and as a result, the tax collects only $75,000 per month, which is represented by the shaded area in **B** in Box 9. Nonetheless, the tax collected from sellers is still fully paid by buyers because the price of gasoline increases by just enough to cover the tax. In general, if the supply of a good is infinitely elastic, sellers can shift any tax collected from them to buyers by reducing the amount they supply until price increases by the full amount of the tax.

In reality, it's highly improbable that the price elasticity of demand for a good will be zero. Although it's possible that price elasticity of supply will be close to infinity over long periods, this too is improbable over shorter periods. Suppose, then, that neither the price elasticity of demand nor the price elasticity of supply takes on extreme values of zero or infinity. In this case we can easily show that the tax will be *shared* by the buyers and sellers of the good. This case is illustrated in the graph in Box 10. The initial market equilibrium is at point *E,* which corresponds to a market price of $1 per gallon and monthly sales of 1 million gallons. As before, the tax shifts the supply curve up by 10¢ per gallon. The new market equilibrium corresponds to point *E',* at which the market price paid by sellers increases to $1.04 and the quantity demanded declines to 850,000 gallons per month. After they pay the 10¢ per gallon tax, the net price sellers receive is $1.04 − $0.10 = $0.94. The total tax revenue collected is $85,000 per month, which is equal to the 10¢ per gallon tax multiplied by the 850,000 gallons per month sold. In effect, sellers pay 6¢

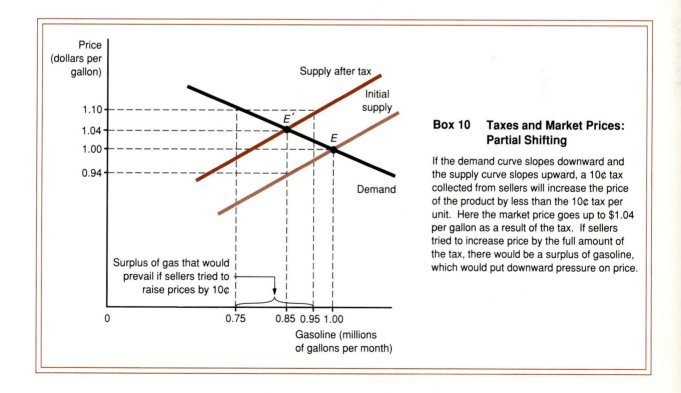

Box 10   Taxes and Market Prices: Partial Shifting

If the demand curve slopes downward and the supply curve slopes upward, a 10¢ tax collected from sellers will increase the price of the product by less than the 10¢ tax per unit. Here the market price goes up to $1.04 per gallon as a result of the tax. If sellers tried to increase price by the full amount of the tax, there would be a surplus of gasoline, which would put downward pressure on price.

of the 10¢ per gallon tax because the price they receive per gallon falls from $1 to 94¢ after the tax. The remaining 4¢ per gallon tax is shifted to buyers as a 4¢ per gallon increase in the market price.

What would happen in this case if sellers tried to pass the full 10¢ per gallon tax on to buyers by increasing price to $1.10? To find out, go to the graph in Box 10 and follow the dashed line from the price axis at $1.10 to the demand curve and the supply curve that prevail after the tax is imposed. Note that the quantity demanded at that price would be only 750,000 gallons per month, while the quantity supplied would be 950,000 gallons per month. There would therefore be a surplus of gasoline that would serve to push the market price down until it reached $1.04 per gallon.

The conclusion of this analysis is straightforward: *Sellers in competitive markets are subject to the laws of supply and demand when it comes to shifting taxes; only in the unlikely case when demand is perfectly inelastic or when supply is perfectly elastic will sellers succeed in raising the price by the full amount of the tax.*

Summary

1. Price elasticity of demand is a number that gauges the sensitivity of quantity demanded of a good to each 1% change in its price. It is calculated by dividing the percentage change in quantity demanded of a good by the percentage change in price that caused it.

2. Price elasticity of demand is a number that can range from zero to an infinitely large negative number. Demand for a good is characterized as inelastic if the number indicating its price elasticity is less than 1, ignoring the minus sign. Demand for a good is unit elastic if the number indicating its elasticity is exactly equal to 1, ignoring the minus sign. When the number indicating price elasticity exceeds 1, ignoring the minus sign, demand is characterized as elastic.

3. Price elasticity of demand for a good is influenced by the availability of substitutes for it, the proportion of their income consumers spend on it, and time.

4. Price elasticity of demand cannot be easily gauged from the slope of demand curves. For example, a downward-sloping demand curve with constant slope at all points will become more elastic as price increases.

5. A perfectly inelastic demand curve is a vertical line, while a perfectly elastic demand curve is a horizontal line.

6. The way total expenditure by consumers and total revenue of sellers change as price changes can be forecast if the price elasticity of demand for the good is known. If demand is elastic, price increases will decrease total revenue. If demand is inelastic, price increases will increase total revenue.

7. Income elasticity of demand is a number that gauges the sensitivity of demand for a good to changes in consumer income. Cross-elasticity of demand is a number used to measure the sensitivity of demand for a good to changes in the prices of related goods.

8. Price elasticity of supply is a number that measures the sensitivity of changes in quantity supplied to each 1% change in the price of a good. It is calculated by dividing the percentage change in quantity supplied of a good by the percentage change in price that caused it.

9. When price elasticity of supply is greater than 1, supply is elastic. When the number is equal to or greater than zero but less than 1, supply is inelastic. When the number is 1, supply is unit elastic.

10. A perfectly inelastic supply curve is a vertical line, while a perfectly elastic supply curve is a horizontal line.

Key Terms and Concepts

Price elasticity of demand
Elastic demand
Inelastic demand
Unit elastic demand
Total revenue
Total expenditure
Income elasticity of demand
Cross-elasticity of demand

Normal goods
Inferior goods
Price elasticity of supply
Elastic supply
Inelastic supply
Unit elastic supply
Tax shifting

Problems and Applications

1. The price elasticity of demand for furniture you sell is estimated to be −3. What will be the effect on the quantity you sell if you lower your prices by 10% next month? What will happen to the total revenue you take in next month as a result of the price cut?

2. The price elasticity of demand for Brussels sprouts is estimated to be −0.5. Government authorities want to increase consumption of Brussels sprouts by 15%. By what percentage must the price to consumers fall to achieve the objective of increasing Brussels sprout consumption by 15%? What will happen to total consumer expenditure on Brussels sprouts as a result of the price reduction?

3. The price of a package of Reese's Peanut Butter Cups increases from $1 to $1.25. As a result, the weekly quantity of Reese's demanded falls from 10,000 to 9,000 packages. Calculate the price elasticity of demand using the average of the initial and new prices and quantities as the basis for figuring the percentage changes.

4. Suppose that for each 25¢ increase in the price of Reese's Peanut Butter Cups, the demand curve is such that the quantity demanded falls by 1,000 packages per week. Plot the demand curve for Reese's on a set of axes. Show that the demand for Reese's becomes more elastic as the price increases.

5. Suppose Susan decides she'll spend $30 per month on Taco Supremes no matter what the price. Assuming she sticks by her decision, show that her demand for Taco Supremes is unit elastic at all possible prices.

6. Draw the demand curve for a good that has a unit elastic demand at all possible prices.

7. The supply of pencils decreases, but there's no change in the quantity demanded. Draw the demand curve for pencils and comment on its price elasticity. What will happen to total expenditure on pencils as the price increases?

8. The income elasticity of demand for furniture is 3. A recession reduces consumer income by 10%. What will happen to furniture sales? Explain why fluctuation in the demand for soap will be much less responsive to a reduction in income than demand for furniture if the income elasticity of demand for soap is only 0.2.

9. The cross-elasticity of demand for bacon with respect to the price of eggs is −2. What does this tell you about the way consumers perceive the relationship between bacon and eggs?

10. The price elasticity of demand for cigarettes is -1.2. The price elasticity of supply is estimated to be 1. Will a 15¢ tax per pack of cigarettes increase the price of cigarettes by 15¢ per pack?

Suggested Readings

David N. Hyman, *Modern Microeconomics: Analysis and Applications,* 2nd ed., Homewood, Ill.: Richard D. Irwin, Inc., 1989. Chapters 5 and 8 contain technical analyses of the concept of elasticity.

Donald S. Watson and Malcolm Getz, *Price Theory in Action,* 4th ed., Prospect Heights, Ill.: Waveland Press, 1987. This anthology contains a number of essays showing how the concept of price elasticity is estimated and used in economic analysis.

Beth V. Yarbrough and Robert M. Yarbrough, *The World Economy: Trade and Finance,* Chicago: The Dryden Press, 1988. This is a textbook on the economics of international trade. Chapter 10 discusses the market for foreign exchange of currencies and the relevance of the concept of price elasticity of demand for trade imbalances and their correction.

A Forward Look

In the next part of the book we take an in-depth view of the forces underlying supply and demand in competitive markets. In Chapter 8 we begin this task with an analysis of the logic underlying consumer choices.

Career Profile

SAM WALTON

He bounds around Wal-Mart inquisitive and full of energy, eager to help an employee with a line at the cash register or to share doughnuts with the crew on the loading dock. It may not sound like a typical day for the richest man in America, but for Sam Walton, founder and chairman of the Wal-Mart Stores empire, it's a way of life.

He doesn't act like a billionaire in other ways either. He lives with his wife in a modest home in Bentonville, Arkansas, drives a pickup truck, works in an office covered with inexpensive paneling, gets $5 haircuts, and eats at Fred's Hickory Inn, the home of ribs and cheesecake. Yet this small-town folk hero is estimated to be worth $4.5 billion, and the company he started posts annual profits of more than $627 million on nearly $16 billion in sales.

By motivating employees, keeping expenses low, and satisfying its customers, Walton's chain of discount stores has become the nation's third largest retailer, expanding more than 35% annually in the past decade. In addition to Wal-Mart Discount City stores, the company operates more than 80 Sam's Wholesale Clubs and has begun opening Wal-Mart Supercenters, which sell everything from frozen food to electric drills.

Walton earned a degree in economics from the University of Missouri-Columbia in 1940. After serving in the Army, he began buying five-and-dime stores. Having studied discount stores, he opened the first Wal-Mart Discount City in Rogers, Arkansas, in 1962. Even though he has retired from his position as the company's chief executive officer, Walton continues to visit the more than 1,000 Wal-Marts nationwide to make sure his customers and employees are happy. Famous for dancing the hula on Wall Street when the company far surpassed profit forecasts, he leads the pep rallies at new store openings and frequently travels with his two pointer dogs, just in case he comes upon an opportunity for some good quail hunting.

Product Markets:
Microeconomic Analysis

Consumer Choice
and the Theory of Demand

As a consumer, you make decisions each day about how to spend your limited income. What motivates your choices? Why do you choose to buy another T-shirt or pair of jeans, and what do you sacrifice by doing so? In analyzing consumer choices, economists assume that buyers are rational. This means that as buyers we have a clear-cut goal of obtaining as much personal benefit as possible from purchasing goods and services. To understand adequately the demand side of the market, we need to make a thorough analysis of the logic of consumer choice. In this chapter we'll use marginal analysis to help you understand the important influences on consumer choices.

We briefly analyzed consumer choice in Chapter 2, when we introduced the notion of rational behavior. Because marginal analysis is so useful in understanding how consumers decide how much of each good to buy, you'll find it helpful to review the marginal analysis of consumer behavior in Chapter 2 before reading this chapter. Against that background, we can further investigate the logic of consumer choices to gain insights that help explain market demand. As you'll see, the law of demand is firmly rooted in a model based on rational behavior by consumers.

A main goal of this chapter is to show you how all of us as consumers must reconcile our likes and dislikes with our budgets. You often buy fewer goods or services than you would if your income were higher or the prices of goods were lower. For example, when dining in a restaurant, you might very well rather have prime rib than hamburger. However, given your available income and the prices of these two items, you often choose the hamburger over the prime rib.

Economists recognize that as consumers we differ greatly in our likes and dislikes and that we aren't always rational and consistent. However, by assuming that the marginal benefit of goods declines as more are purchased and by assuming rational choices, we can obtain important insights into market demand. These simplifications help us establish cause-and-effect relationships between changes in prices of goods or changes in income and the willingness of consumers to buy certain goods. In fact, in this chapter we'll actually derive demand curves and show that they're consistent with rational behavior by consumers.

Concept Preview   *After reading this chapter, you should be able to:*

1 Explain the difference between the concepts of total and marginal utility and show how the way marginal utility varies with purchases can reflect a person's preferences.
2 Describe the conditions for consumer equilibrium as expressed by the equimarginal principle for purchases.
3 Show how the concepts of total and marginal benefit are related to total and marginal utility.
4 Demonstrate that buying any particular good up to the point at which its marginal benefit equals its price maximizes the total net benefit of giving up money to purchase the good.
5 Analyze the impact of changes in prices and incomes on consumer choices.
6 Derive a demand curve for a good for an individual consumer from data on marginal benefit and show how marginal benefit, and therefore demand, shifts when income changes.
7 Derive a market demand curve from the demand curves of individual buyers.

Utility and Consumer Equilibrium

Preferences:
Individual likes and dislikes.

We differ widely in our preferences; one person's pleasure is another's pain. **Preferences** represent individual likes and dislikes. Don't confuse preferences with actual choices. To use our restaurant example, you may prefer prime rib over hamburger but end up *choosing* the hamburger over the prime rib because the latter is too expensive for your budget. The theory of consumer choice assumes that preferences are determined independently of our income and independently of the prices of goods. We must reconcile our dreams with our actual budgets.

Utility:
The satisfaction consumers receive from items they acquire, activities they engage in, or services they use.

Utility is the term economists use for the satisfaction consumers receive from items they acquire, activities they engage in, or services they use. Utility measures the intensity of a person's desire for an item. One way to determine someone's preferences is to ask her questions about the utility, or satisfaction, she expects from various items available for consumption. For example, if she receives more utility from a glass of orange juice than from a can of Coke, this means she *prefers* orange juice to Coke. Someone who says he gets no utility from classical music would be unlikely to purchase classical recordings in a store. If he did so, he'd give up the opportunity of using his income to buy John Cougar Mellencamp records or any other item that would give him positive utility. Giving up something of value for something of no utility would be irrational.

Total Utility and Marginal Utility

Total utility:
The total satisfaction enjoyed from consuming any given quantity of a good.

The **total utility** received from a good measures the total satisfaction enjoyed from consuming any given quantity. Of course, it's very difficult to measure total utility because it's a *subjective concept*. Only the person concerned can estimate the satisfaction he obtains from consuming, say, 20 Big Macs a week. What units would be used to measure total utility? This too is a difficult problem. Even if it could be solved, how would we compare the satisfaction, in utility units, of any one person with that of another? Can the utility of one person be added to the utility of another person and be meaningful? Questions of actual measurement of utility have plagued economists for years. However, as you'll see soon, it really isn't necessary to measure utility to make the concept useful in explaining consumer choices.

The way *increases* in utility vary with the amount of any good consumed is likely to follow a similar pattern for *all* consumers. The *extra* satisfaction a person receives over a given period by consuming *one extra unit* of a good is called the **marginal utility** of that good. The marginal utility of a good to you is likely to decline as you consume more over a given period. For example, the marginal utility of Big Macs— your extra satisfaction from each additional Big Mac—is likely to decline as you consume more per week. This is because you eventually tire of the sensation you obtain from consuming more Big Macs. The marginal utility of a Big Mac to you might be quite high if you haven't eaten any at all this week. However, a second Big Mac adds less to total utility than does the first. After about 10 Big Macs in a week, you're likely to get very little marginal utility from still another one. You approach a point of satiation for Big Macs as you eat more in a week.[1] The **law of diminishing marginal utility** states that the marginal utility of any item tends to decline as more is consumed over any given period.

Marginal utility:
The extra satisfaction received over a given period by consuming one extra unit of a good.

Law of diminishing marginal utility:
States that the marginal utility of any item tends to decline as more is consumed over any given period.

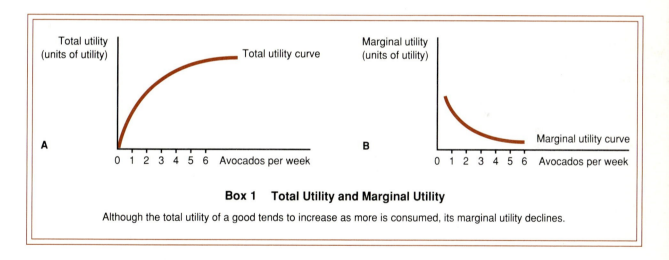

Box 1   Total Utility and Marginal Utility
Although the total utility of a good tends to increase as more is consumed, its marginal utility declines.

Box 1 contains a curve showing how economists assume that total utility *(TU)* and marginal utility *(MU)* vary as more of a good is consumed over any period. **A** shows the total utility a consumer receives from avocados as more are consumed each week. Notice that the curve becomes flatter as more avocados are consumed. The slope of the curve steadily decreases, and the number of avocados consumed in-

[1]At the point of satiation, the marginal utility of a good would be zero. Because marginal utility declines, going beyond the point of satiation means that marginal utility would be negative. If the marginal utility of Big Macs were negative, eating one more would give you a bellyache! Rational people never choose to consume a good in amounts for which marginal utility is negative because they would decrease total utility by doing so.

creases. The slope of the curve at any point can be thought of as the *extra* utility obtained from an extra avocado, which is the marginal utility of avocados:

$$\text{Slope of total utility curve } = \frac{\Delta TU}{\Delta Q} = MU$$

Change in total utility/Change in number of avocados consumed =
Marginal utility of avocados

In Box 1, **B** plots the marginal utility of avocados. The marginal utility declines as more avocados are consumed, reflecting the fact that the slope of the total utility curve diminishes. Notice how marginal utility decreases even when total utility is increasing. More avocados can increase your total utility even though the marginal utility you get from avocados is declining. Remember, marginal utility is the *extra* utility of additional avocados. As long as the marginal utility is positive, your total utility from avocados will increase as you consume more. The dollar value you and other consumers place on the *marginal utility* of a good is a crucial determinant of your decision to buy it.

Consumer Equilibrium for Purchases: The Equimarginal Principle

As a consumer, you have limited income available to spend on the goods that provide you with utility. Your problem is to allocate your income (say per month) among the items you want. The opportunity cost of spending some of your income on any one good is represented by the price of that good. As you spend more on one good, you forgo the opportunity to spend that income on the next best alternative.

Each time you buy more of an item you simultaneously obtain extra utility, which is the marginal utility of the item, and sacrifice the opportunity to purchase other goods. Assuming you can buy as much of an item as you want at the market price, the sum of expenditure on other goods you sacrifice for each unit of a particular good is constant. For example, if hot dogs and ice cream cones both cost $1, you'll have to give up one hot dog each time you buy another ice cream cone. However, the marginal utility of ice cream cones will decline as you buy more per month. The marginal utility *per dollar* of ice cream cones will therefore be less as you buy more cones per month.

As a rational consumer, you presumably seek to obtain the greatest possible utility from spending your limited monthly income. You'll gain utility each month by consuming more hot dogs if your marginal utility *per dollar* of hot dogs exceeds your marginal utility per dollar of ice cream cones. For example, if your units of marginal utility *per dollar* are 5 for hot dogs and 3 for ice cream cones, it's easy to see that you can enjoy a gain in utility by consuming more hot dogs instead of cones. If you choose not to buy a cone so you can buy another hot dog, you forgo the opportunity of getting 3 units of utility for your dollar. Instead you enjoy 5 units of utility from spending the dollar on the hot dog. Your net gain from using the dollar to consume the hot dog *instead of* the ice cream cone is 2 units of utility.

We can generalize this principle: As long as the marginal utility per dollar is not the same for all goods consumed, the consumer can gain by reallocating income to buy more of the goods that have higher marginal utility per dollar than others. Of course, when you consume more goods with high marginal utility per dollar, the marginal utility per dollar of those goods declines. Consuming fewer goods with low marginal utility per dollar increases their marginal utility per dollar. Adjusting marginal utility per dollar in this way by controlling the purchase of particular goods enables you to maximize your satisfaction from spending your income.

A **consumer equilibrium** is attained when a consumer purchases goods (say weekly) until the marginal utility per dollar is the same for all goods consumed. In general, the marginal utility per dollar for any good can be obtained by dividing the marginal utility the consumer places on that good by the price of the good. For example, if the marginal utility of a sweatshirt is 50 units and the price of sweatshirts is $25, its marginal utility per dollar is 2. The conditions for consumer equilibrium can therefore be expressed as:

$$\frac{MU_{\text{A}}}{P_{\text{A}}} = \frac{MU_{\text{B}}}{P_{\text{B}}} = \frac{MU_{\text{C}}}{P_{\text{C}}}, \text{ and so on for all goods.}$$

In this formula, *MU* is the marginal utility of the good indicated by the subscript and *P* is the price of the good indicated by the subscript. The equation illustrates the **equimarginal principle** for consumer purchases, which states that to maximize utility, consumers must equalize the marginal utility per dollar spent on each good.

Placing Dollar Values on Utility: Total Benefit and Marginal Benefit

The problems of measuring utility in consistent units can be sidestepped by asking consumers questions that force them to place a *dollar value* on goods and services they consume. The maximum sum of money a consumer would give up to obtain a certain quantity of a good measures the **total benefit** the consumer receives from that quantity. The advantage of using dollar values instead of utility units is that it allows us to compare the value the consumer receives with the dollars he or she must give up to buy the good. However, total benefit measures *willingness and ability to pay* for a certain quantity of a good. Your willingness and ability to pay for an item depend on both the utility you obtain from the item and the amount of income you have available to spend.

The *marginal benefit* of a good, which we first discussed in Chapter 2, is the maximum sum of money a consumer is willing and able to give up to obtain another unit of a good. *The marginal benefit is therefore the dollar value the person places on the marginal utility enjoyed from a good.* The *law of declining marginal benefit* states that people with a given budget will give up fewer and fewer dollars for additional units of a good over any given period because the marginal utility, or additional satisfaction, they obtain from each extra unit also becomes less and less. The budget must be kept fixed because a change in a person's income can affect his or her *ability* to pay for a good and therefore influence the marginal benefit of the good.

The table in Box 2 shows how marginal benefit is related to total benefit for a person consuming avocados—let's say it's you. The first column in the table shows the number of avocados you consume per week, which varies from 0 to 10. The second column provides a measure of the dollar value of the total utility of avocados to you. We can obtain this value only by asking you how much of your weekly income you'd be willing and able to give up for each basket of avocados containing the number indicated in the first column. The second column therefore shows the total benefit of avocados to you.

Consumer equilibrium: Attained when a consumer purchases goods over a period until the marginal utility per dollar is the same for all goods consumed.

Equimarginal principle: States that to maximize utility, a consumer must equalize the marginal utility per dollar spent on each good.

Total benefit: The maximum sum of money a consumer would give up to obtain a certain quantity of a good.

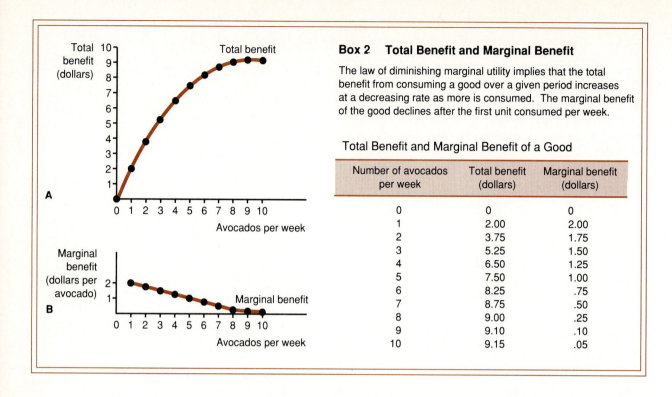

Box 2 Total Benefit and Marginal Benefit

The law of diminishing marginal utility implies that the total benefit from consuming a good over a given period increases at a decreasing rate as more is consumed. The marginal benefit of the good declines after the first unit consumed per week.

Total Benefit and Marginal Benefit of a Good

Number of avocados per week	Total benefit (dollars)	Marginal benefit (dollars)
0	0	0
1	2.00	2.00
2	3.75	1.75
3	5.25	1.50
4	6.50	1.25
5	7.50	1.00
6	8.25	.75
7	8.75	.50
8	9.00	.25
9	9.10	.10
10	9.15	.05

We can calculate the marginal benefit from the data on total benefit in Box 2. To obtain the marginal benefit of each avocado, calculate the change in total benefit, ΔTB, and divide this by the change in the number of avocados consumed, ΔQ.

$$MB = \frac{\Delta TB}{\Delta Q}$$

The marginal benefit of the first avocado is the extra total benefit you obtain when your weekly consumption increases from zero to 1. This represents the monetary value to you of the first avocado you consume that week. This is $2, the total benefit of one avocado per week, minus zero, the total benefit of no avocados. The marginal benefit of the first avocado is therefore $2.

The marginal benefit of the second avocado is the total benefit you enjoy when you consume two per week, minus the total benefit you'd enjoy if you consumed only one per week. This is $3.75 − $2.00 = $1.75. This represents the maximum sum of money you'd give up to get another avocado that week after you've already consumed one. Similarly, we can obtain the marginal benefit of each extra avocado by subtracting the total benefit of a given quantity from the total benefit you'd enjoy if you consumed one less than that quantity per week. Notice that the marginal benefit of avocados declines as you consume more. Assuming your income is held constant, the marginal benefit of avocados must decline as you buy more because the marginal utility declines as you consume more.

In Box 2, **A** plots the total benefit of avocados and **B** plots the marginal benefit. Notice that total benefit increases, but at a decreasing rate. This is because of the decrease in marginal benefit: the addition to total benefit from each extra avocado you consume per week. The marginal benefit represents the increase in the total benefit resulting from each extra avocado. As the marginal benefit gets smaller and smaller, the increase in total benefit also gets smaller and smaller.

Purchasing a Good to Maximize the Net Benefit

You'll always buy more of a good if the value of the marginal utility measured in dollars you receive exceeds the number of dollars you must give up for that unit. Remember, the dollar value of the marginal utility of a good is its marginal benefit to you. This implies that as a rational person, you consume goods up to the point at which the marginal benefit of each good equals its respective price. If P is the price of a good and MB is its marginal benefit, you'll buy each good up to the point at which:

$$P = MB$$

The price represents the marginal cost to you of each extra unit of a good. As a rational consumer, you'll stop buying a good when its marginal benefit falls just below the price of an additional unit.

In Box 3, **A** graphs the marginal benefit of avocados for you based on the data in Box 2. Also plotted on the same set of axes is a horizontal line representing the price of avocados, which is assumed to be 49¢ each. It's clear that you can gain by purchasing a basket containing one avocado because the marginal benefit of $2 you obtain by doing so exceeds the 49¢ price that is the marginal cost of an avocado to you. Similarly, a second avocado added to the basket is a good deal for you because that avocado, which is worth $1.75 to you, can be purchased for only 49¢. Whenever marginal benefit exceeds price, you can enjoy a *net gain* from buying an additional avocado.

When you've purchased seven avocados during the week, the marginal benefit of avocados will have fallen to 50¢, as you can see in the table in Box 2. This means that the seventh avocado you buy is worth just 1¢ more than it cost you. What would happen if you bought an eighth avocado? The table in Box 2 shows that the eighth avocado has a marginal benefit of only 25¢. Because the avocado is priced at 49¢ it costs you more than it's worth, and you choose not to buy it. As a rational consumer, you'll never buy more of a good when its price exceeds its marginal benefit. In this example, as a rational consumer you choose to purchase seven avocados per week, which corresponds to point E in graph **A** of Box 3, at which the marginal benefit of avocados falls to the point at which purchasing an additional avocado would exceed the marginal benefit of doing so.

Net benefit:
The total benefit of the quantity of a good purchased less the dollar sacrifice necessary to purchase that quantity.

The **net benefit** of purchasing a good is the total benefit of the quantity purchased less the dollar sacrifice necessary to purchase that quantity. In Box 3, **B** shows that the net benefit from buying avocados varies as you buy more avocados per week. For example, if you buy one avocado per week, you obtain a total benefit of $2 at a cost of 49¢ to provide a net benefit of $1.51. This is the difference between the marginal benefit of $2 you receive and the market price of 49¢. Similarly, buying another avocado gives you an additional benefit of $1.75 at a price of 49¢, resulting in an increase of $1.26 in the net benefit of exchanging cash for avocados.

The table in Box 3 shows the net benefit from consuming any given number of avocados per week. We obtain this by subtracting the total expenditure for any given quantity of avocados from the total benefit. The last column shows the net benefit, which is then plotted in **B**. In **B**, a smooth line has been traced through the points corresponding to the net benefit for the various possible numbers of avocados con-

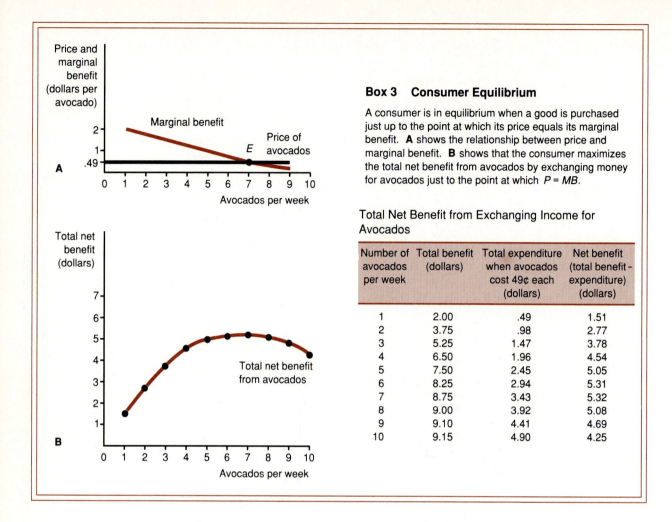

Box 3 Consumer Equilibrium

A consumer is in equilibrium when a good is purchased just up to the point at which its price equals its marginal benefit. **A** shows the relationship between price and marginal benefit. **B** shows that the consumer maximizes the total net benefit from avocados by exchanging money for avocados just to the point at which $P = MB$.

Total Net Benefit from Exchanging Income for Avocados

Number of avocados per week	Total benefit (dollars)	Total expenditure when avocados cost 49¢ each (dollars)	Net benefit (total benefit – expenditure) (dollars)
1	2.00	.49	1.51
2	3.75	.98	2.77
3	5.25	1.47	3.78
4	6.50	1.96	4.54
5	7.50	2.45	5.05
6	8.25	2.94	5.31
7	8.75	3.43	5.32
8	9.00	3.92	5.08
9	9.10	4.41	4.69
10	9.15	4.90	4.25

sumed per week. Notice how the net benefit reaches a maximum at seven avocados per week. Net benefit increases whenever marginal benefit exceeds price. It decreases as marginal benefit falls below price. *It follows that, by purchasing each good up to the point at which the marginal benefit falls to equal the price of the good, a rational consumer is acting in a way that maximizes the net benefit of giving up money for goods.*

Consumer Surplus

Notice from the data in the table in Box 3 that the total benefit you receive from seven avocados per week is $8.75. However, because avocados cost 49¢ each you have to pay only $3.43 to obtain these seven avocados. In other words, you obtain goods whose total utility is valued at $8.75 for an outlay of only $3.43! Because the value to you of the goods you bought during the week exceeds the expenditure necessary to obtain them, you enjoy a surplus of benefit over expenditure. **Consumer surplus** is the difference between the total benefit of a given quantity purchased by a consumer and the expenditure necessary to purchase that quantity.

Consumer surplus:
The difference between the total benefit of a given quantity purchased by a consumer and the expenditure necessary to purchase that quantity.

Consumer surplus is the same as the *net benefit* you obtain from buying a given quantity of a good. The last column of the table in Box 3, which shows the net benefit of each quantity of avocados, also measures the consumer surplus.

You can see how the concept of consumer surplus applies to all of your purchases. When you budget your expenditures for a year, you might have to decide how many pairs of new jeans to add to your wardrobe. When you go shopping, you have some idea of how much you'd be willing to pay for new jeans rather than do without them. Suppose you'd pay $40 for only one pair per year. That $40 is the marginal benefit to you of buying jeans when you buy only one pair per year. If the market price of jeans is only $29.99, you'd enjoy a consumer surplus of $10.01 if you bought only one pair.

Suppose, after already buying one pair of jeans, you're willing to pay $35 for a second pair rather than get along with only one pair this year. You could add $5.01 to your consumer surplus by buying the second pair because its marginal benefit to you exceeds its price. *Whenever the marginal benefit of a good exceeds its price, a consumer can add to consumer surplus by purchasing more.* If the marginal benefit of a third pair to you were $30, you'd also be better off buying a third pair because you'd augment your consumer surplus by 1¢. However, a fourth pair is worth only $25 to you, so you can't add to your consumer surplus by buying four pairs per year when the price is $29.99. If you bought a fourth pair, your consumer surplus would decline by $4.99.

The graph and table in Box 4 show that consumer surplus is the difference between the sum of the marginal benefit you obtain from each of the three pairs of jeans you purchase and your total outlay for jeans of $89.97. This is represented by the portion of the three bars in the graph above the $29.99 price. Your consumer surplus per year from jeans in this case is $15.03 when you buy three pairs per year.

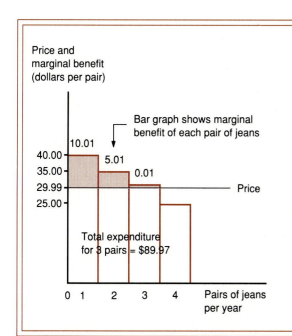

Price and marginal benefit (dollars per pair)

Bar graph shows marginal benefit of each pair of jeans

10.01
5.01
0.01
40.00
35.00
29.99 ——— Price
25.00

Total expenditure for 3 pairs = $89.97

0 1   2   3   4   Pairs of jeans per year

Box 4   Consumer Surplus

Consumer surplus is represented by the portion of the bar graphs showing marginal benefit lying above the price line. The consumer surplus on the three pairs of jeans purchased is $10.01 + $5.01 + $0.01 = $15.03. By purchasing a good up to the point at which its marginal benefit falls to just equal its price, the consumer maximizes consumer surplus.

Calculation of Consumer Surplus

Pairs of jeans purchased per year	Marginal benefit (dollars per year)	Total benefit (dollars per year)	Expenditure on jeans @ $29.99 per pair (dollars per year)	Consumer surplus (dollars per year)
1	40	40	29.99	10.01
2	35	40 + 35 = 75	59.98	10.01 + 5.01 = 15.02
3	30	75 + 30 = 105	89.97	15.02 + 0.01 = 15.03
4	25	105 + 25 = 130	119.96	15.03 − 4.99 = 10.04

The concept of consumer surplus shows that the value of goods to you and other consumers *exceeds* the expenditure you incur to buy those goods. For example, if a strike of textile workers made it impossible to buy jeans during the year, the loss to you and other jeans wearers would be the consumer surplus you earned by buying jeans. Because jeans wouldn't be available, the income you would have spent on jeans would be used for other purposes and wouldn't be lost. Instead, the social loss of not having the jeans available is the consumer surplus that's lost for the year by those who would have bought jeans.

You can see how the concept of consumer surplus can be applied in policy analysis when you realize that many government regulations affect the quantity of a good available to consumers. For example, government regulations in all states prohibit people under age 21 from purchasing alcoholic beverages. An estimate of the consumer surplus these people would have earned from buying alcoholic beverages measures the *social* cost of the prohibition. The loss in consumer surplus can then be compared with the gains possible in the form of reduced traffic deaths and other benefits from a legal drinking age of 21.

Concept Check

1   How does the total utility of a certain quantity of a good differ from its marginal utility? How are the concepts of total and marginal benefit related to those of total and marginal utility?

2   Explain why you as a consumer consider both the prices and marginal utilities of all goods in making your choices. What is the equimarginal principle, and how is it relevant to consumer equilibrium?

3   What must you as a consumer do to maximize your net benefit from purchasing goods?

Using the Theory of Consumer Choice

Choosing Items on a Menu: How Prices Induce You to Choose a Lower-Valued Alternative Over a Higher-Valued One

Now we can use the theory of consumer choice to investigate more fully the way prices affect choices. To begin, examine how you choose to order meals when you look at a menu in a restaurant. Suppose the restaurant includes fine wines and gourmet foods along with the standard fare of hamburgers and soft drinks. You eat at the restaurant regularly and prefer the prime ribs of beef as your main dish to the hamburger. This means that the marginal benefit you place on any given number of prime rib dinners per month exceeds the marginal benefit you place on that *same number* of hamburger dinners.

In Box 5, **A** shows your marginal benefit curve for prime rib dinners per month, while **B** shows your marginal benefit curve for hamburger dinners per month. Suppose the price of a prime rib dinner is $15.95 while the price of a hamburger dinner is $4.95. Assuming you have a certain income each month, the declining marginal benefit of each good reflects the declining marginal utility you receive from each of the dinners.

Now we can use consumer choice theory to show how prices often induce you to choose a lower-valued alternative over a higher-valued one. In other words, it

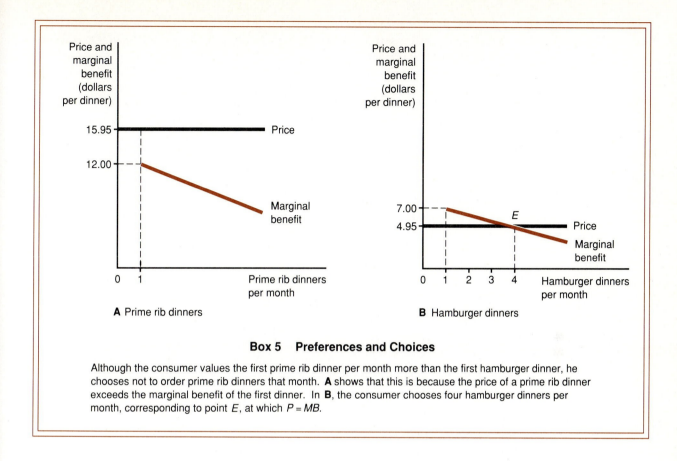

Box 5   Preferences and Choices

Although the consumer values the first prime rib dinner per month more than the first hamburger dinner, he chooses not to order prime rib dinners that month. **A** shows that this is because the price of a prime rib dinner exceeds the marginal benefit of the first dinner. In **B**, the consumer chooses four hamburger dinners per month, corresponding to point *E*, at which *P = MB*.

shows why your preferences often differ from your choices. The marginal benefit of the first prime rib dinner per month is $12, which exceeds the maximum marginal benefit of $7 you get from the first hamburger dinner of the month. *But the $12 marginal benefit of the first prime rib dinner is less than the price of $15.95 you must pay to get it.* To buy even one prime rib dinner would provide less benefit than it costs. You'd get $12 worth of benefit for $15.95—a bad deal! You therefore buy no prime rib dinners that month.

In Box 5, **B** shows that the marginal benefit you get from the first hamburger dinner is $7. You'll be better off exchanging your $4.95 for the hamburger dinner because you'll get $7 worth of benefit for only $4.95—a good deal! You'll continue to buy hamburger dinners that month until the marginal benefit falls to the $4.95 price in **B**. This occurs at point *E,* at which you consume four hamburger dinners per month.

Even though you prefer the prime rib dinner to the hamburger dinner, you choose four hamburger dinners when going to the restaurant that month and don't consume any prime rib dinners. The reason is that the price of the prime rib dinner exceeds the maximum amount of expenditure on other goods you'd be willing to give up for even the first dinner that month. The value you place on the marginal utility of hamburger dinners, although lower than the value you place on the corresponding number of prime rib dinners, exceeds the price until you consume four hamburger dinners that month.

Your choices are therefore influenced by the price you must pay. High prices force you to forgo highly valued alternatives when those prices exceed the marginal benefit you obtain from the alternatives.

The Paradox of Value: Why Water Is Cheaper than Diamonds

Paradox of value:

People are willing to give up zero or very small amounts of money to obtain certain items that provide them great total benefit.

Have you ever noticed that some items of great value, like air and water, are free while apparently useless items like diamond jewelry can be sold at astronomically high prices? The **paradox of value** is that people are willing to give up zero or very small amounts of money to obtain certain items that provide them great total benefit. For example, the total benefit obtained from one gallon of drinking water per day is great because we can't survive without water each day. The total benefit of diamonds, however, is likely to be lower because we can survive without diamonds.

The key to unraveling this apparent paradox is to look at the marginal benefit you or any person receives from these two goods. Water is very abundant in most regions. This means that at the current quantity available, the marginal benefit you receive falls to a level close to zero. However, diamonds aren't very abundant relative to the desire for them. Given the availability of diamonds, most of us have so few that the gems' marginal benefit remains quite high. Your willingness to give up more money for one more diamond per year than for one more gallon of water per year is therefore rooted in the fact that diamonds are scarcer than water.

You can see this in the graphs in Box 6; **A** shows the marginal benefit you receive from water. Given the amount of water you already have available, represented by the vertical line, the marginal benefit of water is close to zero. Graph **B** shows the

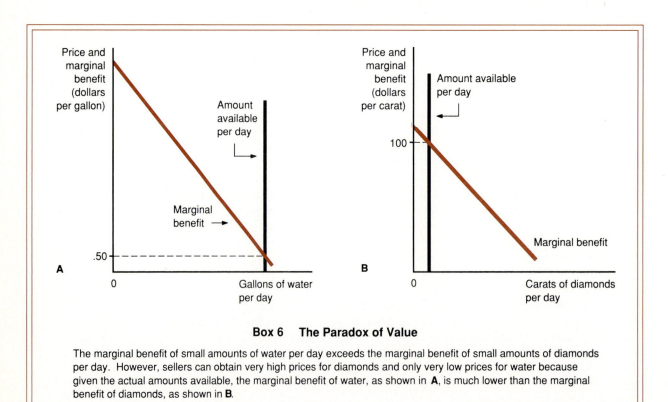

Box 6   The Paradox of Value

The marginal benefit of small amounts of water per day exceeds the marginal benefit of small amounts of diamonds per day. However, sellers can obtain very high prices for diamonds and only very low prices for water because given the actual amounts available, the marginal benefit of water, as shown in **A**, is much lower than the marginal benefit of diamonds, as shown in **B**.

marginal benefit of diamonds. Note that the maximum amount of money you'll give up for one diamond is less than the amount you'd give up for water *if only one gallon of water were in fact available*. Given the number of diamonds you currently have, you'd be willing to give up more for an extra diamond than for an extra gallon of water. This is why sellers of diamonds can get higher prices for their goods than can sellers of drinking water. Given the quantities actually available, the marginal benefit of diamonds exceeds the marginal benefit of water for most of us. This holds even though the *total* benefit we obtain from water exceeds the total benefit we obtain from diamonds.

Also note that this doesn't mean that everyone will buy diamonds. Because diamonds are rare, their current market price is likely to exceed the marginal benefit of even the first diamond for many consumers!

How Changes in Income Change the Dollar Value Consumers Place on Items of Given Utility

Changes in income affect the *ability* of you or any other consumer to pay for any given amount of a good. Your income can change, of course, while your preferences remain the same. Although the total utility you might get from an item like a taxi ride is the same at any income level, your ability to give up income for the taxi ride is enhanced as your income increases. The dollar value you place on various alternatives of given utility will therefore change when your income changes. For example, you might be willing to give up a maximum of $4 for a taxi ride from school to home when you have low income. If your income were to double, you might be willing to give up $6 for the same ride even though it provides you with exactly the same utility as before.

Recall that the marginal benefit is the *maximum* sum of money you'd be willing and able to give up for one more unit of a good. This amount depends on the amount of money you *actually have* over that period. *In other words, the dollar value you place on the marginal utility you receive from a good depends on your income as well as your preferences.*

For most goods, an increase in income is likely to result in increases in demand and marginal benefit. Recall from Chapter 7 that *normal goods* are those for which any increase in income results in an increase in the amount of that good purchased. To illustrate the effect of an increase in income on a normal good, recall the example of prime rib dinners used earlier. The marginal benefit of even the first prime rib dinner in the example exceeded its price, causing you to consume no such dinners that month. Now suppose the prime rib dinners are a normal good for you. Assume as well that you finally graduate from college and find a great job that increases your monthly income substantially! The increase in your income will increase the marginal benefit, which is the maximum amount of money you'd give up for any given number of prime rib dinners per month.

The graph in Box 7 shows the effect of the increase in income on your consumption of prime rib dinners each month, assuming the price is still $15.95 per dinner. The initial marginal benefit curve is labeled MB_1. Your increase in income increases your willingness to pay for each dinner, thereby shifting the marginal benefit curve upward. This also implies that at any given price you'd be willing to buy more prime rib dinners. To see this, draw a horizontal line from any point on the vertical axis and note that it intersects the new marginal benefit curve, labeled MB_2, at a point corresponding to more prime rib dinners per month on the horizontal axis.

As shown in the graph, your increase in income causes the marginal benefit of

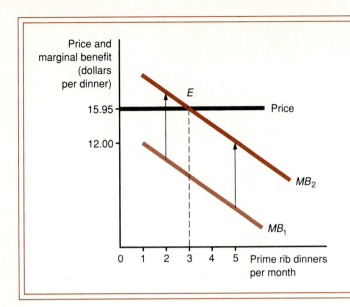

Box 7   The Effect of an Increase in Income on Consumption of a Normal Good

An increase in income increases a consumer's willingness to pay for a normal good. An increase in income therefore shifts the marginal benefit curve upward from MB_1 to MB_2. The new consumer equilibrium at the higher income corresponds to point E, at which three prime rib dinners per month are consumed.

the first prime rib dinner to exceed its price. The new consumer equilibrium occurs at point E on the graph, at which the marginal benefit along the new curve just equals the $15.95 price. With your new job you choose to consume three prime rib dinners per month!

As you also learned in Chapter 7, *inferior goods* are those a consumer chooses to purchase less of as a result of increases in income. Inferior goods are generally low-quality items like cheap cuts of meat and used clothing.

Suppose hamburger dinners are inferior goods for you. This means that your willingness to pay for these dinners goes down as your income increases. Understandably, the dollar value of the marginal utility you get from hamburgers is lower when you're rich than when you're poor! This decreases the marginal benefit you receive from any given quantity of hamburger dinners. The graph in Box 8 shows that any increase in income *decreases* the marginal benefit for any quantity of an

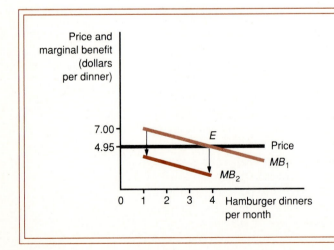

Box 8   The Effect of an Increase in Income on the Consumption of an Inferior Good

An increase in income decreases a consumer's willingness to pay for an inferior good. The increase in income shifts the marginal benefit curve for hamburger dinners downward from MB_1 to MB_2. Because the marginal benefit of even one hamburger dinner per month is now less than the price, this consumer reduces monthly consumption from four dinners to zero.

Principles in Practice

Using Marginal Analysis to Understand the Choice to Have Children

There's more to life than buying and selling! We can use marginal analysis of consumer choice to obtain valuable insights into many choices that don't directly relate to buying of goods in markets. For example, for couples engaging in family planning, the decision to have children involves both marginal benefit and marginal cost. There's a "price" to be paid for each child in terms of material goods, services, and time per year for their own use that parents must sacrifice to raise the child. This price represents the marginal cost of a child. The marginal benefit of a child is the dollar value parents place on the marginal utility they obtain from children.

In choosing to have children, couples compare the marginal benefit, as they evaluate it, with the price, as measured by their estimate of what they must sacrifice for each child. The graphs show how two different couples might make different choices about childbearing. Assume that both couples evaluate the annual price per child at $10,000. The first couple, whose marginal benefit curve is depicted in **A,** chooses not to have chil-

dren. This is because the marginal benefit of the first child is less than the "price" they'd have to pay. The second couple, in **B,** places a higher marginal benefit on children. This couple is in equilibrium when they have one child.

Any changes in economic conditions or preferences that influence either the "price" or the marginal benefit of children to couples are likely to affect choices to have children. The important economic variables that could affect the choice to have children, and therefore the birth rate, include family income and the value of time. The value of time to couples is an important determinant of the "price" of children.

Since 1950 there's been a reduction in the size of the family in the United States and other nations. Increased employment opportunities for women have affected the choice to have children by increasing the value women place on their time. Increases in the value of time therefore shift the price line upward, as shown in **C.** This could reduce the number of children per family or cause some to remain childless.

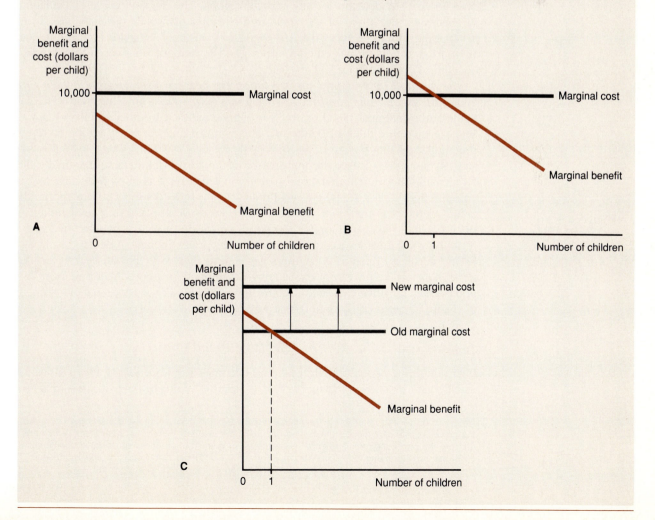

inferior good. In fact, as you can see in the graph, the increase in income allows you to afford enough better food to drop hamburger dinners completely from your monthly budget! After your increase in income, the marginal benefit of even the first hamburger dinner is below its price. You therefore consume no hamburger dinners.

Concept Check

1 Use the concept of marginal benefit to explain why people choose not to consume any of a good even though the marginal and total utility of the good are positive.

2 Why is an item like gold jewelry likely to have high marginal benefit to many consumers?

3 What is the distinction between normal and inferior goods?

Deriving Demand Curves

The Demand Curve for an Individual Consumer

Now we can explain the law of demand using the theory of consumer choice. Concentrate on your demand for any particular good. The demand curve is a relationship between the price of the good and the quantity you'll purchase at various prices, other things being equal. The theory of consumer behavior argues that over any period, a person will buy any given good in amounts that cause the marginal benefit to fall to the price.

The demand curve represents a relationship between the marginal benefit of a good and the quantity consumed, other things being equal. In other words, we can think of the marginal benefit curve for a good as the consumer's demand curve.[2] You can therefore think of points on your own demand curve for a good as representing the maximum sum of money you'll give up for various available amounts of an item. Now you can see the importance of the law of diminishing marginal utility for demand theory. The maximum price you'll pay for a good will decline as you consume more because the marginal utility of goods declines as you buy more. The law of demand is therefore rooted in the law of diminishing marginal utility. As price declines, you buy more of the good so that the marginal benefit you receive from the good declines to equal the new lower price. The law of demand is, in fact, based on the idea that as consumers we seek to maximize the satisfaction, or total net benefit, we receive from exchanging our money for goods. You buy more of a good when its price falls because the lower price allows additional net benefit, through increased consumption, that wasn't previously possible.

Income and Substitution Effects of Price Changes

When the price of a good falls, the good becomes a more attractive buy and we can usually gain by consuming more. This is because at the lower price, we must buy

---

[2] We must qualify this statement by pointing out that when the price of a good changes and the purchasing power of a fixed budget is affected substantially, the marginal benefit curve will shift. When this is the case the individual's demand curve is composed of points on a number of marginal benefit curves, each one corresponding to a different price for the good. The demand curve would be obtained by connecting the points corresponding to the marginal benefit of each possible quantity.

more to decrease marginal benefit to the new lower price. However, as the price of a good changes, the purchasing power of your income can also be affected. The increase in the purchasing power of a fixed dollar income caused by a price decline can cause a marginal benefit curve to shift in the same way that a change in money income can cause such a shift.

The change in the purchasing power of income resulting from a price change in a good depends on the extent of the price change and the portion of your income you spend on that good. For example, if the price of pencils declines by 50%, the increase in the purchasing power of fixed money income will be negligible because most of us spend only a small portion of our income on this good. If, for example, you spend $1 per month on pencils, a decline in price to 50¢ will increase the purchasing power of your money income by only 50¢ if you don't buy more pencils when the price falls. However, if you spend one third of your income on housing and the price of housing declines by 50%, you get a whopping increase in the purchasing power of your income. For example, if you spend $500 per month on rent, a 50% decline in your rent will increase your money income available for spending by $250 per month. The increase in available income can itself affect your marginal benefit (willingness and ability to pay) for housing.

Economists find it useful to divide the effect of a change in price on purchases of a good into two separate components. The **income effect** is a change in consumption of a good *only* as a result of the variation in the purchasing power of money income caused by a price change. For example, the income effect of a decrease in the price of gasoline is the change in the purchases of gasoline caused only by the increase in the purchasing power of income resulting from the price decline.

Recall that an increase in income increases your ability to pay for all normal goods. If gasoline is a normal good, the income effect of a fall in its price will increase its monthly consumption. Similarly, if the price of gasoline were to increase, the income effect would decrease the ability of consumers to pay for this good and act to decrease its monthly consumption.

An increase in income *decreases* your willingness as a consumer to pay for an inferior good. For example, if hamburger is an inferior good for you, a decrease in its price would result in an income effect, decreasing your monthly consumption of hamburger. Similarly, an increase in the price of an inferior good *increases* your willingness to pay for this good because it *decreases* the purchasing power of your income (making you poorer). The income effect of a price increase for an inferior good is an increase in its consumption.

The **substitution effect** of a price change is a change in consumption of a good only as a result of a change in its price relative to the prices of other goods. *This effect measures the change in the quantity of the good purchased, say, per month that would be observed if the consumer's money income were adjusted so that he was neither better nor worse off as a result of the price change.* We could observe the substitution effect of a price decline if enough income were taken away from the person to make him just as well off as he was before the price went down. Similarly, for us to observe the substitution effect of a price increase, the person's income would have to be increased enough to make him just as well off as he was before the price went up. The variations in income would remove the income effect.

For example, suppose you were given the opportunity to fly at half fare on a certain airline. If you spend a substantial amount of your income on air travel, this could result in a rather large increase in the purchasing power of your income. However, suppose you must join a special club to obtain the bargain airfare. The

Income effect:
A change in consumption of a good *only* as a result of the variation in the purchasing power of money income caused by a price change.

Substitution effect:
A change in consumption of a good only as a result of a change in its price relative to the prices of other goods.

annual dues of the club are $200. Suppose this annual payment is just enough to make you as well off as you were before you had the option of flying at half fare. The annual dues would therefore reduce your income just enough to eliminate the income effect. The resulting change in your consumption of air travel, assuming you actually pay the dues to join the club, would be the substitution effect.

The substitution effect *always* acts to increase the consumption of a good whose price declines and to decrease the consumption of a good whose price increases. *This is because if there is no change in the purchasing power of a person's income as a result of the price change, the marginal benefit of the good can decline only if more of the good is consumed.* Therefore you *must* consume more of a good when its price declines to lower the marginal benefit so as to set it equal to the lower price. The lower price definitely increases the net gain from buying more when the income effect is negligible. As long as the law of diminishing marginal utility holds, the substitution effect will increase the quantity you buy of a good whose price declines while other determinants of demand are unchanged. The opposite, of course, is true for a price increase.

The income effect of a decrease in the price of a normal good increases the marginal benefit of any given quantity. This increases the net gain possible at any given price and induces you to buy more to enjoy the additional gains not previously possible. The income effect of a price decline for an inferior good acts to decrease the consumption of such a good because it decreases the marginal benefit of any given quantity of the good.

Understanding the income and substitution effects gives you further insight into why you and other consumers adjust your purchases of a good when its price changes. The substitution effect indicates that it's advantageous for you to substitute the good whose relative price declines for other goods given your available budget and the constant purchasing power of a dollar over a period. The income effect indicates that when a price change results in a change in the purchasing power of a fixed amount of income, the marginal benefit of any given quantity of a good is affected as well. As your ability to pay is changed, you adjust still further your consumption of the good whose price changes. For normal goods both the income and substitution effects of price declines act to increase the quantity demanded.

Deriving Market Demand Curves from Individual Demand Curves

Are bell-bottom jeans coming back into style? Is the popularity of four-wheel drive vehicles declining? Could a chain of Chinese fast-food shops succeed?

Market demand for consumer products is of great interest to business firms and investors. Ultimately, the success or failure of businesses depends on their ability to satisfy consumer demands. Astute investors anticipate changes in market demand for products and profit by doing so. A successful marketing and sales program for any business is based on comprehensive studies of the demand for the product. Predicting the pattern and level of consumer demand is a prerequisite to forecasting business conditions.

A **market demand curve** shows the relationship between the price of a product and the total quantity demanded by *all* consumers willing and able to purchase the product at each price, other things being equal. We derive a market demand curve from individual demand curves for a given product by adding the quantity demanded by each buyer in the market at each possible price. Because, as we've just

Market demand curve: Shows the relationship between the price of a product and the total quantity demanded by *all* consumers willing and able to purchase the product at each price, other things being equal.

Principles in Practice

Demographics and Market Demand: The Aging of America

There's no sure-fire way to get rich—but an ambitious person who studies demographic trends might profit from learning about some dramatic changes in the mix of the U.S. population that are affecting the demand for products:

1. *The proportion of the population accounted for by single people living alone has increased.* Between 1950 and 1980 the divorce rate in the United States increased from 2.6 to 5.3 per thousand population. During the same period the number of marriages per thousand population remained about the same at 11 per thousand. This has contributed to an increase in the number of people living alone. This in turn probably means an increase in the demand for convenience-food services and for apartments and condominiums. It could even contribute to an increase in the demand for pets as substitutes for children!

2. *The average age of heads of households in the United States has been increasing and will continue to increase throughout much of the twenty-first century.* Evidence indicates that expenditures on furniture, appliances, housing, and automobiles in a nation tend to decrease as the average age of household heads increases.* Also, as the elderly drop out of the labor force and begin to live on pensions, their spending often declines relative to what it was in their middle years.

3. *The percentage of the population accounted for by persons over the age of 65 has been increasing and will continue to increase throughout the first half of the twenty-first century.*

The table shows how the proportion of the population accounted for by elderly persons is projected to increase throughout much of the twenty-first century. Notice that the most dramatic increases are anticipated in the proportion of the population expected to be 85 years of age and older! Persons over the age of 85 accounted for just over 1% of the population in 1985 but are expected to make up nearly 6% of the population by the year 2080. In the year 2080 it's projected that about one in four people living in the U.S. will be over the age of 65!

There's little doubt that business firms developing products that are likely to be in demand by elderly people will prosper in the twenty-first century. Medical specialties that satisfy the demands of the geriatric population will certainly be profitable enterprises. The demand for rest-home services, false teeth, pacemakers, and leisure activities also is likely to increase as a result of the aging of the population.

Actual and Projected Population, Persons Over Age 65 and Over Age 85: Selected Years 1975 - 2080 (in millions)

Year	Total U.S. population	Persons aged 65 and over	Percent of total	Persons aged 85 and over	Percent of total
1975	216.0	22.7	10.5%	1.8	0.8%
1980	227.7	25.7	11.2	2.3	1.0
1985†	238.6	28.6	12.0	2.7	1.1
Projections					
2000	268.0	34.9	13.0	4.9	1.8
2010	283.2	39.2	13.8	6.6	2.3
2030	304.8	64.6	21.2	8.6	2.8
2080	310.8	73.1	23.5	18.2	5.9

Source: U.S. Census Bureau.
†Estimated.

*For a discussion of these effects, see Philip Musgrove, *U.S. Household Consumption, Income, and Demographic Changes, 1975-2025,* Washington, D.C.: Resources for the Future, 1982.

proved, individual demand curves are downward sloping, market demand curves will also be downward sloping.

We can illustrate the principle for deriving a market demand curve by showing how the quantity demanded by a few consumers can be added along the horizontal axis. The table in Box 9 shows the demand schedules for gold-nibbed luxury fountain pens for three consumers: Al, Bob, and Carol. Each individual's demand curve

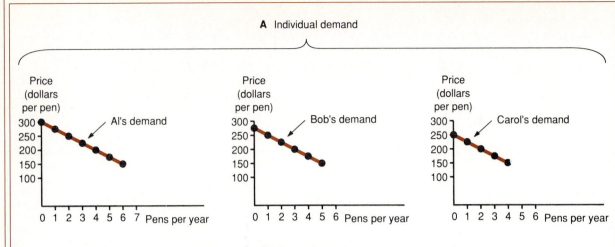

A Individual demand

Al's demand

Bob's demand

Carol's demand

B Market demand

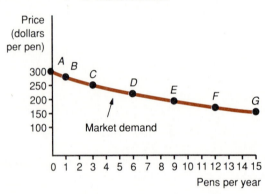

Market demand

Deriving a Market Demand Curve

Price of a pen (dollars per year)	Al	Bob	Carol	Total	Point on market demand curve
300	0	0	0	0	A
275	1	0	0	1	B
250	2	1	0	3	C
225	3	2	1	6	D
200	4	3	2	9	E
175	5	4	3	12	F
150	6	5	4	15	G

Box 9   Derivation of a Market Demand Curve

A market demand curve is obtained by adding the quantities demanded at each price of all consumers willing and able to purchase the good at those prices.

for the fountain pens is drawn separately in Box 9. These separate demand curves show how many pens each of the three consumers will buy per year at various prices.

The table in Box 9 shows that the total quantity demanded at each price is the sum of the quantities demanded by each of the three consumers at each possible price. If these were the only consumers in the market, the total quantity demanded by all three would be the market quantity demanded. The market demand schedule would be the last column of the table. This would show how market quantity demanded varies with price.

In **B** in Box 9 we derive the market demand curve by adding the quantities demanded by each consumer per year at each possible price along the horizontal axis. At any price above $275, total sales would be zero because no single consumer will buy the pens when the price exceeds this sum. As the price falls to $275, Al decides to buy one of the pens. At that price one pen per year would be sold (to Al) and point B in graph **B** would be the corresponding point on the market demand curve. At a price of $250, Al would buy two pens per year and Bob would buy one pen per year. Total quantity demanded would be three pens per year, and the corresponding point on the market demand curve would be C. As the price falls to $225, Carol also buys, and the fourth row of the table in Box 9 shows that total quantity demanded would be six pens per year, corresponding to point D on the market demand curve. Similarly, the table shows how the quantities demanded of the three consumers can be added at other prices to obtain other points on the market demand curve. As you can see in **B,** the market demand curve represents the sum of the quantities demanded of all three consumers at each possible price.

In a typical market, the quantity demanded by any one buyer at any given price is likely to be a very small share of total quantity demanded. An important influence on market demand is the number of consumers willing to purchase the good at each possible price. The number of buyers served by the market is therefore a major determinant of market demand. For example, if the U.S. could expand its markets for cars overseas, the additional buyers would increase the demand for U.S. cars.

Population and its composition are also very important determinants of market demand. As the age composition of the population changes, the prospects for marketing various types of products will change as well (see Principles in Practice box on p. 163).

Are There Exceptions to the Law of Demand?

Remember that a demand curve shows the relationship between price and quantity demanded for a good assuming there's no change in money income, quality of the good being sold, the prices of related goods, expectations of future price, and consumer preferences. When prices change, there are inevitable (but usually small) changes in the purchasing power of available money income. These changes in purchasing power can cause changes in the willingness to pay for goods through the resulting income effects.

For inferior goods the income effect of a price decline decreases the quantity demanded. It's therefore conceivable that the demand curve for an inferior good could be upward sloping if the income effect of a price change were very strong. For this to be the case the consumer would have to spend a very large portion of income on such a good. This exception to the law of demand is possible but very unlikely. Historically, Sir Robert Giffen (1837-1910), a British statistician and economist, claimed to observe very poor workers increase their consumption of cheap starchy foods like bread when price increased. These workers spent large portions of their income on bread, which was apparently an inferior good to them. When the price of bread rose, the income effect could have been so strong as to force them to drop meat and other expensive foods from their diet and consume more bread instead. A *Giffen good* is an inferior good whose demand curve would slope upward. In the modern world, Giffen goods are rare because consumers are unlikely to spend high proportions of their income on goods they regard as inferior.

It's possible, however, that other influences on demand can change along with prices. This might make it appear that the law of demand has been violated. However, in such cases the law of demand remains valid because other things assumed to be constant change with price. Remember, a demand curve shows a relationship between price and quantity demanded when *all other influences on the willingness and ability to purchase a good are unchanged.*

For example, an antique dealer might notice that she sells more goods when prices of all the items in stock are doubled! Is this really an exception to the law of demand? The answer is no, because it's likely that consumers think *quality* is higher when price is higher. In other words, changes in price are associated with a change in an important factor that affects the willingness of consumers to pay for a given amount of a good.

Demand curves might also appear to slope upward in periods of high inflation. In those periods consumers might view a current increase in the price of a good as indicative of a future price increase. Because an increase in price is associated with a *change in price expectations,* the demand curve will shift outward each time price goes up. This increase in willingness to pay because of the expectation of future price increases could offset the tendency to buy more as price declines. This isn't really an exception to the law of demand because, once again, "other things" are not unchanged when prices change.

We can therefore conclude that the law of demand is an economic principle based firmly on the notion that all of us maximize the net benefit we obtain from purchasing goods and services.

Concept Check

1 How is the law of demand related to the tendency of the marginal benefit of a good to decline as more is consumed?

2 What is the distinction between the income and substitution effects of price changes?

3 How is a market demand curve derived from individual demand curves?

Summary

1. Preferences represent a person's likes and dislikes. Utility is a concept that can be used to gauge preferences. Utility measures a person's intensity of desire for goods and services. Higher-utility alternatives are preferred to ones that provide less utility. Utility is a subjective concept.
2. Total utility measures the total satisfaction obtained from a certain quantity of a good consumed over a given period. The marginal utility of a good is the extra utility obtained from an extra unit of the good.

3. The law of diminishing marginal utility is a general principle that states that the marginal utility obtained from an item tends to decline as more is consumed over a given period.

4. Consumers are assumed to seek the most utility possible from exchanging their limited income for goods and services available in markets. A consumer equilibrium is attained when a consumer buys goods over a given period in such a way as to equate the marginal utility per dollar for all goods purchased. The equimarginal principle expresses the conditions for consumer equilibrium by indicating that the marginal utility of each good divided by its respective price must be the same for *all* goods.

5. The total benefit of a certain quantity of a good is the dollar value a person places on the utility of that quantity. Total benefit measures the willingness to pay for a certain amount of a good.

6. The marginal benefit of a good is the maximum sum of money a person will give up for another unit of it.

7. The net benefit of purchasing a good is the difference between the total benefit obtained from the amount purchased and the sum of money given up to purchase it.

8. A rational consumer purchases each good up to the point at which its marginal benefit falls to its price.

9. A consumer's choices depend on both the marginal benefit and the price of each alternative. Because marginal benefit measures *willingness and ability to pay* for additional units of a good, it can change as a person's income changes.

10. Normal goods are those for which an increase in income results in increased purchases, while inferior goods are those for which increases in income result in decreased purchases.

11. The demand curve of an individual consumer for a good is generally downward sloping because the marginal benefit of the good tends to decline as more is consumed. When the price of a good falls, a consumer buys more until the marginal benefit falls to the new lower price.

12. The income effect of a price change is the change in purchases of the good resulting *only* from the change in purchasing power of money income caused by the price change. The substitution effect of a price change is the change in purchases of a good resulting *only* from the change in the relative price of a good.

13. A market demand curve is obtained by adding quantities demanded for all consumers at each possible price. Market demand curves slope downward because individual demand curves slope downward and because, at lower prices, more consumers are willing and able to buy.

14. The law of demand is firmly based on the notion that people maximize the benefit they obtain from purchasing goods and services.

Key Terms and Concepts

Preferences	Total benefit
Utility	Net benefit
Total utility	Consumer surplus
Marginal utility	Paradox of value
Law of diminishing marginal utility	Income effect
Consumer equilibrium	Substitution effect
Equimarginal principle	Market demand curve

Problems and Applications

1. This month you've gone to four movie shows. You estimate that the total utility you've received from the movies is 1,000 units. When you go to a fifth movie, your total utility increases to 1,100. What is the marginal utility of movies when you've consumed (attended) five per month? Assuming that the law of diminishing marginal utility holds, what will happen to total and marginal utility when you go to a sixth movie this month?

2. The marginal utility to you of meals at fast-food restaurants has fallen to zero. Draw your total utility and marginal utility curves for these meals and show that total utility is at a maximum. What will happen if you buy one more meal this month at a fast-food restaurant?

3. The price of both hamburgers and pizza is $1 per serving. You estimate that you currently enjoy a marginal utility of 10 from hamburgers and 20 from pizza. Have you reached a position of consumer equilibrium? Explain your answer.

4. The price of steak is $7 per pound, and the price of chicken is $2 per pound. Your mother currently receives a marginal utility of 14 from consuming steak this week and 6 from consuming chicken this week. The marginal utility of chicken is therefore less than that of steak. Does this imply that she should buy less chicken this week?

5. The total benefit you've enjoyed from the two mystery novels you've purchased this month is $20. You estimate that your total benefit from mystery novels this month will increase to $25 if you purchase another one. Suppose the price of mystery novels is $6. Will you buy another one this month? Explain your answer.

6. The following table shows how the total benefit your best friend gets from hamburgers varies with the number purchased per week:

Number of hamburgers per week	Total benefit (dollars)
1	5
2	8
3	10
4	11

Suppose the price of hamburgers is $2. Forecast how many hamburgers your friend will buy and calculate the net benefit he would obtain from that amount. What would happen to your friend's choice and net benefit from hamburgers if the price fell to $1?

7. You're currently in the market for a new car. The marginal benefit you place on a BMW 325i is $15,000, while the marginal benefit of a Toyota Corolla is $10,000. The current market price of the Toyota is $9,500, while the BMW sells for $16,000. Which one will you choose?

8. Suppose that just as you're about to make your choice of cars you receive an unexpected gift from your parents that increases your income. Assuming that both the BMW and the Toyota are normal goods, the marginal benefit you place on the BMW increases to $20,000, while the marginal benefit of the Toyota increases to $11,000. Assuming you buy only one car and the prices are the same as in question 7, which one will you now choose?

9. Travel by bus is an inferior good for you. Show what will happen to your marginal benefit curve for bus travel when your income increases. Assuming that the price per mile of bus travel doesn't change when your income goes up, show what will happen to the amount you choose to buy. Under what circumstances will you drop bus travel completely?

10. The market for Rolls-Royces currently consists of three buyers in a small town. The current price for these magnificent cars is $100,000. At that price each of the buyers will purchase one car this year. If the price were $120,000, only one of the buyers would buy the car this year. Use this information to derive the market demand curve for Rolls-Royces in this town.

Suggested Readings

Gary S. Becker, *A Treatise on the Family,* Cambridge: Harvard University Press, 1981. This book applies the economic analysis of rational behavior to choices that affect such important family and demographic factors as childbearing, marriage, and divorce.

Eric N. Berkowitz, Roger A. Kerin, and William Rudelius, *Marketing,* 2nd ed., Homewood, Ill.: Richard D. Irwin, Inc., 1989. This is a textbook about the practical aspects of making products available to buyers in markets and doing so profitably.

David N. Hyman, *Modern Microeconomics: Analysis and Applications,* 2nd ed., Homewood, Ill.: Richard D. Irwin, Inc., 1989. Chapters 3 to 5 consider the theory of market demand in depth. Students interested in more advanced analysis of consumer choices and additional applications will find these chapters useful.

Louise B. Russell, *The Baby Boom Generation and the Economy,* Washington, D.C.: The Brookings Institution, 1982. This is an interesting analysis of the impact of the baby boom generation on market demand.

A Forward Look

In this chapter we've examined the logic of consumer choice to isolate the forces underlying market demand. In the appendix that follows we look at consumer choices in greater depth. In the next chapter we begin an analysis of influences on market supply by examining the business firm as an organization and considering its goals.

8

Indifference Curve Analysis

Indifference curve analysis:
A technique for explaining how choices between two alternatives are made.

Market basket:
A combination of goods and services.

Indifference curve analysis is a technique for explaining choices between two alternatives. The analysis can show how consumers choose one combination of goods and services, called a **market basket,** over another available for consumption over a given period. An advantage of the more sophisticated approach presented in this appendix is that it allows us to explicitly consider the consumer's budget and the tradeoffs involved in making choices.

Indifference Curves

A basic underlying assumption of indifference curve analysis is that consumers can *rank* market baskets. This means they can compile a list of market baskets and order them with the most desired basket ranked first and the least desired basket ranked last. *Of any two market baskets, the consumer is assumed to prefer one to the other or to be indifferent between the two.* When a consumer is *indifferent* between two market baskets, it means that the two provide equal satisfaction and are therefore equally desirable.

Indifference curve:
A graph of various market baskets that provide a consumer with equal utility.

An **indifference curve** is a graph of various market baskets that provide a consumer with equal utility. Recall that utility is an indication of the satisfaction a consumer obtains from any given alternative. The table in Box 1 shows four weekly market baskets of two goods, apples and bananas, among which a consumer is indifferent. In the graph in Box 1, the points corresponding to these market baskets, labeled *I, II, III,* and *IV,* are plotted on a set of axes with the number of apples consumed per week plotted on the horizontal axis and the number of bananas consumed per week plotted on the vertical axis. A smooth curve has been traced through the points.

Different individuals will naturally rank market baskets according to their own tastes. However, economists assume that there are certain characteristics common to all consumer rankings that are reflected in the shape of the indifference curve.

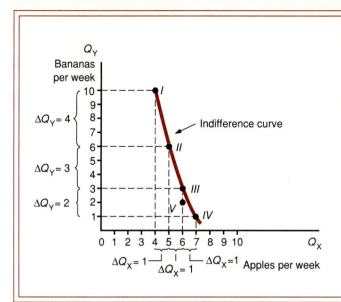

Box 1 An Indifference Curve

The consumer is indifferent among all the market baskets on an indifference curve. The marginal rate of substitution of apples for bananas is the slope of the indifference curve multiplied by minus one. The marginal rate of substitution of apples for bananas declines as apples are actually substituted for bananas each week.

Data for an Indifference Curve

Market basket	Q_Y (bananas per week)	Q_X (apples per week)
I	10	4
II	6	5
III	3	6
V	1	7

Indifference Curves Slope Downward

Indifference curves for any two alternative goods are negatively sloped. This is because it's assumed that consumers prefer more of each good to less of it. If confronted with two different market baskets of apples and bananas, you'll always prefer the one that has more apples, provided each basket has the same number of bananas. Similarly, when confronted with two baskets, each containing apples, you'll naturally prefer one that has more apples to one that has fewer. And, of course, you'll prefer a basket that has more of both apples and bananas to another basket with fewer of both fruits.

To see why this implies negatively sloped indifference curves, imagine you currently have the weekly market basket III. This basket consists of three bananas (the *Y* good) and six apples (the *X* good) per week. If one banana per week were removed from the basket, you'd be made worse off. Thus market basket V in the graph in Box 1, consisting of two bananas and six apples per week, will provide less satisfaction than is provided by market basket III. It therefore can't be on the same indifference curve as market basket III. To return you to the same indifference curve, the reduction in the weekly number of bananas consumed must be offset by the addition of some number of apples.

In general, a reduction in the amount of good *Y*, measured on the vertical axis, by any amount, $-\Delta Q_Y$, from your market basket must be replaced with the addition of a positive amount of good *X*, measured on the horizontal axis, $+\Delta Q_X$, to remain on a given indifference curve. It follows that the slope of indifference curves, $\Delta Q_Y/\Delta Q_X$, will always be negative because its numerator and denominator will always be opposite signs.

The Shape of Indifference Curves: Diminishing Marginal Rate of Substitution

Indifference curves become flatter as the good on the horizontal axis is substituted for the good on the vertical axis while the consumer remains on the same indiffer ence curve. This means you'll give up less and less of the good on the Y axis for each extra unit of X as X is actually substituted for Y while you maintain the same level of utility.

Marginal rate of substitution:
The quantity of one good a consumer would give up to obtain one more unit of another good while being made neither better off nor worse off by the trade.

The **marginal rate of substitution** (MRS_{XY}) of X for Y is the quantity of good Y that a consumer would give up to obtain one more unit of good X while being made neither better off nor worse off by the trade. Giving up more than the amount of Y represented by MRS_{XY} for another unit of X would make you worse off. Giving up less than this amount for another unit of X would make you better off. *The marginal rate of substitution therefore measures the willingness of a consumer to exchange one good for another while neither gaining nor losing utility in the process.* You can think of MRS_{XY} as measuring the marginal benefit of good X in terms of the amount of good Y you're willing to give up in exchange for that unit of X. The curvature of the indifference curve in Box 1 implies that the quantity of bananas (or any other good, Y) you're willing to give up for another unit of apples (or any other good, X) diminishes as more of the X good is substituted for the Y good in your market basket.

To see this, move along the indifference curve illustrated in Box 1. If you neither gain nor lose satisfaction (utility) by giving up some weekly consumption of Y to get additional weekly consumption of X, it follows that you remain on the same indifference curve. Identify as ΔQ_Y the maximum amount of weekly consumption of good Y you'll give up to obtain another unit of good X. The gain in weekly consumption of one unit of X is $\Delta Q_X = 1$. The amount of Y that you'll exchange for a unit of X between any two points along the indifference curve can therefore be written as $\Delta Q_Y / \Delta Q_X$. This is the slope of the indifference curve along which you move by exchanging X for Y. However, the slope of the indifference curve is negative. The marginal rate of substitution is defined as a *positive* amount of Y you're willing to give up for an additional amount of X. It's therefore the slope of the indifference curve multiplied by minus one:

$$MRS_{XY} = -\frac{\Delta Y}{\Delta X}$$

The curvature of the indifference curve illustrated implies diminishing marginal rates of substitution of X for Y. Notice how its slope changes as you substitute the X good for the Y good along the curve. The marginal rate of substitution between points *I* and *II* on the indifference curve illustrated in Box 1 is 4. This means you'll give up 4 units of Y (bananas) to get another unit of X (an apple) when there are 10 bananas and only 4 apples in the market basket.

Suppose instead you have the market basket of goods represented by point *II* (6 bananas and 5 apples). You'd now be willing to give up only 3 bananas in exchange for another apple each week while still remaining on the same indifference curve. The marginal rate of substitution has declined as you moved from market basket I to market basket II because the indifference curve becomes flatter as X is actually substituted for Y along the curve. The convex shape of the indifference curve therefore implies that, as your market basket contains fewer bananas and more apples, the quantity of bananas you're willing to trade for more apples declines. When you have the weekly market basket represented by point *III* in Box 2, you enjoy only 3 bananas each week but would consume 6 apples each week. Under those circumstances, the marginal rate of substitution of apples and bananas would only be 2. You'd be willing to give up only 2 bananas per week to get another apple in the

Box 2 Marginal Rate of Substitution

Market basket	Q_Y	Q_X	MRS_{XY}
I	10	4	4 units of Y per unit of X
II	6	5	3 units of Y per unit of X
III	3	6	2 units of Y per unit of X
IV	1	7	

weekly market basket. The table in Box 2 summarizes the data used to calculate the marginal rates of substitution at various points on the indifference curve.

Diminishing marginal rates of substitution of X for Y constitute an important assumption made about the shapes of indifference curves. As good X is substituted for good Y along the curve, the curve becomes less steep. Individuals differ in their preferences. Differences in preferences imply differences in the amounts of one good they would be willing to exchange for another while neither gaining nor losing satisfaction. However, the marginal rate of substitution of good X for Y will tend to decline as more X is substituted for Y along any consumer's indifference curve.

A look at your own experience might convince you that this assumption is quite reasonable. Suppose you were given a market basket each week consisting only of food. You'd exchange that food for other goods like entertainment and clothing only if you wouldn't be made worse off by the exchange. Isn't it reasonable that at first you'd be willing to exchange fairly large amounts of food to get other items of which you have little? If you're naked but have a lot to eat, you'll give up a fair amount of food to get some clothes on your back. However, as your food stock dwindles and you obtain more of other goods that month, you'll become less willing than before to surrender food to get one more unit of any other good.

Diminishing marginal rates of substitution:
The marginal rates of substitution of good X for Y will tend to decline as more X is substituted for Y along any consumer's indifference curve.

Indifference Maps

The fact that the consumer is assumed to prefer more of any good to less of it can be used to derive additional indifference curves. For example, basket VI, consisting of 10 bananas and 5 apples per week, is preferred to basket I, as shown in the graph in Box 3. This is because basket VI has one more apple per week than basket I and the same number of bananas per week. It's now possible to find those market baskets among which you'd be indifferent when compared to basket VI. This allows us to trace out another indifference curve through point VI, as shown in Box 3.

By the same token, we could draw an indifference curve through point V corresponding to market basket V that consists of 2 bananas and 6 apples per week in Box 3. We could draw an indifference curve through the point corresponding to any given market basket on the graph.

The indifference curves that can be drawn in this way constitute an **indifference map,** which is a way of describing a consumer's preferences. An indifference map for apples and bananas is illustrated in Box 3. Market baskets lying on indifference curves further away from the origin must be preferred to those on curves closer to the origin.

Indifference map:
A way of drawing indifference curves to describe a consumer's preferences.

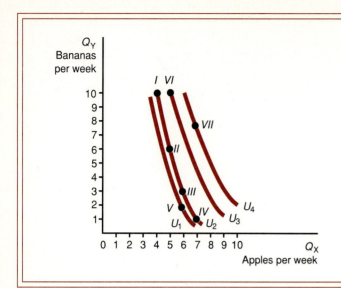

Box 3   An Indifference Map

An indifference map is a way of describing a person's preferences. An indifference curve can be drawn for any market basket on the graph.

Each indifference curve corresponds to a given level of utility. In Box 3 the indifference curves are labeled U_1, U_2, U_3, and U_4, with market baskets on U_4 giving more utility than those on U_3 and market baskets on lower curves providing less utility than those on higher curves. This follows from the assumption that all of us prefer more to less. For example, removing bananas from the market basket labeled *II* must make you worse off if the bananas aren't replaced by some number of apples. This would move you to a lower indifference curve, thus providing you less satisfaction.

Market baskets corresponding to a given quantity of X goods are preferred according to the quantity of Y goods in the basket. Similarly, market baskets with a given quantity of Y are ranked according to the quantity of X in them. Market basket VII is preferred to any market basket on the indifference curve going through *II* because it has more of *both* X and Y than contained in basket II. All market baskets on the indifference curve going through point *VII* are therefore preferred to those on the indifference curve going through *II*.

Indifference Curves Cannot Intersect

Indifference curves cannot intersect. To see why this is so, consider the implications of having two indifference curves intersecting, such as those illustrated in Box 4. Market basket A is at the point of intersection common to both indifference curves. Since market basket A is on indifference curve U_1, it follows that you'll be indifferent between A and B. Similarly, basket C is on curve U_2 along with basket A. Therefore you're indifferent between A and C as well. It must follow that you'll also be indifferent between baskets B and C.

It's easy to see, however, that you'll prefer basket C to basket B. The reason is that basket C corresponds to more of both X and Y than basket B. Reading off the coordinates in the graph in Box 4, you can see that basket C has 3 units of good Y and 6 units of good X, while basket B contains only 5 units of X and 2 units of Y. Since you can't simultaneously prefer C to B and be indifferent between the two, the intersection of the two indifference curves implies a contradiction.

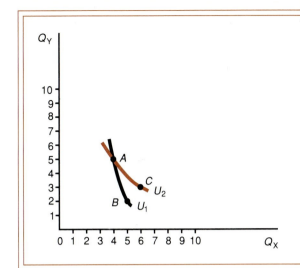

Box 4   Intersecting Indifference Curves Imply a Contradiction

Because basket *A* is on the intersection of indifference curves U_1 and U_2, it follows that the consumer is indifferent among the market baskets represented by *A* and *B* and *C*. But basket *C* has more of both good *X* and good *Y* than basket *B*. It follows that basket *C* must be preferred to basket *B*, which contradicts the result that the consumer is indifferent between baskets *B* and *C*.

The Budget Constraint

A budget tells you how much money you have available to spend in a given period, such as a month. This amount of money is your income. How much that income will buy depends on the prices of the goods and services you want. A consumer's income and its purchasing power define the **budget constraint,** which indicates that income must equal expenditure.

Assume you spend your entire income on goods *X* and *Y*. The sum of your expenditure on good *X* and your expenditure on good *Y* must equal your income. *I* is your income (say per week). P_X is the price of good *X,* and P_Y is the price of good *Y.* The symbol Q_X represents the quantity of good *X* you consume, and Q_Y represents the quantity of good *Y* you consume. It follows that $P_X Q_X$ is the amount you spend on good *X*, while $P_Y Q_Y$ is the amount you spend on good *Y*. The budget constraint may therefore be written as:

$$I = P_X Q_X + P_Y Q_Y$$

or

$$\text{Income} = \text{Expenditure}$$

Budget constraint: As defined by a consumer's income and its purchasing power, indicates that income must equal expenditure.

Suppose you budget $5 per week to spend on fruit. The only fruits you consider for purchase are apples and bananas. Assume that apples can be purchased for $1 each while bananas cost 50¢ each. The table in Box 5 shows the various combinations of apples and bananas you can buy with the $5 of budgeted income per week.

If you spent all of the budgeted $5 on apples, the most apples you could buy per week at a price of $1 would be 5. This is represented by the market basket for which you buy 5 apples and no bananas. At the other extreme is a market basket for which you spend all of the budget on bananas each week and consume no apples. The maximum number of bananas you could buy would be 10 per week when their price is 50¢ each. The table in Box 5 shows 6 possible market baskets of apples and bananas you can purchase with a $5 weekly allowance given the $1 price of apples and the 50¢ price of bananas.

These combinations are graphed in Box 5. The resulting line is called the *budget line,* which shows all those market baskets you can buy if you spend all of your budget on apples and bananas. All market baskets represented by points on or below the line are possible alternatives given your budget. Market baskets represented by points above the line require you to budget more income per week for fruit purchases. For example, the market basket represented by point Z consisting of 8 apples and 4 bananas per week would require a weekly budget of $10 ($8 to buy the apples and another $2 for the bananas). This exceeds your current $5 fruit allowance.

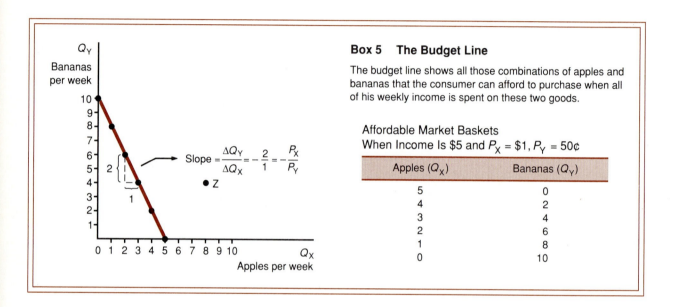

Box 5   The Budget Line

The budget line shows all those combinations of apples and bananas that the consumer can afford to purchase when all of his weekly income is spent on these two goods.

Affordable Market Baskets
When Income Is $5 and $P_X = \$1, P_Y = 50¢$

Apples (Q_X)	Bananas (Q_Y)
5	0
4	2
3	4
2	6
1	8
0	10

Notice that in the table in Box 5, you gain the possibility of consuming 2 bananas for each apple you give up. When you give up the opportunity to consume an apple, you free $1 of your budget. You can then use this amount to buy 2 bananas. The number of extra bananas you can buy each time you give up 1 apple is the price of apples divided by the price of bananas ($1/$0.50 = 2).

In general, the extra amount of good Y you can purchase by sacrificing a unit of good X depends on the relationship between the price of X and the price of Y. By giving up one unit of X you'll be able to purchase P_X/P_Y units of Y. This represents the extra Y you can add to your market basket for each unit of X you remove, which is the slope of the budget line ($\Delta Q_Y/\Delta Q_X$) multiplied by minus one. Since the budget line is linear, it will have the same slope at all points. You must always give up some of one good to gain the possibility of adding more of the other good to your market basket.

Because the slope of the budget line is $\Delta Q_Y/\Delta Q_X$, it follows that:

$$-\frac{\Delta Q_Y}{\Delta Q_X} = \frac{P_X}{P_Y}$$

Also note that your income can be expressed in terms of either apples or bananas. If you chose to spend your entire $5 weekly fruit allowance on apples, the number you could buy would be $I/P_X = \$5/\$1 = 5$. Expressing income in terms of

APPENDIX Indifference Curve Analysis

the maximum number of apples that money income would purchase is a way of measuring your *real* (as opposed to money) income. Similarly, your real income in terms of bananas is $I/P_Y = \$5/\$0.50 = 10$.

Consumer Equilibrium

As a consumer, you're assumed to choose the quantities of X and Y that maximize your utility given your budget constraint. The economic variables the model seeks to explain are the quantities of goods X and Y you choose to buy over a given period.

In Box 6 a typical consumer's indifference map is superimposed on the same set of axes as that consumer's budget line. Let's say you're this typical consumer. We can now use the model to determine your choice of weekly consumption of apples and bananas. The quantities chosen represent your equilibrium market basket. We can view this equilibrium basket as maximizing your utility level subject to the constraint that you can spend no more than the available income per time period. This gives your most preferred weekly purchases of goods X and Y given your income and the prices of X and Y.

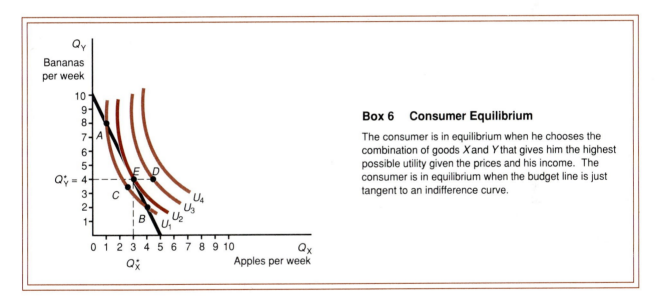

Box 6   Consumer Equilibrium

The consumer is in equilibrium when he chooses the combination of goods X and Y that gives him the highest possible utility given the prices and his income. The consumer is in equilibrium when the budget line is just tangent to an indifference curve.

Look first at a point like A corresponding to a market basket of one unit of good X (apples) and eight units of good Y (bananas) per week. This basket of goods gives you a utility level of U_1. Similarly, the market basket corresponding to point B where $Q_X = 4$ and $Q_Y = 2$ also gives you a utility level of U_1.

But neither point A nor point B can be an equilibrium. By moving along the budget line from A to the market basket represented by point E, you can increase your utility by moving to higher indifference curves. You do this by substituting good X for good Y in your weekly market basket. Keep in mind that even though they haven't been drawn, there's an indifference curve going through each and every point on the budget line. Similarly, by moving toward point E from point B, you become better off.

A market basket corresponding to a point, like C, inside the space below the budget line and the axes provides you with lower levels of utility than the equilibrium market basket at point E. This is because market baskets like the one at point C must lie on lower indifference curves than the one going through E. Market baskets corresponding to points above the budget line, like the one represented by point D, provide more utility than is provided by the market basket corresponding to point E. However, the former are unaffordable because they require more income than your budget permits.

You achieve the maximum utility from your budget when you consume the combination of goods corresponding to the point where the budget line touches the highest possible indifference curve. The combination of goods X and Y corresponding to this market basket, $Q_X^* = 3$, $Q_Y^* = 4$, is your equilibrium market basket of goods. No other combination will give you more utility or satisfaction given your available income. The *consumer equilibrium* represents that combination of goods purchased that maximizes utility subject to the budget constraint.

Geometrically, the equilibrium can be described as that combination of goods corresponding to the point at which the budget line is just tangent to the highest attainable indifference curve in the consumer's indifference map. At that point the slope of the budget line is just equal to the slope of an indifference curve. The slope of the budget line is $-P_X/P_Y$. The slope of the indifference curve at any point is the marginal rate of substitution of X for Y multiplied by minus one. The equilibrium condition can therefore be written as:

$$\frac{-P_X}{P_Y} = -MRS_{XY}$$

or

$$\frac{P_X}{P_Y} = MRS_{XY}$$

This condition, when achieved, implies that the consumer is maximizing utility subject to the budget constraint.

Marginal Utility Analysis of Consumer Choices

It's possible to relate the marginal rate of substitution along an indifference curve to marginal utilities of the goods on each axis. Removing ΔQ_Y units of Y from your market basket makes you worse off. The loss of utility is $\Delta Q_Y MU_Y$ where MU_Y is the marginal utility of Y to you. Replace this lost Y with enough X added to your market basket to make you just as well off as you were previously. The gain in utility would be $\Delta Q_X MU_X$ where MU_X is the marginal utility of the added X. If you are to return to the same indifference curve, the gain in utility from the added X must exactly equal the loss in utility from the Y removed from the market basket:

$$\Delta Q_X MU_X = -\Delta Q_Y MU_Y$$

Therefore

$$\frac{-\Delta Q_Y}{Q_X} = \frac{MU_X}{MU_Y} = MRS_{XY}$$

The marginal rate of substitution of X and Y can therefore be thought of as the ratio of the marginal utility of X to the marginal utility of Y. This also implies that:

$$MRS_{XY} = \frac{MU_X}{MU_Y} = \frac{P_X}{P_Y}$$

or

$$\frac{MU_X}{P_X} = \frac{MU_Y}{P_Y}$$

This says that a consumer who maximizes utility buys goods so that the marginal utilities per dollar are equal. This is the *equimarginal principle* for consumer purchases, which was discussed in Chapter 8. Both the marginal utility and the indifference curve approaches therefore reach the same conclusion about the purchases of a utility-maximizing consumer. However, the indifference curve approach doesn't need to assume that utility is measurable.

Using Indifference Curves

How Changes in Income Affect Consumer Choices

Given your preferences, as represented by the shapes of indifference curves in your indifference map, a change in your income will affect your equilibrium market basket. An increase in income allows you to buy market baskets of goods that you previously couldn't afford. It therefore shifts the budget line outward, as shown in Box 7. Note that the slope of the budget line doesn't change. The slope of the budget

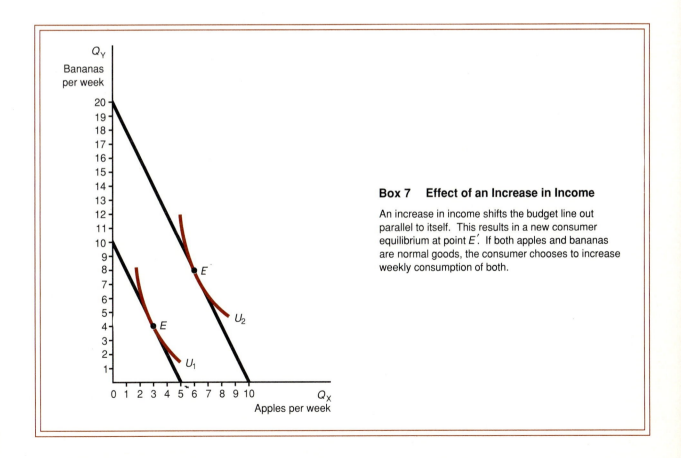

Box 7   Effect of an Increase in Income

An increase in income shifts the budget line out parallel to itself. This results in a new consumer equilibrium at point E'. If both apples and bananas are normal goods, the consumer chooses to increase weekly consumption of both.

line depends only on the prices of the goods you consume and is independent of your income. An increase in income shifts the budget line out parallel to itself. Similarly, a decrease in income will result in an inward shift of the budget line.

Referring to the table in Box 5, suppose your fruit budget were to double from $5 to $10 per week. The number of bananas and apples you could buy in each market basket would also double, provided there was no change in their prices. As long as prices are constant, an increase in money income is equivalent to an increase in purchasing power. Similarly, a cut in your budget would reduce the quantities of goods you could consume. You should also note that the budget line would shift out parallel to itself if your money income were constant but the prices of goods X and Y fell by the same proportion. For example, if the prices of both apples and bananas in Box 5 were cut in half, the effect on your consumption options would be exactly the same as if your money income were to double.

The graph in Box 7 shows the possible impact of an increase in your income on your consumption of apples and bananas. As the budget line shifts out, the original equilibrium at point E no longer gives you the greatest possible satisfaction *given your new higher level of income*. The new equilibrium corresponds to point E', at which you choose to buy more apples and bananas each week. This means that both apples and bananas are normal goods for you.

The graph in Box 8 shows how you would react if apples were an inferior good. Under these circumstances the new equilibrium at point E' corresponds to a market basket for which you choose *fewer* apples.

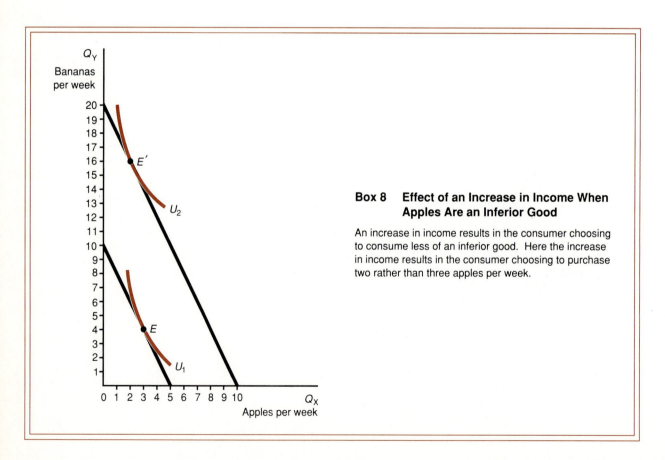

Box 8   Effect of an Increase in Income When Apples Are an Inferior Good

An increase in income results in the consumer choosing to consume less of an inferior good. Here the increase in income results in the consumer choosing to purchase two rather than three apples per week.

How Changes in Relative Prices Affect Consumer Choices

A change in the price of apples relative to bananas will change the slope of the budget line. This is because the slope of the budget line is, as we have seen, the ratio of the price of apples to the price of bananas. Suppose the price of apples declines. This will rotate the budget line along the horizontal axis without changing its intercept on the vertical axis, as shown in **A** in Box 9. If you were to spend all your income on apples, you'd be able to buy more at the lower price. The intercept on the vertical axis remains unchanged, provided the price of bananas doesn't change. Similarly, a decrease in the price of bananas, assuming no change in the price of apples, will shift the intercept on the vertical axis upward by rotating the budget line upward as shown in **B** in Box 9. An increase in the price of bananas, other things being equal, will shift the intercept of the budget line and the vertical axis downward.

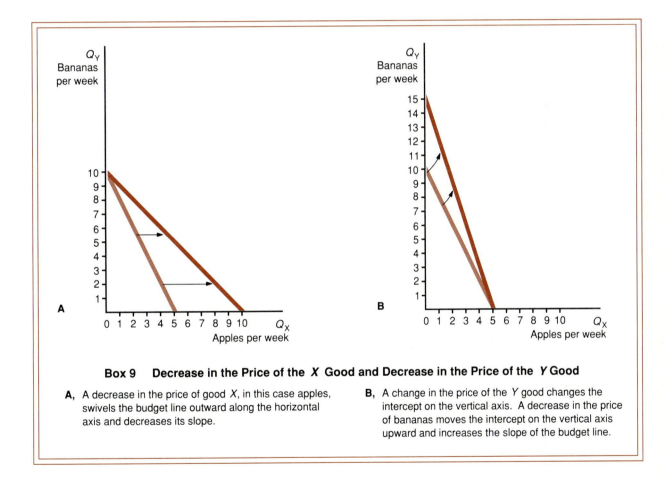

Box 9   Decrease in the Price of the *X* Good and Decrease in the Price of the *Y* Good

A, A decrease in the price of good *X*, in this case apples, swivels the budget line outward along the horizontal axis and decreases its slope.

B, A change in the price of the *Y* good changes the intercept on the vertical axis. A decrease in the price of bananas moves the intercept on the vertical axis upward and increases the slope of the budget line.

A change in the price of any good affects your equilibrium market basket. For example, if the price of apples were to fall, thereby rotating your budget line outward as shown in Box 10, the initial equilibrium at *E* would no longer provide you the greatest possible satisfaction. Instead you'd be induced to move to point *E'*, at which the *new budget line* is just tangent to a higher indifference curve. The lower

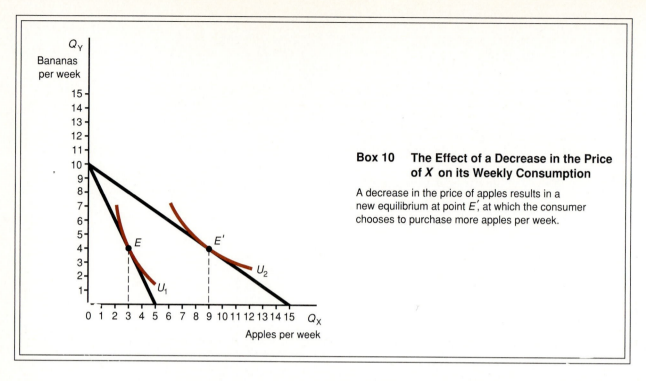

Box 10   The Effect of a Decrease in the Price of X on its Weekly Consumption

A decrease in the price of apples results in a new equilibrium at point E', at which the consumer chooses to purchase more apples per week.

price allows you to enjoy market baskets that weren't possible at the higher price; and by consuming more apples per week, you increase your weekly satisfaction.

Deriving the Demand Curve

We can easily derive a demand curve for a good from indifference curve analysis. A demand curve gives a relationship between price and quantity demanded *given* the prices of other goods, the consumer's income, and the consumer's preferences. To derive your demand curve, allow the price of the good on the horizontal axis, apples, to fall while the prices of all other goods, including that of bananas, are held fixed. Also assume that your income is fixed and your preferences, as reflected by your indifference curves, are known.

Initially, as shown in **A** in Box 11, you're in equilibrium at point E_1 and choose to consume 3 apples per week. *This is the quantity demanded at the initial price, say P_1, per apple.* The price, P_1, is plotted on the vertical axis of **B** in Box 11. The corresponding quantity demanded, 3, is plotted on the horizontal axis.

Now assume the price of apples falls to P_2 and nothing else changes. The reduction in price shifts your equilibrium point from E_1 to E_2. The new quantity demanded is 5. The quantity demanded increases as the price falls, as is consistent with the law of demand. Similarly, if price were to fall to a still lower level, P_3, the budget line would swivel out still further. The new equilibrium would be at point E_3, at which quantity demanded increases again to 8.

In Box 11, **B** plots the coordinates of each quantity and price pair and traces a curve through them to draw the demand curve. *The law of demand is therefore consistent with a model in which consumers maximize satisfaction from their budget and in which the marginal rate of substitution of any one good for another decreases as more of the first good is consumed.*

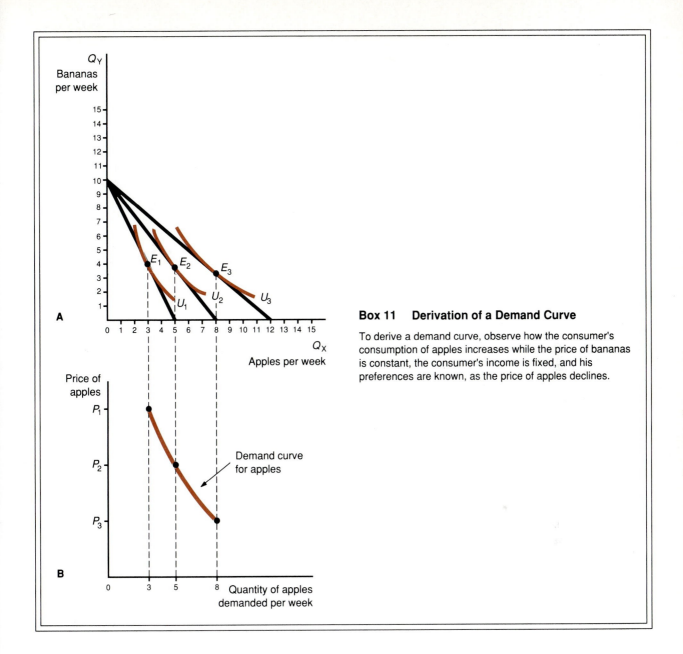

Box 11   Derivation of a Demand Curve

To derive a demand curve, observe how the consumer's consumption of apples increases while the price of bananas is constant, the consumer's income is fixed, and his preferences are known, as the price of apples declines.

Key Terms and Concepts

Indifference curve analysis
Market basket
Indifference curve
Marginal rate of substitution

Diminishing marginal rates of substitution
Indifference map
Budget constraint

The Business Firm: A Prologue to the Theory of Market Supply

Do you work part-time or have a summer job? If so, you know you don't work just for the fun of it. You may enjoy your job, and it may be giving you the opportunity to learn skills that will be valuable to you in your post-college career. But whether you need your income for college expenses or are working to provide yourself with extras, as a rational person your primary objective in working is to earn income.

By the same token, business firms don't make goods and services available in markets for the pleasure of doing good deeds. Instead, their purpose is to earn income for their owners. Like your personal goals, the goals of a business firm can be multifaceted. However, much of economic theory about the behavior of business firms assumes that their primary goal is to make profits—just as your primary goal as a rational consumer is to maximize your satisfaction.

In their quest for profits, owners of business firms often face many competitors. Just think how many different companies manufacture jeans, cassette tapes, and hair-care products! The opportunities a firm has to make profits depend on the demand for its product, its competition, and its cost of making products available. In this chapter we examine the characteristics of business firms and the way profit is measured. We discuss the functions of the business firm and its organization, and we consider the simplifications necessary to construct a model that explains the firm's behavior. From a practical standpoint we also look at the advantages and disadvantages of different forms of business organization.

1 Explain the functions of business firms and how various aspects of production and distribution are integrated within a single firm.
2 Outline the advantages of alternative forms of business organization: the sole proprietorship, the partnership, and the corporation.
3 Describe a simplified view of the business firm that is useful in constructing a model that explains market supply.
4 Show how the concept of opportunity cost must be applied to accurately measure the profit of a business firm.

The Business Firm

A **business firm** is an organization under one management set up for the purpose of earning profits for its owners by making one or more items available for sale in markets. The terms *firm, business,* and *enterprise* are often used interchangeably to mean the same thing.

In the early 1980s there were over 17 million business firms operating in the United States. Firms operate out of one or more **plants,** which are physical structures or locations at which a firm's owners or employees conduct business. In the case of a manufacturing firm like General Motors, the plant is one or more factories. For a restaurant like Taco Bell, the plant is the structure in which employees produce and serve meals to customers. A farmer operates an agricultural firm, and the plant is the location or locations at which the farmer has fields, barns, tractors, and other equipment.

Some firms operate many similar or identical plants: A & P Supermarkets, J.C. Penney, and Western Auto. Some large firms operate different plants for various stages of production. For example, your supermarket might own a dairy and a bakery and sell their products in its stores. A firm producing petroleum products, such as gasoline and lubricants, might own oil wells and supertankers. The term used to describe the ownership of plants used in various stages of its production by a single firm is **vertical integration.** These firms operate different kinds of plants to provide themselves with raw materials, parts, and services they need to produce their final product. Finally, many modern business firms operate plants that produce very different kinds of goods. For example, CBS produces television programming, makes records, and has other operating subsidiaries. A firm operating plants that produce many different kinds of goods and services is called a **conglomerate.**

Industries

An **industry** is a group of firms that sell a similar product in a market: for example, cars, soybeans, lead, cigarettes, and construction.

However, drawing neat industry lines isn't always easy. For example, should business firms that specialize in producing athletic footwear be placed in the same industry as firms that specialize in producing leather shoes? Should fast-food restaurants be placed in the same industry as full-service luxury restaurants serving

Business firm:
An organization under one management set up for the purpose of earning profits for its owners by making one or more items available for sale in markets.

Plant:
A physical structure in which a firm's owners or employees conduct business.

Vertical integration:
A term used to describe a firm that owns plants used in various stages of its production.

Conglomerate:
A firm operating plants that produce many different kinds of goods and services.

Industry:
A group of firms selling a similar product in a market.

gourmet dishes and fine wines? Defining a group of firms as an industry requires arbitrary judgments.

Corporate vs. Noncorporate Firms

Sole proprietorship:
A business owned by one person.

Just as these are different types of industries, there are different forms of business organization. The most basic type of business enterprise is the **sole proprietorship,** which is a business owned by one person. Not all sole proprietorships are small; some are large firms with many employees and hired managers.

The sole proprietorship is by far the most popular form of business organization in the United States, accounting for about 70% of all business firms in the country in the early 1980s. The number of sole proprietorships in the United States ranges from 10 million to 13 million. Nonetheless, numbers can be misleading. Although about 70% of all firms in the United States are sole proprietorships, they account for less than 6% of the sales revenue of all business firms. This is because, on average, proprietorships are smaller than other types of firms, such as corporations.

Partnership:
A business owned by two or more persons, each of whom receives a portion of any profits.

A **partnership** is a business owned by two or more persons, each of whom receives a portion of any profits. Sometimes one of the persons is actually an organization, such as a corporation or an estate. Partnerships allow two or more persons to pool their resources. Because more than one person is involved, a partnership has more opportunity to expand than a sole proprietorship, where one person is responsible for raising money and assumes all the risks of the enterprise. However, partnerships are the least popular form of business organization in the United States, accounting for approximately 10% of all firms and less than 4% of annual sales revenue in the early 1980s.

In both sole proprietorships and partnerships, the owners are personally liable for the firm's debts and for any judgments imposed by a court of law. There's no limit to these owners' liability, and both their personal and business assets are exposed to it.

Corporation:
A business that is legally established under state laws that grant it an identity separate from its owners.

The alternative to sole proprietorships and partnerships is the corporation. A **corporation** is a business that is legally established under state laws that grant it an identity separate from its owners. A corporation is a *legal fiction*. This is a term used by lawyers to describe a preposterous or impossible state of affairs that everyone accepts. From a legal standpoint a corporation *is* a person. By incorporating, owners of the firm create an organization that can legally own property, incur debts, and is otherwise granted many of the legal rights of a citizen, including the right to engage in litigation. Any group of people can form a corporation by obtaining a corporate charter from one of the 50 states. This requires paying a fee and filing the appropriate forms.

In the early 1980s there were nearly 3 million active corporations conducting business in the United States. Although these corporations represented less than 20% of all firms in the nation, they accounted for 90% of the total sales revenue of all U.S. firms.

The bar graphs in Box 1 show how U.S. businesses were organized in 1983. In **A** you can see the breakdown by number of firms, while **B** shows the breakdown by percentage of annual sales revenue.

The form of organization can affect the cost of running a business and therefore influence its profits. To understand why the corporate form might be preferable to other forms of business organization, we'll need to analyze the impact of incorporation on the costs of production and transactions.

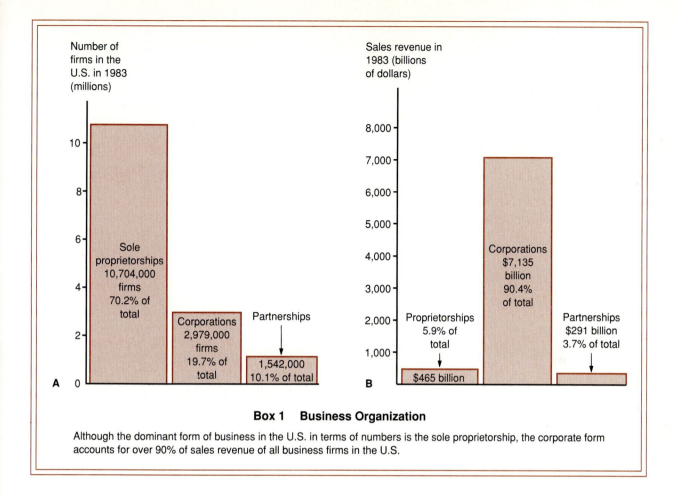

Box 1   Business Organization

Although the dominant form of business in the U.S. in terms of numbers is the sole proprietorship, the corporate form accounts for over 90% of sales revenue of all business firms in the U.S.

The Corporate Form of Business

The corporate form of business has a number of distinct characteristics that set it apart from sole proprietorships and partnerships. The distinctive features of the corporation are:

1. *The corporation is owned entirely by its stockholders, who have purchased shares of ownership in the corporation.* These shares are called *stocks.* For example, suppose a corporation has 10,000 shares of stock. If you own 1,000 shares, your share of ownership in the corporation would be 10%. Stockholders, as the owners of the corporation, have certain rights. They can vote for the directors of the corporation, who manage it, and on other issues. The number of votes a stockholder can cast depends on the number of shares owned.

2. *As owners of shares of a corporation, stockholders are entitled to a share of the corporation's income.* The portion of any profits earned by a corporation paid to its stockholders is called **dividends.** Dividends are paid to stockholders on a per-share basis. The corporation typically retains a portion of its profits as a source of funds to make investments and expand the corporation's capacity to earn income. The portion of corporate profits not paid out as dividends is called **retained earnings**

Dividend:
The portion of a corporation's profit paid to its stockholders.

Retained earnings:
The portion of corporate profits not paid out as dividends.

A corporation isn't required to pay dividends each year and always has the option of retaining all of its earnings.

3. *Stockholders cannot be held personally liable for the debts of the corporation.* **Limited liability** is a legal provision that protects the owners of a corporation (its stockholders) by putting a ceiling equal to the purchase price of their stock on their liability for debts of the corporation. If a corporation goes bankrupt, no stockholder can lose any more than he or she has invested in the firm.

Limited liability:
A legal provision that protects the owners of a corporation (its stockholders) by putting a ceiling equal to the purchase price of their stock on their liability for debts of the corporation.

Limited liability is an advantage that reduces the risk of investing in a corporation and makes it easier for such firms to raise large sums of money. This advantage isn't available to owners of sole proprietorships and partnerships, who place their personal assets (such as their homes) at stake when they start a business.

4. *Everyone who works for a corporation is an employee.* The concept of the owner-operator isn't applicable to a corporation. Everyone, from the president down to the janitors, is on the corporation's payroll. The ownership and management of the corporation are clearly separate. This isn't always the case in sole proprietorships and partnerships, where it's common for the owners to act as managers without actually receiving a salary. As owner-operators, they earn profits if they are successful.

The officers, directors, and managers of a corporation serve at the pleasure of the stockholders. They can be—and sometimes are—voted out of a job. Typically executives own some stock in the corporation, but this is usually a small percentage. The existence of many stockholders makes it difficult for any single stockholder to control the firm's day-to-day management decisions. It sometimes happens that there's a conflict between the interests of the corporation's officers and its stockholders.

Corporate vs. Noncorporate Business: Pros and Cons

Most big businesses in the United States are corporations. Although sole proprietorships outnumber corporations by about four to one, corporate business revenues in a typical year exceed the revenues of sole proprietorships by about 10 times! Big business is corporate business. How can we explain the popularity of the corporate form of business?

There are both pros and cons to organizing a business as a corporation. For large firms, the pros often outweigh the cons. The opposite is frequently true of small firms.

The pros:
1. *The corporate form of business allows the firm to issue both stocks and bonds as a means of raising revenue.* Remember, the corporation has many of the rights of an individual citizen. It can borrow in its own name rather than in the names of its owners. Corporations can borrow directly from banks or issue corporate bonds to be sold to investors. (A bond is a promise by a corporation to pay the bondholder a certain amount of money by a specified future date and obligates the corporation to pay interest to the bondholder.) In addition, the corporation can obtain funds to finance its operations and expansion by selling more stock. By issuing stocks and bonds, the corporation has a way to obtain large sums of money that a noncorporate firm would have difficulty raising.
2. *The owners of the corporation, its stockholders, have limited liability.* Because they risk no more than the funds they invest in the corporation, they're more willing to supply those funds. Once again, this helps the corporation raise the large sums

Principles in Practice

Modern Corporations and Their Chief Executive Officers

How many billions make a big corporation? How big are the bucks earned by the people who run the top firms? And, perhaps most important to you, what college majors did these business leaders choose?

Each year *Fortune* magazine compiles a list of the largest U.S. industrial corporations. Firms are ranked according to their annual sales revenue. In 1986 the largest corporation in the United States based on annual sales revenue was General Motors, which took in revenue of more than $100 billion that year. The second biggest corporation in terms of sales was Exxon, which had sales worth nearly $70 billion that year. The table shows the top 10 industrial corporations in the Fortune 500 ranked according to 1986 revenue. Also shown are their 1986 profits as a percentage of sales revenue.

The people who exercise leadership of large corporations are called *chief executive officers* (CEOs). *Fortune* magazine conducted a survey of chief executive officers of the Fortune 500 largest industrial and 500 largest service companies in 1985.* The average age of a CEO in 1985 based on responses to the *Fortune* survey was 58. Chief executive officers in the major industrial companies are very well compensated. The CEOs of the top 100 industrial companies earned median compensation of $931,000 in 1985. Their compensation is an amalgam of salary, bonuses, and profit sharing. In 1985 Lee Iacocca, chairman of the Chrysler Corporation, received compensation estimated to be worth $11.4 million!

These handsome rewards usually require far more than the standard 40-hour work week. Nearly half of the CEOs responding to the survey said they put in a work week of 55 to 64 hours. Another 22.3% of the respondents said they worked over 65 hours per week.

The modern CEO is better educated than those of the past. In the *Fortune* survey, nearly one third of CEOs had master's degrees and about 12% had Ph.D. degrees. Nearly all of those responding had at least a bachelor's degree. Education ranked high among concerns of the CEO, as shown by the fact that over 40% of them wished they had received *more* academic training.

One third of the CEOs majored in business as undergraduates, while about one quarter were engineering majors. Economics was the third most often listed undergraduate major for the group, accounting for about 17.5% of those responding, while humanities was the major of another 15.3%. Business, law, and engineering were the dominant fields of graduate study. Over half of the CEOs listed business as their main field of graduate study. About 21% studied law, while about 11% studied engineering.

Profit is the key goal of the chief executives in the survey. When asked to list their goals, 36.7% of the CEOs listed as their key goal maintaining or improving profits of the company. The profit goal outranked all other objectives. The runner-up to profit as an objective was company growth, which is probably related to long-term profits.

Top 10 Industrial Corporations in the Fortune 500, 1986

Company	Sales revenue (billions of dollars)	Profit as a percentage of sales revenue
General Motors	102.8	2.9
Exxon	69.9	7.7
Ford Motor	62.7	5.2
IBM	51.3	9.3
Mobil	44.9	3.1
General Electric	35.2	7.1
AT&T	34.1	0.4
Texaco	31.6	2.3
E.I. du Pont de Nemours	27.1	5.7
Chevron	24.4	2.9

*Maggie McComas, "Atop the Fortune 500: A Survey of the C.E.O.s," *Fortune*, April 28, 1986, pp. 26-31.

of money it needs to expand. Owners of noncorporate businesses have unlimited liability for debts because their *personal* as well as business assets are at risk.

3. *It's relatively easy for stockholders to sell their rights of ownership.* Corporate stocks are sold in the stock market. This gives investors in a corporation more flexibility than is enjoyed by investors in sole proprietorships and partnerships.

The cons:

1. *The separation of owners from managers in the corporate structure has the potential for conflicts of interest between these two groups.* Sometimes managers of a corporation try to protect their jobs at the expense of stockholders' profits. Of course, this can be a problem for a sole proprietorship or partnership if an absentee owner hires a manager to run the business. However, the larger number of owners in a corporation increases the costs associated with remedying such conflict.

2. *In the United States, the corporation is subject to a separate income tax.* The corporate income tax subjects profits earned by corporations to double taxation. Profits are taxed annually as they're earned by the corporation. Then the portion of profits paid out as dividends is taxable as personal income to stockholders. In addition, when stockholders sell their shares, they pay a tax on the difference between the selling price and the purchase price.

Do the Pros Outweigh the Cons?

The major advantage of the corporate form of business over the noncorporate form is its ability to raise funds. To conduct its business and grow, a large firm needs a way to raise large sums of money. The costs and risks of raising money are greatly reduced by incorporation. It's for this reason that the corporation is the dominant form of business enterprise for large firms. This also explains the fact that large corporations dominate business in the United States, employing about 25% of the labor force and accounting for nearly 90% of business revenue.

Concept Check

1   What is an industry?

2   What are the major differences between corporate and noncorporate business firms?

3   How would you decide whether or not to incorporate a business that is currently a sole proprietorship?

The Functions of Business Firms

Whether they make microwave pizzas or space shuttles, all firms are first organizations of *people*. As such, they must make daily decisions about how to deal with other firms that supply them with goods and services and with workers they hire. They must also decide how to market their products.

Production of Goods and Services to Be Sold

Manager:
A person who coordinates decisions within a firm.

A **manager** is a person who coordinates decisions *within* a firm. Managers make decisions about methods of producing goods and services. They also help decide *what* and *how much* to produce and how the firm will adapt to change and new technology. The firm's managers and owners hire workers and assign them various tasks. The managers must also decide which tasks to have the firm's workers perform and which tasks to fulfill by purchase (or contract) with other firms. For example, as the manager of a restaurant you can buy equipment and hire workers to launder tablecloths, napkins, and uniforms. Alternatively, you can send these items out to a laundry.

Assignment of Tasks to Workers vs. Contracting with Other Firms: Determining the Degree of Vertical Integration

A fully *vertically integrated firm* doesn't purchase the goods or services of any other firms in the process of making its products available to consumers. Such a firm supplies itself with materials, parts, and all other services. A fully vertically integrated firm is a rarity. Managers of most firms find it cheaper to rely on specialized firms for at least some materials and services.

A key factor in determining the degree of vertical integration of a firm is the transaction costs involved in contracting with other firms to provide services needed for the production or marketing of the firm's output. Firms try to keep their transaction costs, as well as production costs, as low as possible to earn a higher profit. Managers are always looking for ways to lower the costs of operating the firm. For example, a department store manager can hire and train workers as security guards. Alternatively, she can obtain guard services under contract with a specialized firm. To a great extent she'll base her choice on the costs of these two methods.

It stands to reason that a firm's own employees perform some tasks more reliably, more conveniently, and, most important, at lower cost than outsiders. This is why there's at least some degree of vertical integration within firms. However, conditions change over time, and both managers and stockholders are always on the alert for ways to increase profits by reducing costs and possibly by providing new services to other firms.

When a firm is vertically integrated, it has within its organization divisions that perform the same functions as independent businesses existing elsewhere in the economy. There are a number of reasons why a firm may choose to integrate operations that could be performed by or purchased from other firms:

1. To ensure a reliable flow of materials and services as inputs. By controlling its own production, a manufacturer can reduce or eliminate delays that might prevent it from shipping its orders on time. Of course, each firm has to calculate whether integration of such an operation within the firm actually does reduce uncertainties in input supply.
2. To put rival firms at a disadvantage by controlling a key input. For example, if an aluminum manufacturer acquires all the bauxite mines that exist, it gains control of a key input into the production of aluminum. Control of this input could prevent rival firms from producing the good.
3. To improve communication in ways that might reduce costs or improve the quality of output. Many managers believe that integrating their advertising operations rather than purchasing services from another firm results in higher-quality advertising. This is because the firm can keep its own advertising people informed about the development of new products at a lower cost than would be possible if the firm used an outside advertising agency.
4. To adapt more easily to changing technology. Changes in the technology of producing parts and components can have a significant effect on the way a firm assembles its output. By constantly communicating with an integrated division

Principles in Practice

Vertical Integration and Business Profits

Vertical integration of production processes can contribute to increased business profits by reducing transaction costs. Many factory production operations involve movement of unfinished goods through various stages until the final product is ready for shipment. Vertical integration of the stages of production within a single business firm can reduce transportation and storage costs for materials and ensure a steady supply of these inputs.

For example, ownership of bauxite deposits and construction of plants to refine the bauxite to obtain aluminum at the same site enable a firm to reduce its transaction costs. A refinery designed to produce aluminum must be constructed to meet the particular characteristics of the bauxite from which the aluminum will be extracted. In addition, bauxite deposits are widely scattered and the material itself is very expensive to transport. Aluminum producers can therefore economize on both refinery costs and transportation costs by vertically integrating bauxite mining with their refining and smelting operations. They can build a plant designed specifically for the type of bauxite they mine themselves at the site. This way they avoid the need to transport bauxite to refineries located elsewhere, and they're assured the use of a particular type of bauxite. The storage costs of bauxite are also reduced by mining directly at the same site as the refining plant.*

The Toyota Motor Corporation of Japan has developed a unique way of accomplishing the goals of vertical integration of the production process for the passenger automobile. The company is able to lower transaction costs without actually establishing divisions in the company. The company does buy raw materials such as plastics and steel from other firms. It also buys tires, batteries, and other car components. The company builds engines and body components, and assembles as well as paints the final product within the firm.

However, many key components such as piston pins, castings, transmissions, and other items designed specifically for cars are obtained from about 230 specialized companies that have a unique relationship with Toyota. The 230 companies are called the *Kyohokai,* which means "Toyota Cooperation Association." About 60% of Toyota's outlay for materials and parts is accounted for by purchases from these companies. Directors of Toyota usually serve as directors of the *Kyohokai* companies, and Toyota usually owns a good proportion of the corporate stock of these suppliers.

Although Toyota deals with companies other than those in the *Kyohokai,* its unique relationship with these companies allows it to coordinate planning and other considerations to reduce transaction costs. It also helps Toyota achieve the goals of its *Kan-ban* system (see Chapter 3) so as to reduce inventory storage costs. The detailed planning with its affiliated companies allows Toyota to synchronize delivery of supplies and get car components from affiliated companies "just in time." This system of quasi-vertical integration through control and planning, rather than full ownership of suppliers, has significantly reduced costs for the company.†

Of course, vertical integration of various stages of production isn't always successful in increasing profits. In many cases companies give up the advantages of specialization and large-scale production when they try to become their own suppliers. Before a firm can assess the impact of vertical integration on profits, it must carefully weigh the gains from lower transaction costs against possible increases in costs from these diseconomies.

*See Oliver E. Williamson, *The Economic Institutions of Capitalism,* New York: The Free Press, 1985, pp. 118-119.
†See Toyohiro Kono, *Strategy & Structure of Japanese Enterprises,* Armonk, N.Y.: M.E. Sharpe, Inc., 1984, pp. 125-128.

supplying materials, the firm's managers might more easily keep abreast of these changes.

What's the most desirable degree of vertical integration for a firm? It boils down to a question of cost and quality of product. The advantages of vertical integration are likely to differ from industry to industry and from firm to firm. It's not unusual to see firms with varying degrees of vertical integration competing with one another in the same industry. When deciding whether to deal with other firms or establish internal divisions in the firm to make inputs available, owners and managers consider the costs of searching for the best price, negotiating contracts with suppliers, taking on risks associated with contractual arrangements, and other transaction costs.

The Division of Labor and Personnel Management

Managers must determine the appropriate division of labor and assignment of specialized tasks to workers. They must also check to make sure that workers actually accomplish their assigned tasks. In modern industrial firms there's a complex division of labor. A worker rarely completes a product alone. Instead, firms use mass production techniques that involve many workers doing separate tasks and operating as a team.

Personnel management is the process by which managers monitor worker performance and provide rewards for workers who perform efficiently. Good managers choose productive workers and motivate them to perform up to their potential. Good personnel management procedures ensure the maximum possible output per worker over any given period. For example, Japanese personnel management techniques, including lifetime employment, have been very effective in motivating Japanese workers to perform in ways that keep production going and costs low. Policies that don't motivate workers to advance or that result in high absenteeism can substantially increase costs of production and make it difficult for a firm to compete with its rivals. Offering incentives for advancement, providing on-the-job training, and rewarding productive workers for their efforts ultimately can result in greater profits for the firm's owners.

Personnel management:
The process by which managers monitor worker performance and provide rewards for workers who perform efficiently.

Some Simplifications

It's clear from the preceding analysis that the organization and functions of the modern business firm are multifaceted and complex. To analyze the behavior of business firms, we need to make a number of simplifications so we can concentrate on the essential features of a firm's activities. The economic model of the firm we'll develop in detail in the next two chapters involves quite a bit of abstraction from reality. The simplified firm of economic theory is one that produces only one product and seeks to maximize profits.

In reality, the modern business firm produces more than one product. For example, a pharmaceuticals company might have thousands of *product lines*. In addition to prescription and over-the-counter drugs, it might produce cosmetics, perfume, and toothbrushes. A **multiproduct firm** is one that produces several different items for sale in markets. An important problem faced by the management of a multiproduct firm is the allocation of scarce productive resources among the various product lines.

Multiproduct firm:
A firm that produces several different items for sale in markets.

The economic model of the firm that we'll use in the chapters to follow is based on a **single-product firm** that produces only one type of item for sale in markets. By analyzing the operations of a single-product firm, we can understand most of the important managerial decisions relating to production, resource use, and profits.

Single-product firm:
A firm that produces only one type of item for sale in markets.

Profit is the difference between the revenue a firm takes in over any given period and the costs incurred in operating the firm over the same period. To explain how firms supply products and hire inputs, the behavioral assumption usually made is that firms seek to maximize profits. Of course, it's possible that the owners or managers have other goals as well. They could be concerned about the firm's image, its sales, or the price of its stock and the dividends it pays to stockholders. Managers might be concerned about their salary and prestige, and they could have goals that conflict with those of the firm's owners.

Profit:
The difference between the revenues a firm takes in over any given period and the costs incurred in operating the firm over the same period.

Economists recognize that firms are complex organizations and that their owners or managers can have more than one goal. They also realize that there's a great deal of risk and uncertainty involved in making business decisions. Managers of firms don't have crystal balls to tell them whether their decisions will achieve the intended objectives. Nevertheless, models based on the assumption that those who operate firms seek to maximize profits have proved to be very fruitful. These models have consistently yielded hypotheses that have been supported by empirical evidence. Models based on the assumption that firms maximize profits are useful in explaining the law of supply and possible exceptions to this law.

Concept Check

1 **What are the functions of a business firm?**
2 **What influences the degree of vertical integration within a firm?**
3 **What simplifications are made in the economic model of a business firm?**

Measuring Cost and Profit

Because of the importance assigned to profit as a motivating force for business firms, our first step in analyzing market supply is to make a careful analysis of the way profits are measured. To do this, we need to analyze the differences in the way economists measure costs and the way costs are currently measured according to standard accounting practices. The equation for a firm's profit over a certain period can be written as:

$$\text{Profit} = \text{Total revenue} - \text{Total cost}$$

The total revenue for a single-product firm would be the total units of output sold over the period multiplied by the price per unit:

$$\text{Total revenue} = \text{Price} \times \text{Quantity sold}$$

Total cost is obtained by summing the value of all input services used to make the good available to buyers. In making this calculation, we must be careful to include the monetary value of inputs supplied by the firm's owners rather than purchased.

Economic Cost vs. Accounting Cost

Economic cost:
The monetary value of all inputs used in a particular activity or enterprise over a given period.

Economic cost is the monetary value of *all inputs* used in a particular activity or enterprise over a given period, say a year. The idea behind economic cost is that the sum of dollars representing the value of resources used must accurately reflect the opportunity cost of those resources. Remember, the opportunity cost of a resource used in a particular activity is its value in its next best use. When firms hire or purchase inputs in markets, the market price in most cases reflects the value of those resources to others. Owners of firms give up funds to buy these resources; and if they're rational, they consider the opportunity cost of not using those funds in their next best uses.

However, in many cases owners of firms use *their own resources* in producing goods and services instead of purchasing these services from others in markets. For example, the owner of a firm might work 40 hours a week managing his business. Similarly, a large corporation typically owns structures, equipment, vehicles, and

Principles in Practice

Corporate Takeovers: The Price of Failing to Maximize Profit

Even if you're not a regular reader of business news, you're probably familiar with the term "corporate raider." Unlike Indiana Jones, these raiders wear pinstripes and ride in limousines. But in temperament they're usually adventurous, keen, and capable of swift action. These modern-day swashbucklers are a major force in the current wave of merger activity in today's business world. Let's look at some of their targets—and tactics.

In recent years corporate takeovers and mergers have been making front-page news. In the 10-year period from 1975 to 1985 the dollar value of annual mergers increased tenfold. Hostile takeovers take place when an outside investor acquires a controlling interest in a company despite the opposition of management. Corporate raiders like T. Boone Pickens are ready to swoop down and acquire a company when they believe they can gain by doing so.

The market value of a corporation is represented by the value of its outstanding corporate stock. The price of a corporation's existing stock on any given day depends on the demand for and supply of shares traded. The willingness of stockholders to sell the stock of a corporation depends on their assessment of the profitability of holding the stock relative to interest rates and the return they can earn on alternative investments. If a company is poorly managed so that its prospects for future profits aren't encouraging, many stockholders may choose to sell their stock and use the funds thus obtained to purchase an alternative asset. This increases the supply of the stock and puts downward pressure on its price.

Naturally, a decline in a company's profit potential also puts downward pressure on the value of its outstanding stock. Corporate raiders look at the *market value* of a company's outstanding stock and compare it with their estimate of the market value that would prevail *were the company better managed.* If they believe the current stock price understates the value of the corporation with improved management, they're likely to attempt a takeover.

The raiders might make a *tender offer,* which involves a bid to obtain a controlling interest in the company, by offering stockholders a price per share well in excess of the current market price. The raiders might also seek to obtain proxies rather than actual stock ownership. This would give them the power to vote in their own company directors at the next corporate stockholders' meeting. If a takeover attempt succeeds, heads usually roll as the new owners begin to cut costs and replace management in an effort to increase profit and raise the value of the company's stock. Typically raiders borrow considerable sums to finance a takeover. A newly acquired corporation therefore often has a higher ratio of debt to assets.

An extreme form of takeover might involve liquidation of a company and its assets. This would occur if the raiders reasoned that the market value of the company's capital, land, and other marketable assets exceeded the current market value of its outstanding stock. Under such circumstances both the stockholders and raiders can gain by dismantling the company and selling off its assets!

Corporate takeover threats can act as a constraint on managers that prevents them from pursuing policies that don't maximize profit. In this way, the corporate raiders argue, they actually protect stockholders of a company from incompetent managers. If a firm fails to maximize profits, the corporate raiders come in, buy the company, and put in their own presumably more adept managers! Managers who don't maximize profits are therefore likely to be replaced by managers who do.

---

land. Owner-supplied inputs aren't purchased from others in markets. However, these input services must be valued in dollar terms at their highest value in their next best use so the firm can accurately measure its economic costs. The costs of nonpurchased inputs are called **implicit costs.** These are costs to which a cash value must be imputed (estimated and assigned) because the inputs aren't purchased in a market transaction.

For example, the implicit cost of the labor hours the owner of a business devotes to running it are the earnings he forgoes by not working for someone else or the value he places on the leisure time he gives up—whichever is higher. The implicit cost measures the opportunity cost of the owner's time spent working for his own business.

The implicit cost of tying up funds in a business enterprise is the highest return that could have been earned on those funds had they been invested elsewhere. For

Implicit costs:
The costs of nonpurchased inputs, to which a cash value must be imputed because the inputs are not purchased in a market transaction.

example, to run a bicycle manufacturing business requires materials, machines, and other capital equipment. Suppose the owner uses her own funds instead of borrowing to acquire these assets. The opportunity cost of money used in this way is the return she could earn by investing that sum in the next best alternative, say, corporate stocks. Suppose the owner ties up $50,000 of her own funds in the business and forgoes the opportunity to earn a 10% annual return on the funds in the stock market. The annual opportunity cost of those funds would therefore be $5,000. To calculate the economic cost of the enterprise, we have to add implicit costs of $5,000 to the firm's actual cash outlays that year.

Costs as measured by accountants don't include the opportunity cost of inputs supplied by a firm's owners. **Accounting cost** measures the explicit costs of operating a business. Explicit costs don't include the value of nonpurchased inputs. Accounting cost provides valuable information. Those who own businesses, however, are aware of the shortcomings of this measure and actually base their decisions on economic cost, including implicit costs, to accurately measure their opportunity costs. Business owners always compare the desirability of remaining in that particular enterprise with what they forgo by doing so. Economists therefore assume that decisions made by business firms are always based on economic cost, which is a complete measure of the opportunity cost of using economic resources in a business.

Because there are no owner-supplied labor services in a corporation, the implicit cost of a corporation is represented by forgone interest on funds tied up in the firm by stockholders and any rental income on equipment, land, and structures that's forgone when the corporation uses these inputs. The *equity* of a corporation is the difference between the value of its assets (including the cash that could be obtained if its equipment and real estate were sold rather than rented) and its debt. For example, if a corporation has equity of $1 million and the interest rate is 10%, the implicit cost of funds tied up in the corporation will be $100,000 per year.

Opportunity Costs vs. Accounting Costs: An Example

Accounting costs are different from opportunity costs because accounting costs don't include the value of the services of inputs owned by the business firm. Accounting costs include only explicit costs involving monetary outlays. An example will make the distinction between economic cost and accounting cost clearer. Suppose Melissa owns her own monogramming and embossing business and devotes 40 hours a week to personalizing and decorating sweaters, sweatshirts, and T-shirts. At the end of the year her accountant provides information on the costs of operating the firm.

The information supplied by the accountant is summarized in the table in Box 2. Melissa has three full-time employees to whom she has paid $40,000 in wages during the year. She has also borrowed money from the bank to finance her purchase of a store and embossing equipment, garments, transfers, and acrylic paints. She incurs total interest payments of $10,000 per year. The original cost of this capital (store, fixtures, machinery, and equipment) was $100,000. Its current market value is estimated to be $80,000.

In computing the annual cost of this equipment, the accountant spreads the original purchase price over a number of years. This accounting practice is called *depreciation*. The accountant assumes the embossing equipment will last five years before it has to be replaced. He therefore takes one fifth or 20% of the value of the equipment as depreciation. This is $20,000.

Accounting cost:
Measures the explicit costs of operating a business—those that result from purchases of input services.

Box 2   Accounting Cost vs. Economic Cost: An Example

Item	Accounting cost	Economic cost
Wages and salaries	$40,000	$40,000
Interest paid	10,000	10,000
Depreciation (1/5 of the value of capital)	20,000	20,000
Miscellaneous (garments, transfers, acrylic paints, thread, etc.)	20,000	20,000
Implicit wage of owner	0	30,000
Implicit wage of owner's spouse	0	10,000
Implicit rent	0	40,000
Implicit interest of owner's equity	0	3,000
Total cost	$90,000	$173,000

In measuring cost, the accountant also includes all other cash outlays such as those for insurance, materials, and utilities. These extra costs as measured by the accountant amount to $20,000. Total accounting costs are therefore $90,000, as shown in the table in Box 2.

Melissa appreciates the information supplied by the accountant. However, she's more concerned with the economic cost of running her store than with the accounting cost. To find the economic cost, Melissa estimates implicit costs. Her next best alternative other than running the monogramming shop is working as a monogrammer for someone else. She figures she could earn $30,000 per year managing someone else's shop. She includes this as her implicit wage. She must also impute a wage to her husband, who works 20 hours a week in the shop. Her husband's next best alternative for these 20 hours per week would pay $10,000 annually. This is her husband's implicit wage.

Melissa also forgoes the opportunity of renting her store to someone else when she uses it herself. If the annual market rent on her store is $40,000, she forgoes that amount by using the store herself. This is the opportunity cost of using the store for her own business and represents the implicit rent.

Finally, the market value of Melissa's equipment is $80,000. She owes the bank $50,000. If Melissa were to sell her equipment and pay off her bank loans, she'd have $30,000 in cash left over. By remaining in her monogramming business she forgoes the opportunity of investing these funds elsewhere. If she could earn 10% on these funds in her next best investment, the opportunity cost of those funds is $3,000 per year. This $3,000 is included in costs as implicit interest. This must be added to the depreciation expense calculated by the accountant to get the full cost of capital.

Adding all implicit costs to those figured by the accountant gives the opportunity cost, or economic cost, of Melissa's annual operations. As shown in the table in Box 2, Melissa's total economic costs for the year are $173,000, which is almost double the accounting costs.

The extent to which opportunity costs diverge from accounting costs varies with the amounts and kinds of inputs supplied to a firm by its owners. Typically, large corporations pay all employees wages even if those employees are also stockholders. It's rare, therefore, to have implicit wages in corporations. However, corporations usually have considerable amounts of cash tied up in capital equipment and land. The costs of these corporate funds are implicit interest and implicit rents.

Normal Profit vs. Economic Profit

Normal profit:
That portion of a firm's cost that is not included in accounting cost. A measure of the implicit costs of owner-supplied resources in a firm over a given period.

Economic profit:
Profit in excess of the normal profit; the difference between total revenue and the opportunity cost of all inputs used by a firm over a given period.

Normal profit is that portion of a firm's cost that is not included in accounting cost. Normal profit is a measure of the implicit costs of owner-supplied resources in a firm over a given period. Profit in excess of the normal profit is called **economic profit.** *When a firm is earning economic profit, its revenues exceed the sum of its accounting cost and the implicit costs of owner-supplied inputs.* Economic profit is the difference between total revenue and the opportunity cost of all inputs used by a firm over a given period. *Throughout this book, when a firm is said to be earning profits, it will mean that it earns economic profits.*

Because current accounting practice doesn't include implicit costs of owner-supplied inputs, accounting costs, as we've shown, underestimate economic costs. As a result, accounting profits based on accounting costs overestimate profits by underestimating costs. For example, suppose the annual sales revenues taken in by Melissa in the preceding example were $200,000. Because annual accounting cost was $90,000, the accountant would report an annual profit of $110,000! Melissa, being shrewd, would realize that her actual economic profit was only $27,000 that year. The normal profit for Melissa's store is $83,000, the opportunity cost of her owner-supplied inputs. Suppose her annual sales revenues were instead only $100,000. The accountant would report a $10,000 annual profit. However, Melissa would realize that she actually lost $73,000 based on her economic costs that year! She would go out of business as soon as possible if she didn't expect an improvement in sales.

Because economists always measure costs as opportunity costs, normal profit is always included as a cost of operating the firm. When measuring costs, remember that the normal profit is included in those costs because it's a measure of the value of owner-supplied resources.

Concept Check

1   How do accounting costs differ from economic costs?

2   Explain why profits calculated on the basis of accounting costs won't always accurately measure a firm's economic profits.

Summary

1. A business firm is an organization under one management set up for the purpose of earning profits for its owners by making one or more items available for sale in markets.

2. Business firms can be grouped according to industries selling similar products. Each firm might operate more than one physical facility, called a plant.

3. Sole proprietorships, partnerships, and corporations are different types of business organizations. Sole proprietorships and partnerships are owned by individuals, while corporations have a legal identity separate from their owners. A corporation is owned by its stockholders.

4. Limited liability is a legal provision that protects stockholders by putting a ceiling equal to the purchase price of their stock on their liability for debts of the corporation.

5. Both corporate and noncorporate business firms fulfill similar functions, including production of goods and services, assignment of tasks to workers, contracting with other firms, and personnel management.

6. Firms that supply themselves with all materials and services at all stages of production are vertically integrated. The degree of vertical integration of a firm is influenced by the transaction costs of contracting with other firms for materials and services.

7. In analyzing supply decisions by firms, it's useful to make some simplifications by assuming that firms produce a single product and seek to maximize profits.

8. Profit over a certain period is the difference between a firm's total revenue and total cost over that period.

9. Economic cost is the monetary value of all inputs used in a particular activity or enterprise over a given period. Economic cost exceeds accounting cost by the value of the services of owner-supplied inputs. The value of the services of owner-supplied inputs is called implicit cost. Economic profits are always based on economic costs. Normal profit is the part of the firm's costs that is included in profit when profit is calculated on the basis of accounting cost instead of economic cost.

Key Terms and Concepts

Business firm	Manager
Plant	Personnel management
Vertical integration	Multiproduct firm
Conglomerate	Single-product firm
Industry	Profit
Sole proprietorship	Economic cost
Partnership	Implicit costs
Corporation	Accounting cost
Dividend	Normal profit
Retained earnings	Economic profit
Limited liability	

Problems and Applications

1. How would you determine how to group business firms into industries? How can you use the concept of elasticity of demand to help establish industry groups?

2. Suppose you're a management analyst for a fast-food chain. Assuming this chain sells meals similar to those sold by McDonald's, make a list of the firm's inputs and outputs.

3. A major automobile producer hires you to evaluate the desirability of acquiring a firm that produces tires. The firm would be vertically integrated into the automobile firm and would produce tires *only* for use in new cars manufactured for sale by the company. What factors would you consider when making your evaluation of the acquisition?

4. Write an equation to calculate total revenue for a single-product firm. How

would you calculate total revenue for a multiproduct firm? How would you calculate total profit for both of these firms?

5. A corporation earns $100,000 profit. None of this profit is paid out as dividends to stockholders. What does the corporation do with the profits?

6. A corporation has assets valued at $5 million. It also has debts of $2 million. What is the corporate equity? The next best use of funds tied up in the corporation is an investment that would earn a 10% annual return. What is the normal profit for the corporation?

7. If you were starting a new business, what factors would you consider before choosing to organize as a sole proprietorship or a partnership?

8. Your firm's accountant calculates that its annual profit is $10,000. Under what circumstances will the firm's economic profit also be $10,000?

9. You own a small retail clothing store that you manage yourself. You rent your facilities, but you have $30,000 of your own funds tied up in the firm after making allowance for your debts. How would you calculate your implicit costs? How would you use these costs to supplement information provided to you on accounting costs?

10. "Normal profit really is a cost; that's why it isn't included in economic profit." Do you agree with this statement? Why or why not? What can cause normal profit to differ among firms?

Suggested Readings

Alfred Chandler, *Strategy and Structure,* Cambridge: The MIT Press, 1962. This is a classic analysis of the impact of business organization on performance and cost.

Toyohiro Kono, *Strategy & Structure of Japanese Enterprises,* Armonk, N.Y.: M.E. Sharpe, Inc., 1984. This is an intriguing and well-written analysis of the organization and goals of firms in Japan.

William G. Nickels, *Understanding Business,* St. Louis: Times Mirror/Mosby, 1987. This is a comprehensive textbook on all aspects of business enterprise. Chapter 4 goes into detail on the forms of business organization, and Chapter 5 discusses the practical problems involved in starting a small business.

Oliver E. Williamson, *The Economic Institutions of Capitalism,* New York: The Free Press, 1985. Chapters 4 and 5 discuss issues in vertical integration of firms, while Chapters 11 and 12 examine issues relating to the modern corporation.

A Forward Look

In the following chapter we begin the analysis necessary to understand the supply decisions made by business firms. We look carefully at the process of production and the costs of production. Cost is an important component of a firm's profits, and we must understand the relationship between productivity and cost so we can gauge the way cost is likely to vary over short periods when input prices and technology are fixed. In the chapters that follow we'll assume a single-product firm motivated to maximize profits.

Production and Cost

Have you ever been struck with what seemed to be a brilliant inspiration for a product or service that would make you a millionaire? Chances are, if you took your idea beyond the fantasy stage, you discovered that when it comes to producing an item, there's no free lunch. Whether you've come up with a hot new bumper-sticker slogan or found a way to make delectable ice cream without calories, the hard reality is that getting your product to consumers is going to cost you money.

In this chapter, as a first step toward understanding the process of supply in markets, we'll examine the production and cost of goods and services. We'll see how the supply decisions made by managers of business firms are influenced by production and cost considerations that affect the profitability of making goods available to consumers in markets.

Cost is a measure of the value of alternatives forgone when inputs are used to make goods or services available. Cost depends in part on input prices, such as hourly wages, hourly rental rates for equipment, and the unit prices of materials. However, cost also depends on the way output varies with input use. The productivity of inputs is a key determinant of the cost per unit of output. In deciding how much to produce, managers consider not only the output they can get from using various combinations of inputs, but also the prices of those inputs.

In a broad sense the process of production involves the use of inputs to create useful products. The products can be tangible goods like VCRs and frozen pizzas or intangible services like education and insurance. Economic theory assumes that no matter what's being produced—Porsche 944s or hair-styling services—there are certain basic principles of production that govern the way output varies with inputs used. Perhaps the most famous principle of production is that of *diminishing marginal returns,* which we'll discuss later in the chapter.

Concept Preview

After reading this chapter, you should be able to:

1 Analyze production relationships and show how the law of diminishing marginal returns implies a certain pattern of variation in output in the short run when the use of some inputs cannot be varied.
2 Explain the distinction between variable cost and fixed cost and describe the pattern of variation in total cost and other cost concepts as a single-product firm varies production.
3 Explain the relationship between cost and productivity of inputs.
4 Show how marginal cost is affected by changes in input prices.

Production Relationships

Production:
The process of using the services of labor and capital together with other inputs, such as land, materials, and fuels, to make goods and services available.

Inputs:
The labor, capital, land, natural resources, and entrepreneurship that are combined to produce products and services.

Production function:
Describes the relationship between any combination of input services and the maximum attainable output from that combination.

Short run:
A period of production during which some inputs cannot be varied.

Variable input:
An input whose quantity can be changed.

Fixed input:
An input whose quantity cannot be changed over the short run.

Long run:
A period of production long enough that producers have adequate time to vary *all* the inputs used to produce a good.

Production is the process of using the services of labor and equipment together with other inputs to make goods and services available. **Inputs** are the labor, capital, land, natural resources, and entrepreneurship that are combined to produce any output: cars, insurance policies, hair styling, hamburgers. For example, to produce a rock concert the inputs would be the concert hall, electricity, and the services of promoters, musicians, sound technicians, equipment transporters, security guards, ticket takers, ushers, and refreshment-stand workers. To produce pizzas, the inputs are the labor of one or more cooks, pizza ingredients, pans, ovens, boxes, delivery vans, and drivers.

The relationship between any combination of input services and the maximum output obtainable from that combination is described by a **production function.** Production functions are defined for a given technology. An improvement in technology increases the maximum output obtainable from any combination of inputs and therefore results in a new production function.

The Period of Production

The **short run** is a period of production during which some inputs cannot be varied. A **variable input** is one whose quantity can be changed. For example, because managers can hire more or fewer workers to produce compact discs in a factory, labor is a variable input. A **fixed input** is one whose quantity cannot be changed over the short run. For example, if a factory has a certain number of machines occupying a specified amount of floor space that can't be changed over a short period, the machines and floor space are a fixed input.

The short run can be best thought of as a period of production during which the firm is confined to a given plant. It has some flexibility to vary input use within that plant, but it can't vary *all* inputs simultaneously. Typically, labor inputs are more variable in the short run than are capital inputs, such as structures. A firm can work a factory around the clock in periods of peak demand by using both day-shift and night-shift workers. However, it takes more time than is available in the short run to increase the plant size by building additions to existing facilities or constructing new facilities. *In effect, in the short run there's a limit to production because there's only limited plant capacity available.*

The **long run** is a period of production long enough that managers have time to

Technology on the Move: New Materials Improve Productivity

There's a revolution of sorts going on in the field of materials. The new field of materials science is developing advanced replacements for steel, copper, and other metals. In many cases the new materials allow machines to last longer and work more efficiently, and machines can be engineered for a specific purpose, such as for use in aircraft engines. New materials are also used as coatings for cutting tools.

The new technology of materials enables industries to reduce their reliance on natural resources and traditional metals in a way that's never before been possible. The availability of new materials at lower prices in the future will undoubtedly represent a shift in production functions that will substantially increase productivity in many industries.*

Advanced materials currently are used in many industries, ranging from aerospace and aircraft to automobiles and electronics. Many new materials reduce the weight of vehicles without sacrificing strength, thus improving fuel economy. New materials used in aircraft engines allow those engines to burn fuel at higher temperatures. In some cases ceramic materials will replace alloys used in engine rotors.

The use of new materials in manufacturing often allows a shift to a more mechanized method of production that reduces cost per unit of output. For example, production of automotive connecting rods by conventional forging methods is currently estimated to cost $3.62 per rod. Shifting to new technology utilizing powder-metallurgy forging, a new system that uses rapidly solidified metal powders, is estimated to reduce the cost per rod to $3.22. The new system involves the use of a new forging tool that's more precise than older methods and results in less waste of material. Labor costs per part are only about 10% of total costs under the new system, compared to approximately 20% under conventional forging.†

The new technology of materials is likely to result in substitution of new materials for many scarce natural resources. For example, copper has already been replaced by optical fibers to conduct electrical impulses in communications. Electrically active polymers are now being developed as a substitute for copper in conducting electrical energy. New plastics are likely to replace steel in automobile bodies of the future. Plastic is corrosion resistant and is also more resistant to minor damage like dents and scratches. Assuming that an acceptably strong plastic can be developed at reasonable cost, substitution of the new material for steel could increase fuel economy and lengthen the useful life of an automobile.

The materials revolution is likely to have significant effects on productivity as well as the quality of products we enjoy as consumers. The change in technology is therefore likely to affect the lives and well-being of all of us.

*See Joel P. Clark and Merton C. Flemings, "Advanced Materials and the Economy," *Scientific American,* 255,4, October 1986, pp. 51-57.
†Clark and Flemings, p. 52.

vary *all* the inputs used to produce a good. In the long run there are no fixed inputs. It's clear that producers have more flexibility in the long run than they do in the short run.

The actual period of time encompassing the long run is likely to vary from one industry to another. For example, the owner of a hot-dog stand might be able to increase all of its inputs in a month. However, an oil company could take years to increase the capital inputs, such as refineries, required to produce more output. We can think of the long run as a planning period in which managers contemplate future changes in the use of currently fixed inputs. For example, in the long run the manager of a waterbed factory can consider expanding by acquiring more floor space and machinery.

Production in the Short Run: The Law of Diminishing Marginal Returns

Before you can understand the relationships between output and cost, you first need to understand the physical relationships between inputs used and outputs. To begin the analysis, we'll examine the relationship between the quantity of one variable input used and the quantity of output. You can think of managers as being confined to one plant of given size with a given number of machines.

The **law of diminishing marginal returns** states that the extra production obtained from increases in a variable input will eventually decline as more of the variable input is used together with the fixed inputs. This law implies that there's a certain predictable pattern of variation in output as more of a variable input is used in the short run.

The law of diminishing marginal returns means, for example, that in a factory with a given amount of space and a given number of machines, there's a limit to the extra production that can be obtained by hiring more workers. Eventually the extra output obtained over any period from an extra worker peters down to near zero. You can actually reach a point where adding another worker to the factory would result in a decrease rather than an increase in output! This might occur because the worker would have no equipment to work with and his presence could actually impair the functioning of other workers, thereby reducing their effectiveness.

The Total Product Curve and the Marginal Product Curve

A **total product curve** describes how output varies in the short run as more of any one input is used together with fixed amounts of other inputs under current technology. Points on a total product curve give the output that's obtainable, given current technology, from any quantity of the variable input used with the fixed inputs.

The table in Box 1 provides data that show how weekly output is likely to vary in the short run as a firm hires more workers (each working a 40-hour week) to operate a given amount of equipment in a given size plant. Suppose the factory produces running shoes, and you're the manager. The **total product of a variable input,** such as labor services, is the amount of output produced over any given period when that input is used along with other fixed inputs. The first column of the table shows the number of workers employed per week in your factory. The second column shows the greatest possible output that can be produced with that number of workers, assuming nothing else is varied when more workers are employed.

The first line of the table shows that if no workers were employed, your plant's weekly output would be zero. You need at least some workers before the equipment and other facilities of your factory can be productively utilized. When you hire 1 worker working a 40-hour week, the total product of labor is 7 pairs of running shoes each week. Hiring a second worker results in a sharp increase in weekly output, from 7 to 18 pairs of shoes.

The **marginal product** of an input is the increase in output from one more unit of that input when the quantity of all other inputs is unchanged. The marginal product of labor (MP_L) is 7 pairs of shoes per week when you hire 1 worker because production increases from zero to 7 units when you hire the first worker. The marginal product of labor when you hire 2 workers per week is $18 - 7 = 11$ pairs of shoes per week. In other words, by hiring a second worker your firm adds 11 units of output to its weekly production. Hiring a third worker to work a 40-hour week increases output to 33 pairs per week. The marginal product of labor when 3 workers are employed, as shown in the third column of the table, is 15 pairs of shoes per week.

Law of diminishing marginal returns:
States that the extra production obtained from increases in a variable input will eventually decline as more of the variable input is used together with the fixed inputs.

Total product curve:
Describes how output varies in the short run as more of any one input is used together with fixed amounts of other inputs under current technology.

Total product of a variable input:
The amount of output produced over any given period when that input is used along with other fixed inputs.

Marginal product (of an input):
The increase in output from one more unit of an input when the quantity of all other inputs is unchanged.

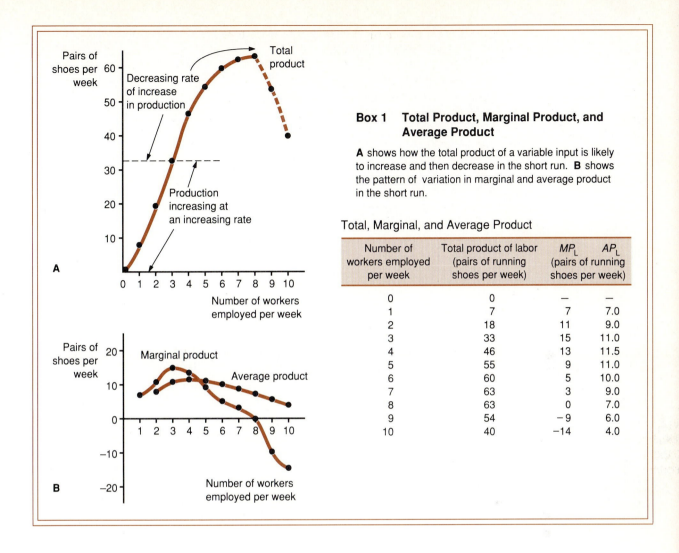

Box 1   Total Product, Marginal Product, and Average Product

A shows how the total product of a variable input is likely to increase and then decrease in the short run. **B** shows the pattern of variation in marginal and average product in the short run.

Total, Marginal, and Average Product

Number of workers employed per week	Total product of labor (pairs of running shoes per week)	MP_L (pairs of running shoes per week)	AP_L
0	0	—	—
1	7	7	7.0
2	18	11	9.0
3	33	15	11.0
4	46	13	11.5
5	55	9	11.0
6	60	5	10.0
7	63	3	9.0
8	63	0	7.0
9	54	−9	6.0
10	40	−14	4.0

Now notice what happens when you hire the fourth worker: weekly output increases to 46 pairs of shoes; however, the marginal product of labor declines to 13 pairs of shoes per week. Thereafter the data in the table show that as your firm continues to hire more workers, the marginal product of labor continually declines. In fact, hiring an eighth worker doesn't increase weekly production at all! The marginal product of labor when 8 workers are employed per week is zero. If you were to hire more than 8 workers, the data show that your firm's weekly production would actually decline. The marginal product of labor when more than 8 workers per week are hired would be negative!

Graph **A** in Box 1 plots the data for the total product of labor from the table in Box 1. The vertical axis corresponds to the total output of running shoes per week. The horizontal axis shows the number of workers hired per week. A smooth curve is drawn through the points showing the pattern of variation in weekly output as labor input is increased while all other inputs are held constant. Notice how production initially increases at an increasing rate as the curve becomes steeper, up to the point at which 3 workers are hired per week. When more than 3 workers per week are hired, the rate of increase in output decreases. You can see this in the fact that the curve becomes flatter as more workers are hired. Eventually, when 8 workers are hired, the rate of increase in output is zero. At this point the total product curve is at a maximum. This implies that there's a maximum amount of weekly output you can squeeze out of your plant. Thereafter, hiring additional workers would actually decrease output. This is shown in the dotted portion of the total product curve. As a manager who seeks to maximize profits, you'll *never* operate your plant in the downward-sloping portion of the total product curve. If you did so, you'd be paying additional workers to *decrease* total production. This implies higher costs *and* less output to sell, and therefore less revenue. The increase in costs and decrease in revenue would both act to reduce your profits.

In Box 1, **B** plots the marginal product of labor from the data in the table. You'll notice that marginal product increases at first and then decreases. You can also see that when marginal product is decreasing, the rate of increase in total product is declining. This is because the marginal product of labor *is* the slope of the total product curve. Marginal product (MP_L) is

$$MP_L = \frac{\Delta TP}{\Delta L}$$

where ΔTP is the change in the total product of labor and ΔL is the increase in the number of workers hired per week. When the marginal product of labor is zero, total product is at its maximum value per week. This is because at the point at which MP_L is zero, hiring another worker doesn't add to production anymore, and hiring still one more worker would begin to reduce output. When marginal product is *negative,* additional workers *decrease* weekly production.

Average Product

Average product (of an input):
The total output produced over a given period divided by the number of units of that input used.

The **average product** of an input is the total output produced over a given period divided by the number of units of that input used. We can calculate the average product of labor from the data in the table in Box 1 simply by dividing the total weekly output of running shoes by the number of workers. The average product of labor is therefore total product *(TP)* divided by the number of workers *(L):*

$$\text{Average product of labor} = \frac{TP}{L}$$

The average product measures output per worker, which is an indication of the *productivity* of workers in a plant. The average product of labor is shown in the last column of the table in Box 1.

The pattern of variation in the average product of labor is similar to that in the marginal product of labor. The average product of labor increases at first, reaches a maximum, then decreases. Although the average product of labor becomes smaller and smaller, it never reaches zero.

The Relationship Between Average and Marginal Products of a Variable Input

In Box 1, **B** plots the average product of labor on the same set of axes as the marginal product of labor. You'll notice that when the marginal product exceeds the average product, the average product increases. This is because the marginal product is the *last number* added in to compute the average product. When the marginal product exceeds the average product, the average product has to go up. A good way to understand this is to think about your average of test grades at any point. Until the end of the semester, your average changes each time you take another test. The grade on each extra test is your *marginal* grade. Suppose you have an 80 average on the first two tests. What happens to your average if you get an 85 on the third test? Your average must increase because the last number, your grade on the third test, exceeds your previous average. By the same token, your average will fall if you get a grade of less than 80 on the last test.

Graph **B** in Box 1 reflects this relationship between average and marginal numbers for an average that is continually recomputed as the number of workers is increased. Average product increases when marginal product exceeds it. Average product declines when marginal product is below it. Finally, this implies that the marginal product curve must intersect the average product curve at the latter's maximum point.

How Product Curves Illustrate the Law of Diminishing Marginal Returns

The total, marginal, and average product curves drawn in Box 1 reflect the law of diminishing marginal returns. It's possible that the marginal product of labor can increase for a while when the quantity used is low. *However, the law of diminishing marginal returns implies that the marginal product eventually declines.* The **point of diminishing returns** corresponds to the level of usage of a variable input at which its marginal product begins to decline. In Box 1, the point of diminishing returns corresponds to employment of 3 workers per week because hiring more than 3 workers results in a decline in the marginal product of labor. The marginal product of labor in some cases could actually become zero and even negative, as shown in Box 1.

Because the marginal product of a variable input will approach zero, it will eventually fall below the average product of the variable input. *Remember: when the marginal product falls below the average product of an input, the average product declines. This means the law of diminishing marginal returns also implies that the average product of a variable input will eventually decline as more of that input is used together with fixed inputs.* The average product of labor in a factory of given size inevitably declines as more workers are hired, unless more space, equipment, and other inputs can be supplied to complement the extra labor services.

Reasons for Diminishing Marginal Returns

It's easy to comprehend the reasons for the law of eventually diminishing marginal returns. Inputs complement one another. You can't increase production indefinitely by hiring more workers to work with a fixed number of machines and a fixed amount of materials in a facility of given size. Eventually you'll have too many workers relative to other inputs. Some workers will have nothing to do because they'll lack space or equipment to do their jobs. You'll soon cram so many workers into a given amount of space that they might actually impair each other's productivity by bumping into or distracting each other. This could result in a negative marginal product of labor. On the other hand, when you hire too few workers relative to the equipment and space available in your factory, it isn't possible to assign workers

Point of diminishing returns:
Corresponds to the level of usage of a variable input at which its marginal product begins to decline.

specialized tasks that contribute to increased productivity. In effect, when too few workers are hired relative to a plant's capacity, capital equipment and space are wasted. This is why the productivity of workers increases in early stages of production when output is low and the plant's facilities are underutilized.

You can also understand the implications of the law by asking yourself what the consequences would be if it didn't hold. For example, if marginal returns didn't eventually decline from using more labor to farm an acre of land, there would be no limit to the amount of food workers could produce on an acre. Adding more workers to farm the acre would always increase output under any given technology. It would therefore be feasible to produce the entire world supply of food on one acre. This, of course, is impossible. As you can see, the hypothesis of diminishing marginal returns is quite reasonable. Throughout the book we'll assume that this law holds.

Concept Check

1 What is a production function?

2 What is the distinction between variable inputs and fixed inputs? Explain why there are no fixed inputs in the long run, and list the important distinctions between the short run and the long run as periods of production.

3 How are the concepts of total product, marginal product, and average product of a variable input related to each other? Use these concepts to describe the implications of the law of diminishing marginal returns.

Short-Run Cost Curves for the Single-Product Firm

Our next step is to examine how costs of production vary with output over any given period. *Cost measures the dollar value of inputs used over any given period to produce an item.* Remember that economic cost also includes the implicit cost of nonpurchased inputs (see Chapter 9). Actual cost depends on the prices of input services hired (or the monetary value of input services supplied by the firm itself), the quantity of those inputs used, and the productivity of those inputs. In this section we analyze the variation of cost with inputs in the short run when some inputs are variable while others are fixed.

Variable Costs, Fixed Costs, and Total Cost

Fixed costs:
Costs that do not vary as a firm varies its output. Also called *overhead costs.*

In the short run, costs are divided into two basic categories. **Fixed costs** (FC) are those that do not vary as a firm varies its output. Managers often refer to their fixed costs as *overhead costs.* These are costs that must be incurred in the short run even if the firm doesn't produce anything. Examples of fixed costs are rents on leased property, interest on borrowed funds, salaries of managers (who must be employed to oversee the affairs of the firm even if the firm shuts down and produces no output for a short period), and depreciation on capital equipment. The monthly value of fixed inputs is a firm's monthly fixed cost.

Variable costs:
Costs that change with output. Variable costs are the costs of variable inputs.

Variable costs (VC) are those that change with output. These are the costs of variable inputs. Examples of variable costs are the monetary value of the services of most workers, fuel, materials, and machinery or equipment that is rented on a

Principles in Practice

Measuring Fixed Costs: An Example

The common business term for fixed costs is *overhead costs.* Fixed, or overhead, costs are all those costs that don't vary with output. The following data show how fixed cost can be measured. These data are based on cost estimates for a fish processing plant.* The plant dresses mountain trout for shipment to urban fish markets. The plant will cost $67,782 to construct. Total equipment cost will be $60,337. The cost of acquiring the land for the plant is $7,500. The plant is designed to produce 2,304 pounds of dressed trout per day.

Fixed costs include depreciation on plant and equipment, property taxes, insurance, repairs, maintenance, and forgone interest on cash invested. In addition, the plant manager's salary may be regarded as a fixed cost. Irrespective of the output level, he must be paid his salary to oversee operations or to manage the plant's affairs if it is to be shut down.

In calculating depreciation, we assume the plant has a 20-year life and equipment has a 10-year life before it will have to be replaced. A straight-line depreciation of these assets uses one twentieth of the plant cost and one tenth of the equipment cost

as a measure of annual capital cost. Forgone interest is estimated at 9% of one half of the total investment in land, building, and equipment. Annual fixed, or overhead, costs are:

Depreciation	
Plant	$3,389
Equipment	6,034
Total	9,423
Forgone interest	6,103
Property tax	1,356
Insurance	1,239
Repairs and maintenance	1,922
Manager's salary	15,325
Total fixed cost	$35,368

Property taxes are estimated at 1% of investment in land, building, and equipment. Insurance is estimated at a bit less than 1% of investment in building and equipment, whereas repairs and maintenance are estimated at 1.5% of the same amount.

*J.E. Easley, *Costs and Returns of Alternative Mountain Trout Processing Facilities,* Economics Information Report No. 47, Department of Economics and Business, North Carolina State University at Raleigh, June 1976.

monthly or hourly basis. To produce more goods and services per month, a firm requires more of the services of these variable inputs. As it hires more of these inputs, its variable costs will increase. Variable cost is therefore dependent on weekly or monthly output.

Total cost (TC) is the sum of the value of *all* inputs used over any given period to produce goods. Total cost is the sum of fixed costs and variable costs:

$$TC = VC + FC$$

Total cost:
The sum of the value of *all* inputs used to produce goods over any given period; the sum of fixed costs and variable costs.

Input Substitution and Variable Cost

In using variable inputs, managers of a firm must choose the combinations so as to produce any given output at the lowest possible variable cost. Remember that there's usually more than one way to accomplish any production objective. For example, as the manager of a running-shoe factory, you could produce a certain number of shoes of given quality with a great deal of labor, using hand tools and very little machinery. Alternatively, you could produce the same number of shoes with lots of machinery and very little labor. *To produce efficiently, managers seek to produce any given output using the combination of variable inputs that costs the least.* In choosing inputs in this way, managers must consider both the price and the marginal product of each input.

The appendix to this chapter provides a technical analysis of how managers choose inputs to minimize variable cost. However, we can easily use a numerical example to illustrate the general principle involved in choosing input combinations to keep the total cost of a given output as low as possible. Suppose your objective as manager is to fill orders for a certain number of running shoes per month. If some inputs were variable and could be substituted for each other to perform similar tasks, you'd have to examine how costs could be reduced by, say, substituting machines for workers.

For example, suppose you can rent an extra machine for $100 per hour. Assume the machine could replace 10 workers who currently produce 20 pairs of shoes per week. Each worker gets paid $20 per hour. By renting the machine, you could replace the 10 workers without any reduction in weekly output. Because the 10 workers cost a total of $200 per hour and the machine can be rented for only $100 per hour, the firm's costs will fall by $100 per hour if you substitute the machine for the 10 workers. The reduction in hourly costs would reduce the total cost of producing shoes.

The actual cost saving from substituting capital for labor depends in part on the hourly rental rate for the machine compared to the hourly wage of workers. For example, if the workers were paid $5 per hour, the total hourly labor cost for 10 workers would be only $50. In this case it would *not* pay you to rent the machine and dismiss the workers, because the $100 per hour cost of the machine would now exceed the $50 per hour cost of workers who can produce the same 20 pairs of shoes.

The marginal products of the machine and the workers are important in your choice of the input combination. If each machine could produce only 10 pairs of shoes per week instead of 20, you'd need 2 machines to do the work of the 10 workers. If the machine still rents for $100 per hour, you'd now have to incur hourly costs of $200 to replace the 10 workers. If they're paid $10 per hour, you'd enjoy no cost savings from replacing the workers with two machines. This is because the $200 hourly cost for the 2 machines would just equal the $200 hourly cost for the 10 workers.

As you can see, managers must look at the marginal product and the price per unit of inputs to decide which combinations to use. In our analysis of costs we always assume that managers choose the lowest-cost combination of variable inputs to produce a given output.

Average Cost

Average cost:
Total cost divided by the number of units of output produced over a given period. Also called *average total cost* or *unit cost*.

Average cost (AC) is total cost divided by the number of units of output produced over a given period. It's also called *average total cost*. Managers often refer to average cost as their *unit cost*:

$$AC = \frac{TC}{Q}$$

Average variable cost:
Variable cost divided by the number of units of output produced over a given period.

Average variable cost (AVC) is variable cost divided by the number of units of output produced over a given period:

$$AVC = \frac{VC}{Q}$$

Average fixed cost (AFC) is fixed cost divided by the number of units of output produced over a given period:

Average fixed cost:
Fixed cost divided by the number of units of output produced over a given period.

$$AFC = \frac{FC}{Q}$$

It's easy to show that average cost is the sum of average variable cost and average fixed cost. Remember that total cost is the sum of variable cost and fixed cost. It follows that:

$$\frac{TC}{Q} = \frac{VC}{Q} + \frac{FC}{Q}$$

because dividing both sides of an equation by the same variable doesn't disturb the equality. The first term of the equation just given is AC. The two terms on the other side of the equal sign are AVC and AFC, respectively. It follows that:

$$AC = AVC + AFC$$

The Relationship Between the Total Cost Curve and the Total Product Curve

It's now possible to derive a total cost curve for your running-shoe firm, whose total product curve was drawn in Box 1, by making a few simplifying assumptions. First, let's assume your firm uses only two inputs in the short run: labor, a variable input, and capital, a fixed input. Lumped into capital are the services of all machines, structures and land, the inventory of materials the firm keeps on hand, and any other equipment. Assume that the monthly cost of all capital is $1,000. This is your firm's monthly fixed cost.

The only variable input is labor services. Assume that as the firm's manager you can hire all the workers you desire at the going market wage of $300 a week. It's now possible for us to use the data on production in the table in Box 1 to calculate the firm's total cost and show how that cost varies with output in the short run. The table in Box 2 shows how costs vary with output as your firm produces more by

Box 2 Calculating Total Cost

Number of workers employed	Total output (pairs of running shoes per week)	Fixed cost (dollars)	Variable cost (dollars)	Total cost (dollars)
0	0	1,000	0	1,000
1	7	1,000	300	1,300
2	18	1,000	600	1,600
3	33	1,000	900	1,900
4	46	1,000	1,200	2,200
5	55	1,000	1,500	2,500
6	60	1,000	1,800	2,800
7	63	1,000	2,100	3,100
8	63	1,000	2,400	3,400
9	54	1,000	2,700	3,700
10	40	1,000	3,000	4,000

hiring more workers. The first column shows the number of workers, and the second column shows the output per week that can be produced with that number of workers and the fixed inputs. These data are identical to the data in the table in Box 1. The third column of the table in Box 2 shows the fixed costs of production. These costs amount to $1,000 per week no matter how much is produced. For example, the first entry in the third column shows that fixed costs are $1,000 *even if the factory shuts down for the week* by laying off all workers and producing no shoes.

The fourth column shows the variable costs of production. In this case the only variable cost is the cost of hiring workers. To obtain the variable cost, we simply multiply the number of workers hired per week by the weekly wage of $300. For example, weekly variable cost is $300 when only one worker is hired. As more output is produced and more workers are hired, weekly variable cost increases by $300 for each extra worker. (Of course, you could hire part-time workers for added flexibility in the production process.) Finally, the last column of the table in Box 2 shows total cost, which we obtain simply by adding variable cost and fixed cost for each row of the table.

The graph in Box 3 plots the data for variable cost. The vertical axis measures the variable cost, while the horizontal axis measures the corresponding weekly output of running shoes. It's easy to show how the variable cost curve is related to the total product curve drawn in **A** in Box 1. The total product curve shows how output varies with the number of workers hired per week and reflects the law of diminishing marginal returns. The variable cost curve shows the relationship between labor cost and output produced. Because the weekly wage doesn't change as more workers are hired, the variable cost curve reflects the way output varies with labor input. *The shape of the variable cost curve mirrors the shape of the total product curve.* To prove this to yourself, turn the book so that Box 3 is on its side and hold it up to a mirror. You'll see that the shape of the variable cost curve looked at in this way parallels that of the total product curve drawn in **A** in Box 1, except it doesn't include the variable cost levels corresponding to points at which the marginal product of labor would be negative.

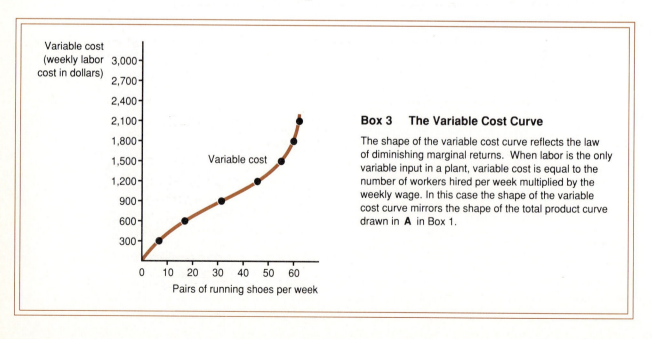

Box 3   The Variable Cost Curve

The shape of the variable cost curve reflects the law of diminishing marginal returns. When labor is the only variable input in a plant, variable cost is equal to the number of workers hired per week multiplied by the weekly wage. In this case the shape of the variable cost curve mirrors the shape of the total product curve drawn in **A** in Box 1.

Notice in Box 1 that the maximum possible output of running shoes in your factory is 63 pairs per week. Accordingly, if you tried to hire more labor to produce more than 63 pairs per week, variable cost would increase but output could not increase. As a manager who seeks to maximize profit, you won't hire more labor if you can't increase saleable output by doing so. Therefore the variable cost curve in Box 3 isn't extended upward after your firm reaches a weekly output of 63 pairs of shoes.

The pattern of variation in variable costs reflects the pattern of variation in the total product of labor in the short run. In general, when there's more than one variable input, the shape of the variable cost curve will reflect the variation in the total product of all these inputs.

To obtain the total cost curve from variable cost, simply add fixed costs to variable costs. Because fixed costs are always $1,000 per week, no matter how much your firm produces or how many workers it employs, total costs will always be $1,000 more than variable costs. The graph in Box 4 shows the fixed cost curve as a horizontal line intersecting the vertical axis at the point corresponding to $1,000.

As you can see, the total cost curve has exactly the same shape as the variable cost curve but is higher up on the axes. Also note that both total cost and variable cost increase at a *decreasing rate* at first but then increase at an *increasing rate* as weekly output increases.

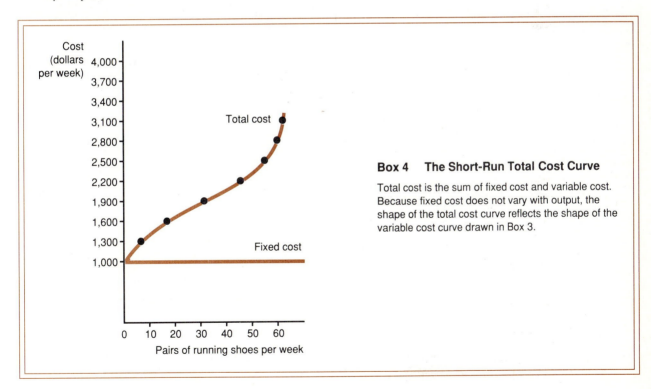

Box 4   The Short-Run Total Cost Curve

Total cost is the sum of fixed cost and variable cost. Because fixed cost does not vary with output, the shape of the total cost curve reflects the shape of the variable cost curve drawn in Box 3.

Deriving Average Cost Curves

The table in Box 5 shows how average fixed cost, average variable cost, and average cost can be calculated from the data in Box 2. In drawing up the table we assume that no rational manager would hire more than 7 workers per week because additional workers beyond that number don't increase weekly output above 63 pairs of

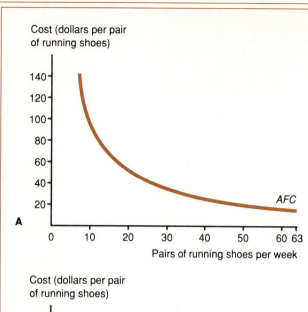

A

Cost (dollars per pair of running shoes)

AFC

Pairs of running shoes per week

Box 5 Average Cost Curves

Average fixed cost continually declines as output expands, as shown in **A**. Because of the law of diminishing marginal returns, both average variable cost and average cost decrease at first, then increase as more output per week is produced in the plant, as shown in **B**.

Calculating Average Cost

Total output (pairs of running shoes per week)	Average fixed cost (dollars)	Average variable cost (dollars)	Average cost (dollars)
0	—	—	—
7	142.86	42.86	185.72
18	55.56	33.33	88.89
33	30.30	27.27	57.57
46	21.74	26.09	47.83
55	18.18	27.27	45.45
60	16.67	30.00	46.67
63	15.87	33.33	49.20

Cost (dollars per pair of running shoes)

AC

AVC

B

Pairs of running shoes per week

shoes. We obtain average fixed cost simply by dividing the $1,000 weekly fixed cost by the number of pairs of shoes produced per week. Similarly, dividing the data for variable cost and total cost in Box 2 by weekly output gives us the average variable cost and average cost, respectively. Note that the sum of average fixed cost and average variable cost is equal to average cost in all cases.

In Box 5, **A** shows the average fixed cost curve while **B** shows the average variable cost and average cost curves on the same set of axes. Smooth curves have been fitted on the axes from the data. First note the shape of the average fixed cost curve. *As more output is produced per week, average fixed cost continually declines.* Business managers sometimes refer to this phenomenon as *spreading of overhead costs.* Because fixed costs (overhead costs) don't vary with output, it's inevitable that the amount of these costs per unit of output will decline as weekly output goes up.

Both average variable cost and average cost decline at first as weekly production increases, reach a minimum level, and then increase, giving each a U shape. Note that the average variable cost curve reaches its minimum before the average cost curve reaches its minimum.

The shape of both the average variable cost curve and the average cost curve reflects the law of diminishing marginal returns. To see this, recall the shape of the average product curve drawn in **B** in Box 1. The average product of labor increases at first, reaches a maximum, then decreases when more workers are hired to work in a plant of given size.

To see how the average variable cost is related to the average product of labor, remember that the average product of labor is output, Q, divided by the number of workers employed, L:

$$\text{Average product of labor} = \frac{\text{Output}}{\text{Number of workers}}$$

Because the only variable cost in the plant used in this example is labor cost, average variable cost is simply labor cost divided by output. Weekly labor costs are obtained by multiplying the number of workers by the weekly wage. Average variable cost is therefore:

$$AVC = \frac{(\text{Weekly wage})(\text{Number of workers})}{\text{Output}}$$

Because the average product of labor is output divided by the number of workers, the expression for average variable cost can also be written as:

$$AVC = \frac{\text{Wages per time period}}{\text{Output/number of workers}} = \frac{\text{Wages per time period}}{\text{Average product of labor}}$$

For example, using the data in Box 1, note that if your firm uses 3 workers per week, it will produce 33 pairs of running shoes per week. The average product of labor will be 11 pairs of shoes per week. Using the formula just given, and noting that the weekly wage is $300, we find that average variable cost is $300/11 = $27.27, which agrees with the data in Box 5.

With the formulas just presented, we also can show how data on productivity of labor can be used to calculate average variable cost and average cost at varying wage rates. For example, suppose data for a steel mill show that it takes 6 hours of labor to produce 1 ton of steel. This represents the variable input (labor) per unit of output, which is the inverse of the average product of labor. If the wage is $20 per hour and labor is the only variable input, then variable cost per ton of steel will be $120, which is the hourly wage multiplied by the labor it takes to produce a ton of steel. If fixed cost per ton of steel is $1,000, then average cost will be $1,120, which is the sum of average variable cost and average fixed cost. In general, when labor is the only variable input:

$$\text{Average cost} = w(\text{Labor per unit of output}) + \text{Average fixed cost}$$

where w is the wage per time period (for example, per hour or per week).

It's now easy to see why the *AVC* and *AC* curves must fall at first and then increase if the law of diminishing returns holds. This is because as you hire more workers to produce more output in your plant, their average product increases at first, *decreasing* average variable cost, and then decreases, *increasing* average variable cost.

We can derive the average cost curve simply by adding average fixed cost to average variable cost. The vertical distance between the *AVC* and *AC* curves must get smaller and smaller as output is increased, reflecting the fact that average fixed cost gets smaller and smaller as output is increased. This is because the vertical distance between the two curves is average fixed cost.

Marginal Cost

Marginal cost (MC) is the extra cost of producing one more unit of output. There is no accounting concept that parallels marginal cost. However, all good business managers have an idea of their marginal cost and use their estimates of marginal cost of production to make decisions.

We can calculate marginal cost from the data in Box 6. As is common in many businesses, the data show increases in weekly output associated with additional workers rather than increases in cost for *each unit* of output. However, we can approximate marginal cost from the data by recalling that marginal cost can be thought of as the change in cost associated with any given change in output. Marginal cost for the batch of output associated with each extra worker can be calculated from the following formula:

$$MC = \frac{\Delta TC}{\Delta Q}$$

where ΔTC is the change in total cost associated with any given change in weekly output, ΔQ.

The table in Box 6 calculates marginal cost from the data on total cost and output in Box 2. The second column in the table in Box 6 shows the change in total cost associated with each change in output as more workers are hired. For example, the change in total cost when the first worker is hired is $\Delta TC = \$1,300 - \$1,000 =$

Box 6   Calculating Marginal Cost

Output (pairs of shoes per week)	Change in total cost (ΔTC) (dollars)	Change in output (ΔQ) (pairs of shoes per week)	Marginal cost $= \frac{\Delta TC}{\Delta Q}$ (dollars per pair)
7	1,300−1,000 = 300	7− 0 = 7	300/ 7 = 42.86
18	1,600−1,300 = 300	18− 7 =11	300/11 = 27.27
33	1,900−1,600 = 300	33−18 =15	300/15 = 20.00
46	2,200−1,900 = 300	46−33 =13	300/13 = 23.08
55	2,500−2,200 = 300	55−46 = 9	300/ 9 = 33.33
60	2,800−2,500 = 300	60−55 = 5	300/ 5 = 60
63	3,100−2,800 = 300	63−60 = 3	300/ 3 = 100

$300. The change in output is $\Delta Q = 7 - 0 = 7$. Marginal cost for the batch of shoes produced by the first worker is therefore approximated as $300/7 = $42.86. Notice that marginal cost depends *only* on changes in variable cost. *Because fixed cost doesn't change as output changes, fixed cost doesn't influence marginal cost.* Marginal cost is influenced only by variable cost. For example, here fixed cost is $1,000. As output increases, fixed cost *remains* $1,000. Only labor cost, which is the variable cost, increases as output increases.

Marginal cost decreases at first and then increases. The eventually increasing marginal cost of output reflects the law of diminishing marginal returns. As more of the variable input is hired, the extra output obtained eventually becomes smaller and smaller. This means that it eventually takes more and more of the variable input to produce each extra unit of output. Given the price per unit of the variable input, this implies increasing marginal cost.

The marginal cost curve plotted in Box 7 therefore has a U shape. Note that the marginal cost curve must intersect *both* the average variable cost curve and the average cost curve at the minimum point of each of these curves. This is because the marginal cost is the last number added into both *AVC* and *AC* when each average is calculated. When *MC* is below either of these averages, the average will decline. Similarly, when it's above the average, the average will increase. Note that this means the *AVC* curve must reach its minimum before the *AC* curve reaches its minimum. This is because when *AVC* = *MC*, *MC* is *below AC* because *AVC* is always less than *AC* by an amount equal to *AFC*. Average cost must therefore still be falling to its minimum when average variable cost begins rising above its minimum. You can see this in Box 7.

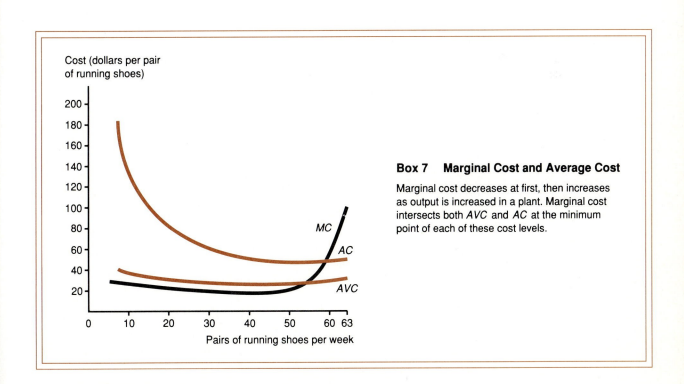

Box 7   Marginal Cost and Average Cost

Marginal cost decreases at first, then increases as output is increased in a plant. Marginal cost intersects both *AVC* and *AC* at the minimum point of each of these cost levels.

1 Assuming that all inputs are variable, what would you have to consider when choosing the minimum-cost combination of inputs to produce a given output?

2 Write down the formulas for average cost, average fixed cost, and average variable cost and explain why if you know the value of any two of these, you can calculate the third. Why does the distance between the average variable cost curve and the average cost curve become smaller as output is increased over a certain period?

3 Assuming constant input prices, how does the law of diminishing marginal returns explain the way variable, total, average, and marginal cost vary as a firm increases its weekly production? Explain why marginal cost must equal average cost when average cost is at a minimum.

Long-Run Cost Curves

Over the long run, production managers can think about expanding or contracting operations. They can move to larger plants or smaller plants by varying the amounts of *all* inputs. Remember: in the long run *all costs are variable*. At any point in time, however, the firm is confined to a plant of given size. Within that plant, costs will vary according to the pattern described for the short run. At any given time short-run costs are relevant.

Long-run cost:
The minimum cost of producing any given output when all inputs are variable.

The **long-run cost** of any given output is the minimum cost of producing that output when *all inputs are variable*. The basic difference between the long run and the short run is flexibility. In the long run producers have options that aren't available in the short run. In the long run managers can control output and costs not only by varying the intensity of operation of a given plant but also by varying the *size* and *number* of plants operated.

Variation in Plant Size

Suppose your firm that manufactures running shoes can consider only five possible plant sizes. As the manager of the firm, your options are plants designed to operate most efficiently at weekly outputs of 50, 100, 150, 200, and 250 pairs of shoes.

Box 8 contains the short-run cost curves for each of the five plants. As a manager seeking to operate efficiently, you must determine the minimum possible level of average cost for each possible output. Points satisfying this requirement are shown on the long-run average cost curve.

Look at weekly outputs ranging from zero to 75 pairs of shoes. At any output below 75 pairs, your firm can produce at lower average cost in the first plant. For example, the average cost of a weekly output of 65 pairs is $21 in the first plant, whose short-run average cost curve is labeled AC_1. In the second plant, whose short-run average cost curve is labeled AC_2, it would cost $30 per unit to produce the same output. If you tried to produce this output in the second plant, much of its capital equipment would be underutilized. It's cheaper to produce the 65 pairs in the smaller plant.

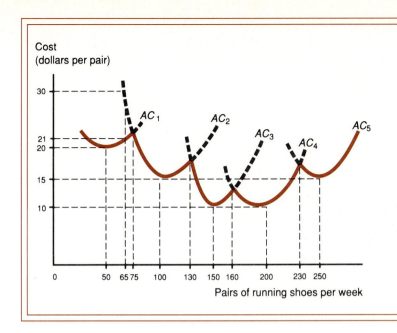

Cost
(dollars per pair)

Box 8 Long-Run Average Cost

The long-run average cost curve drawn at left is derived from five short-run cost curves, each corresponding to a larger plant size. Only the portions of the curves below their intersection are relevant for long-run decisions.

At outputs below 75 pairs per week, the relevant points on the long-run average cost curve are those that fall on AC_1. Beyond the point where AC_1 and AC_2 intersect on the graph, it becomes cheaper to produce in the second plant. Only points on the short-run average cost curves below these points of intersection will also be points on the long-run average cost curve. This holds for all points of intersection on the curve. For example, beyond a monthly output of 130 pairs, corresponding to the point at which AC_2 and AC_3 intersect, it becomes cheaper to produce in the third plant. *The long-run average cost curve for all five possible plant sizes is the portions of all five short-run cost curves below each point of intersection.* The dashed portions of each short-run average cost curve aren't included in the long-run average cost curve because they don't correspond to the *minimum* possible cost of producing output when all inputs are variable.

A smooth long-run cost curve exists when it's possible to vary plant size so that the output corresponding to minimum possible average cost for each plant is one unit greater than the output of the previous plant. This would be the case if it were possible for you as manager to expand by adding one square foot and the smallest fraction of a machine hour whenever you wished. In the previous example we assumed that additional capital had to be acquired in large "lumps" that limited your options to only five plants of widely varying capacities.

When managers have more flexibility to expand to a greater variety of plant sizes, the long-run average cost curve becomes smooth rather than lumpy, as shown in Box 9. As the intersection points of the short-run cost curves come closer and closer together, they trace out a smooth long-run average cost curve. Each point on the curve corresponds to a slightly larger plant. The graph shows some of the short-run cost curves and how the long-run average cost curve touches each of them. The minimum possible long-run average cost is achieved when you choose the plant whose short-run cost curve is AC^* and produce Q^* units per week.

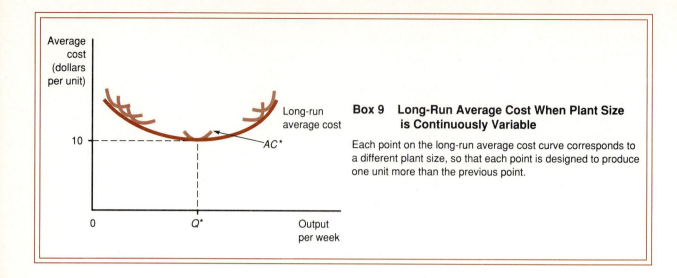

Average cost (dollars per unit)

10

0   Q*

Output per week

Long-run average cost

AC*

Box 9   Long-Run Average Cost When Plant Size is Continuously Variable

Each point on the long-run average cost curve corresponds to a different plant size, so that each point is designed to produce one unit more than the previous point.

Explaining the Shapes of Long-Run Average Cost Curves

In Box 9 the long-run average cost curve was drawn U-shaped. The pattern of variation in average cost in the long run when all inputs are variable can't be explained by the law of diminishing marginal returns, which applies only when it's impossible to increase all inputs in the same proportion. However, we have a number of reasons to expect that average costs of production will decline, at least at first when a firm expands in the long run, and then increase.

Economies of scale:
Reductions in unit costs resulting from increased size of operations. Also called *increasing returns to scale* or *economies of mass production.*

Economies of scale (sometimes called increasing returns to scale or economies of mass production) are reductions in unit costs resulting from increased size of operations. The scale of a firm's operation increases as a firm becomes bigger by operating out of larger plants. Economies of scale can be the result of increases in the productivity of inputs caused by increased specialization and division of labor as the firm builds more or bigger factories. This is quite common, particularly as a firm initially expands production. With only one worker and one machine, there's little opportunity to allocate specialized tasks to labor. When there are two workers and two machines, one worker can specialize in machine operations and the other can specialize in hand-finishing operations.

Economies of scale also result from the fact that a larger scale of operations doesn't require a proportionate increase in all inputs. For example, to double his grazing area, a farmer doesn't have to double the amount of fencing. This is because the perimeter of his farm doesn't double when its area doubles.

Finally, economies of scale can result from shifts in the method of production as a firm expands productive capacity in the long run. Expanding operations also permits use of more sophisticated machinery and allows workers to specialize in certain tasks. Some production processes aren't feasible to use when firms are small. However, as a firm grows in the long run its greater productive capacity makes it economical to use new production processes that are too expensive to use when output is low. Typically a firm shifts to a more capital-intensive (meaning more equipment per worker) production process as it expands. The use of more capital per worker increases labor productivity and helps reduce cost per unit of output.

For example, a cabinet shop that can ship only 100 units per month might find it too expensive to use a machine that lacquers its cabinets. At low levels of output, the cheapest way to finish the cabinets is likely to be by hand. However, when the shop expands and has the capacity to ship 1,000 units per month, the machine becomes the lowest-cost method of lacquering.

Finally, a firm may be able to purchase certain inputs at lower prices per unit when it buys in greater volume. This helps reduce average costs of production.

Economies of scale are eventually exhausted in the long run. As a firm becomes large, it's likely to encounter **diseconomies of scale** (also called *decreasing returns to scale*), which are increases in average costs of operation resulting from problems in managing large-scale enterprises. It's hard to pinpoint the exact time at which diseconomies of scale set in or the reasons for their occurrence. However, as a firm expands, communication between managers and workers often is impaired. Workers sometimes shirk their duties, and the firm can become more difficult to manage. However, the level of managerial skill varies from firm to firm, and it's not at all certain that diseconomies of scale will occur in all enterprises.

Most businesses are likely to enjoy a fairly long range of output for which average costs neither increase nor decrease in the long run. **Constant returns to scale** prevail when economies of scale no longer exist and when average costs do not increase as a result of diseconomies of scale in the long run. If constant returns to scale prevailed at all possible outputs in the long run, the long-run average cost curve would be a horizontal line in the long run. The long-run average cost curve for the case of constant returns to scale is illustrated in Box 10. If constant returns to scale prevailed from zero output on, large-scale firms would have no cost advantage over small-scale firms.

Diseconomies of scale:
Increases in average costs of operation resulting from problems in managing large-scale enterprises. Also called *decreasing returns to scale*.

Constant returns to scale:
Prevail when economies of scale no longer exist and when average costs do not increase as a result of diseconomies of scale in the long run.

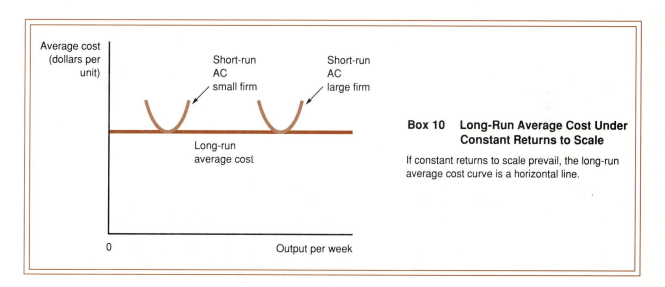

Box 10   Long-Run Average Cost Under Constant Returns to Scale

If constant returns to scale prevail, the long-run average cost curve is a horizontal line.

Economies of Scale and the Size of the Firm

The existence of economies of scale is an important determinant of the size of firms in various industries. When economies of scale exist, a firm can produce at lower average cost as it gets larger. This gives it a competitive edge. Because expansion reduces average cost, firms tend to expand until economies of scale are exhausted. This is because lower average cost, other things being equal, increases profits. For

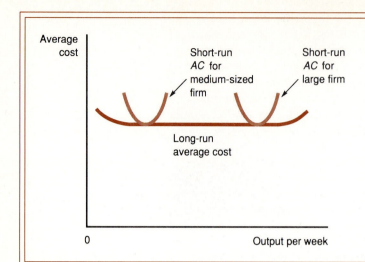

Box 11   A Long-Run Average Cost Curve With a Lengthy Stage of Constant Returns to Scale

The long-run average cost curve at left is U-shaped but has a flat bottom because of a lengthy stage of constant returns to scale after economies of scale are exhausted. Eventually a stage of decreasing returns to scale is encountered and *LRAC* increases.

example, in electric power generation, economies of scale exist over a long range of output, which explains why power companies tend to be very large.

If constant returns to scale are present for a long range of output before any diseconomies of scale increase average costs, an industry will be composed of firms of various sizes. For example, if the long-run average cost curve looks like the one shown in Box 11, medium-sized firms would be able to produce at the same minimum possible average cost as large firms in the long run. This state of affairs is common in retailing, farming, and manufacturing of electronic components, clothing, and other goods. Many studies of manufacturing industries have shown that there's an extensive range of constant returns to scale.

In industries where economies of scale are quickly exhausted and diseconomies of scale set in rapidly, firms tend to be small. Examples of such industries are shoe repairing and dry cleaning.

Concept Check

1 How does a long-run average cost curve differ from a short-run average cost curve?

2 How does a producer vary the scale of operations? What are economies of scale? How does the existence of economies of scale affect the size of firms in industries?

3 Explain why the long-run average cost curve would be a horizontal line if constant returns to scale always prevailed in the long run.

Summary

1. Production is the process of using inputs to make goods and services available. A production function is a relationship between any combination of inputs and the maximum output obtainable from that combination under current technology.

2. The short run is a period of production during which only some inputs are variable while others are fixed. In the long run all inputs are variable.

3. The theory of production assumes that there's a limit to the increase in output that can be obtained by using more of any one input while other inputs and technology are fixed.

4. A total product curve describes the way output varies in the short run as more of any one variable input is used together with fixed amounts of other inputs. The average product of a variable input is the total output divided by the number of units of the variable input when that variable input is used together with a certain number of units of fixed input. The average product of labor is a measure of the productivity of labor expressed as output per worker or per labor hour. The marginal product of a variable input is the extra output that results from using an extra unit of the variable input.

5. According to the law of diminishing marginal returns, the average product and marginal product of a variable input will increase at first and then decrease. The marginal product of the input equals the average product of the input when the average product is at a maximum. When the marginal product of an input falls below its average product, this results in decreases in the average product (or productivity) of a variable input.

6. Cost measures the dollar value of inputs used over any given period to produce an item. Total cost is the sum of fixed cost and variable cost. Variable cost is the cost of variable inputs, while fixed cost measures inputs that don't change as the firm increases or decreases output in the short run. To produce efficiently, managers must seek to produce any given output with the lowest-cost combinations of variable inputs.

7. Average cost is total cost divided by total output. Average cost is the sum of average variable cost and average fixed cost in the short run.

8. Given input prices, the shape of cost curves reflects the fact that the marginal product of variable inputs tends eventually to decline as more are used. The U-shaped average cost curve and eventually increasing marginal cost reflect the law of diminishing marginal returns in the short run.

9. In the long run all costs are variable—there are no fixed costs. In the long run firms can build larger plants or duplicate existing plants at other locations. Economies of scale result in decreases in average cost in the long run, while diseconomies of scale increase average cost. When constant returns to scale prevail, expansion of output in the long run involves no increase or decrease in average cost.

Key Terms and Concepts

Production	Fixed costs
Inputs	Variable costs
Production function	Total cost
Short run	Average cost
Variable input	Average variable cost
Fixed input	Average fixed cost
Long run	Long-run cost
Law of diminishing marginal returns	Economies of scale (increasing returns to scale)
Total product curve	
Total product of a variable input	Diseconomies of scale (decreasing returns to scale)
Marginal product	
Average product	Constant returns to scale
Point of diminishing returns	

Problems and Applications

1. Suppose you run a retail stereo store. In operating the store you have expenses for insurance, depreciation on business property, rent, and interest on borrowed funds. Explain why these payments represent prices for fixed inputs rather than variable inputs. Make a list of the variable inputs you're likely to use in operating the store.

2. As the manager of a fast-food restaurant, you estimate that the total product of labor used to make meals available varies each day according to the following data:

Number of workers per day	Total product of labor (meals per day)
1	30
2	70
3	100
4	120
5	130
6	135
7	140
8	140

   Calculate the marginal product and the average product of labor as the number of workers hired increases.

3. Plot the total product, average product, and marginal product curves for the data in the table given for problem 2. Explain why you'll never hire more than seven workers if you seek to maximize profits. How does the shape of the curve you've drawn illustrate the law of diminishing marginal returns?

4. The average product of workers in a textile factory you manage is estimated to be 50 yards of fabric per labor hour. The marginal product of labor is estimated to be 60 yards of fabric per labor hour when the average product of labor is 50 yards. What will happen to the average product of labor if additional labor is used now in the factory? What would the relationship between the average and marginal products of labor have to be to maximize the productivity of workers in the factory?

5. Your T-shirt manufacturing plant currently produces 2,000 shirts per day. Fixed costs for the plant are estimated to be $10,000 a day. Variable costs are $30,000 per day. Calculate total cost and average cost at the current output level. Calculate average fixed cost and average variable cost.

6. As the owner of a dry-cleaning establishment, you're considering the rental of a new pressing machine. The machine can be rented for $200 per day and will press 200 garments per day. You currently pay $40 per day to each worker who hand presses 50 garments per day. Assuming your firm seeks to press garments at the lowest possible cost, will you choose to rent the machine? How would your answer differ if the machine could be rented for only $150 per day?

7. The average product of 3 hair stylists employed by the small beauty shop you manage is 5 hair cuttings per day. Assuming labor is the only variable input used in hair styling and the hair stylists are paid $20 per hour, calculate the average variable cost of a haircut. If daily fixed cost is $100, calculate the minimum price that your shop must charge to cover its average cost when it schedules 15 appointments per day.

8. As the owner of a firm producing towels, you estimate that the average cost of production in your factory is $2. You also estimate that marginal cost is $2 at the current level of output. Explain why average cost must be at a minimum but average variable cost must be increasing.

9. Use the data in Box 3 to recalculate variable cost and total cost when the fixed cost in column 3 increases suddenly to $1,200 per week. Recalculate marginal cost and average cost for the various levels of output. Show how the average cost, average variable cost, and marginal cost curves are affected by the increase in fixed cost. Why is marginal cost unaffected by the increase in fixed cost?

10. Your firm estimates that whenever it doubles all the labor, capital, land, and any other inputs in the long run, its output also doubles. Assuming input prices don't increase or decrease as your firm expands, draw the firm's long-run average cost curve.

Suggested Readings

"A Special Report: Technology in the Workplace," *The Wall Street Journal*, June 12, 1987, Section 4. This report provides a review of new technology and its application in a variety of industries.

Bela Gold, "Changing Perspectives on Size, Scale, and Returns: An Interpretative Survey," *Journal of Economic Literature*, 19,1, March 1981, pp. 5-33. This article surveys economic research on how output varies with a firm's scale of operations.

David N. Hyman, *Modern Microeconomics: Analysis and Applications,* 2nd ed., Homewood, Ill.: Richard D. Irwin, Inc., 1989. Chapters 6 and 7 provide a more advanced analysis of production and cost.

A Forward Look

In the following chapter we use the cost relationships we developed in this chapter along with the behavioral assumption of profit maximization to derive short-run supply curves. By doing so, we can understand the reasons for the law of supply. This means we can isolate and understand the forces influencing market supply in the short run and those that cause short-run supply curves to be upward sloping.

Isoquant Analysis: Choosing the Method of Production

What influences the input combination a firm's managers choose to produce the items they sell? In other words, what forces determine *how* goods are produced?

Managers are well aware of the fact that there are alternative production methods. For example, the degree of mechanization used to produce furniture varies. A table can be produced entirely by a worker using hand tools. The same table can be produced in a highly mechanized factory with sophisticated machinery substituting for labor. A farmer can produce a crop of 10,000 pumpkins with relatively little land and labor and lots of fertilizer, machinery, and insecticide. He could produce the same crop with less machinery, fertilizer, and insecticide but with more labor and land substituted for those inputs.

In this appendix we'll develop a technique for analyzing the choice of a production method for any given item. In developing the model, we make the behavioral assumption that producers seek to minimize the cost of producing any given amount of output over any given period.

Isoquants

The table in Box 1 shows five alternative methods that can be used to produce 300 pairs of western boots per month in a small factory. Thanks to your experience managing the running-shoe factory in Chapter 10, you've just been named manager of the boot factory. A table like this might be drawn up by an industrial engineer to show you alternative production methods, each of which is capable of producing a maximum of 300 pairs of boots per month.

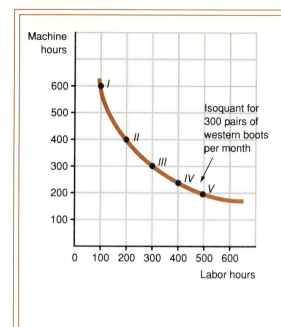

Machine hours (y-axis), Labor hours (x-axis)

Isoquant for 300 pairs of western boots per month

Box 1   An Isoquant

An isoquant is a curve that shows alternative combinations of inputs that can be used to produce a given output.

Production Methods for 300 Pairs of Boots and the Marginal Rate of Technical Substitution of Labor for Capital

Method	Machine hours	Labor hours	ΔK	ΔL (Hours)	$MRTS_{LK} = \dfrac{-\Delta K}{\Delta L}$ (Machine hours per hour of labor)
I	600	100			
			−200	100	2
II	400	200			
			−100	100	1
III	300	300			
			−70	100	0.7
IV	230	400			
			−30	100	0.3
V	200	500			

Method I involves the use of enough capital equipment in the plant to provide 600 hours of machine use. If this much capital is used, the 300 pairs of boots can be produced with only 100 hours of labor per month. This is a very *capital-intensive* method because it involves 6 hours of machine use for each hour of labor use. Alternatively, you could choose to use less capital and more labor to produce 300 pairs of boots during the month. For example, method II involves the use of 400 machine hours but uses 200 instead of 100 labor hours during the month. This is a less capital-intensive method of production than method I because only 2 machine hours are used together with each hour of labor. You can *substitute* 100 labor hours for 200 machine hours *without* reducing production when you switch from method I to method II. The table shows three other production methods capable of producing 300 pairs of boots per month.

An **isoquant** is a curve showing all combinations of variable inputs that can be used to produce a given quantity of output. The isoquant for 300 pairs of western boots is illustrated in Box 1. This isoquant is obtained by plotting the combinations of labor and capital corresponding to each production method in the table in Box 1 and tracing a smooth curve through the points. Points on the curve represent all possible combinations of labor and capital that can produce a maximum of 300 pairs of boots per month given available technology.

The isoquant shows you there are many ways to produce a given quantity of output. The highly mechanized production method I is represented by point *I* on the isoquant, which corresponds to 600 machine hours and only 100 labor hours. Alternatively, the same quantity of boots could be produced per month using fewer machines and more labor, as would be the case at point *V*, which corresponds to enough capital to provide only 200 machine hours of service per month but uses 500 labor hours. As you move along the isoquant from point *I* to point *V*, labor is

Isoquant:
A curve showing all combinations of variable inputs that can be used to produce a given quantity of output.

substituted for capital and there's a decline in the proportion of machine hours to labor hours used in production.

Properties of Isoquants

Common sense and observation of actual production suggest that isoquants are likely to have certain properties. For example, you know that if you use fewer machine hours each month, other things being equal, production will fall. However, you can make up for the reduced use of capital by hiring more labor to prevent production from declining. For any reduction in capital input, $-\Delta K$, the corresponding change in labor input, ΔL, must be positive to prevent output from declining. It follows that along the isoquant, the slope, $\Delta L/\Delta K$, must be negative because the signs of the numerator and the denominator are always opposite when labor is substituted for capital and output remains constant.

Marginal rate of technical substitution of labor for capital:
A measure of the amount of capital each unit of labor can replace without increasing or decreasing production.

The **marginal rate of technical substitution of labor for capital** ($MRTS_{LK}$) is a measure of the amount of capital each unit of labor can replace without increasing or decreasing production. The marginal rate of technical substitution along the isoquant at any point is the slope at that point multiplied by minus one:

$$MRTS_{LK} = \frac{-\Delta K}{\Delta L}$$

The table in Box 1 calculates the marginal rate of technical substitution of labor for capital as labor is substituted for capital in 100-hour increments along the isoquant.[1] This calculation approximates $MRTS_{LK}$ based on 100-hour (rather than 1-hour) changes in labor use as labor is substituted for capital.

At first each hour of labor can replace 2 hours of capital while keeping production fixed at 300 pairs of boots per month. However, as labor use is increased and capital use is decreased, the number of machine hours that can be replaced by each labor hour declines. For example, when 400 labor hours are used with only 230 machine hours per month, it takes only 0.3 machine hour to replace each labor hour when labor use is increased to 500 hours. The marginal rate of technical substitution of labor for capital tends to decline as labor is substituted for capital.

You can think of diminishing marginal rates of technical substitution of labor for capital as implying that increasing numbers of machine hours are required to substitute for successive reductions in labor hours if output is to remain constant. Moving from point *V* to point *IV* on the isoquant in Box 1, you can see that only 30 machine hours would be required to make up the output lost by withdrawing 100 labor hours from production when the method of production currently used involves 200 machine hours and 500 labor hours per month. However, if as manager you want to move from point *II,* where 400 machine hours and 200 labor hours are

---

[1]The marginal rate of technical substitution depends on the marginal products of labor and capital and the way these marginal products vary. To remain on the same isoquant, the decline in machine hours must be replaced with enough labor hours to get back to a point on the original isoquant. The gain in production is ΔL multiplied by its marginal product. Because the gain in production equals the loss in production, it follows that:

$$\Delta L(MP_L) = -\Delta K(MP_K)$$

Solving for the slope of the isoquant:

$$MRTS_{KL} = \frac{-\Delta K}{\Delta L} = \frac{MP_L}{MP_K}$$

where MP_K is the marginal product of capital and MP_L is the marginal product of labor.

used to produce the same monthly output, to point I by withdrawing 100 labor hours from use, 200 machine hours will be required to make up the output lost from 100 labor hours. The convex shape of the isoquant drawn in Box 1 reflects the declining marginal rate of technical substitution of labor for capital as labor is actually substituted for capital along an isoquant.

The reason for declining marginal rates of technical substitution is that inputs tend to complement each other. Each input has the capability of doing something the other either can't do or can do only imperfectly. In most activities, labor and capital are not perfect substitutes for each other. When labor hours are reduced, each additional reduction requires progressively more machine hours to replace the lost workers. The curvature of the isoquants indicates the difficulty with which one input can be substituted for the other without sacrificing production. This varies from activity to activity. It may, for example, be relatively easy to substitute labor for machines in a boot factory, but it may be virtually impossible to substitute labor for capital in the production of complex chemicals like antifreeze.

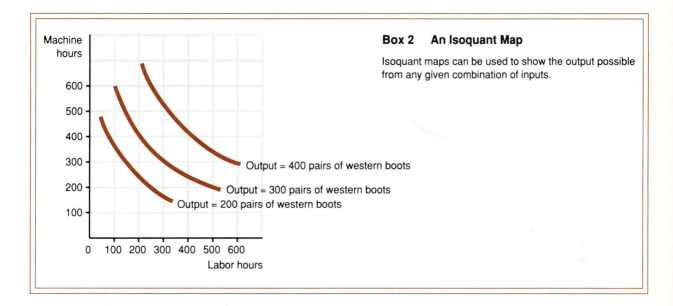

Box 2   An Isoquant Map

Isoquant maps can be used to show the output possible from any given combination of inputs.

Isoquants can be drawn for 400 or 200 pairs of boots per month as well. Naturally, it will take more labor and capital to produce more output. Box 2 contains an **isoquant map** for western boot production that shows the combinations of labor and capital that can be used to produce several possible output levels. Isoquants further from the origin correspond to higher output levels than isoquants closer to the origin. Each isoquant gives alternative combinations of inputs of labor and capital that can be used to produce the indicated output.

Isoquant map:
Shows the combinations of labor and capital that can be used to produce several possible output levels.

Cost of Production

Assume that labor and capital are the only two variable inputs used and that the prices of their services per hour are P_L and P_K, respectively. The total cost, TC, of any amount of these two inputs used is

$$TC = P_L L + P_K K$$

where L is measured as labor hours and K is measured as machine hours. P_L is the hourly wage of labor and P_K is the hourly rental rate for the machines. For example, if the price of labor were $10 per hour while the price of capital were $20 per hour, the total cost of production method III in Box 1, which uses 300 labor hours and 300 machine hours, would be

$$TC = \$10\,(300) + \$20\,(300) = \$9,000$$

Isocost Lines

Isocost line:
Gives all combinations of labor and capital that are of equal total cost.

An **isocost line** gives all combinations of labor and capital that are of equal total cost. Suppose, for example, that the price of labor services (wages) is $10 per hour, whereas the price of capital services (the machine rental rate) is $20 per hour. A monthly input combination consisting of 500 labor hours and 200 machine hours, corresponding to production process V in Box 1, would therefore cost $9,000. This input combination lies on the same isocost line as one corresponding to production process III. An isocost line can be drawn between the two points corresponding to production processes III and V, as is done in Box 3. Any other monthly input combination costing $9,000 would lie on the isocost line drawn through points *III* and *V*.

There's a different isocost line for each level of total cost. This is shown in Box 3, where each line is labeled according to the cost of input combinations lying on it. Isocost lines farther out from the origin involve more input use and therefore more cost than lines closer to the origin.

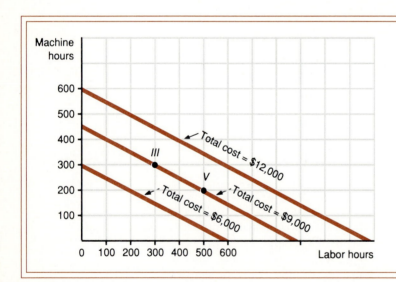

Box 3   Isocost Lines

Points on a given isocost line show alternative production processes of equal cost. The family of isocost lines at left prevails when the price of a machine hour is $20 and the price of a labor hour is $10.

The Slope of Isocost Lines Depends on Input Prices

When the price of labor is $10 per hour and the price of capital is $20 per hour, labor use must be reduced by 2 hours to free the $20 necessary to purchase each machine hour. The slope of any isocost line in the family is

$$\frac{-\Delta K}{\Delta L}$$

When labor use is reduced by $-\Delta L = 2$ hours, the manager can rent 1 extra hour of machine use $\Delta K = 1$ using the $20 released without increasing total cost. It follows that along the isocost line,

$$-\frac{\Delta L}{\Delta K} = \frac{1}{2} = \frac{\$10}{\$20} = \frac{P_L}{P_K}$$

Note that $\Delta L/\Delta K$ is the slope of the isocost line, which in this case would be $-1/2$. The slope of the isocost line therefore varies according to the price of labor relative to the price of capital.[2] The higher the ratio of the price of labor to the price of capital, the less labor use must be reduced to purchase each hour of capital without changing total cost, and the steeper the isocost line.

For example, if the price of labor were only $5 per hour, then it would take 4 hours of labor reduction to free the funds to rent 1 machine hour when machine hours cost $20 per hour. In that case the slope of the isocost line would be

$$-\frac{\$5}{\$20} = -\frac{1}{4}$$

If labor and capital both cost $20 per hour, only 1 labor hour would have to be sacrificed to buy an hour of capital without changing cost. In this case the slope of the isocost line would be

$$-\frac{\$20}{\$20} = -1$$

and the isocost line would be steeper than when the price of labor was only $5 per hour.

A change in the price of either labor or capital changes the slope of a whole family of isocost lines. For example, an increase in the price of labor given the price of capital will make each of the isocost lines in the family steeper. In Box 4, **A** shows how an increase in the price of labor relative to capital will make one isocost line in a family steeper. The graph labeled **B** shows that an increase in the price of capital given the price of labor will make any one isocost line in a family flatter. When the price of capital increases relative to that of labor, therefore, all isocost lines in a family become flatter.

The Minimum-Cost Input Combination for a Given Output

Box 5 reproduces the isoquant for producing 300 pairs of western boots. The family of isocost lines corresponding to wages of $10 per hour and an hourly machine rental rate of $20 per hour is superimposed on the same set of axes as that used for the isoquant.

As manager of the boot factory, what production method will you choose if you want to produce the 300 pairs at the lowest possible total cost? The table in Box 5

---

[2]You can also see this by writing the equation for total cost in terms of K:

$$K = -\left(\frac{P_L}{P_K}\right) L + \frac{TC}{P_K}$$

In this case

$$\frac{P_L}{P_K} = \frac{\$10}{\$20} = \frac{1}{2}$$

The slope of the isocost line is therefore $-1/2$.

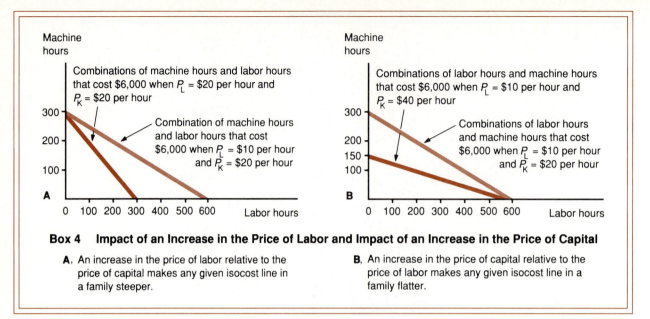

Box 4   Impact of an Increase in the Price of Labor and Impact of an Increase in the Price of Capital

A, An increase in the price of labor relative to the price of capital makes any given isocost line in a family steeper.

B, An increase in the price of capital relative to the price of labor makes any given isocost line in a family flatter.

shows the total cost of the five possible methods of production. You can see from the table that production method IV, which involves 230 machine hours and 400 labor hours per month, costs $8,600, which is less than any of the other methods shown when the price of labor is $10 per hour and the price of capital is $20 per hour.

Using isoquant analysis, it's easy to show the influences on the choice of the least costly production method. The graph in Box 5 shows that method I is not the least costly method because it corresponds to a point on the isocost line for which total cost is $13,000. By substituting labor for capital, you can move to lower isocost lines without decreasing output when first at point *I*. Similarly, production method II, which corresponds to a total cost of $10,000, is not the least costly method because by still further substituting labor for capital, you can move to a lower isocost line. By the same token, production method V is not the least costly because you can move to a lower isocost line from point *V* by substituting machine use for labor use.

The minimum-cost production method corresponds to the point at which the isoquant for 300 pairs of boots is just tangent to an isocost line. This condition is met at point *E*, which corresponds to production method IV. At that point it's not possible to reduce cost still further by substituting one input for another.

A tangency of the isoquant and an isocost line implies that the slope of the isoquant equals the slope of the isocost line at that point. Because the slope of the isoquant is $-MRTS_{LK}$ and the slope of the isocost line is $-P_L/P_K$, the condition for minimizing the cost of producing a given output can be written as

$$\frac{P_L}{P_K} = MRTS_{LK}$$

This equation shows that, as manager, your choice of the least costly production method is influenced by the prices of variable inputs and by the marginal rate of technical substitution between variable inputs. The marginal rate of technical substitution associated with any given input combination on an isoquant depends on technology. However, you're free to substitute inputs for each other given technology by varying production methods until input use is adjusted to meet the above con-

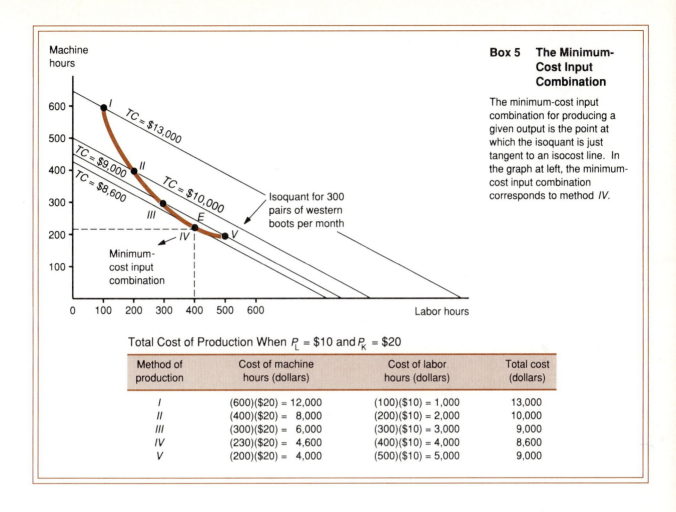

Box 5 The Minimum-Cost Input Combination

The minimum-cost input combination for producing a given output is the point at which the isoquant is just tangent to an isocost line. In the graph at left, the minimum-cost input combination corresponds to method *IV*.

Total Cost of Production When P_L = $10 and P_K = $20

Method of production	Cost of machine hours (dollars)	Cost of labor hours (dollars)	Total cost (dollars)
I	(600)($20) = 12,000	(100)($10) = 1,000	13,000
II	(400)($20) = 8,000	(200)($10) = 2,000	10,000
III	(300)($20) = 6,000	(300)($10) = 3,000	9,000
IV	(230)($20) = 4,600	(400)($10) = 4,000	8,600
V	(200)($20) = 4,000	(500)($10) = 5,000	9,000

dition. The actual production method you choose depends on *both* input prices and technology affecting the marginal rates of technical substitution. Changes in technology change the shape of the isoquants and cause movement to a new least costly production method.

Given the same technology available to two nations, you wouldn't expect to see capital-intensive methods used to produce goods and services in nations where labor is cheap relative to capital, as is the case in China. On the other hand, in the United States labor is expensive while capital equipment is relatively abundant. It's therefore not surprising to see highly mechanized apparel manufacturers in the United States, while in China the same clothes are produced with less capital-intensive techniques—even though both nations have access to the same technology.

Note that changes in the price of labor or capital will change the slope of the isocost lines. When this occurs, assuming no change in technology affecting the shape of the isoquant, managers will respond by adjusting their production method until the isoquant is just tangent to one of the new isocost lines. For example, if the price of machine rental in China were to decrease relative to the price of labor, isocost lines would become steeper and the minimum-cost production methods would become more capital intensive. The impact of a decrease in the price of capital relative to labor is shown in Box 6.

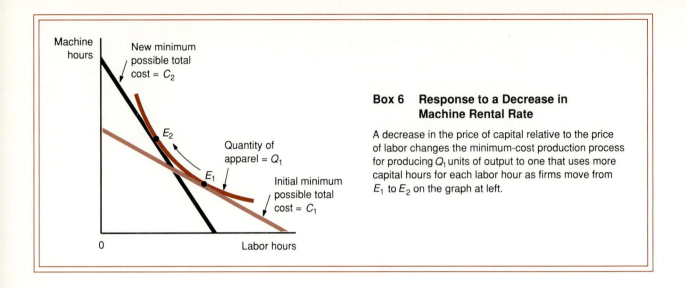

Box 6   Response to a Decrease in Machine Rental Rate

A decrease in the price of capital relative to the price of labor changes the minimum-cost production process for producing Q_1 units of output to one that uses more capital hours for each labor hour as firms move from E_1 to E_2 on the graph at left.

Expansion Paths

Expansion path:
Shows how the use of inputs by a producer will vary as the firm expands output.

An **expansion path** shows how the use of inputs by a producer will vary as the firm expands output. Assuming that the producer minimizes the cost of producing any given output, we can derive the expansion path by connecting points of tangency of isoquants and isocost lines. Such an expansion path is illustrated in Box 7.

Only a few isoquants have been drawn and labeled according to the amounts of monthly output to which they correspond. The minimum possible cost of producing each output is given by the tangency of each isoquant and an isocost line. Points on the variable cost curve can be derived simply by plotting the monthly cost of each output level. Each point on the variable cost curve gives the minimum cost of producing that output given input prices and technology.

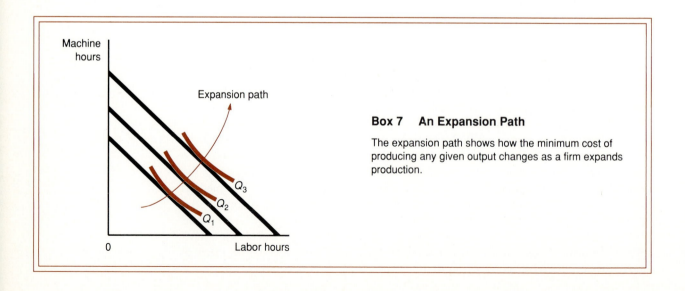

Box 7   An Expansion Path

The expansion path shows how the minimum cost of producing any given output changes as a firm expands production.

Notice how the expansion path drawn in Box 7 bends upward as output is increased by moving to higher and higher isoquants. This shape of the expansion path implies that the ratio of capital input to labor input is increasing as output expands. The ratio of labor to capital would be constant only in the case of a straight-line expansion path.

The expansion path shown in Box 7 is quite realistic for most enterprises in the long run because production methods often become more capital intensive as an enterprise grows. This is because, as firms become larger, they tend to become more mechanized by increasing the ratio of machine hours to labor hours used to produce any given amount of output.

Key Terms and Concepts

Isoquant
Marginal rate of technical substitution
   of labor for capital

Isoquant map
Isoquant line
Expansion path

The Profit-Maximizing Competitive Firm and Market Supply

People just like you have good product ideas every day. And the stroke of inspiration for the next hot craze could very well be yours. Having read Chapter 10, however, you're now aware that manufacturing even a popular item like running shoes involves a lot of cost considerations.

How high a production cost can a firm incur and still make a profit by supplying its goods to consumers? In this chapter we begin an investigation of the theory of supply in business firms. As you'll see, cost is an important influence on a firm's supply decisions because it affects the profitability of making products available to buyers in markets. The goal of the firm is assumed to be the maximization of profits. At this point it's a good idea for you to review the analysis of profits in Chapter 9 to make sure you understand how economists define profits and how economic profits can differ from accounting profits.

In the analysis in this chapter, we also assume that firms produce a single product and that they *react to* rather than control the price of their product. Firms of this type are usually very small and sell their products in a market in which many competing sellers offer identical products to buyers. Your local farmers' market is a good example. In a typical farmers' market there might be 20 or 30 sellers of tomatoes or watermelons of the same quality. If any one seller raises the price of his produce above the market price, he'll find that buyers will choose to buy their tomatoes from his competitors.

Marginal analysis, which we introduced in Chapter 2, is the key tool we use in this chapter to show how firms make supply decisions to maximize profits. We can use marginal analysis to isolate the marginal benefit and marginal cost of business decisions. By doing so, we can develop a rule for profit maximization. This rule will help us establish the cause-and-effect relationship between changes in price and changes in quantity supplied that's necessary to derive a supply curve. We then can use the analysis to show how changes in input prices and other factors affecting cost can cause shifts in supply. Once we've derived the individual firm's supply curve, it's easy to show how market supply curves are related to individual supply curves.

After reading this chapter, you should be able to: *Concept Preview*

1   Explain the concept of perfect competition in markets.
2   Explain why the demand curve for the product of a competitive firm is perfectly elastic at the market equilibrium price.
3   Explain how the total profit a competitive firm can earn over a given period varies with the output actually sold given the market price of the product.
4   Use marginal analysis to explain how the firm chooses its output so as to maximize profits.
5   Use graphs to show the actual profits a firm earns and to show how the market price of the product affects the profitability of the firm.
6   Explain under what conditions a firm will cease operations in the short run.
7   Show how a supply curve can be derived for a competitive firm that maximizes profit from selling a single product and how the market supply curve can be derived from the supply curves of individual firms in an industry.
8   Demonstrate how changes in input prices affect the supply curves in the short run.

Profit, Price, and Output in the Short Run for a Competitive Firm

To develop a theory of supply, we begin by making a number of simplifying assumptions. Although these assumptions may seem quite unrealistic to you, they allow us to develop a model that uncovers the basic forces that underlie supply by profit-maximizing firms in markets. In this instance, as is the case for all economic models, you'll find that unrealistic assumptions will yield useful insights into the way the economy actually functions. The purpose of the model we'll develop in this chapter is to allow us to use marginal analysis to explain how quantity supplied to a market in the short run is related to the price of a product, assuming that sellers maximize profit.

Perfect Competition

The theory of supply is based on the simplifying assumption of "perfect" competition in a market for a product. A **perfectly competitive market** exists when the following conditions prevail:

1. There are *many sellers* in the market. In a perfectly competitive market the number of sellers usually exceeds 100 and is often in the thousands.
2. The products sold in the market are *homogeneous*, which means that the product of each seller is identical to that of other sellers. A homogeneous product

Perfectly competitive market:
Exists when (1) there are many sellers in the market; (2) the products sold in the market are homogeneous; (3) each firm has a very small market share of total sales; (4) no seller regards competing sellers as a threat to its market share; (5) information is freely available on prices; (6) there is freedom of entry and exit by sellers.

Economic Thinkers

FRIEDRICH VON HAYEK

The name Friedrich von Hayek is synonymous with the Austrian school of economics because he has been one of its most powerful and influential supporters. The Austrian school focuses on how markets adjust to changing circumstances. Within this general area, von Hayek has been particularly interested in the problem of how markets transmit information to participants. In 1945 he presented a theory of how this transfer of information takes place in his classic work, *The Use of Knowledge in Society*.

Von Hayek concludes that participants are informed of changes in market conditions not by the media or by the government, but rather through changes in the market prices of goods. He believes this to be an efficient mechanism of communicating information because the majority of market participants never need to know the exact cause of the change, but are still able to adjust to it. Participants can concentrate on their own activities, but have enough information about opportunity costs through market prices that they are able to make the correct decisions.

The market acts as a single unit, according to von Hayek, not because members are constantly surveying the whole market, but rather because each individual's activities overlap just enough to relay relevant information to all through changing prices.

Von Hayek faults economists who quibble over perfect versus imperfect competition. He argues that competition is a process and industries should be judged on whether they conform with the characteristics of the process. If the process is working, people will get the best possible product at the lowest possible price.

In addition to his contributions in these areas, von Hayek has worked in the areas of monetary theory, capital theory, and business cycle theory and has gained a reputation as a political philosopher through books like *The Road to Serfdom, The Constitution of Liberty,* and *Law, Legislation and Liberty*.

---

is one that is standardized. Grade A eggs are an example, as are bushels of soybeans of given quality. Buyers view the product sold by any one seller in the market as a perfect substitute for that of any other seller.

3. Each firm has a *very small market share* of total sales. Market share is the percentage of total sales over any period accounted for by a single seller. Generally in a perfectly competitive market no seller has a market share exceeding 1%.

4. No seller in the market regards competing sellers as a threat to its market share. *Firms therefore are unconcerned about their competitors' marketing or production decisions.*

5. *Information is freely available* on prices, technology, and profit opportunities, and resources are mobile. (See Economic Thinkers box on Friedrich von Hayek.)

6. There is *freedom of entry and exit* by sellers of the standardized good. This means there are no restraints preventing firms from entering the industry, nor are there difficulties involved in ceasing operations.

In a perfectly competitive market an *individual* seller cannot influence the market price of its product. Because each seller's product is a perfect substitute for that of any other seller in the market, buyers have no reason to prefer the product of one seller to that of any other. A firm that tries to charge more than the going market price for its product will lose all its customers to competing sellers.

In a perfectly competitive market no individual firm can shift the market supply sufficiently to make the good scarcer or more abundant. Even if one firm withholds its entire production from the market, this won't cause the good to become scarcer and therefore won't result in an increase in the market price. If the firm floods the market with its output, the good won't become sufficiently more abundant to result in downward pressure on market price. This means that no seller in the market can affect the price of the product by offering to sell either more or less.

A **competitive firm** is one that sells its product in a perfectly competitive market. *A competitive firm is characterized as a "price taker" because it can only react to the market price and cannot by itself cause the market price to go up or down.* In a perfectly competitive market the number of sellers is responsive to the profitability of selling the industry's product. Free entry and mobility of resources ensure that the number of sellers, and therefore market supply, will increase when it's profitable to sell the product in the market.

Competitive firm: One that sells its product in a perfectly competitive market in which it is a price taker.

The key idea underlying the notion of perfect competition is that individual firms *react to* rather than influence prices of the products they sell. The model is relevant to markets where prices are set largely by impersonal forces of supply and demand and in which firms more or less take the market price as given.

In fact, in many agricultural markets, such as that for wheat, the conditions of standardized products, many sellers, and small market shares are often approximated. For example, in 1982 there were nearly half a million wheat sellers in the United States. Even though a small percentage of large wheat farms accounted for about half of total production, the top 3% or so of wheat producers amounted to many thousands of independent firms. The model also will be useful in other cases where there's great similarity between the products of competing sellers and sellers have reasonably small market shares.

Demand as Seen by a Competitive Firm

The market demand curve for the product sold by a competitive *industry* composed of many firms selling a homogeneous product is downward sloping. Market price is determined by demand and supply in the competitive market, in which prices adjust until quantity demanded by the many buyers equals quantity supplied by the many sellers.

For example, suppose firms in a segment of the furniture industry produce a standard-size futon (you know—those comfortable, economical couch substitutes that are a basic in Japanese decor). Assume there are 1,000 firms in the industry and consumers regard the product of any one firm as a perfect substitute for that of any other. The market in which these firms sell their futons is perfectly competitive, and each firm can be considered a price taker. Each individual firm in the industry is very small and operates out of a very small plant in which it can produce a small number of futons each day.

In Box 1, **A** shows how the market price is determined by supply and demand and how this influences the demand as seen by any single competitive firm in the industry. The market demand and supply curves for the futon intersect at point *E*. The corresponding market equilibrium price is $150 per futon, and the equilibrium quantity sold per day at that price is 8,000.

The graph labeled **B** shows the demand curve as seen by any firm in the industry. This demand curve is a horizontal line. We can easily understand the reason for this by considering the short-run productive capacity of each firm in the industry. Suppose each firm can produce no more than 15 futons per day in its existing plant.

Principles in Practice

Are Markets Competitive?

As you know, the notion of a perfectly competitive market is an abstraction. However, in many cases the conditions existing in actual markets closely approximate those assumed for perfect competition among sellers.

Perhaps the best examples of markets in which sellers can be regarded as price takers are those in which agricultural commodities are sold. Agricultural commodities, such as wheat, corn, soybeans, tobacco, cattle, and whole milk, are highly standardized products. It's rare for a buyer to see much difference between the product of one farmer and that of another. In addition, there are thousands of independent sellers of agricultural food products in U.S. markets. For example, in 1982 there were nearly 1.4 million producers of cattle and calves. Slightly over 500,000 farms produced and sold soybeans in 1982. The table that follows shows the number of firms selling major categories of agricultural products in 1982.

Number of Firms Producing Selected Agricultural Products, 1982

Product	Number of sellers
Cattle and calves	1,354,992
Corn	937,704
Soybeans	511,229
Wheat	446,075
Dairy products	197,369
Tobacco	179,141
Peanuts	23,046
Rice	11,445

Source: U.S. Department of Commerce, Bureau of the Census, Census of Agriculture, 1982.

Two of the basic conditions necessary for firms to be price takers—standardized products and large numbers of sellers—clearly are satisfied for most agricultural products. However, doubt is often expressed about whether or not sellers actually do have small market shares. After all, in recent years large corporate farms, often covering thousands of acres, have become more prevalent. The average farm size in the United States is less than 400 acres. However, large farms with 1,000 acres or more account for 40% of all farm acreage in the United States. For example, the top 2% of wheat producers have accounted for more than 50% of wheat production in the United States in recent years. The largest 2% of broiler chicken producers in recent years have accounted for about 70% of market sales.* Does this mean that a few sellers could make certain products scarce enough to increase market price?

The answer to this question is "No." The reason is that the top 2% of producers selling an agricultural product amount to a very large number of independent firms. For example, the top 2% of grain producers that account for 50% of grain sales in the United States represent 27,000 independent sellers! It's therefore unlikely, despite the growth of very large farms in recent years, that any one seller has a large enough market share of sales to be able to shift supply significantly. Agricultural firms thus are likely to be price takers.

In addition, it's easy for firms to enter and leave agricultural markets as sellers. However, there are exceptions. Agricultural markets often have price floors and limitations on output established and enforced by government. For example, for many years government regulations have limited the number of tobacco producers.

In nonagricultural markets, product standardization is the exception rather than the rule. Producers of many consumer products differentiate their product by brand name and by quality. In some markets, such as those for new automobiles, one or a few sellers have large market shares and could affect price by controlling supply. Nonetheless, despite product differentiation among sellers, the products of one seller are often very good substitutes for those of others. A full-size Ford has many similarities to a full-size Chevrolet.

As the following table shows for selected industries, the condition of large numbers of sellers in markets often prevails. For example, in 1982 there were nearly 1.4 million independent sellers of contract construction services. In many markets for nonagricultural products, therefore, the notion of firms as price takers is likely to be reasonable. Although the idea of perfect competition doesn't apply to all markets, it's an abstraction that's useful in explaining the behavior of firms in many different markets. Counting firms in a market is, of course, not the best way to determine whether the market is competitive. However, it provides some insight into the question of whether or not individual sellers in the market are likely to have the power to influence the price of their product. Firms must be price takers for the theory of competitive supply to be relevant.

Number of Nonagricultural Firms Selling Selected Products in the United States, 1982

Contract construction	1,389,309
Lumber and wood products	30,381
Apparel	22,018
Electric and electronic equipment	13,701
Furniture and fixtures	9,227
Iron and steel	1,438
Footwear	751

Source: U.S. Department of Commerce, Bureau of the Census, Census of Manufacturers, 1982, and Census of Construction Industries, 1982.

*Daniel E. Suits, "Agriculture," in Walter Adams, ed., *The Structure of American Industry*, 6th ed., New York: Macmillan, 1982.

The most any one firm can add to (or subtract from) market supply is therefore 15 units per day. Even if any one firm adds or subtracts this maximum amount, the shift in the supply curve will be imperceptible. There would therefore be no perceptible effect on market price. To see this, go to **A** in Box 1 and note how removing 15 futons per day from the market quantity supplied of 8,000 at the $150 price won't noticeably change the quantity supplied. No firm has the capacity to make the good appreciably more abundant or scarce. This means that any firm can sell all it wants at the market equilibrium price. This being the case, there's no incentive to sell at any price lower than the market price. A firm that lowers its price won't be able to sell more than it would otherwise. The decrease in price would therefore lower revenue but have no effect on the quantity of futons sold and the cost of production. Selling at a price below the market equilibrium price would therefore decrease a firm's profit.

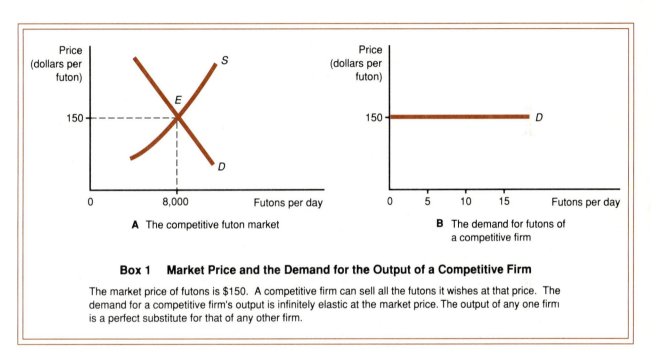

A The competitive futon market

B The demand for futons of a competitive firm

Box 1 Market Price and the Demand for the Output of a Competitive Firm

The market price of futons is $150. A competitive firm can sell all the futons it wishes at that price. The demand for a competitive firm's output is infinitely elastic at the market price. The output of any one firm is a perfect substitute for that of any other firm.

The standardized product sold by any one competitive firm is a perfect substitute for that of any other competing seller. The horizontal demand curve of each firm in a competitive industry is perfectly elastic at the market price. (See Chapter 7 for an explanation of why a horizontal demand curve is perfectly elastic.)

How Profit Varies as a Competitive Firm Increases Output

You'll recall from Chapter 9 that profit can be calculated as the difference between total revenue (*TR*) and total cost (*TC*) per sales period:

$$\text{Profit} = TR - TC$$

Total revenue is the price (*P*) of the good sold multiplied by the amount produced (*Q*). The total cost of production includes all implicit costs. This means that profit is measured as economic profit (see Chapter 9 for a discussion of how accounting profits often overestimate economic profits by not including normal profit as a cost).

The price is beyond the influence of a competitive firm. Therefore the only way a competitive firm can influence its revenues is by varying the amount it produces. However, as output changes, so does cost. The current market price of standard-size futons is $150. Notice that the price of futons can also be expressed as total revenue divided by output. Total revenue *per unit* of a good sold is called the **average revenue** of the good. It's easy to show that average revenue is just another name for the price of a good:

Average revenue:
Total revenue per unit of a good sold.

$$\text{Average revenue} = \frac{\text{Total revenue}}{Q}$$

where Q is output.

Because total revenue is $P \times Q$, it follows that:

$$\text{Average revenue} = \frac{PQ}{Q} = P$$

Therefore average revenue, or revenue per unit, *is* the price of a product.

The table in Box 2 provides hypothetical data on output, revenue, cost, and profits for a typical futon producer selling in a competitive market. Let's call the firm the

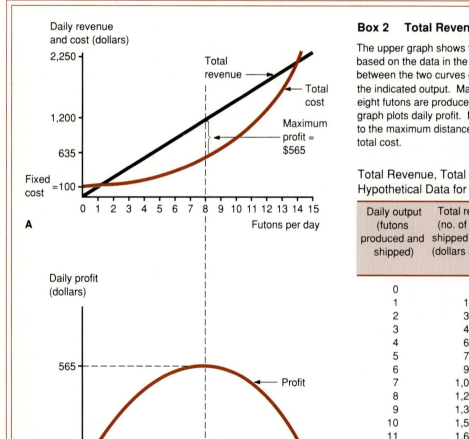

A

Daily revenue and cost (dollars)

Total revenue

Total cost

Maximum profit = $565

Fixed cost = 100

Futons per day

B

Daily profit (dollars)

565

0

−100

Profit

Futons per day

Box 2 Total Revenue, Total Cost, and Profit

The upper graph shows total revenue and total cost based on the data in the table below. The difference between the two curves gives the profit per day for the indicated output. Maximum profit occurs when eight futons are produced each day. The lower graph plots daily profit. Maximum profit corresponds to the maximum distance between total revenue and total cost.

Total Revenue, Total Cost, and Profit: Hypothetical Data for a Competitive Firm

Daily output (futons produced and shipped)	Total revenue (no. of futons shipped × $150) (dollars per day)	Total cost (dollars per day)	Profit (dollars per day)
0	0	100	−100
1	150	160	−10
2	300	200	100
3	450	230	220
4	600	270	330
5	750	320	430
6	900	390	510
7	1,050	490	560
8	1,200	635	565
9	1,350	815	535
10	1,500	1,015	485
11	1,650	1,245	405
12	1,800	1,495	305
13	1,950	1,775	175
14	2,100	2,095	5
15	2,250	2,495	−245

Futon Factory, and let's appoint you as its manager. We assume the firm has fixed costs of $100 per day and the pattern of variation of short-run costs reflects the law of diminishing marginal returns we discussed in Chapter 10.

The first column of the table shows the daily output of futons ranging from zero to 15. To obtain the total revenue from that output, just multiply output by the market price, which is assumed to be $150. The second column shows the total revenue, PQ, of all the output levels shown. The third column shows total cost. Notice that your firm incurs $100 in fixed cost even if output is zero. Finally, profits are shown in the fourth column. Profits are simply the difference between total revenue and total cost at each possible output level.

Graph **A** in Box 2 plots total revenue and total cost for the data in Box 2 and shows profits graphically as the difference between the two curves. Graph **B** plots daily profit. Total revenue increases by $150 each time an extra futon is sold. The graph of total revenue is therefore a straight line through the origin of the two axes with a slope of $150 because the change in total revenue (ΔTR) is always $150 when another futon is sold. The total cost curve has the shape typically assumed to exist in the short run. Its shape reflects the law of diminishing marginal returns. *The vertical distance between the total revenue and total cost curves gives profit at each level of production.* This difference is plotted directly below the total revenue and total cost curves.

You'll note that at low levels of output, the Futon Factory would lose money. *If it were to produce nothing, its losses would be equal to fixed costs.* As production begins, profits increase, eventually reaching a maximum level. Maximum possible daily profits are earned when the firm sells eight futons per day. If the firm were to produce more than eight futons per day, profits would steadily decline and eventually become negative again. Given the price of its product and the way its cost varies as more is produced, the competitive firm therefore finds that its profit varies as it produces more and more per day. At low levels of output it can expect to incur losses because it will earn little revenue but still incur fixed costs. As output increases, profits tend to rise at first but then fall as the law of diminishing marginal returns comes into play. As the firm approaches its daily capacity to produce futons, the rapid increase in costs tends to decrease daily profits.

Concept Check

1 Draw the demand curve for the output of a single-product competitive firm and explain why it differs from the industry demand curve. Explain why the competitive firm is a price taker.

2 Draw a curve to show how total revenue will change as a competitive firm sells more output.

3 Explain how profit will vary with output for a competitive firm in the short run. What accounts for the pattern of variation in profits as firms increase output in the short run?

Using Marginal Analysis to Choose the Profit-Maximizing Output: The Theory of Short-Run Supply

Business managers are seldom confronted with a neat graph like the one drawn in Box 2 showing how profits vary with output. Managers usually grope for maximum profits by comparing the extra gains possible from additional production each day with the additional costs they incur. Marginal analysis, as we saw in Chapter 2, is ideally suited to show how benefits of actions are compared with costs to achieve certain objectives. In this case your objective as the manager of the Futon Factory is assumed to be the maximization of profit each day. To achieve this objective, as a rational manager you must compare the gain from producing and shipping more futons with the cost of doing so. The gain to your firm of selling more futons is the *extra revenue* from selling an additional futon. The cost of doing so is the *extra cost* of making the futon available.

Marginal Revenue, Marginal Cost, and Marginal Profit

Marginal revenue:
The extra revenue obtained from selling an additional unit of a good.

The extra revenue obtained from selling an additional unit of a good is called the **marginal revenue** (MR) of output. We can compute marginal revenue for any given output by calculating the change in total revenue (ΔTR) associated with any given change in output sold (ΔQ):

$$MR = \frac{\Delta TR}{\Delta Q}$$

Because a competitive firm can sell all the output it wishes at the market price, it's easy to show that its marginal revenue will *always* equal the price of its product and therefore equal its average revenue. For example, if futon producers can sell all the futons they wish at the market price of $150, the *extra* revenue they'll take in for each *extra* futon they sell will be $150. As long as the price is unaffected by the amount the firm sells, the marginal revenue of selling an additional futon will be its price. Because price is also average revenue, this means that for a competitive firm, $P = AR = MR$. It follows that the additional gain, or *marginal revenue*, a competitive firm enjoys from selling output is measured by the market price of its product. In this case the marginal revenue is always $150.

The table in Box 3 shows daily output, total revenue, and marginal revenue, assuming the price of futons is $150. You can now convince yourself that marginal revenue equals price by observing that total revenue increases by $150 each time an additional futon is sold.

The *marginal cost* is the extra cost of selling an additional unit of a good. In the table in Box 4, the marginal cost is obtained by calculating the extra cost associated with each extra futon produced and shipped. Notice how marginal cost decreases at first but then steadily increases as the firm approaches its short-run capacity output of 15 futons per day. This pattern of variation in marginal cost reflects the law of diminishing marginal returns as the firm tries to produce more in the short run.

In choosing the profit-maximizing output, managers can be thought of as comparing the marginal cost with the marginal revenue for each extra futon sold. When marginal revenue exceeds marginal cost, selling an additional futon will increase profits. The marginal cost influences the willingness of firms to sell more. When marginal revenue falls short of marginal cost, sale of an additional futon will decrease profits.

Marginal profit:
The change in profit from selling an additional unit of a good, representing the difference between the marginal revenue from that unit and its marginal cost.

The **marginal profit** is the change in profit from selling an additional unit of a good, representing the difference between the marginal revenue from that unit and its marginal cost. The marginal profit represents the net gain to the firm of making an additional futon available. When the marginal profit is positive, the firm adds to total profits by selling more futons. When the marginal profit is negative, the firm will reduce its profits by selling more futons.

Box 3 Output, Total Revenue, and Marginal Revenue for a Competitive Firm (Hypothetical Data)

Daily output (futons produced and shipped)	Total revenue (dollars per day)	Marginal revenue (dollars per futon)
0	0	–
1	150	150
2	300	150
3	450	150
4	600	150
5	750	150
6	900	150
7	1,050	150
8	1,200	150
9	1,350	150
10	1,500	150
11	1,650	150
12	1,800	150
13	1,950	150
14	2,100	150
15	2,250	150

Box 4 Marginal Cost Calculated from Total Cost for a Competitive Firm (Hypothetical Data)

Daily output (futons produced and shipped)	Total cost (dollars per day)	Marginal cost $= \dfrac{\Delta TC}{\Delta Q}$ (dollars per futon)
0	100	–
1	160	60
2	200	40
3	230	30
4	270	40
5	320	50
6	390	70
7	490	100
8	635	145
9	815	180
10	1,015	200
11	1,245	230
12	1,495	250
13	1,775	280
14	2,095	320
15	2,495	400

Profit Maximization: Choosing the Output

The table in Box 5, which is based on the data in previous tables, shows how marginal revenue, marginal cost, and marginal profit vary as more output is made available for sale. The next to last column of the table calculates marginal profit from the following formula:

$$\text{Marginal profit} = MR - MC$$

A firm maximizes profits by continuing to produce up to the point at which marginal revenue just equals marginal cost. The condition for maximum profit is therefore

$$MR = MC$$

Whenever marginal revenue exceeds marginal cost, producing more will result in extra revenue that exceeds the extra cost. This will cause increases in profit, and marginal profit will be positive. Whenever marginal cost exceeds marginal revenue, the extra output will cost more than the revenue it brings in and profit will fall. Marginal profit in this case would be negative. *Marginal analysis therefore shows that a firm can continue to increase profits up to the point at which marginal revenue equals marginal cost.*

Box 5 Marginal Analysis for Profit Maximization

Daily output (futons produced and shipped)	Marginal revenue = price (dollars per futon)	Marginal cost (dollars per futon)	Marginal profit (dollars per futon)	Total profit (dollars per day)
0	–	–	–	−100
1	150	60	90	−10
2	150	40	110	100
3	150	30	120	220
4	150	40	110	330
5	150	50	100	430
6	150	70	80	510
7	150	100	50	560
8	150	145	5	565
9	150	180	− 30	535
10	150	200	− 50	485
11	150	230	− 80	405
12	150	250	− 100	305
13	150	280	− 130	175
14	150	320	− 170	5
15	150	400	− 250	− 245

Because price (P) is equal to marginal revenue for a competitive firm, maximum profits for such firms occur when output has been adjusted to the point at which:

$$P = MC$$

The equilibrium output of a profit-maximizing competitive firm is therefore attained when the firm produces enough to adjust marginal cost to the point at which it rises to equal the price of the product. Any output below this level will mean that the firm can increase profits by producing more. Any output greater than that corresponding to the point at which marginal cost equals the price of the product implies that the firm can increase profits by producing less.

The table in Box 5 shows that the Futon Factory can continue to increase profits by producing more futons until it produces eight futons per day. Up to that point the $150 marginal revenue from selling futons exceeds the marginal cost of making those futons available. If the firm produces a ninth futon per day, its marginal cost would rise to $180. This would exceed the marginal revenue of $150 that could be obtained from selling that futon. The firm would therefore reduce its profits by selling the ninth futon. The last column of the table shows that profit would fall from the maximum of $565 per day to $535 per day if the firm were to produce and sell a ninth futon. Notice how the firm's choice of output depends on *both* the market price of futons and the way the marginal cost of making futons available to buyers varies as more futons are actually produced.

In Box 6, **A** shows the Futon Factory's choice of the profit-maximizing output. Along the competitive firm's demand curve, $P = MR = \$150$. The marginal cost curve intersects the firm's demand curve at point B. Equilibrium output corresponding to that level of marginal cost is eight futons per day. If the firm were to produce one unit more than eight futons per day, marginal cost would exceed marginal

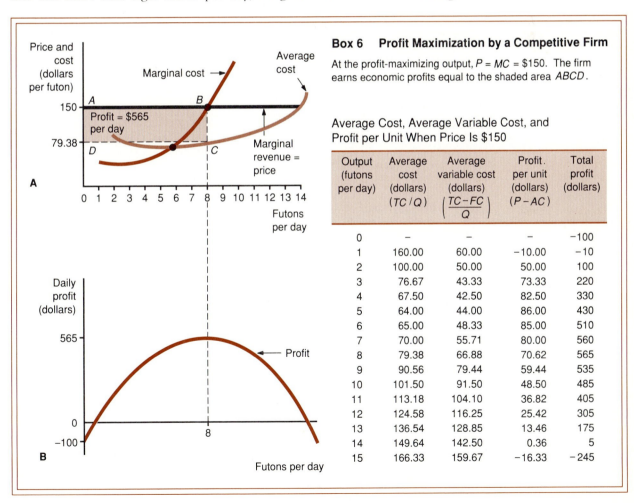

Box 6   Profit Maximization by a Competitive Firm

At the profit-maximizing output, $P = MC = \$150$. The firm earns economic profits equal to the shaded area $ABCD$.

Average Cost, Average Variable Cost, and Profit per Unit When Price Is $150

Output (futons per day)	Average cost (dollars) (TC/Q)	Average variable cost (dollars) $\left(\dfrac{TC-FC}{Q}\right)$	Profit per unit (dollars) $(P-AC)$	Total profit (dollars)
0	–	–	–	−100
1	160.00	60.00	−10.00	−10
2	100.00	50.00	50.00	100
3	76.67	43.33	73.33	220
4	67.50	42.50	82.50	330
5	64.00	44.00	86.00	430
6	65.00	48.33	85.00	510
7	70.00	55.71	80.00	560
8	79.38	66.88	70.62	565
9	90.56	79.44	59.44	535
10	101.50	91.50	48.50	485
11	113.18	104.10	36.82	405
12	124.58	116.25	25.42	305
13	136.54	128.85	13.46	175
14	149.64	142.50	0.36	5
15	166.33	159.67	−16.33	−245

revenue and profit would decline. In Box 6, **B** shows the profit curve based on the data in Box 2. Notice how maximum profit is achieved at exactly the point at which eight futons per day are produced. This is the output level for which output has been increased just to the point at which marginal cost equals the market price.

Profit per Unit vs. Total Profit

The table in Box 6, based on the data in Box 2, shows how average cost, average variable cost, and profit per unit of output vary as your firm produces more futons. The firm's daily profit at the equilibrium output is represented by the area of the rectangle *ABCD* in Box 6. The height of the rectangle is $(P - AC)$. This is the profit per unit of output sold. The width of the rectangle is the quantity produced. Total profit is equal to profit per unit multiplied by the number of units sold:

$$\text{Total profit} = (\text{Profit per unit})(\text{Output sold}) = (P - AC)Q$$

According to the data in the table in Box 6, at a price of $150 per futon, the profit per futon is a healthy $70.62 at the profit-maximizing output. Selling eight futons per day at this price gives the Futon Factory a total profit of $565 per day. Notice that the maximum-profit output is *not* the output for which *profit per unit* is highest. It would be a mistake, therefore, for managers of a profit-maximizing firm to use profit per unit as an indication of total profit. For the data in the table, maximum profit per unit is $86, which occurs when a daily output of only five futons is sold. Note that maximum profit per unit corresponds to the output for which average cost is at a minimum. However, at the point of actual maximum profits, profit per unit is only about $70.62 and output is eight futons per day. *This points out that the output at which profits are maximized is not necessarily the one at which the plant is operated to achieve minimum possible average cost of production.* To maximize profits, a business manager must carefully gauge marginal costs. Comparing average cost instead of marginal cost with marginal revenue doesn't guide the manager to the point of maximum profit.

How Maximum Possible Profit Depends on Market Price

When the market price is greater than the average cost of production at the profit-maximizing output, as is the case in the graphs in Box 6, the firm earns profits. Suppose instead that the price of the product were lower. For example, suppose a decrease in the market demand for the standardized futon produced by the Futon Factory causes its price to fall to $64. Assume nothing else changes that might affect the firm's cost curves. Notice in Box 6 that the *minimum possible average cost* of producing futons is also $64. Also note that the profit-maximizing output is five futons per day at a price of $64. To see this, return to Box 4 and note that marginal cost is $50 when five futons are produced but that it rises to $70 when a sixth futon is produced per day. At the new $64 price, the Futon Factory therefore maximizes profits by producing only five futons per day. At that output the firm *just covers its economic costs.*

As you'll recall, *economic profit* is the difference between a firm's total revenue and total economic cost. A firm earns zero economic profit when it takes in just enough revenue to cover its explicit and implicit costs. When price falls to the minimum possible average cost, the firm's owners are earning just as much as they could in their next best alternative.

Remember that economic costs differ from accounting costs when some inputs are supplied by owners of the firm. It's therefore possible for profits as measured by an accountant to be positive when economic profits are zero. The difference between total revenue and accounting costs is the implicit costs of owner-supplied inputs. The implicit costs that show up as profit on the accountant's books are sometimes called *normal profits*. When economic profit is zero, a firm's owners therefore earn a normal profit, which is just enough to keep them from transferring their resources to an alternative use in the long run. When economists use the term *profit*, they always mean *economic profit*.

The actual market price influences the maximum possible profits a firm can earn. A market price above the minimum possible average cost of production will allow the firm to enjoy profits. If price falls to the minimum possible average cost, the firm will just cover its economic cost and not earn any profit at the equilibrium output. The profit a firm earns always varies with output no matter what the market price of its product. However, the level of the market price for the product sold by the competitive firm affects the *level* of actual profits at the output for which marginal revenue just equals marginal cost.

Box 7 illustrates the case of a firm that's earning zero economic profits. This firm

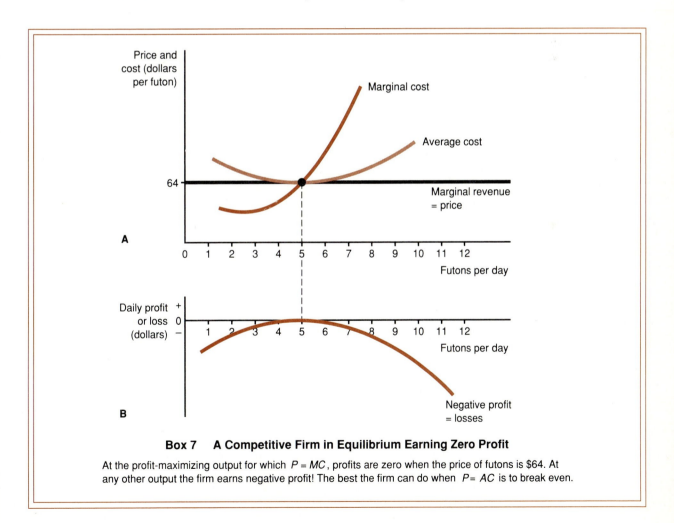

Box 7   A Competitive Firm in Equilibrium Earning Zero Profit

At the profit-maximizing output for which $P = MC$, profits are zero when the price of futons is $64. At any other output the firm earns negative profit! The best the firm can do when $P = AC$ is to break even.

is earning just enough revenue to cover all its economic costs. Since price equals average cost, the profit per unit is equal to zero. The area $(P - AC)Q$ also becomes zero. Because marginal cost equals average cost at the latter's minimum point, $P = MC = AC$ at the point of minimum average cost. Graph **A** in Box 7 therefore shows that a competitive firm, one for which the demand curve is horizontal, breaks even (meaning that it earns enough revenue to cover all its costs) at the level of output corresponding to minimum average cost. This would occur at a price of $64 per futon based on the data in the second column of the table in Box 6. Graph **B** in Box 7 shows how profits vary with output when the market price is $64. At any output other than the equilibrium output, profit will be negative! At the $64 price the best the Futon Factory can do is make zero profits. If it were to produce more, its profits would evaporate into losses. If it were to produce less, its profits would become negative as well. *The marginal analysis remains foolproof: The level of output for which* MR = MC *still gives maximum profits. In the case for which price also equals minimum possible average cost, maximum possible profits are zero.*

Using Marginal Analysis to Choose Output When Market Price Is Below Minimum Possible Average Cost

What happens if price falls below the level corresponding to the minimum possible average cost of production? For example, if the market price of the futon in this example were to fall below the minimum possible average cost of $64, what would you as manager of the Futon Factory choose to do? At any price below $64 you couldn't cover your economic costs. This means you'll incur losses rather than profits at the level of output for which marginal revenue equals marginal cost. You can earn more by employing your inputs elsewhere. In the short run, however, producers often find they lose less by remaining in business than by shutting down! A shutdown firm produces nothing but still incurs fixed costs in the short run.

The graphs in Box 8 show the case of a firm in the unfortunate position of incurring losses at the market price of its output. At a price of $45 a unit the firm incurs economic losses because that price is below the minimum possible average cost of $64. By still producing up to the output level at which $MR = MC$, you can *minimize* those losses. The output corresponding to the point of minimum loss is four futons per day. The loss at that level of output is represented by the area *ABED* in **A** in Box 8. Graph **B** shows that positive profits aren't possible at any output when the price is at such a low level. The firm would incur greater losses if it produced any output greater or less than the one for which marginal revenue just equals marginal cost. *When positive profits are not possible, marginal analysis can be used to pick the option that results in the smallest losses!*

If the Futon Factory produces four futons per day and sells them at a price of $45 each, it generates $180 in revenue per day. Its total cost of producing the futons (from Box 2) is $270. The loss it incurs is therefore $90 per day. If it produces any other quantity of futons, the firm loses still more per day, as you can see in **B** in Box 8.

If you choose to shut down the factory you'll have zero variable costs and produce zero output. However, you'll still incur losses in the short run because you'll have to pay the firm's fixed cost until its leases and other commitments expire. In this case fixed cost per day is $100.

If you were shut down, you'd have no revenue to offset your $100 fixed cost. Your losses would therefore be $100 per day. If, on the other hand, you continue to operate, producing the output for which $MR = MC$, you'd generate enough rev-

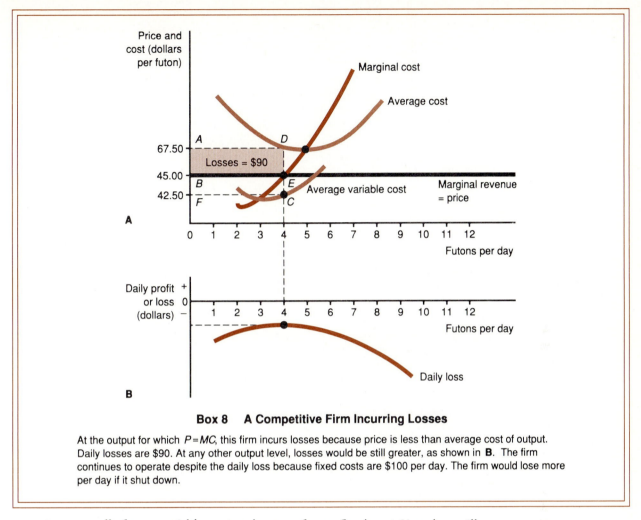

Box 8   A Competitive Firm Incurring Losses

At the output for which *P=MC*, this firm incurs losses because price is less than average cost of output. Daily losses are $90. At any other output level, losses would be still greater, as shown in **B**. The firm continues to operate despite the daily loss because fixed costs are $100 per day. The firm would lose more per day if it shut down.

enue to cover *all* of your variable cost and some of your fixed cost. Your loss will only be $90 if you continue to operate. For a profit-maximizing firm, losing $90 a day is a better alternative than losing $100 a day! You therefore continue to operate.

The Decision to Shut Down in the Short Run

As long as the market price exceeds the minimum possible average variable cost of production, the Futon Factory will continue to operate at a loss in the short run rather than shut down. To see this, recall that the vertical distance between the *AC* and *AVC* curves is average fixed cost (*AFC*). Therefore, at an output of four futons per day, fixed cost can be represented by the rectangle *AFCD* in Box 8. The height of this rectangle is *AFC*, while its length is the equilibrium quantity of output (*Q*). By shutting down, your firm would generate no revenue to offset its fixed costs. Short-run losses would therefore be equal to fixed costs if the firm ceases operations.

By continuing to operate, the Futon Factory loses the amount of money represented by the area *ABED* in Box 8. The distance *DE* represents (*AC* − *P*), the daily loss per unit of output. The distance *BE* is the output. Multiplying these two distances gives total losses. As long as price is greater than the average variable cost at the output for which $MR = MC$, the loss from remaining in business will be less than fixed cost, which is the short-run loss incurred by shutting down.

The graph in Box 9 shows that if price falls below the minimum possible average variable cost, the Futon Factory will shut down immediately. When price has fallen to a level below that which just allows the firm to cover its minimum possible average variable cost, the firm is at the **shutdown point.** When price has fallen to minimum possible average variable cost, the loss per unit is equal to average fixed cost. The loss from continuing to operate will exactly equal fixed cost. In Box 9, the loss per futon is equal to the distance DC, which also represents average fixed cost. It follows that losses from remaining in operation exactly equal fixed cost of $100 per day, which is represented by the area $AFCD$ in Box 9.

Shutdown point:
The point a firm reaches when price has fallen to a level below that which just allows the firm to cover its minimum possible average variable cost.

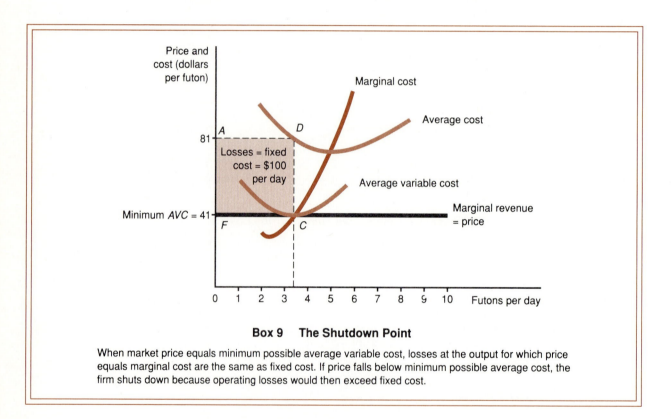

Box 9   The Shutdown Point

When market price equals minimum possible average variable cost, losses at the output for which price equals marginal cost are the same as fixed cost. If price falls below minimum possible average cost, the firm shuts down because operating losses would then exceed fixed cost.

If price were to fall below the minimum possible AVC, losses from remaining in operation would exceed fixed cost and the Futon Factory would cease operating. At any price below minimum possible AVC, the loss per unit $(AC - P)$ would exceed average fixed cost. This is because the vertical distance between the firm's demand curve and its average cost curve would exceed the vertical distance between AC and AVC.

The minimum possible average variable cost is $41, which occurs when between three and four futons per day are shipped. At any price below that, the Futon Factory can do better by shutting down instead of continuing to operate at the output for which $MR = MC$. For example, at a price of $40 per futon the firm could produce two futons per day. It would earn $80 and incur costs of $200. Its daily loss would therefore be $120. Because this exceeds the daily fixed cost of $100, the firm will lose less in the short run by shutting down.

To sum up, the firm elects to continue operating at a loss in the short run only if total revenue exceeds variable costs. This allows the firm to generate revenue to cover some of its fixed costs.

The Competitive Firm's Short-Run Supply Curve

As you know, a supply curve shows a relationship between price and quantity supplied. A competitive firm always adjusts output until price is equal to marginal cost so as to maximize profits. The marginal cost curve therefore gives the relationship between price and quantity supplied by the competitive firm. Price must exceed minimum possible average variable cost of production; otherwise the firm will cease operations. Quantity supplied by the firm at any price below minimum possible AVC will be zero. *The competitive firm's* **short-run supply curve** *is therefore that portion of its marginal cost curve above the minimum point of its average variable cost curve*. This is illustrated in Box 10.

Short-run supply curve: The portion of a competitive firm's marginal cost curve above the minimum point of its average variable cost curve.

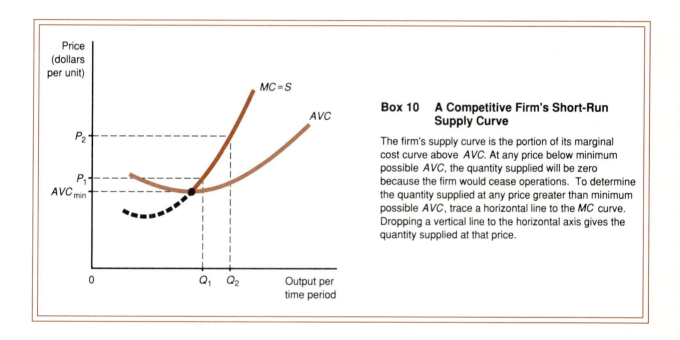

Box 10   A Competitive Firm's Short-Run Supply Curve

The firm's supply curve is the portion of its marginal cost curve above AVC. At any price below minimum possible AVC, the quantity supplied will be zero because the firm would cease operations. To determine the quantity supplied at any price greater than minimum possible AVC, trace a horizontal line to the MC curve. Dropping a vertical line to the horizontal axis gives the quantity supplied at that price.

Short-run supply curves slope upward because the firm's marginal costs tend to increase as output is increased. When firms operate within a fixed plant or facility, marginal cost eventually increases. To induce a profit-maximizing firm to supply more output, market price must rise to cover increased marginal cost as the firm increases output.

To determine quantity supplied by the competitive firm at any price, draw a horizontal line from that price to the marginal cost curve. At any price below minimum possible AVC, quantity supplied in the short run is zero. For example, at a price P_1 quantity supplied is Q_1. At a higher price, P_2, quantity supplied is Q_2. You can see this in Box 10.

Market Supply

Market supply curve:
Gives the sum of the quantities supplied by all firms producing a product at each possible price over a given period.

A **market supply curve** gives the sum of the quantities supplied by all firms producing a product at each possible price over a given period. Such a curve can be derived from the supply curves of competitive firms. To do this, assume that input prices and technology are given. In particular, assume that prices of variable inputs used to produce the good are independent of the total quantity produced by all sellers. If this is the case, the market supply curve is the horizontal summation of the marginal cost curves of all firms producing the standardized product.

Assume there are 1,000 small firms producing exactly the same standardized futon. Suppose as well, for simplicity, that all firms are the same size and have exactly the same cost curves. At a price of $150 per futon, each firm will supply eight futons per day. Total quantity supplied at that price will be 8 (1,000) or 8,000 futons per day, corresponding to point E on the market supply curve in Box 11, where the market demand curve intersects the market supply curve. Similarly, to find the market quantity supplied at any other price, find the quantity supplied by each firm at that price and multiply that quantity by the number of firms selling in the market. To maximize profits under perfect competition, each firm adjusts output until price equals marginal cost of production. The market supply curve is upward sloping because each firm's individual supply curve slopes upward.

When firms are of equal size and have exactly the same cost curves, we obtain the quantity supplied to the market by multiplying the output of a typical firm by the number of firms supplying the product. If firms are not of equal size or have differing marginal cost curves, simply add the quantity supplied by all firms to obtain the quantity supplied to the market at each price.

The determinants of market supply are:

1. The number of firms in the industry selling in the market
2. The average size of firms in the industry measured by the average productive capacity of individual firms
3. The prices of variable inputs used by firms in the industry
4. The technology employed by firms in the industry

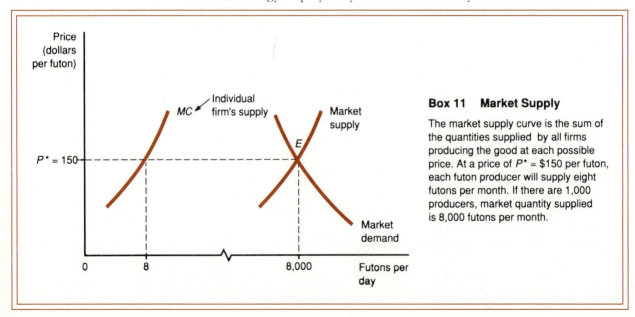

Box 11   Market Supply

The market supply curve is the sum of the quantities supplied by all firms producing the good at each possible price. At a price of $P^* = \$150$ per futon, each futon producer will supply eight futons per month. If there are 1,000 producers, market quantity supplied is 8,000 futons per month.

The last three determinants affect the marginal cost of individual firms. For example, larger firms employ more fixed inputs, which means their physical production facilities are designed to produce higher output. This means larger firms achieve the minimum possible average cost and minimum possible average variable cost at a higher output level than do smaller firms. As a result, the marginal cost curves lie further out from the origin for larger firms than for smaller firms. Accordingly, the larger a firm, the greater the quantity supplied at any given price. Therefore, the greater the average size of firms supplying a product to a market, the greater the quantity supplied at any given price. The higher the prices of variable inputs, the higher the marginal cost associated with any given output. This means that an increase in the prices of variable inputs tends to shift the marginal cost curves of firms upward. As this occurs, firms will produce less output at any given price. It follows that an increase in the prices of variable inputs will decrease supply. Finally, when firms in an industry employ a new technology that reduces the marginal cost of production, the marginal cost curve of each firm will shift downward. The downward shift in marginal cost will increase the quantity supplied by each firm at each price. An improvement in technology that shifts marginal cost curves downward for firms in a perfectly competitive market will therefore contribute to an increase in supply.

Concept Check

1   Assuming that marginal cost eventually increases as more is produced in the short run, show that profit is at a maximum when marginal revenue is just equal to marginal cost. Why will marginal profit equal zero when profits are at a maximum? Explain why marginal revenue equals the price of the product sold by a competitive firm.

2   Draw a typical firm's short-run cost curves and show how maximum possible profit changes when there's a change in the price of the product produced by the firm. Identify the firm's supply curve on your graph.

3   Under what circumstances will a profit-maximizing firm choose to continue operating in the short run even if the best it can do is produce an output level that results in losses? Why does a profit-maximizing firm cease operating when price falls below the minimum possible average variable cost in the short run?

Using the Theory of Competitive Supply

A Reduction in the Price of a Variable Input: How a Decrease in Materials Prices Affects Market Supply and Market Price

A change in input prices will affect costs of production. This will affect both the competitive firm's supply curve and the market supply curve. Suppose the price of fabric used in the production of futons declines. A decrease in the price of any variable input used by producers, other things being equal, decreases variable costs. The short-run effect of a decrease in the price of this variable input on the market price of futons and the quantity produced and on a typical competitive firm is illustrated in Box 12.

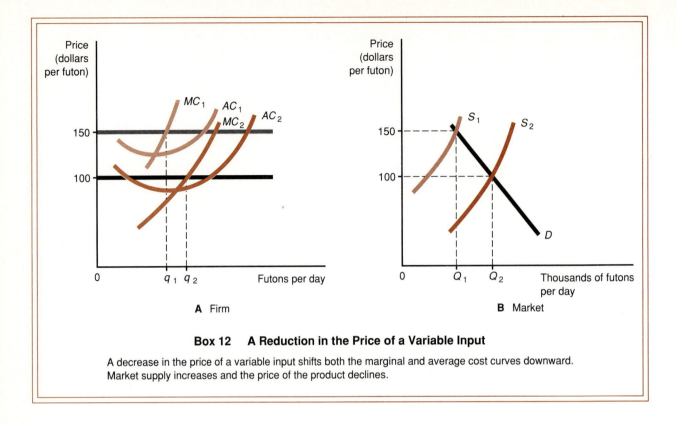

Box 12   A Reduction in the Price of a Variable Input

A decrease in the price of a variable input shifts both the marginal and average cost curves downward.
Market supply increases and the price of the product declines.

The decrease in the price of the variable input causes a downward shift in average variable costs, average costs, and marginal costs. Graph **A** in Box 12 shows the impact of the decrease in the price of fabric on AC and MC for a typical competitive firm like the Futon Factory. The decrease in the price of the variable input shifts the average and marginal cost curves downward from MC_1 to MC_2 and from AC_1 to AC_2. If the market price were to remain at \$150 a futon, its initial level, each competitive firm would increase production until MC_2 equaled \$150. However, as all firms increase production in response to the decrease in marginal cost, the market supply increases from S_1 to S_2, as shown in **B** in Box 12. Given the level of demand, this results in a decrease in the market price of futons from \$150 to \$100. In equilibrium, at the new price, each firm produces the output corresponding to the point at which MC_2 equals \$100. The output corresponding to this is q_2. As all firms increase output, the market equilibrium quantity increases from Q_1 to Q_2, as shown in **B** in Box 12. A decrease in the price of a variable input for all producers therefore results in a decrease in market price as market supply increases.

A Change in the Price of a Fixed Input: The Short-Run Impact of License Fees and Fixed Annual Subsidies

A change in the price of a *fixed input* affects fixed costs and average costs. However, it has no effect on variable costs or marginal costs. As you'll see, this has some interesting implications for policies that affect the prices of fixed rather than variable inputs.

Suppose the market for contractors' services in your state is competitive. The state government, in an effort to raise extra revenue, decides to triple contractors' license fees from $1,000 to $3,000 per year. A license is a fixed input in the practice of an occupation or activity. It represents an annual fee that must be paid independent of the amount of services sold. In the short run, therefore, an increase in such fees is equivalent to an increase in fixed costs.

Graph **A** in Box 13 assumes that the price per square foot of construction is initially $50. At that price contractors just break even, earning zero profit. Before the increase in the license fee, price is just equal to the minimum possible average cost and firms just cover their economic costs at their equilibrium output at which $P = AC = MC$. The increase in the license fee has no effect on variable costs. It does, however, increase average costs. As the average cost curve shifts upward, the distance between the AVC curve and the AC curve increases, reflecting the increase in average fixed costs at any level of output. Because marginal cost depends only on variable cost, the increase in the license fee has no effect on that curve. The market supply curve doesn't shift because the license fee doesn't affect the marginal cost curve. The price of construction services therefore remains at $50 per square foot, as shown in **B** in Box 13.

Each construction firm continues to produce the same level of output, q_1 square feet per year, where $MC = \$50$. Market equilibrium output remains Q_1 square feet per year. Nothing changes *except* the profit earned by contractors. The typical contractor was assumed to just be breaking even before the increase in AC. The in-

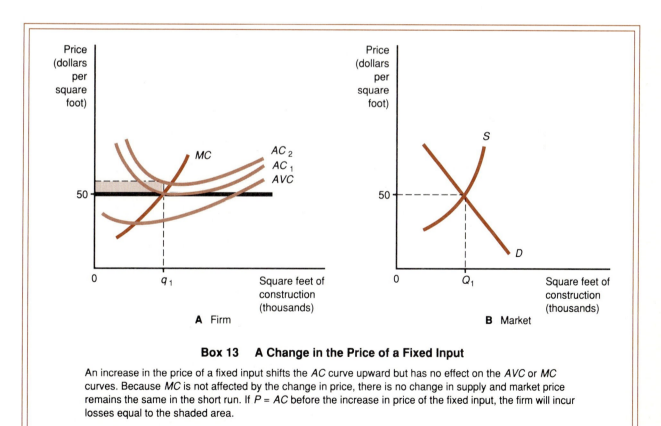

Box 13   A Change in the Price of a Fixed Input

An increase in the price of a fixed input shifts the AC curve upward but has no effect on the AVC or MC curves. Because MC is not affected by the change in price, there is no change in supply and market price remains the same in the short run. If $P = AC$ before the increase in price of the fixed input, the firm will incur losses equal to the shaded area.

creased fee therefore results in losses equal to the shaded area in **A** in Box 13. Price remains above *AVC* because neither *AVC* nor *MC* is affected by the license fee increase. The short-run impact of the increased license fee is therefore confined to the profits of contractors. Neither price nor marginal cost is affected.

A similar analysis holds for a *decrease* in fixed costs. Any factors decreasing fixed costs won't influence either price or supply in a competitive market in the short run. For example, if the government *reduces* license fees for the purpose of increasing construction, there will be no effect on the amount supplied in the short run. If authorities want a rapid increase in the amount of construction services supplied, they must reduce the price of a *variable* input used by contractors.

For example, suppose a government offers farmers a fixed subsidy of $10,000 a year in an effort to get them to produce more food. This would be a windfall to farmers. It would decrease their average costs of operation while having no effect on their variable or marginal costs. Accordingly, their profits would increase but there would be no increase in the quantity of food supplied in the short run. Over the long run, however, there would be an increase in supply as more individuals are encouraged to enter food-related businesses.

Marginal Analysis: Key Insights and Conclusions

Our marginal analysis of decisions made by profit-maximizing firms shows that, in the short run, market supply curves in competitive markets are upward sloping. The reason for this is rooted in the law of diminishing marginal returns, which implies that marginal costs of production eventually increase in the short run. Competitive firms are in equilibrium when they produce the output corresponding to the point at which price equals marginal cost, provided price is higher than average variable cost at that point. The price is the marginal revenue for a competitive seller. Because marginal cost tends to increase as more output is made available in the short run, the firm will increase quantity supplied only if price rises. The increase in price causes marginal revenue to exceed marginal cost at the existing output. This allows additional profits from increased quantity supplied. Firms then increase output until marginal cost increases to equal the higher price. Supply curves therefore slope upward because marginal cost increases with output in the short run.

In gauging the profitability of producing more output, firms must estimate marginal costs. Knowing average cost down to the penny isn't enough. *The marginal cost is the relevant figure to calculate before deciding to increase or decrease output if the goal of the firm is to maximize profit.* As is the case in most marginal analysis of behavior, the key to using it is to find out how changes in economic conditions affect marginal gains and costs. Increases in market demand tend to increase market prices and thereby increase marginal revenue to sellers. To understand and forecast shifts in supply, firms must forecast the impact on marginal cost of changes in such conditions as input prices and technology.

The theory of supply in perfectly competitive markets isolates the cause-and-effect relationship between price and quantity supplied. The simplifying assumptions of the model of perfect competition are clearly unrealistic. Nonetheless, the model gives us useful insights in cases where a firm has enough competitors and sells a product very similar (but not identical) to those of its competitors. The model is relevant as long as it's reasonable to assume that firms largely react to prices set by broad forces of supply and demand in a market, without the ability to influence those prices appreciably by producing more or less by themselves. Hypotheses based on the model of perfect competition are widely supported by evidence. As the price of a product like personal computers goes up, the quantity supplied increases. Similarly, decreases in variable costs of producing computers caused by improved technology tend to increase supply. The insights we obtain from the model of supply in perfectly competitive markets therefore are useful, despite the fact that few markets conform exactly to the assumptions of the model.

Summary

1. Competitive firms react to prices. A competitive firm is a price taker in the sense that it considers the price of its output as beyond its influence.
2. A perfectly competitive market consists of many sellers and buyers. Each seller has a small market share and sells a standardized product also sold by its many competing sellers in the market. Information is freely available in such a market, and both buyers and sellers can freely exit or enter the market as they choose.
3. The demand curve for the output of a perfectly competitive firm is infinitely elastic at the market price of the product. However, the demand curve for the product of the industry to which the competitive firm belongs is downward sloping.
4. Profit in the short run tends to increase and then decrease as a firm produces and sells more of its product. At very low and very high levels of output in the short run, profit is likely to be negative. If a firm were to cease operating in the short run, its losses would be equal to its fixed costs.
5. Marginal revenue is the extra revenue obtained from selling an additional unit of output. If a seller can sell all it wishes at the market price, as is the case for a competitive firm, marginal revenue is equal to price. Another term for price is average revenue, which is total revenue divided by the quantity of output sold.
6. A firm can increase total profit by selling more as long as marginal cost doesn't exceed marginal revenue. Marginal profit is zero when marginal revenue just equals marginal cost. At the point at which marginal revenue equals marginal cost, profit is at a maximum because additional sales would decrease profit.
7. The equilibrium output of a profit-maximizing competitive firm corresponds to the output for which marginal revenue equals marginal cost.
8. Profit per unit is highest at the output level for which average cost is at a minimum. However, the profit-maximizing output depends on price and marginal cost. The output corresponding to maximum profit therefore often is not the one for which profit per unit is at a maximum.
9. A profit-maximizing firm will operate at a loss in the short run as long as the market price exceeds the minimum possible average variable cost. However, when price falls below minimum possible average variable cost, the firm will cease operating because at so low a price its losses would exceed its fixed costs at the output for which marginal revenue equals marginal cost. The firm is just at the shutdown point when price equals the minimum possible average variable cost of production.
10. The firm's short-run supply curve is the portion of its marginal cost curve lying above its average variable cost curve. Short-run supply curves tend to be upward sloping because the marginal cost of production tends to increase as more goods are made available for sale in markets. Short-run market supply is ob-

tained by adding the quantities supplied by all sellers in the market at various prices.

11. Changes in the prices of variable inputs will shift marginal cost curves and will therefore result in changes in supply in the short run. However, because changes in the prices of fixed inputs don't affect variable costs, they result in no shifts in marginal cost curves and therefore no changes in supply in the short run.

Key Terms and Concepts

Perfectly competitive market	Marginal profit
Competitive firm	Shutdown point
Average revenue	Short-run supply curve
Marginal revenue	Market supply curve

Problems and Applications

1. The market equilibrium price of wheat is currently $2.50 a bushel. Assuming that wheat is produced by firms in a perfectly competitive industry, draw the industry demand and supply curves. Draw the demand curve for the wheat produced by a *single* wheat producer and explain how it differs from the industry demand curve.

2. Draw a curve that shows how total revenue will vary as a typical wheat producer sells more wheat per season at the market equilibrium price of $2.50 per bushel. What is the average revenue from selling wheat? Assuming that the wheat producer has fixed costs of $50,000 per season, draw a total cost curve. (Also assume constant input prices and assume that the law of diminishing marginal returns governs the way cost increases with output.) Show how profit will vary with output as more wheat is sold per season.

3. Suppose the marginal cost of producing wheat for a farmer is $1 per bushel when 10 acres are planted. The farmer wants to maximize profits from selling wheat this season. Assuming that the market price is expected to be $2.50 per bushel, would you advise the farmer to plant more wheat this season? Explain your answer.

4. Suppose the price of futons in Box 2 increases to $200. Assuming that nothing else changes, recalculate profit at the daily output level shown in the table. How many futons will a profit-maximizing firm produce daily after the price increase?

5. Given the price of a firm's product, show that profit per unit of output is always at a maximum when the average cost of producing the product is at a minimum. Prove that a profit-maximizing firm will choose to produce the output for which profit per unit is at a maximum only in the case for which the market equilibrium price just equals the minimum possible average cost. Show that in such a case both the profit per unit and total profit will be zero!

6. The current market price for a standardized wire cable produced by a competitive firm is $1 per foot. The firm produces cable each month up to the point at which its marginal cost increases to $1 per foot of cable. At the output for which marginal cost equals $1, the average cost of the cable is $1.25 per foot. Draw the firm's cost curves and the demand curve for cable as seen by the firm. Show that the firm is losing money each month at the output for which marginal cost equals $1. Explain why a firm can incur losses while seeking to maximize profits

and why it might still fill orders for its product even though it can't make profits by doing so.

7. Suppose the minimum possible average variable cost of producing wire cable for the manufacturer in problem 6 is $1.10 per foot. Under these circumstances, what would you advise the owner of the firm to do assuming the price of cable is $1 per foot? Explain your answer.

8. The current equilibrium price of residential housing construction is $50 per square foot. A new government subsidy program designed to encourage new housing construction promises to pay contractors a grant of $10 per square foot for new construction. Show how the subsidy will reduce the marginal cost of construction. Use graphic analysis to show how each individual contractor will want to increase construction per year after the subsidy. Show how the subsidy will affect market supply and the price of residential construction.

9. Instead of a subsidy paid per square foot of new construction, suppose the government simply gives residential construction contractors a flat $1,000 per year subsidy. Explain why such a subsidy will be ineffective in increasing the supply of new construction in the short run.

10. Suppose two manufacturers of tables in a perfectly competitive industry each operate a factory of the same size. However, one of the manufacturers is located close to a cheap source of hydroelectric power that results in lower variable costs of production. Prove that, other things being equal, the quantity supplied by the producer with lower variable costs will always exceed that of the other producer at any given price for tables.

Suggested Readings

Walter Adams, ed., *The Structure of American Industry*, 6th ed., New York: Macmillan, 1982. This book looks at various industries in the United States. The first essay is on agriculture and shows how perfect competition is likely to prevail in this industry. Other industries discussed include petroleum, steel, beer, banking, and major-league sports.

Evan J. Douglas, *Managerial Economics: Theory, Practice, and Problems*, 3rd ed., Englewood Cliffs, N.J.: Prentice-Hall, 1987. This book emphasizes practical aspects of managing business firms. Chapters 7 and 8 discuss some of the problems involved in estimating cost and predicting the profitability of new business ventures.

A Forward Look

In this chapter we've concentrated on short-run supply. In the following chapter we'll look at the process of long-run supply. In the long run firms have more flexibility in expanding or contracting their operations. The lure of profit and the avoidance of losses affect the number of firms in a perfectly competitive industry. In the long run changes in the number of firms in an industry are an important determinant of quantity supplied and profits.

Long-Run Supply in Competitive Markets

Suppose your college gets a surge of enrollment. To accommodate the larger student body, the college hires more instructors and schedules more classes in the late afternoon and evening. However, over a relatively short period of time the college can't add more classrooms and lecture halls to accommodate the increased demand for classes. Over the long run the college can think about building more facilities to accommodate the increased enrollment. Just like a college, over the long run business firms have more flexibility in supplying goods and services than they do in the short run. Remember that in the short run firms are confined to a plant with given capacity. The limited capacity of firms in an industry to respond to price changes makes supply relatively inelastic in the short run compared to the long run. In the short run firms can't even go out of business because they lack adequate time to liquidate their assets and alter their contractual obligations, such as leases for plants and equipment. Although firms can cease operating in the short run, it takes more time for their owners to transfer their resources to alternative uses.

In this chapter we analyze long-run supply in competitive markets. In the long run the market supply of a good is more responsive chiefly because the *number of sellers* in an industry can change when markets are free and competitive. The profit motive is as important in analyzing supply in the long run as it is in the short run. But the interesting conclusion that emerges when analyzing long-run supply in a competitive market is that profits or losses can only be temporary. Profits and losses are *signals* that owners of firms respond to in ways that change supply in the long run. The changes in supply caused by opportunities for profit and the actions taken to avoid losses cause changes in product prices that act to *eliminate* those profits or losses in the long run. A system of competitive markets is fueled by profits and honed by losses in the long run.

For example, an increase in the demand for exercise equipment creates profit opportunities for those who produce exercise bikes, weight-lifting devices, and jogging shoes. Over the long run new firms are likely to enter this industry, attracted by the opportunity to earn profits. The result will be an increase in the supply of exercise equipment, which will eventually put downward pressure on price. As price falls, so does profit. As you'll see, profits plant the seeds of their own destruction when free entry exists in a market, as is the case under perfect competition.

After reading this chapter, you should be able to: *Concept Preview*

1 Explain the concept of long-run competitive equilibrium in a market and analyze the characteristics of this equilibrium for product prices.
2 Show how profits and losses act as signals that cause shifts in market supply in the long run.
3 Derive long-run supply curves for products sold in perfectly competitive markets and show how long-run supply differs from short-run supply.
4 Analyze the long-run impact of taxes and subsidies on prices and quantities traded in perfectly competitive markets.
5 Evaluate outcomes in markets in the long run using normative criteria.

Long-Run Competitive Equilibrium

In the short run, a firm is confined to a plant of fixed size. Managers of a single-product firm can adjust production in the plant to achieve the goal of maximum profits. However, the plant's limited capacity eventually causes average and marginal costs to increase sharply as the firm tries to produce more and more. In the long run, the firm's managers have the flexibility to build larger or additional plants if they can increase their profits by doing so. However, the opportunity to earn profits lures new firms into the market in the long run. By the same token, firms will tend to leave the industry in the long run if losses prevail.

A **long-run competitive equilibrium** exists in an industry when there is no tendency for firms to enter or leave the industry or to expand or contract the scale of their operations. New firms will enter the industry if profits are possible, and existing firms will leave the industry if they can't cover their opportunity costs. Similarly, firms will tend to expand if they can increase their profits by doing so. All opportunities to earn profits or eliminate losses must be exhausted for an industry to attain a long-run competitive equilibrium. Profits must therefore be zero for an industry to be in equilibrium. When economic profits are zero, firms just cover their explicit and implicit costs, and there's no tendency for any sellers to enter or leave the market. When sellers cover their opportunity cost, they can't earn more in their next best alternative. They therefore have no incentive to leave the market. By the same token, new sellers won't enter the market because they can't earn more than they currently enjoy in their existing enterprise.

Long-run competitive equilibrium:
Exists in an industry when there is no tendency for firms to enter or leave the industry or to expand or contract the scale of their operations.

Moving Toward Long-Run Equilibrium When Firms in an Industry Earn Profit

The process by which long-run competitive equilibrium is attained can be illustrated with a simple example. Suppose the market for bicycles is perfectly competitive. The current price of bicycles is $200 each. To simplify the analysis, assume there are currently 100 firms in the market selling a standardized bike. Assume that the long-run costs of producing bicycles are the same for all producers in the industry and that new entrants in the industry can easily acquire the machinery and labor to produce the product at the same cost as existing firms. Finally, assume that at the current price of bicycles, each seller in the industry is enjoying economic profits. The price of bikes therefore exceeds their current average cost of production.

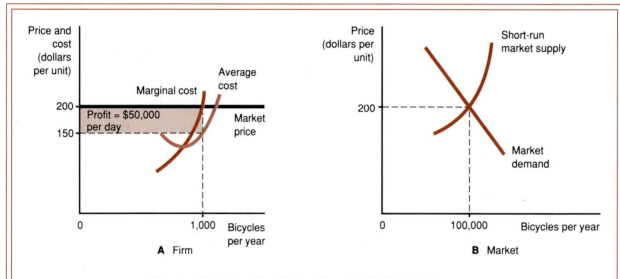

Box 1 Short-Run Equilibrium in a Profitable Market

At the current market price for bicycles of $200, firms in the industry can earn profit. The firm whose cost curves are illustrated above earns $50,000 per year economic profit by selling bicycles in the market. The industry has not reached long-run equilibrium because the profit will induce new firms to enter and existing firms to expand.

The graphs in Box 1 show the average and marginal cost curves prevailing over the short run for a typical bicycle producer, along with the market demand and supply curves for the product. Each seller currently maximizes profit by producing the number of bikes annually for which price equals marginal cost. The annual output that maximizes profit is 1,000 units for each producer, as you can see in Graph **A.** Because there are 100 sellers in the market, each maximizing annual profit by selling 1,000 bikes per year, industry output is 100,000 bikes per year. Graph **B** in Box 1 shows the market demand curve and the existing *short-run* market supply curve for bicycles. At the current market equilibrium price of $200, the equilibrium quantity is 100,000 bikes per year. Remember that the short-run supply curve reflects the marginal cost of producing the item. At a $200 price the marginal cost of bikes is also $200 for each seller.

The graphs in Box 1 also show that firms in the industry earn profits. The average cost of producing bicycles is only $150 at the output for which price is equal to marginal cost. This means each firm earns a profit of $50 on each bike sold. The $50 represents the difference between the market price of a bike and the average cost of producing it. Because each firm sells 1,000 bikes per year, annual profit will be $50,000 for each seller, which is represented by the shaded area in graph **A.**

Now it's easy to illustrate the process by which a competitive industry moves toward equilibrium in the long run. Because the opportunity to earn profit exists in the bicycle industry, new firms will be attracted into it. The new firms can earn more than their opportunity costs by producing bikes. To set up their firms, the new sellers have to acquire machinery and workers and build the plants they need to start producing bicycles. The increased demand for these inputs could increase their prices. However, if the inputs used to produce bikes are also used in other industries, it's unlikely that bike producers will have a significant effect on overall market demand for such resources. If this is the case, the long-run average cost curves won't shift up as new firms enter the industry because there will be no change in input prices. In other words, new sellers will have the same cost curves shown in Box 1 as they begin to operate their plants in the long run.

However, the entry of new firms into the market as sellers will increase market supply. This will result in a new short-run market supply. The increase in market supply caused by the increased number of firms will put downward pressure on price. The graphs in Box 2 show how the increase in the number of firms selling the product shifts the short-run supply curve to the right as new firms enter, thereby increasing quantity supplied and decreasing market equilibrium price. But how far will market price fall?

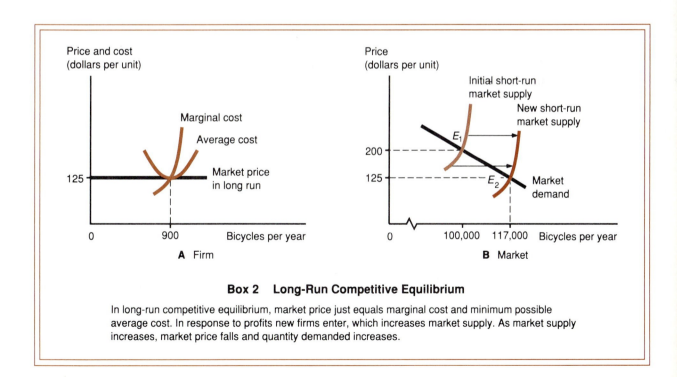

Box 2   Long-Run Competitive Equilibrium

In long-run competitive equilibrium, market price just equals marginal cost and minimum possible average cost. In response to profits new firms enter, which increases market supply. As market supply increases, market price falls and quantity demanded increases.

Price Equals Minimum Possible Average Cost in Long-Run Equilibrium

As long as profit is possible in the bicycle industry, the number of firms will continue to increase or existing firms will expand by building new plants. This means that the opportunity for profit will result in increases in supply that continually put downward pressure on price. This downward pressure will stop only when profit falls to zero, that is, when price has fallen to a level that just allows sellers to recover their average cost. When the profit per bike is zero, any further increases in supply would push price down to levels that will result in losses. At the level for which price just equals average cost, total annual profit will therefore be zero for all sellers.[1] Firms remain in the industry even though they earn zero economic profit because they cover their implicit costs as well as their explicit costs.

The graphs in Box 2 show that profit per unit is zero only when price has fallen enough to equal the *minimum possible average cost of producing the good in the long run*.[2] The minimum possible average cost of producing bicycles is $125. If price were higher than this sum, at the level of output for which price was just equal to marginal cost, the profit per unit would be positive. The annual profits this would make possible would attract new sellers. At any price above $125, marginal cost will exceed average cost, and this will allow profit opportunities for new sellers.

Entry of new firms into the industry will therefore continue until price has fallen to the minimum possible average cost of making bicycles available in the long run. In **B** in Box 2, the market supply has increased enough for the price of bikes to fall to $125. The graph shows that at that price, profit per unit, and therefore total profit, equals zero for each firm. Suppose price falls to $125 after the number of firms in the industry increases to 130.

Notice in **B** in Box 2 that market quantity supplied at the $125 price is 117,000 bikes per year—an increase of 17,000 over the initial quantity supplied. Also notice that after enough firms have entered the market to push profits to zero, each firm produces *less* than it did initially. Output per firm falls from 1,000 to 900 units per year. However, total market output increases because the number of firms increases to 130. Total industry output rises to 117,000 per year even though each firm in the industry now produces less than before.

We can use the analysis for this example to reach a number of important conclusions about the characteristics of long-run competitive equilibrium:

1. In the long run, competitive equilibrium prices equal the minimum possible average cost of making the good available.
2. When prices equal minimum possible long-run average cost, they also equal marginal cost because marginal cost equals average cost when average cost is at a minimum. The maximum profit attainable for the competitive firm is therefore equal to zero when long-run equilibrium has been reached. This is because profit per unit equals zero at the profit-maximizing output (the one for which price equals marginal cost) for each firm when marginal cost equals average cost.

---

[1]This assumes that the minimum possible average cost of production is the same for all sellers.
[2]The average cost curves drawn in this chapter are long-run cost curves. When a firm produces at the minimum possible average cost in the long run, it has adjusted its plant size so that it is producing at minimum average cost.

Long-Run Impact of Changes in Demand

Suppose the bicycle industry is initially in long-run equilibrium, as was illustrated in Box 2. How would the industry react to a decrease in the demand for bikes? Because bikes are currently being produced at the minimum possible average cost of $125, the decrease in demand will cause price to fall below average cost. The graphs in Box 3 show how the decrease in demand causes the price to fall to $105. Notice how in the short run there's a decrease in quantity supplied as the firms currently in the industry decrease quantities supplied by moving down along the initial short-run supply curve. Each firm cuts back production to the point at which marginal cost declines to $105. The corresponding output for each firm is 800 bikes per year. Because there are 130 firms in the industry when it's in equilibrium, total quantity supplied equals 104,000 bikes per year.

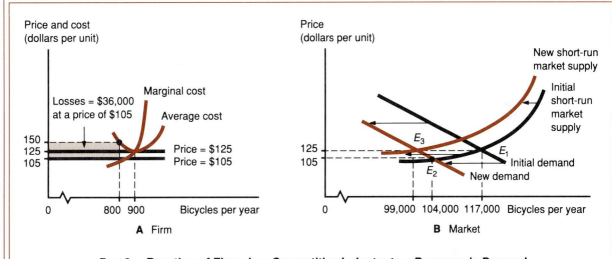

Box 3   Reaction of Firms in a Competitive Industry to a Decrease in Demand

At the initial market equilibrium at E_1, the industry is in equilibrium. In response to a decrease in demand, market equilibrium shifts to E_2, at which price falls to $105. At that price firms in the industry incur losses. In the long run firms in the industry leave the market. This decreases supply and results in a final equilibrium at E_3, at which price is $125 and firms earn zero economic profits.

The graphs in Box 3 show that firms in the industry can't cover their opportunity costs at the new price. Average cost of production for 800 bikes per year is $150. Each firm therefore loses $45 per bike sold for a total annual loss of $36,000. In the long run, firms will begin to leave this industry because they can earn more by selling their equipment and using the cash to set up other types of businesses.

But as firms begin to leave the industry in the long run, the short-run market supply curve will shift to the left. Firms will continue to leave until supply has shifted just enough to push price back up to $125. The final long-run equilibrium therefore occurs, as illustrated in **B** in Box 3, at the point at which the new short-run supply curve corresponding to the reduced industry size intercepts the new demand curve. At that price each firm in the industry once again is producing 900 bikes per year, but the number of firms in the industry has declined to 110. Total industry output is now 99,000 bikes per year. Notice that as long as changes in the number of firms in the industry don't result in changes in input prices that cause the cost curves to shift, the price of bikes returns to its initial $125 level.

We also can trace out the industry reaction to an increase in demand. Suppose, as before, that initially there are 130 firms in the industry, each producing 900 bikes per year, for a total industry output of 117,000 bikes per year at a market equilibrium price of $125 that just covers average cost of production. The increase in demand increases market price to $175. In response to the increase in price, each of the 130 firms in the industry increases quantity supplied by producing more in its existing plants until marginal cost increases to $175. This occurs when each firm produces 950 bikes per year for a total industry output of 123,500 per year, as shown in the graphs in Box 4. This corresponds to the point at which the new market demand curve intersects the existing short-run supply curve in **B** in Box 4.

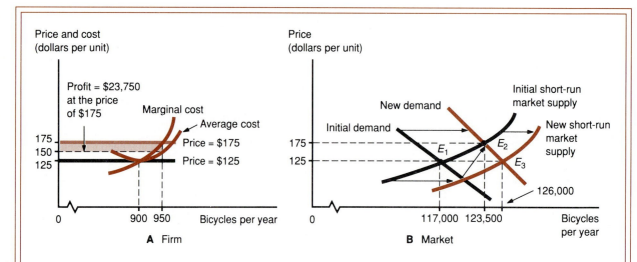

Box 4   Reaction of Firms in a Competitive Industry to an Increase in Demand

The initial equilibrium corresponds to point E_1. At the corresponding price of $125 the industry is in equilibrium. The market equilibrium shifts to point E_2 in response to an increase in demand. As the market price increases to $175, firms earn profits. In the long run new firms enter the industry, shifting the market supply curve until price falls once again to $125.

However, at the new market price firms in the industry can earn profits. The average cost of producing 950 bikes per year is $150. This allows a $25 per unit profit for a total profit of $23,750 per year. This profit will lure new firms into the industry. Once again assume no change in input prices resulting from the entry of new firms in the market in the long run. As this occurs the short-run supply curve shifts to the right until price falls once again to $125. At that level, price equals minimum possible average cost and the number of firms in the industry increases to 140 with each firm producing 900 bikes per year. Total industry output is therefore 126,000 bikes per year at the equilibrium price of $125. This corresponds to the point at which the new short-run supply curve intersects the new demand curve in **B** in Box 4.

Profits, Losses, and Long-Run Supply

In the examples illustrating the process by which long-run competitive equilibrium is reached, notice how profits and losses are zero in the long run. One question that might have entered your mind is, "Why do firms continue to produce if they can't earn profits in the long run?" The answer to this question lies in the fact that when economic profits are zero, firms cover both their explicit and *implicit* costs. Implicit costs show up as accounting (or normal) profit on a firm's income statement and reflect the opportunity cost of owner-supplied inputs. Recall that normal profit equals the imputed costs of owner-supplied inputs. For example, suppose the only owner-supplied input for the bicycle firms is the capital equipment used to make the bikes. Assume that the annual value of this capital, represented by the structures, machines, other equipment, and materials in inventory, is $1 million for each firm and that each seller has no current debt. If the opportunity cost of this capital is 10% in its next best use, each firm must earn 10% of $1 million or $100,000 per year when economic profits are zero. It follows that even though economic profits are zero in the long-run competitive equilibrium, firms earn an accounting or normal profit that just covers their opportunity cost of staying in the industry.

You'll also want to notice another interesting result of the analysis of long-run equilibrium in the examples we've used. In all cases the price of bicycles returns to $125 in the long run. As long as nothing happens to change the minimum possible long-run average cost of producing bicycles as the number of firms in the industry changes, the market price will always return to $125. In general, minimum possible average cost will not change as the number of firms in the industry changes if input prices are not bid up or down as a result of entry or exit of firms in the industry. A **constant-costs industry** is one for which input prices are unaffected by the quantity of a good produced or the number of firms in the industry. For such an industry, minimum possible average cost of producing the good doesn't change as firms enter or leave the industry, other things being equal.

Constant-costs industry:
One for which input prices are unaffected by the quantity of a good produced or the number of firms in the industry.

For the constant-costs industry, price always returns to the same level in the long run as the number of firms changes. You can confirm this by examining the graphs in Boxes 3 and 4 once again. In the long run, changes in the number of firms in the industry cause shifts in the short-run supply curves that change equilibrium output until price falls back to minimum possible average cost. Of course, changes in technology or changes in input prices that occur for reasons other than changes in the number of firms in the industry could affect minimum possible average cost. However, the important point is that for an industry of constant costs, given technology and given influences on input prices other than the number of firms in the industry, minimum possible average cost will be unchanged as the industry expands or contracts in the long run.

The graph in Box 5 plots the points of long-run competitive equilibrium for the bicycle industry based on our previous examples. Connecting these points gives a **long-run industry supply curve,** which is a relationship between price and quantity supplied *for points where the industry is in long-run competitive equilibrium*. Each point on a long-run supply curve corresponds to the minimum possible average cost of producing the good. Point E_1 on the long-run supply curve corresponds to the initial long-run equilibrium first illustrated in Box 2. Point E_2 corresponds to the long-run equilibrium that ultimately resulted from the decrease in demand illustrated in Box 3. Finally, point E_3 corresponds to the long-run equilibrium that resulted from the increase in demand traced out in Box 4.

Notice that the long-run supply curve is a horizontal line for an industry of con-

Long-run industry supply curve:
A relationship between price and quantity supplied for points where the industry is in long-run competitive equilibrium.

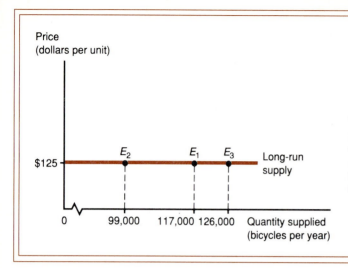

Price
(dollars per unit)

$125

E_2 E_1 E_3

Long-run
supply

0   99,000   117,000 126,000   Quantity supplied
(bicycles per year)

Box 5   The Long-Run Supply Curve for an Industry of Constant Costs

The long-run supply curve gives quantity supplied at prices for which the industry is in equilibrium. For the case of constant costs, price must always return to minimum possible average cost as the industry expands and contracts. Given input prices and technology, the supply curve is a horizontal line.

stant costs. This is because the minimum possible average cost of producing the good doesn't change as the industry expands or contracts. Given input prices and technology, industry output is infinitely elastic at the price corresponding to minimum possible average cost for an industry of constant costs. Any price increases above minimum possible average cost can only result in temporary short-run equilibriums and won't be included as points on the long-run supply curve for the industry. Although increases in price are necessary to increase quantity supplied in all cases in the short run, the long-run supply curve for a constant-costs industry will be flat.

When Are Long-Run Supply Curves Upward Sloping?

A long-run supply curve for an industry will be upward sloping when input prices increase as a direct result of increases in the number of firms in the industry. This will prevail if firms buy a large proportion of the total supply of a particular input, such as a certain type of skilled labor. For example, if the bicycle industry is the chief employer of certain skilled mechanics, then its expansion will tend to bid up the wages necessary to attract more mechanics. By the same token, a contraction of the bicycle industry would cause these mechanics' wages to decrease.

An **increasing-costs industry** is one for which the prices of at least some of the inputs used increase as a direct result of the expansion of the industry. For such an industry, expansion will *increase* the minimum possible cost of producing the output while contraction will *decrease* the minimum possible cost of producing the output. The long-run supply curve for an industry of increasing costs will be upward sloping. This is illustrated in Box 6. For example, suppose the initial price of bicycles was $125 and that an increase in demand increases their price in the short run so as to allow profits and ultimately increase the number of firms in the industry in the long run. If the industry were one of increasing costs, the increased demand for specialized inputs used in the industry would result in an increase in the prices of these inputs. As a result, the minimum possible average cost of producing bicycles would increase in the long run. Suppose the number of firms increased sufficiently to shift the short-run supply curve out enough to reduce price to its initial level of

Increasing-costs industry:
One for which the prices of at least some of the inputs used increase as a direct result of the expansion of the industry.

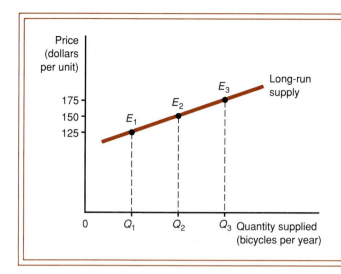

Box 6   The Long-Run Supply Curve for an Industry of Increasing Costs

In an industry of increasing costs, the minimum average cost of producing output increases as the industry expands. The long-run supply curve is therefore upward sloping.

$125. If this is an increasing-costs industry, firms would incur losses because the minimum possible average cost would now exceed $125 as a result of the industry's expansion. If the new minimum possible average cost is $150, the market price would have to increase to this level in the long run as the industry expands.

The graph in Box 6 shows three points of long-run equilibrium for an industry of increasing costs: E_1, E_2, and E_3. Each point corresponds to a higher minimum possible average cost represented by the corresponding higher price.

Concept Check

1   Briefly trace out the process that would eliminate profits in a competitive industry in the long run. How would the process operate in reverse to eliminate losses?

2   Explain why the price of a product sold in a perfectly competitive market must equal the minimum possible average cost of making that good available in long-run equilibrium. Why do firms in competitive industries remain in business in the long run despite the fact that the maximum profits they can hope to earn are zero?

3   How does a long-run supply curve differ from the short-run supply curve for a competitive industry? Under what circumstances can a long-run industry supply curve be expected to slope upward?

Applications of the Model: Changes in Costs or Technology and Long-Run Competitive Equilibrium

Changes in technology and other changes affecting the minimum possible cost of making a good available to buyers in a market can disturb the equilibrium of a competitive industry. As changes in costs affect the profitability of the industry, firms will enter or exit. The insights possible from the competitive model allow you to go

Principles in Practice

How Limits to Entry Affect a Competitive Industry: The Case of Taxis in New York City and the Soaring Price of Taxi Medallions

The taxi industry in large cities is one that seems to meet many of the requirements for perfect competition. The service is more or less standardized. There are usually thousands of independent firms offering taxi services, and it's rare for one taxi seller to have a large market share in a big city. However, in many cities entry into the taxi industry is restricted by government controls.

If you've ever hailed a cab on the streets of New York City, you might have noticed the metal medallion affixed to the hood of the vehicle. The taxi medallion is the license that gives those who own the cabs the right to pick up street passengers. If you live in New York, you can't enter the taxi industry just by painting your car yellow. You must also purchase a taxi medallion. In 1986, for the first time, a New York City taxi medallion sold for over $100,000!

A taxi medallion is a transferable license to operate a taxi in the City of New York. In the late 1930s the city issued one license per cab to people already in the taxi business. When the medallions were issued, they were auctioned off and initially sold for $10! Since then the city has never issued another medallion. The only way to obtain a medallion is to buy it from someone who owns one. There were just under 12,000 medallions outstanding in 1986—not a huge number.

The medallion can be thought of as a government-created fixed input required to engage in the sale of taxi services. Its purpose is to provide a stable supply of taxi services over time. Before the medallion system was implemented in New York, the supply of taxi services would decrease sharply during economic expansions when the opportunity cost of operating a taxi was high in terms of forgone wages in other jobs. Conversely, the supply of taxi services would increase in periods of recession when the opportunity cost of using time to operate a taxi was low for those who would otherwise be unemployed.

The fixed costs of operating a taxi are very low. The vehicle itself has alternative uses to its owner and can easily be withdrawn from the industry on short notice with little loss. By the same token, it's at least theoretically easy to enter the taxi industry because most people have the requisite fixed input—a passenger car.

Because the supply of medallions is *perfectly inelastic,* their price is determined solely by the level of demand, as shown in the graph. The demand, of course, depends on the profitability of selling taxi services.

It's easy to see how the medallion increases the fixed costs of operating a taxi. After acquiring a medallion, its owner is also required to pay a $150 fee each year to maintain the right to operate a cab. However, the real opportunity cost of the medallion is the forgone interest on its $100,000 market price. If, for example, the owner of a medallion forgoes 8% interest by purchasing the medallion, the opportunity cost will be 8% of

$100,000, which is $8,000 per year. This becomes part of the fixed cost of operating a taxi.

The medallion system is an effective limit on entry into the taxi industry that strictly controls the number of cabs on the street. The profits can't act as a lure to increase the supply of taxi services because the number of taxis is limited by the fixed number of medallions. However, this doesn't mean taxi owners will enjoy tremendous economic profits. This is because as the profitability of taxi services increases, the market price of a medallion goes up. The opportunity cost increases in terms of forgone interest income, thereby increasing the costs of operating the taxi. This contributes to higher prices for taxi services—but not to higher profits.

Of course, the medallion owners benefit from the increased profitability of taxi services by having the option to sell their medallion for much more than they paid for it. Someone who bought a medallion as an investment in the 1930s for $10 would have done quite well by holding on to it and selling it in 1986 for $100,000!

In recent years many people have bought medallions as investments rather than to operate a cab themselves. They then lease the right to use their cab to someone else, thereby earning a cash flow from their investment. They hope to be able to sell the medallion at a good profit in the future. In fact, if you had bought a medallion in early 1986 for $75,000 you could have sold it 3 months later for $100,000. This is a 33% return in 3 months, which amounts to an annual return of 132% per year—a handsome profit by any standard!

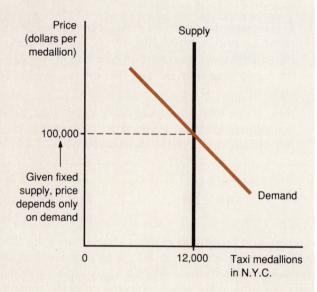

behind the mechanism of supply and demand to better understand the process of adjustment to changes in the cost of making goods available in markets.

Improvements in Technology in a Competitive Industry

Many industries, particularly those producing microelectronic products, have experienced rapid technological improvements in recent years. These improvements have allowed sellers to produce items such as personal computers at lower average costs. We can use the model of long-run competitive equilibrium to show how these technology-induced cost decreases must be passed on to consumers in the form of lower prices if perfect competition prevails.

The market for personal computers provides a useful illustration of how changes in technology affect market equilibrium. Personal computers like the IBM PC and the IBM clones that use the same software as the IBM PC are close to being standardized products. There are also many sellers in the market, and free entry has prevailed, so the conditions of perfect competition are closely approximated. Suppose the current competitive equilibrium price is $2,000 per unit, as shown in Box 7. At that price each of the many firms in the industry earns zero economic profit, as you can see in **A** in Box 7, which shows the cost curves of a typical firm in the industry. Also assume that the industry is one of constant costs.

Now assume there's an improvement in technology that sharply lowers the cost of producing the standardized personal computer. The long-run average cost curve shown in **A** in Box 7 will shift downward. Assume that the new minimum possible

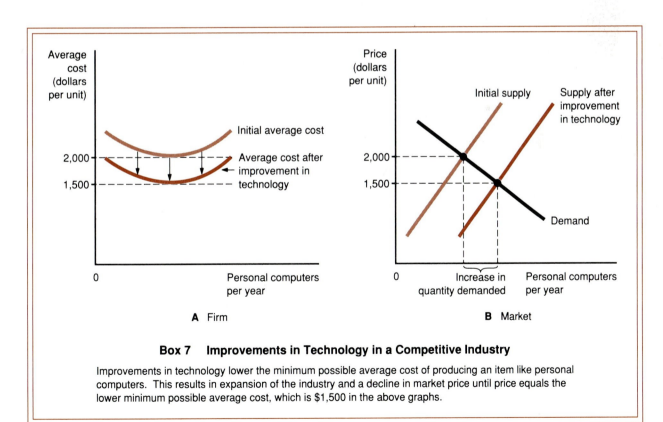

Box 7   Improvements in Technology in a Competitive Industry

Improvements in technology lower the minimum possible average cost of producing an item like personal computers. This results in expansion of the industry and a decline in market price until price equals the lower minimum possible average cost, which is $1,500 in the above graphs.

Principles in Practice

Prices and Competition in the Personal Computer and Home Electronics Industries: How Entry of New Firms Increases Supply to Help Lower Prices

You know those little personal AM-FM radios you can buy for $5.99 in any chain drugstore or supermarket? They're convenient, they're cheap, and they usually provide pretty good sound quality.

It was a different story when your parents were teenagers. Back then, these miniature music machines were brand new and very costly toys. They were called transistor radios, they usually had only an AM band, and because they cost about $50, your parents were more likely to get one as a graduation gift than to pick it up in the supermarket express checkout.

What caused the price of these electronic marvels to decline while the quality actually improved? Technology!

The industries that produce personal computers and home electronics products like color TVs and VCRs are characterized by rapid changes in technology that reduce average costs of production. The cost reductions create opportunities for new and existing firms, which adopt the new technology to make additional profit by supplying more goods to the market.

The combination of ease of entry into the market, rapidly changing technology, and a fairly standardized product has contributed to sharply reduced prices for personal computers. In 1983 the market was dominated by five companies that accounted for 70% of all personal computer sales: IBM, Apple, Tandy, Hewlett-Packard, and Digital Equipment. However, by 1986 there were over 100 manufacturers of IBM "clone" computers. These computers run on software designed for the IBM PC, have a similar keyboard, and perform more or less identically to the IBM product. As a result of the entry of many new sellers into the world market, including Japanese and South Korean firms, the price of personal computers plummeted in 1986—just as the theory in this chapter suggests! For example, an IBM PC system that cost $3,500 in 1983 could easily be bought for about $1,500 in 1986.

The ultimate winner in a competitive market is the consumer, who enjoys quality products at the lowest possible price equal to the minimum possible average cost of production. At least in the short run, manufacturers may be losers. The year 1986 was a terrible one for IBM stockholders. The increased competition forced IBM to cut prices to maintain sales, and as a result profits fell. This is just what the theory of long-run equilibrium suggests.

In the long run even a giant like IBM must be content with zero economic profits. In 1986 the long run was clearly approaching for IBM. Of course, one way to increase profits is to innovate. IBM is well aware of this, and in 1987 it introduced a "new and improved" personal computer in the hope of regaining its market share. IBM also tried to eliminate the standardization that enabled the clones to use software that was specifically designed for IBM machines. IBM's approach was to introduce some twists in the Intel chip that runs its new model, in an effort to make it difficult for IBM software to run smoothly on clone machines.

If you bought any electronic home entertainment products in 1986 and 1987, you enjoyed similar price reductions. The marvels of modern technology, such as VCRs, stereo TV monitors, and compact disc players, can make your living room rival theatres and concert halls! The market for these products in the past was dominated by Japanese firms. However, the South Koreans have emerged as keen competitors eager to adopt new technology and supply more electronic gizmos to consumers. As a result, the market is characterized by falling prices *and* improved quality. Features like picture-enhancing circuitry once available on only the highest-quality VCRs are now standard even on lower-priced models. For about $450 you can buy a color TV equipped with stereo sound, digital displays, and other features that a few years ago were found only on models selling for over $600. Once again you see how you and other consumers benefit from free and competitive markets. In the long run the lower costs that result from improved technology inevitably end up as lower prices to consumers when market conditions approach those of perfect competition.

average cost is $1,500. *Any price above $1,500 per unit will encourage new firms to enter the industry.* It follows that short-run market supply, as shown in **B,** will increase until the quantity of computers available per year is increased sufficiently to drop the price to $1,500 per unit. At that lower price, quantity demanded increases substantially, as shown in **B.** The assumption of constant costs means that the decline in average costs induced by the improvement in technology won't be offset in part by any increases in input prices as the number of firms in the industry increases. Entry of new firms under perfect competition therefore guarantees that consumers will benefit from the improvement in technology through lower prices for personal computers. In fact, the number of firms producing computing equipment in the United States increased from 58 in 1977 to 1,520 in 1982! Thanks to improvements in technology, the prices of personal computers have fallen in recent years.

This conclusion can be generalized: Any change that *decreases* the minimum possible average cost of making a good available to consumers in markets will ultimately lower prices. In the long run, the decrease in minimum possible average cost will be fully passed on to consumers in the form of a decrease in the equilibrium price of the good in a competitive market.

We also can apply the insights of this analysis to the question of international competition. The reason improvements in technology lower the minimum possible average cost of production is that they increase the productivity of inputs. When more output can be squeezed from a given combination of inputs of given cost, the cost *per unit* of output tends to decline. Failure to adapt quickly to new technology therefore means that industries forgo the opportunity to produce goods at lower cost.

For example, if the U.S. electronics industry competes with Japanese electronics firms in domestic and world markets, the U.S. firms won't have a competitive edge unless they keep up with technological change. If the Japanese develop and apply new technology before the U.S. firms, they'll be able to sell at lower prices in world markets and increase their share of total sales at the expense of U.S. firms. The secret of remaining competitive in world markets is therefore quick response to changes in technology that allow firms to reduce average costs of production!

Taxing the Output of a Constant-Costs Competitive Industry

Any change that increases the minimum possible average cost of making an item available will set up a process that ultimately causes a competitive industry in equilibrium to achieve a new equilibrium at a higher price. One change that can increase the minimum possible average cost of selling a good is a tax collected from sellers of the good.

Suppose the trucking industry is perfectly competitive and in equilibrium at a price of $1 per pound of freight shipped. A new tax is imposed on trucking firms equal to 10¢ per pound of freight shipped. *From the truckers' point of view, the tax is equivalent to a 10¢ increase in the cost of each pound shipped.* The cost curves of all firms in the industry will therefore shift upward. Any change in the prices of inputs used in trucking (such as an increase in the price of fuel) would have a similar effect. The graphs in Box 8 illustrate the long-run effect of the tax.

Because the industry was initially in equilibrium, the increase in the minimum possible average cost caused by the tax will result in economic losses. In the long run firms will exit the industry. Firms will continue to exit until the supply of trucking services has decreased enough to increase price to the minimum possible average cost of production, including the tax per pound shipped. In the long run price rises to $1.10, which equals minimum long-run average cost, including the tax. *If the taxed industry is one of constant costs, the price per pound must rise by the amount of the tax.* This is because the increase in the minimum possible average cost is equal to the tax per pound shipped.

Graph **A** in Box 8 shows that the industry is initially in equilibrium at point E_1, where the demand for trucking services intersects the long-run supply curve. Each point on the initial long-run supply curve corresponds to the $1 minimum possible average cost. Initially the price of freight shipped by truck is $1 per pound.

As shown in **A** in Box 8, the minimum possible average cost of shipping freight increases to $1.10 per pound after the tax. As a consequence, the long-run supply curve shifts upward by 10¢ per pound shipped. The new long-run competitive equilibrium would be at point E_2, where the quantity of freight shipped declines from Q_1 to Q_2 pounds per month and price rises to $1.10 per pound. The entire 10¢ per pound tax is reflected in the price paid by shippers in the long run. *If the price didn't rise to $1.10 per pound to cover the full tax, price would fall short of minimum possible average cost.* After payment of the added 10¢ per pound tax, firms *must* receive $1 per pound to cover their average costs of production. Otherwise firms would leave the industry until the long-run quantity supplied decreased enough to allow firms to receive $1 per pound after payment of the 10¢ per pound tax. This requires that the price paid by shippers increase to $1.10 per pound.

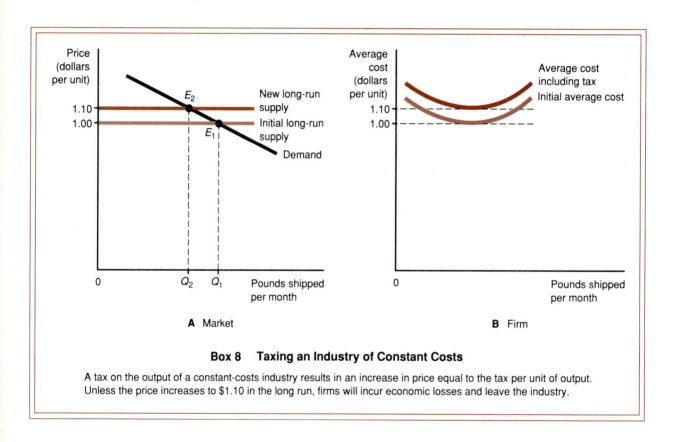

Box 8   Taxing an Industry of Constant Costs

A tax on the output of a constant-costs industry results in an increase in price equal to the tax per unit of output. Unless the price increases to $1.10 in the long run, firms will incur economic losses and leave the industry.

The tax is fully reflected in the price paid by shippers only for the case of constant costs. If increasing costs prevailed in the industry, the prices of some of the inputs used by truckers would fall as firms exited. The decrease in input prices would offset the upward pressure of the tax on prices. In general, prices would then rise by *less* than the tax in the increasing-costs case.

CHAPTER 12 Long-Run Supply in Competitive Markets

1   Explain why improvements in technology ultimately result in lower prices for goods produced under conditions of perfect competition.

2   Why will a tax on the output of an industry of constant costs cause the price of the product to rise by the full amount of the tax?

3   A government policy pays half the labor costs of a competitive industry. Explain how the resulting decrease in average cost will affect the market price of the product for an industry of constant costs. How would the result differ for an industry of increasing costs?

Long-Run Competitive Equilibrium and Efficiency

Allocative Efficiency

Allocative efficiency is achieved when resources are allocated in ways that allow the maximum possible net benefit from their use. When an efficient allocation of resources is attained, it's not possible to make any person in a society better off without making someone else worse off. No change in productive methods or further exchange of goods and services can result in additional net gains if resources are efficiently allocated.

It's easy to show that a system of competitive markets has the potential to achieve allocative efficiency. To see this, concentrate on a single competitive industry that produces bread. A net gain is possible if the maximum price someone is willing to pay for more bread exceeds the minimum price a seller is willing to accept to make that additional bread available. You'll remember that the maximum price a buyer will pay for another unit of a good is the *marginal benefit* of the good. The minimum price a seller will accept for making another unit of the good available is its *marginal cost.* The marginal cost represents the value of resources necessary to make one more unit of a good available. The marginal cost is based on the method that produces the output at minimum possible cost, meaning that productive efficiency is attained. This amount will just cover the opportunity cost of making more of the good available, which means that those whose resources are used won't be made any worse off if the good is provided to consumers.

The graph in Box 9 plots the marginal benefit of bread, along with the marginal cost of making it available. The marginal benefit is assumed to decline with consumption of bread, while the marginal cost is assumed to increase.

A net gain is possible from making more bread available as long as the marginal benefit of bread exceeds its marginal cost. Go to the point on the horizontal axis in Box 9 that corresponds to 50,000 loaves of bread per day. Now follow the vertical dotted line from that quantity up to both the marginal benefit and marginal cost curves. This line intersects the marginal benefit curve at point *B* and intersects the marginal cost curve at point *A.* The marginal benefit of 50,000 loaves of bread per day is $3, and the marginal cost is $1.

It's now easy to show that net gains are possible from making more than 50,000 loaves of bread per day. The marginal benefit of bread exceeds its marginal cost at that daily output. This means that the maximum price consumers are willing and able to pay exceeds the minimum sum of money that's necessary just to compensate the owners of resources used to make that bread available. The difference between

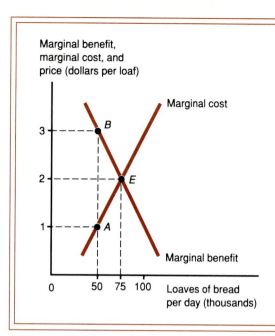

Marginal benefit, marginal cost, and price (dollars per loaf)

Box 9   Efficient Output of a Good

The efficient output of bread per day corresponds to point *E*, at which the marginal benefit of bread just equals the marginal cost.

the marginal benefit of $3 and the marginal cost of $1 is the *net gain* from making another unit of bread available when 50,000 loaves of bread per day are currently produced.

When one more loaf is produced after 50,000 loaves have already been produced, *that extra loaf is worth more to buyers than it is to those whose resources are used to make it available.* This is the basis for the gain from exchange. If consumers were to get the loaf for $3, they would be no worse off from exchanging their dollars for the bread. Those who make the bread available would be better off because they would receive more than the opportunity cost of making that extra bread available. Similarly, if the bread were made available for $1, those who make it available would just cover their opportunity cost for the extra loaf and be made no worse off. Consumers, on the other hand, would now be better off because they would obtain bread they value at $3 for only $1.

If the bread were made available for a price anywhere between $1 and $3 when 50,000 loaves per day are produced, there would be *mutual gains* possible. This is because consumers would get the bread at a price below the maximum they would be willing to pay. Similarly, those whose resources are used to produce the bread would receive a sum that exceeded the minimum they would accept. Additional mutual gains from exchange will always be possible by producing more of the good whenever the marginal benefit of the good exceeds its marginal cost. The output of 50,000 loaves per day is not efficient because, as we've just shown, at that output it would be possible to make consumers better off without harming producers. Similarly, our analysis has shown that at that output it would be possible to make producers better off without harming consumers. Finally, because mutual gains from more daily output are possible, *both consumers and producers can be made better off when more bread is made available each day.*

As long as the marginal benefit of bread exceeds its marginal cost, a net gain will be possible by making more available. *Efficiency requires that bread be produced just up to the point at which its marginal benefit equals its marginal cost.* In Box 9 the marginal benefit of bread just equals its marginal cost when 75,000 loaves per day are produced. If more than this amount were made available, the marginal cost would exceed the marginal benefit. This means that the maximum sum a consumer would pay for one more loaf would fall short of the value of resources necessary to provide that loaf. The bread couldn't be made available without making resource owners worse off. The efficient output of bread is therefore 75,000 loaves of bread per day.

We can generalize the results of this example: *Efficiency requires that all goods be made available just up to the point at which their marginal benefit equals their marginal cost.*

Competitive Markets and Efficiency

A system of competitive markets in which all useful goods and services are traded under conditions of perfect competition is capable of achieving efficiency. The market demand curve is the marginal benefit curve. This is because each point on a market demand curve reflects the maximum sum of dollars some consumer would give up to get more of a good given its current availability. The portion of the marginal cost curve lying above the average variable cost curve is the short-run market supply curve for bread produced by a competitive industry.

If bread were traded in a competitive market, the equilibrium would therefore occur at point *E* in graph **A** in Box 10, at which the marginal benefit and marginal

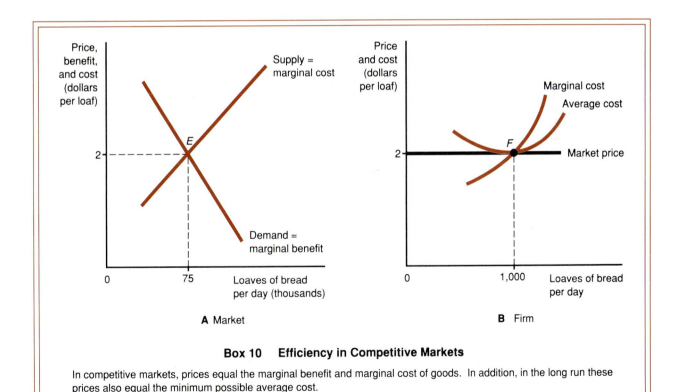

Box 10   Efficiency in Competitive Markets

In competitive markets, prices equal the marginal benefit and marginal cost of goods. In addition, in the long run these prices also equal the minimum possible average cost.

cost curves intersect. The market equilibrium price of bread would be $2 per loaf. The quantity demanded at that price would equal the quantity supplied, which would be 75,000 loaves per day—which is also the efficient output!

The market price of a good in a competitive market equals both the marginal cost and the marginal benefit of the good. To see this, remember that each seller can make more profits by producing more of a good whenever price exceeds marginal cost. Each seller therefore adjusts output of bread until marginal cost rises to equal the market price of the good:

$$\text{Price} = \text{Marginal cost} = \$2$$

In this case the marginal cost equals $2.

Similarly, buyers can gain whenever their marginal benefit exceeds the market price of the good. Buyers therefore continue purchasing bread until the marginal benefit they receive falls to equal the market price:

$$\text{Price} = \text{Marginal benefit} = \$2$$

In this case the marginal benefit equals $2. Because both the buyers and sellers adjust their respective marginal benefits and marginal costs to equal the $2 market price, marginal benefit and marginal cost will both equal $2, resulting in the efficient output of 75,000 loaves per day.

This leads us to an important conclusion: A system of competitive markets, as rare as it might be, receives high marks on the basis of efficiency. In this sense the competitive market system is capable of squeezing the greatest net gain from making goods available given the willingness of consumers to pay for goods. Changes in the marginal benefit of goods caused by changes in tastes or changes in the way income is distributed will result in changes in demand. These changes in demand will change market prices and result in a new efficient resource allocation. In this sense the competitive market system is *responsive* to changes in the value consumers place on various goods. Similarly, changes in the marginal cost of making goods available will shift market supply curves. This will change the market prices of goods and once again result in a new efficient resource allocation. The system is therefore also responsive to changes in the value of productive resources.

In a system of perfectly competitive markets, prices simultaneously equal marginal cost and marginal benefit of goods in equilibrium in both the short and long run. One other desirable feature of the system is attained only in the long run. As we have shown, in long-run competitive equilibrium, prices also equal the *minimum possible average cost* of a good. In the long run, therefore:

$$\text{Price} = \text{Minimum possible average cost} = \text{Marginal cost}$$

This means consumers can buy goods at the lowest possible price that covers both the average and marginal costs of production. This is illustrated in **B** in Box 10, in which a typical bread producer's cost curves are drawn. The $2 market price just covers both the marginal cost of bread and its minimum possible average cost at point *F*.

In a system of competitive markets, the greatest net benefit would be squeezed out of available resources because marginal benefit equals the marginal cost of each good. Finally, assuming that perfect competition prevails in markets for the production of each and every good, the price of each good will reflect its minimum possible average cost. This means the system will economize on resource use because *each good* will be produced at the minimum possible unit cost. This conclusion is really remarkable because it comes about as a result of competition in a system in which each producer seeks nothing more than to maximize profits. However, the final outcome is a resource allocation for which net benefits are the maximum possible from using available resources and prices that are just barely high enough to cover the opportunity costs of sellers.

Concept Check

1   Under what conditions can efficiency be attained in an economy?

2   Show that additional gains are not possible by producing more of a good for which actual production is currently at the level that equates marginal benefit with marginal cost of the good.

3   Why do perfectly competitive markets have the potential to achieve efficiency?

Perfect Competition: From Abstraction to Reality

Perfectly competitive markets are capable of achieving efficiency. For this reason economists take perfect competition as a benchmark against which to compare actual market performance. Although the notion of perfect competition is an abstraction, it's useful not only as a benchmark but also as a basis for providing an understanding of the way actual markets function. The model shows how the pursuit of profit by sellers and net benefits by consumers results in outcomes that maximize the total net gains possible from resource use. Adams Smith's "invisible hand," first discussed in Chapter 2, does its work superbly in perfectly competitive markets.

But alas, the world seldom conforms to theoretical ideals. We therefore must evaluate actual market performance and outcomes on an *ad hoc* basis. As you'll see, there are many cases in which markets fail to achieve outcomes that can measure up to the standard of efficiency. When this is the case, government policies can often result in additional net gains that otherwise wouldn't be possible.

Summary

1. A long-run competitive equilibrium exists in an industry when there's no tendency for firms to enter or leave the industry or to expand or contract the scale of their operations.

2. In the long run new firms will enter an industry whenever the market price of the good produced by that industry exceeds the minimum possible average cost of producing the good. When price exceeds minimum possible average cost, profits are possible because new entrants can earn more than their opportunity costs by entering the industry. Similarly, when price is below minimum possible average cost, firms will exit the industry because they can earn more by using their resources elsewhere.

3. In perfectly competitive markets, profits and losses are eliminated in the long run through changes in supply that change product prices. Increases in supply caused by entry of new firms, and expansion of existing firms in response to profit opportunities, are factors that cause prices to fall. As prices fall, profits are eventually eliminated. Similarly, decreases in supply caused by the exit of firms

from industries where losses prevail put upward pressure on product prices that eventually eliminate losses.

4. In the long run in a competitive industry, prices equal the minimum possible average cost of producing goods, and economic profits are zero at the output for which price equals marginal cost for each firm. In the long run firms just cover their opportunity costs, which include normal profit.

5. A long-run industry supply curve shows a relationship between price and quantity supplied for prices at which the industry is in long-run competitive equilibrium. The long-run supply curve for a constant-costs industry is a flat line that's infinitely elastic at the price equal to the minimum possible average cost of producing the good. Long-run supply curves are upward sloping for industries of increasing costs. An increasing-costs industry is one for which input prices increase as a direct result of the industry's expansion. A constant-costs industry can purchase all the input services it demands without affecting input prices.

6. Improvements in technology lower the minimum possible average cost of producing goods and services. This results in lower product prices in the long run as the industry expands and supply increases in response to the profit opportunities caused by lower costs.

7. In competitive markets, increases in the minimum possible average cost of production resulting from increases in input prices or taxes ultimately cause increases in product prices. Unit taxes on the output of an industry of constant costs are ultimately reflected in price increases that exactly equal the tax per unit of output.

8. Efficiency prevails in an economy when all net gains from resource use have been achieved. Efficient resource allocation requires that each good be made available just up to the point at which its marginal benefit equals its marginal cost. When efficiency is attained, it's not possible to make any individual better off without harming another individual.

9. Competitive markets can achieve efficiency because firms make goods available up to the point at which their marginal costs rise to equal market prices. Buyers adjust to the same market prices that sellers face and consume goods up to the point at which their marginal benefits decline to equal the market price. In this way efficiency is achieved because the marginal benefits of goods are set equal to their marginal costs. In addition, in the long run resource use is economized because market prices also equal the minimum possible average costs of production for each good. This allows maximum satisfaction to be squeezed from available resources in the economy.

10. Perfectly competitive markets represent a benchmark against which to compare actual market performance. Actual markets are rarely perfectly competitive.

Key Terms and Concepts

Long-run competitive equilibrium   Long-run industry supply curve
Constant-costs industry   Increasing-costs industry

Problems and Applications

1. An industrial engineer calculates that the minimum possible average cost of producing roach poison is $10 per gallon under current technology. The current market price of roach poison is $15 per gallon. Assuming the roach poison is

produced under conditions of perfect competition, use graphic analysis to show what will happen to its market supply and price in the long run.

2. Suppose a sharp decrease in demand for roach poison occurs that lowers its price to $8 per gallon. Using the data from problem 1 and assuming the industry is initially in equilibrium, trace out the industry's response. What will the price of roach poison be in the long run, assuming a constant-costs industry?

3. Suppose wheat is produced under conditions of perfect competition. Assume the wheat industry has attained long-run competitive equilibrium at a price of $3 per bushel. What are the average and marginal costs of producing wheat? If a typical wheat producer has $200,000 of capital equipment and this is the only owner-supplied input, calculate economic and accounting profits assuming that the opportunity cost of capital invested in wheat farming is 10%.

4. The industry that produces cables for personal computers is perfectly competitive. Firms in this industry can obtain all the input services they demand without affecting the market prices of those inputs. Derive three points on the industry's long-run supply curve by using graphs to show the long-run equilibrium points in response to increases and decreases in demand. Assume that the minimum possible average cost of producing cable is 5¢ per foot.

5. A firm's short-run supply curve is the portion of its marginal cost curve lying above its average variable cost curve. Explain why points on a long-run supply curve for a competitive market equal *both* marginal cost and the minimum possible average cost of making the product available.

6. Suppose the trucking industry is perfectly competitive and currently in equilibrium. A new procedure is introduced that lowers the minimum possible average cost of shipping freight by truck from 2¢ per pound each mile to 1¢ per pound each mile. Show how the procedure will affect the price of shipping freight per mile if the trucking industry is one of increasing costs.

7. Suppose both American and Japanese firms compete in perfectly competitive markets to sell laser discs. The U.S. firms adopt a new technology that permits them to produce more discs without increasing costs. Show that in the long run U.S. companies will be able to sell the discs at lower prices than Japanese companies, assuming the new technology isn't available in Japan.

8. Show that a 10¢ per gallon subsidy to gasoline sellers will ultimately reduce the price of gasoline to consumers by 10¢ per gallon if gasoline is sold in perfectly competitive markets and if the gasoline industry is one of constant costs.

9. The marginal benefit of automobiles is currently $15,000, but the marginal cost is only $10,000. Is the efficient quantity of automobiles being sold?

10. Currently the market price of a standardized microwave cart produced by firms in a perfectly competitive industry is $100. A tax of $10 is levied on the sale of each cart. The tax increases the market price of microwave carts in the long run to $106. The net price received by sellers after paying the tax is therefore $96. Show that efficiency isn't attained in the competitive microwave cart market after the tax is introduced.

Suggested Readings

Walter Adams, ed., *The Structure of American Industry,* 6th ed., New York: Macmillan, 1982. By reading the essays in this book, you can judge for yourself whether or not perfect competition is approximated in various industries.

David N. Hyman, *Modern Microeconomics: Analysis and Applications,* 2nd ed., Homewood, Ill.: Richard D. Irwin, Inc., 1989. Chapter 9 discusses long-run competitive equilibrium at a more advanced level.

A Forward Look

As we've pointed out in this chapter, actual markets rarely are perfectly competitive. The following chapter looks at the opposite extreme of a competitive market: monopoly. In a monopoly market a single seller is the only source of supply to consumers. In actuality, you'll discover, competition among firms in markets falls between the two extremes of perfect competition and monopoly.

Monopoly

Have you ever played the popular board game of Monopoly®? If so, you know that the object is to gain control of as many neighborhoods, railroads, and utilities as possible, put up as many hotels as you can afford, and bankrupt your opponents with astronomical "rental" fees.

What exactly *is* a monopoly, and does a real-life monopoly bear any resemblance to the game version? In this chapter we'll examine the characteristics of a monopoly and observe how markets function when a monopoly prevails.

If you attend college in a small town, you might find that there's only one store where you can buy books, paper, and other supplies. In such a case you and your fellow students are rival buyers in a market for which there's only *one* seller. If the store managers knew that new sellers couldn't enter the market, they'd be free to control supplies and set prices. They could seek to maximize their profits without any worry that high profits would attract new sellers. When a market is dominated by a single seller, buyers are likely to pay higher prices than would be the case if many sellers competed for business. This means that if you must deal with only one store whose owner seeks to maximize profits, you can expect to pay higher prices for your books and other course supplies than if there were more competition in the market.

In reality, markets often have only a few sellers, and free entry of additional sellers into the market is sometimes impossible. In this chapter we examine outcomes in markets in which there is only a *single* seller and for which entry of additional sellers isn't possible. In such markets the sale of the product is *monopolized* by a single firm. As you'll see, markets in which a single profit-maximizing firm monopolizes the supply are unlikely to result in the efficient outcomes we expect in perfectly competitive markets.

Firms that control the entire market supply of a good can also control the price of that good. This is because they can make the good either significantly scarcer or more abundant, thereby influencing the price buyers are willing to pay. Absence of free entry into a market controlled by a monopoly prevents prices from falling to the minimum possible average cost in the long run because the number of sellers and supply in the market won't increase in the long run if the single seller earns profits.

For example, the world supply of diamonds offered for sale each year is more or less monopolized by a large syndicate. This company markets most of the new diamonds produced in the world. The company, as you'll see soon, uses its control over supply to influence the price of diamonds.

Concept Preview	After reading this chapter, you should be able to:

1 Explain the concept of pure monopoly and how it can be maintained in a market.
2 Show how the demand curve for a product sold by a monopoly firm implies that the firm can control the market price.
3 Show how the marginal revenue from a monopolist's output is less than the price the monopolist charges for its product, and show how the marginal revenue is related to the price elasticity of demand for the monopolist's product.
4 Show how a profit-maximizing monopoly seller chooses how much of its product to make available to buyers in markets, and demonstrate how the decision of how much to sell is inseparable from that of how much to charge.
5 Compare market outcomes under pure monopoly with those that would prevail under perfect competition.
6 Discuss the social cost and possible social benefit of monopoly.

Pure Monopoly

Pure monopoly:
Occurs when there is a single seller of a product that has no close substitutes.

A **pure monopoly** occurs when there is a single seller of a product that has no close substitutes. Buyers who want to consume the product of a monopoly firm have only one source of supply for that particular good. As you know, perfect competition is characterized by the inability of individual sellers to control price. No individual firm produces a large enough share of the total market supply to affect price. Monopoly, on the contrary, is characterized by concentration of supply in the hands of the owners of a single firm.

In actuality, it's rare for a national or world market to have only one seller. The De Beers Company of South Africa, through its syndicate called the Central Selling Organization, accounts for about 85% of the annual sales of diamonds. Although by the definition just given De Beers can't be regarded as a pure monopoly firm, it's pretty close to one. When De Beers offers more diamonds for sale per month, other things being equal, the price of diamonds will fall. Although De Beers isn't a pure monopoly firm, it sells a very large share of the uncut diamonds purchased each year. It can influence diamond prices by controlling the amount it offers for sale (see Principles in Practice box).

Monopoly power:
The ability of a firm to influence the price of its product by making more or less of it available to buyers.

A firm has **monopoly power** if it can influence the market price of its product by making more or less of it available to buyers. Although pure monopoly is very rare, monopoly power is quite common.

The Central Selling Organization: Monopolizing the Sale of Diamonds

Why are people willing to pay vast sums of money for diamonds, which are enchanting but not essential, while the same people balk at paying small municipal charges for water, an undeniable necessity? You'll remember that in Chapter 8 we considered this "paradox of value" and concluded that the marginal benefit of water is low because water is abundant, while diamonds, being scarce, have a much higher marginal benefit.

One reason diamonds are scarce is that the market supply is rigidly controlled by one firm: a virtual diamond monopoly.

De Beers Consolidated Mines, Ltd., is a large diamond mining firm that operates in South Africa. The company accounts for only 15% of annual world diamond production. However, the De Beers Company, through its Central Selling Organization (CSO), headquartered in London, *controls the marketing of over 85% of all diamonds sold in the world*, including those produced in the Soviet Union, Australia, Zaire, Botswana, and Namibia.*

The CSO *buys* as well as sells diamonds. By holding on to stockpiles of the gems it can threaten to dump diamonds on the market to lower prices and thus ruin any independent sellers. For example, in 1981 sellers from Zaire attempted to market their diamonds independently. The CSO reacted by flooding the market with diamonds similar to those sold by Zaire. The price Zaire was obtaining for its diamonds plummeted, and the nation abandoned its plans to sell diamonds independently of the CSO. By buying diamonds CSO can increase demand to maintain price and can add to its stockpiles in periods of recession when

diamond sales fall. In the early 1980s, when the price of diamonds plunged because of flagging demand, the CSO bought many of the gems unloaded by speculators to prevent the price from falling too steeply. As you can see, the CSO acts to control the price of diamonds so as to maximize profits of members that sell diamonds through its auspices.

De Beers and the CSO also act to create demand for diamonds. The CSO's annual advertising budget exceeds $120 million. You've probably noticed some of its slick magazine ads, extolling diamonds as a "gift of love."

The results of the CSO's marketing efforts are sometimes astonishing. For example, in the 1970s the CSO began advertising diamonds aggressively in Japan. The tradition of diamond engagement rings wasn't strong in Japan, where in the late 1960s only 6% of engaged couples bought diamond rings. By the mid-1980s, however, 70% of Japanese engagements resulted in the purchase of a diamond ring! After a sophisticated and skillful advertising campaign launched by the CSO using Japanese advertising agencies, sales of diamond rings were running at $4.3 billion per year in the mid-1980s.

CSO sales during the first half of 1986 rose by 45%, and De Beers profits increased to $161 million. Naturally, with strong demand, the organization has taken the opportunity to raise the price of diamonds. The wholesale price for a one-carat D-flawless diamond increased from $12,600 to $14,500 in March 1986 alone. However, you'll be pleased to know that this raw diamond is still a good buy compared to its record peak price of $63,000 in 1980!

*See Steve Lohr, "Why a Diamond Cartel Is Forever," *The New York Times*, Sunday, September 7, 1986, p. 4 F.

Local monopolies are more common than national monopolies, and local markets often are served by single sellers. However, there are few if any products that have no substitutes. A local electric power company may be the sole seller of electricity in an area, but electricity in its multitude of uses does have substitutes. When the price of electricity rises, there's a decline in the quantity demanded for its use as a means of heating. Natural gas and oil furnaces are good substitutes for electric heat. Similarly, the U.S. Postal Service is the single supplier of letter delivery. However, telecommunication, including electronic transmission of messages, is a substitute for the mail service.

In most regions where local monopolies provide public utility services, the seller can't set the price it charges for service. Most local monopolies that provide electricity, natural gas, and transportation services to regions are regulated by state and local government agencies. In evaluating rates charged by utility monopolies, these regulatory agencies are influenced by political as well as profit considerations. In fact, in many cases these monopolies are actually owned and operated by government agencies. The undesirable outcomes we expect when a pure monopoly firm has freedom to set its prices lead to political intervention to control the monopolist's pricing policies.

How Monopoly Is Maintained: Barriers to Entry

In Chapter 12 you saw how profits serve as a signal to attract new suppliers in competitive markets. If a pure monopoly firm earns economic profits, new entrants will be tempted to compete with the monopolist by producing a similar product. Maintenance of a monopoly requires that new sellers be prevented from entering a market to compete with the monopoly firm. A **barrier to entry** is a constraint that prevents additional sellers from entering a monopoly firm's market. If free entry were possible in monopolistic markets, economic profits earned by monopoly firms would attract new sellers. Supply would increase, as would the number of sellers. The monopolist's control over price would eventually disappear as the market became competitive. The major barriers to entry of new sellers in a monopoly market are discussed in the following sections.

Barrier to entry:
A constraint that prevents additional sellers from entering a monopoly firm's market.

Government Franchises and Licenses

Some barriers to entry are the result of government policies that grant single-seller status to firms. For example, local governments commonly give the right to install cable television systems to a single firm. Governments typically establish monopolies for the rights to sell transportation and communication services, electric power, water and sewer service, and natural gas service. In France, since 1904 the funeral business has been controlled by General Funerals, a government-supported monopoly firm that sells coffins and funeral services. In many cases in the United States, the most notable being the U.S. Postal Service, government-supported enterprises act as monopolists. Many states run monopoly liquor stores, and some states are the sole legal source of gambling through state-run lotteries.

Patents and Copyrights

Patents and copyrights are another government-supported barrier to entry. They give creators of new products and works of literature, art, and music exclusive rights to sell or license the use of their inventions and creations. Patents and copyrights provide monopoly protection for only a specified number of years. After the patent expires, the barrier to entry is removed. For example, the Polaroid Corporation has patents on the instant-picture camera (see Principles in Practice box).

The idea behind patents and copyrights is to encourage firms and individuals to innovate and produce new products. This is done by guaranteeing exclusive rights to the profits from new ideas to their orginators through establishment of monopoly supply for limited periods.

Ownership of the Entire Supply of a Resource

A monopoly can also be maintained as a result of ownership of the entire source of supply of a particular input. The De Beers Company has monopoly power in the diamond market because it controls the sale of over 85% of uncut gem diamonds through its Central Selling Organization. The Aluminum Company of America had a monopoly in the U.S. aluminum market until the end of World War II. Its monopoly was attributable in part to its control of bauxite ore, which is the source of aluminum, and its control of a few excellent sources of low-cost power.

Principles in Practice

Patents and Monopoly: Kodak vs. Polaroid

Anyone who was alive and alert in the 1950s knows that one of the most exciting and innovative consumer products to hit the market was the instant-picture camera developed by Polaroid. This bulky and cumbersome device performed a feat that was close to miraculous: just one minute after the shutter was snapped, out came the picture you'd just taken!

This camera (and its later refinements) were the photographic sensation of the decade. As the holder of key patents for instant photography, Polaroid had a monopoly in the market. But, as you discovered in this chapter, patents don't last forever—and Polaroid found its monopoly threatened by an eager rival.

In 1976 some of Polaroid's instant-photography patents expired, and so, apparently, did its monopoly on instant-picture cameras. After the patents expired, Eastman Kodak entered the instant-camera market with its own cameras and film. By the mid-1980s, Kodak accounted for 25% of the annual sales of instant-picture cameras. During the 10-year period from 1976 to 1985 Kodak sold 16.5 million of the devices.

Polaroid, however, wasn't relinquishing its monopoly gracefully. Claiming patent infringement, the company went to court seeking to block Kodak's marketing of instant-picture cameras.

In October 1985, a federal judge ruled that in entering the instant-picture market as a producer and seller, Eastman Kodak had infringed on no fewer than seven Polaroid patents that were still in force! A court injunction was issued that ordered Kodak to cease producing and selling instant-picture cameras. The injunction took effect during the second week in January 1986, when an appeals court in Washington, D.C., upheld the order for Kodak to cease producing *both the cameras and the film.* Kodak, although maintaining its innocence, decided to get out of the instant-picture business, which represented less than 5% of its total annual sales. However, Kodak said it still intended to appeal the verdict to avoid being hit with damage payments to Polaroid in the neighborhood of *$1 billion.*

Kodak's decision to stop producing film for its instant-picture cameras meant that people who owned the cameras wouldn't be able to use them. Kodak offered to exchange the cameras, which originally sold for $25 to $75, for other Kodak products, certificates to buy Kodak products, or one share of Kodak stock.

The results weren't good for Eastman Kodak, which estimated that the exchanges would cost $200 million and that it would incur additional costs in shutting down its instant-picture operations. Needless to say, the Polaroid Corporation and its stockholders were delighted. Once again, the company that gave the world the instant-picture camera had a monopoly in the market.

Unique ability or knowledge can also create a monopoly. Talented singers, artists, athletes, and the cream of the crop of any profession have monopolies on the use of their services. Firms with secret processes or technologies have monopolies if other firms can't duplicate the techniques.

Cost Advantages of Large-Scale Operations and the Emergence of Monopolies

Monopolies might also arise naturally out of cost or technological advantages associated with large-scale production or marketing of products. *Economies of scale* (see Chapter 10) are cost savings that result from large-scale production. These cost savings favor the establishment of monopolies because bigger firms in industries for which economies of scale prevail can produce at lower average cost than smaller competitors.

If firms can continually reduce average costs of production and profits by expanding in the long run, one firm will eventually emerge as the dominant supplier. Perfect competition would result in much higher average costs of production because its maintenance would require many small firms with small market shares. If perfect competition existed initially, it would end soon as existing firms would merge or one firm would purchase their assets and consolidate them. To achieve lower average costs, one firm must dominate. Once it dominates, new firms can't enter because they would be too small initially to achieve the low average costs the dominant firm enjoys by virtue of producing the entire market supply in very large plants.

Natural monopoly:
A firm that emerges as a single seller in the market because of cost or technological advantages contributing to lower average costs of production.

The term **natural monopoly** is sometimes used to describe a situation in which a firm emerges as a single seller in a market because of cost or technological advantages contributing to lower average costs of production. Competition among firms in such an industry results in one large firm supplying the entire market demand at lower cost than two or more smaller firms. A natural monopoly can produce the entire quantity demanded by buyers at any price at lower average cost than would be possible for each firm in the industry if more than one firm existed. For example, a local electric company might be regarded as a natural monopoly firm if the average cost of producing the quantity of electricity currently demanded would be higher if more than one firm sold this product.

The Demand for a Monopolist's Product

A common mistake made by people who criticize monopoly is to assume that the demand for a monopolist's product is perfectly inelastic. This assumption is without foundation. In fact, as you'll see shortly, a monopolist seeking to maximize profits will try to *avoid* serving markets in which demand is inelastic! Consumers always have the alternative of doing without a monopolist's product when its price is increased. For example, if your local electric monopoly raises its price, you and other consumers can cut down on your use of electricity. You might use your air conditioners less or be more careful about turning out lights when leaving a room.

If there were only one seller of automobiles in the United States, we'd still react by buying more cars when the monopoly seller lowered prices, and buying fewer when prices increased. The managers of a monopoly firm take this fact into account when deciding on their price. They know that the amount they'll sell depends on the price they choose. Because there's only one seller in a pure monopoly market, there's no distinction between the market demand curve and the demand curve for the firm's product. The output of a pure monopoly firm *is* the market output. *The demand curve for the pure monopolist's product is the downward-sloping market demand curve that would be faced by an entire competitive industry.* For this reason the monopolist's pricing decision is inseparable from the decision about how much to offer for sale. The higher the price it sets, the lower the quantity it will sell.

The Monopolist's Marginal Revenue

For a competitive firm, marginal revenue is the same as price. For example, if bread is sold by many rival firms in a competitive market, each individual seller can sell as much as it wishes each day without reducing price. If the price of bread is $2 a loaf, any one firm will take in an extra $2 each time it sells an additional loaf. A monopolist, on the other hand, must *decrease* the price of the product to sell more. This follows from the fact that the demand curve for a monopolist's product is downward sloping. The marginal revenue of additional sales by a monopolist is always less than the price.

A numerical example will help you understand this. Suppose you're a popular entertainer on a par with Michael Jackson or Cyndi Lauper. You're the single seller of live concerts with you as the principal performer. Your fans see no close substitute for your voice and appearance. They're crazy about you. You are, in short, a monopolist in the sale of your services. You can set your price for a concert.

What Price Stardom?

The superstars of Hollywood are box-office magnets who can set their price per film—and the prices are often astronomical. Sylvester Stallone received $15 million plus a percentage of the box-office revenues for his role in *Rocky IV*. Producers gladly pay such incredibly high salaries because they know that millions of moviegoers will line up to see films that feature their idols. The charisma of the superstars gives them a degree of monopoly power that they can exploit to control the price they receive for making a movie.

The acknowledged box-office champion of 1986 was Stallone, who received at least $12 million in salary for 8 weeks' work on the production of *Over the Top*. Other stars also set hefty salaries for their services, as shown in the table.

Published salary figures often understate the actual sum of money a star obtains from a film because the top stars also receive a percentage of box-office revenues. For example, Clint Eastwood often earns as much as $20 million for a film because his contracts specify large percentages of the revenue earned. A contract like that could make your day!

Star	1986 price per feature film
Robert Redford	$7.5 million
Clint Eastwood	$7 million
Dustin Hoffman	$6 million
Warren Beatty	$6 million
Jack Nicholson	$5 million
Eddie Murphy	$5 million
Barbra Streisand	$5 million
Paul Newman	$4 million
Harrison Ford	$4 million
Meryl Streep	$3.9 million
Diane Keaton	$2.5 million
Jessica Lange	$2.5 million
Madonna	$1.6 million

*The salaries and other figures are based on Ivor Davis, "Salaries of the Stars Are Astronomical," *The News and Observer*, Raleigh, N.C., Sunday, September 7, 1986, Section E, p. 1.

The table in Box 1 provides data on the price per performance and the number of appearances you can sell at each price per year. At a price of $1 million per performance, only one concert hall would be willing to buy your services. Your total output of concerts per year thus will be one, and your total revenue per year will be $1 million. Remember that marginal revenue is the *extra revenue* for each *extra* unit of output. It's the change in total revenue divided by the change in quantity sold. The third column calculates annual total revenue from the sale of your services to the concert halls. Your marginal revenue is simply the change in total revenue for each extra concert.

Marginal revenue = Change in total revenue/Change in number of concerts

The marginal revenue of your first concert is $1 million because you'd have zero revenue if you gave zero concerts. If you want to give two concerts per year, you must lower your price to $900,000 per concert. Your total revenue will then be $1,800,000 per year. The marginal revenue of the second concert is therefore $1,800,000 minus $1 million, which equals $800,000. The marginal revenue of the second concert is $100,000 less than the price you received. Notice that you must announce your price in advance. You can give two concerts only if your price is $900,000 for each concert. This assumes you don't have the option of charging $1 million for the first concert and $900,000 for the second. The only way the quantity demanded of your services will increase to two concerts per year is if you lower the price you're willing to accept for *each* concert.

The decrease in price results in downward pressure on your revenue because you lost the opportunity to sell one concert at $1 million. However, the extra sales

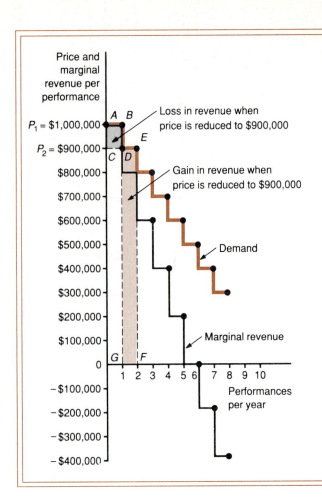

Box 1 Monopoly Demand and Marginal Revenue for Performances

For each $100,000 reduction in price, marginal revenue declines by $200,000. For example, when price is reduced to $900,000, two performances are sold and marginal revenue declines from $1,000,000 to $800,000. Marginal revenue of the second performance is the area *DEFG* minus the area *ABCD*. *ABCD* is the loss in revenue on the first concert that could have been sold at a higher price.

Demand and Marginal Revenue for a Monopoly

Number of performances per year	Price	Total revenue	Marginal revenue
0	More than $1,000,000	0	—
1	$1,000,000	$1,000,000	$1,000,000
2	900,000	1,800,000	800,000
3	800,000	2,400,000	600,000
4	700,000	2,800,000	400,000
5	600,000	3,000,000	200,000
6	500,000	3,000,000	0
7	400,000	2,800,000	−200,000
8	300,000	2,400,000	−400,000

resulting from the lower price result in upward pressure on revenue. *The marginal revenue is the difference between the loss in revenue due to the lower price and the gain in revenue due to the increase in the quantity sold.* Lowering your price gives you $900,000 in revenue from the second concert that you wouldn't have had the opportunity to give had you kept your price at $1 million. The graph in Box 1 shows your gain in revenue from the extra concert when you reduce the price from $1 million to $900,000 per concert. At the same time, you lose the extra $100,000 you could have earned on the first concert had you kept your price at $1 million. The loss in revenue from the decrease in price is also illustrated in Box 1. The net gain in revenue from lowering price is therefore $900,000 less the $100,000 forgone on the first concert. Your marginal revenue from the second concert is $800,000.

The table in Box 1 calculates marginal revenue for each price and quantity. After the first concert, successive reductions in price increase the difference between price and marginal revenue. At a price of $500,000 per concert, marginal revenue becomes zero. At any price below $500,000, marginal revenue is negative. Giving more than six concerts per year will decrease rather than increase your total revenue!

A monopoly seller can be regarded as a *price maker rather than a price taker.* The seller is a price maker whether or not it wants to be! The fact is that a pure monopolist *must* lower its price if it wants to sell more. This is because its demand curve is the entire market demand curve.

Concept Check

1 Under what circumstances would a seller enjoy a pure monopoly in a market? How are monopolies established and maintained?

2 Explain why the demand curve for a monopolist's output is not a horizontal line.

3 How is the marginal revenue from a monopolist's sales calculated? Explain why the marginal revenue is always less than the price the monopolist receives for any quantity sold.

Profit Maximization by Monopoly Firms

A competitive firm, which can't influence the price of its product, maximizes profit by merely adjusting the amount it produces at the market price until marginal revenue equals marginal cost. Although a monopoly seller can influence the market price of its product, the principle of profit maximization is the same for a monopolist as for a competitive firm. Maximization of profits implies that marginal revenue must equal marginal cost at the output produced. *However, the marginal revenue of additional output for a monopolist is less than the price at which that output is sold.*

The table in Box 2 provides data on the costs incurred for your concert performances. Total cost per year of all your performances is shown in the third column of the table. The fourth column shows the average cost of each performance. The marginal cost is calculated in the fifth column as the change in total costs for each extra performance. The sixth column shows your total revenue, while the seventh column reproduces data on marginal revenue from the table in Box 1.

Box 2 Costs and Determination of Profit-Maximizing Monopoly Output

Price	Output (performances per year)	Total cost per year ($)	Average cost ($ per performance)	Marginal cost (MC) ($ per performance)	Total revenue per year ($)	Marginal revenue (MR) ($ per performance)	Total profit (TR−TC) ($ per year)	Marginal profit (MR−MC)
More than $1,000,000	0	$100,000	—	—	0	—	$−100,000	—
$1,000,000	1	500,000	$500,000	$400,000	$1,000,000	$1,000,000	500,000	$600,000
900,000	2	1,000,000	500,000	500,000	1,800,000	800,000	800,000	300,000
800,000	3	1,550,000	516,666	550,000	2,400,000	600,000	850,000	50,000
700,000	4	2,250,000	562,500	700,000	2,800,000	400,000	550,000	−300,000
600,000	5	3,150,000	630,000	900,000	3,000,000	200,000	−150,000	−700,000
500,000	6	4,150,000	691,666	1,000,000	3,000,000	0	−1,150,000	−1,000,000
400,000	7	5,550,000	792,857	1,400,000	2,800,000	−200,000	−2,750,000	−1,600,000
300,000	8	7,550,000	943,750	2,000,000	2,400,000	−400,000	−5,150,000	−2,400,000

Your fixed costs are $100,000 per year. These consist of depreciation and interest on capital equipment such as musical instruments, sound equipment, costumes, and vehicles used to transport you and your entourage (including bodyguards) to each performance. Even if you give no concerts in a year, you still incur these costs. The next to last column, total profit, thus shows that you'll lose $100,000 per year if you choose not to give any concerts. If you price your performances at over $1 million each, there will be no buyers. You'll therefore lose an amount equal to your fixed costs.

If your price is $1 million, you'll find a buyer for one concert per year. Your total costs will be $500,000, so you'll make a $500,000 profit on that concert. The marginal cost of the first concert is $400,000. This is equal to the average variable cost of that concert. It consists of wages paid to your assistants, accompanying musicians, bodyguards who protect you while on the road, and fuel for the vehicles that get you from location to location. The marginal revenue of the first concert is equal to $1 million. Marginal profit, shown in the last column of the table, is therefore $600,000. Recall that marginal profit is the difference between marginal revenue and marginal cost.

After the first concert, marginal revenue falls below price because you must lower your asking price to have the opportunity of giving more performances. The total revenue of two concerts is $1.8 million. You must price your concerts at $900,000 each if you want to sell two per year to the promoters. The total cost of two concerts is $1 million. The marginal cost of the second concert is therefore $1 million less $500,000 divided by 1. Because marginal revenue of the second concert is $800,000, your marginal profit is positive. In this case your marginal profit is $300,000 and your total profit increases from $500,000 to $800,000 per year.

As long as marginal revenue exceeds the marginal cost of a concert, your profits will increase. Profits begin to decrease as soon as marginal cost exceeds marginal revenue. You'll increase your annual profits if you increase your output to three concerts per year. This is because the marginal cost of the third concert is $550,000 while its marginal revenue is $600,000. Your marginal profit for the third concert is therefore $50,000, and your total profits increase to $850,000 per year. If you want to give three concerts per year, you have to price each concert at $800,000.

Will you be interested in reducing your price below $800,000? If you cut your price to $700,000, you'd be able to give four concerts per year. But it wouldn't be worth it! The marginal cost of the fourth concert would be $700,000. Its marginal revenue would only be $400,000. Your marginal profit would therefore be minus $300,000. By cutting your price to $700,000 you'd actually reduce your profits from $850,000 to $550,000 per year.

As the table in Box 2 shows, any output greater than three concerts per year will cost more than it brings in revenue. Your equilibrium price is therefore $800,000 per concert. The equilibrium quantity that will be demanded at that price is three concerts. Any price above or below $800,000 per concert would result in either more or less than the profit-maximizing number of concerts.

Your profits at that price are $850,000 per year. The marginal cost of concerts at that output is $550,000. *At the equilibrium output, therefore, marginal cost is less than price.* This follows from the fact that marginal revenue is less than price under monopoly.

The price set by the monopoly firm therefore determines the quantity demanded. For example, a monopoly electric company can't easily increase or decrease the availability of electricity. However, it can nonetheless influence the quantity demanded by manipulating its price until quantity demanded adjusts to the level at which marginal cost just equals marginal revenue.

As long as the price exceeds average cost at the output for which marginal revenue equals marginal cost, a monopoly will be profitable. The monopoly price of concerts was $800,000 in the example we just considered. The average cost of a concert was a bit less than $516,666 (the average cost shown in Box 2 has been rounded to the nearest dollar) when you gave three concerts per year. Profit per concert, which is the difference between price and average cost, was therefore $283,334. Multiplying this by 3 gives approximately $850,000.

How much profit a monopolist actually makes depends on both costs and the demand for the product. Having a monopoly doesn't guarantee that you'll earn profits. Monopolists can and do go out of business when the demand declines for the product they sell. Owning the only genuine Turkish bath house in town won't be profitable if no one is willing to pay for Turkish baths anymore. If demand and marginal revenue decline, it can be impossible to make a profit.

The graph in Box 3 draws the cost curves, the demand curve, and the marginal revenue curve for a profit-earning monopolist. Suppose the firm monopolizes the supply of bread in a nation. The output for which marginal revenue equals marginal cost is 50,000 loaves per day. The monopolist prices bread at $3 per loaf to sell this amount. The average cost of producing 50,000 loaves per day is $2.25. The monopolist therefore earns a daily profit equal to 75¢ per loaf. At the daily output of 50,000 loaves, total profit is $37,500 per day, shown as the shaded area in the graph in Box 3.

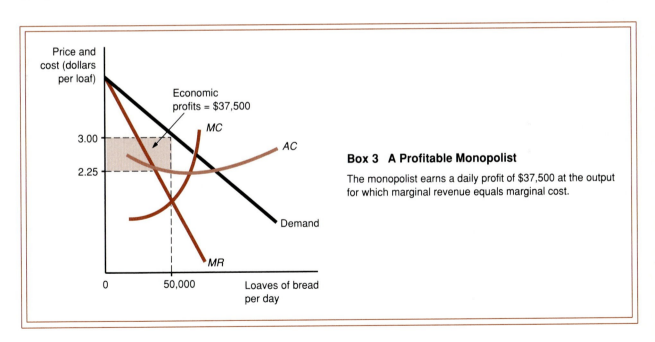

Box 3 A Profitable Monopolist

The monopolist earns a daily profit of $37,500 at the output for which marginal revenue equals marginal cost.

The graph in Box 4 shows a monopoly Turkish bath house that incurs losses at the profit-maximizing output corresponding to the point at which marginal revenue equals marginal cost. The profit-maximizing output for Turkish baths is five per day, and the corresponding price is $10. However, the average cost of five baths per day is $20. Because average cost exceeds price at the profit-maximizing output, the firm

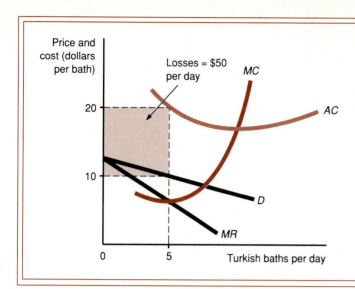

Box 4   A Monopoly Firm Incurring Losses

The monopoly bath house loses $50 per day at the output of five baths sold per day corresponding to the point at which marginal revenue equals marginal cost. Despite the monopolization of this service, demand is insufficient to allow a profit.

incurs losses of $50 per day. *It follows that having a pure monopoly doesn't always guarantee that the monopoly will be profitable!*

Also notice that it's not in the interest of a monopoly firm to charge the highest possible price. The monopolist that maximizes profits realizes it loses sales by increasing price and considers this in making its price decisions. *Monopoly firms maximize profits by always setting price to achieve the output over any period for which marginal revenue equals marginal cost.*

Elasticity of Demand and Monopoly Pricing

The graph in Box 5 shows a linear demand curve and the corresponding marginal revenue curve for a monopoly firm. Recall that demand is elastic when a decrease in price results in an increase in total revenue (see Chapter 7). If total revenue increases when price decreases, marginal revenue must be positive. We therefore can conclude that whenever the marginal revenue resulting from a price decrease is positive, demand is elastic. By the same token, if the marginal revenue from the extra sales resulting from a price decrease is negative, it follows that demand must be inelastic. This is because negative marginal revenue implies that the price decline results in a decrease in total revenue. Finally, when marginal revenue is zero, a change in price doesn't change total revenue, and demand is unit elastic. The lower part of the graph in Box 5 shows how total revenue for the monopoly firm varies as price is reduced. *Maximum total revenue occurs where marginal revenue is equal to zero.* At that point on the linear demand curve, demand is unit elastic.

Monopolists are assumed to maximize profits instead of revenue. To maximize profit the firm must produce the output corresponding to the point at which marginal revenue equals marginal cost. Marginal cost, of course, is always positive because more resources must be used to produce additional output. It follows that marginal revenue at the profit-maximizing output must also be positive. A positive marginal revenue means that demand for the product is elastic. *Surprisingly, a monopoly firm will always price its product to ensure that the demand is elastic!*

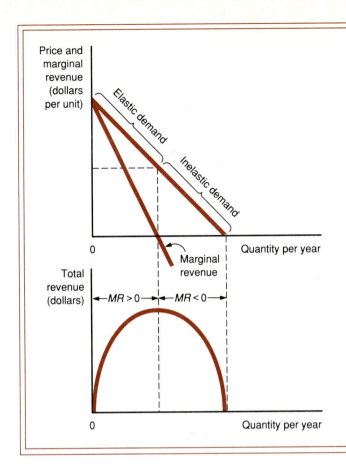

Box 5   Monopoly Demand, Marginal Revenue, Total Revenue, and Elasticity

For a linear demand curve, marginal revenue declines twice as quickly as price when more is sold. When marginal revenue is positive, total revenue increases. When marginal revenue is negative, total revenue declines. Total revenue is at a maximum when $MR = 0$. When $MR > 0$, demand is elastic; when $MR < 0$, demand is inelastic. Demand is unit elastic when $MR = 0$.

Monopoly Supply

A supply curve shows a relationship between price and quantity supplied by a firm or an industry. Competitive firms simply react to prices. A monopolist, however, is a price maker. It chooses the price that maximizes its profits and lets consumers decide how much to buy at that price. A monopoly firm does not react to a price.

A monopoly firm decides how much to produce on the basis of information it has on the demand for its product. Given this information, it prices its product so that marginal revenue equals marginal cost.

Even though a monopoly firm has an upward-sloping marginal cost curve at any point in time, it doesn't necessarily increase quantity supplied when the demand for its product increases. Sometimes a monopoly firm reacts to an increase in demand by raising the price of its product rather than increasing quantity supplied! The change in quantity supplied by a monopoly firm depends on the shift in its marginal revenue curve when demand increases. For example, if the demand for a monopolist's product increases, the monopolist might find it can increase profits more by raising price rather than increasing the quantity supplied. In deciding how to respond to an increase in demand, the monopolist examines the way the price elasticity of demand has changed to figure the new marginal revenue associated with each possible output. It then adjusts price to maximize profit given the new marginal revenue curve by choosing the price that allows sale of the output for which under the new demand $MR = MC$.[1]

Concept Check

1 Explain why the price a monopolist sets for its product will exceed the marginal cost of making the profit-maximizing output available.

2 What determines the actual profit a monopolist earns? Under what conditions will a monopolist incur losses at the output for which marginal revenue equals marginal cost?

3 Explain why a monopolist will never sell in a market in which the demand for its product is inelastic.

Evaluating Market Outcomes Under Pure Monopoly

Pure Monopoly vs. Perfect Competition

The differences in market outcomes under monopoly and perfect competition can be illustrated by making a few simplifying assumptions. Suppose that in the long run the average cost and marginal cost of producing raisin bread are constant and equal to $2 per loaf. Small firms as well as large firms can produce at an average and marginal cost of $2 per loaf. This means that there's no inherent cost advantage available to a single firm serving the entire market demand. If the good were produced under perfect competition, the long-run supply curve would be a horizontal line that intersects the price axis at $2, as illustrated in the graph in Box 6. This line corresponds to both the average and marginal cost of bread.

Suppose the market is currently served by 1,000 small, independently owned and operated bakeries. Each bakery sells raisin bread in a perfectly competitive national market in which price is determined by the forces of supply and demand. In Box 6 the market equilibrium would correspond to point E, at which the market demand curve intersects the market supply curve. The equilibrium output would be 100,000 loaves of raisin bread per day, and the equilibrium price would be $2 per loaf. The price of raisin bread would equal both the average and marginal cost of raisin bread. If the price exceeded $2, new firms would enter the market as sellers and quantity supplied over the long run would increase until price fell to $2, which is the minimum possible average cost.

Now suppose that in a dramatic move, all of the 1,000 independent bakeries are taken over by a single seller that now monopolizes the sale of raisin bread in the nation. Naturally, the new monopoly owner seeks to maximize profits. To do so it estimates the marginal revenue from selling raisin bread in the market. The marginal revenue curve corresponding to the market demand is illustrated in Box 6. The marginal cost of producing raisin bread for the new monopoly firm is always $2, as it was when the industry was competitive. The marginal revenue of selling raisin bread equals the marginal cost of raisin bread at point A, which corresponds to an

---

[1] It can also be shown that two or more prices can correspond to the same quantity supplied for a monopoly. This means that a unique one-to-one relationship between price and quantity supplied cannot be drawn up for a monopoly. For proof of this proposition, see David N. Hyman, *Modern Microeconomics: Analysis and Applications,* 2nd ed., Homewood, Ill.: Richard D. Irwin, Inc., 1989, Chapter 10.

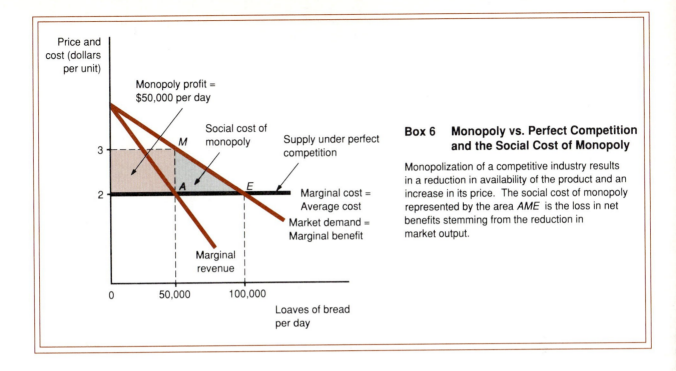

Price and cost (dollars per unit)

Monopoly profit = $50,000 per day

Social cost of monopoly

Supply under perfect competition

M

3

A

2

E

Marginal cost = Average cost

Market demand = Marginal benefit

Marginal revenue

0   50,000   100,000

Loaves of bread per day

Box 6   Monopoly vs. Perfect Competition and the Social Cost of Monopoly

Monopolization of a competitive industry results in a reduction in availability of the product and an increase in its price. The social cost of monopoly represented by the area *AME* is the loss in net benefits stemming from the reduction in market output.

output of 50,000 loaves per day. To maximize profits, the monopolist would therefore have to cut back output to half of its previous level of 100,000 loaves that prevailed in the competitive market! The reduced availability of raisin bread resulting from the monopolist's cutback in output will result in a higher price. At a daily output of 50,000 loaves, competition among buyers results in a market price of $3 per loaf, corresponding to point *M* on the market demand curve.

At the $3 price, the monopolist will enjoy a daily profit of $1 per loaf because the average cost of raisin bread remains $2 after output is cut. Given the daily output of 50,000 loaves, the monopolist earns a daily profit of $50,000, shown by the shaded rectangular area in Box 6. You and other raisin bread lovers will therefore pay $1 per loaf more than you were paying prior to the monopoly takeover. Under perfect competition each of the 1,000 independent bakeries just covered its opportunity costs of remaining in business and earned zero economic profits. The monopoly, on the other hand, raises the price above the average cost of raisin bread and earns a handsome profit each day at the expense of consumers, who now pay more.

To reduce output the monopolist is likely to shut down plants. This means it will dismiss workers and sell off land and equipment. The monopoly firm will shut down a substantial number of the 1,000 bakeries it acquired in the takeover. The remaining bakeries will be operated at the minimum possible cost of $2 per loaf, producing a total daily output of 50,000 loaves.

Now note the following differences between the monopoly equilibrium and perfectly competitive equilibrium:

1. *The monopoly price exceeds the competitive price, and the monopoly output falls short of the competitive equilibrium output.*
2. *The price set by the monopolist exceeds the marginal cost of its product.* Price always exceeds the monopolist's marginal revenue. When the monopolist

chooses the output that sets marginal revenue equal to marginal cost, price will also exceed marginal cost.

3. *The monopoly firm earns economic profit by charging a price that exceeds the minimum possible average cost of production.* Absence of free entry of sellers into the market ensures that supply won't increase, thereby causing price to fall. The monopoly firm enjoys economic profits while competitive firms have no economic profits in equilibrium.

To sum up, monopolists produce less and price their product higher than do firms under the benchmark competitive equilibrium. Other things being equal, as consumers we're better off when we can buy products in a competitive market instead of a monopoly market. The higher prices paid under monopoly enrich its owners at the expense of consumers who, other than consuming less, have no alternative but to pay the higher prices. In short, monopoly control over price is used to redistribute income from consumers of the product to the owners of the monopoly.

The Social Cost of Monopoly

Profit-maximizing monopolies can prevent efficiency from being achieved. Remember that points on a demand curve represent the marginal benefit of various quantities of a good to consumers. As you discovered in Chapter 12, the efficient output is the one at which the marginal benefit of a good just equals its marginal cost. At that output it's impossible to make consumers better off by producing more of a good without harming those whose resources are used to make more of the product available. At the efficient output the net gains from making the good available are at a maximum. The efficient output of raisin bread is 100,000 loaves per day in Box 6. This corresponds to point E on the graph, at which the marginal cost and marginal benefit curves intersect.

The monopoly market fails to achieve the efficient output of 100,000 loaves per day. At the monopoly output of 50,000 loaves per day, the marginal benefit of bread is $3 while the marginal cost is only $2. Because the marginal benefit exceeds the marginal cost of bread at the monopoly output, less than the efficient output of bread is made available each day.

Social cost of monopoly:
A measure of the loss in potential net benefits from the reduced availability of a good stemming from monopoly control of price and supply.

The **social cost of monopoly** is a measure of the loss in potential net benefits from the reduced availability of a good stemming from monopoly control of price and supply. The graph in Box 6 can be used to show how the social cost of monopoly can be measured. Because the marginal benefit exceeds the marginal cost at the monopoly output, additional net benefit is possible from producing more raisin bread each day. This net benefit could accrue either to buyers of bread or to resource owners whose inputs are used to produce bread. For example, if one more loaf of bread were made available after 50,000 per day were already produced, the maximum price that at least one buyer would pay for the loaf would be $3. This is the marginal benefit of raisin bread corresponding to point M in Box 6. The minimum price necessary to cover the opportunity cost of making that loaf available is $2. This is the marginal cost of bread corresponding to point A on the graph. This means either that buyers can be made better off without harming sellers or that sellers of the additional bread can just cover their opportunity cost while buyers are made better off.

The sum of the additional net gains possible from increases in daily output of raisin bread from 50,000 to 100,000 loaves, the efficient output, is represented by the area AME in Box 6. *This area represents potential net gains to buyers or addi-*

tional sellers of bread that are prevented by the monopoly control over supply and price. The area *AME* therefore represents the social cost of monopoly. If barriers to entry were removed and if the single seller of raisin bread were replaced by many competing sellers, price would fall to the competitive level of $2 per loaf and these additional net gains would be realized.

There have been attempts to actually measure the social cost of monopoly in particular industries. In the 1960s the automobile market in the United States was dominated by General Motors, which accounted for nearly 50% of domestic production at a time when imports had a very small share of the U.S. market. One study estimated that the social cost of monopoly control over price exercised by GM at that time equivalent to the area *AME* in Box 6 amounted to over $1 billion per year.[2] This amount was about 4% of the value of GM's revenues per year. Assuming this estimate is accurate, the exercise of monopoly influence on price at the time amounted to a 4% tax on consumers by GM that was added to its profits. Of course, since the 1960s there has been much greater competition in the automobile industry from imports, which now account for over 30% of sales in the United States. The monopoly control of price by GM has substantially diminished since the 1960s.

Are There Any Benefits from Monopoly?

In some cases a firm attains a monopoly position in a market by virtue of technological or cost advantages that wouldn't be possible if many smaller firms supplied the good. Under those circumstances there could be benefits associated with monopoly power that offset part of the social cost of its control over supply and price. Price is still higher than the marginal cost and minimum possible average cost of production in this case, assuming the monopoly firm maximizes profits. However, the level of average cost made possible by the monopoly firm's large-scale operation or technological superiority is lower than would be possible if more than one firm served the market.

It's also sometimes argued that monopolists protected against competition from new entrants tend to be more innovative than sellers with many rivals. This is because they know the profits from their innovations won't be competed away in the long run. Greater innovation means more technological progress, which in turn leads to lower average costs. However, the hypothesis that larger firms tend to be more innovative than smaller firms hasn't been supported by facts. Many innovations are made in highly competitive industries. In many cases new entrants to industries are the most creative innovators.[3]

Concept Check

1 What would happen to prices and output made available to buyers in a market if a perfectly competitive industry were monopolized through a merger of all sellers?

2 How would you measure the social cost of monopoly power?

3 What possible advantages might be associated with monopoly?

---

[2] Keith C. Cowling and Dennis C. Mueller, "The Social Costs of Monopoly Power," *Economic Journal,* 88, December 1978, pp. 722-748.
[3] For a discussion of evidence both supporting and rejecting the hypothesis that monopoly or large market share tends to result in more innovation, see F.M. Scherer, *Industrial Market Structure and Economic Performance,* 2nd ed., Boston: Houghton Mifflin, 1980, pp. 421-438.

Some Surprising Conclusions About Monopoly Markets

Reaction of a Firm with Monopoly Power to Taxes on the Sale of Its Product

Recall that in Chapter 12 we showed that a tax on the output of a perfectly competitive industry of constant costs is fully shifted to buyers. In such an industry the minimum possible average cost doesn't increase as the industry grows or contracts. In industries of constant costs in which firms can't individually control price, all of a tax on the product is paid by buyers as the market price increases in the long run. Paradoxically, in an industry in which a monopoly firm *can* control price, less of the tax will be passed on to buyers.

Suppose a firm with monopoly power produces cigarettes. The current monopoly price of cigarettes is 80¢ per pack and 5 million packs per year are sold at that price, as shown in the graph in Box 7. Now levy a 10¢ per pack tax. The graph shows that the tax will shift the horizontal average cost curve (which is also the marginal cost curve when costs are constant) by 10¢. The average cost of production is now 70¢. The new equilibrium monopoly price is 85¢ per pack. This is the price corresponding to output of 3.25 million packs, which corresponds to point B where the marginal revenue curve intersects the higher marginal cost curve. The initial output of 5 million packs per year corresponds to point A.

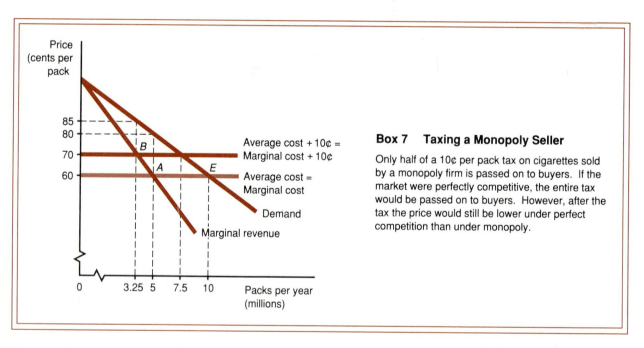

Box 7 Taxing a Monopoly Seller

Only half of a 10¢ per pack tax on cigarettes sold by a monopoly firm is passed on to buyers. If the market were perfectly competitive, the entire tax would be passed on to buyers. However, after the tax the price would still be lower under perfect competition than under monopoly.

Price increases by an amount less than the 10¢ tax. If instead cigarettes were produced by a perfectly competitive industry, initial output would be 10 million packs per year, corresponding to point E in Box 7. The tax would reduce output to 7.5 million packs per year until price rose to 70¢ per pack and the entire tax was passed on to consumers.

Why does a monopoly firm pass on less of a tax than a competitive industry despite its control over price? *The reason is that any change in marginal cost moves the monopoly firm along its marginal revenue curve instead of the demand curve.* The resulting change in output for the monopoly firm is always less than would be the case under perfect competition because the reduction in the availability of the good is less. Because the monopoly output is less responsive to changes in costs, the corresponding change in price is less.

Price Ceilings and Monopoly Output

Price ceilings have some very surprising effects on the way a monopoly firm behaves. Remember that a price ceiling is a legal maximum price that can be charged in the market for an item. The inevitable effect of price ceilings in a competitive market is a decrease in quantity supplied that contributes to a shortage. This is always the case provided the ceiling is below the equilibrium price.

Suppose, however, that all the fiberglass in the United States is produced by one firm. The government levies a ceiling on the price of this good. Normally the price would be 40¢ per pound. The ceiling price is 25¢ a pound. Assume the ceiling isn't so low that it falls short of minimum possible average cost. This means the monopoly firm doesn't incur losses as a result of the ceiling.

The impact of the price ceiling is shown in the graph in Box 8. In the absence of any ceiling a profit-maximizing seller would produce 10,000 pounds of fiberglass per year. This is the output for which marginal revenue just equals marginal cost. At that output price would be 40¢ per pound. The price ceiling prevents the firm from charging the monopoly price. Its managers must take the ceiling price as given. The remarkable conclusion is that the monopoly firm now behaves as if it were a perfectly competitive firm! It can sell all the fiberglass it likes at 25¢ per pound up to 15,000 pounds per year, which corresponds to point *B* on the demand curve. If it wants to sell more than this, it will have to lower the price below 25¢ per pound. The marginal revenue of additional output between 10,000 and 15,000 pounds per year is therefore 25¢ when the ceiling is in effect. Because marginal cost is 20¢ at

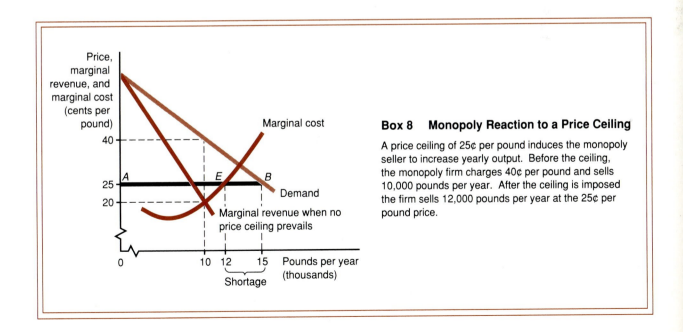

Box 8   Monopoly Reaction to a Price Ceiling

A price ceiling of 25¢ per pound induces the monopoly seller to increase yearly output. Before the ceiling, the monopoly firm charges 40¢ per pound and sells 10,000 pounds per year. After the ceiling is imposed the firm sells 12,000 pounds per year at the 25¢ per pound price.

the current output of 10,000 pounds per year, the monopoly firm can increase profit by making more fiberglass available. The monopoly firm actually *increases* its output of fiberglass in response to the ceiling until marginal cost increases to 25¢ at point E on the graph. After the ceiling is imposed the monopoly firm therefore increases output from 10,000 to 12,000 pounds per year.

Whereas a price ceiling leads to a decrease in the quantity supplied in a competitive market, it can actually increase quantity supplied in a monopoly market. However, a shortage still results.[4] At the price ceiling of 25¢ per pound the quantity demanded is 15,000 pounds per year, which exceeds the quantity supplied by the monopoly firm of 12,000 pounds per year.

Price Discrimination

In some cases a profit-maximizing monopoly firm can charge different prices for the same good or service to different buyers. When this is the case some lucky consumers will be able to purchase the monopolist's product at a price that's just equal to the marginal cost of the good!

Price discrimination: The practice of selling a certain product of given quality and cost per unit at different prices to different buyers.

The practice of selling a certain product of given quality and cost per unit at different prices to different buyers is called **price discrimination.** Price discrimination is often practiced by public utilities, which charge higher rates to businesses than they do to household users. Many drugstores, restaurants, and movie theatres offer discounts to senior citizens. Airlines are notorious price discriminators, as shown by the multitude of fares available for similar seats on a given flight.

To engage in price discrimination a seller must meet the following conditions:

1. *The seller must be able to control the price of its product.* A monopoly firm can engage in price discrimination because it can control prices.
2. *The product that will be sold at more than one price must not be resalable.* It isn't possible to charge different prices to different buyers if the good is resalable. Individuals who buy it at low prices could resell it to people who would pay higher prices. Eventually such a process would lead to the establishment of a single price in the market. This is because resale would continue until it was no longer possible for those who bought at a low price to resell at a higher price to another buyer. Automobiles, for example, are resalable products. It would be difficult for a monopoly firm in a given country to charge different buyers different prices. People who could buy cars at low prices would turn around and sell them to people who would pay high prices. Medical services are nonresalable. If you got a deal on your appendectomy, you can't turn around and sell it to your friend at a higher price!
3. *The seller must be able to determine how willingness and ability to pay vary among prospective buyers.* Price discrimination will result in some people paying more and some paying less than would be the case if one price were announced for the product. The seller must be able to distinguish among buyers in a way that allows it to charge higher prices only to buyers whose marginal benefit for the good would exceed the single price.

Monopolists engage in price discrimination when they can increase their profits by doing so. A simple example will convince you that a monopoly seller that can

[4] This conclusion is true only if the ceiling is also below the price corresponding to the point where the marginal cost curve intersects the demand curve.

meet the conditions required for price discrimination can in fact increase its profit by engaging in the practice.

Suppose there's only one neurosurgeon in the world capable of performing a rare brain operation. Anyone wanting this operation must come to this physician. The surgeon is therefore a monopolist. The medical service is clearly nonresalable. Also assume that the surgeon requires all those who wish to have the operation to fill out an elaborate questionnaire that enables the surgeon to determine the maximum sum of money the patient would pay for the operation.

The graph in Box 9 shows the demand curve for operations along with the marginal revenue curve. For simplicity we assume that the marginal cost of the operation is constant and equal to $40,000. If the surgeon behaves like a regular profit-maximizing monopolist, he'll want to do 20 operations a year because this is the quantity for which the marginal revenue would just equal the marginal cost of operations (at point C). The market price he would have to announce to get quantity demanded equal to 20 operations per year would be $50,000. Because marginal cost equals average cost when marginal cost is constant, the average cost of an operation would also be $40,000. The surgeon would therefore earn a $10,000 profit per operation for a total annual profit of $200,000.

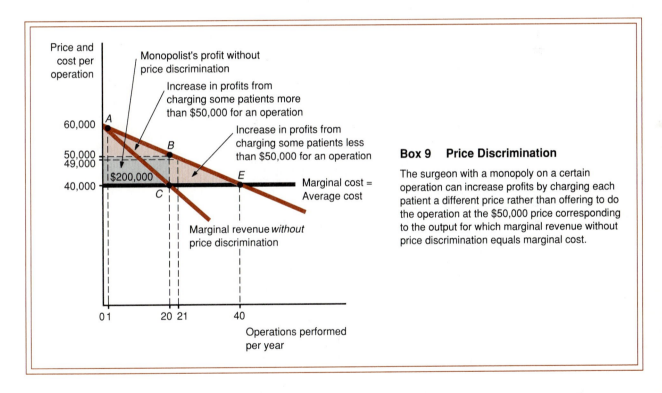

Box 9   Price Discrimination

The surgeon with a monopoly on a certain operation can increase profits by charging each patient a different price rather than offering to do the operation at the $50,000 price corresponding to the output for which marginal revenue without price discrimination equals marginal cost.

But the surgeon can earn more profits if he engages in price discrimination! For example, go to the point on the horizontal axis corresponding to 1 operation per year. The marginal benefit of that first operation to some patient is $60,000 (at point A). Someone would be willing to pay that much to have the operation. Because the surgeon's elaborate questionnaire allows him to identify this patient, he can charge her $60,000. This means he would earn a profit of $20,000 instead of $10,000 on that operation. Similarly, the surgeon can charge more than $50,000 for all patients whose marginal benefit exceeds that amount. By doing so he can increase his profits by the indicated triangular area in Box 9.

Will the surgeon charge any patients *less than* the $50,000 price he would set if he sold the operations at a single price? To find out, ask yourself whether he can increase his profits by doing so. For example, going to the point on the demand curve corresponding to 20 operations per year shows you that some patient would be willing to pay $49,000 for the operation after the surgeon has already performed 20 operations on those willing to pay more. Because the marginal cost of the operation is still $40,000, the surgeon can increase his profits by $9,000 per year by performing the twenty-first operation. Similarly, as long as the marginal benefit of the operation exceeds $40,000, the surgeon can increase his profit by charging the patient a price equal to his marginal benefit. This would increase his profits by the indicated triangular area in Box 9.

The marginal benefit of the operation declines to the $40,000 marginal cost when 40 are performed per year. At that output the surgeon can't increase his profit by performing more operations because the maximum price anyone else would pay falls short of the $40,000 marginal cost.

The output in this case increases to the point at which its marginal benefit equals its marginal cost. This is the same amount of output that would be produced under competitive equilibrium. *However, only the last purchaser gets the service at the price of $40,000 that would prevail under perfect competition. All other buyers pay higher prices than would prevail under perfect competition.*

In fact, physicians and lawyers often set their fees on the basis of ability to pay, thereby engaging in price discrimination. The preceding analysis suggests that they actually gain as a result of the practice. An entire industry that routinely uses price discrimination is airlines, which discount round-trip fares to passengers who agree to a minimum or maximum stay involving at least one Saturday night at the destination. If you buy such a ticket, you can't resell it or use it for a trip of different duration. If you try to fly home before or after the cutoff date, you'll be in for a rude surprise: you'll have to pay the regular fare, which could be twice as much as the discount rate! Airlines offer these discounts to encourage people whose marginal benefit from airline travel is low to take flights they wouldn't take at higher prices. This allows airlines to earn extra revenue they wouldn't enjoy if they charged all travelers the same price. Instead airlines charge high prices to travelers who make short trips, believing that these are largely business trips for which marginal benefit (and therefore willingness to pay) is quite high. As a result, a business traveler sitting next to a tourist on the same flight could be paying twice the tourist fare.

Concept Check

1 Explain why establishment of a price ceiling below the current price charged by a monopolist can increase the availability of a good.

2 What is price discrimination?

3 When does a monopoly firm engage in price discrimination?

Summary

1. A pure monopoly is a single seller of a product that has no close substitutes.
2. In a market in which a profitable monopoly firm sells a product, a barrier to

entry must exist to prevent additional sellers from entering to compete for sales. Monopolies often arise as a result of cost or technological advantages that aren't enjoyed by smaller firms. A natural monopoly firm is one that attains its position as a single seller in a market by virtue of cost advantages.

3. A monopolist's demand curve is the market demand curve. Monopolists can sell more by lowering prices. By the same token, when they increase the price of their product they can expect to sell less. Unlike a perfectly competitive firm, a monopolist can't sell all it wishes at a given price. The price the monopolist receives depends on the amount of its product it makes available.

4. Marginal revenue is the extra revenue a monopolist receives for selling additional output. For any amount sold, the marginal revenue received by a monopolist is less than the price it receives for the product.

5. A monopolist maximizes profits by setting the price that allows it to sell the amount for which marginal revenue equals marginal cost over any period. Marginal revenue is positive only when demand for the monopolist's product is elastic. A monopoly firm never sells in a market in which demand for its product is inelastic because sales in such a market would decrease rather than increase revenue.

6. The price set by a profit-maximizing monopoly firm exceeds the marginal cost and minimum possible average cost of the product in the long run. A monopoly firm that can't earn profit at the output for which marginal revenue equals marginal cost goes out of business in the long run. Monopolization of a competitive industry would result in an increase in product prices and a reduction in quantity supplied to buyers.

7. The social cost of monopoly is the loss of net gains to buyers and additional sellers of a product resulting from the control of supply and price by the monopoly firm. Monopolists prevent efficiency from being attained by pricing their product at a level that exceeds its marginal cost.

8. When the output of a monopoly firm is taxed, the reduction in output is less than would result if the output were sold by many rival firms in a competitive market.

9. Monopolists react to price ceilings in certain cases by increasing quantity supplied.

10. Monopolists sometimes find it profitable to engage in price discrimination by selling the same product at different prices to different buyers, even though the cost per unit is the same. When monopolists engage in price discrimination, they sell more than would be possible if they charged a single price for all buyers.

Key Terms and Concepts

Pure monopoly	Natural monopoly
Monopoly power	Social cost of monopoly
Barrier to entry	Price discrimination

Problems and Applications

1. The average cost of a kilowatt hour of electricity is lower in a single plant designed to serve 100,000 customers than in two plants that serve the same market with each plant satisfying 50,000 customers. Draw the long-run average cost

curve for firms producing electricity and explain why a single seller building a single plant in a city of 100,000 is likely to emerge as a natural monopoly.

2. A dealership in a small city enjoys a monopoly in the sale of Rolls-Royces. The market demand schedule for Rolls-Royces in the city corresponds to the following data:

Price (dollars)	Quantity demanded per month (number of Rolls-Royces)
120,000	1
110,000	2
100,000	3
90,000	4
80,000	5
70,000	6
60,000	7
50,000	8

Calculate the total revenue and marginal revenue from selling Rolls-Royces.

3. Using the data from the demand schedule in problem 2, draw the demand curve, the marginal revenue curve, and the total revenue curve. For each price indicate whether the demand is elastic, inelastic, or unit elastic.

4. The dealership estimates that the marginal cost of selling Rolls-Royces each month varies according to the following schedule. The marginal cost consists of the wholesale cost of each Rolls-Royce plus the cost of other variable inputs such as salesperson salaries, advertising, and other publicity necessary to sell additional vehicles each month.

Quantity sold per month (number of Rolls-Royces)	Marginal cost (dollars)
1	70,000
2	75,000
3	80,000
4	85,000
5	90,000
6	100,000
7	120,000
8	150,000

Assuming the dealer seeks to maximize profits, predict what price he'll set for Rolls-Royces and indicate the quantity he'll succeed in selling at that price.

5. Suppose the marginal cost of selling any given quantity of Rolls-Royces doubles. What would the monopoly dealer do?

6. Currently bubble gum is supplied by many competing sellers in a nation. The market for bubble gum is perfectly competitive. In a massive takeover effort, a large conglomerate corporation buys out all the assets of current bubble-gum producers and establishes a monopoly. Draw the market demand and supply curves for bubble gum prior to the takeover, assuming the market equilibrium price of bubble gum is $1 per large pack and the equilibrium quantity supplied is 5 million packs per month. Show what would happen to the price of bubble gum and the quantity supplied as a result of the takeover, assuming the new bubble-gum monopoly maximizes profits.

7. Use the graph you drew in answer to problem 6 to show the social cost of the monopoly takeover.

8. Use the graph you drew in answer to problem 6 to show how a tax of 10¢ per pack collected from bubble-gum sellers will result in a smaller monthly decrease in quantity sold when the industry is a monopoly than would be the case if the industry were competitive.

9. Suppose a monopoly firm supplies plywood in a small town. The monopoly firm maximizes profits and currently charges $20 for a standard ¾-inch sheet. The government imposes a price ceiling of $15 per sheet. Show how the price ceiling could induce the monopoly firm to increase its monthly output. Use a graph to show how a shortage of plywood develops after the ceiling is imposed.

10. List goods and services for which price discrimination is possible. Under what circumstances will a monopoly firm engage in price discrimination?

Suggested Readings

Manley R. Irwin, "The Telephone Industry," in Walter Adams, ed., *The Structure of American Industry*, 6th ed., New York: Macmillan, 1982. This author offers an analysis of the monopoly position of AT&T prior to its breakup.

David Koskoff, *The Diamond World*, New York: Harper & Row, 1981. This is an interesting account of the De Beers Company and how it maintains a near monopoly in the diamond market through its elaborate syndicates.

F.M. Scherer, *Industrial Market Structure and Economic Performance*, 2nd ed., Boston: Houghton Mifflin, 1980. This is a text on industrial organization that analyzes the extent of monopoly in the United States.

A Forward Look

In the real world, markets are rarely perfectly competitive and are seldom served by a pure unregulated monopoly firm. In the following chapter we take a look at models that more closely approximate competitive conditions in actual markets. These models represent refinements of the basic models of perfect competition and pure monopoly.

14

Monopolistic Competition and Oligopoly

At this point what you're probably wondering is: How do markets function in the real world?

Perfect competition and pure monopoly are both abstractions that are useful in explaining basic forces that influence market prices and quantities. In reality, markets are somewhere between the extremes of perfect competition and pure monopoly. **Imperfect competition** exists when more than one seller competes for sales with other sellers of similar products, each of whom has some control over price. Individual sellers in such markets have a degree of *monopoly power,* which means they can influence the price of their product by controlling its availability to buyers.

Imperfect competition: Exists when more than one seller competes for sales with other sellers of competitive products, each of whom has some control over price.

In this chapter we analyze two forms of imperfect competition. In one case control over price is a result of the fact that competing firms in a market don't sell a standardized product. Differences in product quality and appearance, the firms' reputations for service, and other factors make the output of each seller in such a market unique. The uniqueness of its product gives each seller a measure of monopoly power over price.

Meals in restaurants are a good example of a product that's differentiated. The quality of restaurant food runs the gamut from greasy to gourmet. Service can be sullen, so-so, or suave. Prices range from pocket change to a week's pay. The manager of any restaurant can charge higher prices than competing restaurants without losing all his patrons. The demand for a restaurant's product is likely to be quite elastic—but not perfectly elastic, as would be the case if the market were perfectly competitive. Product differentiation by brand also gives sellers some control over price. Loyal buyers of brands like Coca-Cola, Bayer aspirin, and Häagen-Dazs ice cream gladly pay prices above those of generic (unbranded) supermarket products.

In other cases individual sellers gain control over price by having large market shares. In these markets each seller produces a large enough portion of total market output to significantly influence supply and therefore price. A few firms with power to influence the price of their output dominate the market. For example, in the United States during the early 1980s there were only five companies producing lead. Because each of these firms had a large market share, changes in their supply decisions would have affected the market price of lead.

In many markets, firms gain control over price by a combination of product differentiation and large market shares. The markets for cigarettes and beer fall into this category. The U.S. cigarette market is dominated by four firms that together account for about 80% of sales. The four largest brewers in the United States account for about 77% of total beer sales in the country.

As refinements of the basic models of perfect competition and pure monopoly, the models of imperfectly competitive markets we'll discuss in this chapter will add to your knowledge of how markets actually work. However, the basic lessons you've learned from the theories of perfectly competitive and pure monopoly markets will remain useful in helping you understand the underlying forces of supply and demand.

After reading this chapter, you should be able to:

1 Explain the concept of monopolistic competition in markets and show how outcomes in such markets differ from those expected under perfect competition and pure monopoly.
2 Explain the concept of oligopoly and analyze market outcomes under oligopoly.
3 Explain the concept of a cartel and show how it differs from a pure monopoly.
4 Understand the impact of competition through advertising and improvements in product quality in imperfectly competitive markets, and explain how imperfectly competitive firms decide to price their products.

Monopolistic Competition

Monopolistic competition exists when many sellers compete to sell a differentiated product in a market in which entry of new sellers is possible. In a monopolistically competitive market:

1. *There are relatively large numbers of firms, each satisfying a small but not microscopic share of the market demand for a similar but not identical product.* The market share of each rival firm is generally larger than that which would prevail under perfect competition. Each firm in the industry has a market share of over 1% of the total sales over any period, but it's unlikely that any one firm satisfies more than 10% of market demand.

2. *The product of each firm selling in the market is not a perfect substitute for that sold by competing firms.* Each seller's product has unique qualities or characteristics that cause some buyers to prefer it to products of competing firms. For example, you might be willing to pay higher prices for Reeboks if you believe

Monopolistic competition:
Exists when many sellers compete to sell a differentiated product in a market in which entry of new sellers is possible.

they're more comfortable than other sports shoes. Similarly, you may be willing to pay premium prices for the clothing produced by Calvin Klein or Forenza because you like the way it's cut or the quality of the detailing. Although each seller's product is unique, there's enough similarity among particular kinds of products to group sellers into broad categories similar to an industry. A **product group** represents several closely related, but not identical, items that serve the same general purpose for consumers. The sellers in each product group can be considered competing firms within an industry. An example of a product group is footwear. Another example is women's dresses.

Product group:
Represents several closely related, but not identical, items that serve the same general purpose for consumers.

There are problems, however, in clearly defining product groups. Is the footwear industry, for example, to include all types of footwear including men's shoes, women's shoes, children's shoes, boots, athletic shoes, rubber overshoes, and so on? Arbitrary decisions are necessary to define a product group. Restaurant services could constitute a product group. But are the providers of fast-food services like McDonald's and Hardee's to be considered members of that product group? The answer isn't clear. Many buyers don't think the meals served by these firms are good substitutes for meals in a full-service restaurant. Similarly, it might be argued that Chinese, Italian, and Pakistani restaurants constitute another product group.

3. *Firms in the industry don't consider the reaction of their rivals when choosing their product prices or annual sales targets.* This is in part a consequence of the relatively large number of firms in a monopolistically competitive industry. The managers of any one firm reason that their actions can't significantly reduce the market share of their rivals. For example, if a single firm cuts the price of its shoes by 20% to gain more sales, these extra sales are likely to come at the expense of many other firms rather than just a few rivals. These other firms experience only a small decrease in sales and are therefore unlikely to react by cutting their prices also. The managers of the first firm know this, so they don't bother to consider any possible reaction from competitors.

4. *Relative freedom of entry by new firms exists in monopolistically competitive markets.* It's easy to set up new firms in monopolistically competitive markets. By the same token, it's relatively easy to exit the market. Entry may not be quite as easy as it is in perfect competition because new firms with new brands or product features might initially have difficulty establishing their reputations. Existing firms with established brands and reputations for service are likely to hold some competitive edge over new entrants.

Free entry means that profitable conditions in the industry are likely to attract new sellers. In the long run the magnet of profits will serve to increase supplies of the product sold by the industry. This in turn will put downward pressure on both price and profits.

5. *Neither the opportunity nor the incentive exists for firms in the industry to cooperate in ways that decrease competition.* This means the firms don't cooperate to fix prices so as to increase their group profits. It also means that firms in the industry can't effectively prevent new entrants from responding to profit opportunities by opening rival enterprises.

In the analysis to follow, we assume that it's possible to draw clear industry lines in monopolistically competitive markets. If a firm within a given industry raises its price above that of competing firms, it can expect to lose a significant amount of sales to many competitors because the demand for its product is quite elastic.

Examples of Monopolistically Competitive Markets

Monopolistic competition is similar to monopoly in that individual firms have some power to control the price of their product. It's similar to perfect competition in that each product is sold by many firms and free entry and exit prevails in the market.

Monopolistic competition is likely to prevail in retail trade. In any region there are many retailers of a given good. Retailers can differentiate their product by quality of service, location of showrooms, and convenience of operating hours. Hair styling is likewise provided by many firms and is differentiated by the personal services offered to clients. Many manufactured goods like clothing, shoes, and furniture are sold in markets that can be considered monopolistically competitive. In all of these industries, entry by new sellers is relatively easy, the products of individual firms are differentiated, and there's a relatively large number of sellers.

The table in Box 1 shows the market shares of the top four and top eight firms in selected manufacturing industries in which monopolistic competition is likely to prevail. The *concentration ratios* shown in the table measure the total shipments to the market accounted for by the four or eight largest domestic shippers in 1982, along with the number of firms in each product group. The value of imported goods isn't included in the total shipments, which means the total market share of the domestic firms is overstated in the table.

Box 1 Shipments by Largest 4 and 8 Firms in Selected Industries in Which Monopolistic Competition Prevails, 1982

Industry	Number of sellers	Percentage of annual shipments accounted for by	
		4 largest companies	8 largest companies
Women's & misses' dresses	5,489	6	10
Bottled & canned soft drinks	1,236	14	23
Hosiery	376	20	29
Men's & boys' shirts & nightwear	535	19	29
Upholstered household furniture	1,129	17	25
Mattresses & box springs	786	23	31
Book publishing	2,007	17	30
Footwear (except rubber)	167	28	45
Jewelry (precious metals)	2,159	16	22

Source: U. S. Department of Commerce, Bureau of the Census: 1982 Census of Manufacturers, MC82-S-7, Subject Series, *Concentration Ratios in Manufacturing.*

In most monopolistically competitive industries, the four largest firms account for less than 25% of domestic shipments and the eight largest firms account for less than 50% of domestic shipments. For example, in 1982 there were 5,489 producers of women's and misses' dresses. The four largest firms in this industry accounted for 6% of domestic shipments, and the eight largest firms accounted for 10% of shipments.

Concept Check

1 Under what conditions would a market be regarded as monopolistically competitive?

2 List some products that are likely to be sold in markets under conditions of monopolistic competition.

3 What is the source of monopoly power for a firm in a monopolistically competitive market?

Market Outcomes Under Monopolistic Competition

Short-Run Equilibrium of the Firm Under Monopolistic Competition

The demand curve as seen by a monopolistically competitive firm is downward sloping, as you can see in the graph in Box 2. This means that marginal revenue is less than price for any given output, as is the case for a pure monopoly. The demand for any particular firm's product tends to be quite elastic, but it's not perfectly elastic, as is the case for a perfectly competitive firm. The demand for the output of a monopolistically competitive firm is more elastic than that for a monopoly firm. This is because many very good substitutes, sold by many rival firms, exist for the product sold by any one firm in the industry.

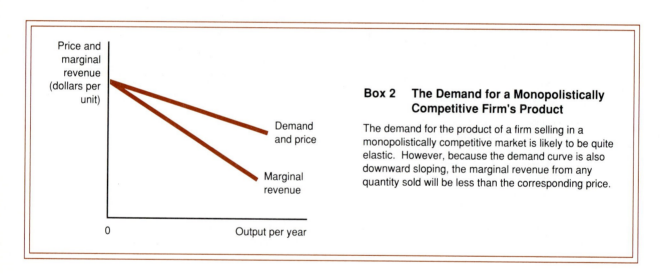

Box 2 The Demand for a Monopolistically Competitive Firm's Product

The demand for the product of a firm selling in a monopolistically competitive market is likely to be quite elastic. However, because the demand curve is also downward sloping, the marginal revenue from any quantity sold will be less than the corresponding price.

It's important, however, to understand why the firm's demand curve is downward sloping despite the fact that there are many competing firms. An example will help illustrate this point. Suppose you run a small firm that produces fashionable women's dresses. Your product is differentiated from those of your competitors by your unique styling and detailing. You have a clientele of devoted customers who go into retail outlets and ask for your brand of dresses. However, you also compete with many other producers of similar but not identical dresses.

Because your product is differentiated from those of competitors, you can raise the price of your dresses without losing all of your customers. Depending on the price elasticity of demand for your product, however, you can expect to lose some customers when you raise your prices. By the same token, you can expect to attract more customers when you lower your prices.

Demand and marginal revenue for your dresses also depend on the prices set by competing firms in your product group. If rival firms were to reduce their prices, you wouldn't be able to sell as many dresses at your set prices as you would have otherwise. The reverse would be true if competitors raised their prices. In the following analysis we concentrate on the decision of a single firm. The prices of other firms are beyond the control or influence of any one firm.

The short-run equilibrium of the firm facing monopolistic competition is illustrated in Box 3. Assuming that you seek to maximize profits from annual sales of dresses, the short-run equilibrium output is the one for which marginal revenue equals marginal cost. *This is exactly the same way a monopolist chooses its price and output.* The marginal cost curve intersects the marginal revenue curve at an annual output of 10,000 dresses. To sell this quantity you must set a price of $100 per dress. Any price lower than this would result in an annual quantity demanded greater than 10,000. Similarly, a higher price would result in a quantity demanded that falls short of the profit-maximizing output of 10,000 dresses per year.

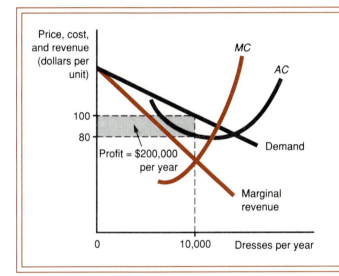

Box 3   Short-Run Equilibrium of the Firm Under Monopolistic Competition

The firm maximizes profit by selecting the output for which marginal revenue equals marginal cost. It then chooses the price that allows it to sell the profit-maximizing output. In the short run the firm whose costs, output, and price are illustrated at left earns annual profit of $200,000.

As you can see in Box 3, the average cost of dresses when you sell 10,000 per year is $80. At the $100 price, therefore, you earn a profit equal to $20 per dress. Total profit from the 10,000 dresses sold per year is $200,000, which is represented by the shaded area in the graph. If you enjoyed a pure monopoly in the production of these dresses, a barrier to entry in the market would prevent additional sellers from competing with you. Under monopolistic competition, however, your handsome profits are likely to disappear in the long run. To find out why, we have to show how entry of new firms as sellers in the market affects demand for your dresses.

Long-Run Equilibrium Under Monopolistic Competition

You must be doing something right to be earning such handsome profits! This means your competitors are going to be very interested in copying your styling. In addition, if all firms in the dress industry are earning similar profits, new entrants are likely to be attracted into the industry. You see this process going on all the time. If a firm introduces a new and improved type of toothpaste and its innovation is successful in earning profits, you can be sure that existing competitors and new firms will soon introduce similar products. When Crest came out with a tartar-control formula that increased its profits in 1985, other companies soon followed suit with their own tartar-control toothpastes.

Your hefty $200,000 annual profit will attract new firms that will market similar but not identical dresses. As more firms produce these dresses, the available supply will increase, thereby putting downward pressure on price. This will reduce the maximum price and marginal revenue you can expect from any given annual quantity of shipments. The demand curve and the marginal revenue curve for your product will shift downward. It's also likely that the demand for your product will become more elastic. This is because in the long run, the entry of new sellers into the market will *decrease* your market share. More sellers also means there will be more substitutes for your product, which will make demand for your dresses more elastic.

The graph in Box 4 illustrates the long-run equilibrium that can be expected for a firm under monopolistic competition. The average cost curve shows the average cost of alternative outputs in the long run. As long as firms can charge a price that exceeds average cost of production at the profit-maximizing output, profits will be possible. Under those circumstances new firms will seek to earn profits by supplying a similar product to buyers in the market. The demand and marginal revenue curves for your product can be expected to shift down until the price you can charge to induce your buyers to purchase the profit-maximizing quantity equals your average cost. When price just equals average cost, your profit per unit, and therefore your total profit, will be zero. In the long run you can expect to do no better than cover your opportunity costs!

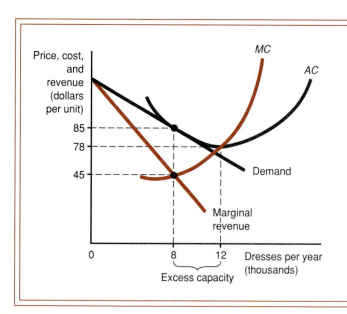

Box 4   Long-Run Equilibrium of the Firm Under Monopolistic Competition

In the long run, entry of new firms decreases the demand for any one firm's product to eliminate profit. At a price of $85 per dress for the output for which marginal revenue equals marginal cost of 8,000 dresses per year, the firm just covers its costs. The firm does not expand production in the long run to the output for which average cost is at a minimum because it would reduce its profit by doing so. The firm has excess capacity of 4,000 dresses per year.

As you can see in Box 4, your equilibrium output in the long run will be 8,000 dresses per year. The price you must charge to get customers to buy that quantity is $85 per dress, which is exactly equal to the average cost of producing 8,000 dresses per year. *In long-run equilibrium the demand curve for the product of each firm in the industry is just tangent to the firm's average cost curve.* Free entry prevents firms from earning economic profits in the long run. When this is the case, there's no tendency for sellers to either enter or leave the market.

Suppose the demand for the output of any firm in the industry were to decrease so that the firm couldn't make a profit in the long run. In the graph in Box 5, demand for your firm's output has shifted so far downward that it lies below the average cost curve. The price you set to induce consumers to buy the output for which marginal revenue just equals marginal cost is now $70. However, the average cost of producing the corresponding output of 7,000 dresses per year is $90. You're losing $20 per dress for a total annual loss of $140,000, represented by the shaded area in the graph. This means you won't be able to cover your opportunity costs in the long run. Because other firms are also likely to be sustaining losses, some firms will leave the industry in the long run. As this happens, the demand for the output of the remaining firms will increase and the generally decreased availability of the product will act to raise the price that all firms can charge for their products. The demand and marginal revenue curves for the remaining firms will then shift upward. This will continue until existing firms can once again cover their opportunity costs.

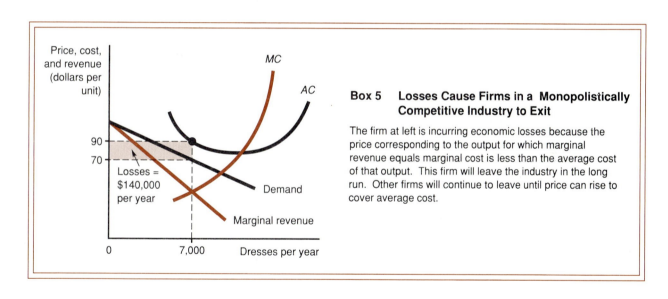

Box 5   Losses Cause Firms in a Monopolistically Competitive Industry to Exit

The firm at left is incurring economic losses because the price corresponding to the output for which marginal revenue equals marginal cost is less than the average cost of that output. This firm will leave the industry in the long run. Other firms will continue to leave until price can rise to cover average cost.

Losses in Efficiency Under Monopolistic Competition: Excess Capacity and Market Prices that Exceed Marginal Cost

When looking at the graph in Box 4, you'll notice some characteristics of long-run equilibrium under monopolistic competition that indicate inefficiency. Remember that to guarantee efficiency the price of a product must equal its marginal cost and also equal its marginal benefit. If marginal benefit exceeds marginal cost at the equilibrium output, additional net gains from making more of the good available will be possible (see Chapter 12).

Principles in Practice

Product Variety, Information Costs, and How to Differentiate a Chicken: Something Good About Monopolistic Competition

When they're not wearing feathers, it's hard to tell one chicken from another. Exactly how *would* a chicken producer go about convincing buyers that his naked chickens are better than someone else's? For that matter, what can the manufacturer of any product do to make you reach for his olive jar, soap bar, or luxury car—and not that of his competitors? Let's take a look at how the miracle of differentiation is wrought.

Supermarkets often carry generic (unbranded) items that are less expensive than the brand-name items. Many of us are suspicious of new and generic brands of goods because information about them is scarce. We often don't know if a product we buy will perform or otherwise provide satisfaction in the way we expect. Many of us use brand names and other aspects of product differentiation as a way of ensuring the reliability of products we buy.

Firms in monopolistically competitive markets invest resources in advertising, showrooms, and other specific expenditures designed to signal the superior quality of their products. This means that product differentiation and branding can serve a useful social purpose. It acts as a *signal* for quality. As buyers, we're willing to pay higher prices for the benefits of such signaling. This suggests that the higher prices and excess capacity resulting from monopolistic competition reflect the value of information. The price premiums are a way of ensuring product reliability. We use them to reduce the transaction costs associated with buying products.

For many products, standardization is impossible. Perhaps the best example is the used car. We may pay more for a used car sold by a dealer if it's guaranteed for a period of time. Similarly, we may want to deal with a particular seller to be sure of quality service. We're often willing to pay a price premium for the assurance of reliable service.

The costs of "image-creating" activities can't be recovered if the firm fails. Monopolistically competitive firms can make more profits after they establish their reputation by lowering the quality of their products. This will allow lower production costs. However, when we as buyers become aware of the lower qual-

ity, we're likely to boycott the product. This causes the firm to lose not only its reputation, but also the value of the costs it has incurred to build up its reputation. This gives the firm an incentive to perform reliably.*

Franchising chains attempt to signal quality in this way. The thousands of franchised hamburger stands on the road are independently owned. However, as consumers we know exactly what the standard of cleanliness and the quality of the food will be at each one. The franchises act to control the quality. If you don't get a bellyache from eating the food at your local McDonald's, you can be pretty sure you won't have a problem with a McDonald's 500 miles from home. Controlling quality ensures repeat business and holds the value of the franchise. Those who sell the franchise inspect establishments regularly, and they're prepared to revoke the franchise if quality isn't upheld. If they didn't do so, they'd have difficulty maintaining the market price of their franchises. Product variety confers monopoly power on certain sellers. The higher prices they charge, however, can be viewed as necessary to offset the benefits of signaling.

Firms sometimes achieve remarkable success by differentiating a previously unbranded item. One of the most successful entrepreneurs of recent times is Frank Perdue, who created a fortune by putting his brand name on chickens! Perdue used modern marketing techniques to create an image of high quality for his brand of chickens. Perdue chickens are always well plucked and grade A! The poultry business has been one of rapidly improving technology in which new feeds and other techniques have reduced the cost per pound. In addition, chicken has lower cholesterol than red meat. Perdue chickens cost more, but more consumers believe they get a higher-quality product with less fat.

By advertising on TV and in magazines, Perdue was able to create the image of a quality-controlled product that ended up with a large share of the growing market for poultry products. In 1984 Perdue Farms sold 270 million chickens and took in nearly $750 million in revenues. Yes, you can differentiate one chicken from another, and it's profitable to do so!

*See Benjamin Klein and Keith B. Leffler, "The Role of Market Forces in Assuring Contractual Performance," *Journal of Political Economy,* 89, 4, August 1982, pp. 615-641.

The graph in Box 4 shows that in long-run equilibrium, the market price charged by a monopolistically competitive firm will exceed the marginal cost of making the equilibrium output available. The price charged for dresses in long-run equilibrium is $85. Buyers will therefore continue to purchase dresses until the marginal benefit declines to $85 per year. However, the marginal cost of dresses at the equilibrium output of 8,000 per year for your firm is only $45.

Because profits are already zero, you and other firms you compete with have no incentive to produce more so as to increase marginal cost and make marginal benefit decline until the two are equal. *Under monopolistic competition, free entry in the long run results in profits declining to zero before prices fall to a level that just allows firms to cover their marginal costs.* The marginal benefit of the output produced by firms under monopolistic competition will exceed marginal cost in long-run equilibrium. This implies that less than the efficient output will result from exchange in markets in which monopolistic competition prevails.

Also notice in Box 4 that, although price equals average cost in equilibrium, average cost is not equal to the *minimum possible amount.* Because the demand curve slopes downward, it can't be tangent to the average cost curve at the latter's minimum point. Profits fall to zero in the long run *before* the output of each firm increases enough to result in the minimum possible average cost of production. The difference between the output corresponding to minimum possible average cost and that produced by the monopolistically competitive firm in the long run is called **excess capacity.** Excess capacity results in higher consumer prices. It's a cost of product variety.

In Box 4 the minimum possible average cost of production is $78 per dress. In long-run equilibrium the average cost of dresses is instead $85. Profits are zero because the market price of the dress set by sellers will also be $85 in the long run.

Excess capacity means that buyers don't enjoy the opportunity to consume products at minimum possible average cost. It also means that fewer firms in the industry could produce the same output. For example, suppose that in equilibrium each firm produces 8,000 dresses per year at an average cost of $85. If there are 1,000 firms in the product group, total output will be 8 million dresses per year. The graph in Box 4 shows that, if each firm in the industry were to produce at minimum possible average cost, total output per firm would increase to 12,000 dresses. Under these circumstances only 667 firms could produce the total annual output of 8 million dresses.

Monopolistically competitive industries tend to be crowded, with each firm operating its plant at a level below that corresponding to minimum possible average cost. The firms in the industry therefore underutilize their plants. Too many firms in the industry and underutilization of plants result in inefficient resource use.

Excess capacity:
The difference between the output corresponding to minimum possible average cost and that produced by the monopolistically competitive firm in the long run.

Advertising and Product Development in Monopolistically Competitive Markets

Product differentiation is the hallmark of monopolistically competitive markets. In many cases firms incur costs either to make the unique characteristics of their products known to consumers or to convince consumers that their product really is different from those of its rivals. Monopolistically competitive markets are characterized by brand names and by continual product development and improvement. For example, many of us use the brand name Clorox synonymously with liquid bleach. The long-standing image of Clorox allows the company to charge significantly higher prices for its product than those prevailing for rival brands. Similarly, some of us use the brand names Band-Aid and Windex as synonyms for all products in a product group and are willing to pay higher prices for the familiar names. You've probably noticed in supermarkets that famous brands of a variety of products are priced higher than lesser-known brands. You may be one of the many consumers who are convinced that the brand-name products are of higher quality than supermarket or generic brands.

Firms are often more likely to compete by improving their products or developing new products rather than by cutting prices. A firm that improves its product can enjoy temporary profits until its improvement is copied by existing rivals or new entrants. Product improvements are often criticized as being superficial rather than substantive. Nonetheless, firms do compete in this way, and many of us respond to the changes in products' quality and characteristics.

Selling costs:
All costs incurred by a firm to influence the sales of its product.

Advertising and promotion of products is a costly process. **Selling costs** are all costs incurred by a firm to influence the sales of its product. These costs include advertising expenses, salaries for sales personnel, and other promotional expenses. Firms incur these expenses in the hope of increasing revenues from sales of their products. When selling costs are added to production costs, they increase the average cost of making goods available. The graph in Box 6 shows how selling costs shift average cost curves upward. To give you an idea of how much firms are willing to spend to boost their sales, advertising expense in the United States in recent years has been over $100 billion annually.

Advertising can affect the level of demand for a firm's product and the price elasticity of that demand. *Keep in mind that advertising is an alternative to price reduction as a means of selling more per year and increasing profits.* In the long run, however, free entry ensures that these profits will disappear. New entrants and the firm's existing rivals will copy its advertising or promotional campaign. This means it will become more costly to gain additional sales through advertising.

As a result of advertising, each monopolistically competitive firm produces more than it would otherwise. The excess capacity in the industry is reduced. This, however, doesn't benefit consumers because the price doesn't fall to reflect the lower average costs of production. Instead selling costs are now added to production costs. This results in the overall increase in average cost at any level of output illustrated in Box 6. Consumers buy more of the advertised goods. However, resources are diverted from the production of other goods to provide the advertising.

There are both benefits and costs associated with advertising. In a monopolistically competitive industry no firm gains from advertising in the long run. Economic profits are zero in long-run equilibrium both with and without advertising. Advertising can, however, serve a useful social purpose by providing consumers with information.

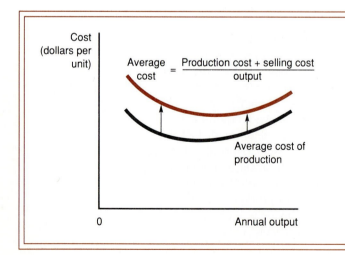

Box 6   The Impact of Advertising and Other Selling Costs on Average Cost

Advertising and other costs incurred to sell more of a product without reducing its price must be added to production costs to compute average cost of a product. Selling costs increase average cost and contribute to higher prices.

A Recap

The monopolistically competitive equilibrium is like the pure monopoly equilibrium in that prices exceed marginal costs of production. Under pure monopoly, however, price can also exceed average cost in the long run because of barriers to entry of new sellers. Under monopolistic competition, entry of new firms will prevent economic profits from lasting. Profits serve the function of a lure that attracts new firms and keeps prices below the levels that would prevail were the market supplied by a single seller. Monopolistic competition is therefore like perfect competition in the sense that prices fall to equal average costs in the long run. However, although prices equal average costs in long-run equilibrium under monopolistic competition, they don't equal the minimum possible average cost. This means resources are wasted in the sense that the same output could be made available at lower cost. Firms operate their plants at levels for which minimum possible average cost can't be achieved. There is excess capacity in the industry. The same output could be produced at lower cost by fewer firms.

Finally, monopolistic competition is characterized by heavy costs for product development and advertising. There are advantages and disadvantages to this process. One advantage is that consumers are offered a variety of brands and types of products within a given product group. However, the variety of brands is often bewildering, and consumers may end up spending more time trying to decide what to buy. In addition, the process of product development and advertising is costly. Advertising increases the average costs of making goods available, thus contributing to higher prices.

Concept Check

1   Explain why a firm won't earn profit in long-run equilibrium under conditions of monopolistic competition.

2   In what ways can long-run equilibrium in a monopolistically competitive market be considered inefficient?

3   What is the role of advertising in monopolistically competitive markets?

Oligopoly

Oligopoly is a market structure in which a few sellers dominate the sales of a product and where entry of new sellers is difficult or impossible. The product sold by oligopolistic firms can be either differentiated or standardized. An example of an oligopoly where the product is standardized is the market for aluminum. In that market sales in the United States are dominated by ALCOA, Reynolds, and Kaiser. Automobiles, cigarettes, beer, and chewing gum are examples of differentiated goods whose market structures are oligopolistic.

Oligopoly:
A market structure in which a few sellers dominate the sales of a product and where entry of new sellers is difficult or impossible.

Oligopolistic markets typically are characterized by high market concentration. Usually the four largest producers of the good account for over half the domestic shipments. Using this as an indication of oligopoly, the table in Box 7 shows industries that can be regarded as oligopolistic. Keep in mind, however, that the concentration ratios are based on domestic shipments only and don't include shipments of goods produced in foreign countries. For this reason the market power of the four largest domestic producers is overstated in the data.

Box 7 Shipments by Largest 4 and 8 Firms in Selected Oligopolistic Industries, 1982

Industry	Number of sellers	Percentage of shipments accounted for by	
		4 largest companies	8 largest companies
Aluminum	15	64	88
Lead	5	99+	100
Steel	211	42	64
Automobiles & car bodies	28	92	97
Cereal breakfast foods	22	86	98
Flour	91	58	74
Pet food	222	52	71
Corn sugar	19	65	91
Chewing gum	9	95	99
Malt beverages (beer)	67	77	94
Roasted coffee	118	65	76
Cigars	54	60	82
Woven carpets & rugs	59	71	85
Soaps & detergents	642	60	73
Tires	108	66	86
Plumbing fixtures	41	63	85

Source: U. S. Department of Commerce, Bureau of the Census: 1982 Census of Manufacturers, MC82-S-7, Subject Series, *Concentration Ratios in Manufacturing.*

For example, the four largest domestic automobile producers in recent years have accounted for over 90% of domestic shipments. However, throughout much of the 1980s about 30% of *total* supply in the automobile market has been accounted for by foreign producers. Therefore the market isn't as concentrated as the statistics on domestic shipments imply. The largest domestic automobile producer is General Motors, which during the mid-1980s accounted for about one third of all car sales in the United States.

In oligopolistic markets at least some firms can influence price by virtue of their large shares of total output produced. Sellers in oligopolistic markets know that when they or their rivals change either their prices or outputs, the profits of all firms in the market will be affected. The sellers are aware of their interdependence with their rivals. Each firm knows that a change in its price or output will cause a reaction by competing firms. The responses an individual seller expects from its rivals are a crucial determinant of its choices, and they also influence equilibrium in oligopolistic markets.

Let's review the characteristics of oligopolistic markets:

1. Only a few firms supply the entire market with a product that may be standardized or differentiated.
2. At least some of the firms in the oligopolistic industry have large market shares and thus can influence the price of the product.
3. Firms in the industry are aware of their interdependence and always consider the reactions of their rivals when selecting prices, output goals, advertising budgets, and any other business policy.

Barriers to Entry and Cost Advantages: How Oligopolies Arise and Are Maintained

In many cases oligopolies are protected by barriers to entry similar to those we discussed for monopoly firms. Oligopolies sometimes arise because of inherent cost or technological advantages associated with large-scale production. In such cases a few firms can supply the entire market output at lower long-run average cost than can many firms. In such an industry, small firms would eventually merge with rivals to achieve the lower average costs associated with larger factories. Alternatively, a few firms would buy out existing small firms and combine their assets into large factories.

Conscious Rivalry: Oligopolistic Price Wars and Contestable Markets

We'll begin our analysis of oligopoly by investigating the consequences of conscious rivalry among a few firms selling a standardized product. The price policy of any given firm depends in part on how that firm believes its rivals will react when it changes its price. Suppose each firm seeks to maximize profits and assumes its rival will set a price and stick to that price. Each firm that lowers the price of its product conjectures that its rivals won't cut their prices in response. Under such circumstances the temptation to cut prices is irresistible. After all, firms know that by lowering prices they can gain a substantial increase in sales, at the expense of their competitors. Of course, that gain is possible only if the competitor doesn't react by also lowering his prices.

A **price war** is a bout of continual price cutting by rival firms in a market. It's one of *many* possible consequences of oligopolistic rivalry. For example, a group of gas stations serving a local market might on occasion engage in a price war. Price wars are great for consumers but bad for the profits of sellers.

Suppose your town has only two gas stations and there's no possibility a new station will ever open. Also assume each seller faces constant costs and the marginal and average cost of gasoline equals 65¢ per gallon. If gasoline were distributed by a monopoly gas station, assume that the price would be $1 per gallon.

Suppose both Jones and Smith are currently charging a price of $1 per gallon and each is selling half the total amount of gasoline in the market. Jones decides he can do better by cutting his price to 95¢ per gallon and assumes Smith won't respond by lowering his price. At first Jones sells much more gasoline per day at the lower price.

However, Smith promptly reduces his price to 90¢. He gains back all his lost sales and the bulk of Jones' sales. The process of price cutting continues in this way during the war. Equilibrium occurs when neither firm can benefit further from a price cut. This is when price is equal to average cost and profits fall to zero. Cutting price below this level will result in losses. Because each firm assumes the other won't change price, there's no incentive to increase price. To do so would result in a loss of all sales to the rival firm, which is assumed to keep its price fixed at the minimum possible average cost. The price war therefore goes on and on until price falls to the average cost of 65¢ per gallon. In equilibrium both firms charge a price just equal to the minimum possible average cost. This is the same price that would result under perfect competition!

Prices can also be expected to be close to minimum possible average cost when firms in an oligopolistic market fear that high profits will encourage new firms to enter the market. A **contestable market** is one in which entry of sellers is easy and

Price war:
A bout of continual price cutting by rival firms in a market; one of many possible consequences of oligopolistic rivalry.

Contestable market:
A market in which entry of sellers is easy and exit is not very costly.

exit isn't very costly. A seller can enter a contestable market quickly whenever it's profitable to do so. It can leave the market just as quickly without incurring high transaction costs or losses.

An unregulated air travel market could easily be contestable. If transaction costs of gaining access to a route are negligible, an airline exercising monopoly power and earning economic profits on a particular route can expect those profits to attract competing airlines. It's relatively easy for an airline to allocate its planes to the most profitable routes. As new airlines enter the market, the supply of air travel on the route increases, which puts downward pressure on air fares. Air fares must fall to the minimum possible average cost to discourage further entry. Airlines with monopoly power on routes are likely to keep their prices close to minimum possible average cost to avoid attracting competing sellers into the market.

The fear of entry into the market by foreign sellers makes the market contestable for domestic firms with monopoly power and serves to keep prices close to minimum possible average cost of production in the long run. Free trade can therefore help keep domestic markets contestable and benefit consumers by ensuring them prices that don't exceed average cost of production in the long run.

In a contestable market, even low profits will encourage new entrants. As the new entrants come in, supply increases and price falls to eliminate profits. Oligopolistic firms selling in such a market know they can gain little in the long run from using their monopoly power to raise prices. If they do raise prices, a new firm (such as a foreign supplier) might enter the market. The new firm may eventually become a major supplier, thus reducing the existing firm's market share.

Collusion and Cartels Under Oligopoly: Organizing to Keep Prices High and to Prevent Price Wars

The disastrous effect of price wars on profits of firms in oligopolistic markets provides an incentive for sellers to collude to keep profits up. Such collusion is illegal in most nations, and governments may prosecute firms that collude to fix prices at high levels or at temporarily low levels to force competitors out of business.

Cartel:
A group of firms acting together to coordinate output decisions and control prices as if they were a single monopoly.

A **cartel** is a group of firms acting together to coordinate output decisions and control prices as if they were a single monopoly. Cartels are illegal in the United States.

International cartels, however, do exist. Perhaps the best known is OPEC: Organization of Petroleum Exporting Countries (most of which are Middle Eastern nations). It seeks to regulate its members' output of crude oil with the goal of controlling price to maximize group profits. The Central Selling Organization of the De Beers Company, described in Chapter 12, also functions as a cartel by enabling a few sellers of diamonds to market their product through a single syndicate.

A cartel is a group of firms rather than a single firm. The basic problem faced by a cartel is coordinating decisions among the member firms and establishing a system of restrictions for those firms.

Forming a Cartel: Directions

Suppose several producers of bricks in your county want to form a cartel. Assume there are 15 suppliers of bricks and the product is standardized. Because of previous price wars, each firm is charging a price equal to minimum possible average cost. Each firm is afraid to raise its price for fear the others won't follow suit. Any single seller assumes it will lose all of its business if it raises its price above the current equilibrium level.

Here are the four steps necessary to form the cartel:

Step 1: Make sure there is a barrier to entry to prevent other firms from selling bricks after the price is increased. If free entry were possible, an increase in price would attract new producers if the market is contestable. The supply of bricks would increase and price would fall below the monopoly level the cartel seeks to maintain.

Step 2: Organize a meeting of all brick producers to establish a target level of output. To do this, estimate market demand and calculate marginal revenue at all output levels. Choose the output for which marginal revenue just equals marginal cost.

The monopoly output will maximize the group profits of all 15 sellers. You can see this in the graphs in Box 8. Before the cartel is organized, the market price of bricks under perfect competition is 2¢ each. As you can see in the right part of graph **A,** each firm just covers its minimum possible average cost at that price as-suming this cost is the same for each producer. Total industry output is 15,000 bricks per day, and each firm in the market produces 1,000 bricks each day. Because the price is equal to the minimum possible average cost, each seller just covers its opportunity costs.

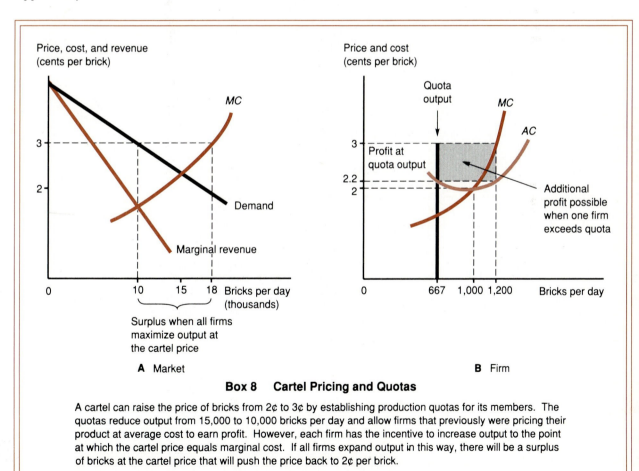

Box 8   Cartel Pricing and Quotas

A cartel can raise the price of bricks from 2¢ to 3¢ by establishing production quotas for its members. The quotas reduce output from 15,000 to 10,000 bricks per day and allow firms that previously were pricing their product at average cost to earn profit. However, each firm has the incentive to increase output to the point at which the cartel price equals marginal cost. If all firms expand output in this way, there will be a surplus of bricks at the cartel price that will push the price back to 2¢ per brick.

Principles in Practice

OPEC: A Cartel in Distress

Gasoline rationing. . . skyrocketing oil prices. . . OPEC. For a good part of 2 years—1973 and 1979—the once-routine task of filling up a gas tank became frustrating, complex, and sometimes impossible. What is OPEC, and what did its members do to cause such a panic at the pumps in our country—and what happened to its power over oil prices in the years that followed?

The Organization of Petroleum Exporting Countries (OPEC) is a cartel formed in 1960. By 1973 it appeared to have limitless power to raise the price of crude oil in world markets. In that year members of the cartel sharply cut back shipments, and the price of oil tripled. By 1979 the price of a barrel of crude oil averaged over $30. However, by the mid-1980s there was a glut of crude oil on the market, and the price of oil plummeted to less than $10 a barrel in response to the surplus at OPEC prices. In late 1986 OPEC was struggling to raise the price of oil to $18 by instructing its members to begin cutting back production by 7%. The experts of the 1970s had argued that OPEC would eventually drive the price of oil up to $100 a barrel. What happened between 1973 and 1986 to diminish OPEC's ability to keep oil prices high?

One problem was that OPEC never was able to establish a barrier to entry into the crude oil market. In response to higher prices, non-OPEC nations increased their development and production of petroleum throughout the 1970s and early 1980s. By the early 1980s, production from North Sea, Mexican, and Alaskan oil wells was putting downward pressure on crude oil prices. In addition, since 1970 the demand for oil has become more elastic. Consumers have learned that there are good substitutes for petroleum products. Fuel conservation, improved insulation of homes, and more energy-efficient automobiles have sharply decreased the demand for crude oil in the 1980s.

OPEC's attempt to reassert its market power in the 1980s met with some short-run success as the price of oil rose to about $22 per barrel. However, it's not clear that all of the price increase can be attributed to OPEC policies. For example, the demand for oil increased substantially in 1987 as some buyers sought to stockpile it in anticipation of future price increases resulting from the Iran-Iraq war that year. The success of OPEC in forcing the price of crude oil up depends on its ability to enforce the quotas it establishes. At their meeting in late 1986 there was considerable squabbling among members, particularly between Iran and Iraq (which had been engaged in a protracted war), about quotas. Iraq succeeded in getting its producers exempted from quotas.

The table that follows shows the daily production quotas established for OPEC members in December 1986.

OPEC quotas for member nations, first half of 1987 (thousands of barrels per day)

OPEC nation	Quota
Saudi Arabia	4,153
Iran	2,255
Iraq	No quota
United Arab Emirates	902
Kuwait	948
Qatar	285
Venezuela	1,495
Nigeria	1,238
Indonesia	1,133
Libya	948
Algeria	635
Ecuador	210
Gabon	152
Total	14,334

Source: *New York Times*, December 21, 1986.

The reduced quotas were expected to reduce output by about 7% from over 15 million to about 14.3 million barrels per day. Each member nation had the capacity to produce much more than its daily quota. Because the estimated daily output capacity of member nations is nearly twice the sum of the quotas, the potential for cheating can easily prevent the cartel from raising the price of crude oil to its target level. For the present at any rate, the oil sheiks of OPEC appear to have lost their power over America's petroleum prices.

The output corresponding to the point at which marginal revenue just equals marginal cost is 10,000 bricks per day. If total daily output can be reduced to this level, the market price will increase to 3¢ per brick. To see this, note that when only 10,000 bricks are available each day, the corresponding point on the demand curve, shown on the left part of graph **A**, indicates that buyers will pay 3¢ instead of 2¢ per brick. The cartel organizers will succeed in getting this higher price only if they can get each of the individual sellers to agree to decrease output.

Step 3: Set up quotas for each member of the cartel. Divide up the agreed-upon cartel output among the firms. For example, each firm could be instructed to deliver one fifteenth of the agreed-upon output each day. This means each firm would have to reduce current output by one third from its daily current production level of 1,000 bricks. A quota of about 667 bricks per day for each seller would succeed in raising the price of bricks to 3¢ and maximizing group profits.

Step 4: Make sure no firm exceeds its quota. This step is crucial to make the cartel work. It's also difficult to enforce. The reason is that each firm has incentives to sell more than its assigned quota at the cartel price. If all firms sell more than their quotas, the cartel is doomed because price will fall right back down to 2¢.

This can easily be demonstrated. Graph **B** in Box 8 shows the marginal and average costs of a typical brick producer. At the cartel price of 3¢ per brick, each producer earns profits because the average cost of bricks is 2.2¢ when daily output is at the cartel level of about 667 per seller. This is an improvement for each seller over the pre-cartel arrangement, for which profits were zero.

But there will be a temptation for each seller to *exceed* its quota. This is because at the cartel price of 3¢ per brick, each *individual* seller can increase its profits by selling more than its assigned quota. In fact, if each seller assumes it won't appreciably lower the market price below 3¢ by selling more, it will tend to expand output until its marginal cost increases to about 3¢. In **B,** this occurs when the firm sells 1,200 bricks per day. By selling more than its quota, it increases its profit by the shaded area *provided the price of bricks doesn't fall.*

One firm may be able to get away with exceeding its quota without reducing market price appreciably. Suppose, however, all 15 brick companies exceed their quota by increasing daily production to 1,200 just as the first firm did to earn more profits. If this happened, total output would be 18,000 bricks per day. But industry output must be restricted to 10,000 bricks per day to keep the price at 3¢! The increase in quantity supplied would put downward pressure on price as all of the firms exceed their quotas. Price will fall until the surplus of 8,000 bricks per day at the 3¢ price is eliminated. As price falls, quantity demanded will increase and quantity supplied will decrease until there is no longer a surplus. If all firms cheated on their quotas, it's likely they would find themselves right back where they started with a price of 2¢ per brick, just equal to the minimum possible average cost of production.

Cartels usually try to set penalties for firms that cheat on their assigned quotas. The fundamental problem is that once a cartel price is established, individual firms maximizing profits at that price can make more by cheating. If all cheat, the cartel breaks up because economic profits fall to zero.

Cartels also experience problems in deciding on the monopoly price and output level. This problem is particularly acute if firms disagree on their estimates of market demand or its price elasticity, or have different costs of production. Firms with higher average costs favor higher cartel prices. Firms are also likely to squabble about how to divide up territories. If a firm thinks its quota is too low, it has all the more reason to risk a penalty by cheating.

Other Oligopoly Models

In the preceding analysis of oligopoly we considered only the possibility of price wars and the tendency of firms to collude to maximize group profits. *There are many other possible outcomes in oligopolistic markets.* Each outcome depends on how firms regard their rivals, on their willingness to collude with their rivals, and on the penalties they might pay for illegal collusion.

Let's look at two other possibilities in oligopolistic markets: *price leadership* and *price rigidity.*

1. *Price leadership.* Under these circumstances one dominant firm in the industry sets its price to maximize its own profits and other firms simply follow its lead by setting exactly the same price. The dominant firm is called the **price leader.** There's no collusion or quota setting among firms. For example, in banking markets one or two large banks typically set the prime rate, which is the interest on loans to large corporations. Other banks quickly follow the large banks' lead and adjust their own interest rates.

Price leadership was believed to prevail in the steel industry in the United States during the 1960s. One dominant firm set prices, and smaller firms followed its lead. However, because of increased competition from foreign steel producers, observers of the steel industry believe that no single firm currently dominates the domestic steel industry.

Price leadership can be explained in terms of fear on the part of smaller firms of retaliatory reactions by the dominant firm. This is particularly true when the dominant firm can produce at lower average cost than its smaller rivals. When this is the case, the smaller firms might hesitate to undercut the dominant firm's price. They would reason that although they would temporarily gain sales, they would ultimately lose a price war. This is because the larger firm could make economic profits at a price lower than their break-even price. Pricing policy designed to put rival firms out of business and to establish monopolies is called *predatory pricing,* and this is illegal in the United States.

Smaller firms in an oligopolistic industry sometimes act as price followers because they believe larger firms have superior information on market demand. They're unsure of the future demand for their output. They view the large firm's price change as indicating a change in their own demand in the future. This may explain price leadership in the banking industry. Small banks may view a large bank's increase in the prime rate as indicative of a general excess demand for loans at the current interest rate.

2. *Price rigidity.* Price rigidity in oligopolistic markets can occur if individual firms believe that any increase in their price won't be matched by their rivals. At the same time they believe their rivals will match their price *decreases.* Under such circumstances, the demand curve as seen by any particular firm has a strange shape.

For example, suppose the market price of a chocolate bar is 75¢. Chocolate bars are produced by only a few firms. Assume firms in the industry think the demand for their product will be very elastic if they raise their price. This is because they expect their rivals *not* to follow the price increase. However, if they lower their price, they conjecture demand will be less elastic because they expect rival firms to follow their price cuts. The sharp change in elasticity of the firm's demand curve at the established price gives it a kinked shape.

The graph in Box 9 shows the kinked demand curve along with the marginal revenue curve corresponding to it. Notice the sharp drop in marginal revenue when price falls below 75¢, which is the established price. This is caused by the sharp drop-off in revenue that the firm expects when it reduces its price since it

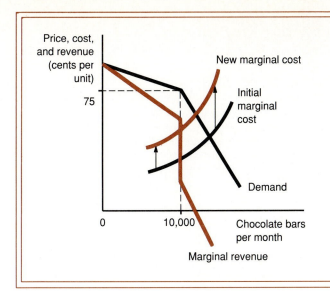

Price, cost, and revenue (cents per unit)

75

New marginal cost

Initial marginal cost

Demand

0   10,000   Chocolate bars per month

Marginal revenue

Box 9   Oligopolistic Price Rigidity

If the demand curve for the product of a firm selling in an oligopolistic market has a kink in it, prices will be rigid. An increase (or decrease) in marginal cost in the vertical section of the marginal revenue curve will not cause the firm to adjust the profit-maximizing price or output.

expects to gain little in sales because its rivals also reduce their prices.[1]

The price rigidity will be maintained only for cost increases that result in shifts of the marginal cost curve within the vertical segment of the marginal revenue curve. A larger increase in costs will result in a new price. There will then be a new demand curve with a new kink. The kink remains only if firms maintain the same beliefs about their rivals' price reactions after the new price is established.

Maximum profits correspond to the output of 10,000 chocolate bars per month, at which marginal revenue equals marginal cost. Suppose there's an increase in the price of one of the inputs necessary to produce chocolate bars. This shifts the marginal cost curve upward. If after the increase the marginal cost curve still intersects the marginal revenue curve in its vertical segment, the firm will change neither output nor price. Similarly, a decrease in marginal cost could result in no change in price or output.

Concept Check

1 What is the likely outcome of an oligopolistic price war in which each rival thinks its competitors will keep their prices fixed? How can price rigidity be explained in oligopolistic markets?

2 What is a contestable market? Why are prices likely to remain close to marginal and average cost in a contestable market?

3 Why are cartels likely to be difficult to maintain?

[1]The marginal revenue curve can be derived by recognizing that up to output Q^*, marginal revenue corresponds to the less elastic portion of the demand curve. When output exceeds Q^*, the marginal revenue corresponding to the more elastic demand prevails.

Principles in Practice

Cost-Plus Pricing: Price Leadership or Collusion?

A practice often observed in imperfectly competitive markets is *cost-plus pricing*, in which a firm adds a percentage markup to average variable costs to set a price for its product. For example, if the average cost of an automobile were $10,000 and sellers used 30% markups, they would add $3,000 to average cost and price their vehicles at $13,000.

Cost-plus pricing can be viewed as an attempt by firms to ensure *at least* a normal profit to cover the opportunity cost of stockholders' invested capital (equity). A problem with implementing this procedure is that the average cost of production can vary with output volume in the short run. Firms usually set a target level of annual output. Then they add a sufficient percentage to average cost to make sure they earn the target level of accounting profit as a percentage of *invested funds*. Of course, if they set the price too high to achieve their target output, they can be in for a rude surprise because lower sales volume means less revenue and *higher* average costs.

General Motors Corporation is one well-known business that has used cost-plus pricing in the past. GM's objective has been to earn a 15% return after taxes on its capital. To achieve this objective GM might assume it will sell 100,000 Oldsmobile Cutlasses during the year, a number that would correspond to roughly 80% of plant capacity. It would then calculate the average cost of each Cutlass at the estimated annual output. Finally, a markup of, say, 50% would be applied to the car based on an estimate of what it would take to get that product line to contribute to the 15% annual return on capital. For example, if the average cost of the Cutlass were $10,000 at the target output, a 50% markup would result in a $15,000 list price. The pricing decision would be reviewed during the year and could be revised depending on actual market conditions.

The rationale for cost-plus pricing lies in uncertainties about the level of average costs and the demand for a firm's product over the year. It represents a pragmatic way of dealing with the problems of estimating marginal revenue and marginal cost on a day-to-day basis. However, a firm's revisions in its estimates of average cost and sales volume over the year in effect are new annual estimates of marginal revenue and marginal cost. This means cost-plus pricing might have results that don't diverge much from those the economist would predict if firms set price to produce the output that equates marginal revenue and marginal cost.

Cost-plus pricing can also lead to price leadership. If firms in an oligopolistic industry take a large firm's announced price as the one necessary for them to also earn at least a normal profit, they too will use the markup price set by the leader. Cost-plus pricing can therefore be regarded as yet another way firms tend to tacitly collude to set prices at levels that guarantee them economic profits.

The Risk of Inefficient Outcomes

Outcomes in both monopolistically competitive and oligopolistic markets can be inefficient. In the case of monopolistic competition, a clear case can be established that prices will exceed minimum possible average cost and the marginal cost of production. However, oligopoly is much more difficult to analyze. Price wars and fear of new entrants in markets can serve to keep prices close to minimum possible average cost in oligopolistic markets. The big risk in oligopolistic markets is that, in an effort to keep output low and prices high, firms will cooperate in ways that restrict competition. If this occurs, oligopoly can be as bad as pure monopoly in terms of efficiency. Collusion among firms in oligopolistic markets will result in prices that exceed minimum possible average cost and marginal cost.

As we observed earlier, the markets for many basic products, like automobiles, tires, and basic metals, can be regarded as oligopolistic. Governments generally use their powers to discourage collusion among firms in such markets. Government regulation of markets is of great importance because it can prevent the exercise of monopoly power and thereby minimize losses in efficiency.

Summary

1. Under imperfect competition there are rival sellers, each of which has some measure of control over the price of the product they sell.

2. Monopolistic competition exists when many rival sellers compete to sell a differentiated product in a market in which there is free entry of new sellers. The product each firm sells is a close but not perfect substitute for the products of competing firms.

3. The demand curve for the product of a monopolistically competitive firm slopes downward. The price of the product exceeds the marginal revenue of any given quantity. The firm maximizes profits by selecting the output for which marginal revenue equals marginal cost. The corresponding price necessary to get consumers to buy the profit-maximizing output exceeds the marginal cost of producing the item.

4. Because free entry is possible in a monopolistically competitive market, prices in such markets tend to decrease when it's possible for new entrants to earn profits. In equilibrium the demand curve for a firm's product tends to be tangent to its average cost curve. Entry of new firms continues until economic profits fall to zero.

5. There can be losses in efficiency even in the long run under monopolistic competition because prices exceed marginal cost and plants are not operated at the output corresponding to the minimum possible average cost. Excess capacity is the difference between the output corresponding to minimum possible average cost and the output produced by a monopolistically competitive firm in the long run.

6. Monopolistically competitive firms commonly engage in advertising to help differentiate their product and increase demand for it. Selling costs are all costs the firm incurs for the purpose of influencing the sales of its product. Advertising is an alternative to reducing price as a means of increasing sales.

7. Oligopoly is a market structure in which a few sellers dominate the sales of a product and where entry of new sellers is difficult or impossible. Firms in oligopolistic markets can influence market price because they have large shares of total market sales. In choosing prices and sales goals, oligopolistic firms consider the reactions of their rivals.

8. A price war is a bout of continual price cutting by rival firms in a market. Price wars push prices down to the average costs of production. Prices in oligopolistic markets also are likely to be close to average costs when the market is contestable. A contestable market is one in which ease of entry and exit attracts new firms when prices are high enough to permit profits.

9. A cartel is a group of firms acting together to coordinate output decisions and control price as if they were a single monopoly. Cartels tend to be unstable because maximization of group profits is inconsistent with maximization of profits by individual members at the high cartel price. Firms tend to cheat on their cartel quotas to earn extra profits. If all firms cheat, the market supply increases and prices decline.

10. In an oligopolistic market, one firm might emerge as a price leader. This firm sets prices to maximize profits, and other firms also set that price.

11. Price rigidity occurs in oligopolistic markets when firms believe their rivals will follow price cuts but not follow price increases.

Key Terms and Concepts

Imperfect competition   Oligopoly
Monopolistic competition   Price war
Product group   Contestable market
Excess capacity   Cartel
Selling costs   Price leader

Problems and Applications

1. A soft-drink firm sells its particular brand of cola and has a loyal following of consumers who believe the company's cola is better than those of its competitors. The cola company prices its product so as to maximize profits. Currently the marginal cost of a liter of the cola is $1 at the profit-maximizing output. Draw a graph to show that the price of the cola will exceed $1 per liter.

2. Suppose the cola company, through a new advertising campaign, succeeds in making the demand for its product more inelastic. This means that the price corresponding to any given marginal revenue will now be greater than before. Assuming that the marginal cost at the profit-maximizing output is still $1, use the graph you drew in answer to problem 1 to show that the price the firm sets will now be higher.

3. The jeans business is booming. There are many firms marketing jeans with their own distinctive labels and styles. Each firm uses advertising to establish an image for its product. Makers of brand names like Jordache and Guess Jeans make skillful use of advertisements in selected magazines to market their product. Suppose the typical firm in the jeans industry is making a profit. Use a graph to illustrate the process by which those profits will be eliminated in the long run.

4. Suppose the minimum possible average cost of producing designer jeans is $20. Use a graph to show that the price of jeans set by firms producing the various brands will exceed $20 even after long-run equilibrium has been achieved in the industry.

5. Show how advertising affects a firm's cost curves and contributes to higher prices in a monopolistically competitive industry.

6. There are only five firms producing lead in the United States. Assume that each firm produces at least 10% of the current quantity of lead demanded each year. Draw the market demand curve for lead and show how any one firm in the industry can raise the price of lead by significantly cutting back production. Show what would happen to the price of lead if all five firms agreed to cut back production by 50%.

7. Suppose a price war for gasoline breaks out in a small town in which there are four gas stations. Assuming each firm believes its rivals won't follow its price cuts or price increases, show how the price of gasoline will equal both the marginal and minimum possible average cost of making it available.

8. The marginal cost of providing an additional flight from New York to San Francisco is $100,000. Suppose the current fares charged on this route allow revenue of $200,000 per flight. Assuming the market for air travel between New York and San Francisco is a contestable one, explain why air fares will fall until the marginal revenue of flights between these two points equals $100,000.

9. A cartel of 20 lumber producers sets a price of 20¢ per board foot of 2 × 4 lumber. Each firm in the cartel reasons it can sell as much lumber as it chooses at that price without significantly lowering the price. Show how a surplus of

lumber will result at the cartel price if all producers disregard quotas set by the cartel management and seek to maximize profits at the cartel price. What measures must a cartel take to ensure that the price it sets is maintained?

10. The marginal cost of producing tires increases by $2. However, none of the 15 firms in the industry raises its price. How can you explain the behavior of these firms?

Suggested Readings

Walter Adams, ed., *The Structure of American Industry,* 6th ed., New York: Macmillan, 1982. A collection of essays in this book discusses market structure in such imperfectly competitive industries as beer, professional sports, and steel.

Eric N. Berkowitz, Roger A. Kerin, and William Rudelius, *Marketing,* 2nd ed., Homewood, Ill.: Richard D. Irwin, Inc., 1989. Chapters 16 and 17 discuss selling costs and practical aspects of marketing products.

William S. Comanor and Thomas A. Wilson, "The Effect of Advertising on Competition: A Survey," *Journal of Economic Literature,* 17, 2, June 1979, pp. 453-476. This article looks at the pros and cons of advertising and the impact of advertising in markets.

A Forward Look

Losses in efficiency and higher prices can result from unfair business practices that limit competition in markets. In the United States, the U.S. Department of Justice enforces antitrust legislation whose purpose is to prevent unfair business practices that limit the ability of rivals to compete in markets. In the following chapter we examine antitrust policy in the United States and other government policies that regulate business.

14

Oligopoly Strategies and the Theory of Games

Theory of games:
Analyzes the behavior of individuals or organizations with conflicting interests.

The **theory of games** analyzes the behavior of individuals or organizations with conflicting interests. The payoff to their decisions depends not only on their choices but also on those of their competitors. The theory of games can be applied to the pricing strategy of oligopolistic firms. Without going into its richness or complexity, the following example will show you the insights we can obtain from game theory.[1]

The Payoff Matrix

In the example of a price war we discussed in this chapter, each firm assumed in making its pricing decision that its competitor would hold price fixed. Suppose the firm's managers are more sophisticated. They don't stubbornly adhere to the belief that their rival will pursue the strategy of stonewalling it on price. The managers realize that when they lower their price, the rival firm may either keep its price constant or lower its price too. The firm's profits depend on the reaction of the rival. Suppose the rival firms are the Adams and Baker Brick companies. In determining their prices and outputs, these firms use more sophisticated techniques than those employed by the two gas station operators we discussed earlier.

The managers of both firms calculate the profits they can earn when they lower price or keep price constant. They do this for two contingencies: the case in which their rival lowers price, and the case in which their rival doesn't lower price. The result is a **payoff matrix,** which shows the gain or loss from each possible strategy for each possible reaction by the rival player of the game. Deciding to begin a price

Payoff matrix:
Shows the gain or loss from each possible strategy for each possible reaction by the rival player of the game.

[1]The theory of games was originally formulated in the 1940s. See John Von Neumann and Oskar Morgenstern, *The Theory of Games and Economic Behavior,* New York: Science Editions, Wiley, 1964. For applications to oligopoly, see James W. Friedman, *Oligopoly and the Theory of Games,* Amsterdam: Elsevier, North Holland, 1977.

war is like making the opening move in a game. How much a player can win or lose depends not only on his own strategy but also on the strategy used by his opponent.

The table in Box 1 shows the payoff matrix for the two brick companies. The Adams Company is concerned only with the change in its profits. It knows that if it cuts the price of bricks by 1¢, it will gain sales only if the Baker Company doesn't match its price cut. The first row in the payoff matrix shows the consequences of Adams' price cut. If Baker also cuts price by 1¢ per brick, profit will decline by

---

Box 1   Payoff Matrix for a Price War

	Baker's strategies*		Adams' maximum losses
	Cut price by 1¢ per brick	Maintain price	
Adams' strategies* **Cut price by 1¢ per brick**	Change in Adams' profits = −$5,000 Change in Baker's profits = −$5,000	Change in Adams' profits = +$15,000 Change in Baker's profits = −$10,000	− $5,000
Maintain price	Change in Adams' profits = −$10,000 Change in Baker's profits = +$15,000	Change in Adams' profits = 0 Change in Baker's profits = 0	− $10,000
Baker's maximum losses	−$5,000	− $10,000	

*Maximin strategy for Adams: cut price. Maximin strategy for Baker: cut price. *Both* make less profit by cutting price than they can by colluding to maintain price. However, if one maintains price, the rival is always better off to cut price.

$5,000 per month. If Baker maintains its price at the current level, profit will increase by $15,000 per month.

Adams' alternative strategy is to maintain price. If it does so, it will suffer a $10,000 loss in monthly profits if Baker responds by cutting its price. There will be no change in profits if the rival firm maintains its price.

The payoff matrix also shows the change in Baker's profits for each of its possible strategies. If the Adams Company knew for sure that when it cut price its rival would maintain price, it would know that a price cut would increase its profits by $15,000. This is the highest payoff to Adams in the matrix. However, the managers know that Baker might match the price cut. They therefore look at Adams' payoff for that contingency as well since it would lose $5,000 per month as a result of the price cut.

Managers of the two companies can pursue various strategies in their attempt to maximize their profits. One possibility is to assume that the worst possible outcome will occur for any strategy. The last column of the matrix shows the *worst* that can happen as a result of any strategy for the Adams Company. If it cuts price, the worst possible outcome would be for Baker also to cut price, resulting in a $5,000 decrease in profits. Similarly, observe that the worst possible outcome for Adams if it

Maximin strategy:
The strategy that maximizes the minimum (or worst) outcomes of all possible strategies.

maintains price would be for Baker to cut its price. This would result in a decrease in profits of $10,000 per month. The strategy that results in the smallest decrease in profits is called the **maximin strategy.** It maximizes the minimum (or worst) outcomes of all possible strategies. Other strategies are possible. However, the advantage of the maximin strategy is that it provides protection of profits. In effect, it places a floor on profits. By choosing this strategy, each of the firms can be sure that its profits won't fall below a certain level. Accordingly, we'll assume each firm pursues this strategy.

As long as it doesn't know for sure what the Baker Company will do, the Adams Company will cut its price. The worst that can happen if it does so is that it will lose $5,000. The worst that can happen if it maintains its price is that it will lose $10,000.

The management of Baker makes similar calculations. It too will lose $10,000 in the worst scenario if it maintains price and the Adams Company cuts price. It loses only $5,000 if it cuts price and Adams maintains its price. It therefore chooses the price-cutting strategy as well.

Each firm hopes the other will maintain price so it can increase profits by $15,000 a month. However, if *both* firms try to avoid the worst by pursuing the maximin strategy, each decides to cut price. The firms therefore start a price war, and both firms end up losing $5,000 rather than increasing profits. One firm can increase profits only if the other firm pursues a strategy of maintaining price. When both firms employ the protective maximin strategy, neither can gain as a result of the price war but both choose to lower price anyway.

Both firms would be better off by maintaining price. Their rivalry and their desire to avoid the worst possible outcome ensure that neither can gain from a price cut. If they realize this, they can collude and agree to maintain prices. Such an agreement will neither increase nor decrease profits. It will, however, avoid the inevitable losses that result when any one firm tries to cut price.

Key Terms and Concepts

Theory of games
Payoff matrix
Maximin strategy

Problem

In your small town there are only two beer distributors. State laws make it impossible for new distributors to enter the market. The Anderson Beer Distributing Company estimates it can increase profits by $2,000 per month if it cuts prices by 5%, provided that its rival, the Bull Beer Distributing Company, maintains its price. On the other hand, if the rival cuts price, Anderson will lose $1,500 per month. Assuming Bull Beer makes exactly the same calculations, set up the payoff matrix and indicate the maximin strategy for each firm.

Career Profile

SANDRA DAY O'CONNOR

Her pioneer grandfather built up a huge ranch in southern Arizona. A pioneer herself, Sandra Day O'Connor may not be staking out land, but she's certainly carving out new territory for women as the first female justice of the U.S. Supreme Court.

Possessing a unique combination of fairness, intelligence, integrity, and a calm temperament, O'Connor serves as a role model for women and as a symbol of their changing status. But those qualities also make an extremely good judge, and even though O'Connor lacked extensive court experience she was unanimously confirmed by the Senate when President Ronald Reagan appointed her to the Supreme Court in 1981.

Born in 1930, she grew up on the 155,000-acre Lazy B Ranch her grandfather founded. She attended boarding school in El Paso and earned her undergraduate degree in economics from Stanford University, where she also attended law school, graduating third in her class (Chief Justice William Rehnquist was first that year). When she went looking for a job, she found prejudice against women at the law firms in Los Angeles and San Francisco where she interviewed. Most had never hired a female lawyer and were unwilling to do so. One even offered her a job as a legal secretary.

O'Connor set her sights on public service and since 1952, when she worked as a county deputy attorney, she has rarely worked in the private sector. As an Arizona state senator, she was elected majority leader, the first woman in the nation to hold that office in any state. Her colleagues praised her precise and concise mind, her meticulous approach to the details of legislative duty, her demand for accuracy, and her ability to motivate others.

Diligence, sternness, and fairness characterized O'Connor as a judge, both at the Superior Court, to which she was elected in 1974, and at the Arizona Court of Appeals, to which a Democratic governor appointed the moderate-to-conservative Republican in 1978.

As a Justice, O'Connor votes with other conservative Republican appointees on many issues. However, on cases involving freedom of information, sex discrimination, and traditional civil rights issues, she tends to vote differently, showing that she brings a fresh perspective to the high court.

Government as a Regulator in Markets and as a Provider of Services: Microeconomic Analysis

CHAPTER

15

Antitrust Policy and Regulation of Markets

Remember the opening of Chapter 13, when we asked if you've ever played Monopoly®? If you have, you know that there are almost no restrictions on the types and numbers of properties you can acquire. In theory, if you have the cash and the dice are rolling in your favor, you could end up owning everything from low-rent Mediterranean Avenue to glitzy Boardwalk. The name of the game is unrestricted wheeling and dealing.

As you'll see, business as it was conducted in the United States a century ago bore a strong resemblance to a game of Monopoly. In fact, thanks in large part to the competitive excesses of that period, government now is an ever-present force affecting the way the economy operates each day. Because markets seldom function perfectly, government intervention can often help achieve efficiency and other goals. Dissatisfaction with and distrust of market outcomes lead many people to support government policies that regulate or modify the freedom of sellers to do as they please in markets. Monopoly and the use of monopoly power are not illegal in the United States. However, the federal government does set policies to restrain business firms from engaging in certain practices that make it difficult for rival sellers to compete in the market.

In some cases large-scale firms that dominate a market have cost or technological advantages that provide benefits that couldn't be enjoyed if perfect competition prevailed. When this is the case, governments allow a single monopoly firm to operate but regulate the price the monopoly firm can charge for its product. Because of concern about the exercise of monopoly power to control price and maximize profit, governments regulate monopolies such as local power and telephone companies.

If government regulation of markets to control monopoly power is effective, it can provide net benefits to market participants and result in more output at lower prices. The net benefits can accrue to sellers that would otherwise be excluded from competing in markets and to consumers, who can benefit from lower prices. When regulation succeeds in eliminating the exercise of monopoly control over price, the profits of the monopoly firm in effect can be transferred to consumers in the form of lower prices.

In practice, government regulation often is used to influence both prices and the conditions for entry of sellers into markets. In this chapter we examine the process of government regulation of markets. As you'll see, regulation has both costs and benefits. When governments intervene in markets, inevitably some people gain while others lose. Regulations don't always succeed in lowering prices and in some cases may actually make them higher! In recent years there's been a trend toward deregulation of some markets. For example, government regulation of entry and exit in air travel markets was eliminated completely in the early 1980s. Markets for trucking, communication, banking, and railroad services have also been significantly deregulated in recent years. These instances of deregulation give us an opportunity to investigate what happens when government eliminates regulations that prevent free entry in markets.

After reading this chapter, you should be able to:

Concept Preview

1   Describe how governments use the law and the courts to prevent establishment of monopoly positions through unfair business practices. Also, discuss antitrust laws and how they affect business behavior and mergers.

2   Explain the behavior of natural monopoly firms and discuss alternative policies of government control over the prices such firms are permitted to charge for their products. Also, demonstrate understanding of the concept of "fair-rate-of-return" pricing.

3   Describe the impact of government policies that limit the freedom of sellers to choose their own prices and to enter markets. Also, discuss the impact of eliminating government controls on prices and competition in markets.

Using the Law and the Courts to Prevent Business Practices that Limit Competition: Antitrust Policy

The U.S. government tries to limit the use and growth of monopoly power by outlawing certain business practices that prevent competition among sellers. **Antitrust statutes** seek to prevent "unfair" business practices that give rise to monopoly power. The threat of prosecution can deter firms from exercising monopoly power. The main goal of government antitrust policy is to prevent sellers from engaging in activities intended to exclude rivals from competing in markets.

Antitrust statutes:
Seek to prevent "unfair" business practices that give rise to monopoly power.

The antitrust laws are enforced by the U.S. Department of Justice. However, the extent of active enforcement depends on political as well as economic considerations. For example, the Reagan Administration was notably lax in pursuing and initiating antitrust lawsuits.

The threat of an antitrust suit and the high costs of legal defense against such suits are in themselves a powerful deterrent to activities that limit competition. For example, in defending itself in a prolonged antitrust case, IBM spent over $100 million in legal fees over a 13-year period! (The Justice Department eventually dropped the case because its lawyers believed there was little chance of winning.) In the past, antitrust laws have been successfully used against the nation's largest corporations, including Standard Oil, the Aluminum Corporation of America (AL-COA), and the American Telephone and Telegraph Corporation (AT&T). The Department of Justice also acts to prevent mergers of large firms when it can be shown that such mergers will lessen competition in a market.

The ability to initiate an antitrust suit against a company or to hold up a merger is a powerful government weapon to prevent the exercise of monopoly power. This weapon is a double-edged sword. When used carefully it can benefit consumers, but it can harm them when used indiscriminately. When action is taken against firms for which a good case can't be established, the only winners are the lawyers who collect the awesome legal fees that pile up in such proceedings.

Controlling the Trusts: Background for the Enactment of Antitrust Legislation in the United States

The first major antitrust legislation in the United States was enacted in the late nineteenth century. Trusts were large business organizations of the period, many of which used tactics intended to drive their competitors out of business and to establish monopoly positions in markets. For example, the Standard Oil Company, under the leadership of John D. Rockefeller, established a near-monopoly position in the market for refined oil chiefly by getting the railroads to provide it with kickbacks on freight rates. The kickbacks enabled Standard to sell oil at lower prices than its competitors and eventually put them out of business. Once the rivals were out of the way, Standard Oil was free to control the price of its product to maximize its profits. The Standard Oil Trust was established in 1882 to coordinate the operations of a number of associated firms in the industry. The trust closed down refineries and limited output of oil to achieve its goal of increasing the market price to maximize profits.

Trusts also were formed to control output and discourage rivalry in the markets for lead, sugar, and whiskey. Nineteenth-century business leaders like J.P. Morgan had a reputation for using force to limit competition in markets. By the end of the nineteenth century, the time was ripe for laws to prohibit unscrupulous business practices.

Antitrust Laws

The first major antitrust law was the *Sherman Act* of 1890, which sought to prohibit contracts, combinations, and conspiracies in restraint of trade. Although the act established penalties for those convicted of violations, it didn't include any provisions for enforcement. Monopoly and large market shares, as such, were not declared illegal. Instead the legislation outlawed the use of unfair practices to exclude rivals. The possession of monopoly power through superior skill or cost advantages wasn't and still isn't considered illegal.

In 1914 additional antitrust legislation was enacted to supplement the Sherman Act. The *Clayton Act* broadened the government's antitrust powers to outlaw specific business practices and further restrain the growth of monopoly power. The practices outlawed by the Clayton Act are:

1. *Price discrimination that lessens competition*. Price discrimination (see Chapter 13) is the practice of charging different prices to different buyers of the same product. Under the Clayton Act, this practice is permitted only when the price differences reflect differences in cost or quality. This provision outlawed practices like the railroad rate kickback scheme that helped John D. Rockefeller establish the Standard Oil Trust.
2. *Tying contracts*. These contracts are agreements between a supplier and a client firm that prevent a purchaser from using the products of a competing supplier. When used specifically for the purpose of reducing competition, such contracts are illegal.
3. *Interlocking directorates*. These exist when the same person sits on the boards of directors of two or more firms. The Clayton Act prohibits interlocking directorates in cases where firms are large and compete with each other.
4. *Corporate stock acquisition for the purpose of reducing competition*. An antimerger provision of the Act prohibits a firm from acquiring the stock of a competing supplier when the acquisition is for the purpose of reducing competition.

Also enacted in 1914, the *Federal Trade Commission Act* established and empowered a commission to police markets and regulate methods of competition. The legislation didn't offer a specific definition of what constitutes an "unfair" competitive practice. In recent years, however, the commission has acted to prevent false and deceptive advertising.

The *Robinson-Patman Act* of 1936 was passed to protect small independent sellers, particularly those engaged in wholesale and retail activities, from unfair competition by large firms. This act prevents the granting of special price discounts for supplies to firms that buy large quantites of an item unless it can be proved that the discounts are offered to meet an equally low price of a competitor. However, such discounts are permitted if it can be shown they are justified by lower costs.

A final concern of the antitrust laws is the impact of mergers of firms in an industry on competition and the exercise of monopoly power. Although the Clayton Act contains provisions designed to prevent one company from acquiring the stock of another to lessen competition, it doesn't specifically control mergers that lessen competition. The *Celler-Kefauver Antimerger Act* was passed in 1950 to control mergers that might substantially reduce rivalry among sellers in a way that would contribute to higher prices in an industry. This legislation specifically prohibits one corporation from acquiring the assets of another if the purpose of the acquisition can be shown to be the creation of a monopoly.

Use of Antitrust Policy to Control Price Fixing

Among the prime monopolistic practices discouraged by the antitrust laws are price-fixing agreements. Any conspiracy among competing firms to fix prices is illegal. Explicit price-fixing agreements among firms in an industry are subject to both civil and criminal penalties. In many cases the legal issue is whether or not closeness or similarity of prices among firms is evidence of intent to fix prices. An example of this occurred in the government's 1946 case against the three major tobacco producers in the U.S. cigarette industry. American Tobacco, Reynolds, and Liggett & Myers were convicted of violating antitrust acts because their retail prices were identical. In addition, the firms had pressured retailers not to lower their prices. As a result, in the depths of the 1930s Depression retail prices for cigarettes were rising, while at the same time both tobacco-leaf prices and labor costs were falling. Although there was no evidence that the companies had communicated to create a conspiracy, they were found guilty of price fixing. In issuing a pronouncement on this case (which it refused to review), the Supreme Court argued that no formal agreement is necessary for proof of conspiracy. The court concluded that conspiracy may be inferred from the acts of the accused.[1]

However, there's often a thin line between price fixing and price leadership. The courts in this country have ruled that price leadership in general is not illegal. This is upheld as long as the price followers aren't coerced in any way into following the leader. This principle was established in two key cases in the 1920s, one involving U.S. Steel and the other in which the defendant was International Harvester.

The Rule of Reason

Rule of reason:
Holds that acts beyond normal business practice that unduly restrain competition for the purpose of excluding rivals can be used to infer intent to monopolize an industry.

In 1911 the Supreme Court ruled that the Standard Oil Company of New Jersey engaged in illegal business practices with the intent and purpose of excluding other sellers from the market. This decision established the **rule of reason,** which holds that acts beyond normal business practice that unduly restrain competition for the purpose of excluding rivals can be used to infer intent to monopolize an industry. This rule broke up the Standard Oil Trust of John D. Rockefeller, which at the time controlled over 90% of the market for refined oil. It was shown that the company had used railroad rates, rebates and discounts, business espionage, control of supplies to rivals, and price warfare specifically designed to drive rivals out of business or to weaken them for takeover by the Standard Oil Company. The Supreme Court viewed these practices as unusual and unfair. Between 1911 and 1920 the rule was also applied in cases breaking up the Tobacco Trust and the Powder Trust and in cases against the Eastman Kodak Company and other trusts.

In a 1920 case against U.S. Steel, however, the Supreme Court ruled that the company was not guilty of monopoly violations of the Sherman Act despite evidence of price leadership. It was argued that the company didn't exercise its monopoly power to exclude rivals and that its size alone wasn't evidence of abuse of monopoly power. This case established the legal principle that size, a high market share of output, or oligopolistic price leadership is not by itself illegal. The case also made it clear that dominant firms in an industry could expect antitrust action only if they used their power actively and aggressively to exclude or damage rivals.

Another significant case was decided in 1945 when a Supreme Court decision found the Aluminum Company of America (ALCOA) guilty of monopolization and ordered it broken up. In that case the court ruled that ALCOA possessed a monopoly of primary aluminum ingots and had used its knowledge of demand to expand capacity before rivals had a chance to enter the market. Expansion of capacity was viewed as intent to monopolize the market. This decision established the precedent of inferring illegal monopolization from acts other than unreasonable business practices designed to drive competitors out of business.

The Relevant Market

The outcome of many antitrust cases depends on disputes concerning definition of the relevant market. The 1945 case against ALCOA hinged on the definition of the

---

[1] For an economic analysis of this case, see William H. Nichols, "The Tobacco Case of 1946," *American Economic Review,* 39, May 1949.

product market. ALCOA had been organized in 1888. Although there were some attempts by new firms to enter the market before 1940, ALCOA held a monopoly position by virtue of its ownership or control of most of the high-grade bauxite reserves used to derive aluminum. The court considered aluminum to be a metal with unique properties that put it in a separate product group from other metals. They were convinced that copper and steel were poor substitutes for aluminum. In evaluating the company's market share of aluminum ingots, the court used primary production and didn't include aluminum ingots produced from recycled scrap. Using that definition, the court concluded that ALCOA's 90% market share constituted a monopoly.

In 1956 the Supreme Court found the E.I. du Pont de Nemours Company innocent of monopolizing cellophane production. Although du Pont did in fact have a monopoly in cellophane production, it was able to convince the court that there was a high cross-elasticity of demand between cellophane and alternative packaging materials. You'll recall that cross-elasticity of demand (see Chapter 7) is the percentage change in the quantity of a good that consumers demand in response to each 1% change in the prices of related goods. A high cross-elasticity of demand for cellophane with respect to the prices of alternate packaging materials means that cellophane has some very close substitutes. The Supreme Court held that the cellophane substituted for other wrappings to a sufficient degree to accept the broader definition of the product market.

Another case where definition of the relevant market was a major issue was the Justice Department suit against IBM, which was initiated in 1969. This case lingered in the courts until 1982 when it was finally dropped by the Justice Department. The government argued that IBM used unreasonable business practices to prevent entry and protect its market share. The government defined the relevant product group as general-purpose electronic digital computing systems. Defining the market in this way gave IBM a 72% share of total shipments. IBM argued that its share was little more than 30% of the market that included military computers, programmable calculators, leased computers, and other information processing products and services.

One of the unfair business practices IBM was charged with was bundling of hardware, software, and maintenance services at a single price. These practices, the government claimed, made it difficult for independent programming and servicing firms to enter the market. It also argued that IBM engaged in practices to put out of business firms that leased IBM machines to others. Other practices cited were redesigning computers so they couldn't use accessories produced by competing companies, and cutting prices to put competitors out of business.

IBM argued that its high market share was the result of superior products and service. It claimed that its practices resulted in better service to customers and that customers benefited from the lower costs that IBM passed on in the form of lower prices. In 1982 the government dropped its case against IBM after concluding it was virtually unwinnable.[2]

Are High Market Concentration and High Profit Synonymous with the Exercise of Monopoly Power?

The potential to use monopoly power as a means of controlling price and maximizing profit is a source of concern to consumers, who will have to pay higher prices

[2]See "After the IBM Case," *New York Times,* Sunday, May 13, 1984, Section 3. Also see Franklin M. Fisher, John J. McGowan, and J.E. Greenwood, *Folded, Spindled, and Mutilated: Economic Analysis of U.S. vs. IBM,* Cambridge, Mass.: MIT Press, 1983.

Principles in Practice

The Courts and Business: The "De-monopolizing" of Telephone Service and Football Telecasts

Several years ago, the long arm of the Justice Department reached out and touched what was perhaps our country's best-known monopoly, thus sounding the death knell for Ma Bell. Not long afterward, the U.S. Supreme Court found the National Collegiate Athletic Association guilty of illegal blocking—of college football telecasts. Let's look into the facts and results of these two key cases.

The AT&T Case and Its Aftermath

In 1974 the Justice Department accused the Bell System and its parent organization, American Telephone and Telegraph Corporation (AT&T), of illegally monopolizing telecommunications service. In 1982 the AT&T case was settled by an agreement between the government prosecutor and the firm. The court decree implementing the agreement caused a radical change in the structure of the company. In 1984 AT&T divested itself of its 23 operating telephone companies. The companies became seven regional entities that independently provide local telephone service and access to long-distance lines operated by AT&T and competing companies.

As a consequence of the decree, AT&T now competes with other telecommunications companies. It faces competition not only for long-distance telephone service but also for manufacturing and sales of equipment. In 1982 AT&T accounted for about 90% of long-distance traffic. It now competes with several other suppliers. Consumers have freedom of choice in the telephone equipment they use and in the installation of phone jacks. AT&T also faces competition for the installation of switching systems for large institutions.

Although the price of long-distance telephone service has fallen as a result of increased competition stemming from the AT&T breakup, the price of local service has risen sharply. The price of interstate long-distance calls dropped by about 17% from January 1984 to October 1986. However, from December 1983 to June 1984 the price of local telephone service increased on average by nearly 13%. From January 1984 to October 1986 local telephone service rates increased by an additional 40%.

Why has the breakup of AT&T increased the price of local telephone service? In the past the Federal Communications Commission regulated long-distance rates while state commissions regulated local telephone rates. A portion of local plant, equipment, and facilities was considered part of the capital costs of providing long-distance service. This made the costs of long-distance service appear to be high. In effect, AT&T recovered part of its expenditures for local service through long-distance revenues. Long-distance rates actually exceeded their marginal costs. The FCC policy resulted in a subsidy from long-distance users to local users. Under the new policy, adopted after the 1982 court agreement, AT&T's primary line of business is interstate long-distance service. This eliminates the subsidy of local service from long-distance service revenues. The goal of the new regulatory policy is to make the prices of both long-distance and local telephone service more accurately reflect their marginal costs of production.* You're paying more for local service—but long-distance rates really look like a bargain!

The NCAA Case: Ending Monopoly Control of Collegiate Football Telecasts

"Offside," said the U.S. Supreme Court in 1984 when it settled a suit charging the National Collegiate Athletic Association with illegal monopoly control of college football telecasts. The suit was initiated in 1981 by the board of regents of the University of Oklahoma and the University of Georgia Athletic Association. The court judgment stated that the NCAA acted as a "classic cartel," using its power to control the number of TV appearances by a college team. The court viewed this as an "unreasonable restraint of trade" in violation of the Sherman Antitrust Act. By limiting the number of games that networks could televise, the court ruled, the NCAA exercised monopoly power to set artificially high prices for television rights.

The NCAA rules and contracts with major television networks had limited the telecasts of games of any one college team to six times in a 2-year period. Networks also were required to schedule appearances of at least 82 teams in each 2-year period. Individual colleges were prohibited from negotiating television rights on their own.

In its defense, the NCAA used the typical "relevant market" argument. NCAA lawyers held that it lacked market power to affect price because college football telecasts competed with many other forms of television entertainment. The Supreme Court threw a flag on the play and resoundingly rejected this defense.

---

*Craig M. Newmark, "The Breakup of Bell: Present Concerns and Future Prospects," *Tar Heel Economist*, Department of Economics and Business, Agricultural Extension Service, North Carolina State University, November 1984.

when monopoly power is exercised. However, the threat of entry of new firms and the threat of government regulation and antitrust action could decrease the incentive of firms to use that power.

What explains high market concentration of sales and high profits by a few firms in an industry? High concentration could be the result of economies of scale, and a firm could be making high profits because of lower average costs. Even if the firm charges a price that exceeds its average and marginal cost, its prices might be lower than those that would prevail under perfect competition.

A firm could also enjoy high profits and a substantial share of market sales because its products are better. If a firm can always produce at lower prices than competitors and offers products that consumers regard as superior, it will be rewarded with a high market share. This is the outcome of competition.

Also, we shouldn't jump to the conclusion that a firm that consistently earns high profits is exercising monopoly power in its industry. Remember, there's a difference between accounting profit and economic profit. Accounting profit includes normal profit, which is really a *cost* of production. The profits firms report to their stockholders and to tax authorities are their *accounting profits*. To determine a firm's economic profit, we need to deduct normal profit from accounting profit.

Normal profits can vary from industry to industry because the value of owner-supplied inputs, particularly capital, varies substantially. Firms in industries in which stockholders or owners of the firm supply significant amounts of their own funds to acquire new capital will have higher normal profit than other firms. For example, suppose firms in two industries earn $100,000 accounting profit. If one firm has $1 million of capital supplied by stockholders and the interest rate stockholders can earn in their next best investment is 10%, then normal profit will be $100,000. Economic profit for this firm will actually be zero, even though the firm reports a $100,000 accounting profit. On the other hand, if the second firm has capital worth $200,000 supplied by stockholders, then at a 10% interest rate its normal profit will be only $20,000. The second firm therefore earns $80,000 economic profit. An adjustment like this must always be made to see if a firm's revenues actually do exceed the opportunity costs of doing business.

As you can see, the dominance of one or a few firms in an industry earning high accounting profits isn't sufficient evidence to prove the exercise of monopoly power. The normal profit must be deducted from accounting profits to measure the actual economic profits enjoyed by owners of firms.

In looking at domestic concentration ratios (the percentage of shipments accounted for by the four or eight largest firms in an industry), we need to consider the extent of actual or potential foreign competition by gauging the share of the market represented by imports. Similarly, a low *national* concentration ratio doesn't necessarily imply that monopoly power is not exercised in local markets.

A situation in which monopoly power is exercised implies that a firm actually earns economic profits by charging its customers a price that exceeds average and marginal cost, and that entry of new firms into the market is barred. Under those circumstances customers do pay higher prices as a result of the exercise of monopoly power. Economic policy that ensures free entry into markets prevents this power from being exercised. If entry is possible, a firm can't earn economic profits over a prolonged period because new firms would eventually enter the market and increase supply to put downward pressure on price. High market shares don't prove that a firm is earning economic profit, nor do they necessarily imply that entry of new firms is barred. *The right question to ask when diagnosing exercise of monop-*

oly power is: Would a high market share survive an attempt to charge high prices and earn economic profits?[3]

Mergers

The decade of the 1980s has been characterized by numerous mergers and take-overs of large corporations. Mergers have always been a matter of concern in anti-trust policy because in many cases they result in increased market shares and re-duced competition. Without antitrust regulations, a group of firms could avoid charges of price fixing simply by merging into one firm. Mergers that can be shown to reduce competition can result in government action under the provisions of the Celler-Kefauver Act. All types of mergers are scrutinized by the Justice Department and the Federal Trade Commission.

Horizontal merger:
Occurs when competing sellers in the same market merge into a single firm.

Vertical merger:
A merger of a firm with its suppliers.

Conglomerate merger:
A merger of firms selling goods in unrelated markets.

A **horizontal merger** occurs when competing sellers in the same market merge into a single firm. The merger of two steel-producing firms, like the merger of Republic Steel and Jones & Laughlin Steel to form LTV Steel in 1984, is an example of a horizontal merger. A merger of a firm with its suppliers is called a **vertical merger,** while a merger of firms selling goods in unrelated markets is called a **conglomerate merger.** An example of a vertical merger is the purchase of an electronic component manufacturer by a manufacturer of computers. An example of a conglomerate merger is the purchase of a liquor company by a cigarette manufac-turer.

The trend toward mergers has been particularly strong in manufacturing indus-tries. In 1947 the 50 largest manufacturing firms in the United States accounted for only 12% of the total value of production by all manufacturing companies. By 1982 this figure had doubled to 24%. There have been as many mergers in the 20 years between 1960 and 1980 as in the 60 years between 1900 and 1960. Over 75% of the mergers in the period 1960 to 1980 have been conglomerate.

One concern about merger activity is that it concentrates economic power in the hands of a few corporations. For example, in the mid-1980s, 12% of U.S. corpora-tions accounted for 94% of total corporate assets. Many people express concern that this concentration of market power affects the ability of corporations to influence both prices and political outcomes.

Of course, mergers of two competing firms needn't necessarily cause prices to rise. Mergers can result in cost decreases and improved management policies that lower prices. Evaluating the impact of mergers on the ability to exercise monopoly power is therefore tricky. For example, if a market is contestable in the sense that new firms can easily enter, an attempt by a new firm created by a merger to increase prices is likely to attract new competition that would ultimately put downward pres-sure on price. Antitrust policy seeks to thwart mergers that decrease competition while not preventing mergers that reduce average costs of production through bet-ter management or economies of scale.

In general, the Department of Justice doesn't oppose mergers in industries where the market share of the largest firms is relatively low. It also doesn't prevent mergers of firms in markets where entry of new sellers is easy. Under the Reagan Adminis-tration, the Justice Department relaxed its opposition to large corporate mergers on the grounds that such mergers are necessary to meet foreign competition. In effect,

[3]Franklin M. Fisher, "Diagnosing Monopoly," *Quarterly Review of Economics and Business,* 20, Summer 1979, pp. 7-33.

Economic Thinkers

JOHN KENNETH GALBRAITH

The man who can claim the title of most literate and most widely read economist can also claim the title of most critical. In an age when most economists are focusing on increasingly narrower aspects of the field, John Kenneth Galbraith takes on the entire range of economic and social problems facing so-

ciety, making himself one of the leading social critics of American life.

The epitome of the twentieth century liberal, Galbraith attacks contemporary social and economic values and the institutions that enforce them. In *The Affluent Society* he states that, rather than responding to consumer demands, modern corporations create consumer tastes and preferences through advertising. In *The New Industrial State* he declares that large corporations are run not by principles of profit maximization but rather through elaborate planning mechanisms that insulate the companies from market pressures.

In *Economics and the Public Policy* and other works, Galbraith asserts that, by focusing on the interaction of supply and demand in markets, contemporary economic theory ignores the role of power in the economy: power wielded not only by large corporations but also by strong labor unions and government bureaucracies. It is Galbraith's belief

that, far from being controlled by the market, corporations in fact control the market.

Because of this and what he considers to be other misconceptions on the part of conventional economists, Galbraith believes they have adopted policy positions that are inconsistent with reality.

A prominent figure in the Democratic Party at one time and a leading voice against the Vietnam war, Galbraith relishes political involvement. He has been the U.S. ambassador to India, has received the Medal of Freedom, and has been a frequent speaker before congressional committees.

Galbraith received his Ph.D. in agricultural economics from the University of California at Berkeley in 1936. During the 1940s he worked for the U.S. government and later taught at Harvard for more than 25 years. The author of best-selling books, he is the only economist who is a fellow in literature of the National Institute of Arts and Letters.

---

this argument is based on the presumption that the contestability of the market through foreign competition is great enough to offset reduced domestic competition. It's also based on the belief that in many cases mergers result in cost and productivity advantages that help reduce prices and make U.S. industry more competitive in world markets. This policy was in part responsible for the jump in corporate acquisitions in the 1980s.

Possessing considerably less faith in the unfettered operation of markets is controversial economist John Kenneth Galbraith (see Economics Thinkers box).

Concept Check

1   What are the goals of antitrust policy in the United States? List the major antitrust laws on which U.S. policy toward business competition is based.

2   What is the "rule of reason"?

3   If you were a judge in an antitrust case, how would you determine the "relevant market" for a product a defendant was charged with illegally monopolizing? Does a high market share for a firm in an industry always imply that the firm is exercising monopoly power?

Regulation of Pricing: The Case of Natural Monopoly

Bigness isn't all bad. Antitrust policy recognizes that a merger of firms into one large supplier can allow technological and cost advantages that wouldn't be possible if the industry were composed of many competing sellers. In many cases government allows pure monopolies to operate but regulates their pricing.

We first discussed the concept of natural monopoly in Chapter 13. You'll recall that a *natural monopoly* occurs when a firm can supply the entire market demand for a product at lower average cost than would be possible if two or more smaller firms supplied the market. Natural monopolies can prevail for the local provision of electric power, gas, and telephone service. The industries that provide these services are sometimes called *public utilities*.

Changes in technology can change cost conditions. For example, long-distance telephone service was once regarded as a natural monopoly but is no longer considered so because of changes in technology. Satellite communication systems and other technological advances have made it possible for a number of firms to compete for long-distance business. The market is no longer dominated by one large seller that has the advantage of lower average costs.

Cost Curves and the Profit-Maximizing Output for a Natural Monopoly

The cost curves for a natural monopoly firm are shown in Box 1. Assume that in the absence of any government intervention in the market, the monopoly firm will try to set a price that allows it to earn maximum profit. Given the demand for its product, the profit-maximizing monopoly firm produces the output for which marginal revenue equals marginal cost. The profit-maximizing monopoly output is Q_M, and the monopoly firm selects a price of P_M to induce its customers to buy that amount annually. For example, if the natural monopoly firm is a power company, it will select a price per kilowatt hour that induces its customers to purchase Q_M kilowatt hours of electricity per month.

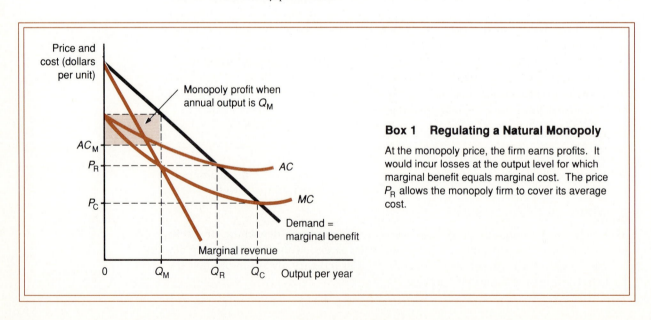

Box 1   Regulating a Natural Monopoly

At the monopoly price, the firm earns profits. It would incur losses at the output level for which marginal benefit equals marginal cost. The price P_R allows the monopoly firm to cover its average cost.

The monopoly firm earns economic profits equal to the shaded area in Box 1. Notice that the firm could lower average costs of production further by producing beyond Q_M. Its objective, however, is to maximize profits, not continually reduce average costs. You should also note that allocative efficiency isn't attained when the monopoly sets its price so as to maximize profits. Remember that efficiency requires that output be made available up to the point at which its marginal benefit just equals its marginal cost. When the monopolist charges price P_M, consumers buy the good until their marginal benefit just equals P_M. However, the marginal cost of the corresponding quantity demanded, Q_M, is less than P_M. You can see this by following the dotted line running from Q_M to the marginal cost curve. The output is inefficient because the price the monopolist sets to maximize profits exceeds the marginal cost of making that output available.

Marginal-Cost Pricing to Achieve Efficiency: A Policy Dilemma

Natural monopolies and government-franchised monopoly firms are commonly subject to the authority of government commissions that regulate prices for the services of monopoly suppliers in their jurisdiction. In determining what price they allow the monopolist to charge for its product, commissions usually consider the input prices that monopoly firms pay and the interests of consumers.

Suppose government intervenes to get the monopoly firm to produce the efficient output. This will require an increase in output until the marginal cost and marginal benefit of the good to consumers fall to the point at which the two are equal. This means monthly output would have to increase to Q_C, for which the demand curve just intersects the marginal cost curve. To induce consumers to buy the corresponding quantity labeled Q_C on the graph, the firm would have to charge price P_C. If government intervened to require the monopolist to set a price of P_C, efficiency would be attained. This is because at that price the quantity sold would be Q_C, for which both the marginal cost and the marginal benefit would also be P_C. Remember that points on the demand curve reflect the marginal benefit, or the maximum price buyers will pay for available quantities. Government intervention in the market to help attain efficiency therefore requires that price be controlled to equal the marginal cost of output at the point at which the marginal benefit of the good has declined to equal its marginal cost.

The policy of marginal-cost pricing to achieve efficiency, however, runs into a snag when a natural monopoly produces the good. At Q_C, average cost exceeds marginal cost. Setting price equal to marginal cost therefore results in losses for the seller. If a natural monopoly firm were forced to charge a price equal to its marginal cost, it would need a government subsidy to remain in business. The government could simply allocate a certain amount of revenue to cover the monopolist's losses. Alternatively, the government could nationalize the monopoly, as is done quite often, and absorb the loss itself.

It also would be unrealistic to expect the efficient output to emerge if the industry were perfectly competitive. This is because perfect competition requires many competing sellers. No single small firm under perfect competition would be able to enjoy economies of scale in such a competitive market. Thus it would be impossible for prices to fall to the marginal cost level for which the market demand curve intersected the marginal cost curve of the single monopoly producer. Regulators seeking to achieve efficiency in the market therefore know that breaking up the monopoly into smaller firms isn't the solution because average cost and marginal cost of production would rise as a result. They also know the monopoly firm wouldn't cover its opportunity cost and thus wouldn't voluntarily serve the market if it were forced to charge a price low enough to induce consumers to buy the efficient quantity. What should the regulators do to solve the problem?

The Solution: Average-Cost Pricing

Regulatory commissions rarely attempt to make public utilities establish a price that equals both the marginal cost and marginal benefit of the service. Commissions generally try to let the firm at least cover its accounting costs and the opportunity costs of capital invested in the firm.

Suppose the commission approves a price that allows the owners of the natural monopoly to just cover their opportunity costs. The graph in Box 1 shows that the price that allows zero economic profits is P_R. This price corresponds to the point where the demand curve intersects the average cost curve. When the price is P_R, the quantity demanded is Q_R. The price that is approved by the rate commission is P_R, which equals the average cost corresponding to the quantity Q_R. At this price economic profits are zero because the profit per unit is zero. However, price exceeds marginal cost. But any price lower than P_R will result in economic losses for the natural monopoly. P_R *is therefore the minimum price that will allow the monopoly firm to operate privately without subsidy.* Consumers are better off than they would be if there were more competition in the industry because average costs are lower. However, they aren't as well off as they would be if price were set lower until it fell to equal marginal cost and marginal benefit at the output Q_C.

Note that the firm's owners would be better off if they could charge P_M, corresponding to the output where marginal revenue equals marginal cost. If the commission selects this price, the owners of the monopoly can earn maximum economic profits. Similarly, a price above P_R and below P_M will permit the firm's owners to enjoy more than the normal profit.

Average-cost pricing seeks to allow the owners of the monopoly to earn a "fair rate of return" just equal to the normal profit. Remember that the normal profit is a cost of production equal to the value of owner-supplied inputs. Because most large natural monopolies, such as telephone and electric power companies, are corporations, the main owner-supplied input is capital. To figure the fair rate of return, regulators measure the value of the firm's capital. For example, suppose an electric company has $100 million of capital. Suppose stockholders in the corporation on average could earn 10% on the funds in their next best investment. The opportunity cost of holding on to their share of capital in the monopoly is 10% of $100 million, which is $10 million per year. The rate commission would add all the accounting costs for the corporation and then include the $10 million fair return before computing the average cost of the output.

Government Regulation of Natural Monopolies in Practice

Implementing a policy that allows natural monopoly firms to just cover their costs is easier said than done. Regulators don't have neat graphs like the one in Box 1 with which to calculate average cost, Q_R, and P_R. Accurately determining average costs of production at the level of output for which price equals average cost is a difficult problem. Another area of serious dispute concerns the incentives that regulators establish for the regulated firms. Regulation of electric rates in recent years

Principles in Practice

Why Do Electric Companies Want You to Use *Less* Electricity?

Believe it or not, back in the 1960s electric utility companies throughout the country were actually encouraging their customers to consume *more* electricity. Many local companies offered free installation of power lines to an "all-electric" home that heated and powered all its appliances with electricity. Going a step further, some power companies advertised electrical appliances and urged customers to buy the latest kilowatt-consuming contraptions. In these halcyon days, power was not only plentiful but delightfully cheap.

Expecting sharp increases in demand for electricity in the 1970s and 1980s, many companies invested heavily in nuclear power plants. They expected to sell lots and lots of electricity to an ever more affluent population. This optimistic scenario turned out to be considerably less cheery.

In the projections they made in the 1960s, the power companies assumed electricity would remain cheap and expansion of capacity in the industry would lower average costs still further. However, steep hikes in the prices of oil and coal in the 1970s, accompanied by safety woes and new regulations that significantly increased the costs of building nuclear power plants, markedly raised the average cost of electricity. Consumers responded by conserving power. Houses were built to be energy efficient. Having constructed more capacity than they could use, many power companies found themselves saddled with expensive nuclear plants that generated more electricity than was demanded. The companies petitioned their regulatory commissions for rate increases to cover the higher-than-expected capital costs of their nuclear plants. The resulting rate hikes aggravated the problem by further decreasing the quantity of electricity demanded.

Although nuclear power plants have high fixed costs because of extensive capital requirements, the marginal cost of generating electricity in such plants is quite low. In a typical nuclear plant, electricity can be generated at a cost of less than 1¢ per kilowatt hour. In some of the older non-nuclear plants, electricity costs over 12¢ per kilowatt hour! When demand increases beyond the capacity of a nuclear plant, most companies have computerized controls that automatically turn on the more expensive non-nuclear sources of power. Naturally, profits go down when the price per kilowatt hour is fixed by a regulatory commission and the company shifts to a higher-cost source. This means that for a typical company with at least one nuclear power plant, the marginal cost of electricity can rise quite sharply with peak demand as older plants are put into operation to meet the demand.

Many power companies believe the solution to this problem is demand management. Many companies now offer low-interest loans to households installing storm windows and other energy-saving devices. Some firms offer a discount to homes that are fully insulated. Advertisements by electric companies in the 1980s are light years removed from the consumption-boosting messages of the 1960s. Today's ads stress one theme—conservation—and consumers are listening.

Power companies are also petitioning regulatory commissions to allow "peak load" pricing that would increase the price per kilowatt hour as marginal costs increase. Some companies use a time-of-use policy that gives customers a discount on electricity used during certain hours of the day when demand is usually slack.

Despite these changes in policy, many electric power companies are still in financial difficulty because of past investment decisions. Should the regulatory commissions make customers pay higher prices to allow a fair rate of return to investors on investments that didn't pan out as expected? Or should the stockholders of the electric companies take the loss? If this route is chosen, it may be more difficult for power companies to raise funds for future expansion and maintenance through issuance of corporate stock. On the other hand, to what extent can consumers be forced to pay for decisions in which they had no voice?

---

provides a good example of these controversies. Critics of the regulatory process have argued that consumers rather than stockholders are being forced to pay for poor management decisions that resulted in higher average costs of production. The alleged management blunders include overinvestment in nuclear power plants and overexpansion of facilities.

By increasing the amount of capital used, the monopoly can increase the dollar amount of normal profits. Some economists have argued that this results in more capital-intensive production techniques relative to those that would prevail in the absence of regulation. Choice of relatively inefficient capital-intensive production methods results in average costs that are higher than would otherwise prevail.[4]

[4]Harvey Averch and Leland L. Johnson, "The Behavior of the Firm Under Regulatory Constraint," *American Economic Review,* 52, December 1961, pp. 1053-1069.

The average-cost pricing rule provides no incentives for utilities to minimize their cost of production. They face no competitors, and any increase in cost resulting from blunders won't affect the rate of profit they earn on their investment as long as the commission sets a price that allows them a normal profit. Political opposition to average-cost pricing in recent years has attempted to shift at least part of the burden of mismanagement from consumers to stockholders of the regulated firms. Managers counter this argument by pointing out that if they can't make a normal profit, they'll have difficulty attracting additional investors. They claim that service quality will decline or rates will increase still more to cover interest costs as firms are forced to borrow because they find few buyers for their stock.

Other critics of the policies of regulatory commissions argue that political interests favorable to the natural monopoly tend to gain control of the commissions. When this is the case, the regulated prices set by the commissions often allow the natural monopoly to come close to enjoying the price it would set to maximize its profits.

Concept Check

1   How would you determine whether a firm is a natural monopoly?

2   Explain why a natural monopoly firm wouldn't be able to cover its costs if it were told to increase output until price fell enough to equal marginal cost of production.

3   What are the advantages and disadvantages of the average-cost pricing method of regulating a natural monopoly?

Regulating Pricing and Entry in Markets Served by Competing Sellers

In the United States, regulation of pricing isn't confined to markets in which there's a single seller. In many cases, particularly for transportation industries, in which there are a number of competing sellers, the federal government has traditionally controlled both pricing and entry and exit of sellers into markets. For example, airlines in the past required government approval to enter markets for service between two airports. Railroads have to obtain government permission to abandon rail services and lines. Many state governments regulate the rates set by insurance and financial firms.

Regulation of pricing and entry in markets in which there's more than a single seller has been supported as a means of guaranteeing at least minimum levels of service to some routes or clients and of preventing the establishment of monopoly power. In recent years critics of the regulatory process have argued that in fact regulation of transportation industries has contributed to monopoly power and high prices. This has led to political support for deregulation of certain industries, most prominent of which may be air travel.

The Regulatory Commissions

Rate regulation in the United States began in 1887 with the establishment of the Interstate Commerce Commission to regulate railroad rates. The ICC currently regulates not only railroad rates but also rates charged by other freight shipping firms, including barges, pipelines, and some types of trucking. The Civil Aeronautics Board, which was established in 1938 to regulate airline fares and entry into air routes, was abolished in 1984 when most airline regulation was eliminated. The Securities and Exchange Commission regulates brokerages and other aspects of the sale of stocks. Other regulatory commissions organized in the 1930s include the Federal Power Commission, the Federal Communications Commission, and the Federal Maritime Commission.

The regulatory commissions have pursued policies that tended to keep prices high and stable and to limit entry of new firms. The goal in part was to ensure stable supplies or service and to control price fluctuations in certain markets by assuring sellers that they would receive at least a *minimum* price for their services. The policies of the rate commissions have been criticized for being too restrictive and for keeping prices higher than they would be if more competition were allowed. In some cases airlines were forced to serve unprofitable routes but in return were given protection against competition on profitable routes. The result was lower fares and more service on some routes but higher fares on others than would prevail without regulation.

Regulatory agencies also sought to stabilize rates to prevent sharp shifts that might result in business failure and erratic service to the market. For example, fluctuations in railroad rates that cause abandonment of lines could result in high costs in the future to restart service. Regulatory agencies have sought to allow railroads to cover their marginal cost of operation.

Deregulation: Domestic Air Travel Markets

One way to look at the actual effects of rate regulation in industries in which natural monopoly doesn't prevail is to examine what happens when regulation is eliminated. In recent years regulation has been eased or eliminated in the trucking, railroad, and telecommunications industries. The industry in which deregulation has been most extensive is commercial aviation, where virtually all fare, entry, and exit regulations have been eliminated.

The Airline Deregulation Act of 1978 reduced government-established barriers to entry into air travel markets and allowed airlines complete autonomy in pricing their services. Before deregulation the Civil Aeronautics Board (CAB) was the government agency that controlled entry into air travel routes and regulated airfares. Under the 1978 deregulation legislation, the CAB lost its authority over domestic routes after 1981. On January 1, 1983, the CAB lost its authority over airline pricing, mergers, and acquisitions. Finally, at the end of 1984, the CAB itself ceased to exist! The era of airline regulation thus came to a complete end in 1985. The result of airline deregulation since 1978 has been a complete restructuring of the industry. There's been a change in the way airlines do business that has affected all airline travelers through changes in fares, service quality, and stability within the industry.

Deregulation clearly has broadened the market for air travel. More people than ever are flying at discount fares that have made air travel competitive with travel by bus and car. Air traffic is up sharply, and there often are long delays at many key airports. The quality of service at airports and by the airlines, according to many seasoned travelers, has seriously deteriorated. It's clear that there are both costs and benefits associated with airline deregulation.

Between 1976 and 1983 the number of certified air carriers of both freight and passengers nearly tripled.[5] Most existing carriers expanded their route system using a "hub-spoke" technique. This schedules a large number of flights into key airports at certain periods of a day during which passengers change planes for turnaround departures. The new system resulted in expanded competition in one-stop markets for air travel. More passengers traveled relatively long distances on a single airline, making one plane change along the way without changing air terminals. Much of the increased competition from deregulation appears to have been in these one-stop markets as opposed to the nonstop markets.[6]

It does appear that deregulation has increased entry into (and exit from) air travel markets and, at least for long-haul service, has increased competition. The number of passengers traveling increased from 292 million in 1980 to an estimated 392 million in 1986. The number of flights increased from 14.7 million in 1980 to an estimated 19.2 million in 1986.

The impact of deregulation on air fares on average has been favorable to consumers. From 1976 to 1982, the average fare per mile, adjusted for inflation, fell 8.5%. However, deregulation ushered in a new era of complexity in air fares. As you may have noticed, there are now a myriad of discount fares. Travel agents need complex computer programs to keep up with the rapidly changing fares, advance booking requirements, and penalties. Nonetheless, a number of clear trends have emerged in air fares. Much of the decline in air fares has occurred in long-haul trips and trips between major urban centers. The number of passengers using discount fares, which usually have advance purchase and other restrictions, has skyrocketed. Between 1976 and 1983, discount coach fares fell by about 20% on major long-haul routes. Discount fares on major short-haul routes fell by over 30% during the same period. In the major markets, the number of people paying discount fares increased from about 25% of all passengers in the 1970s to 75% of all passengers in the early 1980s. The fare decreases came in a period of sharply increasing fuel costs for airlines.

The benefits of deregulation to consumers have thus been lower fares, increased availability of discount fares, and more service on certain routes. What about the costs? There are clear indications that the quality of service has declined—something you may have noticed even if you're not a frequent flier. There's more congestion in both airports and airplanes since deregulation. Airlines have modified planes used for long-haul routes to cram in more passengers. The average percentage of seats occupied per flight has also increased since deregulation. On average, the number of passengers per plane has increased by 25%.[7] However, the number of passengers per plane on short-haul flights has declined. Airlines have shifted to smaller aircraft on these routes. The increased congestion on long-haul flights and the shift to smaller aircraft on short-haul flights have reduced comfort for many passengers. Another indication that the quality of air service has declined can be seen in the fact that between 1976 and 1982 airline spending per passenger mile fell by 14% after adjustment for inflation.[8] Many passengers—perhaps you're one of them—complain that the quality of food in flight has deteriorated. There were increased complaints in 1986 of instances of overbooking, dirty cabins, long runway delays, and poor treatment by airline attendants.

It's clear that deregulation has greatly benefited the vacation traveler and low-

[5]Thomas G. Moore, "U.S. Airline Deregulation: Its Effects on Passengers, Capital, and Labor," *Journal of Law & Economics,* 29, April 1986, pp. 1-28.
[6]Moore, pp. 7-8.
[7]Moore, pp. 11-12.
[8]Moore, p. 13.

income people who traditionally used other modes of transport. In July of 1986, 90% of all passengers were flying at discount fares.[9] The benefits have been greater on long-haul trips compared to short-haul trips. On average, fares for short trips and trips from small towns have increased. A major effect of deregulation has been to change the clientele of the airlines. Before deregulation, U.S. airlines primarily served business and middle-income travelers. Today airlines serve more moderate-income people and vacation travelers.

One post-deregulation sour note is the large number of airline failures and mergers in recent years. This has led some economists to predict that deregulation will ultimately decrease competition on some routes.[10] For example, TWA, which dominates travel from its St. Louis hub, accounted for nearly 90% of the total passengers handled out of the St. Louis airport in 1987. Airport capacity is strained in many areas, as is air traffic control capability. This makes it more difficult for airlines to obtain landing rights and could serve as a barrier to entry. It's clear that thus far the chief benefit of deregulation has been lower fares. The lower fares must be balanced against alleged decreases in the quality of service and increased monopoly power that could lead to higher prices in the future.

Government Regulation: Pro and Con

Government regulation of pricing, conditions of entry, business practices, and mergers can produce net gains when the regulations prevent the exercise of monopoly power. However, where regulation exists, politics as well as the profit motive becomes an important influence on prices in markets. Firms exercising monopoly power are likely to defend their right to do so because they fear losing economic profits. The outcome that emerges under regulation depends on political interaction among various special-interest groups.

The failures of markets to achieve allocative efficiency aren't always easily corrected by government policies, as the case of airline deregulation shows. Even the enforcement of antitrust laws is influenced by political considerations, as could be seen in the anti-interventionist policies of the Reagan Administration.

In evaluating existing and proposed government regulation of markets, we must look at the goals of the policies and then evaluate the regulatory process to determine whether those goals are likely to be achieved given the political and economic realities.

Summary

1. Antitrust statutes are laws that seek to prevent unfair business practices that give rise to monopoly power. The antitrust laws are enforced by the U.S. Department of Justice.
2. The first antitrust laws were enacted in the United States to control certain practices engaged in by large business organizations to put rivals out of business and thus establish a monopoly.
3. Among the business practices outlawed in the United States are collusion to fix

[9]"Frequent Flyers Finding the Skies Less Friendly," *The News and Observer,* Raleigh, N.C., Sunday, September 28, 1986, p. 7D.
[10]See Peter Capelli, "Settling Inexorably into an Oligopoly." *The New York Times,* Sunday, September 7, 1986, p. 2F.

prices by firms selling in a market, price discrimination to lessen competition, tying contracts that prevent a purchaser from using the products of a competing supplier, and mergers for the purpose of lessening competition.

4. The "rule of reason" holds that acts beyond normal business practice that unduly restrain competition can be used as evidence in court to infer intent to illegally monopolize an industry.

5. One problem in proving that a firm actually has monopoly power is defining the relevant market. A firm actually monopolizes the supply of an item only if it's the dominant supplier in the market. Proving that a firm is the dominant supplier involves showing that it has the dominant share of sales in a market. The relevant market can be a matter for debate because firms often contend that their products are substitutes for a broad range of products.

6. High concentration of market sales by one or a few firms is not sufficient to prove the exercise of monopoly power. A firm actually exercising monopoly power is charging high prices that allow it to earn economic profits that could be eliminated through increased rivalry. It's possible that a firm with high market share is keeping prices close to its average and marginal costs but that its costs are lower than those a rival would incur.

7. Mergers can reduce competition in a market. Horizontal mergers are those of competing sellers in a market into a single firm. In recent years over 75% of mergers have been of the conglomerate type between firms selling goods in unrelated markets. Vertical mergers are those of firms with their suppliers.

8. A natural monopoly is a firm that can supply the entire market demand for a product at lower average cost than would be possible if two or more smaller firms supplied the market. The average cost of production for a natural monopoly tends to fall as more output is produced.

9. A natural monopoly won't be able to cover its average cost of production if it produces an output large enough to result in a market price that falls to equal its marginal cost of production. This is because when average cost is declining, it exceeds marginal cost.

10. Firms that are franchised to serve the entire market for a good such as electric power or natural gas are commonly regulated by government commissions. These commissions generally seek to control pricing to allow the monopoly supplier to cover its accounting costs and earn a "fair rate of return" equal to the opportunity cost of capital invested in the firm. In practice, average-cost pricing policies might provide little incentive for firms to control costs and could provide incentives to overinvest in capital inputs.

11. Government regulation of pricing and entry in markets served by a number of sellers has been used as a means of guaranteeing minimum levels of service and of preventing the exercise of monopoly power. However, this type of regulation often results in higher prices because of the limits it places on entry into markets. In recent years, dissatisfaction with this type of regulation has led to deregulation of certain industries.

12. Deregulation of the airline industry in the United States has broadened the market for air travel through increased competition and discount fares. Deregulation has resulted in a sharp increase in air traffic. While the fares on long-haul trips on average have declined substantially, average fares on short trips and trips between small towns have increased since deregulation went into effect in 1978.

Key Terms and Concepts

Antitrust statutes   Vertical merger

Rule of reason   Conglomerate merger

Horizontal merger

Problems and Applications

1. Do the antitrust statutes in the United States actually outlaw monopoly? How does the existence of antitrust statutes affect the incentive firms have to exercise monopoly power? Explain why indiscriminate antitrust suits can actually cause more harm than good.

2. Suppose an organization of real estate agents orders all real estate firms to charge a 6% commission on sales. Firms that refuse aren't permitted to use the services provided by the organization that make it easier to sell homes. In addition, firms that charge less than a 6% commission are considered to be engaging in "unethical behavior" and aren't allowed to belong to the organization. How would this arrangement be viewed by the U.S. Department of Justice?

3. On a route between Detroit and Providence, an airline deliberately sets fares below a level that permits it to cover its costs. As a result of this pricing policy, a rival airline goes out of business. After the rival airline leaves the market, the remaining airline jacks up its fares. Is this firm guilty of an antitrust violation?

4. Defenders of IBM in an antitrust case argued that the government's claim of the firm's high market concentration was a result of improper definition of the product group in which IBM products compete. How would you define the market for computer products?

5. A cigarette company merges with a company producing breakfast cereals. Is this type of merger likely to increase monopoly power in either of the markets served by the two firms?

6. How can a merger of two steel firms lead to lower prices? What guidelines are used by the U.S. Department of Justice in approving mergers?

7. Suppose the average cost of producing electric power declines continually as more is made available to buyers. If a power company can be induced to charge a price of 2¢ per kilowatt hour, the quantity demanded would be great enough to allow a reduction in marginal cost to 2¢. Use a graph to show that the electric company wouldn't cover its opportunity cost at that price.

8. An electric power company invests in a new nuclear power plant. This increases the amount of capital owned by the company. Explain why firms have an incentive to build capital-intensive means of production under average-cost pricing regulation. Show how an increase in average cost is likely to result in a decrease in the quantity demanded of electricity under an average-cost regulatory policy.

9. Explain why deregulation of the airline industry resulted in an increase in fares on some routes but a decrease in fares on other routes.

10. Why have regulatory commissions in the past sought to limit entry into markets? How have the commissions traded off low prices for stable prices? Has deregulation of the airline industry resulted in stable prices and predictable service on all routes?

Suggested Readings

William S. Comanor, "The Political Economy of the Pharmaceutical Industry," *Journal of Economic Literature,* 24, 3, September 1986, pp. 1178-1217. This is a thorough study of issues and policies in an industry often characterized as exercising monopoly power. The analysis illustrates the tools economists use to evaluate markets for the purpose of diagnosing the exercise of monopoly power.

Franklin M. Fisher, "Diagnosing Monopoly," *Quarterly Review of Economics and Business,* 19, 2, Summer 1979, pp. 7-33. This article offers an analysis of traditional means of measuring monopoly power and their shortcomings.

Thomas G. Moore, "U.S. Airline Deregulation: Its Effects on Passengers, Capital, and Labor," *Journal of Law and Economics,* 29, April 1986, pp. 1-28. This is a readable account of the impact of deregulation on a major industry.

Sidney Saltzman and Richard E. Schuler, eds., *The Future of Electrical Energy,* Westport, Conn.: Praeger, 1986. This is a collection of essays on the electric utility industry that discuss costs of production, nuclear power, and other issues affecting the regulation of firms generating electricity in the United States.

F.M. Scherer, *Industrial Market Structure and Economic Performance,* 2nd ed., Boston: Houghton Mifflin, 1980. This is a textbook that analyzes industrial market structure, public policy, and court action to control the exercise of monopoly power.

A Forward Look

The role of government in markets is much broader than merely regulating competition. In the following chapter we look at the key causes of market failure to achieve efficiency and examine the role of government in correcting for the inadequacies of the price system.

Market Failure and the Role of Government in Allocating Resources

How do you feel about government involvement in the economy? For most of us, this is a very personal and subjective issue—and while we may oppose the *idea* of government intervention in markets, we don't usually object to such intervention when it works to our own benefit.

Because we live in a less than perfect world, the fact is that markets often fail to allocate resources efficiently even when there's adequate competition among sellers. Polluted air and water, congestion in cities, inadequate provision of cultural and educational services, business fluctuations, and the persistence of poverty are problems we face even when markets are free and competitive. The pursuit of private gains through market exchange of goods inevitably results in some unfortunate side effects, such as environmental damage and neglect of social problems. Despite the awesome productive potential of the modern market economy, there are many socially useful services that can't be profitably provided through markets. Both business firms and consumers often are blind to the side effects of their dealings in markets. We typically look to government to help us cope with the social and environmental problems of the modern economy.

You learned in Chapter 6 that *market failure* exists when exchange between buyers and sellers in unregulated markets doesn't result in an efficient outcome. When markets fail to achieve efficiency, government intervention in the economy can provide us additional net benefits by influencing resource allocation in ways that affect the kinds and quantities of goods and services available. In Chapter 15 we saw how government intervenes in markets to control the exercise of monopoly power. In this chapter we concentrate on causes of market failure in competitive markets. We'll focus on government's attempts to correct the consequences of market failure. In a sense, economics and politics are inextricably intertwined: We look to both government and the marketplace as a means of satisfying our desires for goods and services.

Concept Preview

After reading this chapter, you should be able to:

1 Explain the concept of an externality and show how externalities prevent free and competitive markets from allocating resources efficiently.
2 Describe the causes of externalities and show how government can help achieve efficiency by intervening in markets when externalities exist.
3 Explain the concept of a public good and show how provision of public goods by government can result in net gains to consumers.
4 Describe and evaluate social regulation by government to correct for market failure.

Externalities: A Common Cause of Market Failure

The major causes of market failure to achieve efficiency under perfect competition are discrepancies between the marginal benefits and costs on which private decisions are based and the actual marginal *social* benefits and costs. When these discrepancies exist, market prices don't accurately reflect marginal social benefits and marginal social costs. For example, firms often dispose of their wastes in the air or water without paying for the damage that these wastes ultimately cause by polluting the environment. In such a case the marginal cost of production will fall short of the actual marginal social cost. Similarly, as consumers we don't always consider the fact that when we buy a certain item, that item might provide benefits to others. For example, if you're a tenant in a large apartment building who's considering buying a smoke detection system for your apartment, you don't consider the benefit this provides to your neighbors by reducing the probability of spread of fire. You base your decision on your own marginal benefit rather than the marginal social benefit, including the benefit received by your neighbors.

You'll recall from Chapter 6 that *externalities* are costs or benefits of market transactions that aren't reflected in prices. Externalities represent the impact of market transactions on third parties who don't participate as buyers and sellers in a market. When externalities are present, important information pertaining to the value of resources exchanged is *external* to the market price.

Negative externality:
A cost associated with the use of resources that is not reflected in prices. Also called *external cost.*

A **negative externality,** sometimes called an *external cost,* is a cost associated with the use of resources that is not reflected in prices. A competitive firm whose manufacturing operations pollute the environment, causing damage to recreational and other environmental resources, is causing a negative externality. These damages could impair people's health by decreasing the quality of the air they breathe or the water they drink. The marginal cost on which the owners of the firm base their production decisions doesn't include the **marginal external cost** (MEC), the extra cost imposed on third parties as a result of the firm's operations. In the case of

Marginal external cost:
The extra cost imposed on third parties when a negative externality is present.

---

pollution, the marginal external cost is the extra damage to the environment for which the producer isn't charged when production is increased. When a negative externality exists, to achieve efficiency the marginal costs of production must be adjusted upward to include the marginal external cost. For example, the actual marginal social cost for the manufacturing firm causing pollution damage will be the firm's marginal cost *plus* the marginal external cost of its operations over a given period. A negative externality can result from consumption as well as production. For example, you pollute the air when you drive your car. If you are not charged for the damage you do, you are responsible for a negative externality.

A **positive externality,** also called an *external benefit,* is a benefit associated with the use of resources that is not reflected in prices. Third parties to market transactions, other than buyers and sellers, benefit when a positive externality exists. Fire prevention is an activity that generates positive externalities. If you lived in an apartment building or a group of attached condominiums, you'd be willing to contribute to fireproofing efforts by your neighbors. Similarly, good sanitation practices benefit people other than the buyers and sellers of these services by reducing the risk of spread of disease.

When a positive externality is present, the marginal benefit on which we as consumers base our decisions falls short of the marginal social benefit. The **marginal external benefit** (MEB), that accruing to people other than consumers, must be added to the marginal benefit to obtain the actual marginal social benefit.

Positive externality:
A benefit associated with the use of resources that is not reflected in prices. Also called *external benefit.*

Marginal external benefit:
The extra benefit that accrues to third parties when a positive externality is present.

How Negative Externalities Prevent Exchange in Competitive Markets from Achieving Efficiency

The graph in Box 1 shows how a negative externality prevents the attainment of efficiency in a competitive market. The demand and supply curves reflect the marginal benefit and marginal cost of the product sold. Assume that the marginal benefit accurately measures the marginal social benefit. This demand curve therefore is the marginal social benefit curve. However, because of the negative externality, the marginal cost curve of sellers doesn't fully reflect the marginal social cost of making the good available.

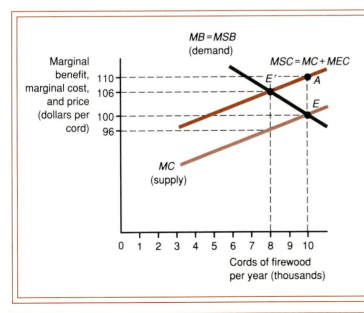

Box 1   How a Negative Externality Prevents Efficiency from Being Attained in Competitive Markets

The competitive market equilibrium corresponds to point E. At the corresponding output of 10,000 cords per year, more than the efficient amount is sold because the marginal social cost of the output, $MSC = MC + MEC$, exceeds its marginal social benefit. The efficient output corresponds to point E', at which $MSB = MSC$.

In Box 1 the item whose use results in the negative externality is firewood and the negative externality is $10 per year per cord (a cord is 128 cubic feet of firewood). This means that each cord of firewood burned results in $10 worth of damage to people other than those who buy or sell the wood. The damage could be in the form of impaired health (such as respiratory disease) or increased cleaning expenses for people whose property is damaged by wood smoke. Assume that firewood is sold in a perfectly competitive market and the current equilibrium amount sold per year in a city is 10,000 cords at an equilibrium price of $100 per cord. This equilibrium corresponds to point E in Box 1. At point E, the demand curve, which is the marginal social benefit curve, intersects the supply curve, which is the marginal cost curve of sellers. The marginal external cost associated with each cord of firewood is always $10 per year.

The market equilibrium output is 10,000 cords per year. At that output follow the dashed line up to point A on the marginal social cost curve. Now note, by following the dashed lines from points A and E to the vertical axis, that at the equilibrium output the marginal social cost of firewood exceeds its marginal social benefit. Marginal social cost is $110 per cord when 10,000 cords are produced per year. We obtain the marginal social cost of firewood simply by adding the $10 marginal external cost to the marginal cost of sellers at any output. Marginal social benefit is only $100 per cord when 10,000 cords are consumed.

The efficient output corresponds to point E', at which the marginal social benefit and marginal social cost curves intersect. At that point annual output is only 8,000 cords, and the market price would be $106 per cord. Because of the negative externality, *more* than the efficient output results from the market sale of the good.

The results of this example can be generalized: *When a negative externality exists, competitive market equilibrium results in more than the efficient output and a market price that falls short of the actual marginal social cost of the product.* Under such circumstances an excessive amount of resources is allocated to produce the good whose sale results in the negative externality.

How Positive Externalities Prevent Efficiency in Competitive Markets

Positive externalities also prevent efficient outcomes from emerging in competitive markets. Suppose a positive externality is associated with college enrollment. This means that third parties other than college students and owners of educational institutions gain when students enroll in college. For example, an increase in the general level of education might cause the crime and accident rates to fall, which would benefit everyone.

Assume that college education is supplied by a competitive higher education industry. Independent colleges and universities provide a standardized curriculum and instruction. The graph in Box 2 shows the competitive equilibrium in the market for college education. The horizontal axis measures the number of full-time students enrolled per year. Currently 5 million students are enrolled and the equilibrium annual tuition is $2,500. The supply curve in Box 2 reflects the marginal cost incurred by sellers in producing college instruction. Assume that this accurately measures the marginal social cost. The demand curve for college instruction reflects the marginal benefit received by students. However, the marginal benefit falls short of the actual marginal social benefit because of the positive externality. Suppose the marginal external benefit, *MEB,* of college instruction is $1,000 per student per year. To obtain the marginal social benefit, we must add $1,000 to the marginal benefit

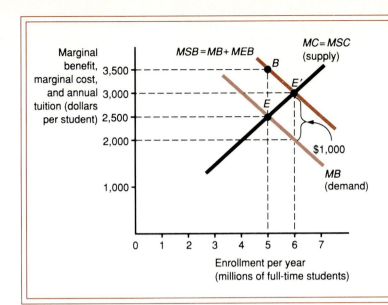

Box 2   Impact of a Positive Externality

The market equilibrium at point *E* corresponds to less than the efficient output because the marginal social benefit of 5 million students enrolled per year exceeds the marginal social cost. To achieve the efficient output, net tuition paid by the students (after receiving the $1,000 subsidy) must fall to $2,000 per year. So although tuition rises to $3,000 in the graph at left, the actual cost paid by the students is only $2,000. At that price, the number of students enrolled will be 6 million per year and marginal social benefit will equal marginal social cost.

received by students. This gives us the marginal social benefit curve, shown in Box 2. This curve is $1,000 higher than the marginal benefit curve on the graph.

Now it's easy to show that the market equilibrium is inefficient. At the market equilibrium output of 5 million students enrolled per year, the marginal social benefit of college education is $2,500 plus $1,000, which is $3,500 per year (at point *B*). This exceeds the marginal social cost of $2,500 when 5 million students per year are enrolled. Because marginal social benefit exceeds marginal social cost at the market output corresponding to point *E* on the graph, *less* than the efficient annual enrollment results from market sales of college instruction. The efficient outcome corresponds to point *E'* on the graph. At that point the marginal social benefit curve intersects the marginal social cost curve. The efficient annual enrollment corresponding to that point is 6 million students. At that point both the marginal social cost and marginal social benefit of enrollment are $3,000. Note, however, that to induce 6 million students to enroll each year the market tuition would have to *fall* to $2,000 because students use their own marginal benefit rather than the marginal social benefit to decide whether or not to attend college.

Once again, we can generalize the result: *When a positive externality exists, sale of a good or service in a competitive market results in less than the efficient output and a market price that is too high.* Less than the efficient amount of resources is devoted to producing goods and services whose use results in positive externalities.

Concept Check

1   What are externalities? Give an example of a positive externality and a negative externality.

2   Why does an unregulated market for a good for which a negative externality prevails not attain an efficient outcome?

3   Explain how positive externalities result in an output level that doesn't include all net gains from resource use.

Coping with Externalities: Causes and Cures

Property Right Disputes

Negative externalities result from competing uses for resources for which property rights are in dispute. The issue is the right of buyers and sellers to impose costs on third parties. The third parties are harmed by the externalities resulting from exchanges between buyers and sellers of, say, chemicals. Do the chemical producers have the right to dump their wastes in streams without paying for that right? The problem is that no one owns the streams. The firms can dump their wastes without payment because no one person has the right to charge for the use of a stream.

People who are harmed by chemical wastes have a competing claim on the use of the stream for alternative purposes. For example, these people might want to fish, swim, or use the stream as a source of drinking water. The use of the stream as a chemical dump diminishes its usefulness in such competing uses. One way to resolve the externality is for government to step in and arbitrarily assign the third party the property rights to the stream. The government does so by passing a law guaranteeing people the right to pollution-free water. This nips the pollution in the bud. Dumping of wastes is simply banned. The examples of negative externalities we discussed earlier implicitly assumed that the property right assignment was the reverse of this. In such cases the chemical firms would have the right to dump wastes in any stream they wished without charge.

For positive externalities, the property rights of those who benefit third parties are not established. There's no means for them to extract payment for those benefits. This results in underproduction of the good. A positive externality could be corrected if a way could be developed for the people who receive the positive externalities to make payments to those who generate them. For example, an externality associated with college enrollment could be removed if students could receive a discount on tuition equal to the marginal external benefit of their college credits. The third-party beneficiaries would thus finance the tuition discount.

Internalizing Externalities

Internalization of an externality:
Occurs when the marginal cost or marginal benefit of a good has been adjusted so that market sale of the item results in the efficient output.

Internalization of an externality occurs when the marginal cost or marginal benefit of a good has been adjusted so that market sale of the item results in the efficient output. In the case of a negative externality, internalization would require that the marginal cost incurred by sellers be *increased* by an amount equal to the marginal external cost of the good. This would increase the market price of the good and reduce the equilibrium quantity demanded. In other words, *internalizing an externality results in the efficient output by altering incentives to buy and sell the good.*

Internalization of a positive externality could be accomplished by a payment to consumers equal to the marginal external benefit associated with purchase of the good. This would encourage consumers to buy the good. The resulting increase in demand would encourage suppliers to devote more resources to production of the good so as to help achieve the efficient output. In other words, a subsidy to users can internalize a positive externality. Subsidizing students is one way to encourage them to go to college, thereby helping increase consumption of a service that many of us believe generates positive externalities. Alternatively, a subsidy to sellers would increase the market supply of the good. This would reduce the price to consumers, thus increasing the quantity of the good demanded and internalizing the externality.

Using a Corrective Tax to Internalize Negative Externalities

The basic problem that exists for negative externalities, such as those that result in less than the efficient amount of pollution control, is that a resource is used without charge. In the case of environmental pollution, firms and others use environmental resources without having to consider the marginal external costs of disposing of their wastes in the air and water and on the land. A **corrective tax** is one that is levied on polluters to simulate a charge equal to the marginal external cost of their actions. In principle, a corrective tax raises the marginal cost incurred by producers up to a level that reflects the true marginal social cost of production.

The idea behind a corrective tax is easy to demonstrate in theory. However, the practical problems involved in implementing such a tax are quite formidable. To implement the tax, it would be necessary to identify all people who emit pollutants. Then the marginal external cost associated with the pollution would have to be measured.

We can illustrate the principle of the corrective tax by using the example of air pollution from burning of firewood, assuming it's easy to identify the polluters and measure the damage from the smoke. In fact, in many communities pollution from firewood is a very serious problem. The move to wood stoves, encouraged by high energy prices in the 1970s, has resulted in a shift from relatively nonpolluting methods of heating homes with natural gas, oil, and electricity to firewood, which has a number of adverse effects.

The graph in Box 3 shows the market demand and supply curves for firewood based on the data from the example used to illustrate the negative externality. The total pollution damage from the use of firewood is $10 multiplied by 10,000 cords per year, which is $100,000 per year. This is represented by the rectangular area *BAEF*. A corrective tax won't eliminate the pollution. However, if the practical problems of administering the tax can be solved, the tax can help achieve the efficient amount of pollution control.

Corrective tax:
A tax levied on polluters to simulate a charge equal to the marginal external cost of their actions.

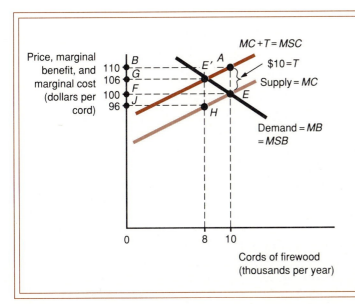

Box 3   Controlling Pollution with a Corrective Tax

A corrective tax of $T = $10 per cord of firewood can internalize the externality by increasing the marginal cost of firewood to its marginal social cost. The tax reduces emissions and collects $80,000 revenue per year, corresponding to the area *GE'HJ*, that can be used to compensate for the remaining pollution damage.

Remember that the marginal external cost of the wood smoke in the example was assumed to be constant at $10 per cord. Suppose government authorities levied a corrective tax of exactly $10 per cord to be collected from sellers of firewood. *To internalize the externality, the corrective tax must be set exactly equal to the marginal external cost associated with the use of the product.* As a result of the tax, the marginal cost of selling firewood is $10 higher for each cord sold. The marginal cost now equals the marginal social cost of firewood. The supply of firewood will therefore decrease as a result of the tax.

The decrease in the supply of firewood results in a new market equilibrium at point E' in Box 3. *At that point the marginal social cost of firewood is exactly equal to its marginal social benefit.* The market price of firewood rises to $106 per cord as a result of the tax. At the higher price the quantity demanded declines from 10,000 to 8,000 cords per year. Because annual sales decline, pollution declines as well. At the new output, pollution costs, which are still $10 per cord per year, fall from $100,000 to $80,000 per year. Finally, because the tax collects $10 per cord, total revenue from the tax will be $80,000 per year at the equilibrium output.

You should note the following desirable results that stem from use of the corrective tax:

1. The tax internalizes the negative externality by raising marginal cost of production to marginal social cost. As a result, the efficient annual output is attained.
2. When the negative externality is internalized, the output of the good whose use generates it is reduced. This illustrates an important tradeoff between cleaner air and other goods. The prices of goods whose use generates a negative externality rise when the externality is internalized. The higher price causes a decrease in consumption of the good. Cleaner air is attained by sacrificing some of the goods whose production or use generates the externality.
3. The tax collects enough revenue to pay for damages from the pollution after the efficient output is produced. In this case the tax collects $80,000 per year, which is exactly equal to pollution damages at the efficient annual output. *If the people incurring these damages could be identified and the damages incurred by each calculated, then they could be fully compensated for those damages.* If identification is impossible, the tax revenues can be used to reduce reliance on other taxes or increase government expenditures. This will result in other benefits to people that will offset the pollution damage.

Finally, note that the corrective tax provides more incentives for pollution control than indicated by this simple example. Firms seek to maximize profits in the long run. They're likely to look at the short-run payment of the tax as a temporary solution. In the long run they might find they can make still more profits by changing their production process in ways that actually reduce or eliminate the emissions that cause the pollution. A reduction in emissions would reduce the marginal external cost and result in a lower corrective tax for the firm. For example, a corrective tax on production of electricity in plants burning coal might induce these firms to change their method of production. In the long run producers might sharply reduce emissions by installing devices in their smokestacks that absorb pollutants. If the marginal external cost associated with their output then declines to zero, they would have no liability under a corrective tax.

Using a Corrective Subsidy to Internalize a Positive Externality

A positive externality could be internalized in a similar fashion. However, the problem with a positive externality is that *less* than the efficient amount of the good is produced. To internalize a positive externality, the government could use a **corrective subsidy** equal to the marginal external benefit of the item. The subsidy would increase consumer demand for the good, thereby increasing the equilibrium quantity so as to approach the efficient output.

Corrective subsidy:
An amount paid to consumers or producers of a good equal to the marginal external benefit of the good.

For example, to internalize the externality associated with college enrollment, the government could pay students $1,000 per year if they enroll as full-time students in a college. When deciding whether or not to attend college, students will now consider both their own personal marginal benefit *and* the $1,000 annual payment that reflects the marginal external benefit. The subsidy would have the effect of increasing the demand for higher education as it's added to the marginal benefit students receive. Referring to the graph in Box 2, this will have the effect of shifting the market equilibrium from point *E* to point *E',* and annual enrollment will increase from 5 million to 6 million students per year. The total subsidy necessary to internalize the externality would be $6 billion, which is the $1,000 per student multipled by the 6 million students who will be enrolled after the subsidy. The market tuition will rise to $3,000. But because of the $1,000 subsidy, students will pay a net tuition of only $2,000.

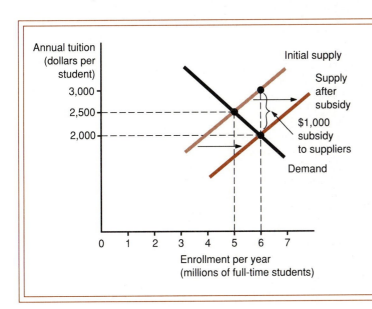

Box 4   Using a Subsidy to Suppliers to Internalize a Positive Externality

A $1,000 subsidy to suppliers of education increases market supply and lowers market tuition from $2,500 to $2,000 per year. The decrease in annual tuition increases the equilibrium enrollment from 5 million to 6 million students annually, which is the efficient level.

The same result could be obtained if a $1,000 subsidy were paid to suppliers of education. However, in this case the supply of education (rather than the demand for it) would increase after the subsidy, thereby decreasing the market tuition paid by students to $2,000 per year. The graph in Box 4 shows how an increase in supply caused by a subsidy to the higher education industry can internalize the positive externality. The funds to pay the subsidy could be collected from those third parties who gain from the consumption of education. If members of society at large benefit from college enrollment, then the government might decide to finance the subsidy out of its general revenues. In fact, a good portion of the cost of higher education in the United States is subsidized by general government revenues.

1 How do property right disputes give rise to negative externalities?

2 What must be done to internalize an externality?

3 Explain how corrective taxes and subsidies can be used to internalize externalities.

Public Goods and Their Provision by Governments

Markets work well for goods or services that can easily be packaged and sold to consumers. To be easily salable in a market an item must be *rival in consumption,* meaning that consumers know they must compete with others to obtain the available amount of the item. For example, a loaf of bread sold in a market provides benefits only to the person who consumes it. If a given number of loaves is baked each day, the more loaves that go to any one consumer, the fewer are available to others.

Goods that are sold in markets must also have the characteristic of being easily withheld from consumers who don't pay. This is called the *exclusion property of a good.* For example, automobiles are subject to the exclusion property because people who don't pay a price agreeable to the seller can't acquire title to an automobile. **Private goods** are goods whose benefits are rival in consumption and for which exclusion of those who refuse to pay is relatively easy. Private goods are easily sold in markets.

> Goods whose benefits are rival in consumption and for which exclusion of those who refuse to pay is relatively easy.

Public Goods

As we saw in Chapter 6, *public goods* are goods whose units of production can be consumed collectively by everyone whether or not they pay. Public goods are *non-rival in consumption.* People who don't pay for the units of a public good they consume *can't easily be excluded from enjoying the benefits of such goods purchased by others.* Unlike bread, which is a good example of a private good, a public good will benefit many people when it's made available to any one person. National defense and police protection are public goods. When a baby is born, that baby is protected by police and national defense services without appreciably diminishing the protection available to others. Additional consumers can enjoy the benefit of a given quantity of a public good at *zero marginal cost* because no additional output is necessary to accommodate more users.

The reason markets are likely to fail to efficiently supply public goods lies in the nonexclusion property of these goods. Public goods benefit everyone when they're supplied to one person. It's difficult and costly to establish a price for these goods because firms can't prevent those who refuse to pay from enjoying the good. For example, air pollution control is a public good. If the air quality is improved as a result of government policies, everyone will benefit. However, it will be impossible to prevent any one person from breathing the cleaner air even if that person refuses to pay. There's no way to package the benefits of air pollution control services and sell them by the unit like loaves of bread in a supermarket! Once a certain amount of a public good is produced, it's extremely difficult to exclude consumers from benefiting from the good by charging them a fee.

The characteristics of public goods make it difficult for profit-maximizing firms to supply them efficiently. In fact, such public goods as national defense or snow removal might never be made available if free enterprise in markets were relied on to supply them. It's not surprising that in almost all societies, governments provide defense, environmental protection, police and firefighting services, air traffic control, and other services that benefit everyone.

But the neat distinction between public and private goods rarely exists in reality. For example, television programming is nonrival because additional viewers can enjoy a given amount of programming without decreasing the enjoyment of existing viewers. However, as cable TV has demonstrated, it *is* possible to prevent those who don't pay from enjoying the service.

The ability to price a good depends in part on current technology. Some people hook into cable TV programming illegally. However, as electronic devices make it easy to detect such cheaters, the incentives to cheat diminish. Recently cable TV companies have succeeded in scrambling program transmissions that were previously available to satellite dish antenna owners for free. With this innovation, the companies can now require antenna owners to purchase an unscrambling device and pay the monthly fee for reception of programming.

Efficient Output of Pure Public Goods

A **pure public good** is one that provides benefits to *all* members of a community as soon as it is made available to any one person. Such a good is collectively consumed by everyone in a community, and it's impossible to charge for the use of the good. For example, you can think of fireworks displays in a small town as a pure public good for people in that town. If you decide to shoot off fireworks for your own amusement, provided they go high enough in the air, anyone else in the town would be able to enjoy the display without having to pay.

Pure public good:
A good that provides benefits to all members of a community as soon as it is made available to any one person.

A simple example will show why we often turn to government for provision of goods that have characteristics similar to pure public goods. Suppose your community consists of 200 people, each of whom places a value of $10 on a fireworks display if only one is to be made available per year. This is the marginal benefit *to each person* of one fireworks display per year. Naturally, if more than one display were made available per year, its marginal benefit to any person, representing the maximum sum of money that person would pay for an additional display, would be less. The graph in Box 5 shows this by drawing a person's downward-sloping marginal benefit curve for fireworks displays. For simplicity, assume each person in the community has exactly the same marginal benefit curve. This means there are 200 marginal benefit curves identical to the one drawn in Box 5.

Suppose a standard fireworks display can be arranged for $1,000. Residents of your community can contract with a private pyrotechnics firm to enjoy as many displays per year as they wish for $1,000 per display. The marginal cost of each fireworks display is therefore $1,000. Assume there are no negative externalities associated with fireworks displays, so $1,000 can also be regarded as the marginal social cost of fireworks displays.

Now look at the graph and ask yourself: "How many fireworks displays would be available to my community if displays were sold in a market to individual buyers?" To answer the question, first look at the marginal benefit curve on the graph. The marginal benefit of one display per year for each individual is $10. *This represents the maximum sum of money any one person would give up to enjoy one display*

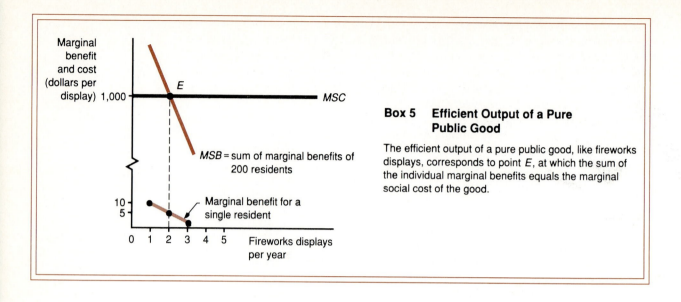

Box 5   Efficient Output of a Pure Public Good

The efficient output of a pure public good, like fireworks displays, corresponds to point *E*, at which the sum of the individual marginal benefits equals the marginal social cost of the good.

per year. Now look at the horizontal marginal social cost curve for fireworks displays. *This curve tells you that the minimum sum of money sellers of fireworks displays will accept is $1,000 per display.* Because the maximum price any buyer will pay falls considerably short of the minimum price sellers would accept, the market equilibrium number of fireworks displays per year for your community would be zero. No individual would buy any displays at the $1,000 price sellers need to cover their opportunity costs. The market therefore fails to make any fireworks displays available to your community.

Is the market equilibrium efficient? A bit of thought will convince you that the answer to this question is "No." Keep in mind that because fireworks displays are pure public goods, everyone will enjoy a display when it's provided for any one person. The marginal benefit will be the $10 enjoyed by the person whose marginal benefit curve is drawn in the graph, plus an additional $10 marginal benefit for each of the community's 199 other residents. *The marginal social benefit of a pure public good is therefore the sum of the individual marginal benefits enjoyed by all consumers.*

It follows that the marginal social benefit of the first fireworks display is $2,000, which is the sum of the $10 marginal benefits of that display to the 200 residents. The graph in Box 5 also plots the sum of the marginal benefits for each of the first three fireworks displays per year. Notice that when two fireworks displays per year are provided, the marginal benefit for each person is $5 per display. The sum of the marginal benefits for each of the 200 persons is therefore $1,000. This is exactly equal to the marginal social cost of fireworks displays. It follows that the efficient number of fireworks displays is two per year for your community. If more than two displays per year were provided, the marginal benefit for each person would fall below $5 and the sum of the marginal benefits would be less than $1,000. In Box 5 the marginal social benefit curve intersects the marginal social cost curve at point *E*, which corresponds to two displays per year.

You can now see that the market sale of fireworks, assuming this is a pure public good, results in less than the efficient number of displays per year. Because the benefits of fireworks displays are collectively enjoyed, an efficient means of financing

CHAPTER 16 Market Failure and the Role of Government in Allocating Resources them is for beneficiaries to *share* the costs. For example, if each person could be induced to *voluntarily* contribute $5 per display to obtain two displays per year, the total contribution would exactly cover the $2,000 cost. Each person would be no worse off by making such a contribution because $5 per display is each person's marginal benefit for two displays. Each person therefore would kick in $10 ($5 × 2) as his or her share for two displays per year, and the 200 people would contribute a total of $2,000. Such a cooperative solution would achieve the efficient output of fireworks displays each year. Each resident is better off than would be the case if fireworks displays were available through individual market purchase. *Many useful public goods would not be provided, or would be provided in less than efficient amounts, if they were made available for individual purchase in markets.*

The Free-Rider Problem

There is, however, a fly in the ointment that often prevents voluntary cost sharing from working as a way to finance public goods. The fly stems from the fact that we're often better off by not contributing but instead attempting to enjoy the amounts of a good provided and paid for by others. Remember, you can't be excluded from the benefits of a pure public good even if you fail to help finance its cost. All of us know this. Therefore we all hope others will pay enough to make the good available. A person who seeks to enjoy the benefits of a public good without contributing to its costs is called a **free rider.** Of course, if everyone behaves this way, not a cent is provided to finance the costs of the good. The free-rider problem therefore prevents voluntary cost sharing from achieving the efficient output of a public good. In fact, if everyone tried to be a free rider, then no fireworks displays or any other public good could be financed by voluntary contributions.

Free rider:
A person who seeks to enjoy the benefits of a public good without contributing to its costs.

The free-rider problem gives you a clue as to why we often look to government to provide public goods. While there's no guarantee that this will achieve the efficient output, government can overcome the free-rider problem by using tax financing. It can also use its authority to make sure that essential public goods like national defense and pollution control are provided when they can't be profitably sold in markets.

Concept Check

1 What are the characteristics of public goods?

2 What conditions must prevail to achieve the efficient output of a pure public good?

3 How does the free-rider problem prevent voluntary cost-sharing arrangements from achieving the efficient output of a pure public good?

Coping with Other Types of Market Failure: Social Regulation

There are still other reasons why competitive markets might not result in efficient outcomes even if there were no externalities or public goods. One problem stems from inadequate information about product quality and job characteristics. In practice, one of the most difficult problems you face when buying goods and services is that you never know if a product you buy will perform exactly as you expect. You

Principles in Practice

Social Regulation of the Automobile in America: What It Costs

If you own a car, chances are you think of it as your big ticket to freedom. In some ways that's exactly what it is: you can hop into your car and drive to school, work, a party, or the beach. But if you turn over this ticket, you'll see some fine print on the other side that's considerably less cheery.

The private automobile has been called the greatest generator of externalities ever invented. The contraption pollutes the air, and its use and misuse are a major cause of death and injury. It's not surprising that the automobile is one of the most regulated products in the United States. Since the mid-1960s the federal government has been imposing a variety of standards on the manufacture of new cars.

The goals of the three major regulatory programs affecting automobiles are cleaner air, reduced deaths and injuries on the highway, and fuel conservation. Instead of corrective taxes or other measures that take effect through the price system, the regulatory approach operates by issuing directives to the manufacturers of new automobiles.

All three programs have affected both the costs of producing new cars and the costs of operating cars produced after the regulations went into effect. *One estimate indicates that the total cost of the emissions control and safety programs in 1981 was as much as $2,500 per new automobile in that model year.* [*] This figure reflects the costs imposed on manufacturers and estimates the cost of increased maintenance and diminished vehicle performance resulting from the standards. Safety costs amount to 30% to 39% of the total estimated costs. The cost of government-mandated equipment was estimated to be as high as $1,400 per car, with about two thirds of this cost passed on to buyers of new cars after a 1-year lag.[†]

One undesirable impact of these programs is that they have caused many motorists to postpone replacing older-model cars that are less safe and more polluting than the more expensive newer models. In addition, regulations that achieve one goal often make the other goals more difficult to attain. For example, safety regulations add to the weight of a vehicle, thereby making it more difficult to achieve fuel economy standards. In many cases emissions standards have reduced fuel economy, which has made the goal of achieving fuel economy standards more costly.

Analysis of safety regulations for automobiles indicates that the benefits exceed the costs.[‡] However, even though emissions standards for automobiles have improved air quality, a careful study of the program suggests that the costs of achieving the reduction in emissions exceed the benefits obtained.[§] A problem with the emissions standards approach that decreases its effectiveness is that, on average, new cars do not actually meet the standards. In addition, the emissions control systems often deteriorate more rapidly than expected, which decreases their effectiveness in curbing pollution. As a result of these problems, some critics suggest alternative approaches, such as annual inspection of cars and corrective taxes levied according to emissions from each vehicle. Movement to a system of corrective taxes that operates through the price system might be more effective than the current system in cleaning up our air at lower costs. What do you think?

[*]Robert W. Crandall, Howard K. Gruenspecht, Theodore E. Keeler, and Lester B. Lave, *Regulating the Automobile*, Washington, D.C.: The Brookings Institution, 1986.
[†]Crandall, pp. 39-40.
[‡]Crandall, Chapter 4.
[§]Crandall, Chapter 5.

---

might also doubt the accuracy of information supplied by sellers about the risks associated with the use of the product.

When the marginal benefit that buyers associate with a product is based on inaccurate information, inefficient outcomes are likely. To cope with the difficult problems associated with evaluating product quality and risk, many people demand government action. Similarly, to help reduce risk at work, people have demanded and gotten government regulation of working conditions.

Social regulation is the use of government power to intervene in markets so as to reduce the risk of accidents and disease and to achieve other social goals such as equality of opportunity for all persons. For example, the Food and Drug Administration evaluates new drugs before allowing them to be sold in markets. The Consumer Product Safety Act passed in 1972 empowers the federal government to set and

Social regulation:
The use of government power to intervene in markets so as to reduce the risk of accidents and disease and to achieve other social goals such as equality of opportunity for all persons.

enforce safety standards for hazardous products such as lawn mowers, bicycles, and automobiles. The Occupational Safety and Health Act of 1970 established government regulation of working conditions to protect workers from hazards. The Equal Employment Opportunity Act of 1967 is an example of government intervention in markets to prevent discrimination against minority groups. In the next chapter we'll discuss a host of regulatory programs administered by the Environmental Protection Agency that are designed to improve environmental quality.

In addition to using regulation to cope with market failure to supply information, governments also seek to supply information directly to consumers. For example, there are government programs to inform people about the hazards associated with using tobacco, alcohol, and other substances.

Government Failure: How Politics Can Prevent Efficiency

If trading between independent buyers and sellers in markets fails to achieve efficiency, can the government do better in allocating resources? This is a key question we must address in evaluating the role of government in a market economy. Unfortunately, however, there's no clear answer to this question. Even for governments, the path to efficiency is riddled with pitfalls. Of course, efficiency is an ideal that's seldom approximated in the real world. Government provision of goods and services and regulation of markets are subject to political influences. Special interests may use government power in ways that result in redistribution of income for private gain. In Chapter 18 we'll discuss the economics of special-interest groups and how political action by such groups can result in approval of policies that cost more than the benefits they provide.

Like the market, the mechanism for supplying public goods, regulations, and social policies isn't perfect. Unequal distribution of political power can affect the outcomes of the political process. We need to scrutinize the results of economic policies to determine whether their costs justify the gains they provide. We also must examine the distribution of benefits and costs of government programs to allocate resources.

Despite these problems, however, few of us would be content to have all goods and services provided through markets. Market failure to efficiently provide such valuable goods and services as environmental protection, economic and social stability, and other important services is a fact of life. For many of us, the benefits we receive from government policies that redistribute income in our favor are worth the personal loss in benefits from not enjoying an efficient economy. Efficiency, if attained, maximizes the size of the pie that represents national well-being from available resources. As individuals, however, we're often more concerned with our own slice of the pie than with the overall size of the pie. In many cases, under inefficient policies, some of us can enjoy larger slices even though the pie is smaller!

Summary

1. Market failure exists when exchange between buyers and sellers in unregulated markets doesn't result in efficient resource use.
2. Market failure often results when there are discrepancies between the marginal benefits and costs on which private decisions are based and the actual marginal social benefits and costs. Under such circumstances the price system fails to attach a monetary value to the use of certain resources.

3. Externalities are costs or benefits of market transactions that are not reflected in prices.
4. A negative externality is a cost associated with resource use that is not priced. A positive externality is an unpriced benefit of resource use.
5. When a negative externality is associated with the sale of a good, exchange of that good in a competitive market results in more than the efficient amount of resources being allocated to its production.
6. When a positive externality is associated with the sale of a good, exchange of that good in a competitive market results in less than the efficient amount of resources being allocated to its production.
7. Negative externalities result from competing uses for resources in cases for which property rights to resource use are in dispute. When negative externalities exist, there are third parties to market exchanges whose property rights to resource use are not considered by the buyers and the sellers. Government assignment of property rights to resource use can help settle such disputes.
8. An externality is internalized when the marginal cost or marginal benefit of the good has been adjusted so that market sale of an item results in the efficient output. In effect, internalizing an externality involves pricing its costs or benefits.
9. A corrective tax can be used to internalize a negative externality when the tax is set equal to the marginal external cost. Similarly, a corrective subsidy can be used to price the marginal external benefit of the sale of an item to internalize the externality. Corrective taxes and subsidies alter incentives to trade a good by making traders consider all the social costs or benefits of their actions.
10. Private goods are goods that are easily sold in markets because their benefits can easily be priced. The benefits of private goods are rival in consumption because the more of the good purchased by one consumer, the fewer the benefits available to others. Similarly, it's easy to withhold the benefits of private goods from those who don't pay the price.
11. Public goods are nonrival in consumption and have benefits that can't be easily withheld from those who refuse to pay. Public goods purchased or provided by others can be enjoyed by those who don't buy the items. A pure public good benefits all members of a community as soon as it's made available to any one person.
12. The marginal social benefit of a pure public good is the sum of the individual marginal benefits enjoyed by all consumers of a given quantity of the good. Efficient output of a pure public good requires sharing its costs and allocating resources toward its production up to the point at which the sum of the marginal benefits received by all consumers of the good equals its marginal social cost.
13. Voluntary contributions to finance provision of public goods often fail because of the free-rider problem. Free riders are people who seek to enjoy the benefits of public goods provided by others without contributing to the costs. The free-rider problem causes an underallocation of resources to production of a good.
14. Market failure to allocate resources efficiently can stem from inadequate information about product quality and job characteristics. Social regulation is the use of government power to intervene in markets so as to reduce the risk of accidents and disease and to achieve other social goals such as equality of opportunity for everyone.
15. Although it's easy to establish causes of market failure to achieve efficiency, there's no guarantee that government intervention to correct for the effects of market failure will achieve efficiency.

Key Terms and Concepts

Negative externality
Marginal external cost
Positive externality
Marginal external benefit
Internalization of an externality
Corrective tax

Corrective subsidy
Private goods
Pure public good
Free rider
Social regulation

Problems and Applications

1. Suppose that whenever you buy and use a gallon of gasoline, the marginal external cost is 5¢. Use a graph to show why sale of gasoline in a competitive market will result in more than the efficient output of gas. Assume the current market price of gasoline is $1 per gallon and 10 million gallons per month are sold at that price.

2. On the graph you drew in answer to problem 1, show the *total* external cost per month resulting from gasoline consumption. List the types of damage that can result from air pollution by gasoline exhaust.

3. The market price of inoculations against the flu is $20. There's a marginal external benefit of $10 per flu shot. Will sale of inoculations in a competitive market achieve the efficient output?

4. Suppose the marginal external benefit from flu shots falls as more shots are sold per year. This is, in fact, a likely occurrence because the positive externality of flu shots (in the form of reduced spread of flu) is enjoyed by the portion of the population that isn't inoculated. More inoculations reduce the hosts for the disease and therefore reduce the probability that noninoculated persons will catch it. Suppose the marginal external benefit falls to zero when 20 million flu shots are sold per year. Use a graph to show that sale of flu shots in competitive markets will fail to achieve the efficient output only when the quantity demanded at the market price is less than 20 million inoculations per year.

5. Suppose the right to pollution-free water is granted to fishermen who use a stream to catch trout. A paper plant wants to use the stream to dispose of its wastes. Under what circumstances would the fishermen give up their right to clean water to the paper company?

6. Explain why internalizing a negative externality is likely to raise the market price of a good and make both buyers and sellers of the good worse off. Who gains when a negative externality is internalized?

7. The current market equilibrium price of paper averages $200 per ton. There's a marginal external cost of $20 per ton resulting from water pollution associated with paper production. Current sales of paper amount to 100 million tons per year. Use a graph to show how a corrective tax can internalize the negative externality associated with paper production. Show how the tax affects the market equilibrium price and quantity. Does the tax reduce the pollution from paper production to zero? Under what circumstances are paper producers likely to eliminate the pollution rather than pay the tax?

8. Suppose the corrective tax on paper producers collects $800 million in revenue per year. If the people who bear the cost of the remaining amount of pollution can be identified, can you suggest a use for the tax revenue collected?

9. Explain why a positive externality is likely to be associated with purchase of smoke detectors. Can you suggest a policy to internalize the externality?

10. Security protection is a pure public good for the 1,000 residents of your apart-

ment complex. Each resident obtains a marginal benefit of $10 per month from each security guard when 20 guards are employed per month. What is the marginal social benefit of security protection for the residents when 20 guards are employed? If each guard costs $1,000 per month, is 20 guards the efficient number?

Suggested Readings

William J. Baumol and Wallace E. Oates, *Economics, Environmental Policy, and the Quality of Life,* Englewood Cliffs, N.J.: Prentice-Hall, 1979. This is a lively and relevant application of the theory of externalities to the problems of environmental policy.

Ronald Coase, "The Problem of Social Cost," *Journal of Law and Economics,* 22, April 1970, pp. 141-162. This is a classic analysis of the problem of market failure that emphasizes the connections between legal and economic issues.

Robert W. Crandall, Howard K. Gruenspecht, Theodore E. Keeler, and Lester B. Lave, *Regulating the Automobile,* Washington, D.C.: The Brookings Institution, 1986. This is a thought-provoking analysis of the costs and benefits of regulations such as emissions standards, safety standards, and fuel economy standards that are imposed on automobiles sold in the United States.

David N. Hyman, *Public Finance: A Contemporary Application of Theory to Policy,* Chicago: The Dryden Press, 1987. Chapter 3 provides an in-depth analysis of market failure, externalities, and government policies designed to internalize externalities. Chapter 4 develops the theory of public goods.

Charles Wolf, Jr., "A Theory of Non-Market Failures," *The Public Interest,* 55, Spring, 1979, pp. 114-133. This is a readable analysis of some of the difficulties governments encounter in correcting for market failure to achieve efficient resource use.

A Forward Look

A symptom of negative externalities commonly observed in market economies is overuse of the environment for disposal of wastes. The resulting pollution of the air and water is a social problem with serious health costs. In the following chapter we apply the theory of market failure to analyze policies designed to cope with environmental pollution.

Externalities and the Environment: Policy Analysis

In a perfect world, not only would there be perfect competition, but we'd also enjoy breathing fresh, pure air and drinking sparkling, untainted water. But in our less than perfect real-life world, pollution is one of the prices we pay for owning cars, wearing clothes, and using miracle drugs.

How high a price are we paying? The answer to that question depends in large part on whom you ask: the manager of a firm that pollutes, or a physician who treats the victims of that pollution.

In any case, all of us can agree that environmental pollution is a serious health problem. Pollution is also an economic problem because it results from the use of environmental resources as a means of disposing of wastes. These wastes damage the environment in ways that make it less valuable for alternative uses. The more polluting exhausts emitted by cars, factories, and households in a city, the lower the quality of the air we breathe and the higher the risk of disease from breathing it. Environmental degradation is a negative externality associated with the production and use of goods and services. Critics of the market system argue that the pursuit of profit by business firms results in many forms of damage for which firms are not held liable. Critics also contend that shortsighted business managers interested in short-term profits overuse limited natural resources such as land, minerals, and petroleum.

However, the problems of environmental pollution and the economics of natural resources are often poorly understood. We can use economics to look carefully at the issues involved in resolving political disputes over the rights of firms to pollute and to use natural resources, and the rights of people to clean air and water. Like most economic issues, those relating to the environment involve tradeoffs. In this *chapter we look at those tradeoffs and discuss alternative policies to allow net gains in well-being while resolving disputes concerning the natural environment.*

Concept Preview

After reading this chapter, you should be able to:

1 Explain the costs and benefits of pollution control and the tradeoffs involved in government policies designed to protect the environment.
2 Discuss some of the problems involved in estimating the costs and benefits of pollution control and choosing policies that result in the efficient level of environmental protection.
3 Describe actual and proposed policies designed to control pollution and evaluate their impact on the environment and resource allocation.
4 Describe economic incentives to use natural resources and discuss policies that prevent overuse or depletion of these resources.

The Economics of Pollution

The problem of pollution has plagued societies since early times. Waste disposal and public sanitation were a serious health problem in medieval cities. Air pollution was common even in preindustrial cities where wood was burned for heat and cooking. Poor sanitation practices polluted rivers and streams. Today, as you know, pollution is a widespread problem affecting all regions of the earth. Fear of the effects of pollution on aquatic life and climatic conditions has become a serious concern.

Pollution:
Waste that has been disposed of in the air, in water, or on land and that reduces the value of those resources in alternative uses.

Pollution is waste that has been disposed of in the air, in water, or on land and that reduces the value of those resources in alternative uses. All of us have experienced pollution. You've undoubtedly been in large cities where the air was barely fit to breathe because of gases and other particles emitted as exhaust. You've probably lamented the fact that once-pristine streams are strewn with beer cans and plastic bags. And you may be worried about the possible damage to the usefulness of land and water resources in the event of malfunction of a nuclear reactor.

Emissions vs. Pollution

It's common to confuse emissions of waste products with pollution. Emissions aren't necessarily pollutants if they don't cause damage. For example, you can emit the most noxious gas imaginable in an unpopulated desert and do virtually no damage. The amount of damage done by emissions of any kind into the air or water depends on the concentration of those emissions and on the human beings, material, and natural resources in the vicinity.

For example, auto exhaust is much more hazardous in an underground garage than it is in a coastal area where winds circulate the air. This is because the emissions of carbon monoxide, sulfur dioxide, and other gases that damage human health are much higher *per cubic foot* of air in the garage than in the coastal area. Dumping a given amount of chemical wastes in the ocean does less harm than dumping the

---

same amount of wastes in a small lake. This is because the wastes will disperse more widely in the ocean than they will in the lake. Similarly, a given quantity of emissions of a certain gas does more damage in an urban area than in a rural area simply because the density of population and capital is higher per square mile in the city.

In evaluating the cost associated with a given quantity of emissions, it's therefore necessary to take into account the rate of dispersion of the emissions. It's also necessary to consider the amount of damageables in the vicinity of the emissions.

Although pollution is both unattractive and hazardous to health, the fact is that disposal of wastes in the atmosphere, in water, or on land decreases the cost of producing goods and services. Under current technology, fuels can't be consumed without generating waste particles and gases. If all wastes could be recycled and then reused to produce energy or other useful products, there would be no pollution problem. However, as long as there are useless wastes, it's inevitable that the waste must be placed somewhere. For example, you pollute the air when you drive your car because your exhaust discharges gases and other harmful combustion wastes into the air. The simplest way to eliminate the exhaust completely would be to ban driving! Few of us, however, would support a move back to the Stone Age as a way to clean up pollution.

You can think of pollution control as an economic good that has both benefits and costs. The benefits are improved human health and reduced damages from pollution. The costs are higher prices for goods and services as production costs increase because of pollution controls. *Pollution is an economic problem.* Resolving the problems associated with pollution involves weighing the benefits of pollution control against the costs.

The Efficient Amount of Pollution Control

It might seem like a great idea simply to ban all pollution. However, this would mean that all damaging wastes that couldn't be recycled would be outlawed! You could produce wastes, but you couldn't dispose of those wastes in the air (say by burning), in the water, or by burying them. Because the technology isn't available to recycle all wastes, such a complete ban on pollution would probably bring our industrial society to a screeching halt! Factories would have to shut down, and truck and automobile use would be forbidden. It's likely that a ban on pollution would cause many deaths because it would prevent the production of many basic goods and services and raise the prices of others as manufacturers moved to more expensive production methods to meet the ban. Few of us would be willing to pay the costs of a pollution-free society.

This scenario can be contrasted with one in which no restraints at all exist on the rights of firms to emit wastes. Naturally, all firms that seek the minimum-cost method of production would dispose of their wastes by dumping or burning. There would be little incentive to keep the air, water, or landscape clean. Our cities would be immersed in smog, and water supplies would have to be checked regularly for contamination. This scenario is undoubtedly just as unacceptable to you as the first.

The efficient level of pollution control strikes a balance between the social benefit and social cost involved in decreasing pollution. You'll recall from Chapter 13 that the efficient amount of any good is the amount for which the marginal social benefit (MSB) just equals the marginal social cost (MSC). Because pollution control is itself an economic good, the efficient amount per year is that for which the marginal social benefit just equals the marginal social cost.

The graph in Box 1 shows how, in principle, we could determine the efficient amount of pollution control. The horizontal axis measures the percentage reduction in polluting emissions each year as a result of controls. Shortly we'll discuss the actual methods used to reduce pollution. At this point just think of the government as policing each potential polluter and preventing emission of more than a certain amount of damaging wastes each year. The vertical axis measures the marginal social benefit and marginal social cost of reducing polluting emissions each year.

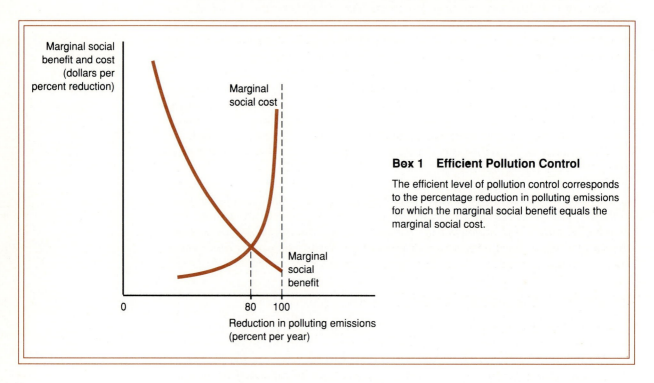

Box 1   Efficient Pollution Control

The efficient level of pollution control corresponds to the percentage reduction in polluting emissions for which the marginal social benefit equals the marginal social cost.

The marginal social benefit of pollution control is assumed to decline. Remember, the marginal social benefit of a good is the *extra* benefit associated with extra amounts of the good. The marginal social benefit of pollution control is the extra benefit associated with each extra 1% reduction in polluting wastes emitted per year. Although the total social benefit of pollution control always increases, its marginal social benefit tends to decrease. This means each extra 1% reduction in polluting wastes per year is worth less to us than the previous 1%.

The marginal social cost of pollution control, on the other hand, tends to increase for each additional 1% reduction in wastes emitted per year. In fact, empirical evidence indicates that after substantial amounts of polluting emissions have already been reduced, extra waste reduction is much more costly than previous reductions. One study estimated that elimination of 85% to 90% of water pollution in the United States would cost about $61 billion over a 10-year period. The marginal social cost of increasing the elimination of water pollution by an additional 10% was estimated to be $58 billion over the same period. The last 10% would cost almost as much as the first 90%![1]

[1]Allen V. Kneese and Charles L. Schultze, *Pollution, Prices, and Public Policy,* Washington, D.C.: The Brookings Institution, 1975.

The graph in Box 1 shows a downward-sloping marginal social benefit curve and an upward-sloping marginal social cost curve for pollution control. *The efficient amount of pollution control is that for which the marginal social cost of reducing wastes just equals the marginal social benefit.* This means no additional net gains are possible from changing the annual amount of pollution control. In the graph the efficient amount of pollution control is an 80% reduction in damaging wastes emitted per year.

Assuming the marginal social benefit of pollution control declines while its marginal social cost increases, the extremes of no pollution control or complete control will be inefficient. To see this, look at points on the graph corresponding to very little reduction in polluting emissions per year. Notice how the marginal social benefit of pollution control would far exceed its marginal social cost at such points. This indicates that substantial net gains in well-being are possible by applying more stringent pollution control measures. Also look at the point on the graph corresponding to close to 100% pollution control. At that point the marginal social cost of pollution control would far exceed its marginal social benefit. This means that more than the efficient amount of pollution control has been undertaken. Additional net gains are possible in this case by making pollution controls less stringent.

Estimating the Costs and Benefits of Pollution Control

It's no easy task to estimate how the marginal social benefit and marginal social cost of pollution control vary with the actual percentage of waste reduction. There's considerable disagreement about the costs of pollution and therefore about the benefits of reducing it. These disagreements stem both from difficulties in determining actual damage from pollution and from difficulties in placing a dollar value on these damages.

Similarly, estimating the actual marginal social cost of pollution damage is also quite difficult because it requires predicting the impact of pollution on production costs, product prices, and output.

The benefits of pollution control are measured by the reduction in damages caused by pollution. Pollution damages consist of those discussed in the following sections.

Damage to Human Health

Pollution causes diseases such as cancer and emphysema, and it also has been linked to heart disease. Damage to human health means human suffering, hours of work lost because of sickness, and premature death. To measure the social benefit of pollution control, a value must be placed on health damage. Human health damage caused by pollution is likely to be substantial. However, there's great debate among economists about how to measure such damages.

One approach is to give people information on the possible costs of pollution damage to their health. They could then be asked in a survey how much they would be willing to contribute for each extra 1% reduction in pollution. Although this would provide an estimate of the marginal benefit of pollution control, this estimate might not be very reliable, since people might try to behave as free riders (see Chapter 16) and not respond truthfully about how much they would be willing to pay.[2]

---

[2]For a discussion of the controversy regarding valuation of human life, see Steven E. Rhoads, "How Much Should We Spend to Save a Life?" *The Public Interest,* 51, Spring 1978, pp. 74-92.

Damage to Material Inputs, Natural Resources, and Agricultural Resources

Pollution causes materials to corrode. The destructive effects of pollution on historical monuments in Rome and Athens are a case in point. Much of the limestone and other materials used to construct ancient buildings has been severely damaged by automobile exhausts and other pollutants. Closer to home, pollutants can cause the paint on your house to deteriorate more quickly than it would otherwise. Pollution also damages natural resources like parkland and forests. Acid rain has been blamed for the death of trees and of fish in streams. Agricultural yields are adversely affected by pollutants that are absorbed by plant and animal tissue. By damaging natural resources, pollution involves costs in terms of reduced recreational and other benefits from natural areas. The aesthetic and recreational damages of pollution are especially difficult to value, as is the loss of such resources as wildlife and natural vegetation.

Negative Externalities and Efficient Pollution Control

The efficient amount of pollution control, as we've just seen, is unlikely to be 100%. Another, more dramatic way of stating this proposition is that there is an efficient amount of pollution. It's wrong to think of pollution as an evil that must be eliminated no matter what the cost. Of all the economic principles you've learned, the one that's most important to remember is that no gain can be considered desirable without evaluating the cost.

We can apply the theory of externalities to understand some of the concerns and tradeoffs involved in dealing with pollution as a social issue. Production of goods and services for sale in unregulated markets is likely to result in *more than the efficient amount of pollution*. This is because in most unregulated markets there's no mechanism for charging polluters a fee equal to the marginal external damage of their emissions. If the negative externalities associated with harmful emissions of wastes could be internalized by corrective taxes, there would be less pollution. However, pollution would not fall to zero. As we saw in Chapter 16, use of a corrective charge to *internalize* a negative externality reduces the amount of the damage but doesn't necessarily eliminate it. However, a corrective charge would generate enough revenue to pay for the damage caused by the emissions.

Concept Check

1 In what sense is pollution indicative of both a waste disposal and a resource use problem?

2 Why is it likely to be inefficient to attempt to eliminate *all* pollution? What are the costs and benefits associated with reducing pollution?

3 What is the distinction between emissions of waste and pollution?

Emissions Control Policies in Practice

In practice, governments use a number of techniques to control pollution. These techniques range from charges for the right to emit polluting waste to regulations that impose limits on the quantity of such wastes that can be emitted. In this section we look at policies governments use to cope with environmental problems and evaluate their impact on resource use.

Emissions Charges

Emissions charges are prices established for the right to emit each unit of a pollutant. For example, each ton of sulfur dioxide might be subject to a $10 charge. Modern electronics makes it feasible to install devices on smokestacks that accurately measure the kinds and amounts of pollutants emitted. An industrial firm could be billed by the month according to the marginal external cost of each type of pollutant.

Emissions charges: Prices established for the right to emit each unit of a pollutant.

The advantage of charging for polluting emissions rather than taxing firms is that the charge directly internalizes the externality by pricing the use of the environment to dispose of various types of waste. To accurately internalize the externality, the charge must reflect the marginal external cost of the damaging emissions. Assuming these emissions could be accurately measured, the charge could be varied from location to location depending on the actual opportunity cost of using the environmental resource.

Emissions charges have been used in some countries to deal with water pollution problems. For example, governing authorities in the Ruhr River basin in West German are successfully using such charges to control industrial wastes dumped in the river. In some areas of the United States similar charges, called *effluent fees,* are levied for the right to dump industrial wastes in municipal water-treatment facilities.

One study has estimated that emissions charges on sulfur dioxide, a harmful air pollutant, and other harmful emissions from factories and power plants in the United States would have raised nearly $9 billion in 1982.[3] This revenue would have allowed a reduction in other taxes or in the federal deficit while helping internalize a negative externality.

Regulation

The dominant method of controlling pollution in the United States is through government regulations. **Emissions standards** are limits established by government on the annual amounts and kinds of pollutants that can be emitted into the air or water by producers or users of certain products. For example, legislation enforced by the Environmental Protection Agency (EPA) places limits on the amounts and kinds of automobile exhaust emissions per vehicle. The limits specify the allowable number of grams per mile, per vehicle, of hydrocarbons, nitrogen dioxide, and carbon monoxide. Manufacturers must meet these standards or face stiff fines. Most manufacturers satisfy emissions standards by equipping their cars with catalytic converters. While reducing harmful emissions, these devices contribute to higher prices for cars and other motor vehicles.

Emissions standards: Limits established by government on the annual amounts and kinds of pollutants that can be emitted into the air or water by producers or users of certain products.

There are a number of disadvantages to emissions standards compared to emissions charges. The standards allow emission of less than the permitted levels *at no charge.* In other words, under standards polluters can pollute for free *up to a point.* After the maximum emissions are reached per firm, per vehicle, or other unit, *further emissions are strictly outlawed.* This means firms have incentives to meet but not to perform better than the standards. In addition, rather than allowing firms to choose the least-cost method of complying with emissions standards, the regulations often strictly specify the method of compliance. This gives firms no incentive to seek more efficient, less costly, means of satisfying the standards.

Another problem with standards is that they don't take into account the differ-

[3]David Terkla, "The Efficiency Value of Effluent Tax Revenues," *Journal of Environmental Economics and Management,* 11, June 1984, pp. 107-123.

ences among firms in costs of eliminating polluting emissions. If pollution control is to be efficient, it should be undertaken up to the point at which its marginal social benefit just equals its marginal social cost. The marginal social cost of pollution control for a firm depends on existing technology for reducing such emissions. This is likely to vary from firm to firm. For example, if the goal is to reduce emissions of sulfur dioxide by 20% nationally, it's unlikely to be efficient to require *all* polluters to cut down emissions by 20%. The reason is that in one firm a 20% reduction could cost $1 million per year, while in another firm the $1 million would buy a 50% reduction. If you want to minimize the cost of pollution control, you'll get more control per dollar by requiring the firms with low emissions control costs to reduce harmful emissions.

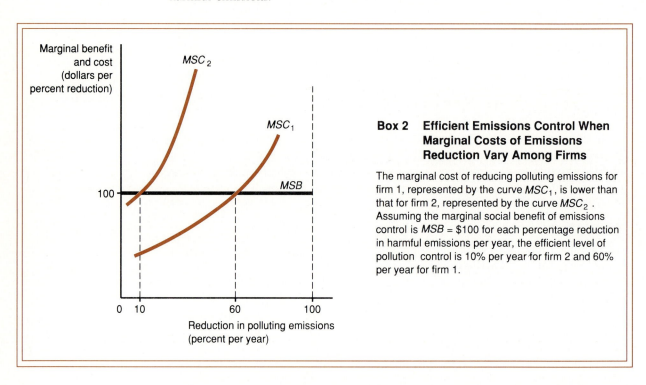

Box 2   Efficient Emissions Control When Marginal Costs of Emissions Reduction Vary Among Firms

The marginal cost of reducing polluting emissions for firm 1, represented by the curve MSC_1, is lower than that for firm 2, represented by the curve MSC_2. Assuming the marginal social benefit of emissions control is MSB = $100 for each percentage reduction in harmful emissions per year, the efficient level of pollution control is 10% per year for firm 2 and 60% per year for firm 1.

You can readily see this in the graph in Box 2, which shows the marginal social benefit and marginal social cost curves of polluting emissions reduction for two firms. For simplicity, assume the marginal social benefit of each 1% of such emissions reduction is a constant equal to $100 per year. As you can see, the marginal social cost of any given percentage reduction is higher for firm 2 than it is for firm 1. The efficient amount of pollution reduction for each firm corresponds to the amount for which its marginal social cost of reducing polluting emissions just equals the $100 marginal social benefit. This means it's efficient to expect the first firm to reduce harmful emissions by 60% while the second firm reduces such emissions by only 10% per year.

It's also easy to show that strict and uniform regulations are inefficient if the marginal social benefit of pollution control varies regionally. For example, there might be less social benefit from each 1% reduction in polluting emissions for firms located in isolated rural areas than for firms in densely populated urban areas. This is simply because there are more people and capital to bear damages per square mile in the city than in the country. To see why this is so, assume the marginal social cost of pollution reduction is the same for two firms. One firm operates in an urban area while the other operates in a rural area. The marginal social benefit of each 1% of emissions reduction is lower in the rural than in the urban area. In the graph in Box 3 this is reflected in the fact that the marginal social benefit curve for rural pollution reduction is lower than that for urban pollution reduction. Once again we assume that the marginal social benefit of pollution reduction is constant at each location for each 1% reduction. Each 1% reduction in polluting emissions in urban areas is worth $200, while each 1% reduction in rural areas is worth only $100.

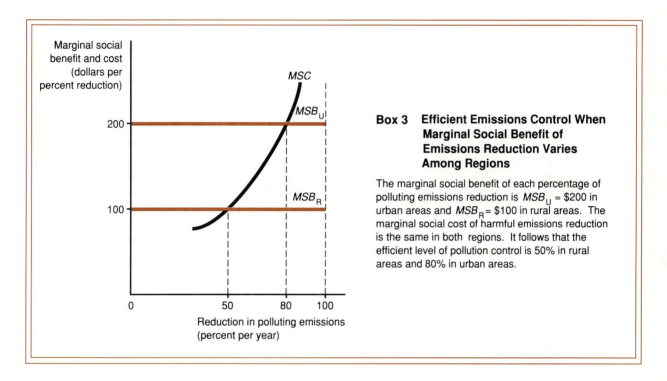

Box 3 Efficient Emissions Control When Marginal Social Benefit of Emissions Reduction Varies Among Regions

The marginal social benefit of each percentage of polluting emissions reduction is MSB_U = $200 in urban areas and MSB_R = $100 in rural areas. The marginal social cost of harmful emissions reduction is the same in both regions. It follows that the efficient level of pollution control is 50% in rural areas and 80% in urban areas.

The efficient amount of such emissions reduction is 80% in the urban area. This corresponds to the point at which the marginal social cost of emissions reduction in that area just equals $200. Similarly, the efficient amount of emissions reduction at the rural location is 50%. This corresponds to the point at which its marginal social cost of emissions reduction equals $100.

Uniform standards therefore are unlikely to achieve efficient pollution control. Flexible standards, if they could be enforced, would be more desirable. Why, then, are standards and regulations so widely used in the United States? The reason has to do with some of the practical problems involved in administering fees and charges. First of all, in many cases there's concern about underestimating the long-term costs of pollution. Many environmentalists prefer stringent control to charges because they believe the charges would be set too low. Others argue that it would be impossible to meter polluting emissions to enforce charges. However, you might also argue that if this is so, it might be difficult to track down violators of emissions standards. For example, some motorists disconnect their catalytic converters so they can use cheaper leaded gasolines.

Pollution Rights

Still another method of pollution control involves pricing the *right* to pollute. You'll recall that the basic source of negative externalities is the lack of clearly defined property rights to use resources. With no constraints or charges, a zero charge for the right to pollute results in emissions up to the point at which their marginal benefit to the emitter is zero. You can see this in the graph in Box 4. The horizontal axis measures the tons of annual emissions of a given type of pollutant per year. The vertical axis shows the price and the marginal benefit of emitting wastes. The marginal benefit curve indicates the maximum sum that those who use the environment would pay to dump any given quantity of harmful wastes per year. Because the actual price to emit wastes is assumed to be zero, firms continue to emit until the marginal benefit of emissions is zero. This occurs at point E_1, at which 200,000 tons of waste per year are emitted.

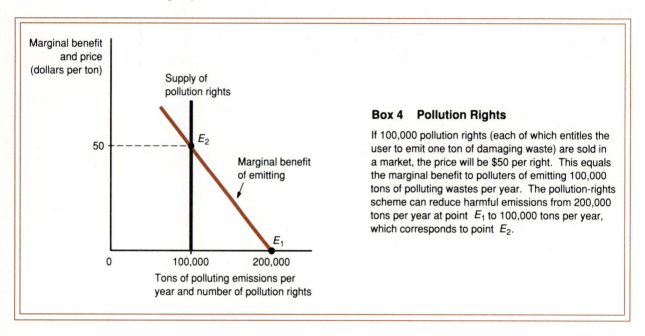

Box 4   Pollution Rights

If 100,000 pollution rights (each of which entitles the user to emit one ton of damaging waste) are sold in a market, the price will be $50 per right. This equals the marginal benefit to polluters of emitting 100,000 tons of polluting wastes per year. The pollution-rights scheme can reduce harmful emissions from 200,000 tons per year at point E_1 to 100,000 tons per year, which corresponds to point E_2.

Pollution right:
A government-issued certificate allowing a firm to emit a specified quantity of polluting waste.

Now suppose regulatory agencies told firms they would have to purchase the right to emit each ton of waste. A **pollution right** would be a government-issued certificate allowing a firm to emit a ton of polluting waste. These rights would be offered for sale in a market. Once purchased, they could be resold to others by the initial buyer. The agency enforcing the pollution-rights system would have to police firms to make sure no one emitted wastes without the required number of pollution rights.

Suppose the government issues 100,000 pollution rights and *never issues any more*. The supply of rights available in any year would therefore be fixed at 100,000. The supply curve is drawn as a vertical line in the graph in Box 4. Competition among firms and other polluters for the rights would establish a price of $50. This corresponds to point E_2, at which the supply curve intersects the demand curve. The demand curve is the marginal benefit curve for polluting emissions. At that price harmful emissions are immediately reduced from 200,000 to 100,000 tons per year. How does the reduction occur? Some firms will go out of business rather than pay the price to obtain pollution rights. Other firms will find it cheaper to cut back their output or install emissions control devices rather than pay for pollution rights. Each time a firm that already has purchased pollution rights goes out of business or reduces harmful emissions, it can sell its pollution rights to another firm for extra revenue. If the demand for pollution rights moved up or down, of course, the price of pollution rights would change.

One advantage of issuing pollution rights is that regulatory authorities could control the amount of pollution by controlling the outstanding number of pollution rights. They could, for example, buy back existing rights if they wanted to reduce pollution. Given the market price of the rights, firms could choose to purchase the permits and pollute, or to reduce harmful emissions and save the cost of the rights. They also would have an added incentive to clean up polluting emissions because they could sell previously purchased pollution rights to gain extra revenue.

Recent EPA Policies: Bubbles and Offsets

The Environmental Protection Agency recently has taken steps to make its regulations less rigid. This came about partly because of political pressures in response to the adverse effects of strict EPA regulations on regional economic development. For example, the EPA has the power to prevent firms from locating in certain regions if those firms would increase pollution above allowable levels. To prevent the imposition of such outright limits on regional growth, the EPA has moved to policies that are similar to the pollution-rights scheme we just discussed.

For example, in many regions of the country the EPA now uses an *emissions offset policy*. This policy allows new firms to enter areas in which air quality is such that additional polluting emissions resulting from the firm's operations normally would prevent the firm from being approved by the EPA. Under the offset policy, the new firm must induce other firms in the area to reduce their harmful emissions. The new firm usually does this by making cash payments to the existing firms. For example, the EPA permitted General Motors to build a new plant in Oklahoma City after the local Chamber of Commerce made arrangements for oil firms in the area to reduce their hydrocarbon emissions to offset GM's anticipated emissions.[4] Offset arrangements like this are exactly equivalent to sales of existing pollution rights!

The EPA has added flexibility to its regulations by using a scheme that has been dubbed "the bubble." The bubble is an imaginary enclosure placed over a firm. Within this bubble, emissions of various types are monitored. If the firm exceeds emissions standards for one type of pollutant, the EPA will look the other way, *provided the firm reduces emissions of another pollutant by more than the current standard*. This added flexibility in meeting standards results in considerable cost savings to firms.

The EPA recently moved yet another step closer to a pollution-rights scheme by allowing *banking* of emissions reductions in excess of current standards. A firm that emits less than the specified level of a pollutant is given a credit that allows it to exceed the standards at some time in the future. As an added incentive, *the firm is also allowed to sell these credits for cash to other firms that wish to exceed the standards*. This system not only encourages firms to reduce polluting emissions but also rewards them with a marketable credit that will increase their revenues and profits.[5]

[4]Joseph J. Seneca and Michael K. Taussig, *Environmental Economics,* 3rd ed., Englewood Cliffs, N.J.: Prentice-Hall, 1984, p. 232.
[5]See Wallace E. Oates, "Markets for Pollution Control," *Challenge* 27, May/June 1984, pp. 11-17.

Principles in Practice

Coping with a Negative Externality: Wood Stoves and Wood Smoke

The glowing warmth of the old-time pot-bellied stove . . . the cheery crackle of well-aged logs . . . the tangy aroma of wood smoke on the crisp winter air. . . .

Sounds inviting, doesn't it? Is it possible that this sturdy, enduring symbol of rural America is actually a negative externality?

Because of increased prices for oil, electricity, and natural gas, many families in the United States have turned to an older technique for heating their homes: the wood stove. According to the Environmental Protection Agency, there were 12 million wood stoves in use in the United States in 1986. Alas, the smoke and other gases emitted from use of the stoves are hazardous to your health! To deal with the problem, the EPA would like to place emissions limits on stoves similar to those used to control emissions from automobiles and factories.

In some parts of the country where wood stoves are very popular, the air is already thick with wood smoke. Some local communities, like Amherst, Massachusetts, have begun to levy license fees on wood-stove users to help internalize the externality. Users are subject to a $500 fine if they allow their stoves to put out too much smoke. In Telluride, Colorado, a town of 1,000 people located in a canyon, a permit is required to equip a new home with a wood stove. A builder can obtain the permit only if two other residents can be persuaded to give up their stoves. In 1986 it took $1,000 to get an existing permit owner in Telluride to give up his right to the stove to a permit seeker. Because of wood smoke, air quality is so poor in Telluride that the town government itself is offering anyone who uses a wood heating system $750 to replace that system with natural gas. Other communities are limiting the right of stove owners to burn wood when atmospheric conditions are conducive to concentration of pollutants. The state governments of Oregon and Colorado ban the sale of wood stoves that don't meet state standards.*

As you can see, even without federal government action the health hazards of wood-smoke pollution have prompted communities to enact regulations and charges in an effort to internalize the externality. It's likely that new EPA regulations will soon require that wood stoves be equipped with catalytic converters similar to those mandated for cars! The converters are likely to add as much as $300 to the cost of a wood stove. How do you think this requirement will affect the demand for these relics of Americana?

*See Matthew L. Wald, "Wood Stoves Facing Curbs as Polluters," *The New York Times*, Sunday, November 30, 1986, p. 1.

Political Reality

Many of the political issues surrounding pollution control involve disagreements concerning the short-run and long-run costs of pollution damage. As a result, determining the efficient amount of pollution control and agreeing on emissions charges or standards is often difficult in practice.

There are additional political problems in pollution control policy. If those who are harmed by pollution aren't actually compensated when pollution is reduced, they'll want further pollution control. They won't be satisfied with reduction of pollution to its efficient level because they'll still bear pollution costs for which they aren't compensated. Of course, producers and consumers of goods whose production or consumption results in pollution are made worse off as a result of pollution control. Firms' profits are reduced, and in some cases firms are forced out of business if regulations or payment of emissions charges or taxes cause their operations to become unprofitable. Thus, to the extent to which they don't gain from a cleaner environment, business interests often oppose pollution control policies.

Finally, you should note that emissions control policies often provide more incentives for pollution control in the long run than they do in the short run. Firms seek to maximize profits in the long run. They're likely to look at short-run compliance with regulations or payment of emissions charges as a temporary solution. In the long run they might find they can make still more profits by changing their production process in ways that actually reduce or eliminate the polluting emissions. For example, an emissions charge on the production of electricity in coal-burning plants might induce these firms to change their method of production. In the long run producers might sharply reduce harmful emissions by installing devices in their smokestacks that absorb pollutants if doing so reduces the annual emissions charge. If the marginal external cost associated with their output then declines to zero, they would have no liability under an emissions charge.

Concept Check

1 How can emissions charges help internalize a negative externality that results in pollution?

2 Why do regulations that set emissions standards often fail to actually internalize the externalities that cause pollution?

3 How can the issuance of transferable "pollution rights" help reduce pollution and internalize the externality that is responsible for pollution?

The Economics of Exhaustible Resources

One of the fundamental propositions of economics is that resources are scarce. Perhaps this is most obvious in the case of natural resources. Are the economics of natural resources, such as mineral and petroleum deposits, any different from the economics that apply to other goods and services? There are good reasons for us to discuss the economic characteristics of mineral deposits, timber, and other natural resources. For example, in some cases these resources must be searched for. The price at which the resources can be sold influences the willingness of entrepreneurs to explore for and extract them, as well as the incentives of consumers to seek out substitutes.

It's very misleading to use trend lines, based on current supplies and current consumption, to project future stocks of natural resources. These calculations assume that no new stocks will be uncovered in the future, that technology will remain fixed, and that the price of the resource will be unchanged as its availability diminishes. None of these assumptions is likely to hold over time. In fact, so-called crises in the availability of resources have a way of curing themselves over time. For example, doomsday prophets predicted that the world would run out of petroleum products and that the price of crude oil would soar to over $100 a barrel during the energy "crises" of the 1970s. Yet in 1986 the world was literally swimming in oil as prices plummeted to about $10 a barrel.

Markets for Depletable Natural Resources

The role of price is crucial in analyzing resource use. Failure to understand the price mechanism can result in misleading projections of future reserves and rates of consumption.

A **depletable resource** is a resource for which there is a given amount of known reserves available at any point in time. Only some of the reserves are profitable to exploit at current prices. *Proven reserves* are reserves that can be profitably

Depletable resource:
A resource for which there is a given amount of known reserves available at any point in time.

extracted for sale in markets. For example, petroleum is known to exist in shale rock. However, under current technology the cost of extracting oil from shale is very high. At the current price no shale oil will end up being exploited. At higher prices it might become profitable to extract this resource.

The graph in Box 5 shows the short-run supply curve for a typical depletable resource, such as oil. Suppose the current price of oil is $15 per barrel. Over time, assuming there are no new discoveries, the short-run supply of oil will tend to decrease as known reserves are depleted. Also over time, because of normal economic growth, the demand for oil tends to increase. Both of these factors result in upward pressure on the market price. In Box 5, at the new equilibrium price of $20 per barrel, equilibrium quantity declines to Q_2 from the initial quantity Q_1 given the shifts in demand and supply.

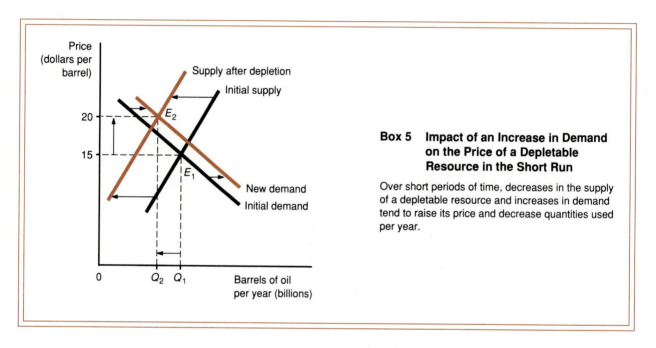

Box 5   Impact of an Increase in Demand on the Price of a Depletable Resource in the Short Run

Over short periods of time, decreases in the supply of a depletable resource and increases in demand tend to raise its price and decrease quantities used per year.

However, in the long run the high price of a depletable resource is likely to encourage additional exploration for and development of the resource. As the number of firms involved in exploration and development increases, the supply of the natural resource eventually increases. Decreases in demand can also occur as substitutes for the resource are developed. These two effects can combine to decrease the price of the resource and increase the quantity used, as illustrated in Box 6 where the initial equilibrium price of $20 at E_2 falls to $10 at E_3, while quantity increases from Q_2 to Q_3. Here, increased supply puts downward pressure on price. However, if the decline in demand is stronger than the increase in supply, equilibrium quantity can decline along with equilibrium price.

For example, in the early 1980s the price of oil peaked at about $33 per barrel. Much of the price increase at that time was attributed to the control of a large portion of the supply by the OPEC cartel. However, by 1986 the price of oil had plunged to about $10 per barrel. The higher prices of oil in the 1970s encouraged exploration and development of new supplies. This tended to increase the supply of oil reserves. In addition, at higher prices it was profitable to develop some known

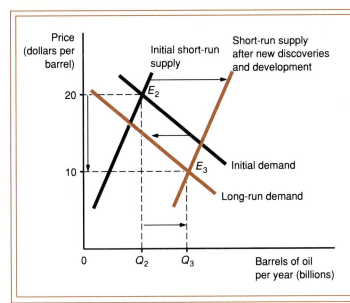

Box 6 **How Increases in Supply and Decreased Demand in the Long Run Can Lower the Price of a Depletable Resource**

In the long run, increased exploration and development of new reserves can increase supplies of a depletable resource. Decreases in demand can occur as substitutes for the resource are developed. These two effects can combine to decrease the price of the resource and increase the quantity used. If, however, the decline in demand is stronger than the increase in supply, price can decline and quantity used will decline as well.

reserves that were unprofitable to exploit at lower prices. This also increased the supply of oil.

There was also a profound demand-side effect over time as people reacted to the initial increase in the price of oil by cutting down their usage. Automobiles became more energy-efficient as average gas mileage per car went up. New homes were built with better insulation. People shifted to wood stoves and other means of heating that decreased the demand for petroleum. You're probably familiar with these and other responses to higher energy prices. In the long run these higher prices resulted in the development of substitutes for oil use. As a consequence, the demand for oil actually decreased, or at least didn't grow as quickly as it otherwise would have. In the long run the demand for a resource is likely to be more elastic than in the short run. As a result of the growth in supply and decrease in demand in the long run, the price of oil actually declined. Also contributing to the decline in price was the fact that new producers, such as Mexico and the United Kingdom, were not members of the OPEC cartel. This decreased OPEC's apparent control over price. The lower price of oil in the mid-1980s led many producers to abandon extraction of certain reserves because they were no longer profitable to exploit at the lower prices.

Property Rights and Renewable Natural Resources

A **renewable resource** is a natural resource that can be restocked in time, such as timber, fish, and wildlife. A basic problem with many renewable resources is that the natural resources from which they are obtained, such as the ocean, lakes, or common hunting lands, are not the private property of any one person. Fishermen, for example, don't have to pay a fee for the right to fish in the ocean. An input like the ocean, whose use is not priced because property rights have not been established is called a **common property resource.** Because fees are rarely paid for the right to use the ocean for fishing, the costs of fishing appear lower than they actually are and there's a tendency to overexploit the ocean as a source of fish. This

Renewable resource:
A natural resource that can be restocked in time, such as fish, timber, and wildlife.

Common property resource:
A resource (such as the ocean) whose use is not priced because property rights for payment of services have not been established.

is like using land and not paying rent. When you don't pay for the right to use land, you tend to use more than you would if you paid a price equal to the opportunity cost of that land in an alternative use.

In this case a negative externality exists. Fishermen don't consider the fact that as they catch more fish, fish become scarcer in the future because the breeding stock is reduced. The source of the externality is the lack of a price for the right to use the common property resource. Fishermen can be forced to consider the effects of overfishing by being made to pay a yearly fee for the right to use the water resources.

Other examples of common property resources are the atmosphere, common grazing lands, and hunting areas. As the services these resources yield become scarcer, the failure to price the services can have disastrous consequences. A typical result is the possible extinction of hunted species. A secondary effect of this type of externality is higher prices for goods produced with common property resources.

Finding a way to price the services of common property resources often improves efficiency and increases future stocks of the renewable resource. For example, one study showed that restrictions on the right to trap lobsters in waters off the coast of Maine resulted in a doubling of the catch.[6]

Concept Check

1 Why does the annual consumption of a depletable resource tend to decline as the reserves available decline?

2 How does a renewable resource differ from a depletable resource?

3 Why is there a tendency to make more than efficient use of a common property resource like the ocean as an input into such activities as fishing?

Summary

1. Pollution is waste that has been disposed of in the air, in water, or on land that reduces the value of those resources in alternative uses.
2. Pollution is an economic problem because it stems from competing uses for scarce environmental resources.
3. Pollution control is an economic good whose benefits are improved human health and reduced damage to structures, materials, and natural and agricultural resources.
4. The efficient level of pollution control balances the marginal costs of reducing pollution against the marginal benefits by adjusting the amount of cleanup to the point at which the marginal social benefit equals the marginal social cost.
5. Not all emissions of wastes are necessarily pollution. A pollutant causes damage to competing uses of a resource. When emissions disperse before achieving concentrations high enough to cause damage, they never actually become pollutants. Similarly, when emissions occur in regions in which alternative uses of environmental resources are not damaged, they are not pollutants.
6. More than the efficient amount of pollution results when a negative externality

[6]James A. Wilson, "A Test of the Tragedy of the Commons," in Garret Hardin and John Baden, eds., *Managing the Commons,* San Francisco: W.H. Freeman & Co., 1977.

exists. An emissions charge can be used to internalize negative externalities that result in overuse of the environment for waste disposal. An emissions charge set equal to the marginal external cost of pollution damage can cause a firm to achieve an efficient level of pollution.

7. Emissions standards are limits established by governing authorities on the annual amounts and kinds of pollutants that can be emitted into the air or water. Emissions standards allow emission of polluting wastes at no charge up to the permitted levels. Thereafter, further emissions are strictly outlawed. The standards don't usually consider the differences among firms in costs of eliminating harmful emissions or regional differences in the benefits of pollution control.

8. Pollution can also be controlled by the issuance of transferable pollution rights that price the right to pollute at a level that reflects the marginal social cost of pollution. Recent Environmental Protection Agency policies to modify rigid standards allow firms to purchase the right to pollute from other firms already in the area through emissions offsets. The EPA also allows firms to exceed standard emissions rates for one pollutant if they reduce emissions of another pollutant by an amount that exceeds the current standard.

9. Depletable natural resources are those for which there is a given quantity of known reserves available at any point in time. Proven reserves of a depletable resource are those that can be profitably extracted for sale in markets. As demand for a resource increases and reserves decline, the price of the resource increases. This provides incentives to develop previously unprofitable reserves for extraction and to search for more reserves. The higher price also encourages consumers to conserve the resource. In this way the price system economizes on the use of depletable resources.

10. Renewable resources are natural resources such as timber, fish, and wildlife that can be restocked in time. Common property resources, like the ocean, used in producing renewable resources are difficult to price and are usually overexploited relative to the usage that would be efficient. Finding a feasible method of pricing a common property resource can improve efficiency and increase future stocks of the renewable resource.

Key Terms and Concepts

Pollution
Emissions charges
Emissions standards
Pollution right

Depletable resource
Renewable resource
Common property resource

Problems and Applications

1. An environmental activist argues that all pollution should be banned because this will save lives and preserve the natural beauty of the environment. An industrialist argues that there should be no restraints on the right of firms to emit pollutants. Why are both of these extreme positions on the issue of pollution control likely to result in inefficient resource use if they are enacted?

2. Why would a ban on all pollution cause deaths just as surely as unrestricted pollution is responsible for deaths?

3. The marginal social benefit of pollution control is currently estimated to be $5 billion per year at a level of 80% of emissions abated. The marginal social cost

of pollution control at that level of abatement is $8 billion per year. Is the level of pollution control efficient? If not, what must be done to achieve the efficient level of pollution control?

4. How would you go about estimating the marginal social benefit of pollution control? How would you estimate the marginal social cost of pollution control?

5. A firm that produces chemicals operates a plant in a remote desert area. No one lives within 50 miles of the plant. The plant emits a noxious chemical waste into the air. Under what circumstances would these emissions not be regarded as pollutants? Should an emissions charge be imposed on the firm to reduce the pollution?

6. A firm emitting nitrogen dioxide waste into the atmosphere is subjected to a $5 per ton emissions charge, which equals the marginal external cost of nitrogen dioxide in the area. The firm's smokestack is monitored electronically, and it's easy to accurately levy the charge. After the charge is imposed the firm reduces its emissions by only 10%. Why is the charge ineffective in completely eliminating the emissions? Would it be efficient to reduce this firm's emissions to zero?

7. Suppose instead that the firm described in problem 6 was told to meet an emissions standard that required it to reduce emissions by 50% of their current levels. Why would this emissions standard not lead to efficiency?

8. The marginal external cost of sulfur dioxide emissions is estimated to be $20 per year in urban areas and $10 per year in rural areas. Current emissions standards limit emissions to 200 tons per year for all firms irrespective of their location. Why are such standards not likely to achieve the efficient level of pollution control?

9. The government issues 100,000 pollution rights and sells them at auction. It's announced that no more pollution rights will ever be issued. The competition for the rights establishes a price of $50. After the rights have been sold to all firms wishing to pollute, a rich philanthropist buys up 20% of the rights outstanding and keeps them in a bank vault. What will happen to the price of pollution rights and the amount of pollution as a result of this purchase?

10. a. Conservationists are very concerned about excessive killing of deer in a hunting area. How can the price system be employed to decrease the incentive to hunt deer on common property hunting grounds?

    b. A student calculates that the consumption of a certain mineral is equal to 500 tons per year. Given the proven reserves of this mineral, the student estimates that at the current rate of annual consumption the reserves of the mineral will be depleted in 20 years. Why is his prediction almost certainly wrong?

Suggested Readings

Myrick A. Freeman III, *The Benefits of Environmental Improvement,* Baltimore: Johns Hopkins University Press, 1979. This book discusses the benefits of pollution control and develops techniques for estimating those benefits.

Wallace E. Oates, "Markets for Pollution Control," *Challenge* 27, May/June 1984, pp. 11-17. This is a readable account of how recent EPA policies are moving the nation toward a system of exchangeable pollution rights.

Joseph J. Seneca and Michael K. Taussig, *Environmental Economics,* 3rd ed., Englewood Cliffs, N.J.: Prentice-Hall, 1984. This is a textbook that uses economics to analyze environmental policy.

CHAPTER 17 Externalities and the Environment: Policy Analysis

A Forward Look

In this chapter and the one preceding it we've concentrated on the role of government in correcting for market failure to price resource use. Many of the demands placed on government to influence resource use stem from dissatisfaction with the price system as a means of allocating incomes. In the following chapter we focus on the role of government in subsidizing agriculture and industries and show how special-interest groups compete for government programs that increase their incomes. We analyze the impact of these programs on resource use.

CHAPTER

18

Subsidizing Agriculture and Industries: The Economics of Special-Interest Groups

Modern government isn't unlike the royal courts of bygone days in which sovereigns were petitioned for favors by a horde of special interests. Today in the United States many different groups compete for subsidies, tax breaks, and other special favors from governing authorities. The cast of characters for this drama includes labor unions, industrial associations, organizations of farmers, and a host of sophisticated political action groups that promise to deliver votes to candidates who support certain programs. There are also government agencies that administer programs designed to benefit particular interests. The U.S. Department of Agriculture, for example, operates programs to support the incomes of farmers.

In this chapter we look at the economics of special-interest groups. Agriculture, which seems to be an industry in perpetual crisis, is often singled out for special treatment by U.S. government authorities. We'll examine some of the special problems of agriculture and the consequences of agricultural price supports. We'll also analyze the impact of subsidies and special tax breaks for other particular industries and in general.

After reading this chapter, you should be able to:

1   Discuss special-interest groups, their goals, and the impact of programs that benefit these interests on prices and resource allocation.
2   Describe the process of rent seeking, in which people compete for government subsidies and other programs that increase their incomes.
3   Evaluate the impact of agricultural policies that subsidize farmers in the United States.

Special-Interest Groups

A **special-interest** group is an organization that seeks to increase government expenditures or induce government to take other actions that benefit particular people. These groups represent industries, ethnic and racial groups, regions, cities, environmentalists, or taxpayers in general. In recent years special-interest groups have become potent political forces. They encourage their members and others to vote for certain candidates for elective office. Successful special-interest groups manage to obtain government subsidies, reduce taxes, or manipulate government regulations and international trade policies to benefit their constituents.[1] One of the most powerful lobbies in the United States represents farmers, a group that comprises fewer than 6 million Americans.

An increase in government spending (or a reduction in taxes) that makes one group better off usually means that someone else pays more taxes or enjoys less government expenditure, at least in the short run. However, if pressure groups manage to obtain changes in policies that move the economy to a more efficient resource allocation, then it will be possible for government to make those groups better off without harming anyone else in the long run. Subsidies like those designed to internalize positive externalities discussed in Chapter 16 can actually help the economy allocate resources more efficiently. In this chapter we concentrate on subsidies whose purpose is to increase the incomes of certain groups and that don't necessarily internalize a positive externality. A society doesn't automatically enjoy net gains from these subsidies or from other policies that affect prices in ways that increase the incomes of some groups while reducing the money incomes or purchasing power of others.

You might think that the more people a special-interest group represents, the more powerful the group. However, a little thought will convince you that in fact the opposite is likely to be true! The reason for this is that the smaller the group, the lower the tax per taxpayer necessary to finance a given dollar subsidy per group member. For example, if farmers number 1 million, then a $3,000 per farmer annual subsidy requires an annual outlay of $3 billion. If there are 100 million taxpayers, the tax per taxpayer to finance this outlay will be only $30 per year. This is a sum small enough to be barely noticed by the average taxpayer. If instead farmers numbered 20 million, then the same $3,000 per farmer subsidy would require an annual

Special-interest group: An organization that seeks to increase government expenditures or induce government to take other actions that benefit particular people.

[1]See Gary S. Becker, "A Theory of Competition Among Pressure Groups for Political Influence," *Quarterly Journal of Economics,* 98, August 1983, pp. 371-400.

outlay of $60 billion. Assuming 100 million taxpayers, the tax per taxpayer to finance the subsidy to farmers would now be $600 per year—hardly a negligible sum.

In the case of agriculture this hypothesis seems to be supported by the facts. Agriculture enjoys heavy subsidies in nations where it's a very small sector of the economy, as is true in the United States and Japan. On the other hand, agriculture is quite heavily taxed in nations where it's a very large economic sector, as is the case in many African nations, the Soviet Union, and Poland.[2]

Special-interest groups contribute to the growth of government. Many people would be *no worse off* if the subsidies they receive and the taxes they pay to subsidize others were reduced in equal amounts. However, because taxes and subsidies distort choices in ways that prevent markets from achieving efficient outcomes, there would be a net gain in efficiency by reducing *both* taxes and subsidies in equal amounts.

Rent Seeking

Economic rents:
Earnings that exceed the opportunity cost of an activity.

Economic rents are earnings that exceed the opportunity cost of an activity. When you earn economic rent from working in a particular occupation, you receive a higher labor income than you can earn in your next best alternative. Many people seek to use the power of government to create economic rents that allow them to obtain higher incomes than would otherwise be possible. Governments can create economic rents by limiting the right to engage in certain activities. They could require licenses to sell certain goods or services. These licenses would be designed to limit the number of persons selling the good or service. Governments might require licenses for farmers to grow certain crops. The license would limit the number of growers or the amount of land that could be placed in production. For example, to market tobacco, farmers in the United States must have a tobacco allotment. The allotments represent the right to sell leaf tobacco and serve to limit the acreage devoted to tobacco production. This tends to limit the supply of tobacco. When demand increases, price goes up while supply is prevented from increasing in the long run through the entry of new farmers. This tends to increase the incomes of the growers fortunate enough to have the allotments. People who own tobacco allotments have a valuable asset created by government policy that can be leased to others who actually grow the tobacco or that can be sold at the going market price.

Rent seeking:
The process by which people compete to obtain government favors that increase the economic rents they can earn.

Rent seeking is the process by which people compete to obtain government favors that increase the economic rents they can earn. Rent seeking includes competition for monopoly privileges granted by government, such as exclusive franchises to run transportation routes. The transaction costs involved in using resources to try to obtain economic rents can be substantial. These costs include the time and effort of lobby groups that use employees, computers, office equipment, and real estate for the purpose of persuading politicians to support policies that grant them special privileges. One study concluded that the transaction costs and losses in efficiency of resource use resulting from rent seeking accounted for between 10% and 60% of sales in six major industries in the United States.[3]

---

[2]See Becker.
[3]Richard A. Posner, "The Social Costs of Monopoly and Regulation," *Journal of Political Economy,* 83, August 1975, pp. 807-827.

1   What are the goals of special-interest groups, and how do they seek to attain these goals?

2   Under what circumstances can subsidies and other policies benefiting special-interest groups result in net gains rather than income redistribution?

3   Why is rent seeking likely to result in a redistribution of income and prevent efficient use of resources?

Agricultural Policy

As observed earlier, an industry that enjoys heavy subsidies in the United States is agriculture. Over the years, concern about the welfare of farmers, coupled with the desire for a stable domestic source of food, has led to the enactment of controls on supply, direct subsidy payments, and price supports.

In 1984 the farm sector of the economy contributed $68 billion to national production and accounted for 2.7 million jobs. In that same year farmers enjoyed various government subsidy payments amounting to $8.4 billion, which was 12% of the market value of farm production. By 1985 federal spending to support farmers had increased substantially, to over $18 billion. Provisions of the Food Security Act of 1985 sharply increased total federal support to farmers to a record $25 billion in 1986.

Despite the many government programs to assist farmers, in the mid-1980s the profitability of farming appeared to plummet. Agricultural land values fell, and the newspapers were loaded with stories of farmers sinking into bankruptcy. Farmers faced increased competition in foreign markets, which resulted in sharp declines in agricultural exports. Prices of agricultural commodities fell.

Although their industry is heavily subsidized, many farmers blame the federal government for the financial problems they've experienced in the 1980s. Others criticize farm subsidies as welfare for the rich because they appear to give more to wealthy farmers than to poor ones.

Agriculture offers us an excellent opportunity to look at the economics of subsidies and the consequences of government intervention in markets. Why, despite payments totaling $25 billion in 1986, is U.S. agriculture still in such bad shape? Is this, many ask, a case of government failure?

Goals of Agricultural Support Programs in the United States

In the United States, government policy to assist farmers has been a political reality for over 200 years. Farmers represent an active and successful special-interest group. The basic objectives broadly accepted as part of U.S. farm policy are[4]:

1. Maintain farming as a free and independent business
2. Maintain an adequate supply of food at reasonable prices
3. Encourage agricultural exports

[4]See Wayne D. Rasmussen, "Historical Overview of U.S. Agricultural Policies and Programs," in U.S. Department of Agriculture, *Agricultural-Food Policy Review: Commodity Program Perspectives*, Economic Research Service, Agricultural Report No. 530, July 1985.

In our country's early years, agricultural products made up about 80% of total exports. Today agricultural commodities amount to less than 20% of exports. In 1862 concern about the viability of agriculture led to the enactment of legislation that established the U.S. Department of Agriculture, homesteads for settlers, and land grants for the formation of agricultural colleges. Recognizing the importance of farm products as a source of foreign exchange, politicians supported legislation designed to help keep agriculture financially healthy.

Agriculture as a Special Interest

The political power of farmers and their effectiveness in rent seeking gained considerable strength in the late 1800s when farming interests organized the Populist party to represent them. The party advocated free coinage of silver and government control of monopolies. The source of farmers' problems was price volatility of their products and increased production resulting from improved methods of farming. Gains in agricultural productivity increase supply, putting downward pressure on farm prices. Because the demand for food is inelastic, the decrease in prices results in decreases in farm revenues, which result in lower profits.

Farmers prospered during World War I when farm prices rose and exports increased. However, farm prices collapsed in the 1920s and continued to decline through much of that decade. The decline in farm prices and incomes during the 1920s is often cited as one of the underlying causes of the Great Depression of the 1930s. In fact, many doomsayers have drawn parallels between the farm situation of the 1920s and that of the 1980s. However, before you lose sleep over such analogies, you should remember that farming is a much smaller sector of the economy today than it was in the 1920s.

In the 1920s and 1930s, the major pressure group to champion the interests of farmers in the political arena was the American Farm Bureau Federation, which lobbied for federal legislation to support farm prices and incomes. Eventually Congress passed the Agricultural Adjustment Act of 1933, which was signed into law by President Roosevelt. This act sought to maintain farm incomes chiefly by controlling the amount of acreage in production and the prices paid to farmers. These methods of supporting farm incomes remain the major means of subsidizing agriculture in the United States today. These programs involve a constant struggle, and expenditure of government funds, to keep surplus agricultural commodities from being offered for sale in markets where they will lower prices and therefore reduce incomes of farmers. What's more, as you can see in the Principles in Practice box, agricultural price support programs may involve a delicate balancing of opposing interests.

The Goal of Parity

Parity:
The idea that the prices of agricultural commodities must rise as fast as the prices of goods and services on which farmers spend their income.

The purpose of **parity,** often stated as a goal of agricultural price supports, is to keep the prices of agricultural commodities high enough to guarantee constant purchasing power from the sale of given amounts of commodities. Parity means that the prices of agricultural commodities must rise as fast as the prices of goods and services on which farmers spend their income. Because the relative price of agricultural commodities has tended to fall compared to other goods and services, the goal of parity has required price supports for farmers. The period usually used to measure parity is 1910 to 1914, which was considered the golden age for American agriculture because the price of agricultural products was high relative to other goods. If

The Consequences of Agricultural Price Supports: Price Floors on Milk Induce the Government to Turn Dairy Cows into Hamburger!

Whether you favor or oppose government support of farm prices, you have to admit that price supports can have some unexpected—sometimes even bizarre—consequences, as in this case of turning Bossy into beef.

Price supports have aided dairy farmers for many years. From 1949 to 1983, price support levels were above equilibrium prices for milk products. During that period there were no restrictions on dairy production levels, nor were there any incentive payment programs to reduce production. The result was a tremendous surplus of dairy products. The U.S. Department of Agriculture bought the surplus—at the support prices—in the form of butter, cheese, and powdered milk products.

The stockpiles of cheese and other storable products reached incredibly high levels by the mid-1980s, when the Department of Agriculture was purchasing about 10% of the total production of U.S. dairy farmers. During the early 1980s, outlays to support dairy farmers were costing taxpayers over $2 billion annually. The surplus and outlays to buy it remained at high levels after 1983 despite other policies designed to discourage production. When the warehouses began to burst at the seams with cheese, the government went into low-income neighborhoods and discreetly gave cheese out free to needy families!

In 1985 a so-called "Milk Production Termination Program" was enacted as part of the Food Security Act of 1985.* The program represented an attempt to reduce the chronic surplus of dairy products by turning milk cows into hamburger!

Here's how the program worked:

1. The federal government paid dairy farmers a total of $1.8 billion for agreeing to sell their herds. The cows, heifers, and calves were sold for slaughter during 1986 and 1987. Farmers selling their herds promised to keep their milking facilities idle and to stay out of all dairy activities for a period of 5 years.

2. Price support levels were cut, and special assessments were levied on all dairy farmers to finance some of the costs of the new buyout program.

3. The sellout of herds was voluntary. Producers submitted bids to the U.S. Department of Agriculture stating the price they were willing to accept to sell out their herds. The 14,000 dairy farmers whose bids were accepted had produced 12.3 billion pounds of milk in 1985, which represented close to 9% of U.S. production. The productive capacity of these farmers was removed as a source of supply for 5 years.

4. The animals sold to the government were slaughtered or exported. This did not please beef and hog producers, who feared the program would lower the price of their output in 1986 and 1987. To mollify these producers, the federal government promised to purchase an additional 400 million pounds of red meat during the period of the buyout. This will keep beef and pork prices from falling too much but will add to the costs borne by taxpayers.

The Milk Production Termination Program was expected to reduce but not eliminate the surplus of dairy products. Increases in productivity measured by milk per cow will offset some of the reduction in the stock of animals.

*For additional details see G.A. Benson, "The Dairy Herd Buyout Program," Agricultural Extension Service, Department of Economics and Business, North Carolina State University, July 1986.

farm prices were at 100% of parity, a bushel of wheat would sell for a price that would allow the farmer to buy the same quantity and quality of goods and services he could have enjoyed in, say, 1914 by selling the same amount of wheat. Note that parity is a goal that relates only to the prices of agricultural products and not to the profits of farm owners. Maintenance of price parity doesn't guarantee that farming will be profitable because farming profits depend on costs as well as revenues. However, achievement of parity prices means government intervention makes farming more profitable than it would be without such intervention.

The **parity price ratio** is the ratio of an average of prices of goods sold by farmers to an average of prices of goods on which farmers spend their income. In the 1930s and 1940s, much of the legislation to support farmers sought to keep agricultural prices between 75% and 90% of parity. The parity price ratio fell to nearly 60% in the 1930s and rose to 120% during World War II. Except for a brief

Parity price ratio:
The ratio of an average of prices of goods sold by farmers to an average of prices of goods on which farmers spend their income.

period in the early 1970s when it increased to nearly 100%, the parity price ratio has declined steadily since 1950. *In the mid-1980s the parity price ratio reached an all-time low of less than 60%.*

Agricultural Price Supports and the Farm Surplus Problem

Price Supports

Government policy in the United States has supported agricultural incomes by guaranteeing farmers a minimum price for their commodities. For example, in 1986 the federal government guaranteed farmers $2.40 for each bushel of corn. As you saw in Chapter 5, a price support for an agricultural commodity is a price floor that contributes to a surplus of the commodity when it exceeds the market equilibrium price. Because the support price for corn in 1986 was well above the market equilibrium price of about $1.60 per bushel that year, the result was a surplus of corn. In fact, in 1986 and 1987 the grain elevators were just about bursting at the seams with corn stored by the government as a result of the surplus. In 1987 the government spent a total of $11.9 billion subsidizing corn growers! Taxpayers pay the costs of acquiring the surplus crop. The annual cost of storing surplus corn was estimated to be $900 million in 1987. When stored grain owned by the government is sold, it provides revenue to the government. However, grain is fragile. After 9 months in storage its quality declines, and sometimes stored corn is ruined by mold and turns to useless dust.

Agricultural support prices are established through federal *nonrecourse loan* programs. Under these programs farmers pledge crops in storage as collateral for a government loan. For example, if the loan rate for corn is $2.40 per bushel the Commodity Credit Corporation, which acts as the government agent in these transactions, is required to take title to corn pledged by farmers if the farmers choose to forfeit their collateral. If farmers choose this option of paying off their loan, they keep the cash they borrowed from the government, which was $2.40 per bushel, while the Commodity Credit Corporation has no recourse but to take title to stored commodities. In effect, this loan program obligates the government to buy commodities at the established price floor. Nonrecourse loan programs are available for wheat, corn, cotton, peanuts, rice, tobacco, sorghum, barley, oats, rye, soybeans, and sugar. Farmers choose to sell rather than forfeit the stored commodities only if the market price exceeds the loan rate.

The table in Box 1 shows the loan rates prevailing for selected agricultural commodities in 1984. The table in Box 2 shows the relationship between the parity price, the loan rate, and the market price for wheat and corn from 1951 to 1983. As you can see, the loan rates for these two crops have been considerably below the parity price since 1971. You should also note that the loan rate isn't always above the market price.

Acreage Control Programs

Acreage control programs: Provide cash payments to farmers who agree to take some of their land out of production for certain crops.

Acreage control programs provide cash payments to farmers who agree to take some of their land out of production for certain crops. Farmers earn income by agreeing *not* to produce certain commodities! Some of the land taken out of agricultural production is put into conservation uses.

Box 1 Price Supports for Selected Agricultural
Commodities, 1984

Commodity	Loan rate (national average)
Corn	$ 2.55 per bushel
Soybeans	5.02 per bushel
Wheat	3.30 per bushel
Cotton	0.55 per pound
Sorghum	4.32 per cwt.
Rice	8.00 per cwt.

Source: *Statistical Abstract of the United States*, 1987.

Box 2 Parity Prices, Loan Rates, and Market Prices for Wheat and Corn:
Selected Years Between 1951 and 1983

Year	Parity price	Loan rate	Market price
Wheat			
1951	2.40	2.18	2.11
1956	2.42	2.00	1.97
1961	2.38	1.79	1.83
1966	2.58	1.25	1.63
1971	2.91	1.25	1.34
1974	3.95	1.35	4.09
1976	4.87	2.25	2.73
1981	7.07	3.20	3.65
1982	7.26	3.55	3.50
1983	7.39	3.65	3.54
Corn			
1951	1.77	1.57	1.66
1956	1.76	1.50	1.29
1961	1.61	1.20	1.10
1966	1.62	1.00	1.24
1971	1.99	1.05	1.08
1974	3.04	1.10	3.02
1976	3.45	1.50	2.15
1981	5.04	2.40	2.50
1982	5.06	2.55	2.62
1983	5.17	2.65	3.30

Source: U.S. Department of Agriculture, Economic Research Service, Agricultural Economic
Report No. 53, July 1985, *Agricultural-Food Policy Review: Commodity Program
Perspectives,* p. 131.

The prospect of a payment not to use land increases the opportunity cost of using that land to plant the crop eligible for the acreage control program. The goal of the program, of course, is to reduce the supply of certain commodities. By doing so it raises the prices of those commodities received by farmers, thereby raising the parity price ratio for those crops.

The graph in Box 3 shows the impact of acreage restriction on market supply and market equilibrium price. If enough land is taken out of wheat production, the supply curve shifts sufficiently to increase the market equilibrium price from $1.75 to $3 per bushel.

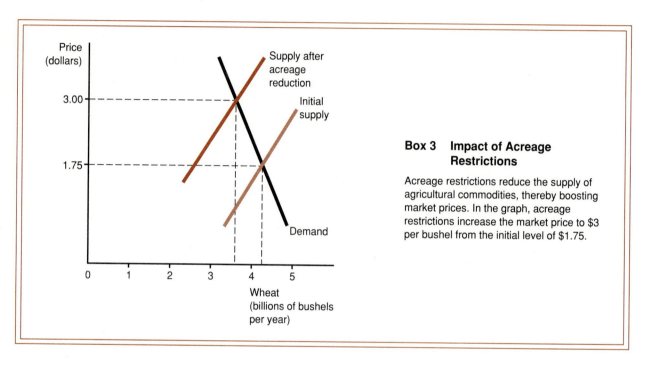

Box 3   Impact of Acreage Restrictions

Acreage restrictions reduce the supply of agricultural commodities, thereby boosting market prices. In the graph, acreage restrictions increase the market price to $3 per bushel from the initial level of $1.75.

The advantage of the acreage control policy is that it prevents the production of surplus commodities that then have to be purchased by the government and stored. However, to induce farmers to voluntarily take land out of production, the subsidy per acre must be high enough to cover their opportunity cost of not planting. As taxpayers we foot the bill for the direct payments to farmers. As consumers we end up paying higher prices for agricultural commodities.

What Does the Government Do with Surplus Agricultural Commodities?

To keep prices of agricultural commodities above market equilibrium levels when support prices result in surpluses, the government must keep grain and other commodities it acquires off the market. In recent years, for example, the government has held about one third of the total world stocks of grain to keep grain prices at support levels. By holding on to its enormous stocks, the government stabilizes commodity prices. If it were to dump its stocks on the market, the tremendous increase in supply would cause world prices of many commodities to plummet.

Using Production Quotas to Deal with Agricultural Surpluses:
A Lesson from the Peanut Program

"It's just peanuts to me." We use that slang phrase to mean that something isn't worth much. To peanut farmers, however, peanuts aren't pocket change–they're a source of income and profits. Let's look at an innovative system the federal government uses to support prices received by peanut farmers.

Two problems exist with current methods of maintaining farm incomes in the United States: overproduction and high prices that decrease the competitiveness of U.S. farm products abroad. One method to support farm incomes and keep U.S. farm products competitive abroad is the use of quotas to restrict production and a system that allows producers who exceed quotas to sell their crops at the market price. Such a system has been used for many years to support the incomes of U.S. peanut growers.

Peanut farmers have a quota on the number of pounds of peanuts they can grow at support prices. For example, a peanut farmer with a 50,000-pound quota in 1986 knew she could sell that volume of peanuts for a guaranteed price of $607 per ton under the price support that prevailed that year. By establishing the quota for the amount of the crop that will be under support prices, the government reduces the likelihood of overproduction at the support price. It also sets a cap on the amount of payments to be made to growers during the year.

However, peanut growers are *not* prohibited from growing more than their allotted quota. If they do so, however, they must sell the nonquota peanuts at market equilibrium prices. In 1986 the equilibrium price for peanuts on world markets ranged from $335 to $340 per ton. Although this wasn't much more than half the support price, farmers often chose to sell more than their allotted quota. Apparently the marginal cost of selling additional peanuts beyond the quota amount is less than the market equilibrium price, and farmers can increase their profits by planting more than their quota.

This two-price system and use of quotas are apparently working well in supporting farmer incomes and encouraging exports of peanuts. Farmers like having the option to exceed their quotas when it's profitable to do so. Policymakers like the fact that the program encourages exports. The supply management approach reduces the need to store peanuts. The peanut program is in fact one of the less costly agricultural programs in the United States, accounting for expenditures of only $4 million in 1985.

The quota system is likely to be considered for other crops, such as wheat, corn, and soybeans, for which support prices have created incentives to overproduce and have flooded government storage facilities with surplus crops.

In certain cases the reserved food is used to provide foreign aid to less developed nations. The Food Security Wheat Reserve Act of 1980 authorized a reserve of 147 million bushels to be used for emergency and humanitarian purposes in less developed nations. However, the amounts of commodities that can be allocated to these programs must be limited if the government is to achieve its objective of keeping world and U.S. prices from plummeting. Our government must be careful not to increase supplies to such an extent that normal market incentives to produce are disrupted.

One novel use of the stored commodities was the recent *Payment-in-Kind (PIK) program*. Although the program is no longer active, it's interesting to look at its effect. This program tried to kill two birds with one stone by using surplus commodities as payment to farmers for acreage reduction. Under the PIK program, farmers were promised payment in the form of surplus wheat, corn, rice, and cotton if they agreed to cut back plantings of these commodities. The program was designed to increase agricultural prices through acreage reductions that would decrease supply while not requiring tax-financed cash subsidies to farmers. When the program began in 1983, farmers eagerly signed up for it and took about one third of farm land out of production of eligible crops.

Unfortunately, the program coincided with a record drought. The drought plus the incentive of the payment in kind contributed to a 50% decline in U.S. corn production in 1983 and resulted in higher than expected market prices. Farmers accepted their payments in surplus commodities, which they were then able to sell at high market prices. The price of corn rose from $2.60 per bushel in 1982 to about $3.30 in 1983. The price of cotton also rose about 20% in 1983. As a result of the PIK program, food prices increased substantially.

The market value of the commodities given to farmers under the PIK program in 1983 was about $12 billion. By allowing farmers, rather than taxpayers, to benefit from the sale of these commodities, the government lost that much revenue. However, it cost the government more than that because of handling and transportation costs to restock the surplus commodities.

Recent Policies: Target Prices and Direct Subsidies

The Food Security Act of 1985 sharply reduced the loan rates for many agricultural commodities with the goal of lowering prices that farmers will accept for their crops. This was designed to make U.S. crops more competitive in international markets, thereby increasing agricultural exports. To prevent a sharp drop in farmer incomes, the act increased direct subsidies to farmers and increased the limit on payments that can be enjoyed by individual farmers.

Target price:
Guarantees sellers of agricultural commodities a minimum price per unit of output.

The method most recently used to support the incomes of grain producers is the imposition of a **target price,** which guarantees sellers a minimum price per unit of output. Unlike the price supports that function as price floors, target prices do *not* directly increase the market price paid by buyers. Instead the entire quantity supplied by farmers at the target price is dumped on the market. The resulting price depends on the demand for the commodity. Farmers are then subsidized by the government for each bushel sold through a payment equal to the difference between the target price and the price paid by buyers.[5]

At the beginning of each crop year the U.S. Department of Agriculture announces the target prices for various crops and the eligibility requirements to participate in the target price program. For example, in 1987 the target price for wheat was $4.38 per bushel. To be eligible for the target price program, farmers typically are required to hold a certain percentage of their acreage idle. In 1987 farmers had to hold 25% of their land out of production.

The graph in Box 4 uses supply and demand analysis to analyze the impact of the target price on farmers, consumers, and taxpayers. Two supply curves are illustrated. The supply curve labeled S_1 shows the relationship between price and the quantity of a crop, say wheat, that would be supplied per year in the absence of any acreage controls. Given the demand curve for wheat, the market equilibrium price per bushel would be $2 and the equilibrium quantity would be Q_E bushels per year without acreage restrictions, corresponding to point C in the graph.

The acreage restriction serves to decrease the supply of wheat so that the new supply curve is the one labeled S_2. The quantity supplied in any year depends on the target price guaranteed to farmers, assuming the price exceeds the anticipated market equilibrium price with the acreage restrictions. In Box 4 the quantity supplied at the target price is Q_T bushels, which corresponds to point A on the supply curve with acreage restrictions. Note that despite the acreage restrictions supply is not fixed because farmers can vary the quantity produced on remaining acreage by working the land with varying amounts of labor, machinery, and fertilizer.

[5]Actually, the program is a bit more complicated in that there is also a support price established through government loan programs that places a limit on the extent to which the price paid by buyers can fall.

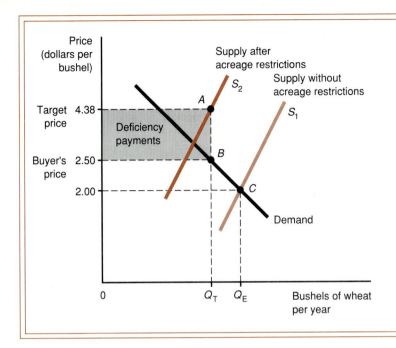

Box 4 **Impact of Agricultural Target Prices**

The target price results in quantity supplied of Q_T bushels of wheat per year, corresponding to point *A* on the supply curve after acreage restrictions. This amount is sold on the market at the price buyers will pay. The buyer's price corresponds to point *B* on the demand curve. Farmers receive deficiency payments corresponding to the shaded rectangle, which are financed by tax revenues. Without any acreage restrictions, the price to buyers corresponding to point *C* could be lower than the price at point *B*.

Unlike the price support programs established through nonrecourse loans, the government doesn't purchase the surplus that would prevail at the target price. Instead the entire quantity supplied is offered for sale to buyers in the market. At quantity Q_T, the price buyers are willing to pay corresponds to point *B* on the demand curve. As a result, buyers are able to purchase wheat at $2.50 per bushel instead of the target price of $4.38. However, farmers do receive the target price because the government pays them an amount equal to the difference between the buyer's price and the target price. In Box 4 this payment, which is a government subsidy that varies with quantity sold by farmers, corresponds to the distance *AB*. With a target price of $4.38 and a buyer's price of $2.50, the deficiency payment is $1.88 per bushel. Total deficiency payments to all farmers are represented by the shaded rectangle in the graph, the area of which equals the deficiency payment per bushel multiplied by the Q_T bushels supplied over the year. The cost to taxpayers of the target price program is represented by the total deficiency payments to farmers.

As consumers we're clearly better off under the target price program than we would be under a price floor of $4.38 per bushel. In fact, one of the justifications for the target price program in recent years has been that it does contribute to lower prices for U.S. crops, thereby increasing the ability of U.S. producers to compete in international commodity markets. However, because of the acreage restrictions that go along with the program, prices can be higher than would be the case without subsidies. In Box 4 the market equilibrium price in the absence of any government subsidies or price supports would be $2 per bushel, which is lower than the $2.50 per bushel that prevails under the target price program. Subsidizing farmers in this way therefore transfers income from taxpayers in general to farmers but doesn't necessarily result in lower commodity prices to consumers compared to those that would prevail in a free market. The United States isn't the only nation that subsidizes farmers in ways that increase quantities supplied. Other countries have their own

Target Prices and Farmers' Choices

After reading this chapter you may have the impression that, thanks to government subsidies and price supports, a farmer's choices aren't very difficult and in fact are pretty attractive. In reality that's definitely not the case. Let's see why.

The target price mechanism for subsidizing farmers has been used for many years. However, the target price hasn't always been above the loan rate. The decisions farmers make about how much of various crops to plant are influenced in a complex way by the relationship between the loan rate, the target price, and the market price for crops. The target price and loan rate are set each year by the U.S. Department of Agriculture. For example, in 1977 the target price and loan rate for corn were equal. When this is the case and the market price exceeds the loan rate, there are no deficiency payments available for farmers.

In addition, the tying of eligibility for target price programs to acreage reduction, as we discussed earlier, converts part of the deficiency payments made under the target price program to compensation for keeping acreage idle. In other words, rather than being an income support, the deficiency payments in part represent compensation to farmers for reduced revenue from planting less of a crop.

Farmers are usually subject to a limit on the acreage eligible for deficiency payments under target prices. In addition, in recent years a cap has been placed on the amount of deficiency payments per farm. However, this limit is sometimes circumvented when farmers deed the title to portions of their farms to family members.

The target price program and other programs in use during the 1980s have encouraged expansion of farms beyond that which would have occurred had market forces been operating freely. The programs encouraged farmers to invest in capital equipment and more land in the early 1980s. Increased supplies of agricultural commodities accompanied by decreased demand in the 1980s then put downward pressure on commodity prices and farmland, resulting in a financial crunch for farmers.

---

subsidy programs that tend to raise prices received by their farmers above the equilibrium level. The result of these programs in recent years has been a glut of grain on international markets, which has sharply reduced prices. Farmers in nations without subsidy programs have suffered. For example, in Canada, where farm subsidies are below those in other nations, many farmers have been forced out of business.

The Food Security Act of 1985 gave the Secretary of Agriculture more discretion in lowering the loan rates for agricultural commodities. The law is designed to move loan rates closer to market prices while still providing farmers income support through deficiency payments based on target prices. The ultimate objective is to lower prices of U.S. agricultural commodities in world markets below the previous support prices so as to increase U.S. exports.

The Farm Debt Problem

One of the most dramatic problems faced by U.S. farmers in recent years has been the financial difficulties of the mid-1980s that caused increasing numbers of farmers to go bankrupt. The problem has been particularly acute for small and mid-sized farms with less than $400,000 annual gross receipts, because they tend to have higher average costs of production than larger farms.[6] The debt problems of farmers, however, were caused by high interest rates rather than low commodity prices.

---

[6]See Luther Tweeten, "Farm Financial Stress, Structure of Agriculture, and Public Policy," in Bruce L. Gardner, ed., *U.S. Agricultural Policy: The 1985 Farm Legislation,* Washington, D.C.: American Enterprise Institute for Public Policy Research, 1985.

The high interest rates have had a pronounced effect on many agricultural communities and have contributed to the failure of banks with high proportions of their assets in loans to farmers.

Farmers are hard hit by high interest rates because the ratio of capital to labor in agriculture is double that in other industries. High interest rates also keep the value of the dollar high in terms of foreign currencies. This tends to decrease the attractiveness of U.S. agricultural commodities in world markets and thus decreases international sales. The decrease in export sales in the mid-1980s significantly reduced farm profitability and also tended to lower agricultural land values. The decline in the price of the dollar in terms of foreign currencies in 1987 and 1988 helped U.S. farmers boost export sales. This in turn generated revenues that eased the farm debt crisis.

The new target price program we discussed earlier is designed to decrease prices of U.S. agricultural commodities in foreign markets. Lower interest rates and depreciation of the dollar in foreign markets are likely to improve the financial position of many U.S. farmers.

Concept Check

1   List the major goals of agricultural policy in the United States.

2   The parity price ratio in farming falls to 50%. What does this imply about the purchasing power of income obtained from a bushel of wheat?

3   Explain how target prices contribute to lower prices of crops eligible for the target price program.

The Economics of Subsidies and Tax Breaks

Agriculture, of course, isn't the only sector of the economy to benefit from government subsidies. The federal government often dispenses loan guarantees to other industries. In addition to direct subsidies, many industries are more profitable because special tax provisions indirectly subsidize their operations. Also, workers and corporations in many industries are protected against competition from foreign firms by federally imposed tariffs and import quotas. We'll discuss tariffs and import quotas in a later chapter. In the analysis that follows, we concentrate on direct subsidies and indirect subsidies through tax breaks.

Direct Subsidies

Subsidies that increase revenue in a particular industry can be given either to consumers of a product or to sellers. The effect is the same in either case. Suppose, for example, that people who buy insulation receive a payment from the federal government.

The graph in Box 5 shows the impact of a direct subsidy on the market for insulating materials. Assume these materials are sold in a perfectly competitive market. The initial price is $1 per pound. At that price, 10 million pounds per month are sold. The government then announces that buyers of insulation will receive a 10¢ per pound subsidy payment. The payment is made after proof of purchase is sent to the government, in much the same way as we redeem rebate coupons from manufacturers.

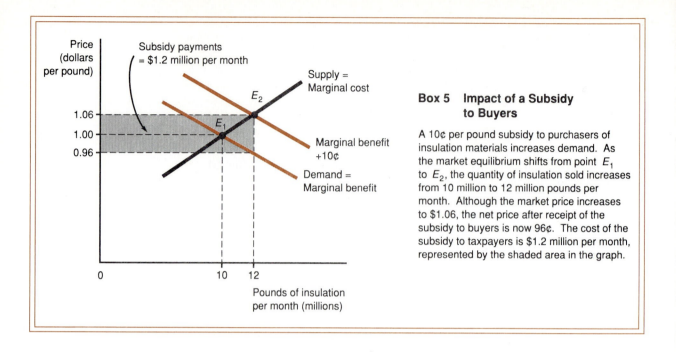

Price
(dollars
per pound)

Subsidy payments
= $1.2 million per month

Supply =
Marginal cost

E_2

E_1

1.06
1.00
0.96

Marginal benefit
+10¢

Demand =
Marginal benefit

0

10   12

Pounds of insulation
per month (millions)

**Box 5   Impact of a Subsidy
to Buyers**

A 10¢ per pound subsidy to purchasers of insulation materials increases demand. As the market equilibrium shifts from point E_1 to E_2, the quantity of insulation sold increases from 10 million to 12 million pounds per month. Although the market price increases to $1.06, the net price after receipt of the subsidy to buyers is now 96¢. The cost of the subsidy to taxpayers is $1.2 million per month, represented by the shaded area in the graph.

When making a buying decision, you add the 10¢ per pound subsidy to the marginal benefit you get from purchasing the insulation. This increases the maximum price you'll pay for the item. As a result of the subsidy, the demand for insulation increases. Monthly equilibrium quantity sold increases from 10 million to 12 million pounds. Assuming an upward-sloping supply curve (at least in the short run), the market equilibrium price also increases. As you can see in Box 5, the increase in demand for insulation after the subsidy is announced increases its market price from $1 to $1.06 per pound. The higher price is necessary to induce sellers to supply more, at least in the short run. After receiving their 10¢ per pound subsidy from the government, consumers pay a net price of only 96¢ per pound. Sellers receive the full price of $1.06 per pound. As long as the supply curve is upward sloping, the increase in demand resulting from the subsidy tends to raise the price received by the seller. The higher price tends to attract more resources into production of insulation in the long run. If the insulation industry is one of increasing costs, the incomes of suppliers of specialized inputs increase as the prices of these inputs rise. For example, there could be an increase in the price of fiberglass, an important input in the production of insulation.

The cost of the program to the federal government would be $1.2 million, which is the 10¢ per pound subsidy multiplied by the 12 million pounds per month sold after the subsidy is enacted. In Box 5 the monthly subsidy payments are represented by the shaded rectangular area. The cost of the monthly subsidy would be paid by taxpayers.

Notice that the subsidy benefits consumers by reducing the price per pound of insulation. However, it also benefits sellers by increasing the price of insulation and by increasing their monthly sales. As a result of the subsidy, monthly revenues for sellers of insulation increase from $10 million to $12.72 million. Those who own specialized inputs used to make insulation are also likely to gain as increased demand for those inputs puts upward pressure on the prices they receive.

The impact of the subsidy would be the same if it were paid directly to the suppliers of insulation instead of to buyers. You can see this in the graph in Box 6. The subsidy to sellers would reduce the marginal cost of producing fiberglass by 10¢ per pound. This would shift the supply curve, which is the marginal cost curve under perfect competition, downward by 10¢. The market price would fall to 96¢, and the quantity sold would increase from 10 million to 12 million pounds per month in response to the increase in supply. The price received by the sellers *after* receipt of the 10¢ per pound subsidy payment from the government will be $1.06 per pound, which is exactly the same price they received when the subsidy went to buyers. Note that both the price received by sellers and the price paid by buyers are exactly the same as those that prevailed when the subsidy was paid to buyers.

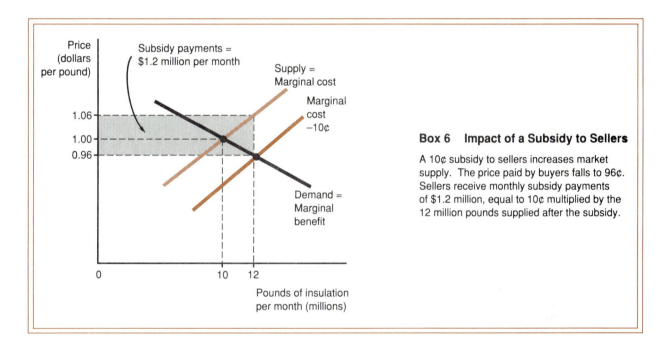

Box 6   Impact of a Subsidy to Sellers

A 10¢ subsidy to sellers increases market supply. The price paid by buyers falls to 96¢. Sellers receive monthly subsidy payments of $1.2 million, equal to 10¢ multiplied by the 12 million pounds supplied after the subsidy.

Indirect Subsidies: Tax Credits and Tax Preferences

Many industries and consumers of selected goods benefit from indirect subsidies that stem from special provisions in the federal tax code. Direct subsidies of the kind we just discussed are relatively rare. Instead government usually provides subsidies through tax credits or other forms of preferential tax treatment. A **tax credit** is a reduction in the tax liability for a person or corporation making certain purchases or engaging in certain activities. Instead of a cash reward for making the purchase, the government gives the person a reduction in taxes at the end of the year. Tax credits have more or less the same effect as direct subsidies, but they don't require outlays of funds by the government. Instead the government reduces its collection of taxes.

For example, up until 1987 business firms received an investment tax credit for purchases of new capital equipment. The credit was in the form of a reduction in taxes equal to a certain percentage of the outlays for the new equipment. Similarly, an energy tax credit was available in the late 1970s and early 1980s for homeowners

Tax credit:
A reduction in the tax liability for a person or corporation making certain purchases or engaging in certain activities.

who installed such energy-saving improvements as insulation, solar water heaters, and storm windows. Governments also provide indirect subsidies through special tax deductions and exclusions that we'll discuss shortly. The effects of tax credits are equivalent to those of direct subsidies.

A **tax preference** is an exemption, deduction, or exclusion from income or other taxable items in computing tax liability. Tax preferences are subsidies just like those we discussed in the previous section. They are likely to benefit both buyers and sellers in certain industries. The losses in revenue to the federal government as a result of these tax breaks are called **tax expenditures.**

The graph in Box 7 shows how tax preferences affect market equilibrium. In the absence of any preferential tax treatment, suppose the average price of a home in the United States would be $100,000. Assuming that homes are supplied in perfectly competitive markets and that there are no externalities associated with home ownership, the market equilibrium would be efficient. At point E, the marginal benefit of home ownership would just equal its marginal cost and annual sales would be Q_1. With the tax preference, home buyers consider not only the marginal benefit they receive from buying a home but also the tax benefit. The tax benefit is likely to vary from person to person depending on income, the tax rate paid, and other personal circumstances. However, it's clear that the demand for homes will increase because the tax benefit will be added to the marginal benefit of home owning. The *marginal tax benefit* represents the tax saving over time from deciding to purchase a home. Because owning a home will lower the buyer's tax burden, the willingness and ability of buyers to pay for homes increases accordingly. When the marginal tax benefit is added to the marginal benefit, the demand for housing shifts upward. Assuming an upward-sloping supply curve, the increase in demand increases the market price of housing and increases the quantity sold.

Just like a direct subsidy, the tax preference benefits both buyers and sellers of homes. Specialized inputs used to construct housing increase in price, benefiting owners of these inputs. In Box 7 you can see how the special treatment of housing

Tax preference:

An exemption, deduction, or exclusion from income or other taxable items in computing tax liability.

Tax expenditures:

The losses in revenue to the federal government as a result of tax breaks granted to individuals and corporations.

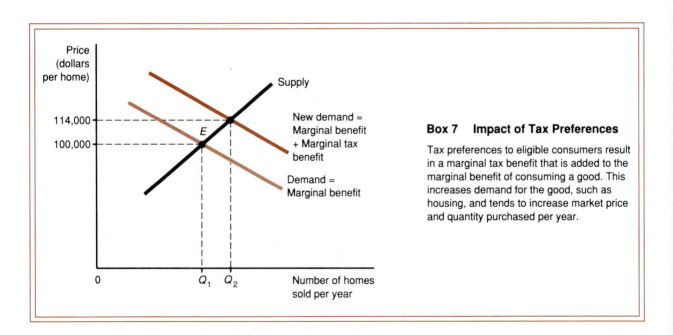

Box 7   Impact of Tax Preferences

Tax preferences to eligible consumers result in a marginal tax benefit that is added to the marginal benefit of consuming a good. This increases demand for the good, such as housing, and tends to increase market price and quantity purchased per year.

in the tax code increases the price of housing and increases annual sales, assuming the supply curve of housing is upward sloping.

The special tax treatment of homes influences the choice between renting and owning. It therefore influences the allocation of resources between rental and owner-occupied housing. It's been estimated that preferential treatment of housing in tax policy explains nearly 25% of the growth in the proportion of home ownership in the United States from the end of World War II up through much of the 1970s.[7] It's also been estimated that if preferential tax treatment of housing were to be eliminated, the price of a typical home would decline by about 14%.

Deduction of interest on mortgages in the United States in 1987 resulted in a loss in tax revenue of nearly $24 billion. As you can see, the cost of the indirect subsidy to housing is quite substantial. If the loss in revenue from not taxing economic rents earned by owner-occupiers were added to the loss in revenue from interest deductions, the tax expenditure would be much higher.

Major tax preferences benefit buyers and sellers of other products. For example, employees can exclude from taxable income the value of employer contributions for medical insurance and life insurance. This exclusion indirectly subsidizes insurance companies. The tax expenditure for this subsidy was over $33 billion in 1987.

Deduction of interest on consumer credit in 1987 resulted in a loss of $10.8 billion in revenue to the federal government that year. This tax preference subsidizes debtors and financial institutions that extend consumer credit. The Tax Reform Act of 1986 eliminated many tax preferences and provides for a phase-out of the deduction of interest on consumer credit. However, many tax preferences, including those that subsidize home ownership, still remain in the tax code.

Hidden Subsidies

Politicians are often skillful at concealing the cost of subsidies to special-interest groups they favor. Many subsidies don't involve current cash outlays. Tax preferences and tax credits are examples of such hidden subsidies to businesses and consumers. However, tax expenditures are estimated annually and published in the federal budget, although they aren't included in calculating government outlays.

There are still other types of indirect subsidies that are rarely counted as part of government spending. For example, the use of government loan guarantees for private industry won't result in any cash outlay unless there's an actual default on the part of the borrower. However, the guarantee reduces the risk of making the loan and allows a corporation to borrow at a lower interest rate. The risk is transferred to taxpayers, who would have to pay increased taxes only if the loan were defaulted.

Sometimes the government acts as an insurer either directly or indirectly when private firms find it unprofitable to provide such insurance. For example, federal flood insurance is available in coastal areas. This is subsidized insurance that private firms can't supply profitably at the same premium rate charged by the federal government. Critics of this type of subsidy argue that it encourages construction in areas that are likely to be flooded. In the event of a major storm, federal outlays for insurance compensation are likely to be quite high. Similarly, some states require private insurance companies to insure all drivers, even those with poor driving records. Because it's unprofitable to insure bad drivers, these insurance companies

---

[7]Harvey S. Rosen and Kenneth T. Rosen, "Federal Taxes and Homeownership: Evidence from Time Series," *Journal of Political Economy,* 88, February 1980, pp. 59-75.

often lose money. Regulatory commissions frequently pass these losses on to all drivers by allowing the insurance companies to charge higher premiums to safe drivers. In effect, the safe drivers subsidize insurance coverage for poor drivers.

Concept Check

1   A subsidy in the form of a $200 tax credit per car is given to domestic automobile manufacturers. Use supply and demand analysis to show how the subsidy affects the market price of cars and the quantity sold.

2   Who is likely to benefit from a subsidy for automobile production? Would it make any difference if the $200 tax credit were given to buyers instead of sellers of automobiles?

3   What are tax preferences and how do they affect incentives to engage in certain activities?

Impact of Subsidies to Industries: A Generalization and Conclusion

Government subsidies, whether direct or indirect, always have a cost to us as taxpayers. The cost is either higher taxes to finance a direct subsidy, or a reduction in government revenue or services if an indirect subsidy is used. On the other hand, the subsidy benefits both the buyers and sellers of the subsidized good. In other words, subsidies act to redistribute income among individuals. In addition, subsidies can improve efficiency when they're used to internalize positive externalities. For example, subsidies to encourage installation of fire protection devices or to encourage students to enroll in college can improve efficiency because these activities are likely to result in positive externalities. By adding subsidy payments to the marginal benefit consumers receive from these goods we derive the marginal external benefit. This helps improve efficiency by encouraging more consumption of goods whose use results in positive externalities.

Let's recap what we've learned about subsidies:

1. Subsidies result in increased consumption and production of certain goods. This provides gains to both buyers and sellers of the subsidized items.
2. Subsidies reduce the well-being of the people who finance their costs. Direct subsidies result in increased tax bills to certain people, while indirect subsidies cause government tax collections to decline. The reduction in taxes collected either contributes to budget deficits or causes cutbacks in government services.
3. In certain cases subsidies can benefit people other than the buyers or sellers of the subsidized items. These benefits are in the form of improved efficiency when positive externalities are internalized.

Summary

1. Special-interest groups are organizations that seek to increase government expenditures or induce government to take actions that benefit their members. Much of the gain these groups achieve comes at the expense of losses incurred

by others. Special-interest groups act mainly to redistribute income to their constituents.

2. Many programs that benefit special-interest groups cause losses in efficiency. The competition among special-interest groups to obtain the favors of government also involves resource use as part of the transaction costs to gain approval of programs. These transaction costs divert resources from more productive uses.

3. Economic rents are earnings that exceed the opportunity cost of an activity. Rent seeking involves competing with others to obtain approval of government programs that increase economic rents.

4. In the United States, agriculture represents a relatively small sector of the economy. This industry has been successful in obtaining substantial subsidies that benefit its constituents. The costs of the subsidies are distributed among taxpayers and food consumers, who pay higher prices for agricultural commodities as a result of price supports. Federal spending to assist farmers amounted to over $25 billion in 1986.

5. Many programs to aid farmers support prices at levels above market equilibrium prices. One goal of agricultural policies is that of parity, which seeks to keep the prices of agricultural commodities high enough to guarantee farmers constant purchasing power from the sale of a given quantity of commodities. The goal of parity is elusive because in recent years agricultural prices have fallen relative to those of other goods and services. In the mid-1980s agricultural prices averaged less than 60% of parity.

6. Nonrecourse loan programs guarantee farmers a certain price for their crops. The support price is called the loan rate. When the market price is below the loan rate, farmers forfeit crops they have pledged as collateral for government loans at the loan rate. The fact that the loan rate has exceeded the market equilibrium price for many crops has created large agricultural surpluses that are stored by the Commodity Credit Corporation.

7. Recent policies have reduced agricultural loan rates to make U.S. crops more competitive in export markets. To prevent a sharp drop in agricultural incomes resulting from lower crop prices, the government has made farmers the beneficiaries of direct subsidies paid according to output.

8. Target prices maintain agricultural prices and reduce agricultural surpluses when accompanied by acreage restrictions. However, the target price program involves increased costs to taxpayers through deficiency payments that are based on the difference between the target price and the loan rate (or market price).

9. The farm debt problem stems from the fact that the ratio of capital to labor in agriculture is double that in other industries. High interest rates are therefore particularly burdensome to farmers, who borrow heavily to acquire capital equipment. In recent years this problem has been most severe for farms with less than $400,000 annual gross receipts because these farms have higher average costs of production than larger farms.

10. Many industries receive subsidies in the form of tax credits that reduce the tax liability of firms that make specified purchases or engage in certain activities. Tax credits and direct subsidies tend to reduce the market price paid by consumers and increase the quantity sold. As a result, subsidies benefit both buyers and sellers of the subsidized good or service.

11. Tax preferences are exemptions, deductions, and exclusions from income (or other taxable sums) in computing tax liability. Tax preferences are really indirect

subsidies. Tax preferences cause losses in government revenue that are called tax expenditures. Like any subsidy, tax preferences encourage allocation of resources toward the tax-preferred activities. Tax preferences affect the market prices of tax-preferred goods and services and benefit both buyers and sellers of these items.

12. Subsidies can result in net gains through more efficient resource use. However, in most cases tax preferences and other subsidies to special-interest groups result in gains to some groups that are offset by losses to other groups that pay higher taxes (or receive less benefit from government expenditures) to finance the subsidies.

Key Terms and Concepts

Special-interest group   Acreage control programs
Economic rents   Target price
Rent seeking   Tax credit
Parity   Tax preference
Parity price ratio   Tax expenditures

Problems and Applications

1. A special-interest group represents 300 workers who produce a rare herb used for medicinal purposes. This group succeeds in getting a program enacted that provides a benefit of $50,000 per year per worker. The cost of the program is distributed equally among 100 million taxpayers. Calculate the annual cost per taxpayer and explain why the program is unlikely to be opposed.

2. Explain why rent seeking by special-interest groups is likely to absorb substantial amounts of resources but results in little *net gain* in overall well-being in a nation.

3. Explain why achievement of the goal of parity requires government price supports to increase the prices farmers receive for their crops. Draw a graph showing shifts in demand for and supply of agricultural commodities that have caused the prices of crops to drift below a 100% parity price ratio. Explain why the supply of agricultural commodities has increased so substantially in recent years, thus decreasing the prices of these commodities relative to those on which farmers spend their income.

4. Suppose you're a farmer growing soybeans. The loan rate for soybeans is $5 per bushel. Use supply and demand analysis to show how you decide how many bushels of soybeans to produce. Suppose at the end of the season the world market equilibrium price for soybeans turns out to be $3 per bushel. What will you do with your soybean crop?

5. Show how a loan rate of $5 per bushel of soybeans will result in a domestic surplus of soybeans when the equilibrium price is $3 per bushel. Use supply and demand analysis to show the cost to taxpayers of purchasing the surplus and indicate the increase in consumer expenditure for soybeans as a result of the price support programs.

6. Suppose the price support program administered by the Commodity Credit Corporation is completely abolished. In its place a target price program is used that makes payments to farmers per bushel of soybeans whenever the market price is below the target price. Show why such a program won't eliminate the surplus

of soybeans. What will happen to the surplus if the government refuses to purchase it? Use a graph to show the cost of the program to the government assuming that farmers produce 7 million bushels of soybeans during the season.

7. Show how skillful use of a combination of acreage controls and target prices can eliminate agricultural surpluses. What information would policy makers need to estimate the acreage controls necessary to eliminate the surpluses? What would be the cost to taxpayers of such an acreage control–target price program?

8. Show how an acreage control program alone can act to raise the market prices of agricultural commodities and eliminate surpluses. Such a program would maintain farmer income and increase the parity price ratio. Assuming that farmers voluntarily participate in the acreage control program, who will bear its cost?

9. A tax credit equal to $5 per sheet is given to producers of plywood. The current market equilibrium price of plywood is $20 per sheet. Show the impact of the subsidy on the market equilibrium price of plywood and the price received by sellers. Assuming the supply curve of plywood is upward sloping, show how the subsidy benefits both buyers and sellers. How would owners of specialized inputs used to produce plywood benefit from the subsidy?

10. Suppose all medical expenditures were tax deductible. Show how this tax preference would influence the demand for medical services and the market equilibrium price and quantity of medical services, assuming an upward-sloping supply curve. Why would the American Medical Association be likely to support legislation to allow tax deductibility of all medical expenditures?

Suggested Readings

Gary S. Becker, "A Theory of Competition Among Pressure Groups for Political Influence," *Quarterly Journal of Economics,* 98, August 1983, pp. 371-400. This is a technical analysis of the impact of special-interest groups on resource allocation.

James M. Buchanan, Robert D. Tollison, and Gordon Tullock, eds., *Toward a Theory of the Rent-Seeking Society,* College Station, Tex.: Texas A & M University Press, 1980. This is a collection of essays on the economics of rent seeking.

Bruce L. Gardner, ed., *U.S. Agricultural Policy: The 1985 Farm Legislation,* Washington, D.C.: American Enterprise Institute for Public Policy Research, 1985. This is a collection of essays on recent and perennial problems in U.S. agriculture and policies designed to deal with these problems.

U.S. Department of Agriculture, *Agricultural-Food Policy Review: Commodity Program Perspectives,* Washington, D.C.: Economic Research Service, Agricultural Economic Report No. 530, July 1985. This is a collection of articles providing background information to evaluate U.S. farm policies.

A Forward Look

In this chapter and the two preceding chapters we concentrated on the role of government as a regulator in markets. In the following chapter we take an overview of government's role in the economy by discussing government expenditures, revenues, and the political process by which public choices are made.

The Government Sector of the Economy: Expenditures, Revenues, and Public Choice

If you've read Orwell's classic *1984*, you're familiar with his now-famous metaphor for government, Big Brother—as in "Big Brother is watching!"

Whether or not you believe Big Brother is watching, there's no question that government is a lot more involved in your daily life than it was in the lives of your grandparents when they were your age.

In 1929 total federal government spending in the United States amounted to a minuscule 2.3% of the value of all goods and services produced that year. By the mid-1980s federal spending on all programs, including national defense, Social Security, and welfare, was close to 25% of the value of total annual production. This represents a tenfold increase in the relative importance of the federal government as measured by the share of total production that it spends in various ways. The federal government currently spends over $1 trillion annually. Since 1975 the total of federal, state, and local government spending has averaged a bit more than one third of the value of total production. One out of every three dollars spent in the United States is accounted for by government programs.

Taxes:
Compulsory payments associated with income, consumption, or holding of property that individuals and corporations are required to make each year to governments.

The bulk of government spending is financed by **taxes,** which are compulsory payments associated with income, consumption, or holding of property that individuals and corporations are required to make each year to governments. Taxes have become one of the most important items in the budgets of most households in the United States. On average, as U.S. citizens we allocate 25% of our annual income to pay taxes that help finance government goods and services.

The purpose of this chapter is to provide an overview of the role of government in modern societies. In the previous two chapters we've emphasized the role of government in correcting for market failure. In actuality, what governments do depends on the political process. Governments are called on to redistribute income, provide important public goods, and regulate people's private activities.

In the political process we vote for politicians who seek to represent us in executive and legislative government positions. In most cases elections are decided on the basis of majority rule, in which a proposal or candidate must receive more than half the votes cast. In this chapter we'll consider the differences between political and market supply of goods and services.

After reading this chapter, you should be able to:

1 Describe the economic functions of modern governments.
2 Explain how governments raise revenue and describe the major categories of expenditure for the federal, state, and local governments in the United States.
3 Explain principles used to evaluate taxes.
4 Explain the process of public choice under majority rule.

Government Goods and Services

Government is a major force in modern economies. Both business firms and households rely on the federal government, the 50 state governments, and thousands of local governments to provide them with essential services. The United States has a **federal system of government** in which numerous levels of government, each with its own powers, provide services and regulate private affairs. Over the years a division of responsibility has evolved among levels of government in the United States. For example, the federal, or central, government has as its major functions the provision of national defense and income redistribution. State and local governments have primary responsibility for education, roads and other transportation facilities, hospitals, and other health services.

Federal system of government:
Numerous levels of government, each with its own powers, exist to provide services and regulate private affairs.

The basic functions of government are:

1. *The establishment of rights to use productive resources and the regulation of private actions.* Governments guarantee rights and enforce contracts. Disputes between private citizens concerning property rights and contractual obligations are resolved through the courts of the government judicial system. In effect, government serves as a rule maker and a rule enforcer in the economy.

Government rules facilitate trade in markets. Governments also use their powers to regulate the way goods and services are produced and what can or cannot be sold in markets.

2. *Provision of goods and services.* Governments purchase input services to provide national defense, education, roads, health services, and many other services that benefit citizens. About one fifth of the work force in the United States is employed by government.

3. *Redistribution of income.* Governments establish and administer programs that

---

redistribute income among citizens. Welfare programs provide assistance to the poor. Government pensions redistribute income from workers to retirees. Government also subsidizes workers and producers in certain industries, such as agriculture, to stabilize supplies and put floors on incomes.

Government transfers:
Payments made directly to certain people or organizations for which no good or service is received in return at that time. Transfers usually are financed by taxes.

Government transfers are payments made directly to certain people or organizations for which no good or service is received in return at that time. Government transfers are usually financed by taxes. Social Security pensions are transfers from workers who pay Social Security taxes to retired workers and their dependents. Welfare payments to the poor are government transfers from taxpayers to eligible low-income people.

4. *Stabilization of the economy.* The federal government pursues policies designed to affect the overall level of demand and supply in the economy so as to control economic fluctuations. This is accomplished through control of government spending and taxation and through control of the nation's supply of money and credit.

Categorizing Government-Provided Goods

Government goods and services can be divided into two broad types:

1. *Goods that are made available to all citizens free of charge, the costs of which are financed by taxes or borrowings.* These goods often have the characteristics of public goods (see Chapter 16 for a discussion of public goods). Included in this category are national defense, police and fire protection, public health, sanitation services, roads, bridges, national parks, and museums. Some of these goods, such as roads, bridges, and some recreational and health services, can feasibly be priced. For example, we pay a toll to use some roads and bridges, and admission is often charged for the right to enter government-provided recreational and cultural facilities.

2. *Goods and services that are tax financed but are available only to certain individuals meeting predetermined eligibility criteria.* Often these goods have certain characteristics of public goods in that some of their benefits are enjoyed by everyone, not just the recipients of the services. However, these goods clearly are subject to exclusion because the government can withhold the benefits from people who don't meet established criteria. Examples of goods in this category are education, Social Security pensions, and welfare benefits. Public education is provided only to people in a certain age group who are required to attend school until they reach a certain age. To be eligible for a Social Security pension, you must have worked in a job covered by Social Security for a period of about 10 years and have attained a specified minimum age or become disabled. Usually this means that you and your employer will have paid a minimum amount of Social Security taxes.

In many cases governments provide services, like pensions, that are also provided by private firms. Public and private schools and universities exist side by side, and people are free to choose between them, assuming they're able to pay the higher costs of private education.

Many government transfer programs, such as Social Security and the various welfare programs, are designed primarily to help particular people rather than provide a service to all of us. However, many people believe these programs do provide a public good in that any of us, if and when we become eligible, could take advantage of the benefits. Also, by placing a floor on the incomes of many people, such programs decrease poverty. This could provide a public good to everyone in the form of a more stable and humane society.

Government Expenditures

One way we can understand what governments actually do is to look at their expenditures for various functions. In 1987 the federal government spent over $1 trillion on its activities. This tremendous sum of money represents over $4,000 for every resident of the nation! The table in Box 1 shows how federal government expenditures in 1987 were distributed among various functions.

Box 1 Federal Government Expenditures by Type and Function, 1987

Item	Amount (billions of dollars)	Percent of total
National defense	282.00	26.4
Social Security	207.35	19.4
Net interest	138.57	13.0
Income security	123.25	11.5
Medicare	75.12	7.0
Health	39.97	3.7
Agriculture	27.36	2.6
Education, training, employment, and social services	29.72	2.8
Transportation	26.23	2.5
Veterans' benefits	26.79	2.5
International affairs	11.65	1.1
Natural resources and environment	13.36	1.3
General service, space, and technology	9.22	*
Community and regional development	5.05	*
Administration of justice	7.55	*
General government	7.57	*
Energy	4.11	*
Commerce and housing credit	6.18	*
All other and offsetting receipts	−28.05	
Total	1069.1	

*Less than 1%

Source: *Economic Report of the President*, January 1988, and *Survey of Current Business*, January 1988.

The two largest categories of federal government expenditures are national defense and Social Security. National defense accounted for 26.4% of federal government spending in 1987, while 19.4% was spent on Social Security. Social Security expenditures are mainly transfers to retired workers. Income security, which involves expenditures for a variety of programs that mainly aid the poor, accounted for 11.5% of federal government spending in 1987.

In recent years interest payments have emerged as a major category of federal government expenditures. In 1987 interest paid to holders of government bonds and other interest-paying debt obligations amounted to 13% of expenditures. This means that about 13¢ of each dollar spent by the federal government went to compensate the nation's creditors instead of to provide government goods and services to citizens. Of course, many of those creditors are U.S. business firms that obtained a source of income from their purchase of government bonds and other government securities.

The table in Box 1 also shows spending on other government programs. Medicare, which is a government-subsidized program of medical insurance for people over age 65, accounted for 7% of federal expenditures in 1987. No other item in the table accounted for more than 4% of federal spending in 1987. For example, expenditures in 1987 on general science, space, and technology accounted for less than 1% of total federal spending that year.

The table in Box 2 shows the distribution of state and local government expenditures by type and function in 1986. State and local government in the aggregate typically spend only a little more than half the amount spent by the federal government. Total state and local government spending in 1986 amounted to $605.8 billion. This amount includes $99 billion of spending financed by federal grants that is also included in federal spending. The most important function of state and local governments is education, which accounts for nearly 35% of their expenditure. In the United States the bulk of the responsibility for primary and secondary education falls on local governments. State governments provide considerable financial support to local governments and also supply higher education.

State and local governments spend considerable sums on income support for the poor. Income support, social insurance, and welfare account for 12.5% of state and local government expenditure. State and local governments also are responsible for provision and maintenance of roads, and transportation represents 8.2% of their expenditure. State and local governments run hospitals and provide other health services. They also provide police and fire protection and incur expenditures for judicial activities. All activities other than education, highways, and income support accounted for 44.5% of state and local government outlays in 1986.

Box 2 State and Local Government Expenditures* by Function, 1986

Item	Amount (billions of dollars)	Percent of total
Total	605.8	
Education	210.8	34.8
Income support, Social Insurance and welfare	76.0	12.5
Transportation and highways	49.4	8.2
Other (includes health, hospitals, civilian safety, legislative and judicial, housing, community services, recreation and culture, agriculture, national resources, and interest paid)	269.6	44.5

Source: U. S. Department of Commerce, *Survey of Current Business*.

*Includes expenditures financed by federal grants of $99 billion. These expenditures are also included in various categories of federal expenditure in **Box 1**.

As you can see from the data in Boxes 1 and 2, a division of functions exists between the federal and other levels of government in the United States. Over three quarters of federal expenditures are accounted for by income redistribution programs and national defense programs. On the other hand, the major state and local government function is education, which accounts for nearly 35% of their expenditures.

Government Revenues

In 1987 the federal government raised $916.5 billion in revenue. Because total federal expenditures that year were $1,069.1 billion, revenues fell short of expenditures by $152.6 billion in 1987. The **budget deficit** is the amount by which government expenditures exceed government revenues in a given year. Since the 1970s, chronic federal budget deficits have been a matter of great concern. In 1986 legislation was enacted that will require the federal government to eliminate its budget deficit by the early 1990s. In 1986 the mammoth deficit of $220 billion amounted to 20% of federal expenditures. This means that one out of every five dollars spent by the federal government in 1986 was borrowed! The government borrows to cover its debt when the Treasury Department issues bonds and other interest-yielding Treasury obligations that are sold to the public.

Budget deficit:
The amount by which government expenditures exceed government revenues in a given year.

Box 3   Federal Government Revenues, 1987

Item	Amount (billions of dollars)	Percent of total
Personal income taxes	395.3	43.0
Payroll taxes	348.4	38.0
Corporate profits tax	110.3	12.0
Excise taxes	32.5	3.5
Other	30.0	3.3
Total	916.5	

Source: U. S. Department of Commerce, *Survey of Current Business*, January 1988.

Taxes accounted for about 99% of the revenue raised (rather than borrowed) by the federal government. The table in Box 3 shows the sources and amounts of federal government revenues in 1987. The major types of federal taxes are the following:

1. *Personal income tax.* This tax accounts for over 40% of federal revenues. It's levied on most sources of income, including wages and salaries, interest, rents, and profits of proprietorships and partnerships. The rules for calculating personal income tax administered by the Internal Revenue Service are quite complex. Despite a major reform of the personal income tax in 1986 that reduced tax rates, there are still many special tax preferences or "loopholes." These tax preferences are deductions, exemptions, and exclusions from income that reduce the tax bills of taxpayers who engage in specific activities.

2. *Payroll taxes.* These are taxes levied on wages that are usually collected from

both employees and employers. The payroll tax is actually a separate tax on labor income. In 1987 this tax accounted for 38% of federal revenues. The tax is levied on wages up to a certain limit, and the proceeds are earmarked for a specific use. Payroll taxes are used to finance Social Security pensions and other Social Security benefits. In 1987 payroll taxes earmarked to finance Social Security benefits were levied on wages of each worker up to a maximum of $43,800 per worker per year. The maximum amount of wages as well as the tax rate changes from year to year. Payroll taxes also are used to finance unemployment insurance benefits. The share of federal revenues accounted for by payroll taxes has increased dramatically in recent years.

3. *Corporate profits taxes.* Corporations are subject to a special income tax. In 1987 corporate profits taxes accounted for 12% of federal revenues.

4. *Excise taxes.* Excise taxes are levied on the sale of specific goods or services. The federal government imposes excise taxes on cigarettes, gasoline, liquor, telephone service, tires, and a variety of other goods and services. Excise taxes accounted for only 3.5% of federal government revenues in 1987.

The table in Box 4 shows state and local government revenues in 1987. As you can see, these revenues totaled $652.5 billion. Because state and local government expenditures were only $607 billion in the same year, these governments in the aggregate raised $45.5 billion more than they spent. A **budget surplus** is an excess of government revenues over government expeditures in a given year. When a budget surplus exists, government can use the extra revenue to pay off previous borrowing at a quicker rate or can build up reserve funds to finance future deficits.

Budget surplus:
An excess of government revenues over government expenditures in a given year.

Box 4   State and Local Government Revenues, 1987

Item	Amount (billions of dollars)	Percentage of total
Sales taxes	149.8	23.0
Property taxes	122.6	18.8
Federal grants	104.7	16.0
Income taxes	81.8	12.5
Fees and charges	65.3	10.0
Payroll taxes	46.1	7.1
Other	82.2	12.6
Total	652.5	

Source: U.S. Department of Commerce, *Survey of Current Business*, January 1988.

The major sources of state and local revenues are:

1. *Sales taxes.* Almost all states have a retail sales tax that is levied as a certain percentage of retail purchases collected from sellers. In 1987 the retail sales tax amounted to 23% of state and local revenues. These taxes are the chief source of revenue for state governments, and the tax is also used by many local governments.

2. *Property taxes.* These are chiefly taxes on real estate. The property tax is the

main source of tax revenue for cities, towns, counties, and other local governments. Property taxes accounted for 18.8% of state and local government revenue in 1987.

3. *Federal grants.* State and local governments rely heavily on the federal government for financial assistance to provide education, roads, health, and a variety of other community services. The federal government gives local governments cash grants, most of which must be spent on specific types of services. Federal grants accounted for 16% of state and local government revenue in 1987.

4. *Income taxes.* While income taxes are the most significant source of revenue for the federal government, they are much less important for state and local governments. In 1987 only 12.5% of revenue was raised through income taxes by state and local governments.

5. *Fees and charges.* State and local governments rely on nontax sources of revenue to a greater degree than does the federal government. Various types of fees and charges in 1987 amounted to 10% of state and local government revenues. Fees include those charged for admission to public museums, for sewer hookups, and for other government services. They also include charges for the services of such government enterprises as state liquor stores and municipal water and sewer service. Also included in nontax revenue are fines levied on people who break the law.

6. *Payroll taxes.* Like the federal government, state and local governments use payroll taxes to finance social insurance benefits. However, payroll taxes account for a much smaller percentage of state and local government revenues than is the case for the federal government.

Concept Check

1 What are the major functions of governments in the United States?

2 How do government transfer programs differ from programs like national defense that benefit all citizens?

3 List the major types of taxes used in the United States. What means other than taxation do governments employ to finance their expenditures?

Principles of Taxation

Nobody enjoys paying taxes. Unlike prices, which are paid for the right to acquire or consume a good or service, taxes are compulsory payments that aren't a prerequisite for the right to consume a good. Naturally, any of us would like to pay as little tax as possible while still receiving the benefits of government goods and services. Most of us have some idea of what we consider a fair distribution of taxes. Taxes are therefore usually evaluated according to fairness or *equity*. However, taxes also affect our incentives to work, save, invest, and buy goods and services. The fairest taxes aren't always those that are the most efficient in terms of affecting incentives.

Tax Equity: Different Points of View

There are many different points of view about how to evaluate tax equity. Many people believe taxes should be levied according to ability to pay. In this view, people with higher incomes should pay higher taxes than people whose incomes are lower.

In fact, taxes are commonly evaluated according to how they vary with respect to income. A **regressive tax** is one for which the fraction of income used to pay it decreases as income increases. For example, the federal payroll tax can be regarded as a regressive tax. This is because it's levied as a flat percentage of labor income only up to a certain maximum. For example, the payroll tax was 7.15% in 1987, but wages in excess of $43,800 per year weren't subject to the tax. If your father had labor income of only $20,000 in 1987, he would have paid $1,430 under the payroll tax in 1987, which is 7.15% of his labor earnings. If your mother had the same labor income and also had $20,000 of nonlabor income that year (such as income for rents or interest), she would also have paid $1,430 in payroll tax. This amounts to only about 3.6% of her total income of $40,000.

The maximum wage subject to payroll taxation also contributes to the regressivity of the tax. For example, suppose your mother earned the maximum of $43,800 in labor income in 1987. She would have had 7.15% or $3,131 deducted from her labor earnings to pay the payroll tax that year. Your uncle, with $100,000 in labor earnings in 1987, would also have paid $3,131 in payroll taxes that year. For your uncle, however, the tax would be only 3% of wages. Because the fraction of income paid in payroll taxes tends to decline as income rises, such taxes are regarded as regressive.

A **progressive tax** is one for which the fraction of income used to pay it increases as income increases. The federal income tax is a progressive tax because tax rates tend to rise as income rises. Under the federal income tax, income is taxed at a 15% rate until it reaches a certain level. Income above that level is taxed at 28%. Because the tax rates increase with income, upper-income people pay higher percentages of their income in taxes than lower-income people.

A **proportional tax** is one for which the percentage of income paid in taxes is the same no matter what the taxpayer's income. A flat 20% tax rate on all income would be a proportional tax. Note, however, that a proportional tax results in people with higher income paying more in taxes than people with lower income. For example, under a 20% flat-rate income tax your cousin with income of $10,000 would pay only $2,000 per year in taxes while your aunt with a $100,000 income would pay $20,000 in taxes.

We also evaluate taxes by looking at the amounts paid by people with similar ability to pay. If taxes are to vary with ability to pay, people with the same income should pay the same amounts in taxes.

Another common criterion used to evaluate taxes holds that taxes should vary with the benefits received from government services. This principle is very hard to administer because of the difficulty involved in allocating the benefits of government services to individual taxpayers. However, the federal gasoline tax is earmarked to finance roads and other transportation services. The idea is that the benefits we receive from transportation services vary with the amount of gasoline we consume. By taxing gasoline the government establishes a rough linkage between the use of roads and the taxes paid to build and maintain roads.

Tax Rates: Average and Marginal

When discussing taxes, it's important to be clear on the meaning of the tax rate. The **average tax rate** is the amount of taxes paid divided by the dollar value of the item

---

Regressive tax:
A tax for which the fraction of income used to pay it decreases as income increases.

Progressive tax:
A tax for which the fraction of income used to pay it increases as income increases.

Proportional tax:
A tax for which the percentage of income paid in taxes is the same no matter what the taxpayer's income.

Average tax rate:
The amount of taxes paid divided by the dollar value of the item taxed.

Principles in Practice

The Tax Reform Act of 1986

They said it couldn't be done. But to the surprise of many observers, the Congress in 1986 passed a major overhaul of the federal income tax. The new legislation introduced two major changes in the tax system that affect the distribution of the tax burden and the economic decisions we make as taxpayers. The major provisions of the new law are:

1. *New marginal tax rates.* There are now only two marginal tax rates—15% and 28%—used to figure the taxes owed by most taxpayers. Prior to the new law a taxpayer was subject to as many as 15 different marginal tax rates that increased with taxable income. Also, many low-income people won't be subject to federal income tax. In 1989 a married couple with two dependent children is allowed to earn $13,000 before its income becomes subject to the 15% marginal tax rate. The table that follows shows the new tax brackets, which are the amounts of taxable income subject to each of the new marginal tax rates.

Tax Brackets and Marginal Tax Rates, 1989

Single taxpayers with less than $43,150 taxable income

Tax bracket	Marginal tax rate
$0 to $17,850	15%
$17,850 and above	28%

Married taxpayers filing jointly with less than $43,150 taxable income

Tax bracket	Marginal tax rate
$0 - $29,750	15%
$29,750 and above	28%

People with income above the limits in this table are subject to a 5% surcharge on their taxable income, which will raise their marginal tax rate to 33% on a portion of their income. This provision is designed to phase out the benefit of the low 15% tax rate for high-income taxpayers. As a result of this complex provision of the new law, the richest Americans will end up paying a flat-rate tax of 28% on *all* their taxable income. Your taxable income depends on actual income from all sources that are subject to tax less your personal exemptions and deductions.

Except for very high-income people, all taxpayers are eligible for personal exemptions for themselves and their dependents. A personal exemption in 1989 is worth a $2,000 subtraction from income. As a single taxpayer, you may elect to subtract a standard deduction of $3,000 from your taxable income or to make a listing of itemized deductions that you can subtract instead. The expenses eligible for deduction include state and local income and property taxes, interest on certain mortgage debt, and certain medical expenditures. Obviously, if your itemized deductions exceed the $3,000 standard deduction allowed to a single taxpayer, you can reduce your taxes by itemizing.

2. *Elimination of many deductions, exemptions, and exclusions from taxable income.* The new tax law will change the behavior of many Americans because it eliminates many "loopholes" that have allowed taxpayers to reduce their tax bills by engaging in certain *tax-preferred* activities and purchases. One of the tax preference items getting the ax is the exclusion from taxation of a portion of long-term capital gains. Long-term capital gains are the difference between the purchase price and selling price of assets like stocks, bonds, and artwork that have been held at least 6 months. Under the old law, 60% of such gains realized from the sale of assets were excluded from taxation. Under the new law, *all capital gains* earned on assets sold will be taxed just like ordinary income. However, special provisions still exist for deferring and excluding from taxation portions of capital gains earned from selling your principal residence.

Also no longer excludable from taxable income are unemployment compensation, many scholarships and fellowships, certain prizes and awards, and income placed in Individual Retirement Accounts for many taxpayers.

Finally, the new law eliminates many time-honored deductions taken by people who itemized their deductions. These include state and local sales taxes, a portion of medical expenses, and personal interest expense for credit-card balances, car loans, educational loans, and most personal loans. The deduction for personal interest is being phased out gradually and will be completely eliminated by 1991.

The effects of the new tax law will be complex. The reduction in tax rates will affect incentives in various ways. The elimination of old tax preferences will also change behavior as people find that there's less marginal tax benefit from engaging in an activity. In general, because under the old law the marginal tax rates were as high as 50% for many taxpayers, they'll get to keep more of their earnings after taxes at the new lower 28% marginal tax rate. Lower marginal tax rates for upper-income taxpayers also imply that exclusions, exemptions, and deductions from income are worth less. Before the new law, a dollar's worth of itemized deductions was worth 50¢ in reduced taxes for a taxpayer in the highest tax bracket. Now that same dollar of deductions will be worth only a 28¢ reduction in taxes.

taxed. For example, suppose your income is $25,000 per year. If you pay $5,000 per year in income tax, your average tax rate would be:

$$\text{Income taxes paid/Income} = \$5,000/\$25,000 = 20\%$$

The average tax rate is an important factor in evaluating the fairness of a tax because it shows how taxes vary as a percentage of income among taxpayers with differing incomes.

Marginal tax rate:
The extra tax paid on extra income or the extra dollar value of any other taxed item.

The **marginal tax rate** is the *extra* tax paid on extra income or the extra dollar value of any other taxed item. Under the federal income tax there are two positive marginal tax brackets for most taxpayers. Under a flat-rate tax there's no difference between the marginal and average tax rates. For example, if income were subject to a flat 20% tax rate, total taxes paid divided by total income would always be 20%. Under a flat-rate tax, both the average and marginal tax rates are the same. However, when a progressive tax structure is used, the marginal tax rate often exceeds the average tax rate. For example, if you were a single person earning exactly $17,850 after all exemptions, exclusions, and deductions, you'd pay $2,677.50 in tax. Your average tax rate expressed as a percent of your taxable income would therefore be 15%. However, the marginal tax rate *increases* to 28% on taxable income in excess of $17,850. This means that for each dollar of taxable income over $17,850, you'll pay 28¢ rather than 15¢ in taxes. Also, under the federal income tax law for 1988, if your taxable income exceeded $43,150 you would pay a surtax of 5%, which would raise to 33% the marginal tax rate on a portion of your income above $43,150.

Naturally, when deciding whether to work or engage in any other activity that increases your income, you look at your *marginal* rather than average tax rate. This is because the marginal tax rate tells you how much of your *extra* earnings subject to tax you can keep.

Taxes and Efficiency

Taxes distort choices. For example, an income tax is likely to distort the choice between work and leisure by affecting the *net wage* you can keep after payment of taxes. As you certainly know if you work, you don't receive the full amount of your salary because of the payroll and income taxes withheld from your paycheck. When you decide how many hours to work per week or year you look at your net wage, which will vary with your marginal tax rate. For example, if your marginal tax rate were 28% you'd get to keep only 72% of the additional gross wages you earned.

Because they reduce net wages, income taxes can cause changes in our behavior as we make choices that differ from those we'd make if our wages weren't subject to tax. If you're subject to a high marginal tax rate, you might choose to work less than you would otherwise. The tax causes a substitution of leisure for work and results in a loss of efficiency in labor markets. This decreases production in the economy and results in less output from available resources. Taxes on interest income likewise can result in efficiency losses. If you earn 10% interest and are subject to a 15% marginal tax rate, you'll receive net interest of only 8.5% after taxes. The tax therefore lowers the interest rate received by you and other savers, and this could induce you to substitute spending for saving. This results in less funds available for investment, which reduces the economy's production potential.

Of course, the actual reduction in efficiency depends on how responsive we are as taxpayers to tax-induced changes in net wages, net interest rates, and other prices.

The actual impact of taxes on efficiency is therefore a subject for empirical investigation.

The **excess burden** of a tax is the loss in net benefits from resource use caused by the tax-induced distortion in choices. For example, suppose the federal income tax collects $300 billion in revenue. In addition, suppose that as a result of reduced output the tax indirectly causes losses in net benefits estimated to be $10 billion per year. This is the excess burden of the tax over and above the $300 billion it raises.

Taxes with a low excess burden are likely to be those levied on goods that are very unresponsive to changes in price. An example is a tax on basic food items. However, many people would oppose such a tax on the grounds it would be regressive. This is because the percentage of income we spend on basic food items tends to decline as our income rises. As we observed earlier, the most efficient taxes aren't always the most equitable ones.

Excess burden:
The loss in net benefits from resource use caused by the distortion in choices resulting from taxation.

Concept Check

1 How would you determine whether or not a tax is progressive?

2 What is the distinction between the marginal tax rate and the average tax rate for an income tax?

3 What is the excess burden of a tax?

Public Choice and Voting Under Majority Rule

The process through which government provides goods and services differs significantly from the process through which goods and services are provided in markets. **Public choices** are those made by voting. As you know, each nation has its own unique political institutions, which are rules for reaching public choices on the role of government and government activities. **Simple majority rule** is a means for reaching public choices that enacts a proposal if it obtains affirmative votes from more than half the voters casting ballots in an election. James Buchanan, winner of the 1986 Nobel Prize in economics, is the architect of a controversial theory of public choice (see Economic Thinkers box).

Public choices:
Choices made by voting.

Simple majority rule:
A means for reaching public choices that enacts a proposal if it obtains affirmative votes from more than half the voters casting ballots in an election.

Voting

When public choices are made, each of us has the opportunity to vote on proposals. In fact, politics is complicated because we differ sharply in our demands for various government activities.

Our first step in understanding public choices is to examine individual voting decisions. In voting for a proposed alternative, we assume you'll vote "no" if enactment of the alternative would make you worse off. In this analysis we assume that people seek to maximize their own well-being, as they see it, in making their voting decisions. To understand a voter's choice, we therefore need to analyze the marginal benefit and marginal cost to him of a proposal.

The marginal cost of a proposal to a voter is the extra tax or other cost the voter will bear if the proposal is enacted. Suppose the members of your community must vote to decide the number of fireworks displays to make available each year and

Economic Thinkers

JAMES BUCHANAN

Chance has a lot to do with James Buchanan's success as an economist. By chance he entered the University of Chicago's graduate economics program. By chance he learned German, and by chance one day in the library he discovered a slim book written in German in 1896 by a Swedish author. It was the dissertation of Knut Wicksell, a Swedish economist known for his theoretical

work in monetary policy. A portion of that book became one of the main planks of Buchanan's theory of public choice.

Buchanan believes that individuals in politics act to maximize net gains just as they would in markets: they pursue their own interests. For politicians, this means responding to the interests of their own constituents so that they can remain in office. Buchanan believes legislators trade votes to obtain enactment of laws that benefit the special interests they represent, and this "loyalty" results in bulging government budgets.

This theory helps explain why budget deficits seem to be chronic and uncontrollable. Buchanan says that Keynesian economics has destroyed the constraints on politicians' appetite to spend without the apparent necessity to tax. His ideas have made him unpopular with more liberal economists and politicians. When he received a Nobel Prize in economics in 1986 for his work, a stir of controversy arose. His critics claimed his

award reflected political fashion rather than meritorious scholarship. Buchanan admits his ideas are "not standard," but says many academics have failed to use common-sense solutions even when they are appropriate.

Buchanan grew up on a farm in Tennessee, and when he is not teaching at George Mason University, he runs a 400-acre farm outside Blacksburg, Virginia. He learned how the eastern establishment can discriminate against outsiders while he was in officer's school in the Navy before World War II. Judging by the reaction to his award, he remains outside that establishment even today.

Buchanan says that to control government spending, we should change the rules surrounding government policy makers. He favors a balanced-budget amendment to the Constitution, which would outlaw deficit spending except in cases of national crisis. He may be on the conservative end of the spectrum of economic thought, but he is certainly thriving.

finance with taxes. Assume each person in the community places a different marginal benefit on the various possible numbers of fireworks displays per year, which are assumed to be a pure public good.

Let's say seven voters are told they each will have to pay a certain annual tax for each fireworks display. Suppose the standard fireworks display costs $700 and each voter is told he'll pay a tax of $100 per display per year. Each extra display per year will cost each voter an additional $100 per year, which is the marginal cost for each unit of the public good for *each* voter. Also note that the tax is equally apportioned among voters and that $700 will be collected to finance each display. The budget will therefore be in balance.

Now look at the voting decision of a particular voter—let's say it's you. Assume that the marginal benefit of fireworks displays declines as more are made available. The graph in Box 5 plots your marginal benefit curve. Also shown on the graph is the tax per fireworks display, representing your $100 marginal cost per display. If the marginal benefit of a fireworks display to you exceeds its marginal cost, represented by your tax for that display, you'll be made better off if that display is approved. This is because the dollar gain from the display, represented by the marginal benefit, will exceed the dollar cost, represented by the tax. For example, in the graph in Box 5, your marginal benefit for the first annual display is $200. Because

Principles in Practice

Payroll Taxes and the Social Security System: How Taxes on Workers Pay the Pensions of Retirees

Hard as it may be to imagine, someday you'll be getting ready to collect your gold watch for faithful service and begin what we'll hope is a leisure-filled retirement. If you haven't won the lottery or inherited a fortune, what will you live on when you're not working? When you retire, you can probably count on receiving a pension from the federal Social Security system, depending on how many years you worked and how much eligible compensation you were paid. What exactly is Social Security? How does it work, and can you look forward to receiving a tidy monthly sum when you retire? Let's find out.

The Social Security system in the United States administers many programs that provide pensions, disability payments, unemployment compensation, and health benefits. By far the most expensive Social Security programs are those that provide Old Age, Survivors, and Disability Insurance (OASDI). These benefits go primarily to people who are over age 65. In 1986 OASDI accounted for expenditures of $198 billion, while expenditures for Medicare (federal health insurance for the elderly) were an additional $70 billion. Social Security pensions alone represent over 20% of federal government spending.

The Social Security pension system is really a government transfer program. This might surprise you because the taxes paid to finance the system are often referred to as Federal Insurance Act "Contributions" (FICA). These are actually payroll taxes levied on wages and paid by both workers and employers. The taxes imposed on your wages aren't invested to provide an income for you in your old age. Instead the bulk of the taxes paid by you and other workers are transferred directly to retirees now receiving Social Security pensions. When you eventually retire, your pension will be paid for by taxes on workers still in the labor force. Social Security pensions therefore represent a *transfer* of income from workers to retirees.

Payroll taxes to finance Social Security pensions have been the fastest-growing taxes in the United States. In 1990 workers earning up to a maximum of approximately $50,000 per year will be subject to a payroll tax of 7.65% of their earnings. Their employers will pay an additional 7.65% on those wages. The combined tax rate of employees and employers will therefore be 15.3% of wages. Wages in excess of the maximum taxable amount will not be subject to the payroll tax.

To give you some idea of the magnitude of the taxes involved, suppose you're lucky enough to have a $50,000 job in 1990. You'd pay 7.65% of your wages in FICA payroll taxes, for a total of $3,825 per year. Your employer would pay the same amount. Your salary would therefore generate a total of $7,650 per year in payroll taxes to be transferred to retired workers. If you were married and your spouse also earned $50,000 in 1990, your combined salaries would generate $15,300 per year in Social Security taxes.

There's considerable variation in pensions paid under Social Security, depending on your earning history and your dependents. A worker earning maximum wages subject to Social Security payroll taxes over a full career in the labor force would get a Social Security pension in the range of $15,000 per year in 1990 if the worker had a dependent spouse in 1990. You and your spouse, each earning maximum wages subject to the payroll tax, would therefore pay enough taxes to pay the Social Security pension for a retired high-income worker in 1990! In fact, by the early twenty-first century there will be one retiree for each two workers in the labor force. As you can see, the aging of America means that a tax-financed Social Security system will result in higher taxes per worker.

Unless the level of benefits enjoyed by Social Security retirees is reduced or the retirement age is increased, the scenario just sketched will be a fact for much of your working life. You can expect to pay substantial taxes over your lifetime to finance the pensions of retired workers. You'll have to hope that the political climate in the year you retire will be conducive to workers paying high taxes to support *your* pension!

---

this exceeds the marginal cost of $100 imposed on you by the tax, you'll be made better off if that display is approved. Similarly, you'd vote in favor of a second and a third display because the marginal benefit of these displays exceeds their marginal cost.

What's your best alternative, given your annual assigned tax? The answer is four displays per year. This is the annual number of displays that just sets your marginal benefit equal to your marginal cost, or tax, per display. If five displays per year were provided, you'd be made worse off because the marginal benefit of the fifth display is below its marginal cost. A voter's **most-preferred political outcome** is that alternative for which the marginal benefit just equals the tax the voter would pay if

Most-preferred political outcome:
That alternative for which the marginal benefit just equals the tax a voter would pay if he were able to purchase the good or service in a market at a price equal to his assigned tax per unit.

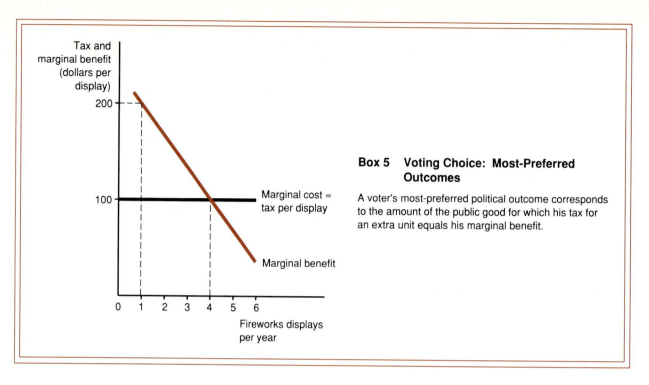

Box 5 Voting Choice: Most-Preferred Outcomes

A voter's most-preferred political outcome corresponds to the amount of the public good for which his tax for an extra unit equals his marginal benefit.

he were able to purchase the good or service in a market at a price equal to his assigned tax per unit.

As a voter, your most-preferred political outcome depends on your tax per unit of the public good. For example, if as the voter whose marginal benefit curve is drawn in Box 5 you had an assigned tax share of $200 instead of $100, your most-preferred political outcome would be one display per year instead of four. This points out a very important fact: A voter's willingness to vote for a proposal depends in part on the marginal cost he would incur if the proposal is enacted. The marginal cost is largely determined by the extra taxes the person would pay if the extra units of the public good are approved. *If you change a voter's tax, or the way the tax varies with output of a public good, you'll change the voter's voting behavior and the voter's most-preferred outcome.*

Also note that your tastes, as reflected in your marginal benefit for a public good, affect your voting behavior and your most-preferred political outcome. The graph in Box 6 shows the marginal benefit curve of another voter—let's say it's your sister. She doesn't place as high a value on fireworks as you do, as shown in your marginal benefit curve in Box 5. Your sister's most-preferred outcome, given her tax share of $100 per display, is one display per year. Note that if your sister's tax per display were increased above $100 per year, she would vote against even one display per year.

As we observed earlier, voters are likely to differ in terms of the marginal benefit they place on proposals for increased government activity. *Differences in preferences, as reflected in differences in the marginal benefit placed on public goods in various quantities, are therefore an important determinant of voting choices.* Also note that the marginal benefit you place on a fireworks display varies with your income. If fireworks are a normal good, the marginal benefit you associate with a fireworks display will increase as your income increases.

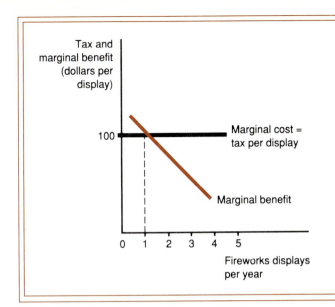

Box 6   Marginal Benefit and Voting Choice

Differences in marginal benefits from public goods account for differences in voting choices. The voter whose marginal benefit curve is drawn at left has a most-preferred political outcome corresponding to one fireworks display per year. Compare this to the case of the voter whose marginal benefit curve is drawn in Box 5, whose most-preferred outcome is four displays per year. Differences in taxes per display can also explain differences in most-preferred outcomes.

Political Equilibrium Under Majority Rule

A **political equilibrium** is an agreement on the quantity of a public good to be supplied through government, given the rule for making the public choice and given the taxes per unit of the public good for each voter. It's easy to show how a political equilibrium for a pure public good, such as fireworks displays, can be established under majority rule.

Political equilibrium:
An agreement on the quantity of a public good to supply through government, given the rule for making the public choice and given the taxes per unit of the public good for each voter.

Assume that each of seven voters in your community has a different most-preferred political outcome, ranging from one to seven displays per year. Recall that each voter is assumed to have exactly the same tax share of $100 per display and that the cost per display is assumed to be $700. The graph in Box 7 plots the marginal benefit curves of all seven voters on the same set of axes and shows how their most-preferred outcomes range from one to seven.

Suppose the voters get together in a room and successively propose approval of various numbers of fireworks displays per year beginning with one. Any proposal that receives a majority, meaning at least four affirmative votes, is approved. Look first at the alternative proposed: to have only one fireworks display per year. This is the most-preferred outcome of the voter whose marginal benefit curve is labeled MB_1. Naturally this voter votes in favor of this alternative because it's her first choice. All other voters will also vote in favor of one fireworks display per year because the marginal benefit of the first display exceeds the tax per display for each of the remaining six voters. The alternative of one display per year passes by unanimous agreement!

Now look at the alternative of two displays per year. If this is proposed, all voters except the voter whose marginal benefit curve is labeled MB_1 will vote in favor of it. The first voter votes no because the marginal benefit of the second display for her falls short of the extra tax she would have to pay if it's approved. No other voter's marginal benefit falls below the $100 tax share for this alternative, so it passes with six votes in favor and one opposed.

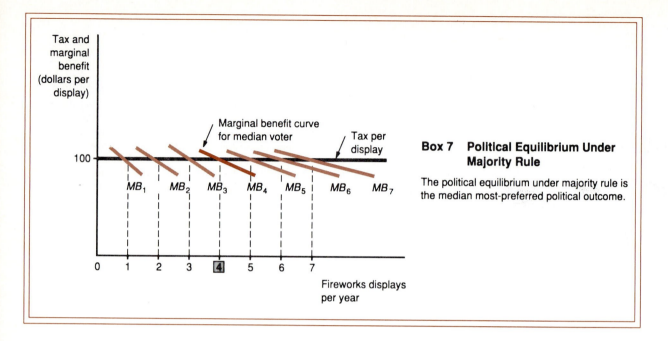

Tax and
marginal
benefit
(dollars per
display)

100

Marginal benefit curve
for median voter

Tax per
display

MB_1 MB_2 MB_3 MB_4 MB_5 MB_6 MB_7

0   1   2   3   [4]   5   6   7

Fireworks displays
per year

**Box 7   Political Equilibrium Under
Majority Rule**

The political equilibrium under majority rule is
the median most-preferred political outcome.

Similarly, the alternative of three displays per year will pass with five votes in favor and two opposed. The voter whose marginal benefit curve is labeled MB_2 votes against this alternative along with the first voter. The proposal to have four displays per year will also pass with four votes in favor and three votes against. However, given the tax of $100 and the marginal benefit curves in the graph, any proposal to have five or more displays per year won't receive the four votes necessary to satisfy the majority rule. It follows that up to four fireworks displays per year can be approved under majority rule. The alternative of four displays per year will emerge as the political equilibrium under majority rule.

The Median Voter Rule

Median voter:
Given an odd number of voters, the voter whose most-preferred outcome is the median of all the most-preferred outcomes.

Median voter rule:
States that when the marginal benefit of a pure public good declines for each voter as more of the good is made available, the political equilibrium under majority rule always corresponds to the median most-preferred outcome when there is an odd number of voters.

Notice that the political equilibrium under majority rule in the preceding example has an interesting property: exactly three voters have a most-preferred outcome that exceeds the political equilibrium. Also, exactly three voters have a most-preferred political outcome that's less than the political equilibrium number of displays per year. The alternative of four displays per year is the median most-preferred outcome. The voter whose marginal benefit curve is MB_4 in Box 7 is called the **median voter** because his most-preferred outcome is the median of all the most-preferred outcomes. *The **median voter rule** says that when the marginal benefit of a pure public good declines for each voter as more of the good is made available, the political equilibrium under majority rule always corresponds to the median most-preferred outcome when there is an odd number of voters.*

This result has an important lesson for politicians. If an election deals with a single issue, such as the quantity of a pure public good to provide, and there's a variety of most-preferred outcomes, the median most-preferred outcome will always emerge as the victor. A politician who sticks his neck out to support an extreme of very little or a great deal of a public good is likely to lose an election when there's a wide variation in most-preferred outcomes.

Market Outcomes vs. Political Outcomes

It's also useful to highlight the distinctions between market outcomes and political outcomes. In general, it's a great advantage to have nonpublic goods made available through markets. This is because each of us could buy as much or as little of such goods as we wanted. We'd simply purchase the good up to the point at which the marginal benefit received fell to equal the market price. The market therefore would achieve efficiency, assuming no externalities, by allowing each of us to set our own marginal benefit equal to market price. Under perfect competition, market price in turn would reflect the marginal social cost of the good. Each of us, given our willingness and ability to pay as reflected in the marginal benefits we receive from alternative quantities, and given the market price of the good, can choose our most-preferred quantity by adjusting our purchases until marginal benefit equals price.

Under majority rule, not every voter gets to enjoy his most-preferred outcome. *Given marginal taxes per unit of the public good or service and marginal benefit, which measures willingness to pay, only the median voter enjoys her most-preferred outcome.* All voters must consume exactly the same quantity of pure public goods in equilibrium. For example, in Box 7, under majority rule each voter ends up consuming four fireworks displays per year. If, however, each of the seven voters were able to purchase fireworks displays in a market at a price of $100 each, each voter would be able to enjoy his or her most-preferred outcome. Of course, it's not possible to buy fireworks displays at the $100 price because each display actually costs $700. The only way the voters can obtain the display is to share the costs.

Finally, notice that *if every voter had the same most-preferred outcome,* then under majority rule any voter could be considered to be the median voter. The degree to which voters are dissatisfied with the results of majority rule, because they don't enjoy their most-preferred outcome, depends on the dispersion of most-preferred outcomes from the median most-preferred outcome.

Concept Check

1 How does a rational person choose to vote yes or no on an issue to be considered in an election?

2 What could change a voter's most-preferred political outcome?

3 What does the median voter rule imply about the political equilibrium under simple majority rule?

Shaping the Role of Government

Through politics and voting we determine the size of the government sector in our economy. The way you vote on a proposal depends on the marginal benefit you expect from it if it's enacted and on the marginal cost, such as taxes, you'll pay as a result of its passage. Over the past 50 years government expenditures and activities have broadened and expanded. Under a system of majority rule, voters have consented to more and more government programs. It's difficult to evaluate whether the current allocation of resources between government goods and services and other goods and services is efficient. Many government programs are approved simply to redistribute income among citizens. In addition, government taxes result in losses of efficiency in markets by distorting choices in ways that reduce net benefits from national production.

Government failure:
Exists when voters approve programs for which marginal costs exceed marginal benefits.

Although government seeks to correct for market failures, we also must evaluate the actual impact of government on resource use. The specter of government programs whose costs exceed their benefits is a distinct possibility. When voters approve programs for which marginal costs exceed marginal benefits, a **government failure** exists. Government failure results in losses in efficiency by allocating resources to uses for which the net gain is negative. The efficiency of government expenditures can be improved if we as voters are provided with accurate information on both the marginal costs and marginal benefits of proposed programs.

Summary

1. Annual spending by all levels of government in the United States accounts for about one third of the value of national production.

2. The basic functions of government are the establishment of property rights and the regulation of private actions, provision of goods and services, redistribution of income, and stabilization of the economy.

3. Government goods and services are usually made freely available to everyone and financed with taxes or borrowings. In some cases government services are available only to certain individuals who meet predetermined eligibility criteria.

4. In the United States, the federal government spends a large proportion of its budget on transfer programs that tax some people to provide income support to others. Social Security and welfare programs are examples of transfer expenditures. National defense is another important government expenditure; it accounts for over one quarter of all federal government expenditures each year. Education accounts for more than one third of expenditures by state and local governments.

5. When government revenues fall short of expenditures, there is a budget deficit. The government covers the deficit and meets its expenditures by borrowing through issuance of bonds that are sold through financial markets.

6. Taxes represent the bulk of revenues raised by governments in the United States. The personal income tax accounts for over 40% of federal revenues. The sales tax is the most important tax for state governments, while local governments rely chiefly on property taxes to raise revenues.

7. Taxes affect our incentives to work, save, invest, and purchase goods and services. However, we also evaluate taxes in terms of their fairness or equity as well as in terms of distortions they cause in resource use.

8. A progressive tax is one that collects higher fractions of income from taxpayers as their income rises. A proportional tax is one for which the percentage of income paid in taxes is the same no matter what the taxpayer's income. A regressive tax collects smaller fractions of income from high-income taxpayers than it does from low-income taxpayers.

9. The average tax rate is the amount of taxes paid over a certain period divided by the dollar value of the item taxed. The marginal tax rate is the extra tax paid on a dollar of additional income or an extra dollar's worth of any other taxed item. The average tax rate is useful in evaluating the equity of a tax because it can indicate the proportion of a person's income paid in taxes. The marginal tax rate is useful in evaluating the impact of a tax on incentives because it shows how much extra earnings (or extra dollars' worth of other activities) a person has to give up in taxes.

10. Taxes distort choices and the ability of the price system to allocate resources

efficiently because they cause decisions to be made on prices that are distorted by taxes. The excess burden of a tax is the loss in net benefits from production caused by the tax-induced distortion in choices.

11. Public choices are those made by voting. When a rational person votes on a proposal, he compares the marginal benefit he expects from the proposal with the marginal cost. The marginal cost depends on the extra taxes the voter must pay to finance the additional government activity. A person's most-preferred political outcome is the alternative for which the marginal benefit just equals the extra tax the person must pay to enjoy the additional government expenditure.

12. A political equilibrium is an agreement on the quantity of a public good to supply through government action. Under simple majority rule, the political equilibrium often corresponds to the median most-preferred outcome of all voters. Generally, not all voters enjoy their most-preferred outcome under majority rule.

Key Terms and Concepts

Taxes	Marginal tax rate
Federal system of government	Excess burden
Government transfers	Public choices
Budget deficit	Simple majority rule
Budget surplus	Most-preferred political outcome
Regressive tax	Political equilibrium
Progressive tax	Median voter
Proportional tax	Median voter rule
Average tax rate	Government failure

Problems and Applications

1. Give an example of a government-provided service that benefits you. Why are Social Security pensions a transfer?

2. Estimate the amount of taxes you and your family pay each year. Are the benefits you receive from these taxes worth the taxes you pay?

3. In markets, goods and services are sold at a price determined by the forces of supply and demand, and we make buying decisions according to our willingness and ability to pay. Are government goods and services distributed in this way? Choose four government-provided services and describe the method of making each service available to consumers.

4. How are government deficits financed? How can budget deficits be eliminated? Explain why interest payments by government go up when budget deficits increase.

5. A flat-rate income tax of 20% is levied on all citizens with no allowable tax preferences. Show that both the average and marginal tax rate equal 20%. How would you evaluate the equity of this tax?

6. Suppose you have a job in which you earn $10 per hour. Will you base your decision to work on the wage your employer pays you when you must pay a 20% flat-rate income tax? How will the tax affect your incentive to work?

7. A state levies a sales tax of 5% on cars, but the tax is imposed only on the first $10,000 of the purchase price. Is the tax proportional, progressive, or regressive?

In your answer assume that people with higher incomes buy more expensive cars.

8. Suppose the following tax rate schedule is used to collect income taxes:

Annual income	Marginal tax rate
0 - $4,000	0%
$4,000 - $29,000	15%
$29,000 - $70,000	25%
Above $70,000	35%

Calculate the average tax rate for people with annual incomes of $4,000, $29,000, and $70,000. Is this tax progressive, regressive, or proportional?

9. Your community holds a local election to decide whether to hire an additional police officer. You estimate that your marginal benefit from the extra officer is $150 per year. Under what circumstances will you vote against the proposal?

10. Suppose candidates running in an election can be ranked on a political spectrum from conservative to liberal, and voters' most-preferred political outcomes are evenly distributed between liberal and conservative. Explain why a moderate candidate will defeat an ultraconservative or ultraliberal opponent.

Suggested Readings

James M. Buchanan, *Public Finance in Democratic Process,* Chapel Hill: University of North Carolina Press, 1967. This is a classic economic analysis of public choice by a Nobel Prize–winning economist.

Harold Groves, *Tax Philosophers,* Madison: University of Wisconsin Press, 1974. This book offers a review of the philosophies of taxation.

Joseph A. Pechman, *Who Paid the Taxes: 1966-1985?* Washington, D.C.: The Brookings Institution, 1985. This analysis of the distribution of taxes among households in the United States provides information to evaluate the equity of taxes.

A Forward Look

A major concern of each us is our personal income and the incomes of others. In the next part we begin to explore input markets and how input prices influence resource use and personal incomes. We open this inquiry in the next chapter by analyzing the forces influencing the demand for inputs and employment of inputs by profit-maximizing business firms.

Career Profile

REGINALD LEWIS

Bored with his legal career, the man who founded the first black law firm on Wall Street decided it was time to try a new game. Reginald Lewis, lawyer and venture capitalist, has proved himself an excellent player in the takeover game, earning Wall Street's attention with a 90–1 return on his first big play.

In 1984 Lewis purchased McCall Pattern Company through his TLC investment company. He bought the firm on a leveraged buyout, using $1 million in cash and $24 million in borrowed funds. Emphasizing higher quality, decreased costs, and improved cash flow, he revitalized the company by doubling profits in 3 years. He then sold the company for $63 million to a British firm, which also agreed to assume $32 million in debts owed by McCall.

The deal established Lewis's reputation on Wall Street as an intense and demanding perfectionist who hates to lose—and so far hasn't. His next move was even bigger: a $985 million acquisition of Beatrice International Foods, a group of 64 overseas companies that operate in 31 countries. In a big-league leveraged buyout, Lewis beat out firms like Citicorp and Pillsbury to get the deal. Most of the money came from Drexel Burnham Lambert, an investment firm that will get a 35% share in the business.

Lewis now controls the largest black-owned business in the country, and the deal shattered traditional patterns for black enterprise. Most black businesses are anchored in the black community, and until Lewis, Wall Street had not taken blacks seriously. Now analysts are speculating that others may follow in his footsteps, attracting big Wall Street capital for their enterprises.

A tough, aggressive businessman, Lewis originally planned to become a professional athlete until a shoulder injury sidelined his career as a quarterback at Virginia State University. There he fell in love with economics, and later studied securities law at Harvard.

In both of his major purchases, Lewis has demonstrated the ability to spot a pot of gold behind a firm's financial data. In his metamorphosis from athlete to lawyer to venture capitalist to takeover artist, Lewis has always showed tremendous resolve, a passion for hard work, and a keenly analytical mind.

Input Markets and Incomes:
Microeconomic Analysis

Input Markets and the Demand for Resources

If you own something someone else wants, whether it's your flawless economics lecture notes or your 1976 Chevy Nova, you can offer it to that person for a sum of money. In the same way, owners of economic resources such as labor, land, or capital equipment can offer the services of those inputs to others to employ in the production of goods and services. The proceeds received from selling the services of productive resources are a major source of income for most of us. An **input market** is one used to trade the services of productive resources for income payments. For example, you might enter the labor market, which is a market for the sale of labor input, as a seller of labor services. The payment you receive for your services is wages, which represent the *price* of labor services. Like most prices, wages depend on supply and demand in markets.

Input market:
A market used to trade the services of productive resources for income payments.

If you're fortunate, you might have other valuable resources you can sell in input markets for employment in production. If you own land, you can rent its services to people who might use it for farming or business. Rent per acre of land per month represents the price that must be paid to use land. You might also earn income from interest payments you receive on savings deposits or bonds. Interest is also a price.

From the viewpoint of employers of economic resources, input prices are an important influence on the cost of production. Wages affect the labor costs of producing goods and services, while rents affect the cost of employing land.

Interest rates affect the costs of borrowing loanable funds to finance new equipment and expansion of business enterprises. In this chapter we examine the decisions made by profit-maximizing firms in employing inputs. By analyzing hiring decisions, we can better understand the influences on the demand for inputs. Then, by analyzing the supply of inputs, we can show how the forces of supply and demand act together to influence prices.

From the viewpoint of *sellers* in input markets, wages, rents, and interest represent important influences on their incomes. Your income depends on both the prices of inputs and the amount you actually have available to sell. For most of us, the dominant source of income is the sale of labor services. In the United States, income from the sale of labor services accounts for about 75% of total annual income earned. Rental income is a mere 2% of total income earned each year, while about 10% typically is interest earnings. The remaining 13% consists of business profits.

After reading this chapter, you should be able to:

1   Explain the concept of a perfectly competitive input market.
2   Show how much of a particular input, like labor, a profit-maximizing firm chooses to buy over a certain period in a competitive market.
3   Show how a firm's demand for an input depends on the productivity of the input and on the price the firm receives from selling the product of the input.
4   Show how the market price of an input depends on its supply and demand.

Competitive Input Markets

The laws of supply and demand are as relevant to input markets as they are to product markets. A **competitive input market** is one in which neither individual buyers nor individual sellers can influence the prices of input services. In such markets both buyers and sellers are price takers. This means that no one firm buys a large enough share of the total amount of a particular input to be able to affect the market demand for it. Individual firms can buy all they like at the market price. Similarly, sellers can't affect the overall market supply of the input, no matter how much they sell at the market price.

In addition to lack of control over price, *perfectly* competitive input markets have the following characteristics:

1. *There is free entry and exit of sellers into the market.* For example, suppose labor services of a given skill and quality are paid higher wages in service industries (such as life insurance) than in manufacturing. Under these circumstances we can expect workers to be attracted into service jobs from manufacturing jobs until the wages in the two types of occupations are equal.

2. *Owners of economic resources can transfer their resources from one use or location to another in response to differences in prices.* This means resource owners can maximize their income by adjusting quickly to changes in the prices they can obtain from the sale of their resources. For example, people who have loanable funds can easily transfer the funds from a bank in Switzerland to one in New York to take advantage of a higher interest rate.

The two conditions just cited imply that in a competitive input market, a resource of given quality will always be sold at the same price if it's employed under similar conditions in all uses and locations. For example, in a perfectly competitive labor market, wages for male and female workers of equal skill and experience employed in the same occupation under the same working conditions would be expected to

Competitive input market:
A market in which neither individual buyers nor individual sellers can influence the prices of input services.

be equal. If a labor market imperfection exists, such as discrimination against women, women would earn wages below those of men in similar occupations with similar skills. Such wage differences couldn't persist in a perfectly competitive market because competition among employers for the underpaid women would bid their wages up while the wages of men fell. Women would be expected to flock to the higher-paying jobs of men until the wage differential disappeared.

Operation of Perfectly Competitive Input Markets

The forces of supply and demand determine input prices in a perfectly competitive input market. In such a market, input prices, like wages, serve as *signals* for resource owners to reallocate the use of their resources. Any difference in input prices for a *given type and quality of resource* among regions or uses can only be temporary in a perfectly competitive market.

For example, as a nation industrializes, the wages of workers in manufacturing industries typically begin to rise above those of agricultural workers. Suppose *all* workers are of the same quality, possessing skills that are equally useful in both agriculture and manufacturing. Suppose that initially equilibrium wages in both agricultural and manufacturing jobs are $2 per hour. The upper two graphs in Box 1 show the initial equilibrium in the labor market for both agricultural and manufacturing workers. Initially there are L_A workers employed in agriculture and L_M workers employed in manufacturing.

Suppose now that demand increases for manufacturing workers. This will put upward pressure on wages in manufacturing. The higher wages attract more workers to accept manufacturing jobs. In fact, some of these workers will come from the agricultural sector of the economy. As long as wages are higher in manufacturing than in agriculture, workers will leave agricultural jobs, assuming free entry and exit and perfect mobility, to accept manufacturing jobs. This also assumes that working conditions are similar in both industries so that wages are the only factor workers consider in taking jobs. You'll see in the following chapter that differences in working conditions can explain wage differentials even in competitive labor markets.

As workers leave agricultural jobs, the supply of labor for agriculture decreases. The supply curve will continue to shift to the left in agricultural jobs until wages rise to equal the higher wages possible in manufacturing jobs. In the final equilibrium, the wages of both agricultural and manufacturing workers must be equal if workers are equally capable of doing farm and factory jobs. The lower graphs in Box 1 show that in the final equilibrium, wages rise to $3 per hour in *both* agricultural and manufacturing labor markets.

We can conclude from this analysis that in competitive labor markets, *all* workers of given skill benefit by enjoying higher wages when the demand increases for workers in one use or location. Thus both agricultural and manufacturing workers benefit from the increased demand for manufacturing workers.

Derived Demand

Derived demand:
The demand for an input that is derived from the demand for the product that the input is used to produce.

The example we just discussed highlights the importance of shifts in product demand in affecting input prices such as wages. The demand for input services is derived from the demand for the products consumers want to buy. Employers of inputs have a **derived demand** for inputs because they purchase input services for the purpose of making another product. The number of labor hours or machine

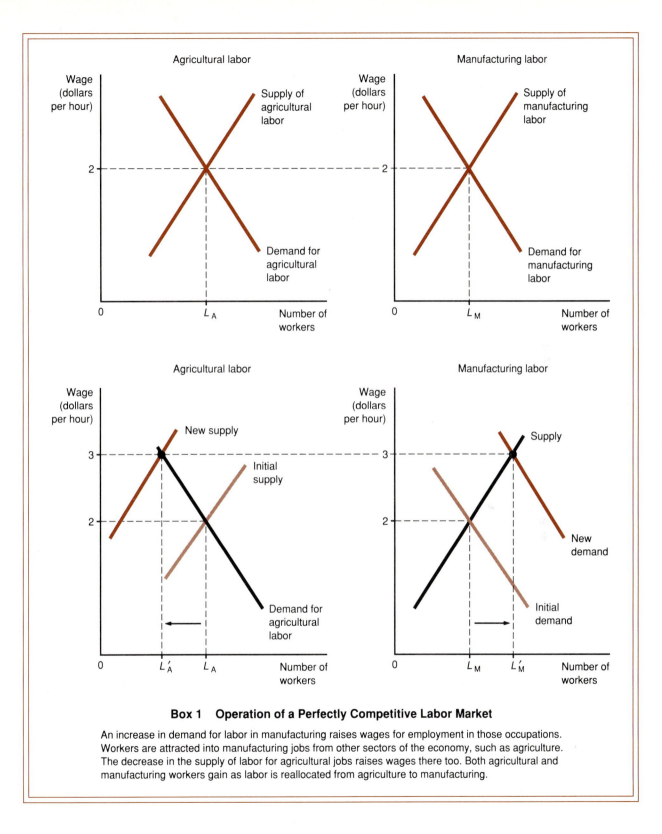

Box 1   Operation of a Perfectly Competitive Labor Market

An increase in demand for labor in manufacturing raises wages for employment in those occupations. Workers are attracted into manufacturing jobs from other sectors of the economy, such as agriculture. The decrease in the supply of labor for agricultural jobs raises wages there too. Both agricultural and manufacturing workers gain as labor is reallocated from agriculture to manufacturing.

hours or the amount of land business firms employ depends in part on the revenue they can obtain from the items they sell. For example, there would be no demand for the services of automobile workers if no one demanded cars. The demand for health care affects the demand for physicians and nurses. An insurance firm's demand for leased computer time depends on the data processing it needs to sell and service its insurance policies.

When a business firm hires labor or any other type of input, it does so for the obvious purpose of making more of its product available to its customers. Hiring additional workers allows the firm to sell more of its output and to generate additional revenue. In deciding how much input to use, business managers weigh the extra revenue they obtain from using more of an input against the extra cost they incur to pay for the use of the input. Naturally, a firm will be willing to pay more for an input if it's more productive. This is because the more productive an input, the greater the extra output it provides for the firm to sell.

The firm's willingness to pay for an input also depends on the price of the product that the input is used to produce. For example, suppose that hiring an additional worker allows a manufacturing firm to produce 100 more radios per week. The additional worker will be more valuable to the firm when those radios can be sold at $50 each than when they can be sold at only $20 each. Accordingly, the derived demand for input services is stronger when product prices are high than when product prices are low.

Concept Check

1   What are the characteristics of a competitive labor market?

2   Suppose the market for plumbers is perfectly competitive. What is likely to occur over a period of time if the market wage for plumbers in New Jersey is $20 per hour while the market wage for plumbers in Maryland is only $8 per hour?

3   What is likely to influence the derived demand for an input?

The Hiring Decision: Marginal Analysis

Productivity, Product Prices, and Input Demand: Marginal Revenue Product

The influence of input productivity and product prices on input demand can best be illustrated with a simple example. Suppose you manage a restaurant selling a standardized pizza pie that's also sold by hundreds of other restaurants in your city. In a competitive product market you can sell as many pizzas as you choose at the going market price of $5 a pie. Your restaurant has a given amount of capital equipment—square footage, ovens, chairs, tables, fountain equipment, and so on. You must decide how many workers to employ per day. (Although this example deals with labor, we can apply its conclusions to all inputs in the short run.) Assume that as the manager you seek to maximize profits.

The table in Box 2 shows that your restaurant's productivity and profitability will vary with the number of workers you hire each day. The first column of the table shows the number of workers, while the second column shows the total product produced with that number of workers. The *total product of labor* is the total output of pizzas per day produced by the corresponding number of workers using the available equipment and space in your restaurant. The third column of the table shows the *marginal product of labor,* which measures the *extra* production that's possible when an *extra* worker is hired. To obtain the marginal product for an additional worker, just subtract the total product that's possible when one less worker is used from the total product that's possible when the extra worker is hired. The data in the third column of the table show, for example, that when you employ only one worker, your restaurant can produce 45 pizzas per day. If you employ a second worker, daily production will increase to 75 pizzas per day. The marginal product of labor when you employ two workers is therefore 30 pizzas per day. This is because hiring a second worker when one is already employed allows you to make 30 more pizzas available each day. The hypothetical data in the table assume that diminishing marginal returns to additional workers set in after you hire the first worker. This means the marginal product of workers declines as you hire more. The marginal product of labor falls to 20 when you employ three workers per day. Hiring an additional worker after you have already hired two thus will allow you to produce only 20 more pizzas per day. The marginal product of labor steadily declines as you hire more workers and would actually become negative if you employed more than 7 workers per day.

Box 2 Marginal Revenue Product, Marginal Input Cost, and Profitability of Hiring Workers for a Competitive Firm

(1) Number of workers per day	(2) Total product (pizzas per day)	(3) Marginal product of labor	(4) Price of pizza	(5) Total revenue from sale of pizza	(6) Marginal revenue product of labor	(7) Marginal input cost (daily wage)	(8) Change in profit per day
0	0	0	$5	$ 0	$ 0	$ 0	—
1	45	45	5	225	225	32	$193
2	75	30	5	375	150	32	118
3	95	20	5	475	100	32	68
4	102	7	5	510	35	32	3
5	105	3	5	525	15	32	−17
6	106	1	5	530	5	32	−27
7	106	0	5	530	0	32	−32
8	101	−5	5	505	−25	32	−57

Column 4 of the table shows that the price of pizza is always $5 no matter how many pizzas you produce per day. Column 5 shows how your total revenue from the sale of pizzas will vary as you hire more workers, assuming you can sell all the pizzas you produce at the $5 price. Column 6 shows the change in your total revenue per day that results each time you hire an additional worker. The **marginal revenue product** of an input is the change in total revenue that results when one more unit of that input is hired. The marginal revenue product of labor is calculated in the sixth column of the table. For example, when you hire a second worker after

Marginal revenue product (of an input): The change in total revenue that results when one more unit of that input is hired.

you've already employed one worker, your daily revenue from the sale of pizzas increases from $225 to $375. The marginal revenue product when you employ two workers is therefore $150 ($375 − $225). When you employ a third worker, the marginal revenue product is $100 because total revenue increases to $475 per day.

Weighing the Benefits and Costs of Additional Workers

Suppose the workers you hire will be doing general chores and waiting on tables. You purchase the services of these workers in a competitive labor market. You can hire any number of labor hours per day at the going market wage of $4 per hour. The cost to the restaurant of hiring a worker for a standard 8-hour shift will be $32 at the $4 hourly wage.

The graphs in Box 3 show the demand for and supply of general restaurant workers in the labor market for such workers. The market demand for their services, as you'll see soon, depends in part on the number of industries hiring these workers. The market supply of workers is upward sloping because at higher wages more workers can be attracted to make themselves available for employment. The equilibrium daily wage corresponds to the point at which the market demand curve intersects the market supply curve. In Box 3 the equilibrium wage is $32 per worker for a standard 8-hour work day.

The supply curve of labor for any single firm hiring workers in a competitive labor market is the horizontal line in the right-hand portion of the graph. The horizontal line indicates that your restaurant can hire all the workers it wants at the $32 daily wage. Whenever you hire more workers, you don't shift the *market* demand

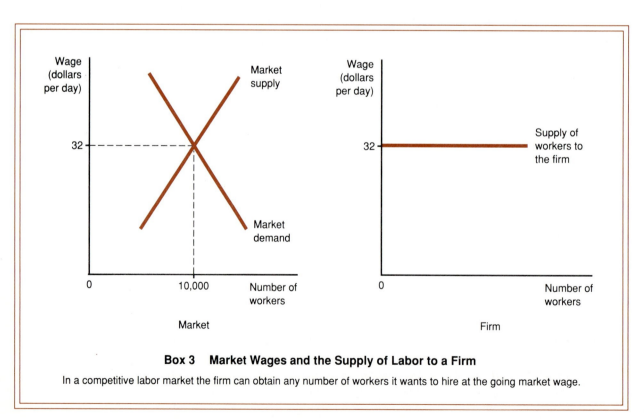

Box 3   Market Wages and the Supply of Labor to a Firm

In a competitive labor market the firm can obtain any number of workers it wants to hire at the going market wage.

curve out enough to raise the market wage. No matter how many workers you hire per day, the wage remains $32 for an 8-hour work day. Wages do change when *market* supply or *market* demand changes. However, an increase in the demand for workers by any one firm has no effect on market wages.

Competitive *output* markets allow a firm to *sell* as much as it likes at the going market price. If a firm operates in competitive output *and* input markets, it can both buy as many input services and sell as much output as it chooses at the going market prices. A fully competitive firm can influence neither its output price nor its input prices.

As the manager of a profit-maximizing firm, you compare the extra revenue you can earn from added labor services with the extra cost you incur by hiring those services. This means we can use marginal analysis to predict how much labor a firm will choose to employ. The extra revenue is the marginal revenue product of labor. The **marginal input cost** is the extra cost associated with hiring one more unit of an input. In this case the daily wage represents the marginal input cost of hiring another worker. *As long as the marginal revenue product of labor exceeds its wage, additional workers will add more to revenue than they will to costs.* When the marginal revenue product of labor exceeds the marginal labor cost, hiring additional workers will increase the firm's profit. As a profit-maximizing manager you'll therefore hire more workers until the marginal revenue product of labor falls to equal its marginal input cost. The rule for hiring any variable input is:

Marginal revenue product = Marginal input cost

The data in Box 2 illustrate how following this rule will maximize profit for your pizzeria. The daily wage is always $32 for an 8-hour day, independent of the number of workers you hire. When you hire only one worker, the marginal revenue product of labor is $225. The extra labor cost, shown in the next to last column of the table, is $32. By hiring one worker you increase your daily profits by $193 ($225 − $32). You can see this in the last column of the table.

When you employ two workers, the marginal revenue product of labor is $150. Daily marginal labor costs remain $32. Profits therefore increase by $118 per day, as shown in the last column of the table. Similarly, the marginal revenue product of labor exceeds the wage when you employ three workers. When you employ four workers, the marginal revenue product of labor is $35 per day. Your extra profit from hiring a fourth worker is $3 per day. Profits would decline if a fifth worker were employed. The marginal revenue product of labor when you hire five workers is only $15 per day. Since the wage is $32 per day, your profits would decline by $17 per day if you increased the number of workers from four to five. Similarly, the marginal revenue product of labor continues to decline when you employ more than five workers. In fact, the marginal product of labor when seven workers are employed is zero. Given the amount of fixed inputs in the restaurant in the short run, employing more than seven workers would actually decrease the number of pizzas you could serve per day.

The marginal input cost of labor services to a firm is the daily wage when labor is hired in a competitive labor market. When a firm can hire all the labor it wants at a given wage, the firm maximizes profit by hiring workers up to the point at which the marginal revenue product of labor falls to equal the wage. The rule for maximizing profit when hiring labor in a competitive market is therefore to hire workers until

Marginal revenue product of labor = Market wage

Marginal input cost:
The extra cost associated with hiring one more unit of an input.

The equilibrium number of workers for your pizzeria is illustrated graphically in Box 4. The supply of labor for your restaurant is represented by the horizontal line that intersects the vertical axis at $32. Also plotted on the same set of axes are the points showing how the marginal revenue product of labor declines as you hire more workers. These data come from the sixth column of the table in Box 2. The equilibrium number of workers corresponds to the point at which the marginal revenue product curve just intersects the labor supply curve at point *E*. You employ four workers per day. If you hired more workers per day, the table shows that your profits would begin to decline. For example, hiring a fifth worker per day would reduce your daily profits by $17, as you can see in the last column of the table.

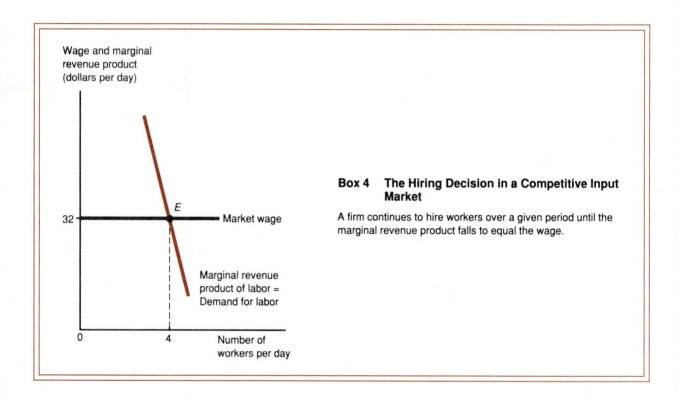

Box 4   The Hiring Decision in a Competitive Input Market

A firm continues to hire workers over a given period until the marginal revenue product falls to equal the wage.

The Marginal Revenue Product Curve: A Firm's Demand Curve for an Input Hired in a Competitive Market

A firm's input demand curve shows a relationship between input prices and the quantity of the input demanded by the firm. When a firm can hire all the input it desires at the market wage, its marginal revenue product curve is its input demand curve. To see this, just remember that a profit-maximizing firm hiring labor (or any other input) in a competitive market will continue hiring until the marginal revenue product of the input equals its price.

For example, to find out how many workers your pizzeria will hire at a given daily wage, just extend a dotted line from the corresponding wage to the marginal revenue product curve in Box 4. Dropping a vertical dotted line to the horizontal axis gives the number of workers demanded at that wage. The marginal revenue product curve therefore describes the relationship between the input price (in this case the wage) and the quantity of input demanded for a firm purchasing input services in a competitive market. In this case, therefore, the marginal revenue product curve *is* the input demand curve. There's an inverse relationship between wages and the number of workers that will be hired because of the declining marginal product of labor. Input demand curves, like output demand curves, slope downward.

What Can Cause a Firm's Input Demand to Change?

A **change in input demand** is a shift of an entire input demand curve caused by a change in one of the determinants of input demand other than price. In addition to the price of the input, the major determinants of input demand are:

Change in input demand: A shift of an entire input demand curve caused by a change in one of the determinants of input demand other than price.

1. *The demand for the firm's output.* Remember that the demand for any input is derived from the demand for the product it's used to produce. An increase in the demand for pizza is likely to increase its market price. An increase in the market price of pizza will increase the marginal revenue product associated with each number of workers hired. This will result in an upward shift of the demand curve for labor. Such a shift in demand is illustrated in Box 5. After the increase in demand for workers, the number employed increases from four to six, assuming the wage remains $32 per worker per day. Similarly, a decrease in the price of the product would decrease the demand for labor.

For example, if a sharp increase in the market demand for pizza were to double its price from $5 to $10, the marginal revenue product of labor, shown in the sixth column of the table in Box 2, would also double. To verify this, substitute $10 for $5 as the price in the fourth column and recalculate both total revenue and the marginal revenue product of labor. When you plot the data, you'll see that the mar-

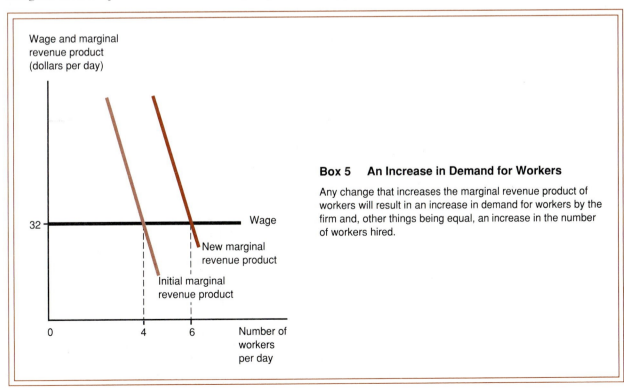

Box 5   An Increase in Demand for Workers

Any change that increases the marginal revenue product of workers will result in an increase in demand for workers by the firm and, other things being equal, an increase in the number of workers hired.

ginal revenue product curve has shifted up and out, indicating an increase in demand for labor to produce pizza. *When an increase in demand for a product increases its price, the demand for inputs used to make that product also increases.* An increase in the price of fine-quality furniture caused by increased demand will increase the demand for skilled furniture workers. By the same token, a decrease in the price of petroleum products caused by a decrease in demand is likely to decrease the demand for chemical engineers whose services are used to produce petroleum products. There also will be a decrease in demand for workers in regions that produce petroleum products. In fact, a decrease in the demand for oil in the mid-1980s caused sharp increases in unemployment in Texas and Louisiana, where oil production was a major industry.

2. *The prices and quantities of substitute and complementary inputs.* Suppose the price of labor-saving kitchen equipment declines. This is likely to decrease the demand for labor as a firm substitutes capital for labor in response. For example, dishwashing equipment is a *substitute input for labor.* If your pizzeria acquires more dishwashing equipment, its demand for labor will decline, meaning that its demand curve will shift inward.

On the other hand, if your pizzeria expands in the long run and acquires more tables to accommodate a stronger demand for its pizzas, then your demand for labor will increase because you'll need more workers to serve the additional tables. This will shift your demand curve for labor outward. Tables are a *complementary input* for labor in your restaurant.

3. *Technological change affecting the marginal product of an input.* If an improvement in technology increases the marginal product of any given number of computers employed, the marginal revenue product curve will shift upward. This means that for any given rental rate for computer hours, the quantity demanded will increase. An increase in the marginal productivity of an input at each possible level of employment therefore results in an upward shift in its demand curve for each firm, similar to the upward shift shown in Box 5.

Hiring More than One Input for Profit Maximization

To maximize profits from the use of *all* inputs, a firm must hire each variable input just up to the point where the price of the input equals its marginal revenue product. For example, suppose your pizzeria also rents equipment on a daily basis. You could rent vehicles to deliver pizzas or pay a daily rent for ovens and other equipment leased from other firms. Assume you can acquire as many delivery vehicles as you want at a daily rental rate of $50. You'll therefore hire vehicles up to the point at which the marginal revenue product per day equals the daily rental.

The principle for hiring the profit-maximizing amount of capital equipment is exactly the same as that for hiring the profit-maximizing number of workers per day. The marginal revenue product of each and every input must be adjusted by hiring either more or less of that input until the marginal revenue product of each input equals the input price. If the marginal revenue product of any input exceeds its price, the firm can increase its profits by hiring more of that input.

Industry Demand for Labor

The industry demand for labor is the relationship between the price of labor and the quantity demanded by all firms in an industry. However, when an industry hires more labor in response to a decrease in the price of labor, the price of the industry's *product* is likely to be affected. Think about what would happen if wages fell for factory workers producing televisions. This would induce all employers in the industry to hire more labor. As more labor was hired, the supply of televisions would increase. Other things being equal, an increase in the supply of televisions puts downward pressure on their price. As the price of TVs falls, so does the marginal revenue product of any given quantity of labor.

If the input prices of one firm in an industry were reduced, the firm's increased output wouldn't significantly affect market supply if it sold its output in a competitive market. However, as an entire industry hires more of an input whose price has declined, product prices must decline because of the increased market supply of output.

The Hiring Decision of a Monopoly Firm

A firm with monopoly power in its product market has a degree of control over the price of its product. These firms face a downward-sloping demand curve for their product. Remember that a monopolistic firm tends to supply less to buyers, other things being equal, than would a competitive firm. It naturally follows that if a competitive industry were monopolized, the monopoly firm would tend to reduce employment of labor and other inputs because reduction in input use is necessary to reduce output.

The impact of monopolization of an industry on the demand curve for a particular input can be easily demonstrated. Suppose there's only one pizzeria in your town. This restaurant has a monopoly in supplying residents of the town with pizza. Because it satisfies the entire local market demand for pizzas, it can't sell all the pizza it wants without reducing the price. As it produces more pizzas each day, it must lower the price to sell all its output. *The decline in price as more pizzas are produced per day causes the marginal revenue product of labor to decline more rapidly as additional workers are hired.*

We can understand the impact of a more rapidly declining marginal revenue product on labor demand by examining the hiring decision of this monopoly pizzeria. In the table in Box 6 it's assumed that the monopoly pizzeria has exactly the

Box 6 Marginal Revenue Product, Marginal Input Cost, and the Profitability of Hiring Workers for a Monopolist

(1) Number of workers per day	(2) Total product (pizzas per day)	(3) Marginal product of labor	(4) Price of pizza	(5) Total revenue from sale of pizza	(6) Marginal revenue product of labor	(7) Marginal input cost (daily wage)	(8) Change in profit per day
0	—	0	$5.00	0	—	$ 0	—
1	45	45	4.75	$213.75	$213.75	32	$181.75
2	75	30	4.50	337.50	123.90	32	91.90
3	95	20	4.30	408.50	71.00	32	39.00
4	102	7	4.15	423.30	14.80	32	−17.20
5	105	3	4.05	425.25	1.95	32	−30.05
6	106	1	4.00	424.00	−1.25	32	−33.25

same square footage and capital equipment as the competitive pizzeria you manage. The only difference is that the monopoly pizzeria can't sell all the pizza it produces at a price of $5. The price declines as daily pizza output increases. The total and marginal productivity of workers are exactly the same as they are for the competitive pizzeria. However, as the monopoly pizzeria hires more workers and increases its output, the price of pizza falls.

The first three columns of the table in Box 6 show how the total product and marginal product of labor vary as the monopoly pizzeria hires more workers per day. These data are the same as those in Box 2. The fourth column of the table in Box 6 shows how the price of pizza varies as output is increased. Notice how price declines steadily from $4.75 to $4 per pizza as the number of workers employed increases from one to six per day. The fifth column shows the total revenue from selling pizzas as more workers are hired. The sixth column shows the marginal revenue product of labor and how it decreases as more workers are employed. Compare this column with the corresponding column in Box 2 and notice how the marginal revenue product declines more rapidly.

The seventh column shows that this monopoly pizzeria, like its competitive counterpart under your management, can obtain all the workers it wants at a daily wage of $32. In other words, this pizzeria hires workers in a competitive labor market even though it has a monopoly in its product market.

The principle of profit maximization is the same for the monopoly pizzeria as it is for the competitive pizzeria: workers must be hired up to the point at which their marginal revenue product falls to equal the wage, which is the marginal input cost. For the monopoly pizzeria, notice that the marginal revenue product of the third worker exceeds the wage. However, the marginal revenue product of the fourth worker is only $14.80, which is less than the $32 wage. The monopoly pizzeria will

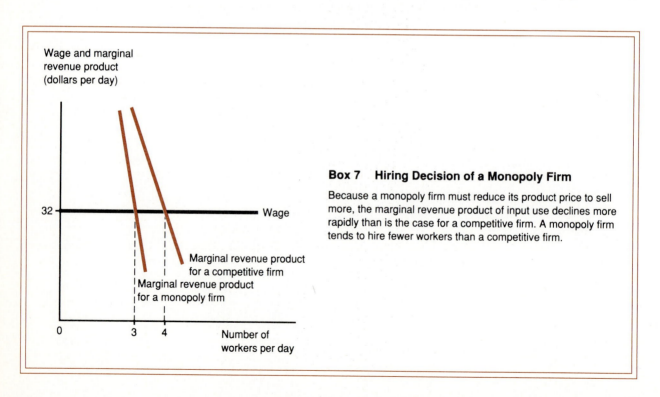

Box 7   Hiring Decision of a Monopoly Firm

Because a monopoly firm must reduce its product price to sell more, the marginal revenue product of input use declines more rapidly than is the case for a competitive firm. A monopoly firm tends to hire fewer workers than a competitive firm.

therefore hire fewer than four workers. Your competitive pizzeria, which can sell all the pizza it wants at $5, hires four workers (see Box 2).

The graph in Box 7 plots the marginal revenue product curves for both the competitive and monopoly pizzerias. It's assumed that both pizzerias can hire all the workers they want at the $32 daily wage. Notice that the marginal revenue product curve of the monopoly pizzeria is steeper and lies to the left of the corresponding curve for the competitive pizzeria. The monopoly pizzeria therefore has a weaker demand for labor input and hires fewer workers than the competitive pizzeria.

Concept Check

1   Explain why an increase in the demand for a product sold by a firm will increase that firm's demand for labor.

2   A new machine doubles the marginal product of any quantity of labor used to produce televisions. Assuming wages are constant and the price of the TVs doesn't fall after the machine is introduced, show how a typical firm's hiring decision is affected. Explain why an improvement in the productivity of workers in an industry might not always increase employment of workers in the industry.

3   Why does the marginal revenue product of input use by a monopoly firm decline more quickly as more workers are hired than is the case for a competitive firm?

Market Demand for and Supply of Inputs and the Concept of Economic Rent

Market Demand for an Input

Market demand for an input is the sum of the quantities demanded by *all industries* and other employers using that input at any given price. The market demand for unskilled workers is the sum of the demands of the pizza industry, other restaurants, and all other industries using this type of labor. All these industries compete for the services of workers in the same regional labor market. At any given wage, the sum of the number of labor hours used by all these industries in the region must equal the quantity supplied. The more workers used in one industry, the fewer are available to work in other industries at any given wage.

Suppose unskilled workers in a region are employed only in the restaurant, retailing, and construction industries. The graph in Box 8 shows the demand for labor for these three industries. The regional market demand is the sum of the quantities demanded by all three industries at any wage.

The market demand for an input is obtained in the same way as the market demand for an output. At each price the quantity demanded by each industry is summed to obtain the market quantity demanded. The more industries using a particular type of labor, the stronger the market demand for that labor. In general, the demand for the input by each industry depends on the marginal revenue product of labor and the way the price of the product changes as the supply of the product increases.

> **Market demand for an input:**
> The sum of the quantities demanded by all industries and other employers using that input at any given price.

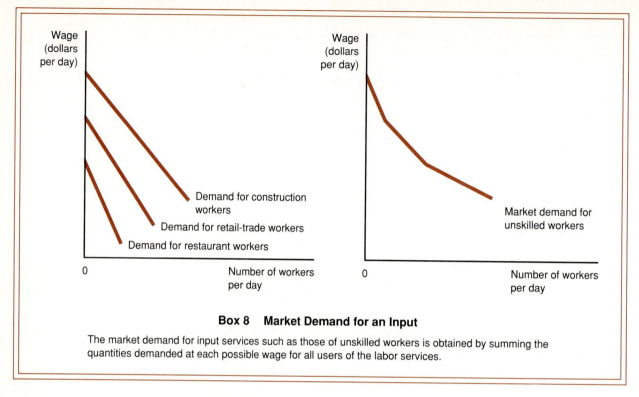

Box 8   Market Demand for an Input

The market demand for input services such as those of unskilled workers is obtained by summing the quantities demanded at each possible wage for all users of the labor services.

Market Supply of an Input

Market supply of an input:
A relationship between the price of the input and the quantity supplied for employment in all industries and other uses.

The **market supply of an input** is a relationship between the price of the input and the quantity supplied for employment in all industries and other uses. When all industries using a particular input demand more, the price of the input's services will tend to rise. The willingness of an input owner to sell the services of that input depends on the opportunity cost of doing so. For most inputs the seller's marginal cost of supplying more input to the market tends to increase. This implies that higher input prices are necessary to induce resource owners to increase the quantities they supply to the market.

In the same way, higher wages are necessary to make additional workers enter the labor force and to induce employed workers to work longer hours. The supply curve of labor services therefore tends to be upward sloping. In some cases labor supply curves might be very inelastic. Empirical evidence indicates that this is true in the United States. We'll discuss the shapes of labor supply curves in the following chapter.

Market Equilibrium and Economic Rent

The market equilibrium price of an input in a competitive market is the one for which quantity demanded equals quantity supplied. For example, in Box 9 the market equilibrium wage for the type of labor whose demand and supply curves are drawn is $4 per hour. At that wage the quantity of labor demanded and supplied equals Q hours per month.

Economic rent, which we first discussed in Chapter 17, is the difference between the payments made for input services and the *minimum* amount that would be required to induce the suppliers to make those services available. The minimum amount required for an input supplier to agree to sell any quantity of input services is the marginal cost of those services to the supplier. Economic rent is therefore the difference between actual payments for input services and the marginal cost of those services. The marginal cost of using an input for a particular purpose is the payment the owner can earn in the input's next best use.

Economic rent is a surplus over the opportunity cost of supplying an input. Workers who have skills or talents that are highly valued only in a particular occupation tend to earn very high rents. This is because there's a vast difference between the wages paid for their services in the occupation or job for which they're best suited and the wages they can earn in their next best alternative. For example, suppose the annual wage of a 7-foot-tall basketball player is $1 million when he's employed by a professional basketball team. If the wage the player can earn in his next best alternative job is only $20,000, then his annual economic rent is $980,000.

The graph in Box 9 illustrates economic rent earned in a competitive input market. At any price below P^*, no one would be willing to supply the input for hire. For example, if the input is labor services, P^* might be $1. At an hourly wage below $1, no one would be willing to work. As the wage increases above this minimum amount, labor hours are supplied to employers. At a wage of $1 per hour, Q^* hours of work would be supplied per month. That wage, as low as it is, is sufficient to induce some workers to supply labor services. These are the workers with the lowest opportunity cost of working. The supply curve of the input reflects the marginal cost to workers. It therefore represents the minimum price at which workers will supply additional hours.

Suppose the market equilibrium wage is $4 per hour. This means that the workers who would be willing to work for $1 per hour earn $3 economic rent per hour. All workers who would supply labor services at a wage below the market wage of $4 per hour earn economic rent. The economic rent of all workers is the shaded area in Box 9.

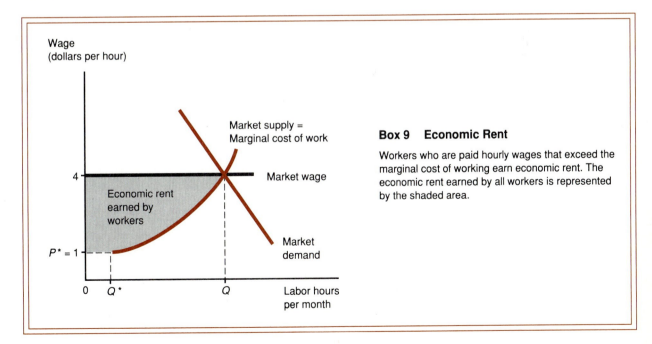

Box 9   Economic Rent

Workers who are paid hourly wages that exceed the marginal cost of working earn economic rent. The economic rent earned by all workers is represented by the shaded area.

Economic rents earned by input suppliers can be removed without influencing the incentive to supply those services. For example, if it were possible to identify the workers who would work for less than the market wage, a tax on their rents would result in no change in the number of hours they supply. As long as they cover their opportunity costs, they're no better off doing anything other than working in their current job. For example, suppose the 7-foot-tall basketball star mentioned earlier paid $970,000 in taxes. His after-tax wages would be $30,000. Because this wage is still higher than the $20,000 per year he can earn in his next best alternative, the star remains in the basketball profession. On the other hand, if the wage of workers who earn zero rent is taxed, they'll reduce the number of hours they work or switch occupations. For example, suppose another basketball player who earns only $200,000 a year also has the skills to be a lawyer and can earn slightly less than $200,000 a year in that profession. If this player's wages from basketball are taxed, he'll be likely to switch to the legal profession, assuming his wages as a lawyer aren't taxed.

Concept Check

1 How is the market demand for an input derived?

2 Why is the market supply curve for an input upward sloping?

3 What is economic rent?

Key Facts About Input Markets

What follows are some simple conclusions about input markets that you'll want to keep in mind as we move into our study of the workings of specific input markets in the next chapter.

1. *The prices of resources used as inputs in production are determined by conditions of supply and demand in input markets.* Of course, the scarcer an input of a given quality, the higher its market equilibrium price. For example, the services of highly skilled lawyers and physicians are in relatively scarce supply. Given the demand for the services of these professionals, the wages they enjoy are quite high. On the other hand, the pool of workers who can do restaurant work is quite large. Given this fact and given the value of their marginal product, these workers' wages tend to be low relative to those of skilled lawyers and physicians.

Supply conditions do change in markets and, just like changes in demand, can cause changes in input prices. An increase in the supply of skilled physicians or lawyers can be expected to put downward pressure on their wages and incomes. Similarly, a decrease in the supply of workers available for restaurant work will tend to increase their wages. The gap between the labor incomes of full-time lawyers and full-time restaurant workers could narrow if both these shifts in supply occur at the same time.

2. *The price of an input always equals its marginal revenue product in a competitive input market.* However, the marginal revenue product of an input depends on how much is available to be employed. Workers with essential jobs, such as sanitation workers, often have very high value to the community in terms of the value of their total product. After all, you wouldn't want to live in a city where no one was available to collect the garbage! However, given the supply of workers able

and willing to supply sanitation pickup services, their *marginal* revenue product tends to be low even though the *total* product they generate has very high value. They'll therefore be paid low wages in a competitive market. A decrease in the supply of sanitation workers will increase their marginal revenue product and raise their wages, thus increasing the income they can earn. You can see this in the graph in Box 10. At the initial market equilibrium, the equilibrium wage is $5 per hour, which equals the marginal revenue product of workers when 1,000 workers are employed per week. After the supply of workers decreases, the market equilibrium wage rises to $7 per hour. At that wage only 900 workers are employed per week. The employers are willing to pay these workers $7 per hour because the decrease in workers employed has increased their marginal revenue product to $7 per hour.

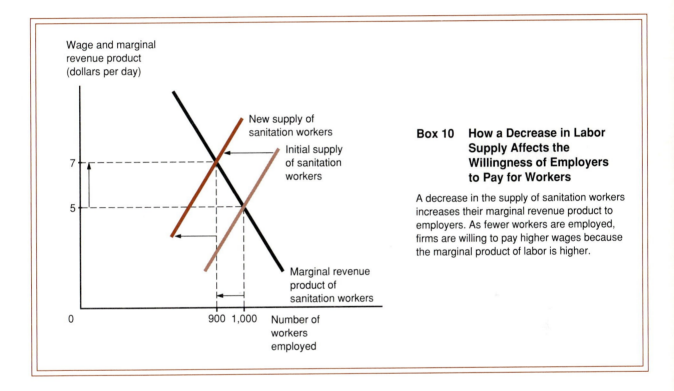

Box 10   How a Decrease in Labor Supply Affects the Willingness of Employers to Pay for Workers

A decrease in the supply of sanitation workers increases their marginal revenue product to employers. As fewer workers are employed, firms are willing to pay higher wages because the marginal product of labor is higher.

3. *The demand for inputs is a derived demand.* When the demand for output in the economy is strong, so is the demand for the use of resources as inputs. Now you can understand why fluctuations in output demand can lead to fluctuations in input prices. For example, in periods of slack overall demand, the demand for labor will also be slack. As a result, you can expect downward pressure on wages in labor markets and a reduction in employment. By the same token, in periods of expansion when the demand for products is strong, the demand for labor will also be strong. This means you can expect wages and employment to be increasing when the economy is enjoying strong demand for products.

4. *A key determinant of input prices is the productivity of inputs.* Other things being equal, improvements in input productivity increase the prices of inputs and therefore increase the incomes of those who sell the input services. For example, improvements in the productivity of factory workers increase the wages employers

Principles in Practice

Why Do Women Earn Less than Men? The Issue of Comparable Worth

Women earn less than men. For example, 1984 hourly wages of women in the United States averaged 30% less than wages paid to men. The gap in total labor earnings between the sexes is even wider because on average women on full-time schedules work fewer hours per week than men. Female workers had median labor earnings in 1984 that were only about 65% of earnings by males.

The gap between male and female earnings varies with age. The gap between the labor earnings of young women and young men is much smaller than the gap between middle-aged women and men. For example, in 1984 women between the ages of 16 and 24 earned nearly 90% of the wages earned by men in the same age group.[*]

It's also clear that jobs in which women are concentrated pay less. The higher the proportion of workers in an industry who are women, the lower the average wages. Industries in which 70% of the employees were women had average hourly earnings of $5.71 in 1982. In contrast, industries in which women accounted for less than 10% of the employees had average hourly earnings of $11.56 in 1982.[†]

Why do women earn less than men? Is the marginal product of workers lower in industries in which women constitute the bulk of the labor force? Or are the differences in wages explained by prejudice, discrimination, and traditional labor market practices that confine women to particular jobs and prevent their advancement? Because discrimination in employment on the basis of sex is illegal, this issue is of great concern. Supporters of the doctrine of "comparable worth" argue that government intervention in markets is necessary to force employers to pay equal wages for equal jobs. This approach would require job evaluations to indicate which jobs require comparable skills and effort. Employers would be forced to use the evaluations to make sure that women aren't paid less than men who do comparable work. Under this approach, in cases for which discrimination can be proved, wages would be set by the government rather than the marketplace.

It's important to understand the causes of the pay gap between men and women so we can evaluate the impact of government intervention in markets to increase the wages paid to women. Unfortunately, however, there's no consensus among economists about the causes of the gap. One view argues that women on average have chosen low-paying jobs in which workers have low marginal products so they can enjoy the freedom of entering and exiting the labor force often. Women are in fact concentrated in jobs that require little training. The opposing view is that women are barred by traditional labor market practices from entering all-male jobs for which higher wages prevail.

At least half of the wage gap between men and women has been explained by differences in age and educational background that affect work skills and experience and are therefore likely to reflect differences in the marginal product between men and women. The fact that women in the past have tended to enter and leave the labor force to have children has reduced their years of experience relative to men. The smaller gap in earnings for younger men and women could reflect these women's greater commitment to work and build careers that will help eliminate the gap in the future. However, much of the gap

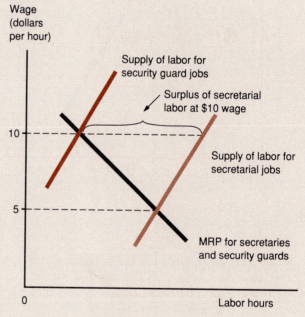

*Henry J. Aaron and Cameran M. Lougy, *The Comparable Worth Controversy*, Washington, D.C.: The Brookings Institution, 1986, pp. 8-9.
†Aaron and Lougy, p. 9.

hasn't been adequately explained and could be the result of discriminatory labor market practices. It's this conjecture that has spurred the calls for government action.

What would happen if governments did intervene in markets to increase the wages paid to women? One possibility is that earnings for women as a group might actually *decline*. An increase in wages decreases the quantity of labor input demanded. This could result in decreased employment as the rate of hiring new workers declines. If the government wage exceeds the market equilibrium wage, a surplus of workers in the market could result. The impact of increased wages could be offset by a reduction in hours of work demanded, which could contribute to lower earnings!

A basic problem with implementing a comparable-worth program is the fact that wage differentials between two jobs depend not only on the marginal revenue product of labor but also on the supplies of labor for those jobs. For example, consider two jobs: secretary and security guard.

The graph shows the marginal revenue product of labor in security guard and secretarial jobs. The two jobs are of "comparable worth" in the sense that the marginal revenue product of any given quantity of labor in each job is the same. In other words, the marginal revenue product curve for both jobs is identical. However, because the supply curve of labor for security guard jobs lies to the left of the supply curve for secretarial jobs, wages are higher for security guard jobs. In market equilibrium, security guards earn $10 per hour while secretaries earn $5 per hour. The difference in equilibrium wages between the two jobs stems from differences in supply.

Now suppose comparable-worth legislation raises the wages of secretaries to $10 per hour. As a result, the quantity of labor hours demanded in the market for secretaries will decline while the quantity of labor hours supplied will increase. The result will be a surplus of labor. Those secretaries fortunate enough to keep or find jobs at the higher wage will clearly be better off. However, because of the government-mandated wage for secretaries, fewer secretaries will be employed, and some who previously had jobs will find themselves out of work.

This analysis suggests that comparable-worth legislation, although well intentioned, could have effects that harm women. Over the long run, enforcement of laws outlawing discrimination and changes in training, experience, and job choices by women are more likely to eliminate the male-female wage gap.

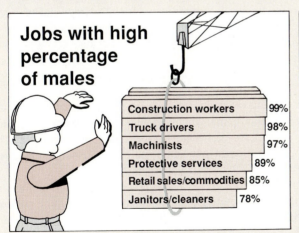

Jobs with high percentage of males

Construction workers	99%
Truck drivers	98%
Machinists	97%
Protective services	89%
Retail sales/commodities	85%
Janitors/cleaners	78%

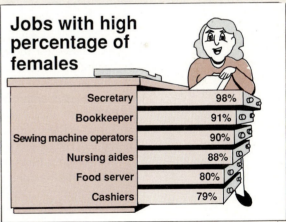

Jobs with high percentage of females

Secretary	98%
Bookkeeper	91%
Sewing machine operators	90%
Nursing aides	88%
Food server	80%
Cashiers	79%

Source: National Commission on Working Women
By Marcy Eckroth Mullins, USA TODAY

are willing to pay these workers. Productivity of labor and other inputs generally increases when more capital equipment is used to complement these resources. For example, a backhoe or bulldozer operator is paid more per hour than a ditch-digger working with a shovel because the marginal revenue product of the equipment operator is greater. For the same reason, the rent paid for an acre of land that has a high-rise structure on it is higher than that for an acre of land that only has a single-family house on it.

5. *In a perfectly competitive input market, any attempt to pay a resource owner a price less than the marginal revenue product of the input in its current use will fail.* An employer who paid a worker less than the marginal revenue product of labor input would lose the services of that worker to a rival buyer in the labor market. Competition among firms ensures that each worker of a given skill receives a wage equal to the marginal revenue product of that type of labor. This is because an employer can always increase profits by hiring more workers whenever the wage is less than the marginal revenue product. This tends to bid wages and other input prices up to equal their marginal revenue products.

Summary

1. Input markets are those used to trade the services of productive resources. The prices of input services are a major determinant of income in a market economy. Input prices are wages, rents, and interest.
2. A competitive input market is one in which neither individual buyers nor individual sellers can influence the prices of input services. In a perfectly competitive input market, there's free entry and exit of sellers, and productive resources are mobile geographically and among industries. In a perfectly competitive input market, differences in prices for an input of given quality among regions or uses can only be temporary. Shifts in input supply in response to regional or occupational price differentials will eventually eliminate those differentials.
3. Employers of inputs have a derived demand for inputs because input services are purchased for the purpose of making another product. The derived demand for an input depends on the revenue that can be generated by business use of the input.
4. A profit-maximizing firm's hiring decision depends on the marginal benefit and marginal cost of using the input. The marginal benefit a firm receives from using an input is the extra revenue it can generate from employing more of it. The marginal cost of the input is the extra payments the firm must make to input owners when it hires more.
5. The marginal revenue product of an input is the change in total revenue that results when one more unit of that input is hired. The marginal revenue product of an input depends on the marginal product of the input and the price at which that product can be sold.
6. When hiring an input, such as labor, in a competitive market, a firm can continue to increase its profits up to the point at which the marginal input cost just equals the marginal revenue product. In a competitive market the wage paid to labor will equal the marginal input cost because the firm can hire all the labor it wishes at the market wage.
7. The marginal revenue product curve for an input is the firm's demand curve for the input. An increase in the demand for a firm's product will increase the price of the product and increase the marginal revenue product of using inputs. This

will increase the demand for inputs. An increase in the marginal productivity of using any given quantity of an input will also increase the demand for that input, provided the price of the product doesn't fall as a result of increased supply.

8. To maximize profits a firm must hire each input up to the point at which the marginal revenue product of the input equals its marginal cost.

9. The marginal revenue product of an input used by a monopoly firm tends to decline more quickly than that for a competitive firm because the monopoly firm must lower its product price to sell more.

10. The market demand for an input is the sum of quantities demanded by all industries using that input at each possible input price. The supply curve of an input for a particular industry will be a horizontal line if the industry doesn't buy a large market share of the input. In general, the market supply curve of an input is upward sloping because resource owners tend to incur increasing marginal costs of making their resources available for use as inputs by employers. For example, higher wages are necessary to induce existing workers to work longer hours and to induce more workers to enter the labor force. Input prices are determined by the forces of supply and demand. In a competitive market the price of an input equals its marginal revenue product.

11. Economic rent is the difference between the payments made for input services and the minimum sum that would be required to induce suppliers to make the services available. Economic rent represents a surplus over the opportunity cost of supplying an input to the market. Economic rent can be taxed without reducing the incentive of resource owners to make their services available to employers.

Key Terms and Concepts

Input market
Competitive input market
Derived demand
Marginal revenue product

Marginal input cost
Change in input demand
Market demand for an input
Market supply of an input

Problems and Applications

1. Credit markets are markets for exchange of the use of loanable funds. Assuming that the market for credit is perfectly competitive, draw the market demand and supply curves for loanable funds when the market rate of interest is 9% and the quantity of funds exchanged per year is $400 billion. Draw the supply curve for credit to a single borrower, such as General Motors. Show what happens to the market interest rate if GM increases its demand for credit.

2. Assume that the market for carpenters is perfectly competitive and that all carpenters are of equal skill. A sudden decline in economic activity in Houston, Texas, decreases the demand for carpenters and causes the equilibrium wage in that city to decrease from $20 to $12 per hour. However, the decline in demand is only regional. The demand for carpenters is still strong in other regions, such as the Southeast, where wages remain $20 per hour. Explain what is likely to occur over the long run in the market for carpenters in Houston.

3. Use the data in Box 2 to show that the marginal revenue product of labor could be calculated by multiplying the marginal product of labor by the price of pizza as more workers are hired.

4. Suppose the demand for pizza suddenly plummets. This lowers its market price

to $3. Assuming that only the price of pizza changes, use the data from Box 2 to recalculate the marginal revenue product of labor. Draw the new marginal revenue product curve and predict the change in the pizzeria's hiring decision as a result of the change in the price of pizza.

5. A new minimum-wage law increases the daily wage employers must pay for unskilled workers. Suppose the daily wage the pizzeria must pay for workers increases to $40. Assuming the price of pizza is $5 per pie and there's no change in the productivity of workers, use the data from Box 2 to forecast the employer's response to the increase in the minimum wage.

6. A new system of work rules for safety instituted by the government has an adverse effect on the productivity of restaurant workers. After the new rules go into effect, the productivity of workers employed by a restaurant is:

Number of workers	Total product of labor per day
1	35
2	55
3	65
4	70
5	70
6	65

Calculate the marginal product of labor. Assuming the price of pizza is $5 and the daily wage is $32, how many workers will the firm hire? If the decrease in productivity affects all pizzerias, what is the likely impact on the price of pizza?

7. Suppose all the shirt factories in the United States are taken over by a single firm that monopolizes the supply of shirts. Assuming that unskilled workers are employed in shirt production and that shirt production employs only a small share of the total available number of these workers, forecast the effect of the monopoly takeover on employment in the shirt industry.

8. An increase in population results in an increase in the supply of unskilled workers available for employment. Show the likely effect of this in the labor market for the services of these workers and on the employment of these workers in various industries.

9. A general increase in the education and training level of workers in a nation increases their productivity. Other things being equal, show the impact of the increased productivity on wages and the demand for labor.

10. Suppose a basketball player earns an annual salary of $200,000 before taxes. His next best alternative is working as the manager of a restaurant, which would pay an annual salary of $40,000 after taxes. Assume the player receives only monetary benefits from playing basketball as reflected in his salary. Would he change jobs if the annual tax on his basketball earnings were $100,000? Calculate the economic rent earned by the basketball player and indicate what level of annual taxes on his basketball salary would induce him to change jobs.

Suggested Readings

Henry J. Aaron and Cameran M. Lougy, *The Comparable Worth Controversy*, Washington, D.C.: The Brookings Institution, 1986. This is an analysis of the differences in wages between men and women in the United States and the causes of the differentials. Policies proposed to establish equal pay for equal work are evaluated.

Ronald G. Ehrenberg and Robert S. Smith, *Modern Labor Economics: Theory and Public Policy,* 2nd ed., Glenview, Ill.: Scott, Foresman & Co., 1985. This is a textbook on labor markets and the economics of work. The essentials of a firm's hiring decisions are covered in depth.

A Forward Look

The most important source of income in most economies is wages and salaries. In view of the importance of labor resources as both a source of income and a cost of production, economists pay particular attention to the forces of supply and demand in labor markets. In the following chapter we analyze the decision to work, labor supply, and other influences on wages and the productivity of workers.

Labor Markets, Labor Productivity, and Personnel Management

Ours is a nation of workers. Wages and salaries constitute about three quarters of personal income in the United States. Economists have developed a special branch of economics, called labor economics, to analyze how the forces of supply and demand influence labor incomes. Studying labor markets in depth can help us answer such questions as why some workers earn more than others. Analysis of labor markets can also help us understand the link between productivity, the demand for labor, and wages. Finally, by understanding the forces influencing the demand for and supply of labor, we can learn why some people voluntarily choose not to participate in the labor force and can identify the causes of unemployment.

In 1987 the average earnings of workers in the United States were about $9 per hour. However, there was considerable variation in wages among industries. For example, construction workers had average earnings of over $12 per hour in 1987, while retail trade workers earned about $6 per hour in that year. Surgeons and other skilled professionals and managers earn incomes from their services that are much higher than those of workers in basic industries. It's not uncommon for the chief executive officer of a major corporation to earn well over $1 million per year. For example, in 1985 Lee Iacocca, chairman of Chrysler Corporation, received compensation estimated to be over $11 million! A goal of labor economics is to understand the reasons for wage differentials among professions, occupations, and regions.

The impersonal exchange of labor services in markets is one of the hallmarks of modern industrial nations. Labor, however, is unique in that it is a *human* resource. Only its services can be traded. Unlike a machine or a plot of land, human beings cannot be sold outright in free societies. Workers voluntarily enter into contracts to sell their services to employers only if the wage or salary is mutually agreeable.

Personnel managers must consider the preferences and feelings of workers. One of the keys to achieving increases in labor productivity is to provide workers appropriate incentives.

Labor markets differ greatly in their degree of organization. In many local labor markets, communication between potential employees and employers begins with the simple placement of "help wanted" signs in windows or classified advertisements in newspapers. In more formal markets, trade journals and direct links with professional schools serve as the medium of communication. At the very top levels, corporate "headhunters" recruit executives in the rarefied six- and seven-figure salary range.

Firms in some industries hire labor services by negotiating with organizations of workers called *labor unions*. Because unions control large blocks of workers, they often can influence the wages received by their members. In the next chapter we'll discuss the potential impact of labor unions on wages, working conditions, and worker productivity. In this chapter we'll consider only perfectly competitive labor markets, in which no worker or employer can influence wages.

After reading this chapter, you should be able to:

Concept Preview

1 Analyze the choice to work and show how a person's labor supply curve depends on his preferences and other influences, such as nonlabor sources of income.
2 Show how the market supply of labor services is influenced by population and other demographic variables.
3 Explain why different wages are paid for different jobs, occupations, or skills.
4 Show how labor productivity is a key determinant of the average level of wages in a nation.
5 Show how personnel management techniques can be used to motivate workers and increase the marginal revenue product of labor.

Labor Supply

The supply of labor services available for employment depends on the opportunity cost of work. You engage in work by giving up some of your own time for use by an employer who compensates you with pay. When you decide whether or not to work, you weigh the value of the alternative uses of your time in nonemployment against the wages you'll receive from working. Time you don't use in work for pay can be used for recreation, sleeping, eating, productive tasks at home, or any activity other than remunerative work.

Because we value our own use of time in various leisure activities and other nonpaying pursuits, we need monetary compensation to induce us to give up some of our time for the use of an employer. In general, the opportunity cost of time for work increases as we work more in a given period. The more time we devote per week (or day) to work activities in paying jobs, the more precious is the remaining time. For example, if you put in more hours at your part-time job each week, you give up more time for leisure activities like going to the movies. Because the opportunity cost of additional work tends to increase as more work is undertaken in a given period, extra pay per hour is usually necessary to induce people to work overtime.

Higher wages also induce *more* people to give up their time to enter the labor force. For example, many people, like yourself, decide not to work so they can attend a college. You might be quite content to study full time when the hourly wage you forgo in a job is only $5. However, you might think twice about continuing your education if you could obtain a satisfying job paying $50 per hour without your college degree!

Keep in mind that the money wage isn't the only remuneration workers receive. Many workers also enjoy fringe benefits such as employer-provided insurance for medical and dental services and the guarantee of a pension at retirement. In addition, workers consider nonmonetary aspects of their jobs, including safe working conditions, flexibility of hours, and benefits like cafeterias and child-care facilities.

Workers are also concerned about the amounts of goods and services their money wages can buy. Changes in the price level can affect the willingness of workers to work by changing the purchasing power of their wages.

Equilibrium Allocation of Time to Work: Marginal Analysis

The number of hours per week or year that you're willing to work is influenced by the nonlabor income you have available, and your preferences between income and leisure or other nonpaying activities. For example, if you received a yearly allowance of $100,000 from an inherited trust fund, you'd be less likely to supply labor hours for employment than a similar person without such an allowance. **Nonwage money income** includes pensions, welfare payments and subsidies, interest, dividends, allowances, and any other type of income that is available independent of work.

In deciding how much time to devote to work, each worker compares the value of extra leisure time given up with the extra income received from extra work. (For simplicity in our analysis of the choice to work, all activities other than work for pay will be considered "leisure.") The value of extra leisure time given up to work is the **marginal cost of work.** The extra income received from extra work, including any nonmonetary satisfaction a worker obtains from a job, is the **marginal benefit of work.** To maximize the *net benefit from work,* a worker continues to work up to the point at which the marginal benefit of work just equals its marginal cost. In this analysis we assume that workers have considerable flexibility in the number of hours they can work. Although this is a simplifying assumption, the fact is that even workers who choose jobs with a standard 40-hour week have ways of varying the hours they work on average over a long period. Absenteeism, periods of unemployment, leave without pay, and early retirement all are ways to vary the quantity of labor supplied on average over a long period.

In a competitive labor market, each worker is a price taker who takes the hourly wage as given. The graph in Box 1 shows a typical worker's equilibrium allocation of time, on average per day, to work over a given year. Let's assume this worker is your younger sister, who's working full time this year to earn money for college. The graph assumes that the hourly wage fully reflects the marginal benefit your sister receives from her job. Because her wage is independent of hours worked, it is drawn as a horizontal line. The marginal cost of hours worked per day increases because as total leisure hours given up per day increase, your sister places a higher

Nonwage money income:
Includes pensions, welfare payments and subsidies, interest, dividends, allowances, and any other type of income that is available independent of work.

Marginal cost of work:
The value of extra leisure time given up to work.

Marginal benefit of work:
The extra income received from extra work, including any nonmonetary satisfaction obtained from a job.

value on her remaining leisure hours. Her equilibrium is at point *E,* at which her wage just equals her marginal cost of work. This corresponds to an average over the year of 8 hours of work per day. If your sister were to work more than 8 hours per day, she would become worse off than at *E* because the marginal cost of work would exceed the marginal benefit.

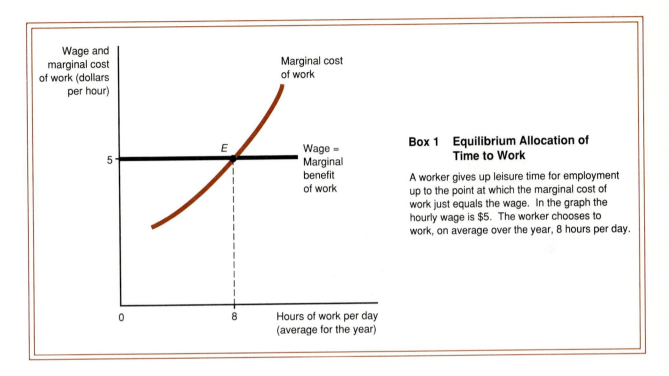

Box 1   Equilibrium Allocation of Time to Work

A worker gives up leisure time for employment up to the point at which the marginal cost of work just equals the wage. In the graph the hourly wage is $5. The worker chooses to work, on average over the year, 8 hours per day.

A **labor supply curve** for a particular individual shows the relationship between hourly wages and labor hours supplied for work over a given period. Because a person always works up to the point at which the marginal cost of work increases to equal the wage, the marginal cost of work curve drawn in Box 1 is the labor supply curve. An increase in wages raises the marginal benefit of work. Workers respond by increasing hours worked over the period until the marginal cost of work increases to equal the higher wage.

Labor supply curve:
Shows a relationship between a worker's hourly wages and labor hours supplied for work over a given period.

Income and Substitution Effects of Wage Changes

As wages rise, work becomes more attractive because each hour of leisure given up will now result in more income. The opportunity cost of an hour of leisure is higher when wages increase. For example, the opportunity cost of using an hour during the day for leisure or other nonpaying activities is only $5 when your hourly wage is equal to $5. However, it will cost you $20 to take an hour of leisure during the day if you can work at a $20 hourly wage. The **substitution effect of a wage change** is the change in hours worked resulting only from a change in the oppor tunity cost of an hour of leisure. The substitution effect of an increase in wages i an increase in hours worked as work is substituted for leisure and other nonpaying activities. The substitution effect of a wage increase is therefore favorable to work.

Substitution effect of a wage change:
The change in hours worked resulting only from a change in the opportunity cost of an hour of leisure.

Similarly, the substitution effect of a decrease in wages would decrease the opportunity cost of an hour of leisure. This induces the individual to substitute leisure for work and therefore supply fewer hours of work to employers. If the substitution effect were the only impact of a change in wages, labor supply curves would always be upward sloping.

Income effect of a wage change:
The change in hours worked stemming from the change in income caused by the wage change.

There is, however, another effect. The **income effect of a wage change** is the change in hours worked stemming from the change in income caused by the wage change. For example, if hourly wages increase from $5 to $7 for your sister, who currently works 8 hours a day, she'll enjoy higher income even if she doesn't choose to work more hours. This increase in income, even if there's no change in hours worked, induces your sister to consume more of all normal goods. You'll recall that a normal good is one that we want more of when our income increases. Even though it's not sold in a market, leisure (or other nonpaying uses of our time) can be regarded as a positively valued normal good. If in fact leisure is a normal good for your sister, an increase in her wages results in an income effect that induces her to consume more leisure hours and thus to work less. The income effect of a wage increase conflicts with the substitution effect.

We therefore have ambivalent feelings about working more when wages increase. The higher wages allow us to enjoy the same income while working fewer hours. For those of us who regard leisure as a normal good, the income effect provides a temptation to work less. However, the increase in wages makes it more costly to devote an hour to nonwork activity because the number of dollars sacrificed is greater at higher wages. This increases the opportunity cost of leisure and other nonwork activities. The substitution effect of higher wages therefore provides an inducement to work more.

Backward-Bending Labor Supply Curves

Backward-bending labor supply curve:
Implies that the substitution effect on a worker's labor services outweighs the income effect only at relatively low wages.

A **backward-bending labor supply curve** for a person's labor services implies that the substitution effect outweighs the income effect only at relatively low wages. As wages increase, the income effect becomes stronger and eventually overtakes the substitution effect, causing the individual to work less as wages increase. Some people prefer to work less when their wages increase so they'll have the time to enjoy spending their higher wages and income on leisure activities. As people become more affluent they tend to spend their higher incomes on vacations, to pursue hobby activities at home, and to enjoy the luxury of relaxing. All of this requires more leisure time.

The graph in Box 2 illustrates a backward-bending labor supply curve for an individual—let's say it's your sister. After the wage reaches w^* dollars per hour, additional wage increases result in fewer labor hours supplied. Note that there's a portion of the labor supply curve for which labor hours supplied to the market are unresponsive to the change in wages when wages are between w_1 and w^*. The labor supply is perfectly inelastic for this range of wages. When this is the case, the income effect of wage changes is exactly offset by the substitution effect of wage changes. A number of empirical studies of labor supply have indicated that a large segment of males in the U.S. labor force behave as though the income effect of wage changes is just offset by the substitution effect.[1]

[1]For example, see Jerry A. Hausman, "Labor Supply," in Henry J. Aaron and Joseph J. Pechman, eds., *How Taxes Affect Economic Behavior,* Washington, D.C.: The Brookings Institution, 1981.

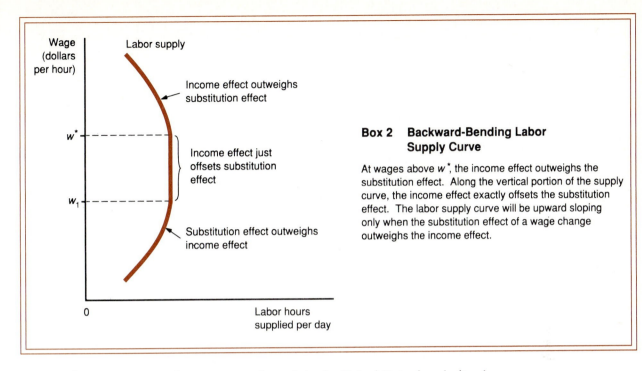

Box 2   Backward-Bending Labor Supply Curve

At wages above w*, the income effect outweighs the substitution effect. Along the vertical portion of the supply curve, the income effect exactly offsets the substitution effect. The labor supply curve will be upward sloping only when the substitution effect of a wage change outweighs the income effect.

Over the past 100 years the average work week in the United States has declined from about 70 hours to about 40 hours. This provides support for the hypothesis that the market supply of labor has been backward bending over the long run for the major increases in wages that have occurred in the twentieth century.

Concept Check

1   List the important influences on the number of hours per year a person chooses to work.

2   Use marginal analysis to show how an increase in market wages is likely to induce an increase in hours worked on average per day over a year.

3   Explain how the income and substitution effects of wage changes influence labor supply decisions.

Market Demand for and Supply of Labor

Market Supply of Labor Services: Population Effects on Wages

The market supply of labor services for a particular type of labor at a given wage is the sum of the amounts supplied by each worker. Summing total individual labor hours for each possible wage gives the total market supply of labor services. Total labor supply in the economy depends on population and the willingness of individuals to sell their labor services to employers. Total population depends on the birth rate, the death rate, immigration, and emigration.

An increase in population over time tends to increase the supply of available workers. Other things being equal, this puts downward pressure on wages. There's another reason why population growth tends to lower wages. Growth in population increases the proportion of younger workers in the labor force. Younger workers are less experienced. Experience is one of the most important determinants of labor productivity. A less experienced labor force is a less productive labor force. A decline in the average age of workers tends to decrease the marginal revenue product of labor, which contributes to lower average wages.

The "baby boom" generation of the 1950s began entering the labor force in the 1970s, and by 1977 the proportion of 20-year-olds in the population was 44% higher than it was in the early 1960s.[2] This large influx of inexperienced workers into the labor force resulted in a 12% to 15% decline in the wages of new workers when compared to adults. The increase in inexperienced workers also served to sharply reduce the growth rate of productivity in the economy. Slower growth of productivity results in slower growth of wages adjusted for changes in the price level. Higher proportions of inexperienced workers in the labor force also contribute to an increase in the unemployment rate. This is because younger workers are more likely than older workers to quit their jobs in search of better ones. At any point in time, therefore, there will be more younger workers "between jobs" than older workers.

The decline in the growth rate of productivity is likely to be reversed in the 1990s. By that time the baby boomers will be middle aged. They'll contribute to higher average wages as the proportion of experienced workers in the labor force increases. Because of declines in the birth rate in the 1970s, the proportion of inexperienced workers in the labor force in the 1990s will be relatively low.

Labor Productivity: A Key Determinant of Labor Demand and Market Wages

A key determinant of the average level of wages in a nation is labor productivity, which measures the average output per labor hour of workers in the economy. Labor productivity is correlated with the marginal product of labor, which is a major factor affecting the willingness of employers to pay for labor services.

What influences the productivity of workers in a nation? Productivity depends on a variety of factors, including the skills, experience, training, and motivation of workers. A key factor is the amount and sophistication of the capital equipment with which employers supply their workers. Capital equipment, such as machines and automated devices, complements labor services and helps increase the average, and therefore the marginal, product of workers. As better equipment enhances labor productivity, employers become more willing to pay higher wages.

Improvements in labor productivity increase wages and salaries, which constitute the major source of income in a nation. These improvements therefore are major determinants of progress in a nation's standard of living. The graph in Box 3 shows how improvements in productivity over time can increase wages paid to the average worker, even if the supply of labor is increasing. Suppose the average wage of factory workers this year is $15 per hour. Next year new workers enter the labor force, looking for work in factories. This increases the supply of labor. Other things being equal, the increase in the supply of labor depresses wages and would cause them to fall to $14 per hour. The fall can be counteracted if business firms continually reinvest in their plants to update equipment and technology. Capital investment has

---

[2]Ronald G. Ehrenberg and Robert S. Smith, *Modern Labor Economics: Theory and Public Policy,* 3rd ed., Glenview, Ill.: Scott, Foresman, & Co., 1988, pp. 41-42.

the effect of increasing the marginal revenue product of workers as it increases their productivity. This *increases* the demand for labor. The demand for labor can also increase with growth in population because this increases the demand for goods and services. In Box 3 the increase in demand for labor is sufficient to offset the depressing effect on wages of the increase in labor supply. As a result, wages increase to $16 per hour despite the increase in the supply of workers.

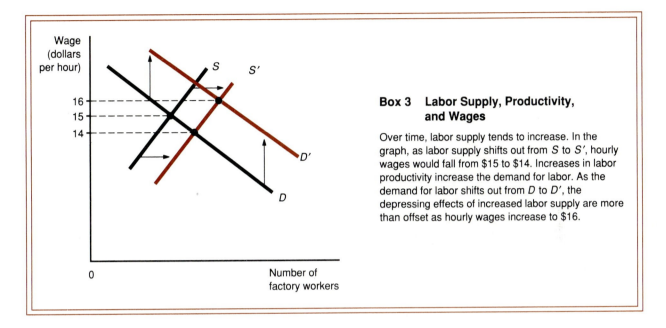

Box 3   Labor Supply, Productivity, and Wages

Over time, labor supply tends to increase. In the graph, as labor supply shifts out from *S* to *S'*, hourly wages would fall from $15 to $14. Increases in labor productivity increase the demand for labor. As the demand for labor shifts out from *D* to *D'*, the depressing effects of increased labor supply are more than offset as hourly wages increase to $16.

Sustained investment by business firms is therefore important to all workers because it ensures that wages, and thus labor income, will continually increase. However, we should qualify this statement by pointing out that investment in *human beings* as well as in machines is important to achieve this goal. Increased levels of education, training, and experience are another prime determinant of worker productivity. **Human capital** represents the skills and qualifications of workers that stem from education and training. Investment and saving, which provide funds for investment, are thus important determinants of a nation's standard of living.

Human capital:
Represents the skills and qualifications of workers that stem from education and training.

Explaining Differences in Wages Among Workers and Jobs

There are many different competitive labor markets. At any point in time there are markets for various kinds of labor services, from those of talented athletes to those of kitchen workers. The wages for each type of labor service are determined by the demand for and supply of workers offering that service. If demand is strong relative to supply, the wages offered will be high. For example, suppose the annual marginal revenue product generated by talented 7-foot-tall professional basketball players is extremely high. Also assume there are few people available with the qualifications for this job. As shown in **A** in Box 4, the high marginal revenue product combined with the scarcity of workers will result in a very high equilibrium annual wage for the few lucky standouts. As you can see, the equilibrium annual wage for the star basketball players is $1 million.

On the other hand, the marginal revenue product of kitchen helpers is much lower than that of professional basketball stars. In addition, the number of workers willing and able to be kitchen helpers is quite high. As shown in **B** in Box 4, the abundant supply and relatively low marginal revenue product of these workers combine to result in annual wages of only $10,000.

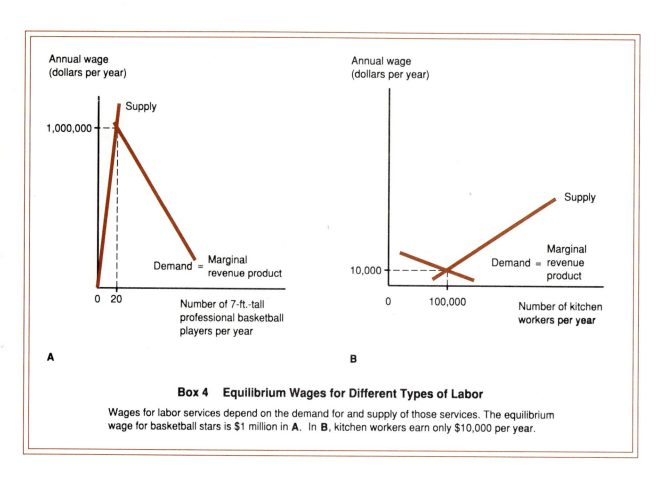

Box 4   Equilibrium Wages for Different Types of Labor

Wages for labor services depend on the demand for and supply of those services. The equilibrium wage for basketball stars is $1 million in **A**. In **B**, kitchen workers earn only $10,000 per year.

Quality Differences in Labor Services

As just suggested, differences in talents, intelligence, skills, training, and experience can account for wage differentials. These differences establish separate labor markets. Suppose that 7-foot-tall professional basketball players actually do earn $1 million per year. If you happen to be 5 feet tall, nearsighted, and lacking in athletic ability, you cannot enter that profession. The number of people with the talent to play professional basketball is limited by physical differences among individuals. Each of us has talents and skills not possessed by others. If these skills are in strong demand and scarce, they can be sold at high wages. However, for unique skills to result in high wages, the skills must be valuable to employers. No one would pay high wages for basketball players unless there were people interested in basketball and willing to pay to see games.

Another factor affecting quality differences in labor is the extent to which workers are trained to do certain tasks. This is because training increases the marginal product of workers and therefore increases the willingness of employers to pay for their services. Training is costly in terms of both time and money. In deciding to pursue training, we weigh the opportunity cost of the time and money against the extra returns we expect to receive. Without significant positive wage differentials, many people would be unwilling to undertake the 8 years or more of postgraduate work necessary to enter certain medical specialties. Wage differentials therefore serve the purpose of attracting people into certain occupations and compensating them for their training costs. Long training periods have high marginal cost to workers in terms of forgone income over the period of training. This probably discourages many people from entering professions with extensive training requirements. This in turn contributes to the scarce supply of people with skills like those required for medical specialties.

This is not to say that those who spend long years studying are guaranteed high wages. If you spend 8 years studying Slavic literature, you could have trouble finding a job if there's little demand for someone with your expertise.

Differences in Working Conditions

Differences in the quality of working environments can also affect wages. In choosing a job, workers consider factors other than money wages. An important nonmonetary factor is working conditions. Assume you're considering two jobs, both of which require the same level of skill and training. Also assume perfect mobility and information. In a competitive labor market, wages would be the same in both jobs. Suppose, however, that working conditions are *not* the same in the two jobs.

Suppose one job involves hazards not present in the other, such as risk of exposure to disease or radiation. Other things being equal, you're likely to prefer the safe job to the hazardous job. This is because, after deducting the negative value of the hazard, total compensation per hour of work is higher in the safe job. For total compensation to be the same in both jobs, money wages must be higher in the unsafe job. **Nonpecuniary wages** are the nonmonetary aspects of a job that must be added to or subtracted from money wages to obtain total compensation per hour of work.

Nonpecuniary wages: The nonmonetary aspects of a job that must be added to or subtracted from money wages to obtain total compensation per hour of work.

Compensating Wage Differentials

A **compensating wage differential** is a difference in money wages necessary to make the total compensation for similar jobs equal when nonpecuniary wages are not equal to zero. These differentials will be positive for jobs whose nonpecuniary wages on average are negatively valued. This is the case for hazardous jobs. The differentials will be negative for jobs with nonpecuniary wages that on average are positively valued.

For example, workers who agree to work on mid-sea oil drilling rigs obtain much higher wages than workers with similar skills working inland. The difference is the compensating wage differential for the isolation and risk of working on a floating rig. The military also offers compensating wage differentials for hazardous duty, such as serving on Navy submarines.

Similarly, if labor is mobile and information is freely available on job conditions, employers offering work in unsanitary conditions will pay higher wages if alternative

Compensating wage differential: A difference in money wages necessary to make total compensation for similar jobs equal when nonpecuniary wages are not equal to zero.

Principles in Practice

Motivating Workers: You Get What You Pay For!

Setting aside advertising hype and fleeting fads, it's usually true that the more you pay for an item, the better its quality. In your time you've probably bought a few "unbeatable bargains" that ended up in the trash can: $1 T-shirts that shredded after one washing; plastic hubcaps that cracked when you put them on; a "waterproof" watch that drowned in the shower.

In labor markets, just as in department stores, the old saying is true: "You get what you pay for."

Increases in the marginal productivity of workers in an organization benefit both employees and employers. Higher marginal productivity means higher revenue for a firm from a given labor force and higher wages for workers. There's certainly a connection between wages and productivity. Firms that pay higher wages can often attract the most productive workers in the labor force. Conversely, a firm that pays low wages often can keep only the poorest workers. A low-wage policy is by no means always the best policy. A firm that pays lower wages than its competitors will have trouble competing because it will suffer from low productivity.

Personnel managers are constantly seeking ways to motivate workers to increase their productivity. One of the first such methods was developed in the early twentieth century by Frederick Taylor, whose *Principles of Scientific Management* was published in 1911. Taylor advocated a scientific method: using *time-motion studies* to find the best matches of equipment and workers to accomplish a given task. First he used a stopwatch to determine the time needed to accomplish tasks in various ways. He then used these time-motion studies to set standards for productivity goals.

Although scientific methods to increase productivity are still used, economic analysis of productivity and personnel management emphasizes the importance of incentives in influencing worker productivity. Employee compensation is therefore important in attracting high-productivity workers, providing incentives to increase productivity and avoid shirking, and keeping turnover low so as to minimize the loss of highly productive trained workers to competing firms.

Employee compensation often amounts to more than the wages paid. Fringe benefits include sick pay, paid vacation time, employer pension contributions, and employer-paid Social Security taxes. Fringe benefits in the United States average nearly $7,000 a year per employee, which is close to 40% of wage costs.

Some fringe benefits are specifically designed to increase worker productivity. For example, many companies pay bonuses based on performance. Workers and managers jointly establish production or sales goals. When performance exceeds the goals, the extra revenue earned goes into a bonus fund. At the end of the year typically 75% of the money in the fund is distributed to employees and the remainder is added to the firm's profits.

The ultimate technique for aligning the interests of workers and firm owners is the *employee stock ownership plan.* Under such an arrangement, employees acquire partial or total ownership of the firm in which they work. The workers become the capitalists! In this case it's the workers themselves who bear the cost of shirking and lagging productivity in terms of reduced profit. Workers have incentives to increase productivity under such a plan because they share in the company's profits. However, the results from use of these plans are mixed. In some cases employees complain that they get ownership but still don't participate in decision making. In cases for which stock ownership is given *in lieu* of wage increases or to finance wage cuts, worker morale and productivity sometimes fall rather than rise.

---

jobs exist where working conditions are better. Here the compensating wage differential gives the employer an incentive to provide decent working conditions.

Research by Thaler and Rosen has confirmed that positive wage differentials are associated with the risk of death on the job. The analysis indicates that on average in 1967, workers received $176 in extra annual wages for each 1 out of 1,000 workers who died in that job during the year. For example, lumberjacks on average earned about $450 more per year than workers of comparable skill in other jobs. The annual death rate on the job for security guards was about 2.7 per thousand in 1967. Security guards therefore earned a compensating wage differential of $470 that year.[3] Adjusting this figure for inflation shows us that the wage differential for security guards would have been over $1,000 per year in the mid-1980s.

Nonpecuniary Job Benefits

When jobs have positively valued nonpec   ary wages, money wages will be lower than those in comparable jobs with valued nonpecuniary wages. For two jobs with given skill and training requirements, the one that offers such benefits as flexible working hours, opportunities for advancement, and safe and pleasant surroundings will pay lower money wages than the job that doesn't provide these benefits.

Nonpecuniary benefits also are associated with jobs at particular locations. They can explain regional wage differentials that arise from such positively valued amenities as climate, recreational opportunities, and city size. Employers locating in "sun belt" areas where the climate is warm can attract labor services at lower wages because of the value workers place on the pleasant climate. If money wages were equal in sun belt and other areas, migration would continue to the sun belt areas until money wages fell.

Studies confirm that wages for the same job and level of skill are higher in larger cities than in smaller cities. These results hold even after careful adjustment for differences in the cost of living associated with city size. The cause of the city size differential hasn't been completely explained. A likely reason is that smaller cities offer a better quality of life. The differential could reflect less congestion, less pollution, and less exposure to crime in smaller cities.

Compensating wage differentials are most pronounced when all individuals have the same tastes. If some individuals enjoy exposing themselves to hazards and others dislike what would commonly be regarded as amenities, the differentials will be correspondingly less.

Concept Check

1 Other things being equal, show how an increase in population is likely to put downward pressure on wages.

2 Why have wages risen even after adjustment for inflation despite increases in labor supply over the past 50 years?

3 What can explain differences in wages among workers and among jobs?

Signaling, Screening, and Personnel Management

Not all workers are alike. Some workers are more motivated and tend to be more productive than others. Similarly, workers differ in terms of their basic skills, reliability, and receptiveness to on-the-job training. Employers typically invest significant amounts of time and resources in training workers and seek to reduce turnover so as to avoid increases in costs associated with new workers. *Personnel management*

---

[3]Richard Thaler and Sherwin Rosen, "The Value of Saving a Life: Evidence from the Labor Market," in Nestor E. Terleckyj, ed., *Household Production and Consumption,* New York: National Bureau of Economic Research, 1975, pp. 265-298. Also see Robert S. Smith, "Compensating Wage Differentials and Public Policy: A Review," *Industrial and Labor Relations Review,* 32, April 1979, pp. 339-352.

Principles in Practice

Big Blue and White Shirts: IBM Personnel Policies

The giant IBM Corporation, or "Big Blue," as it's affectionately known among its thousands of employees, has developed personnel management policies to cover almost any contingency. For many years, in fact, IBM's stringent dress code required male employees to wear white shirts to work!

When it comes to staffing, however, the company is considerably more flexible. How does this huge and widespread organization manage its vast work force?

IBM has a 50-year-old standing policy of not laying off workers. However, the company maintains flexibility in its work force in other ways. First, it makes use of temporary and part-time personnel. These workers are often let go when the company experiences decreases in the demand for its products, as was the case in 1986. Also, in periods of slack demand, hiring is reduced. Normal attrition of workers through quits and retirement then acts to reduce the labor force. For example, in 1986 IBM expected to hire only about 3,000 workers compared with 18,400 workers hired in 1984.*

The company regularly retrains workers in response to changes in the pattern of demand for its products. For example, workers in manufacturing might be retrained in robotics if the company believes this field will grow in the future. Workers who take additional courses are given opportunities to train for higher-level jobs in the company. Retraining, of course, is an expensive program for the company.

IBM also regularly asks workers to relocate to create a better distribution of the work force as market conditions change. This has led many IBM employees to comment wryly that the company's initials really stand for "I'll Be Moved." Workers are typically asked to volunteer for moves.

However, in many cases moves from one job to another or one location to another involve changes in positions that workers don't regard as desirable. This can cause poor performance that may ultimately lead to dismissal or provide workers with incentives to quit.

IBM still has a very low attrition rate compared to most firms. Less than 3% of IBM's employees leave each year. However, many observers believe that IBM, which has a mammoth work force of nearly 250,000 in the United States, will have to rethink its employment policies unless its earnings picture improves.

*See Ellen Grissett, "IBM sticks to policy of no layoffs," Raleigh, N.C., *News and Observer,* Sunday, July 13, 1986, p. 6D.

deals with the tasks of staffing, training, providing appropriate compensation, and motivating workers to achieve maximum productivity.

Workers respond to both monetary and nonmonetary aspects of their jobs. Successful personnel management provides a working environment that gives workers incentives to work up to their peak potential. It involves pairing the right workers with the right jobs. Effective workers must be rewarded to provide incentives to increase productivity and to prevent them from quitting and taking their experience to a competing firm. Ineffective workers must get the message that they either improve or risk losing their job. Personnel management requires a means of predicting and evaluating worker performance.

The Problem of Staffing: Signals and Screens

Staffing:
The process of recruiting and hiring workers to perform the various tasks required to produce goods and services.

Staffing is the process of recruiting and hiring workers to perform the various tasks required to produce goods and services. This process involves certain costs, such as advertising the positions, evaluating applicants, and ranking them according to their qualifications before selecting employees. Staffing also involves orientation and on-the-job training. Given their staffing requirements, employers seek to keep hiring costs as low as possible to maximize profits.

All of you will eventually enter the labor market as sellers. At that time you'll probably prepare a resume, which is a list of your educational accomplishments, experience, and skills. Many of the items you'll place on your resume will be seen by employers as predictors of your future success in your job. **Signals** are indicators displayed by job applicants and used by prospective employers to predict an applicant's future satisfaction and productivity. Employers realize that signals aren't a substitute for careful evaluation of each applicant's characteristics and that they may not accurately reflect a candidate's motivation, ambition, or dependability. What signals do offer is a quick, cheap way to evaluate applicants.

Signals also aid employers in **screening,** which is the process of limiting the number of applicants for a job to those the employer believes are most likely to succeed in the company. For example, an employer might consider only college graduates for certain positions. By screening, firms hope to cut the costs involved in hiring and also to select new employees from a pool of the most qualified workers.

Promoting Workers: The Internal Labor Market

An **internal labor market** exists *within* a firm when it fills positions by using its own employees, rather than hiring new employees, to fill all but the lowest-level jobs. Only the most promising employees are considered for upper-level jobs through the internal labor market. After the productivity of screened employees in low-level jobs is evaluated, the best workers are promoted to the upper-level positions. This serves the dual purpose of minimizing hiring costs and providing incentives for existing employees to perform well in their current jobs so as to advance to better-paying positions. For example, to obtain a position with a package-delivery firm, a worker might first have to work in the freight terminal as a laborer or sorter. If the worker performs this task well and dependably, the firm is likely to promote her to delivery driver or supervisor at significantly higher pay.

On-the-Job Training

On-the-job training increases the marginal product of workers. Firms try to economize on training costs by using existing employees to work overtime to accommodate temporary increases in demand. When a trained employee quits, the firm often must incur training costs to replace him.

Firms prefer to provide *firm-specific* training that increases the marginal product of the worker only in that firm. This provides the worker with skills that aren't readily salable to competing firms. The worker who receives firm-specific training also usually receives an increase in wages. The firm can pay higher wages because the trained employee has a higher marginal product.

Many observers of Japanese labor markets say that Japanese firms make firm-specific investments and offer workers upward mobility through the internal labor market. This decreases worker quit rates to close to zero. Firms can then provide workers with both firm-specific and more general training with confidence that these workers won't take the skills they learn to competing firms.

Monitoring Workers to Avoid Shirking: The Principal-Agent Problem

As a practical matter, firms must incur costs to make sure that workers actually perform their assigned tasks to the best of their ability. **Shirking** is behavior by workers that prevents a firm from achieving the maximum possible marginal product of labor over a given period. Shirkers are of concern to a firm because they

Signals:
Indicators displayed by job applicants and used by prospective employers to predict the future satisfaction and productivity of an applicant.

Screening:
A process in which an employer limits the number of applicants for a job to those it believes are most likely to succeed in the company.

Internal labor market:
Exists within a firm when it fills positions by hiring its own employees, rather than new employees, to fill all but the lowest-level jobs.

Shirking:
Behavior by workers that prevents a firm from achieving the maximum possible marginal product of labor over a given period.

increase costs and decrease the productivity of other workers who must make up for the shirkers' lack of effort. A chief objective of personnel management is to minimize incentives to shirk.

To accomplish this task requires *monitoring,* or observing workers, to compare the performance of each worker with objective standards of productivity. Monitoring is necessary when the goals of workers and firm owners differ. The owners of a firm are sometimes referred to as *principals,* while their workers and managers are their *agents.* It's reasonable to assume that the goal of a firm's principals is to maximize profits. If workers had the same goal, personnel management would be a trivial problem. Unfortunately, this often is not the case. Many workers seek to minimize their work loads or to minimize stress on the job rather than working effectively with their co-workers to ensure profit maximization.

When the goals of workers and employers conflict, a *principal-agent problem* exists. This forces the firm to incur extra costs to observe the work force in action. The firm must balance these extra costs against the gain it receives from added productivity and lower production costs when shirking is reduced. The cost and worker resentment involved in monitoring lead many firms to choose other methods to deal with the principal-agent problem. The most common and perhaps most effective technique is the institution of a *profit-sharing plan.* Profit sharing is a way of reducing the differences between the goals of workers and employers by giving workers a share of profits as a supplement to wages.

For example, managers of corporations typically are given *stock options* as part of their compensation. A stock option allows the manager to buy stock in the company at a set price as of a given date. Because the price of a stock is favorably influenced by a firm's long-term potential to earn profits, the stock option gives the manager an incentive to increase the company's profitability. The manager can buy the stock and then sell it to convert its increased value into cash. Assembly-line workers may be given a pro-rata share of company profits. Professional athletes may earn bonuses based on annual paid admissions to games. This presumably motivates the athletes to perform their best so as to win games and maximize attendance.

Another way of dealing with the principal-agent problem is through performance-based contracts. For example, production workers and sales representatives might be given certain annual output or sales quotas. After they achieved their quotas, they would be given cash bonuses based on the additional output or sales they generated. This provides an incentive-based rather than a monitoring-based solution to the principal-agent problem.

Concept Check

1 What signals and screens are used in the process of staffing?

2 What is meant by an internal labor market?

3 List some of the techniques used in personnel management to increase worker productivity.

Summary

1. The market supply of labor services depends on the opportunity cost of work. Because people value their own use of time in nonpaying activities, they require

monetary compensation to work for an employer. The supply of labor is also influenced by nonwage money income available to an individual.

2. Rational workers give up their own time for labor income up to the point at which the marginal cost of work just equals its marginal benefit. In a competitive labor market, the monetary marginal benefit of work is the wage.

3. A person's labor supply curve shows a relationship between hourly wages and labor hours supplied for work over a given period.

4. The substitution effect of a wage change is the change in hours worked resulting only from a change in the opportunity cost of an hour of leisure. The income effect of a wage change is the change in hours worked stemming from the change in income caused by the wage change. Because people generally want more leisure when their income increases, the income effect of a wage increase tends to decrease hours worked. The substitution effect increases the price of an hour of leisure and increases hours worked. When wages increase, people have ambivalent feelings about working more because the income and substitution effects work in opposite directions on work incentives.

5. Labor supply curves can be backward bending when the income effect of a wage change outweighs the substitution effect. When the two effects exactly offset one another, the labor supply curve will be perfectly inelastic.

6. Labor supply in the aggregate is influenced by population and labor force participation rates. Increased labor supply puts downward pressure on wages. This can be offset by increased productivity of workers that increases the demand for labor and puts upward pressure on wages. Improvements in labor productivity are also the major sources of improvements in a nation's standard of living.

7. Differences in wages among workers and jobs can be explained by differences in the quality of labor services, differences in working conditions, and compensating wage differentials that adjust the monetary wages of a job to account for nonpecuniary benefits and hazards.

8. Personnel management deals with the tasks of staffing, training, compensating, and motivating workers to maximize their productivity. In staffing a firm, managers read the signals displayed by prospective employees and screen candidates to choose those most likely to succeed in their jobs.

9. An internal labor market exists within a firm when the firm uses its own employees to fill all but the lowest-level jobs. Firms use on-the-job training to provide workers with skills. Firms seek to compensate and motivate workers not to shirk because shirking prevents the achievement of maximum possible labor productivity.

Key Terms and Concepts

Nonwage money income
Marginal cost of work
Marginal benefit of work
Labor supply curve
Substitution effect of a wage change
Income effect of a wage change
Backward-bending labor supply curve
Human capital

Nonpecuniary wages
Compensating wage differential
Staffing
Signals
Screening
Internal labor market
Shirking

Problems and Applications

1. As a student you estimate the marginal cost of giving up your time to an employer at $7 an hour when you don't work at all. Currently the jobs you're qualified for are jobs paying $4 an hour. Draw a graph to show how you rationally choose not to work at all.

2. Use the graph you drew in answer to problem 1 to show how you'll choose to work at least part time if the market wage for the jobs you're qualified for increases to more than $7 per hour.

3. Suppose you currently work an average of 40 hours a week at a job that pays $10 per hour. Because of your excellent performance you receive a raise that increases your hourly wage to $15. Under what circumstances might you choose to work *less* than an average of 40 hours a week after the wage increase?

4. A fortunate worker receives an inheritance that provides her with $50,000 of tax-free nonwage money income per year. Explain why this person is likely to work less per year after the inheritance if leisure is a normal good for her.

5. The labor supply curve for men between the ages of 25 and 55 appears to be perfectly inelastic over the range of wage increases enjoyed over the past 20 years. What does this imply about the relative magnitudes of the income and substitution effects of those wage increases?

6. An increase in the population of working-age people and an increase in labor force participation of the population are expected to increase labor supply in the next 10 years. Productivity growth is expected to slow down. Show how the slowdown in productivity growth coupled with the increase in labor supply could act to reduce market wages.

7. Two chemical engineers graduate from the same college with the same grades. Both are likely to be equally productive at their jobs because their skills and training are identical. One of the engineers takes a job with an oil company and agrees to work in a branch located in a Middle Eastern nation with an unstable and potentially dangerous political situation. The other engineer takes a job with the home office of the same company. Explain why the engineer taking the foreign job is likely to earn a higher salary than his colleague working at the home office.

8. You have a choice between two jobs in two cities. Both jobs involve the same type of work and offer the same possibility for advancement, and the cost of living in the two cities is the same. However, one city, located in the "sun belt," has a mild climate and is uncongested, while the other city is located in an area subject to cold weather and rain and is heavily congested and polluted. Why might you rationally accept the job in the sun belt city even though it pays considerably less?

9. Suppose you were the personnel director of a large corporation. What signals would you read from applicants to screen them for jobs?

10. List some ways of compensating workers that business firms might use to maximize productivity.

Suggested Readings

Belton M. Fleisher and Thomas J. Kniesner, *Labor Economics: Theory, Evidence, and Policy*, 3rd ed., Englewood Cliffs, N.J.: Prentice-Hall, 1984. This textbook will introduce you to the field of labor economics. The book covers many topics in the demand for and supply of labor.

William G. Nickels, *Understanding Business,* St. Louis: Times Mirror/Mosby, 1987. Part V of this book provides an applied analysis of personnel management. The appendix to Chapter 17 actually helps you improve your signaling by offering hints on how to prepare a resume!

Robert S. Smith, "Compensating Wage Differentials and Public Policy: A Review," *Industrial and Labor Relations Review,* 32, April 1979, pp. 339-352. This essay analyzes wage differentials among jobs and occupations and the implications for public policy.

A Forward Look

Labor markets are not always perfectly competitive. In the following chapter we examine the implications for wages and employment when an employer or an organization of employers purchases a large enough portion of the labor supply to affect its market price. Labor unions can act to influence wages on the sellers' side of the market. Labor unions are complex organizations whose goals and influence in labor markets we'll also explore in the next chapter.

Imperfectly Competitive Input Markets: Labor Unions, Monopsony, and Bilateral Monopoly

If you were a star athlete, you would probably be in great demand by professional sports teams. But what would be the effect on your earnings if you could offer your services to only one team? Would you join a labor union to protect your interests as a worker? How is competition restricted in markets where labor unions and employers' associations exist?

In a competitive input market there are many buyers and sellers of resource services. In such markets no single buyer or seller can influence the price of input services. Input markets are *imperfectly competitive* if either individual buyers or sellers, or organizations of buyers or sellers, can influence input prices.

Imperfections can exist in input markets when independent sellers act in concert to monopolize the supply of an input available to employers. To exert more influence over their wages and working conditions, workers often band together in groups similar to cartels to control labor supply. A **labor union** is an organization formed to represent the interests of workers in bargaining with employers for contracts concerning wages, fringe benefits, and working conditions. Although their objectives are complex, labor unions have the potential to restrict the supply of labor in particular markets in ways that increase wages. Key goals of unions are raising the wages and improving the working conditions of their members.

Control over the prices of input services can also exist on the *buyers'* side of the market. This occurs if a single buyer or organization of buyers buys a significant share of the total available amount of a particular input service. Whereas a monopoly

Labor union:
An organization formed to represent the interests of workers in bargaining with employers for contracts concerning wages, fringe benefits, and working conditions.

exists when there is a single seller in a market, a **monopsony** exists when there is a single buyer with no rivals in an input market. Monopsony is the analogue of monopoly for the buyers' side of a market.

Monopsony:
Exists when there is a single buyer with no rivals in an input market.

It's relatively rare to observe a market in which there is only a single employer of an input service such as labor. However, it's not uncommon for a firm to employ a very large share of the total available supply of a certain resource. For example, suppose a private university employs 70% of the labor force of a small town. If the university were to increase its demand for labor, it would probably have to pay higher wages to attract workers from other towns or local workers who are currently out of the labor force. Similarly, if an aircraft producer employed 90% of the workers in a town, a slowdown in its business would sharply reduce wages in the region as its demand for labor declined. Firms like these must operate with the knowledge that the level of demand for labor will affect the wages they must pay to hire workers. As you'll discover in this chapter, profit-maximizing firms that employ large shares of the available supply of an input are likely to pay prices that fall below the marginal revenue product of that input. Wages in such noncompetitive input markets are therefore likely to be lower than those that would prevail in a competitive input market, other things being equal.

Organizations of employers sometimes act in concert to reduce competition for input services so they can pay lower wages without fear of losing low-paid employees to competing employers. For example, an arbitrator recently ruled that major-league baseball owners have acted in collusion to keep the salaries of free-agent players below the levels that would prevail with competitive bidding.

When a firm with monopsony power trades input services with a seller or organization of sellers that have monopoly power over those input services, the confrontation of power is on a par with that when Godzilla meets King Kong! When a powerful labor union confronts an equally powerful employers' association in a wage dispute, the result can be a long struggle to agree on wages, combined with disruptive work stoppages that can adversely affect the whole economy.

After reading this chapter, you should be able to:

Concept Preview

1 Describe the goals and purposes of labor unions.
2 Show how labor union practices can influence wages and affect the productivity of workers.
3 Describe the hiring practices of a monopsony firm and show how such a firm sets input prices.
4 Show how conflicts in input markets arise when monopoly and monopsony are simultaneously present.

The Economics of Labor Unions

Labor unions act as workers' agents to bargain with employers on matters related to employment. The process of negotiating for wages and improvements in working conditions between a union and employers is called **collective bargaining.** This process substitutes one labor negotiator for many independent negotiators. Many industrial relations specialists claim that the collective bargaining process can con-

Collective bargaining:
The process of negotiating for wages and improvements in working conditions between a labor union and employers.

tribute to higher labor productivity. Collective bargaining provides information to management on the production process and factors influencing worker morale that would otherwise be unavailable. This could contribute to improved managerial efficiency. Collective bargaining is viewed as more effective than individual bargaining in achieving the objectives of improved pay and working conditions. Individual workers fear employer retaliation and job loss and are therefore often unwilling to individually pursue actions that would benefit all workers.

Labor unions can also be viewed as organizations with potential monopoly power in the sale of labor services. A union is like a cartel of many independent sellers of a particular type of labor service. For example, a successful plumbers' union would control the entire market supply of plumbing services in a region. It would have the power to set the price of plumbing services. Whether labor unions actually have or use monopoly power is a subject for empirical investigation. Many experts argue that the monopoly power of labor unions is minimal.[1]

Unions that successfully raise wages above competitive levels for particular firms in a competitive industry will cause those firms to fail. This is because in a competitive product market, price is equal to minimum possible average cost of production in the long run. Suppose only a few firms in a competitive industry must pay higher wages to workers because of union agreements. These firms will go out of business in the long run because they won't be able to cover their costs when the price is set on the basis of the minimum possible average cost and competing sellers use nonunion labor. Unions can succeed only by unionizing workers in an entire competitive industry.

Similarly, unions can be successful in raising wages without causing firms to fail when they negotiate higher wages with firms that can control the prices of their products. This is because firms with monopoly power can raise prices to cover higher union wages without the fear of losing business to competing sellers. Under these circumstances union-negotiated wage increases in excess of any productivity gains do not necessarily place firms at a competitive cost disadvantage.

Organizational Problems Faced by Labor Unions

A labor union faces many of the problems a cartel confronts in establishing a monopoly position in a market. The first step to ensure the union's success is to establish a barrier to entry. The union must block entry into any job or occupation for which it succeeds in raising wages above the competitive level. Like cartels, labor unions also are potentially unstable. To maintain their power and the wages they set, they must prevent workers from negotiating independently with employers.

Labor unions are complex organizations, and it's difficult to determine their actual goals. The analogy between a labor union and a cartel is, of course, a simplification. Labor unions, unlike business firms, cannot be regarded as maximizing profits. The workers themselves are the beneficiaries of any wage increases the union secures above the competitive level. Unions seek to increase the well-being of their members. They can accomplish this task by keeping their members employed. They can also pursue a variety of strategies designed to increase the labor income of their members. In the analysis to follow we assume that labor unions seek to increase wages earned by their members.[2] We also consider the possibility that union activity affects labor productivity.

[1]See Richard B. Freeman and James L. Medoff, *What Do Unions Do?* New York: Basic Books, 1984, Chapter 3.
[2]For a more complete analysis of unions' objectives, see Freeman and Medoff.

Economic Thinkers

SAMUEL GOMPERS

As president of the American Federation of Labor, Samuel Gompers was the spokesman for the American labor movement for more than four decades. As one of the movement's founders, he shaped the path unions would take long after his death.

Gompers believed unions should be formed by workers who share some skill, not on industry lines, and that their goal should be to improve the lot of union members, whether it be through higher pay, better working conditions, shorter hours, or other changes. He firmly believed that unions should be nonpolitical. Whether this was because he feared socialists would take over any political activity or for other reasons, his determination on this point has made the American labor movement even today less political than its counterparts in other nations.

Free collective bargaining without government interference was another of his goals. Unlike the socialist elements of the movement, he was convinced that capitalism was permanent and believed unions should work with, not against, the system.

Born in a London tenement in 1850, Gompers immigrated to the United States after serving an apprenticeship to a cigar maker. He became president of the cigar makers' largest local union in New York City in 1873. Later he moved up to the national level as president of a constitutional committee for the Federation of Organized Trades and Labor Unions, which was an attempt to unite craft unions of all types across the United States and Canada. The attempt failed, but it laid the groundwork for the formation of the American Federation of Labor (AFL) in 1886. Gompers became president of the organization, and except for one year was reelected to that position until his death in 1924.

Gompers guided labor unions through many of their earliest crises—the Homestead and Pullman strikes, the open shop campaign, adverse court decisions, World War I, and the Red Scare following the Russian Revolution, among others. He led the movement conservatively through a period when the United States was bitterly hostile to labor unions, attempting to make trade unionism a respectable alternative to radicalism.

It's a good idea to keep in mind that labor unions realize that the demand for labor is derived from the product workers produce. Unions therefore often pursue policies designed to increase the demand for the product of unionized industries. For example, unions have been strong supporters of quotas and tariffs on imported goods to prevent the loss of union jobs.

Labor Unions in the United States

The first labor unions in the United States were formed late in the eighteenth century. Unions didn't achieve significant power in this country, however, until the 1930s. The modern American labor movement began in 1886 when Samuel Gompers (see Economic Thinkers box) founded the American Federation of Labor (AFL). Gompers and others in the movement sought to improve working conditions in many industries. The movement acted to reduce working hours and unreasonable pressures on the job. At first, most American unions were organized to include workers with specialized skills or who were involved in specialized crafts. **Craft unions** are organizations of workers in particular skilled jobs, such as plumbers, electricians, carpenters, and musicians. Unions belonging to the American Federation of Labor were craft unions and didn't include unskilled workers.

Craft union:
An organization of workers in a particular skilled job, such as plumbers, electricians, carpenters, or musicians.

The antitrust laws, like the Sherman Antitrust Act of 1890, were often used to restrain the activities of unions prior to the 1930s. During the Depression years of the 1930s, labor unions gained political power. The Norris-LaGuardia Act of 1932 identified unfair labor practices and limited the powers of the federal courts to intervene in labor disputes. The Wagner Act, which was passed in 1935, established the National Labor Relations Board to investigate and protect workers against unfair labor practices. This act also guaranteed workers the right to form unions. Child labor was outlawed with the passage of the Fair Labor Standards Act in 1938.

Another major milestone of the labor movement was the founding of the Congress of Industrial Organizations (CIO) by John L. Lewis in 1935. The CIO was an organization of **industrial unions,** each of which represented all workers in a specific industry, regardless of their craft or skill. The United Mine Workers and the United Automobile Workers are examples of industrial unions. The CIO merged with the AFL in 1955 to form the AFL-CIO.

Industrial union:
A union that represents all workers in a particular industry, regardless of their craft or skills.

A political backlash against unions occurred in 1947 with the passage of the Taft-Hartley Act. This legislation outlawed specific labor practices it deemed unfair. For example, the law prohibited **closed shops**—union arrangements with employers that permitted hiring only of union members. The law also allowed states to establish *right to work laws.* These laws were used in individual states to ban arrangements that required workers in certain jobs to eventually join a union. Another practice outlawed was *featherbedding,* a term used for arrangements that resulted in union workers being paid for work they didn't actually do or for unnecessary tasks. Featherbedding is a difficult charge to prove. For example, the use of firemen on diesel locomotives was often cited as featherbedding. The fireman's job was to stoke coal on steam locomotives, a function that was no longer necessary when railroads shifted to diesel locomotives. Firemen and engineers insisted that firemen in diesel locomotives improved safety by helping the engineer. Train operators viewed the practice as featherbedding, arguing that the firemen served no useful function. The practice persisted for many years despite the provisions of the Taft-Hartley Act.

Closed shop:
A union arrangement with an employer that permits hiring only of union members.

Perhaps the most significant feature of the Taft-Hartley Act was the provision that gave courts the right to issue injunctions to delay strikes for an 80-day *cooling-off period.*

Union Shops and Labor Union Membership

The arrangement most preferred by unions today is the union shop, in which workers don't have to belong to the union to be hired but must agree to become members after a certain period of employment. An alternative to the union shop is the open shop, in which union membership is voluntary for both new and existing workers. Workers who aren't members of the union in an open shop aren't required to pay union dues.

Union membership in the United States peaked in the 1950s at about 26% of the labor force. Since then the proportion of union workers has declined to less than 20%. In 1984 only 16.1% of the workers in the U.S. labor force belonged to unions.

In the United States unions are strongest in manufacturing, construction, mining, and transportation industries, where they account for more than 40% of workers. They represent much smaller percentages of employment in wholesaling, retailing, service industries, and financial industries.

However, the pattern of union membership has been changing in recent years. Union membership in such traditional strongholds as steel, clothing and textiles,

Box 1 Trends in Union Membership: Selected Years 1920-1984 (in thousands)

Year	U.S. membership	% of U.S. labor force unionized	% of nonagricultural workers unionized
1920	4,823	11.7	17.6
1939	6,491	11.8	21.2
1953	16,310	25.9	32.5
1960	15,516	22.3	28.6
1970	20,990	25.4	29.6
1975	22,207	23.7	28.9
1980	22,556	19.6	23.2
1984 (P)	18,306	16.1	19.4

P: Preliminary

Source: Leo Troy and Neil Sheflin, *Union Sourcebook*, 1st ed., 1985, West Orange, N. J.: Industrial Relations Data and Information Services, 1985.

U.S. Membership in AFL-CIO Affiliated Unions by Selected Union, 1971-1985 (in thousands)

Labor organization	1971	1975	1979	1983	1985
Boilermakers	121	123	199	119	110
Bricklayers	121	143	106	103	95
Carpenters	714	712	629	609	609
Clothing and textiles	440	377	308	253	228
Communication workers	415	476	485	573	524
Electrical workers	760	856	825	820	791
Firefighters	101	123	150	142	142
Hotel and restaurant	300	421	373	340	327
Oil, chemical, atomic	149	145	146	124	108
Postal workers	169	249	245	246	232
Retail, wholesale, dept. store	122	120	122	110	106
Service	406	490	537	589	688
State, county, municipal	458	647	889	959	997
Steelworkers	950	1,062	964	707	572
Teachers	194	396	423	456	470

Source: *Statistical Abstract of the United States,* 1987.

and oil has been declining, in part because of the general decrease in employment in these industries. On the other hand, union membership in service and government jobs has been increasing. For example, between 1971 and 1985 union membership in the hotel and restaurant industries increased by some 9%. Union membership for teachers, firefighters, postal workers, and other government employees has also been on the rise. The table in Box 1 shows some recent trends in union membership in selected occupations and industries.

Union Control Over Labor Supply

Unions can use their power of control over labor supply to establish wages above the competitive equilibrium wage. Assume a union sells labor services to many in-

Principles in Practice

Unions in Decline: Employment and Wage Effects

The once-mighty union movement in the United States is losing strength. Between 1970 and 1984 the proportion of the U.S. labor force that is unionized declined from 25.4% to 16.1%. During that period unions experienced increasing difficulty in organizing workers. Import competition, high unemployment rates, deregulation in transportation industries, increased resistance to unions by employers, and other factors all have been detrimental to union strength. Whereas unions once demanded and won hefty wage increases and benefit packages, in the 1980s industrial relations between unions and manufacturing firms have largely concerned wage cuts!

Particularly hard-hit by the forces of change has been the steel industry. Membership in the United Steelworkers of America has been cut in half, from 1.4 million dues-paying workers in 1970 to 572,000 members in 1985. The demand for steel products has plummeted since the 1970s. Currently about one quarter of the steel used in the United States is imported. New products, such as an array of high-tech plastics, substitute for steel in a variety of uses. The steelworkers spend much of their time these days negotiating contracts to maintain jobs, to minimize reductions in wages, and to prevent changes in work rules that favor employers. This is a far cry from the union's heyday when it could threaten to strike and grind virtually all U.S. heavy manufacturing to a halt if its demands weren't met.

Although wages for steelworkers in 1985 of over $22 per hour were still high, these workers' wages have declined in the 1980s. Agreements worked out with LTV Steel, National Steel, and Bethlehem Steel in 1986 resulted in wage and fringe benefit reductions ranging from 99¢ to $3.15 per hour, coupled with the possibility of offsetting gains to workers in the form of profit-sharing or stock ownership benefits.* In 1986 USX, formerly known as U.S. Steel, sought union concessions that would reduce worker compensation by a whopping $7 per hour, thus inducing the union to call a strike.

Despite the concessions made by unions in certain industries, recent research indicates that up through 1984, the union wage differential in the United States had not declined substantially. Richard Edwards and Paul Swaim have analyzed data on union and nonunion wages from 1979 to 1984 and have observed that the wage premium enjoyed by union workers over their nonunion counterparts has not narrowed since 1979. They conclude that nongovernment unions have been content with maintaining wages at the expense of losing members as nonunion labor is substituted for union counterparts.† However, Edwards and Swaim concede that the gap in wages might be chiseled away soon if union wage concessions continue.

In some cases union members themselves resist wage increases to avoid a job loss. For example, the 400 members of Local 32 of the International Association of Heat and Frost Insulators and Asbestos Workers recently demanded a substantial reduction in wages and fringe benefits to preserve jobs. The union thought management was offering *too much in wages* as part of a collective bargaining package. They reasoned that at higher wages, the firm would have its product priced over the competition and an excuse to start hiring nonunion members!

Another industry in which unions have been in decline is construction. One estimate by Steven G. Allen is that the proportion of unionized construction workers fell from about one half in 1966 to less than one third in 1984. More and more union construction workers work in open shops at nonunion wages. Allen estimates that the wage gap between union and nonunion workers has narrowed substantially since 1977. He also estimates that the productivity advantage enjoyed by union contractors in the past has been eliminated.‡

*See A.H. Raskin, "The Steelworkers: Limping at 50," *The New York Times,* Sunday, June 15, 1986, p. F29.
†Richard Edwards and Paul Swaim, "Union-Nonunion Earnings Differentials and the Decline of Private Sector Unionism," *American Economic Review,* 76, 2, May 1986, pp. 97-102.
‡Steven G. Allen, "Declining Unionization in Construction: The Facts and the Reasons," Faculty Working Paper No. 79, North Carolina State University, Raleigh, N.C.

dependent firms, each of which is normally a price taker. This means each firm can normally hire as great a quantity of labor services as it desires at the competitive wage.

Assume that a union of plumbers in a large city establishes a wage for the labor services of its members above the competitive equilibrium wage. This is illustrated in the graph in Box 2. The union wage is $20 per hour, and the competitive equilibrium wage is $10 per hour. The competitive wage corresponds to the intersection of the demand for and supply of labor. Without union influence, the market wage

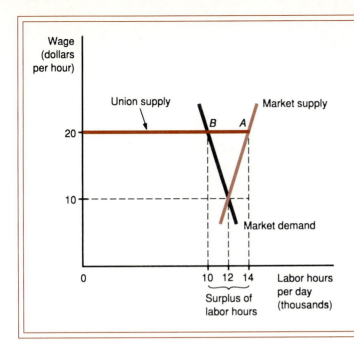

Box 2   Union Wages vs. Market Wages

When a labor union negotiates a contract that sets wages above the market equilibrium level, there will be a surplus of labor hours at the union wage. In the graph the union guarantees that employers can hire all the workers they wish at a $20 union wage. Because the union wage exceeds the $10 market equilibrium wage, there is a surplus of labor hours.

would be $10 per hour and 12,000 labor hours per day would be sold at that price. At the union wage, the quantity of labor services demanded falls to, say, 10,000 hours a day. The quantity supplied increases to 14,000 hours a day as plumbers from other areas flood the city in search of work at the higher wage. This causes a daily surplus of 4,000 labor hours.

To achieve the objective of increasing wages above the market equilibrium level, the union must prevent competition among workers from causing wages to fall. One way the union can accomplish this is to negotiate a wage agreement with employers. The plumbers' union agrees to supply all the labor services employers desire up to 14,000 hours per day at the union wage. The labor supply curve *to the employers* now becomes a horizontal line at the $20 wage until it hits the actual labor supply curve at point *A*. Of course, employers hire fewer plumbers at $20 per hour than they do at $10 per hour, the competitive wage. Employers choose to hire 10,000 hours of plumbing service per day because that is the number for which the horizontal line drawn from the point corresponding to the $20 wage on the vertical axis intersects the demand curve at point *B* in Box 2. This is the point at which the marginal revenue product of labor equals $20. What happens to the labor surplus? These plumbers might join the union, but they will not be guaranteed work.

Another way the union can achieve its goal of higher wages is by limiting the number of union members. The union negotiates a contract that requires employers to use union labor only through the establishment of a closed shop. The impact of a closed shop is illustrated in Box 3. The union neither sets nor negotiates a wage. Instead it strictly controls union membership. This results in a perfectly inelastic supply of labor at 10,000 hours per day. The union supply curve is the vertical line drawn at 10,000 labor hours per day. Given the demand for labor, this results in an equilibrium wage of $20 per hour. At that wage there is again a surplus of labor. This is because $20 exceeds the market equilibrium wage. For closed shops that raise wages above the equilibrium wage there will be a waiting list of workers to

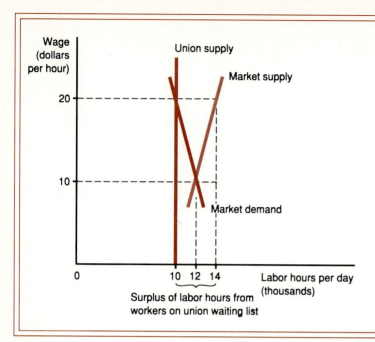

Wage (dollars per hour)

Union supply

Market supply

20

10

Market demand

0   10   12   14   Labor hours per day (thousands)

Surplus of labor hours from workers on union waiting list

Box 3   Impact of a Closed-Shop Arrangement on Wages

In a closed shop only union members can work and the labor union controls the number of workers in the union. By rigidly restricting union membership to ensure that only 10,000 labor hours are available each day, the union raises the wage above the market equilibrium level of $10 per hour to a level of $20 per hour.

join the union. Union membership acts as the control to prevent entry. The result is the same as setting wages equal to $20 per hour as in Box 2. Many states have taken advantage of the provisions of the Taft-Hartley Act to outlaw closed shops.

Waiting lists can be long. For example, in the mid-1970s public employee unions in New York City used their power to raise the wages of city sanitation workers. The union wages were 60% higher than those received for equivalent work elsewhere in competing jobs. As a result, there was a waiting list of nearly 37,000 workers while total sanitation jobs were less than one third of this number.[3]

Collective Bargaining

Collective bargaining sessions between management and unions represent the process of give and take through which agreements are established on contracts stipulating wages and working conditions. These sessions cover the whole range of issues relating to employee compensation, including fringe benefits, working hours, work rules, holidays, and retirement age. Fringe benefits include employer-provided insurance for health and other purposes, pensions, child care, employee discounts, and meals. Other important issues are wage increments for overtime work and procedures for settlement of employee grievances. Unions are also very sensitive to the issue of *seniority,* which is a measure of a worker's length of service as a union member. Seniority is usually used as a basis for determining promotion in union work rules. In addition, priority for laying off workers is established by seniority. During periods of declining demand, the workers with the highest seniority are laid off last and are recalled first when business conditions improve.

There's often considerable give and take in these collective bargaining sessions. Employers are frequently willing to meet union demands for higher wages and im-

[3]Ronald G. Ehrenberg and Robert S. Smith, *Modern Labor Economics: Theory and Public Policy,* 3rd ed., Glenview, Ill.: Scott, Foresman & Co., 1988, p. 48.

proved fringe benefits in return for changes in work rules designed to increase labor productivity.

An important fact to note about contracts that are reached through collective bargaining is that they often are very detailed and specify wage levels and fringe benefits for a number of years. Typically, contracts are in effect for 2 to 3 years. For this reason unions and management are very careful in the negotiating process.

Often the negotiators reach a stalemate. When this occurs, there are a number of alternatives. The union and management officials can submit to a process by which a third impartial party settles their disputes. This process is called *arbitration*. Arbitration is sometimes required by law. In other cases an impartial *mediator,* often a government official, is sent in to try to speed up the process of reaching an agreement. The last resort is a strike, in which workers leave their jobs to pressure employers to agree to the union demands. Sometimes employers themselves shut down the plant, resulting in a *lockout* of workers to pressure the union to accept their offer.

The Impact of Unions on Wages

Empirical studies confirm that union workers in the United States on average enjoy higher wages than their nonunion counterparts of equal skill. Estimates of the positive average wage differential for union workers fall in the range of 10% to 20%.[4] In some cases the differentials are much higher. For example, one study indicated that in the mid-1970s the union wages for electricians and plumbers working in construction were 55% to 70% higher than wages for their nonunion counterparts.[5] However, these estimates ignore the fact that unions may actually depress wages of nonunion workers. If unions are successful in increasing wages above the competitive equilibrium level, they create a surplus of workers, as you saw in Box 2. These workers seek employment in alternative nonunion jobs while hoping some day to obtain a union job. The increase in the supply of labor hours to nonunion work, other things being equal, decreases wages in these jobs and occupations. Some nonunion workers, on the other hand, could benefit from union efforts to organize labor. The threat of unionization can cause many employers to pay higher wages and provide better working conditions to their nonunion employers than they would otherwise.

The Impact of Unionization on Labor Productivity

What do employers get in return for the higher wages they pay to union workers? For one thing, higher wages cause firms to use fewer workers. The marginal revenue product of labor therefore increases as firms reduce the amount of labor input used in production. In the long run there's a tendency to substitute capital for labor to adjust further to the higher wages. An increase in the capital-labor ratio could contribute to making union workers more productive than their nonunion counterparts. However, if union restrictions on labor supply in particular occupations or industries *increase* the supply of labor to nonunion jobs and industries, the marginal revenue product of labor in these sectors of the economy will decline, as will wages.

[4]C.J. Parsley, "Labor Unions and Wages: A Survey," *Journal of Economic Literature,* 18, March 1980, pp. 1-30.
[5]Martin E. Personick, "Union and Nonunion Pay Patterns in Construction," *Monthly Labor Review,* 97, 8, August 1974, pp. 71-74.

It also appears that the working environment of union members is more structured than that of nonunion workers. While some union work rules can contribute to decreased worker productivity, other aspects of union control can increase productivity. Work is generally at a faster pace, and there's less employee control of overtime hours. One study found evidence supporting the hypothesis that unionized construction workers are more productive than their nonunion counterparts.[6]

On the other hand, unions often require minimum-size work crews that increase costs of production to employers. For example, musicians' unions often require that orchestras used in theatrical performances have a minimum number of musicians. In some cases unions seek to limit the ability of employers to substitute capital for labor. For example, for many years printers' and typographers' unions strongly resisted introduction of new technology that sets type by computer because such an innovation would eliminate many of their jobs. Before new technology could be applied, agreements had to be worked out with the union to protect existing jobs and incomes of union members.

Evidence indicates that union work forces are more stable and reliable than nonunion labor. Unions are effective in reducing worker quit rates. This reduces training costs for employers.[7] The collective bargaining process can also contribute to increased productivity. Workers often point out improvements in the production process that mutually benefit employers and employees. Whether the social gains associated with unionization of workers exceed the social costs of monopoly power of unions remains an area of controversy.[8]

Concept Check

1 In what sense is a labor union similar to a cartel? List some of the goals of labor unions.

2 What techniques can labor unions use to raise wages for their members?

3 Why will increases in wages in unionized industries be likely to reduce wages in nonunionized industries?

Monopsony

Pure monopsony:
Exists when a single firm buys the entire market supply of an input that has few, if any, alternative employment opportunities.

A **pure monopsony** exists when a single firm buys the entire market supply of an input that has few, if any, alternative employment opportunities. A monopsonist has the power to set the price of the input services it purchases.

Pure monopsony is as rare as pure monopoly. It can conceivably exist in small towns where a single firm employs all workers. A single mining firm that employs all workers in mining jobs in an isolated frontier town is an example of a pure monopsony. The U.S. government as sole purchaser of many defense-related materials like nuclear weapons is a pure monopsonist for those inputs. Similarly, some agencies of the federal government are monopsonists in certain labor markets. For example, the Federal Aviation Administration (FAA) is the sole employer of air traffic

[6]Steven G. Allen, "Unionized Construction Workers Are More Productive," *Quarterly Journal of Economics,* May 1984, pp. 251-273.
[7]See Ehrenberg and Smith, pp. 485-490.
[8]Freeman and Medoff provide evidence that the gains outweigh the losses. Other economists disagree with their findings.

controllers. This gives the FAA the authority to set wages. This power was clear when President Reagan fired all air traffic controllers rather than grant their demands for higher wages and changes in working conditions after they engaged in an illegal strike. The controllers who lost their jobs had no alternative but to enter different occupations because there was only a single employer of air traffic controllers.

Professional sports in the United States is a good example of an industry in which a few firms can act in concert as if they were a monopsony firm. Athletes can sell their services to a small number of buyers. There are usually 20 to 30 teams in each professional sport. Most professional sports leagues have some agreed-upon mechanism for reducing competition that would bid up the salaries of athletes. The result is similar to a cartel. The group of teams acts together as if they were a single buyer. Draft rules typically limit the negotiation rights of a single player to a single team in a league. Each team has its "quota" of players, and the system prevents one team from acquiring all the best new players.

In some sports, players can become "free agents" after a certain number of years of service to a team. Free agents are not subject to the rules that limit their negotiation rights to a single team. Instead they can invite competing teams to bid for their services. Free agency has resulted in sharp increases in salaries for sports stars (see Principles in Practice box on p. 468.) Nonetheless, critics of the sports industry argue that teams still collude to keep the salaries of free-agent players lower than would be the case if teams competed actively. In 1987 an arbitrator ruled that the 26 major-league baseball owners colluded illegally to avoid bidding up the salaries of players who were free agents.

Marginal Input Cost for Monopsony Firms

Monopsony power is the ability of a single buyer to influence the price of an input service it purchases. As firms with monopsony power buy more inputs, the price they have to pay increases. Because it buys a significant portion of the total market supply of an input, a firm with monopsony power cannot acquire all the input services it wants at a given price. The supply curve of input services to a firm with monopsony power is upward sloping. To acquire more input services, firms with monopsony power must pay higher prices.

Monopsony power:
The ability of a single buyer to influence the price of an input service it purchases.

The data in the table in Box 4 illustrate the effect of monopsony power on labor cost. The data are for a hypothetical coal mining firm in an isolated frontier region. The firm is the sole employer of workers. All workers are coal miners, and there are no quality differences among their labor services. To attract additional workers the mining firm must increase wages. An increase in wages attracts workers from other regions or induces those currently not working to enter the labor force.

Columns 1 and 2 of the table show how wages paid per day increase as additional workers are hired. When the firm employs 100 miners it pays a wage of $40. It cannot, however, obtain additional workers at that wage. Currently everyone who wants to work at that wage is employed by the mining firm. If it wants to attract additional labor services, the firm must pay higher wages.

The **marginal input cost** (MIC) is the change in total input cost associated with a change in input services hired:

Marginal input cost:
The change in total input cost associated with a change in input services hired.

$$\text{MIC} = \text{Change in input cost/Change in input services}$$

Marginal input cost for a monopsonist increases as the firm employs more of an input's services.

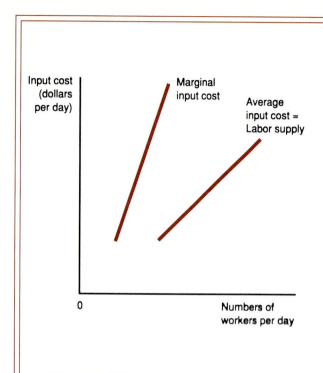

Input cost (dollars per day)

Marginal input cost

Average input cost = Labor supply

0

Numbers of workers per day

Box 4 Marginal and Average Input Cost for a Monopsony Firm

For any given quantity of input use, marginal input cost exceeds average input cost for a firm with monopsony power in the input market.

Marginal Input Cost and Marginal Revenue Product for a Monopsony

Number of workers per day	Average input cost = Wages per day	Total labor costs	Marginal input cost	Marginal revenue product
100	$40	$4,000	–	–
101	41	4,141	$141	$200
102	42	4,284	143	180
103	43	4,429	145	165
104	44	4,576	147	150
105	45	4,725	149	148
106	46	4,876	151	140
107	47	5,029	153	130
108	48	5,184	155	115
109	49	5,341	157	100

In a competitive input market the marginal input cost equals the price of the input's services. Because a firm hiring labor services in a competitive market can obtain all the workers it wants per day at the market wage, the marginal input cost of labor is equal to the daily wage for firms without monopsony power.

The table in Box 4 shows how the marginal input cost, in this case for labor, increases as more workers are hired. If the mining firm wants to increase the labor force to 101 workers per day, it must raise daily wages to $41. Keep in mind that all workers are paid the same daily wage. When the firm hires more workers (each working an 8-hour day), it must pay more to *all workers,* not just the last worker it hires. If it didn't do so, some workers would quit and the firm wouldn't be able to maintain a daily work force of 101 workers.

The table shows how wages will increase as the firm's management hires between 100 and 109 workers per day. Total labor costs when the firm hires 100 workers at a daily wage of $40 are $4,000 per day. Because the employer must increase wages to $41 per day when it wants to increase the daily work force to 101, total labor costs rise to $4,141 per day. The marginal input cost associated with the services of an extra worker is therefore $141. The marginal input cost of labor greatly exceeds the wage paid to workers. This is because all 100 workers must be paid an extra dollar per day when the work force is increased to 101 workers. The marginal input cost is the sum of the wages of the last worker and the additional wages paid to existing employees.

As the calculations in the table show, the marginal input cost always exceeds the wage as additional workers are hired. For any given quantity of labor, the marginal input cost exceeds the price of an input when a firm has monopsony power. The price of an input represents the **average input cost** (AIC). In this case the average

Average input cost:
The price of an input.

input cost is the wage. The curve showing how the average input cost (or wage in this case) must increase to hire more workers is the labor supply curve for the monopsony firm. The marginal input cost always exceeds the average input cost for a monopsonist. For a firm hiring an input's services in a competitive input market, marginal input cost always equals average input cost because input prices are constant. The graph in Box 4 shows the firm's marginal and average input cost curves based on the data in the adjacent table.

Hiring Decisions in Monopsonistic Input Markets

A firm with monopsony power maximizes profits by hiring an input's services up to the point at which the marginal input cost just equals the marginal revenue product of the input:

Marginal input cost = Marginal revenue product

The marginal revenue product measures the contribution of the extra input services to the firm's revenues. The marginal input cost is the extra cost of an extra unit of the input. As we have seen, the marginal input cost exceeds the price of the input for a monopsonist.

As long as the marginal revenue product of labor exceeds the marginal input cost of labor for the coal mining firm, it can increase profits by hiring more workers. As shown in the table in Box 4, marginal input cost begins to exceed the marginal revenue product of labor when more than 104 workers are hired each day. Maximum profits are realized when the firm hires 104 workers. If the firm were to hire an additional worker to increase the size of its labor force to 105, the marginal

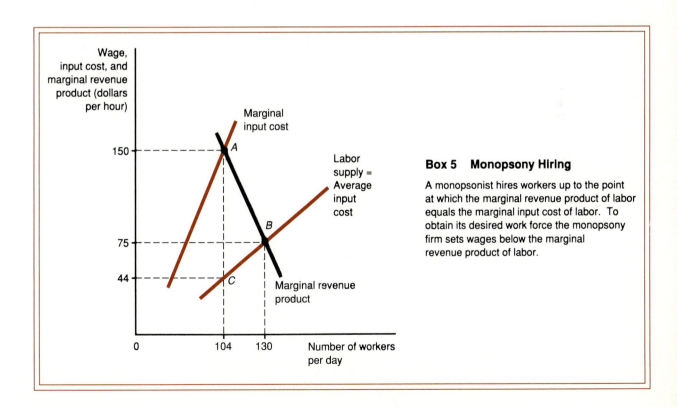

Box 5   Monopsony Hiring

A monopsonist hires workers up to the point at which the marginal revenue product of labor equals the marginal input cost of labor. To obtain its desired work force the monopsony firm sets wages below the marginal revenue product of labor.

Principles in Practice

Monopsony Power and Athletes' Salaries: Are Sports Stars Underpaid?

In 1982, while swinging a bat for the California Angels, Reggie Jackson was paid a salary of $975,000. The Angels posted pretty impressive results that year, and the marginal revenue product of Jackson as a player was estimated to be $1.5 million for 1982. This is based on an estimate of how much of the attendance at games and other revenues earned by the team was attributable to Jackson's drawing power as a player.

To estimate the marginal revenue product of a particular player, economists estimate the contribution of that player to games won and then estimate the extra revenue from extra games won. Using this technique, one economist estimated that Jackson's marginal revenue product in 1982 was considerably above his salary that year.* In other words, Jackson was well worth a salary of close to $1 million in 1982 because he contributed much more than that to team revenues.

A wage that is below the marginal revenue product of labor suggests that the employers have monopsony power. In fact, as we saw in the text, major-league baseball teams did have monopsony power before players were allowed to act as free agents. An analysis of career marginal revenue products and salaries by George Scully indicated that players did in fact earn salaries that were only about 15% of their marginal revenue products in 1977!† The graphs show how this implies a monopsony situation in the market.

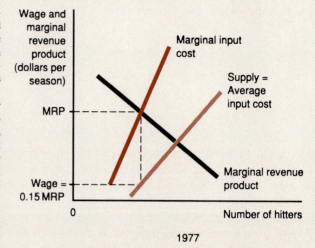

Elimination of reserve clauses allowed free agents to increase their salaries. As the case of Reggie Jackson indicates monosony power hasn't been completely eliminated in baseball. However, it has lessened considerably. One estimate indicates that hitters in the 1982 season had salaries that equaled 75% of

*See Timothy Tregarthen, "Are Professional Athletes Worth the Price?" *The Margin,* November 1985, pp. 6-8. The estimates of Reggie Jackson's marginal revenue product are based on the work of Howard University economist John Leonard quoted in the article.
†George Scully, "Pay and Performance in Professional Sports," *American Economic Review,* 64, December 1974.
‡See Tregarthen, *The Margin,* November 1985.
§See Tregarthen, p. 8. This too is based on estimates by John Leonard.

revenue product of labor would fall to $148 while the marginal input cost would rise to $149. Because the marginal input cost of labor exceeds the marginal revenue product of labor when 105 workers are employed, the firm would suffer a decrease in profit by hiring this extra worker.

What wage does the monopsonist set to obtain a work force of 104 workers each day? To find out, go to the second column of the table in Box 4 and notice that wages must be set at $44 per day to hire 104 workers each day. If the employer were to pay less than this, it couldn't attract that many workers.

The profit-maximizing hiring decision of the firm with monopsony power is illustrated graphically in Box 5. The marginal input cost curve just intersects the marginal revenue product curve at point *A.* The corresponding profit-maximizing number of workers per day is 104. The firm sets the wage it pays at $44 per day. Follow the vertical dashed line from point *A* and note that it intersects the labor supply curve at point *C.* Now follow the horizontal dashed line from point *C* to the vertical axis.

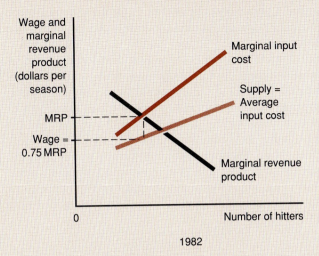

Wage and
marginal
revenue
product
(dollars per
season)

Marginal input
cost

Supply =
Average
input cost

MRP

Wage =
0.75 MRP

Marginal revenue
product

0

Number of hitters

1982

new contracts surprisingly received *no offers* from any team but the one for which they were currently playing. The eight players, who were called the "untouchable eight," were Rich Gedman, Ron Guidry, Tim Raines, Doyle Alexander, Bob Horner, Andre Dawson, Lance Parrish, and Bob Boone, all of whom had just become free agents. Most of the players re-signed with their original teams that year at salaries well below the levels they were seeking. The 26 team owners claimed they weren't in collusion but that the high price of players had caused their profits to decline (as might be expected in a competitive input market) and they chose not to bid so as to prevent further declines. A federal arbitrator disagreed with the team owners' defense.

On September 22, 1987, the arbitrator ruled that major-league baseball owners colluded to prevent bidding for free agents. The arbitrator saw evidence of collusion in the absence of competitive offers in 1985, when 62 free agents were in the market and only a handful were signed in competitive bidding. To the players' delight, the arbitrator ruled that the owners had entered into a scheme designed to destroy the free-agency system!

One case in which athletes are clearly underpaid is in college sports, where under NCAA rules star players *cannot* be paid salaries. One study indicates that a star college athlete has a marginal revenue product to his college in the range of $100,000 per year! However, that athlete is rarely paid more than a $5,000 scholarship. In this sense the NCAA rule can be interpreted as permitting college teams to enjoy monopsony power for college-age athletes and pay them less than their marginal revenue product.§ Student athletes are indeed a good bargain for colleges!

their marginal revenue product.‡ The graphs show that the decline in the gap between marginal revenue product and wages means that the gap between wages and marginal input cost is also smaller. When monopsony power is reduced, marginal input cost for employers rises less rapidly and diverges less from the wage.

In 1987 there was further evidence suggesting that major-league baseball team owners were colluding to prevent wages of free agents from increasing. That year free agents seeking

This line intersects the vertical axis at a daily wage of $44. This indicates that when the firm pays wages of $44 per day it will be able to maintain a daily work force of 104 workers.

The marginal revenue product of labor when 104 workers are employed is $150 per day. However, the wage paid to workers by the monopsonist is only $44 per day! The marginal revenue product of labor exceeds the wage paid to workers by about $106 per day. *This means that the monopsony firm increases its profits at the expense of its workers, who are paid less than the marginal value of their production to the firm*

A monopsony firm hires less input services and pays lower wages compared to the benchmark competitive input market equilibrium. In a competitive input market, equilibrium occurs when labor is hired up to the point at which the marginal revenue product of the input equals the price of the input. If there were many mining companies competing for the services of miners in the town, equilibrium would occur at a point like *B* in Box 5. Market wages would be $75 per day, and 130 workers per day would be hired at that wage. Each firm would be able to hire as many miners as it chose at the $75 competitive wage. Wages for miners would be higher than monopsony wages, and *more* workers would be hired. The wage of the miners would equal the marginal revenue product of their labor if the market were competitive. In Box 5, the marginal revenue product of labor is $75 per day when 130 workers per day are employed.

Workers are better off in a competitive labor market than in a labor market in which a monopsony firm does the hiring. In the competitive market, the forces of supply and demand determine the wage. If any employer tries to pay workers less than the market equilibrium wage in the competitive market, it will be unable to attract workers. By the same token, if a worker is paid less than the marginal revenue product of labor by one firm, another firm can always increase its profits by hiring that worker at a slightly higher wage. The competitive process would bid up the wages of workers under such circumstances until they rose to equal the marginal revenue product of labor. Only when wages equal the marginal revenue product of labor for all workers will it be impossible for a firm to increase its profits by hiring workers from its competitors.

The Market for Professional Athletes: An Example of the Exercise of Monopsony Power

Professional sports leagues typically cooperate to prevent competition for players from driving up salaries. Special reserve clauses in contracts often prevent players from negotiating with teams other than the one they have signed with. The team holding the player's contract has exclusive rights to the contract. The team can, of course, trade its contract rights to another team. Typically this is done for a cash payment, in exchange for the contract rights of another player, or a combination of the two. Once a player is traded, his reserve clause once again prevents him from negotiating with any other team except the one to which his contract has been traded.

Depending on the sport, veteran players may be able to gain freedom to negotiate with rival teams by playing out their contracts with a given team for 1 or 2 years. In some sports a player must have a certain number of years of experience before he can offer his services to other teams. Once freed from the reserve clause, he becomes a free agent. He can contract with any team he wishes and bargain for salary and benefits. However, the team that acquires the free agent's contract must pay compensation to the team that loses the player. This limits the salary the new team can offer the free agent.

In effect, reserve clause contracts establish monopsony power in the market for athletes. Since 1975 the baseball industry has had a liberal free-agency system. Players who exercise their option to become free agents now can obtain much higher salaries than they could before 1975. The new system sharply reduces the compensation that must be paid to the team that loses the free agent by the team that acquires his contract. Professional basketball teams adopted a similar system in 1981. However, professional football has a system that makes it quite difficult for its players to become free agents. During the 1987 season the average salary of professional football players was $215,000. A salary of nearly a quarter million dollars for playing football might seem generous to you. However, when compared with the 1987 average salaries of over $400,000 for professional baseball and basketball players (where free agency has been more effective in raising wages), it seemed quite low to gridiron stars.

Breaking the monopsony power of the baseball teams has led to sharply increased salaries for players. In 1970, under the old system, the average salary was about $45,000 per year. In 1980 the average salary was more than four times that amount. The Philadelphia Phillies, for example, paid their players an average of over $200,000 a year in 1980. Their star player, Pete Rose, earned $800,000 that year. Many of the players had declared themselves free agents. Philadelphia was able to retain them by paying salaries competitive with what they could have earned playing for other teams.[9]

In 1987 baseball players' average salary had risen to $431,000—nearly 19 times the average in 1970. Dave Winfield signed a 10-year contract in 1980 for $20 million. In 1986 and 1987 there were free agents playing for the Kansas City Royals with contracts guaranteeing them salaries in excess of $1 million per year for their lifetime as players! As a result of competitive bidding, free agents also enjoyed such fringe benefits as free life insurance, stock options, and other extras not reflected in their salaries. Prior to the free-agent system, star baseball players were paid salaries below their estimated marginal revenue products.[10]

Concept Check

1 Why is the marginal input cost for a monopsonist in a labor market greater than the wage it pays its employees?

2 Show that a profit-maximizing monopsonist will pay wages that are less than the marginal revenue product of labor.

3 Suppose textile manufacturers form an employers' association to hire workers. If this association acts as though it is a monopsonist, what will happen to wages in the industry?

Bilateral Monopoly

Bilateral monopoly exists when only one buyer and one seller trade input (or output) services in a market. Both the buyer and the seller have the power to control the price of the input's services. The graph in Box 6 illustrates the case of bilateral monopoly in which a single firm purchases the entire market supply of a certain type of labor service. The labor is sold through a powerful labor union that monopolizes the supply.

Bilateral monopoly:
Exists when only one buyer and one seller trade input (or output) services in a market.

The labor supply curve shows the input price necessary to attract any quantity of the input's services. Because the firm purchasing the labor services is a monopsonist, it will want to pay the wage necessary to attract the input quantity corresponding to the intersection of the marginal input cost curve with the marginal revenue product curve. This intersection occurs at point *A*. At that point the firm will want to hire 10,000 hours of labor services per day. The wage necessary to hire this number of labor hours per day is $8 per hour. To see this, simply note that $8 per hour is the wage corresponding to point *B* on the labor supply curve, at which the quantity of labor services supplied is 10,000 hours per day. If the labor market were competi-

[9]See Roger G. Noll, "Major League Sports," in Walter Adams, ed., *The Structure of American Industry,* 6th ed., New York: Macmillan, 1982.
[10]Gerald W. Scully, "Pay and Performance in Professional Sports," *American Economic Review,* 64, December 1974.

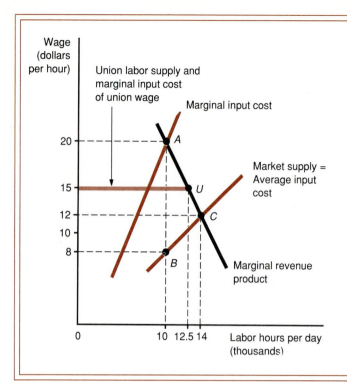

Wage
(dollars
per hour)

Union labor supply and
marginal input cost
of union wage

Marginal input cost

20 ─ ─ ─ ─ ─ ─ ─ ● A

Market supply =
Average input
cost

15 ━━━━━━━━━━━ ● U

12 ─ ─ ─ ─ ─ ─ ─ ─ ✕ C
10 ─

8 ─ ─ ─ ─ ─ ─ ─ ●
                  B

Marginal revenue
product

0   10 12.5 14   Labor hours per day
                          (thousands)

Box 6   Bilateral Monopoly

When a monopsony firm confronts a union that monopolizes labor supply, there is no equilibrium in the market because the profit-maximizing wage set by the monopsonist will be far below the wage the union seeks to set. If, however, the union succeeds in negotiating a wage that exceeds the monopsonist's profit-maximizing wage, it is possible that the monopsony firm will increase its employment of labor hours per day.

tive, market wages would be $12 per hour. This corresponds to point *C* on the graph, at which the demand for labor curve (which is also the marginal revenue product curve) intersects the labor supply curve. At the competitive wage, 14,000 labor hours per day would be supplied.

The labor union naturally wants to set a wage that exceeds the market equilibrium wage of $12 per hour. Suppose the union demands an hourly wage of $20. There's a $12 difference between the union's desired hourly wage and the monopsony employer's profit-maximizing wage.

As a result, there's no equilibrium in the market, and no trading can take place until there's an agreement on price. The outcome depends on the bargaining strategies of the buyer and seller. Eventually the traders will agree on an input price somewhere between the $20 hourly wage demanded by the union and the $8 profit-maximizing hourly wage of the monopsonist. Each side will employ tactics to fool the other. They may try to hide the price they find most favorable to their own interest. The union might threaten a strike. At the same time the employer might threaten to lock out the workers by shutting down the plant until they agree on a wage. However, neither side has any alternative but to deal with the other because the market has only one buyer and one seller.

Pure bilateral monopoly is rare. It's occasionally encountered when a government monopolist (such as for tobacco or liquor) purchases goods from a single seller franchised to sell the product in the country. In labor markets, strong unions often deal with equally strong employers' associations that act in concert as if they were a monopsony firm. For example, the Bituminous Coal Owners' Association is a national employers' association that deals principally with two major unions of employees, one of which is the United Mine Workers. Trucking Management, Inc., is a national association of truckers that bargains with the Teamsters Union.

An employers' association could attempt to set the wage at a low level to maximize its members' profits. If the union didn't agree to the wage, the employers would cease operations and lock workers out. The union would demand a wage higher than that which would prevail in a competitive labor market, which also would be considerably higher than the wage offered by the employers' association. The union would threaten to strike unless its demands were met. If the difference between the wage demanded by the union and the wage offered by the employers' association were great, a long strike or lockout of workers could result. The costs of either action to both workers and employers would eventually result in a compromise agreement.

Bilateral monopoly of this type is also quite common in professional sports, in which an organization of team owners bargains with a players' union to set wages and working conditions over a contract period. For example, the National Football League Players Association (NFLPA) bargains with the Management Council of the National Football League, which represents the team owners. When the two groups cannot agree on salary and working conditions, the result is often a strike. For example, NFLPA players walked off the job in the fall of 1987 when the two groups couldn't agree on salary and other issues relating to free agency of players. The NFLPA, whose members earned an average salary of $230,000 per season, wanted to set a $90,000 minimum salary for players, escalating to $320,000 for players with 13 years of experience. The NFL Management Council wanted to set a $60,000 minimum salary, escalating to $180,000 for 13-year players and $200,000 for 15-year players. There were other issues of contention in this confrontation between the union and the employers' association. Because a compromise agreement couldn't be reached at the outset, players went out on strike in the fall of 1987. However, the strike fizzled out and players eventually returned to their jobs without winning their demands.

How a Labor Union Can Increase Both Wages and Employment When Dealing with a Monopsony Firm

In some cases unionization of workers employed by a firm can actually lead to an increase in both wages and hiring of workers if the employer is a monopsonist. For example, imagine a case in which a textile firm that currently has a nonunion labor force acts as a monopsonist. The monopsonist sets a profit-maximizing wage of $8 per hour corresponding to point B in Box 6 and currently employs enough workers to provide 10,000 labor hours each day. A union moves in and organizes the labor force, acting as a monopoly seller. Suppose a shrewd labor leader manages, through carefully planned bargaining tactics, to get the monopsony textile firm to accept the $15 per hour wage demanded by the union. You'd normally expect the higher wage to result in a decrease in labor hours demanded by the textile firm. However, in this case the surprising result is that the employer will increase employment of workers at the union wage!

To see why this is so, first assume the union guarantees the employer that it can hire all the labor hours it wants at the $15 union wage. The employer therefore knows that the marginal input cost of labor will always be $15 an hour. The union contract enables the employer to hire more workers, up to a point, without having to increase hourly wages to do so. It can now maximize profits by hiring workers up to the point at which the wage equals the marginal revenue product of labor. The marginal revenue product of labor is $15 per hour at point U, at which the firm hires 12,500 labor hours per day. Employment increases from the 10,000 hours per day the monopsonist would hire at $8 per hour if it were to maximize profits without having to worry about the union. This shows that if a union wins a confrontation with a monopsonist, it can succeed in raising both wages *and* employment for union members!

Concept Check

1 Under what circumstances will bilateral monopoly prevail in a market?

2 Suppose a strong labor union goes on strike against an equally strong employers' association. Why is it difficult to predict the outcome of the strike?

3 Under what circumstances can unionization of an employer's work force increase *both* wages and employment?

Summary

1. Input markets are imperfectly competitive if either individual buyers or sellers, or organizations of buyers or sellers, can influence input prices.

2. Labor unions are organizations formed to represent the interests of workers in bargaining with employers for contracts concerning wages, fringe benefits, and working conditions. Raising the wages and improving the working conditions of their members are key goals of labor unions. The process of negotiating for such improvements between representatives of labor unions and employers is called collective bargaining.

3. A successful labor union acts like a cartel by controlling labor supply and conditions of entry into jobs so as to raise wages. However, unions have other goals, including increased labor productivity and protection of jobs. If unions succeed in raising wages above the market equilibrium, there will be a surplus of workers seeking union jobs or trying to become union members. These workers will seek work in nonunion jobs or occupations, which will put downward pressure on wages in those labor markets. The gains obtained by union workers can therefore be offset by losses to other workers.

4. Empirical studies indicate that union workers in the United States earn wages that are 10% to 20% higher than wages earned by nonunion workers of equal skill. Some studies indicate that union work rules often increase worker productivity.

5. A pure monopsonist is a single firm that buys the entire market supply of an input that has few alternative employment opportunities. Monopsony power is the ability of a single buyer to influence the price of an input it purchases.

6. Marginal input cost tends to increase as more input services are hired by a monopsonist. For any quantity of the input used, the marginal input cost exceeds the average input cost. A monopsony employer has to pay higher wages to all workers when it wants to increase the size of its work force.

7. A profit-maximizing monopsonist hires workers up to the point at which the marginal input cost equals the marginal revenue product of labor. To hire its desired number of workers, the monopsonist sets a wage that is *less* than the marginal revenue product of labor. Under monopsony, workers are paid a wage that is less than their marginal contribution to a firm's revenue.

8. Bilateral monopoly exists when only one buyer and one seller trade input (or output) services in a market. Bilateral monopoly exists in labor markets when a

---

single employers' association using a certain type of labor bargains with a union that controls the supply of this labor. There is likely to be wide disparity between the wage most favored by the employers' association and that most favored by the union.

Key Terms and Concepts

Labor union	Pure monopsony
Monopsony	Monopsony power
Collective bargaining	Marginal input cost
Craft union	Average input cost
Industrial union	Bilateral monopoly
Closed shop	

Problems and Applications

1. Suppose that the textile industry producing corduroy fabric is perfectly competitive. Currently workers in the industry are not unionized. A successful organizing campaign results in unionization of workers employed by one firm in the industry. Assume that once this union is in power it succeeds, through collective bargaining, in raising the wages of workers employed by this firm. If the industry is currently in long-run equilibrium and each nonunionized firm has the same costs, predict what will happen to the unionized firm.

2. Suppose there is a single monopoly seller of corduroy fabric in the nation. How will the result of unionization of workers in this firm differ from the result in your answer to problem 1? Explain why the result might be different if the monopoly seller faces the threat of foreign competition.

3. How can labor unions increase the wages of their members by increasing the demand for the product produced by their employers instead of directly negotiating wage increases?

4. Suppose that in the absence of union bargaining, the market equilibrium wage for electricians in a large eastern city would be $10 per hour. A craft union manages to increase wages for electricians to $15 per hour. Assuming there's no change in the marginal revenue product curve for workers, show that not all electricians will be able to find work at that wage even if they join the union.

5. After the union negotiates the $15 wage in the large city, predict what might happen to the wages earned by electricians in neighboring areas where electricians are not unionized.

6. The following schedule shows the labor supply curve for workers in a small town:

Number of workers available for work per day	Daily wages
50	$30
51	31
52	32
53	33
54	34
55	35

Calculate the marginal input cost for a monopsonist that is the sole employer in the town.

7. Suppose the marginal revenue product schedule for the monopsony employer described in problem 6 in the town is as follows:

Number of workers employed per day	Marginal revenue product
50	$100
51	85
52	83
53	80
54	70
55	60

How many workers will the monopsonist employ? What wage will the monopsonist set?

8. Suppose the monopsonist whose marginal input schedule and marginal revenue product schedule were shown in problem 7 is broken up into a number of smaller firms that cannot influence wages. What will happen to wages and employment in the town?

9. In the town in which hiring is done by a monopsonist, what would happen to wages if workers formed a labor union?

10. In what sense can a monopsonist be said to "exploit" workers?

Suggested Readings

Belton M. Fleisher and Thomas J. Kniesner, *Labor Economics: Theory, Evidence, and Policy*, 3rd ed., Englewood Cliffs, N.J.: Prentice-Hall, 1984. Chapters 6 and 7 discuss noncompetitive labor markets and labor unions in detail.

Richard B. Freeman and James L. Medoff, *What Do Unions Do?* New York: Basic Books, 1984. This is a comprehensive and balanced analysis of the role of labor unions in the United States. The authors cite many empirical studies regarding the impact of labor unions on wages, fringe benefits, and productivity. They also discuss political activity by U.S. labor unions.

C. J. Parsley, "Labor Union Effects on Wage Gains: A Survey of Recent Literature," *Journal of Economic Literature*, 18, 1, March 1980, pp. 1-31. This is a thorough survey of the literature on the impact of unions on wages. It includes studies done for both the United States and the United Kingdom.

A Forward Look

In the next chapter we discuss the markets for nonlabor inputs. We'll analyze the markets for loanable funds borrowed by firms that seek to purchase new capital, and we'll study the market for land. In addition, we'll investigate the sources of profit for entrepreneurs who assume the risks of organizing and operating business enterprises.

Interest, Rents, and Profit

If you're fortunate enough to have funds in your savings account, then you know that the bank pays interest on your account. You also know that you have to pay interest on funds you borrow. For example, if you've borrowed to pay your tuition, you'll have to pay interest to the lender. *Interest* is a payment for the use of funds lent by one person for the use of others. Interest represents a price for the use of funds in the same way that wages represent a price for the use of labor. The rate of interest is usually expressed as a percentage per dollar made available for others to use. For example, if you can obtain 8% annual interest by making a loan, you'll earn 8¢ for each dollar you allow others (such as a bank) to use when interest is computed once at the end of the year. A $100,000 loan at 8% annual interest will provide the lender with $8,000 annual income at the end of the year.

A price called **rent** must be paid for using the services of land. Although land rents represent less than 1% of total income in the United States, they are crucial influences on the uses to which land is put. The chief factor affecting land rents is location. When land rents increase, the use of land is economized by building taller structures on each acre of land.

Rent:
The price that is paid for the use of land.

Developing and marketing new goods and services is risky business. Profits are earned by successful entrepreneurs who undertake the risks of introducing new products or techniques. Economic profit is a residual enjoyed by an entrepreneur after subtracting all the opportunity costs of doing business, including those of the entrepreneur's own labor and funds and other resources supplied to the enterprise.

In the United States, income from interest, rents, and profits constitutes only about one quarter of all income earned. However, it's impossible to overestimate the importance of interest and rents as prices influencing incentives to produce and to expand the productive capacity of the nation or a region. Also, the opportunities to earn profit motivate entrepreneurs to innovate so as to improve resource use and respond to consumer demands. In this chapter our goal is to understand the function of interest rates, land rents, and profit as influences on resource use and as a source of income.

After reading this chapter, you should be able to:

1 Explain the concepts of capital and investment and show how the interest rate represents a crucial price influencing investment in new capital.
2 Analyze investment decisions and show how the interest rate affects those decisions.
3 Outline the influences on the supply of and demand for loanable funds that affect the equilibrium interest rate for various types of loans in a competitive market.
4 Explain how land rents are determined in competitive markets.
5 Understand how profit opportunities arise in an economy and how entrepreneurs seize those opportunities for personal gain.

Capital, Investment, and the Interest Rate

The interest rate is an important influence on total expenditure in an economy because it represents the price of borrowing funds to make purchases. The interest rate also affects the opportunity cost owners or corporate stockholders incur by tying up their own funds in their firms. When interest rates are high, investors give up more interest income by using their funds in their business than when interest rates are low. From the business perspective, the interest rate is a *price* that influences the incentive of firms to acquire or replace inventories of materials and parts, equipment, vehicles, and structures.

Investment, Saving, and Capital Stock

Capital is an input created by people for the purpose of producing goods and services. Physical capital consists of tools, machinery, vehicles, structures, raw materials, and inventories in various stages of production. Physical capital can be thought of as a certain amount of equipment and materials that will last for a certain period of time. For example, an inventory of parts might last for 3 months, during which time the parts are used to make a firm's final product. A structure might last 50 years, during which time it will be used to provide space and facilities for a firm to conduct its business. Similarly, various types of vehicles, machines, and tools can last for periods ranging from a few months to many years, during which they will be used to produce goods and services.

Human capital consists of skills such as those of medical practitioners created for the purpose of producing goods or services. Also included in human capital are such nonmaterial items as technological know-how and the skills, talents, and experience of workers. Be sure to read the Economics Thinkers box on economist Gary Becker of the University of Chicago. In his classic *Human Capital*, he examines the profitability of investment in education in terms of individual earnings and productivity.

Investment:
The process of replenishing or adding to capital stock.

The capital of a firm represents a *stock* or inventory that can be drawn on to produce goods or services without additional outlays of funds other than for maintenance and repairs. **Investment** is the process of replenishing or adding to capital

Economic Thinkers

GARY BECKER

Can economic theory be used to determine the impact of discrimination on employment, or to measure the rate of return on a high school or college education? Gary Becker thinks so. This innovative economist has gone beyond the traditional focus on how physical capital contributes to productivity and economic growth and has instead applied microeconomic theory to investments in people, or human capital.

Born in 1930 in Pottstown, Pennsylvania, Becker received his Ph.D. from the University of Chicago in 1955 and became an assistant professor there that same year. Before 1957, when Becker published his pioneering work, *The Economics of Discrimination,* something as irrational as prejudice was thought to be beyond the realm of a rational science like economics. Becker proved the conventional wisdom wrong by presenting a general theory for analyzing the impact of discrimination in the marketplace. He described economic discrimination as a situation where members of a certain group earn less than their skills are worth because some other market participant is willing to pay to avoid dealing with them. His work laid the foundation for research in the economics of discrimination in the 1960s and 1970s.

In 1957 Becker joined the faculty of Columbia University and the staff of the National Bureau of Economic Research. There he began to measure the dollar rates of return on high school and college educations by studying government statistics on income and education costs to find out how profitable investment in education was in terms of individual earnings and productivity. This research culminated in the publication of his classic, *Human Capital,* in 1964. Becker found that the return on education was substantial. In one group of white males, college graduates earned about 60% more than high school graduates by the age of 50, a rate of return close to 14.5% for their investment in education. Most important, the widely acclaimed book developed a theoretical foundation to explain the costs and returns of investing in people through education, on-the-job training, and health measures. In 1967 Becker's work earned him the John Bates Clark Award, granted by the American Economic Association to the "outstanding economist under 40."

Becker has also applied economic analysis to such nontraditional areas as crime prevention, an individual's allocation of time, and even the selection of a marriage partner and the decision to have children. Since returning to the University of Chicago in 1970 as professor of economics, Becker has written a number of books and articles, such as *The Economic Approach to Human Behavior* (1976) and *A Treatise on the Family* (1981), which many economists regard as his most significant contribution to the field to date.

---

stock. Investment represents a *flow* of new capital in a given year. Individuals can add to their human capital by undergoing additional education and training. In many cases business firms undertake the expense of training their employees.

The capital of a firm is used up in production. Inventories of materials are drawn down, and machines eventually wear out or become obsolete and have to be replaced. The rate at which machines and structures wear out is called *depreciation*. If the new capital created in a nation each year is less than the depreciation of the existing capital stock, the total capital stock will decline. A decrease in capital stock implies that investment is *negative*. You can think of a nation's capital stock as the level of water in a bathtub. The bathtub has a slight leak, representing depreciation and drawing down of inventories. If the level of water in the tub is to rise, investment, which is the flow of new capital, each year must exceed depreciation and declines in the stock of inventories. Gains in productivity associated with rising standards of living require continual investment to create new capital. This is why economists are so concerned with annual investment as well as the amount and state of repair of a nation's capital stock.

Saving:
The amount of income not consumed in a given year.

The amount of income not consumed in a given year, called **saving,** can be supplied to investors who use the funds to create new capital inputs. In some cases the people who save are the same people who make the investment. For example, the owner of a small business might plow some of her profits back into her enterprise, rather than consuming them, to expand by acquiring new structures, vehicles, or equipment. Similarly, corporations often save in this manner by retaining their earnings to finance investments rather than paying them out as dividends. Such business saving provides a considerable amount of funds for new investment.

Specialized financial markets for the trading of bonds and corporate stocks provide a means of channeling savings as loanable funds to those who wish to make investments. Banks and brokerage houses arrange transactions involving the use of funds for payments of interest. For convenience, in this chapter all markets for the use of credit are referred to as *loanable-funds markets*. These markets are also sometimes called credit markets or capital markets.

How the Interest Rate Affects Investment Decisions

To make investments, a business firm must make outlays of funds *today* to acquire capital that will provide productive services over *a period of time in the future*. When making an investment, the firm must weigh the extra revenue it obtains over a number of years from the productive services of new capital against the opportunity cost of using funds to acquire that capital.

A profit-maximizing firm will compare the marginal revenue product from the acquisition of new capital with the marginal input cost of borrowing or tying up its own funds to make the investment. To compare the marginal revenue product of an investment with the market rate of interest, the firm must estimate a percentage rate of return on the investment. For example, suppose you own a computer company that's considering investing $1 million in a new inventory of electronic chips. You estimate the chips will generate sales that will raise an additional $1.2 million in revenue over the year. To evaluate this investment, you must answer the following question: *What annual percentage return would result in $1 million growing to $1.2 million at the end of 1 year if this sum were deposited in a bank?* The answer to this question is easy. The annual percentage return on the $1 million would have to be 20% for it to grow to $1.2 million after 1 year:

$$\$1 \text{ million} + 20\%(\$1 \text{ million}) = \$1.2 \text{ million}$$

Once you've estimated the percentage return on the investment, you must compare this return with the market rate of interest. Suppose you can arrange a 1-year loan at 10% interest. Will you invest in the electronic-chips inventory that yields a 20% return after 1 year? If you're rational, you'll go to it! It would cost you $100,000 in interest to borrow the funds for a year to finance the inventory. At the end of the year, the revenue made possible by the new inventory would return the $1 million cost and an additional $200,000. Your net profit on the investment would be the $200,000 return less the $100,000 interest, which equals a nifty $100,000! If you seek to maximize profits, you'll certainly acquire this inventory because you can gain by doing so! In fact, as long as the percentage return on an investment exceeds the interest rate on borrowed funds, a firm can add to profits by making the investment.

In general, calculating the percentage return on an investment becomes more complicated as the number of years involved increases. For example, suppose your firm is considering investing in a new computer system that will last 5 years before becoming obsolete. You'll have to estimate the marginal revenue product of the new system for each of 5 years. Next you'll look at the cost of the new system. Suppose it costs $10 million. The next step is to determine the percentage return that would result in an annual *stream* of increases in revenue equal to the annual marginal revenue product of the new system if the $10 million were deposited in a bank.

Business Demand for Investment Funds and the Investment Decision: Marginal Analysis

The **marginal return on investment** is the percentage rate of return on investment of additional sums of money to acquire more capital. The marginal return on investment in a given year tends to decline as more investments are made. This is because the marginal product of new capital decreases as more is acquired. The law of diminishing marginal returns applies to acquisition of new capital just as it applies to acquisition of additional labor services. A firm with a given amount of labor and other inputs finds that the marginal return on investment in a given year tends to decline. Naturally, managers of a firm seek to make the most profitable investments first. A profit-maximizing firm would undertake an investment with a 20% annual return before it undertook one with a 15% annual return.

There's still another reason why the return on more investment in a given year tends to fall. As all firms in an industry make more investments in a given year, output in the future tends to increase as the new investments increase the market supply of goods and services. The increased future supply will put downward pressure on the prices of goods produced by the industry. Anticipated price declines for a product tend to reduce estimates of the industry's future annual marginal revenue products. This in turn tends to reduce the estimated return on the investment.

The graphs in Box 1 show how a firm decides how much investment to undertake in a given year. The market rate of interest depends on the market demand for and

Marginal return on investment:
The percentage rate of return on investment of additional sums used to purchase more capital.

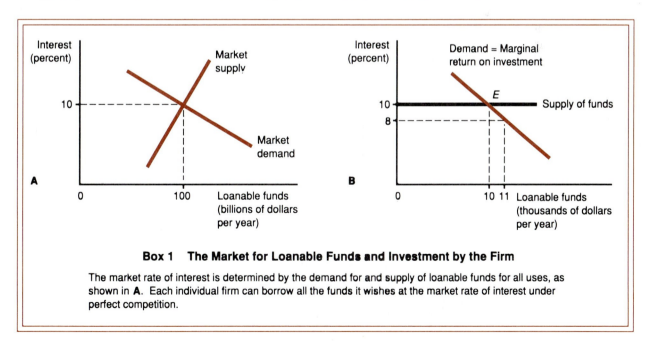

Box 1   The Market for Loanable Funds and Investment by the Firm

The market rate of interest is determined by the demand for and supply of loanable funds for all uses, as shown in **A**. Each individual firm can borrow all the funds it wishes at the market rate of interest under perfect competition.

supply of loanable funds. The graph labeled **A** shows that the equilibrium interest rate is 10%. An individual firm can borrow all the funds it wants at 10% under perfect competition. The supply of loanable funds to the firm is therefore a horizontal line that intersects the vertical axis in graph **B** at the market rate of interest. The firm will borrow additional funds as long as the annual marginal return on investment exceeds the interest rate. The firm will therefore borrow funds (or use its own funds) to make investments up to the point at which the marginal return it can earn on investment falls to equal the market rate of interest. Graph **B** in Box 1 shows that the marginal return on investment equals the market rate of interest at point *E*. The corresponding amount of investment for the firm is $10,000 per year.

The firm's investment demand curve is the curve that shows how the marginal return on investment varies with the dollar amount of loanable funds invested per year. You can see this by imagining that the interest rate declines to 8%. The firm will find that additional investments that were unprofitable at 10% interest now are profitable. For example, making an investment with only a 9% return wouldn't be profitable at a 10% interest rate because the firm would suffer a net loss of 1 percentage point on the funds used to acquire the new capital. On the other hand, as the market interest rate falls to 8%, the investment with the 9% return will yield a profit of 1 percentage point on the funds used to acquire the new capital. The firm will borrow additional funds to finance more investment until the marginal return on investment falls to 8%.

Calculating the Present Value of a Stream of Future Annual Payments[1]

Investment decisions involve comparing sums of money received at different points in time. Dollars received in the future are worth less than current dollars. The reason for this is that any sum to be received in the future could be obtained by depositing a *smaller* sum in a bank account earning the market rate of interest. The sum in the account would grow to equal the future dollar amount as the interest was earned. For example, the sum of $1 received 1 year from today is worth only about 91¢ in current dollars when the interest rate is 10%. This is because at 10% interest, 91¢ is all that is needed to have $1 at the end of the year after the interest is taken into account. The **discounted present value** of funds to be received in future periods is the current value of those funds. The sum of 91¢ is the discounted present value of $1 received at the end of 1 year when the interest rate is 10%.

Discounted present value:
The current value of funds to be received in future periods.

Because capital assets result in a flow of current and future revenue to their owners, the value of these assets today must be computed as a discounted present value. The price of a capital asset traded in a perfectly competitive market is determined by its present and future earning potential, its useful life, and the market rate of interest.

Present Value

It's easy to derive a simple formula that can be used to compute the discounted present value of a revenue-producing asset. This formula is also useful in helping decide whether the acquisition of such an asset is worth the cost.

[1]This section can be skipped by students and instructors not interested in the financial calculations necessary to determine the profitability of investments.

Suppose a capital asset, such as 50 gallons of stored wine, is expected to sell for $990 after 1 year in storage. The market rate of interest is currently 10%. The maximum amount you as an investor would pay to buy the stored wine is the sum of money, V, that would grow to $990 at the end of the year. The following equation shows that the principal and interest on V at the end of the year equal $990:

$$V(1 + 0.10) = \$990$$

Solving for V gives:

$$V = \$990/(1.10) = \$900$$

If you paid more than $900 for the wine, you'd make less than you could earn by simply lending that amount to someone else at 10%.

In general, the present value, V, of R received after 1 year is:

$$V = R/(1 + i)$$

where i is the market rate of interest.

The present value of an asset with a given annual dollar return to be received in the future declines when the market rate of interest increases. Suppose the interest rate increases from 10% to 20%. The present value of $990 received 1 year from now is $PV = 990/1.20 = \$825$.

Similarly, the present value of R received in 2 years can be calculated from the following formula:

$$V = R/(1 + i)^2$$

where i is the market rate of interest. V in this case is the sum of money that must be lent out at the market rate of interest to end up with R dollars after 2 years when interest is computed once annually at the end of the year. For example, the present value of $10,000 revenue from an investment to be realized after 2 years when the market rate of interest is 10% is $\$10,000/(1.10)^2 = \$8,264.46$. This sum represents the amount that would have to be deposited in the bank today to grow to $10,000 after 2 years under simple interest computed at the end of each year. To see this, note that after the first year at 10% interest, $8,264.46 would be:

$$\$8,264.46\,(1.10) = \$9,090.91$$

After the second year this sum would be:

$$\$9,090.91(1.10) = \$10,000$$

Because $9,090 can be written as $8,264.46(1.10), the expression just given can also be written as:

$$\$8,264.46\,(1.10)^2 = \$10,000$$

The present value of $10,000 received after 2 years is therefore:

$$V = \$8,264.46 = \$10,000/(1.10)^2$$

This means that in terms of *current dollars,* $10,000 received after 2 years is worth only $8,264.46.

In general, the present value of a sum of R received n years in the future when the market rate of interest is i is:

$$V = R/(1 + i)^n$$

Because the denominator of the equation gets bigger each time n increases, you can

Principles in Practice

Corporate Finance: The Issuance of New Stock to Raise Funds for Expansion

The stock market with which you're probably most familiar consists of a number of markets at particular locations, such as the New York Stock Exchange and the American Stock Exchange, both of which are located on Wall Street in lower Manhattan. Stock exchanges are places at which holders of *previously issued* stock can sell their holdings and those interested in buying previously issued stock can do so through brokers that are members of the exchanges.

The market for *newly issued stock* is one that involves communication between underwriting firms and the public. This market is not at a particular location. There are a limited number of underwriting firms, including such well-known companies as Merrill Lynch and Goldman, Sachs, that advertise new public offerings of stock and manage sales. The underwriter in effect guarantees sale of the corporation's new stock at the agreed-upon price by promising to purchase all stock not sold to the public at the set price. A stock offering is accompanied by a prospectus that provides financial information about the company issuing the stock and the use to which the new funds raised will be put. For example, if a newly formed corporation issues 20,000 shares of stock in a public offering at $10 per share, it will raise $200,000 that can be used to finance capital projects.

People who purchase shares often receive voting rights in the corporation along with the right to receive dividends, which are payouts of earnings to stockholders. However, purchase of a stock doesn't guarantee that the holder will earn dividends because the corporation is under no legal obligation to pay dividends. The payment of dividends depends on profits the corporation earns and how the board of directors chooses to distribute profits between dividends and *retained earnings*, which are also called *undistributed profits*. A corporation that needs funds for expansion can use retained earnings instead of borrowing funds or issuing additional stock. U.S. corporations rely heavily on retained earnings as a means of financing their expansion.

---

conclude that the further in the future $R is received, the smaller the present value of $R. For example, at a 10% interest rate, $10,000 received in 10 years is worth only $10,000/(1.1)^{10} = $3,855.44.

If you have an investment that will yield revenue for each of 4 years, you can calculate its present value from the following formula:

$$V = \frac{R_1}{(1 + i)} + \frac{R_2}{(1 + i)^2} + \frac{R_3}{(1 + i)^3} + \frac{R_4}{(1 + i)^4}$$

where R_1 is the revenue from the investment in the first year, R_2 is the revenue in the second year, and so on.

For example, suppose you're given the opportunity to make a sure-bet investment that promises you $20,000 revenue after the first year, $30,000 after the second year, $40,000 after the third year, and $50,000 after the fourth year. In later years the investment will no longer provide revenue. If you have the option of putting your money in the bank to earn 8% interest and the amount of money you must put up to make the investment is $100,000, is it a good deal? To find out, all you have to do is compute the present value of the stream of revenue at an 8% interest rate:

$$\begin{aligned} V &= \$20{,}000/1.08 + \$30{,}000/(1.08)^2 + \$40{,}000/(1.08)^3 + \\ &\quad \$50{,}000/(1.08)^4 \\ &= \$18{,}518.52 + \$25{,}720.17 + \$31{,}753.34 + \$36{,}751.47 \\ &= \$112{,}743.50 \end{aligned}$$

The investment *is* a good deal because its present value exceeds the cost of $100,000. However, you should note that the investment might not be a good deal at an interest rate higher than 8%. Remember that the interest rate is the opportunity cost of tying up funds in an investment. When the interest rate increases, fewer investments are profitable. To convince yourself of this, calculate the present value of the $100,000 investment when the interest rate is 20%. Would you undertake this investment if the opportunity cost of tying up your funds were 20%?

You should also note that the formula for calculating the present value of an investment can be used to calculate its marginal return. For example, suppose you know that an investment will cost $100,000. You also have an estimate of the annual revenue or marginal revenue product (R) of the investment in each year. To calculate the marginal return on the investment, all you have to do is find out what interest rate would make the present value of the marginal revenue product over time equal $100,000. You do this by substituting $100,000 for V in the equation and then, using the estimated Rs, solving the equation for i. Most spreadsheet programs for personal computers have a special routine that solves the equation and gives the value of i representing the marginal return on the investment.

Equilibrium Price of a Capital Asset

A *capital asset* is a particular capital good such as a machine or a building that will last for a certain period and can be used to generate revenue over that period. *In a perfectly competitive capital market, the price of a capital asset must equal the present value of future net revenue that can be earned from using it.* If the price falls short of the present value of the asset, buyers can make a profit by purchasing it. This increases the demand for the asset and causes the price to rise until it equals the asset's present value. For example, if the interest rate is 10% and the stored wine in the previous example sold for less than its present value of $900, investors would compete to buy stored wine. This is because by investing in the wine they could make more than the market rate of interest. At any price below $900, the wine would be bid up by increased demand until the price reached $900. Similarly, at a 10% interest rate, any price above $900 would mean that those who held the wine would be earning less than 10%. They would sell the wine. As the supply of stored wine offered for sale increases, its price will fall to $900.

In the long run, the price of a capital asset must equal both its present value and its average cost of production, assuming the asset is sold in competitive markets. If price were below average cost, producers of new capital couldn't cover their opportunity costs. The supply of the capital asset would decrease, and price would rise. Similarly, if price were above average cost, new entrants would increase the supply of the capital asset and the price would fall. Finally, the price of any capital asset depends on the market rate of interest. The higher the rate of interest, the lower the price of any capital asset.

Concept Check

1   What is the relationship between physical capital, investment, and depreciation?

2   Suppose the market interest rate is 10%. Use marginal analysis to show how a decrease in the interest rate to 8% will increase investment by a corporation.

3   Explain why the equilibrium price of a capital asset must equal the discounted present value of its marginal revenue product over the life of the asset.

Supply of and Demand for Loanable Funds

In actuality no one individual or business firm, not even the largest of corporations, borrows a significant portion of the total funds supplied per year. Borrowers may be business firms seeking to finance new capital and consumers who want to finance purchases of homes and automobiles. Governments also borrow to cover budget deficits and fund new public facilities. The interest rate is determined by the supply of funds from savings and the demand for loanable funds by all borrowers. Each year in the United States, well over a trillion dollars is deposited and loaned out by individuals and financial institutions to governments, businesses, and households who compete in the loanable-funds market for available supplies of credit.

Market Demand for Loanable Funds

The market demand for loanable funds is the sum of the quantities of loanable funds demanded by all borrowers at each possible interest rate. As is the case for most demand curves, the demand curve for loanable funds is downward sloping. As the interest rate declines, the quantity of funds demanded for all uses increases.

The graphs in Box 2 show how the market demand for loanable funds is derived. The graph labeled **A** shows business demand, consumer demand, and government demand for funds in a given year. Graph **B** shows the market demand for funds.

The demand for loanable funds can shift in response to changes in economic conditions. For example, improved confidence in the future of the economy could increase business demand for investment. This is because the marginal revenue product of new capital is higher when business firms expect to sell more in the future or when they expect prices of their products to rise. Improvements in technology also affect the business demand for funds. Improvements in technology that increase the productivity of new capital increase the marginal revenue product of new capital. This tends to increase the marginal return on investment, which shifts the entire investment demand curve outward.

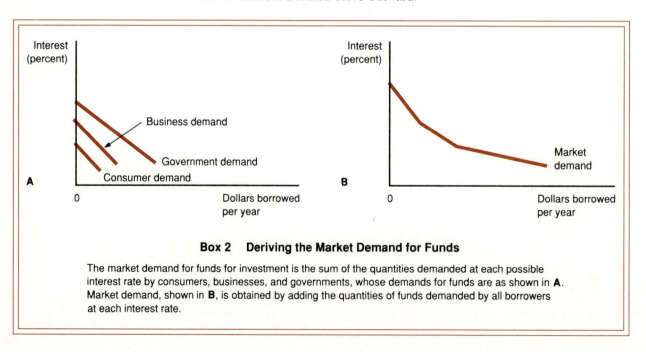

Box 2   Deriving the Market Demand for Funds

The market demand for funds for investment is the sum of the quantities demanded at each possible interest rate by consumers, businesses, and governments, whose demands for funds are as shown in **A**. Market demand, shown in **B**, is obtained by adding the quantities of funds demanded by all borrowers at each interest rate.

The demand for loanable funds also depends on the willingness of consumers to incur debt to finance purchases of homes and other goods. Consumer demand for credit is influenced by tax rules for deducting interest on borrowing and by general attitudes toward going into debt. Finally, government borrowing to cover budget deficits tends to increase the demand for loanable funds.

Market Supply of Savings

The market supply of savings is the relationship between interest rates and the quantity of loanable funds willingly supplied by all savers. Other savers in addition to individuals are corporations, governments, and foreign holders of domestic currency. Savers temporarily loan out excess funds they choose not to use to make purchases in the current year. The total quantity of savings supplied to the market for loanable funds at each possible interest rate is the sum of the funds supplied by all individuals, corporations, governments, and foreign holders of domestic currency.

The higher the market rate of interest, the greater the quantity of loanable funds supplied. There are a number of reasons why the supply of loanable funds curve is upward sloping. Keep in mind that individuals forgo the opportunity to buy something this year for their own use when they save some of their income. The more saved, the greater the amount of current consumption that is given up during the year. *People generally require more than one dollar's worth of future consumption to compensate them for giving up a dollar's worth of current consumption.* The higher the market rate of interest, the greater the compensation for giving up the opportunity to immediately consume income. Lending part of your income is more attractive when the interest rate is 20% than when it's 10%! Higher interest rates increase the gains possible from saving and induce an increase in the quantity of loanable funds supplied to the market. At higher market rates of interest, the quantity of loanable funds supplied by households therefore tends to increase. *In addition, the higher market rate of interest induces business firms to make more of their profits and other idle funds available for loan to others. This is because it's less attractive for firms to use these funds for their own investments when market interest rates increase.*

As observed earlier, the supply of loanable funds depends on the willingness and ability of households to save. This is highly correlated with income in a nation. The supply curve of savings tends to shift outward as income increases in a nation. The supply of savings also depends on a nation's system of banking and the amount of funds channeled into banks and other financial institutions that specialize in making loans.

Determining the Market Rate of Interest in Competitive Markets

The market rate of interest depends on both the market demand for and the market supply of loanable funds. In the graph in Box 3 the quantity of loanable funds demanded per year equals the quantity supplied at a market interest rate of 10%. The equilibrium amount of funds loaned at that rate is $1,000 billion per year. This sum represents the amount borrowed that year for all uses, including purchase of goods and services by consumers, business investment, and government borrowing to finance new projects and to cover budget deficits. In equilibrium the quantity of funds demanded for all purposes equals the quantity supplied from all sources. If the market interest rate were higher than 10% in Box 3, there would be a surplus of loanable funds and the market rate of interest would decline. If the interest rate were less than 10%, there would be a shortage of loanable funds and the market interest rate would rise.

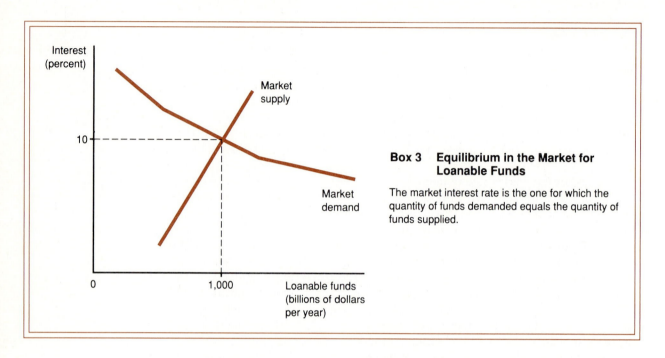

Box 3 Equilibrium in the Market for Loanable Funds

The market interest rate is the one for which the quantity of funds demanded equals the quantity of funds supplied.

An increase in the demand for loanable funds will increase the market rate of interest. Increased demand for credit by government, households, or business firms, other things being equal, shifts the demand curve outward. As the market rate of interest increases, the quantity of loanable funds supplied also increases. Similarly, a decrease in the demand for loanable funds would alter the market rate of interest. Of course, changes in the supply of loanable funds would also affect the interest rate.

Investment Risk

Investment decisions to acquire new capital involve spending money today on projects whose returns will be received in the future. Investors estimate the returns from investments, but they can't know for sure that those returns will be realized. A new computer system might not work as anticipated. The system therefore might not earn an investor as much revenue as expected. Similarly, the demand for output can change in the future. A firm might invest in aging cheese or wine, expecting to receive a certain price when these items are sold after a certain period. If the price is lower than expected, the firm can't realize the expected return. In other words, the firm may inaccurately estimate the marginal revenue product of particular investments over their useful lives. Such inaccuracy stems from differences in the anticipated and actual future marginal products of new capital or differences in anticipated and actual product prices.

Risk measures the variation of actual outcomes from expected outcomes. Suppose two investments are expected to yield a marginal return of 15%. However, investors know from experience that the marginal return on one of the investments is more variable than that on the other. For example, assume one of the investments is in new firms producing computer software. On average these investments yield 15%. Some companies do very well, and an investor can earn as much as 50%. Others do very poorly, and investors can end up earning nothing or even losing money. On the other hand, for an investment in a "blue-chip" company, the variation in the return will be much lower. On average, investors can earn 15% in these investments. However, investors can expect to earn as much as 18% and as little as 10%. The software investment is riskier than the blue-chip investment because there's greater variation in its return from the amount expected.

An investor is said to be **risk averse** if, given equal expected returns, he or she would choose an investment with lower risk. This means that, other things being equal, an increase in the riskiness of an investment makes the investor worse off. Given the risk of an investment, an increase in its expected return makes the investor better off.

The hypothesis of risk aversion can explain differences in the rates of return of alternative investments. If investors are on average risk averse, higher returns on riskier investments are necessary to compensate them for the added risk. The argument here is analogous to that used to explain wage differentials between jobs that are safe and unsafe. Safe investments, like government bonds, have low returns. Riskier investments, like those in speculative stocks, have higher average returns, but much greater variation in returns over time and among companies.

Risk:
Measures the variation of actual outcomes from expected outcomes.

Risk averse:
Describes an investor who, if given equal expected returns, would choose an investment with lower risk.

Differences in Interest Rates

It's an abstraction to talk about *the* interest rate in an economy because there's significant variability in interest rates for loans of different types and made to different borrowers. However, the general *level* of all interest rates tends to increase with shifts in the supply of and demand for loanable funds in the economy.

Interest rates on federal government securities are typically lower than those on consumer credit. For example, in 1986 the interest rates on short-term government bonds were less than 6%. Mortgage interest rates available to homeowners in that year averaged about 10%. However, consumer credit available from banks or through the use of credit cards ranged anywhere from 10% to 18% and even higher!

Interest rate differentials among loans can be explained by differing characteristics of the loan or the borrower. The federal government can borrow funds at much lower rates than households because the risk of its not being able to repay is virtually nil. After all, the federal government has the power to tax and even to print money to repay its debts! Lenders are reluctant to make funds available to borrowers who are likely to have trouble repaying the loan. However, some lenders will take the risk of loaning funds to less creditworthy borrowers for higher interest rates. Just as jobs with less favorable working conditions have higher wages, so do riskier loans command higher interest rates because the supply of funds for such loans is scarcer.

Collateral, which is an asset pledged as security for a loan, typically reduces the risk to the lender. When you pledge your car or home as collateral for a loan, the lender can seize and sell the asset to claim the balance on the loan if you default. The interest rate on mortgages and automobile loans is generally lower than that on

Principles in Practice

More on Stocks: The Discounted Present Value of Corporate Earnings and the Volatility of Prices

If you could accurately predict the ups and downs of the stock market, you could make a fortune. The willingness of investors to pay for either newly issued or existing stock in a corporation ultimately depends on their assessment of the corporation's profitability. The price of a stock represents buyers' assessment of the discounted present value of the company's future earnings divided by the number of outstanding shares of stock. Variations in stock prices therefore in part reflect changing assessments of the company's current and future ability to earn profits. Changes in expectations about movements in interest rates also influence stock prices because the market rate of interest affects the discounted present value of the company's future stream of earnings.

One factor investors consider in deciding whether to purchase existing or new corporate stock is the company's *price-earnings ratio,* which is simply the current market price of a share divided by total annual earnings per share. For example, suppose the price of a share of a certain corporation is currently $10. If the earnings per share are $1 per year, then the price-earnings ratio is 10. A price-earnings ratio of 10 corresponds roughly to an annual *current* rate of return of 10% in current earnings per share. The higher the price-earnings ratio, the lower the current rate of return per share. A price-earnings ratio of 20 means that earnings are currently only 5% of the current price per share. The willingness of investors to purchase stocks with high price-earnings ratios is an indication that they think future profits will exceed current profits. They're willing to accept a low current return in the hope that they'll enjoy a high future return.

The return stockholders earn is in the form of either dividends or capital gains. Dividends are portions of corporate profits paid out to stockholders. A capital gain is an increase in the value of the stock over the original purchase price. If investors believe the profitability of the stock has increased, the demand for the existing stock will increase, and this will bid up its price. The stockholder can sell the stock and convert its increased price into cash, thus obtaining a realized capital gain. Many stockholders who are fortunate enough to earn capital gains on their holdings don't sell their stocks because they still believe their holdings will give them good future returns compared to alternative investments. Unrealized capital gains are gains that are not converted into cash by selling assets.

Stock prices are volatile because assessments of the profitability of investing in stocks relative to other assets are revised daily. New information causes changes in the demand for existing stocks that often spur wild gyrations in averages of stock prices and in the prices of the shares of particular companies. Increases in interest rates generally cause declines in the average price of stocks traded on stock exchanges. This is because higher interest rates make debt instruments such as bonds and mortgages a more attractive alternative to stocks. In addition, higher interest rates are likely to affect the future profitability of corporations. This compounds the decrease in demand for stocks caused by the higher yields on interest-earning debt that substitutes for stocks in investor portfolios. Similarly, declines in market interest rates generally send stock prices upward on stock exchanges. A shrewd investor carefully follows the daily and weekly course of interest rates and makes investment decisions with interest rates in mind.

---

consumer loans for which no collateral is offered. Another factor that can affect the risk of a loan is its duration. Longer-term loans are generally regarded as riskier to lenders than short-term loans.

A factor affecting the interest rate a lender would be willing to accept for a loan is the tax treatment of interest on the loan. Lenders make their decision on the basis of the net interest they receive after payment of any taxes. For example, if all interest is subject to a tax of 28%, lenders would realize only 72% of gross interest earned. Suppose, however, that interest earned on loans to municipal governments is tax free. In equilibrium, the gross interest charged to these governments will be lower than that charged on other loans of equal risk. If it were not, there would be an increase in the supply of funds available for this investment (and a decrease in funds for other investments) until the after-tax interest that could be earned on all loans became equal.

Box 4   Selected Market Interest Rates, Last Week in January 1986 (Percent per Year)

Home mortgages	10.01
Corporate AA industrial bonds	8.50
30-year Treasury bonds	7.45
Tax-exempt bonds	6.52
Passbook savings	5.50

The table in Box 4 shows interest rates on various types of loans and financial obligations in early 1986. Notice how government bonds pay a lower interest rate than mortgage loans. Also notice how the interest paid on tax-exempt bonds is lower than that on corporate bonds, on which the interest is fully taxable.

Concept Check

1   What could cause the demand for loanable funds to increase in credit markets? What effect will the increased demand have on the market rate of interest?

2   Why is the supply curve for loanable funds in credit markets likely to be upward sloping?

3   What does it mean to be risk averse? How does risk aversion explain differences in interest rates on different kinds of loans?

Land Rents, Profit, and Resource Allocation

Land is unique as an input because it's immobile. The total amount of land available at a given location is fixed. The total supply of usable land in a nation is fixed. The rent that can be charged for the use of land depends on its marginal revenue product in the highest use. There's usually more than one competing use for land. If landowners seek to maximize profits, they'll try to rent their land to the highest bidder. Of course, if the highest bidder bids less than the opportunity cost of letting someone else use the land, the landowner holds on to the land for personal use. For example, if you own the land on which your house is located, you'll rent the land to someone else only if the rent you can obtain per year exceeds the value you place on the land as a place to live.

Location, Land Use, and Land Rents

The supply of land at a particular location is perfectly inelastic. If land rents at that location increase, the quantity of land supplied at that location cannot increase. Because the supply of land at a given location is fixed, the price of land depends entirely on the level of demand for land at that location.

Differences in land rents arise from a number of influences on the willingness of buyers to pay for land. In agricultural areas, land that's more fertile will be bid up to higher rents than less fertile land. In nonagricultural areas, improvements on the land such as roads, sewers, water supplies, and landscaping can increase the rent tenants will pay. Structures on the land also increase a parcel's marginal revenue product and contribute to higher land rents. In fact, it's often difficult to separate the rent on the land from the rent paid to use a structure on the land. Rents per apartment or per square foot of office space reflect an amalgam of a payment for the land location and a payment for the use of the capital such as the space, rooms, and facilities in the structure.

The main determinant of land rents in nonagricultural areas is location. Rents have reached astronomical levels in places like midtown Manhattan because of the locational advantage of that land and the amount of capital (structures) that has been (or can be) placed on the land at those locations.

Locational advantage depends on the proximity of a parcel of land to centers of work, recreation, and shopping. It also depends on the amenities of the neighborhood such as the streets, public facilities (for example, water and sewer service), the types and state of repair of surrounding structures, and other factors.

At sites closer to centers of work and other activities, rents rise to offset the advantages of transportation cost savings at those locations. For example, if you live far out in the suburbs and must commute 30 miles one way to work every day, you'll spend a lot on gasoline or transportation fares. Other things being equal, you'd be willing to pay higher monthly rent for an identical site and home only 5 miles from the city center. Competition among land users tends to bid rent up at more central sites to compensate for the advantage of transportation cost savings.

Consider two parcels of land in a region. One parcel is located 2 miles due north of the city center. The other parcel is 5 miles due south of the city center. There are 50 usable acres at the first site and 40 usable acres at the second site.

The graphs in Box 5 show how the rent per acre is established at each of these locations. The graph labeled **A** shows that four different types of users are interested

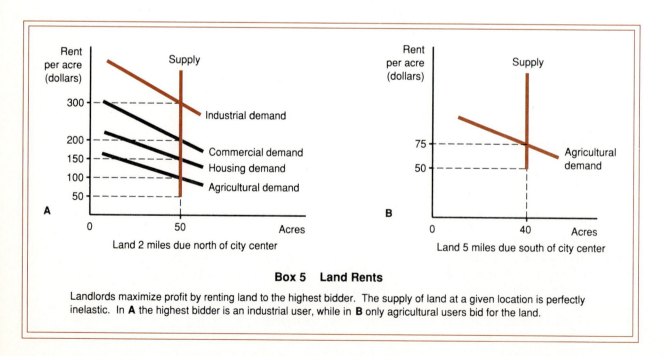

Box 5   Land Rents

Landlords maximize profit by renting land to the highest bidder. The supply of land at a given location is perfectly inelastic. In **A** the highest bidder is an industrial user, while in **B** only agricultural users bid for the land.

in the land located north of the city. The four demand curves show the maximum rent each of these users would pay per acre per month. The minimum rent the landowner will accept is $50 per acre per month. The four competing uses indicated by the four demand curves are agriculture, housing, commerce (such as retailing), and industry (a factory). The rent per acre offered in each use depends on the monthly marginal revenue product of the land to the user. Farmers offer $100 per acre per month for the fixed supply of 50 acres. The site has a marginal revenue product of $150 per acre in housing. This means a developer estimates that if developed as an apartment complex, the 50-acre site would generate a marginal revenue product of $150 per acre per month. In commercial use, a developer estimates that establishment of a retail shopping center on the 50 acres would generate a marginal revenue product of $200 per acre per month. Finally, an industrial user considering the site as a place to build a new factory estimates the marginal revenue product to be $300 per acre per month. To what use is the land put? The landowner naturally rents to the highest bidder. This happens to be the industrial user. The land therefore is leased to be used as a factory site. Of course, instead of leasing the land, the company building the factory could purchase it outright. The purchaser would thus become the landowner and would retain the land in industrial use because no competing user would be willing to pay more per acre in rent.

In Box 5, **B** shows the market for land use at the southern site. The only users interested in the land there are farmers. The rent is therefore $75 per acre per month for the 40 acres at that site. This is the rent corresponding to the intersection of agricultural demand and the supply of land at that site. If land were mobile, owners of land 5 miles south would move their land to the location 2 miles north of the city to earn the higher rents. The supply of land at various sites would adjust until rents were equal at all locations. Of course, this cannot happen. The land is fixed. It cannot be moved. Differences in land rents are the rule, not the exception, in land markets. Each site at each location has its own unique characteristics that affect its rent and therefore its price. Only a change in demand at that site can change the rent. The price that will be paid to purchase rather than rent a parcel of land also depends on the marginal revenue product per acre. In general, the higher the marginal revenue product per acre to a particular user, the higher both the rent and the price the user would pay for outright purchase of the site.

The rent for land changes whenever the demand for land changes. The demand for land changes when the marginal revenue product from using it changes. For example, in the early 1980s prices plummeted for agricultural commodities such as grains. This decreased the marginal revenue product of agricultural land. Not surprisingly, the result was a sharp drop in agricultural rents and land prices.

Taxing Land Rents

Suppose the government were to estimate the market rent of land and tax it away irrespective of whether the owners or renters used the land. Landlords couldn't avoid the tax. They couldn't reduce the amount of land available. It would be in their interest to rent the land at the market rent per acre to generate the revenue to pay the tax.

The tax on land rents wouldn't cause an increase in market rents. This is because the rent could increase only if land were made scarcer as a result of the tax. Because there's a fixed supply of land, the quantity supplied can't decrease in response to a decrease in the after-tax rent earned by landlords.

Because of the factors just cited, the land tax is a very efficient source of revenue. Henry George, a noted nineteenth-century advocate of land taxes, proposed levying very high taxes on the market rent of land and doing away with other taxes. George reasoned that the tax on land rents would have no effect on the use to which land was put. Landlords would have no choice but to rent the land to the highest bidder to generate the revenue to pay the tax based on the market rent. Because a tax on land rents still encourages landlords to rent their land to the user with the greatest willingness to pay, it would result in no loss in efficiency. This is because landlords would behave in the same way even in the absence of such a tax.

Land Use Conversion

Agricultural land is converted to housing, retailing, office, or industrial use when the marginal revenue product in these alternative uses rises above the marginal revenue product in agricultural uses. For example, a new road in an area might increase the marginal revenue product of industrial use of an agricultural land parcel. This occurs because the new road decreases the cost of getting materials to the site and the cost of delivering the firm's product to customers. This change in the area will increase the rent or price per acre that would be paid to use the land as the site of a factory.

Similarly, growth in the population of a neighboring city increases the demand for housing in the area. This increases the marginal revenue product of agricultural sites for housing developments. The graph in Box 6 shows how a change that results in a new demand for land induces farmers to rent or sell their land to others. The increased marginal revenue product of a current agricultural site in an alternative use results in a new bidder for the land. If the marginal revenue product of the land is now higher in housing or industrial use than it is in farming, the farmer would be better off renting the land to someone else or selling it. The graph in Box 6 shows that if the marginal revenue product for a 40-acre site south of the city rises to $100 per acre per month, then the land will be converted to housing use. This is because the farmer who owns the land can earn more per month by converting its use to housing than by farming. Unless the farmer gets a nonmonetary reward for farming that exceeds $25 per acre per month, he'll choose to convert his land from agricultural to housing use to enjoy the extra $25 per acre rent.

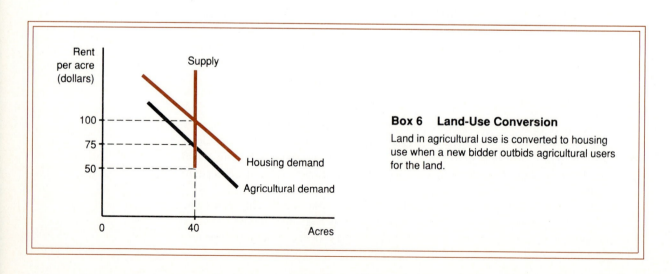

Box 6   Land-Use Conversion

Land in agricultural use is converted to housing use when a new bidder outbids agricultural users for the land.

Profit

The role of profits in the price system under perfect competition is an issue we discussed extensively earlier in the book. In a perfectly competitive system, economic profits are merely temporary rewards for innovations and for those entrepreneurs who anticipate changes in the pattern of consumer demand.

When discussing profit, we must be careful to distinguish between economic profit and normal profit. You'll recall that normal profit is a cost of production that equals the opportunity cost of all owner-supplied inputs. An important component of normal profit is the opportunity cost of owner-supplied funds used to acquire physical capital. This cost represents the interest income that stockholders and proprietors of business firms forgo by tying their own funds up in their business. When market interest rates are high, the normal profit is also high.

In the United States, corporate profits account for about 10% of the national income. The income earned by owners of proprietorships and partnerships comprises an additional 5% of national income. It therefore appears as though business profits account for 15% of national income. Beware, however: that appearance can be misleading!

The problem with the official statistics on profit is that they include both normal and economic profits. Much of the profit earned by corporations is really accounted for by the opportunity cost of owner-supplied funds. Similarly, much of the income earned by owners of sole proprietorships includes wages of owner-supplied labor and the opportunity cost of owner-supplied funds invested in the firm. Actual profits, as a percentage of national income, are therefore significantly lower than 15%. This also implies that official statistics on labor income and interest income understate the amounts actually earned because these statistics don't include imputed wages and interest earned by owners of business enterprises.

Sources of Economic Profit

Economic profits are only temporary rewards in competitive markets. However, when monopoly exists or when barriers to entry prevent new firms from entering markets, profits can be maintained over longer periods. The following sources of economic profit can be identified:

1. *Innovations and anticipation of consumer demands.* This is a source of short-term profit even under perfect competition. Those who market new products and are shrewd enough to predict changes in the pattern of consumer demand will earn temporary economic profits. Of course, under perfect competition, free entry will reduce these profits to zero in the long run. However, shrewd entrepreneurs continually shift their funds around to support expansion of growing industries while removing their funds from declining industries. This is what playing the stock market is all about! Investors with the skills to supply funds to finance expansion of industries with the right ideas at the right time can turn temporary profits into a permanent source of income. Financial support of those who innovate represents the drive that keeps the capitalist system moving.

2. *Risk taking.* Innovations more often than not involve risks. Profit can be regarded as a payment to entrepreneurs for taking risks. As you're well aware, not everyone who plays the stock market succeeds in making a profit. Only a few shrewd or lucky investors strike it rich by always buying the stock of the

right company just as that company begins to earn economic profits, and then selling it just when those profits fall to zero. There are thousands of other investors who make little profit or lose money by taking risks. In effect, investing and starting new enterprises are a bit like gambling. The rewards can be viewed as profits.

3. *Exercise of monopoly power.* The exercise of monopoly power can be a source of long-term profits in an industry. For this to be the case there must be a barrier to entry in the industry that prevents the market from becoming contestable. In monopolistic markets, barriers to entry result in profits that are more than temporary rewards for innovation. These profits are a source of concern to consumers and policymakers because they stem from prices that are higher than the marginal cost of producing goods. Increased competition can eliminate monopoly profits and result in net gains in well-being as production increases and prices fall to the minimum possible average cost. Often governments cooperate with firms to allow monopoly profits to be earned by granting exclusive franchises and enacting policies that set up barriers to entry in industries.

Concept Check

1 How does land differ from other productive inputs?

2 Show how competition among users of land determines land rents.

3 What are the sources of economic profit?

Summary

1. Interest is a payment for the use of funds. The interest rate represents the price of obtaining credit to make purchases.

2. Capital is an input created by people for the purpose of producing goods and services. The capital stock of a nation consists of equipment, materials, structures, tools, vehicles, and human skills that will last for a number of years. Physical capital stock, however, does wear out, and the rate at which it does so is called physical depreciation. Investment is the process of replenishing or adding to capital stock.

3. Savings is the amount of income that is not consumed in a given year and can be supplied to investors to help them purchase or create new capital. Specialized financial markets channel savings as loanable funds to those who wish to make investments.

4. An investment decision involves an outlay of funds today to acquire capital that will provide revenue over a period of time in the future. The market rate of interest must be compared with the marginal return on an investment to gauge the profitability of the investment. This involves estimating future increases in revenue from an investment and calculating the annual percentage return represented by that stream of returns based on the sum of money needed for the investment. A firm invests up to the point at which the marginal return on investment each year falls to the market rate of interest.

5. The interest rate is influenced by both the supply of loanable funds and the

demand for credit. Market demand for loanable funds is the sum of the quantities demanded by businesses, consumers, and governments at each possible interest rate. Savers generally require more than one dollar's worth of future consumption to compensate them for giving up a dollar's worth of current consumption. The quantity of loanable funds supplied tends to increase as interest rates go up. This is because people tend to save more as compensation increases for giving up current consumption in exchange for future consumption.

6. Risk measures the variation of actual outcomes from expected outcomes. The more variable the possible return on an investment, the greater the risk. A risk-averse investor is one who chooses the investment with less variation in return given a choice between two that have the same expected return.

7. Interest rates on loans and securities such as bonds vary with the characteristics of the loan or the borrower, the collateral pledged, and tax treatment of the interest. In general, the riskier the loan, the higher the interest rate.

8. Land is an immobile input. Rent is the price paid for the use of land. A major determinant of land rents is location. The more capital built up on land, the greater the marginal revenue product of the land parcel and the higher the rent.

9. Because land is in perfectly inelastic supply, a tax on rent for land in all uses will not make it any scarcer. Because the supply of land cannot decrease in response to a tax, a tax on land will not increase land rents. A landowner will bear the full brunt of a land tax and will not be able to raise rent to recoup the tax from tenants, provided all land is subject to the tax.

10. Changing demand for land use results in conversion of land from one use to another.

11. Economic profit is the return to entrepreneurship. It can result from innovations and anticipation of changes in consumer demand. Risk taking and the exercise of monopoly power can also explain profit.

Key Terms and Concepts

Rent	Discounted present value
Investment	Risk
Saving	Risk averse
Marginal return on investment	

Problems and Applications

1. List the capital that would be used in a retail store. What type of capital is used in an automobile factory? What capital equipment is used by an airline? What influences the rate of depreciation of the capital used by each of these firms?

2. Suppose you operate a shoe store. You're considering investing in a substantial increase in your inventory. The investment will involve an outlay of $100,000. You expect that this outlay will enable you to increase your revenue by $130,000 by the end of the year. The market rate of interest you must pay to borrow funds is 10%. Will you choose to make the investment?

   Suppose instead of the 10% interest rate in problem 2, the interest rate is 15%. Also suppose you anticipate a reduction in sales because of a general economic downturn during the year. As a result of the downturn you expect your $100,000 in inventory to move more slowly and therefore to generate only $110,000 in revenue by the end of the year. Will you still make the investment in new inventory?

4. Would your answers to problems 2 and 3 be different if instead of borrowing the money to finance the new inventory you used your own funds?

5. The best investment your family's textile firm can make in a certain year is calculated to yield a marginal return of 14% on the funds needed to acquire the new capital. Draw a graph to show that your textile firm won't make any investments at all if the market rate of interest is 15% that year. Show how a decrease in the interest rate to 10% will result in at least some investment by the firm.

6. The federal government borrows a significant amount of funds each year to cover its budget deficit. Because of the considerable amount of credit required to finance the deficit, the government cannot be regarded as a price taker in credit markets. Use a graph to show the impact on the market rate of interest of a significant increase in the government's demand for loanable funds.

7. Use a graph to show how the market demand for loanable funds can be derived from the demand curves for credit by business, household, and government borrowers. Show how the increase in demand for credit by the federal government you showed in answer to problem 6 affects the *quantity of loanable funds demanded* by households and by businesses.

8. The current interest rate paid on unsecured personal loans is 15%. The interest rate on 30-year U.S. Treasury bonds is 8%. What accounts for the 7-percentage-point spread between these two types of loans?

9. Municipal zoning laws control land use in a city by specifying the types of uses to which land parcels in various locations can be put. The goal cited in zoning is often to allow the "highest and best use" for land. How does the marketplace determine the "highest and best use" for a parcel of land? Suppose the maximum rent offered for land in an area of the city bordering a residential subdivision is $1,000 per acre per year. This bid is by an industrial user. The next highest bid is $800 per acre per year by a user who plans to build apartments on the site. Suppose you're the owner of this parcel of land and a zoning law is proposed that will prevent use of the land by industry. If you owned 1,000 acres in the area, would you support the zoning law?

10. Use a graph to show how increased demand for housing as a city grows is likely to result in conversion of land from agricultural to housing uses.

Suggested Readings

William J. Baumol, *The Stock Market and Economic Efficiency,* New York: Fordham University Press, 1965. This is a classic analysis of the role of the stock market in allocating resources.

David N. Hyman, *Modern Microeconomics: Analysis and Applications,* 2nd ed., Homewood, Ill.: Richard D. Irwin, Inc., 1989. Chapter 15 contains a more technical analysis of investment decisions, savings decisions, and interest rates.

Burton G. Malkiel, *A Random Walk Down Wall Street,* New York: W.W. Norton & Co., 1973. This is an analysis of variation in corporate stock prices and the difficulties involved in forecasting changes in stock prices.

William G. Nickels, *Understanding Business,* St. Louis: Times Mirror/Mosby, 1987. Chapters 21-23 discuss practical aspects of financial management and both corporate and personal finance.

A Forward Look

The distribution of income is never perfectly equal. Some people are rich and others are poor. In the following chapter we investigate income inequality in the United States. The startling fact is that a substantial portion of the U.S. population is officially classified as living in poverty. In the next chapter we also discuss poverty in the United States and the programs designed to alleviate it.

The Distribution of Income and the Economics of Poverty

"Standard of living" is a term almost everyone hears, sees, and uses in conversation—but what does it really mean?

Your standard of living, measured in terms of the goods and services you can enjoy over a given period, is largely determined by your income. The distribution of well-being among people in a nation is influenced by the distribution of ownership of capital, land, and natural resources, and the distribution of talents, skills, and abilities. Resource owners' incomes also depend on their willingness to sell the services of their inputs to others and on the market prices of those inputs. In the previous four chapters we've seen how the prices of the services of economic resources are determined and how those who take risks and innovate earn profits. One of our major objectives in this chapter is to analyze the facts about the *differences in annual income* among people in a nation.

In every country there's significant variation in people's annual incomes. In the United States, as in other parts of the world, some people live in luxury while others earn barely enough income to survive. Some people are fortunate enough to inherit capital and land that provide them with nonlabor income. Many other people couldn't survive without cash assistance through government programs or charity. In all nations there's considerable *inequality* of income among individuals.

Income inequality isn't necessarily an undesirable outcome. If everyone were guaranteed the same income by government authorities no matter how hard they worked or how they employed their nonlabor resources, the incentive to use resources in the most productive way would be impaired. A reduction in income inequality through government policies can therefore cause reductions in total national production. The familiar tradeoff between equity and efficiency is never more obvious than when policies are considered to distribute income more equally.

Although few people would support programs to ensure income equality, many people do support programs to increase the incomes of the poorest individuals in a society. In the United States, federal government statistics classified nearly 15% of the population as living in poverty in the mid-1980s. This means these people's annual money income, including government cash assistance, was less than the amounts government authorities estimated as necessary for a minimum standard of living. As you'll see in this chapter, the actual measurement of poverty is a controversial subject. In any case, a major criticism of the U.S. economy is that it cannot eliminate the paradox of poverty in the midst of affluence. Despite an array of government programs seeking to alleviate poverty, it remains a serious social problem whose causes must be understood before it can be eliminated.

After reading this chapter, you should be able to: *Concept Preview*

1   Discuss the facts about income distribution in the United States.
2   Document the extent of poverty in the United States.
3   Discuss government assistance programs to the poor and the impact of these programs on incentives and well-being of recipients.
4   Explain the causes of income inequality and evaluate the impact of policies designed to reduce poverty and alter income distribution.

Income Inequality in the United States

On average, the standard of living of American citizens has improved vastly since the 1950s. The median income of married couples increased from $4,599 per year in 1955 to approximately $30,000 in 1987. Adjusting for the effects of inflation, this represents an increase of more than 30% in living standards. This means that on average the income earned by a married couple in the United States in 1987 bought about one third more goods and services than it did in 1955!

A median income of $30,000 for married couples means half of the married couples in the country earned *less* than that sum and half earned more. Data on the *distribution* of total income earned indicate the variation in standards of living within the nation. From these data we can learn the percentage of U.S. citizens earning very low incomes and the percentage earning very high incomes. Once we have such information we can make judgments about policies designed to alter the distribution of income. This helps us evaluate the *equity* or fairness of an economic system with respect to the distribution of well-being.

Income Shares

How unequal is the distribution of money income in the United States? The facts show that there's considerable inequality in income among households. One way we can see this is to divide all families into groups ranked according to actual income earned. We can then compare the percentages of *total money income* of these groups. A family is defined for statistical purposes as a group of two or more persons related by birth, marriage, or adoption and residing together in a household.

The first group will be the one fifth of families with the lowest incomes in the nation. The second group will be the one fifth of families with the second lowest incomes. In this way we can divide the population into five groups, with the fifth group including only those families with the highest annual money incomes.

The table in Box 1 shows the share of total money income of each fifth of households in the United States for selected years from 1947 to 1984. Money income includes all labor earnings, nonlabor earnings, and cash payments, including welfare assistance to the poor and Social Security pensions. The data reveal significant and persistent income inequality in the United States. If income were equally distributed, each one fifth of the population would account for exactly one fifth, or 20%, of total national income. Instead the lowest one fifth of families—the poorest fifth—accounted for less than 5% of money income in 1984. The highest or richest fifth of families accounted for nearly 43% of money income! In other words, the richest 20% of the families in the United States have annual incomes that exceed those of the poorest 20% by almost nine times! Similarly, the fifth of the population with the second lowest income enjoys total annual income twice that of the poorest fifth. There's even a wide gap between the poor and the near poor! The third or middle-income fifth enjoys an annual income more than three times that of the poorest fifth. Finally, the fourth fifth, representing the upper-middle income group, enjoys five times the annual income of the poorest fifth. Also note that the highest fifth enjoys about as much income as the middle- and upper-middle income groups combined.

One other interesting fact stands out from the data in Box 1. *The distribution of money income shares among the five segments of the population has been remarkably stable from 1947 to 1984.* This observation needs to be qualified in two ways. First, the data in Box 1 don't include the value of government assistance to the lowest-income groups in the form of food and medical care. Second, the data don't include the influence of taxes on disposable income. Soon we'll discuss these two factors and estimate their effects.

Box 1 Percentage Share of Aggregate Money Income of Each One Fifth of Families, Selected Years, 1947–1984

Year	Lowest fifth	Second fifth	Third fifth	Fourth fifth	Highest fifth
1947	5.0	11.9	17.0	23.1	43.0
1967	4.0	11.1	17.6	24.6	42.7
1969	4.1	11.0	17.5	24.5	42.8
1971	4.1	10.7	17.3	24.5	43.4
1973	4.3	10.6	17.2	24.4	43.5
1974	4.4	10.6	17.0	24.5	43.5
1976	4.3	10.4	17.0	24.7	43.6
1978	4.3	10.3	16.9	24.7	43.9
1983	3.9	10.0	16.5	24.6	45.0
1984	4.7	11.0	17.0	24.4	42.9

Source: U.S. Department of Commerce, Bureau of the Census, *Money Income of Households in the United States*, Current Population Reports, Series P-60, various years.

The Lorenz Curve

A **Lorenz curve** is a plotting of data showing the percentage of income enjoyed by each percentage of households ranked according to their incomes. A Lorenz curve can be plotted directly from the data in Box 1. The vertical axis plots the percentage of national income, with the scale running from zero to 100. The horizontal axis plots the percentage of families ranked according to their amount of income. In the graph in Box 2, the curve is enclosed in a square. The first point on the curve is the origin. This is because zero percent of the families naturally earn zero percent of national income. The last point in the box corresponds to point Z with coordinates of 100% on both axes. At point Z, 100% of families naturally account for 100% of national income. The other points in the box correspond to the data in Box 1. For example, point A indicates that the lowest 20% of families had only 4.7% of income in 1984. To see this, go from the point on the horizontal axis corresponding to 20% up to the Lorenz curve. Then draw a horizontal line to the vertical axis and note that it intersects that axis at 4.7%.

Lorenz curve:
A plotting of data showing the percentage of income enjoyed by each percentage of households ranked according to their incomes.

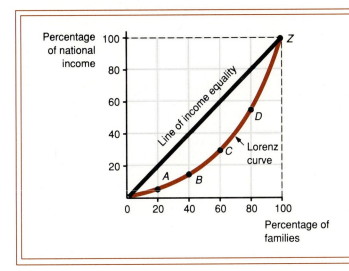

Box 2   Lorenz Curve for the United States, 1984

The horizontal axis shows the percentages of families ranked according to their annual income. The points on the Lorenz curve show the percentage of national income earned by each cumulative percentage of families in the United States.

The other points on the curve are a bit trickier to interpret. Go first to point B. This point corresponds to 40% on the horizontal axis and 15.7% on the vertical axis. This means that the cumulative share of income going to the families in the lowest 40% of the population is 4.7% + 11.0%, which equals 15.7%. Similarly, point C shows the cumulative share going to the lowest 60% of the population, which equals 32.7%. Finally, point D corresponds to the cumulative share of national income going to the lowest 80% of families. The graph shows that this corresponds to 57.1% of national income. It follows that the richest 20% of families earn (100% − 57.1%) of income, which is 42.9%. As you can see, this agrees with the data in Box 1.

What would the Lorenz curve look like if there were no income inequality? Absence of income inequality means that each 20% of the population earns exactly 20% of income. If this were the case, 40% of the population would earn 40% of national income, 60% of the population would earn 60% of the income, and 80% of the population would earn 80% of the income. The Lorenz curve would therefore be a diagonal line through the square, called the *line of income equality.* The lower the position of the Lorenz curve with respect to the line of income equality, the less equal the income distribution in a nation.

Is Affluence on the Rise? The Declining Middle Class and the Impact of Two-Earner Families

To Americans who grew up in the 1950s and 1960s, "middle class" probably described most people they knew, including themselves. Back then, the middle class was a comfortable cloak worn by just about everyone from President Eisenhower to Beaver Cleaver. Today's middle class wears a noticeably different face. Let's look at how it's changed and consider some of the implications of the changes.

In 1985, families earning between $15,000 and $38,000 accounted for 39% of all income in the United States. Although this is a substantial chunk of total income, it represents a significant decline in the share earned in past years by the middle-income group. In 1970 the group of families represented by the same income class accounted for 46% of income, after adjustment for inflation. It appears that more American families are moving into the upper-income classes while the ranks of the middle-income classes are declining.

In the 1980s the two-earner household became commonplace. Households in which both husband and wife pull in a salary have increased the well-being of many families. For example, if a husband and wife both work and earn a fairly modest $24,000 each per year, their total family income of $48,000 would just put them into the *top fifth* of all families ranked according to income in 1985.

The table shows the median income for selected groups of families in 1985. For all families the median income was $27,735 in that year. This means that half of all families earned more than this amount while half earned less. The median income for families in which both the husband and wife worked was $36,431 per year. On the other hand, the median income for families in which only the husband worked was $24,556. Note that the median *female-headed* family with no husband earned an income of $13,660, which was about half the median income of all families in 1985. The median family headed by college graduates earned $46,423, which is 67% more than the median income of all families.

The trend toward two-earner families has been growing, and the salaries earned by women have been increasing. More and more women are entering the professions and securing managerial positions. Women currently account for 20% of all physicians, and this figure is likely to increase because one third of all students in medical school are females. Because high-income men tend to marry high-income women, this tends to increase the ranks of the families in the top fifth of the income distribution.[*]

Rising divorce rates and increases in the number of women having children out of wedlock tend to swell the ranks of the poor, who constitute the lowest fifth of the income distribution. The Census Bureau estimated that half of the 7.2 million poor families in the United States in 1985 were headed by females with no husband. The unfortunate consequence of this development is a higher proportion of children living in poverty. About 20% of all children lived in poverty in 1985 compared to 15% of all children in 1970.

The growth in the number of upper-income families also has implications for the marketing of products. More firms are developing products that appeal to upper-income groups. Luxury goods and foods were selling briskly in the mid-1980s, while firms that catered to middle-income groups were experiencing trouble. For example, Sears, Roebuck had a clientele with average income close to the median of all families. Sears' market share has declined in recent years. Stores like Gimbels in New York City, which also catered to the middle-income group, suffered such a decline in sales in the 1980s that they closed down.[†] Let's hope that the newly affluent will retain enough of their taste for bargains that a few discount stores will survive!

Median Family Income by Family Group, 1985

Group	Income
All families	$27,735
Married couples, both spouses working	36,431
Female-headed family, no husband present	13,660
Families headed by college graduate	46,423

Source: U.S. Bureau of the Census.

[*]See David Wessel, "Growing Gap: U.S. Rich and Poor Increase in Number; Middle Loses Ground," *The Wall Street Journal,* September 22, 1986.

[†]Wessel, *Wall Street Journal.*

Economic policies can be used to reduce the degree of income inequality in a nation. Taxes that take proportionately more from the rich than the poor can result in an after-tax Lorenz curve that's closer to the line of income equality. Programs that provide cash assistance to the poor can increase the income shares going to the lowest fifth of the population and also move the Lorenz curve in the direction of income equality.

Income inequality in the United States appears to be more pronounced than in other countries, such as Japan, Sweden, and socialist and communist nations.

Distribution of Families Earning Incomes in Various Ranges

Another way we can gauge inequality of income is to look at the percentages of families that earn income within certain ranges. This gives each family a way to see how it fares financially relative to other families. In 1984 the median family income in the United States was $26,433. This means that half the families enjoyed *more* than this annual money income while half enjoyed less. The table in Box 3 shows that 15.8% of families had annual incomes over $50,000 in 1984. On the other hand, only 5% of families had less than $5,000 income that year.

Box 3 Percentage Distribution of Family Money Income in the United States, 1984

Annual income level (dollars)	Percentage of families
Under 5,000	5.0
5,000 – 9,999	9.4
10,000 – 14,999	10.8
15,000 – 19,999	10.8
20,000 – 24,999	10.7
25,000 – 34,999	19.0
35,000 – 49,999	18.4
50,000 and over	15.8

Source: U.S. Department of Commerce, Bureau of the Census, *Statistical Abstract of the United States*, 1986.

To see where your family stood in terms of money income relative to other families in 1984, compare your family's 1984 income with the data in the table. For example, if your family had 1984 pretax income of $50,000, you enjoyed higher income than was received by 84.2% of the U.S. population! This is because only 15.8% of families, as shown in Box 3, had a 1984 income of $50,000 and over.

Concept Check

1 If the median income of married couples in the United States is $30,000, what can you conclude about the distribution of income?

2 What information is conveyed by points on a Lorenz curve?

3 Explain why the Lorenz curve for the United States is not a straight line.

The Economics of Poverty

The most unpleasant social consequence of income inequality is poverty. In 1985 there were 33 million Americans—a number corresponding to 14% of the entire population—officially listed as living in poverty! The human misery endured by poor families is a source of concern to all of us. However, in designing policies to cope with poverty and improve circumstances for the poor, care must be taken to avoid removing incentives of the poor to work and seek training and education to make themselves more productive.

In discussing the social issues relating to poverty, we must look into both the causes and consequences of poverty. We must also come to grips with the inevitable tradeoff between equity and efficiency involved in aiding the poor.

Defining Poverty and Measuring Its Extent

What is poverty? The standards for considering a person poor vary from one society to another. Similarly, the standards of poverty vary over time. The standard of living of even the poorest U.S. citizens is much higher than that of average citizens of many Asian, African, and Latin American nations. Also, the standard of living of the poorest people in the United States today is much higher than that of the poorest Americans living 100 years ago. Many poor Americans today enjoy electricity, central heating, television, radio, and a diversified diet, all of which would have been inconceivable to poor, and even nonpoor, Americans during the 1890s!

Poverty income threshold:
The income level below which a person or family is classified as being poor.

The federal government classifies a person as poor if his or her income is lower than three times the annual cost of a diet that is considered *minimally acceptable*. Based on prices for food prevailing in 1984, the cost of this minimal diet for a family with two adults and two school-age children was $2.32 per person per day. If you multiply the cost of this diet by 3, you obtain the poverty income threshold that prevailed in 1984. The **poverty income threshold** is the income level below which a person or family is classified as being poor. For example, the poverty income threshold for a four-person family was $2.32 × 3, or about $7 per person per day in 1984. The total daily income required by this family to avoid being considered poor is $28 per day. Based on 1984 prices, therefore, the family would have needed an annual income of $28 × 365, which equals about $10,220 per year, to avoid being considered poor. The poverty income threshold for a family of four in 1986 was $11,203. In 1986 a single person under age 65 would have been considered poor if his annual income was less than $5,701. The poverty income threshold is adjusted each year for the effects of inflation.

The table in Box 4 shows the number of people and percentage of the population classified as poor from 1959 to 1985 according to the definition just given. In computing the number of people living in poverty *only cash income is used, including government cash assistance to the poor*. The cash value of special services available to the poor, such as food stamps, free medical assistance, and government-financed rent reductions, is *not* included in income.

The table in Box 4 shows that there was a sharp drop in the number of people classified as poor from 1959 to 1985. In 1959 nearly 40 million Americans, amounting to 22.4% of the population, were classified as poor. In 1985 there were 34 million poor Americans, or 14% of the population. However, a disturbing increase in the number and percentage of the population classified as poor has occurred since 1980. In part this trend reflects cutbacks in government cash assistance programs to the poor since 1980.

Box 4 Persons Below the Poverty Level, 1959–1985

Year	Number	Percentage of population
1959	39,490,000	22.4
1960	39,851,000	22.2
1961	39,628,000	21.9
1962	38,625,000	21.0
1963	36,436,000	19.5
1964	36,055,000	19.0
1965	33,185,000	17.3
1966	28,510,000	14.7
1967	27,769,000	14.2
1968	25,389,000	12.8
1969	24,147,000	12.1
1970	25,420,000	12.6
1971	25,559,000	12.5
1972	24,460,000	11.9
1973	22,973,000	11.1
1974	23,370,000	11.2
1975	25,877,000	12.3
1976	24,975,000	11.8
1977	24,720,000	11.6
1978	24,497,000	11.4
1979	26,072,000	11.7
1980	29,272,000	13.0
1981	31,822,000	14.0
1982	34,398,000	15.0
1983	35,266,000	15.2
1984	33,700,000	14.4
1985	33,064,000	14.0

Source: U.S. Bureau of the Census, *Characteristics of the Population Below the Poverty Level*, Current Population Reports, Series P-60, various years.

Although they indicate considerable progress in reducing poverty since 1959, the official statistics *understate* the actual progress. This is because, as observed earlier, the official statistics don't include *noncash* benefits that many poor people receive from the federal government. If an estimate of the *cash value* of food stamps, medical services, and subsidized housing is included in income, a Census Bureau study has indicated that the poverty rate in the United States would fall to as low as 10% of the population.[1]

Who Are the Poor?

The incidence of poverty in the United States is higher among blacks and people of Spanish origin than among whites. In 1984, 11.5% of all white people were classified as poor. However, in that year 33.8% of all black people and 28.4% of all Hispanics were classified as poor. In the 1980s the incidence of poverty among these minority groups was nearly three times as high as among whites.

[1]See U.S. Department of Commerce, Bureau of the Census, Public Information Office, Release No. CB84-30, February 24, 1984.

The incidence of poverty for people living in families headed by a female with no husband present is also much higher than average. In 1984, 34% of the people living in such households were classified as poor. The incidence of poverty among children is also higher than the average for the entire population. In 1984 slightly over 20% of the children in the United States were classified as poor.

The population group that has shown the greatest advances in reducing its rate of poverty in recent years is the elderly. In 1959 over 35% of all people over age 65 were classified as poor. In 1985 only 12.4% of the people in this age group were poor. The great strides against poverty made by the elderly are mainly the result of improved pension benefits, particularly those enjoyed under Social Security.

Finally, the incidence of poverty declines with increases in the head of household's years of schooling. In 1984 over 25% of people with fewer than 8 years of schooling were classified as poor. However, only 9.5% of those with 12 years of schooling were poor, and only 4.8% of people with at least 1 year of college were poor.

To sum up, on average in the United States, whites are less likely to be poor than blacks and Hispanics. Women with children but no husband are much more likely to be poor than other people. Children are more likely to be poor, and the elderly are slightly less likely to be poor. A person with more education is less likely to be poor than is a person with less education.

Government Assistance to the Poor

There's reason for all of us to be concerned about the problem of poverty. One way to cope with it is through private charity. Religious institutions and philanthropic organizations have traditionally tried to raise funds to benefit the poor. However, many people don't contribute to charity in the hope or belief that others will help the poor. Because of this "let George do it" attitude, charitable contributions are an unreliable means of assisting the poor. Charitable contributions are also unstable. This is because in periods of decreased employment and income, when the number of poor is likely to increase, the ability and willingness of others to contribute is likely to decline.

The unreliability of private charity has led government to establish programs to assist the poor. People support such programs for a number of reasons:

1. They believe there are benefits to all when the number of poor in the society is reduced. A society with masses of poor people is ripe for revolution and turmoil. Most people are well aware of this and support government programs to ensure that everyone has a certain minimum standard of living. In addition, most people have genuine compassion for the poor and support programs of assistance on humanitarian grounds.
2. Programs of assistance to the poor are viewed as "safety nets," providing assurance to everyone that their standard of living won't fall below minimally acceptable levels. If they should experience a catastrophe in their life that sends them into poverty, people know that their support of poverty assistance programs would provide benefits to them.

Eligibility for Government Assistance to the Poor in the United States

In the United States, the government programs that have emerged to assist the poor have strict eligibility standards. These standards, although subject to guidelines set by the federal government, vary from state to state. **Welfare programs** are government programs designed to assist the poor in the United States who are unable to work. The groups eligible for such assistance include the disabled, the aged, and families with dependent children headed by females or disabled males. Single people without dependent children, even if they are poor, are not eligible for the major programs of government assistance if they are not also disabled or elderly. Similarly, able-bodied males heading a family are not usually eligible for government assistance.

People in the groups just mentioned become eligible for assistance if their income is below certain levels. A **means test** establishes the fact that people in the groups eligible for welfare payments have incomes and property below the amounts that are minimally acceptable. People who are in the eligible groups and also pass the means test are *automatically entitled to government assistance*. Government welfare programs are sometimes called *entitlement programs* because people are entitled to benefits if they pass the means test and meet eligibility requirements.

Welfare programs:
Government programs to assist the poor in the United States who are unable to work.

Means test:
Establishes the fact that people in the groups eligible for welfare payments have incomes and property below the amounts that are minimally acceptable.

Federal Programs to Aid the Poor in the United States

Federal programs to assist the poor in the United States can be divided into two broad categories: programs of *cash* assistance and programs of *in-kind* assistance. The first type of program simply provides eligible people with financial support in the form of money income. The recipients can spend their welfare checks as they please. The second type of program provides those who qualify with services or assistance to purchase a certain good or service. Some in-kind assistance allows eligible people to rent government-supplied housing at a reduced price. People must pass a means test to be eligible for benefits from these programs. The following programs are specifically designed to aid the poor:

1. *Major programs of cash assistance.* There are two major programs of cash assistance (or transfers) to the poor in the United States: *Aid to Families with Dependent Children* (AFDC) and *Supplemental Security Income* (SSI).

The first program is designed mainly to aid families headed by one parent, usually a female, that have dependent children. The program is jointly run and funded by the federal government and state governments. On average the federal government bears about 54% of the cost of AFDC payments. Eligibility requirements and the actual amount of cash assistance under this program vary from state to state.

Under the AFDC program, there's a maximum benefit in each state for workers who have no earnings. As a recipient earns income after a certain point, welfare payments decline. In 1987 the maximum cash benefit for a family of four ranged from $144 per month in Mississippi to $833 per month in Alaska. As a percentage of the estimated median monthly income of a family of four, payments ranged from a low of 6.6% in Alabama to a high of 26% in New York and California. There were 11 million people, representing one third of the country's poor, receiving benefits under the AFDC program in 1987.

You should observe that these AFDC benefits are modest compared to the poverty income level. For example, a family consisting of a mother and two dependent children receiving the maximum average benefit under AFDC would have had a cash income of $4,600 in 1987, which was only slightly more than half of the 1987 poverty income threshold of approximately $8,800 for a family of three.

The second major program of cash assistance to the poor, Supplemental Security Income, is federally funded and benefits the aged, the blind, and the disabled. In

1984 the maximum SSI benefit paid to a single person with zero earnings was $314 per month, while a married couple received $472 per month. In 1984, 3.4 million people received aid under the SSI program. This represented less than 10% of the people classified as poor in that year.

2. *Major programs of in-kind assistance.* Government in the United States each year pays out more to eligible poor people in the form of in-kind assistance or transfers as opposed to cash benefits. For example, total cash assistance to the poor in 1986 through the AFDC and SSI programs amounted to $20 billion. In that same year, in-kind assistance, chiefly in the form of programs to help the poor acquire medical services, food, and housing, totaled $55 billion. The three major government programs of in-kind assistance to the poor in the United States are:

Medicaid. This is a program that pays for medical services to eligible poor people under age 65 who pass a means test. Everyone who receives cash benefits from AFDC and SSI is automatically eligible for Medicaid.

Medicaid has been the single most expensive of all government programs to aid the poor in the United States. In 1986 outlays by federal and state governments to pay for Medicaid amounted to nearly $25 billion.

Food Stamps. This is a federally financed program administered by state governments that provides the poor with stamps that can be redeemed for food and related items. The cash value of the stamps received varies with the eligible recipient's earned income. The maximum value of stamps received by a family of four in 1984 was $264 per month. In 1986 federal outlays for food stamps were $12.6 billion.

Housing Assistance. A number of federally financed programs provide subsidies to help the poor pay for housing. The programs include government-provided housing at subsidized rents and payments to assist people who rent private housing. These programs provided $11.6 billion worth of housing assistance to the poor in

Box 5   Major Federal Government Expenditures to Provide Income Support to Aid the Poor, Fiscal Year 1986

	Billions of dollars	Percentage of total
Cash transfers		
AFDC	9.9	12.9
SSI	10.2	13.3
Other	1.8	2.3
Subtotal	21.9	
In-kind transfers		
Medicaid	24.6	32.0
Food stamps	12.6	16.4
Nutrition programs	6.2	8.1
Housing subsidies	11.6	15.1
Subtotal	55.0	
Total federal assistance to the poor under major programs	76.9	

Source: Budget of the United States Government, Fiscal Year 1988.

1986. However, this level of expenditure wasn't sufficient to provide benefits to all eligible people. Only one person in four eligible for housing assistance actually receives benefits. There are often long waiting lists to obtain government-subsidized public housing.

The table in Box 5 summarizes the major cash and in-kind assistance programs available in the United States to people who pass a means test.

Impact of Government Assistance on Incentives and Well-Being of the Poor

Cash and in-kind assistance from government or other sources raise the standard of living of the poor people who receive the aid. However, the availability of welfare payments can reduce the incentives of recipients to work. The availability of in-kind assistance can distort choices made by the poor in ways that cause losses in efficiency.

There are two ways that government assistance programs can decrease work incentives. First, the programs provide income to recipients *independent of work*. This means the poor know they can survive without working. Naturally, this gives some people an incentive to work less and encourages others to refuse offers of work so they can be eligible for government assistance. In the United States, this effect is minimized by limiting welfare payments to those groups that are least likely to be in the labor force. These are children and their mothers in single-parent families, the elderly, and the disabled. In addition, the actual level of cash assistance received by eligible people is quite low. In most cases the assistance is not sufficient to raise recipients' incomes to levels that exceed the poverty income threshold. For those able to work, incentive still exists to earn more to raise their standard of living above the poverty level.

Second, because both in-kind and cash benefits are *reduced* as the earnings of recipients increase, the poor are subjected to a trap that makes it hard for them to get ahead by working. For example, under the AFDC program, welfare mothers are allowed to earn a modest amount of income per month, usually in the range of $100 to $125, without any reduction in their welfare benefits. *After more than this amount is earned, the cash benefits received under AFDC are reduced by 67¢ for each $1 of earnings.* The welfare recipient is also subject to some taxes when she works, and in most cases benefits under other programs, such as food stamps, are reduced as her earnings increase. This means that for each dollar of earnings, her net increase in income is often as little as 20¢ because of the reduction in welfare payments! Would you be eager to work if you could keep only 20¢ of each dollar you earned?

The Welfare Trap: An Illustration

Imagine you're the head of a household receiving welfare benefits. If you're a typical recipient, you're a single mother with three dependent children, you don't work, and you receive a cash benefit of $400 per month in 1986 dollars, or $4,800 per year. This sum is approximately equal to the average annual cash payment received in 1986 by families of four eligible for Aid to Families with Dependent Children. You'd also be eligible for food stamps that would buy about $2,400 worth of food in 1986, assuming you had zero earnings and thus received the maximum dollar amount of food stamps. Medicaid benefits, which have an estimated cash value of

$2,400 per year, would raise the sum of your cash income and the estimated value of in-kind benefits to $9,600. You might also be eligible for other government programs, such as free school lunches or subsidized housing, which would push your total income over $10,000. Note, however, that if you were eligible only for Aid to Families with Dependent Children, Medicaid, and food stamps, your annual income, assuming no work, would still be below the poverty threshold. These benefits vary from state to state. However, on average welfare recipients don't receive enough government assistance to push them over the poverty threshold.

The data just given assume you don't work. What happens if you begin accepting part-time work? Keep in mind that if you're the typical welfare recipient, you lack the education, skills, and experience to qualify for high-paying jobs. The most you can hope for is a job paying a minimum wage of, say, $3.35 per hour. Most states will allow you to earn about $150 per month before they start reducing your welfare benefits. In addition, some federal programs in the past have given the poor earned income credits, a kind of subsidy for working. However, the most you can expect to earn before your welfare benefits start being reduced is about $1,200 per year.

After you earn the permissible maximum, your AFDC payments decline by 67¢ per dollar of earnings. You'll also have to pay some taxes on your wages. The dollar amount of food stamps you receive also eventually declines as your income increases. Finally, after you earn about $6,000 per year, your Medicaid benefits will be cut off! This means your real income declines by the $2,400 value of medical benefits as soon as you hit the Medicaid cutoff point.

After you reach a certain level of income, your total welfare benefits fall to zero and you're on your own. How well off will you be compared to when you didn't work at all? The answer is: not very. The table in Box 6 shows how you would fare as your earnings increased to various levels. The figures in this table are based on hypothetical but realistic data for the typical welfare recipient of the mid-1980s.

If you obtained part-time work during the year to earn $4,000, your cash payments from government would be only $2,000. You'd also have the privilege of paying taxes. Because there are generous deductions and exclusions under the income tax, the only actual tax you'd pay would be payroll taxes of $200. The food stamps you received would decline modestly to about $2,300 worth, and you'd still retain your Medicaid benefits. Your total real income after taxes would be $10,500.

Box 6 Earnings, Transfers, and Real Income for Welfare Recipients

Annual earnings	Cash payments from gov't.	Taxes [a]	Value of food stamps	Value of medical services (Medicaid)	Total income (including in-kind benefits)
0	4,800	0	2,400	2,400	9,600
4,000	2,000 [b]	200	2,300	2,400	10,500
6,000	100 [b]	400	2,200	0	7,900
8,000	250 [b]	550	1,800	0	9,500
10,000	0	1,000	1,200	0	10,200

[a] Includes Social Security taxes and some state income tax.
[b] Earned income credit paid at the end of the tax year.

Principles in Practice

Work for Welfare Recipients: Is It the Solution to the Welfare Mess?

A popular country-western song of the 1970s entitled "The Welfare Cadillac" detailed the lavish, free-spending life-style of welfare recipients who rolled up to the government payment window in Detroit's finest.

Although the song unquestionably was a mean-spirited exaggeration, it did capture the frustration of many Americans with a welfare system that just doesn't seem to be working.

Speaking of working, is this what welfare recipients should be doing? A number of people say "yes." Let's see why.

At a recent governors' conference, strong political support was expressed for the concept of "work for welfare." Under such a system, welfare recipients would have to do some type of work to continue receiving their welfare benefits. Budget cuts and other economy measures have the governors of the states, which pay part of the costs of the welfare programs, seeking a way to get people off welfare. Some supporters of government assistance to the poor like the idea of work for welfare because they believe it will increase political support for programs that aid the poor.

In a recent analysis of the work for welfare idea, Frank Levy and Richard Michel make some interesting observations about the people on welfare in the United States.* Any program of work for welfare must confront harsh facts. These facts are:

1. *The proportion of the lowest-income fifth of the families who work to provide themselves with at least some support has declined precipitously in recent years.* In 1959 the lowest fifth of families in the income distribution received 70% of their income from earnings. In 1983 earnings provided families in this group with only 42% of their income. This suggests that cash transfers have become the most important source of money income to the poor. Cuts in these programs will sharply reduce their already low standard of living.

2. *The dominant type of family on the welfare rolls is headed by a female.* In 1959 female-headed families accounted for only 23% of poor families. By 1984 this figure had doubled to 46%. To be able to work, these women must have child-care services. However, their low incomes make it difficult for them to afford such services. It's also highly likely that the AFDC program has increased the formation of female-headed families.

The proportion of females heading families who work at least some of the time during the year was 38% in 1984. Only 13% of these women currently work year round. Typically such women either work full time, dropping off welfare completely, or don't work at all. It's difficult to prove that the availability of welfare benefits is the chief cause of nonwork. Cash welfare benefits are quite low in many states.

3. *Welfare benefits diminish the incentive of females in poverty to marry.* Although welfare benefits are quite low, they're higher than the incomes that are earned by many men in the low-income groups. This suggests that young women find the alternative of going on welfare more attractive than marrying. Providing more job opportunities to low-income young men might be a fruitful way of getting women off the welfare rolls because this would give the poor more incentive to form two-parent families.

In evaluating a work for welfare plan, the ultimate question we must ask is: How much is it going to cost to put the poor to work? Training and government-supported child-care programs might end up costing more than the existing system of transfers unless they actually do succeed in turning welfare recipients into productive full-time workers!

*Frank S. Levy and Richard C. Michel, "Work for Welfare: How Much Good Will It Do?" *American Economic Review*, 76, 2, May 1986, pp. 399-404.

Your $4,000 annual earnings increase your actual income by only $900! This means that you really keep only one in four of the dollars you earn. How much incentive would you have to voluntarily accept part-time work under those circumstances?

Suppose you obtain a full-time job. Given your skills, you can't hope to earn more than $4 per hour. Let's say you earn $8,000 per year. That's enough income to make you ineligible for welfare payments. At the end of the tax year you'll still get from the government a modest payment of $250, called the earned income credit. You'd have about $550 in payroll taxes deducted from your pay. You'd still be eligible for $1,800 worth of food stamps, but your Medicaid benefits would be terminated! If you didn't receive employer-provided health insurance, you'd now be responsible for your own medical bills. Assuming you don't have health insurance, your real income after taxes is now $9,500. This is $100 less than your income when you didn't work at all!

The table in Box 6 also shows how you would fare with earned income of $6,000 and $10,000 per year under programs existing in the mid-1980s. As you can see, the welfare system is a bitter trap for those who are eligible. It's hard to get ahead by working. Recipients therefore are reluctant to accept jobs voluntarily. Some new policies adopted in the late 1980s *required* able-bodied welfare recipients to accept jobs so as to offset this lack of incentive to work.

Of course, the incentive to work could be increased if the welfare benefits weren't reduced as much as the poor began to work. However, this would greatly increase the number of welfare recipients and therefore increase the burden of taxes needed to pay for welfare programs.

Losses in Efficiency Caused by In-Kind Transfers

In addition to losses in production from reduced work incentives, welfare programs also can cause overconsumption of subsidized goods. Some in-kind welfare benefits, like food stamps, give eligible recipients the right to consume a certain amount of food per year. The cash these people would have spent on food thus is freed for other uses. If the value of food stamps is no more than the recipients would have spent on food anyway, then the stamps are just like cash to the recipients. However, if the recipients receive stamps whose cash value *exceeds* the amount they want to spend on food, then the stamps are worth *less* than their cash value to the recipients. In this case the recipients would be better off if they were able to sell the stamps for cash that they could use for items other than food. If the recipients do spend the entire value of the stamps on food, then some of them are forced by the program to spend more on food then they wish. The value of food stamps received by most recipients is at such a modest level, however, that most recipients would spend that much on food anyway. Economists therefore believe that the food-stamp program causes little if any overconsumption of food.

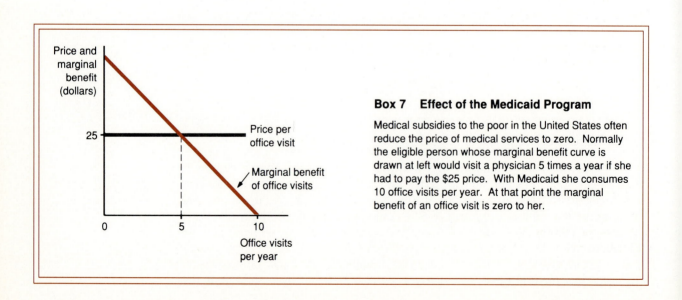

Box 7 Effect of the Medicaid Program

Medical subsidies to the poor in the United States often reduce the price of medical services to zero. Normally the eligible person whose marginal benefit curve is drawn at left would visit a physician 5 times a year if she had to pay the $25 price. With Medicaid she consumes 10 office visits per year. At that point the marginal benefit of an office visit is zero to her.

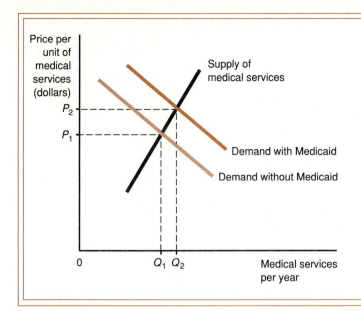

Box 8   The Effect of Medical Subsidies to the Poor on the Price of Medical Services

Medical subsidies to the poor that increase their consumption of medical care at any given price increase demand for those services. If the supply of medical services is upward sloping, this puts upward pressure on medical service prices. In the graph, Medicaid increases overall consumption of medical services from Q_1 to Q_2. The nonsubsidized price of a unit of medical service increases from P_1 to P_2.

The Medicaid program is fundamentally different in its effect on incentives than the food-stamp program. Rather than giving recipients the right to consume a certain amount of services, the program allows recipients to consume almost all the medical services they desire at *zero price*. The graph in Box 7 shows the impact of the Medicaid program on the choices made by recipients. Given the price of medical services, such as an office visit at $25, a typical low-income person would consume five visits per year if she had to pay. This is the number of visits for which her marginal benefit just equals the $25 price. At zero price she chooses to consume 10 visits per year. This is the number for which the marginal benefit of a visit equals zero. The availability of Medicaid *increases* consumption of medical services by all those eligible by breaking the link between the price of the services and the right to enjoy their benefits. This tends to increase the overall demand for medical services and is likely to raise the price of these services to other consumers. You can see this in Box 8.

Concept Check

1   How does government compute the poverty income threshold used to count the number of people living in poverty in the United States?

2   What programs are available to assist the poor in the United States? Are these programs available to all the poor? Why is private charity an unreliable method of assisting the poor?

3   Why are government programs to assist the poor likely to decrease the recipients' incentives to work? Why do in-kind transfer programs result in losses in efficiency?

Equity vs. Efficiency: The Inevitable Tradeoff

Policies in the United States designed to reduce income inequality represent a combination of taxes and transfers to the poor. Upper-income people are subjected to higher federal income tax rates. Under the Tax Reform Act of 1986, most families with incomes close to or below the poverty line are entirely exempt from federal income taxes. The use of taxes and transfers to alter income distribution can also affect incentives to work, invest, and use resources in the most efficient way. In the preceding section we discussed the impact of programs of assistance to the poor on their incentives. In this section we look at the inevitable tradeoff between efficiency and equity that prevails for the economy as a whole when policies redistribute income to create a more equitable society.

Reducing income inequality requires reducing the income of those with the highest earnings and greatest wealth. Such income reduction, say through taxation by government, can be used to finance increases in the income of the lowest-income groups. Unfortunately, as we have seen, there's no easy way to accomplish this task without reducing the incentive of low-income people to work. There's also another side of the coin: Those who pay the taxes to finance increases in income for low-income groups are also likely to have reduced incentives to work and save. When taxes are increased for upper- and middle-income people, they get to keep less of their earnings. The taxes they pay are therefore likely to distort their work and investment choices in ways that cause losses in the efficiency of resource use.

One way to minimize the loss in efficiency is to have only programs of income redistribution that modestly reduce income inequality. This is apparently the course we Americans have chosen. Most studies of the net effect of both taxes and transfers on income redistribution show that the overall impact of U.S. government policies is only a modest inward shift of the Lorenz curve, as you can see in Box 9. Many studies conclude that except for the lowest-income groups, who pay little if any taxes, and some of the richest taxpayers, who pay more than the average percentage of their income in taxes, most taxpayers use the same percentage of their income to pay *all* federal, state, and local taxes.[2] The combined effect of taxes and all transfer

[2]See Joseph A. Pechman, *Who Paid the Taxes, 1966-1985?* Washington, D.C.: The Brookings Institution, 1985.

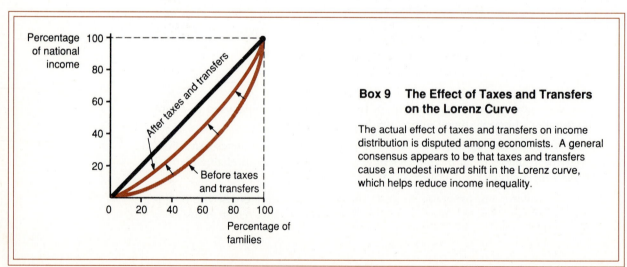

Box 9   The Effect of Taxes and Transfers on the Lorenz Curve

The actual effect of taxes and transfers on income distribution is disputed among economists. A general consensus appears to be that taxes and transfers cause a modest inward shift in the Lorenz curve, which helps reduce income inequality.

programs is probably a modest inward shift of the Lorenz curve, as illustrated in Box 9.

The Negative Income Tax and Longer-Term Solutions to Eliminate the Causes of Poverty

The Negative Income Tax

Poverty remains a serious problem in the United States, with close to 15% of the population, many of them children, classified as poor when only money income is counted. Including in-kind benefits in the income of the poor suggests that only 10% of the population can be classified as poor. A significant increase in taxes to finance more generous payments to the poor can eliminate poverty. However, this course of action could subject the most productive members of society to very sharp increases in taxes.

One proposal to deal with poverty is to place a floor on incomes through a **negative income tax** that would provide government payments to people whose income fell below certain levels. These payments would be financed by taxes on other people whose income was above the cutoff level of government payments. This program would provide a *minimum-income guarantee* to all citizens. If a person had zero earned income, the government would give him a payment equal to the income guarantee. The government payments to each person would decline as his earnings increased. For example, suppose the income guarantee were set at the poverty income threshold. If the threshold were $12,000 for a family of four, each such family would be guaranteed an income of that amount even if they had zero earnings. The family's government payments would be reduced by, say, 50¢ for each dollar earned. The reduction in payments as earnings increase is the *phaseout rate* for transfers to low-income groups. For example, if this family earned $10,000, its government payment would be reduced by $5,000. The family's total income would be $10,000 earnings plus a $7,000 payment from the government for a total of $17,000 per year. The family wouldn't become subject to taxes until it earned $24,000. At that level of earnings the government payment would finally be reduced to zero. The table in Box 10 shows how a negative income tax plan would work.

Negative income tax:
Provides for government payments to people whose income falls below certain levels.

Box 10	A Negative Income Tax Plan (Income Guarantee = $12,000; Phaseout Rate = 50¢ per Dollar of Government Payments for Each Dollar of Earnings)	
Earned income	Payments received from government	Total money income
$ 0	$12,000	$12,000
4,000	10,000	14,000
8,000	8,000	16,000
12,000	6,000	18,000
16,000	4,000	20,000
20,000	2,000	22,000
24,000	0	24,000

The problem with the negative income tax is that it would be very expensive. For example, if a $12,000 income guarantee were used along with a phaseout rate of 50¢ on the dollar, all families of four with earnings of less than $24,000 per year would be eligible for welfare payments. This would probably amount to 40% of the population! Some people might *choose* not to work so as to be eligible for government payments. This could reduce median income and increase the percentage of the population eligible for welfare. Needless to say, the tax rates on the remaining 60% of the population would have to skyrocket to generate revenue to pay the negative income taxes and finance other goods and services.

Although it's an appealing idea, the negative income tax is likely to run into the equity-efficiency tradeoff problem, which probably explains why it hasn't been adopted in the United States.

Eliminating the Causes of Poverty

After examining ways to help our country's poor, it's interesting to reflect on the reasons for low incomes. Remember that labor income accounts for more that three quarters of all income earned. Poverty can be viewed as the result of the lack of marketable skills or the inability to work. In the long run, to eliminate the causes of poverty, government must pursue policies that provide educational opportunities or decrease discrimination against minority groups in labor markets. Ultimately, a successful antipoverty program makes the poor self-sufficient by increasing their ability to earn income on their own. Programs that support equality of opportunity, economic growth, education, and effective training of workers to increase their productivity represent long-term solutions to poverty.

As we discovered earlier, the burden of poverty is disproportionately borne by blacks, Hispanics, and families headed by women. Is discrimination against these groups a possible cause of their poverty? **Discrimination in labor markets** occurs when minority-group workers with skills, experience, and training comparable to those of workers in other groups are paid lower wages and have less opportunity for employment and advancement.

Do employers in the United States discriminate against minority-group members despite the fact that the Civil Rights Act of 1964 outlawed discrimination in hiring on the basis of race, religion, sex, or national origin? The fact is that women on average earn less than men in the United States. Blacks and Hispanics earn less than whites. But is the earnings gap for these groups the result of discrimination or the result of experience, education, and other factors that influence productivity?

One study found that over 24% of the difference in labor earnings between men and women in the United States can be attributed to factors other than discrimination. It also concluded that about 40% of the difference in earnings between blacks and whites is explained by factors other than discrimination.[3] For example, blacks on average are younger than whites. Experience is a major influence on earnings. To actually *prove* the practice of discrimination it must be shown that *two workers who are equally productive receive different wages for the same work.* The presence of discrimination might be indicated by the fact that not all the differences in earnings between minority-group members and others can be explained by differences in the characteristics of their work.

Discrimination in labor markets:
Occurs when minority-group workers with skills, experience, and training comparable to those of workers in other groups are paid lower wages and have less opportunity for employment and advancement.

[3]Ronald Oaxaca, "Theory and Measurement of the Economics of Discrimination," in *Equal Rights and Industrial Relations,* Madison, Wis.: Industrial Relations Research Association, 1977.

Discrimination can also take the form of restricting minority-group members from entering higher-paying occupations or from acquiring the skills necessary to earn higher wages. For example, women are concentrated in certain occupations such as nursing, clerical work, and retailing in which wages are lower than average. Exclusion of minority-group members from occupations for which they are qualified is wasteful. It keeps wages higher for certain groups who are shielded from competition by qualified minority-group members. Because the supply of workers in these occupations is smaller than it would be otherwise, wages are higher. By the same token, crowding minority-group members in certain occupations makes wages lower by increasing the supply of labor for these occupations. If discrimination is practiced, therefore, there are both gainers and losers.

Elimination of occupational discrimination results in an increase in the value of production. This is because minority workers would be transferred from jobs in which their marginal revenue product is low to those in which their marginal revenue product is higher. At the same time, the increase in the supply of workers in the higher-paying occupations reduces wages in those jobs while the decrease in the supply of labor for the low-paying occupations increases wages there. Low-income workers remaining in the low-paying jobs therefore benefit. Workers previously suffering from discrimination also enjoy higher wages. The workers who lose are those in the protected occupations in which discrimination was practiced.

The existence of discrimination in labor markets remains difficult to prove. However, a long-term solution to raise incomes of minority-group members clearly requires equality of opportunity for education, training, and jobs. Efficiency is improved when each worker can work to the best of his or her capability.

Concept Check

1 How will an increase in the number of people receiving income assistance and an increase in welfare benefits affect the people who aren't receiving welfare?

2 What are the basic components of a negative income tax plan?

3 Suppose a negative income tax plan guarantees all families an annual income of $12,000 and uses a phaseout rate of 40¢ on the dollar for the transfers. At what level of income will families stop receiving transfers?

Summary

1. The standard of living of American families has increased substantially since the 1950s. However, the distribution of income going to each fifth of families ranked according to their income has been quite stable. There is considerable income inequality in the United States. The richest 20% of families have annual money income that accounts for over 40% of national income. The poorest 20% of families have annual money income that is less than 5% of national income.

2. In the United States 15% of the population is officially classified as poor. The poverty income threshold is three times the cost of a minimal diet for a family. In computing the number of families officially considered to be poor, only money income, including cash transfers, is included in income. In-kind transfers, which also increase the well-being of the poor, are not reflected in the official figures. In that sense the official statistics on poverty overstate the percentage of the population that is poor.

3. Private charity is an unreliable means of assisting the poor because many potential contributors seek to be free riders on the contributions of others. In addition, in periods of economic decline, when the numbers of poor are likely to swell, contributions typically decline. Government programs to assist the poor provide collective benefits to all members of society and compensate for the unreliability of private charity. Such programs also provide a "safety net" of insurance to all citizens should they be unfortunate enough to fall into poverty.

4. To be eligible for government welfare programs, recipients must pass a means test. Welfare is available only to certain demographic groups such as the aged, the disabled, and families with dependent children headed by a single parent.

5. Government programs to assist the poor in the United States offer both cash and in-kind assistance. The major programs of cash assistance are Aid to Families with Dependent Children and Supplemental Security Income. Major programs of in-kind assistance are Medicaid, food stamps, and housing assistance.

6. Government assistance to the poor affects their incentives to work and to consume goods. The availability of income support without work is a powerful work disincentive. To minimize this effect, welfare support levels tend to be quite low in the United States. In addition, as a recipient of government assistance begins earning income, welfare payments, including in-kind benefits, are phased out. This phaseout of benefits amounts to a tax on the earnings of recipients and further decreases their incentive to work.

7. In-kind transfer programs can cause losses in efficiency by distorting the incentive of the poor to consume goods that are subsidized. The Medicaid program causes the poor to consume medical services beyond the point at which the marginal cost equals the marginal benefit.

8. Programs of income redistribution inevitably must decrease the incomes of some people so that others can enjoy higher incomes. Some of the population must be taxed to provide transfers to others eligible for the programs. Income redistribution programs can affect the work incentives of taxpayers as well as recipients of transfers in ways that cause losses in efficiency.

9. The negative income tax is a program that would establish an income guarantee to everyone. The reason for a person's low income would not be a consideration in establishing eligibility for transfers. As a recipient earned income, the transfers received would be phased out at the rate of, say, 50¢ on the dollar. After reaching a certain level of earnings, the recipient would become a taxpayer instead of a welfare recipient. The basic problem with such a scheme is that if the guarantee is set close to the poverty income threshold and the tax rate is set low enough not to impair work incentives, a very large portion of the population will be eligible for transfers.

10. Discrimination in labor markets occurs when minority-group workers with skills, experience, and training comparable to those of workers in other groups are paid lower wages and have less opportunity for employment and advancement. Elimination of discrimination can improve efficiency and reduce poverty for low-income members of minority groups.

Key Terms and Concepts

Lorenz curve	Means test
Poverty income threshold	Negative income tax
Welfare programs	Discrimination in labor markets

Problems and Applications

1. Suppose the percentages of money income going to families in a nation correspond to the following data:

Income group	Percentage of income
Lowest fifth	5
Second fifth	10
Third fifth	15
Fourth fifth	25
Highest fifth	45

   Plot the Lorenz curve for the nation.

2. Suppose a new tax program for this nation cuts the share of income going to the highest fifth of families to only 35% of total income. If all the taxes paid by this group are distributed in equal portions to the lowest two fifths of the population, show how the Lorenz curve shifts.

3. Suppose the cost of a minimally acceptable diet is estimated to be $4 per person per day. Calculate the official poverty threshold annual income for a family of four.

4. How is noncash income considered when calculating the number of people in the United States whose income is below the poverty income threshold? Calculate the income of a worker who works full time at the minimum wage of $3.35 per hour. Assuming this person is the head of a family of four, will the family be above the poverty income threshold, as calculated in problem 3, on the basis of that annual income?

5. Suppose the Medicaid program is revised to require recipients to pay a modest charge for office visits to physicians after a certain number of visits have been consumed free during the year. Draw a graph to show how this revision is likely to decrease the number of office visits by Medicaid patients and decrease the gap between the efficient number of visits and the number consumed under the program.

6. Suppose that in the long run the supply of medical services is infinitely elastic. Under those circumstances, will a program like Medicaid increase the price of medical services in the long run to people not eligible for benefits?

7. Suppose an AFDC mother is allowed to earn $150 per month without any decrease in her AFDC payment. Above that amount her payment is reduced by 67¢ for each dollar of earnings. She is eligible for a $400 per month AFDC payment when she doesn't work at all. At what level of monthly income will her AFDC payment be reduced to zero?

8. Suppose a welfare recipient's payment is $200 per month if she doesn't work at all. The payment will be reduced by 33¢ instead of 67¢ as her earnings increase to above $150 per month. Why is a welfare recipient receiving these basic benefits likely to have more incentive to work than the AFDC mother whose benefits were described in problem 7?

9. Tom would normally spend $150 per month on food. He is eligible for food stamps of $250 per month. If instead Tom had received $250 in cash, he would spend $200 per month on food. Explain why the food stamps would be worth less than their face value to Tom. Explain why, even though food stamps can only be spent on food, they also increase recipients' consumption of other goods.

10. Suppose the median income for families in the nation is $30,000 per year. A

negative income tax plan is adopted to provide a $15,000 income guarantee and a 50¢ phaseout rate for transfers. What proportion of families in the nation will be receiving negative tax payments (transfers) from the government?

Suggested Readings

David N. Hyman, *Public Finance: A Contemporary Application of Theory to Policy,* 2nd ed., Chicago: The Dryden Press, 1987. Chapter 7 has a more advanced and detailed analysis of welfare programs in the United States.

Sar A. Levitan, *Programs in Aid of the Poor,* 5th ed., Baltimore: Johns Hopkins University Press, 1985. This is a thorough description and analysis of all major government assistance programs to the poor in the United States.

John L. Palmer and Isabel V. Sawhill, eds., *The Reagan Record,* Cambridge, Mass.: Ballinger Publishing Co., 1984. This is a discussion of major changes in welfare programs during the first Reagan Administration and the effects of these changes on income distribution.

A Forward Look

The overall performance of the economy is a major determinant of the income of families and the number of families that live in poverty. In the following chapters we begin a macroeconomic analysis of the economy to gain understanding of the causes of the ups and downs of economic activity, job opportunities, and the price level.

Career Profile

SCOTT McNEALY

The latest bad boy of the computer business, Scott McNealy looks and often acts more like the head of a college fraternity than the chief executive officer of a Fortune 500 company that's rocking the computer industry.

McNealy received his economics degree from Harvard in 1976. He helped found the company 2 years out of business school, and he and other company officials are boldly going where other companies have feared to tread, attempting to revolutionize the entire computer industry.

McNealy's company, Sun Microsystems, Inc., is a fast-growing manufacturer of computer workstations that win rave reviews among engineers, scientists, and analysts who want high-powered systems at low cost. If that isn't enough to irritate competitors, McNealy is suggesting that the industry adopt standard hardware and software and calmly offers a package that his company and AT&T have put together as the best possible choice.

Sun Microsystems designed the hardware for the new system, which is based on a company-developed microprocessor chip that is cheaper and easier to make than conventional microprocessors and acts as the brain of the computer. The computer operates on a software package developed by AT&T, which tells the brain what to do.

At present in the computer industry, hardware and software from different companies are incompatible. If many industry leaders adopt McNealy's idea of a standard system, businesses will be able to buy machines and software from various companies and use them together in a package.

McNealy has led his company through a period of phenomenal growth—nearly 30% every quarter. Currently, sales top $538 million annually and profits exceed $36 million, and McNealy is the company's biggest cheerleader. With more than 6,500 employees behind him, he says he focuses on pulling everyone together to have fun while they get the job done. His competitors may call him a presumptuous youngster, but McNealy's exuberance rubs off on his company, which has weekly dress-down days and monthly beer bashes.

PART VI

National Income, Production, and the Price Level: Macroeconomic Analysis

Gross National Product and the Performance of the National Economy

Did you know that your well-being is tied to the performance of the national economy? The fact is, your job prospects, income, and the purchasing power of your hard-earned dollars all depend on the performance of the economy as a whole. How can we keep tabs on the economy to evaluate its performance and its ability to provide jobs? Is it possible for a nation's economic policies to guarantee a stable and growing economy that allows steady improvement in living standards and job opportunities?

If you follow the news about the economy, you know there are periods during which the economy appears to be bursting at the seams. At those times business firms can't keep up with orders. When the economy approaches full steam there's usually inflation, and interest rates often rise as well. At other times the economy's performance is sluggish, so that inventories of unsold goods build up and workers seeking employment have difficulty finding jobs. When production declines in the economy, factories and offices are not fully utilized, workers are laid off, and incomes fall.

The economy is a dynamic mechanism. Each day the decisions of managers, workers, politicians, and government officials mesh to keep the economy functioning. *Macroeconomics* is the study of the overall performance of the economy as measured by national production and income earned each year and by fluctuations in income, purchases, employment, and the level of prices. In macroeconomics we focus on the total value of all production in a nation, ranging from safety pins to oil drilling rigs and from haircuts to coronary bypass surgeries. Rather than looking at the purchases of one household alone, as we did in microeconomics, we'll examine influences on total consumption by all households and purchases by business firms of tools, equipment, structures, and goods to hold in inventory. We'll examine the influences on movements in the prices of a market basket of goods and services purchased by consumers and seek to understand the forces that influence the cost of living in a nation on average. Rather than discussing the demand for and supply of particular goods, we'll analyze the forces influencing the *aggregate* demand for and *aggregate* supply of *all* goods and services produced nationally.

Macroeconomics focuses on two major problems: unemployment and inflation. In macroeconomics we develop techniques to measure the performance of the economy and to help formulate policies to keep unemployment and inflation under control and ensure adequate growth of job opportunities and incomes.

The three chapters in this part of the book will show how the performance of the economy is measured. You'll see how employment opportunities and national income depend on the level of production in the economy. The concepts of gross national product, recession, inflation, and unemployment, which are of key importance in macroeconomics, will be defined and analyzed.

In this chapter we outline the basic logic underlying the system of national income and product accounting used to measure economic performance in the United States. The goal of this chapter is to show you how production and income in a nation are related. You'll also see how the forces of demand and supply in the aggregate influence production and the cost of living.

After reading this chapter, you should be able to: *Concept Preview*

1 Explain what GNP is and how it is measured and discuss the shortcomings of GNP as a measure of national well-being.
2 Understand the distinction between final products and intermediate products. Explain how GNP can be measured as the sum of value added at each stage of production and how value added must equal the earnings accruing to owners of resources used in production.
3 Understand the distinction between nominal GNP and real GNP and how real GNP can be used to measure aggregate production over time.
4 Show how GNP can be viewed as either a flow of expenditures or a flow of income.
5 Use a circular flow analysis to understand the interrelationships in the economy among households, business firms, financial transactions, governments, and international trade and explain how leakages and injections of spending affect the economy.
6 Understand how supply and demand analysis is used in macroeconomics and show how changes in aggregate demand or aggregate supply can cause real GNP and prices to change.

Gross National Product

Gross national product (GNP):
The market value of an economy's final goods and services produced over a period of 1 year.

In reading the newspapers and watching television news reports, you've undoubtedly been exposed to the term "gross national product." **Gross national product (GNP)** is the market value of an economy's final goods and services produced over a period of 1 year. The goods and services included in GNP are items produced as *end products* for final use rather than for use as materials, parts, or services to be incorporated in the value of other items that will then be resold as final products.

Gross national product is a key economic variable that is closely watched in gauging the performance of the economy. In 1987 the gross national product in the United States based on market prices prevailing that year was $4.5 trillion. The importance of gross national product stems from the fact that both job opportunities and earnings in a nation are linked to production. When the output of final products in the economy grows, so will income and job opportunities. This is because more production means greater use of inputs; and as more inputs are used, the earnings of those who supply the inputs also go up, as do the opportunities for employment.

Every 3 months the U.S. Department of Commerce issues new statistics on GNP and its components. This event is eagerly awaited by business managers, investors, and policymakers in government agencies. The data on GNP and its components are compiled as part of the elaborate and sophisticated **National Income and Product Accounts (NIPA),** which is the official system of national accounting to measure the flows of income and expenditure in the United States. Literally thousands of decisions by business firms and governments hinge on the ups and downs of the numbers in this complex system of accounts.

National Income and Product Accounts (NIPA):
The official system of accounting to measure the flows of income and expenditures in the United States.

The National Income and Product Accounts help us determine how well the economy is doing and where it is headed. The accounts can be used to ascertain whether national production has increased or decreased over a certain period. Data from the accounts can be used to chart the course of the economy and get some idea of its ability to provide jobs and generate income in the future. Without data on GNP, it would be impossible to formulate policies to help control unemployment and inflation or to test hypotheses about the causes of unemployment and inflation.

The task of actually developing the system of national accounting was a monumental one. In fact, one economist, Simon Kuznets, was awarded the Nobel Prize in economics for his pioneering work during the 1930s that helped build the foundation for the National Income and Product Accounts. Professor Kuznets helped create the system that has become the basis for charting the course of the economy.

GNP as a Measure of the Market Value of Aggregate Production

Aggregates:
Broad totals of economic variables such as production or unemployment.

In analyzing the performance of an entire economy in macroeconomics, the focus is on **aggregates,** which are broad totals of economic variables such as production or unemployment. Gross national product is a measure of the *monetary value* of aggregate production. There's no meaningful way to add loaves of bread, computers, tickets to football games, pizzas, televisions, new homes, new cars, bulldozers, drill presses, aircraft, insurance, and medical and other services produced each year. Any attempt to measure aggregate physical quantities of goods inevitably runs into difficulties because different goods are measured in different units. Also, the mix of goods changes yearly (even daily). Thus arbitrary judgments must be made to decide whether aggregate production has gone up or down if, for example, the economy produces 50,000 fewer cars and 100,000 more insurance policies in a given year.

The best that can be done is to measure the *dollar value* of the nation's aggregate production of output. This is accomplished by first multiplying the quantity of each individual type of product measured over the period by its market price. The dollar values of all products derived in this way are then added to obtain a sum that equals the *market value* of the economy's aggregate production.

Purely financial transactions are excluded from GNP. Because GNP is a measure of the market value of aggregate production, transactions that don't involve production aren't included in it. For example, the value of sales of stocks and bonds is *not* part of GNP. This is because these transactions don't involve actual production of goods and services. Changes in the value of existing assets are also excluded from GNP because they don't represent production of new goods and services. The value of used goods sold during the year likewise is not part of GNP because the value of these goods was counted in prior years. Finally, goods and services not sold through markets in most cases are not reflected in GNP.[1] For example, if you clean your own apartment or cook your own meals, the value of these productive services you provide to yourself rather than purchase in a market will not be included in GNP.

Intermediate Products vs. Final Products: GNP as Total Value Added

In measuring GNP it's important to exclude the market value of production that is not for final use to avoid overestimating aggregate production. **Intermediate products** are those produced by business firms for resale by other firms or for use as materials or services that will be included in the value of resold goods. For example, steel purchased by General Motors from the USX Corporation is *not* considered part of the final product of the economy. This is because the steel will be used by General Motors as an input in the production of automobiles. If the value of the steel and the value of the automobile it is used in are *both* counted in GNP, the value of the steel will be counted twice. In effect, the value of the steel is already included in the value of the automobile. The steel sold for use in automobile bodies is an intermediate rather than a final product.

Intermediate products: Products produced by business firms for resale by other firms or for use as materials or services that will be included in the value of resold goods.

Total value added in a nation is the difference between the market value of *all* products of business firms and the market value of all intermediate products:

$$\text{Total value added in a nation} = \text{Market value of all products} - \text{Market value of intermediate products}$$

Total value added in a nation: The difference between the market value of *all* products of business firms and the market value of all intermediate products. Equivalent to GNP.

The market value of all products includes the value of both final and intermediate products. When the value of intermediate products is subtracted from this sum, the result is therefore the market value of the nation's final product. *Because the market value of final products is GNP, it follows that GNP can be viewed as total value added in a nation over the year.*

A simple example will show you how value added is computed at each stage of production and how it is related to the receipts and payments of a business firm. There are a number of transactions involved in making a product available. For example, to make a pair of jeans available in product markets, the cotton grown by farmers that goes into annual production of jeans must first be sold to weavers.

---

[1] An important exception is the value of housing services received by owners of their own homes. Those who live in their own homes are viewed as purchasing housing services from themselves even though no actual market purchase of services takes place.

Assume that farmers produce cotton without purchasing any materials or services from other firms. If this is the case, the value added by farmers equals the market value of their sales of cotton. This is because in the preceding formula for value added, the value of the intermediate products would be zero.

Suppose annual sales of the cotton to be used in producing jeans are $1 million. The value of these sales must be fully accounted for by the sum of profit and costs incurred by the farmer. Because farmers don't purchase anything from other firms, it follows that the value of wages paid to workers, rent paid to land and equipment owners, and interest paid to lenders must be reflected in the $1 million sales receipts. Any part of the $1 million that is not reflected in these costs must be the profit of farmers. *Note that the value added of the farmer represents the income generated by the sale of cotton.* The first line of the table in Box 1 shows the sales transactions of farmers. The line also shows that the farmers have no intermediate purchases and that their value added is therefore equal to their sales revenue.

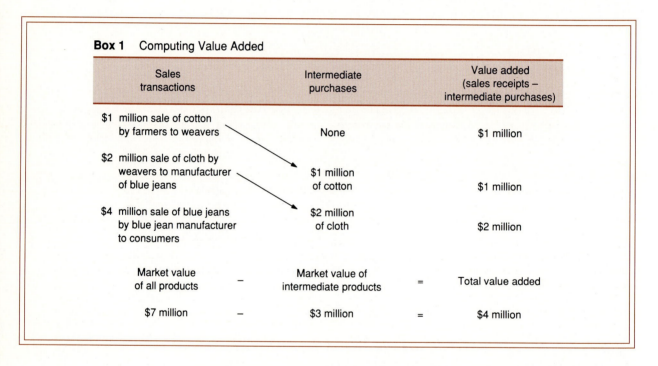

Box 1 Computing Value Added

Sales transactions	Intermediate purchases	Value added (sales receipts – intermediate purchases)
$1 million sale of cotton by farmers to weavers	None	$1 million
$2 million sale of cloth by weavers to manufacturer of blue jeans	$1 million of cotton	$1 million
$4 million sale of blue jeans by blue jean manufacturer to consumers	$2 million of cloth	$2 million
Market value of all products	– Market value of intermediate products	= Total value added
$7 million	– $3 million	= $4 million

All of the cotton is purchased by weavers who convert the cotton to cloth. The weavers' only intermediate purchase is that of the $1 million worth of cotton they obtain from farmers. After the cotton is processed into cloth, they sell the cloth for $2 million to a manufacturer of jeans. The value added by the weavers is therefore the $2 million in sales less the $1 million purchase of cotton. The logic of the concept of value added should be clear to you now. Value added *at each stage of production* is the difference between the value of the product at that stage and the cost of products purchased from other firms for use as inputs. The value added by the weavers represents the worth they have added to the cotton by processing it into cloth. This worth must reflect the value of the inputs *not* purchased from other firms that are used to process the cotton into cloth. Line 2 of the table in Box 1 shows that value added by the weavers is therefore $1 million per year. The $1

The Value Added Tax: A New Way to Tax GNP or Its Components

From the hallowed halls of Congress to the local diner, there's an ongoing debate about government spending and income taxes. Should we cut spending? Raise income taxes? Neither? Both?

Amid all the controversy, a new source of government revenue is being considered: the value added tax. What is it? Where is it being used? And how does it work?

The sum of value added at each stage of production over the year is equal to the market value of a nation's final product. In European nations it's common to tax value added. Value added taxes account for over 20% of tax revenue in most Western European nations. Such a tax has often been proposed as a means of providing additional revenue for the federal government without raising income tax rates. However, because total annual value added is equal to gross national product, a tax on value added would really be a tax on earnings in a nation. In other words, adoption of a value added tax would simply be another way of increasing the taxes on the major components of aggregate income.

A value added tax (VAT) is sometimes called a national sales tax because it's levied on every transaction as both final and intermediate products are sold. Under the value added tax used in European nations, almost every transaction in the economy is subject to tax. Sellers must add the tax to the value of the goods they sell at each stage of production. Business firms that collect the tax then make tax payments quarterly on their value added over the period.

In European nations the "invoice method" is used to collect the tax. Under this method no taxpayer has to compute value added (or understand what it is)! Each business adds up the tax it has collected during the period as recorded on its sales invoices, where the tax is itemized. At the same time the firm gathers all the invoices for the purchases it made during the period from other firms. The value added taxes on these transactions are also itemized on the bills the firm has paid. The firm's accountants then sum the amounts of tax it *paid* on intermediate purchases from other firms. The firm's tax liability is the difference between the tax it collected from sales to other firms and the tax it paid on purchases from its suppliers:

Tax liability =

Tax payable on sales − Tax paid on purchases from other firms

If the tax rate on each transaction is 20%, then the firm's tax liability is

20% (Sales receipts − Purchases from other firms)

Because the difference between a firm's sales receipts and its purchases of materials, parts, and services from other firms is its value added, the tax liability will be 20% of its value added:

Tax liability = 20% of value added

If *every* purchase is taxed at 20%, the government will collect 20% of GNP in tax revenue. Even the federal government's own purchases would be subject to the tax. In other words, if a value added tax is levied on all the components of expenditure in GNP, the federal government will collect the tax from itself as well as from state and local governments. The buyers of the final products will find that the price they pay for goods increases by 20% because the 20% tax is levied on all final sales as well as on intermediate sales. The tax will therefore collect 20% of the market value of the nation's final products, which is 20% of GNP.

In practice, the value added tax as used in most European nations is not levied on most investment purchases and government purchases. In this case the value added tax is really a tax on purchases of consumption goods! If the European version of the value added tax were introduced in the United States it would be equivalent to a national sales tax on consumption goods. Any purchaser of investment goods would have the tax rebated on such purchases. The federal government either would not collect the tax on purchases made by state and local governments or would rebate the tax they paid.

Viewing GNP as total value added in a nation thus helps us understand how a VAT would affect the economy. If a VAT that excludes investment and government purchases from taxation were introduced in the United States, those who allocate high percentages of their income to consumption would end up paying higher percentages of their income in taxes.

million value added must be fully accounted for by the weavers' labor costs and any costs other than purchases of cotton. Any difference between the weavers' costs and value added represents their annual profits.

Now the manufacturers of blue jeans sell the product they produce with the cloth to consumers who wear the jeans. Assume that the only intermediate purchase made by the blue jean manufacturer is the $2 million purchase of cloth. If the total market value of the jeans sold by the manufacturer is $4 million, then the value added at this final stage of production is $4 million less $2 million, which equals $2 million. Once again the $2 million value added by the blue jean maker must equal the sum of incomes of workers and other input owners whose resources are used to produce the blue jeans, plus the manufacturer's profit.

The table in Box 1 shows that the sum of product sales, including those of intermediate products, is $7 million, which is obtained by adding the numbers in the first column. The sum of the market value of all intermediate purchases is $3 million, obtained by summing the dollar values of sales in the second column. The sum of value added is $4 million. Now notice this very interesting point: *The sum of the value added associated with the production of jeans at its various stages exactly equals the market value of the final product sold by the jean makers to consumers.* Value added *is* the value of the final products because it nets out the value of intermediate transactions from *all* transactions.

GNP can be viewed as the sum of value added in all transactions involving new production in a nation over a year. Value added also equals the sum of payments to the owners of all resources used to produce the goods and services included in GNP and the profit of business firms. This is because value added at each stage represents the sum of payments to labor, capital, land, and all other inputs. When value added goes up in a nation, so will income in the nation.

Nominal GNP and Real GNP

Nominal GNP:
The market value of a nation's aggregate production of final output based on current prices for the goods and services produced during the year.

Nominal GNP is the market value of a nation's aggregate production of final output based on *current prices* for the goods and services produced during the year. Nominal GNP is of only limited use in measuring changes in aggregate production over time. This is because nominal GNP can rise from one year to the next as a result of increases in the market prices of goods even when the nation's aggregate production of final products does not increase. In fact, nominal GNP can increase as a result of substantial increases in a broad array of market prices even when the nation's aggregate production of final output actually declines! Similarly, if market prices were to fall substantially during a year, nominal GNP might fall even if the nation's aggregate production goes up.

Real GNP:
A measure of the value of a nation's aggregate output of final products obtained by using market prices prevailing for products during a certain base or reference year.

Real GNP is a measure of the value of a nation's aggregate output of final products obtained by *using market prices prevailing for products during a certain base or reference year*. Real GNP indicates the expenditure in dollars necessary to buy the economy's final products during a given year if they were sold at prices prevailing in the base year. The U.S. Department of Commerce, which gathers the data and actually calculates real GNP, now uses 1982 as its base year. Calculation of real GNP allows more accurate measurement of changes in aggregate production in the economy over time by adjusting nominal GNP for the effects of inflation.

Calculating Nominal and Real GNP: A Simple Example

A simple numerical example will make clear the distinction between nominal and real GNP. Imagine an economy where only two final products are produced each year: pizzas and jeans. The table in Box 2 shows how both nominal and real GNP can be computed for this imaginary economy for different years. Suppose that in 1982 the economy's final products were 2 million pizzas and 1 million pairs of jeans. The market price of a pizza in 1982 is $5, and the market price of a pair of jeans is $20. The table shows that the market value of pizzas that year is therefore $10 million, while the market value of jeans amounts to $20 million. Nominal GNP is the sum of the market values of pizzas and jeans, which in this case is $30 million. The $30 million sum represents the market value of the economy's aggregate production using current prices prevailing during the year. Nominal GNP in the United States is calculated in a similar fashion by estimating the production of each industry and then multiplying units of production by current market prices and summing the market values of all the many products.

Box 2 Nominal and Real GNP for a 2-Product Economy

Calculation of 1982 nominal GNP

Final products	1982 price	Market value
2 million pizzas	$5	$10 million = (2 million)($5)
1 million pairs of jeans	20	20 million = (1 million)($20)

Nominal GNP = $30 million = $10 million + $20 million

Calculation of 1990 nominal GNP

Final products	1990 price	Market value
4 million pizzas	$6	$24 million = (4 million)($6)
2 million pairs of jeans	25	50 million = (2 million)($25)

Nominal GNP = $74 million = $24 million + $50 million

Calculation of 1990 real GNP using 1982 prices

Final products	1982 price	Market value based on 1982 prices
4 million pizzas	$5	$20 million = (4 million)($5)
2 million pairs of jeans	20	40 million = (2 million)($20)

Nominal GNP = $60 million = $20 million + $40 million

The table in Box 2 also shows how nominal GNP is computed for the same economy in 1990. The output of both pizzas and jeans is significantly greater in 1990 than it was in 1982. As you can see, production of both these goods has doubled over the 8-year period. Also note that the 1990 market prices of the two goods have increased from their 1982 levels. As the calculation in the table shows, based on the $6 market price prevailing in 1990, the market value of the 4 million pizzas produced that year is $24 million. Similarly, the market value of the 2 million pairs of jeans produced in 1990 is $50 million based on the price of $25 per pair prevailing that year. The market value of the economy's aggregate production of final products is therefore $74 million based on 1990 market prices.

If you now compare nominal GNP between 1982 and 1990, you can see why nominal GNP gives a misleading picture of the change in aggregate production between the two years. The output of each of the two products in the economy has doubled from 1982 to 1990. However, between 1982 and 1990 nominal GNP has more than doubled. The discrepancy between growth in output and growth in nominal GNP stems from the fact that the growth in nominal GNP represents an amalgam of the changes in the prices of the products and the growth in output.

It's easy to obtain an accurate estimate of the change in aggregate production by valuing products produced in 1990 at the prices that prevailed in 1982. Using 1982 as the base year for comparing changes in production, the table in Box 2 shows how real GNP is calculated by valuing output at base year prices. The market value of pizza in 1990 based on the $5 price that prevailed in 1982 is $20 million, while the market value of jeans produced in 1990 valued at the $20 price that prevailed in 1982 is $40 million. Summing these two market values gives a real GNP of $60 million, which is twice the real GNP that prevailed in 1982. The doubling of real GNP reflects the doubling of aggregate production. Note that 1982 nominal GNP is also 1982 real GNP when 1982 is used as the base year.

You can see the relevance of the distinction between real GNP and nominal GNP if you look at the changes in the values of these two measures between 1981 and 1982 in the United States. Nominal GNP in 1981 was equal to $3,052.6 billion. In 1982 nominal GNP went up to $3,166.0 billion. However, 1982 was a very bad year for the economy because the nation's aggregate production actually declined from the level prevailing in 1981. You can easily see this by noting that when aggregate production of the economy for *both* 1981 and 1982 is valued at prices prevailing in

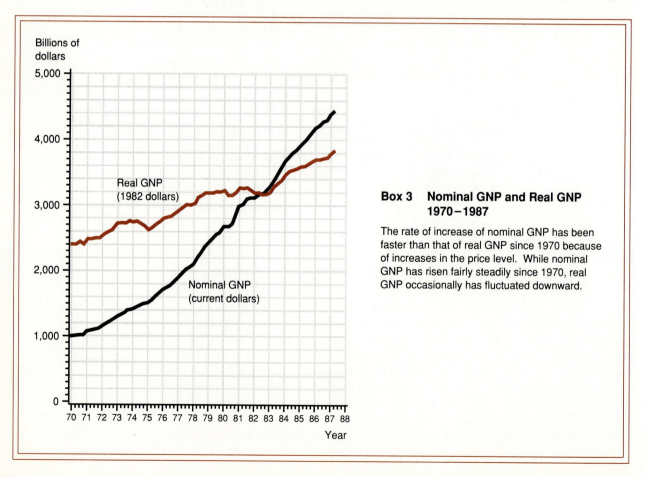

**Box 3   Nominal GNP and Real GNP
1970 – 1987**

The rate of increase of nominal GNP has been faster than that of real GNP since 1970 because of increases in the price level. While nominal GNP has risen fairly steadily since 1970, real GNP occasionally has fluctuated downward.

1982, *real* GNP fell from $3,248.8 billion in 1981 to $3,166.0 billion in 1982. The decline in real GNP in 1982 caused considerable disruption in the operation of the economy as unemployment increased and household incomes declined because of the cutback in production that year.

The graph in Box 3 charts both real GNP and nominal GNP for the economy from 1970 to 1987. Note that nominal GNP increases at a more rapid rate over time than does real GNP. Nominal GNP has grown more quickly than real GNP since 1970 because prices have risen on average since that time. Also note that real GNP is more apt to decline than is nominal GNP. The graph shows sharp declines in real GNP during the periods 1973-1975 and 1981-1982. During these two periods production declined, and as a consequence job opportunities were reduced. As a result, many workers lost their jobs and suffered declines in income.

How Good Is GNP as a Measure of National Well-Being?

How does GNP rate as a measure of the overall well-being of Americans? How does exclusion of nonmarket services affect the accuracy of GNP as an index of national well-being? Does GNP account for *decreases* in the quality of the environment that result from pollution? In this section we discuss important items that affect our well-being that are not included in GNP.

1. *Nonmarket goods.* Many useful services are produced by members of households for the benefit of themselves or their families. Husbands and wives perform useful services for themselves and their families when they prepare meals, make household repairs, and handle their own financial affairs. The value of these services is *not* included in GNP because they do not represent services purchased through market transactions. The value of work people do at home for themselves and their families has been estimated to be about one third of GNP.[2] If this estimate is correct, GNP significantly undervalues the total output of the nation by excluding nonmarket household production. The 1985 GNP of slightly less than $4 trillion is worth $5.3 trillion if this estimate of the value of household production is added to it. Perhaps you can see this more graphically if you imagine each husband paying his wife for her services and each wife paying her husband for his services. These services would now become market services and would be included in GNP. Similarly, if more people remain single and hire housekeepers to do work that spouses would normally do without monetary compensation, GNP will increase!

Some nonmarket transactions, however, are included in GNP. For example, homeowners who live in their own homes enjoy the housing services their homes provide. In the National Income and Product Accounts, these owner-occupiers are viewed as being in the business of renting their homes to themselves. An estimate of the value of housing services enjoyed in this way *is included in GNP*. The estimated value of housing services, called imputed rent, earned by owner-occupiers of nonfarm housing was $296 billion in 1986. Intermediate goods and services of $40.7 billion were deducted from this, resulting in value added of $255.3 billion included in 1986 GNP.

In addition, GNP accountants impute values to farm products consumed on farms, and food, clothing, and lodging furnished to employees. The imputed market values of these goods and services *are* included in GNP. Of course, the goods and services

[2]See Oli Hawrylyshyn, "The Value of Household Services: A Survey of Empirical Estimates," *The Review of Income and Wealth*, 22, 2, June 1976, pp. 101-131; and Reuben Bronau, "Home Production—A Forgotten Industry," *Review of Economics and Statistics*, 63, 3, August 1980, pp. 408-416.

made available by governments, such as national defense, are not sold in markets. However, the value of these services is reflected in GNP because government purchases of labor and products necessary to perform its functions are a component of GNP.

2. *The value of leisure.* All of you place some value on your time. You sell some of your time to employers for labor income. However, you retain much of it for your own use as leisure. Some of this leisure is used to produce household services that, as we discussed earlier, escape inclusion in GNP. The satisfaction you get from recreational activities and other uses of your leisure time also escapes inclusion in GNP. The National Income and Product Accounts make no attempt to value leisure time.

3. *Cost of environmental damage.* Costs are associated with pollution and other aspects of industrial activity that damage the environment. The costs of environmental damage are not subtracted from the market value of final products when GNP is calculated. We Americans may be able to enjoy more and better goods and services each year, but we also must put up with more congestion, dirty air, polluted waters, and other environmental costs that decrease the quality of our lives. In fact, costs incurred to clean up pollution damage (like an oil spill) actually *increase* GNP because they are treated as final services in the accounts. Some economists therefore believe that GNP overestimates the value of output by failing to account for environmental costs of production.

4. *The underground economy.* The United States has a vast *underground* economy, which consists of transactions that are never reported to tax and other government authorities. The underground economy includes transactions for the sale of illegal goods and services, such as narcotics, gambling, and prostitution. These illegal goods and services are final products that are not included in GNP!

The transactions of the underground economy also include activities by people who don't comply with tax laws, immigration laws, or government regulations and who don't report their income to authorities. For example, a person might obtain a job and be paid in cash without paying any Social Security taxes or income taxes on his earnings. This type of transaction is never reported to the Internal Revenue Service, and because no record of the transaction is transmitted to governing authorities, the final product of the transaction often goes unvalued in GNP.

Estimates of the value of transactions that take place in the underground economy and are not included in GNP range as high as one third of GNP. However, one recent study concludes that previous studies have overestimated the value of unreported transactions from the underground economy. This report concludes that GNP is understated by no more than about 1.5% when underground transactions are excluded.[3]

[3]Carol S. Carson, "The Underground Economy: An Introduction," U.S. Department of Commerce, *Survey of Current Business,* July 1984, pp. 106-117.

Concept Check

1   What is measured in GNP? What are the defects of GNP as a measure of national well-being?

2   How is value added related to the market value of all production in the economy and to the earnings of owners of economic resources?

3   Why is real GNP a better measure of variation in aggregate production over time than nominal GNP?

The Expenditure and Income Components of GNP

The National Income and Product Accounts were designed to be used to help evaluate the performance of the economy. For that reason the accounts can be disaggregated into various components that can be used to measure purchases of goods and services used for various purposes. The accounts can be used to chart fluctuations in consumption and investment purchases over time. In addition, the accounts measure government purchases and purchases of products exported from the United States as well as domestic purchases of imported goods. Thus data on real GNP can be used to examine how aggregate production fluctuates from year to year, and it can also show who purchases the final products produced during the year.

We can also use data on the composition of real GNP to see how the mix of final products changes in the economy from year to year. For example, the NIPA can be used to show how the aggregate output of service industries, such as banking, has changed over time relative to the aggregate output of manufacturing industries, such as steel. In this way the data on value added in various industries from the GNP accounts can provide a picture of how the structure of the economy changes in terms of its mix of industry output.

Finally, annual expenditure for the goods and services produced in the economy each year, as measured by GNP, must also equal the aggregate income of the nation. The value of final goods and services produced each year must ultimately be accounted for in the compensation of workers, the rents earned by landlords and owners of capital, the interest earned by savers and lenders, and the profits of both incorporated and unincorporated businesses. The equality between national expenditure on final products and aggregate income in a nation stems from the fact that whatever is spent during the year ultimately becomes income. You saw this earlier in the analysis of value added. Value added represents the value of final products, but total value added during a year must also equal the sum of payments to all input owners during the year.

Total income earned annually in a nation is a major influence on well-being and is an important determinant of the ability of households and businesses to purchase goods and services. Real GNP represents the value of final products produced during the year after adjustment for inflation. You now can see that real GNP also represents the **aggregate real income** of a nation, which is its nominal (money) income adjusted for inflation.

Aggregate real income: The nominal (money) income of a nation, adjusted for inflation. Equivalent to real GNP.

The aggregate market value of a nation's final products (value added), aggregate expenditure on final products, and aggregate income from the sale of final products are therefore all useful ways of viewing GNP.

The Expenditure Side of GNP

Annual expenditure can be divided into four broad categories: consumption expenditures (C), investment expenditures (I), government purchases of goods and services (G), and any excess of expenditure on exports over imports, which is called **net exports** (NE). Exports represent the expenditure on U.S. final products by citizens of foreign nations. Imports, representing the value of goods and services produced in foreign nations and purchased by Americans (and therefore included in aggregate expenditure), must be netted out of total expenditures to accurately reflect the purchases of goods and services produced domestically. When the value of imported goods and services exceeds the value of exported domestic goods and ser-

Net exports: Any excess of expenditure on exports over imports.

vices, net exports will be negative, as has been the case in recent years in the United States.

Aggregate expenditure is the sum of consumption expenditures, investment expenditures, government purchases, and net exports during the year. The expenditure side of GNP can be expressed as the following identity:

$$GNP = C + I + G + NE$$

To help you understand the demand for the economy's aggregate production, it's useful to outline the kinds of expenditures included in each separate component of GNP.

1. *Consumption.* **Personal consumption expenditures,** the official name for consumption purchases in the NIPA, include household and individual purchases of *both* durable and nondurable goods and services. Consumer durable goods include automobiles, kitchen appliances, furniture, and similar items. Nondurable goods include food, clothing, and gasoline. Services are nonmaterial items consumed by households. For example, annual rental payments for housing services are a major component of personal consumption expenditures. Household operating services such as electricity, gas, and water also account for substantial consumption expenditure. Other services are those of physicians and hospitals, lawyers, mechanics, banks, insurance companies, hotels, and so on.

Over 50% of personal consumption expenditures in 1987 were for services, including housing. The table and pie chart in Box 4 show the breakdown of 1987 personal consumption expenditures into various types.

Aggregate expenditure:
The sum of consumption expenditures, investment expenditures, government purchases, and net exports during the year. Equivalent to real GNP.

Personal consumption expenditures:
Household and individual purchases of both durable and nondurable goods and services.

Box 4   Personal Consumption Expenditures by Type (1987)

Item	Nominal amount (billions of dollars)	Percent of total
Total durable goods	413.9	14.0
Motor vehicles and parts	194.5	6.6
Furniture and household equipment	146.3	4.9
Other	73.1	2.5
Total nondurable goods	980.4	33.0
Food	514.5	17.3
Clothing and shoes	176.5	5.9
Gasoline and oil	79.9	2.7
Other nondurable goods	209.6	7.1
Total services	1,571.6	53.0
Housing	469.2	15.8
Household operation	182.2	6.1
Transportation	105.4	3.6
Medical care	350.9	11.8
Other	463.9	15.6
Total	2,966.0	

Source: U.S. Department of Commerce, *Survey of Current Business,* January 1988.

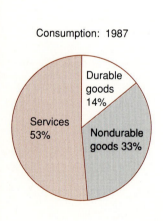

Consumption: 1987

Durable goods 14%

Services 53%

Nondurable goods 33%

Personal consumption expenditures were nearly $3 trillion in 1987, which amounted to 66% of GNP in that year. You can now understand the importance of the consumer in the U.S. economy. Two thirds of the value of final products included in nominal GNP in 1987 was produced for the use and enjoyment of American consumers! If we as consumers decided to spend less, the demand for goods and services would decline; and because of reduced sales, aggregate production also would decline.

2. *Investment.* **Gross private domestic investment,** the official name for investment purchases by business firms in the NIPA, includes expenditure on new machinery and equipment (producer durables), the value of new residential and nonresidential construction, and the change in business inventories during the year. Gross investment represents the acquisition of new capital goods by businesses, including changes in inventories of unsold goods, materials, and parts over the year.[4] Purchases of investment goods by governments are *not* included as investment in the accounts. Instead all government purchases are lumped together into a single category, whether it be consumption of food or an investment purchase of a new structure.

Only domestic investment, that which takes place within the United States, is included in the accounts because investment goods purchased in foreign nations are not part of current domestic production. For example, if IBM invests in a new plant in Mexico, this investment is *not* included in GNP except to the extent that IBM purchases machinery in the United States for use in its Mexican plant.

Finally, investment is *gross* because it doesn't deduct that amount of purchases necessary to replace capital that wears out or becomes obsolete during the year. **Depreciation** (also called the capital consumption allowance) is an estimate of the value of capital goods that wear out or become obsolete over the year. In effect, depreciation represents expenditure by business firms to replace worn-out or obsolete equipment during the year rather than expenditure to add to their capital stock. Deducting depreciation from gross private domestic investment gives **net private domestic investment.** If net private domestic investment were zero during a year, it would imply that after allowance for the capital that has simply been replaced during the year, there has been no net addition to or decline in the capital stock available in the nation.

Be sure you understand the difference between the common use of the term *investment* and its use in economics and in the National Income and Product Accounts. Your purchase of shares of corporate stock is *not* investment in the sense that the term is used in economics. *Investment is the purchase of final products by business firms for use in production or as additions to inventories.*

Gross private domestic investment totaled $716.4 billion in 1987, an amount equal to 16% of GNP. The table and pie chart in Box 5 show the components of gross domestic private investment in 1987. In 1987 investment purchases for durable equipment, structures, and residential housing accounted for 94% of total gross private domestic investment. When there is an increase in stocks of unsold goods or unused materials or parts during the year, the increase is added to investments in durable equipment, business structures, and residential housing purchased during the year to obtain gross private domestic investment. When inventories decrease during the year, the decrease is subtracted from investment.

Gross private domestic investment:
Investment purchases by business firms: expenditure on new machinery and equipment (producer durables), the value of new residential and nonresidential construction, and the change in business inventories during the year.

Depreciation:
An estimate of the value of capital goods that wear out or become obsolete over the year. Also called the *capital consumption allowance.*

Net private domestic investment:
Gross private domestic investment less depreciation.

---

[4]Purchase of a home by an individual is also part of investment. The NIPA accounts view those who live in their own homes in effect as businesses that produce housing services for themselves.

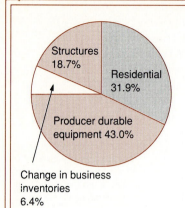

Box 5 Gross Private Domestic Investment 1987

Item	Nominal amount (billions of dollars)	Percent of total
Structures	134.1	18.7
Producer durable equipment	308.0	43.0
Residential	228.5	31.9
Change in business inventories	45.7	6.4
Total	716.4	

Source: U.S. Department of Commerce, *Survey of Current Business,* January 1988.

The logic of treating business inventories in this way should be clear to you. When inventories increase from one year to the next, they represent goods that have been produced during the year but have not been sold. To accurately measure the market value of production over the year, these goods must be included in GNP. Similarly, when inventories decline during a year, the decline represents goods that were produced in *previous* years but sold during the current year. To accurately represent *current* GNP, the decline in inventories must be subtracted from investment.

The data on changes in business inventories do not, however, indicate whether or not the change in business inventories was intentionally planned. For example, business inventories can grow during the year because firms intentionally stock up in anticipation of strong sales. But inventories could just as well build up because the current year was terrible and the firms got stuck holding products they had expected to sell!

The change in business inventories each year is an extremely unstable component of gross private domestic investment. In some years the change is positive; in others it's negative.

3. Government purchases of goods and services. **Government purchases of goods and services** include expenditure on final products of business firms and all input costs, including labor costs, incurred by all levels of government in the United States. Each paper clip, computer, fighter plane, filing cabinet, and Saturn rocket purchased by the government is included in the government purchases component of GNP. Also included is the entire payroll of all governments in the United States (state, local, and federal), representing government purchases of labor services. Increases in government inventories of crops under agricultural support programs are treated as government purchases. However, transfer payments made by government are *not* included in government purchases, although they are part of government expenditure.

Transfer payments are payments for which no good or service is currently received in return and therefore do not represent expenditures for the purchase of final products. For example, Social Security pensions are a transfer payment from government to retired workers. Welfare payments to the poor are another transfer to members of households. Similarly, subsidy payments by government to agricultural firms are transfers. Other examples of government transfer payments are veterans' benefits and interest paid on government borrowings.

Government purchases of goods and services:
Expenditure on final products of business firms and all input costs, including labor costs, incurred by all levels of government in the United States.

Transfer payments:
Payments for which no good or service is currently received in return and that therefore do not represent expenditures for the purchase of final products.

Although transfer payments don't reflect production of goods and services, they are spent by recipients and therefore end up as part of the consumption or investment component of GNP. In effect, transfer payments are negative taxes representing payments by governments to individuals instead of payments by individuals to governments.

Governments themselves *do* produce valuable goods and services, such as national defense, police and fire protection, roads, bridges, and space exploration. However, government services like national defense are not sold in the marketplace. Services like national defense, public education, and garbage pickup are indirectly valued in computing GNP because the cost (including labor) to make the services available is included in GNP.

Government purchases amounted to $923.8 billion or 21% of GNP in 1987. The table and pie charts in Box 6 show the breakdown of government purchases between federal and nonfederal (state and local) governments. Also shown is the

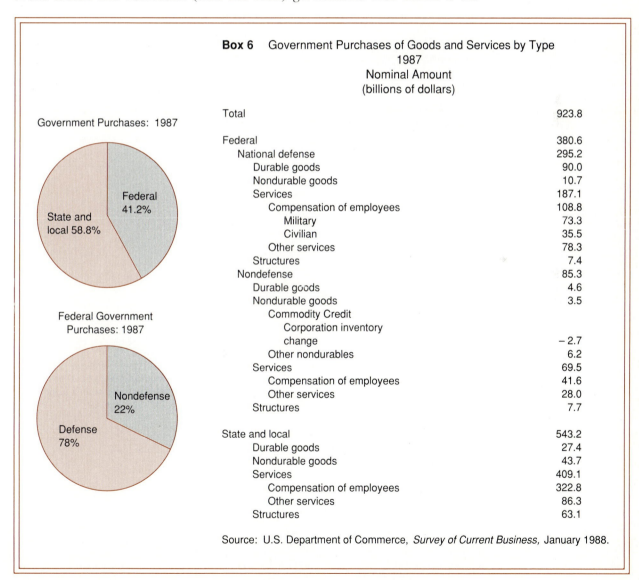

Box 6 Government Purchases of Goods and Services by Type
1987
Nominal Amount
(billions of dollars)

Government Purchases: 1987

State and local 58.8%

Federal 41.2%

Federal Government Purchases: 1987

Defense 78%

Nondefense 22%

Total	923.8
Federal	380.6
National defense	295.2
Durable goods	90.0
Nondurable goods	10.7
Services	187.1
Compensation of employees	108.8
Military	73.3
Civilian	35.5
Other services	78.3
Structures	7.4
Nondefense	85.3
Durable goods	4.6
Nondurable goods	3.5
Commodity Credit Corporation inventory change	−2.7
Other nondurables	6.2
Services	69.5
Compensation of employees	41.6
Other services	28.0
Structures	7.7
State and local	543.2
Durable goods	27.4
Nondurable goods	43.7
Services	409.1
Compensation of employees	322.8
Other services	86.3
Structures	63.1

Source: U.S. Department of Commerce, *Survey of Current Business,* January 1988.

breakdown of government purchases between defense and nondefense items. Defense-related items accounted for 78% of all federal government purchases of goods and services in 1987. Remember that government purchases don't include transfers, so expenditures for programs like Social Security and welfare are not reflected in the G component of GNP.

4. *Net Exports.* Net exports measure the extent to which foreign spending on U.S.-produced goods and services exceeds spending by Americans on foreign-produced goods and services. When the value of spending on imports exceeds the value of U.S. exports, net exports are negative. Under such circumstances GNP is less than the sum of consumption, investment, and government purchases. In fact, in 1987 the value of imports did exceed the value of exports by $119.9 billion, and that amount was subtracted from the sum of consumption, investment, and government purchases to obtain GNP.

Charting the Expenditure Components of GNP

The various components of real GNP differ in terms of their stability. Personal consumption expenditures are the most stable component of GNP. Since 1950 annual personal consumption expenditures in the United States have risen quite steadily from about $700 billion to nearly $2,500 billion per year in 1987 when measured in 1982 dollars to adjust for inflation. The lack of major fluctuation in personal consumption expenditures can be readily seen in the graph in Box 7, which plots personal consumption expenditures over time from 1950 to 1987. Remember that real

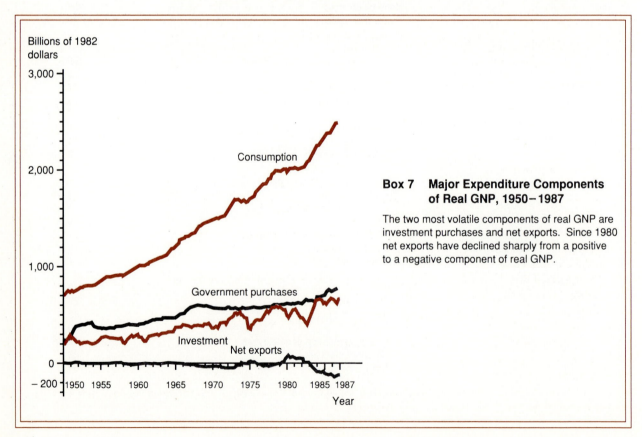

Box 7   Major Expenditure Components of Real GNP, 1950–1987

The two most volatile components of real GNP are investment purchases and net exports. Since 1980 net exports have declined sharply from a positive to a negative component of real GNP.

consumption expenditures reflect an increase in aggregate production consumed. The physical quantities of goods and services consumed in the aggregate in the United States have therefore more than tripled since 1950, reflecting a general improvement in the standard of living.

The graph in Box 7 also shows government purchases of goods and services over time, measured in 1982 dollars. Noticeable blips in government purchases occur during periods of war, reflecting increases in military purchases. Government purchases increased sharply during the Korean War in the early 1950s and again in the late 1960s during the buildup for the Vietnam War.

The two most volatile components of real GNP are investment and net exports. For example, net exports often swing from a positive component of GNP to a negative component. Investment purchases are quite volatile from year to year, often plummeting and then increasing sharply. Fluctuations in aggregate expenditure, except during periods of war, are therefore largely explainable by fluctuations in gross private domestic investment and net exports.

The Income Side of GNP

GNP can also be broken down into components of the aggregate incomes of individuals and corporations. The major components of a nation's income are compensation of employees, proprietors' income, corporate profits and capital consumption allowances, interest, and rents.

1. *Compensation of employees.* Compensation of employees represents the income from sale of labor services in the United States during the year. This is the largest income component of GNP, accounting for $2,647.5 billion in 1987 or about 60% of GNP. Total compensation of employees includes *fringe benefits,* such as employer-provided insurance and pension contributions. The figures in the GNP accounts are designed to measure the total labor cost of goods and services.

2. *Proprietors' income.* This measures the income earned by owners of unincorporated businesses. This income represents payments for the labor services, capital, and entrepreneurial ability of persons who own their businesses. In 1987 proprietors' income amounted to $327.82 billion, which was about 7.3% of GNP.

3. *Corporate profits.* Corporate profits represent the income earned by all corporate businesses in the nation. In 1987 corporate profits, which include dividends and retained earnings before taxes, amounted to $305.3 billion or 6.8% of GNP. (Dividends are the portion of corporate profits paid out to shareholders over the year. The portion of corporate profits not paid out to shareholders or as taxes is retained earnings.)

   Corporate profits represent the most volatile income component of GNP. For example, corporate profits before tax fell from $181.5 billion in 1981 to $129.7 billion in 1982, which was a recession year. Then in 1983 pretax corporate profits increased to $159.3 billion.

4. *Net interest.* This represents the dollar earnings of savers and other suppliers of loanable funds for investment purchases. Interest paid by governments is treated as a transfer payment because it is financed by taxes rather than productive investment. The interest paid by governments is therefore excluded from net interest. Net interest earned in 1987 amounted to about 7.5% of GNP.

5. *Rental income.* Rental income is earned by those who supply the services of land,

Principles in Practice

How the Bureau of Economic Analysis Calculates GNP Every 3 Months

There are two teams and a match. But there's no competition. The teams are composed of staff members of the Bureau of Economic Analysis of the U.S. Department of Commerce. One team measures GNP from the expenditure side, while the other measures it from the income side. When the two teams finish their independent work, a group of 15 economists meets to reconcile the two estimates.* Aggregate expenditures on final products must equal aggregate income earned. On occasion the results don't match, and when the economists can't explain the source of the difference it shows up as a statistical discrepancy on the GNP accounts.

The team that estimates GNP from the expenditure perspective uses data collected by the U.S. Bureau of the Census and other organizations. The group estimating GNP from the income side uses the results of a number of income surveys.

In making estimates of real GNP, the Bureau of Economic Analysis staff members must value final products at prices prevailing in a base year. This often creates some serious problems when new products are developed or the quality of products changes over time. For example, in the early 1980s the base year used to estimate real GNP was 1972. However, by 1980 the economy was producing products like personal computers that didn't exist in the early 1970s. There was no 1972 price for personal computers because the product wasn't sold in markets at that time! To resolve such problems, the Bureau of Economic Analysis looks at how prices of similar products such as electric typewriters change over time and then deflates the current price of the new product to match the trend. For example, if electric typewriters in 1972 were priced at 70% of their 1980 market price, the Bureau would value personal computers at 70% of their 1980 selling price when computing real GNP that year.

Quality changes in products also create headaches for the people who measure real GNP. Suppose a car sells for $18,000 in 1989 and the same model of that car sold for $14,000 in the 1982 base year currently used to estimate real GNP. However, the 1989 model has anti-lock brakes, a stereo cassette system, auto-lock doors, and other features as standard equipment that weren't available in 1982. To adjust for the quality change, the Bureau must add on the market value of these features by estimating their value in 1982. Many judgments about the value of quality changes must be made in computing real GNP.

The preliminary estimate of GNP is released 15 working days after the end of each calendar quarter. The quarterly figures are adjusted for seasonal variation and then multiplied by 4 to obtain GNP at an annual rate. The President is privileged to obtain the estimate 1 day before its official release. Revised estimates of GNP are released 45 days after the preliminary estimate. The revised estimates reflect the inclusion of new data that sometimes are unavailable for the preliminary estimates.

*See Timothy Tregarthen, "How to Count: The Making of the GNP," *The Margin*, 1, 1, September 1985, pp. 18-20.

---

mineral rights, and structures for the use of others. Also included in rental income is an estimate of the imputed (in-kind) rent earned by homeowners less the expenses of maintaining their homes. As observed earlier, homeowners are viewed as renting their homes to themselves. GNP estimates the net income of these owner-occupiers.

Rental income is the smallest component of GNP, accounting for only $18.5 billion in 1987, which is less than 1% of total GNP.

6. *Other income components of GNP.* A portion of income earned by businesses during the year is set aside to fund investment purchases that replace worn-out and obsolete capital. Business firms deduct depreciation, the capital consumption allowance, as a cost of production before they compute their profits and pay for inputs used in production. In effect, the capital consumption allowance represents *business saving*. This form of saving is a sizable chunk of GNP, amounting to $479.4 billion or more than 10% of GNP in 1987.

Indirect business taxes:
Taxes levied on business firms that increase their costs and are therefore reflected in the market value of goods and services sold.

Another aspect of total expenditure that is not directly accounted for in the incomes earned by individuals and corporations is **indirect business taxes.** These are taxes levied on business firms that increase their costs and are therefore reflected in the market value of goods and services they sell. Included in indirect business taxes are sales taxes, excise taxes, and certain business property taxes. Although these taxes are included in business receipts, they are paid to governments instead of to members of households. To maintain the equality between expenditure and income, these must be added to the income side of the GNP accounts as income to government. **Corporate profits taxes** are those amounts corporations pay as taxes to governments out of their annual receipts from the sale of goods and services. These payments are not income to owners of corporations but are instead revenue for government.[5]

Corporate profits taxes: Those amounts corporations pay as taxes to governments out of their annual receipts from the sale of goods and services.

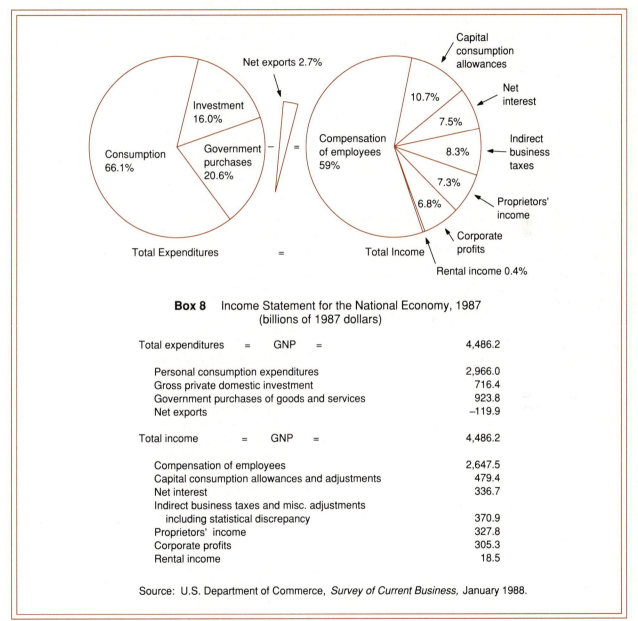

Box 8 Income Statement for the National Economy, 1987
(billions of 1987 dollars)

Total expenditures	=	GNP	=	4,486.2
Personal consumption expenditures				2,966.0
Gross private domestic investment				716.4
Government purchases of goods and services				923.8
Net exports				−119.9
Total income	=	GNP	=	4,486.2
Compensation of employees				2,647.5
Capital consumption allowances and adjustments				479.4
Net interest				336.7
Indirect business taxes and misc. adjustments including statistical discrepancy				370.9
Proprietors' income				327.8
Corporate profits				305.3
Rental income				18.5

Source: U.S. Department of Commerce, *Survey of Current Business,* January 1988.

[5]A portion of the income included in GNP is earned by U.S. citizens working or holding property in foreign nations, while income earned by foreigners who own resources located in the United States is not included in GNP. For example, the income of a U.S. citizen working in Italy is included in GNP while the income earned by Toyota's U.S. operation is not included in U.S. GNP. Gross domestic product (GDP) measures the market value of final products produced within the boundaries of the United States by netting out U.S. earnings abroad from GNP while adding in foreign earnings in the United States.

The table and pie charts in Box 8 show the income statement for the national economy in 1987. In effect, in the NIPA the economy is viewed as an enormous household. Income *must* equal expenditure. As the table shows, total income does equal total expenditure after inclusion of capital consumption allowances and indirect business taxes and various adjustments to make the accounts balance.

The Circular Flow of Expenditure and Income

National income and product accounting demonstrates that expenditure on final products generates income. But this is not a one-time affair. Instead the income in turn generates purchases of final products, which then result in more income as the process goes on and on. We can illustrate the continual flow of expenditure and income with a *circular flow diagram* similar to the one used in Chapter 6. However, with our enhanced knowledge of the NIPA accounts, we now can further investigate the relationship between the sources and uses of income by showing how the financial system, governments, and international trade affect the economy.

The enhanced circular flow diagram is drawn in Box 9. The upper loop of the big circle represents expenditures generated by purchases of final products, while the lower loop represents a flow of income generated by the purchases. Where does the expenditure that generates income originate? To find out, let's start at the box marked "households."

Households purchase about 65% of GNP for consumption (C). Now move along the upper loop and notice that investment purchases (I) add to the flow of expenditures as funds from the nation's financial system are used to finance acquisition of producer durables, new structures, and other investment goods. Then as you reach the top of the loop, government purchases (G) represent another addition to the flow of spending. Finally, moving down along the upper loop toward the box marked "business firms," notice that some spending is for import purchases (M) from international trade. Expenditures by U.S. buyers for such goods as Japanese computers and televisions, German automobiles, and Korean shoes end up as receipts to foreign sellers rather than to U.S. businesses. The spending for imports is therefore removed from the circular flow and does not end up as income to U.S. businesses and households. However, purchases of U.S. exports (E) represent foreign purchases of U.S. products that help generate income in the United States from international trade. The difference $E - M$ represents net exports (NE). By the time you get to the box marked "business firms," the total spending has grown to the sum $C + I + G + NE$, which you now know represents GNP expressed as a sum of its expenditure components.

The expenditure on GNP generates the national income earned by owners of business firms and members of households. This income is paid out as compensation to employees, net interest on funds borrowed, and rents, and a portion is set aside by business firms as capital consumption allowances. The remainder represents proprietors' income and corporate profits.

We can now trace the uses of national income by moving along the lower loop of the circle. Some of the income earned "leaks out" of the lower loop to pay taxes to governments. A portion of the taxes paid by U.S. households and businesses is used to finance transfers that are added to income and thus become available for spending. However, **net taxes,** which are the difference between taxes and transfers, are positive because taxes exceed transfers. Thus there is a net withdrawal of spending power that is not available to households at this point in the lower loop.

Net taxes:
The difference between taxes and transfer payments.

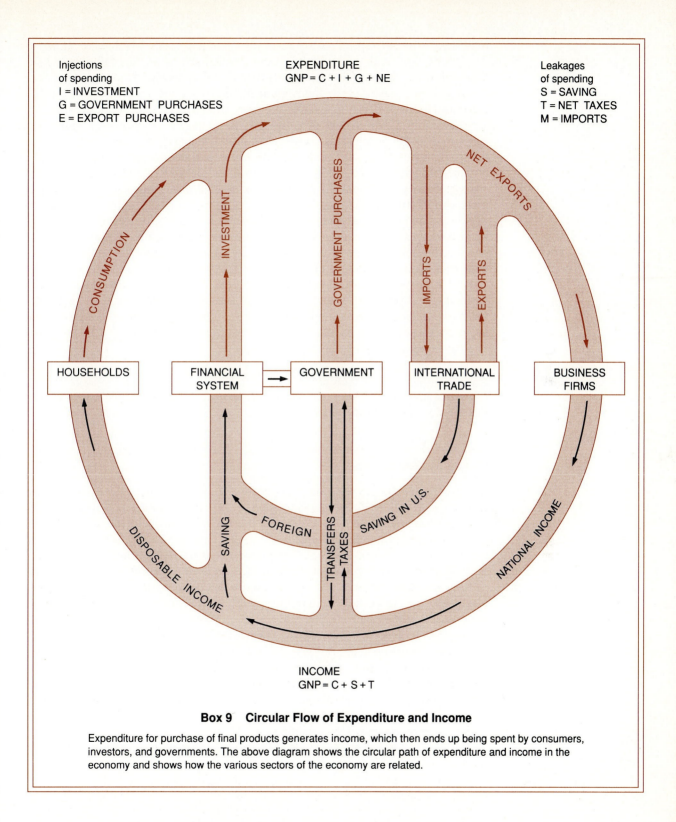

Injections
of spending
I = INVESTMENT
G = GOVERNMENT PURCHASES
E = EXPORT PURCHASES

EXPENDITURE
GNP = C + I + G + NE

Leakages
of spending
S = SAVING
T = NET TAXES
M = IMPORTS

CONSUMPTION

INVESTMENT

GOVERNMENT PURCHASES

NET EXPORTS

IMPORTS

EXPORTS

HOUSEHOLDS

FINANCIAL SYSTEM

GOVERNMENT

INTERNATIONAL TRADE

BUSINESS FIRMS

DISPOSABLE INCOME

SAVING

FOREIGN

SAVING IN U.S.

TRANSFERS

TAXES

NATIONAL INCOME

INCOME
GNP = C + S + T

Box 9   Circular Flow of Expenditure and Income

Expenditure for purchase of final products generates income, which then ends up being spent by consumers, investors, and governments. The above diagram shows the circular path of expenditure and income in the economy and shows how the various sectors of the economy are related.

Net taxes (T) are then used to finance government purchases, which were shown in the upper loop. Finally, a portion of income earned also flows out of the lower loop as saving, which is channeled to the financial system to provide funds for investment purchases. Personal saving is the portion of household income that is not used to make purchases or to pay taxes over the year. The financial system does not merely serve investors. Governments also absorb some of the saving during the year when they run a budget deficit. This occurs when insufficient taxes are collected to finance government purchases and transfers. When this is the case the government must borrow through the financial system, as shown by the flow of funds from the financial system to government. In the 1980s the federal government was absorbing as much as $200 billion of annual savings to finance its enormous deficits.

Disposable income:
The amount of income available for households to spend after receipt of government transfer payments and payment of taxes.

Now you're back to the box marked "households," and the process begins all over again as you move to the upper loop. Expenditure on final products during the year has provided households with the income necessary to finance their consumption. **Disposable income** is the amount of income available for households to spend after receipt of government transfer payments (such as Social Security pensions and welfare payments) and payment of taxes. Disposable income either can be used by households to purchase goods for consumption or can be saved. It follows that disposable income represents the sum of household consumption and saving.

GNP expressed as the sum of uses of income is

$$GNP = C + S + T$$

Income is used for consumption purchases, saving, or to pay the difference between taxes and government transfers (net taxes).

The Balance of International Trade and Foreign Saving in the United States

In recent years the U.S. economy has become more dependent on trade with the rest of the world. In 1987 Americans spent $119.9 billion more on imported products than foreigners spent on exports of the products of U.S. firms. The excess of payments for imports over receipts from exports amounted to 2.7% of nominal GNP that year. When the dollar value of imports exceeds the dollar value of exports in a given year, the domestic receipts from foreign trade fall short of the payments made to foreign sellers. When this is the case, there is a *balance of trade deficit* because foreigners earn more dollars than they return to U.S. businesses for purchases of exports during the year.

The excess of dollars accumulated during the year by foreigners in international trade transactions ends up as dollar deposits in U.S. banks. These dollars then enter the U.S. financial system as foreign saving in the United States, as is shown in the circular flow diagram in Box 9. These funds end up as loans to U.S. investors or to governments in the United States or as direct investment in the United States by foreigners. For example, in recent years foreigners have used some of the excess dollars to purchase new U.S. structures.

The flow of funds into the hands of foreigners resulting from international transactions is exactly offset by an inflow of foreign saving in the United States.[6] For

---

[6]Foreign saving in the United States typically exceeds the balance of trade deficit for goods and services. This is because foreign holders of dollars also earn interest income on their U.S. investments, and some foreigners also receive transfer payments from governments in the United States. For example, in 1986 the balance of trade deficit was $105.5 billion, but the excess of dollars earned by foreigners over their expenditure on U.S. products that year was $148.7 billion.

Principles in Practice

Who Owns America? How Foreign Saving and Investment Are Changing the United States

The great American supermarket is something with which you're all familiar. Many of you at one time or another have shopped in an A & P. But did you know that as of early 1988, 52% of A & P was owned by West Germany's Tengelmann A.G.? During the 1980s some of America's best-known corporations have come under the control of foreign investors. For example, the CertainTeed Corporation, famous for roofing materials, was controlled by Saint Gobain, a French firm, as of early 1988.

The growth of foreign investment in the United States in the 1980s is the direct result of the soaring U.S. balance of trade deficit. As the circular flow analysis in this chapter has shown, negative net exports imply that foreign ownership of U.S. assets must increase. And the Japanese, German, French, and Dutch magnates, to name a few, don't particularly like to keep their spare dollars sitting in the bank. Instead they're using those dollars to purchase U.S. real estate, corporate stock, and U.S. government and corporate bonds. In short, U.S. debt to foreigners and foreign ownership of U.S. assets must increase each year that the United States runs a balance of trade deficit.

How much of the vast wealth of the United States is controlled by foreigners? No one really knows, but most estimates indicate that less than 1% of U.S. assets were foreign owned in 1988. However, depending on your perspective, it might seem like a whole lot more. For example, Japanese investors own a large share of the real estate in downtown areas on the West Coast. You might end up getting a job at the U.S. subsidiary of Honda or Canon! In the 1980s both excess dollars accumulated through international trade and a favorable exchange rate for the dollar in terms of foreign currency have made investing in

the United States an attractive option for many foreigners.

There's something good for Americans about foreign ownership of U.S. assets. Americans save very little of their disposable income. The low supply of savings from U.S. households makes funds for investment scarce and puts upward pressure on interest rates. Foreign saving offsets the low rate of U.S. saving and puts downward pressure on interest rates by increasing supplies of loanable funds. By purchasing U.S. government securities such as Treasury bonds, notes, and bills, foreign savers keep the huge federal budget deficit from exerting still more upward pressure on interest rates. By making direct investments in U.S. industries, which is what they do by acquiring ownership of U.S. firms and plants, foreigners in the long run will help U.S. business compete in international markets. This is because funds supplied by foreign investors will help U.S. firms acquire new equipment and technology that will enable them to produce at lower cost in the future. And foreign producers are finding it in their interests to use the U.S. dollars they acquire in trade to build their own plants in the United States. The Toyota Camry you buy may very well have been produced in Georgetown, Kentucky, where Toyota has a plant. Honda also has plants in the United States. Since 1982 manufacturing costs per unit have fallen in the United States, while they have risen in other nations. This makes direct investment in the United States a good deal for foreign producers, who in the late 1980s actually found in many cases that they could *reduce* their labor costs by producing in the United States instead of at home! On the flip side, the more U.S. assets owned by foreigners, the more income earned in the United States will accrue to foreign instead of U.S. citizens in the future.

---

example, when the Japanese sell more products to U.S. buyers than U.S. firms sell in Japanese product markets, the excess of dollars paid by U.S. buyers to Japanese firms over the dollars Japanese buyers spend on U.S. products ends up as deposits in U.S. banks. These dollars represent Japanese saving in the United States that the Japanese supply to the U.S. financial markets. The Japanese-owned dollars might eventually end up as purchases of stocks or bonds in the United States or as direct investments in the United States. Whenever the United States has a balance of trade deficit with Japan, the Japanese will have assets denominated in dollars that they save in the United States rather than use to buy U.S. exports of final products during the year.

Of course, if the United States were to earn export receipts that exceeded the dollar value of import purchases, there would be a *balance of trade surplus*. In this case the United States would earn more foreign currency from export sales than it used to buy imports from foreign markets. Firms that earned foreign currency would use these funds to finance loans in foreign financial markets. In this case there would be U.S. saving in foreign nations rather than foreign saving in the United States.

Leakages and Injections of Purchasing Power and the Demand for U.S. Final Products

Leakage (of spending):
A portion of income that is not used to purchase domestically produced goods during the year.

Injection (of spending):
A purchase made by business firms, governments, or foreign buyers that increases the flow of income in a nation.

A **leakage** of spending represents a portion of income that is not used to purchase domestically produced products during the year. An **injection** of spending is a purchase made by business firms, governments, or foreign buyers that increases the flow of income in a nation. There are three types of leakage of spending power from the circular flow:

1. Net taxes—the difference between total taxes paid to governments and transfer payments made by governments
2. Saving
3. Import purchases

Leakages of spending from the circular flow cause decreases in the demand for U.S. final products. Other things being equal, the more saving, the greater the difference between taxes and transfers, and the greater the import purchases, the less national income is used to buy U.S. goods and services.

Injections of purchasing power for purposes other than consumption by U.S. households increase demand in the economy. The injections illustrated in the circular flow diagram are:

1. Investment
2. Government purchases
3. Exports

A reduction in business investment purchases during the year or a decline in export purchases could spell trouble for the economy by causing a reduction in income. On the other hand, an increase in government purchases will increase the demand for goods and services.

You can think of real GNP as a volume of liquid flowing through the tubes of the circular flow diagram in Box 9. When the injections of spending exceed the leakages of spending, the volume of liquid in the tubes will increase, meaning that real GNP will increase. On the other hand, when the injections of spending fall short of the leakages of spending, the volume of liquid in the tubes will decline, meaning that real GNP will decrease. The task of macroeconomic theory is to understand the economic forces that influence these leakages and injections so as to forecast changes in real GNP and develop policies that stabilize fluctuations in real GNP.

Concept Check

1 What are the expenditure components of GNP?

2 What are the income components of GNP? What are the leakages of income from the circular flow?

3 Why is foreign saving in the United States positive when there is a balance of trade deficit? Under what circumstances will foreign saving in the United States be negative?

Supply and Demand Analysis in Macroeconomics: A Brief Preview

The principles of supply and demand you learned in studying microeconomics will be of use as well in macroeconomics. In macroeconomics we'll study how wages, interest rates, and the international value of the dollar depend on supply and demand in labor, financial, and foreign exchange markets.

In macroeconomics we also make use of *aggregate supply and demand analysis,* which will be developed in detail in a later chapter. Here we offer a brief preview of how shifts in aggregate supply and demand can cause real GNP to fluctuate and how the resulting fluctuations can affect employment opportunities and inflation.

In Box 10 we illustrate how a slump in the demand for goods and services can cause the economy to slip into an economic downturn that can cause unemployment rates to soar. A decrease in demand for a nation's products can result from a reduction in consumer spending (meaning that consumers increase the portion of their disposable income allocated to saving—an increase in the leakage of spending from the circular flow). A decrease in business investment or government spending could also cause a decrease in the general level of demand in the economy. Finally, either a decrease in demand for U.S. exports or an increase in U.S. demand for imported products would also serve to decrease the general level of demand in the economy.

The demand curve drawn in Box 10 is called an *aggregate demand curve,* which shows how demand for U.S. final products is related to an average of prices of U.S. goods and services. The price level, which is plotted on the graph's vertical axis, can be thought of as the *cost of living,* which is the price of purchasing a certain market basket of goods and services during the year compared to the cost of doing so in a base year. (In the chapter entitled "Inflation and Its Consequences" we'll show how the price level is actually measured in the United States, and in the following chap-

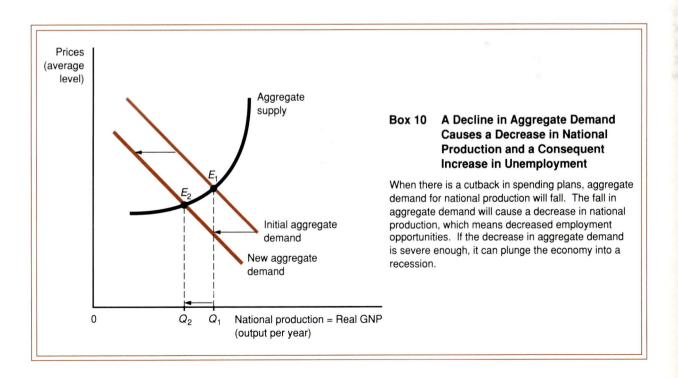

Box 10   A Decline in Aggregate Demand Causes a Decrease in National Production and a Consequent Increase in Unemployment

When there is a cutback in spending plans, aggregate demand for national production will fall. The fall in aggregate demand will cause a decrease in national production, which means decreased employment opportunities. If the decrease in aggregate demand is severe enough, it can plunge the economy into a recession.

ter we'll explain how an aggregate demand curve is derived and how it differs from the demand curve for a particular product.) The horizontal axis on the graph plots real GNP, which, as you've already learned, is a measure of aggregate national production.

The supply curve drawn in Box 10 is an *aggregate supply curve*, which shows how national production for the economy as a whole is related to the price level. Initially the economy is in equilibrium at point E_1, at which the aggregate demand and aggregate supply curves intersect. At the point of equilibrium there is a balance between the willingness of buyers to purchase goods and services and the willingness of sellers to make them available. When the economy achieves equilibrium, there are on average neither widespread shortages nor widespread surpluses in product markets.

A decrease in the demand for U.S. products moves the economy down along its aggregate supply curve. As this occurs, real GNP declines from Q_1 to Q_2 as the economy moves from equilibrium at E_1 to equilibrium at E_2 in Box 10. A decline in real GNP means less production, which in turn means fewer job opportunities, layoffs of factory workers, and a general reduction in aggregate real income. In other words, a decrease in aggregate demand means bad times for the economy. For example, the Great Depression of the 1930s resulted mainly from a massive decline in aggregate demand. Consumer spending, investment purchases, and demand for U.S. exports plummeted during the Depression. The decline in aggregate demand resulted in both decreased production and decreased income, and as a result one out of every four workers was unemployed. The price level also fell during the Great Depression.

The graph in Box 11 shows how increases in aggregate demand can cause inflation. An increase in aggregate demand means an outward shift in the aggregate demand curve. When aggregate demand increases each month and year, the result

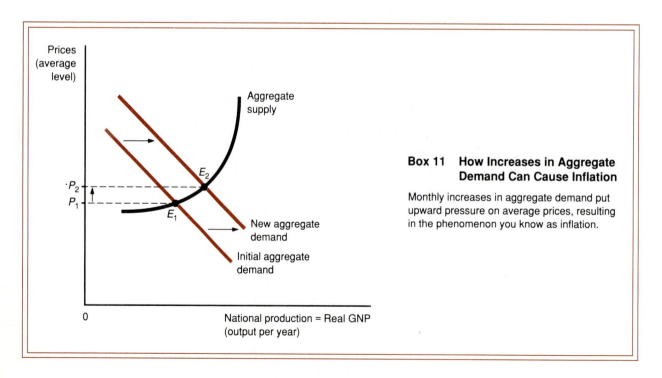

Box 11 How Increases in Aggregate Demand Can Cause Inflation

Monthly increases in aggregate demand put upward pressure on average prices, resulting in the phenomenon you know as inflation.

is continual upward pressure on prices in the economy. This increase in the general level of prices over time is what we mean by inflation. For example, increased availability of money and credit in the economy can cause a surge in aggregate demand. As aggregate demand increases in Box 11, the economy moves from the initial equilibrium at E_1 to a new equilibrium at E_2, at which the price level increases.

Analysis of the role of aggregate demand also suggests a way in which economic policy can be used to control inflation and unemployment. If aggregate demand is forecast to decline, policies that increase spending on U.S. goods and services can be used to offset the decline in spending. For example, government can act to lower interest rates, make credit easier to obtain, or increase government spending (or reduce taxes) to inject spending into the circular flow. Similarly, if aggregate demand is surging, thereby putting upward pressure on prices, the inflation that would result could be reduced if policies are pursued that restrain spending. Policies that seek to influence aggregate demand through their effects on interest rates, credit availability, government spending, and taxes can therefore be used to stabilize aggregate demand. Unfortunately, such policies are not always successful, and the economy inevitably suffers from bouts of high unemployment and high inflation.

You shouldn't get the impression that shifts in aggregate demand are the only culprits in causing inflation and high unemployment. As you'll see in subsequent chapters, shifts in aggregate supply can also cause the economy to contract or overheat. The aggregate supply curve, like a market supply curve, will shift when input prices rise. For example, a sharp rise in unit costs of production caused by an increase in the price of a key input such as labor or fuel can cause a decrease in aggregate supply. The graph in Box 12 shows the impact of a decrease in aggregate supply on the economy. The decrease in aggregate supply results in both a decrease in national production and an increase in prices as the economy moves from equilibrium at point E_1 to point

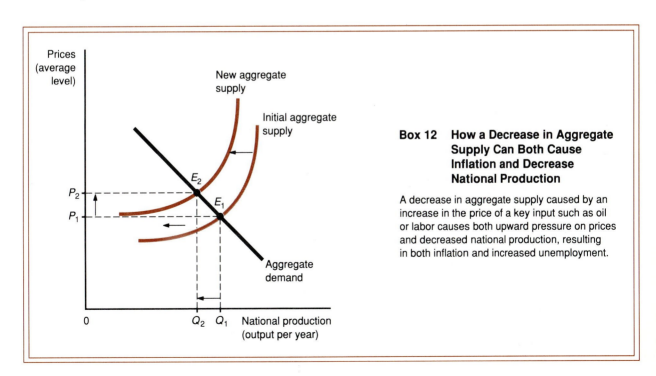

Box 12 How a Decrease in Aggregate Supply Can Both Cause Inflation and Decrease National Production

A decrease in aggregate supply caused by an increase in the price of a key input such as oil or labor causes both upward pressure on prices and decreased national production, resulting in both inflation and increased unemployment.

E_2 in Box 12. As you'll see, decreases in aggregate supply are particularly harmful to the economy because they can result in both inflation and increased unemployment, an unfortunate combination dubbed "stagflation."

This brief introduction gives you an idea of how the concepts of supply and demand you learned in earlier parts of the book can be adapted to understand the overall functioning of the economy. In the next two chapters you'll learn how unemployment and inflation are measured and the consequences of their fluctuations. After you've mastered how the performance of the economy is measured and the consequences of fluctuations in production, income, unemployment, and prices, we can begin to investigate the causes of those fluctuations in detail.

Summary

1. Macroeconomics is the study of the overall performance of the economy as measured by total national production and income each year and fluctuations in income, employment, and prices.
2. Gross national product is the market value of the final goods and services produced in a nation over a period of 1 year. GNP is an imperfect measure of well-being in a nation because it does not include the value of nonpurchased goods and services produced within households. GNP does not include the value of leisure time in a nation, nor is it adjusted for the costs of environmental damage caused by consumption and production.
3. The National Income and Product Accounts represent the official system of national accounting in the United States. Statistics on these accounts are published quarterly by the U.S. Department of Commerce and are used to measure the performance of the national economy.
4. Total value added in a nation over the year is the difference between the market value of all products of business firms and the market value of all intermediate products and is equivalent to GNP. Value added at each stage of production is the worth added to items purchased from other firms.
5. Aggregate expenditure must reflect annual income in the nation because whatever is spent during the year ultimately becomes income to some individual or organization. Therefore GNP must be equal to the sum of all income payments to workers, landlords, owners of equipment and structures, and profits of business enterprises.
6. From an expenditure standpoint, GNP is the sum of consumption, investment, government purchases, and net exports. Net exports are the difference between exports and imports of goods and services over the year. Exports are the dollar value of U.S.-produced goods sold abroad. Imports are the portion of expenditures accounted for by U.S. purchases of goods produced in foreign nations. When imports exceed exports, net exports are negative.
7. From the income standpoint, GNP is the sum of annual compensation of employees, proprietors' income, corporate profits, net interest, rental income, capital consumption allowances, and indirect business taxes. Capital consumption allowances are a form of business saving to fund the replacement of depreciated capital. Capital consumption allowances, indirect business taxes, and corporate profits taxes are not paid out as income to members of households.
8. Nominal GNP is the market value of a nation's aggregate production of final goods and services based on current prices, while real GNP measures the value of aggregate production using base year prices. Changes in real GNP reflect

changes in aggregate production over time more accurately than do changes in nominal GNP.

9. The circular flow of expenditure and income in an economy stems from the fact that expenditures on final products end up as income, which is then used to make purchases. Disposable income is the income available to households for spending or saving after payment of taxes.

10. The forces of supply and demand in the aggregate influence real GNP and the cost of living in a nation. Fluctuations in real GNP and prices can be caused by shifts in either aggregate supply or aggregate demand.

Key Terms and Concepts

Gross national product (GNP)
National Income and Product Accounts (NIPA)
Aggregates
Intermediate products
Total value added in a nation
Nominal GNP
Real GNP
Aggregate real income
Net exports
Aggregate expenditure
Personal consumption expenditures

Gross private domestic investment
Depreciation
Net private domestic investment
Government purchases of goods and services
Transfer payments
Indirect business taxes
Corporate profits taxes
Net taxes
Disposable income
Leakage (of spending)
Injection (of spending)

Problems and Applications

1. During the year a small nation produces the following final products: 1 million automobiles, 5 million outfits of clothing, 10 million pounds of food, rental of 2 million dwelling units, 1 million hours of attorneys' services to households, and 2 million hours of medical services to households. The current market prices for these products are:
   - $10,000 per automobile
   - $100 per outfit of clothing
   - $2 per pound of food
   - $4,000 per year per dwelling unit
   - $20 per hour of attorneys' services
   - $30 per hour of medical services

   Calculate the nation's gross national product at current prices.

2. Suppose nominal GNP in the U.S. economy increases from $5,000 billion in 1990 to $5,500 billion in 1991. Can you conclude that aggregate production, income, and job opportunities have increased as well? Explain your answer.

3. Explain why GNP would be overestimated if the market values of both final products and intermediate products were included in it.

4. The market value of all sales in an economy, including those of intermediate products, is $10,000 billion. If the market value of intermediate products is $6,000 billion, what is the total value added in the nation? Why is the value added equal to gross national product?

5. GNP is currently equal to $4,500 billion. Consumption is $3,000 billion, and government purchases are $1,000 billion. If net exports are zero, how much is

gross private domestic investment? What are the major components of gross private domestic investment? Under what circumstances would net private domestic investment be negative?

6. During 1985 total government expenditures in the United States amounted to $1,400 billion. In the same year the government purchases component of GNP was only $815 billion. Explain why the government purchases component of GNP falls short of actual government expenditures. List some of the important government expenditures that are not included in the government purchases component of GNP. What is the logic of excluding these expenditures?

7. GNP is $5,000 billion in the current year. During the year employee compensation is $3,000 billion, net interest earned is $300 billion, and rental income is $50 billion. Calculate the sum of corporate profits and proprietors' income, assuming that capital consumption allowances are $400 billion and indirect business taxes are $300 billion.

8. Suppose investment, government purchases, and exports are expected to decline this year. Can you conclude that real GNP will also decline? Why would you look at growth in disposable income to predict changes in consumer spending?

9. Real GNP is currently $5,000 billion. How will a decrease in aggregate supply affect real GNP?

10. Explain why, other things being equal, a decrease in aggregate demand will decrease real GNP.

Suggested Readings

Albert T. Sommers, *The U.S. Economy Demystified,* Lexington, Mass.: Lexington Books, 1985. Chapters 1 and 2 provide an in-depth analysis of the national economic accounting system. Chapter 3 shows how to use the data as indicators of business conditions.

U.S. Department of Commerce, Bureau of Economic Analysis, *Survey of Current Business,* Washington, D.C.: U.S. Government Printing Office, monthly. This periodical is the official source of data on the National Income and Product Accounts. Each issue contains a review of the current business situation, economic analysis of topics related to national economic accounting, and a wealth of data on the performance of the economy.

A Forward Look

Fluctuations in economic performance can be gauged by ups and downs in real GNP. In the following chapter we examine the consequences of gaps between real GNP and the potential output of the economy. When an economy fails to operate at its potential, the result is excessive unemployment. A major goal of the next chapter is to develop measures of unemployment and analyze the factors that cause the unemployment rate to fluctuate.

Other National Income and Product Account Concepts

The National Income and Product Accounts include other measures of aggregate production and income that serve particular purposes. This brief appendix introduces the concepts of net national product, national income, and personal income as they are defined in the NIPA. You'll also see how these concepts are related to the concepts of GNP and disposable income discussed in the preceding chapter.

Net National Product

Because GNP does include investment purchases reflecting replacement of existing capital goods (including residential structures), it is a *gross* estimate of the value of production. To account for *net* additions to capital stock, a measure of depreciation of the existing capital stock, the capital consumption allowance, must be deducted from new capital produced. Netting out capital consumption allowances from GNP gives a measure of **net national product (NNP):**

Net national product (NNP):
Gross national product less capital consumption allowances (depreciation).

$$\text{Net national product} = \text{GNP} - \text{Capital consumption allowances}$$

Net national product measures the sum total of consumption, government purchases, net exports, and investment for *net additions to capital,* excluding any purchases for replacement of worn-out capital.

National, Personal, and Disposable Income

The accounting adjustment required to make total income equal total expenditure gives a misleading view of actual income available for spending by members of households. To address this problem, a number of additional income concepts are reported in the National Income and Product Accounts.

Let's begin with *national income*.

National income (NI):
Net national product less indirect business taxes.

1. *National income.* **National income (NI)** equals net national product less indirect business taxes. When compared to GNP, national income as defined in the National Income and Product Accounts is smaller because it excludes capital consumption allowances of business firms (a form of business saving to finance worn-out and obsolete capital) and indirect business taxes. It's a measure of the income actually earned by members of households who supply the inputs necessary to produce the goods and services included in GNP. Indirect business taxes must be subtracted from NNP because they don't reflect actual payment for input services. *National income is the best measure in the NIPA of the household and business earnings from the use of productive resources over a year.* National income amounted to $3,635.9 billion in 1987.

Box 1   From GNP to Disposable Income Step by Step

			Nominal amount in 1987 (billions of dollars)
Step 1	Gross national product		4,486.2
	Less:	Capital consumption allowances	− 479.4
	Equals:	Net national product	4,006.8
Step 2	Net national product		4,006.8
	Less:	Indirect business taxes and other adjustments[a]	− 370.9
	Equals:	National income	3,635.9
Step 3	National income		3,635.9
	Less:	Social Security payroll taxes	− 394.4
		Corporate income taxes	− 137.5
		Undistributed corporate profits	− 43.3
	Plus:	Transfer payments and other adjustments[b]	+ 685.1
	Equals:	Personal income	3,745.8
Step 4	Personal income		3,745.8
	Less:	Personal taxes	− 564.7
	Equals:	Disposable income	3,181.1

[a]Other adjustments are a deduction of business transfer payments such as pensions, a statistical discrepancy, and an addition of subsidies less current surplus of government enterprises. These additional adjustments amounted to $29.5 billion in 1987.

[b]Includes additional interest income not received for productive services and business transfer payments such as pensions.

Source: U.S. Department of Commerce, *Survey of Current Business,* January 1988.

2. *Personal income.* **Personal income** is national income plus government transfer payments and income received from sources other than sale of productive services, less Social Security payroll taxes, corporate profits taxes, and undistributed corporate profits. *Personal income is the best measure of income available to households for spending before personal taxes are paid.* Government transfer payments must be added to national income to obtain this measure because these represent income to those who don't sell input services. Similarly, undistributed corporate profits and corporate profits taxes are part of the income of corporations that isn't paid out to stockholders during the year. This income is unavailable for spending by stockholders and must therefore be subtracted from national income to obtain a measure of spendable income. Personal income in the United States was $3,745.8 billion in 1987. *Personal income exceeds national income because the value of government transfers exceeds Social Security taxes, corporate profits taxes, and undistributed corporate profits.*

Personal income:
National income plus government transfer payments and income received from sources other than sale of productive services, less Social Security payroll taxes, corporate profits taxes, and undistributed corporate profits.

3. *Disposable personal income.* **Disposable personal income,** which is also simply called disposable income, is personal income less personal taxes. *Disposable income is the best measure of money income that individuals have available to spend on market goods and services.* Disposable income in 1987 amounted to $3,181.1 billion.

Disposable personal income:
Personal income less personal taxes. Also called *disposable income.*

If all spending by individuals is deducted from disposable personal income along with all interest payments (including mortgage interest), the result is **personal saving.** Personal saving was $120.2 billion in 1987, which was 2.7% of GNP.

The table in Box 1 summarizes all the steps necessary to derive disposable income from GNP. Data for 1987 nominal GNP and its components are included in the table.

Personal saving:
Disposable personal income less all spending by individuals and all interest payments.

Concept Check

1 Why is net national product less than gross national product?

2 What is measured by national income, personal income, and disposable income?

3 Explain why personal income exceeds national income but disposable income is less than national income.

Key Terms and Concepts

Net national product (NNP)
National income (NI)
Personal income

Disposable personal income
Personal saving

Business Cycles and Unemployment

Unemployment can be a devastating experience. Not only does your income fall when you're unemployed, but so do your morale and health. Macroeconomic policies seek to minimize unemployment and help the economy accommodate jobs for a growing labor force. You've undoubtedly heard the terms "recession" and "economic expansion" talked about on the nightly news. During a recession, unemployment typically increases. Expansions, on the other hand, are characterized by growth in real GNP and expanding employment opportunities. The ups and downs of real GNP affect both aggregate real income and job opportunities. The fact is, your future can depend on how well the economy performs.

A major goal of this chapter is to show how employment is measured and how some unemployment is normally expected each month in a dynamic economy that doesn't instantaneously adjust to change. We'll also develop some benchmarks called the *natural rate of unemployment* and *potential GNP* against which actual economic performance can be evaluated. We'll discuss the problem of inflation in detail in the next chapter. In later chapters we'll investigate the actual causes of and cures for excessive unemployment, along with policies that seek to minimize fluctuations in the economy.

Although the historical trend has been for real GNP to grow, there have always been periods of instability during which real GNP falls short of the national potential to produce goods and services. In these times there is excessive unemployment of workers and other resources. For example, during a severe recession in 1982, unemployment of the nation's labor force reached levels of over 10%.

When excessively high numbers of workers are unemployed, it's difficult for new entrants to the labor force to find jobs, and more people have difficulty meeting their expenses. Excessive unemployment is wasteful because the labor services of idle workers are not being used to produce goods and services. Lack of employment can be a demoralizing experience that disrupts the lives of families and threatens the social fabric of the nation. Because unemployment is seldom evenly distributed among regions of the nation, it disrupts some localities more than others. For example, in early 1986 nearly 8% of the U.S. labor force was unemployed. However, during that same period the proportion of the labor force unemployed in Louisiana, a state hard hit by the reduced demand for petroleum, was nearly 12%! In contrast, the unemployment rate in Massachusetts in early 1986 was only about 4%.

Concept Preview

After reading this chapter, you should be able to:

1 Discuss the record of fluctuation in real GNP in recent years and understand the consequences of declines in real GNP.
2 Discuss the phases of the business cycle and give examples of recent periods of recession and expansion of the U.S. economy.
3 Understand the concept of the unemployment rate and discuss different possible causes of fluctuations in the unemployment rate.
4 Define the concept of full employment and show how it is related to the natural rate of unemployment. Also, show how the actual unemployment rate is the sum of the natural unemployment rate and the cyclical unemployment rate.
5 Discuss the social costs of unemployment and programs designed to cushion those costs.
6 Understand the concept of potential GNP and the difficulties involved in estimating it.

Fluctuations in Real GNP: The Historical Record

Increases in real GNP from one year to the next indicate that the economy's aggregate production of final products also increases. More production means more goods and services available for people to consume. Given a growing population, increases in real GNP are necessary to maintain the standard of living as measured on average by goods and services per person. When real GNP falls from one year to the next, final output per person will also fall, implying reduced standards of living. When output falls from one year to the next, employers won't use as much input as they did the year before. This means some workers will lose their jobs and new entrants into the labor force will have difficulty finding jobs. *Declines in real GNP therefore also imply declines in income, employment opportunities, and the standard of living on average in a nation as output per person falls in the economy.*

The Business Cycle

Business cycle:
The term used to describe the fluctuations in aggregate production as measured by the ups and downs of real GNP.

Unfortunately, real GNP doesn't steadily increase year after year. There are irregular fluctuations in real GNP over time that have consequences for you and for everyone in the nation. The **business cycle** is the term used to describe the fluctuations in aggregate production as measured by the ups and downs of real GNP.

The phases of the business cycle, although not subject to easy predictability or regularity, can be readily identified. Box 1 contains a stylized graph depicting the recurrent phases of the business cycle that shows the periodic ups and downs of real GNP. Real GNP is estimated quarterly by the U.S. Department of Commerce.

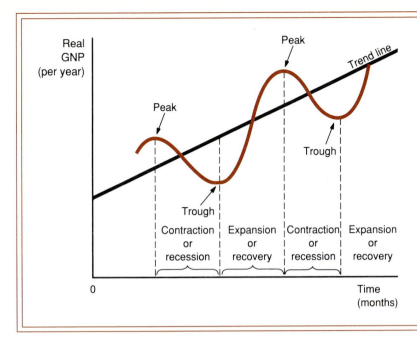

Box 1   The Business Cycle

The business cycle is characterized by peaks and troughs of real GNP fluctuating about an upward trend line. The fluctuations, of course, are not as regular as those illustrated in the stylized graph.

The quarterly estimate is then multiplied by 4 (after adjusting for normal seasonal variation) to obtain the annual rate of GNP over the 3-month period.[1]

The phases of the business cycle are:

1. *Peak.* The *peak* is the highest level of real GNP in the cycle. Each peak (two are illustrated in the graph) is characterized by an economy operating at close to full capacity so that national product and national income correspond to a very high degree of utilization of labor, factories, and offices. During a peak of the cycle there are likely to be shortages of labor, parts, and materials in certain markets. On occasion the economy might be booming to such a degree during a peak that factories and offices are being utilized around the clock with two or more shifts of labor. During such boom periods the economy can actually exceed its normal capacity.

2. *Contraction or recession.* A **contraction** is a downturn from peak economic activity in the business cycle during which real GNP declines from its previous value. During a contraction real GNP and therefore earnings also decline in the nation. During a contraction business profits typically decline. As profitability falls, so does business demand for investment goods.

Sometimes the decline in real GNP that occurs during a contraction is particularly severe or prolonged. The U.S. Department of Commerce usually considers a contraction to be a **recession** when the decline in real GNP measured at an annual rate occurs for two consecutive 3-month reporting periods.

Recessions that have occurred in the United States since the end of World War II typically have lasted for about 10 to 12 months. In 1982, which was a recession year, real GNP fell by 2.5% of its 1981 value. As a consequence of a decline in real GNP, the percentage of the work force classified as unemployed usually rises by anywhere

Contraction:
A downturn from peak economic activity in the business cycle during which real GNP declines from its previous value.

Recession:
Exists when the decline in real GNP measured at an annual rate occurs for two consecutive 3-month reporting periods.

[1]In some quarters real GNP is normally expected to be higher because of seasonal production patterns. To avoid overestimating the *annual* rate of GNP during quarters when GNP is higher because of seasonal increases, actual data are adjusted downward before multiplying by 4 to obtain annual real GNP. A similar upward adjustment is made for quarters during which real GNP is normally expected to be lower.

Principles in Practice

What Is a Recession, and Who Can Predict When One Will Arrive?

Who decides whether the United States has had the misfortune to be in a recession? Surprisingly, there is no official definition of a recession. Instead the Business Cycle Dating Committee, which meets under the auspices of the National Bureau of Economic Research, dates the beginnings and ends of recessions after they have actually occurred. The Committee consists of seven experts, including Geoffrey Moore of the Center for International Business Cycle Research at the Columbia University Business School.

A recession is usually defined as a period in which output, income, and employment decline nationally over a period lasting at least 6 months. Most economists agree that a 2-quarter decline in real GNP is a recession. During a recession there is a widespread contraction of economic activity affecting many sectors of the economy. Orders for new plants and equipment and for materials and inventories typically plummet. Real GNP, industrial production, and personal income usually decline, while unemployment increases. Almost all recessions are preceded by a decline in stock market prices, but not all declines in stock market prices result in a recession.

Predicting when a recession will start isn't easy, and the record of economists in forecasting the major recessions of the past 20 years hasn't been good. Most forecasters failed to predict the two worst recessions of the 1970s and 1980s—the recessions of 1974-1975 and 1981-1982.

What do you look for when trying to spot a recession brewing? Most economists look for overexpansion of business investment—overstocks of parts and materials as a prelude to a coming contraction. Sudden increases in the prices of key inputs, such as oil, can also precipitate a recession. How to spot a coming recession became a popular sport in 1988 after the stock market crash of 1987 and rising interest rates in early 1988 gave rise to fears that bad times were around the corner. The 6-year expansion from 1982-1988 made many business cycle forecasters fear that the next recession was overdue.* Yet despite the stock market decline, 1988 came in with a boom as the economy approached full employment with the official unemployment rate falling to 5.5%. The stock market decline once again failed to forecast a recession.

*See Sylvia Nasar, "How to Spot a Recession," *Fortune*, March 28, 1988, pp. 63-68.

---

from 2 to 4 percentage points. In a typical nonrecession year only 4% to 6% of the labor force might be unemployed, while during a recession it's not uncommon to observe 1 out of every 10 workers unemployed.

The increased unemployment during a recession can turn families topsy-turvy. As earnings fall, so do living standards. Work routines are broken up, and the idleness that goes with joblessness often leads to mental illness. Typically during a recession, divorces and suicides increase along with the increase in unemployment. From an economic standpoint, the waste of labor and other resources capable of both producing goods and services and earning incomes for their suppliers is lamentable.

3. *Trough.* A *trough* is the lowest level of real GNP observed over the business cyle. Two troughs are illustrated in Box 1. The trough is reached when the economy begins pulling out of a period of contraction or recession. When the economy is in a trough, there is an excessive amount of unemployment and idle productive capacity. Business failures are likely to be prevalent during a trough because of low demand for their products.

Although the trough is the pits, it's also the point at which things start looking up. Once a trough is reached, things can't get much worse and the economic health of the nation begins to take a turn for the better.

4. *Expansion or recovery.* An **expansion** is an upturn of economic activity between a trough and a peak during which real GNP increases. During an expansion, aggregate demand increases and real GNP rises as firms expand production, hire more workers, and begin to purchase more investment goods. Employment opportunities increase during a period of expansion. The expansion in economic activity

Expansion:
An upturn of economic activity between a trough and a peak during which real GNP increases.

after a trough is called a **recovery** if it follows a period of contraction severe enough to be classified as a recession. During an expansion the economy moves toward a new peak where the cycle begins again.

Recovery:
The term used to describe an expansion in economic activity after a trough if the expansion follows a period of contraction severe enough to be classified as a recession.

The cycle of peak-contraction-trough-expansion-peak is never as regular and predictable as in the graph shown in Box 1. However, the fluctuations in real GNP do actually occur even though they don't do so in a clear pattern.

An upward-sloping trend line has been fitted through the peaks and troughs of the cyclical pattern of real GNP. Although real annual GNP fluctuates, the trend is upward over the long run.

Actual Fluctuations and Trend for Real GNP in the United States

The graph in Box 2 shows the actual variation in real GNP over time. A trend line has been fitted through the data to reflect the average rate of increase in real GNP over time. The graph in Box 3 shows the fluctuations in American business activity between 1860 and 1986.

The general upward trend in real GNP is clear in Box 2. On average from 1900 to 1987, real GNP grew by 3.1% per year. *Real GNP has increased more then tenfold since 1900.* However, the growth has not been steady. There are clearly ups and downs in real GNP that can be identified as peaks, contractions, troughs, and expansions in national economic performance. However, the cyclical fluctuations in real GNP are not as regular as those shown in the stylized graph in Box 1.

The purpose of showing the historical record for real GNP is to demonstrate that it fluctuates irregularly and that it has an upward trend. A number of historical periods have been identified on the graph.

1. *The Great Depression.* The Great Depression of the 1930s is clearly identifiable in the graph as a prolonged recession with a deep trough. The Great Depression was unquestionably the trough of troughs.

The Great Depression hit in 1929 as a stock market crash late that year wiped out

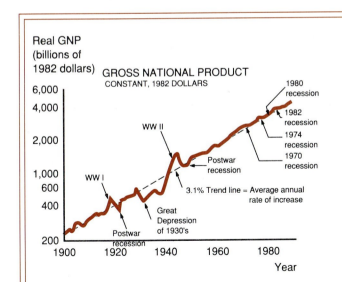

Box 2   The Ups and Downs of U.S. Real GNP

The graph shows that, although real GNP has had its ups and downs since 1900, the trend on average has been upward. The average annual growth rate of real GNP since 1900 has been 3.1%. A number of historical periods are shown on the graph. The scale used to measure real GNP uses the same vertical distance for each doubling of real GNP.

Source: *1986 Historical Chart Book*, Board of Governors of the Federal Reserve System.

a substantial portion of the nation's accumulated savings. From the end of 1929 through 1933, real GNP fell by nearly one third of its 1929 value. Although you're used to living in a world of inflation, during many severe recessions it isn't uncommon for prices on average to fall. From the end of 1929 through 1933, prices fell to only 75% of their 1929 level. Those who could spare a dime in 1933 knew it was worth more then than it had been in 1929.

During the Great Depression there were virtually no business investment purchases. The decline in real income made the prospects for selling goods bleak. Given the gloomy outlook, few investors were willing to build new plants or purchase new equipment.

But the worst part of the Depression was the unemployment. One out of every four workers in the labor force was jobless in 1933. Imagine the terrible waste of having one quarter of the able-bodied workers in the nation without jobs. You can also imagine the plight of the unemployed at the time in a nation that didn't have the unemployment insurance and welfare programs we take for granted today. If you think there are a lot of street people today, you should have been around in the 1930s. The increased unemployment in the early 1930s is all the more dramatic when you realize that in 1929 only 3% of the labor force had been unemployed.

To anyone who lived through it, the Great Depression was a period of social unrest as well as economic contraction. The Depression was worldwide, and the

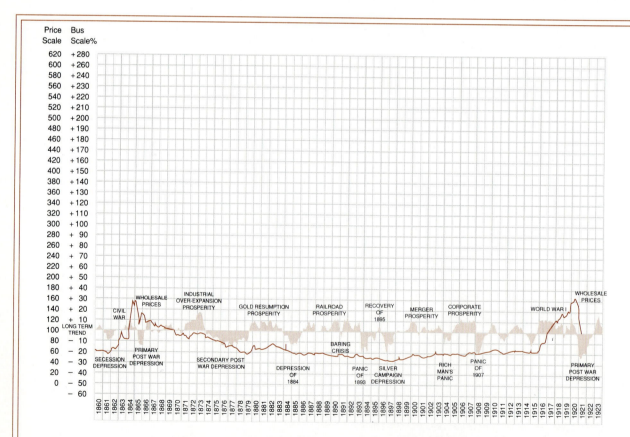

Box 3   The Ups and Downs of U.S. Business Activity

The graph shows the ups and downs of U.S. business activity along with a measure of prices on average since 1860.

social instability in Europe helped spawn the Nazi party and bring Hitler to power. As you'll see in the next part of the book, the Great Depression also affected the thinking of economists, most of whom thought prior to the 1930s that recessions would quickly cure themselves without assistance from government authorities. This led to the birth of macroeconomics as a policy-oriented branch of economics designed to help formulate government programs to prevent severe recessions in which the economy could stagnate for years.

The Great Depression of the 1930s taught economists a great lesson. Macroeconomic policies are designed to help prevent a repeat performance of such an extreme contraction and deep trough in the business cycle.

2. *Wartime prosperity and the Post-WW II expansions.* You might also observe that peaks have been identified for the years when the economy was working at full steam producing goods for the war effort during World War I, just before the 1920s, and during World War II in the early 1940s. Typically after a war ends there is a recession as the economy readjusts.

There was a period of prolonged and markedly steady growth in real GNP in the 1950s. However, the postwar expansion wasn't entirely uninterrupted by contractions and recessions. Immediately after World War II there was a recession, and there were also recessions in 1949, 1954, 1958, and 1961. However, these four recessions were remarkably mild and much shorter than recessions of the past.

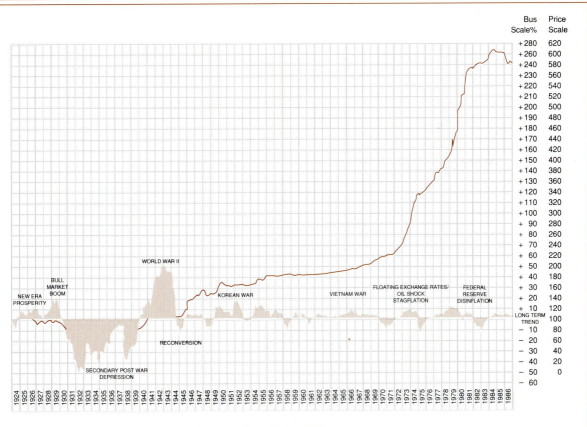

Box 3, Cont'd.

Source: American Trust Co., Cleveland.

3. *The booming sixties.* After the recession of 1961 ended, the economy moved into a period of expansion until a recession hit in 1970. The 1960s were a period of military expansion and the Vietnam conflict. The increase in government purchases fueled the economy and also resulted in rising inflation.

4. *The curious seventies.* The 1970s came in with a recession. Although the recovery from this recession began in 1971, something strange happened to the economy in 1973. At that time the Organization of Petroleum Exporting Countries (OPEC) instituted an embargo of oil shipments to the United States and other nations. Inflation increased, and the price of petroleum products in particular skyrocketed. However, not only did inflation go up in the 1970s, so did unemployment! By 1974 the economy was buffeted by double-digit inflation and a severe recession. This was viewed as highly unusual because in the past inflation usually eased up during a recession and sometimes prices actually fell, as was the case in the Great Depression. Real GNP fell substantially between 1973 and 1975, and unemployment soared to 9% of the labor force. However, it was all over by the end of 1975 as the economy recovered and an expansion led to a 5% growth in real GNP in 1976. Inflation continued at a rampant rate in the remainder of the 1970s, but the nation avoided another recession until the 1980s.

5. *The expanding eighties.* Like the 1970s, the 1980s came in with a recession. The recession of 1980 was brief, lasting only 6 months, but extraordinary in the sense that it took place when inflation was still in double digits. As was the case for the 1974 recession, inflation and high unemployment sat side by side. The recession of 1980 was quite mild with real GNP declining by only 0.2% that year. However, inflation remained a serious problem for the economy, running at 10% annual rates. At the end of 1982 the economy was plunged into the deepest recession it had experienced since the Great Depression of the 1930s. In that year real GNP fell by 2.5%, and the unemployment rate soared to 11% of the labor force.

But the recession ended in late 1982, and the economy was well on its way to recovery. The years between 1982 and 1987 were a period of expansion for the economy. However, by 1988, after the stock market crash of 1987, many economists began to worry that the 1980s would end with still another recession. Despite this concern, in early 1988 real GNP was still growing at a rate in excess of 4% per year.

Concept Check

1 How are living standards in a nation affected by a decline in real GNP from one year to the next when population is growing?

2 How would you identify the phases of the business cycle from quarterly data on real GNP?

3 What has the trend been for growth of real GNP in the United States since 1900?

Unemployment

When real GNP declines over a period, businesses reduce their output. Cutbacks in production inevitably mean that firms will use less labor and materials. This means some workers will lose their jobs and those seeking new jobs will have a harder time finding employment. Increased unemployment is therefore a major consequence of cyclical declines in real GNP during periods of contraction or recession. Workers in some industries are more apt to be unemployed during recessions than others. Those who are engaged in the production of producer durable goods, consumer durable goods, and construction typically are hard hit by economic contractions and recessions. This is because investment purchases by businesses and purchases of durable goods by consumers decline during recessions. However, unemployment is not limited to a few industries. As unemployed workers cut back on their spending, workers in service and other industries soon find their jobs in jeopardy.

Some unemployment naturally exists even during periods of peak economic activity. The portion of unemployment attributable to a cyclical downturn or production below the economy's potential can, however, be identified once agreement is reached on what constitutes "normal" unemployment. In this way the concept of "full" or high employment for the economy can be defined.

Macroeconomic stabilization policies seek to minimize excessive unemployment. However, to intelligently formulate such policies, it is first necessary to understand what unemployment is and how it is measured. In this way excessive or cyclical unemployment can be distinguished from normal unemployment.

The Unemployment Rate

The total **labor force** is the sum of the number of persons over the age of 16 with jobs and workers who are actively seeking a job but currently do not have one. The **unemployment rate** measures the ratio of the number of people classified as unemployed to the total labor force. An **unemployed person** is defined as one over the age of 16 who is available for work and has actively sought employment during the previous 4 weeks. Note that this definition does not include people who *choose not* to have or seek jobs and therefore are not part of the labor force. For example, full-time students over the age of 16, people who choose to devote their time to household chores or to raising their children, retired people, people unable to work because of disability, and people in mental or correctional institutions, although they are not working for pay, are not considered to be unemployed. These groups by definition are not part of the labor force.

The table in Box 4 shows the labor force, number of people unemployed, and

Labor force:
The total number of persons over age 16 with jobs and workers who are actively seeking a job but currently do not have one.

Unemployment rate:
Measures the ratio of the number of people classified as unemployed to the total labor force.

Unemployed person:
A person over age 16 who is available for work and has actively sought employment during the previous 4 weeks.

Box 4   Labor Force and Unemployment, 1985*

Total labor force [a]	108,856,000
Labor force as a percent of noninstitutional U.S. population aged 16 years and over	65.1
Unemployed workers	8,312,000
Unemployed workers as a percent of labor force	7.1

* Annual average of monthly data.
[a] Includes members of resident armed forces.

Source: U.S. Department of Labor, Bureau of Labor Statistics, *Employment and Earnings* , March 1986.

---

the unemployment rate in 1985 based on averages for each month of the year. The year 1985 is chosen as a typical year of the 1980s for which there was no recession but for which unemployment was regarded as excessive. In 1985, 7.1% of the U.S. labor force was unemployed on average each month.

The official unemployment statistics do include people who are temporarily let out of service without pay by their employers but are waiting to be recalled to work in the same job. These people, though not actively seeking a *new* job, are counted among the ranks of the unemployed. A **layoff** is the temporary suspension of employment without pay for a period of 7 consecutive days or more. Workers who are on layoff are not fired. Instead they are let go because of reduced demand for the product they are employed to produce. Layoffs are a consequence of cyclical declines in aggregate demand. A worker who is laid off has some expectation of being recalled by his or her employer should business pick up again. Of course, some layoffs end up being permanent, in which case the worker must search for a new job to regain employment.

The U.S. Department of Labor estimates the unemployment rate each month with a sample of about 60,000 households. The households in the sample are changed periodically. A person is classified as unemployed if he or she did not do any work the previous week, part time or full time. Note that people who have suffered reductions in paid work *hours* because of employer work cutbacks are *not* counted as unemployed. For example, a person whose work hours were cut from 40 to 20 a week because of slack demand for the product his employer manufactures would not be counted as unemployed. However, each two workers who suffer a 50% reduction in paid hours of work amount to the loss of a 40-hour work week for the economy! This type of loss in work isn't picked up by the unemployment statistics. In this sense, because the statistics don't measure the "underemployment" of workers who are not working full time but would like to be, they tend to underestimate actual unemployment.

The U.S. Department of Labor's monthly survey asks those in the sample whether they are actively looking for work. Some of the people who answer "no" to this question would be looking for work in the labor market if wages were higher. Similarly, some of those classified as unemployed because they answer "yes" to the question might have unrealistic ideas about the value of their services and the wages they can reasonably expect. They might therefore be holding out for a job that they are unlikely to ever be offered.

A **discouraged worker** is one who leaves the labor force (stops actively seeking a job) after unsuccessfully searching for a job. It's not unusual for more than 1% of those surveyed by the Department of Labor to respond that they aren't looking for a job because they don't believe one can be found. It's difficult to objectively determine why workers respond in this way. However, by not counting discouraged workers among the ranks of the unemployed, the official unemployment statistics tend to *underestimate* actual unemployment. Because of the way it treats part-time and discouraged workers, the official unemployment rate therefore is only an imperfect indicator of actual unemployment as a percentage of the labor force.

Who Are the Unemployed?

The table in Box 5 shows the unemployment rate experienced by various demographic groups in the labor force during February 1986, a month in which the economy was generally agreed to be operating below its potential. At that time nearly 9

Layoff:
The temporary suspension of employment without pay for a period of 7 consecutive days or more.

Discouraged worker:
A worker who leaves the labor force (stops actively seeking a job) after unsuccessfully searching for a job for a certain period.

Box 5 Unemployed Persons 16 Years of Age and Over by Marital Status, Race, and Sex (February 1986)

	Number of persons	Unemployment rate (percent)
Male workers		
All	5,161,000	8.0
Married, spouse present	2,168,000	5.3
Widowed, divorced, separated	667,000	10.3
Single, never married	2,326,000	13.7
Female workers		
All	3,880,000	7.6
Married, spouse present	1,595,000	5.7
Widowed, divorced, separated	841,000	8.2
Single, never married	1,444,000	11.1
White males		
All	4,033,000	7.2
Married, spouse present	1,824,000	5.0
Widowed, divorced, separated	522,000	9.7
Single, never married	1,687,000	11.9
Black males		
All	976,000	15.8
Married, spouse present	274,000	9.1
Widowed, divorced, separated	128,000	13.5
Single, never married	574,000	25.6
White females		
All	2,921,000	6.7
Married, spouse present	1,347,000	5.4
Widowed, divorced, separated	621,000	7.5
Single, never married	952,000	9.0
Black females		
All	926,000	14.0
Married, spouse present	192,000	8.7
Widowed, divorced, separated	235,000	11.3
Single, never married	500,000	21.9
Teenagers (16-19 yrs. old)		
All	1,443,000	20.1
White	1,115,000	17.8
Black	297,000	38.4

Source: U.S. Department of Labor, Bureau of Labor Statistics, *Employment and Earnings*, March 1986.

million workers were unemployed.[2] The unemployment rate for males, 8%, was a bit higher than the corresponding figure for females. The table also shows some interesting patterns that tend to hold most of the time. First note that the unemployment rate for married males or married females living with a spouse is lower than

[2] This figure is not seasonally adjusted.

the corresponding rate for single persons or other persons without or not living with a spouse. In fact, the unemployment rate for single males in February 1986 was 13.7%, which is close to three times the corresponding rate for married males living with a spouse! The unemployment rate for single females of 11.1% was nearly twice the rate for married females living with a spouse.

The table also breaks down the unemployment rate by race. Notice that unemployment rates for blacks are typically much higher than those for whites. The overall unemployment rate for black males in February 1986 was about 16%, which is about twice the corresponding unemployment rate for white males. The unemployment rate for single blacks is quite high. About one in four single black males was unemployed in early 1986, and about one in five single black females was unemployed during the same period.

The unemployment rate for teenagers (ages 16-19) is typically much higher than the unemployment rate for adults. For example, in February 1986 over 20% of all teenagers in the labor force were unemployed. The unemployment rate for black teenagers was 38.4%.

Types of Unemployment

Frictional, Structural, and Cyclical Unemployment

Job separation:
Occurs when a worker leaves a job for any reason: quitting, being fired, or being laid off.

Job search:
The process of looking for suitable work either by those just entering the labor force or by those having just experienced a job separation.

Job finding:
Occurs when an unemployed worker accepts an offer of a new job.

Frictional unemployment:
Represents the usual amount of unemployment resulting from people who have left jobs that did not work out and are searching for new employment, or people who are either entering or reentering the labor force to search for a job.

Structural unemployment:
Unemployment resulting from shifts in the pattern of demand for goods and services or changes in technology in the economy that affect the profitability of hiring workers in specific industries.

When a worker leaves a job for any reason, a **job separation** occurs. Job separation can result when a worker quits, is fired, or is laid off. Job separations are always to be expected because of poor matches of workers to jobs and changes in the pattern of demand for goods and services. Few of you, especially at the outset of your careers, would be willing to sign a lifetime contract with an employer. Similarly, employers can't be expected to retain workers who don't perform up to a minimum standard.

Unemployment would always be zero if the time between a job separation and the discovery of a new job for each worker were zero and if new entrants and reentrants into the labor force immediately found a job. The time, effort, and transaction costs involved in gathering information to find a new job guarantee that there will always be some unemployed workers looking for jobs. **Job search** is the process of looking for a suitable job either by those just entering the labor force or by those having just experienced a job separation. **Job finding** occurs when an unemployed worker accepts an offer of a new job.

Members of the labor force search for jobs that best suit their skills and preferences. Workers and employers make mistakes in the process of matching workers to jobs. It's normal for workers to leave jobs they find unsuitable and for employers to fire workers who aren't performing their tasks up to required standards. **Frictional unemployment** represents the usual amount of unemployment resulting from people who have left jobs that didn't work out and are searching for new employment, or people who are either entering or reentering the labor force to search for a job. For example, if you were to graduate and spend 6 months looking for the right job, you would be counted among the frictionally unemployed during that period. If a worker who is dissatisfied with a job managing a fast-food restaurant quits and takes 2 months to find a new job, that worker would be among the frictionally unemployed for that period.

Structural unemployment is unemployment resulting from shifts in the pattern of demand for goods and services or changes in technology in the economy that affect the profitability of hiring workers in specific industries. Structural unemployment often requires that workers who lose their jobs learn new skills or move to another location to find a satisfactory new job. When the demand for goods decreases, some workers will naturally be dismissed as production of those goods declines. For example, a decline in the demand for petroleum products causes a decrease in the demand for oil field and refinery workers. Oil workers who lose their jobs as a result of this reduction in demand are said to be structurally unemployed. Similarly, if a decrease in demand for Chevrolets and Chryslers occurs because consumers choose to buy more Mazdas and BMWs, then U.S. auto workers who lose their jobs will be part of structural unemployment.

To regain employment, some workers in the pool of the structurally unemployed will have to find jobs in new industries requiring different skills. As noted earlier, a change in technology can also cause structural unemployment. More automation in the automobile industry will imply a reduction in the demand for auto workers.

The economy is always in flux in the sense that the pattern of demand and technology changes almost monthly. Both the industrial and regional patterns of demand for workers also change, implying that some workers will lose their jobs and have to search for new ones as a result of normal changes in the economy.

It's inevitable that a certain percentage of the labor force will experience job separation over the year. Forcing workers to stay in a job forever and preventing employers from ever cutting back employment, going out of business, or firing or laying off workers would involve losses in efficiency just as surely as excessive unemployment would result in waste.

Some unemployment, however, is attributable directly to cyclical declines in real GNP. **Cyclical unemployment** is the amount of unemployment resulting from declines in real GNP during periods of contraction or recession when the economy fails to operate at its potential. The increase in unemployment that is observed during recessions is cyclical unemployment. In macroeconomic policy analysis, cyclical unemployment receives the greatest amount of attention. This is because cyclical unemployment is viewed as controllable. Policies that help prevent cyclical declines in real GNP can prevent cyclical unemployment. When cyclical unemployment is present, the economy is not utilizing its labor force to the extent possible. This means not only that workers are unemployed but also that aggregate production and aggregate real income are below the levels the economy is capable of supporting.

The total amount of unemployment in any month is the sum of frictional, structural, and cyclical unemployment. Frictional and structural unemployment result from natural and perhaps unavoidable occurrences in a dynamic economy. Cyclical unemployment, however, is the result of imbalances between aggregate purchases and the aggregate production corresponding to full employment.

Cyclical unemployment:
The amount of unemployment resulting from declines in real GNP during periods of contraction or recession or in any period when the economy fails to operate at its potential.

The Natural Rate of Unemployment

The **natural rate of unemployment** is the percentage of the labor force that can normally be expected to be unemployed for reasons other than cyclical fluctuations in real GNP. In other words, the natural unemployment rate is the sum of frictional and structural unemployment expected over the year. When the economy operates so that there is only structural and frictional unemployment, it is viewed as achieving its potential productive capacity that is normally expected at the peak of the business

Natural rate of unemployment:
The percentage of the labor force that can normally be expected to be unemployed for reasons other than cyclical fluctuations in real GNP.

Full employment:
Occurs when the actual rate of unemployment is no more than the natural rate of unemployment.

cycle.[3] When the actual rate of unemployment is no more than the natural rate of unemployment, the economy operates at **full employment.** *Because the natural rate of unemployment is not zero, full employment does not mean zero unemployment!*

The natural rate of unemployment depends on the rate of job separation expressed as a percentage of the labor force, and the rate of job finding expressed as a percentage of the number of workers unemployed. Given the size of the labor force and the rate of job finding, the lower the rate of job separation resulting from poor matches of employees and employers or changes in the structure of demand and technology, the lower the natural rate of unemployment. Given the size of the labor force and the rate of job separation, the higher the rate of job finding by the unemployed, the lower the natural rate of unemployment.[4] The natural rate of unemployment is generally believed to be in the range of 4% to 6% per year.

In 1985 the natural rate of unemployment was generally believed to be about 6%.[5] If this was the case, cyclical unemployment would have been 1.1% because the actual unemployment rate that year, based on monthly averages, was 7.1%.

Analysis of data on the reasons for unemployment provides some support for the hypothesis that the natural rate of unemployment was close to 6% in early 1986. The table in Box 6 shows the percentage distribution of unemployed persons in early 1986 by reason for unemployment. Over half the unemployed at that time lost their

---

Box 6   Unemployed Persons by Reason for Unemployment (February 1986)

	Percent Distribution
Job losers	53.3
On layoff	16.7
Other job losers	36.6
Job leavers	11.0
Reentrants	25.2
New entrants	10.5
Unemployed as a percentage of the civilian labor force	
Job losers	4.2
Job leavers	0.9
Reentrants	2.0
New entrants	0.8

Source: U.S. Department of Labor, Bureau of Labor Statistics, *Employment and Earnings*, March 1986.

---

[3]Another way to define the natural rate of unemployment is as the unemployment rate that would prevail if all wages and prices were instantaneously adjustable to changes in market conditions.

[4]Actually it's a matter of simple arithmetic to calculate the natural rate of unemployment when there are no movements of workers in and out of the labor force. The natural rate of unemployment, U, under these circumstances is the rate of job separation, s, divided by the sum of the rate of job finding, f, and the rate of job separation: $U = s/(f + s)$. For example, if 1% of the labor force experiences job separation during the year and 15% of the unemployed find jobs, the natural rate of unemployment is $0.01/0.16 = 6.2\%$. See Robert J. Barro, *Macroeconomics,* New York: John Wiley & Sons, 1984, p. 207.

[5]See, for example, Robert J. Gordon, *Macroeconomics,* 4th ed., Boston: Little, Brown, 1987, Chapter 11.

Principles in Practice

What Influences the Natural Rate of Unemployment?

Changes in the natural rate of unemployment can easily be mistaken for cyclical unemployment. For this reason it's important to understand the forces influencing the natural rate of unemployment in an economy. The natural rate of unemployment is related to the willingness of workers to voluntarily separate from a job, job loss, duration of periods of unemployment, and the rate of change in the pattern of demand and technology for the economy.

Younger workers are more likely to quit their jobs than older workers. It simply takes some time for a younger worker to find a good match of skills with employment. It's therefore reasonable to assume that the younger the average age of workers in the labor force, the higher the natural rate of unemployment, because frictional unemployment increases when job separations increase. Teenagers in particular are likely to quit their jobs after only a short period. The higher the percentage of teenagers in the labor force, therefore, the higher the natural rate of unemployment.

The high unemployment rates observed in the United States in the late 1970s were partially the result of the entry of a disproportionately high number of younger workers into the labor force. At that time those of the baby boom generation born in the early 1950s were in their 20s. These younger workers had higher quit rates than older workers, and there were a lot of them. If this reasoning is correct, it implies that the natural rate of unemployment will fall in the 1990s as the bulk of the baby boomers hit age 40 and are snugly matched to the right job. Workers over 40 are much less likely to quit their jobs than younger workers.

Increased fluctuation in the pattern of aggregate demand for domestic goods increases structural unemployment and in turn contributes to a higher natural rate of unemployment. For example, the increase in energy prices that occurred in the mid-1970s disrupted hiring in many U.S. industries. Increased foreign competition also hurt the U.S. automobile and steel industries at that time. One researcher has estimated that the changes in the structure of demand in the late 1970s increased the natural rate of unemployment by 1 to 2 percentage points.*

Rapid changes in technology designed to cut costs can also result in greater job separation of workers. In an effort to compete more effectively with foreign firms, many U.S. firms have shifted to new technology that requires fewer workers per plant and results in slower hiring of new workers.

A worker in a two-earner family is more likely to quit a job than a worker in a single-earner family. In recent years the number of married women in the labor force has increased sharply, thereby increasing the number of two-earner families. The existence of a second income in a family prevents income from falling to zero when one of the spouses quits a job to search for a better one. Also, the second income allows a longer period to find a new job than would otherwise be possible. Thus an increase in the number of two-earner families tends to increase the natural rate of unemployment because it increases the tendency for job separation through quitting and also increases the duration of unemployment.

Tendencies to move in and out of the labor force can also affect the natural rate of unemployment. This is because such movements can affect the rate of job separation and job finding in the future. Workers who frequently move in and out of the work force have a high rate of job separation because they're less experienced than other workers. As a result, they're more likely to quit or be fired from a job.

*David M. Lilien, "Sectoral Shifts and Cyclical Unemployment," *Journal of Political Economy,* August 1982, 90, 4, pp. 777-793.

---

jobs instead of quitting. The majority of those job losers were not laid off in early 1986. This means that the bulk of the unemployed at that time could be expected to be searching for a new job rather than return to their old job. Job leavers, those who quit their jobs, constituted only 11% of the unemployed, while those who reentered the labor force accounted for 23.2% of the unemployed. Only slightly more than 10% of the unemployed were people searching for a first job. *The bulk of the unemployed are typically persons who lose their jobs for reasons other than being laid off.* Layoffs are the major consequence of cyclical fluctuations in real GNP. The table in Box 6 also breaks down unemployment into its components. Job losers amounted to 4.2% of the labor force in early 1986, while reentrants into the labor force searching for new jobs accounted for 2% of the labor force.

There is a predictable pattern of quits vs. layoffs as a source of unemployment. Layoffs tend to increase, as you would expect, during contractions and recessions. Typically during a recession around 3% of the labor force will be unemployed because of layoffs. In February 1986 less than 1% of the labor force was unemployed because of layoffs. However, in 1982, which was a recession year, about 3% of the labor force was unemployed as a result of layoffs. The unemployment rate in 1982 averaged over 9% for the 12 months. The 1982 unemployment rate can be thought of as the sum of a natural rate of about 6% and the cyclical rate of 3%. Layoffs represent the cyclical component of the unemployment rate.

Unemployment resulting from quitting a job tends to drop during recessions but increases during expansions. Obviously, you wouldn't want to quit a job when the probability of finding another one is low, as it is during a recession. However, when times are good, you and many workers like you take the chance and quit to find a new job. In February 1986 less than 1% of the labor force was unemployed because they quit their jobs. In a period of expansion, however, quit rates typically are as high as 3% of the labor force.

The pie charts in Box 7 show the distribution of unemployment by reason for a typical year of peak economic activity and a typical recession year corresponding to a trough in the business cycle. During a peak in the business cycle, the percentage of unemployed workers losing their jobs because of layoff is typically not more than 12% of the unemployed. For example, the left-hand chart in Box 7 shows that during 1978, which was a year generally classified as one of peak economic activity, only 11.5% of the job losers were on layoff. During peak years the percentage of the unemployed who quit their jobs (job leavers) also tends to increase. In 1978, for example, 14.1% of the unemployed voluntarily left their jobs.

During a recession year such as 1982, which was a particularly severe period of recession, the proportion of unemployed who are on layoff approaches 20%. People who voluntarily have left their jobs account for a much smaller percentage of the unemployed during a recession period. For example, in 1982 only 7.9% of the unemployed were people who left their jobs voluntarily.

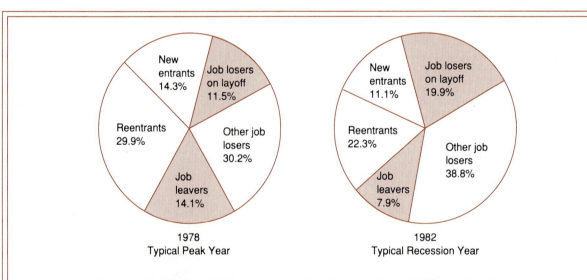

Box 7   Distribution of Unemployment by Reason: Peak and Recession Years

As the economy moves from peak economic activity to a recession, the percentage of the unemployed on layoff typically rises while the percentage who are unemployed because they voluntarily left their jobs goes down.

Source: *Economic Report of the President*, 1983.

Unemployment Rates Since 1970

Since 1970 there has been a general upward trend in the unemployment rate. Much of this can be explained by demographic and structural changes in the economy since that time that have tended to increase the natural rate of unemployment. For example, the 1970s was a period marked by a large influx of younger workers into the labor force. Because younger workers tend to change jobs more often than older workers, this could increase frictional unemployment. Similarly, the 1970s and early 1980s were periods of dynamic change in the U.S. economy during which increased foreign competition, higher energy prices, and a change in the pattern of demand away from goods and toward services caused many workers to lose their jobs and return to the labor market to search for new ones.

Box 8   Unemployment Rates 1950–1987

The official unemployment rate in the United States follows a cyclical pattern with ups and downs over time.

Source: *1987 Historical Chart Book*, Board of Governors of the Federal Reserve System.

The graph in Box 8 plots unemployment rates from 1950 to 1987. Periods of peak unemployment occur during recessions. As recovery from a recession begins, the unemployment rate declines. The ups and downs in the unemployment rate are caused by the business cycle. From 1970 to 1982 unemployment rates rose on average. Since 1982, however, unemployment rates have begun to decline. As the labor force ages, it's likely that the natural rate of employment will decline. In 1988 many economists believed that the natural rate of unemployment was falling from 6% to 5.5%.

Concept Check

1   Under what circumstances is a person officially classified as unemployed in the United States?

2   Why is the economy considered to be operating at full employment when as much as 6% of the labor force is unemployed?

3   The decrease in the price of oil in the mid-1980s resulted in sharp increases in unemployment in Texas, Louisiana, and Oklahoma. Would you classify the high unemployment in these states as cyclical unemployment?

Potential GNP, Cyclical Unemployment, and the GNP Gap

Potential Real GNP

Potential real GNP:
The level of GNP that would prevail if the economy achieved the natural rate of unemployment over a period.

Declines in real GNP and increased unemployment go hand in hand. As the economy plunges into recession, output falls below its potential level. **Potential real GNP** is the level that would prevail if the economy achieved the natural rate of unemployment over a period. During recessions and other periods of nonpeak performance for the economy, the unemployment rate rises above the natural rate. When the economy is booming at peak capacity, it's even possible for the economy to produce more than potential real GNP.

Potential real GNP is a measure of the quantity of final products the economy is capable of producing when it operates at peak capacity. Although the concept of peak capacity output for an economy is simple to comprehend, actually measuring the level of real GNP that corresponds to it is riddled with pitfalls.

The first step in measuring potential real GNP is to select the level of unemployment that corresponds to the natural rate. This is not easy because the natural rate of unemployment can vary from time to time, and a precise estimate of its value is probably impossible (see Principles in Practice box). In the past, various percentage rates of unemployment have been used as estimates of the natural rate. For example, the U.S. Department of Commerce and the Council of Economic Advisers to the President estimated that the natural rate of unemployment in the mid-1950s was 4% of the labor force. By 1973 the natural rate of unemployment was commonly believed to be in the range of 5%. In recent years, because of shifts in the composition of the labor force, the most commonly used estimate of the natural rate of unemployment has been 6%; and, as pointed out earlier, by 1988 many economists were using 5.5% as their estimate.

Once an estimate of the natural rate of unemployment is agreed upon, the next step is to estimate the number of annual labor hours that would be utilized in the economy if the natural rate of unemployment were achieved. Arriving at such an estimate is also difficult because of the way unemployment is defined. Remember that part-time workers are considered to be employed in the official unemployment statistics. To arrive at an estimate of the number of hours of labor that would be utilized when the economy reaches its potential therefore requires an estimate of the average number of hours worked per person employed. *Full-employment labor hours* are equal to:

$$
\begin{array}{c}
\text{Average no. of} \\
\text{hours worked} \\
\text{per worker} \\
\text{per year}
\end{array}
\times
\begin{array}{c}
\text{Number of workers} \\
\text{employed when the} \\
\text{natural rate of unemploy-} \\
\text{ment is achieved}
\end{array}
$$

The final number necessary to estimate potential real GNP is output per labor hour, which is a measure of labor productivity. Here again there are conceptual problems in making an accurate estimate because labor productivity is likely to vary with the degree of capacity utilization in the economy. Labor productivity tends to fall eventually as more labor is used in factories and offices of given size. As the economy approaches its peak, productivity measured by output per labor hour is likely to decline relative to the levels that prevail when there is some slack in capacity utilization. Some judgments must therefore be made in translating actual output per labor hour figures to accurately reflect productivity that would prevail at full employment.

Full-employment productivity is measured as real GNP per labor hour that would prevail when the natural rate of unemployment is achieved. This measure is obtained by valuing the aggregate of final products produced per labor hour at full employment at base year (in this case 1982) prices.

Once an estimate of output per labor hour is made, all that is necessary to arrive at the estimate of full-employment real GNP is to multiply the estimate of real GNP per labor hour by the number of labor hours measured at the level of employment that would prevail when the natural rate of unemployment is achieved:

Potential real GNP = Real GNP per labor hour at full employment ×
Number of labor hours utilized at full employment

For example, suppose that in 1992, 300 billion labor hours would be utilized if the natural rate of unemployment is achieved. If it is estimated that labor productivity at full employment would be $20 per labor hour on average for the economy when measured in 1982 dollars, then potential real GNP would be

300 billion labor hours × $20 per labor hour = $6,000 billion

As you can see, a number of arbitrary judgments must be made to arrive at the estimate of potential real GNP. For this reason many economists don't believe an accurate estimate of potential real GNP is possible.

The GNP Gap

The **GNP gap** is the difference between potential and actual real GNP. This gap can be measured by estimating the natural rate of unemployment and then estimating potential real GNP using a method such as that described earlier. The difference between actual and potential GNP can then be calculated to estimate the loss in aggregate final output measured in base year dollars stemming from cyclical unemployment. The GNP gap is therefore an estimate of the cost of cyclical unemployment measured in terms of lost real GNP.

GNP gap:
The difference between potential and actual GNP.

The graph in Box 9 shows estimates of potential and actual real GNP from 1960 to 1986 based on estimates of the natural rate of unemployment prevailing in each of the years.[6] Whenever two lines intersect, the actual performance of the economy is presumed to have matched its estimated potential. For example, based on Commerce Department estimates, the economy was operating at peak capacity in 1964, 1973, 1978, and 1979. Between 1960 and 1964 the economy operated below its potential because actual GNP fell below estimated potential GNP. Even though there were no economic contractions during this period, the economy had considerable slack in it. However, in the period after 1964 up to 1974, during which the United States began a military buildup and became involved in an armed conflict in Vietnam, actual GNP was estimated to exceed potential GNP. Not surprisingly, this was a period of surging demand and upward pressure on prices, resulting in double-digit rates of inflation. During this period the GNP gap was negative.

---

[6] These estimates are published in conjunction with calculations of federal government receipts and expenditures. For example, see U.S. Department of Commerce, Bureau of Economic Analysis, *Survey of Current Business,* 66, 3, March 1986, pp. 11-17.

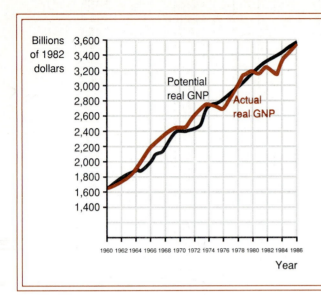

Billions of 1982 dollars

Potential real GNP

Actual real GNP

1960 1962 1964 1966 1968 1970 1972 1974 1976 1978 1980 1982 1984 1986

Year

Box 9   Potential Real GNP and Actual Real GNP 1960–1986

Potential GNP represents real GNP that would prevail if the natural rate of unemployment is achieved. The graph is based on estimates of the natural rate of unemployment in various years. In some years the economy exceeds its potential and actual real GNP is greater than potential real GNP. From 1982-1986 actual GNP was less than potential GNP.

The 1974 recession caused actual real GNP to plunge below potential real GNP. The GNP gap remained positive until full employment was restored in 1978. The economy operated close to its potential from 1978 until the 1982 recession. From 1982 to 1986 the economy continued operating below its potential despite the ongoing expansion.

The Capacity Utilization Rate

Another statistic that can be used to gauge the performance of the economy is the *capacity utilization rate,* which estimates the percentage of total industrial capacity utilized per month. The capacity utilization rate is published monthly by the Board of Governors of the Federal Reserve System, the nation's central bank. The graph in Box 10 shows the capacity utilization rate for U.S. industry based on monthly averages from 1967-1987. In periods of peak economic activity the capacity utilization rate usually is about 85% or higher. When an economic contraction sets in, the capacity utilization rate plunges to only about 70%. For example, in the boom year of 1967 the capacity utilization rate for industries in the United States was estimated at 87%. In the recession year of 1982 the capacity utilization rate was only 72%.

Okun's Law: Relating the Unemployment Rate to Changes in Real GNP

Okun's Law:
States that each 1% increase in the unemployment rate is associated with a 2.5% reduction in real GNP.

A rule of thumb based on the historical relationship between unemployment and changes in real GNP is that each 1% increase in the unemployment rate is associated with a 2.5% reduction in real GNP. The relationship between changes in the unemployment rate and real GNP is called **Okun's Law** after the man who uncovered it, Arthur M. Okun, a chairman of the Council of Economic Advisers in the early 1960s.[7]

Okun's Law can be used to provide a rough indication of the loss in real GNP

[7]Arthur M. Okun, "Potential GNP: Its Measurement and Significance," reprinted in Arthur M. Okun, *The Political Economy of Prosperity,* Washington, D.C.: The Brookings Institution, 1970.

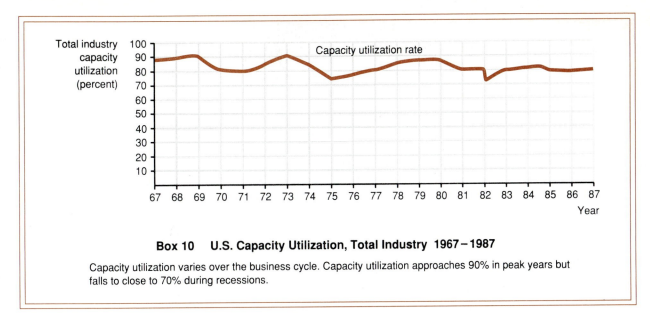

Box 10   U.S. Capacity Utilization, Total Industry 1967–1987

Capacity utilization varies over the business cycle. Capacity utilization approaches 90% in peak years but falls to close to 70% during recessions.

attributable to cyclical unemployment. This law provides a handy way to estimate the GNP gap in any given year without going through the calculations described earlier. However, because Okun's Law is based on historical patterns, it could prove inaccurate if the underlying forces influencing real GNP should change in the future. In 1985 the actual unemployment rate was 7.1%. If the natural rate of unemployment was 6%, then this implies cyclical unemployment of 1.1% for the year. Okun's Law implies that the loss in real GNP from this cyclical unemployment would be 2.5(1.1)%, which is 2.75% of potential real GNP. This means actual GNP that year was only 97.25% of its potential.

In 1982, which was a recession year, the actual employment rate was over 3 percentage points higher than the natural rate of 6%. The 9% actual unemployment rate that year meant that GNP would have been only 92.5% of its potential. The loss in that year, measured in 1982 dollars, would have been close to $300 billion worth of real GNP.

The Costs of Unemployment

Unemployment means a drop in national production. This implies a reduction in income for the nation. When business receipts decline and firms have unused capacity, profits decline. When workers lose their jobs, they also lose the labor income they would have otherwise earned. The loss in wages and profits is part of the cost of unemployment. As income and business revenues decline during a recession, governments also suffer because they experience a decline in their tax revenues from income taxes, sales taxes, and payroll taxes.

But there is still more cost associated with unemployment. Unemployment can be a depressing experience. Research provides some evidence that increases in the cyclical unemployment rate are associated with increased suicide, crime, mental illness, and physical illness.[8] During recessions the average period of unemployment tends to double from the normal 2-month duration. Also during recessions, it's more

[8]See Barry Bluestone and Bennett Harrison, *The Deindustrialization of America,* New York: Basic Books, 1982, Chapter 3.

probable that in many families both spouses will lose their jobs. This tends to compound the stress and other social problems stemming from unemployment.

Cushioning the Costs of Unemployment: Unemployment Insurance

Unemployment insurance available to eligible workers cushions the loss of income associated with temporary unemployment. Benefits vary from state to state, but they average about 50% of previous earnings. Some states pay certain workers as much as 60% to 75% of previous earnings and even provide extra funds for workers with dependents. Usually benefits last for a maximum of 26 weeks. Because the average duration of unemployment is only about 8 weeks, workers seldom collect for the full period. However, during a recession the duration of unemployment increases dramatically to over 4 months. During periods of unusually high unemployment Congress extends benefits for an additional 13 weeks.

Unemployment insurance was established in the United States as part of the Social Security Act of 1935. The program is managed by individual states, each of which has a separate trust fund used to support unemployment insurance benefits. Tax collections to finance the program are administered by the federal government. The tax is collected from employers, and the federal government returns most of the funds to states for deposit in their trust funds.

For those eligible, unemployment insurance puts a floor on income and eases the costs of unemployment. But unemployment insurance is not available to all the unemployed. Eligibility varies from state to state. However, in all states only covered workers are eligible. How does a worker obtain coverage under unemployment insurance? He or she must have worked for a specified period at a job for which an employer paid the payroll tax for unemployment insurance. Currently close to 95% of workers are in jobs covered by unemployment insurance. New entrants and reentrants into the labor force are *not* eligible for unemployment insurance. For example, if it takes you 6 months to find a job after graduating from college, don't count on getting unemployment insurance to tide you over till you gain employment!

Job quitters almost without exception are not eligible for benefits, nor in most cases are people who are fired from their jobs because of poor performance. Who then gets the benefits? The answer is mainly people who lose their jobs temporarily because of layoffs or permanently because of shutdowns of business firms or contractions in business operations. In other words, the insurance alleviates the costs of cyclical and structural unemployment.

Finally, to remain eligible for benefits an unemployed worker must be actively looking for a new job and cannot reject an offer of a suitable job. This last provision, however, is hard to enforce.

A major criticism of unemployment insurance is that it tends to lengthen the period of job search and thereby increase the duration of periods of unemployment. Some critics argue that benefits are too high. One study of unemployment compensation in the 1970s indicated that at that time many workers received unemployment insurance benefits in excess of 60% of their previous earnings. Many unemployed workers also receive union benefits or employer-provided benefits that push their income close to previous earnings. For married women, unemployment insurance benefits averaged 75% of previous earnings.[9]

---

[9]Martin Feldstein, "Unemployment Compensation: Adverse Incentives and Distributional Anomalies," *National Tax Journal,* 27, June 1974, pp. 231-244.

Under the provisions of the Tax Reform Act of 1986, unemployment insurance benefits are now included in the taxable income of workers. This decreases the generosity of the program and might help reduce the period of unemployment of workers receiving benefits. Evidence seems to indicate that workers who receive benefits remain out of work longer than workers who don't receive benefits.[10]

Summary

1. The material well-being of citizens in a nation depends on real GNP. Declines in real GNP reduce both national production and national income. In a nation with a growing population, declines in real GNP result in decreases in final production per person.
2. The business cycle describes the periodic fluctuations in national production as measured by the ups and downs of real GNP.
3. Although the phases of the business cycle are not regular, they consist of movements from peaks to contractions and occasional recessions, then to troughs, and then expansions and recoveries from recessions. A recession is a decline in real GNP that occurs over at least a 6-month (two consecutive quarters) reporting period.
4. Despite the ups and downs of the business cycle, there has been a general upward trend in real GNP since 1900. On average, real GNP has grown at the rate of 3.1% per year in the United States since 1900.
5. A consequence of declines in real GNP is excessive unemployment of workers. The unemployment rate measures the ratio of the number of people classified as unemployed to the total labor force, which consists of the sum of employed and unemployed people over the age of 16. An unemployed person is one over the age of 16 who is available for work and has actively sought employment during the past 4 weeks. The unemployment rate is estimated each month from a sample of 60,000 households. Not included in the ranks of the unemployed are people who suffer reductions in hours worked but are employed part time during a period because of production cutbacks.
6. A layoff is the temporary suspension of employment without pay for a period of 7 days or more.
7. A job separation occurs whenever a worker quits, is fired, or is laid off. Job separations are normal occurrences resulting from poor matches of workers to jobs and changes in the pattern of demand for goods and services. Frictional unemployment represents the usual amount of unemployment that occurs when people have left jobs and are searching for new employment or are entering the labor force to search for a job. Structural unemployment is that resulting from shifts in the pattern of demand for goods and services or changes in technology in the economy that affect the profitability of hiring workers in specific industries. Cyclical unemployment is that amount of unemployment resulting from declines in real GNP when the economy fails to operate at its potential. The excessive unemployment that is observed during a recession is cyclical unemployment. Layoffs are the major source of cyclical unemployment.
8. The natural rate of unemployment is the percentage of the labor force that can normally be expected to be unemployed for reasons other than cyclical fluctuations in real GNP. Natural unemployment is the sum of frictional and structural

[10]Stephen F. Marston, "The Impact of Unemployment Insurance on Job Search," *Brookings Papers on Economic Activity,* Washington, D.C.: The Brookings Institution, 1975, pp. 12-48.

unemployment. The economy is viewed as operating at full employment when cyclical unemployment is zero. At full employment the actual unemployment rate is not zero because some frictional and structural unemployment is normal even when the economy is operating at its potential. The natural rate of unemployment varies, but in recent years it has been estimated to be close to 6%.

9. Potential real GNP is an estimate of the level of production that would prevail in an economy if the natural rate of unemployment were achieved. Potential GNP can be estimated by estimating the natural rate of unemployment and the number of labor hours that would be utilized over the year when the economy achieves the natural rate of unemployment. Multiplying full-employment labor hours by the real GNP per labor hour that would prevail at that level of employment provides an estimate of the economy's potential real GNP. A GNP gap prevails when there is a difference between potential and actual real GNP. Each 1% increase in the unemployment rate appears to be associated with a 2.5% reduction in real GNP in the United States.

10. The costs of unemployment include a reduction in national output and tax revenues. It appears that increases in unemployment are associated with increased mental and physical illness and higher crime rates and other social problems. Unemployment insurance cushions the declines in well-being that result from excessive unemployment.

Key Terms and Concepts

Business cycle	Layoff	Cyclical unemployment
Contraction	Discouraged worker	Natural rate of unemployment
Recession	Job separation	Full employment
Expansion	Job search	Potential real GNP
Recovery	Job finding	GNP gap
Labor force	Frictional unemployment	Okun's Law
Unemployment rate	Structural unemployment	
Unemployed person		

Problems and Applications

1. Following are seasonally adjusted data for real GNP for each of 10 quarters:

Period	Quarterly real GNP (billions of seasonally adjusted dollars)	Period	Quarterly real GNP (billions of seasonally adjusted dollars)
1st quarter, year 1	1,000	2nd quarter, year 2	750
2nd quarter, year 1	900	3rd quarter, year 2	850
3rd quarter, year 1	800	4th quarter, year 2	1,100
4th quarter, year 1	700	1st quarter, year 3	1,150
1st quarter, year 2	700	2nd quarter, year 3	1,100

Calculate real GNP at an annual rate for each quarter and plot the points associated with each quarter. Trace a curve through the points to illustrate the phases of the business cycle. Was there a recession over the period covered by the data? How would you calculate the long-term trend in growth in real GNP over the period?

2. Can real GNP decline even though there is no recession? What are the consequences for the economy of declines in real GNP?

3. In January there are 60 million employed workers and 2 million unemployed workers in the economy. Calculate the January unemployment rate.

4. How can the official unemployment rate be criticized for underestimating actual unemployment in the economy?

5. Explain why it is unreasonable to expect the unemployment rate ever to fall to zero for an economy. If an improvement in the job search process decreases the time required for job finding, how can this contribute to a decrease in unemployment?

6. Suppose the natural rate of unemployment in 1993 is 6% and corresponds to 320 billion hours of labor for the year. When that unemployment rate is achieved, output per labor hour is $20 of real GNP measured in 1982 prices. Calculate potential real GNP for 1993.

7. The current unemployment rate is 7%. If the sum of structural and frictional unemployment is 6%, then how much cyclical unemployment prevails? Assuming Okun's Law prevails and potential real GNP is currently $5,000 billion, calculate current real GNP and indicate the size of the GNP gap resulting from cyclical unemployment. Suppose the natural rate of unemployment is reduced from 6% to 5%. Assuming Okun's Law prevails, what will happen to the full-employment level of real GNP?

8. Explain how the pattern of quits and layoffs varies predictably with the business cycle.

9. What can explain the general upward trend in unemployment rates in the United States and other major industrial nations since 1970? Do you think the upward trend will continue?

10. How can unemployment insurance contribute to an increase in the natural rate of unemployment? What are some of the benefits of unemployment insurance?

Suggested Readings

Robert J. Barro, *Macroeconomics,* 2nd ed., New York: John Wiley & Sons, 1987. Chapter 9 provides an in-depth analysis of labor markets and explains how the process of job separation, search, and finding influences the unemployment rate.

Robert J. Gordon, *Macroeconomics,* 4th ed., Boston: Little, Brown, 1987. Chapter 11 of this text provides a more advanced analysis of unemployment.

U.S. Department of Labor, Bureau of Labor Statistics, *Employment and Earnings,* Washington, D.C.: U.S. Government Printing Office. This monthly publication tells you everything you wanted to know about unemployment, the labor force, and labor earnings, but were afraid to ask.

A Forward Look

In the following chapter we examine price instability in the United States. Just as this chapter has defined unemployment, the following chapter will define inflation and show how it is measured. The effects of inflation on incomes and decisions will be emphasized. As you'll soon see, policymakers often must walk a thin line to prevent policies that minimize cyclical unemployment from causing an inflationary spiral!

Inflation and Its Consequences

In the not-so-long-ago 1960s, a hot dog cost about 25¢. Nowadays try to find a decent hot dog for less than $1! The process of inflation means that the prices of the goods and services you buy goes up over time. Just think about how much more you could buy with your allowance or earnings if you were able to buy those items at prices prevailing when you were a kid. Prices of goods and services purchased by a typical urban consumer have more than tripled since 1967. A lunch at the corner greasy spoon that could have been purchased for $1 back then will set you back about $3 today.

In this chapter we discuss the concept of the price level for the economy and show how inflation is measured. But why is there so much concern among politicians and voters about inflation? Who is harmed by inflation, and who gains from it? Is inflation such a threat to our living standard that we should support policies that may cause excessive unemployment so as to keep inflation within reasonable bounds?

Inflation can make it difficult to plan for the future and can adversely affect the purchasing power of our income and savings. When the prices of goods and services we buy are subject to erratic increases over time, the result is distortions in resource use as we seek ways to protect the purchasing power of our dollars. When general inflation adversely affects living standards by reducing the purchasing power of annual income and savings, incentives to work, save, and invest are likely to be impaired in ways that affect the performance of the economy.

The impact of price fluctuations on the economy isn't as easy to understand as the impact of cyclical fluctuations in employment and output. However, inflation (and its opposite, deflation, or falling prices) does quite a bit of damage to the normal functioning of the economy. Inflation can result in arbitrary and often capricious redistribution of income among people. It interferes with the normal functioning of financial markets by distorting incentives to work, borrow, lend, save, and hold cash. Over time erratic inflation can affect market interest rates in ways that prevent the economy from operating at peak capacity. Inflation can also influence unit labor costs in ways that decrease production and can even cause a recession.

Our major task in this chapter is to investigate the consequences of price instability. In the following chapter we'll begin to consider the causes of inflation. Later on in the book we'll evaluate policies designed to prevent inflation.

After reading this chapter, you should be able to:

Concept Preview

1   Understand how price indexes are used to measure the price level.
2   Define the concepts of inflation and deflation and show how they are measured.
3   Distinguish nominal income from real income and nominal wages from real wages.
4   Explain the consequences of inflation for incomes and decisions.
5   Explain how inflation affects interest rates and explain the difference between real and nominal interest rates.

The Price Level and Inflation

Before discussing inflation, we need to define what we mean by the level of prices in the economy in a given year. The **price level** is an indicator of how high or low prices are in a certain year compared to prices in a certain *base year*. Given the bewildering variety of goods and services available in markets, the government chooses a representative group (or aggregate) of goods and services, called a market basket, and calculates the cost of purchasing the items in the basket. The cost of the market basket of goods and services in the current year is then compared with the cost of the same market basket in a certain base year.

Price level:
An indicator of how high or low prices are in a given year compared to prices in a certain *base year*.

A **price index** is a number used to measure the price level. The value of the index is set at 100 in the base year. If the price index in a given year exceeds 100, it means the price level in that year is higher than it was in the base year. Similarly, a price index of less than 100 for a given year means the price level in that year is lower than it was in the base year.

Price index:
A number used to measure the price level. The value of the index is set at 100 in the base year.

Inflation is the rate of upward movement in the price level for an aggregate of goods and services. Inflation occurs when prices on average are increasing over the year. Of course, not all prices increase at the same rate during periods of inflation, and it's quite common for some items to fall in price even during periods when prices on average are rising. For example, during the late 1970s and early 1980s, a period of rapid inflation, prices of televisions and other electronic goods actually declined.

Inflation:
The rate of upward movement in the price level for an aggregate of goods and services.

Rising prices make it difficult to plan for the future and cause distortions in decisions as people seek to protect themselves against the effect of inflation on the purchasing power of their money income and savings.

Although you're probably accustomed to a rising price level, there have been periods in history when the price level actually declined. For example, during the Great Depression of the 1930s there was a sharp decline in prices. **Deflation** is the rate of downward movement in the price level for an aggregate of goods and services.

The Consumer Price Index and Its Use in Measuring Inflation

Inflation is measured as the annual percentage change in the value of a *price index*. A price index varies as the cost of purchasing a certain standard market basket of goods and services varies from the cost of purchasing the same market basket in the base year. A price index is calculated as the ratio of the current cost of a given market basket to the cost of the same market basket in the base year multiplied by 100:

$$\text{Price index} = \left(\frac{\text{Cost of a market basket of products in current year}}{\text{Cost of the same market basket of products in the base year}} \right) 100$$

The value of the index is always 100 in the base year because the numerator and denominator of the equation just given will be the same in the base year.

Consumer price index (CPI):
The price index most commonly used to measure the impact of changes in prices on households. The index is based on a standard market basket of goods and services purchased by a typical urban family.

The **consumer price index (CPI)** is the price index most commonly used to measure the impact of changes in prices on households. This index is based on a standard market basket of goods and services purchased by a typical urban family. The consumer price index does not include exported goods, investment goods, or items purchased by governments. However, changes in the prices of imported goods purchased by the typical urban family are considered when calculating the CPI.

The goods in the CPI market basket are based on a survey conducted once a decade by the Bureau of Labor Statistics. The most recent survey resulted in a revision of the goods in the market basket in 1987 (see Principles in Practice box). The CPI used 1967 as its base year until the beginning of 1988. Since 1988 an average of prices for the years 1982 to 1984 has been used in calculating the base year cost of the market basket.

The CPI is actually a *weighted average* of a number of component price indexes. Price indexes for such items as housing, transportation, food and beverages, and other broad categories of expenditure are computed separately. Then each price index receives a weight that indicates the relative importance of the item in consumer spending. For example, in the CPI in Box 1, housing is presumed to account for 42.6¢ of each dollar spent by the urban family. The index measuring the price level for an aggregate of housing services is therefore multiplied by 0.426 when calculating the "all items" CPI. Entertainment is currently assumed to absorb 4.4¢ of each dollar spent by the typical urban family. The price index for entertainment items will therefore be multiplied by a weight of 0.044 when calculating the "all items" index.

Because the weight attached to housing exceeds the weight attached to entertainment items, a given percentage increase in the price of housing will have a much greater impact on the CPI than the same percentage increase in the price of entertainment items. For the current CPI, a 4% increase in the aggregate price of housing services would receive nearly 10 times as much weight in calculating the "all items" CPI as a 4% increase in the price of an aggregate of entertainment items.

Principles in Practice

The New CPI Market Basket

A couple of generations ago there were no supermarkets or 7-Eleven stores. Back then, a housewife did her weekly shopping on foot, walking from store to store and placing her selections in a large market basket. When she was finished, her basket most likely contained an array of the items a typical family of that time consumed each week.

The shopping cart you steer down the supermarket aisles today probably contains items that differ from those used by a family 50 years ago. For example, most people are buying less red meat and fewer eggs because of health concerns, and disposable shavers have replaced the old-fashioned straight razors every man used to own.

Because consumers' needs and purchases change, every 10 years the consumer price index gets an overhaul. As you've learned, the CPI is designed to measure changes in a weighted average of prices for goods and services purchased by a typical urban family. To account for changes in buying behavior, the Bureau of Labor Statistics every decade updates the goods and services included in the market basket. The way a typical urban family spends each dollar of earnings also changes over time. The weights used in the consumer price index reflect the percentage of each dollar an urban family allocates to particular groups of items. When the CPI is updated, so are the weights given to various prices for groups of products included in the CPI.

The most recent version of the CPI market basket was introduced in January 1987. It was based on interviews with nearly 10,000 American families over the period 1982-1984. The new CPI is calculated for the cost of a market basket that consists of 184 different goods and services consumed by the typical urban family of the 1980s.

The new basket of goods that will be used to measure changes in the cost of living for the next 10 years reflects changes in the working, living, and spending patterns of U.S. citizens since 1978. Families are now smaller, and over half the women living in families are employed ouside the home. As a result, food eaten away from home is now a larger component of consumer budgets than was the case in 1978. People tend to drive less than they did in 1978, so transportation is now given less weight.

In computing the CPI, the item of consumption given the most weight is housing. Of each dollar spent on consumer goods and services, the typical urban family spent 43¢ for housing over the period 1982 to 1984. Housing has become a more important part of all consumer budgets in the past 10 years. In computing base year expenditure for the previous CPI, housing received a weight of only 38¢ for each consumption dollar.

New goods and services creep into the CPI each time it's revised. For example, in the latest model of the CPI, day care for children is included in the index for the first time ever. Personal computers, VCRs, and compact disc players didn't exist in 1978. However, these goods are now purchased regularly by Americans, and they're included in the new CPI. Other new services in the CPI are videocassette rentals, pet services, and home care for the elderly and the disabled.

The table shows the percentage of consumer spending in each major category under the latest model of the CPI. This is compared with the percentage allocated to each category based on the old CPI. These percentages represent the broad category of weights that are used in computing all the items in the CPI from the individual price indexes that represent its components.

Percent Distribution of Consumer Spending Based on CPI Survey

Expenditure	1972-1973	1982-1984
Housing	38.2%	42.6%
Transportation	19.1	18.7
Food and beverages	20.8	17.8
Apparel and upkeep	7.5	6.5
Other goods and services	4.8	5.1
Medical care	5.0	4.8
Entertainment	4.6	4.4

The higher the percentage of income spent on an item based on the CPI survey, the greater the weight given to a change in the price of that item in computing the CPI each month. The CPI is called a base period weight index because the importance of each price in determining the value of the index each month depends on how much income consumers spent on that item *during the base period survey.* In other words, the mix of housing, transportation, and other items in consumer budgets will be assumed to stay at the percentages in the base year survey despite price changes in the future. The survey for 1982 to 1984 is therefore very important because it will influence the way inflation is actually measured from 1987 for 10 years until a new survey is conducted to change the weights once again.

The CPI is published monthly. The data used to calculate the index each month are gathered by about 250 "price collectors" employed by the Bureau of Labor Statistics who check prices at about 18,000 different stores in 56 cities. The average prices for each product included in the index are then computed and combined into the overall CPI using the weights based on the most recent survey. A complicated exercise—but useful!

The table in Box 1 shows the consumer price index and its major components for 1987. In late 1987 the CPI stood at roughly 342, which means the market basket of products consumed by a typical urban family was priced at 3.42 times the 1967 prices for the same market basket of products. If you were born in 1967, this means prices have more than tripled over your lifetime! The all-items CPI shown on the last line of the table represents a weighted average of the individual item price indexes shown above it, with the greatest weight given to the housing price index.

Box 1 The Consumer Price Index and Its Components Seasonally Adjusted August 1987 (1967 = 100)

Component	Value	Weight* (portion of each dollar spent)
Food and beverages	325.4	0.178
Housing	373.1	0.426
Apparel and upkeep	215.0	0.065
Transportation	320.0	0.187
Medical care	466.3	0.048
Entertainment	284.0	0.044
Other goods and services (includes personal care and educational expenses)	373.8	0.051

CPI = Weighted average of all items = 342.6

*Rounded to nearest 1/100 of a cent.

Source: Bureau of Labor Statistics, U.S. Department of Labor.

Annual rates of inflation are measured by the percentage change in a price index, such as the CPI, from one year to the next. For example, the monthly average of the consumer price index in 1987 using 1967 as the base year was actually 340.4. In 1986 the monthly average of the CPI was 328.4. To calculate the percentage change in the CPI, first take the change in the price index over the year, which in this case is (340.4 − 328.4). Next divide the change in the price index by its value in the initial year, 1986, and multiply the result by 100% to convert to a percentage increase. The rate of inflation between 1986 and 1987 was therefore:

$$\left(\frac{\text{CPI in 1987} - \text{CPI in 1986}}{\text{CPI in 1986}} \right) \times 100\%$$

$$\left(\frac{340.4 - 328.4}{328.4} \right) \times 100\% = 3.7\%$$

Changes in the Price Level vs. Changes in Relative Prices

You should always keep in mind that the official inflation rate is a measure of the average rate of change in the prices of a broad aggregate of products. For example, in 1986 when the official inflation rate was 1.9% measured by the percentage change in CPI, energy prices *fell* by 19.7%, which helped pull the average of all prices down. However, food prices rose by 3.7% that year, and the price of medical care rose by

7.7%. The economy rarely experiences **pure inflation,** during which the prices of *all* goods rise by the same percentage over the year.

Pure inflation:
Occurs when the prices of all goods rise by the same percentage over the year.

The *change in the relative price of a good* is a change in its price relative to the prices of an average of all goods (see Chapter 4). If the economy experienced pure inflation, there would be no changes in the relative prices of goods because the price of every good would rise by the same percentage. Under pure inflation, the price of any one good does not change more or less than the average rate. This means that over the year any particular good does not become any cheaper or more expensive relative to other goods than it was at the beginning of the year. Pure inflation therefore does not provide any incentive for consumers to substitute one good for another in their budget, nor does it change the profitability for sellers of one good rather than another. On the other hand, changes in the relative prices of goods in the economy are signals that provide incentives to adapt to changing conditions.

Other Price Indexes and Inflation Measures

Because pure inflation is unlikely, it's often useful to develop price indexes for various sectors of the economy so as to more accurately chart changes in relative prices for broad groups of products. For example, the **producer price index** measures movements in the prices of a broad aggregate of products purchased by producers rather than consumers. This index is designed to measure inflation or deflation of prices for products used to produce other goods. Included in the aggregate of goods that make up the producer price index are industrial materials, chemicals, wood products, raw farm products, fuels such as coal and oil, intermediate products such as steel and cloth, and equipment and machinery. The producer price index has been calculated by the Bureau of Labor Statistics continuously since 1890. Increases in the producer price index are likely to foreshadow increases in the consumer price index. This is because increases in an average of producer prices will increase their unit costs of production and thus put upward pressure on the prices of final products.

Producer price index:
Measures movements in a broad aggregate of products purchased by producers rather than consumers

The **implicit GNP deflator** is an implicit index for all final products, derived as the ratio of nominal GNP to real GNP (multiplied by 100); an index of the average of the prices used to deflate nominal GNP. Remember from the discussion in the chapter on GNP and economic performance that nominal GNP measures aggregate production of final products valued at their current market prices. Real GNP measures the value of aggregate production of final products valued at base year prices. The Department of Commerce currently uses 1982 as the base year in calculating real GNP. The GNP deflator is therefore:

Implicit GNP deflator:
An implicit index for all final products, derived as the ratio of nominal GNP to real GNP (multiplied by 100); an index of the average of the prices used to deflate nominal GNP.

$$\text{Implicit GNP deflator} = (\text{Nominal GNP/Real GNP})100$$

For example, in 1987 the GNP deflator stood at 117.5, which implies that on average a unit of aggregate production that cost \$100 in 1982 would cost \$117.50 in 1987.

The aggregate of products used to compute the GNP deflator differs from that used to compute the CPI. Imported products are not part of GNP because they are produced in foreign nations rather than domestically. A change in the prices of imports will therefore have no impact on the GNP deflator. However, changes in the prices of imported products purchased by a typical urban family, such as Japanese VCRs, will affect the CPI. For example, in 1988 when the prices of imported items rose sharply in the United States, the CPI increased to reflect such price increases but the GNP deflator did not.

The Department of Commerce also computes price deflator indexes for various components of GNP. For example, price indexes are available for durable goods, nondurable goods, services, structures, producer durable equipment, exports, and government goods. By comparing the price indexes of these various components of GNP, you can see which prices are rising relative to the average of prices in the economy. For example, the price deflator for durable consumer goods in 1987 was only 106.6 while the GNP deflator that year was 117.5. This means that prices for consumer durable goods did not increase as much as the average for all goods and services since 1982.

The price index for the consumer services component of GNP was 127.6 in 1987. This means that prices for consumer services increased more than the average of all prices since 1982. A price index is also computed for imports. Looking at the price index for imports in 1987 gives a clue to why Americans imported more goods than they exported in that year. The price index for imports stood at 97.6 in 1987. This means the prices of imported goods actually decreased on average from 1982 while the prices of most other goods were increasing. No wonder imported goods still looked like bargains to American consumers in 1987!

The table in Box 2 shows implicit price deflators for various components of GNP in 1987.

Box 2 Implicit Price Deflators for GNP and Its Components in 1987
(Index Numbers, 1982 = 100)

Gross national product	117.5
Personal consumption expenditures	118.9
Durable goods	106.6
Nondurable goods	111.9
Services	127.6
Gross private domestic investment	
Fixed investment	104.3
Nonresidential	98.9
Structures	107.9
Producers' durable equipment	95.5
Residential	116.5
Net exports of goods and services	
Exports	100.2
Imports	97.6
Government purchases of goods and services	119.5
Federal	112.7
National defense	111.7
Nondefense	116.2
State and local	124.7

Source: U.S. Department of Commerce, *Survey of Current Business*, January 1988.

A History of the Consumer Price Level and Inflation

The graph in Box 3 shows fluctuations in consumer prices from 1913 to 1987. The data are based only on goods in the market basket used to calculate the consumer price index. The base year is 1967. Notice how decreases in the price level occurred occasionally until 1950.

Consumer prices rose sharply during World War I. Immediately after the war

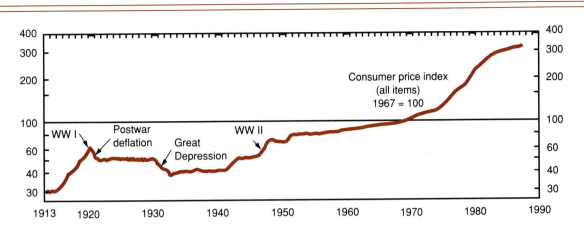

Source: *1987 Historical Chart Book*, Board of Governors of the Federal Reserve System.

Box 3   Consumer Prices 1913-1987
Quarterly Averages, 1967 = 100

Consumer prices have risen steadily since 1950. However, prior to 1950 there were periods in which prices fell. There was a sharp drop in consumer prices during the Great Depression of the 1930s. The scale used to measure prices uses the same vertical distance for each doubling of the price level.

there was a period of deflation followed by price stability during the 1920s. Consumer prices plummeted, however, during the Great Depression of the 1930s. Prices began to increase again in 1933 but at a very slow rate. After World War II began, the price level shot up again. There was a mild deflation of the price level in 1948.

Since 1948 consumer prices have risen. The rate of increase was greatest in the 1970s. During the 1980s prices continued to rise but at a much slower rate than during the 1970s.

The graph in Box 4 shows the percentage change in the consumer price index

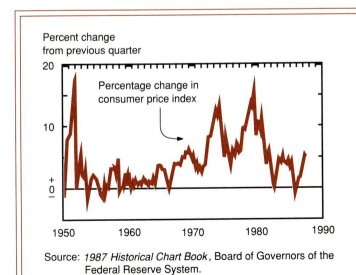

Box 4   Quarterly Percentage Changes in the Consumer Price Index: Seasonally Adjusted Annual Rates 1950-1987

Since 1950 the pattern of inflation has been erratic. Inflation was very high during the period 1974-1975 and between 1978 and 1981.

Source: *1987 Historical Chart Book*, Board of Governors of the Federal Reserve System.

The Price Level and Inflation   587

quarterly from 1950 to 1987. As you can see, the pattern of inflation measured by the annual percentage change in the CPI has been quite erratic since 1950. After a sharp increase in the inflation rate in the early 1950s during the Korean War, the price level was relatively stable with inflation seldom exceeding 5% per year and even a brief period of deflation in the early 1950s. However, the 1970s was a period of high and erratic inflation. During the 1970s the average annual rate of inflation ranged between 3.3% and 11.3%. In 1980 inflation was roaring at an average annual rate of 13.5%.

From 1982 to 1987 inflation averaged less than 3.8% per year based on year-to-year percentage changes in the CPI. In fact, mainly because of sharp drops in the prices of gasoline and other energy-related products, there was even deflation of the price level in some months during 1986. Based on the change in the CPI over the entire year, the rate of inflation was 1.9% in 1986.

Box 5 Average Annual Rate of Inflation
5-Year Averages

Period	Average annual percentage change in consumer price index
1960-1965	1.3
1965-1970	4.2
1970-1975	6.8
1975-1980	8.9
1980-1985	5.9
1985-1987	3.1

Source: *Statistical Abstract of the United States*, 1987, and *Economic Report of the President*, 1988.

The table in Box 5 shows the average annual rate of inflation of consumer prices during 5-year periods from 1960 to 1985 and from 1985 to 1987. As you can see, inflation was quite low in the early 1960s when it averaged 1.3% per year. It peaked in 1975 to 1980 when it averaged 8.9% per year. Between 1980 and 1985 inflation averaged a bit less than 6% per year, and between 1985 and 1987 inflation averaged only 3.1% per year.

Concept Check

1 How is inflation measured?

2 How do the GNP deflator and the CPI differ as measures of the price level?

3 Inflation during the year has been 4%. However, the relative price of clothing fell during the year. Does this necessarily mean that clothing costs less in dollars than it did last year?

The Distortions and Costs of Price Instability

Why all the concern about price instability? Who gains and who loses as a result of inflation or deflation? What distortions in decision making are associated with price instability?

Inflation can significantly affect the national standard of living. It can also cause changes in behavior that can have serious effects on resource use and the functioning of the economy. To analyze the costs of inflation we must examine its effects on both incomes and decisions. Although you might think it would be great to live in an economy in which deflation rather than inflation is the norm, you'll soon see that deflation can be just as damaging to the economy as inflation!

Real Income: Using the CPI to Deflate Nominal Income

Fluctuations in the price level affect the quantity of goods and services that can be purchased with a given sum of money. The **purchasing power of a dollar** (or any other unit of currency) is a measure of how much it can buy. An increase in the price level means a decrease in the purchasing power of a dollar. For example, if the price level were to double over a year, the purchasing power of a dollar would be cut in half because it would take $2 to purchase what in the past could have been bought for $1. In any given year, the greater the rate of inflation, the greater the decline in the purchasing power of a dollar for the year.

Purchasing power of a dollar:
A measure of how much a dollar can buy.

To measure changes in the purchasing power of income over time it is necessary to adjust nominal income for changes in the price level. **Nominal income** is the actual number of dollars of income received over a year. **Real income** is the purchasing power of nominal income. Real income is usually expressed in terms of the market value of final products it can purchase when those products are valued in *base year* rather than current year prices.

Nominal income:
The actual number of dollars of income received over a year.

Real income:
The purchasing power of nominal income.

Real income is obtained by deflating nominal income by the CPI to adjust for rises in the price level since the base year. To deflate nominal income, divide it by the CPI/100.

$$\text{Real income} = (\text{Nominal income})/(\text{Current CPI}/100)$$

For example, suppose your nominal income in 1987 was $10,000. To find out what your *real* income was in 1987, first divide the 1987 CPI of 342 by 100, which gives 3.42. This tells you that the price of a market basket of goods purchased by a typical urban family was 3.42 times higher in 1987 than it was 20 years earlier during the base year of 1967. Your real income is

$$1987 \text{ real income} = \$10,000/3.42 = \$2,923.98$$

Real income is a measure of income in base year (in this case 1967) dollars rather than current year dollars. Your $10,000 nominal income for 1987 has the same purchasing power that $2,933.98 had in 1967! A person who earned $10,000 in 1987 had the same purchasing power as a person who earned less than $3,000 in 1967.

You can also use the preceding formula to deflate $1 to find out the purchasing power of a current dollar after adjusting for inflation since the base year:

$$\text{Purchasing power of a current dollar} = \frac{\$1}{\text{CPI}/100}$$

For example, in 1987 the purchasing power of a dollar was

$$\frac{\$1}{3.42} = 29.2\text{¢}$$

This means that on average each dollar in 1987 would buy what could have been purchased for only about 29¢ in 1967. The 1987 purchasing power of a dollar was a bit less than one third the purchasing power of a dollar in 1967.

The graph in Box 6 shows how the purchasing power of the dollar has varied from 1960 to 1987. Because the price level has increased substantially since 1960, the purchasing power of the dollar has fallen. The more rapid the rate of inflation in a given year, the greater the decline in the purchasing power of the dollar in that year.

Of course, conclusions about the impact of inflation on the purchasing power of dollars available to particular consumers must be qualified because not all consumers buy exactly the same mix of goods. For example, inflation is less of a problem

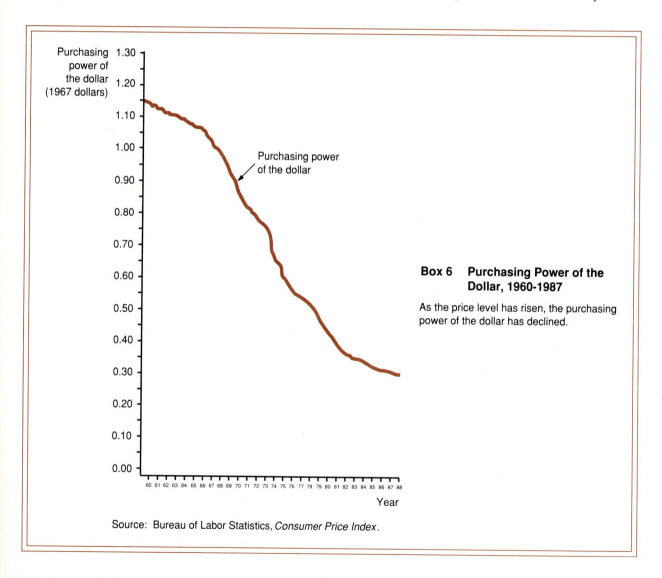

Box 6   Purchasing Power of the Dollar, 1960-1987

As the price level has risen, the purchasing power of the dollar has declined.

Source: Bureau of Labor Statistics, *Consumer Price Index.*

for consumers who spend higher proportions of their income on goods whose prices increase less than average. Suppose you spend more of your income than the average urban consumer on electronic items, such as televisions, calculators, stereo equipment, and other goods whose prices have not increased as fast as the average. If this is the case, inflation is less of a problem for you than for the typical urban consumer.

Also, because not all prices rise by the same percentage during inflationary periods, consumers adjust their buying habits in response to changes in prices. They buy more of goods whose prices have increased less than average and less of goods whose prices have increased more than average. To say that the purchasing power of the dollar in 1987 was one third what it was in 1967 means that a dollar will buy only one third as many goods as it did in 1967 *for the consumer who buys exactly the same goods in the CPI market basket year after year*.

When the rate of inflation of consumer prices exceeds the rate of increase of a person's nominal income, a person buying the standard market basket of goods used to calculate the CPI will find that his money income buys less this year than the year before. *When a person's annual rate of increase in nominal income lags behind the annual rate of increase in the price level, the person's real income will decline.* A decline in a person's real income implies a decline in his material standard of living measured by the quantity of goods and services his income can buy. To find out the effect of inflation on a person's standard of living, we therefore must analyze its impact on that person's real income. As you'll soon see, inflation can have some rather capricious and unpredictable effects on the distribution of real income. Inflation affects everyone but not equally!

Nominal Wages vs. Real Wages

Wages are a measure of both hourly payments by business firms for labor services and hourly compensation to workers. **Nominal wages** are hourly payments to workers in current dollars. **Real wages** are nominal wages deflated to adjust for changes in the purchasing power of the dollar since a certain base year. Real wages give hourly compensation in terms of base year dollars. For example, suppose nominal hourly wages in 1992, including the hourly dollar value of fringe benefits, are $20. If the consumer price index is 400 in 1992 (and 1967 is the base year), then the purchasing power of a 1992 dollar is only one quarter that of a 1967 dollar. It follows that the real wage expressed in terms of 1967 dollars is only $5. To find out whether real wages increased between 1967 and 1992, we then would compare actual wages in 1967 with real wages in 1992.

The graph in Box 7 shows the percentage change in the consumer price index and the percentage change in hourly employee compensation (the hourly nominal wage and the nominal value of hourly fringe benefits) from 1960 to 1987. The graph shows that in most years the percentage change in hourly employee compensation exceeds the percentage change in prices. This means that in most years the rate of growth of nominal wages (including the value of fringe benefits) exceeds inflation. This is because employers compensate workers not only for changes in the price level but also for changes in productivity. The graph shows that, on average, competition for labor services has resulted in a nominal wage growth exceeding the inflation rate. This means that, on average, real wages in the United States tend to increase each year. The increase in the real wage reflects increases in labor productivity.

Nominal wages:
Hourly payments to workers in current dollars.

Real wages:
Nominal wages deflated to adjust for changes in the purchasing power of the dollar since a certain base year.

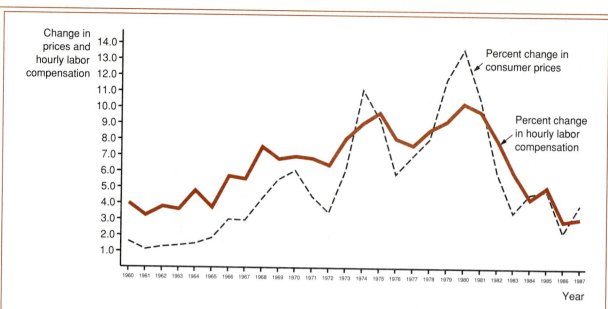

Source: U.S. Bureau of Labor Statistics.

Box 7 **Annual Percentage Changes in Hourly Labor Compensation and in Consumer Prices 1960-1987**

Changes in annual consumer prices and annual hourly labor compensation move together. In some years, however, increases in the prices of consumer products do exceed increases in labor compensation.

You should also observe that the annual percentage change in labor compensation and the inflation rate move together. However, there's often a lag between the increase in consumer prices and the increase in nominal hourly labor compensation. During periods of rapid inflation the rate of increase in consumer prices often exceeds the rate of increase in nominal hourly labor compensation. For example, during the periods of rapid inflation from 1973 to 1975 and from 1979 to 1981, inflation *did* outstrip annual increases in hourly labor compensation. Real wages therefore fell over that period. Similarly, in 1984 inflation outstripped the growth of nominal wages, resulting in a decline in real wages.

During periods of rapid inflation, real wages often do decline. This means workers are harmed by inflation during such periods in the sense that their hourly compensation falls. Who gains during those periods? The answer is employers, who end up paying less in hourly labor costs because real wages decline. *As a result, during periods in which inflation exceeds the percentage increase in nominal wages (hourly labor compensation), there is a redistribution of income from workers to their employers.* This is one of the capricious effects of inflation on the distribution of income.

Workers *do* consider inflation when engaging in contract negotiations that set wages. By and large the growth in nominal wages and inflation move together because workers demand increases in hourly compensation to offset the effects of inflation. Nominal increases in hourly compensation lag behind inflation only in periods when inflation heats up rapidly.

How Inflation Can Redistribute Income and Wealth from Creditors to Debtors

Inflation is great for people who are in debt. Many debts are long-term commitments. For example, mortgages typically have maturities of 15 to 30 years. This means that if a borrower agrees to lend, say, $60,000 to a home buyer at a certain rate of interest, say 9%, over several years the borrower will make monthly payments to repay the outstanding balance at 9% interest. Similarly, many corporate and government bonds have maturities of more than 10 years.

Inflation means that the purchasing power of dollars will decline over the life of the loan. Borrowers will therefore pay back the principal and interest in dollars that are worth less and less each year in terms of purchasing power. *Inflation tends to decrease the burden of paying off the loan because debtors make payments in dollars that have less purchasing power than those they borrowed!* In this way inflation tends to benefit debtors and harm creditors. The burden of a loan to a borrower depends on both the rate of inflation during the repayment period *and* the rate of interest for the loan.

Inflation will decrease the wealth of creditors, who will experience a reduction in the purchasing power of the outstanding balances on loans they carry on their books as assets. By the same token, debtors who borrowed money many years ago will have the real value of their outstanding debt decline as a result of inflation. For example, suppose you borrowed mortgage money in 1967. Assume the outstanding balance on your loan in 1987 was $10,000. Because the purchasing power of a dollar in 1987 was only about one third of its purchasing power in 1967, the outstanding balance valued in 1967 dollars (when the money was spent to buy the house) is only $3,333. In this way inflation redistributes wealth (asset values) from creditors to debtors.

In effect, savers can be regarded as creditors. Those who have savings accounts in banks, such as 10-year certificates of deposit, are harmed by inflation because the purchasing power of their savings will be eroded unless the interest they earn is high enough to compensate them for the effects of inflation. For example, suppose you purchase a 5-year certificate of deposit that yields 10% interest per year. If inflation is 20% per year, you'll lose purchasing power on your savings each year. Although the balance will go up by 10% per year because of interest payments, the inflation of 20% will outstrip the interest payment, and the net effect will be that the purchasing power of your savings will fall.

The heaviest borrower in the nation is the federal government. The outstanding federal debt in the mid-1980s was over $2 trillion. According to one estimate, the purchasing power of the outstanding federal debt in 1980 declined by nearly $70 billion: the net effect of inflation outpacing interest payments on the debt.[1] This means the creditors of the government lost that much while the government gained that much during 1980. In effect, the decline in the value of the debt as a result of inflation could be regarded as an increase in real revenue to the federal government. Inflation therefore has redistributed income from those who hold government debt to other taxpayers who are not creditors of the government. It's also likely that inflation, other things being equal, benefits the young and middle-income groups that tend to be heavily in debt.

[1]Robert Eisner and Paul J. Pieper, "A New View of the Federal Debt and Budget Deficits," *American Economic Review,* 74, March 1984, pp. 11-29.

Inflation and Interest Income: Nominal Interest Rates vs. Real Interest Rates

The preceding analysis of the impact of inflation on debtors and creditors assumed that the interest rate doesn't adjust for the effects of inflation. You should recall the analysis of the impact of inflation on wages. Inflation is considered in the bargains that are struck between workers and employers. By the same token, inflation is considered in the bargains that are struck between borrowers and lenders. When lenders see inflation coming, they are less willing to make loans than they would be otherwise. This is because they know that future inflation will reduce the purchasing power of the dollars that will be repaid on current loans. As lenders anticipate the adverse effects of inflation on the profitability of lending, they decrease the supply of loanable funds and thus put upward pressure on interest rates.

The **nominal interest rate** is the annual percentage amount of money that is earned on a sum that is loaned or deposited in a bank. The nominal interest rate is the contract interest on the face of the loan or deposit and will always be positive. For example, if you buy a $5,000 certificate of deposit that yields 10% annual interest, you are a creditor who loans the bank that sum for a period of time at a 10% nominal annual rate of interest. The **real interest rate**[2] is the actual annual percentage change in the *purchasing power of interest income* earned on a sum of money that is loaned out. When inflation is present, the real rate of interest will be less than the nominal rate. The real rate of interest is the nominal rate adjusted for the decrease in purchasing power that results from inflation.

The earned real rate of interest can be thought of as the nominal interest rate minus the rate of inflation.[3] For example, suppose the nominal interest rate you earned over a 1-year period on a $5,000 certificate of deposit was 9%. If over the same period inflation averaged 6%, then the real interest rate you earned was 3%.

$$\begin{matrix} \text{Real interest earned} \\ \text{on a loan} \\ \text{over its life} \end{matrix} = \begin{matrix} \text{Nominal interest rate} \\ \text{per year} \end{matrix} - \begin{matrix} \text{Inflation rate} \\ \text{per year} \end{matrix}$$

$$3\% = 9\% - 6\%$$

This means that the $5,000 principal plus the interest it earned over the period the bank held it, after adjustment for inflation, was worth only 3% more than it was when you deposited it.

Real Interest Rates Can Be Negative

Although nominal interest rates are always positive, real interest rates can be negative. Real interest rates will be negative when the actual rate of inflation exceeds the nominal interest rate. Lenders will incur losses on loans during periods when the nominal interest rate on the loan is less than the rate of inflation. Of course, given the nominal interest rate, lenders need not incur losses in future years on loans

[2] The definition refers to the "earned" or *ex post* real interest rate. In contrast, the *ex ante* real interest rate is the nominal interest rate minus the anticipated rate of inflation. The "earned" real interest rate is important for calculating the actual real return on a loan outstanding. The *ex ante* real interest rate is important when parties are considering a new loan or investment. *Ex ante* real interest rates are difficult to estimate because "anticipated inflation" is not available in the market.

[3] The real interest rate can be shown to equal the nominal interest rate plus the rate of inflation plus the product of the rate of inflation and the nominal interest rate. However, when both inflation and the nominal interest rate are less than 20%, the product of inflation and the nominal interest rate is so low that it can be ignored.

Nominal interest rate: The annual percentage amount of money that is earned on a sum that is loaned or deposited in a bank.

Real interest rate: The actual annual percentage change in the purchasing power of interest income earned on a sum of money that is loaned out.

CHAPTER 27 Inflation and Its Consequences

made during years when real interest rates are negative. This is because changes in the rate of inflation over the life of the loan will affect the real interest rate earned in future years.

Despite the fact that nominal interest rates soared to double digits in the late 1970s, borrowing was a good deal because roaring inflation at that time actually resulted in negative real interest rates! For example, the real interest rate on 3-month Treasury bills, which represent short-term borrowing by the federal government, in 1978 was estimated to be −1.5%. In periods like this, when nominal interest rates increase less rapidly than prices, borrowers benefit greatly while lenders are harmed.

The graph in Box 8 shows how estimated *ex ante* (or anticipated) U.S. interest rates have varied from 1919 to 1986. The measure of inflation used to estimate the real interest rate is the average percentage change in the CPI over the preceding 2 years. This measure is used as a very rough estimate of inflation anticipated by borrowers and lenders. It's assumed that in making loans, market participants use past inflation as an indicator of future inflation. Subtracting this measure from the nominal interest rate for a composite of U.S. government bonds provides a rough measure of anticipated real interest rates, which was constructed by the staff of the U.S. Council of Economic Advisers. As you can see, U.S. real interest rates were negative during the 1940s and early 1950s and again during the late 1970s. When real interest rates are negative, it's a good time to borrow and a bad time to lend! As you can also see from the chart, estimated real interest rates soared in the early 1980s. Despite the fact that nominal interest rates fell after 1982, real interest rates

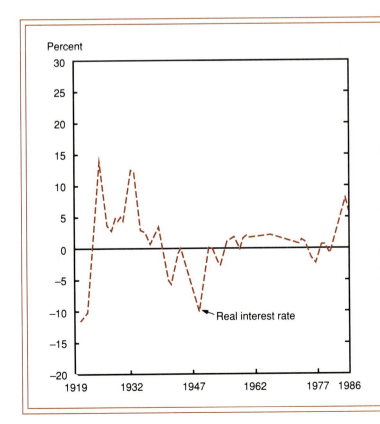

Box 8   Estimated *Ex Ante* (Anticipated) Real Interest Rates, 1919-1986

This estimate of real interest rates over time was computed by the U.S. Council of Economic Advisers. It is obtained by subtracting the inflation rate of the previous 2 years from an average of interest rates paid on U.S. government bonds. Real interest rates as estimated by this proxy measure have fluctuated from positive to negative values over time.

moved up to near historic highs of nearly 10% in 1983. This is why borrowing was more burdensome in 1983 than it was in the late 1970s, despite the decline in nominal interest rates over that period!

You can see that the impact of inflation on borrowers and lenders is a bit more complex than that discussed earlier when interest rates were not assumed to adjust for inflation. It's really quite difficult to predict who gains and who loses as a result of inflation because market forces tend to adjust nominal interest rates as creditors seek compensation for the effects of inflation in the same way that workers seek to protect themselves from inflation.

If all long-term contracts involving loanable funds had clauses allowing automatic adjustment of nominal interest rates for inflation, there would be no redistribution of income from creditors to debtors arising from changes in the rate of inflation. In fact, after the period of rapid unanticipated inflation in the 1970s, many banks became reluctant to make long-term loans (such as mortgages) at fixed interest rates. These were largely replaced by variable-interest rate long-term loans with the rates tied to more volatile current rates. Both individual consumers and business managers learn from their mistakes!

Deflation

In the preceding discussion we concentrated on only one aspect of price instability: inflation. What about deflation, which occurs when prices are unstable on the down side? What are the consequences of reductions in the price level? As is the case for inflation, the impact of deflation on your income depends on how that income varies when the price level falls.

Suppose wages are inflexible in the downward direction when the price level falls in periods of deflation. If this were the case, real wages would increase as a result of deflation. In fact, this is precisely what occurred during the Great Depression of the 1930s, which was also a period of deflation. Betwen 1929 and 1933 the CPI declined by 29% while nominal wages fell by only 18% in manufacturing and 21% overall. As a result, real wages during this period increased by 8% overall and by 11% in manufacturing.[4] However, we can't conclude from this that workers gained from deflation. This is because high unemployment rates during the Depression years of 1929-1933 reduced labor income in the aggregate despite the increase in real wages.

Deflation *increases* the purchasing power of a dollar over time. This has important implications for the distribution of well-being between debtors and creditors. Deflation *harms* debtors by increasing the real value of the outstanding balance on their loans. For example, if you have a mortgage balance of $20,000, the real value of that balance in terms of base year dollars will *increase* when deflation occurs. Deflation also benefits creditors because the dollars they receive as loan payments have higher purchasing power than those they lent.

During periods of deflation, real interest rates tend to soar. For example, if you look back at the graph in Box 8, you'll notice that during the Depression of 1929-1933, real interest rates on government bonds approached 15%.

---

[4]See Martin N. Baily, "The Labor Market in the 1930s," in *Macroeconomics, Prices and Quantities,* James Tobin, ed., Washington, D.C.: The Brookings Institution, 1983, pp. 21-61.

1   Under what circumstances is inflation likely to result in a decline in real wages?

2   Under what circumstances will inflation redistribute wealth and income from creditors to debtors?

3   What is the real interest rate? Under what circumstances will real interest rates be negative?

How Price Instability Affects the Performance of the Economy

Price instability, or more accurately the actions taken in anticipation of it, can adversely affect the performance of the economy. When buyers and sellers try to guess what price instability will do to the purchasing power of the dollar in the future, they also base their decisions in part on the gains or losses they might incur as a result of inflation (or deflation). The resulting shifts in supply and demand in individual markets cause distortions in market prices. There would be little problem if everybody had the same expectation of future inflation and if those expectations were always correct. However, in actuality future inflation differs from what many people anticipate.

Anticipated Inflation

You've undoubtedly gotten used to the fact of inflation over your lifetime. If you're like most people, you've probably made purchases today that you might otherwise have put off to the future because you *anticipated* that inflation would increase the price of the product. For example, if you anticipate a 10% price increase in the stereo system you really want to have for next year when you move out of your dorm into an apartment, you might choose to buy it now rather than next year. Similarly, when signing a lease for an apartment or borrowing money, you've probably considered what inflation would do to the burden of making rent or interest payments. Just like you, business firms, savers, and investors also are likely to consider the possible rate of inflation when engaging in transactions.

Anticipated inflation will affect the choices we make as individuals. Those who correctly anticipate the impact of inflation on their incomes can avoid the reduction in real income that inflation will cause. As the choices of buyers and sellers in markets are affected by their anticipation of inflation, so are the demands for and supplies of goods and services as well as labor and loanable funds. In this way inflation can distort choices and cause changes in relative prices that can impair the functioning of the economy.

When inflation is steady and predictable, many people are likely to correctly anticipate its effects on the purchasing power of the dollar. However, when inflation is erratic, fewer people will succeed in anticipating its effects. The actual impact of inflation on the distribution of income between workers and their employers and between borrowers and lenders will depend on how accurately inflation is anticipated by each of these groups. For example, if lenders correctly anticipate inflation, they can seek to avoid its undesirable effect on their real income by trying to attach an inflation "premium" to the nominal interest rate they charge for new loans.

Inflationary Distortions in Saving and Investment

Erratic inflation is particularly troublesome for long-term contracts. It increases the risk involved in estimating the returns on investment projects by making it difficult to anticipate future input and output prices. This might lead to distortions in decisions to save and invest and cause investment to be reduced below the efficient level.

Inflation also can adversely affect the growth of the economy by reducing the willingness of households to supply funds to businesses for productive investment. Remember that inflation erodes the value of bank deposits and other assets such as bonds that are fixed in monetary value. If inflation soars, savers might seek to liquidate their financial assets and purchase land or items like antiques and other collectibles. This is because during periods of inflation the prices of land and antiques are likely to soar. Unfortunately, this makes less funds available for productive investments like new factories that ensure future increases in labor productivity and increased future employment opportunities for workers. This puts further upward pressure on real interest rates.

Inflation not only distorts current choices but also can decrease confidence in the nation's financial markets, thereby adversely affecting future opportunities as the amount of saving channeled into productive investment is reduced. A nation's real GNP growth rate can be adversely affected if inflation reduces business investment.

Inflation and Purchases

If consumers and businesses anticipate inflation, they may make purchases they wouldn't make if prices were expected to be stable. When there are unpredictable fluctuations in the price level, consumers and businesses purchasing parts and materials have difficulty deciding whether to buy now or wait until later. When higher inflation is anticipated, there's a tendency to purchase some goods today that might otherwise be purchased in later years. For example, businesses might stock up on parts and raw materials in expectation of future price increases. Similarly, you might stock your pantry or freezer with food if you think the prices of storable items will increase as a result of inflation. Under such circumstances, decisions about how much to buy are made not only on the basis of the current price of the item but also on the basis of anticipated inflation.

In addition, inflation makes it hard to collect information about what constitutes a reasonable price for an item. You never know whether prices for a good have gone up because of shifts in the supply of and demand for that item or because of general inflation. This makes it difficult to decide what to buy and when to buy it. Steady inflation does less harm in this sense than erratic inflation because it causes less distortion in choices.

The Disastrous Effects of Hyperinflation

Extraordinarily high rates of inflation are likely to be more costly than modest inflation in terms of loss in efficiency and transaction costs. If people expect very high inflation, they'll try to spend their earnings as quickly as possible and to avoid holding money that will quickly have its purchasing power eroded. For example, if you anticipate that prices will rise 10% per week, you'll be eager to be paid once or twice a day so you can spend your earnings before the purchasing power of the dollar deteriorates!

During the 1920s, inflation in the German Weimar Republic reached such astronomical rates that it was dubbed *hyperinflation*. In 1922 the annual inflation rate in Germany exceeded 5,000%. Prices rose almost hourly that year! German currency became worthless and was used as kindling for stoves. The cause of the inflation was an extraordinarily high rate of money creation as the Weimar government sought to pay its bills by printing money. In 1922 the money stock in Germany grew by about 30% per month. Once people began to anticipate the inflation they tried to unload cash balances, which caused further inflationary pressures by increasing the demand for goods and services. The cost to Germany was tremendous. Credit markets virtually collapsed, as no one was willing to take the risk of lending money. There was a massive redistribution of income that literally wiped out the savings of millions and benefited those who were heavily in debt. People demanded to be paid at least once a day and spent an inordinate amount of time each day trying to unload their earnings before the price level rose again! This is the specter of uncontrolled inflation that policymakers seek to avoid. The ultimate solution for Germany was a monetary reform in 1923 that changed the currency and promised to limit printing of new currency.

Hyperinflation is not a historical relic. In 1985 the rate of inflation in Bolivia was 11,749%! Putting this spectacular rate of inflation into terms you can understand, an item that sold for the equivalent of 50¢ in Bolivia at the beginning of 1985 cost more than $5,000 at the end of the year!

Price Instability as a Distorter of Choices and a Capricious Redistributor of Income

Inflation (and its opposite, deflation) is a distorter of choices and a capricious redistributor of income. Erratic changes in the price level distort choices because people base their decisions not only on the benefits and costs they incur when buying and selling but also on their assessments of changes in the price level. Erratic changes in the price level inevitably cause changes in the distribution of income. There are always gainers and losers as a result of inflation, but it's difficult to predict who will gain and who will lose.

Concept Check

1　How can inflation decrease the supply of credit and contribute to higher nominal and real interest rates?

2　How can inflation influence household allocation of income between current and future consumption?

3　Can the impact of inflation on the distribution of income be easily predicted?

Summary

1. Inflation is the rate at which the general price level increases for goods and services produced in a nation. When inflation exists, the purchasing power of a nation's currency declines over time. This means that a dollar buys fewer goods and services over time as a result of increases in the price level. Deflation is the

opposite of inflation. When deflation prevails, the price level declines and the purchasing power of a dollar increases.

2. The percentage change in the consumer price index (CPI) over a year is the most common measure of inflation. The consumer price index represents a weighted average of the prices of a market basket of goods purchased by a typical urban family relative to an average of the prices of the same basket of goods in a base year. Measured in this way, inflation is an average of the increases in the prices of all goods in the CPI market basket. The greater the weight attached to an item in the CPI, the greater the impact of a change in its price on the CPI.

3. Some goods can actually decrease in price even when inflation is positive. Pure inflation would prevail in an economy if the prices of all goods rose by the same percentage over the year. The relative price of a good increases when its price rises at a more rapid rate than the prices of all goods.

4. Nominal income is the actual number of dollars received as income during a year. Real income is the purchasing power of nominal income measured by the quantity of goods and services that can be bought with money income. Real income is measured in base year prices and can be obtained by deflating current income by dividing it by the CPI/100. When there is inflation in an economy, increases in nominal income do not necessarily imply increases in real income.

5. When the rate of inflation exceeds the growth rate of nominal income, real income declines. The real wage for an hour of work declines if the nominal wage increases at a rate less than the rate of inflation. In the U.S. economy, nominal wages tend to increase with inflation. However, there is also a lag between increases in the price level and increases in nominal wages, particularly during periods of rapid inflation. Under those circumstances workers suffer temporary reductions in real wages.

6. Inflation can result in a redistribution of income and wealth from creditors to debtors. As a result of inflation, borrowers can pay back loans in dollars that have less purchasing power than those they borrowed. This makes debtors better off at the expense of creditors, who are repaid in dollars that are worth less than those they lent. Inflation can also harm savers, who in effect are creditors, because the purchasing power of dollars in savings is decreased as a result of inflation.

7. The effect of inflation on debtors and creditors also depends on how much the nominal interest rate adjusts for inflation. The real interest rate on a loan is the actual annual percentage change in the purchasing power of interest income earned on a sum of money loaned out. As a result of inflation, the real interest rate is less than the nominal rate. The real interest rate earned on a loan can be thought of as the nominal interest rate less the inflation rate annually over the life of the loan. Real interest rates can be negative.

8. Actions taken in anticipation of inflation (or deflation) can adversely affect the performance of the economy. When buyers and sellers try to anticipate inflation, they base their economic decisions in part on the gains or losses they expect to incur as a result of inflation. This can affect the supply of and demand for particular goods and services, thereby distorting market prices.

9. Anticipated inflation can distort consumer choices by causing buyers to purchase more goods today when they might otherwise prefer to purchase those goods in the future. Hyperinflation seriously impairs the functioning of the economy by causing credit markets to collapse and wiping out the purchasing power of accumulated savings in a nation.

10. Inflation is a distorter of choices and a capricious redistributor of income. Erratic inflation has both gainers and losers, but it is difficult to predict who will gain and who will lose.

Key Terms and Concepts

Price level
Price index
Inflation
Deflation
Consumer price index (CPI)
Pure inflation
Producer price index
Implicit GNP deflator

Purchasing power of a dollar
Nominal income
Real income
Nominal wages
Real wages
Nominal interest rate
Real interest rate

Problems and Applications

1. Suppose the consumer price index is 450 in 1995. Assuming the base year is 1967, explain the implication of the CPI for prices and the cost of living in 1995 compared to 1967.
2. Suppose average nominal income for young urban professionals was $10,000 per year in 1967 and $50,000 per year in 1995. Using 1967 as the base year, calculate the real 1995 income of an average yuppie measured in 1967 dollars, assuming the CPI is 450 in 1995.
3. Suppose the rate of inflation is 5%. Does this mean that all the goods you purchase will cost 5% more than they did the year before? How would you determine the rate of inflation for goods and services that are included in your own personal budget? What can cause a decline in the relative price of a good?
4. Suppose the consumer price index goes up from 300 to 310 during the year. At the beginning of the year your nominal wage is $10 per hour. At the beginning of the following year you get a raise that increases your nominal wage to $11 per hour. Calculate your real wage in each year and indicate whether your real wage has gone up or down.
5. How are real wages in the United States affected by inflation on average over a period of several years? What is the implication of a decline in real wages for both workers and their employers? Under what circumstances does inflation redistribute income from workers to employers?
6. A borrower negotiates a $20,000 loan at 3% interest in 1967 when the value of the consumer price index is 100. In 1987 the outstanding balance on the loan is $10,000. If the CPI is 300 in 1987, how much is the outstanding balance of the loan in 1967 dollars? How has inflation since 1967 affected the borrower?
7. In what sense does inflation redistribute income from the holders of the federal debt to current taxpayers?
8. The nominal interest rate on bank deposits is 6%. During the year the inflation rate is 3%. What is the real interest rate earned on bank deposits that year? Suppose depositors and banks anticipated 4% inflation during the year. How did real interest rates differ from those anticipated, and how did the difference between actual and expected inflation affect the distribution of well-being between borrowers and lenders?
9. The nominal interest rate in a certain nation is not permitted to exceed 10%.

During the year most lenders anticipate 14% inflation. Predict the impact of the expectations of high inflation on the decision to lend funds.

10. Suppose you lived in a nation where hyperinflation prevailed. If you were given a choice between two jobs, both paying the same wage and with the same fringe benefits, explain why you would be more likely to choose the job that paid you every week instead of the one that paid you every month.

Suggested Readings

Robert J. Barro, *Macroeconomics,* 2nd ed., New York: John Wiley & Sons, 1987. Part II of this book offers a more advanced analysis of inflation and discusses the relationship between actual and expected inflation and real and nominal interest rates.

Robert J. Gordon, *Macroeconomics,* 4th ed., Boston: Little, Brown, 1987. Chapter 2 contains a more detailed analysis of the consumer price index and its shortcomings as a measure of inflation.

A Forward Look

In the following chapter we begin an investigation of the causes of excessive unemployment and inflation. Analysis of aggregate demand for and aggregate supply of final products will be used to explain the economic forces influencing the price level and real GNP in a given year. You'll see how shifts in aggregate supply and aggregate demand can cause cyclical fluctuations in real GNP and result in price instability. As in this chapter we've examined the consequences of inflation, in the following chapter we'll begin to unscramble its causes.

The Forces of Aggregate Supply and Demand: Investigating the Causes of Cyclical Unemployment and Inflation

You now know how real GNP, the price level, and their fluctuations are measured. You also know that the economy is subject to irregular fluctuations as measured by the ups and downs of real GNP. In the preceding part of the book we also discussed the wasteful and distorting effects of cyclical unemployment and inflation. Historically, recessions have been accompanied by reduced inflation and even deflation, which leads many policymakers to believe there is an inevitable tradeoff between inflation and unemployment. However, in the 1970s and 1980s there have been periods in which the economy has stagnated without growth or has even experienced declines in real GNP while simultaneously inflation roared—an unfortunate marriage that has been dubbed "stagflation."

But what causes excessive unemployment and inflation? How is it possible to avoid contractions and recessions and the cyclical unemployment that goes hand in hand with economic downturns? How can the ravages of inflation be kept under control? How can we explain why an economy sometimes suffers simultaneously from both high unemployment and high inflation, as was the case during recessions in the 1970s and 1980s? In this chapter we begin an investigation of these "whys." The analysis in this part of the book will help uncover the basic forces that influence real GNP and its rate of growth and the price level and its tendency to inflate.

To sensibly formulate macroeconomic policies that help stabilize the economy, it's necessary to understand how the forces of demand and supply in the aggregate affect real GNP and the price level. You have already seen how supply and demand analysis can be used to explain prices and quantities exchanged in individual markets. In macroeconomics the basic tools of supply and demand are adapted to explain aggregate production (real GNP) and the price level (as measured by a price index such as the GNP deflator or the CPI).

Overall supply and demand in the aggregate, and therefore the performance of the economy, are influenced by input prices, interest rates and the availability of money and credit, foreign exchange rates for U.S. currency, expectations about the future, productivity of workers, technological change, and government policies regarding taxes and spending. It's quite a task to understand how the economy functions. This chapter avoids the temptation to explain everything at once. Instead its goal is the modest one of examining the basic forces of aggregate supply and aggregate demand that influence annual output and affect price levels over a year for the economy.

Concept Preview

After reading this chapter, you should be able to:

1   Distinguish an aggregate demand curve from a market demand curve and explain why an aggregate demand curve is downward sloping.
2   Distinguish an aggregate supply curve from a market supply curve and explain the shape of an aggregate supply curve prevailing in the short run.
3   Use aggregate supply and demand analysis to show how we determine the equilibrium level of real GNP and the price level over a given year.
4   Use aggregate supply and demand analysis to show how changes in aggregate demand and aggregate supply affect the equilibrium levels of real GNP and the price level for a given year.
5   Use aggregate supply and demand analysis to explain the possible causes of recessions, excessive unemployment, and inflation.
6   Understand the classical model of macroeconomic equilibrium and explain why the self-correction mechanism implied by the model does not work quickly and reliably in modern economies to ensure full employment.

Aggregate Demand and Aggregate Supply

In macroeconomics, supply and demand analysis is used to help us understand how changes in the economy can result in expansions or contractions and price instability. Rather than trying to explain the quantity of an individual item that is produced over a certain period, the goal of macroeconomics is to explain the forces that influence *aggregate* production as measured by real GNP. Similarly, instead of trying to explain how the price of one good is established in a market, the goal of supply and demand analysis in macroeconomics is to explain how the price *level* is established, as measured by a price index such as the GNP deflator or the CPI.

When you understand the forces influencing aggregate demand and aggregate supply, you'll be in a position to make your own forecasts about where the economy is headed. You can better understand the mysteries of inflation, recession, and stagflation once you've mastered the causes of shifts in aggregate demand and aggregate supply. You'll then be able to comprehend more clearly both newspaper articles and evening news reports and be able to formulate your own ideas about what the government and banking authorities should do to help stabilize the economy.

The Aggregate Demand Curve

What influences the quantity of final goods and services that will be purchased in a given year? It's not always the case that the entire amount produced by U.S. businesses during the year is purchased by buyers. The production and buying plans in the economy don't always match. If producers can't sell all they have produced during the year, their inventories will increase by more than they intended. They'll also find that they're overstaffed relative to what they can actually sell. When this happens, businesses will reduce orders of new materials and are also likely to cut back on personnel. This can spell trouble for the economy because the resulting decline in production, income, and employment causes an economic contraction that can lead to a recession.

On the other hand, if the amount buyers want to purchase in markets exceeds the amount produced over a period, the economy is likely to heat up. This is because inventories of final products will be drawn down more quickly than businesses anticipated and staffs will be inadequate to meet the demand. When this happens, the economy will heat up as firms reorder and seek to hire more workers. In this case the economy can be headed for inflation.

The demand for goods and services is therefore an important influence on the performance of the economy. Demand in the aggregate depends on the willingness and ability of consumers, business firms, and governments to purchase the goods and services produced nationally and available for sale in domestic and foreign markets.

An **aggregate demand curve** shows how the amount of aggregate national production demanded, measured by real GNP, will vary with the price level. The amount of real GNP that buyers are willing and able to purchase at each possible price level is the **aggregate quantity demanded** associated with that price level. The graph in Box 1 shows the downward-sloping aggregate demand curve prevailing

Aggregate demand curve:
Shows how the amount of aggregate domestic production demanded, measured by real GNP, will vary with the price level.

Aggregate quantity demanded:
The amount of real GNP that buyers are willing and able to purchase at each possible price level.

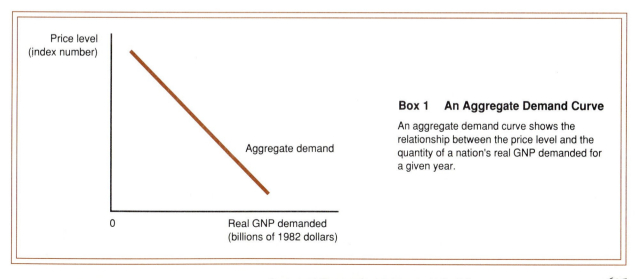

Box 1   An Aggregate Demand Curve

An aggregate demand curve shows the relationship between the price level and the quantity of a nation's real GNP demanded for a given year.

for a given year. The vertical axis measures the price level for the aggregate of final goods and services included in real GNP. The horizontal axis measures the quantity of real GNP demanded measured in base year (1982) dollars, representing the quantity of aggregate production that will be demanded for the year at each possible price level.

The price level is only one of many determinants of the quantity of real GNP that will be demanded in a nation over a given year. *Aggregate demand* represents a relationship between the aggregate quantity of real GNP demanded and the price level, other things being equal. When there is a change in aggregate demand, the entire aggregate demand curve will shift. A change in aggregate demand can occur when there is a change in anything other than the price level that will influence the quantities willingly purchased by consumers, business firms, government, or buyers in foreign markets.

Aggregate demand also can change in response to changes in such economic variables as the confidence we as consumers have that our future income will increase. For example, if we think our income will fall in the future, we'll put off purchases of new automobiles, furniture, major appliances, and other consumer durables. Changes in interest rates or business expectations can affect business firms' planned purchases of new equipment, structures, and vehicles. Changes in the international value of the dollar can cause a change in aggregate demand by changing the prices of U.S. exports to foreigners and affecting the prices of imports in domestic markets. As you'll see later in the book, aggregate demand also can shift in response to changes in the value of assets held by U.S. households and in the stock of money available as measured by currency and deposits in checking accounts.

Influences on aggregate demand will be discussed in detail in chapters to follow as we study in depth the macroeconomic determinants of aggregate demand. When there is a change in aggregate demand, the quantity of real GNP demanded at *each possible price level* for the year will also change.

How an Aggregate Demand Curve Differs from a Market Demand Curve for a Single Product

Although the aggregate demand curve might look like a market demand curve, it's really quite different because it describes a relationship between an *index* of prices and an *aggregate* of final products demanded in a nation. For example, when you move down an aggregate demand curve, there is an increase in an *aggregate* of goods and services demanded in the nation instead of an increase in the quantity of a particular good. Similarly, when the price level falls, it means that the cost of purchasing an aggregate (or "market basket") of many products falls rather than the price of a single item. It's possible that some individual prices may actually rise when the price level itself falls, and vice versa.

Because changes in real GNP mean changes in input use in the nation, income earned in the nation also changes when you move along an aggregate demand curve. Therefore income is not held constant as you move along an aggregate demand curve as it is when you move along the market demand curve for a single product.

The downward-sloping aggregate demand curve means that an increase in the price level will decrease the willingness and ability of at least some buyers to purchase the products included in real GNP. The reasons for the downward slope of an aggregate demand curve are much more complex than those that explain downward-sloping market demand curves for a single product. Three basic reasons for the inverse relationship between the aggregate quantity of real GNP demanded and the price level are:

1. *The real wealth effect: higher prices can decrease real wealth in a nation and reduce consumer spending on final products.* An increase in the price level reduces the purchasing power of some of the assets held by households. The purchasing power of these assets, which constitute the accumulated savings or wealth of households, is an important determinant of the willingness and ability of households to purchase goods and services. The purchasing power of accumulated savings denominated in fixed dollar amounts declines when the price level goes up.

   An example of a household asset whose value is denominated in money terms is currency. For example, suppose you have $100 in cash in a cookie jar in your apartment. If the price level rises, the real value of this currency falls. The reduction in purchasing power associated with the rise in the price level will make you less wealthy and can decrease your willingness and ability to purchase final goods and services. The aggregate reduction in wealth caused by an increase in the price level is likely to decrease the willingness and ability of all consumers to purchase currently produced final products during the year.

   The reduction in the value of assets that results from an increase in the price level might also induce a significant number of households to increase the portion of their current income that they devote to saving. For example, if savers have specific goals such as accumulating enough funds to make a down payment on a house or to finance their children's college education, an increase in the price level can induce them to save more of their current income for those purposes. This is because when the price level rises, they must accumulate more dollars to achieve the same objective. For example, if the goal is to save enough to pay a child's college tuition costs in the future, an increase in the price level that also increases tuition will mean that more dollars now must be saved to achieve the goal. As the desire to save increases as a result of the higher price level, consumer purchases in the *current year* decrease, resulting in a decrease in the quantity of real GNP demanded.

2. *The real interest rate effect: a higher price level can increase interest rates, making credit more expensive and reducing the quantity of investment goods demanded.* The ability of business firms and households to purchase goods and services produced over a given period also depends on the cost of credit, which is measured by the real interest rate. Naturally, at a higher price level the dollar amount of credit necessary to purchase any given quantity of goods and services also increases. The increased demand for credit resulting from the higher price level puts upward pressure on real interest rates. Assuming there is no offsetting increase in the supply of credit, an increase in the price level will act to increase real interest rates. As real interest rates rise, business firms cut back on their purchase of investment goods and households that seek to borrow funds to finance the purchase of homes and cars cut back their spending. These actions decrease the aggregate quantity of goods and services demanded.

3. *Foreign trade effect: a higher price level reduces foreign demand for U.S. exports and increases domestic demand for imports.* An increase in the domestic

price level does not immediately affect the dollar prices of foreign-produced goods that are available as imports. On the other hand, the prices of domestically produced items that are exported do increase over the year as the U.S. price level rises.

Because the higher domestic price level implies that U.S. goods become more expensive relative to foreign goods, consumers in the United States tend to substitute imported goods for domestic goods. For example, rapid increases in the price level over the year mean an increase in the price of U.S. products such as domestically produced cars. Assuming the increase in the price level in the United States has little effect on the dollar prices Korean sellers are willing to accept for cars they export to the United States, there will be a decrease in the quantity of U.S. cars demanded and an increase in the demand for Korean-made imported cars.

The increase in the price of U.S. items in foreign markets decreases the quantity of U.S. exports demanded, other things being equal. The net effect of the increase in the price level is therefore a decline in the demand for the final products of U.S. firms in foreign markets and a further decline in the quantity of final products of U.S. firms demanded in domestic markets as buyers substitute foreign goods for domestic goods. Both the increase in U.S. demand for foreign products and the decrease in demand for U.S. products abroad contribute to a decline in the quantity of real GNP demanded during the year stemming from the increase in the price level.[1]

The Aggregate Supply Curve

Sellers, like buyers, respond to incentives. How much they are willing to produce in a given year depends on their assessments of the profitability of selling their products. Any change in the economy that affects producer assessments of profitability can affect the quantity of final products they are willing and able to supply to product markets.

Aggregate supply curve:
Shows the aggregate output of final products, as measured by real GNP, that will be produced at each possible price level over a given period.

Aggregate quantity supplied:
The quantity of real GNP supplied by producers that is associated with a given price level.

An **aggregate supply curve** shows the aggregate output of final products, as measured by real GNP, that will be produced at each possible price level over a given period. **Aggregate quantity supplied** is the quantity of real GNP supplied by producers that is associated with a given price level. The aggregate supply curve shows a relationship between aggregate quantity supplied and the price level. The graph in Box 2 draws an aggregate supply curve plotting real GNP supplied against the price level prevailing for a given year. An aggregate supply curve is drawn under the assumption that the level of input prices, the quantity of inputs, and technology are given.

Of course, the price level is only one of several influences on actual annual production of final goods and services. *Aggregate supply* is a relationship between the price level and aggregate quantity supplied, other things being equal. Aggregate supply will change in response to changes in input prices. A change in aggregate supply means the entire aggregate supply curve will shift. For example, an increase in nominal (money) wages will increase the unit cost of any given level of aggregate

[1]This analysis assumes that the exchange rate of the dollar for foreign currency does not immediately adjust to cancel out the effect of the increase in the domestic price level. In practice many foreign nations manipulate the demand for and supply of their currencies in ways that prevent the exchange rate of their national currency from changing immediately in response to changes in the U.S. price level.

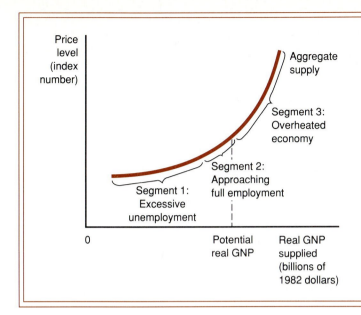

Box 2   An Aggregate Supply Curve

An aggregate supply curve shows the relationship between the price level and real GNP supplied in a given year. Because unit costs of production increase slowly at first, the aggregate supply curve is quite flat at low levels of production, but its slope becomes very steep as the economy's capacity is reached.

output. An increase in the general level of nominal wages in the economy will tend to increase the price level required for firms to willingly supply any given quantity of output. In other words, a change in input prices changes the aggregate quantity supplied associated with each possible price level during the year.

Aggregate supply also depends on the availability of productive resources during the year and on technology and other influences on the productivity of inputs. Recall that the productivity of inputs is a measure of output per unit of input use. For example, labor productivity is a measure of output per labor hour. Increased availability of productive resources or improvements in technology will increase aggregate supply.

An upward-sloping aggregate supply curve implies that an increase in the price level will increase the aggregate of final products measured by real GNP that domestic business firms are willing and able to produce. As was the case for aggregate demand, the shape of the aggregate supply curve cannot be as easily explained as that of a market supply curve for a particular item.

The aggregate supply curve shows a relationship between *aggregate* quantity supplied and an index of a broad array of prices. You know that a market supply curve slopes upward because higher prices imply greater opportunities for profit and also attract new sellers to enter the market over the long run. When we discuss aggregate supply the number of sellers and resources available during the year are more or less fixed, so it's not possible to explain the increase in output in terms of attraction of additional sellers or resources into production.

However, there is reason to believe that profit opportunities from supplying more output do increase in the aggregate, at least over a period of 1 year, when the price level rises. The reason for this is that over a short period a higher price level increases what businesses receive from selling additional output, *while input prices do not increase.* Naturally, as product prices rise but *input* prices remain constant, opportunities arise for additional profit from producing more. This leads producers to produce more until the costs of additional output (this is the marginal cost of output) rise to match the higher prices.

Aggregate Demand and Aggregate Supply

The costs of additional output tend to rise because firms must work their existing facilities more intensely and hire less experienced workers to produce more. As this occurs, unit costs of production tend to rise because of overuse of facilities and the lower skill and productivity of less experienced workers. If you've already covered the microeconomics chapters in this book, you know that the marginal cost of output for a firm tends to increase as more output is supplied. Similarly, the marginal cost of additional *aggregate* production for the economy as a whole tends to increase as quantity supplied increases over a given period.

In the graph in Box 2 the level of real GNP corresponding to potential real GNP is indicated on the horizontal axis. Recall from the preceding chapter that potential real GNP (also called full-employment real GNP) is the level of real GNP that would be produced if the economy were at full employment. As potential real GNP for the economy is approached, factories, offices, and other productive facilities are pushed beyond the levels at which the unit cost of production is at a minimum. When the economy is approaching peak production levels, machines tend to break down more often from heavy use and in general more materials and less experienced workers are used with available facilities, so that the overall level of efficiency of operation is impaired. These factors contribute to the higher unit production costs that occur even though input prices are constant.

In addition, as an economy's potential real GNP is approached, businesses often have difficulty in obtaining all the input they require to produce more. For example, to operate facilities around the clock, firms must use overtime labor, which is often difficult to obtain without paying bonuses. The difficulties in obtaining labor and material inputs also contribute to the rising cost of additional output as the economy approaches the level of real GNP corresponding to full employment. The aggregate supply curve becomes steeper because the costs of producing the additional units of aggregate production increase as output moves toward potential real GNP.[2]

Because business firms must be able to profit by producing more, it follows that prices of additional units of output must rise for firms to cover higher costs of additional units of output as potential real GNP is approached. These higher prices are required before the aggregate quantity supplied can increase.

Segments of the Aggregate Supply Curve

The slope of the aggregate supply curve can differ depending on how much slack there is in the economy at the beginning of a year (or any other production period). The aggregate supply curve drawn in Box 2 has been divided into three distinct segments for corresponding levels of real GNP:

Segment 1: *The economy is operating well below its potential with considerable cyclical unemployment.* When actual real GNP is considerably below the level that corresponds to potential real GNP, there will be cyclical unemployment and idle capacity. Under such circumstances aggregate production can increase without much upward pressure on unit costs of production. If the economy is operating in this segment, business firms can produce more simply by bringing idle plant capacity and equipment back into service. It's also easy to obtain materials and labor under such circumstances so that output can increase with-

---

[2] Just as the marginal cost of output for an individual producer increases when output goes up, so does the marginal cost of real GNP for the economy increase as the economy approaches full employment.

out increasing the costs of additional units of output. In segment 1 of the aggregate supply curve, there is considerable slack in the economy and, other things being equal, little or no increase in the price level will suffice to increase aggregate quantity supplied.

Segment 2: *The economy is close to full employment.* As the idle capacity is eliminated and an economy is approaching the level of aggregate production corresponding to potential real GNP, costs of additional units of real GNP begin to rise more quickly. Under such circumstances more substantial increases in the price level are necessary to induce firms to increase aggregate quantity supplied. It follows that as the economy approaches full employment, inflation will heat up if real GNP supplied increases further.

Segment 3: *The economy is overheated.* In segment 3 of the aggregate supply curve, the level of real GNP supplied would exceed potential real GNP. This means that unit costs of production will rise very rapidly and much higher prices are necessary to cover those higher costs if the economy is to produce more. An economy operating at the beginning of the year in the nearly vertical portion of its aggregate supply curve will be bursting at the seams through overproduction and can be characterized as being *overheated.*

Steady increases in aggregate demand in an overheated economy are likely to result in high inflation. While inflation resulting from outward shifts in aggregate demand will be a minor problem to worry about in segment 1 of the aggregate supply curve, it will be a very serious problem in segment 3 of the curve.

Concept Check

1   Explain why an aggregate demand curve is downward sloping.

2   Explain the likely shape of an aggregate supply curve.

3   Explain how aggregate demand and aggregate supply curves differ from market demand and supply curves for individual products.

Macroeconomic Equilibrium

The preceding analysis of aggregate demand and aggregate supply curves shows that both the amounts buyers are willing to buy and the amounts sellers are willing to produce depend on the price level. But what determines the actual price level and the level of real GNP that will prevail over a given period? Will actual real GNP be equal to potential real GNP over a period? Will increases in aggregate demand cause inflation that will send the price level skyrocketing, or will they merely result in an increase in aggregate production? How will an oil embargo affect the aggregate supply curve and real GNP over the year?

To answer these questions we have to examine whether or not the spending plans of buyers match the production plans of sellers over a given period. We must also examine how changes in aggregate demand and aggregate supply will affect the balance between aggregate quantity demanded and aggregate quantity supplied. In this way we can forecast how changes in the economy will affect unemployment and inflation. We can also examine the way government stabilization policies can affect the economy through their impact on the balance between aggregate quantities demanded and supplied.

Macroeconomic equilibrium:
Occurs when the quantity of real GNP demanded equals the quantity of real GNP supplied.

A **macroeconomic equilibrium** is attained for an economy when the quantity of real GNP demanded equals the quantity of real GNP supplied. When aggregate supply and demand balance at the equilibrium price level, neither is there widespread unplanned buildup of inventories of products produced over a period (but not purchased), nor are inventories unexpectedly being rapidly drawn down because businesses cannot fill orders quickly enough. When a macroeconomic equilibrium is achieved, the aggregate production made available for sale over a given period is on average willingly purchased in markets at the prevailing price level.

The phrase "on average" is important when discussing macroeconomic equilibrium because both the price level and real GNP are aggregates. Be sure you understand that it's always likely that some *individual* markets can be out of equilibrium during the year even when a macroeconomic equilibrium is attained. For example, during a given year the demand for personal computers might fall, resulting in a surplus of computers and unanticipated buildup of inventories for that product. At the same time, an increase in the demand for compact discs during the year might result in a shortage of this product and consequent unanticipated depletion of producer inventories. During the year there would therefore be downward pressure on the price of personal computers and upward pressure on the price of compact discs as these markets move to a new equilibrium.

When a macroeconomic equilibrium exists, there might be shortages in some product markets but there will also be surpluses in other product markets. *In the aggregate* there will be neither upward nor downward pressure on the price level or the level of real GNP once macroeconomic equilibrium is attained.

The graph in Box 3 illustrates the concept of macroeconomic equilibrium using aggregate demand and aggregate supply curves prevailing for a given year. The macroeconomic equilibrium corresponds to the point at which the aggregate demand and aggregate supply curves intersect. The equilibrium level of real GNP corresponding to the point of intersection, *E,* is $5,000 billion. Aggregate production of $5,000 billion (measured in 1982 dollars) will also correspond to the quantity of real GNP demanded at the equilibrium price level of 120 as measured by a price index such as the GNP deflator, which corresponds to point *E*. Because the entire

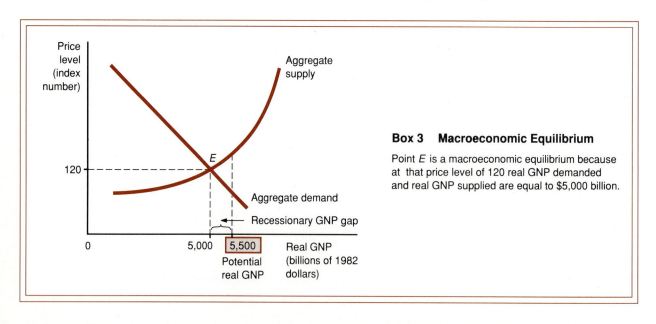

Box 3   Macroeconomic Equilibrium

Point *E* is a macroeconomic equilibrium because at that price level of 120 real GNP demanded and real GNP supplied are equal to $5,000 billion.

real GNP supplied of $5,000 billion of final products is willingly purchased at the current price level of 120, there is no upward or downward pressure on prices or production on average when the macroeconomic equilibrium is attained.

How Unintended Inventory Changes Result in Forces that Move the Economy to Macroeconomic Equilibrium

Suppose the quantity of real GNP demanded did not match aggregate quantity supplied at the existing price level during the year. For example, suppose real GNP demanded fell short of real GNP supplied. Under such circumstances there would be an abundance of unsold goods in markets. Many industries would experience slack demand for the final products produced during the year, and this slack would not be made up by booms in other industries. Manufacturing firms would find that their orders were less than anticipated. As inventories build up, these firms will lay off workers and cut back on orders for materials. Similarly, service firms such as banks, insurance companies, and brokerage houses will find that their staffs are excessive for the volume of business they are doing and they too will lay off workers. Under such circumstances production and employment will begin to fall, and there will also be downward pressure on the price level.

You can imagine a different scenario if real GNP demanded exceeded real GNP supplied. In this case inventories of goods and services would be rapidly drawn down. Manufacturing firms would experience difficulty in keeping up with orders. Firms would seek to hire more workers or work their plants around the clock with existing workers as goods and services are reordered. Service firms would also have difficulty in keeping up with demand and would seek to expand their staffs or offer overtime bonuses to existing workers. In this case there would be upward pressure on the price level and upward pressure on the output of final products as the economy moves to a macroeconomic equilibrium.

The production plans of sellers are based on guesses about the buying plans of buyers. In a market economy no one coordinates the production decisions of business firms with the purchase decisions of buyers over a period. For example, businesses might anticipate a strong holiday selling season. Then an unanticipated event such as a sharp increase in real interest rates or a stock market collapse might cause buyers to buy less than sellers anticipated. As this occurs, business firms that are stuck with lots of inventory cancel their orders for more goods. Similarly, some businesses may revise their investment purchases after the unexpected decline in sales. As orders are canceled, aggregate production will decline and so will aggregate real income. There could also be downward pressure on the price level as sellers stuck with inventories of unsold goods lower prices to move the goods. As this happens, real GNP and possibly the price level will adjust until an equilibrium is attained. Similarly, if sellers *underestimate* the aggregate quantity demanded during a period, there will be upward pressure on real GNP and the price level as reorders of goods and additional hiring of workers increase aggregate quantity supplied and aggregate real income.

Equilibrium Real GNP Is Not Necessarily the Level of Real GNP Corresponding to Full Employment

A macroeconomic equilibrium need not necessarily occur at the level of real GNP that corresponds to potential real GNP. For example, in Box 3 potential real GNP is

$5,500 billion. If that level of real GNP were attained, the economy would be at full employment. However, in Box 3 the level of aggregate demand is not high enough to generate full employment. The equilibrium level of real GNP is $500 billion below potential real GNP, implying that there is some cyclical unemployment in the economy. In other words, if the level of real GNP corresponding to full employment were attained, the result would be widespread buildup of inventory. This would cause decreases in production that would reduce income and spending until an equilibrium was attained at point E, where real GNP falls to $5,000 billion. Only the level of real GNP corresponding to point E could be maintained as an equilibrium given the aggregate demand and aggregate supply curves drawn in Box 3. The difference between the equilibrium level of real GNP and potential real GNP when the economy is operating at less than full employment is called a **recessionary GNP gap.** The recessionary GNP gap in Box 3 amounts to $500 billion.

It's quite possible for the aggregate demand curve to intersect the aggregate supply curve along the latter's flat portion. In this case the macroeconomic equilibrium would correspond to considerable unemployment of workers and idle capacity in the economy.

How Changes in Aggregate Demand Can Affect the Economy

A **change in aggregate demand** is a shift of the economy's aggregate demand curve. Changes in aggregate demand cause the economy to move to a new macroeconomic equilibrium. For example, a decrease in aggregate demand can result in a decrease in equilibrium real GNP and a consequent decrease in earnings and employment in the economy. If the decrease in aggregate demand is severe enough, it can cause the economy to operate well below its potential and thereby result in excessive unemployment. If the decline in aggregate demand is prolonged, it pushes the economy into a recession.

1. A decrease in business demand for investment goods such as machines, equipment, inventories of goods, structures, and other final products purchased for business use.
2. Decreased willingness of consumers to spend their income on the final products of domestic producers. Consumers might want to increase saving during the year, which would mean less current demand for final products.
3. An increase in demand for imports by domestic consumers or a decrease in demand for exports in foreign markets.
4. A decrease in government purchases of final products and input services.

Much of the macroeconomic analysis to follow in the next few chapters will examine in depth the determinants of changes in aggregate demand. At this point we'll examine only the general consequences of such changes, no matter what the cause.

Just as a decrease in market demand means an inward shift of the entire market demand curve, so does a decrease in aggregate demand mean an inward shift of the entire aggregate demand curve. The graph in Box 4 shows the impact of a decrease in aggregate demand in an economy. Suppose the economy is initially in equilibrium at point E_1, at which the price level is 120 and real GNP is at the full-employment level of $5,500 billion. When aggregate demand decreases, the economy moves to an equilibrium at point E_2, at which real GNP declines to $5,000 billion and the price level falls to 115. The decline in real GNP means the economy moves into a

---

Recessionary GNP gap:
The difference between the equilibrium level of real GNP and potential real GNP when the economy is operating at less than full employment.

Change in aggregate demand:
A shift of the economy's aggregate demand curve, causing the economy to move to a new macroeconomic equilibrium.

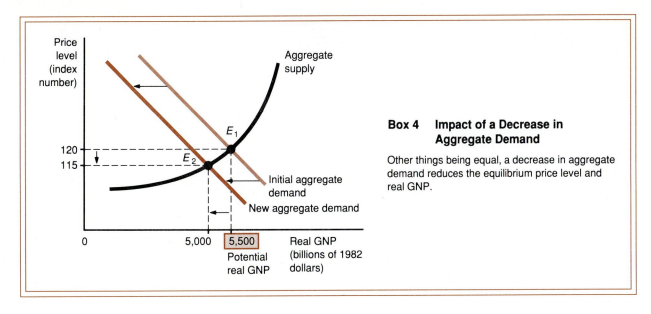

**Box 4   Impact of a Decrease in
Aggregate Demand**

Other things being equal, a decrease in aggregate
demand reduces the equilibrium price level and
real GNP.

contraction as a result of the decrease in aggregate demand. You can now see how
a decrease in aggregate demand can cause a recession and cyclical unemployment.
*A decline in aggregate demand is one possible cause of contractions or recessions
and can explain increases in cyclical unemployment.* We can now begin to unravel
the mysteries of the causes of excessive unemployment and recessions.

Similarly, an increase in aggregate demand means an outward shift of the aggregate demand curve. In response to the increased aggregate demand, there will be
upward pressure on equilibrium real GNP and the price level. The graph in Box 5
shows how an increase in aggregate demand moves the economy to a new macroeconomic equilibrium corresponding to point E_2, at which both real GNP and the

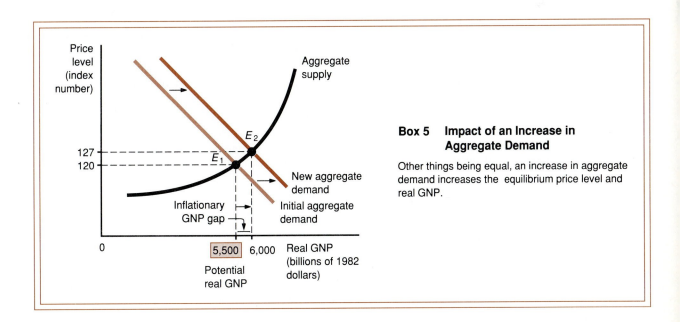

**Box 5   Impact of an Increase in
Aggregate Demand**

Other things being equal, an increase in aggregate
demand increases the equilibrium price level and
real GNP.

Principles in Practice

The Rising Importance of Imports and Exports for Macroeconomic Equilibrium in the U.S. Economy

How many Japanese or other foreign cars were on the American roads 25 years ago? Practically none. There likewise were few foreign TV sets, shoes, or cameras in comparison to what's available today.

In recent years the U.S. economy has become increasingly linked with the rest of the world through international trade. Americans have enjoyed gains from foreign trade as they have been able to buy quality goods at lower prices than would have otherwise been possible. When annual expenditure on imports exceeds annual expenditure on exports, there is a balance of trade deficit. In the 1980s the growth in the value of imported products has exceeded the growth in the value of exported products, which has contributed to huge balance of trade deficits in the United States.

The balance of trade has important implications for aggregate demand. Foreign purchase of U.S. products contributes to aggregate demand and therefore puts upward pressure on real GNP. On the other hand, purchase of foreign products by U.S. consumers means some of the income generated from aggregate production in the United States is being spent on foreign rather than domestic items. Expenditures on imports thus contribute to declines in aggregate demand for U.S. final products and tend to put downward pressure on real GNP.

The overall impact of foreign transactions on aggregate demand is gauged by *net exports,* which is the difference between expenditures on exports of final products and expenditures on imports of final products in a given year. When there's a balance of trade deficit, net exports will be negative. For example, in 1987 negative net exports (the excess of the value of imports over the value of exports in that year) amounted to 2.7% of gross national product measured in current dollars.

The table shows the gross national product, the market value of exports, and the market value of imports along with net exports from 1980 to 1987 based on prices prevailing in each year. In 1980 exports amounted to 13% of the value of GNP, while imports represented 12% of GNP. The sum of imports and exports therefore was equivalent to 25% of nominal GNP in that year. In 1970 international trade (exports plus imports) accounted for only 13% of nominal GNP.

Net exports were positive in 1980, injecting $32.1 billion of aggregate demand into the economy. In 1980 net exports were 1.2% of GNP. Because net exports were positive in 1980, international trade contributed to upward pressure on real GNP and income, and thus increased employment opportunities in the economy.

In 1987 the sum of exports and imports amounted to over 20% of the value of GNP. However, in 1987, as was true for every year from 1983 to 1986, the value of imports exceeded the value of exports. In 1987 net exports withdrew about $120 billion of aggregate demand from the U.S. economy. This amounted to 2.7% of GNP.

Whenever net exports are negative, U.S. international trade acts to put downward pressure on real GNP. This means that some U.S. firms have difficulty selling their products and are forced to cut back production. As they do so they hire less labor and use less of other inputs. The reduction in business receipts and the consequent reduction in national income resulting from the trade deficit are often concentrated in particular industries. In the early 1980s, for example, the automobile industry and U.S. agriculture were hard hit by loss of sales to foreign competitors. This is why there's serious concern about the impact on macroeconomic equilibrium of the rising negative value of net exports.

Imports, Exports, Net Exports, and Nominal GNP in the United States

Year	Nominal GNP (billions) of dollars)	Exports Amount (billions of dollars)	Exports % of nominal GNP	Imports Amount (billions of dollars)	Imports % of nominal GNP	Net Exports Amount (billions of dollars)	Net Exports % of nominal GNP
1980	2,732.0	351.0	13.0	318.9	12.0	+ 32.1	+ 1.2
1981	3,052.6	382.8	13.0	348.9	11.0	+ 33.9	+ 1.0
1982	3,166.0	361.9	11.5	335.6	10.6	+ 26.3	+ 0.83
1983	3,405.7	552.5	16.0	358.7	11.0	− 6.1	− 0.2
1984	3,765.0	382.7	10.0	441.4	11.7	− 58.7	− 1.6
1985	3,998.1	369.9	9.0	449.2	11.0	− 79.2	− 2.0
1986	4,235.0	376.2	8.9	481.7	11.4	− 105.2	− 2.5
1987	4,486.2	426.7	9.5	546.7	12.2	− 119.9	− 2.7

Source: *Economic Report of the President,* 1988.

price level are higher than at the initial equilibrium corresponding to point E_1. Increases in aggregate demand can therefore put upward pressure on the price level as well as increasing real GNP and earnings in the nation.

Demand-pull inflation is inflation caused by increases in aggregate demand. When, given aggregate supply, the aggregate demand curve continually shifts outward, the result is upward pressure on prices, which means inflation. Among the factors that can cause aggregate demand to increase are an increase in household wealth, a decrease in real interest rates (not caused by a fall in the price level), a decrease in net taxes levied by government, or an increase in government purchases. A general increase in the availability of money and credit in the economy is a common cause of demand-pull inflation that we'll investigate later on in the book. Increases in the stock of money measured by currency in circulation and bank deposits can cause a process of inflation through their impact on aggregate demand. For example, over a long period, a doubling of the quantity of money in circulation (other things being equal) is very likely to double prices. Suppose, to give you an extreme case, the government issued an extra dollar to each holder of a dollar of currency and suddenly by decree doubled the dollar value of bank deposits held by households and businesses. Who can doubt that as households and business firms run out to spend the new money that has literally been created out of thin air, aggregate demand and prices would skyrocket? Steady increases in the availability of money and credit in an economy can therefore result in the steady outward shifts in aggregate demand that cause demand-pull inflation.

In Box 5 the increase in aggregate demand is sufficient to overheat the economy. As a result, equilibrium real GNP rises above potential real GNP. In Box 5 there is an **inflationary GNP gap,** which is the difference between equilibrium real GNP and potential real GNP when the economy is overheated.

The extent to which changes in aggregate demand cause changes in aggregate production and the price level depends on how close the economy is to the level of real GNP that corresponds to full employment. Suppose the economy starts the year operating in segment 3 of its aggregate supply curve. This means that factories and offices are already operating around the clock and there is little unemployment. Under such circumstances the main impact of the increase in aggregate demand will be upward pressure on the price level, and there will be little if any effect on equilibrium real GNP. The increase in aggregate demand moves the economy along the portion of its aggregate supply curve that is nearly vertical, as shown in **A** in Box 6. Demand-pull inflation is likely to be a very serious problem in an overheated economy. When the economy is operating in equilibrium above potential real GNP, steady increases in aggregate demand will surely put sharp steady upward pressure on the price level.

On the other hand, if there is considerable unused capacity in the economy and excessive unemployment during the year, then the main effect of the increase in aggregate demand will be an increase in real GNP, with little upward pressure on the price level. Demand-pull inflation is therefore unlikely to be a serious problem for economies operating well below their potential. For example, government stabilization policies that seek to increase real GNP by increasing aggregate demand can do so with little fear of generating inflation in an economy operating in segment 1 of its aggregate supply curve. In such a case the increase in aggregate demand moves the economy along the relatively flat portion of its aggregate supply curve, as shown in **B** in Box 6.

Conversely, if the economy were in equilibrium at a level of real GNP at which

Demand-pull inflation:
Inflation caused by increases in aggregate demand.

Inflationary GNP gap:
The difference between equilibrium real GNP and potential real GNP when the economy is overheated.

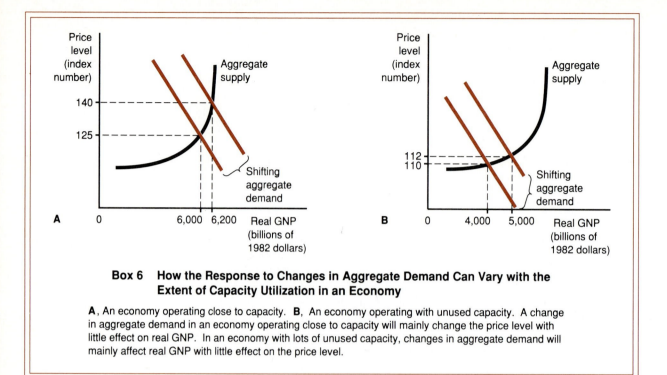

Box 6   How the Response to Changes in Aggregate Demand Can Vary with the Extent of Capacity Utilization in an Economy

A, An economy operating close to capacity. **B**, An economy operating with unused capacity. A change in aggregate demand in an economy operating close to capacity will mainly change the price level with little effect on real GNP. In an economy with lots of unused capacity, changes in aggregate demand will mainly affect real GNP with little effect on the price level.

factories and offices were utilized well below capacity levels and there was excessive unemployment, a decrease in aggregate demand would decrease real GNP with little downward pressure on the price level.

How Changes in Aggregate Supply Can Affect the Economy

A change in aggregate supply can be caused by a change in the level of nominal wages and other input prices, a change in the quantity of inputs available, or a change in technology in the economy. A **change in aggregate supply** means the economy's aggregate supply curve will shift as the relationship is altered between the price level and real GNP supplied. The graphs in Box 7 show the impact on the economy of changes in aggregate supply. Suppose there is a decrease in aggregate supply caused by an increase in the general level of nominal wages or a sharp increase in the price of a key input such as oil. The decrease in aggregate supply is shown in **A** in Box 7. As the curve shifts on the left, the economy moves from its initial equilibrium at point E_1 to a new equilibrium at point E_2.

Note that at the new equilibrium after the decrease in aggregate supply, real GNP is lower than it was initially and the price level is higher. Decreases in aggregate supply are therefore particularly harmful for the performance of the economy because they result in *both* decreased production and upward pressure on the price level. A decrease in aggregate supply thus can simultaneously contribute to increased unemployment *and* increases in the price level that erode the purchasing power of income! For example, if a war disrupts supplies of oil in the year you graduate and start looking for a job, you can expect rapid inflation of the price level that erodes the purchasing power of your savings and can also anticipate difficulty

Change in aggregate supply:

A shift of the economy's aggregate supply curve as the relationship is altered between the price level and real GNP supplied.

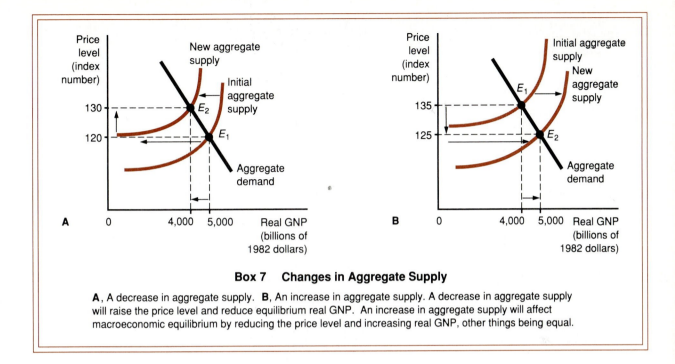

Box 7   Changes in Aggregate Supply

A, A decrease in aggregate supply. **B**, An increase in aggregate supply. A decrease in aggregate supply
will raise the price level and reduce equilibrium real GNP. An increase in aggregate supply will affect
macroeconomic equilibrium by reducing the price level and increasing real GNP, other things being equal.

in finding a job. Decreases in aggregate demand are not the only suspects in our
search for the causes of economic contractions and recessions. You now see how a
recession can be caused by a decrease in aggregate supply as well!

Inflation caused by continual decreases in aggregate supply is called **cost-push
inflation.** An increase in nominal input prices can result in cost-push inflation. For
example, an increase in the general level of nominal wages or salaries in the economy at the beginning of a year can contribute to cost-push inflation. You can now
see that the phenomenon of a stagnating economy along with inflation (stagflation)
can be caused by a decrease in aggregate supply.

On the other hand, an increase in aggregate supply can improve the performance
of the economy by simultaneously increasing production and putting downward
pressure on the price level. An increase in aggregate supply can be caused either by
a reduction in input prices or by application of improved technology that increases
the productivity of inputs. Graph **B** in Box 7 shows how a rightward shift of the
aggregate supply curve affects the economy. Initially the economy is in equilibrium
at point E_1, at which real GNP is $4,000 billion and the price level is 135. As aggre-
gate supply increases, the economy moves to a new equilibrium at point E_2. At that
point real GNP is equal to $5,000 billion, which is its potential level, while the price
level falls during the year to 125.

Increases in aggregate supply are particularly desirable for the economy because
they can reduce cyclical unemployment and keep inflationary pressures down. For
example, in early 1988 the news that the price of oil was decreasing was greeted
very favorably by those who evaluate the economy. Because a decrease in aggregate
demand was feared in 1988, the forecast of a likely increase in aggregate supply was
viewed as reducing the likelihood that there would be a recession in 1988.

Cost-push inflation:
Inflation caused by continual
decreases in aggregate supply.

Leading Indicators: Can They Forecast Changes in Macroeconomic Equilibrium?

You've heard about the "leading indicators" of economic activity—but what exactly are they? What do they indicate? And how accurate are they?

Macroeconomic theory seeks to understand the causes of ups and downs in the economy with the goal of stabilizing economic activity in the nation to avoid extensive contractions and recessions. Timing is crucial in trying to stabilize the economy, so a first step is to determine when a downturn or upturn is likely to occur. For example, one way to counteract a decline in consumer or investment purchases is to increase government purchases so as to increase aggregate demand when it would normally decline. To accomplish this task requires some indicator of when future consumer and investment purchases (or net exports) will be on the downswing.

Experts who try to forecast changes in real GNP keep a close watch on various sectors of the economy. A *leading economic indicator* is an economic variable whose value is normally expected to decline prior to a decline in real GNP and to rise prior to a rise in real GNP. In other words, leading economic indicators can sometimes (but not always) be useful in forecasting economic contractions or expansions. Among the important leading economic indicators watched in the United States are:

1. Net formation of new businesses
2. Building permits for new private housing
3. Common stock prices
4. Initial claims for unemployment insurance
5. Changes in prices of materials used in production
6. Changes in outstanding credit
7. Vendor companies reporting slower deliveries
8. Average work week in manufacturing
9. Net change in business inventories
10. Plant and equipment contracts and orders
11. New orders for manufacturing, consumer goods, and materials
12. Checking deposits and currency in circulation

The U.S. Department of Commerce regularly compiles a composite index of these 12 leading indicators, with 1967 set equal to 100. Some of the indicators enter negatively in the index. For example, an increase in initial claims for unemployment insurance forebodes a decline in real GNP, so the index will go down whenever these claims go up. Similarly, a decline in materials prices will decrease unit costs of production and thus will increase the value of the index. Other components of the index can signify increases in economic activity and real GNP for fairly obvious reasons. For example, an upturn in new business formation, building permits, credit or bank deposits outstanding, the average work week, or the number of new contracts and orders implies more aggregate demand for final products and upward pressure on real GNP. Similarly, if vendor companies have difficulty getting deliveries of parts and equipment, the economy could be approaching a peak level of economic activity. Other components of the index are more difficult to interpret. For example, an increase in business inventories could mean that businesses are stocking up for a surge in aggregate demand, or it could also mean they're having difficulty selling their available stock.

Perhaps the most controversial component of the index is common stock prices. The rationale for including this indicator is that declines in stock prices decrease wealth and can adversely affect aggregate demand. Declines in stock prices can also mean reductions in future business profits. However, stock prices change in response to investor perception of the profitability of holding stocks compared to other assets and can change when investors (rightly or wrongly) believe that real interest rates are going to rise.

A Recap: Economic Fluctuations and Their Causes

You can now see that recessions can be caused by *both* decreases in aggregate demand and decreases in aggregate supply. However, a recession induced by a decrease in aggregate supply differs from one induced by a decrease in aggregate demand in that it is likely to be accompanied by *both* inflation and excessive unemployment.

A recession caused by a decrease in aggregate demand will result in both excessive unemployment and some downward pressure on the price level. However, as you'll soon learn, except for very severe economic contractions (such as the Great Depression of the 1930s), there's usually little if any actual decline in the price level during a typical recession.

You also now have some clues for understanding the causes of inflation. Inflation

1967 = 100 (ratio scale)

Note — Peak (P) indicates the end of business cycle expansion and the beginning of recession (shaded area). Trough (T) indicates the end of business cycle recession and the beginning of expansion. Business cycle peaks and troughs are designated by the National Bureau of Economic Research, Inc.

The index of leading indicators does occasionally decline without a subsequent decline in real GNP, so the index must be used with caution. Forecasting the ups and downs of real GNP is riddled with pitfalls.

The graph shows movements in the index of leading indicators from 1968 to the beginning of 1988. The shaded areas in the graph correspond to periods classified as recessions. Notice how the index tends to turn downward just prior to each recession. The index then begins to rise again after the recession has

run its course and an expansion begins. However, you should also note that in some cases the index declines for an extended period, as long as 1 year, before a recession occurs. In other cases, such as in 1984, there are declines in the index and no recession follows. Typically, once a recession does hit, the index plummets. For example, see how sharply the index dropped during the 1974 and 1982 recessions.

Like any measure employed in forecasting, the index of leading economic indicators is useful, but not infallible.

can be explained by either increases in aggregate demand or decreases in aggregate supply. Both demand-pull and cost-push inflations occur, and sometimes both types of inflation exist simultaneously.

In the chapters that follow we'll be carefully examining the underlying forces that cause aggregate demand and aggregate supply to fluctuate. A good understanding of these forces is essential to help formulate macroeconomic stabilization policies.

The Classical Model of Macroeconomic Equilibrium

One question that might have occurred to you is: "When an economy is in macroeconomic equilibrium with excessive unemployment, why don't the labor market and other markets where there are excess supplies reequilibrate to eliminate the surpluses?" In other words, how is it that an economy can stay locked in a deep depression as it did for years during the Great Depression of the 1930s? This is a problem that in fact perplexed economists for much of the nineteenth and early twentieth centuries.

Economists of the nineteenth century believed that when the level of aggregate demand was insufficient to purchase the real GNP that would provide full employment, the resulting surpluses in input markets would cause input prices to decline. The declines in nominal wages, rents, and other input prices would then increase aggregate supply to increase equilibrium real GNP. The model of macroeconomic equilibrium of the nineteenth-century classical economists maintained that price flexibility in the economy would prevent it from stagnating in a macroeconomic equilibrium with excessive unemployment.

The classical economists, whose ideas paralleled those of Adam Smith, believed that all markets had a very reliable self-regulation mechanism that would quickly eliminate surpluses and shortages. The **classical model of macroeconomic equilibrium** implied that excessive unemployment of workers and unused productive capacity would set up market forces that would eventually result in increases in real GNP and eliminate cyclical unemployment. In other words, this model has as its underlying implication that the economy itself has a self-correction mechanism that can keep the economy working at full employment most of the time. A key assumption of the classical model is that in response to decreases in aggregate demand that cause cyclical unemployment, nominal wages and other input prices would fall sufficiently to shift aggregate supply outward enough to restore full employment quickly.

To see how the classical model concluded that cyclical unemployment would quickly be eliminated, think about why a decrease in aggregate demand reduces equilibrium real GNP and can cause unemployment to increase. Given the level of input prices, a decline in aggregate demand reduces the profitability of supplying final products in markets. The decline in profitability causes firms to reduce output, as was illustrated in Box 4.

Of course, the decrease in real GNP that occurs in response to the decrease in aggregate demand also implies a decrease in the demand for labor and other inputs used to make products available. What would happen if the level of nominal wages and other input prices (measured by some index of *input* prices) *also* fell when the price level fell? Such a decline would reduce the unit costs of any given level of aggregate production and therefore would make it more profitable for firms to supply output.

A decline in nominal wages and other input prices would cause the aggregate supply curve to shift outward. For example, suppose a decrease in aggregate demand moves an economy initially in equilibrium at potential real GNP (implying full employment) at point E_1 in Box 8 to an equilibrium at point E' along the initial aggregate supply curve. According to the classical economists, the equilibrium at point E' would only be temporary. The decrease in aggregate demand that caused real GNP to decline below potential real GNP would result in cyclical unemployment. The resulting surplus of labor would then cause nominal wages to decline. As this happened, the aggregate supply curve would shift outward, as illustrated in Box 8. The increase in aggregate supply would continue until nominal wages declined enough to restore full employment. Downward flexibility of nominal wages would ensure that the equilibrium at point E' would only be temporary and the economy would soon return to a new equilibrium at point E_2. As shown in Box 8, the increase

Classical model of macroeconomic equilibrium:
Implied that excessive unemployment of workers and unused productive capacity would set up forces that would eventually result in increases in real GNP and eliminate the unemployment of workers.

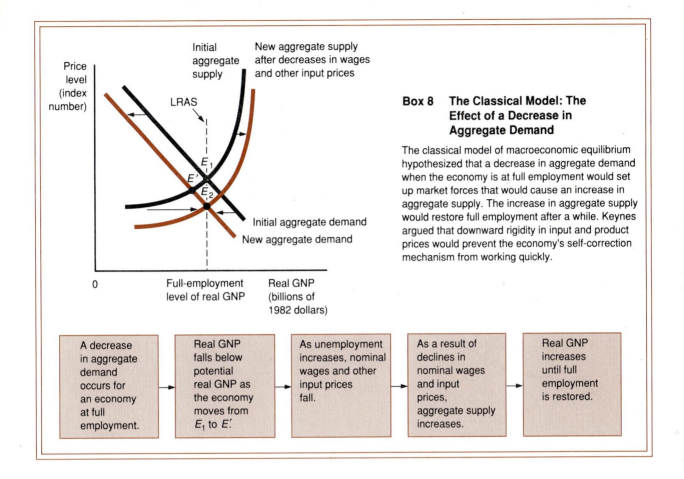

Price level (index number)

Initial aggregate supply

New aggregate supply after decreases in wages and other input prices

LRAS

E_1

E'

E_2

Initial aggregate demand

New aggregate demand

0

Full-employment level of real GNP

Real GNP (billions of 1982 dollars)

Box 8   The Classical Model: The Effect of a Decrease in Aggregate Demand

The classical model of macroeconomic equilibrium hypothesized that a decrease in aggregate demand when the economy is at full employment would set up market forces that would cause an increase in aggregate supply. The increase in aggregate supply would restore full employment after a while. Keynes argued that downward rigidity in input and product prices would prevent the economy's self-correction mechanism from working quickly.

| A decrease in aggregate demand occurs for an economy at full employment. | Real GNP falls below potential real GNP as the economy moves from E_1 to E'. | As unemployment increases, nominal wages and other input prices fall. | As a result of declines in nominal wages and input prices, aggregate supply increases. | Real GNP increases until full employment is restored. |

in aggregate supply puts upward pressure on real GNP and further downward pressure on the price level. This counteracts the unfavorable effects on real GNP of the initial decrease in aggregate demand.

The logical conclusion of the classical model is that equilibrium real GNP can never deviate for long below the level that corresponds to full employment of all labor and other economic resources, as long as *both* product prices and input prices are flexible. As long as nominal wages are flexible, they must fall enough to eliminate cyclical unemployment.

The classical model also implies that *increases* in aggregate demand will only temporarily put upward pressure on real GNP if the increase in aggregate demand causes the economy to overheat. For example, suppose the economy is initially in equilibrium at a level of real GNP corresponding to full employment (potential real GNP). At that point all factories and offices are being operated at capacity. An increase in aggregate demand could cause the economy to exceed its potential real GNP as overtime labor is used and physical facilities are operated around the clock. This would, of course, put upward pressure on the price level. In Box 9 an increase in aggregate demand moves the economy to a temporary equilibrium at a level of real GNP that exceeds the level for which full employment is attained. As a result of the increase in aggregate demand the economy becomes temporarily overheated, moving along its initial aggregate supply curve from point E_1 to point E'. As this occurs, the resulting increase in demand for labor puts upward pressure on nominal wages (and other input prices). Temporary shortages occur in labor markets until nominal wages rise sufficiently. The wage increase continues shifting the aggregate supply curve inward until labor shortages are eliminated. The aggregate supply curve shifts inward until equilibrium is attained at point E_2 in Box 9, at which equilibrium real GNP declines to potential real GNP corresponding to full employment. At the final equilibrium at point E_2, both nominal wages and the price level will have increased.

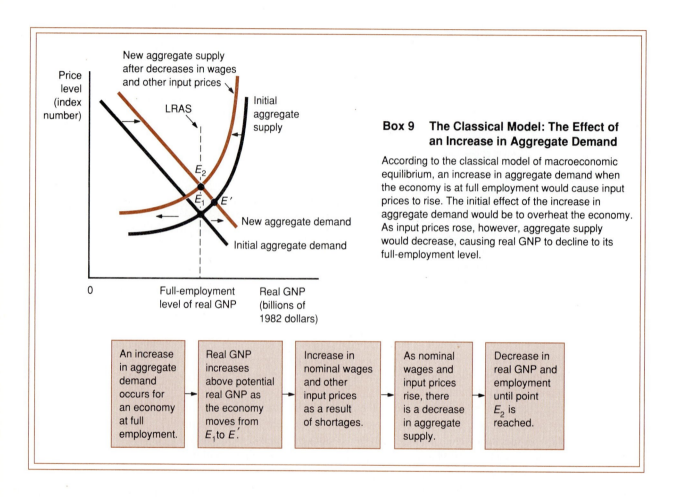

Box 9   The Classical Model: The Effect of an Increase in Aggregate Demand

According to the classical model of macroeconomic equilibrium, an increase in aggregate demand when the economy is at full employment would cause input prices to rise. The initial effect of the increase in aggregate demand would be to overheat the economy. As input prices rose, however, aggregate supply would decrease, causing real GNP to decline to its full-employment level.

| An increase in aggregate demand occurs for an economy at full employment. | → | Real GNP increases above potential real GNP as the economy moves from E_1 to E'. | → | Increase in nominal wages and other input prices as a result of shortages. | → | As nominal wages and input prices rise, there is a decrease in aggregate supply. | → | Decrease in real GNP and employment until point E_2 is reached. |

The Classical Long-Run Aggregate Supply Curve

Long-run aggregate supply curve (LRAS):

Shows the relationship between the aggregate quantity supplied and the price level that would be observed if nominal wages and other money prices were flexible enough to allow the classical self-correction mechanism to work.

According to the classical economists, equilibrium real GNP could deviate from potential real GNP only temporarily. Any recessionary or inflationary real GNP gaps would be quickly eliminated through shifts in aggregate supply that serve to eliminate the discrepancy between equilibrium and potential real GNP. The classical economists therefore argued that except for short-lived temporary episodes, the economy could be expected to achieve equilibrium at full employment. The **long-run aggregate supply curve (LRAS)** shows the relationship between the aggregate quantity supplied and the price level that would be observed if nominal wages and other money prices were flexible enough to allow the classical self-correction mechanism to work. Because equilibrium real GNP over the long run would equal potential real GNP if all prices were flexible, the long-run aggregate supply curve would be a vertical line corresponding to potential (full-employment) real GNP.

The graph in Box 10 shows the long-run aggregate supply curve for the economy. This curve can be thought of simply as indicating the economy's potential real GNP at any point in time. In Boxes 8 and 9 the long-run aggregate supply curve for the economy, labeled LRAS, is the dashed vertical line that intersects the horizontal axis at the level of real GNP corresponding to full employment. Points on the long-run aggregate supply curve (such as E_1 and E_2 in Boxes 8 and 9) correspond to full employment. Points of temporary equilibrium (such as E' in Boxes 8 and 9) are not points on the LRAS.

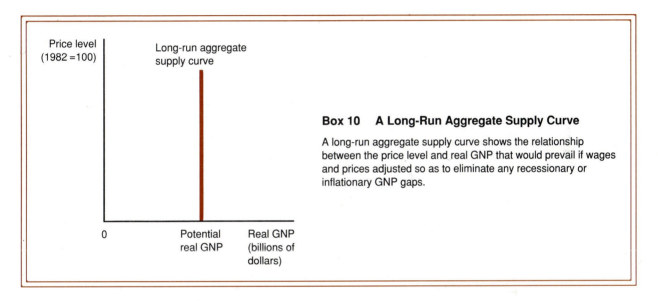

Box 10   A Long-Run Aggregate Supply Curve

A long-run aggregate supply curve shows the relationship between the price level and real GNP that would prevail if wages and prices adjusted so as to eliminate any recessionary or inflationary GNP gaps.

Wage Rigidity and the Keynesian Model of Macroeconomic Equilibrium

Although the logic of the classical model is correct, the evidence indicates that nominal wage levels in the economy are quite inflexible over a period of 1 year. When nominal wages are inflexible in response to declines in aggregate demand, the aggregate supply curve cannot be expected to shift outward when the economy is in equilibrium at a level of real GNP below potential real GNP. This is because unit labor costs in the United States don't fall quickly when the demand for labor falls. Unit labor costs, measured by nominal wages, are an important determinant of aggregate supply in the United States because labor costs constitute over 70% of production costs.

This is not to say that nominal wages never fall in response to sharp declines in aggregate demand. For example, during the Great Depression of the 1930s, nominal wages did fall substantially. There was a 21% drop in nominal wages between the end of 1929 and 1933. However, the decrease wasn't sufficient to shift the aggregate supply curve outward enough to restore full employment.

During the severe recession that occurred in the United States in 1982, equilibrium real GNP fell significantly below potential real GNP but nominal wages actually

Principles in Practice

How Long-Term Labor Contracts Prevent Wage Flexibility in the United States

Although the influence of organized labor on the U.S. economy unquestionably has waned over the last several years, unions still exert considerable power over wage levels in the nation. They accomplish this through the long-term labor contracts they negotiate with employers.

Long-term labor contracts set nominal wages for a period of at least 1 year. Most union contracts in the United States cover a 3-year period. Even though union workers account for less than 20% of the labor force, union wage levels tend to influence wages in nonunion jobs as well. The existence of labor contracts prevents nominal (money) wages from fluctuating daily as prices do in stock markets and commodity markets.

Because of long-term contracts, nominal wages are likely to be quite unresponsive to changes in the price level over a period of 1 year. Most union contracts contain inflation-linked cost-of-living adjustments, but the adjustments usually are made at the *end* of the contract year.

Why do workers agree to contracts that fix nominal wages over a period of 1 year? The reason lies in the costs of the process of negotiating wages. A 3-year contract that specifies wages and allows them to increase yearly according to the contract terms tends to economize on the costs incurred in reaching wage agreements. Such contracts also reduce the losses incurred in strikes by limiting the incidence of strikes and employer lockouts to once every 3 years. For these reasons both workers and employers gain when long-term contracts are negotiated, even though they run the risk that real wages will fluctuate over the contract period.

Similarly, rapid cost-of-living adjustments are rare in most labor agreements in the United States. Firms fear that as the price level increases, rapid and automatic increases in nominal wages will force them to raise the prices of their products. This, they fear, will cause a large reduction in sales volume that will adversely affect their profits. Similarly, unions fear that a reduction in sales resulting from nominal wage increases will cut the demand for labor and increase unemployment. Both workers and employers prefer not to take the risks associated with automatic cost-of-living adjustments.

These labor market practices keep the aggregate supply curve from shifting inward rapidly when the U.S. economy overheats. Over a period of 1 year nominal wages are not only inflexible in the downward direction, they also appear to be inflexible in the upward direction. The rigidity of wages in the U.S. economy implies that over a relatively short period (say 1 year) the economy's self-correction mechanism is unlikely to operate to stabilize real GNP at its full-employment level.

---

increased! Based on past evidence, nominal wages don't appear to fall enough to increase the profitability of production sufficiently to restore full employment when the U.S. economy operates below full employment. As a consequence, declines in aggregate demand do tend to significantly reduce real GNP in the United States without setting up a process of rapid self-correction that restores full employment. In other words, it doesn't appear that declines in aggregate demand when the economy is initially at full employment automatically result in quick outward shifts of the aggregate supply curve.

The reason for downwardly inflexible nominal wages is not completely understood. However, it's believed that labor market characteristics such as long-term wage contracts reached through union negotiation prevent wages from falling quickly in response to declines in labor demand. Wage flexibility also is affected by seniority and other rules that dictate which workers are laid off first. Many workers apparently are willing to accept periods of unemployment when they first enter the labor market in exchange for greater job stability when they gain seniority. Whatever the reasons for downward rigidity of the nominal wage level in the United States and other economies, the phenomenon is quite well documented.

Downward nominal-wage rigidity plays an important role in the theory of macroeconomic equilibrium developed by John Maynard Keynes (1883-1946), whose theories you'll begin studying in the next chapter. Keynes (pronounced KAINS) developed a theory to explain macroeconomic equilibrium at levels well below an economy's productive potential. Keynes believed that an economy could become locked in a macroeconomic equilibrium with high cyclical unemployment and that the classical self-correction mechanism would not work. His theory was based primarily on fluctuations in aggregate demand as the cause of recessions. The **Keynesian** (pronounced KAINSIAN) **model of macroeconomic equilibrium** assumes that because of rigid nominal wages the economy's self-correction mechanism cannot be expected to restore full employment when aggregate demand declines.

The Keynesian model implies that measures to restore aggregate demand to the level that will ensure full employment are necessary to avoid declines in aggregate real income and employment opportunities. Government policies to influence aggregate demand play a major role in the Keynesian model. According to the Keynesian view, when there is considerable slack in the economy, increases in aggregate demand result primarily in increases in real GNP with little upward pressure on the price level.

Modern Keynesians also believe that, because of the way labor contracts are negotiated, over a period of 1 year nominal wages tend to be inflexible upward as well (see Principles in Practice box). This tends to reduce the effectiveness of the economy's self-correction mechanism during periods when the economy is overheated.

Keynesian model of macroeconomic equilibrium:
Assumes that because of rigid nominal wages the economy can be in equilibrium at less than full employment.

Concept Check

1   Under what circumstances will an economy achieve a macroeconomic equilibrium?

2   Explain why unintended inventory buildup during the year implies that the economy has not achieved macroeconomic equilibrium. What will happen to aggregate production and earnings in the economy in such a case?

3   What is the self-correction mechanism for the economy envisioned by the classical economists?

Summary

1. Aggregate demand is a relationship between the price level and real GNP demanded that is depicted by an aggregate demand curve. Aggregate supply is a relationship between the price level and real GNP supplied that is depicted by an aggregate supply curve.
2. An aggregate demand curve slopes downward because increases in the price level can result in decreases in real wealth, increases in real interest rates, and changes in prices of exports and imports that decrease people's willingness and ability to purchase a nation's real GNP.
3. An aggregate supply curve slopes upward because the unit costs of additional production tend to increase as more is produced over a given year. When the economy has considerable slack the aggregate supply curve is quite flat, but it is very steep when the economy is operating above the level of aggregate production corresponding to potential real GNP.
4. A macroeconomic equilibrium is attained for the economy when the quantity of real GNP demanded equals the quantity of real GNP supplied at the prevailing price level. When macroeconomic equilibrium is attained, there is no unin-

tended inventory change that can cause changes in business orders for new goods or services.

5. Decreases in aggregate demand put downward pressure on real GNP and the price level, while increases in aggregate demand put upward pressure on real GNP and the price level. A recession can be caused by a decrease in aggregate demand or a decrease in aggregate supply.

6. Inflation can be caused by continual increases in aggregate demand (demand-pull inflation) or continual decreases in aggregate supply (cost-push inflation).

7. Decreases in aggregate supply put upward pressure on the price level but exert downward pressure on real GNP, while increases in aggregate supply put downward pressure on the price level and upward pressure on real GNP.

8. The classical model of macroeconomic equilibrium is based on the assumption of flexible nominal wages and prices. The classical model suggests that the economy has a self-correction mechanism that guarantees full employment.

9. Downward rigidity in nominal wages prevents the economy's self-correction mechanism from working.

10. The Keynesian model of macroeconomic equilibrium explains how real GNP and aggregate real income are determined in an economy in which there is downward rigidity in nominal wages.

Key Terms and Concepts

Aggregate demand curve
Aggregate quantity demanded
Aggregate supply curve
Aggregate quantity supplied
Macroeconomic equilibrium
Recessionary GNP gap
Change in aggregate demand
Demand-pull inflation

Inflationary GNP gap
Change in aggregate supply
Cost-push inflation
Classical model of macroeconomic equilibrium
Long-run aggregate supply curve (LRAS)
Keynesian model of macroeconomic equilibrium

Problems and Applications

1. An increase in aggregate demand occurs during 1991. Under what circumstances might you expect the increase in aggregate demand to increase real GNP while having little or no effect on the price level for the economy?

2. Potential real GNP is currently $5,000 billion. Equilibrium real GNP in the current quarter is also $5,000 billion. There is a sharp increase in the demand for U.S. exports during the year. Other things being equal, forecast the effect of the increase in export demand on unemployment and inflation in the economy.

3. Suppose all assets held by the public are automatically adjusted for inflation or deflation whenever the price level changes and that there is no international trade in the economy. Also assume that real interest rates do not change when the price level changes. What would the aggregate demand curve for such an economy look like?

4. The economy is currently operating at full employment. At the beginning of the year all nuclear power plants are shut down because of protests about the risk of environmental contamination. As power companies shift to more expensive sources of electricity production, the price of electricity triples. Predict the effect of the power plant closings on macroeconomic equilibrium.

5. Suppose that after a period of labor unrest, all workers in a nation succeed in getting governing authorities to order a 25% increase in nominal hourly wages. Other things being equal, predict the impact of this settlement on macroeconomic equilibrium for the economy. Under what circumstances will the increase in the wage level reduce labor earnings?

6. The economy is in a deep recession. After extensive negotiations, labor unions and all other workers agree to a 25% cut in nominal wages at the beginning of the next year. Use a graph to show the impact of the wage cut on macroeconomic equilibrium.

7. Suppose the aggregate supply curve for the nation is a flat line. What would this imply about the relationship between real GNP and the price level? Show how a decrease in aggregate demand will affect the economy if the aggregate supply curve is a flat line.

8. The economy is currently in a deep recession. The Federal Reserve Banks, which influence the supply of credit, take actions to lower real interest rates. As real interest rates fall, business firms increase their demand for investment goods. Use a graph to show how the increase in demand can pull the economy out of the recession with little or no resulting inflation.

9. What is the underlying logic of the classical model of macroeconomic equilibrium? Explain why the classical model does not fit the facts for the U.S. economy very well.

10. Suppose all input and output prices instantaneously adjust whenever there are shortages or surpluses in markets. Draw the aggregate supply curve for such an economy.

Suggested Readings

Economic Report of the President, Washington, D.C.: United States Government Printing Office, published annually in January. If you're interested in the performance of the economy over the past year, the current *Economic Report of the President* can tell you what happened to real GNP, income, and the price level during that period. The report is loaded with statistics on economic performance.

The Margin. This periodical, also cited in Chapter 1, contains articles about the current state of the economy and shows how changes in economic policies and conditions are likely to shift aggregate demand and aggregate supply.

A Forward Look

The Keynesian model of macroeconomic equilibrium concentrates on understanding the causes of shifts in aggregate demand. Once these shifts are understood, policies can be devised to counteract their undesirable effects. However, to gain a complete picture of how the economy functions we must now turn to an analysis of the components of aggregate demand, which will be the subject of the next two chapters. We'll then discuss supply-side explanations of economic fluctuations.

Career Profile

DALE LANG

Dale Lang has been raising Cain in the magazine business ever since his days as an economics student at the University of Wisconsin, innovating profitable publications that irritate the competition.

Back then it was a poster-type magazine that was attracting advertisers away from the campus newspaper. Its editors were bugged, needless to say, and tried to have his business banned from campus. Lang has been bugging the competition ever since.

When research showed that some products do better in particular regions of the country, Lang acted. In 1968 he persuaded *Time, Newsweek,* and *U.S. News & World Report* to let his company pro-

duce regional advertisements that could be inserted into magazines being shipped to certain areas of the country, bound right in with the main material.

Everyone profited from the deal, which at first they had greeted as crazy. By offering advertisers a chance to pitch products only in certain parts of the country, national magazines such as *Sports Illustrated* are able to tap new sources of revenue.

Lang founded one of the first city magazines in the country in Minneapolis in the late 1950s. Most recently he got in trouble with competitors when he announced that *McCall's* would openly negotiate advertising rates, rather than using the standard rates adopted by the rest of the top women's magazines. Even though other magazines were negotiating rates, most wouldn't admit it and were perturbed by his announcement.

Lang loves to innovate, and that's exactly what Time Inc. wants him to do. He's been their entrepreneur-in-residence since a 1986 deal that split ownership of Lang's *Working Woman/McCall's* group 50-50 with Time. They want his creativity behind an effort to introduce new women's magazines. Competitors are watching the partnership closely because with Time's powerful distribution network and Lang's innovation and knowledge of the market, they're in for a battle.

Working Woman made Lang's reputation as a brilliant force to be reckoned with; it was in bankruptcy when he bought it and now offers advertisers a circulation of almost 1 million. If he could revamp that mess into a success, competitors have to wonder what he'll think up next.

Aggregate Demand and Aggregate Supply: Macroeconomic Analysis

The Components of Aggregate Demand: Consumption, Investment, Government Purchases, and Net Exports

The sad truth is that most Americans save only a small percentage of their annual income. U.S. households are big spenders, and their purchases each year keep the wheels of commerce grinding away. People like you, as well as investors, governments, and those who buy the exports of U.S. businesses, generate the aggregate demand and purchases that provide income each year.

In this chapter we look at the major components of aggregate demand. We must know what factors influence buyers' willingness and ability to purchase final products before we can begin to understand how fluctuations in aggregate demand can cause recessions, excessive unemployment, or inflation.

The Great Depression of the 1930s forced economists to reconsider their idea of a self-equilibrating economy and the role of aggregate demand in influencing macroeconomic equilibrium. John Maynard Keynes, one of the most influential economists of all time, took the initiative to develop a theory that explained how the economy can and does achieve an equilibrium at a level below full employment. In doing so he developed a new model of macroeconomic equilibrium that explained how economies can stagnate in a recession because of weak aggregate demand. Keynes published his influential book entitled *The General Theory of Employment, Interest, and Money* in 1936. In that work he developed a theory to explain the causes of and cures for excessive unemployment that occurs during deep recessions.

The Keynesian analysis provides a basis for suggesting policies that can pull the economy out of a recession—something the economy apparently cannot do by itself!

Keynes's model concentrated on the role of aggregate demand in influencing macroeconomic equilibrium. In this chapter we begin a study of aggregate demand by examining its major components: consumption, investment, government purchases, and net exports. In the following chapter we show how aggregate demand influences macroeconomic equilibrium.

Concept Preview

After reading this chapter, you should be able to:

1 List the determinants of annual consumer purchases in an economy.
2 Use a consumption function graph and the concepts of marginal propensity to consume and marginal propensity to save to show how consumption and saving in a given year vary with disposable income.
3 List the major determinants of business investment purchases and explain why such purchases are extremely unstable from year to year.
4 Discuss how government influences aggregate demand and understand why government purchases in a given year are independent of disposable income.
5 Discuss how exports and imports for a year are likely to vary with disposable income, and draw a nation's net export function graph.
6 Draw an aggregate purchases line and explain how it shows the way purchases of final products that comprise GNP will vary with disposable income in a given year.

Aggregate Demand: Consumption

In many ways the consumer is king in the modern economy because the bulk of production is to satisfy consumer desires. But the consumer is also very predictable. Consumer purchases are largely determined by consumer income over the year. Expenditures for personal consumption purchases account for about two thirds of real GNP in the United States. A first step toward understanding the role of aggregate demand in the economy is therefore to examine the relationship between consumer purchases, consumer income, and other possible determinants of annual consumer purchases.

Income and Consumption

The major determinant of the quantity of goods and services that consumers can purchase in a given year is household income. Just as your income largely determines how much you can buy during the year, so does aggregate income mainly determine aggregate consumer purchases in the economy each year. As income available for spending has increased over time in the United States, so has personal consumption.

Disposable income is the best measure from the National Income and Product Accounts to gauge the income available for spending by members of households. Recall that disposable income is income available for spending by households after payment of personal taxes (see the chapter on GNP and economic performance). There is a clear historical relationship between real disposable income and real consumption in the United States. The graph in Box 1 shows how real disposable income and real consumption (both measured in 1982 dollars) have moved together. Over the 27-year period from 1960 to 1987, Americans on average have used slightly over 90% of their real disposable income annually for consumer purchases. As disposable income increases, so do consumption expenditures.

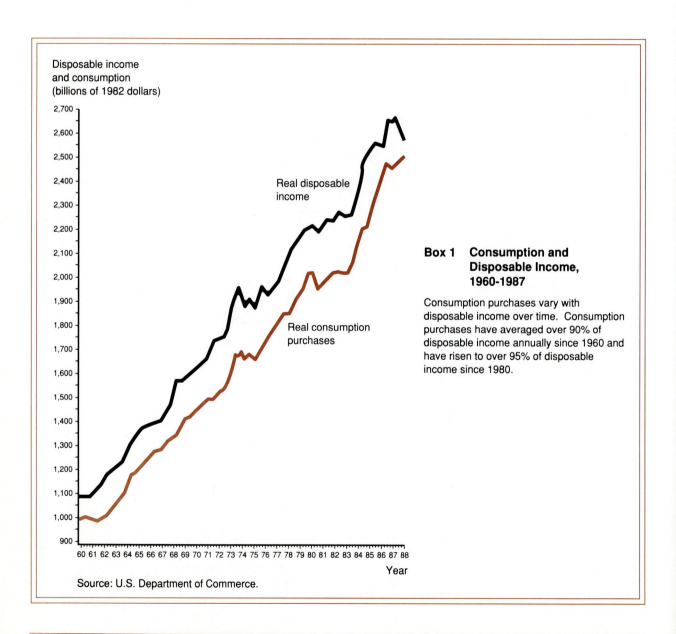

Box 1 Consumption and Disposable Income, 1960-1987

Consumption purchases vary with disposable income over time. Consumption purchases have averaged over 90% of disposable income annually since 1960 and have risen to over 95% of disposable income since 1980.

Source: U.S. Department of Commerce.

CHAPTER 29 The Components of Aggregate Demand

Other Determinants of Consumption: Wealth, Debt, and Expectations

Income is not the only determinant of the amount of consumer purchases in a given year. You can readily understand this if you examine your own behavior. If you have a savings account at a bank, you can use your accumulated savings from past years to finance the purchase of a car or a stereo system this year. If you have a fat bank account of savings accumulated from past earnings, you can actually spend more than your current income on consumer purchases during a year by drawing on your savings. Similarly, many parents finance their children's college educations by drawing down accumulated savings put aside in past years for that purpose.

A person's **wealth** is the sum of the current values of all assets owned. Examples of such assets are bank deposits, corporate stock, bonds, and real estate. Do not confuse wealth with income. Wealth is a *stock* of accumulated purchasing power stored up from past income. It's possible to have a great deal of wealth but very little income. For example, many elderly people have very low incomes and draw on past accumulated savings to make consumer purchases.

Aggregate household wealth is the purchasing power of all assets owned by households. Aggregate wealth is a very important determinant of consumption in the economy. Just as you're more willing to spend out of your current income when you have a fat bank account and a large portfolio of valuable stocks, so is aggregate consumption likely to be greater, at any given annual income, as aggregate household wealth increases. For example, when the stock market goes up, the value of stocks owned by households increases. The resulting increase in wealth is likely to increase annual consumption.

A general decrease in stock prices decreases the wealth of households and is likely to cause them to decrease annual consumption given their current annual income. The sharp rise in stock prices in the United States from 1982 to 1987 helped fuel consumer purchases. Similarly, increases in home prices in the late 1970s increased the wealth of many households and made them more willing to spend their current income on consumer purchases rather than saving. The crash of stock market values in late 1987 caused great concern that consumer purchases would decline, especially for durable goods such as homes and cars. Although the stock market crash of '87 didn't appear to have an immediate major impact on consumer purchases, the more serious stock market crash of 1929 did force many people to sharply reduce consumer purchases.

Changes in the price level can affect household wealth and thereby indirectly affect annual consumption. For example, an increase in the price level erodes the purchasing power of accumulated savings that are fixed in dollar value. Each dollar of savings you hold in certificates of deposit has its purchasing power reduced when the price level goes up. A reduction in the purchasing power of aggregate household wealth caused by an increase in the price level can adversely affect consumer purchases in a given year.

Debt accumulated by households can also influence consumption. The more debt you have, the more of your current income you must allocate to repaying that debt rather than buying goods and services. For example, if your monthly income after taxes is $1,000, you'll have less to spend when you have to make a car payment of $200 each month than you'd have if you had no debt at all. **Aggregate household debt** is represented by the purchasing power of the sums of money outstanding that households have borrowed and are currently obligated to repay. Given aggregate wealth and disposable income in the economy, an increase in debt can reduce both

Wealth:
The sum of the current values of all assets a person owns.

Aggregate household wealth:
The purchasing power of all assets owned by households.

Aggregate household debt:
The purchasing power of the sums of money outstanding that households have borrowed and are currently obligated to repay.

the willingness and ability of households to make consumer purchases out of current income. Increased household debt burdens in the late 1980s gave rise to fears that consumer spending would fall, thereby putting downward pressure on aggregate demand.

Consumer purchases in a given year also depend on household *expectations* about the future course of their income and wealth. The reason for this is very simple: if you think bad times are ahead, you're likely to want to save more of your current income to help you get by in the future. For example, suppose you think there's a good chance you'll be laid off from work or that your employer will go out of business this year. In this case you might want to set aside more of your current income to finance a period of reduced income while you search for a new job. If many workers feel the same way, the resulting loss in confidence about future income will lead to increased saving in the current year, which means less consumer purchases out of current disposable income. On the other hand, if you think your income will rise in the future because of opportunities for overtime work or good raises and that the value of assets you hold also will rise, you might be willing to save very little and indulge in consumer purchases. The greater the expectations of future increases in income and wealth, the greater are consumer purchases in the current year.

The Consumption Function

Consumption function:
A relationship between aggregate consumer purchases and disposable income in a certain year given all other determinants of consumption.

Autonomous consumption:
The portion of annual consumer purchases that is independent of current disposable income.

Induced consumption:
The portion of annual consumer purchases in a given year that responds to changes in current disposable income.

The economy's **consumption function** is a relationship between aggregate consumer purchases and disposable income in a certain year given all other determinants of consumption. The portion of annual consumer purchases that is independent of current disposable income is called **autonomous consumption.** Autonomous consumption is not affected by changes in current disposable income. For example, retired people who draw on accumulated savings to finance some of their purchases account for some annual autonomous consumption. Similarly, in a given year a number of families will be dipping into their accumulated savings to finance college tuition costs or purchase a new car. A change in disposable income during the year will not affect these autonomous consumption purchases.

Induced consumption is the portion of annual consumer purchases in a given year that responds to changes in current disposable income. If current disposable income were zero, induced consumption would also be zero. However, total consumption wouldn't necessarily be zero even if disposable income were zero because there would be some level of autonomous consumption that could be paid for by drawing down accumulated savings.

The table in Box 2 provides data that show the relationship between possible levels of annual disposable income and aggregate consumer purchases for a hypothetical economy. The first column shows possible levels of disposable income *(DI)* for a certain year. The second column shows the consumer purchases *(C)* associated with each possible income level for the year. It's assumed that $400 billion of consumption expenditure is independent of income and would occur during the year even if disposable income were zero. The $400 billion represents the amount of annual autonomous consumption that depends on wealth (or other factors) rather than income. The rest of the data in column 2 is obtained by assuming that each $1,000 billion increase in income available for households to spend would increase annual consumer purchases by $800 billion.

The table also shows how saving would vary with possible levels of disposable

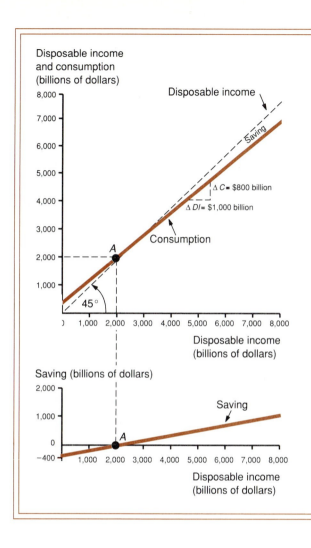

Box 2 **The Relationship Between Disposable Income, Consumption, and Saving for a Given Year (Hypothetical Data)**

The higher disposable income is for a year, the higher consumption and saving will be for that year. However, saving will be negative at low levels of income. Points A and A' show that at a level of disposable income of $2,000 billion for the year, saving would be zero. As disposable income increases above this level, households save some of their income.

Disposable Income (DI)	Consumption (billions of dollars) (C)	Saving (S)
0	400	−400
1,000	1,200	−200
2,000	2,000	0
3,000	2,800	200
4,000	3,600	400
5,000	4,400	600
6,000	5,200	800
7,000	6,000	1,000
8,000	6,800	1,200

income over a given year. Saving is simply the difference between disposable income and consumption expenditures that would be associated with each level of income. Whatever is saved is not spent by consumers on current production. Other things being equal, therefore, an increase in saving decreases aggregate demand.

Saving and consumption are mutually exclusive uses of disposable income. Whatever portion of disposable income is not used for consumption purposes is saved. Note that saving can be negative when households draw more from previously accumulated savings in a given year than they save in the current year. Saving is negative whenever consumer purchases exceed disposable income.

Graphing the Consumption Function and Showing the Relationship Between Income and Saving

The consumption function based on the data in Box 2 is plotted in the upper graph. Notice how consumer purchases increase in any given year when the actual level of disposable income increases that year. The line drawn in the upper graph shows the relationship between possible levels of income and the consumption associated with each of those income levels for *a given year.* In actuality, at the end of the year disposable income will have been at a certain level and the consumption observed would end up being the amount associated with the actual level of disposable income.

The lower graph in Box 2 plots the relationship between saving and income. If disposable income were very low in any given year, households would reduce their savings and might sell some of their assets to maintain their consumption over the year. The table and graphs in Box 2 show that saving in the economy would be negative if disposable income were less than $2,000 billion for the year. As observed earlier, negative saving means people consume more than their current income by converting some of their savings from years past into cash and using it to make purchases during the current year. As disposable income rises during the year, saving increases. The table in Box 2 shows that saving would be zero if disposable income were $2,000 billion for the year. For each $1,000 billion increase in disposable income, saving would increase by $200 billion. Remember that disposable income already has taxes deducted from it. The sum of saving and consumption must therefore equal disposable income at each possible level of disposable income.

Using a 45-Degree Guideline on the Consumption Function Graph to Measure Savings

A 45-degree line from the origin has been drawn in the upper graph in Box 2 to help you see the relationship between the consumption and saving graphs. Remember from the chapter on GNP and economic performance that disposable income can be expressed as the sum of consumption and saving over a period. Disposable income *(DI)* minus consumption *(C)* always equals saving *(S):*

$$DI = C + S$$

therefore

$$S = DI - C$$

You can easily understand the function of the 45-degree line by taking any point on it and drawing a straight line from that point to each of the axes. The result will be a square whose sides are the two lines you drew and a portion of each of the axes of the graph. Because all sides of a square are equal in length, it follows that the length on the horizontal axis corresponding to disposable income equals the distance from the origin to the point at which your horizontal line cuts the vertical axis. The 45-degree line therefore enables you to compare disposable income with consumption. The vertical distance between the consumption line and the 45-degree line represents saving for any given level of disposable income on the horizontal axis.

For example, look at point *A.* At that point the consumption line intersects the 45-degree line. At that point annual consumption of $2,000 billion equals annual disposable income of $2,000 billion. It follows that if the actual level of disposable income were $2,000 billion for the year there would be no saving that year. When disposable income exceeds $2,000 billion per year, annual consumption is less than annual disposable income. This is reflected in the fact that points on the 45-degree line correspond to greater dollar amounts on the vertical axis than points on the consumption line when disposable income exceeds $2,000 billion per year. The vertical difference between the 45-degree line and the consumption line therefore measures annual saving at each possible level of disposable income. You can verify this by looking at the lower graph, in which saving is positive whenever national income exceeds $2,000 billion but is negative when national income is less than $2,000 billion.

Just as consumption increases with income, so does saving. For example, if annual disposable income were $2,000 billion, the percentage of income saved would be zero. If disposable income were $4,000 billion, the fraction of income saved would be $400 billion/$4,000 billion, which is 0.1 or 10% of disposable income. However, if disposable income were $8,000 billion, the fraction saved would be $1,200 billion/$8,000 billion or 15%. The greater the disposable income for a year in the economy, the greater the ability of consumers to save and the higher the percentage of their disposable income they are likely to save.

The Marginal Propensities to Consume and to Save

The **marginal propensity to consume** is the fraction of each additional dollar of annual disposable income that is allocated to consumer purchases. The marginal propensity to consume can be calculated from the following formula:

$$MPC = \frac{\text{Change in consumption}}{\text{Change in disposable income}} = \frac{\Delta C}{\Delta DI}$$

Marginal propensity to consume:
The fraction of each additional dollar of annual disposable income that is allocated to consumer purchases.

where the symbol Δ signifies "change in" the variable it precedes. In Box 2 each $1,000 billion of additional income earned each year would result in $800 billion of additional consumption that year. In this case $MPC = $800 billion/$1,000 billion = 0.8. The hypothetical data in Box 2 imply that the marginal propensity to consume of each extra dollar of disposable income is always 80¢.

The **marginal propensity to save** is the fraction of each additional dollar of annual disposable income that is saved. The formula for calculating the marginal propensity to save is:

$$MPS = \frac{\text{Change in saving}}{\text{Change in disposable income}} = \frac{\Delta S}{\Delta DI}$$

Marginal propensity to save:
The fraction of each additional dollar of annual disposable income that is saved.

In Box 2 each $1,000 billion of additional disposable income earned in a year would result in $200 billion in additional saving. In this case $MPS = $200 billion/$1,000 billion = 0.2. If only 80¢ of each extra dollar is used for consumer purchases, it must follow that 20¢ of each extra dollar of disposable income is saved.

Because additional disposable income available during the year is either consumed or saved, the sum of the marginal propensity to consume and to save is always 1:

$$MPC + MPS = 1$$

You should note that the marginal propensity to consume is the *slope* of the consumption line drawn in the upper graph in Box 2. Each additional dollar of disposable income, ΔDI, will increase consumption by ΔC along the consumption line. The slope of the line is therefore:

$$\text{Slope} = \frac{\Delta C}{\Delta DI} = \frac{\text{Change in consumption}}{\text{Change in disposable income}} = MPC$$

The consumption line has constant slope because the marginal propensity to consume is assumed to be constant at 0.8. Similarly, the marginal propensity to save is the slope of the savings line, which is also drawn in Box 2. The slope of this line is 0.2 because 20¢ of each additional dollar of disposable income is assumed to be saved.

How Changes in Wealth Can Shift the Consumption Line

A consumption function describes the relationship between possible levels of disposable income and consumption for a certain year *given all other influences on consumption.* What would happen if over time there was a change in aggregate household wealth? For example, property values in a nation might soar or stock prices might rise, thus increasing household wealth from one year to the next. If wealth increases, autonomous consumption at each possible level of disposable income will also increase. An increase in aggregate household wealth is therefore hypothesized to shift the consumption line upward, as illustrated in Box 3. Increases in wealth, other things being equal, increase aggregate demand by increasing consumer purchases.

If the consumption line shifts upward, it follows that the savings line, also shown in Box 3, must shift downward. This is because when more of any given level of disposable income is used for consumer purchases, less must be allocated to saving. *An increase in aggregate household wealth therefore tends to increase the consumption but decrease the saving that is associated with each possible level of annual disposable income.*

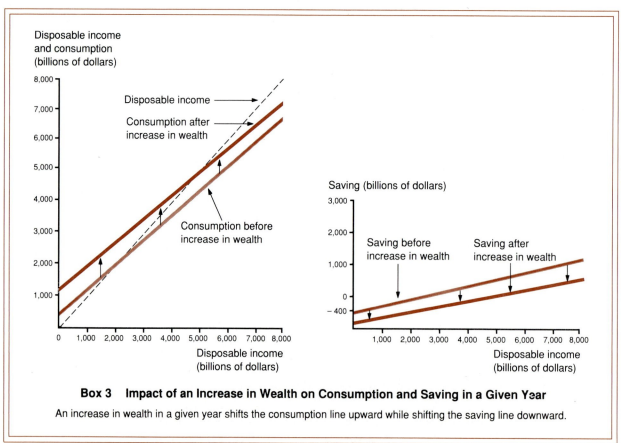

Box 3   Impact of an Increase in Wealth on Consumption and Saving in a Given Year

An increase in wealth in a given year shifts the consumption line upward while shifting the saving line downward.

A decrease in wealth would have opposite effects. For example, the stock market crash of 1987 obliterated $1 trillion worth of aggregate household wealth. Concerns were expressed during the year that if this decline in wealth were not quickly regained through increases in stock prices, it would put downward pressure on consumer purchases and aggregate demand.

How a Change in Household Debt Outstanding Can Affect Current Consumption

Given the value of assets owned by households, an increase in aggregate household debt can reduce households' willingness and ability to consume out of current income. This is because the greater the debt of households, the greater the proportion of current income that must be allocated each month to make payments to creditors. An increase in aggregate household debt is therefore likely to shift the consumption line downward but shift the savings line upward. This is illustrated in Box 4. When consumers devote higher proportions of their current income to paying off previous debts, they are in effect increasing current saving at each level of disposable income because repayment of debt represents a use of disposable income for a purpose other than consumption. Consumers have to decrease current consumption to pay

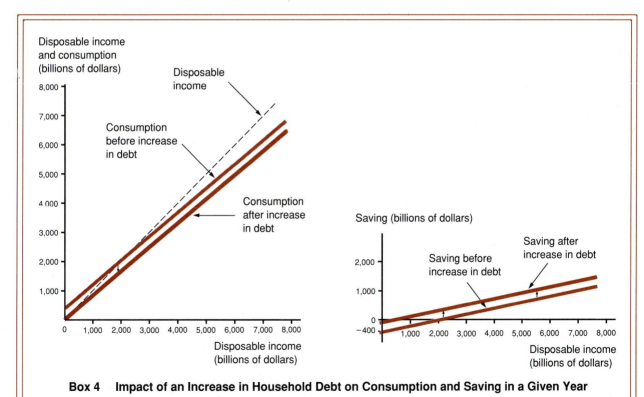

Box 4   Impact of an Increase in Household Debt on Consumption and Saving in a Given Year

An increase in household debt decreases consumption at each possible level of disposable income for a year while having the opposite effect on saving as consumers must devote higher proportions of current income to repaying debt instead of making purchases.

Principles in Practice

Personal Consumption and Saving in the United States: American Households Are Saving Less of Their Disposable Income

For a variety of reasons, Americans are known around the world as big spenders—and our reputation, if not always flattering, is certainly well deserved.

On average over the past 60 years, we Americans have spent approximately 90% of our disposable income each year on consumer purchases. In the last several years we've become even more self-indulgent. In 1987 U.S. households spent approximately 97% of their disposable income on consumer purchases.

American consumers also piled up debt at record levels during the 1980s. Armed with credit cards and mortgage loans, we amassed household debt equal to 86% of disposable income in 1986, when we owed $2.2 trillion to creditors.

From 1975 to 1987 personal saving in the United States declined from nearly 10% of disposable income to a mere 3.8%, as shown in the graph. The personal saving rate in the United States is much lower than it is in Western Europe and Japan. In Western Europe personal saving averages 7% to 10% of disposable income, while in Japan personal saving amounts to 15% of disposable income.

The saving habits of American households have important implications for the functioning of the economy. First of all, consumption constitutes the bulk of aggregate demand, amounting to 65% of purchases of real GNP. High consumption rates therefore help fuel expansion of the economy by bolstering aggregate demand. On the other hand, saving constitutes a source of loanable funds for investment purchases that help stimulate growth in the economy's productive capacity. As personal saving declines, other things being equal, the supply of loanable funds for investment diminishes, thereby putting upward pressure on real interest rates. Higher real interest rates in turn tend to decrease investment purchases.

In recent years the decline in personal saving has been offset by increased foreign saving in the United States, which results when there is a balance of trade deficit (see the chapter on GNP and economic performance). If net exports in the United States eventually become positive, foreign saving will dry up and the low savings rate in the United States could then begin to have unfavorable effects on investment purchases.

The low savings rate in the United States can be explained in part by demographic trends. In the mid-1980s, 30% of the country's population was under age 35. People in this age group tend to be big spenders as they establish their households. Typically the biggest savers are people between the ages of 35 and 65. People over 65 are dissavers who draw down savings accumulated in past years as they retire. It's likely that as the percentage of the population between the ages of 35 and 65 increases by the year 2000, the savings rate will increase in the United States. However, in the twenty-first century the portion of the population accounted for by people over 65 is expected to double from the current level of about 12% to nearly 25%! As the elderly become a larger portion of the population, the savings rate could decline because the elderly tend to be net dissavers. In light of these realities, you might want to think about spending less and saving more!

U.S. saving as a percentage of disposable personal income

Source: U.S. Department of Commerce.

off borrowings that helped them increase consumption in previous years. Conversely, other things being equal, an decrease in consumer debt will shift the consumption line upward and the savings line downward. Fears of the impact of increased consumer indebtedness in the late 1980s led many forecasters to predict that the economy's consumption line would shift downward, thereby putting downward pressure on aggregate demand.

Expectations About the Future Can Influence Current Consumption

Consumers are more likely to be willing and able to consume in the current year if they think the purchasing power of their future income will increase. On the other hand, they're less likely to be willing to spend current income if they think bad times are ahead. Anticipation of bad times is likely to shift the consumption line downward as consumers try to save more of any given level of disposable income to supplement future income. Decreased consumer confidence therefore will result in the shifts of the savings and consumption lines illustrated in Box 4. On the other hand, consumer optimism about future well-being will result in the shifts illustrated in Box 3.

Concept Check

1 What are the major influences on annual consumption expenditures in a nation?

2 How are saving, consumption, and disposable income related in a given year? If the marginal propensity to consume is 0.9, how will a $1,000 billion increase in annual disposable income be used?

3 List three possible causes of an upward shift in a nation's consumption function line and explain why the nation's savings line will shift downward when the consumption line shifts upward.

Investment Purchases

Investment purchases of final products by business firms represent a very unstable component of aggregate demand compared to consumption. Investment purchases include expenditures for new machinery, equipment, structures, and inventories. The graph in Box 5 shows the variation in real disposable income, real consumption, and real gross private domestic investment, each measured in 1982 dollars from 1960 to 1987. Notice how gross private domestic investment jumps up and down over this period while there is a steady clear upward trend in disposable income. Although consumer purchases are closely related to disposable income, investment purchases apparently are not.

The variability of real gross private domestic investment is also obvious when it is expressed as a percentage of real GNP. For example, in 1933 when the economy was in the doldrums, real gross private domestic investment amounted to only 5% of real GNP (measured in 1982 dollars). In the recession year of 1982, real gross private domestic investment accounted for 14% of real GNP. In a typical boom year like 1978, real gross private domestic investment approaches 20% of real GNP.

There is no clear relationship between investment and disposable income over time. Instead movements in investment purchases are quite erratic and not easily predictable. In fact, investment is even more variable than is suggested by the data from the National Income and Product Accounts. The reason for this is that the official accounting system of the United States includes all net additions to or reductions in business inventories as part of gross private domestic investment. This means that additions to business inventories that result from the fact that firms sell *less* than they had anticipated during the year are part of the official statistics on

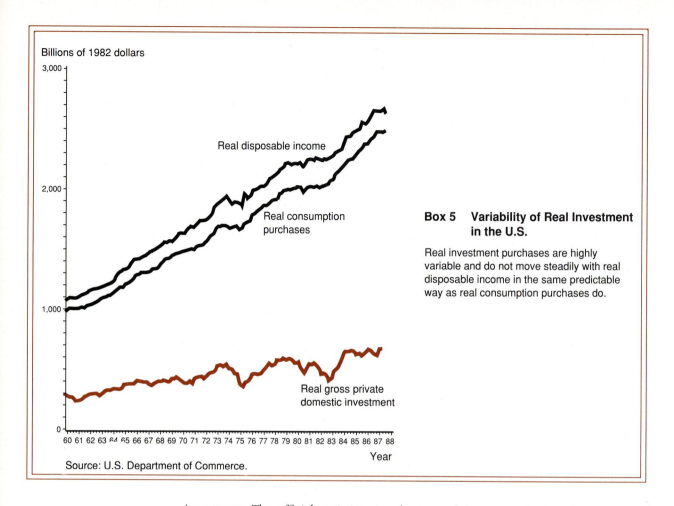

Billions of 1982 dollars

Real disposable income

Real consumption purchases

Box 5   Variability of Real Investment in the U.S.

Real investment purchases are highly variable and do not move steadily with real disposable income in the same predictable way as real consumption purchases do.

Real gross private domestic investment

Year

Source: U.S. Department of Commerce.

investment. The official statistics view business firms as purchasing their own net additions to inventories at the end of the year. This is clearly misleading because some of the increments (or declines) in business inventories occur because businesses end up selling more or less of their stocks of final products than they intended to during the year.

Planned investment purchases:

Purchases of new or replacement residential and nonresidential structures, producer durable equipment, and additions to inventories that business firms intentionally make during the year.

Planned investment purchases are purchases of new or replacement residential and nonresidential structures, producer durable equipment, and additions to inventories that business firms intentionally make during the year. Gross private domestic investment differs from planned investment by the extent to which firms end up with unintended net changes in their business inventories. In discussing the determinants of investment, the relevant economic variable that must be explained is *planned* investment purchases. When planned investment deviates from actual investment, the economy will be in a state of macroeconomic disequilibrium that results in pressure for change in real GNP and/or in the price level (see the preceding and following chapters).

Investment Demand and the Real Interest Rate

When a firm makes an investment, it incurs expenditures for current purchases of investment goods that will be employed to provide future revenue. Business firms typically borrow funds to make an investment and repay their borrowings out of future revenues. Even if they don't borrow, managers know that if they use current revenues to finance investment purchases, they forgo the opportunity to earn interest on the funds allocated to the investment.

The annual opportunity cost of using a dollar to make an investment can therefore be represented by the real interest rate. The real interest rate is the "price" of using a dollar to make an investment purchase that will increase future revenues.

The **real marginal return to investment** is an estimate of the percentage of each dollar invested that will be returned to a firm as additional revenue per year (adjusted for the effects of changes in the price level). Naturally, a firm that seeks to maximize profit compares the marginal return on each dollar's worth of an investment, which is its percentage marginal return, with the opportunity cost of using another dollar for an investment purchase, which is the real rate of interest. As long as the real marginal return to investing a dollar (adjusted for inflation) is higher than the real rate of interest, businesses can add to their profits by increasing annual investment purchases. For example, if you owned a business and thought that by purchasing a new computer system you could earn revenue that returned the price of the system plus an additional 7% after adjustment for inflation over the 3-year life of the system, then you could gain by borrowing to finance the system if the real rate of interest were only 4%.

Real marginal return to investment:
An estimate of the percentage of each dollar invested that will be returned to a firm as additional revenue per year (adjusted for the effects of changes in the price level).

The graph in Box 6 shows the demand for investment goods in the economy as a function of the real interest rate. The lower the real interest rate, the lower the opportunity cost of making investment purchases and the greater the quantity of investment goods demanded. The demand curve for investment goods therefore is downward sloping. In Box 6 the real rate of interest is currently 3% and the equilibrium level of annual investment purchases in the economy is $600 billion. If the real interest rate fell to 2%, investment purchases that were not profitable at the 3% interest rate would be undertaken during the year.

Now that you see how important the real interest rate is in determining investment purchases, you can also begin to understand one source of the instability of investment purchases by looking at the variability of real interest rates. The real

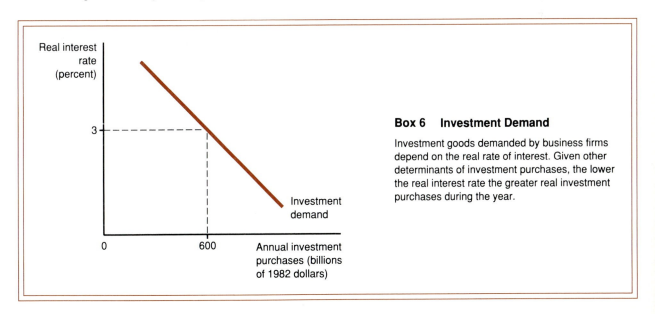

Box 6   Investment Demand

Investment goods demanded by business firms depend on the real rate of interest. Given other determinants of investment purchases, the lower the real interest rate the greater real investment purchases during the year.

interest rate that business firms anticipate paying over the life of an investment depends not only on the nominal rate but also on the fluctuation in the price level over the life of the investment. In the chapter entitled "Inflation and Its Consequences," we discussed the instability of real interest rates. Real interest rates tend to fluctuate widely, often going from positive to negative values. This fluctuation contributes to instability in equilibrium investment purchases, which in turn contributes to instability in aggregate demand. Investment purchases are therefore unstable in part because real interest rates have been quite unstable over time.

Shifts in Investment Demand and Their Causes

Investment demand is notoriously unstable. The investment demand curve shifts inward and outward regularly in response to changes in business perceptions of the future profitability of expansion in productive capacity. When the investment demand curve shifts outward, businesses will invest more dollars each year at each possible real interest rate, as illustrated in Box 7. For example, at a 3% real interest rate, annual investment would rise from $600 billion to $700 billion per year in response to the outward shift in the investment demand curve shown in the graph. Similarly, it would be greater at any other possible interest rate. In view of the importance of investment demand, it's useful to outline influences on business confidence in the future that can contribute to steady outward shifts in the investment demand curve.

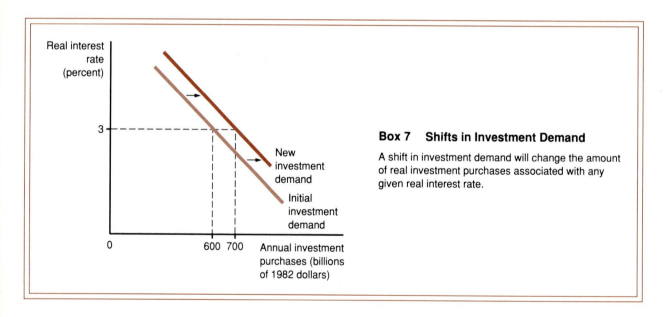

Box 7   Shifts in Investment Demand

A shift in investment demand will change the amount of real investment purchases associated with any given real interest rate.

Among the important influences on investment demand given the level of real interest rates in the economy are:

1. Expectations about shifts in aggregate demand
2. Expectations about input and product prices and other considerations affecting the profitability of adding to productive capacity and inventory
3. Current capacity utilization

4. Technological change in the economy
5. Tax treatment of investment purchases and income

The future revenue from an investment purchase depends on future prospects of sales. If firms expect future declines in aggregate demand, the revenues they anticipate from investment purchases will sag and the demand for investment goods will decline. A decline in investment demand means an inward shift in the investment demand curve. When investment demand decreases in this way, the quantity of investment purchases at any given real interest rate will be less. Conversely, expectation of a future increase in aggregate demand will shift the investment demand curve outward, as illustrated in Box 7.

Business expectations about future prices also affect the demand for investment goods. If businesses believe that input prices will fall relative to output prices, the profitability of supplying output in the future will increase. As a result, they will seek to add to productive capacity when they anticipate declines in input prices that act to decrease marginal cost. Decreases in input prices relative to product prices therefore increase investment demand, while increases in input prices relative to product prices tend to decrease investment demand.

Business investment demand is also likely to be related to current capacity utilization. When there's considerable slack in the economy and existing plants and equipment are not being used, firms are not likely to be thinking about making new investment purchases. For example, during the contraction in economic activity between 1979 and 1982, investment purchases in the United States declined by nearly 20%. On the other hand, when the economy is in a phase of expansion, firms will want to add to inventories and increase plant capacity, thus shifting the investment demand curve outward.

The rate of technological advance is also likely to affect investment demand. This is because as technology advances so do opportunities for profit by making new investments. During periods of rapid change in technology, firms are likely to want to replace obsolete equipment and processes with newer ones that reduce unit and marginal costs of production. Rapid advances in technology therefore shift the demand curve for investment outward at a rapid rate.

Finally, tax treatment of investment purchases and income also affects investment demand. Often the tax codes subsidize investment purchases through generous depreciation rules that allow firms to deduct large portions of their investment outlays from their taxable income. However, tax treatment of investment changes from time to time, and this results in changes in investment demand. For example, the Economic Recovery Tax Act of 1981 introduced very generous depreciation allowances and investment subsidies that encouraged investment at that time. However, the Tax Reform Act of 1986 substantially reduced depreciation allowances and investment subsidies.

You saw in the previous section that investment purchases are unstable first of all because real interest rates are highly variable, often fluctuating from positive to negative values. Now you see that investment purchases also fluctuate because the investment demand curve itself tends to shift inward and outward rather unpredictably in response to changes in business expectations about future revenues, costs, and changes in tax rules.

Planned investment purchases are usually formulated at the beginning of the year based on the current economic outlook for real interest rates and other conditions affecting business demand. In analyzing aggregate purchases, the level of planned

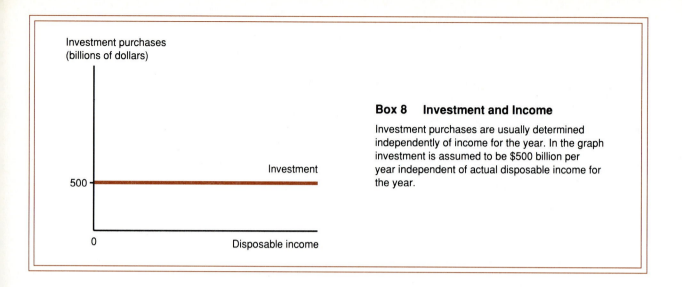

Investment purchases
(billions of dollars)

500

0   Disposable income

Investment

Box 8   Investment and Income

Investment purchases are usually determined independently of income for the year. In the graph investment is assumed to be $500 billion per year independent of actual disposable income for the year.

investment purchases is assumed to be the same no matter what the actual level of disposable income for the year. This assumption is reflected in the graph in Box 8, which shows planned investment purchases as a fixed amount for the year independent of annual disposable income. In Box 8 investment purchases are assumed to be $500 billion for the year no matter what the disposable income for the year.

Concept Check

1   List the major influences on investment purchases.

2   Why will an increase in real interest rates decrease investment purchases?

3   Why are purchases of investment goods more volatile than purchases of consumer goods?

Other Components of Aggregate Demand: Government Purchases and Net Exports

Consumption and investment both fluctuate, but on average they account for about 80% of aggregate demand in a given year. The remaining 20% of aggregate demand comes from government purchases and net exports. In recent years U.S. net exports have actually been negative, thereby putting downward pressure on aggregate demand. In this section we look at the influence of government and international trade on aggregate demand.

Government Purchases and the Influence of Taxes and Transfers on Aggregate Demand

Government purchases of final products and input services are the third major component of real GNP. To provide national security, health, education, transportation, and other essential services, state and local governments and the federal government purchase aircraft, food, clothing, medical supplies, and the services of workers and capital. Governments also purchase new structures and durable goods produced by business firms during the year. The government purchases component of aggregate demand accounted for about 20% of real GNP in 1987.

Government purchases for a given year are determined by political considerations. The actual amounts of purchases for a given year are usually set at the time budgets are approved by the U.S. Congress and in various state legislatures and city or town councils. It's reasonable to assume that government purchases, like investment purchases, are not affected in any clear-cut way by changes in disposable income in a given year. The graph in Box 9 reflects this assumption and shows that actual government purchases in a given year will be the same no matter what the actual level of disposable income in that year. In the graph it's assumed that annual government purchases are $1,000 billion no matter what disposable income is for the year.

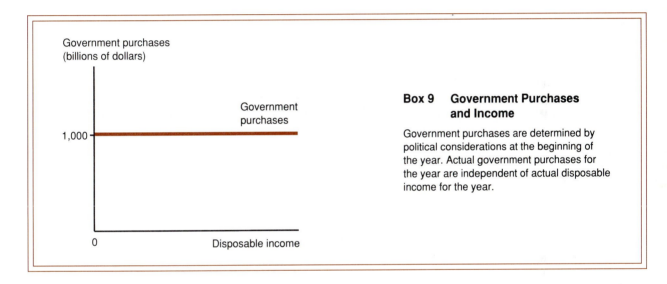

Box 9   Government Purchases and Income

Government purchases are determined by political considerations at the beginning of the year. Actual government purchases for the year are independent of actual disposable income for the year.

You should note, however, that government also affects aggregate demand indirectly through the influence of its tax and transfer policies on disposable income. For example, given government purchases and transfers, an increase in taxes levied on households will decrease the disposable income associated with any given level of real GNP and aggregate real income. Government can therefore affect consumption purchases by changing its tax policy to change the relationship between real GNP and disposable income. Similarly, if government were to increase transfer payments to households while not increasing taxes, it would increase disposable income associated with any level of real GNP and therefore influence consumption. As you saw earlier in the analysis of investment purchases, taxes affecting business income can also affect aggregate demand indirectly by changing investment demand. Both investment and consumer demand are therefore influenced by government policies relating to taxes and transfers.

The ability of government to affect aggregate purchases gives it the opportunity to stabilize aggregate demand. The use of government spending and taxing policy to affect aggregate purchases and equilibrium real GNP is called *fiscal policy* and will be examined in the part of the book entitled "Stabilizing the Economy."

International Trade and Aggregate Demand: Determinants of Net Exports

If you've been following the newspapers and evening news broadcasts, you probably know that the United States has been importing more goods than it has exported in recent years. For example, in 1987 net exports—the difference between the market value of goods imported by U.S. buyers and the market value of exports of U.S. businesses to foreign markets—amounted to nearly $120 billion measured in current dollars. Net exports are negative when imports exceed exports and decrease aggregate demand. But why all the concern about the fact that U.S. buyers spend more on Japanese VCRs, German automobiles, Polish ham, and other foreign goods than U.S. firms earn from selling their goods abroad? The answer is that negative net exports represent a subtraction from aggregate demand.

The graphs in Box 10 show how exports, imports, and the difference between the two are likely to vary with disposable income in a given year. Like consumer

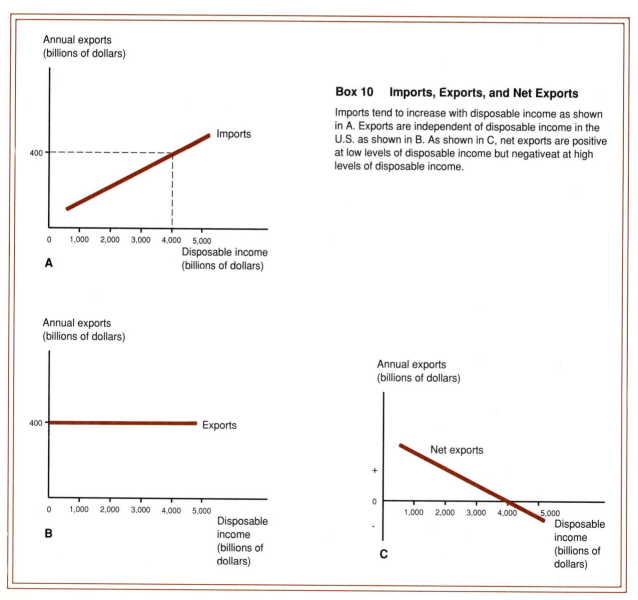

Box 10   Imports, Exports, and Net Exports

Imports tend to increase with disposable income as shown in A. Exports are independent of disposable income in the U.S. as shown in B. As shown in C, net exports are positive at low levels of disposable income but negativeat at high levels of disposable income.

purchases, purchases of imported goods are greater when disposable income is high than when it is low. In Box 10, **A** shows that imports increase with disposable income. Just as you're likely to buy more goods in general when you have a lot of income to spend, so does aggregate spending on imports increase as disposable income increases. In a boom year, other things being equal, BMW, Mercedes, Denon, and other foreign manufacturers are likely to enjoy good sales in the United States. On the other hand, in a recession year when disposable income is low, U.S. consumers are likely to cut back on their purchases of imports as they do on most purchases.

Exports of U.S. goods, however, are unlikely to be related to disposable income in the United States. Instead exports are determined in part by disposable income in foreign nations that purchase our exports. An increase in disposable income in the United States during the year does nothing to increase the ability of Mexicans and Italians to purchase IBM computers and Boeing 767s. This is reflected in **B** in Box 10, where exports for a given year are shown to be constant no matter what disposable income is in the United States that year.

In **C** in Box 10, imports associated with any given level of disposable income are *subtracted* from exports to obtain a graph showing how *net exports*, which are exports minus imports, vary with disposable income. Exports are assumed to be $400 billion no matter what disposable income is for the year. However, when disposable income is relatively low, imports will also be low and exports will exceed imports. As disposable income increases in the United States, imports grow. For example, if disposable income for the year turned out to be $4,000 billion, then imports would be $400 billion (see graph **A** in Box 10). At that level of imports, graph **C** shows that net exports would be zero because exports would also equal $400 billion, as shown in graph **B.** When disposable income is less than $4,000 billion for the year, imports will be less than $400 billion. This means exports exceed imports and net exports are positive. If disposable income were greater than $4,000 billion for the year, imports would exceed exports and net exports would be negative, as shown in graph **C.**

The level of disposable income is not the only determinant of net exports. The quantity of imported products that U.S. buyers will buy at any given level of disposable income also depends on the prices of imported goods relative to the prices of domestically produced substitutes. For example, as you learned in Chapter 4, the prices of imported goods depend in part on the international value of the dollar. When the dollar increases in value relative to foreign currencies, the prices of imports decrease while the prices of our exports in foreign markets go up. This will make the price of Japanese Toyotas fall relative to the price of U.S.-produced Fords. This has the effect of shifting the net exports line downward, as shown in Box 11. This is because imports will increase and exports will decrease as a result of a rise in the price of the dollar. During the period 1980 to 1986 when the price of the dollar went up in most international markets, U.S. import purchases soared while our exports dipped. A similar shift could occur as a result of any other change that makes imports cheaper and our exports more expensive. When the net exports line in Box 11 shifts downward, the level of disposable income associated with zero net exports declines to $3,000 billion. This means that if actual disposable income for the year were $4,000 billion, net exports would be negative.

Similarly, anything that makes imported goods more expensive and makes our exports cheaper in foreign markets will shift the net exports line upward. For example, by early 1988 the decrease in the price of the dollar that occurred in 1987 was beginning to have an effect on net exports. In the first half of 1988, exports

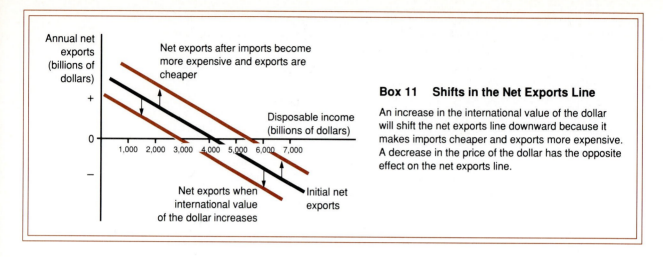

Box 11   Shifts in the Net Exports Line

An increase in the international value of the dollar will shift the net exports line downward because it makes imports cheaper and exports more expensive. A decrease in the price of the dollar has the opposite effect on the net exports line.

increased substantially and the net exports line shifted upward. After the upward shift of the net exports line shown in Box 11, net exports would be positive if disposable income turned out to be $4,000 billion for the year.

Whether net exports are positive or negative in a given year therefore doesn't depend only on disposable income in the United States. It also depends on disposable income in foreign nations and influences on the prices of imports and exports.

Aggregate Purchases: $C + I_P + G + NE$

Aggregate purchases:
The market value of final goods and services that will be purchased at any given level of income.

Aggregate purchases represent the market value of final goods and services that will be purchased at any given level of income. Therefore:

$$\text{Aggregate purchases} = C + I_P + G + NE$$

where I_P are investment purchases planned for the year. Both consumer purchases, C, and net exports, NE, will vary with income. Planned investment and government purchases, G, are assumed to be independent of income, as is likely.

The graph in Box 12 shows how aggregate purchases will vary with income. First

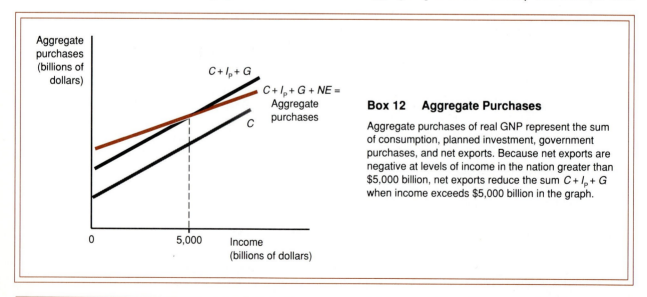

Box 12   Aggregate Purchases

Aggregate purchases of real GNP represent the sum of consumption, planned investment, government purchases, and net exports. Because net exports are negative at levels of income in the nation greater than $5,000 billion, net exports reduce the sum $C + I_P + G$ when income exceeds $5,000 billion in the graph.

the levels of investment and government purchases for the year are added to consumption for each possible level of income. Next net exports are added to the line labeled $C + I_p + G$ for each possible level of income. The sum $C + I_p + G$ is equal to aggregate income when net exports are zero, as is the case in Box 12 when income is $5,000 billion.

When income is less than $5,000 billion in Box 12, net exports will be positive and aggregate purchases will exceed $C + I_p + G$. However, when income is greater than $5,000 billion for the year, net exports will be negative and aggregate purchases will be less than the sum $C + I_p + G$.

You can now see that the level of aggregate purchases in a given year in the economy depends on consumer, investment, government, export, and import purchases for the year. In addition, the actual amount of consumption and net exports for the year depends on the equilibrium level of disposable income.

Now that you know the components of aggregate purchases and aggregate demand, the next step is to investigate the important role aggregate demand plays in determining equilibrium real GNP and income. In the following chapter we examine the Keynesian model of macroeconomic equilibrium by focusing on the role of aggregate demand in the economy.

Concept Check

1   How does the government sector of the economy influence aggregate demand?

2   Explain why net exports will vary with disposable income.

3   What are the components of aggregate purchases?

Summary

1. Consumption is the most important component of GNP, typically accounting for two thirds of annual purchases of real GNP. Annual disposable income is the major determinant of the annual quantity of goods and services that consumers are willing and able to purchase at the current price level.

2. Total annual consumption is the sum of the amount attributable to disposable income and the amount attributable to other influences during the year.

3. A consumption function describes the relationship between annual disposable income and consumption expenditures for the economy in a given year. Annual consumption increases as annual disposable income increases.

4. The marginal propensity to consume is the fraction of each additional dollar of annual disposable income that is consumed. The marginal propensity to save is the fraction of each additional dollar of annual disposable income that is saved. The marginal propensity to consume is the slope of the consumption function line.

5. The consumption function line showing the relationship between annual consumption and annual disposable income will shift upward in response to an increase in annual household wealth, which is the purchasing power of assets owned by households. This implies that an increase in wealth increases consumption but decreases saving associated with each possible level of annual disposable income.

6. Aggregate household debt is the purchasing power of sums of money outstanding that households have borrowed and are currently obligated to repay over

time. Given the value of household wealth, an increase in household debt decreases the willingness and ability to consume out of current income because more of current income must be allocated to repayment of debt. An increase in household debt therefore shifts the consumption function line downward.

7. Expectations about the future are also likely to influence current annual consumption. Consumers are more willing and able to spend on goods and services when they believe their future real income will increase. Consumer confidence about increases in their future real income will shift the consumption function line upward, while the line will shift downward if consumers think hard times are ahead.

8. Planned investment in a given year is a highly unstable component of real GNP. Fluctuations in real interest rates and investment demand explain fluctuations in planned investment purchases. Investment demand shifts in response to changes in expectations about aggregate demand and prices, and in response to changes in capacity utilization, technology, and tax treatment of investment purchases and income.

9. Planned investment during a year represents purchases for new and replacement residential and nonresidential structures, producer durable equipment, and additions to business inventories that firms intentionally make during the year.

10. Government purchases for a given year are determined by political considerations and are likely to be independent of disposable income for the year. Governments also influence aggregate demand indirectly because their tax and expenditure policies influence disposable income and can also influence the profitability of investment.

11. Net exports are the difference between exports and imports. Net exports vary with disposable income because imports tend to increase as disposable income increases. The greater the disposable income for the year, the smaller the net exports component of aggregate demand, everything else being equal. Net exports are also influenced by changes in the international value of the dollar and other factors affecting the prices of exports and imports.

Key Terms and Concepts

Wealth
Aggregate household wealth
Aggregate household debt
Consumption function
Autonomous consumption
Induced consumption

Marginal propensity to consume
Marginal propensity to save
Planned investment purchases
Real marginal return to investment
Aggregate purchases

Problems and Applications

1. The consumption function for households in a certain nation can be expressed by the following equation:

$$C = (\$800 \text{ billion} + 0.7DI)$$

where C is annual consumption and DI is annual disposable income. How much annual consumption is dependent on national wealth and factors other than annual disposable income? What are the nation's marginal propensity to consume and marginal propensity to save?

2. Suppose disposable income is $3,000 billion for the year. Use the consumption function from problem 1 to calculate annual consumption. Calculate annual consumer purchases for annual disposable income of $4,000 billion, $5,000 billion, and $6,000 billion and show how the percentages of income consumed and saved vary as disposable income varies.

3. Graph the consumption function whose equation is given in problem 1. Use your graph to show the level of annual disposable income at which household saving would be zero. How could consumers afford to purchase goods and services even if their annual disposable income were zero?

4. Suppose an increase in household wealth increases the amount of autonomous consumption each year from $800 billion to $1,000 billion. Assuming the marginal propensity to consume remains 0.7, write the equation of the new consumption function and show how the increase in wealth affects the consumption line you drew in answer to problem 3.

5. Suppose the marginal propensity to consume increases from 0.7 to 0.8. Assuming the amount of annual consumption that is independent of annual income remains $800 billion, show the impact of the increase in the marginal propensity to consume on the consumption line you drew in answer to problem 3.

6. The current real rate of interest is 5%. Draw an investment demand curve and show the equilibrium quantity of investment purchases. What is the real marginal return to investment in equilibrium?

7. Assuming no change in the real rate of interest during the year, what can cause investment purchases to increase? Use the graph you drew in answer to problem 6 to show how an increase in investment purchases can come about. What can cause a decrease in investment purchases?

8. Suppose the real rate of interest increases from 5% to 7%. Use the graph you drew in answer to problem 6 to show the impact on investment purchases.

9. Suppose net exports in 1988 are negative for the U.S. economy. Explain how a recession in the United States in 1989 could result in positive net exports that year.

10. Draw an aggregate purchases line and show how aggregate purchases fall short of the sum of consumer, investment, and government purchases when net exports are negative.

Suggested Readings

Economic Report of the President, published annually in January, Washington, D.C.: U.S. Government Printing Office. This report contains analyses and data on the components of aggregate demand and discusses influences that are currently affecting consumption, investment, government spending, and net exports.

Robert J. Gordon, *Macroeconomics*, 4th ed., Boston: Little, Brown, 1987. Chapter 3 provides a detailed technical analysis of the determinants of consumption and investment.

A Forward Look

In the following chapter we analyze the role of aggregate demand in influencing macroeconomic equilibrium. You'll see how declines in aggregate demand can cause recessions and how surges in aggregate demand can heat up the economy and cause inflation. The insights of Keynes into the way the economy works will form the basis of the theory developed in the chapter.

Aggregate Demand and Keynesian Analysis of Macroeconomic Equilibrium

Did you know that your prospects for finding a job in the year you graduate will be tied to the level of spending in the U.S. economy? Will aggregate demand be strong enough to purchase the quantity of final products that corresponds to potential real GNP so that the economy can provide for full employment when you graduate? When the economy is operating at its potential there are more employment opportunities, and naturally under those circumstances it's easier for college graduates to find jobs.

The classical economists believed the income generated from production would create its own demand and that, when aggregate demand was insufficient to generate full employment, price flexibility would soon correct the imbalance. Keynes pointed out that aggregate demand is not always strong enough to generate sufficient aggregate purchases to buy the level of output corresponding to potential real GNP. When this is the case, equilibrium real GNP will be less than potential real GNP.

The Great Depression of the 1930s cast doubt on the ideas of the classical economists that we discussed in the chapter on the forces of aggregate supply and demand. In stating that the economy had a reliable and quickly operating self-correction mechanism that would ensure full employment, the conclusion of the classical model was at odds with the facts. Between late 1929 and 1933 the U.S. unemployment rate rose to 25%! Business investment purchases plummeted during the Depression, and so did real GNP and the price level. It was clear that the economy remained stubbornly in equilibrium at a level of real GNP at which aggregate quantity demanded fell short of the level of real GNP that could provide full employment for workers.

It's become quite clear that the economy does run the risk of attaining a macroeconomic equilibrium at a level of real GNP well below the economy's potential real GNP that corresponds to full employment. Forces are not immediately and automatically set up to push the economy to full employment when a recession hits.

Keynesian analysis concentrates on the role of fluctuation in aggregate demand as a cause of excessive unemployment, recession, and inflation. When the economy is stagnating in a recession, policies that encourage increases in aggregate demand can help reachieve full employment. As you'll see, $1 of new purchases in an economy can increase real GNP by more than $1. In this chapter we examine how an injection of new purchases can start a spending spree that can help pull an economy out of a recession.

Policies that increase aggregate demand in an economy in a deep recession were Keynes's major recommendation to solve the problem of economic stagnation. As long as an economy was operating well below its potential, Keynes argued that there was little risk of inflation from policies that resulted in new purchases to bolster aggregate demand. The increase in aggregate demand could substitute for the defects in the economy's own self-correction mechanism in restoring full employment.

As you saw in the preceding chapter, aggregate demand depends not only on consumer and investment purchases but also on government purchases, exports, imports, and taxes. Aggregate demand can also be excessive in a given year, just as it can be insufficient relative to potential real GNP. When aggregate purchases exceed the full-employment level of real GNP, an economy will overheat and there will be inflation. The model of the economy developed in this chapter will be used to help you understand how shifts in aggregate demand can cause excessive unemployment at some times and inflation at others.

After reading this chapter, you should be able to: *Concept Preview*

1 Explain how an economy can attain a macroeconomic equilibrium at a level of real GNP below the level that will provide full employment, and understand the concept of a recessionary GNP gap.

2 Show how a contraction or recession can result from a decline in aggregate demand.

3 Understand the concept of the multiplier and how it is related to the rate at which income earned is respent.

4 Show how a decline in net exports or a sudden sharp increase in the price level can cause a contraction of economic activity.

5 Derive an aggregate demand curve by showing how the aggregate equilibrium quantity demanded of real GNP is likely to vary with changes in the price level.

6 Understand the concept of an inflationary GNP gap for the economy and how its existence implies that the economy will overheat and cause inflation that will act to reduce equilibrium real GNP.

Aggregate Purchases and Macroeconomic Equilibrium

You now know that aggregate demand is comprised of purchases by consumers, investors, and governments and is also influenced by U.S. purchases of imports and the willingness and ability of buyers in foreign markets to purchase our exports. Fluctuations in any component of aggregate demand can cause changes in macroeconomic equilibrium. The most likely sources of such fluctuations are changes in investment purchases and net exports, which are the most fickle and unpredictable components of aggregate demand. However, even small fluctuations in consumer purchases at any given level of income (changes in autonomous consumption) also can have major effects on aggregate demand because of the fact that consumption accounts for 65% of real GNP.

Keynesian analysis of macroeconomic equilibrium shows how declines in aggregate purchases can cause recessions and cyclical unemployment. The analysis can also be used to show how increases in aggregate purchases can cause inflation when the economy is operating at or close to its potential.

We're now ready to show how changes in aggregate demand can cause real GNP to fluctuate. Keynes assumed that increases in aggregate demand would result in increases in equilibrium real GNP with little or no inflation if the economy were operating below its potential. Aggregate demand is the key determinant of real GNP and therefore of income in the Keynesian analysis.

To simplify the analysis at the outset, we'll assume that aggregate purchases consist only of consumption and investment. We'll also assume that government purchases, net taxes (taxes minus transfers), capital consumption allowances (depreciation), undistributed corporate profits, and indirect business taxes, exports, and imports are all equal to zero in the economy. When we make these simplifying assumptions, we eliminate the distinction between real GNP, national income, and disposable income based on their definitions in the National Income and Product Accounts (see the chapter on GNP and economic performance). We can now view real GNP, which also equals real income earned in a nation, as the major influence on consumer purchases. Real GNP is also the economic variable whose fluctuations we seek to explain in the Keynesian model of macroeconomic equilibrium.

Analysis of Macroeconomic Equilibrium: The Role of Aggregate Demand

The table in Box 1 provides hypothetical data on the components of aggregate purchases that would prevail at alternative levels of income earned in a given year at a given price level. Throughout this analysis we assume the price level doesn't change in response to changes in aggregate purchases. Because the price level is fixed, increases in the value of GNP shown in the first column of the table reflect increases in real GNP, which reflects aggregate production in the economy.

The first column of the table shows possible levels of real GNP during the year. Because of the assumption made earlier, real GNP is also income available for spending.

What level of real GNP (and therefore real income) will emerge as the equilibrium for the year? To find out, we must examine the relationship between aggregate purchases and aggregate production. The second column gives consumption purchases based on the consumption function we discussed in the preceding chapter.

Box 1 Aggregate Production, Aggregate Purchases, and Determination of Macroeconomic Equilibrium Real GNP in a Simple Economy (hypothetical data, billions of dollars)

(1) Aggregate production (real GNP = income)	(2) Consumption puchases (C)	(3) Planned investment purchases (I_p)	(4) Aggregate purchases ($C + I_p$)	(5) Unintended inventory investment	(6) Employment (billions of hours per year)	(7) Pressure on real GNP and employment
1,000	1,200	600	1,800	− 800	50	Up
2,000	2,000	600	2,600	− 600	100	Up
3,000	2,800	600	3,400	− 400	150	Up
4,000	3,600	600	4,200	− 200	200	Up
5,000	4,400	600	5,000	0	250	Equilibrium
6,000	5,200	600	5,800	200	300	Down
7,000	6,000	600	6,600	400	350	Down
8,000	6,800	600	7,400	600	400	Down

Planned investment, shown in the third column, is assumed to be $600 billion per year no matter what the level of real GNP. The fourth column shows the aggregate purchases of final products given the price level prevailing during the year.

Aggregate purchases in this simple economy are the sum of consumer purchases (C) and planned investment purchases (I_p) by business firms during the year:

$$\text{Aggregate purchases} = \text{Consumption} + \text{Planned investment}$$
$$= C + I_P$$

The equilibrium level of real GNP is the one for which the forces of aggregate demand and aggregate supply balance so that there is no upward or downward pressure on real GNP and income. Note from the data in Box 1 that aggregate purchases increase at a slower rate than aggregate production as income increases during the year. This is because a portion of income earned from additional production in a given year is always saved.

The data in Box 1 show that when real GNP is less than $5,000 billion, aggregate purchases (shown in column 4) exceed aggregate production (shown in column 1). This means aggregate quantity demanded would exceed aggregate quantity supplied if real GNP were less than $5,000 billion during the year. Under such circumstances firms will sell more than they produced during the year and will find their inventories unexpectedly depleted. This means there will be unintended inventory reductions, which are shown as negative unintended inventory investment in the fifth column of the table.

Remember from the analysis of macroeconomic equilibrium in the chapter on the forces of aggregate supply and demand that any imbalance between aggregate quantities demanded and supplied will affect both hiring plans and business orders for goods and services. For example, suppose real GNP and income were only $1,000 billion for the year. At that level of aggregate production and income, the table in Box 1 shows that aggregate purchases would be $1,800 billion for the year. Because aggregate purchases would exceed aggregate production by $800 billion, there would be an unanticipated reduction in business inventories equal to this amount, as shown in column 5 of the table. As inventories fall during the year, producers will increase output to replenish their inventories, and real GNP and income will increase. When inventories are unexpectedly being depleted, firms will seek to produce more and hire additional labor to do so. Column 6 of the table shows billions of labor hours utilized at various levels of real GNP.

Similarly, notice that when real GNP exceeds $5,000 billion, aggregate purchases will fall short of aggregate production. This means sellers will be unsuccessful in selling everything they produce at current prices. The unsold goods will pile up as unintended inventory investment, which is shown in the fifth column of the table. When this happens, firms will soon cut back production and real GNP, and income earned in the nation will tend to fall. When this occurs, firms will tend to lay off workers. For example, if aggregate production were $6,000 billion, aggregate purchases would amount to only $5,800 billion. As a result, $200 billion worth of final products would go unsold and firms would cut back production in response to the unintended inventory buildup.

The last column in the table in Box 1 shows how real GNP and income will move according to the relationship between aggregate production and aggregate purchases at each possible level of real GNP, assuming the price level doesn't respond to imbalances between aggregate demand and supply. *Real GNP is in equilibrium, meaning there will be no tendency for it to increase or decrease, when aggregate purchases just equal aggregate production.* This occurs when the quantity of goods supplied at current prices just equals the amount that consumers and businesses are willing to purchase at current prices. When equilibrium is reached, there will be no unintended inventory increase or decrease and there will be no tendency for income and employment in the economy to increase or decrease. In the table in Box 1, equilibrium real GNP is $5,000 billion.

Graphic Analysis of the Movement Toward Equilibrium Real GNP

The graph in Box 2 plots aggregate purchases and shows how they would vary during the year at each possible level of income based on the data from the table in Box 1. The upward-sloping curve representing aggregate purchases is obtained by summing consumption and planned investment corresponding to each level of income. Because planned investment is assumed to be $600 billion no matter what the level of income for the year, the upward slope of the aggregate purchases line reflects the upward slope of the consumption line.

The equilibrium level of real GNP and income is illustrated graphically in Box 2. Points on the aggregate purchases line correspond to the numbers in column 4 of the table in Box 1. The 45-degree line represents aggregate production because points on this line when measured on the vertical axis correspond to the level of real GNP and income on the horizontal axis. Points on the 45-degree line correspond to the sum of consumption and saving at any level of income, as was the case for the 45-degree line drawn in the preceding chapter. Points on the 45-degree line in Box 2 correspond to the numbers in column 1 in the table in Box 1.

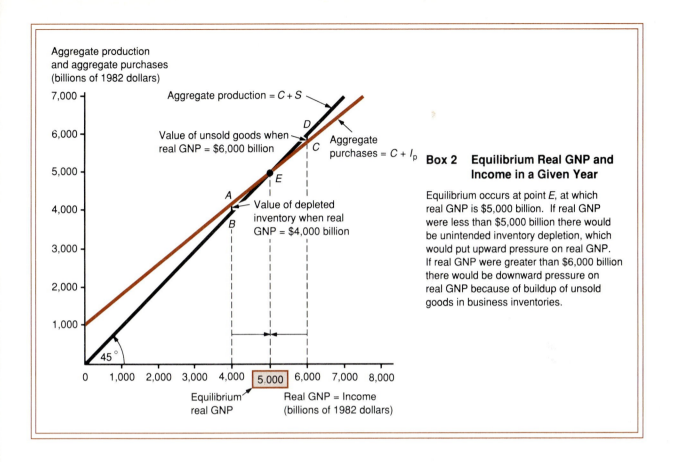

Aggregate production
and aggregate purchases
(billions of 1982 dollars)

Box 2   Equilibrium Real GNP and Income in a Given Year

Equilibrium occurs at point *E*, at which real GNP is $5,000 billion. If real GNP were less than $5,000 billion there would be unintended inventory depletion, which would put upward pressure on real GNP. If real GNP were greater than $6,000 billion there would be downward pressure on real GNP because of buildup of unsold goods in business inventories.

The vertical difference between the aggregate purchases line and the 45-degree line represents unintended inventory investment (positive or negative). For example, if real GNP were $4,000 billion per year, aggregate purchases would be $4,200 billion per year and there would be $200 billion of unintended inventory depletion, shown as the distance *AB* on the graph. Because aggregate purchases would exceed aggregate production when real GNP is $4,000 billion, the consequent reordering of goods and services to replenish inventories would result in upward pressure on real GNP. Similarly, if real GNP were $6,000 billion per year, there would be unintended inventory buildup of $200 billion per year, represented by the distance *DC* on the graph, because aggregate production would exceed aggregate purchases for the year. This would result in downward pressure on real GNP because firms would cut back orders. Only at point *E* are aggregate purchases equal to aggregate production. At that point the forces of aggregate demand and aggregate supply balance, and the corresponding equilibrium level of real GNP and income is $5,000 billion per year.

Conditions for Macroeconomic Equilibrium

The economy is in macroeconomic equilibrium only when unintended inventory investment is equal to zero. Whenever aggregate demand is insufficient to purchase all the goods produced by firms during the year, there will be downward pressure on real GNP. Conversely, whenever aggregate demand is so strong that buyers in

---

product markets want to purchase more than the current aggregate production, there will be upward pressure on real GNP.

It's easy to show that, when macroeconomic equilibrium is achieved in Box 2, saving (which is the portion of income not used to purchase final products in this simple model) equals planned investment purchases. To see this, remember that real GNP must also equal real income, which is either used for consumer purchases or saved:

$$\text{Real GNP} = \text{Income} = C + S$$

In *equilibrium,* real GNP must also equal the sum of consumer purchases plus planned investment purchases (I_P):

$$\text{Real GNP} = \text{Aggregate purchases} = C + I_P$$

It follows that in equilibrium

$$\text{Real GNP} = C + S = C + I_P = \text{Aggregate purchases}$$

Subtracting C from both real GNP and aggregate purchases shows that in equilibrium:

$$S = I_P$$

You can understand this simply by reasoning that whatever households don't spend is saved, assuming that taxes are zero, as is the case in this simple model. Saving provides funds for investment purchases. However, when the amount saved exceeds the amount businesses plan to invest, some of real GNP will not be purchased. Saving constitutes a portion of income that is not used for purchases. Unless the amount saved is exactly matched by planned investment purchases, aggregate supply will not balance aggregate demand and the economy cannot be in equilibrium.

The relationship between saving and planned investment based on the data in Box 1 is shown in the graph in Box 3. Because planned investment is $600 billion, the equilibrium level of saving must also be $600 billion. If saving exceeded $600 billion, aggregate purchases would fall short of aggregate production and there would be downward pressure on real GNP because of unintended inventory accumulation. Similarly, if saving fell short of investment, aggregate purchases would exceed aggregate production because the sum of consumption and planned investment would exceed real GNP. In that case there would be unexpected inventory depletion and real GNP would increase.

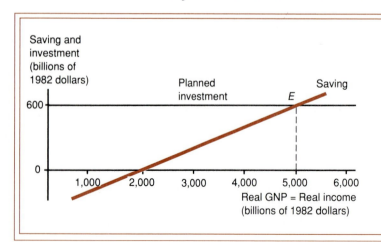

Saving and investment (billions of 1982 dollars)

Planned investment

Saving

E

600

0

1,000   2,000   3,000   4,000   5,000   6,000

Real GNP = Real income (billions of 1982 dollars)

Box 3   Saving and Investment and Macroeconomic Equilibrium

In an economy in which government purchases and net taxes are zero and there is no international trade, macroeconomic equilibrium corresponds to the level of real GNP for which saving equals planned investment purchases. This corresponds to point   E on the graph.

Saving will equal $600 billion based on the data in Box 1 only when real GNP and therefore income is equal to $5,000 billion. It follows that equilibrium real GNP will be $5,000 billion, which is exactly the same conclusion reached by using the aggregate purchases = aggregate production approach.

Concept Check

1   What are the components of aggregate purchases in an economy with no government sector and no international trade?

2   At the end of the year business firms have $200 billion worth of unintended inventory accumulation. Is the economy in macroeconomic equilibrium?

3   Aggregate purchases are currently $5,000 billion for the economy. Real GNP for the year is $4,500 billion. Is the economy in equilibrium?

Keynesian Analysis of the Causes of and Cures for Contractions or Recessions

Remember that potential real GNP is the level corresponding to the natural rate of unemployment. Suppose the equilibrium level of real GNP of $5,000 billion in Box 2 is also potential real GNP. At that level of real GNP, 250 billion labor hours will be employed in the economy during the year. Under such conditions the actual unemployment rate equals the natural unemployment rate and there is no cyclical unemployment.

How a Decline in Planned Investment Can Cause Equilibrium Real GNP to Fall

Suppose business firms revise their plans and decide to spend only $400 billion on new investment purchases instead of $600 billion. The table in Box 4 shows how aggregate purchases would vary with real GNP at the current price level, given the new level of planned investment and assuming no change in the consumption function.

It's easy to see that $5,000 billion will no longer be the equilibrium real GNP after the decline in planned investment purchases. If real GNP were $5,000 billion, aggregate purchases would be only $4,800 billion after the decline in investment demand. *This means there would be unintended inventory investment at potential real GNP.* It follows that aggregate purchases at potential real GNP of $5,000 billion will be insufficient to purchase all the aggregate production. The $200 billion worth of unintended inventory investment results in downward pressure on real GNP. The equilibrium level of real GNP is now only $4,000 billion at the current price level. The economy therefore will be in equilibrium at a level of real GNP that is $1,000 billion below its potential real GNP. The decline in real GNP over the year will mean that the reduction in planned business investment has caused a contraction. The result will be job layoffs, and cyclical unemployment will increase the actual unemployment rate above the natural rate. As real GNP falls to its new equilibrium level, employment in the economy falls from 250 billion to only 200 billion labor hours during the year.

Box 4 Macroeconomic Equilibrium: The Response to a Decline in Planned Investment
(hypothetical data, billions of dollars)

(1) Aggregate production (real GNP = income)	(2) Consumption purchases (C)	(3) Planned investment (I_p)	(4) Aggregate purchases ($C + I_p$)	(5) Unintended inventory investment	(6) Employment (billions of hours per year)
1,000	1,200	400	1,600	− 600	50
2,000	2,000	400	2,400	− 400	100
3,000	2,800	400	3,200	− 200	150
4,000 = Equilibrium real GNP	3,600	400	4,000	0	200
5,000 = Potential real GNP	4,400	400	4,800	+ 200	250
6,000	5,200	400	5,600	+ 400	300
7,000	6,000	400	6,400	+ 600	350
8,000	6,800	400	7,200	+ 800	400

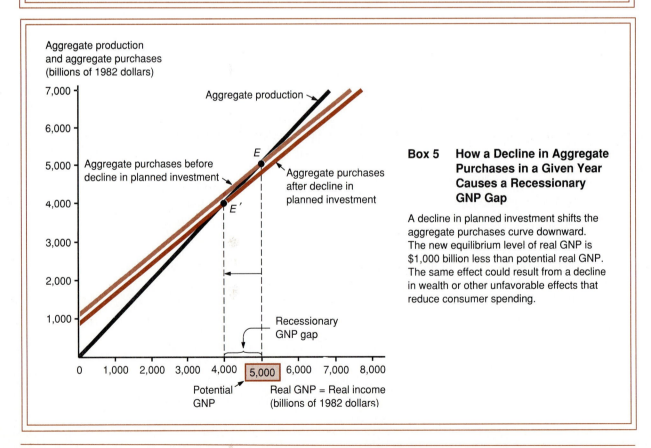

Box 5 How a Decline in Aggregate Purchases in a Given Year Causes a Recessionary GNP Gap

A decline in planned investment shifts the aggregate purchases curve downward. The new equilibrium level of real GNP is $1,000 billion less than potential real GNP. The same effect could result from a decline in wealth or other unfavorable effects that reduce consumer spending.

A decline in planned investment in 1981 caused exactly such a scenario in the United States. As aggregate demand fell, firms found themselves stuck with inventory they couldn't sell. The automobile industry was particularly hard hit that year, and unplanned accumulations of inventories were in evidence at dealerships and manufacturers' lots. As inventories of cars and other goods built up, the recession of 1982 hit with a vengeance and firms began laying off workers as the economy moved to a lower equilibrium level of real GNP.

The impact of the decline in planned investment can also be shown graphically. The graph in Box 5 shows that the decline in planned investment shifts the aggregate purchases line downward. This results in a new equilibrium at point E'. At E' the economy is in equilibrium at the new lower level of real GNP of $4,000 billion for the year. Only at E' is unintended inventory accumulation zero. The *recessionary GNP gap* of $1,000 billion shown on the graph measures the difference between potential real GNP and equilibrium real GNP. Whenever a recessionary gap exists for the economy, there will be cyclical unemployment.

How a Decline in Consumer Spending Intentions Can Cause a Contraction or a Recession

A contraction or recession can also be induced by a decline in the willingness and ability of consumers to spend their income. Suppose that because of a decrease in household wealth, an increase in household debt, or a decline in consumer confidence about future income, autonomous consumption associated with each possible level of real GNP declines by $200 billion. The table in Box 6 shows the impact of a shift in the consumption function and assumes that planned investment is $600 billion as it was initially.

Box 6 Macroeconomic Equilibrium: The Response to a Decline in Consumer Spending (hypothetical data, billions of dollars)

Aggregate production (real GNP = real income)	Consumption (C)	Planned investment (I_p)	Aggregate purchases ($C + I_p$)	Unintended inventory investment	Employment (billions of hours per year)
1,000	1,000	600	1,600	− 600	50
2,000	1,800	600	2,400	− 400	100
3,000	2,600	600	3,200	− 200	150
4,000 = Equilibrium real GNP	3,400	600	4,000	0	200
5,000 = Potential real GNP	4,200	600	4,800	+ 200	250
6,000	5,000	600	5,600	+ 400	300
7,000	5,800	600	6,400	+ 600	350
8,000	6,600	600	7,200	+ 800	400

It's now easy to see that once again the economy cannot be in equilibrium at the level of real GNP that corresponds to full employment. The table in Box 6 shows that the level of aggregate purchases at a real GNP level of $5,000 billion is once again only $4,800 billion. Equilibrium real GNP will therefore decline over the year to $4,000 billion to eliminate the unintended inventory accumulation. The aggregate purchases curve will shift downward as a result of the decline in consumer spending, and as before a $1,000 billion recessionary GNP gap occurs as the economy moves into a contraction. If the contraction is severe enough, the economy can be plunged into a recession as a result of the decline in autonomous consumption.

A recession can be caused by a decline in consumer spending in just the same way that it can be caused by a decline in planned investment spending! This is why the stock market crash of 1987 led many economists to forecast a possible recession in 1988.

The Keynesian Aggregate Supply Curve: Why Recessions Do Not Quickly Disappear

The preceding analysis shows how contractions or recessions are caused by declines in either autonomous consumption or planned investment. When input prices and product prices don't fall as a result of the decline in aggregate demand, the unintended inventory accumulations cannot be sold off quickly. As a result firms cut back production. Why don't prices decline to quickly eliminate any unsold inventory during recessions? A parallel question is: Why don't wages fall to eliminate the surplus of workers looking for jobs when cyclical unemployment exists in the economy?

The answer to this question remains one of John Maynard Keynes's major contributions to economic theory (see Economic Thinkers box). Keynes observed that there is a significant *downward rigidity in prices and wages in modern industrial economies*. The explanation for lengthy recessions that don't cure themselves, according to Keynes, therefore lies mainly in downward price and wage rigidity for the economy.

The core of the Keynesian theory of recessions is that both product prices and wages tend to be downwardly inflexible as a result of market imperfections. Long-term labor contracts, particularly those negotiated by powerful unions, don't allow for quick downward adjustment in wages when aggregate demand slacks off. Similarly, many firms have the power to control the prices of their products and are reluctant to reduce prices even when inventories pile up.

The Keynesian view of recessions contrasted with the prevailing classical view at the time that the economy would eventually pull itself out of recessions through downward pressure on nominal wages and prices. Keynes didn't dispute this view, but he pointed out that "eventually" could in fact be a very lengthy period, as was evident during the Great Depression of the 1930s. Keynes argued that an immediate solution was required to alleviate the misery caused by excessive unemployment during deep recessions. In this regard Keynes's often-quoted remark about the classical prescription of doing nothing for recessions was: "In the long run we are all dead!" By this he meant that the economy's own tendency to self-equilibrate through price adjustment took too long and was too unreliable.

Using aggregate demand and aggregate supply curves, it's easy to illustrate the Keynesian view of macroeconomic equilibrium and recessions. In Keynes's view an economy stagnating in a recession attained a macroeconomic equilibrium in the flat

Economic Thinkers

JOHN MAYNARD KEYNES

In the darkness of worldwide depression, economists might well have expected help to come from someone who had struggled in its bowels. Certainly not from a buoyant, successful British phenomenon who once claimed his only regret was not drinking enough champagne. John Maynard Keynes was a dynamo of sorts who revolutionized economics as did no other in the twentieth century.

This darling of Britain's most avant garde intellectuals wrote a highly acclaimed book on mathematical probability on the side while working for the British government, made a fortune speculating in international currencies and commodities by phoning orders from his bed the first half hour of the morning, climbed mountains, married a beautiful Russian ballerina, and set the economic world on its head with his masterwork, *The General Theory of Employment, Interest and Money.*

Written during the Great Depression, it explained what classical economics could not: perpetual unemployment and a stagnating economy. The most depressing part of the Great Depression was that it seemed without end. Keynes's theory explained how this phenomenon could occur and offered a solution in the form of increased government spending.

Keynes was famous long before this masterpiece was published. He worked for the British Treasury during World War I and saw the conference at Versailles firsthand. He wrote a book, *Economic Consequences of the Peace,* that claimed the treaty would lead to further instability and war in Europe. His perception of the historical consequences of the harsh financial treatment of Germany in reparation for the war was prophetic.

Keynes studied economics at Cambridge University under Alfred Marshall, whom he later lovingly described as an absurd old man. His father was also a noted economist, and Keynes followed in his footsteps teaching at Cambridge.

Ironically, this man who sold champagne at discounted prices to support its consumption was born the year Karl Marx died. Both were revolutionary economists, but while Marx viewed capitalism with despair, Keynes—even in its blackest hour—looked for explanations, hope, and a cure. And being the man he was, he found them.

portion of its aggregate supply curve, as shown in the graph in Box 7. Keynes drew two important implications from the idea of a flat aggregate supply curve for an economy stagnating in a recession. First, it implies that wages and the price level don't fall over a relatively short period in response to declines in aggregate demand. This prevents the self-correction mechanism envisioned by the classical economists from operating to quickly cure a recession by restoring full employment. Because wages didn't decline, there was no incentive for firms to increase production, and surpluses of labor in the economy were not easily eliminated in the labor markets. Second, when an economy is operating in the flat portion of its aggregate supply curve, increases in aggregate demand will increase real GNP and therefore increase income and employment *without* putting upward pressure on the price level. This is because the excessive unemployment and slack in productive capacity that exist in the economy during a recession mean that unused capacity can easily be put back into use without prices rising.

Keynes's insight into the way the economy works not only explained why an economy can stagnate in a recession, it also suggested a way out of recessions. *A recession could be cured by stimulating aggregate demand.* This could be accom-

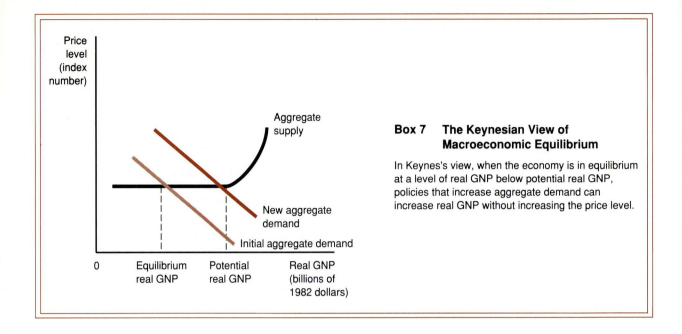

Box 7   The Keynesian View of Macroeconomic Equilibrium

In Keynes's view, when the economy is in equilibrium at a level of real GNP below potential real GNP, policies that increase aggregate demand can increase real GNP without increasing the price level.

plished either by encouraging more private investment or consumer purchases or by using government purchases to bolster aggregate demand. Keynes argued that in a deep recession, business confidence would probably be so low that even decreases in real interest rates could be ineffective in increasing planned investment. After all, when there's a great deal of excess capacity in the economy, business firms are likely to be reluctant to add still more! Similarly, the decline in income and wealth that occurs during a deep recession makes it unlikely that government policies could effectively stimulate consumption.

Therefore Keynes strongly advocated that governments step in to purchase final products and labor services during a recession by engaging in deficit spending if necessary. By doing so, governments could shift aggregate demand outward and move the economy back to full employment with little fear of causing inflation to heat up.

Concept Check

1   At the economy's potential GNP level of $5,000 billion, consumption expenditure is $4,000 billion and planned investment is $500 billion. Will the economy produce at its potential for the year assuming consumption and investment are the only components of aggregate purchases?

2   During the current year $500 billion of goods and services that business firms had planned to sell during the year remain unsold. Explain how downward rigidity in product prices contributes to slow elimination of the unintended increase in business inventories.

3   Suppose a sharp decline in the stock market cuts household wealth in half. How could this contribute to a recession?

The Multiplier: What It Is and How It Works in a Simple Economy

The variability of investment purchases is both a curse and a blessing. On the one hand, it can throw an economy into recession, as was shown earlier, when such purchases suddenly swing down in response to a decrease in business confidence or an increase in real interest rates. On the other hand, increases in investment purchases can help an economy that is stagnating in a recession move up to its potential.

Suppose the economy is in equilibrium at a level of real GNP that is below potential real GNP. As a consequence, there is excessive unemployment and unused productive capacity. One way to increase aggregate demand is to pursue policies that *increase* investment purchases. For example, suppose measures are taken to reduce the real interest rate (you'll soon see how banking authorities in a nation can manipulate interest rates). Also assume that reductions in the real interest rate are effective in increasing the quantity of new investment goods demanded by business firms.

The Multiplier

Remarkably, it's quite reasonable to expect that each $1 increase in investment purchases will increase real GNP and income in the nation by more than $1 for the year! This conclusion stems from the fact that $1 of additional purchases during a year results in increases in income that are *respent* many times.

For example, suppose that after a decline in real interest rates, many business firms put in orders for new investment goods. Auto manufacturers might decide to purchase new machines for their factories. Airlines might decide to order more aircraft to replace their aging fleets and to expand service. Trucking firms might order new tractors and trailers, and railroads might order new locomotives. As the new orders are sent in, production will increase. This means laid-off workers will be recalled and existing staffs might enjoy overtime work as the new orders come in. As earnings increase from the new production, households will increase their own purchases, which in turn will increase aggregate demand for retail goods and services. As the goods start disappearing from the shelves, retailers will put in more orders and hire more staff, which in turn will generate still more income and production. As utilization of labor, plants, and materials increases in response to the new orders, income will increase along with the increase in orders of investment goods.

The **multiplier** is a number that can be used to multiply a change in purchases that results in a shift of the aggregate purchases line to obtain the change in equilibrium real GNP that results from those purchases. **Autonomous purchases** are purchases such as investment or autonomous consumption that cause the economy's aggregate purchases line to shift. For example, a change in planned investment represents a change in autonomous purchases because it will shift the aggregate purchases line. Similarly, a change in wealth can cause a change in autonomous consumption that will shift the aggregate purchases line. As you'll soon see, a change in government purchases or net exports can also shift the aggregate purchases line, and therefore net exports and government purchases are also considered autonomous purchases. The multiplier indicates how many dollars of increase in real GNP can be anticipated from each dollar in new autonomous (meaning independent of

Multiplier:
A number that can be used to multiply a change in purchases that results in a shift of the aggregate purchases line to obtain the change in equilibrium real GNP that results from those purchases.

Autonomous purchases:
Purchases such as investment or autonomous consumption that cause the economy's aggregate purchases line to shift.

income) purchases. For example, if the multiplier were 5 it would indicate that each $1 increase in investment purchases will increase equilibrium real GNP by $5. Any increase in purchases that results in an upward shift of the economy's aggregate purchases line, implying an outward shift in its aggregate demand curve, can result in a multiplier effect on real GNP. The multiplier can be expressed as the following ratio of the change in equilibrium real GNP to the change in autonomous purchases:

$$\text{Multiplier} = \frac{\text{Change in equilibrium real GNP}}{\text{Change in autonomous purchases}}$$

How the Multiplier Works: The Respending Process

The multiplier effect stems from a process through which an initial round of autonomous purchases generates income, which in turn generates more purchases, which then result in more income, and so on. To see how the multiplier works, suppose the initial level of equilibrium real GNP is $4,000 billion and potential real GNP is $5,000 billion. The economy therefore suffers from a $1,000 billion recessionary GNP gap. The marginal propensity to consume measures the extra consumption purchases that result from each extra dollar of disposable income. Suppose that, as in the example in the preceding chapter, the marginal propensity to consume for the economy is 0.8 at all levels of real GNP. Also assume that the only components of aggregate demand are consumer and investment purchases and that there is no international trade and no government purchases or net taxation. Under such circumstances, the only way income will not be respent is if it is saved. This means the marginal propensity to consume also represents the rate at which each dollar of income is respent.

When the marginal propensity to consume is 0.8 in this example, an annual increase in investment of only $200 billion will be sufficient to increase real GNP by $1,000 billion to eliminate the recessionary gap and restore full employment. To see why this is so, think about what happens in the economy as annual investment purchases increase during the year.

The orders for $200 billion worth of new machines, new vehicles, and new structures result in $200 billion worth of real GNP and income as firms hire inputs and earn profits filling the orders. An equal increase in income therefore results from the $200 billion in investment purchases. But the increase in *equilibrium* income is much larger than the initial income generated from the investment purchases. Those who earn the $200 billion income generated from orders for investment goods will spend the income on food, clothing, new cars, insurance policies for new cars, hair styling services, and other items, and some will be saved. If the marginal propensity to consume is 0.8, then 0.8 ($200 billion) or $160 billion will be respent in a second round of spending resulting from the initial orders for investment goods, and $40 billion will be saved. As was the case for the investment purchases, the $160 billion of new consumer purchases will result in reorders by retailers and still more employment opportunities to satisfy the increased demand for consumer goods and services. In the second round of spending, $160 billion worth of consumer purchases will generate an additional $160 billion in income to resource owners. And the process doesn't end here. The $160 billion will result in 0.8 ($160 billion) = $128 billion in consumer purchases and $32 billion in additional saving. The $128 billion in consumer purchases will then generate $128 billion of income, and the spending process will commence again.

The table in Box 8 shows how each additional round of respending of the income initially generated by the investment purchases results in more consumption, more production, and therefore still further increases in income. Each additional increase in income then generates still further increases in consumption and saving as a chain reaction ensues. However, notice that as the process continues, the change in income for subsequent rounds becomes smaller and smaller. The total cumulative increase in real GNP approaches $1,000 billion as the increase in income from subsequent rounds of spending approaches zero. The graph in Box 8 shows the cumulative growth in real GNP at each round of spending. As the process goes on and on, the graph shows that equilibrium real GNP eventually grows by $1,000 billion.

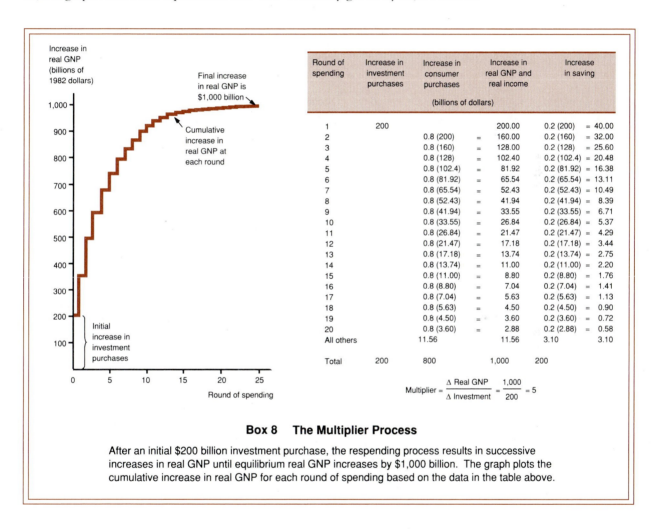

Box 8   The Multiplier Process

After an initial $200 billion investment purchase, the respending process results in successive increases in real GNP until equilibrium real GNP increases by $1,000 billion. The graph plots the cumulative increase in real GNP for each round of spending based on the data in the table above.

In equilibrium, the initial increase in investment purchases will have generated enough additional income to increase saving by $200 billion and increase consumption by $800 billion. The $200 billion increase in saving restores the economy to equilibrium by raising saving by an amount that equals the increase in planned investment that started the respending process. The last column of the table in Box 8 shows the increase in saving resulting from the induced increases in income as the respending process works itself out. The bottom line of the last column of the table shows that the cumulative increase in saving for the economy is $200 billion.

The Multiplier: What It Is and How It Works in a Simple Economy

The Multiplier Effect and Macroeconomic Equilibrium

The graphs in Box 9 show how the multiplier effect results in a new macroeconomic equilibrium for the economy. Initially the economy is in equilibrium at point E_1, at which real GNP is $4,000 billion and the price level is 100. At that equilibrium level of real GNP there is a $1,000 billion recessionary GNP gap. The increase in planned investment purchases shifts the aggregate purchases line upward by $200 billion at each possible level of real GNP for the year. Note that an increase in any type of

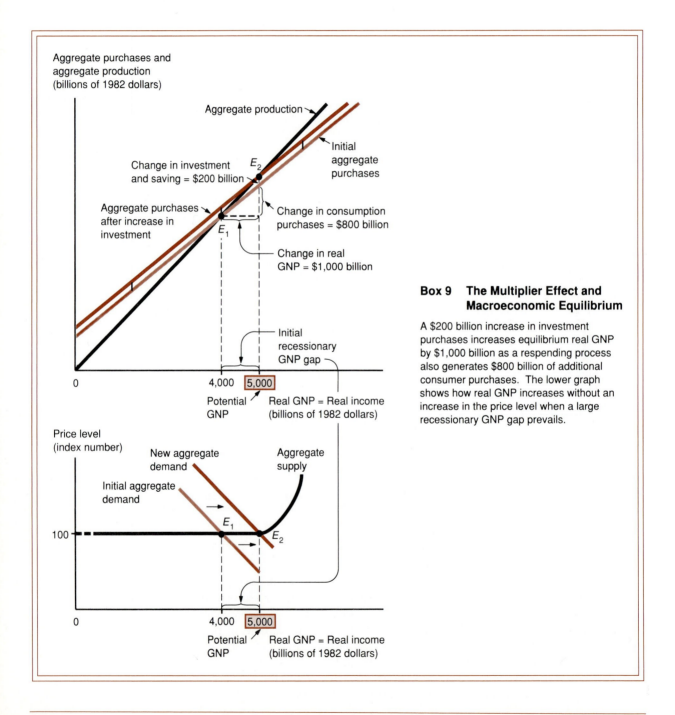

Box 9 The Multiplier Effect and Macroeconomic Equilibrium

A $200 billion increase in investment purchases increases equilibrium real GNP by $1,000 billion as a respending process also generates $800 billion of additional consumer purchases. The lower graph shows how real GNP increases without an increase in the price level when a large recessionary GNP gap prevails.

autonomous purchases would have the same effect. For example, a $200 billion increase in autonomous consumption resulting from an increase in wealth could also shift the line upward. Introduction of $200 billion worth of government purchases would have the same effect.

As the aggregate purchases line shifts upward, $4,000 billion is no longer the equilibrium level of real GNP. This is because, after the new investment orders, aggregate purchases exceed aggregate production at that level of real GNP. As inventories are drawn down, firms reorder and there is upward pressure on real GNP. The economy moves to a new equilibrium at point E_2, at which real GNP increases by $1,000 billion to move to its potential level of $5,000 billion. As the new equilibrium is reached, consumption purchases rise by $800 billion, as shown in the upper graph, and saving increases by $200 billion. The $200 billion increase in investment purchases therefore serves to eliminate the recessionary gap.

The lower graph uses aggregate demand and supply analysis to show how the increase in investment purchases eliminates the recessionary gap. As investment purchases and then consumer purchases increase, the aggregate demand curve shifts outward. If the economy is in a deep recession (as Keynes assumed in his analysis of the multiplier effect), the slack in productive capacity and the excessive unemployment would permit real GNP to grow without putting upward pressure on the price level. As a result, the economy moves from its initial equilibrium at E_1 in the lower graph to the new equilibrium at E_2 as real GNP increases from $4,000 billion to $5,000 billion, and the price level remains at its initial level of 100.

The multiplier works backward as well as forward. Suppose investment orders fell by $200 billion for the year. In this case there would be an initial reduction of $200 billion in real GNP. However, a reduction in orders means that production and therefore income will decline. As workers are laid off, they will have to cut back consumption. As they cancel plans to add to their wardrobes, buy new cars and new TVs, and make other purchases, there will be a second-round effect of a $160 billion reduction in consumer purchases, assuming a marginal propensity to consume of 0.8. In this case the process would work in reverse. If the economy were initially in equilibrium at its potential real GNP of $5,000 billion, a decrease in investment of $200 billion would cause a $1,000 billion decline in real GNP. You can check this reasoning by looking at the example in Box 4 that showed how a $200 billion decline in planned investment resulted in a $1,000 billion decrease in equilibrium real GNP.

A Formula for the Multiplier

The size of the multiplier depends on the extent to which each extra dollar of income earned results in additional purchases of real GNP to generate additional production and income. You can easily see this by looking at the data in Box 8. When the only two uses of income earned are consumption and saving, the marginal propensity to consume equals the rate at which each extra dollar of income is respent. After the initial increase in investment purchases, the additional income resulting from each round of spending would increase as the marginal propensity to consume increases. For example, if the marginal propensity to consume were 0.9 instead of 0.8, the second-round spending in Box 8 would generate $180 billion in income instead of $160 billion.

A formula can be derived to calculate the multiplier to show how its value depends on the marginal propensity to consume when the only alternative to consuming is saving. The sum representing the cumulative increase in real GNP and therefore income can be written as

ΔReal GNP =
$200 billion + 0.8 ($200 billion) + 0.8 [0.8 ($200 billion)] + 0.8 [(0.8) 0.8 ($200 billion)] + . . .

You can see the pattern. At each stage, 0.8 of the previous change in income is respent. At the second round the $160 billion increase in income that results from induced consumption purchases in Box 8 can be written as 0.8($200 billion). Similarly, the $128 billion increase in real GNP and income that results at the third round of spending can be written as $(0.8)^2$($200 billion). The fourth-round increase in real GNP can be written as $(0.8)^3$($200 billion). Note that each successive term in the sum will be smaller than the previous term because the marginal propensity to consume is less than 1. When a number less than 1 is raised to a higher power, it becomes smaller.

A mathematical formula can be used to solve for the end product of such an infinite progression of numbers when the number raised to successively higher powers in the sum is greater than zero but less than 1. In this case the number raised to successively higher powers is the marginal propensity to consume, which is greater than zero but less than 1. The formula for solving for this total increase in real GNP resulting from the $200 billion injection of investment purchases is:

$$\Delta\text{Real GNP} = (\text{Increase in investment purchases})\left[\frac{1}{(1 - \text{Marginal propensity to consume})}\right]$$

Marginal respending rate (MRR):
The extra purchases that result from each extra dollar of income.

where the marginal propensity to consume represents the **marginal respending rate (MRR)** for the economy, which is the extra purchases that result from each extra dollar of income. In this case the increase in investment purchases is $200 billion and the marginal propensity to consume is 0.8, so the increase in national income is

$$\$200 \text{ billion}\left[\frac{1}{(1 - 0.8)}\right] = \frac{\$200 \text{ billion}}{0.2} = \$1,000 \text{ billion}$$

which is the result that was obtained in Box 8.

The formula for the multiplier in an economy with no government sector and no international trade is:

$$\text{Multiplier} = \frac{1}{(1 - \text{Marginal propensity to consume})}$$
$$= \frac{1}{(1 - MPC)}$$

Because the marginal propensity to save *(MPS)* is equal to 1 minus the marginal propensity to consume, the multiplier can also be written as

$$\text{Multiplier} = \frac{1}{MPS}$$

When the marginal propensity to consume is 0.8, the multiplier for a simple economy is 1/0.2 = 5. Notice that the higher the marginal propensity to consume, the smaller the denominator of the formula and the larger the multiplier.

CHAPTER 30 Aggregate Demand and Keynesian Analysis of Macroeconomic Equilibrium

1   A $300 billion increase in planned investment results in a $900 billion increase in equilibrium real GNP over the year. Assuming that income earned is either consumed or saved, what is the multiplier?

2   Calculate the impact of a $300 billion reduction in annual planned investment on equilibrium real GNP, assuming the marginal propensity to consume in the economy is 0.7.

3   A sharp increase in stock prices increases household wealth by 25%. The result is a $100 billion increase in annual autonomous consumption. Assuming the marginal propensity to consume is 0.9, calculate the increase in equilibrium real GNP and use graphic analysis to show how the aggregate purchases line and the aggregate demand curve shift.

International Trade, the Government Sector, and Macroeconomic Equilibrium

In reality, aggregate purchases depend not only on consumption and planned investment but also on government purchases and net exports. It's easy to incorporate government purchases, the impact of taxes and transfers, and international trade into the analysis of aggregate demand and macroeconomic equilibrium.

The graph in Box 10 adds government purchases and net exports associated with

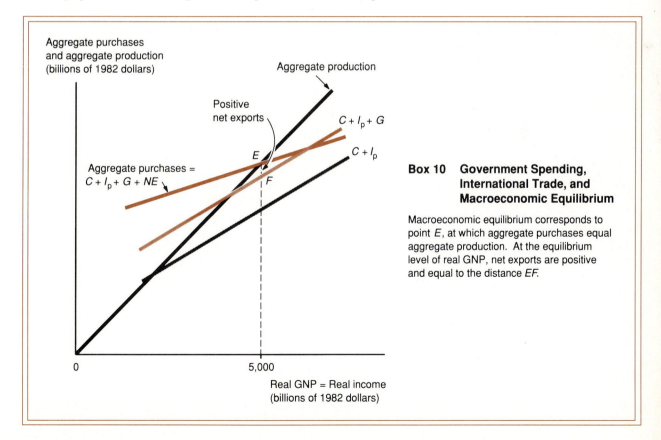

Box 10   Government Spending, International Trade, and Macroeconomic Equilibrium

Macroeconomic equilibrium corresponds to point E, at which aggregate purchases equal aggregate production. At the equilibrium level of real GNP, net exports are positive and equal to the distance EF.

each possible level of income to consumption and planned investment to show how aggregate purchases vary with income. Government purchases are assumed to be a constant amount independent of real GNP and income. Net exports, however, add to aggregate purchases only at relatively low levels of income and must be subtracted from the sum $C + I_P + G$ at relatively high levels of income (see the preceding chapter). The amount of consumption associated with each level of income depends on taxes and transfers because these items affect disposable income. The line labeled aggregate purchases in Box 10 represents the sum of consumption, investment, government, and net export purchases.

Government Purchases, Taxes, International Trade, and Macroeconomic Equilibrium

The principle for macroeconomic equilibrium remains the same even when international trade and government spending and taxation are considered. In equilibrium, aggregate purchases must equal aggregate production. In Box 10 the macroeconomic equilibrium corresponds to point E, at which real GNP and income equal $5,000 billion. Positive net exports at the equilibrium level of real GNP are shown as the distance EF in Box 10.

When international trade and the government sector are considered,

$$\text{Aggregate purchases} = C + I_P + G + (E - M)$$

where E represents purchases of exports and M represents purchases of imports. The difference $(E - M)$ represents net exports.

Aggregate production equals real earnings from goods and services produced. These earnings are used for consumption, saving, or paying taxes. When earnings are saved or used to pay taxes, they are not directly used to purchase final products produced during the year and thus detract from aggregate demand. Aggregate production therefore measures income and can be expressed as:

$$\text{Aggregate production} = C + S + T$$

where C includes purchases of imported products as well as those produced nationally and T represents the difference between taxes paid and transfers received from government during the year.

In equilibrium, aggregate purchases must equal aggregate production; otherwise there will be unintended changes in inventories that will cause real GNP and income to adjust. Therefore real GNP and thus income adjust until

$$\text{Aggregate purchases} = C + I_P + G + (E - M) = C + S + T = \text{Aggregate production}$$

Because C is a component of both aggregate production and aggregate purchases, it can be subtracted from both sides of the preceding equation, showing that

$$I_P + G + (E - M) = S + T$$

By adding M to both sides of the preceding equation we get:

$$I_P + G + E = S + T + M$$

The right side of the equation represents uses of income for purposes other than purchasing current national production. These must exactly equal the sum of planned investment, government, and export purchases in equilibrium. If the preceding equality is not met, the unanticipated changes in inventories will cause changes in aggregate production, which in turn will change income until saving, tax collections, or import purchases adjust to equal the sum of planned investment, government, and export purchases.

The preceding equation is similar to the one derived earlier that showed that macroeconomic equilibrium required that saving equal investment when we ignored government purchases, taxes, transfers, and international trade. In the simpler model, saving was the only possible use of income other than consumption of final products produced domestically. In this more complex and realistic model, income earned during the year is used to pay taxes and purchase imported products as well as being saved. The sum $S + T + M$ therefore represents the portion of income that does not result in purchases that generate aggregate demand for real GNP.

Also in the simpler model, the only alternative to producing consumer goods was production of investment goods. However, in reality, business firms can also produce goods for governments and for export. Unless the amount of income that is not spent on consumer goods is offset by investors (business firms), governments, and buyers in foreign markets purchasing a portion of our real GNP, aggregate production will exceed planned aggregate purchases and real GNP will fall.

We also have to modify our estimate of the multiplier when we consider international trade and taxation. In the simple formula for the multiplier derived earlier, the marginal propensity to consume was the marginal respending rate because the only alternative to consuming income was to save it. However, in this more realistic depiction of the U.S. economy we know that some of the extra income that is earned during the year must go to pay taxes and another portion will be used to buy imported products. The **marginal propensity to import (MPI)** is the fraction of each extra dollar of income used to purchase imported products. The marginal propensity to import is pretty close to 0.1 for the U.S. economy, where 10% of income has been spent on imports in recent years. Because taxes absorb about 20¢ of each extra dollar earned in the United States and imports absorb another 10¢, the marginal respending rate is less than the marginal propensity to consume. Of each extra dollar earned in the United States, about 20¢ is saved,[1] 20¢ must be used to pay taxes, and about 10¢ is used to buy imported products. Only 50¢ of each extra dollar of income earned each year in the United States is respent. Thus the marginal respending rate on national production of each additional dollar earned is only about 0.5. A more realistic estimate of the multiplier for the U.S. economy is therefore:

Marginal propensity to import (MPI): The fraction of each extra dollar of income used to purchase imported products.

$$\text{Multiplier} = \frac{1}{(1 - \text{Marginal respending rate})} = \frac{1}{(1 - 0.5)} = 2$$

How a Decline in Exports or an Increase in the Marginal Propensity to Import Can Cause a Recessionary GNP Gap

Although net exports represent only a small portion of aggregate demand in the U.S. economy, their importance has grown since the 1970s. Many nations, such as Japan and West Germany, rely on the sale of exports for significant portions of their income. Even in the United States exports have become a more important source of income in the past 20 years. Fluctuations in export demand, which is quite unstable, can therefore have a considerable effect on equilibrium real GNP and income in a nation. This is particularly true for many less developed nations that export basic

---

[1]This includes business as well as personal saving. Remember that capital consumption allowances represent business saving.

Principles in Practice

The Export Boom and Macroeconomic Equilibrium

The rust belt of mid-America will rise again! The death sentence for U.S. manufacturing that was passed by many observers in the early 1980s was off the mark. The falling value of the dollar in 1987 and 1988 spurred an enormous export boom. Output of U.S. factories rose by nearly 5% in 1987, and much of the production was for export. Exports accounted for over 11% of real GNP in 1987. The growing demand for U.S. exports abroad, particularly manufactured products, has been an engine of growth in the United States in 1987 and 1988, fueling the economy and helping the unemployment rate fall below 6% for the first time in the 1980s.

U.S. export sales grew by a remarkable 11.4% in 1987, and U.S. manufacturing plants were operating at peak capacity. Industries producing paper, metals, plastics, lumber and wood products, electronics, office equipment, and machine tools enjoyed booming sales in foreign markets in 1987. Over 50% of the total revenue taken in by IBM in the United States was from foreign sales and operations. Even U.S. automakers, which never cultivated foreign sales in the past, were getting into the act. Chrysler Corporation hoped to export close to $1 billion worth of its cars to foreign markets in 1988, and General Motors planned to sell 4,000 cars in Japan that year!

The low value of the dollar is also affecting production decisions of U.S. firms in ways that provide more jobs for U.S. workers. In 1987 the Tandy Corporation shifted assembly operations of its Color Computer 3 from South Korea to the United States, and the Otis Elevator division of United Technologies moved its escalator production operations from West Germany to the United States.*

The changing international trade picture in 1987 and 1988 also affected U.S. markets. Caterpillar Tractor, which had lost much of its share of the U.S. earthmoving equipment market to Japan's Komatsu, regained what it lost. And the U.S. specialty steel industry now finds that as a result of the dollar's decline, its products are more competitively priced in both U.S. and foreign markets.

The U.S. economy of the 1990s will continue to be tied to world markets. To remain competitive, U.S. industries must invest in new technologies that allow productivity gains to keep costs of production low. Tying of the U.S. economy to world trade also means that changes in international currency markets can cause real GNP to fluctuate to a greater extent than was the case in the past.

*See "Big Wheels Turning," *Time*, March 14, 1988, pp. 46-50.

---

materials such as petroleum and tin. It's also true for some prosperous nations like Japan that import much of their raw materials and export a large portion of their real GNP for sale in foreign markets. International transactions account for over 50% of the value of real GNP in West Germany and South Korea. You saw earlier how a contraction or recession could be caused by a decline in planned investment or by a decline in the dollar amount of consumption attributable to influences other than income. It's easy to demonstrate how a contraction (or possibly a recession if net exports are a major component of aggregate demand) could also be induced by a decline in net exports. A decline in net exports associated with each possible level of income for the year results either from a decline in export sales or from an increase in the portion of income that consumers and businesses wish to spend on imports at each level of income. Of course, it can also result from a combination of these two effects. It's not unusual, as you'll see when you study in detail the topic of international trade, for exports to fall just when imports are increasing.

Suppose the initial equilibrium level of income is $5,000 billion and this corresponds to potential GNP so there is no cyclical unemployment. At the beginning of the next year there is a decline in the net exports associated with any given level of real GNP.

It's now easy to show that the equilibrium level of real GNP, other things remaining unchanged for the year, will be below potential real GNP. The decline in net exports associated with each possible level of real GNP causes the aggregate purchases line to shift downward, as shown in the graph in Box 11. This means that over the year there will be unintended inventory accumulation that will put downward pressure on real GNP and income at the full-employment level of $5,000 billion.

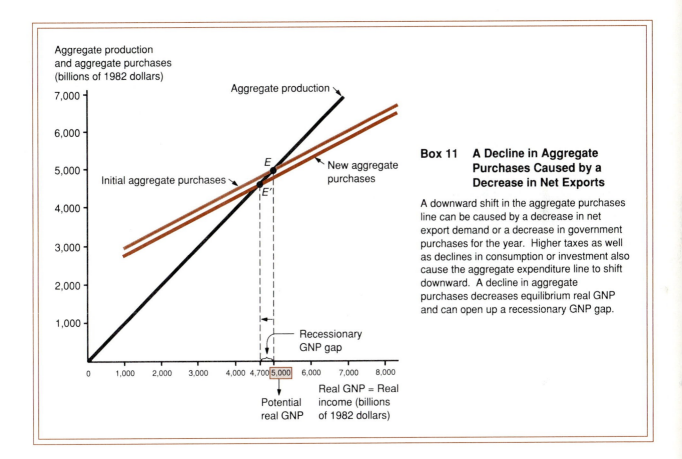

Box 11 A Decline in Aggregate Purchases Caused by a Decrease in Net Exports

A downward shift in the aggregate purchases line can be caused by a decrease in net export demand or a decrease in government purchases for the year. Higher taxes as well as declines in consumption or investment also cause the aggregate expenditure line to shift downward. A decline in aggregate purchases decreases equilibrium real GNP and can open up a recessionary GNP gap.

The equilibrium level of real GNP declines below its potential level, and the equilibrium moves from point E to point E'. The result is a recessionary GNP gap, as shown on the graph. As real GNP falls below its potential level, some cyclical unemployment will result.

You can now begin to understand the concern about the balance of trade deficit in the United States in recent years. Negative net exports put downward pressure on real GNP. In recent years U.S. net exports have been negative, amounting to 4% of real GNP. Other nations, such as Japan, West Germany, South Korea, and many Latin American countries, rely on exports to generate a very large portion of their real GNP and income. Declines in world demand for basic products (such as oil and tin) in recent years have plunged nations like Mexico and Bolivia into deep recessions.

1 What are possible uses for income earned during the year other than for consumption?

2 Explain why an increase in the demand for U.S. exports, other things being equal, will increase equilibrium real GNP.

3 Why is the marginal respending rate for the U.S. economy actually lower than the marginal propensity to consume, and how does that fact affect the value of the multiplier?

The Price Level, Aggregate Demand, and Inflationary Gaps

Thus far the price level has been assumed to be fixed in the Keynesian analysis of aggregate demand. Keynesian analysis of macroeconomic equilibrium argues that shifts in aggregate demand are not only responsible for recessions, but are also the culprit for inflation! At this point we can begin discussing the impact of increases in aggregate demand on the economy. In this section we analyze the effect of changes in the price level on the aggregate quantity of real GNP demanded. In addition, we'll analyze movements in the price level that result when the economy is operating at a level above potential real GNP.

Shifts of the Aggregate Purchases Line Caused by Price Changes

Suppose the prices of *all* goods and services produced in the economy were suddenly *doubled*. In the next part of the book you'll see how a doubling of the money in circulation could cause such a strange phenomenon. These price increases are applicable only to *domestically* produced goods and services that are part of real GNP and don't apply to imported goods, whose prices depend on the price levels in foreign nations.

The increase in the domestic price level is likely to decrease aggregate purchases for the reasons we first discussed in the chapter on the forces of aggregate supply and demand.

1. A higher price level can decrease real wealth in a nation, thereby decreasing consumer purchases of real GNP. As a result of the increase in the price level, the purchasing power of cash will decline (in this example the purchasing power of money will actually be cut in half). This means there will be a decrease in real wealth, which in turn will put downward pressure on consumer purchases, shifting the aggregate purchases line downward.
2. A higher price level can increase real interest rates, making credit more expensive. This occurs because at a higher price level, households and businesses demand larger cash balances to finance their everyday transactions. This decreases the supply of loanable funds, which puts upward pressure on real interest rates. The higher real interest rates in turn cause businesses to reduce the quantity of planned investment purchases for the year.
3. The increase in the price level reduces foreign demand for U.S. exports and increases domestic demand for imports. Assuming the international value of the dollar doesn't immediately adjust to a change in the price level, U.S. goods rise in price relative to foreign substitutes, thus causing an increase in imports and a decrease in exports.

The upper graph in Box 12 shows how an increase in the price level will shift the aggregate purchases line downward. Initially the economy is in equilibrium at a real GNP level of $5,000 billion, corresponding to point E_1 on the graph. As the price level increases from 100 to 200, the aggregate purchases line shifts *downward* for the reasons we discussed earlier. As this happens real GNP declines from its initial equilibrium of $5,000 billion to a new equilibrium of $4,000 billion as the economy moves to a new equilibrium at point E_2.

If the economy was initially in equilibrium at the potential level of real GNP, the increase in the price level will result in a recessionary GNP gap and cause some

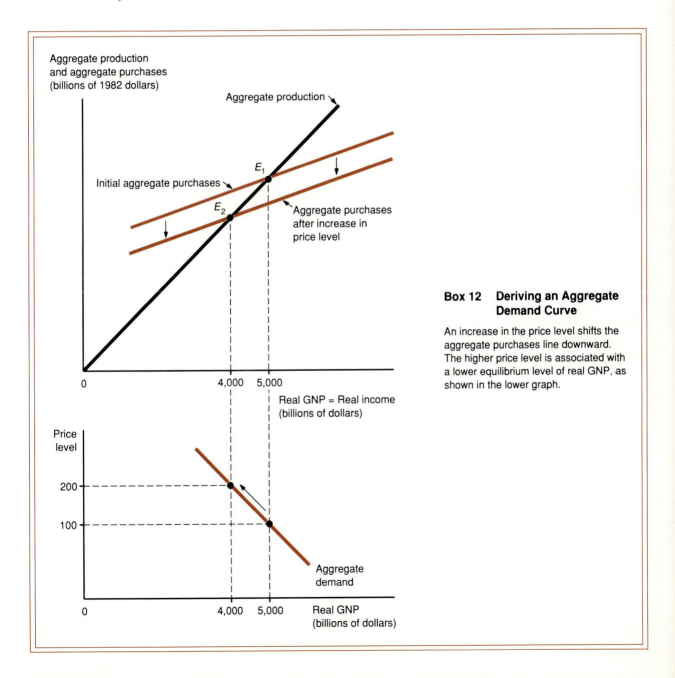

Box 12   Deriving an Aggregate Demand Curve

An increase in the price level shifts the aggregate purchases line downward. The higher price level is associated with a lower equilibrium level of real GNP, as shown in the lower graph.

cyclical unemployment. You can now understand why increases in the price level can cause a cyclical downturn in the economy at least in the short run by decreasing household real wealth, raising real interest rates, and causing net exports to decline. For example, a sudden sharp increase in the price of a basic input like oil would spell trouble for the economy, and a contraction of economic activity could result in a recession.

Deriving the Aggregate Demand Curve

You already know from our analysis of the aggregate demand curve in the chapter on the forces of aggregate supply and demand that a higher price level decreases aggregate quantity demanded. This analysis is in accord with the preceding analysis of the impact of an increase in the price level on aggregate purchases. A higher price level causes a reduction in real wealth, makes imports relatively cheaper for U.S. consumers, and makes U.S. exports more expensive in foreign markets, thus decreasing real GNP and equilibrium purchases of it. Note that when the price level goes up, input prices rise along with output prices. The initial increase in prices doesn't affect income. Although everyone is paying higher prices for the items they consume, they're also receiving higher prices for the input services they sell. It's the reduction in aggregate purchases caused by the higher price level and consequent reduction in wealth that then causes a decline in real GNP and thus income in the nation.

It's now possible to actually derive an aggregate demand curve from our analysis of the impact of changes in the price level on equilibrium real GNP. The preceding analysis of the impact of a change in the price level on aggregate purchases showed how an increase in the price level shifts the aggregate purchases line downward and reduces equilibrium real GNP. The lower graph in Box 12 simply plots the level of equilibrium real GNP associated with the initial price level of 100 and the new price level of 200.

Other things being equal, an increase in the price level, as shown earlier, decreases equilibrium real GNP. Conversely, a decrease in the price level will increase equilibrium real GNP. Connecting the two points in the lower graph traces out the downward-sloping aggregate demand curve.

Aggregate quantity demanded of real GNP decreases as the price level increases because of decreases in wealth, increases in import demand, and decreases in export demand caused by higher prices in the economy, and the reduction in planned investment that results when real interest rates rise.

As you'll see in the next chapter, movements along an aggregate demand curve caused by shifts in aggregate supply are very important in understanding the causes of inflation and unemployment. The changes in real wealth and shifts in net exports and investment demand that result when the price level changes affect the performance of the economy and cause cyclical fluctuations in real GNP.

Inflationary GNP Gaps

Economies can operate at levels of equilibrium real GNP that exceed potential real GNP. However, when an economy is bursting at the seams in this way, there inevitably is upward pressure on the price level that causes aggregate quantity demanded to decline and reduces real GNP. Keynes recognized that although prices and wages are quite inflexible in the downward direction, they are flexible in the upward direction. Increases in aggregate demand can therefore cause inflation when the economy is close to full employment. As a consequence, the economy's self-correction mechanism seems to work much better during periods in which the economy overheats than when it stagnates in a recession.

As you learned in the chapter on the forces of aggregate supply and demand, an *inflationary GNP gap* is the difference between equilibrium real GNP and the level of real GNP corresponding to full employment for an economy that is operating beyond its potential. The graph in Box 13 illustrates the concept of an inflationary GNP gap. The level of potential real GNP is $5,000 billion. However, the economy is in equilibrium at point E_1, at which real GNP is $6,000 billion. This means that equilibrium real GNP exceeds the level of potential real GNP at which full employment is attained. When this occurs, many plants are worked around the clock and overtime work is common. Thus, if full employment implies 250 billion labor hours utilized per year, an economy that is operating beyond its peak might use 300 billion labor hours per year. For example, during the period in which the United States was engaged in the Vietnam war, the economy operated beyond its capacity in this way. The inflationary gap is represented as the distance between the level of potential real GNP and equilibrium real GNP. In Box 13 the inflationary gap is $1,000 billion.

The inevitable result of an inflationary gap is upward pressure on the price level—a bout of inflation. As the price level eventually increases, the aggregate purchases line shifts downward for the reasons we discussed earlier. As this happens,

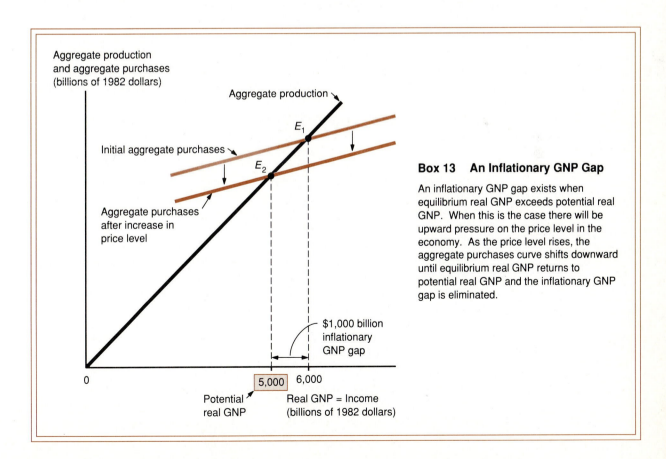

Box 13   An Inflationary GNP Gap

An inflationary GNP gap exists when equilibrium real GNP exceeds potential real GNP. When this is the case there will be upward pressure on the price level in the economy. As the price level rises, the aggregate purchases curve shifts downward until equilibrium real GNP returns to potential real GNP and the inflationary GNP gap is eliminated.

there is downward pressure on real GNP until the economy returns to equilibrium at the level of real GNP corresponding to full employment.

In the following chapter we'll discuss the implications of an inflationary gap and show how a wage-price spiral can result when the economy overheats.

Summary

1. Real GNP is in equilibrium when aggregate purchases equal aggregate production for the year. When real GNP is in equilibrium there is no unintended inventory investment, and there will be no tendency for real GNP and income to increase or decrease.

2. A decline in planned investment or a decline in autonomous consumption can cause a contraction or a recession. When real GNP falls below its potential, the economy suffers from a recessionary GNP gap.

3. When the price level does not fall in response to a decline in aggregate demand, unintended inventory accumulations cannot be sold off quickly. The buildup of inventory caused by downward price rigidity causes firms to cut back production. Lengthy recessions can result when wages and prices do not respond to decreases in aggregate demand.

4. The Keynesian model of macroeconomic equilibrium assumes that the economy operates in the horizontal portion of its aggregate supply curve when stagnating in recession. Because both the price level and wages are assumed to be downwardly inflexible, excessive unemployment is not quickly eliminated and the economy's self-correction mechanism cannot operate. Keynes argued that policies that increase aggregate demand could restore full employment without upward pressure on the price level when the economy is in a recession.

5. The multiplier is the ratio of the increase in real GNP to an increase in autonomous spending such as planned investment. The multiplier implies that an increase of $1 in planned investment or in other types of autonomous purchases will increase real GNP by more than $1.

6. The multiplier effect stems from a respending process as income earned from increased production is spent and respent over a period.

7. Planned investment purchases, government purchases, and exports of final products add to aggregate demand for real GNP, but saving, taxes, and imports decrease aggregate demand for real GNP.

8. A decrease in net exports decreases aggregate purchases and aggregate demand. This decreases equilibrium real GNP and contributes to a recessionary GNP gap.

9. Changes in the price level can cause shifts in the aggregate purchases line for the economy. An increase in the price level reduces the purchasing power of some assets denominated in dollars, like cash, for example. This reduces household real wealth and contributes to a decline in consumption. In addition, an increase in the price level reduces foreign demand for U.S. exports, increases domestic demand for imports, and increases real interest rates. Increases in the price level therefore cause a decrease in aggregate quantity demanded.

10. When an inflationary GNP gap prevails, the economy operates at a level of real GNP that exceeds potential real GNP. An inflationary gap puts upward pressure on the price level, which tends to shift the aggregate purchases line downward, thus restoring the economy to the level of real GNP corresponding to full employment.

Key Terms and Concepts

Multiplier
Autonomous purchases

Marginal respending rate (MRR)
Marginal propensity to import (MPI)

Problems and Applications

1. An increase in real interest rates is forecast to reduce investment purchases by $300 billion next year. Assuming the forecast is correct, what do you predict will happen to real GNP, other things being equal?
2. Use the data in the table in Box 1 to show what would happen to real GNP, income, consumption, and aggregate purchases and employment if planned investment purchases were to double for the year.
3. Suppose autonomous consumption falls by $400 billion. Use the data in Box 1 to show how the fall in autonomous consumption can cause a recession. What will be the new equilibrium real GNP, income, and employment, assuming nothing else changes?
4. Explain why an increase in the amount of saving consumers want to set aside at each possible level of real GNP can cause an economic contraction.
5. Suppose the marginal propensity to consume represents the marginal respending rate of additional income. If the marginal propensity to consume is 0.9, what will happen to real GNP if planned investment increases by $300 billion?
6. Why is the marginal propensity to consume likely to overstate the marginal respending rate in the economy when the impact of government and international trade on the economy is considered?
7. All indications are that consumers plan to devote higher proportions of their income to repayment of debt next year. Business firms have little optimism about the current outlook, and planned investments for next year are down. As an economic forecaster, what is your prognosis for the economy?
8. Why do you think the decline in the international value of the dollar against the yen has the potential to cause a recession in Japan? What effect would a recession in Japan have on U.S. exports to Japan given the current international value of the dollar?
9. Explain how a decrease in the price level in the economy will affect the aggregate purchases line and equilibrium real GNP.
10. Under what circumstances will an inflationary gap prevail for an economy? How would the economy's self-correction mechanism eliminate the inflationary gap?

Suggested Readings

Economic Report of the President, published annually in January, Washington, D.C.: U.S. Government Printing Office. This report contains analyses and data on the macroeconomic setting for the economy and on the components of aggregate demand.

Robert J. Gordon, *Macroeconomics,* 4th ed., Boston: Little, Brown, 1987. Chapter 3 discusses the multiplier and macroeconomic equilibrium.

A Forward Look

When an economy is operating close to full employment, increases in aggregate demand are likely to result in upward pressure on the price level. In the following chapter we analyze aggregate supply in greater detail and show how inflation can exist even when the economy is operating below its potential.

30

A Complete Keynesian Model

In this appendix we extend our analysis by explicitly considering how tax collections and net exports vary with real GNP for a given year. The analysis allows a more precise derivation of the conditions for macroeconomic equilibrium and an equation for the multiplier that shows how import demand and taxation affect the rate at which earned income is respent.

Aggregate Purchases: Explicit Consideration of Taxes, Government Purchases, and International Trade

The table in Box 1 provides data that can be used to derive an aggregate purchases line that explicitly considers how net tax receipts and net exports vary with income. The first column shows possible levels of aggregate production measured by real GNP, which also equals income (Y) earned for a given year. This table is similar to the one drawn up in Box 1 in the preceding chapter. However, because taxes are now explicitly considered, disposable income is no longer equal to income earned during the year.

The second column of the table calculates net taxes at alternative levels of income earned for the year. In making the calculation it's assumed that net taxes are always 20% of income earned. Remember that net taxes are taxes minus government transfer payments. Tax collections are higher at higher levels of real GNP when taxes are proportional to income, as is the case in many modern economies. This means that government net tax collections can vary with real GNP. This is of great importance in balancing government budgets because actual tax collections depend on how close the economy is to its potential real GNP. For example, in 1982 the federal budget deficit turned out to be much larger than government economists anticipated. This occurred because, given the level of government purchases that year, tax collections plummeted when a recession hit and equilibrium real GNP and income fell.

When taxes are considered, income earned in an economy exceeds disposable income. Disposable income represents income less net taxes. The third column of

Box 1 Aggregate Production, Aggregate Purchases, and Macroeconomic Equilibrium (Hypothetical Data)

(1)	(2)	(3)	(4)	(5)	(6)	(7)	(8)	(9)	(10)
Aggregate production (real GNP = real Income) Y	Net taxes $tY = 0.2Y$	Disposable income $DI = (1 - t)Y = 0.8Y$	Consumption purchases $C = 400 + 0.8DI$	Saving $S = DI - C$	Planned investment I_p	Government purchases G	Net exports $NE = 400 - 0.1Y$	Aggregate purchases $C + I_p + G + NE$	Pressure on real GNP
					(billions of dollars)				
1,000	200	800	1,040	−240	500	1,000	300	2,840	Up
2,000	400	1,600	1,680	−80	500	1,000	200	3,380	Up
3,000	600	2,400	2,320	80	500	1,000	100	3,920	Up
4,000	800	3,200	2,960	240	500	1,000	0	4,460	Up
5,000	1,000	4,000	3,600	400	500	1,000	−100	5,000	Equilibrium
6,000	1,200	4,800	4,240	560	500	1,000	−200	5,540	Down
7,000	1,400	5,600	4,880	720	500	1,000	−300	6,080	Down
8,000	1,600	6,400	5,520	880	500	1,000	−400	6,620	Down

the table in Box 1 calculates disposable income by subtracting net taxes from each possible level of income. Notice that because net taxes are 20% of income, disposable income is always 80% of income in the table.

The relationship between income earned and disposable income depends on how net taxes vary with income. In general, disposable income *(DI)* is equal to income *(Y)* less the portion of income paid in taxes. The *marginal tax rate (t)* is the fraction of each extra dollar of income earned in a nation that is collected as taxes.

In the table in Box 1 it's assumed that the marginal tax rate is always equal to 0.2. Although this is a simplifying assumption, it isn't too far off the mark of reality for the U.S. economy. When all federal, state, and local taxes are considered, U.S. taxes do tend to stay within the range of 20% to 30% of earnings for the economy as a whole. Of each extra $1 of national income earned, it's therefore reasonable to assume that 20¢ in the aggregate must be used to pay taxes. This means that $1,000 billion of extra national income would generate extra taxes of $200 billion for households. If the tax rate is a fixed proportion of income earned, as it is in this example, taxes paid at any level of income will be:

$$t(Y) = (\text{Marginal tax rate})(\text{Income}) = \text{Net taxes collected}$$

Disposable income is simply earned income less net taxes collected:

$$DI = Y - (t)Y = (1 - t)Y$$

For example, when $t = 0.2$

$$DI = (1 - 0.2)Y = 0.8Y$$

Disposable income in the third column is therefore always 80% of earned income.

Consumption *(C)* is shown in the fourth column of the table. Consumption is based on the same consumption function used in the chapter on the components of aggregate demand. At each possible level of income, consumption consists of $400 billion in autonomous purchases that are independent of income plus 80% of disposable income. The consumption function is therefore

$$C = (\$400 \text{ billion} + 0.8\,DI)$$

This equation tells how consumption varies with *disposable* income. However, because of taxes, only 80¢ of each $1 of aggregate income, *Y,* is available to households for spending as disposable income. Each $1 of earnings in the aggregate will result in only 80¢ of disposable income. Because the marginal propensity to consume disposable income is 0.8, each $1 of additional earnings will result in (0.8)80¢ or 64¢ of additional consumer purchases.

The extra consumer purchases resulting from an extra dollar of income are therefore $MPC(1 - t)$ dollars where $(1 - t)$ is the proportion of each extra dollar of earnings that ends up as disposable income. In this example $(1 - t)$ dollars is $0.80. You can easily see this by substituting the expression for disposable income into the equation for the consumption function. Because $DI = (1 - t)Y$:

$$C = \$400 \text{ billion} + MPC[(1-t)Y]$$

Because $MPC = 0.8$ and $t = 0.2$:

$$C = \$400 \text{ billion} + 0.64Y$$

Each $1,000 billion of income results in $640 billion more consumption and $200 billion in extra taxes in the table in Box 1. The total of additional consumption and taxes therefore accounts for $840 billion of each $1,000 billion increase in national income. What happens to the remaining $160 billion of national income of each

$1,000 billion increase? Because it's used neither to pay taxes nor to pay for consumption of products, the remainder must be saved. In Box 1, 16¢ of each extra $1 earned ends up as saving. The fifth column of the table shows how saving varies as income increases in the economy for the year. Note that saving is negative at low levels of income but increases by $160 billion for each $1,000 billion increase in income for a given year.

The sixth column of the table shows planned investment (I_P), which is assumed to be $500 billion at all possible levels of national income. Government purchases (G) shown in the seventh column are assumed to be $1,000 billion at all possible levels of national income over the year.[1] Typically government purchases for a year are determined at the beginning of the year independent of economic conditions for the coming year.

How Exports and Imports Affect Aggregate Purchases

To obtain aggregate purchases of domestic final products, export sales must be added to the sum of consumer, investment, and government purchases. However, because purchases also include expenditure on goods produced in foreign nations, imports must be netted out of aggregate purchases to correctly measure aggregate demand for real GNP. This is because expenditure on imports doesn't generate domestic production and therefore doesn't result in income for U.S. firms and households. The difference between expenditure on U.S. exports (E) and U.S. expenditure on imported goods (M) is net exports (NE):

$$NE = E - M$$

Aggregate purchases of real GNP during the year are therefore the sum of consumption, planned investment, government purchases, and net exports:

$$\text{Aggregate purchases} = C + I_P + G + NE$$

Net exports can be positive or negative. In the table in Box 1, net exports have been calculated by assuming that foreign purchases of U.S. products (exports) are $400 billion, independent of the level of real GNP and income in the United States. This is quite realistic because current year demand for U.S. exports is dependent on income and other demand influences in foreign nations that are export customers. Import purchases, however, are assumed to be 10% of income in the United States. *This means that the dollar purchase of imports by Americans will increase as the level of real GNP and income increases for the year.* This assumption is also quite realistic for the United States, where purchases of imports have been close to 10% of real GNP in recent years. As income rises, other things being equal, U.S. consumers typically demand more Toyotas, Volvos, Sony Camcorders, and other foreign goods. Just as consumers purchase proportionately more domestic goods as their income increases, so do they purchase proportionately more imported goods. *In the U.S. economy, imports vary with income earned while exports are independent of income.* This was shown in the chapter on the components of aggregate demand.

---

[1]It should be emphasized that constancy of planned investment and government purchases during the year is a simplification. It is quite possible that both planned investment and government purchases could vary with income as much as consumption does.

As you learned in the preceding chapter, the fraction of each extra dollar of income that is spent on imported goods is called the *marginal propensity to import* (MPI). In this case the marginal propensity to import is 0.1 because 10¢ of each extra dollar of national income is assumed to be spent on goods produced in foreign nations.

Because exports are assumed to be $400 billion no matter what the actual national income during the year while imports are always 10% of income, Y, the following equation can be used to calculate net exports at each possible level of national income:

$$NE = (\$400 \text{ billion} - 0.1Y)$$

As you can see in column 8 of the table, net exports are positive at low levels of national income but become negative at high levels of income as import expenditures outstrip export sales receipts. *Net exports therefore tend to decline as income earned, Y, increases.*

The ninth column of the table gives the aggregate purchases for the year for each possible level of aggregate production. Aggregate purchases are obtained by summing each individual category of expenditure $(C + I_P + G + NE)$ at each possible level of income for the year.

Determination of Equilibrium Real GNP and Income

Despite the added detail, the principle for determining the equilibrium level of real GNP and therefore of income in the economy is just the same as it was in the simple model developed in the preceding chapter. Aggregate purchases at the current price level must equal aggregate production. Aggregate production is represented by real GNP (which also equals real income) in the first column of the table, while aggregate purchases (the sum of consumption, planned investment, government purchases, and net exports) is represented by the numbers in column 9 of the table.

In the table, the equilibrium condition is met when income and real GNP are equal to $5,000 billion for the year, which is assumed to be the level of potential real GNP that will provide full employment. If real GNP were less than $5,000 billion, aggregate purchases would exceed aggregate production at the current price level, and the resulting depletion of inventories would put upward pressure on real GNP. You can see this by comparing the numbers in column 9 with those in column 1. For example, if real GNP were $3,000 billion, aggregate purchases of real GNP would be $3,920 billion and firms would be forced to draw down inventories to meet aggregate demand. The consequent reordering of products to replenish inventories would put upward pressure on real GNP.

Similarly, if real GNP exceeded $5,000 billion, aggregate purchases would fall short of real GNP at the current price level and the unintended inventory accumulation would put downward pressure on real GNP. For example, if real GNP were $6,000 billion, aggregate purchases would be only $5,540 billion and there would be unintended accumulation of inventories. The resulting cutback in production would put downward pressure on real GNP.

At the equilibrium level of real GNP, annual net taxes will be $1,000 billion. Notice from the data in the table that this is exactly equal to government purchases during the year, so the government budget will be balanced. However, if real GNP were lower, tax collections would fall and the budget would be thrown into deficit. For example, if real GNP were $4,000 billion, tax collections would fall to $800 billion. Because the data in the table assume constant government purchases of $1,000 billion, this would imply a budget deficit of $200 billion. This points out an important characteristic of budget balance for the government sector of the economy. The actual state of budget balance (surplus or deficit) is influenced by the level of actual aggregate production in a given year. In the chapter on fiscal policy, you'll study in detail how government tax collections and government purchases actually vary with real GNP.

Also notice that at the equilibrium level of real GNP in this case, net exports are negative. A **balance of trade deficit** prevails when expenditures on imported products over the year exceed receipts by domestic firms from sales of exports. In recent years net exports have been negative, and in 1986 the balance of trade deficit amounted to about 4% of real GNP. The actual level of net exports is sensitive to income because imports typically vary with income.

Balance of trade deficit:
Prevails when a nation's expenditures on imported products over the year exceed receipts by domestic firms from sales of exports.

Income earned in nations in which U.S. firms sell exported products affects the business receipts for exports. In this analysis income in other nations is assumed to be given, so export receipts are also assumed to be fixed and independent of possible levels of U.S. income.[2] If demand for U.S. exports were stronger and/or if the marginal propensity to import were lower, net exports could very well be positive at the equilibrium level of real GNP. Net exports depend on a variety of factors, including economic conditions in foreign nations, the unit costs of U.S. goods compared to the unit costs of competing foreign goods, and the international rates of exchange of the dollar into foreign currencies.

The Balance of Trade, the Government Budget Balance, and the Savings-Investment Balance

Recall from the analysis of the simple economy with no international trade and no government sector that equilibrium required a balance between saving and planned investment. A similar but somewhat more complex condition can be derived for the economy by considering both the balance of international trade and the government budget balance. Aggregate purchases of real GNP are the sum:

$$\text{Aggregate purchases} = C + I_P + G + (E - M)$$

where $(E - M)$ represents net exports, the difference between exports and imports.

Aggregate production, which represents income (Y), is the sum of consumption, saving, and taxes paid over the year:

$$\text{Aggregate production} = Y = C + S + T$$

In equilibrium, aggregate production must equal aggregate purchases, which implies:

$$C + I_P + G + (E - M) = C + S + T$$

---

[2]Once again this is a simplification. An economic downturn in the United States could reduce real income in nations that purchase our exports. If there is such a linkage, U.S. export demand could decline when U.S. national income declines.

Because C is a component of both aggregate production and aggregate purchases, it can be subtracted from both sides of the preceding equation to obtain the following equilibrium condition:

$$I_P + G + (E - M) = S + T$$

This equation can be written in the following form by rearranging terms:

$$(E - M) + (G - T) = S - I_P$$

The term $(E - M)$ represents net exports, which can be positive or negative. When imports exceed exports, net exports are negative. Similarly, the term $(G - T)$ represents the government budget deficit that prevails when net taxes (T) are less than government purchases (G). The equilibrium condition states that the sum of net exports (the balance of trade) and the government budget deficit must equal the difference between saving and planned investment in the economy.

To understand the relevance of this condition, assume that in equilibrium there is a balance of trade deficit and a budget deficit, as has in fact been the case for the U.S. economy in recent years. This implies:

$$\text{Balance of trade deficit} = S - (I_P + \text{Budget deficit})$$

When there is a balance of trade deficit, both sides of the preceding equation will be negative in equilibrium. *This means a balance of trade deficit implies that domestic saving falls short of the sum of planned investment purchases and the budget deficit.* The balance of trade deficit represents foreign saving in the United States (see the chapter on GNP and economic performance) that fills in the gap between domestic saving and the sum of investment and the government budget deficit in equilibrium.

The equilibrium condition just derived suggests that the trade deficit and the budget deficit can be connected. Given planned investment and export demand, an increase in the budget deficit associated with each possible level of real GNP is an expansionary influence on the economy because it increases aggregate purchases. As equilibrium real GNP increases, the increase in income means more saving, and more import demand is generated in the economy. The increased import demand increases the balance of trade deficit. However, the expansionary influence of the budget deficit need not increase the trade deficit if it results in a sufficient increase in private saving or a decline in planned investment.

The way the budget deficit affects saving, planned investment, and therefore the trade balance will be examined in the chapter on the federal budget deficit. Given planned investment, to the extent that the increase in the budget deficit doesn't result in a substantial increase in saving, the difference must be made up by an increase in the balance of trade deficit. In effect this means that increases in income in the economy contribute to a trade deficit because consumers choose to use a higher percentage of their earnings to buy imported products rather than to save. However, as you'll see in the chapter on the federal budget deficit, it's also possible that an increase in the government budget deficit can result in a decline in private investment that also serves to restore macroeconomic equilibrium. The greater the decline in private investment that results from the budget deficit, the less the increase in earnings and the lower the trade deficit because imports will be correspondingly less.

APPENDIX A Complete Keynesian Model

Analysis of Changes in Aggregate Demand and the Multiplier in the Mixed and Open Economy

How the Multiplier Is Related to the Marginal Propensity to Consume, the Marginal Tax Rate, and the Marginal Propensity to Import

An algebraic calculation of the marginal respending rate in general allows us to derive a general formula for the multiplier. The first question to ask in deriving such a formula is: How much of each extra dollar of income earned is spent on consumer purchases? Because taxes are paid on earnings, each $1 of earnings results in less than $1 of disposable income. If the marginal tax rate is t, then the tax on each $1 of additional earnings is some fraction of t, and disposable income resulting from each $1 of extra earnings is

$$(1 - t) Y$$

For example, if the marginal tax rate is 0.2, then each $1 increase in income will result in $(1 - 0.2) = 0.8$ of a dollar or 80¢ of additional disposable income. The extra consumer purchases that result from an extra dollar of income earned are obtained by multiplying the marginal propensity to consume by $(1 - t)$:

$MPC(1 - t) =$ **Extra consumption purchases resulting from each $1 increase in income**

For example, if the marginal propensity to consume is 0.8 and the marginal tax rate is 0.2, then each $1 of extra income will result in $0.8(1 - 0.2) = \$0.64$ of additional consumer purchases.

However, the preceding expression includes consumer purchases of *both* domestically produced and imported final products. Income used to purchase imported goods is not respent on domestic production and thus does not generate domestic income that fuels the respending process. Purchases of imports must therefore be netted out of extra consumption to accurately measure the marginal respending rate in the economy.

The marginal propensity to import (MPI) represents the portion of each extra dollar of earnings that is used to purchase imports. Subtracting MPI from the portion of each dollar respent on consumer purchases gives the extra consumption purchases of *domestic* products resulting from each $1 increase in income, which represents the marginal respending rate (MRR):

$$MRR = MPC(1 - t) - MPI$$

To convince yourself that this is correct, note that when the marginal propensity to consume is 0.8, the marginal tax rate is 0.2, and the marginal propensity to import is 0.1 as it was in the preceding example, the marginal respending rate is

$$MRR = 0.8(1 - 0.2) - 0.1 = 0.64 - 0.1 = 0.54$$

A marginal respending rate of 0.54 means that 54¢ of each extra dollar earned is spent on real GNP and therefore increases income by that amount.

The general formula for the multiplier is:

$$\text{Multiplier} = \frac{1}{(1 - MRR)} = \frac{1}{[1 - (MPC(1 - t) - MPI)]}$$

You can verify that this is in accord with the analysis in the preceding chapter by setting $t = 0$ and $MPI = 0$, which holds when there is no taxation of additional income earned and no international trade. When this is the case, the denominator of the general equation for the multiplier becomes $1 - MPC$, which is the case for an economy with a zero marginal tax rate and no international trade.

The marginal respending rate is influenced by the marginal propensity to consume, the marginal tax rate, and the marginal propensity to import. The greater the marginal respending rate for the economy, the greater the value of the multiplier. In general, the marginal respending rate increases with increases in the marginal propensity to consume, decreases in the marginal tax rate, and decreases in the marginal propensity to import.

The assumptions made in this appendix about the marginal tax rate and the marginal propensities to consume and import are quite close to those that exist for the U.S. economy. The multiplier for injections of spending in the U.S economy is somewhat larger than 2 but less than 3.

Determination of Equilibrium Real GNP: An Algebraic Approach

An algebraic approach can be used to solve for equilibrium real GNP and income. The computations that follow show how to derive a general formula for solving for equilibrium real GNP and income, assuming the price level is fixed and unresponsive to changes in aggregate demand.

The condition for macroeconomic equilibrium is:

$$\text{Aggregate production} = \text{Aggregate purchases}$$

If this condition does not hold, there will be either unintended inventory accumulation or depletion and forces will be set up to either increase or decrease real GNP.

Use the symbol Y for real GNP. Because real GNP is also equal to income, Y also stands for income earned during a year. Aggregate purchases are the sum of consumption purchases (C), planned investment purchases (I_P), government purchases (G), and net exports (NE):

$$\text{Aggregate purchases} = C + I_P + G + NE$$

In equilibrium:

$$Y = C + I_P + G + NE$$

Consumption depends on the consumption function, which may be written in general as:

$$C = A + MPC(DI)$$

where A is autonomous consumption, MPC is the marginal propensity to consume, and DI is disposable income. Assuming the marginal tax rate (t) is constant, disposable income is:

$$DI = (1 - t)Y$$

The consumption function can therefore be written as:

$$C = A + MPC[(1 - t)Y]$$

Both planned investment and government purchases are assumed to be autonomous purchases independent of income. However, net exports, which represent the difference between exports and imports, do depend on Y because imports vary with income. The expression for net exports is:

$$NE = E - MPI(Y)$$

where E is exports and MPI is the marginal propensity to import.

Substituting the preceding equations in the expression for aggregate purchases gives the following equilibrium condition:

$$Y = A + MPC[(1 - t)]Y + I_P + G + [E - MPI(Y)]$$

Solving this equation for Y gives:

$$
\begin{aligned}
Y &= \frac{A + I_P + G + E}{1 - [MPC(1 - t)] + MPI} \\
&= \frac{A + I_P + G + E}{1 - [MPC(1 - t) - MPI]} \\
&= \frac{A + I_P + G + E}{1 - MRR}
\end{aligned}
$$

where MRR is the marginal respending rate for the economy.

To check this formula, substitute the values from the table in Box 1 for the variables in the preceding equation for Y to solve for equilibrium real GNP:

$$Y = \frac{\$(400 + 500 + 1,000 + 400)\text{ billion}}{1 - 0.8(1 - 0.2) + 0.1} = \frac{\$2,300\text{ billion}}{0.46} = \$5,000\text{ billion}$$

which is the same result obtained earlier.

The equilibrium condition derived algebraically shows how real GNP depends on autonomous consumption, planned investment, government purchases, and exports, given the marginal propensities to consume and import and the marginal tax rate in the economy. The equation implies that each extra \$1 of autonomous purchases (A, I_P, G, or E) will result in $1/(1 - MRR)$ dollars of increase in real GNP, which is the multiplier for the economy.

Key Terms and Concepts

Balance of trade deficit

31

Aggregate Supply: Its Influence on Macroeconomic Equilibrium and Economic Growth

What would happen to the economy if our oil supplies were suddenly cut in half? What effect do growing supplies of economic resources, improved technology, and gains in productivity have on macroeconomic equilibrium? How will shifts in aggregate supply over the long run affect your future prosperity? How can the economy suffer from roaring inflation at the same time it's in the throes of an economic contraction or recession? To answer these questions, we must explore macroeconomic supply-side issues.

In the past two chapters we've concentrated on the role of aggregate demand in influencing macroeconomic equilibrium. Aggregate supply also plays an important role in determining macroeconomic equilibrium. In reality, an economy rarely operates in a flat portion of its aggregate supply curve even when it's in equilibrium at a level well below its potential. Steady increases in aggregate demand during a given year are likely to move the economy along the aggregate supply curve that prevails for the year. As this occurs, the outward shifts in aggregate demand will cause inflation when the aggregate supply curve is upward sloping.

Increases in real GNP during recovery periods after mild contractions typically are accompanied by inflation. As an economy moves toward its potential level of real GNP during a year, there is upward pressure on prices. Inflation has persisted in the United States even in periods during which real GNP and employment have been declining!

In this chapter we take an in-depth look at the determinants of aggregate supply and the consequences for the economy of shifts in aggregate supply. We examine influences on aggregate supply over a period of 1 year and over a period of many years. Economic contractions and recessions can be caused by decreases in aggregate supply as well as by decreases in aggregate demand. However, decreases in aggregate supply are also likely to cause the price level to rise. As you'll see, it's quite possible for an economy to suffer from both a recession and inflation when unfavorable shifts in aggregate supply cause an economic contraction!

Shifts in aggregate supply over the long term also imply changes in the economy's potential to produce goods and services. Since 1900 real GNP growth in the United States has averaged 3.1% per year and real GNP per person has risen more than fivefold. Despite the cyclical ups and downs in real GNP over time, there has been a clear upward trend in both productivity and output per person in the U.S. economy over the long haul. Increases in aggregate supply are necessary to allow the output of goods and services to grow in an economy. Short-term shifts in aggregate supply are important in determining cyclical changes in real GNP and the price level. However, long-term shifts in aggregate supply allow the economy to increase its potential to produce goods and services over a period of many years. Such long-term economic growth is necessary to allow improvements in well-being on average while the population is growing.

In this chapter we analyze the sources and consequences of economic growth. We'll see how the social goals of full employment and price stability are important to prevent short-term dislocations in the economy. We'll also see how the social goal of economic growth over the long haul is essential to achieve improvements in the material standard of living in the economy.

After reading this chapter, you should be able to: *Concept Preview*

1   Understand why an increase in aggregate demand can cause the price level to increase even when the economy is operating at a level below full employment.
2   Explain how a wage-price spiral and stagflation can result when an economy overheats.
3   Use aggregate demand and supply analysis to show how an unfavorable supply-side shock can cause a recession and put upward pressure on the price level, thus causing a period of stagflation.
4   Show how an increase in aggregate supply has favorable effects on macroeconomic equilibrium by putting upward pressure on real GNP while at the same time putting downward pressure on the price level.
5   Discuss long-term influences on aggregate supply and explain the economy's long-run aggregate supply curve.
6   Discuss the sources and importance of economic growth as well as its benefits and costs.

The Upward-Sloping Aggregate Supply Curve and Macroeconomic Equilibrium

Typically as an economy moves toward its capacity, unit costs of production will increase. As peak production is approached, it's likely that prices will begin to rise rapidly in a given year in response to steady outward shifts of the aggregate demand curve. This is because the efficiency of plants and offices is impaired as they are operated more intensively. In other words, as you learned in the chapter on the forces of aggregate supply and demand, the aggregate supply curve is likely to be upward sloping.

It's reasonable to assume that increases in aggregate demand will have little effect on the price level when the economy is in a deep recession. However, as aggregate demand increases when the economy moves closer to full employment, it's likely that the equilibrium price level will increase along with equilibrium real GNP.

An upward-sloping aggregate supply curve therefore implies that policies designed to increase aggregate demand and pull an economy out of a recession can also result in inflation, which in turn can cause distortions in decision making that impair the functioning of the economy and result in the capricious redistribution of income we discussed in the chapter entitled "Inflation and Its Consequences."

How an Increase in Aggregate Demand Can Raise the Price Level

The graph in Box 1 depicts the aggregate demand and aggregate supply curves for an economy that is operating below the level of real GNP that corresponds to full employment. The current macroeconomic equilibrium corresponds to point E_1, at which the initial aggregate demand curve and the aggregate supply curve intersect. At the current equilibrium, real GNP is $4,500 billion and the price level is 112 as measured by the value of the GNP deflator that year. The level of real GNP that

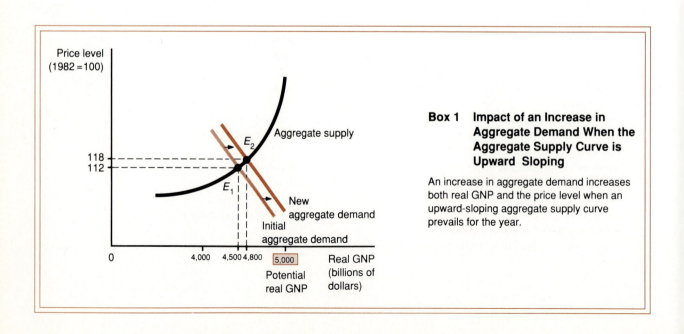

Box 1   Impact of an Increase in Aggregate Demand When the Aggregate Supply Curve is Upward Sloping

An increase in aggregate demand increases both real GNP and the price level when an upward-sloping aggregate supply curve prevails for the year.

corresponds to full employment is $5,000 billion. There is therefore a recessionary GNP gap of $500 billion, reflecting the difference between potential real GNP and equilibrium real GNP. The economy is thus experiencing some cyclical unemployment during the year.

Suppose that at the beginning of the year, because of an improved economic outlook or a reduction in real interest rates, planned investment increases. This shifts the aggregate demand curve outward as aggregate purchases increase, and a multiplier effect on real GNP and real income ensues. However, because the economy is not in a deep recession, it's not possible to expand production during the year without some increase in unit and marginal costs. Therefore the increase in aggregate demand puts upward pressure on the price level. By the end of the year the new macroeconomic equilibrium corresponds to point E_2, at which the price level has increased to 118 and real GNP has increased to $4,800 billion.

As a result of the increase in aggregate demand, the recessionary GNP gap has been narrowed from $500 billion to $200 billion. However, the increase in aggregate demand during the year has also resulted in inflation.[1] The rate of inflation for the year is [(118 − 112)/112]100% = 5.4%. In this case, even though the economy is still experiencing some cyclical unemployment, there has been upward pressure on the price level. The economy is clearly on a recovery path because real GNP increases over the year. Along with the increase in real GNP and the reduction in cyclical unemployment comes inflation of 5.4% as the economy approaches its capacity. It's therefore normal to expect some inflation during the recovery phase for an economy that is approaching its potential real GNP during the year.

Inflationary Gaps and Shifts in Aggregate Supply

Sometimes aggregate demand increases enough so that at the equilibrium level of real GNP, aggregate quantity supplied exceeds potential real GNP. When that happens, the economy booms and inflationary pressures build up. Recall from the preceding chapter that an economy can produce more than its potential real GNP in a year. An *inflationary GNP gap* prevails for the economy when equilibrium real GNP exceeds potential real GNP, which is the level corresponding to full employment in an economy. In the previous chapter you learned that an inflationary gap would put upward pressure on the price level. This in turn would reduce aggregate purchases and aggregate quantity demanded as a new equilibrium was attained, and eventually the inflationary gap would be eliminated. Now, by analyzing shifts in aggregate supply, we can obtain greater insight into what is likely to occur in the economy when an inflationary gap prevails.

The economy operated with an inflationary gap during the late 1960s when the United States was engaged in the Vietnam war. The process of reequilibration that results when an inflationary gap prevails involves shifts in aggregate supply that can cause the economy to experience stagnation or declines in the growth of real GNP at the same time the price level rises.

If the price level increases enough during the year, business firms find it profitable to increase production over the year at levels that actually *exceed* the economy's potential. An economy gets *overheated* when it operates beyond its potential in

---

[1]Recall that the rate of inflation is calculated by taking the difference between the price index for the current year and the price index for the previous year, dividing the result by the price index for the previous year, and multiplying the result by 100 to convert to a percent. In this case the value of the price index in the current year is 118, while its value in the previous year is 112.

---

much the same way an engine can overheat when it's run faster than its potential. When an economy is overheated, factories and offices are worked around the clock. Total labor hours used during the year under such circumstances exceed the level that corresponds to the natural rate of unemployment. This occurs as workers put in overtime and some workers normally out of the labor force are induced to enter as employers are willing to pay bonuses for work during weekends and evenings.

The graph in Box 2 shows the process by which an overheated economy reequilibrates to eventually eliminate an inflationary gap. Suppose at the beginning of the year the economy is in equilibrium at a price level of 120 and a real GNP level of $5,500 billion. Assume that potential real GNP is $5,000 billion. There is now an *inflationary* GNP gap measured by the difference between the equilibrium real GNP of $5,500 billion and the potential real GNP level of $5,000 billion. This $500 billion inflationary GNP gap is illustrated along the horizontal axis. The current equilibrium corresponds to point *E*. During the past year assume that the price level has increased from 112 to 120, implying inflation of just over 7%.

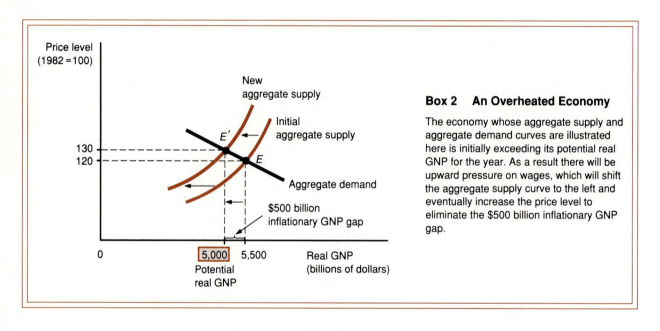

Box 2   An Overheated Economy

The economy whose aggregate supply and aggregate demand curves are illustrated here is initially exceeding its potential real GNP for the year. As a result there will be upward pressure on wages, which will shift the aggregate supply curve to the left and eventually increase the price level to eliminate the $500 billion inflationary GNP gap.

As a result of the higher prices caused by the increase in aggregate demand, workers whose wages have lagged behind the rate of inflation during the past year are likely to demand wage increases as contract talks are opened up again. The labor market is likely to be tight when the economy is overheated, and workers will be in short supply. As a result, employers are likely to grant worker demands for wage increases that allow them to at least keep pace with inflation so their real wages don't decline. Similarly, materials will be in short supply in an overheated economy, and the prices of these inputs will rise over the year. *As a result of increases in wages and other input prices that are likely to take place over the year in an overheated economy, the aggregate supply curve will shift inward.* As this process occurs, the economy will move toward an equilibrium, given the aggregate demand curve, at point *E'*, at which real GNP falls to its potential level. But the decrease in aggregate supply *also* further increases the price level during the following year! Eventually real GNP will decline by $500 billion and the price level will increase from 120 to 130, implying 8% inflation in the next year. Last year's inflation caused the economy to stretch beyond its potential. The wage increases negotiated by workers to keep up with inflation then resulted in cost-push inflation the next year as the aggregate supply curve steadily shifted inward!

Wage-Price Spirals in an Overheated Economy

Whenever aggregate demand is so excessive that it causes an economy to overheat, the result will be an inflationary process. In some cases an economy can remain overheated for a number of years. For example, the U.S. economy was overheated between 1966 and 1968 when the government was engaged in a military buildup for the Vietnam conflict. During those years when equilibrium real GNP exceeded potential real GNP, a process of demand-pull inflation followed by cost-push inflation had the economy in its grips. Between 1965 and 1970 inflation surged. Relatively high inflation continued in 1969 and 1970 despite a brief recession that hit the economy in 1969.

A **wage-price spiral** exists in the economy when higher product prices result in higher wages, which in turn increase prices still further through a decrease in aggregate supply! When a wage-price spiral exists, increases in aggregate demand cause an inflationary GNP gap, which in turn causes wages to increase. The resulting inward shifts of the aggregate supply curve cause further increases in the price level. Further increases in aggregate demand then cause the price level to increase again, and the process starts all over. The process continues until the inflationary gap is eliminated.

The U.S. economy was caught in a wage-price spiral exactly like this during the period from 1966 to 1970. From the beginning of 1966 to the end of 1969 the economy was clearly overheated, with the official unemployment rates over that 4-year period averaging only 3.6%. Workers were in short supply during this period, and it's likely that the economy was exceeding its potential. During this period inflation increased from a mere 2% per year in 1965 to nearly 6% per year in 1970. Each year workers negotiated labor contracts that pushed wages higher. In fact, workers began to anticipate inflation and usually demanded a little more in wages so their nominal wages wouldn't lose purchasing power over the next year. The result was a wage-price spiral. Cost-push inflation followed from the demand-pull inflation that overheated the economy.

Stagflation

Stagflation is the term that has been coined to describe an economy in which real GNP stagnates at a given level or actually declines from one period to the next while inflation ensues at relatively high rates. Stagflation is a combination of stagnation of economic growth in real GNP and rising prices. The process described earlier, as the economy moved from an equilibrium at point E to the one at E' in Box 2, was one of stagflation. After the economy overheated, the consequence was a decrease in aggregate supply, which in turn caused a decrease in real GNP and an increase in the price level, which means stagflation.

Sometimes the decrease in aggregate supply that results after the economy has become overheated can be substantial enough to cause the economy to operate below its level of potential real GNP that corresponds to full employment. As you

Wage-price spiral: Exists when higher product prices result in higher wages, which in turn increase prices still further through a decrease in aggregate supply.

Stagflation: Term coined to describe an economy in which real GNP stagnates at a given level or actually declines from one period to the next while inflation ensues at relatively high rates.

saw earlier, workers often start to anticipate the effect of inflation on their real wages in contract negotiations with employers. When they succeed in getting large nominal wage increases, the aggregate supply curve can shift inward enough to cause equilibrium real GNP to be below potential real GNP. This effect can be compounded, as you'll soon see, when other changes in economic conditions result in further inward shifts of the aggregate supply curve.

Stagflation implies that an economy can suffer from both a recession and inflation at the same time after it has overheated. This is true when the shift in aggregate supply that occurs after a bout of inflation results in an equilibrium real GNP that is below the economy's potential and there is a decline in real GNP over a period of two quarters. For example, during the period 1974-1975 the U.S. economy experienced a recession after achieving huge increases in real GNP of 5% in both 1972 and 1973. In 1974 real GNP declined by 0.5% of its 1973 value, and in 1975 real GNP fell by 1.3% of its 1974 value. The unemployment rate soared to 8.3% of the labor force in 1975. However, at the same time inflation roared at record levels. The rate of inflation measured by the annual percentage change in the consumer price index (CPI) was 11% in 1974 and 9.1% in 1975.

Stagflation occurred again in 1980 when real GNP suffered a slight decline and inflation was in high gear at an annual rate of 13.5%. Then during the severe 1982 recession real GNP fell by 2.5%, and in 1983 unemployment rose to 9.5% while inflation still continued at an annual rate of 6.1% that year.

Stagflation is particularly harmful to consumers because at the same time real GNP declines, so does the purchasing power of the dollar. As people seek to protect themselves against inflation, decision making is distorted in the economy.

To better understand stagflation, our next step is to examine how shifts in aggregate supply can cause a recession.

Supply-Side-Induced Recessions

Supply-side shock:
A sudden and unexpected shift of the aggregate supply curve.

Any shift of the aggregate supply curve prevailing for the economy can influence both real GNP and the price level. In some cases a **supply-side shock** occurs, which is a sudden and unexpected shift of the aggregate supply curve. In 1973, as the economy was reequilibrating from an inflationary gap, it also got socked with a supply-side shock in the form of the OPEC oil embargo that sent the price of a key input skyrocketing.

The reduction in availability of crude oil and the consequent sharp increases in energy prices that followed the oil embargo of 1973 are a prime example of a supply-side shock. The result was an inward shift of the economy's aggregate supply curve. In 1979 higher oil prices caused another unexpected and unfavorable supply-side shock that also raised prices and decreased real GNP.

The graph in Box 3 shows how the economy reacts to an unfavorable supply-side shock. Suppose the economy is initially in equilibrium at a real GNP of $5,000 billion and a price level of 120 at point E. The increase in the price of oil shifts the aggregate supply curve inward. The economy adjusts during the year by moving to a new equilibrium at point E'. At the new equilibrium the price level increases to 140, implying an annual inflation rate of 16.7%.[2] Steady inward shifts of the aggregate supply curve over a year, given aggregate demand, can therefore initiate a process of inflation. At the same time real GNP declines from its initial level of $5,000

---

[2]Rate of inflation = $[(140 - 120)/120]100\% = 16.7\%$.

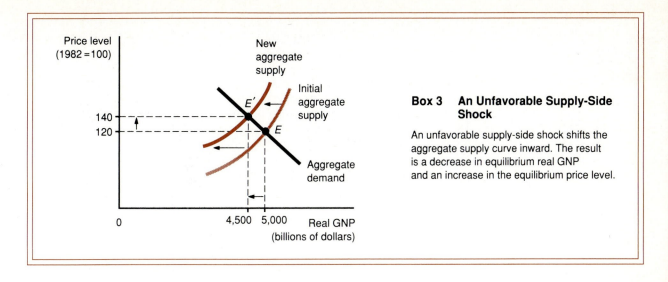

Box 3   An Unfavorable Supply-Side Shock

An unfavorable supply-side shock shifts the aggregate supply curve inward. The result is a decrease in equilibrium real GNP and an increase in the equilibrium price level.

billion to a new level of $4,500 billion. The supply-side shock therefore reduces real GNP, thus contributing to cyclical unemployment at the same time that the annual inflation rate roars at 17%. This type of supply-side shock results in stagflation at its worst. Not only does the economy experience high inflation, it also plunges into a contraction or recession during the year.

Policymakers in the mid-1980s remained concerned about possible future supply-side shocks of this nature because since 1980 the United States had become increasingly dependent on foreign sources of supply for petroleum products. A sharp rise in oil prices in the future could once again result in stagflation!

Favorable Supply-Side Shocks

Supply-side shocks can also be favorable to the economy. For example, increased availability of crude oil in 1986 resulted in lower energy prices. This contributed to

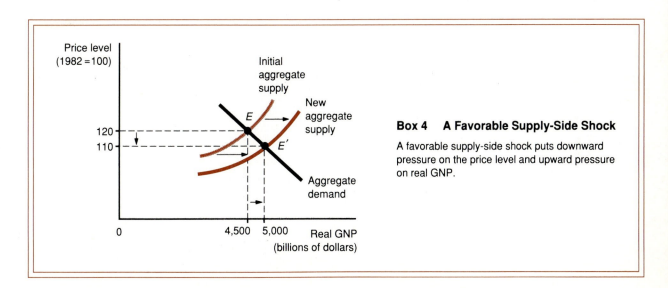

Box 4   A Favorable Supply-Side Shock

A favorable supply-side shock puts downward pressure on the price level and upward pressure on real GNP.

an outward shift of the aggregate supply curve during the year. As a result, inflation moderated in 1986, falling to an annual rate of only 1.9% mainly as a result of declines in the prices of fuels. Remember from the analysis of the causes of shifts in aggregate supply in the chapter on the forces of aggregate supply and demand that any *decrease* in input prices will shift the aggregate supply curve outward just as an increase in input prices shifts it inward. This is because a decrease in input prices increases the profitability of supplying final products for any given price level.

The graph in Box 4 illustrates the effect of a favorable supply-side shock. Such a shift can be caused by a decrease in the price of a key input, discovery of new resources for an economy, or an increase in the supply of labor. The rightward shift of the aggregate supply curve tends to increase real GNP and decrease the price level.

Concept Check

1. Under what circumstances will the price level increase in response to an increase in aggregate demand even when the economy is in a recession?

2. How can stagflation result when an economy becomes overheated? Show how a supply-side shock can cause the economy to suffer from both a recession and inflation.

3. Show the effects of a favorable supply-side shock on macroeconomic equilibrium.

Long-Run Aggregate Supply and How It Shifts: Economic Growth and Its Sources

There are always periods of recession, but their effects tend to be offset occasionally by boom periods during which the economy exceeds its potential. Over a long period *on average* real GNP grows along with growth in potential real GNP. However, because of the tendency for prices to rise more in expansion periods than they fall during periods of contraction, the price level also rises along with the growth in real GNP.

The long-run aggregate supply curve, first discussed in the chapter on the forces of aggregate supply and demand, shows the relationship between the price level and real GNP that would prevail if wages and prices had enough time to adjust so as to eliminate any recessionary or inflationary GNP gaps. This supply curve is a vertical line corresponding to the level of real GNP for which the economy attains the natural rate of unemployment, as shown in the graph in Box 5. This curve is sometimes called the "classical" aggregate supply curve because it is the one the pre-Keynesian classical economists of the nineteenth century assumed would prevail for the economy. These economists mainly analyzed long-term performance of the economy and explained the causes of recessions primarily in terms of delays in downward adjustment of wages and prices. Because adjustments in wages and prices over long periods would eventually return the economy to full employment, the classical economists did not propose policies to deal with eliminating recessionary gaps as Keynes did.

In other words, the long-run aggregate supply curve is the one that would prevail if the economy's self-correction mechanism first discussed in the chapter on the forces of aggregate supply and demand were reliable and had enough time to work.

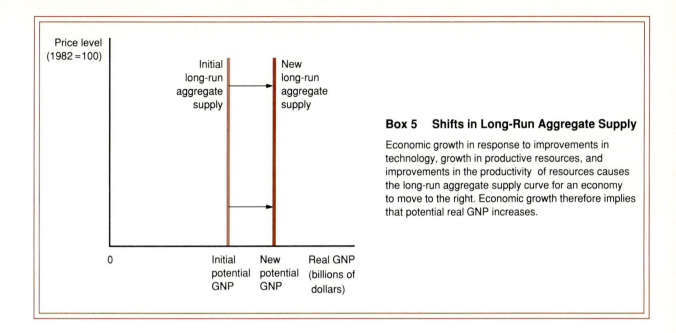

Box 5   Shifts in Long-Run Aggregate Supply

Economic growth in response to improvements in technology, growth in productive resources, and improvements in the productivity of resources causes the long-run aggregate supply curve for an economy to move to the right. Economic growth therefore implies that potential real GNP increases.

A long-run aggregate supply curve *cannot* be used to understand the impact on the economy of short-run cyclical shifts of the aggregate demand curve. The vertical aggregate supply curve shows that on average, increases in aggregate demand will not increase real GNP above the level corresponding to full employment for long periods. Instead, over the long run, increases in aggregate demand that cause the economy to overheat will result in inflation that will increase the price level, as you saw earlier.

In the long run, an increase in real GNP is possible only if potential real GNP increases. When potential GNP increases, the long-run aggregate supply curve shifts outward, as shown in Box 5. In the long run, increases in productive potential arise only from improvements in productivity, resource availability, technology, and other supply-side forces. Although the economy occasionally produces more than potential GNP over the short run when aggregate demand increases, an increase in aggregate demand cannot permanently increase output beyond potential GNP over the long run. Temporary inflationary GNP gaps are eventually eliminated over the long run by increases in wages and prices.

Reductions in aggregate demand might never reduce the price level enough to get to points on the long-run aggregate supply curve! This is because even over relatively long periods, downward rigidity in prices and wages can prevent the economy's self-correction mechanism from working. This is what Keynes had in mind when he said: "In the long run we are all dead." Recessions often require short-run action to increase aggregate demand because the long-run self-correction mechanism of the economy doesn't work well in the downward direction!

Shifts in Long-Run Aggregate Supply: Economic Growth and Its Sources

The long-run aggregate supply curve indicates the nation's potential (or full-employment) level of real GNP. Outward shifts of the long-run aggregate supply curve imply growth in potential and equilibrium real GNP on average over time. *Economic growth* in a nation is the annual percentage increase in its level of real GNP. Economic growth is the key to improvements in a nation's standard of living. Since 1900 real GNP growth in the United States has averaged 3.1% per year. Thus the nation's ability to produce goods and services historically has increased at slightly more than 3% per year since 1900. The table in Box 6 shows the growth rates for real GNP in the United States for selected years from 1933 to 1987.

Box 6   Annual Growth Rate of Real GNP Measured in 1982 Dollars: 1933-1987

Year	Growth rate	Year	Growth rate
1933	−2.1	1965	5.8
1939	7.9	1966	5.8
		1967	2.9
1940	7.8	1968	4.1
1941	17.7	1969	2.4
1942	18.8		
1943	18.1	1970	−.3
1944	8.2	1971	2.8
1945	−1.9	1972	5.0
1946	−19.0	1973	5.2
1947	−2.8	1974	−.5
1948	3.9	1975	−1.3
1949	0	1976	4.9
		1977	4.7
1950	8.5	1978	5.3
1951	10.3	1979	2.5
1952	3.9		
1953	4.0	1980	−.2
1954	−1.3	1981	1.9
1955	5.6	1982	−2.5
1956	2.1	1983	3.6
1957	1.7	1984	6.4
1958	−.8	1985	2.7
1959	5.8	1986	2.5
		1987	2.9
1960	2.2		
1961	2.6		
1962	5.3		
1963	4.1		
1964	5.3		

Source: *Economic Report of the President*, 1988.

Increases in aggregate demand contribute to short-term economic growth. This is because growing aggregate demand gives businesses the confidence necessary to make investments that expand the economy's productive capacity. Annual shifts in aggregate demand therefore exert an influence on the year-to-year performance of the economy. But ultimately the growth of an economy depends on expansion of its productive capacity and is therefore a supply-side phenomenon. Growth in aggregate demand can prevent an economy from falling into a recession and can occasionally cause the economy to exceed its potential temporarily. But the real engine of economic growth is an outward-shifting aggregate supply curve. To understand

Growth in Real GNP per Person and Its Correlation with Growth in Labor Productivity

As Americans, we're fortunate to live in a country where abundant resources and generally steady growth in productivity contribute to improvements in the standard of living. However, our past good fortune shouldn't cause us to be complacent about the future. Some caution may be called for.

The upward trend in real GNP in the United States indicates that on average the economy over time increases its output of goods and services per year. The impact of changes in real GNP on living standards in the nation can be gauged by dividing real GNP by current population in each year. The resulting measure gives real GNP per person and thus provides an indicator of goods and services available per person. More goods and services per person indicate a higher standard of living on average.

The graph shows the growth in real GNP per person measured in 1982 dollars. There's a clear upward trend in per capita real GNP. However, there are also cyclical ups and downs associated with per person output. The deep dip in real GNP per person during the Great Depression of the 1930s is clearly identifiable, as are less serious dips associated with other recessions. Also notice how the upward trend in the curve has been dampened somewhat since the 1974 to 1975 recession.

The table shows growth in real GNP and growth in real GNP per person for three periods since the end of World War II. The data document a disturbing decline in growth rates of real GNP and real GNP per capita. Growth was more rapid between 1948 and 1973 than it has been since. Over that period real GNP grew at a faster rate than its historical average of 3.1% per year. During the same period, real GNP per capita grew by 2.2% per year, which means that on average U.S. citizens enjoyed 2.2% more goods per year over that period. Also note from the table that over the same period, labor productivity growth, as measured by output per hour of all persons employed by business firms, increased at the rate of 2.8% per year.

GNP and Productivity Growth, 1948-86 (average annual percentage change)

Period	Real GNP	Real per capita GNP	Labor productivity*
1948-1973	3.7	2.2	2.8
1973-1981	2.2	1.1	.7
1981-1986	2.5	1.5	1.2

*Output per hour of all persons engaged in the business sector.
Sources: Department of Commerce (Bureau of Economic Analysis), Department of Labor (Bureau of Labor Statistics), and Council of Economic Advisers.

In the period after 1973 there was a very sharp drop in the growth rate of labor productivity. Between 1973 and 1981 labor productivity growth in the business sector averaged only 0.7% per year—one quarter its rate of growth in the previous period. The annual growth in real GNP also fell substantially during that period, and the annual growth of real GNP per person was halved. Since 1981 there has been some recovery in the annual growth rate of labor productivity, but it is still less than half the annual rate of growth that prevailed between 1948 and 1973. Notice, however, how annual growth in real GNP and real GNP per capita also increased after labor productivity growth increased. However, the annual growth in real GNP between 1981 and 1986 remains below the historical annual trend rate of 3.1%. Similarly, the annual growth in real GNP per capita is still below the annual growth rates that prevailed between 1948 and 1973.

Although there are factors other than overall labor productivity in the business sector that influence the growth of real GNP, the correlation between real GNP growth per capita and productivity growth is clear. To maintain the upward trend in growth in real GNP and living standards of U.S. citizens, it is crucial to maintain productivity growth.

Per capita GNP
(1982 dollars)

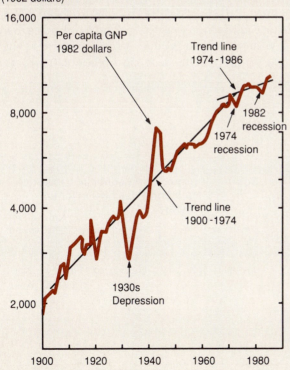

the long-term sources of growth, we therefore need to examine the important influences on a nation's long-run aggregate supply curve.

The major influences on long-run aggregate supply and the nation's potential to produce goods and services are:

1. *The productive resources available to the nation.* The labor, capital equipment, natural resources, and other inputs available in any year influence aggregate supply and productive potential. The more workers and equipment available, given population and natural resources in a nation, the greater the nation's productive potential. An increase in the availability of economic resources will shift the long-run aggregate supply curve outward and increase potential real GNP, as shown in Box 5.

2. *The quality of productive resources available to the nation.* The quality of a productive resource is measured by its **productivity,** which is a measure of output per unit of input. The more productive workers, natural resources (such as agricultural land), and capital equipment are in a nation, the greater the real GNP possible from a given amount of productive resources. Because labor is the dominant productive input, labor productivity growth is a key to economic growth. When output per worker increases in a nation, output per person also tends to go up! Therefore steady growth in labor productivity ensures steady growth in the final products per person and in the material well-being of individuals in the nation. Improvements in the quality of inputs thus can also shift the long-run aggregate supply curve outward.

3. *Improvements in technology.* As technology advances, the output available from a given quantity of productive resources also increases. Technological progress requires investment in research and development.

4. *Improvements in the efficiency with which available inputs are used.* Policies that promote efficiency in resource use allow the economy to obtain the greatest possible output of final products from available resources. Changes in management or policies that reduce waste in production and conserve resources can therefore contribute to increases in the economy's productive potential.

Productivity:
A measure of output per unit of input.

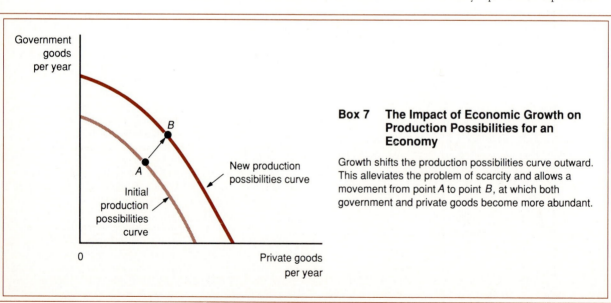

Box 7   The Impact of Economic Growth on Production Possibilities for an Economy

Growth shifts the production possibilities curve outward. This alleviates the problem of scarcity and allows a movement from point *A* to point *B*, at which both government and private goods become more abundant.

A favorable change in any of the preceding factors can be viewed as shifting the nation's production possibilities curve outward (see Chapter 3). As the nation enjoys improvements in the quality of resources, the quantity available, or technology, its potential to produce any combination of goods also increases. The production possibilities curve drawn in Box 7 illustrates the economy's potential to produce two broad classes of goods: private goods available to individuals and business firms for their own exclusive use and government goods whose benefits are shared by all. You can see that growth helps deal with the problem of scarcity by allowing an increase in both government goods and private goods as the economy moves from point *A* to point *B*.

Improvements in Productivity

As suggested earlier, a key to the growth process is annual improvements in labor productivity. Output per worker will go up when worker skills or education improves or when workers have improved tools to work with. Because workers gain more experience as they spend more time on their jobs, productivity growth can also be influenced by the age composition of the labor force. When the percentage of the labor force comprised of younger workers (say, less than 25 years of age) increases, productivity can be adversely affected because of the influx of inexperienced workers.

Improvements in technology allow a given amount of capital or natural resources to be more productive when used by a labor force of given size. The sources of growth just listed therefore are not independent. Steady improvements in the quality of resources depend on steady improvements in technology and steady growth in capital per worker. Improvements in the quality of management of workers can also improve their productivity. Better productive management can improve the division of labor in ways that generate more output from a given work force. Improvements in personnel management procedures can give workers incentives to learn more skills and to produce more efficiently. There is an important *allocative* component to economic growth that is influenced by both business management techniques and public policies. In any given year growth is greater when resources are used in ways that allow maximum output to be squeezed from available inputs.

The Sources of Growth, 1929-1982

According to recent estimates, improvements in labor productivity have accounted for over two thirds of the growth in real GNP over the period 1929 to 1982.[3] The remaining third has been accounted for by increases in the quantity of labor available. Research by Edward Denison indicates that the most important factor influencing improvements in labor productivity over that period has been technological advance. Improvements in the technology of production and of management in the United States have been estimated to account for nearly 40% of the improvement in labor productivity. Keep in mind that it takes considerable business investment to create new technology, so technological advance and investment are not unrelated. Technological improvement results in new and better equipment, machines, and techniques that enhance worker productivity. New computers, machines, and modes

---

[3]Edward F. Denison, *Trends in American Economic Growth 1929-1982,* Washington, D.C.: The Brookings Institution, 1985.

of transport, such as jet travel, have made workers much more productive in recent years.

Increases in the amount of capital available to workers, according to Denison, account for nearly 30% of the increase in labor productivity. Another 21% is accounted for by improved education and training. The bulk of the gains in labor productivity are therefore accounted for by improvements in technology, growth in capital equipment, and better education and training.

Labor Force Participation and the Natural Rate of Unemployment: Influence on Long-Run Aggregate Supply

An increase in labor hours worked per year contributes to growth in real GNP. Potential GNP depends on the availability of workers in the economy and the labor force participation rate. Typically in the United States only 65% of the noninstitutional population aged 16 and over participates in the labor force. The remainder goes to school, is unable or unwilling to work for a variety of reasons, or chooses to engage in full-time household pursuits. Hours worked during the year also depend on the unemployment rate during the year. During recessions output falls and unemployment rises.

However, the economy's potential to produce goods and services depends on the natural rate of unemployment, which is the percentage of the labor force that can be expected to be unemployed for reasons other than cyclical declines in real GNP. The natural rate of unemployment is likely to vary with the age composition of the labor force. Younger workers are more likely to quit jobs than older workers. This is because it naturally takes time for young workers to find the right job. Younger workers are less likely to have families to support and can tolerate longer periods of unemployment than mature workers. The lower the average age of workers in a nation, the higher the natural rate of unemployment.

The natural rate of unemployment was believed to be high in the late 1970s because the "baby boom" generation born during the early 1950s began to enter the labor market. The average age of workers was at an all-time low during the late 1970s. This contributed to high quit rates and higher frictional unemployment. As the baby boom generation ages and the average age of workers goes up in the 1990s, the natural rate of unemployment should fall. This will tend to increase the economy's potential to produce goods and services.

The extent of structural unemployment in the economy also influences potential real GNP. Structural unemployment results from changes in both technology and the pattern of demand that occur in an economy adjusting to changes. For example, as U.S. manufacturing industries adapt to increased foreign competition and the challenge of adopting new technologies, as was the case in the mid-1980s, it's likely that structural unemployment will rise. A rise in structural unemployment means more workers must learn new skills to find employment. In a period of rapid change, therefore, the growth rate of potential real GNP is likely to be slowed because of higher structural unemployment.

Saving, Investment, and Economic Growth

A nation's growth rate is influenced by the portion of national income that is invested. The process of investment involves the sacrifice of current consumption so that resources can be devoted to creating new capital, technology, or skills that will increase productivity and income in the future.

The Costs vs. the Benefits of Economic Growth

Can economic growth in a nation be anything other than a positive development? Can it actually have a down side? Let's see why the answer to these questions is "yes," and let's examine some of the negative consequences of economic growth.

Increases in output per capita benefit people in a nation by allowing higher average levels of material well-being over the long run. Such growth means more job opportunities for workers, and means tax revenue can increase without increases in tax rates. Growth causes an outward shift of the nation's production possibilities curve that allows the economy to have more of both government goods and private goods. This allows a nation the luxury of using government services to deal with social problems without increasing tax rates.

But what about the costs of growth? More output each year can mean more pollution, more stress, and the development of a materialistic philosophy. Preoccupation with growth can prevent social progress that improves job safety and human health. Growth-oriented politicians are likely to oppose social programs that increase business costs if these programs slow growth in output.

Human well-being doesn't depend entirely on growth in real GNP. Many of the amenities of life are not included in real GNP. In fact, some of the costs of economic growth require expenditures of funds to solve problems like congestion and pollution. These expenditures to offset the side effects of growth are actually included in real GNP.

It's clear that social programs designed to cope with pollution, congestion, income inequality, and abuse of worker rights do slow down the rate of economic growth. Estimates by Denison conclude that improvements in the legal and human environment stemming from government regulations and other programs to control the social costs of growth contributed to a decline in economic growth in 1973 and 1976.* A tradeoff clearly exists between growth and policies to correct its undesirable effects. People must decide if they are willing to give up some of the material benefits of economic growth in exchange for increased allocation of resources to correct the social problems of a growing economy.

*Edward F. Denison, *Trends in American Economic Growth 1929-1982*, Washington, D.C.: The Brookings Institution, 1985.

Business investment requires the outlay of funds that are obtained in financial markets or through capital consumption allowances or retained earnings. Capital consumption allowances (depreciation) are a form of saving through which businesses finance investment by setting aside earnings to replace worn-out or obsolete capital. Retained earnings are savings of corporations that are used to finance acquisition of capital goods. Personal saving is also used to finance investment as it is channeled through financial markets to investors who borrow funds to make investments.

Investment in *human* capital often requires that people forgo the opportunity for current income by attending colleges, universities, or training institutes. When people study to obtain new skills they give up the opportunity for current consumption in the hope that the extra education and skills they acquire in school will allow them to enjoy more annual future consumption than they sacrifice per year while in school.

The Tradeoff Between Current and Future Consumption: The Importance of Saving in Encouraging Economic Growth

The process of economic growth depends on the willingness of people in a nation to give up current consumption in exchange for the opportunity for greater future consumption. The funds and labor hours allocated to investment can be used to develop new technology, new factories and equipment, and more productive labor

---

that will increase future real GNP. Of course, all investment entails risks, and the actual payoff to investment is uncertain.

A nation with a greater saving rate each year will be more likely to have a higher growth rate of output per capita over the long run than a nation with a lower saving rate. But a high saving rate can exert downward pressure on aggregate demand in a given year when the business outlook is poor and saving exceeds intended investment. High saving can thus exert downward pressure on equilibrium real GNP in some years because by itself it detracts from aggregate demand. Over the long run, however, when the ups and downs of the business cycle average out, high saving will be matched by high investment rates. High saving over the long run will contribute to growth in productive capacity for the nation and increased future output per capita. It follows that outward shifts in a nation's long-run aggregate supply curve are likely to be correlated with a nation's rate of saving measured by the portion of real income not consumed or used to pay taxes annually.

Macroeconomic Equilibrium in a Growing Economy

The forces that cause the long-run aggregate supply curve to shift to the right will also cause rightward shifts of the aggregate supply curve that prevails for a given year. In a growing economy both the aggregate demand and aggregate supply curves will shift outward to the right yearly. Normally, assuming there are no unanticipated supply-side shocks, the process of economic growth results in fairly steady increases in aggregate supply. There will, of course, be occasional cyclical downturns in aggregate demand. However, as population and income grow, aggregate demand on average also increases as the increased aggregate income in the economy results in more purchases by households, businesses, and government.

In any given year the changes in equilibrium real GNP and the price level depend on how far out aggregate demand shifts relative to the outward shift in aggregate supply resulting from increases in the labor force or increases in labor productivity. This is illustrated in the graph in Box 8. If aggregate supply were fixed, the increase

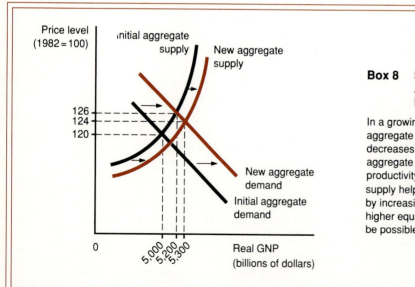

Box 8   Shifts in Aggregate Demand and Aggregate Supply in a Growing Economy

In a growing economy both aggregate demand and aggregate supply increase yearly. Despite cyclical decreases in aggregate demand, on average, aggregate demand increases. Economic growth in productivity means that outward shifts in aggregate supply help dampen inflationary pressures caused by increasing aggregate demand and also result in higher equilibrium real GNP than would otherwise be possible.

in aggregate demand that occurs during the year would increase the price level from 120 to 126 and equilibrium real GNP would increase from $5,000 billion to $5,200 billion. However, because aggregate supply also shifts outward, the price level ends up increasing to only 124 during the year and real GNP increases to $5,300 billion. As you can see, outward shifts in aggregate supply resulting from normal economic growth have favorable effects on macroeconomic equilibrium:

1. Supply-side shifts resulting from economic growth serve to moderate inflationary pressures as outward shifts in aggregate supply offset the upward pressure on the price level resulting from outward shifts in aggregate demand.
2. Supply-side shifts resulting from economic growth increase real GNP beyond the equilibrium level that would result from normal increases in aggregate demand.

Of course, in a given year what actually happens to aggregate demand depends on the spending plans of households, businesses, and governments. In some years aggregate demand shifts outward more quickly than aggregate supply does. When that is the case the inflationary pressures from increased aggregate demand will be strong. In years when there is little economic growth, increases in aggregate demand can result in substantial inflationary pressure that can overheat the economy. Given the rate of growth in aggregate supply, the more rapid the outward shift of the aggregate demand curve for the economy, the greater the rate of inflation and the more likely it is that the economy will overheat.

Increases in productivity and the labor force also tend to increase potential real GNP. When increases in productivity and other positive supply-side influences are shifting the aggregate supply curve outward, it's less likely that an increase in aggregate demand will overheat the economy.

Concept Check

1 Explain why increases in aggregate demand cannot increase real GNP over the long term.
2 List four major influences on economic growth that can cause the long-run aggregate supply curve to shift outward.
3 How can steady growth in aggregate supply moderate inflationary pressures in an economy?

Summary

1. The economy is likely to operate in a flat portion of its aggregate supply curve over a given year only if there is excessive unemployment and excess productive capacity. When the economy is operating closer to its potential, steady increases in aggregate demand are likely to cause inflation during a given year as the economy moves along the upward-sloping portion of its aggregate supply curve.
2. When the economy produces beyond its potential, an inflationary GNP gap prevails. When the economy overheats in this way and workers are in short supply, wage levels are likely to be renegotiated. As wage levels and other input prices increase, the aggregate supply curve prevailing for the year shifts inward. Continual inward shifts of the aggregate supply curve cause a process of cost-push infla-

tion. A wage-price spiral exists when higher prices result in higher wage levels, which then shift the aggregate supply curve inward and result in still higher prices.

3. A supply-side shock is a sudden and unexpected shift of the aggregate supply curve prevailing for the year. A decrease in aggregate supply caused by an increase in the price of a key input can throw the economy into a recession. A favorable supply-side shock shifts the aggregate supply curve outward and puts upward pressure on real GNP and downward pressure on the price level.

4. A long-run aggregate supply curve shows the relationship between the price level and real GNP that would prevail if wages and prices had enough time to adjust so as to eliminate any inflationary or recessionary GNP gaps. As the productive potential of the economy increases, the long-run aggregate supply curve shifts to the right.

5. Economic growth is the annual percentage change in real GNP in a nation.

6. The important sources of economic growth are increases in the quantity and quality of economic resources, improvements in technology, and more efficient resource use.

7. Improvement in labor productivity is a driving force behind economic growth. Improvements in worker skills, education, or the capital that workers use can improve their productivity. Estimates indicate that improvements in labor productivity accounted for over two thirds of the growth in real GNP from 1929 to 1982.

8. Decreases in the natural rate of unemployment can increase potential real GNP, thereby shifting the long-run aggregate supply curve outward.

9. The process of investment involves the sacrifice of current consumption so that resources can be devoted to creating new capital, technology, or skills that will increase productivity and therefore increase real GNP and real income in the future.

Key Terms and Concepts

Wage-price spiral	Supply-side shock
Stagflation	Productivity

Problems and Applications

1. Explain why increases in aggregate demand are more likely to cause a process of inflation in an economy that is close to full employment than in an economy with high cyclical unemployment.

2. Real GNP is currently $4,500 billion, and potential GNP is $4,600 billion. At the beginning of the year new labor contracts are negotiated that increase the general level of wages in the economy by 10%. Other things being equal, show the impact of the new labor contracts on the aggregate supply curve. What effect will the shift in the aggregate supply curve have on macroeconomic equilibrium?

3. An improvement in technology increases labor productivity in the economy. Show the impact of the improvement on the economy's long-run aggregate supply curve. Why is the economy less likely to overheat in response to an increase in aggregate demand after the improvement in technology is adopted?

4. In the next 10 years the average age of workers in the labor force will increase.

Workers are expected to be more experienced and better educated in the future. What effects are the improvements in the quality of the labor force likely to have on aggregate supply and macroeconomic equilibrium?

5. The economy is currently operating with a recessionary GNP gap of about $500 billion. Under what circumstances can economic policies designed to eliminate the recessionary gap cause a wage-price spiral?

6. Potential real GNP is $5,000 billion per year. A surge in aggregate demand causes an equilibrium level of real GNP equal to $5,500 billion for the year. Show how the resulting inflationary gap will be eliminated over a period of time by a shift of the aggregate supply curve.

7. Suppose an international disturbance disrupts shipment of petroleum products into the United States. As a consequence, the price of energy resources increases sharply. Forecast the impact of the increase in energy prices on aggregate supply and macroeconomic equilibrium. Show how, if the price increase is severe enough, it can cause a recession coupled with very high inflation. Why would a nation like Japan have to be very concerned about supply-side shocks resulting from increases in the price of petroleum?

8. Under what circumstances would an economy always achieve a macroeconomic equilibrium corresponding to points on its long-run aggregate supply curve?

9. Suppose wages and prices are completely and instantaneously flexible for the economy. What would happen if aggregate demand increased? How does price and wage rigidity prevent the economy from achieving equilibrium on its long-run aggregate supply curve?

10. Explain why in reality both aggregate demand and aggregate supply tend to increase yearly. Use aggregate demand and supply analysis to show how an increase in the rate of outward shift of the economy's aggregate supply curve prevailing each year will help keep inflation down while putting upward pressure on equilibrium real GNP and potential real GNP.

Suggested Readings

Robert J. Gordon, *Macroeconomics*, 4th ed., Boston: Little, Brown, 1987. Chapter 10 discusses supply-side shocks in detail and analyzes possible policy responses to alleviate their unfavorable effects on the economy.

Arthur M. Okun, *Prices and Quantities: A Macroeconomic Analysis,* Washington, D.C.: The Brookings Institution, 1981. This is an analysis of macroeconomic equilibrium and aggregate supply that evaluates policies to stabilize the economy.

A Forward Look

In the next part of the book we provide an analysis of money, banking, and financial markets. In the following chapter we look at the functions of money and the demand for it. The goal will be to explain how fluctuations in the stock of money available in the economy can affect interest rates, the availability of credit, and aggregate demand.

Career Profile

SAUL STEINBERG

Although he is probably best known to the public for his takeover and investment activities, Saul Steinberg is at heart an insurance man who urges his industry to better educate itself about the fundamentals of its business.

He's made a firm commitment to teaching insurer personnel those fundamentals by pioneering a center for advanced insurance education, which will focus on helping insurance people develop better management skills and more knowledge about the basics of their business. Perhaps because of his background in economics, Steinberg is particularly interested in finding out the exact costs and revenues associated with various parts of the insurance business.

Steinberg has been in the business since 1968 when he bought Reliance Insurance Company. He's built it into Reliance Group Holdings, Inc., a financial services company with 1987 revenues of $3.4 billion. Premiums of life, property and casualty, and mortgage and title insurance accounted for nearly $2.8 billion of that total. He is chairman and chief executive officer of Reliance Group, as well as the company's largest stockholder.

Steinberg is noted for his investment skill. One of his tactics involves Reliance buying significant shares of companies that have the potential for major growth. Sometimes members of Reliance's management serve on the boards of those companies to protect the holding company's investment. In this way Steinberg got involved with the troubled insurance brokerage company, Frank B. Hall, and eventually was named its chief executive officer.

Steinberg is confident he can turn that company around by doing just what he preaches—focusing on the basics. He's planned major education campaigns for all Hall employees, has trimmed down the company's business, and has his eye on the bottom line, which is something he fears many insurers forget to watch.

Steinberg was born in New York in 1939. He earned a bachelor's degree in economics in 1959 from The Wharton School of the University of Pennsylvania, where he currently serves on the Board of Overseers and the Board of Trustees.

In the future, Steinberg hopes to break into the Japanese insurance market by developing partnerships with Japanese companies. For now, insurance, investments, and the many other businesses Reliance is involved in (including a Spanish-language television network and real estate holdings) keep Steinberg more than busy.

PART VIII

Money, Financial Markets, and Macroeconomic Equilibrium

The Functions of Money

Money might not make the world go round, to paraphrase the lyrics of a popular song, but it sure does lubricate the wheels of exchange. Up to this point, little has been said about the functions of money in the economy. In this chapter we'll explore the functions of money and how the amount in circulation can be measured. We'll examine why people and businesses hold money as an asset at any given point in time rather than using it to make purchases of goods or financial assets such as stocks and bonds. You'll also see how, given the demand for money as an asset, changes in the stock of money available can affect interest rates. Because interest rates are important determinants of investment purchases, changes in the demand for money or the amount of money in circulation can affect aggregate demand.

The amount of money in circulation is important because it can affect credit availability, aggregate demand, and the price level in the economy. In the next two chapters we'll show how the nation's banking system affects the quantity of money and credit available. Finally, you'll see how changes in the supply of money can affect the performance of the economy by influencing interest rates over the short run, aggregate demand, and the price level over the long run. The control of the nation's money supply by the Federal Reserve System, the nation's central banking authority, is a major means used to stabilize the economy by influencing aggregate demand.

A prerequisite to understanding the role of money in the economy is an appropriate definition of the concept. Money is often confused with income, capital, and other inputs. The definition of money we develop in this chapter emphasizes the functions it serves. Many items, ranging from precious metals to cigarettes, can be and have been used as money. In most modern societies, however, commodities such as gold or silver are rarely used as money. Instead money usually consists mainly of paper currency issued by governments and deposits in checking accounts at banks that are accepted as a means of making payments for goods and services.

1   List the four major functions of money in the economy.
2   Discuss the major components of the stock of money in an economy.
3   Explain the concept of near money and the official measures of the U.S. money stock and liquid assets held by the public.
4   Discuss the determinants of the demand to hold money.
5   Explain how, given the demand for money, changes in the available stock of money can affect credit and interest rates and influence spending decisions.
6   Explain how, given the stock of money, changes in the demand for money can affect interest rates.

What Is Money and What Are Its Functions?

Money is something you've been familiar with throughout your life. In fact, you may already consider yourself an expert on the subject of money. You regularly use money measures of the value of things you own, and you also hold some of it in the form of currency in your pocket and in bank accounts. It might surprise you to learn that there's a great deal of disagreement among economists about what money is and how to measure it. Money serves a number of functions, and any definition of money must consider all of its functions.

The four major functions of money are:

1. A medium of exchange
2. A standard of value
3. A standard of deferred payment
4. A store of value

It's useful to begin our analysis of the fascinating concept of money by looking into its functions.

1. *Medium of exchange.* As a generally accepted medium of exchange, money eliminates the need for barter. You'll recall that barter is the direct exchange of one item for another (see Chapter 6). Barter is a very inconvenient means of trading because it requires the *double coincidence of wants.* This means that a trader with a good or service to offer must search for a buyer who has exactly what the trader desires. For example, if a baker with a surplus of bread wants meat, he must search for a butcher who wants bread. Because money is generally accepted as payment for any purchase, the baker who sells his bread for money can use the money to buy meat or anything else he wishes. Money facilitates specialization and the division of labor in an economy by avoiding the inconvenience of barter. As a generally accepted medium of exchange, money cuts down on the transaction costs of trading.
2. *Standard of value.* Money provides a unit of account (in the United States it's the dollar) that serves as a standard to measure value. The value of an item is a measure of what a person will sacrifice to obtain it. How much is a 2-week vacation in Hawaii worth to you? If you're like most people, you'll probably respond to such a question by valuing the vacation in dollars—say $2,000—rather

than in terms of other things (like your car) you might give up for the vacation. Money provides a convenient measure of the value of any item. All prices are expressed in monetary units, such as dollars. Whether or not you're conscious of it, you're constantly valuing items in dollars. You measure your income and the value of items you own in terms of dollars. You measure the opportunity cost of most of your purchases in dollar values of expenditure on other things. As a *standard of value,* money allows the addition of values of such diverse items as automobiles, haircuts, and all other goods and services. The concept of GNP would be useless without a standard of value such as the dollar.

3. *Standard of deferred payment.* Many contracts involve promises to pay sums of money in the future. The unit of account for *deferred payment* of debts is also money. For example, if you borrow money to buy a car, the loan contract specifies how much money you must pay back per month and the number of months required to satisfy your obligation to the lender. It would be difficult to obtain credit if money didn't exist. However, money serves its function as a standard of deferred payment only if its purchasing power remains fairly constant over time. If the price level rises, the future purchasing power of money over time will decline. Similarly, a decrease in the price level will increase the future purchasing power of money.

4. *Store of value.* Money can also serve as an asset that provides a store of value that can be quickly converted to goods and services. Money as the actual medium of exchange is completely *liquid,* meaning it can instantaneously be converted to goods and services without any inconvenience or cost. Other assets that serve as stores of value, such as stocks, bonds, or real estate, must first be liquidated (sold) to be converted into a generally accepted medium of exchange. There are often costs (such as brokerage fees) and inconvenience (a time delay) associated with liquidating other assets. Holding money as a store of value thus can reduce the transaction costs involved in everyday business. However, when inflation is present the purchasing power of money declines. In holding money as a store of value, we weigh the gains of doing so against the possibility of loss in its purchasing power from inflation.

We first offered a simple definition of money in Chapter 6 that emphasized its role as a medium of exchange. Now we can offer a more comprehensive definition of money that emphasizes its four functions: **Money** is anything that is generally accepted as payment in exchange for goods or services. It also serves as a standard of value, a standard of deferred payment, and a store of value.

Commodity Money

When you think of money you probably think of the green dollar bills and coins that are used as currency in the United States. Yet throughout history a variety of *commodities* have been used as money. **Commodity money** is an item that serves the functions of money but also has value in uses other than as the medium of exchange. The *intrinsic* value of commodity money is its market value per unit in uses other than as the medium of exchange. In the early days of America, tobacco, corn, and other agricultural commodities were accepted as payment for goods and services. Gold and silver are the commodities that were most commonly used by European and other nations as money throughout much of their history.

Many strange items crop up as commodity money from time to time and from

Money:
Anything that is generally accepted as payment for goods or services. Money also serves as a standard of value, a standard of deferred payment, and a store of value.

Commodity money:
An item that serves the functions of money but also has value in uses other than as the medium of exchange.

society to society. For example, furs were used as money in ancient Russia. Sometimes stamped pieces of leather were used as tokens of the furs and circulated as money. The Zulus of South Africa used cattle as money. The American Indians used *wampum,* which was a form of money consisting of trinkets made out of shells. Recently in Rumania, a communist nation in which many citizens distrust the official money, Kent cigarettes were used as money for black market transactions! It had to be Kent; no other brand would do! The packs themselves were exchanged unopened for the goods. No one would even dream of smoking the cigarettes inside the packs. A Rumanian lighting up a Kent in the mid-1980s would have been considered as crazy as someone who burns dollar bills in the United States. The Kents were more valuable as money than as smokes!

Fiat Money

Fiat money is money that is accepted as a medium of exchange because of government decree rather than because of its intrinsic value as a commodity. The dirty dollar bill in your pocket is really just a piece of high-quality 100% rag paper whose market value as a commodity is virtually nil. But you value the dollar bill you hold because you know that by government decree it will be accepted for a dollar's worth of goods and services at current prices. Even the coins you hold in your pocket aren't made of precious metals. The market value of the metal in a quarter is only a fraction of a cent. In the past U.S. coins were made of silver. However, as the market price of silver increased, the market value of silver in those coins increased above their face value. This meant that a 50¢ piece had more than 50¢ worth of silver in it (see Principles in Practice box). Under such circumstances it would have been profitable to melt down the coins into silver bullion because the coins were more valuable as raw silver than as money!

Paper money was apparently invented by the Chinese in the thirteenth century. If you're fortunate enough to have some paper money in your wallet, pull out a bill and look at it closely. You'll observe, on the dark-colored side, on top of the picture of a famous American, that the bill is a "Federal Reserve Note." This means that it's issued by one of the 12 regional banks of the Federal Reserve System, which is the central banking system of the United States. Toward the upper left corner you'll also see some small print that informs you that "THIS NOTE IS LEGAL TENDER FOR ALL DEBTS, PUBLIC AND PRIVATE." This amounts to a proclamation (or decree) by the government that this piece of paper is the legal medium of exchange in the United States. In effect, whenever you purchase an item you incur a debt to the seller. You can pay off your debt immediately with Federal Reserve notes, which serve as fiat money in the United States.

Fiat money, like Federal Reserve notes, can serve the functions of money simply because it's generally accepted in exchange for goods and services. Again, look at a Federal Reserve note. Nowhere on the note will you find any promise that it will be redeemed by the Federal Reserve Banks for gold, silver, or anything else. Of course, if you take a $20 bill to the Federal Reserve Bank, you might be able to exchange it for two $10 bills. You could also use your money to *buy* gold or silver as you would use it to buy any commodity.

Technically Federal Reserve notes are a liability (or debt) of the Federal Reserve Banks. You'll see in the chapter on the Federal Reserve System that the liabilities of the Federal Reserve Banks are balanced by their assets, which include government bonds and some gold. However, by law the Federal Reserve Banks are not required

Fiat money:
Money that is accepted as a medium of exchange because of government decree rather than because of its intrinsic value as a commodity.

Principles in Practice

Silver Coins in the United States: Good Money, Bad Money, and Gresham's Law

Less than 30 years ago in this country, it was common for people to hand a teller or cashier a $1 bill and ask for "a dollar's worth of silver"—and get it. That's because, up until the 1960s, dimes, quarters, and half dollars actually were made of silver.

Those days are gone. Today the coins used in the United States have value as metal that is far less than their face value. There's no silver in the dimes, quarters, and half dollars used in everyday transactions. Instead these coins are made of an alloy of nonprecious metal that's sandwiched around a layer of copper. Many of the old silver coins still exist, but you're unlikely to find any in your pocket. Instead they're in the hands of coin collectors.

Why did the U.S. government stop minting silver coins?

One problem in using precious metal as money is that it has value in uses other than as money. When the price of the precious metal rises above its face value as money, the metal will become more valuable in alternative uses. Silver dimes, quarters, and half dollars are no longer in circulation because the silver in these coins is worth much more than the denominations of the coins in whose shape they are molded. An enterprising silver firm could find that it's cheaper to obtain silver by melting down coins than by buying it on the commodity market!

Is it true, as some people maintain, that the cheaper alloy coins are worth less than the silver coins of bygone days? Sir Thomas Gresham would answer with a resounding "Yes!"

Gresham's Law argues that "good money" is driven out of circulation by "bad money." Good money, he said, differs from bad money in that it has higher commodity value than bad money. Gresham lived in sixteenth-century England where it was common for gold and silver coins to be debased. Govern-

ments did this by mixing in other nonprecious metals with the gold and silver. The governments could thus make a profit in coinage by issuing coins that had less precious metal than the face value indicated. Because different mintings of coins had varying amounts of gold and silver, even though they bore the same monetary denomination, some coins were *worth more* than others as *commodities*. People who dealt in gold and silver could easily see the difference between the "good" money and the "bad" money. Even the common folk could get a rough idea about the value of a coin by testing its malleability. Because gold and silver are softer than other metals, this was a good test for the precious metal content. Gresham observed that coins with a higher content of gold and silver were hoarded rather than being used in exchange or were melted down for their precious metal.

In the mid-1960s when the United States issued new coins to replace silver coins, Gresham's Law went right into action. Whenever anyone found a silver coin in his pocket he hoarded it or sold it as silver rather than spending it. The old silver coins were worth more as silver than as money! Of course, the old coins were also hoarded because they became valuable as collector's items. In any event, it didn't take long for the new non-silver coins to quickly replace the older ones as old coins were either melted down by dealers or put into coin collections. The "bad" alloy coins drove the "good" silver coins out of circulation, just as Gresham would have predicted!

Inflation will always speed up the action of Gresham's Law when both commodity money and paper money are used. This is because when the price level rises, the money value of silver or gold rises as well. A bout of inflation usually increases the rate at which gold and silver coins are hoarded. Today few nations use gold and silver coins for money.

---

to exchange Federal Reserve notes held by the public for anything other than more currency (either paper money or coins).

When a society loses confidence in its fiat money, as is the case when the value of money is eroded daily by inflation, its functions as a medium of exchange, standard and store of value, and standard of deferred payment will be impaired. Monetary authorities in central banks must be careful to keep confidence in money. When the public loses confidence in the official money of a nation, they seek alternative forms of money. If you thought rampant inflation was on the way, you wouldn't want to hold any money, and whenever you got some you'd quickly exchange it for some commodity whose value would keep up with the rate of inflation.

Checkable Deposits as a Form of Money

Federal Reserve notes, along with the coins minted by the federal government, which constitute the nation's *currency,* are not the only means of paying off debts.

You can also pay by check. A check serves the same function as currency in that it can be used to pay for purchases and pay off debts. **Checkable deposits** represent money deposited in bank accounts that can be used to write checks that are accepted to pay debts, or that can easily be converted to currency. Paying by check has the advantage of safety. A check is made payable to a specific party and must be endorsed by that party before it can be converted to currency or before funds can be transferred from the payer's account to the recipient's account. Paying by check also avoids the risks associated with transporting sums of currency. Thieves find currency a more desirable target than checks, which require endorsement before they can be cashed or deposited.

Checkable deposits are money because they are accepted as a means of payment for goods and services and also perform the other major functions of money. The convenience of paying by check, particularly when large sums of money are involved, explains why, as you'll soon see, the bulk of the money stock is held in the form of checkable deposits rather than currency. Checkable deposits are the liabilities (debt) of the banks that issue them to their depositors.

Checkable deposits are available as accounts offered by various types of specialized firms called *depository institutions*. These institutions are commonly called "banks" and include commercial banks, savings and loan associations, savings banks, and credit unions. **Commercial banks** are firms that acquire funds by accepting checkable deposits and savings deposits of households and business firms and use these funds to make loans for a wide variety of purposes. Commercial banks such as the Chase Manhattan Bank and the Bank of America make both short-term and long-term loans to a variety of businesses and to individuals seeking credit. These banks also extend credit to governments by purchasing government bonds. **Savings and loan associations** are depository institutions that acquire funds chiefly through attracting savings deposits and have in the past specialized in making mortgage loans. **Mutual savings banks** are depository institutions operating in some states that are similar to savings and loan associations in that they primarily attract savings deposits and in the past have specialized in making mortgage loans. Mutual savings banks are owned by their depositors and are concentrated in New York State and the New England states. **Credit unions** are depository institutions whose depositors are called "members" and belong to a particular organization such as a business firm or government. Credit unions make loans only to their members for the purpose of financing homes or personal goods and services (such as cars). Savings and loan associations, mutual savings banks, and credit unions are commonly called "thrift institutions" because they encourage saving by households and small businesses.

Prior to the late 1970s checkable deposits were mainly available at commercial banks in the United States. Up to that time funds in checkable deposits didn't earn interest. Since that time changes and reforms in the U.S. financial industry have allowed thrift institutions to issue checkable deposits and have modified the restrictions on the types of loans all depository institutions can make. Checkable deposits are now available at thrift institutions as well as at commercial banks, and some special checkable deposit accounts pay interest. For example, checkable deposits are available at savings and loan associations and mutual saving banks as *NOW* (negotiable order of withdrawal) accounts that permit check writing on the sums deposited in interest-bearing savings accounts.[1] Commercial banks offer *ATS* (automatic trans-

Checkable deposits:
Represent money deposited in bank accounts that can be used to write checks that are accepted to pay debts, or that can easily be converted to currency.

Commercial banks:
Firms that acquire funds by accepting checkable deposits and savings deposits of households and business firms and use these funds to make loans to businesses and individuals.

Savings and loan associations:
Depository institutions that acquire funds chiefly through attracting savings deposits and have in the past specialized in making mortgage loans.

Mutual savings banks:
Depository institutions operating in some states that are similar to savings and loans associations in that they primarily attract savings deposits and in the past have specialized in making mortgage loans.

Credit unions:
Depository institutions whose depositors belong to a particular organization. Credit unions make loans only to their members.

---

[1]Credit unions also issue checkable deposits similar to NOW accounts. Checkable deposits issued by credit unions are called *share draft accounts*.

fer of savings) accounts that transfer funds from an interest-bearing savings account to a noninterest-bearing checking account when a check is written. The funds in an ATS account therefore earn interest until checks written on the account result in withdrawal of funds and transfer to the checking account. *Demand deposits* are non-interest-bearing checkable deposits held at commercial banks. Over two thirds of demand deposits at commercial banks are held by business firms and largely represent deposit accounts of corporations.

Total checkable deposits in the nation are the sums in demand deposits, NOW accounts, ATS accounts, and other checkable deposits.

What Money Is Not

You should review the preceding discussion of money and its functions and make sure you understand how the functions of money can be used to define money itself. Be careful not to confuse money with other important economic concepts. Although money is a store of value, it is not a productive input. Do not confuse money with capital. Money can be used to purchase investment goods that add to the nation's capital stock. However, this is simply because money *is* the medium of exchange. Also, do not confuse money with bonds and other debts of corporations. These bonds can be sold for money. However, the bonds themselves are not a medium of exchange. **Bonds** are securities issued by corporations and governments representing the promise to make periodic payments of interest and repay a debt of borrowed funds at a certain time.

Do not confuse money with income. Income is measured as a *flow* of dollars over a given period. It's convenient to measure income as a money sum because, after all, money is the standard of value. However, money itself is merely an asset that is held mainly in bank accounts and as currency in people's pockets and purses or in vaults.

Do not confuse credit cards with money. If you've ever used a credit card, you know it's accepted almost as readily as currency as a means to purchase goods and services. However, when you make a purchase with a credit card you really are incurring a debt that must be paid with money at a later time. Most credit card companies give you a specified period in which to repay your loan. After that point you must pay interest on your debt.

You cannot use credit cards as a store of value. But credit cards have allowed many Americans to economize on the amount of money they hold. Rather than having to use money in checkable deposits *each day* for purchases, they can hold more bonds and other interest-bearing assets that they liquidate on a monthly rather than daily basis to pay their credit card bills.

Bonds:

Securities issued by corporations and governments representing the promise to make periodic payments of interest and repay a debt of borrowed funds at a certain time.

Measuring the Stock of Money

Money is a *stock* rather than a *flow*. A stock is a variable that can be measured only at a given point in time. For example, the stock of money can be measured as the amount held by the public on a certain day. The stock of money can vary from day to day with conditions of supply and demand. To delve further into the mysteries of money it's useful to examine the method used to measure the stock of money available for use at a given point in time.

The Money Stock: M1

The stock of money measured by the sum of currency, traveler's checks, and checkable deposits held by the public on a particular day of the year is officially called **M1** in the United States. The table in Box 1 shows the components of the money stock measured as M1 based on daily averages of the amounts actually held by the public during January 1988. You might be surprised to learn that currency constitutes only a bit more than one quarter of the available dollars that can be used as a means of payment. Checkable deposits are by far the most important component of the available stock of money. Demand deposits at commercial banks constituted 38.2% of available money in January 1988. Other checkable deposits, mainly NOW and ATS accounts held at commercial banks, savings and loan associations, and other thrift institutions, accounted for another 34.7% of the money stock. Traveler's checks outstanding (such as those issued by the American Express Company) are a very small part of M1, accounting for approximately 1% of the money stock.

M1:
The stock of money measured by the sum of currency, traveler's checks, and checkable deposits held by the public on a particular day of the year in the United States.

Box 1 The Available Stock of Money
January 1988 – Daily Average (billions of dollars)

Item	Amount	Percent of M1
Currency	198.4	26.1
Demand deposits	289.9	38.2
Other checkable deposits	263.3	34.7
Traveler's checks	7.2	1.0
Total = M1 = 758.9		100.0

M2 and M3: Measures of the Sum of M1 and Liquid Assets

M2 = M1 + (Money market deposit accounts at banks + Money market mutual fund accounts + Savings accounts and small - denomination CDs + Miscellaneous near money)

M2 = M1 + $2,166.1 = $2,925.0

M3 = M2 + (CDs of $100,000 denomination or more)

M3 = M2 + $764.1 = $3,689.1

Source: *Federal Reserve Bulletin*, April 1988.

Adding Near Money to M1: M2

Deposits in noncheckable savings accounts, certificates of deposit, bonds, and other types of financial assets are not usually considered to be money because they cannot readily be used to make payments. These assets must first be *liquidated*, into either currency or demand deposits, before the sum they represent can be used to make a payment. **Near monies** are assets that are easily converted to money because they can be liquidated at low cost and little risk of loss.

Near monies:
Assets that are easily converted to money because they can be liquidated at low cost and little risk of loss.

Because near monies can be easily and quickly converted to money, some economists prefer to include them in a measure of the nation's stock of liquid assets available to make purchases. The Federal Reserve System measures the sum of M1 and certain near monies to obtain a measure of liquid assets held by the public that constitute a store of readily available purchasing power. **M2** is the sum of M1 and certain near monies:

M2:
The sum of M1 and certain near monies; a measure of liquid assets held by the public.

M2 = M1 + Money market deposit accounts at banks + Money market mutual fund accounts + Savings accounts and small-denomination certificates of deposit + Certain other near monies

Money market mutual fund accounts are offered by investment companies and give the owner a share in an account of financial assets that allows him or her limited check-writing privileges on his or her account. Savings accounts are noncheckable savings deposits. Certificates of deposit (CDs) are deposits made in banks for a specified time with a penalty charged for early withdrawal. Savings deposits and certificates of deposit are examples of **time deposits,** which are interest-bearing accounts at commercial banks and thrift institutions for which the bank can legally request a 30-day notice before paying out the funds. In practice banks rarely ask for the 30-day notice, but they do have the legal right to do so. Only insured certificates of deposit in amounts less than $100,000 are included in M2. Certificates of deposit in excess of $100,000 are not insured by an agency of the federal government. The other near monies mainly include certain types of debts issued by commercial banks.

Time deposits:
Interest-bearing accounts at commercial banks and thrift institutions for which the bank can legally request a 30-day notice before paying out the funds.

The table in Box 1 shows the relationship between M1 and M2. In January 1988, average daily balances of funds included in M2 amounted to $2,925 billion or about four times M1! Adding near money to the supply of money measured as M1, we see that total liquid assets available to the public are four times the stock of money narrowly defined as currency and checkable deposits.

Going one step further, you can add the large-denomination certificates of deposit to M2 to obtain still another measure of the stock of liquid assets held by the public called **M3.**

M3:
The sum of M2 and large-denomination ($100,000 and more) certificates of deposit.

M3 = M2 + Large-denomination ($100,000 and more) certificates of deposit

Making this last adjustment shows that the liquid assets held by the public in the United States on average each day in January 1988 amounted to $3,689.1 billion.

Throughout this book we will be referring to M1 when discussing the money stock. Although M2 and M3 are good measures of liquid assets available to the public, they include assets such as saving deposits that cannot readily be used to make payments and therefore cannot fulfill all the functions of money.

Concept Check

1 List the four functions of money and explain how funds in your checking account fulfill these functions.

2 Which functions of money are not fulfilled by funds in your savings accounts?

3 What is included in M1 as a measure of the nation's money stock? How does M2 differ from M1?

The Demand for Money

Why do people desire to hold demand deposits and currency? After all, by holding these two forms of money they give up the opportunity to earn interest on the sum held. Similarly, when money is held in the form of interest-bearing checkable deposits, the interest earned is usually less than can be earned on near monies, bonds, and other less liquid assets that can be purchased with money.

The *opportunity cost* of holding a dollar in money over the year is the interest income that is forgone. For example, if you can earn 8% per year in a savings account, the opportunity cost of holding a dollar in cash is 8¢ over the year assuming interest is computed once annually. The higher the interest rate you can earn on each dollar in the next best alternative you have to holding it as money, such as investing in bonds or certificates of deposit, the greater the opportunity cost of holding money.

People hold money because they receive benefits from doing so. In deciding how much to hold, people consider both the benefits and costs of holding money. In the following sections we analyze the benefits of holding money and look at various motives for choosing to hold money as an asset.

Transaction Demand for Money

At any given level of interest rates, people demand a certain amount of money to carry out the basic transactions associated with everyday business. The level of interest rates is an average of a broad array of interest rates that can be earned on a variety of assets. The greater the dollar volume of transactions during the year, the greater the sum of money each day over the year that is willingly held at each possible level of interest rates.

By holding money you avoid the inconvenience and possible embarrassment of settling your debts late. You also avoid the need to incur other costs involved in liquidating assets to make payments. For example, suppose you have both a savings account and a checking account at a local bank. To pay for your daily and other periodic purchases, you must be sure to have at least a minimum amount of currency and checkable deposits on hand. Your savings deposits do you little good as a means of payment unless you go to the bank and transfer some of the funds to your checking account or withdraw them as currency. The trip to the bank is part of the transaction cost of converting near money to money.

One motive for holding money is the desire to avoid the transaction costs associated with liquidating other assets to make payments. The **transaction demand for money** is the sum of money people wish to hold per day as a convenience in paying their everyday bills. The benefit of holding money in this form is the avoidance of transaction costs of converting other assets to currency and checkable deposits.

Transaction demand for money:
The sum of money people wish to hold per day as a convenience in paying their bills.

Suppose you're paid once a month, your expenses require daily expenditure of money, and you don't borrow to meet any of your expenses. You could deposit *all* of your monthly money income in a savings account on the day you're paid to avoid the loss in interest income associated with holding money. However, every time you needed to pay for an item, you'd have to go to the bank and wait in line to convert some of your savings deposits to checkable deposits or currency. In some cases you might incur penalties for early withdrawal of savings deposits that would reduce your interest income. The time and money costs involved in liquidating these savings deposits are your transaction costs. In managing the money you keep for transactions, you must weigh these transaction costs against the income you forgo by holding money instead of interest-bearing assets. You may decide always to keep a certain sum each month as checkable deposits and currency rather than as less liquid assets. The interest you forgo by doing so is worth less to you than the inconvenience of having to liquidate those assets to make payments every day.

The transaction demand for money for the year in the economy at any given level of interest rates depends on the dollar volume of transactions over the year. In general, the greater the level of nominal GNP over the year, the greater the transaction demand for money. This makes sense. After all, if your monthly bills increase from $1,000 last year to $1,500 this year, you'll need to hold more money to make payments. For example, other things being equal, you'll want to hold more money as transaction balances when your monthly bills are $1,500 than when they're $1,000. Similarly, when nominal GNP increases from $4,000 billion to $5,000 billion per year, the transaction demand for money in the economy will also increase even if interest rates don't change.

Money as an Asset

Money is one of many alternative assets people can choose to hold as a store of purchasing power. In deciding how much of a stock of money to hold, we consider the opportunity cost of holding it as measured by the purchasing power of the interest income we forgo by doing so. However, there are benefits associated with holding money compared to holding alternative assets. In deciding how much of a stock of money to hold, we weigh the marginal benefits of holding additional money against the marginal cost of doing so.

The main advantage of money over alternative assets is its liquidity. Many of us therefore usually find that the benefits of holding money (defined as currency and checkable deposits—M1) as an asset are worth the opportunity cost of doing so. By holding money we have an asset we can quickly and conveniently draw upon to make payments when emergencies arise. In addition to transaction balances, people also hold money because of uncertainty about future flows of income and required payments. Money is held as a *precaution* against lack of synchronization between inflow of income and outflow of payments. You never know when your income over a certain period will fall short of the bills you must meet over that period. Holding some money allows you to make payments quickly even when your income falls short of your expenditures. Would you run the risk of letting your checking account balance run down to zero and encountering embarrassing delays in meeting your bills?

Business firms have a similar precautionary motive for holding money. They do so to ensure a way of quickly paying their bills even when their cash receipts from sales are abnormally low. Because receipts of income and the due dates of bills are rarely completely synchronized, no household or business firm can expect to have income readily available to pay bills exactly at the time the bills come due.

Another reason people hold money has to do with uncertainty about the future level of prices and interest rates in the economy. Although financial assets such as stocks and bonds yield interest income, the prices of these assets fluctuate with economic conditions. Therefore business firms and households evaluate the riskiness of stocks, bonds, and other assets by trying to forecast movements in the prices of these assets. Considering economic conditions, they often find money an attractive alternative to stocks and bonds. In periods during which bond prices are expected to fall, other things being equal, the desired stock of money that people want to hold is likely to increase. The uncertainty concerning future prices of stocks and bonds leads to a *speculative* motive to hold money as an asset.

The Money Demand Curve

The **demand for money** is the relationship between the sums of money that people willingly hold and the level of interest rates in the economy given *all other influences* on the desirability of holding money instead of other assets. Among the other influences on the demand for money, aside from the level of nominal interest rates in the economy, are all those factors that affect the transaction, precautionary, and speculative demand for money. Among these factors are the degree to which payments and receipts can be synchronized in the economy, as well as expectations about future levels of interest rates, stock and bond prices, inflation, and the level of nominal GNP.

A **money demand curve** shows a relationship between the level of interest rates in the economy and the stock of money demanded at a given point in time. In effect, the cost of holding a dollar is measured by the interest rate because the interest forgone on money balances is the opportunity cost of holding money. The higher the level of interest rates in the economy, the greater the opportunity cost of holding money and the lower the quantity demanded.

The graph in Box 2 draws a money demand curve for the economy showing how the stock of money demanded on a given day varies inversely with the level of interest rates. The lower the interest rate, the lower the opportunity cost of holding money and the greater the quantity demanded on any given day as balances in checkable deposits or as currency. The actual responsiveness of the desired stock of money to changes in the level of interest rates is hotly debated among economists. Some economists believe the money demand curve is nearly vertical, implying that changes in the level of interest rates have little effect on the quantity of money demanded.

Demand for money:
The relationship between the sums of money people willingly hold and the level of interest rates in the economy given all other influences on the desirability of holding money instead of other assets.

Money demand curve:
Shows a relationship between the level of interest rates in the economy and the stock of money demanded at a given point in time.

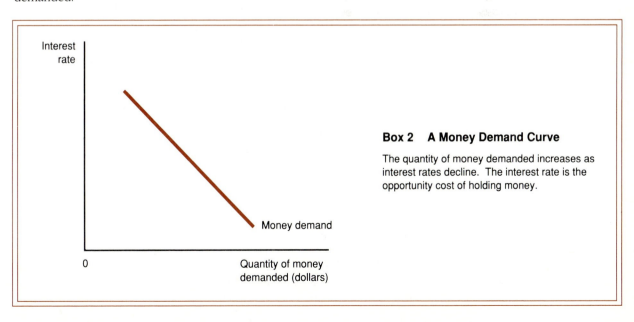

Box 2 A Money Demand Curve

The quantity of money demanded increases as interest rates decline. The interest rate is the opportunity cost of holding money.

Changes in Money Demand

Change in money demand:
A change in the relationship between the level of interest rates and the stock of money demanded in the economy caused by a change in economic conditions.

A **change in money demand** is a change in the relationship between the level of interest rates and the stock of money demanded in the economy caused by a change in economic conditions. When there's a change in money demand, the entire demand curve for money will shift inward or outward. A change in the transaction demand for money at any given interest rate level results in a change in money demand. As pointed out earlier, a change in nominal GNP will result in a change in the transaction demand for money. Nominal GNP will increase either when real GNP goes up or the price level goes up. It follows that either an increase in real GNP or an increase in the price level will shift the money demand curve outward, as illustrated in **A** in Box 3. Similarly, a decrease in real GNP or a decrease in the price level will shift the money demand curve inward, as shown in **B** in Box 3.

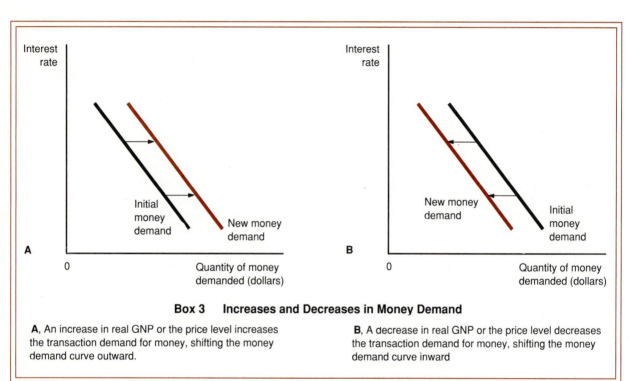

Box 3   Increases and Decreases in Money Demand

A, An increase in real GNP or the price level increases the transaction demand for money, shifting the money demand curve outward.

B, A decrease in real GNP or the price level decreases the transaction demand for money, shifting the money demand curve inward

Given the price level, it's therefore reasonable to expect that an increase in real GNP will increase money demand. This means that during periods of economic expansion, the money demand curve will be shifting outward. Similarly, given the price level, decreases in real GNP will imply decreases in the demand for money. During periods of contraction or recession, it's therefore reasonable to expect that the demand for money will decrease.

The money demand curve can also shift in response to other changes in economic conditions. Suppose financial innovations reduce the transaction cost of converting near money to money. For example, the invention of automatic teller machines has reduced the transaction cost of obtaining currency. With an automatic teller machine you can easily obtain currency from your savings account as you need it, even on evenings and weekends when banks are closed. This innovation is likely to have affected your demand to hold currency and checkable deposits.

The proliferation of credit cards is another financial innovation that has affected the demand for money. With a credit card you can consolidate many bills into one that you can pay each month, and if you pay in full you'll incur no interest expense. By using a credit card, you can keep less money in checkable deposits and hold more in savings accounts or money market accounts that yield interest. You can then withdraw funds from these accounts as needed to meet credit card bills.

A decrease in the transaction cost of converting near money to money will decrease the demand for money. The cost of converting bonds, savings deposits, and other assets to currency and checkable deposits can fall when the time to do so or the penalties involved in doing so are reduced. A reduction in brokerage fees could therefore reduce the demand for money. People hold less money when the transaction costs of converting near money to money fall, because it's less advantageous to hold money in terms of the time and other costs saved by doing so. They therefore shift some of their wealth to bonds and near money. A decrease in the transaction cost of converting near money to money thus will shift the money demand curve inward. Similarly, an increase in the transaction cost of converting near money to money will shift the money demand curve outward.

The demand for money will also change with changes in the risk associated with holding alternative assets other than money. For example, in periods when bond prices are expected to rise, the demand for money is likely to decline as people seek to hold lower money balances at any given interest rate so they can acquire more bonds. If, however, bond prices are expected to fall, the demand for money is likely to increase because money becomes a more attractive asset as the probability increases of incurring a loss from holding bonds. The demand curve for money will therefore shift inward when bond prices are expected to rise and shift outward when bond prices are expected to fall.

Concept Check

1   What is the cost of holding a dollar of currency in your pocket for the year?

2   Suppose nominal GNP is expected to increase next year. Why will the demand for money also increase?

3   What can cause the demand for money to decline?

The Stock of Money, Money Demand, and Interest Rates

The Effect of an Increase in the Available Stock of Money

Given the demand for money, changes in the stock of money available can affect the interest rate level for the economy over short periods of time. To understand the link between the available stock of money and interest rates each day, assume the price level is given and real GNP is fixed in the short run, as are all other determinants of money demand. These assumptions simplify the analysis by ensuring that the money demand curve doesn't shift at the same time the available stock of money does. In the chapters to follow you'll see how the banking system can affect the stock of money available on any given day and how money supplied also varies with the interest rate level.

The graph in Box 4 shows how, given the demand curve for money, an increase in the available daily stock of money will cause interest rates to decline. Suppose the stock of money available on average each day in January is $600 billion and this is exactly equal to the quantity demanded at the current interest rate level of 8%.

In March the available stock of money is up to $700 billion on average each day. If the interest rate remains at 8%, there will be no change in the quantity of money demanded. This means the $700 billion stock of money available will exceed the $600 billion demanded at the 8% interest rate level.

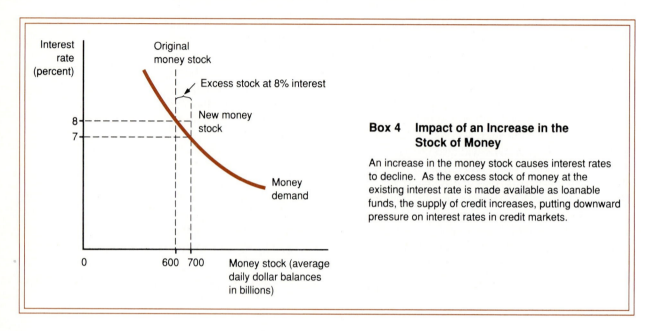

Box 4   Impact of an Increase in the Stock of Money

An increase in the money stock causes interest rates to decline. As the excess stock of money at the existing interest rate is made available as loanable funds, the supply of credit increases, putting downward pressure on interest rates in credit markets.

The graph in Box 4 shows the excess stock of money at the 8% interest rate. What will holders of the excess $100 billion worth of money seek to do with it? They could put the extra funds in savings accounts or use it to buy bonds. Everyone tries to get rid of the excess money, but like a hot potato it always ends up in someone's hands or checking account after it's used to buy bonds. As banks find they have more funds on deposit than they had before the money stock increased, the supply of funds available for loans increases. The increased supply of loanable funds puts downward pressure on interest rates. At lower interest rates the opportunity cost of holding money is also lower and the existing larger stock is willingly held. In the graph in Box 4 the increase in the available stock of money will be willingly held only if the market rate of interest falls to 7%. Other things being equal, an increase in the available stock of money must increase the supply of credit and put downward pressure on the level of interest rates. Over a short period, therefore, given the level of nominal GNP and the price level and other determinants of money demand, the immediate effect of an increase in the available supply of money is a decrease in interest rates in the economy. The lower interest rate will increase aggregate demand and put upward pressure on real GNP as it encourages more purchases of investment goods.[2]

[2]As you'll see in the chapter entitled "Stabilization of the Economy Through Monetary Policy," the long-run effects of an increase in the available supply of money are more complex because over longer periods of time the added money stock could also increase the price level.

The Effect of a Decrease in the Available Stock of Money

Other things being equal, a decrease in the available stock of money will put upward pressure on the interest rate in the short run. Given the money demand curve, a decrease in the available stock of money will result in a shortage (excess demand) of money available at the current interest rate. The graph in Box 5 shows the impact of a decrease in the supply of money from $600 billion per day to $500 billion per day. The initial equilibrium interest rate is 8%. As the available stock of money decreases, the quantity available at the 8% interest rate will fall short of the quantity demanded. There will be a $100 billion excess demand for money. How will the difference between the quantity the public wants to hold and the quantity available be made up? Individuals and corporations will seek to liquidate near money such as bonds to obtain funds to add to their money balances. As the public tries to increase its holdings of money in this way, the funds available for credit and to finance new bonds will decrease. The decrease in the supply of loanable funds will then put upward pressure on interest rates. Interest rates will continue to rise until the reduced stock of money is willingly held without further liquidation of near monies. In the graph in Box 5, interest rates must rise to 9% before the quantity demanded declines to equal the $500 billion of available money per day. Decreases in the stock of money therefore put upward pressure on interest rates in the short run. The higher interest rates reduce the availability of credit in the economy. This is likely to put downward pressure on aggregate demand over a longer period and therefore tends to reduce real GNP.

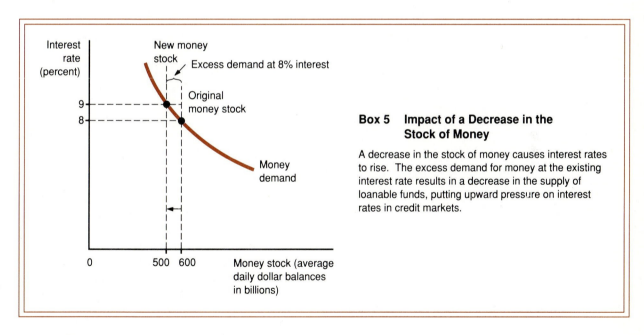

Box 5   Impact of a Decrease in the Stock of Money

A decrease in the stock of money causes interest rates to rise. The excess demand for money at the existing interest rate results in a decrease in the supply of loanable funds, putting upward pressure on interest rates in credit markets.

How Shifts in Money Demand Can Affect Interest Rates

Given the available stock of money, an increase in money demand puts upward pressure on interest rates. An increase in money demand can be caused by an increase in real GNP, an increase in the price level, an increase in the transaction costs of converting other assets into money, or expectations that the prices of bonds and other assets will fall.

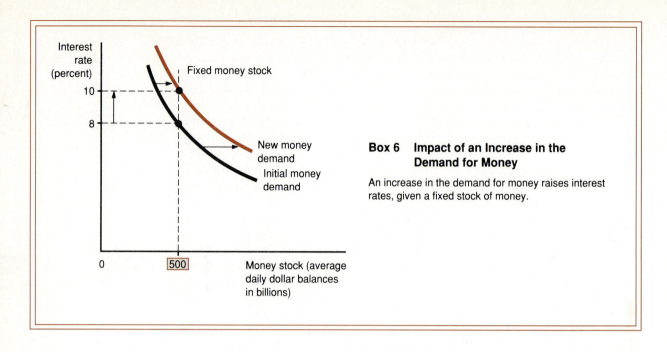

Box 6 Impact of an Increase in the Demand for Money

An increase in the demand for money raises interest rates, given a fixed stock of money.

The graph in Box 6 illustrates the effect of an increase in money demand on interest rates assuming a fixed stock of money. As the money demand curve shifts outward, interest rates tend to rise, other things being equal. For example, an expanding economy in which real GNP is increasing is likely to be characterized by upward pressure on interest rates because the transaction demand for money will be increasing during the expansion. An increase in the price level will also increase money demand and put upward pressure on interest rates.

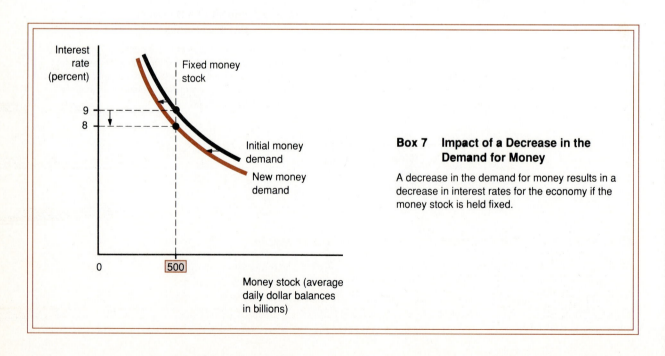

Box 7 Impact of a Decrease in the Demand for Money

A decrease in the demand for money results in a decrease in interest rates for the economy if the money stock is held fixed.

You can expect downward pressure on interest rates as an economy moves into a recession. This is because a decline in real GNP reduces the transaction demand for money and shifts the money demand curve inward. If there is no change in the money stock, the interest rate will fall, as shown in the graph in Box 7. Similarly, a decrease in the transaction cost of converting near money to money will put downward pressure on interest rates over a short period. This is because the decrease in these transaction costs means the demand curve for money shifts inward.

Concept Check

1 Why does an increase in the stock of money put downward pressure on interest rates, given all influences on money demand?

2 Why does a decrease in the stock of money exert upward pressure on interest rates when money demand is fixed?

3 Given the available stock of money (M1), how will money demand and interest rates be affected by an increase in the transaction cost of converting near money to money?

The Need to Understand Changes in the Money Stock

As you can see, the demand for and available stock of money exert an important influence on interest rates in the economy. The impact of changes in the money stock on the economy is complex because changes in interest rates are likely to affect aggregate demand. For example, consumers find it more attractive to borrow as interest rates decline so they spend more on homes, cars, and other durable goods. Similarly, business firms find it more attractive to make investments as interest rates decline. As a result, over longer periods, changes in the national money stock are likely to affect nominal GNP. As nominal GNP changes, so will the demand for money.

The next step in our quest to understand how the economy works is to examine the process by which the money stock changes in the economy. To do this we need to begin an in-depth look at the nation's financial system and to learn how banks conduct their business. We also need to examine how the Federal Reserve System, the central bank of the United States, regulates the financial system and affects the ability of financial institutions to make loans and provide credit in financial markets. Once you understand how the financial system operates, you can begin to see how the policies pursued by the Federal Reserve System can influence macroeconomic equilibrium in the nation. Our goal in the next two chapters therefore is to develop the necessary background for an economic analysis of the impact on real GNP and the price level of policies that affect money supply.

Summary

1. Money serves four basic functions, as medium of exchange, standard of value, standard of deferred payment, and store of value. Currency is the paper money and coins that serve as a medium of exchange. Paper money in the United States is issued by Federal Reserve Banks. Checkable deposits represent money held

in checking accounts that can be used to pay debts or can be converted to currency.

2. M1 is a measure of the money stock that consists of the sum of checkable deposits and currency held by the public on average each day over a certain period.

3. Near monies are assets that can be liquidated at low cost and little risk of loss. An asset is liquidated when it is redeemed for currency or a checkable deposit. M2 represents the sum of M1 and certain near monies.

4. The opportunity cost of holding a dollar of money over a year is the interest income that is forgone by doing so.

5. The demand for money is the relationship between the sums of money that people willingly hold and the level of interest rates, given all other influences on the desirability of holding money instead of other assets. Money is held for precautionary as well as speculative motives and also to facilitate transactions. Money is part of the stock of wealth existing in the economy at a certain point in time.

6. A money demand curve shows a relationship between the level of interest rates in the economy and the stock of money demanded on a given day. The interest rate measures the cost of holding each dollar in terms of the annual interest income forgone.

7. The transaction demand for money is the sum that people wish to hold per day as a convenience in paying their everyday bills. Holding money economizes on the transaction costs of liquidating alternative assets to make payments. In general, the greater the nominal GNP over the year, the greater the transaction demand for money.

8. A decrease in the transaction costs of converting near money to money will decrease the demand for money.

9. Changes in the available stock of money are likely to result in changes in the level of interest rates in the economy, given the demand for money. An increase in the stock of money is likely to increase the supply of loanable funds as holders of money use the excess supply of money at the current interest rate level to buy bonds and extend credit. This puts downward pressure on interest rates. Similarly, a decrease in the stock of money puts upward pressure on the level of interest rates in the economy.

10. The level of interest rates in the economy can be affected by shifts in the demand for money. An increase in money demand puts upward pressure on interest rates, while a decrease in money demand puts downward pressure on interest rates.

Key Terms and Concepts

Money	M1
Commodity money	Near monies
Fiat money	M2
Checkable deposits	Time deposits
Commercial banks	M3
Savings and loan associations	Transaction demand for money
Mutual savings banks	Demand for money
Credit unions	Money demand curve
Bonds	Change in money demand

Problems and Applications

1. What is the difference between commodity money and fiat money? Explain why U.S. currency is fiat money.
2. Explain how currency and checkable deposits fulfill the functions of money for the U.S. economy. What are some of the advantages of currency and checkable deposits over gold and silver as a form of money? What are some of the disadvantages of currency and checkable deposits compared to commodity money?
3. Suppose you open an account with a mutual fund composed of corporate bonds. The company managing the mutual fund gives you a checkbook that allows you to write checks against the market value of bonds in the account. Is the value of the assets held in the mutual fund part of M1?
4. Suppose inflation is expected to heat up in the future. How does inflation affect the function of money as a medium of exchange, standard of value, and store of purchasing power?
5. What can U.S. currency be redeemed for if presented to the U.S. Treasury or a Federal Reserve Bank?
6. The level of interest rates in the economy increases on average over the year from 6% to 8%. What effect will this change have on the quantity of money demanded?
7. Explain how a decrease in the level of interest rates affects the quantity of money demanded in the economy.
8. Nominal GNP is $5,000 billion, and the average daily stock of money measured by M1 during the year is $1,000 billion. What is likely to happen to the demand for money and interest rates if, as a result of an increase in government purchases, nominal GNP increases to $5,500 billion and M1 is held fixed at $1,000 billion?
9. Use a graph to show how a decrease in the demand for money will affect interest rates if the money stock is held fixed.
10. This year there is a 10% reduction in the stock of money measured as M1. Use a graph to show how the reduction in the stock of money will affect the quantity of money demanded and the equilibrium level of interest rates in credit markets. How could such a sharp reduction in the money supply precipitate a recession?

Suggested Readings

William J. Baumol, "The Transactions Demand for Cash: An Inventory Theoretic Approach," *Quarterly Journal of Economics,* 66, November 1952, pp. 545-556. This is a classic analysis of the transaction demand for money.

David Laidler, *The Demand for Money: Theories and Evidence,* 3rd ed., New York: Harper & Row, 1985. This is a survey of both the theory of money demand and empirical research on the relationship between money supply and interest rates.

A Forward Look

In the following chapter we begin an examination of the money supply and the process of money creation. We undertake an in-depth analysis of banking and the incentives for profit-maximizing institutions to make loans to their customers. By studying the basics of banking, you'll begin to understand how the nation's financial system functions.

CHAPTER 33

The Banking System

How old were you when you opened your first savings account? If you were grade-school age, you probably had the common child's-eye view of the bank as a vast place where the coins and crumpled bills you handed the teller were stored in a box neatly labeled with your name. When you wanted to make a withdrawal, the teller would take down your box from a high shelf, remove the amount of money you requested, and replace the box.

You've long since discovered that banks are far more than a cool, dry place to store money. But how exactly do banks function—and where does money come from?

In the previous chapter we saw that the bulk of the money stock at any given point in time is held as checkable deposits in depository institutions. **Depository institutions** are those that make loans and offer checkable deposit and time deposit accounts for use by households and business firms. The term **bank** is generally used to refer to commercial banks and thrift institutions that offer checkable deposits. The remarkable fact is that these institutions can actually *create* checkable deposits by making loans to their customers. In this chapter we show how the depository institutions that comprise the nation's banking system create checkable deposits and influence the stock of money in circulation.

Depository institutions for the most part are business firms motivated to maximize profits. Depository institutions are members of a broad class of firms that seek to make profits by linking savers who supply loanable funds to investors and other borrowers. **Financial intermediaries** are firms that specialize in borrowing funds from savers and lending those funds to investors and others. Depository institutions like commercial banks, savings and loan associations, mutual savings banks, and credit unions (see the preceding chapter) are financial intermediaries. Brokerage houses, mutual fund companies, insurance companies, pension funds, and a host of other institutions and firms also provide financial intermediation services. However, only the banking system can actually create money.

In this chapter we concentrate on the activities of depository institutions. In the following chapter we'll explicitly consider the role in the economy played by the central bank of the United States, the Federal Reserve System.

Depository institutions:
Institutions that make loans and offer checkable deposit and time deposit accounts for use by households and business firms.

Bank:
A commercial bank or thrift institution that offers checkable deposits.

Financial intermediaries:
Firms that specialize in borrowing funds from savers and lending those funds to investors and others.

1. Discuss the origins of banking and explain the concept of fractional reserve banking.
2. Examine bank balance sheets and show how the balance sheets are affected when the bank makes loans.
3. Show how multiple expansion of the money stock can result from an inflow of excess reserves into banks and calculate the reserve multiplier.
4. Discuss bank portfolio management practices.

The Evolution of Banking

The word *bank* is derived from the Italian word for bench, which is *banco*. In the Middle Ages, gold and silver were used as money in most European nations and for international trade. Gold is a very heavy commodity. To avoid the inconvenience (and risk) of carrying around a wheelbarrow full of gold and coins, most merchants preferred to keep it in a safe place. They usually left it with a goldsmith or a money changer. When it was deposited in this way, the gold was first placed on a bench (or counter) so it could be examined and weighed. This practice evolved into what is now known as banking.

The goldsmiths of medieval England and the money changers of medieval Italy assessed the purity of the gold or coins before accepting it as a deposit. The depositor was issued an official receipt with a stamp certifying the deposit in the vault of the establishment. The depositor paid a fee for the storage service, just as you pay a fee for your checking account and other services at your bank. The deposit receipts for the gold soon began to circulate as a medium of exchange. This reduced the transaction costs of market exchanges by avoiding the inconvenience and risk of physically transporting gold in payment for goods and services. Any holder of the receipt could at any time go to the goldsmith and redeem the receipt for the stored gold. In effect, the receipts for the gold became paper currency.[1]

The goldsmiths typically sat at their benches or counters with their ledgers, recording all their transactions. There was a constant inflow and outflow of deposited gold. At first, these early bankers issued no more receipts than the gold they had in the vault. If they had 10,000 ounces stored, the total receipts in circulation were for no more than 10,000 ounces. However, some of the more astute goldsmiths and money changers observed that it was extremely unlikely that all the receipts would be submitted on a given day to be redeemed for all the gold in the vault.

The goldsmiths observed that while receipts were presented each day for redemption of gold, new deposits of gold offset the decline from the outflow and resulted in issuance of new receipts. *This meant the goldsmith could either loan out a portion of the gold on deposit for the use of others or issue more gold receipts than the actual gold available in the vault.* On any given day the inflows and outflows of gold were quite predictable. From experience the goldsmith might know

---

[1] For a discussion of the activities of goldsmiths in medieval England, see A. Andreades, *History of the Bank of England, 1640-1903,* 4th ed., with a new introduction by Paul Einzig, New York: Augustus M. Kelley, 1966 (first published in 1909), pp. 20-26.

that it would be rare for more than 25% of the gold receipts outstanding to end up as net withdrawals of gold on a given day. By making loans the goldsmith could add to profits but would run little risk of being unable to meet the demand for withdrawals.

The goldsmith made loans by issuing more receipts for gold than the actual gold in the vault. *Because the gold receipts circulated as money, the goldsmith actually created money by issuing receipts to his borrowers for more gold than was in the vault!*

Fractional Reserve Banking

Fractional reserve banking: A process by which a banking system creates checkable deposits by making loans in some multiple of the reserves it actually has on hand to pay withdrawals.

The medieval goldsmiths and money changers were the first people to practice **fractional reserve banking,** in which a banking system can create checkable deposits by making loans in some multiple of the reserves it actually has on hand to pay withdrawals. Under *100% reserve banking,* banks always keep enough reserves on hand to pay out *all* their deposits in cash on a given day. For example, when the goldsmith fully backs all his circulating receipts ounce for ounce with gold, he is using a 100% reserve system. Under such a system the goldsmith is unable to issue more gold receipts than the actual amount of gold in his vault.

Suppose instead a goldsmith makes loans equal to *all* the gold he has in the vault. When he does so he will actually create receipts for deposits even though the people receiving the loan proceeds will not have actually deposited gold in the vault. Suppose a goldsmith with 10,000 ounces of gold in the vault makes loans of 10,000 ounces to people who don't actually deposit gold. When the loans are made the goldsmith, who can now be called a banker, credits the accounts of the people receiving the loans with a "deposit" for 10,000 ounces of gold even though the customers don't actually deposit any gold. The borrowers are now free to use receipts for these "created" deposits as money in making purchases.

Fractional reserve ratio: The ratio of actual reserves to total receipts for deposits.

The **fractional reserve ratio** the banker is operating under is the ratio of actual cash reserves (which in this case is the gold) in his vault to total receipts for deposits. In this case the fractional reserve ratio would be:

$$\text{Fractional reserve ratio} = \text{Cash reserves/receipts for deposits}$$
$$= 10,000/20,000$$
$$= 0.5$$

The gold held in the vault is sufficient to pay out only half the actual receipts the banker has issued. The fractional reserve is only 50% of actual deposit receipts. This sounds very risky, but it really isn't. Returning to our example earlier in the chapter, the banker knows from experience that because of daily inflows of new deposits, the new outflow of his reserves is almost never more than 25% of the gold receipts he has issued.

A banker who wants to earn even more interest income on loans might use a lower fractional reserve ratio. Because it's highly unlikely that more than 25% of receipts issued for deposits will be redeemed in gold on any given day, the banker might find it prudent and profitable to loan out *four times* as much gold as is actually in the vault! The fractional reserve ratio for this banker would be 0.25.

A banking system that held 100% cash reserves for currency deposited by its customers would be unable to create checkable deposits to make loans. The 100% reserve system is surely very safe for a banking system because the system can meet its customers' demand for currency in the unlikely event that all customers would simultaneously close their accounts and demand currency for their balances. But like most businesses, banks must weigh safety considerations against profitability. Banks therefore use a fractional reserve system and earn interest income on the checkable deposits they create when they make loans.

In the United States, banking operations and practices are closely supervised by the Federal Reserve System, the U.S. Comptroller of the Currency, the Federal Deposit Insurance Corporation, and a multitude of state regulatory agencies. The purpose is to maintain confidence in the banking system to prevent "panics" that might cause depositors to try to withdraw abnormally high percentages of total deposits on a given day.

How Banks Make Loans and Create Checkable Deposits

The banking industry in the United States consists of about 15,000 commercial banks, 4,000 savings and loan associations (some of which are now simply called savings banks), 400 mutual savings banks, and 20,000 small credit unions that serve the employees of business firms and nonprofit organizations. Each of these institutions offers checkable deposits, time deposits, loans, and other services to its customers. Banks serve useful functions by providing checking accounts, interest-bearing accounts, and certificates of deposit, and by making loans to businesses, consumers, homeowners, and governments and providing other financial services.

The day-to-day operations of a modern banking system are much more complex than those of the ancient banks we just discussed. To understand how the banking system of a modern nation operates, it's useful to begin by analyzing the operations of a single bank in a fractional reserve banking system. By examining the way a single bank accepts deposits and makes loans, you'll begin to understand how a modern banking system can actually create money in the same way the ancient goldsmiths created receipts for gold that circulated as money.

The **reserves** of a modern bank in the United States consist of balances kept on deposit with the Federal Reserve Bank in its district or as currency in its vault. The Federal Reserve System is the nation's central bank, whose operations we'll discuss in detail in the following chapter. There are 12 regional Federal Reserve Banks that serve the function of "banker's bank" in which banks have accounts just as you have accounts at your bank. The Federal Reserve System seeks to control the money stock and, as you'll see shortly, *requires* banks to maintain a certain minimum fractional reserve ratio.

Reserves:
Balances (of a modern U.S. bank) kept on deposit with the Federal Reserve Bank in its district or as currency in its vault.

Using Balance Sheets to Understand Bank Operations

The operations of a bank can be greatly clarified by examining its *balance sheet,* which is a statement of its assets and the claims against those assets. A bank's balance sheet summarizes its financial position by showing the relationship between its loans, property, reserves, and the claims that could be made on the bank by its creditors and owners. A bank's most important creditors are its depositors, who place their funds in the bank for safekeeping and have the right to withdraw those funds. The deposits that customers place in the bank are part of the bank's *liabilities,* which means they are debts of the bank to the depositors.

The bank's *assets* are property, cash, and debts owed to the bank, which include the loans owed to the bank and any marketable securities the bank holds, such as

Treasury bills and other notes of indebtedness. The *net worth* of the bank is the difference between its assets and liabilities. Liabilities and net worth are two types of claims made against a bank's assets. The liabilities of the bank are the claims of its depositors and other creditors who are not owners of the bank. The net worth of the bank is the claim the bank's owners have to its assets after the claims of its creditors have been met. To understand how a bank can create money, we need to examine the relationship between its assets, liabilities, and net worth.

A balance sheet must always balance because its function is merely to divide the claims against assets into two mutually exclusive categories, liabilities and net worth. In other words, the bottom line of a balance sheet always shows that:

$$\text{Assets} = \text{Liabilities} + \text{Net worth}$$

The balance sheet equation is actually an *identity* because it must always hold by definition.

Box 1 shows the balance sheet of a typical bank that has just opened for business. After 1 week in business, the bank has attracted $10 million of deposits. Assume these are all deposits of currency. The deposits don't actually increase the money stock. They simply convert currency to checkable deposits. These deposits are the bank's liabilities. The bank has yet to extend any loans. The $10 million in currency that the bank accepts is deposited as reserves in the bank's own account at its district Federal Reserve Bank. These reserves constitute part of the firm's assets because they are a sum of money owed to the bank. When the bank needs currency to meet the demands of its depositors, it can draw on its account at the Federal Reserve Bank and request a delivery of currency. (Remember that currency is issued by the Federal Reserve Banks.) The bank also has other assets in the form of structures and equipment that constitute its physical plant. Assume the value of the bank's property is $500,000.

Box 1 Bank Balance Sheet
End of Week 1: No Loans

Assets		Liabilities and net worth	
Reserves		Deposits	$10,000,000
Required	$2,000,000		
Excess	$8,000,000	Net worth	
		stockholder shares	$500,000
Loans	$0		
Property	$500,000	Total liabilities	
		and net worth	$10,500,000
Total assets	$10,500,000		

The bank's balance sheet at the end of its first week of business is shown in Box 1. Its assets consist of $10 million of reserves and $500,000 of property. Its liabilities are $10 million of checkable deposits. Its net worth, which is the portion of its assets not owed to creditors or other nonowners, is $500,000. The total assets of $10.5 million exactly equal the sum of liabilities and net worth of $10.5 million, as must always be the case in a balance sheet.

CHAPTER 33 The Banking System

With reserves equal to its deposits, the bank is like the goldsmith who doesn't issue any more receipts than the gold he has on deposit. The bank cannot make any loans as long as it keeps reserves equal to 100% of its deposits. Its only source of income would be the fees it charges its depositors for the services it provides.

Making Loans: Deposit Creation by a Single Bank

Banks, like all financial intermediaries, make most of their profits by making loans to businesses and households and acquiring interest-bearing securities to earn income. During the second week of business, the executives of the newly organized bank in this example will advertise their services and drum up some loan business. But how much can they loan out? Suppose the bank's managers believe it's safe to keep 20% reserves against its deposits. Also assume that the regulatory authorities that oversee bank operations will not permit bank reserves to fall below 20% of deposits. The regulators set a **required reserve ratio,** which is the minimum percentage of deposits that the bank must hold in reserves. *The bank can hold more than this minimum percentage of deposits in reserves if it wishes, but it cannot hold less.* The required reserve ratio is one of the tools the Federal Reserve System can use to control the amount of money in circulation.[2]

Required reserves represent the dollar value of currency and deposits in Federal Reserve Banks that a bank must hold to meet current regulations. For example, for the bank whose balance sheet is shown in Box 1, required reserves are $2 million, which equals 20% of current deposits. **Excess reserves** represent the difference between total reserves and required reserves held against deposits. The bank whose balance sheet is shown in Box 1 currently holds $8 million in excess reserves. This is the excess of its $10 million total reserves over its $2 million required reserves. *An individual bank can make loans in an amount up to the value of its excess reserves.* This bank can therefore make up to $8 million in loans out of its initial deposits of $10 million when it operates under a 20% required reserve rule.

Many local business firms that want funds to finance expansion, inventories, new equipment, and other investments come to the bank and fill out applications for credit. The bank managers carefully examine the applications and choose the most creditworthy businesses as their loan clients. Bank managers must be concerned about the risk of **default,** which is nonrepayment of the principal and interest, on each of its loans. The risk of default must be carefully balanced against the interest income the bank obtains from making any given loan.

After the bank sorts through the applications and makes its decisions, it creates deposits for the clients to whom it makes loans. Usually banks require that their loan clients have an account at the bank. When the loan is approved, the bank simply adds the amount of the loan as a checkable deposit to the client's account.

Banks are usually very cautious about their reserves and seldom loan out all of their excess reserves. However, for simplicity, assume this bank actually does lend out *all* its excess reserves by creating deposits for its clients on the first day of business of its second week of operation. The resulting balance sheet is shown in Box 2. The bank now has $18 million in deposits, of which $8 million represents the proceeds of the loans it has just made. Because the newly created deposits didn't

Required reserve ratio:
The minimum percentage of deposits that a bank must hold in reserves to comply with regulatory requirements.

Required reserves:
The dollar value of currency and deposits in Federal Reserve Banks that a bank must hold to meet current regulations.

Excess reserves:
The difference between total reserves and required reserves of a bank held against deposits.

Default:
Nonrepayment of the principal and interest on a loan.

[2]As you'll see in the following chapter, the required reserve ratio is actually much less than 0.2 for most types of deposits at banks.

result from inflows of currency or from an increase in deposits in the bank's Federal Reserve account, reserves do not increase. Total reserves remain $10 million on the day the loans are made. The bottom line of *both sides* of the bank's balance sheet increases by $8 million on the first day of business of week 2 as the bank acquires assets in the form of loans of $8 million balanced by $8 million of newly created liabilities in the form of deposits. *By making loans in this way, the bank has created $8 million of checkable deposits. It therefore has created money equal to its initial amount of excess reserves.*

Box 2   Bank Balance Sheet
Beginning of Week 2: $8 Million in Loans Not Yet Withdrawn

Assets		Liabilities and net worth	
Reserves	$10,000,000	Deposits	$18,000,000
Loans	$8,000,000	Net worth	$500,000
Property	$500,000		
		Total liabilities and net worth	$18,500,000
Total assets	$18,500,000		

How Checks Drawn on Newly Created Deposits Affect an Individual Bank's Balance Sheet

If the $8 million of newly created deposits were to remain in the bank, required reserves would be $1.6 million, and it would still have $6.4 million of excess reserves. However, the bankers know that the newly created deposits resulting from the $8 million in loans will be quickly withdrawn as the business firms use their loaned funds to finance their investments. *Because there are many banks comprising the banking system, spent loan proceeds are unlikely to be redeposited in the bank that initially created the checkable deposit by making the loan.*

As the businesses draw on their newly created checkable deposits, the checks they write are deposited in other banks throughout the nation. For example, suppose this bank is located in Denver, Colorado. A firm that receives a loan of $1 million uses the funds to purchase a new conveyor system for its factory. The conveyor system is purchased from a firm in Detroit, Michigan. The $1 million check that is written to pay for the conveyor system is therefore deposited in a Detroit bank. When this is done, the Detroit bank sends the check to its district Federal Reserve Bank and requests that it be deposited in its account there. The Federal Reserve Bank will then send the check to the Denver bank's district Federal Reserve Bank where it will reduce the balance in the Denver bank's account by $1 million. When the Denver bank finally gets the check back, it will reduce by $1 million the sum in the account of the firm that wrote the check.

The process of transferring Federal Reserve deposits among banks as checks are paid is called **check clearing.** Because the Federal Reserve deposits held by banks constitute their reserves, the clearing of the $1 million check will reduce the Denver

Check clearing:
The process of transferring Federal Reserve deposits among banks as checks are paid.

bank's reserves by $1 million and increase the Detroit bank's reserves by $1 million. Check clearing, which is handled by specialized firms and the Federal Reserve Bank, usually takes a few days. The Denver bank can expect *all* of its $8 million of newly created deposits to clear through the banking system in this way and end up as deposits in *other* banks. Box 3 shows the Denver bank's balance sheet at the end of the week *after all its newly created deposits have been drawn on by the loan clients and the checks have cleared.*

Box 3 Bank Balance Sheet
End of Week 2: All Newly Created Deposits Drawn
and Paid to Other Banks

Assets		Liabilities and net worth	
Reserves		Deposits	$10,000,000
Required	$2,000,000		
Excess	$0	Net worth	$500,000
Loans	$8,000,000		
Property	$500,000	Total liabilities and net worth	$10,500,000
Total assets	$10,500,000		

Look at the liability side of the balance sheet. The bank now has only $10 million of deposits because its $8 million of newly created deposits has been drawn down and paid to other banks. Its net worth remains $500,000. Its assets now consist of $8 million in loans, $500,000 in property, *and only $2 million in reserves.* What happened to the $8 million in excess reserves that the bank had during its first week? These were paid out to *other* banks as the checks drawn on the loans cleared. The Denver bank had its account at its district Federal Reserve Bank debited by $8 million after all the checks cleared that were written on the newly created checkable deposits. The bank no longer has any excess reserves. It therefore cannot make any more loans at this point. When a bank's excess reserves are zero, the bank is said to be *loaned up.* This bank will remain loaned up unless it obtains more reserves from cash deposits or deposits of checks drawn on other banks that increase the sums in its Federal Reserve account.

There's an important difference between deposits that a single bank creates by making loans and those it obtains from customers who actually deposit cash or from checks drawn on other banks. The latter type of deposits increases the bank's reserves, while created deposits do not. This bank cannot create any more checkable deposits by making loans until it receives more deposits that increase its reserves. In general, its reserves will go up if it receives deposits of cash or of checks that are drawn on other banks. Any type of deposit that increases the cash in the bank's vault or its own deposits at the Federal Reserve Bank will increase the bank's excess reserves and allow it to make more loans.

1   What is fractional reserve banking?

2   What does a bank's balance sheet show?

3   A bank is currently holding reserves equal to 25% of its total deposits of $5 million. Assuming the required reserve ratio is 15%, how much of its deposits can the bank loan out? Why are deposits created by one bank likely to end up as new reserves for other banks?

Multiple Expansion of the Money Stock: The Entire Banking System

The truly amazing fact is that the *entire* banking system can create checkable deposits by an amount equal to a multiple of existing reserves available to all banks. To see how this process works, we need to trace the progress of newly created checkable deposits resulting from loans as they filter their way down through many banks. Suppose the $10 million in deposits that the Denver bank received during its first week of operation represents an increase in *total reserves* for the banking system. The bank might have succeeded in getting all the local misers to take their cash out of their mattresses and put it in banks where it can be used to support loans. In the previous section we saw how this $10 million in deposits supported $8 million of newly created checkable deposits as the Denver bank loaned out its excess reserves. To see how these initial deposits can support still *more* loans and more money creation, assume that *all* of the $8 million of new checkable deposits created by the Denver bank is deposited in the Detroit bank mentioned in the previous section.

The table in Box 4 shows the changes in assets and liabilities of the Detroit bank as a result of these deposits. The $8 million deposited increases the Detroit bank's liabilities by $8 million. As the deposited checks clear, the Detroit bank's reserves also increase by $8 million as $8 million in deposits at the Federal Reserve Banks is transferred from the Denver bank's account to the Detroit bank's account. Remember that the deposits that banks hold at their district Federal Reserve Banks constitute the bulk of their reserves.

The Detroit bank must hold 20% of its new reserves as required reserves against its $8 million in new deposits. This amounts to $1.6 million. The remaining $6.4 million is excess reserves that can be loaned out. *The initial $10 million in deposits at the Denver bank that already has supported $8 million in loans can now be used*

Box 4   Changes in Assets and Liabilities
Detroit Bank

Changes in assets		Changes in liabilities	
Reserves	+$8,000,000	Deposits	+$8,000,000
Required	+$1,600,000		
Excess	+$6,400,000		

to support an additional $6.4 million in loans. As the Detroit bank makes these loans, it will create checkable deposits equal to $6.4 million for its clients, assuming it loans out all its excess reserves. The total expansion in the money stock as a result of the initial $10 million increase in bank reserves is now $8 million plus $6.4 million, which equals $14.4 million.

The process of expansion doesn't stop here! As the checkable deposits created by the Detroit bank are spent by the people who obtain the loans, they will be deposited in other banks. This will increase the reserves of still more banks and will allow additional money creation. For example, suppose all of the $6.4 million is deposited in a New York bank. After the checks clear, the New York bank will find that both its deposits and its total reserves have increased by $6.4 million. This bank must keep 20% of these funds, which is $1.28 million in required reserves, and can loan out amounts up to the excess reserves of $5.12 million as newly created checkable deposits. The initial change in the New York bank's balance sheet is shown in Box 5. Assuming the New York bank loans out all its excess reserves, the money stock will increase by an additional $5.12 million.

Box 5 Changes in Assets and Liabilities
New York Bank

Changes in assets		Changes in liabilities	
Total reserves	+ $6,400,000	Deposits	+ $6,400,000
Required	+ $1,280,000		
Excess	+ $5,120,000		

The Money Creation Process

By now you can probably see how the process works. At each stage, as a result of new loans made by banks, the initial $10 million injection of reserves allows more money creation. However, at each stage the loans that can be made become smaller and smaller in amount because only 80% of the deposits created from new loans end up as excess reserves that can be used to make more loans. The increase in checkable deposits becomes smaller and smaller as the funds work their way through the banking system. Eventually the new loans that can be made approach zero.

The table in Box 6 shows how newly created checkable deposits at each stage decline, assuming that all excess reserves created at each stage of redeposit of loan proceeds are used to make new loans. It's also assumed, in the process of deposit and redeposit of checks among banks, that no reserves leak out of the banking system. For example, at each stage some of the people presenting checks to the banks might not deposit the full amount in their checking accounts. Instead they might ask the bank to give them a portion of the funds in currency. If the currency is held by customers instead of being deposited in banks, the growth of excess reserves at each stage will be less and the amount of new checkable deposits that can be created will also be less.

Box 6 Growth in Checkable Deposits from an Initial $10,000,000 of New Bank Reserves with a 0.2 Required Reserve Ratio (millions of dollars)

Stage	Bank	New reserves acquired	Required reserves	Excess reserves	Checkable deposits that can be created from new excess reserves
1	Denver	10.00	2.00	8.00	8.00
2	Detroit	8.00	1.60	6.40	6.40
3	New York	6.40	1.28	5.12	5.12
4	Chicago	5.12	1.02	4.10	4.10
5	St. Louis	4.10	0.82	3.28	3.28
6	San Francisco	3.28	0.66	2.62	2.62
7	Los Angeles	2.62	0.52	2.10	2.10
8	Seattle	2.10	0.42	1.68	1.68
9	Cleveland	1.68	0.34	1.34	1.34
10	All other				5.36
	Total increase in money stock				40.00

The sum of additional deposits eventually reaches a limit as the additional excess reserves for the banking system that result from redeposit of funds eventually approach zero. The table in Box 6 shows how additional checkable deposits that can be created fall to $4.10 million when the checks drawn on $5.12 million of deposits created by the New York bank are deposited in a Chicago bank. The table also shows how the maximum amount of checkable deposits that can be created becomes smaller as the Chicago bank makes loans and as the funds are then deposited in a St. Louis bank that then acquires $3.28 million in excess reserves. The last column traces out the process for a number of other stages and shows how the maximum sum of new checkable deposits that can be created approaches $40 million. The $10 million of deposits of currency in the new bank therefore can result in a $40 million increase in the money stock when banks find it profitable to loan out all the excess reserves they acquire at each stage of the process.

The Reserve Multiplier

For the entire banking system, an injection of $8 million in new excess reserves can be used to support a maximum of $40 million in new deposits when the required reserve ratio is 0.2! An individual bank can create no more checkable deposits than the amount of excess reserves it acquires. However, the *entire banking system* can create new checkable deposits that amount to a *multiple* of the initial injection of excess reserves into the banking system. Any individual bank is likely to lose excess reserves it acquires when it creates a checkable deposit for a loan customer. However, except for currency withdrawal, the excess reserves are not withdrawn from the banking system. When the new checkable deposits are deposited in another bank, that bank also acquires reserves of which another 80% can be loaned out.

Notice that the money creation process is just like the one described for the multiplier effect in the chapter on Keynesian analysis. The maximum amount of new checkable deposits that can result from a new injection of ΔER dollars of excess reserves into the banking system can be expressed as an infinite geometric progression. After the $8 million in initial deposits created by the initial injection of new excess reserves, the second-round maximum of new deposits that can be created by the Detroit bank is $6.4 million. The $6.4 million can be expressed as (0.8) ($8 million). Similarly, the $5.12 million maximum of new deposits that can be created at the third stage by the New York bank can be expressed as 0.8 [0.8($8 million)], which equals $(0.8)^2$($8 million). In the same way the $4.10 million in maximum checkable deposits that can be created at the fourth stage by the Chicago bank, assuming it loans out all its newly acquired excess reserves, can be expressed as $(0.8)^3$($8 million). The infinite geometric progression is:

Newly created checkable deposits =
$8 million + 0.8($8 million) + 0.8^2($8 million) + 0.8^3($8 million) + 0.8^4($8 million)
$$+ \ldots$$

As the sum continues, each successive term becomes smaller because when any number less than 1 is raised to a higher power it becomes smaller. The maximum possible increase in checkable deposits, and hence the money stock (ΔM), resulting from the initial increase in excess reserves for the banking system can be calculated by using the following formula to solve for the sum of an infinite geometric progression:

$$\Delta M = \frac{\Delta ER}{(1 - 0.8)} = \frac{\Delta ER}{0.2}$$

where ΔER is the change in excess reserves for the banking system. In this example, ΔER is $8 million, which represents the increase in excess reserves resulting from an initial $10 million deposit of currency into the banking system by the public. The maximum increase in the money stock resulting from new checkable deposits that can be created from this amount of excess reserves is therefore

$$\Delta M = \frac{\$8 \text{ million}}{0.2} = \$40 \text{ million}$$

When the required reserve ratio is 0.2, each dollar of excess reserves that enters the banking system can support *five times* as much in new checkable deposits when banks find it profitable to loan out all their excess reserves at each stage of the process. Under these circumstances an injection of $8 million in *new excess reserves* into the banking system can therefore ultimately support $40 million of new money stock in the form of checkable deposits.

The **reserve multiplier** is the maximum amount of new money stock that can be created from each dollar increase in excess reserves available to the banking system. In the example just given the reserve multiplier was 5. In general the reserve multiplier can be calculated simply by dividing the number 1 by the required reserve ratio:

Reserve multiplier:
The maximum amount of new money stock that can be created from each dollar increase in excess reserves available to the banking system.

$$\text{Reserve multiplier} = \frac{1}{\text{Required reserve ratio}}$$

In this case the reserve multiplier is

$$1/0.2 = 5$$

If the required reserve ratio were 0.1 instead of 0.2, the reserve multiplier would be increased to

$$1/0.1 = 10$$

The maximum amount of new checkable deposits, ΔM, that can result from any increase in excess reserves can also be expressed as:

$$\Delta M = \Delta ER(\text{Reserve multiplier})$$

This gives the amount of checkable deposits that the banking system can create from any increase in excess reserves when all excess reserves are loaned out and there is no withdrawal of currency from the banking system. In the previous example the maximum increase in checkable deposits is 5 times $8 million, which is $40 million.

Notice that the maximum possible increase in the money stock depends on *both* the excess reserves injected into the banking system and the required reserve ratio. Other things being equal, the larger the increase in excess reserves or the lower the required reserve ratio, the greater the increase in the money stock. The *actual* increase in the money stock depends on the willingness of banks to lend out excess reserves they acquire as a result of the money creation process and the amount of loan proceeds that end up in other banks (that is, the public's taste for currency). Thus the preceding equation represents the maximum possible creation of deposits; in reality, the amount of money created will be less than is implied by the formula.

As a further illustration of how to use the formula, suppose the Denver bank borrows $5 million from its district Federal Reserve Bank. When it does, the Denver bank's account at the district Federal Reserve Bank will be credited by $5 million. This $5 million represents new bank assets in the form of reserves that are balanced by a liability in the form of a $5 million debt to the Federal Reserve. Since no new deposits were acquired, the entire $5 million becomes excess reserves for the Denver bank. Assuming a required reserve ratio of 0.1, the maximum increase in the money stock that can result from the Denver bank's loan from the Federal Reserve is:

$$\Delta M = \$5 \text{ million}/0.1 = \$50 \text{ million}$$

Assuming that banks find it profitable to loan out all excess reserves at each stage of the money creation process, a $5 million loan to a bank by the Federal Reserve Bank will increase the money stock by $50 million.

Deposit Contraction: The Process in Reverse

The banking system's capacity to create money by making loans is impaired if its reserves are reduced. Suppose misers decide to withdraw $10 million in deposits from banks to stuff back into their mattresses. There will be no change in the money stock at first. The amount of checkable deposits will decline by $10 million, but the amount of currency will increase by the same amount even if the currency stays in mattresses. However, bank reserves will also decline by $10 million as a result of the withdrawal of currency that is not redeposited into the banking system. The $10 million withdrawal from the banking system reduces excess reserves by $8 million.

If the banking system is fully loaned up, it will have to obtain more reserves to make up for its loss or will have to reduce the amount of loans it has outstanding or securities it holds. Certain types of loans can be called in. This means the bank tells the borrowers they must repay their loans. As loans are repaid, the banks in the system find that their deposits decline and the required reserves they must hold also decline. Of course, if there are excess reserves in the system, the decline in deposits wouldn't be as drastic.

In practice, banks rarely have to call in loans when reserves fall because of withdrawals. There's a constant turnover of loans as old loans are paid off and new loans are negotiated. The decline in reserves caused by the withdrawal will force the banks in the system not to renew existing loans as their terms expire. The banks will also make fewer new loans than they would have otherwise as existing loans are paid off. Finally, banks typically supply credit in an impersonal way by buying government securities and other notes of indebtedness. Banks can easily and quickly obtain additional reserves to meet their reserve requirements by selling securities they hold. If government securities are sold to the Federal Reserve Banks, the banks will be credited with an increase in deposits that serve as reserves at the district Federal Reserve Banks.

Assuming a required reserve ratio of 0.2, the maximum reduction in the money stock, ΔM, resulting from an \$8 million withdrawal of excess reserves from the banking system would be:

$$\text{Maximum reduction in checkable deposits} = \frac{\text{Loss in excess reserves}}{\text{Required reserve ratio}}$$

$$\Delta M = \frac{-\$8 \text{ million}}{0.2}$$

$$= -\$40 \text{ million}$$

The maximum decline in the money stock that results from the \$10 million withdrawal from the banking system will therefore be \$40 million. Of course, the decline in checkable deposits will be less if the banking system has excess reserves than would be the case when the bank is fully loaned up.

Bank Demand for Excess Reserves

Why might banks choose to hold excess reserves rather than use those reserves to create checkable deposits for loan customers? Although they give up the opportunity to earn interest income by holding excess reserves, banks often find it convenient to do so. One reason banks hold excess reserves is to meet expected deposit outflows. When a bank has excess reserves available, it doesn't have to call in loans, sell securities, or borrow to meet expected deposit outflows. If a bank anticipates a heavy net outflow of deposits, it's likely to retain more excess reserves so it will be prepared to meet that demand. When excess reserves are on hand, the bank avoids the transaction costs of obtaining the funds in other ways. The savings realized by avoiding these transaction costs often more than offset the forgone interest income on the excess reserves. This is exactly analogous to the idea of transaction demand for money by the public. Also, as a precaution banks might hold excess reserves for unforeseen net outflows of deposits.

A bank's opportunity cost of holding each dollar of excess reserves is the interest income it forgoes by not lending that dollar out. Naturally, the higher the interest rate, the lower the quantity of excess reserves demanded. The lower the interest rate, the greater the willingness of banks to hold excess reserves.

Remember that banks are motivated to make profits. During a recession, interest rates typically decline and business failures tend to rise. It's both less profitable and more risky for banks to make loans in periods of economic downturn than during periods of recovery when aggregate demand and real GNP are increasing. During a recession, banks are therefore more likely to hold excess reserves because lower interest rates and increased risk of loan defaults make lending money less profitable. Similarly, they're less likely to hold excess reserves in periods of recovery when

Principles in Practice

Nonbank Financial Intermediaries

All banks are financial intermediaries, but not all financial intermediaries are banks. What are nonbank financial intermediaries? How do they differ from banks, and what role do they play in the financial system?

Nonbank financial intermediaries are those that make loans and provide other financial services but do not offer checkable deposits included in the M1 definition of money. These intermediaries channel funds from savers to borrowers. Some of these firms also help individuals and firms manage their cash balances in ways that are likely to affect the demand for money balances. Nonbank financial intermediaries include insurance companies, pension funds, mutual funds, and brokerage houses.

Insurance companies invest the premiums paid on policies in government securities, corporate stocks and bonds, mortgages, and real estate. Life insurance companies also allow their policyholders to borrow funds against the cash value of life insurance.

Pension funds invest the contributions of employers and employees in various assets. In effect, these funds channel savings for retirement of workers to finance investment by corporations and other businesses.

There are also finance companies that loan money to consumers and small businesses. These companies raise funds by borrowing on the open market and by issuing their own stocks and bonds. The funds raised in this way are used to finance small loans. General Motors Acceptance Corporation is an example of a finance company set up for the sole purpose of financing cars. There are also consumer finance companies (like Household Finance) that finance the purchase of such consumer durables as furniture and appliances. Finally, business finance firms specialize in providing credit to business firms.

Mutual funds are financial intermediaries that channel the funds of savers into a variety of assets. These firms enable small investors to purchase a share of a diversified portfolio of stocks, bonds, or any variety of assets. One of the most significant recent developments in financial markets has been the organization of *money market mutual funds.* These funds invest in various kinds of short-term debt of business firms and governments and also purchase bank certificates of deposit. These funds were first organized in the late 1970s. By the mid-1980s they held about $200 billion in assets. A unique feature of money market mutual funds is that they often allow their investors to actually write checks on the balances in their mutual fund accounts! In other words, these funds are often as liquid as checkable deposits for the savers who invest in these accounts. They are redeemable at a fixed price per share. However, most of the funds don't permit checks to be written for less than $500 or $1,000.

Money market accounts with check-writing privileges are not legally considered checkable deposits. They are not subject to reserve requirements. Money market funds enable small investors to earn interest on funds they would normally hold in checkable deposit accounts that earn little or no interest. By reducing average daily cash balances that households hold, the funds contribute to quicker turnover of the available money stock. In other words, these financial innovations tend to decrease the demand for money represented by M1.

---

interest rates increase and the risk of loan default declines. The graph in Box 7 illustrates the downward-sloping bank demand curve for excess reserves and shows how changes in the market rate of interest affect bank holdings of excess reserves.

The cyclical fluctuation in bank demand for excess reserves has important implications for the money stock. The more excess reserves that banks wish to hold, the smaller the money stock. This is because by holding excess reserves the banks don't create the maximum possible amount of checkable deposits by making loans. For example, if the required reserve ratio were 0.1, each dollar increase in excess reserves *held by banks* rather than used to make loans or buy securities would prevent the money stock from increasing by $10! This means that during recessions, when banks seek to increase the excess reserves they hold, there will be downward pressure on the money stock. Because, as you'll soon see, the available stock of money influences aggregate demand, the resulting decline in money could further decrease aggregate demand during the recession, thereby causing a further decline in real GNP. By the same token, the eagerness of banks to make loans with their excess reserves during periods of peak economic activity tends to increase the money stock. This puts upward pressure on aggregate demand and could contribute to inflation.

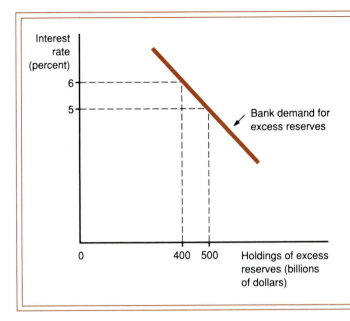

Box 7   Bank Demand for Excess Reserves

The dollar amount of excess reserves banks desire to hold, other things being equal, increases with declines in the market level of interest rates. During an expansion when interest rates typically rise, banks decrease holdings of excess reserves by extending more credit. This fuels the expansion and can cause inflation. During a contraction when interest rates typically fall, banks increase their holdings of excess reserves by cutting back on credit extended, thereby decreasing aggregate demand and making the contraction more pronounced.

The profit-motivated banking system can therefore cause destabilizing swings in aggregate demand that exaggerate the ups and downs of the business cycle. In an attempt to minimize the swings, the Federal Reserve System seeks to manage the total reserves available to the banking system. The role of the Federal Reserve in influencing the money stock in this way is the subject of the following chapter.

Concept Check

1   The required reserve ratio is 0.1. If reserves available to the banking system increase by $10 million, what is the maximum possible increase in checkable deposits that can result?

2   How does a decrease in bank reserves lead to a decrease in the money stock?

3   Why might banks choose to hold some of their assets in the form of excess reserves?

Bank Portfolio Management

The picture of bank deposit creation just presented is highly simplified. In actuality banking is a very complex business. However, you can understand the basic principles of banking from the preceding examples. Banks must be concerned with both the *liquidity* and the profitability of their operations.

Banks earn profits because they can make loans at higher interest rates than the rates they must pay to attract deposits. In fact, for most checkable deposit accounts, the bank pays no interest to depositors. The bank also charges fees for checking services and other financial services. For time deposit accounts, such as savings accounts and certificates of deposit, the bank pays interest to compete with other financial intermediaries and attract deposits.

Principles in Practice

Bank Regulation

Remember the immortal words of outlaw Willie Sutton when he was asked why he robbed banks: "Because that's where the money is!"

Perhaps because banks are where the money is, they're among the most regulated firms in the economy. The reason for stringent regulation by various state and federal agencies is to prevent the horrifying specter of a collapse of the banking system. A *bank failure* occurs when a depository institution cannot meet its obligations to depositors who wish to withdraw funds. Because one bank often has deposits and loans at other banks, a major bank failure could set up a chain reaction that causes chaos in the financial payments system.

A loss of confidence in the banking system can cause a *bank panic* in which depositors flock to banks to convert their deposits to cash. The increase in withdrawals on a given day can deplete the banking system's reserves.

During the Depression of the early 1930s, there were thousands of bank failures that wiped out the savings of millions of persons. In 1934, to prevent future bank failures and to maintain confidence in the banking system, the Federal Deposit Insurance Corporation (FDIC) was established to guarantee bank deposits. The FDIC currently insures all deposits up to $100,000 per account from loss as a result of bank failure. Because many corporations maintain deposit accounts well in excess of $100,000, this insurance provides protection mainly to households. If a bank should fail, the FDIC has the right to dismiss its management and take over the bank to oversee the sale of its assets to pay off depositors. Like any insurance system, the FDIC works if there is a small, predictable number of bank failures in each year. The insurance fund held by the FDIC amounts to about 2% of insured deposits and only a fraction of a percent of total deposits. If a panic spread throughout the banking system, it would be difficult for the FDIC to meet all of its insurance obligations without help from the federal government, which would have to use tax revenues to bail out the banks.

Thrift institutions also have their deposits insured for up to $100,000 per account by the Federal Savings and Loan Insurance Corporation (FSLIC). This agency is similar to the FDIC. In addition, savings and loan associations and mutual savings banks are regulated and examined by the Federal Home Loan Bank Board and by various state agencies.

Unfortunately, bank failures are not a thing of the past. There's increasing concern today about the problem of bank failure because the number of banks that go under has been increasing in recent years. In 1985, 120 banks failed in the United States. In 1984, 70 banks failed. In that year the FDIC worked to prevent the failure of the nation's eighth largest bank, the Continental Illinois National Bank. In the early 1980s this major midwestern bank loaned large amounts of funds to oil companies and other firms in energy-related industries. In 1981 when oil prices began to plummet, Continental Illinois was in trouble as many of the companies to which it had loaned funds went bankrupt. The bank's losses on loans were estimated at over $2 billion. As the rumors about trouble with the bank's loans spread, many large depositors began withdrawing funds, and in 1984 Continental Illinois was forced to borrow $3.6 billion from the Federal Reserve Bank of Chicago. Despite these loans, the bank was still losing reserves because of withdrawals, and its failure appeared imminent.

The FDIC effectively bailed out this institution by taking it over and guaranteeing *all* deposits, not just those amounting to less than $100,000. The bailout of Continental Illinois cost the FDIC $1.5 billion. The FDIC then helped organize a group of 28 banks that loaned Continental $5.5 billion to help meet demands for withdrawals and restore confidence in the institution.

A bank whose management makes loans only to the least creditworthy applicants is likely to be able to charge higher interest rates than if it made safer loans. This will allow the bank to make higher profits provided the customers actually do repay their loans. However, this bank risks the possibility that a high percentage of its loans will default. Loan default means the bank will not earn any interest and will also lose the funds it has lent out. Banks must balance their desire for increased profitability against the risk of default and the risk of having assets that cannot be easily converted to reserves to meet unexpected withdrawals. To do so, most bankers are careful to have a diversified *portfolio,* or mix, of assets.

Typically a bank will make some risky loans at high interest rates. The riskiest types of loans are those that are simply unsecured promises to repay. Consumer loans, such as those on credit card accounts, are an example of this type of risky loan. Banks also make short-term loans to creditworthy businesses at lower interest rates than they charge consumers. The **prime rate** is the interest rate a bank charges

Prime rate:
The interest rate a bank charges its most creditworthy customers for short-term loans of less than 1 year.

its most creditworthy customers, which are usually large corporations, for short-term loans of less than 1 year.

A bank often demands **collateral,** which is an asset a borrower pledges to a lender in case of default. For example, if you borrow money to buy a car, the bank typically asks you to pledge the car as collateral. The bank usually has a formal *lien* on the car, which means you can't sell the car without the bank's permission or repayment of the loan. If you default on the loan, the bank can seize the car and sell it to obtain the outstanding balance on your loan. Similarly, a *mortgage* is a loan a bank makes to finance the purchase of a house or other real estate, with the loan secured by that asset as collateral. The interest rate a bank charges on a loan depends on the collateral offered by the customer, the customer's credit history (as rated by independent credit bureaus), and various other factors. However, in general, loans are not very liquid. Most loans cannot be easily called in to be converted to reserves when the need arises. However, very short-term loans, those made for a period of, say, 1 to 3 months, turn over quickly and give the bank some flexibility in adjusting the amount of loans outstanding when the need for reserves arises.

Most banks carry 10% to 20% of their assets in the form of government securities that can be sold quickly at very low transaction costs to obtain reserves when the bank needs them. **Government securities** are interest-bearing debts of the federal government in the form of Treasury bills, Treasury notes, and Treasury bonds. The interest earned on these securities is typically lower than the interest the bank can earn on loans. However, the liquidity of the assets is worth the loss in profitability to the bank. The business of banking involves careful portfolio management to balance risks, profits, and liquidity.

Commercial Bank Balance Sheets

Box 8 shows the actual balance sheet of all commercial banks in the United States as of January 1988. Assets of commercial banks, the dominant depository institutions in the United States, totaled slightly over $2,800 billion at the beginning of 1988. Notice that actual reserves on deposit at Federal Reserve Banks and other cash items constituted only 7.5% of total assets. The required reserve ratio for commercial banks currently ranges from 0.03 to 0.12, depending on the type of deposit.

Commercial banks typically hold about 20% of their assets in the form of highly liquid government securities. In January 1988 government and other liquid securities accounted for 18.4% of commercial bank assets. These assets can easily be converted to excess reserves. Government securities held by banks are often called **secondary reserves.** The sum of cash and government securities therefore typically amounts to between 25% and 30% of commercial bank assets. This can be viewed as the banking system's *liquidity base* used to meet deposit withdrawal demands.

Loans of various types accounted for over 67% of bank assets in January 1988. The bulk of commercial bank loans is in the forms of commercial and industrial credit to proprietorships, partnerships, and corporations.

On the liability side of the balance sheet, checkable deposits account for about 20% of the sum of all liabilities and net worth. Savings deposits and various certificates of deposit amount to close to 50% of liabilities and net worth. As you can see from the data in Box 8, banks are heavy borrowers. Total borrowings accounted for slightly over 15% of the sum of total liabilities and net worth in January 1988. Banks borrow from the Federal Reserve System, from other commercial banks, and from corporations. The net worth of commercial banks amounts to about 6% of their assets.

Collateral:
An asset a borrower pledges to a lender in case of default.

Government securities:
Interest-bearing debts of the federal government in the form of Treasury bills, Treasury notes, and Treasury bonds.

Secondary reserves:
Government securities held by banks.

Box 8 Balance Sheet: All U.S. Commercial Banks, January 1988 (billions of dollars)

Assets			Liabilities		
	Amount	Percent of total		Amount	Percent of total
Reserves: cash and deposits at Federal Reserve and other banks	209.6	7.5	Checkable deposits	576.0	20.6
Government and other securities	515.2	18.4	Savings and time deposits	1,392.0	49.7
Loans	1,881.6	67.2	Borrowing	443.2	15.8
Commercial and industrial	565.3		Other liabilities and net worth	389.4	13.9
Real estate	588.5				
Individual	330.8				
Other	397.0				
Other assets	194.3	6.9			
Total assets	2,800.7		Total liabilities and net worth	2,800.7	

Source: *Federal Reserve Bulletin*, April 1988.

Balance Sheet of Other Depository Institutions: Savings and Loan Associations and Savings Banks

In recent years the distinction between commercial banks and so-called thrift institutions has blurred. In the past, thrift institutions such as savings and loan associations, mutual savings banks, and credit unions were not able to offer checkable deposits. The Depository Institutions Deregulation and Monetary Control Act of 1980 changed all that. Since that time thrift institutions have been able to issue checkable deposits and compete with commercial banks for these accounts. The law also effectively allows both thrift institutions and commercial banks to pay interest on certain types of checking accounts. Prior to 1980 it was illegal in the United States to pay interest on checkable deposits.

However, major distinctions between commercial banks and thrift institutions still remain, as you can see by looking at the balance sheet of all U.S. savings and loan associations and savings banks shown in Box 9. The dominant thrift institution is the savings and loan association, which accounted for about two thirds of the assets of all thrift institutions in the United States as of November 1987. First look at the asset side of the balance sheet. About 35% of the assets are in mortgage loans or mortgage-backed securities. These are mainly loans to homeowners to finance the purchase of residences. Cash and investment securities, the primary and secondary reserves of the thrift institutions, amounted to 11.5% of their assets in November 1987. These thrift institutions developed primarily to supply credit to homeowners and consumers rather than to business firms. This legacy, although it is changing, still

Box 9 Balance Sheet: All U.S. Savings and Loan Associations and Savings Banks
November 1987 (billions of dollars)

Assets			Liabilities and net worth		
	Amount	Percent of total		Amount	Percent of total
Cash and investment securities	174.6	11.5	Deposits	1,131.4	74.7
			Borrowing	247.1	16.3
Mortgage-backed securities and mortgage loans	524.3	34.6	Other liabilities and net worth	137.1	9.0
Other assets	816.7	53.9			
			Total liabilities and net worth	1,515.6	
Total assets	1,515.6				

Source: *Federal Reserve Bulletin*, April 1988.

dominates the balance sheets of these institutions that have only recently been able to offer checking accounts.

Concept Check

1 How do banks earn profit?

2 What are secondary reserves?

3 Why do banks seek to have a diversified portfolio of assets?

Toward Understanding How the Money Supply Changes

The decisions made by the firms that constitute the nation's banking system exert an important influence on the money stock. In this chapter we've concentrated on the process by which the banking system actually creates money in the form of checkable deposits. As you have seen, the excess reserves available to the system and the willingness of banks to loan out these excess reserves are the major factors influencing daily money supplies.

To understand how the quantity of money available to the public changes, our next step is to examine how changes occur in the reserves available to the banking system. The Federal Reserve System manages the nation's money stock by determining the reserves available to the banking system and thus influencing the level of interest rates in the economy. To understand the role of money in the economy, we must analyze how the Federal Reserve System can control bank reserves and influence the willingness of banks to lend excess reserves.

In the following chapter we examine the operations of the Federal Reserve System. This will give you the necessary background to understand how the monetary policies pursued by the Federal Reserve System can influence macroeconomic equilibrium in the economy.

Summary

1. Financial intermediaries are firms that specialize in borrowing funds from savers and lending those funds to investors and others. The nation's banking system includes those financial intermediaries, such as commercial banks and thrift institutions, that offer checkable deposits.

2. Modern banking originated in the Middle Ages with the practice of issuing receipts for gold on deposit with goldsmiths and money lenders. The receipts began to circulate as money. By observing inflows and outflows of gold deposits, the money lenders realized that only a small fraction of the gold on deposit was likely to be withdrawn on average each day. The issuers of gold receipts, who acted as bankers, ran little risk of running out of gold to meet depositors' demands for withdrawals. As a result they could issue receipts for more than the actual amounts of gold they held in their vaults.

3. Fractional reserve banking allows a banking system to create checkable deposits by making loans in some multiple of the reserves the banks actually have on hand to meet withdrawals. The fractional reserve ratio is actual reserves divided by total deposits.

4. The banking industry in the United States consists of about 15,000 commercial banks, 4,000 savings and loan associations, 4,000 mutual savings banks, and other thrift institutions that offer checkable deposits. The reserves of modern banks consist of cash on hand and balances kept on deposit with the regional banks of the Federal Reserve System, which is the nation's central bank that serves as a bank for bankers.

5. A bank balance sheet is a statement of its assets and the claims against those assets in the form of liabilities and net worth. A bank's liabilities consist mainly of deposit accounts, which represent the debt of the bank to depositors. The bank's major assets are its loans, government securities, and reserves in the form of cash on hand and deposits at the Federal Reserve Banks. Its net worth is the difference between the value of its assets and the value of its liabilities.

6. The required reserve ratio for a bank is the legal minimum percentage of its deposits it must hold in reserves. Required reserves represent the dollar value of currency and deposits in the Federal Reserve Banks that a bank must hold to meet current regulations. Excess reserves represent the difference between total reserves held against deposits and required reserves. A bank can use its excess reserves to make loans.

7. When a bank uses excess reserves to make a loan, it creates a deposit for the borrower. When the borrower spends the newly created deposit, excess reserves are likely to flow out of the borrower's bank and into another bank. The process of check clearing involves transferring of deposits at the Federal Reserve Banks. Excess reserves that one bank loses after making a loan are likely to end up as excess reserves for another bank in the banking system. A bank that uses up all its excess reserves to make loans is said to be loaned up. Banks typically hold at least some of their assets as excess reserves.

8. The banking system can create checkable deposits by an amount equal to a multiple of existing reserves available to all banks. As deposits created through loans are drawn down to make purchases, they increase deposits and reserves in other banks, which can use the excess reserves to make more loans. The reserve multiplier is the maximum number of new dollars in checkable deposits that can be created from each dollar increase in excess reserves available to the banking system. The reserve multiplier is the inverse of the required reserve ratio.

9. Just as an increase in excess reserves has the potential to cause an increase in checkable deposits, a decrease in excess reserves can cause a decrease in checkable deposits. Because checkable deposits are the major component of the money stock, excess reserves available to the banking system are an important influence on the money stock.

10. Banks choose to hold some of their assets as excess reserves rather than using those reserves to make loans. The opportunity cost of holding excess reserves depends on the interest the banks forgo by not using the funds to make loans. The demand for excess reserves typically increases during economic downturns and decreases during economic upturns. The greater the bank demand for excess reserves, the smaller the money stock.

11. Banks are motivated to make profits, but they must also be concerned about the liquidity of their assets so they can make adjustments in the composition of their asset portfolio as business conditions change. Banks also are concerned about the riskiness of their assets and seek to minimize the risk of default on loans. Most banks hold 10% to 20% of their assets in government securities—assets that can be easily liquidated at low transaction cost. In their day-to-day operations, banks balance considerations of profitability, risk, and liquidity.

Key Terms and Concepts

Depository institutions	Excess reserves
Bank	Default
Financial intermediaries	Check clearing
Fractional reserve banking	Reserve multiplier
Fractional reserve ratio	Prime rate
Reserves	Collateral
Required reserve ratio	Government securities
Required reserves	Secondary reserves

Problems and Applications

1. A banker operates under a 20% fractional reserve ratio. What amount of deposits can be supported by $5 million of reserves? In what form does a bank hold its reserves? Explain why the bank is unlikely to ever have to pay out all of its deposits in a single day.

2. Suppose you deposit $3,000 in cash from your mattress in your local bank. Show the impact of your deposit on the bank's balance sheet. Explain why your bank cannot increase loans it makes after it receives your deposit by more than a certain percentage of $3,000. If the required reserve ratio is 0.1, what is the maximum increase in checkable deposits that will result *in the entire banking system* as a result of your deposit of currency into the banking system?

3. Suppose you have accounts at two different banks. During a particular week you write a check on one of your accounts for $1,000 and deposit it in your account at the other bank. Will the money stock increase as a result of your transaction?

4. Suppose the Federal Reserve Bank lends funds to the First National Bank of Toledo. It does so by crediting the Toledo bank's account at the Federal Reserve by $2 million. Show the impact of the loan on the First National Bank of Toledo balance sheet. What will happen to the bank's excess reserves as a result of the loan from the Federal Reserve Bank? If the required reserve ratio is 0.1, what is

the maximum increase in the money stock that can result from the loan?

5. Suppose that during the holiday season households withdraw $10 billion from their accounts in banks to hold as cash in their pockets to facilitate shopping. What will happen to bank excess reserves and the capacity of the banking system to make loans as a result?

6. The required reserve ratio is 0.1 and current available bank reserves are $40 billion. Explain why checkable deposits in the banking system are likely to be less than the maximum possible $400 billion.

7. Following is the balance sheet of the First National Bank of Jonesville:

Assets	*Liabilities and net worth*
Reserves $100 million	Deposits $180 million
Securities $50 million	Net worth $20 million
Loans $50 million	

If the required reserve ratio is 0.1, what is the amount of the bank's excess reserves? How many dollars' worth of additional loans or securities can the bank acquire as assets? How much of an increase in the money stock could be supported by the excess reserves held by the Jonesville bank if all banks in the banking system were to hold zero excess reserves?

8. Suppose the bank demand curve for excess reserves is a horizontal line. What will be the effect on the money stock of an increase in the amount of excess reserves available to the banking system?

9. Explain why bank demand for excess reserves tends to increase during recessions. Why does the fact that bank demand for excess reserves varies with general business conditions tend to destabilize the economy?

10. How do banks choose their portfolio of assets to balance considerations of profitability, liquidity, and risk?

Suggested Readings

Dudley G. Luckett, "Approaches to Bank Liquidity Management," Federal Reserve Bank of Kansas City, *Economic Review,* March 1980. This article uses case studies to illustrate how banks approach the problems of liquidity.

Frederick S. Mishkin, *The Economics of Money, Banking, and Financial Markets,* Boston: Little, Brown, 1987. Chapters 8-15 provide detailed analyses and data on the U.S. financial system.

Dorothy M. Nichols, *Modern Money Mechanics: A Workbook on Deposits, Currency and Bank Reserves,* Federal Reserve Bank of Chicago, 1975. This workbook is loaded with examples that show how multiple deposit expansion by the banking system takes place under a variety of conditions.

A Forward Look

In the following chapter we show how the day-to-day operations of the Federal Reserve System can influence bank reserves and the money stock. The Federal Reserve System exerts a strong influence on aggregate demand and the performance of the economy because its operations affect market interest rates.

The Federal Reserve System and Its Influence on Money and Credit

It's nicknamed "the Fed," and its chairman is a highly visible and powerful person whose pronouncements can change the course of the world's securities markets. It's the Federal Reserve System, and its policies and activities play a central role in the economies of the United States and the world.

In this chapter we continue our analysis of the U.S. monetary system by examining the role of the Federal Reserve System in the economy. As the nation's central banking system, the Fed engages in activities that influence the money stock available in the nation. As you saw in the preceding chapter, the 12 regional Federal Reserve Banks provide deposit accounts for commercial banks and thrift institutions and supply them with currency and check-clearing services. The deposits of banks at the Federal Reserve Banks are part of their reserves.

The Federal Reserve System charges banks fees for its services and earns interest on government securities it holds. However, the Fed isn't motivated to maximize profits like an ordinary bank. It's an independent agency charged with promoting the public interest. In an attempt to promote economic stability, the Fed pursues policies that influence the stock of money in circulation, interest rates, and other macroeconomic variables.

In this chapter we outline the organization and operations of the Federal Reserve System. Our main goal is to see how the Fed can influence the money stock and the level of interest rates in the economy. In the following chapter we'll examine how the Fed's activities can affect aggregate demand in the economy and influence real GNP and the price level.

1 Discuss the organization and structure of the Federal Reserve System.
2 Describe the balance sheet of the Federal Reserve Banks and discuss the techniques used by the Fed to influence the money supply.
3 Show how the Fed's open market operations affect bank reserves, securities prices, interest rates, and the money supply.
4 Analyze the nation's money supply curve and show how desires by banks to hold excess reserves affect the quantity of money supplied.

The Federal Reserve System

The Federal Reserve Act of 1913 established the Federal Reserve System and the 12 regional Federal Reserve Banks. The system was organized in response to a series of bank panics in the late nineteenth and early twentieth centuries. One of the most serious of these panics occurred in 1907. The loss in savings resulting from bank failures at that time led to strong political support for a central banking authority. Since it was established in 1913, the Federal Reserve System has acted in the public interest to promote the stability of the nation's banking and monetary system. Its role in the economy has evolved gradually since its organization. Currently the Fed's day-to-day operations constitute an essential mechanism in the functioning of the economy. To gain a complete understanding of how the economy operates, it's necessary to examine the organization and functions of the Federal Reserve System.

The Federal Reserve System: How It Is Organized

Board of Governors of the Federal Reserve System:
Supervises the operation of the nation's banking system and acts as an authority to regulate the money supply. The Board consists of seven Governors, each appointed by the President to serve a 14-year term.

The **Board of Governors of the Federal Reserve System,** located in Washington, D.C., supervises the operation of the nation's banking system and acts as an authority to regulate the money supply. The Board of Governors consists of seven Governors, each of whom is appointed by the President of the United States, after approval by the Senate, for a 14-year term. One of the Governors serves as Chairman of the Board of Governors. The Chairman is appointed by the President for a 4-year term. The current Chairman is Alan Greenspan, who was appointed by President Reagan in 1987 (see Economic Thinkers box).

The Board of Governors operates as an independent, self-supporting authority. It neither receives funding from Congress nor must take orders from the President or any other political official! The Board has broad policymaking functions. For example, within certain limits the Board makes decisions about reserve requirements for banks.

Regional Federal Reserve Banks:
Perform central banking functions for banks within each of 12 Federal Reserve districts.

The **regional Federal Reserve Banks** perform central banking functions for banks within each of 12 Federal Reserve districts. There are regional Federal Reserve Banks located in San Francisco, Minneapolis, Kansas City, Dallas, Chicago, St. Louis, Atlanta, Cleveland, Richmond, Philadelphia, New York, and Boston. The maps in Box 1 show the boundaries of each of the 12 Federal Reserve districts.

Each of the regional Federal Reserve Banks is a corporation. The banks earn income from assets they hold that more than covers their expenses. The banks are

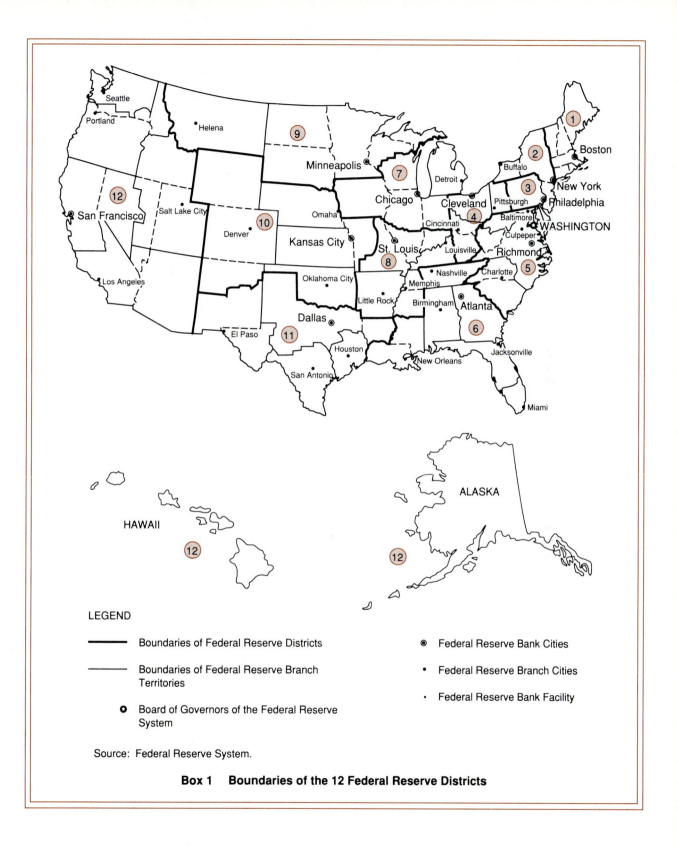

LEGEND

━━━ Boundaries of Federal Reserve Districts

─── Boundaries of Federal Reserve Branch Territories

◎ Board of Governors of the Federal Reserve System

◎ Federal Reserve Bank Cities

• Federal Reserve Branch Cities

· Federal Reserve Bank Facility

Source: Federal Reserve System.

Box 1   Boundaries of the 12 Federal Reserve Districts

Economic Thinkers

ALAN GREENSPAN

Someone once said of former Federal Reserve Board Chairman Arthur F. Burns: "He's more likely to bleed over the numbers than over people." The line also works for Alan Greenspan, a long-time Burns admirer. It's not that Greenspan doesn't care about people; what drives him as an economist is his conviction that policymakers must look beyond palliative actions that may please the public in the short run but hurt it in the long term. He hates and dreads inflation. He is the consummate economic conservative.

"Greenspan believes, as Burns did, that economic stability is best for the people," says Rudolph G. Penner, who was chief economist of the Office of Management and Budget in the Ford Administration. Recalling Greenspan's role as chairman of the Council of Economic Advisers under President Ford, Penner says: "Alan doesn't look at economic policy in terms of one election."

Greenspan looked golden in 1976 when he advised President Ford to cut taxes, and the economy vaulted out of the deep recession caused by the 1973 oil-price explosion. But as the tax stimulus wore out in 1976, and economic growth sagged below 2% for two quar-

ters, Greenspan counseled Ford against taking stimulative action. As Greenspan expected, the economy rebounded on its own toward year end. But Ford's inaction during the economic "pause" damaged confidence in his leadership and, according to some analysts, cost him the 1976 election.

Ford's loss to Jimmy Carter had other causes, not least his pardon of former President Nixon after Watergate. But the defeat was a bitter blow to Greenspan, who took tremendous pride in working for Ford. In 1975 Greenspan said: "I'm not a Keynesian. I'm not a monetarist. I'm a free-enterpriser." It was that belief that got him to Washington and made him a Ford confidant.

Raised in Manhattan's Washington Heights, where he went to the same high school as Henry Kissinger, Greenspan is very much a self-made man. His first love was music, but while playing saxophone in Henry Jerome's swing band in the 1940s along with future Nixon adviser Leonard Garment, he managed between sets to read books on banking.

He returned to school, studied economics, and graduated *summa cum laude* from New York University in 1948. After a stint at the Conference Board, he joined bond trader William Townsend in 1954 in founding Townsend-Greenspan & Co., now a leading economic consulting shop. Garment enlisted him to work for Nixon in the 1968 campaign, but Greenspan rejected bids to leave his $300,000-a-year job and join the Administration until 1974. He was named CEA chairman in Nixon's last days and was asked by Ford to stay on.

Greenspan loved being Ford's chief economic adviser. He had become a "radical conservative" in the 1950s as a friend and follower of Ayn Rand, author

of *Atlas Shrugged.* As such, he opposed federal regulation and other forms of government intervention in economic life. Ford went along with him on most such issues. But almost as important, Greenspan doted on Ford's friendship and trust. He took a childlike delight in being asked to join the sports-minded President at the Army-Navy game in 1974—Greenspan's own tastes ran to listening to Mozart and Bach tapes in his office. He later said in the baritone whisper that makes almost everything he says sound like a state secret: "Can you imagine: The first thing the President asked was, 'How is your mother?' "

Greenspan was a long way from Washington Heights. But sometime in the 1970s he also distanced himself from Ayn Rand's teachings. He retained the belief that capitalism not only is justified on grounds of economic efficiency but also is morally correct. But Wall Street and Washington had turned him away from seeking radical change and toward the centrist pragmatism of the conservative Republican Establishment.

The switch may have cost Greenspan his chance to return to Washington with President Reagan's election in 1980. As a campaign adviser, he induced Reagan to emphasize balancing the budget over tax-cutting in a critical September 1980 speech. Reagan's softening of his supply-side line helped him win and could have brought Greenspan the post of Treasury Secretary. But supply siders did not forgive his opposition to huge tax cuts, and Donald Regan got the job.

Greenspan was not awarded his doctorate in economics until after he had been CEA chairman. As a business economist, he had long hungered for that symbol of academic acceptance. Just as he finally earned the Ph.D., so did he earn the position of Chairman of the Fed.

From Norman Jonas: "Portrait of the Economist as a Consummate Conservative," *Business Week,* June 15, 1987, p. 29.

not government agencies. The stockholders in each corporation are the banks of the region that are members of the Federal Reserve System. All national banks—those with charters from the U.S. Office of the Comptroller of the Currency—must be members of the Federal Reserve System. Commercial banks that have charters approved by state governments can choose to become members of the system. Currently all depository institutions—both commercial banks and thrift institutions—are *required* to keep deposits at their regional Federal Reserve Banks as reserves. All depository institutions have the privilege to borrow funds from the Fed. From the standpoint of the control the Fed exercises over banks, there is little distinction between member and nonmember banks.

The Federal Reserve Banks are very unusual corporations. Member banks can neither sell their shares on the stock market, nor expect to receive a large share of the Fed's profits. Most of the profits earned by the Fed from its operations are given to the U.S. Treasury. Member banks earn a 6% annual dividend on their stock in the Federal Reserve Banks, no matter how much the Fed actually earns in a given year.

The regional Federal Reserve Banks also issue currency. No commercial bank or thrift institution can issue currency. They can, however, draw down their deposit accounts at the Fed in exchange for crisp, clean dollar (or any other denomination) bills when they wish to hold cash. Both currency and the deposits banks hold at their regional Federal Reserve Banks are merely the liabilities issued by the Federal Reserve System.

Another important component of the Fed is the **Federal Open Market Committee (FOMC),** which makes decisions that influence the amount of excess reserves available to banks. The committee issues directives to the Federal Reserve Bank of New York to purchase or sell government securities on the open market. As you'll soon see, adjustments in the amount of government securities held by the Federal Reserve Banks are the major means used by the Fed to influence the stock of money in circulation. The FOMC is therefore the most important policymaking component of the Fed.

The FOMC is composed of the seven Governors of the Federal Reserve System, the president of the Federal Reserve Bank of New York, and presidents of an additional four regional Federal Reserve Banks. The FOMC meets regularly to make important decisions influencing the money supply. The committee's decisions and their implementation are one of the major determinants of interest rates and the availability of credit each day.

There is also the *Federal Advisory Council*, which represents the owners of the Fed—its member banks. This council, which consists of 12 bankers, has virtually no policymaking power. Its function is purely advisory, and its members have no direct influence on the Fed's day-to-day operations.

Box 2 contains a convenient chart that shows how the Federal Reserve System is organized.

Is the Fed Independent of Political Interference?

The intent of the original Federal Reserve Act of 1913 was to diffuse central banking power among the 12 regional Federal Reserve Banks. However, the Federal Reserve System has evolved into an organization with the responsibility to promote economic stability. The Fed's Board of Governors now has a considerable degree of power in establishing policies that affect the performance of the economy. The

Federal Open Market Committee (FOMC): An arm of the Federal Reserve System; affects the amount of excess reserves available to banks by instructing the Federal Reserve Bank of New York to buy or sell government securities on the open market.

Box 2 Major Components of the Federal Reserve System

Board of Governors of the Federal Reserve System

1. Supervises the nation's banking system

2. Regulates the money supply by setting reserve requirements and approving discount rate changes

Regional Federal Reserve Banks

1. Perform central banking services for banks

2. Issue currency and hold bank deposits to serve as reserves

Federal Open Market Committee

1. Makes decisions that influence bank excess reserves by determining open market operations

2. Policy arm of the Fed

Board also can influence the activities of the regional banks and has substantial input in the choice of these banks' presidents. The Federal Reserve System thus has become a much more centralized decision-making organization than was originally intended.

The Chairman of the Board of Governors wields considerable power. That power rests in his control over professional staff members and advisers to the system. This control enables the Chairman to influence the information and analysis upon which actual policy decisions are based.

As noted earlier, each of the seven Governors on the Federal Reserve Board is appointed by the President and must be confirmed by the Senate. In an attempt to eliminate political pressures on the Governors, each is appointed for a *nonrenewable* 14-year term. To avoid possible regional bias, each of the Governors must be from a different Federal Reserve district. The nonrenewable term affords the Governors some degree of political independence: they have little incentive to pursue policies that always please the President or senators. In addition, as pointed out earlier, the Fed is not dependent on Congress for funds. The Fed earns interest income from its holdings of securities and from loans it makes to depository institutions. It earns on average more than $10 billion per year but returns the bulk of these earnings to the Treasury.

Despite these precautions to provide political independence, the Fed is certainly under constant and considerable political pressure. Congress can vote to change the law in ways that would reduce the Fed's independence. The threat of such legislative changes can influence the Fed's behavior, thereby subjecting it to indirect and subtle political interference. For example, in 1975 Congress passed a resolution that requires the Fed to periodically announce its money supply growth targets. The Humphrey-Hawkins Bill passed in 1978 requires the Fed to explain how its objectives coincide with the President's economic policies.

Of course, the President can influence the Board of Governors by appointing Governors and by his choice of the Chairman. The President can also exert political pressure on the Fed in much the same way Congress can.

The issue of the Fed's political independence is highly controversial. Critics of an independent central bank argue that decisions that affect the functioning of the economy should be made by elected representatives rather than long-term appointees. However, those who favor an independent central banking authority argue that political control of the Fed could result in expansion of the money stock and credit in periods before elections to help the dominant political party win. Expansion of the money stock before an election might contribute to short-term increases in aggregate demand that result in expansion of the economy. If this caused the economy to overheat, the result could be a period of inflation after the election.

Balance Sheet of the Federal Reserve System

A quick look at the balance sheet of the 12 Federal Reserve Banks of the Federal Reserve System is useful in understanding the functions of the Fed and how it can influence the equilibrium money stock in circulation. Box 3 shows the consolidated balance sheet of the 12 Federal Reserve Banks as of the end of January 1988.

Box 3 Consolidated Balance Sheet of the Federal Reserve Banks January 1988 (billions of dollars)

Assets			Liabilities and net worth		
Item	Amount	Percent of total	Item	Amount	Percent of total
U.S. government securities	225.9	85	Federal Reserve notes	205.9	78
Loans to banks	0.3	a	Deposits	46.3	17
Other assets[b]	39.0	15	Other liabilities and net worth	13.0	5
Total assets	265.2		Total liabilities and net worth	265.2	

[a] Less than 1%.

[b] Includes assets of the U.S. Treasury held by the Federal Reserve Banks and matched by liabilities in the form of deposits in U.S. Treasury accounts issued by the Fed.

Source: *Federal Reserve Bulletin,* April 1988.

Total assets of the 12 Federal Reserve Banks were a bit over $265 billion as of the end of January 1988. The bulk of these assets are held in U.S. government securities. As you'll recall, these are interest-bearing debts of the federal government in the form of Treasury bills, Treasury notes, and Treasury bonds. Much of the Federal Reserve System's profits come from interest earned on these government securities. As of the end of January 1988, the Fed held $225.9 billion in U.S. government securities. This amounted to about 85% of total assets of the 12 banks.

Loans to banks were $0.3 billion, amounting to less than 1% of assets. There's a big distinction between the Federal Reserve Banks and commercial banks. Federal Reserve Banks hold the bulk of their assets in government securities. In contrast, commercial banks and thrift institutions hold the bulk of their assets in loans.

Also part of the Fed's assets are special accounts for certificates issued by the Treasury Department that are used in making international payments. When these certificates are entrusted to the Fed, they are offset by credits to the Treasury Department deposit accounts at the Federal Reserve Banks that increase the Fed's liabilities. Other Federal Reserve assets consist of coin, cash items in process of collection, bank property and equipment, foreign currencies, and debt obligations of federal agencies.

The major liability of the Federal Reserve Banks is Federal Reserve notes, which constitute the nation's currency. At the end of January 1988, Federal Reserve notes amounted to $205.9 billion or 78% of total liabilities. Whereas the major liability of private depository institutions is deposits, the major liability of the Federal Reserve Banks is currency! Deposits of the Treasury, banks, and foreign nations amounted to $46.3 billion at the end of January 1988, which was 17% of total liabilities and net worth.

Concept Check

1 How is the Federal Reserve System organized?

2 What are the functions of the Fed?

3 How does the balance sheet of the Federal Reserve Banks differ from the balance sheets of the banks they serve?

The Monetary Base and How the Fed Influences It

In the previous chapter we saw that the potential of the banking system to create money depends on the excess reserves available for loans. The Fed uses a variety of techniques to control excess reserves available to depository institutions. The **monetary base** is the sum of currency in circulation and total bank reserves outstanding at any given time. Note that both currency and bank reserves, which consist mainly of vault cash and bank deposits at the Federal Reserve Banks, are the *liabilities* of the Federal Reserve System. The Fed can vary the monetary base by adjusting its liabilities and assets and by regulating banks through control of reserve requirements.

Monetary base:
The sum of currency in circulation and total bank reserves outstanding at any given time.

By controlling the monetary base, the Fed can exert a strong influence on the equilibrium money stock. However, the equilibrium quantity of money held by the public at any point in time depends on a variety of factors, not just the actions taken by the Fed. For example, in the preceding chapter, we saw that banks don't necessarily use all of their excess reserves to create checkable deposits by extending credit. An increase in the monetary base that increases bank excess reserves will increase the money stock only if banks choose to use those reserves to extend credit, thereby creating new deposits. The decisions made by profit-maximizing banks are therefore an important influence on the equilibrium money stock. The equilibrium money stock also depends on the public's demand for money balances. Shifts in the demand for money can affect interest rates and the desire of banks to create checkable deposits by extending credit.

By influencing the monetary base, the Fed can control excess reserves and the potential of the banking system to create money. However, the Fed cannot by its own actions *directly* control the money stock. In this section we concentrate only on the techniques available to the Fed to control the monetary base. Once you understand how the Fed can achieve this objective, the next step is to show how Federal Reserve policies that influence the monetary base also influence the equilibrium money stock and the equilibrium level of interest rates.

The major tools of the Fed to control the monetary base are:

1. Control of *required reserve ratios,* which are the legally mandated ratios of reserves to deposits for banks.
2. Control of the **discount rate,** which is the interest rate Federal Reserve Banks charge member banks for loans.
3. **Open market operations,** which are the Fed's purchases and sales of government securities on financial markets that affect the amount of excess reserves available to banks.

Control of Required Reserve Ratios

The Board of Governors of the Federal Reserve System sets reserve requirements for depository institutions. Within certain limits established by Congress, the Fed can raise or lower the required reserve ratio for checkable deposits, savings deposits, and time deposits at banks. The reserve ratio bounds currently existing were established by the Depository Institutions Deregulation and Monetary Control Act of 1980. As of the beginning of 1988, checkable deposits of up to $40.5 million held by a bank or thrift institution are subject to a 3% reserve requirement. For checkable deposits in excess of $40.5 million at any institution, the Fed can vary the reserve requirement from between 8% and 14%. As of the beginning of 1988, deposits in excess of $40.5 million per institution were subject to a 12% reserve requirement. The $40.5 million cutoff amount is adjusted each year by 80% of the increase of checkable deposits in the United States in that year.

The statutory reserve requirement for noncheckable business time deposits at banks, which are usually large-denomination certificates of deposit, can be varied from 0% to 9%. As of the beginning of 1988 the reserve requirement for these deposits was 3%. The table in Box 4 summarizes reserve requirements for depository institutions that can be set by the Federal Reserve System.

Recall that the maximum amount of checkable deposits that can be supported by any given amount of bank reserves is inversely related to the required reserve ratio. If the average reserve requirement is, say, 10%, the maximum amount of checkable deposits that can be supported by a given amount of reserves available to banks can be computed by dividing the excess reserves by the required reserve ratio. If excess reserves are $20 billion and the required reserve ratio on average is 0.1, a maximum

Discount rate:
The interest rate Federal Reserve Banks charge member banks for loans.

Open market operations:
The Federal Reserve System's purchases and sales of government securities, conducted by the Federal Open Market Committee.

Box 4   Reserve Requirements of Depository Institutions, January 1988

Type of deposit	Statutory limit	Requirement as of January 1988
Checkable deposits		
0 – $40.5 million	3%	3%
Over $40.5 million	8 – 14	12
Business time deposits*	0 – 9	3

*Deposits with maturities of 1 1/2 years or more are exempt from reserve requirements.

Source: *Federal Reserve Bulletin,* April 1988.

of $200 billion ($20 billion/0.1) in checkable deposits can be supported by those reserves. If the required reserve ratio were to fall to 0.05, the maximum amount of checkable deposits that could be supported by the available excess reserves would *double* to $400 billion ($20 billion/0.05).

Checkable deposits at depository institutions are currently about $400 billion. An increase in the required reserve ratio of a mere 0.005 for these deposits would increase required reserves by a whopping $2 billion ($400 billion $\times$ 0.005). This means excess reserves will fall by $2 billion. If the required reserve ratio were 0.1005 after this increase, the potential decrease in the money supply resulting from the increase in the required reserve ratio would be:

$$- \Delta M = - \Delta ER/\text{Required reserve ratio} = \$2 \text{ billion}/0.1005 = \$19.9 \text{ billion}$$

The increase in required reserves would therefore have the potential to reduce the ability of the banking system to create checkable deposits by nearly $20 billion, which is almost 5% of the amount that was outstanding prior to the increase in the required reserve ratio.

Central bankers view the tool of manipulation of reserve requirements as very clumsy. The effects are so powerful and pronounced on excess reserves and money supply that they prevent small adjustments in money stock. For banks with low excess reserves, very small increases in reserve requirements can cause serious disruptions in their loan business as they might be forced to call in loans or clamp down on granting new credit. Changes in reserve requirements, despite their powerful effect on excess reserves, are rarely used in the United States as a tool to influence the monetary base.

Discount Policy: The Fed as Lender of Last Resort

Discount loans:
Bank borrowings from the Federal Reserve System; also called *advances.*

Bank borrowings from the Federal Reserve System are called **discount loans** or *advances.* The *discount window* is the name given to the Federal Reserve facility at which discount loans to banks are actually made.

When Federal Reserve Banks make loans to creditworthy institutions, they create deposits for those institutions. Because deposits at the Fed are part of the reserves of banks, these loans increase reserves available to the banking system. This means that discount loans to banks have the potential to increase the money stock by a multiple of the amounts loaned. Increased willingness of the Federal Reserve to loan funds to banks, as evidenced by a decline in the discount rate, will increase excess reserves and the supply of loanable funds. By the same token, an increase in the discount rate will tend to decrease the potential supply of loanable funds.

The Fed is very careful to regulate banks' use of the discount window. Banks watch the discount rate in relation to the market rate of interest on short-term government securities. For example, if the discount rate is 8% and the market rate of interest that can be earned on 3-month Treasury bills is 10%, banks will be tempted to borrow from the Fed to buy Treasury bills. They'll earn an easy and safe 2% on these transactions without risking any of their own funds. The Fed is well aware of this temptation, and it limits the frequency with which banks can avail themselves of the discount window loan facilities. By borrowing too much for short-term profit opportunities like investing in Treasury bills, a bank runs the risk of being turned down for credit in the future. Regulating the use of the discount window by refusing or discouraging borrowing is sometimes called "moral suasion" by the Fed. The Fed simply uses its discretionary power to say no to banks in this way to keep the supply of reserves down.

The discount window is also used by the Fed to maintain confidence in the banking system. The Fed lets it be known that it is the "lender of last resort." By creating new reserves for a bank when it is in danger of failing, the Fed can maintain confidence in the bank and prevent a bank run. In the past the Fed has prevented financial panic by using the discount window to encourage banks to lend funds to firms in danger of bankruptcy. For example, in 1970 the bankruptcy of the Penn Central Railroad rendered worthless much of that firm's short-term marketable loans, or commercial paper. Other companies that also relied on short-term marketable loans as a means of raising funds had trouble selling their marketable loans in financial markets. The Fed solved this problem by announcing that it would gladly make discount loans to banks willing to make direct loans to firms that had difficulty marketing their commercial paper. This avoided a chain reaction of bankruptcies that might otherwise have developed.

Similarly, immediately after the stock market crash of 1987, the Chairman of the Fed, Alan Greenspan, announced that the Fed would take measures to assure banks of access to the discount window. His motive was to bolster public confidence in the ability of the banking system to obtain funds. Greenspan thereby hoped to prevent fears that banks that couldn't get quick repayment of loans to securities dealers would be unable to meet deposit withdrawal demands.

Changes in the discount rate don't always imply a change in Fed policy to influence the monetary base. Sometimes the Fed might raise the discount rate simply because short-term market interest rates have risen. The Fed's objective might be merely to discourage overuse of the discount window for profit making rather than to slow down economic activity and decrease bank reserves.

Discount loans to banks constitute a fraction of a percent of the assets of Federal Reserve Banks (see Box 3). Discount loans usually amount to less than 2% of the reserves of the banking system.

How Open Market Sales of Government Securities by the Fed Affect Bank Reserves

The most flexible and most commonly used method of controlling the monetary base in the United States is Federal Reserve open market operations. These operations simply consist of daily sales and purchases of government securities by the Federal Reserve Banks. The Fed conducts these transactions in open markets in which its trading partners are securities dealers, banks, other business firms, and the general public. These operations can directly affect the bank reserves available to support loanable funds.

Suppose, for example, that on a given day the Fed decides to reduce its holdings of government securities. This means it will sell more securities than it buys on that day. To see how this affects the reserves available to the banking system, we need to examine both the balance sheet of the Federal Reserve Banks and the consolidated balance sheet of all depository institutions.

Government securities held by the Federal Reserve Banks are part of their assets. When they sell these securities to depository institutions, the Fed's asset holdings decline. As any accountant will tell you, when an entity's assets decline, its liabilities must also fall unless another asset replaces the ones that are sold. But how do the Fed's liabilities decline in this case? The answer is that the depository institutions pay for the securities by writing checks to the Federal Reserve Banks. The Federal Reserve Banks, upon receipt of these checks, draw down the depository institutions' deposits (which serve as banking system reserves) at accounts at the regional Federal Reserve Banks. The Fed's liabilities in the form of deposits of depository institutions decline by the net sales of government securities. As a result, net sales of government securities by the Fed to depository institutions will *decrease bank reserves. It follows that net sales of government securities will decrease the monetary base and the potential of the banking system to create money.*

A $1 billion sale of government securities by the Fed to banks will reduce bank reserves by that $1 billion. If the required reserve ratio is 0.1, the $1 billion sale will reduce the potential amount of checkable deposits in the banking system by $10 billion ($1 billion/0.1). Box 5 shows the effect of the $1 billion net sale of securities on the balance sheets of the Federal Reserve Banks and the banking system. For the Fed the sale of securities reduces both its assets and liabilities by $1 billion. For the

---

Box 5 Changes in Balance Sheets of Federal Reserve Banks and the Banking System as a Result of Net Open Market Sales

Federal Reserve Banks
(billions of dollars)

Assets		Liabilities and net worth	
Government securities	− 1	Reserves of depository institutions	-- 1

Banking System
(Commercial Banks and Thrift Institutions)
(billions of dollars)

Assets		Liabilities and net worth	
Government securities	+ 1	No change	
Reserves	− 1		

---

banking system, $1 billion of assets in the form of reserves are exchanged for $1 billion of assets in the form of government securities. This decreases the reserves in the banking system and thus reduces the banking system's potential to extend credit. There is no direct change in the liabilities of the banking system as a result of the transaction.

Suppose the government securities are sold to the general public instead of the banks. For example, imagine you're a billionaire and decide to purchase all $1 billion of the government securities offered by the Fed for sale on a given day. You'll pay for these securities with a check drawn on your account at your local depository institution. Your check will be made out to one of the Federal Reserve Banks. As the check is presented for payment, the Fed will reduce your bank's account at its regional Federal Reserve Bank. *This reduces bank reserves in exactly the same amount that they would be reduced if banks themselves had bought the securities.*

There are, however, a few distinctions between the Fed's direct transactions with banks and with bank depositors when government securities are sold. If you were to pay for the securities with cash that you normally keep in your mattress rather than in banks, there would be no effect on bank reserves. This is because that cash wasn't part of the banking system's reserves in the first place. There will be no potential for multiple contraction of bank deposits when the public pays for securities purchased from the Fed with cash instead of with checkable deposits. This leads to an important conclusion: Sales of government securities by the Fed will *always* reduce the monetary base. This is because the sales must reduce the Fed's liabilities either in the form of deposits of banks at the Fed or in the form of currency in circulation. However, when the monetary base is reduced in the form of currency in circulation, there is *no effect on bank reserves.* This means the potential impact of the sale on the actual money supply will be correspondingly less.

Also, when the Fed sells securities directly to banks, reserves of the banking system are reduced as a result of the sale of government securities. When instead the Fed sells to the bank's depositors who pay with checkable deposits, *both* bank reserves and bank deposits are reduced by the amount of the sales. This difference is relevant to the impact of the Fed's sales of securities on the *excess reserves* available to banks. The reduction in checkable deposits of the public at banks resulting from purchase of the securities causes a decrease in required reserves. As a result, a $1 billion decrease in reserves will reduce excess reserves by only $0.9 billion assuming a required reserve ratio of 0.1: To see this, recall that the deposit of your $1 billion check at the Fed reduces total reserves in the banking system by $1 billion. Excess reserves available to the banking system equal total reserves less required reserves. In this case the change in total reserves is $-$1 billion, while the change in required reserves is $-$0.1 billion. The change in excess reserves is:

Change in total reserves $-$ **Change in required reserves** $=$ $-$ $1 billion $-$ ($-$ $0.1 billion)
$=$ $0.9 billion

It follows that the sale of securities to the general public, when paid for by checkable deposits, reduces excess reserves of the banking system by a lesser amount than will be the case if the sale of securities is directly to the banks.

How Open Market Purchases of Government Securities Affect Bank Reserves

It's easy to show that the Fed's *purchase* of government securities from banks or the public will increase the monetary base. For example, suppose the Fed buys $1 billion of government securities from the portfolios of depository institutions. The Fed pays for the purchase by crediting the deposit accounts of these banks at regional Federal Reserve Banks. These deposits, of course, are part of the banking system reserves. *The purchase of government securities from banks therefore increases the excess reserves of the banking system.* The creation of these excess reserves has the potential to allow multiple expansion of checkable deposits if the banks are willing to use the excess reserves to make loans. For example, if the required reserve ratio is 0.1, the $1 billion increase in excess reserves can support up to a $10 billion increase in checkable deposits.

The table in Box 6 shows the impact of the Fed's purchase of government securities on its balance sheet and the consolidated balance sheet of the banking system. The purchase of $1 billion of government securities increases the Fed's assets by $1 billion. Of course, whenever assets increase, liabilities must increase by an equivalent amount unless other assets decline. The new liabilities for the Fed in this case are the $1 billion in bank reserves that the Fed creates when it credits the accounts of banks that have sold securities. The Fed could also pay for its purchase of government securities by issuing more Federal Reserve notes. This is another neat trick of the central bank—it can actually create currency. All the Fed needs to do is put in a call to the Bureau of Engraving and Printing and order a crisp clean batch of new $10, $20, $50, and $100 bills to ship out to the banks in payment for the securities. The currency, of course, is just as much a liability of the Fed as the deposits it creates for banks.

Box 6 Changes in Balance Sheets of Federal Reserve Banks and the Banking System as a Result of Net Open Market Purchases

Federal Reserve Banks
(billions of dollars)

Assets		Liabilities and net worth	
Government securities	+ 1	Reserves of depository institutions	+ 1

Banking System
(Commercial Banks and Thrift Institutions)
(billions of dollars)

Assets		Liabilities and net worth
Government securities	− 1	No change
Reserves	+ 1	

Box 6 also shows the change in the balance sheet of the banking system. When the banks sell government securities to the Fed, their assets fall by $1 billion. In exchange, the banks receive new reserves in the form of the $1 billion that the Fed creates for them as deposits at regional Federal Reserve Banks. These are now new excess reserves that the banks can use to make loans and create checkable deposits.

CHAPTER 34 The Federal Reserve System and Its Influence on Money and Credit

Principles in Practice

The Fed's Open Market Operations: A Visit to the Trading Desk

If you read the *Wall Street Journal* (or even if you attended the movie "Wall Street"), you know that securities trading is a fast-paced, high-stakes business that demands keen minds and nerves of steel.

You certainly need those qualities in abundance if you're in charge of trading for the Federal Open Market Committee. Let's see what this job entails.

Policies of the Federal Open Market Committee are executed by the Federal Reserve Bank of New York. The responsibility for actually making the daily purchases and sales of government securities is that of the manager for domestic operations at the trading desk of the New York Fed. The manager supervises a staff of traders who telephone securities dealers to conduct transactions on the open market.

The manager keeps track of available reserves in the banking system and interest rates on loans banks make to each other. The federal funds rate is the interest rate banks charge for overnight loans of funds on deposit at Federal Reserve Banks. The federal funds rate tends to fall when banks have increasing excess reserves, and it tends to rise when excess reserves are decreasing. The manager watches the federal funds rate to get an idea of changes in bank demand for excess reserves.

The manager also contacts major private firms that deal in government securities to track daily trends in the supply of and demand for these assets in the open market. The manager typically also contacts the U.S. Treasury to obtain additional information on supply of and demand for government securities and new issues planned for the period. After collecting data and carefully analyzing trends in bank reserves, the monetary base, and market interest rates, the manager of the trading desk then formulates a plan for buying and selling government securities during the day to meet directives from the Federal Open Market Committee to achieve growth rates in the money stock.

Each day by 11:30 a.m. the traders on the eighth floor of the Federal Reserve Bank of New York begin making their telephone calls to dealers in government securities for price quotations for purchases and sales. The Fed usually collects quotes on prices and makes all its trades by 12:15 p.m.*

*This description is based on Frederick S. Mishkin, *The Economics of Money, Banking, and Financial Markets,* Boston: Little, Brown, 1986, pp. 361-363.

The Fed's purchase of government securities from the general public has a slightly different impact than purchase directly from banks. If you were to sell $1 billion worth of your holdings of government securities to the Fed, the Fed would pay you with a check drawn on one of the Federal Reserve Banks. Where would the Fed get the funds for the check? As is the case when it purchases securities from banks, it creates funds literally out of thin air! When you deposit your $1 billion check at your local bank, the bank's deposits will increase by $1 billion. The bank then presents your check to its regional Federal Reserve Bank. The Fed credits your bank's account by $1 billion. Once again the Fed's purchase of securities has increased bank reserves by $1 billion even though the securities weren't purchased directly from banks!

There is, however, one hitch. If you demand part of the payment for your sale of securities in currency to stuff into your already overstuffed mattress, bank reserves will increase by less than $1 billion. You should also note that when the Fed purchases government securities from the public instead of banks, the increase in the excess reserves of the banking system is less than is the case when all the securities are purchased from banks. The reason for this is that banks must keep some of the newly created reserves as required reserves. For example, suppose the required reserve ratio is 0.1. Here the newly created $1 billion in reserves would result in $9 billion in excess reserves. The remaining $0.1 billion would have to be held as required reserves against your $1 billion deposit.

A Recap: The Operations of the Federal Open Market Committee

The Federal Open Market Committee (FOMC) meets regularly (about once every 6 weeks) in Washington to decide on targets for M1 (currency and checkable deposits) and bank reserves in an attempt to help stabilize economic fluctuations. The FOMC directs the Federal Reserve Bank of New York, which is located in the center of the financial district in Manhattan, to buy or sell securities to achieve the Fed's objectives. The trading desk of the Federal Reserve Bank of New York (located on the eighth floor of the New York Fed, in case you want to visit) is the hub of the Fed's trading of government securities. The manager of the trading desk communicates daily with FOMC members to make sure their objectives are being achieved. If the objective on a given day is to increase bank reserves, the manager will purchase government securities from dealers who act as agents for the banks and the general public. If instead the objective is to decrease bank reserves, the manager will sell government securities.

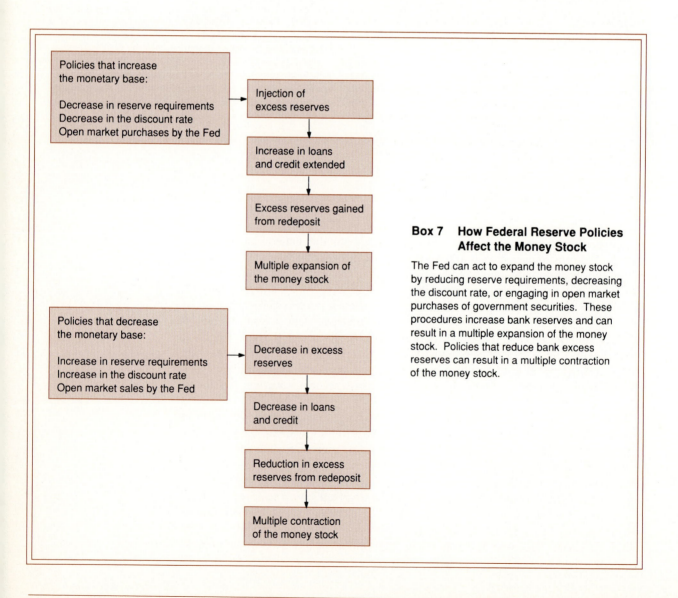

Policies that increase the monetary base:

Decrease in reserve requirements
Decrease in the discount rate
Open market purchases by the Fed

→ Injection of excess reserves

→ Increase in loans and credit extended

→ Excess reserves gained from redeposit

→ Multiple expansion of the money stock

Policies that decrease the monetary base:

Increase in reserve requirements
Increase in the discount rate
Open market sales by the Fed

→ Decrease in excess reserves

→ Decrease in loans and credit

→ Reduction in excess reserves from redeposit

→ Multiple contraction of the money stock

Box 7   How Federal Reserve Policies Affect the Money Stock

The Fed can act to expand the money stock by reducing reserve requirements, decreasing the discount rate, or engaging in open market purchases of government securities. These procedures increase bank reserves and can result in a multiple expansion of the money stock. Policies that reduce bank excess reserves can result in a multiple contraction of the money stock.

Open market operations are the most flexible and direct tool available to the Fed to influence bank reserves and the money supply. For example, open market operations are more direct than discount policy. A reduction in the discount rate doesn't necessarily increase bank reserves. Banks might not respond to the lower discount rate by borrowing significantly more. Another advantage of open market operations is that they are easily reversed. If the manager of the trading desk overshoots the target for bank reserves on a given day by buying too many securities, he can easily correct the mistake the following day by selling a bit more than would otherwise have been offered.

The chart in Box 7 summarizes the policies used by the Fed to influence the monetary base and shows how the impact of such policies on excess reserves affects bank loans and the money creation process.

Concept Check

1 How can the Fed influence the nation's monetary base? How does an increase in the monetary base increase the potential of the banking system to create money?

2 On a given day the Fed purchases $50 billion worth of government securities and sells $20 billion worth of government securities. What is likely to happen to bank excess reserves as a result?

3 Why is an increase in open market sales likely to be a more effective way of decreasing the monetary base than an increase in the discount rate?

Securities Prices, Interest Rates, and the Monetary Base

How Open Market Operations Affect Interest Rates and the Quantity of Government Securities Demanded

One question that might have crossed your mind is: How does the Fed get banks and the public to readily buy or sell securities so that the monetary base and bank reserve targets can be met? The answer lies in the price adjustments that allow securities markets, like all markets, to equilibrate. In fact, much of the trading that takes place is in short-term securities of the U.S. government that don't yield explicit interest. The return earned on these short-term assets depends on the difference between their purchase price and the price at which they can be redeemed when they mature. A financial asset *matures* when its principal, or face value, is repaid by the borrower.

Treasury bills are short-term obligations of the U.S. government with maturities of 3 months to 1 year that are sold at auction without a stated rate of interest. For example, if you buy a $10,000 1-year Treasury bill for $9,500 and hold it for 1 year until it matures, you can redeem it at that time for $10,000. Your effective interest is represented by the $500 *discount* you received from the face value when you bought the bill. In this case the effective annual interest rate would be 5.3% ($500/$9,500)(100%).

When Treasury bill prices decline, their effective interest yield increases. For example, if you could buy a $10,000 1-year Treasury bill for $9,000, your annual interest would be the $1,000 discount from the face value of the bill. The annual interest rate on the bill would now be 11.1% ($1,000/$9,000)(100%). A decrease in the auction price for Treasury bills therefore implies an increase in their effective interest yield. Similarly, an increase in the price of a security means a decrease in its effective yield.

A similar relationship exists between securities prices and effective interest rates for Treasury notes and bonds with fixed yields. A *coupon bond* yields a certain stated percentage interest rate based on its face value. This interest rate is called the coupon yield. For example, a bond with a $1,000 face value and a 10% coupon yield would pay $100 in interest over the year. If market prices of previously issued bonds decrease, the bonds sell at a *discount*. This means that in addition to the coupon yield, a purchaser of a previously issued bond that sells at a discount in effect will earn additional interest when the bond is cashed in on maturity because of the discount in the bond price. For example, if you buy a 1-year $1,000 bond with a 10% coupon yield for $900, you'll earn $100 per year interest plus an additional $100 (which was the discount on the bond) when you cash it in for its face value of $1,000 on maturity. Your effective yield if you hold the bond until it matures will be 22% ($200/$900)(100%).

If the market price of a bond goes up, its effective yield goes down. For example, if the market price of a $1,000 bond with a 10% coupon yield were $1,050, you'd earn $100 interest on the bond. However, you'd still receive only $1,000 when the bond matures. The extra $50 you pay for the bond over its face value is a *premium* that serves to reduce your effective yield on the bond.

With this bit of insight into the relationship between securities prices and their effective interest yields, you can better understand the impact of open market transactions on interest rates and the equilibrium quantity of securities held by banks and the public. On any given day a certain amount of government securities (measured in dollar value) is available to banks and the public as financial assets. The amount held by the Fed is *not* available to the general public and banks as financial

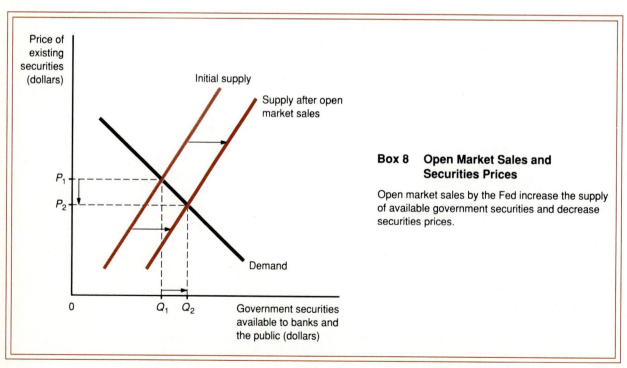

Box 8 Open Market Sales and Securities Prices

Open market sales by the Fed increase the supply of available government securities and decrease securities prices.

assets. The Fed holds such a large amount of government securities that it can influence the prices of these Treasury bills, bonds, and notes by selling or buying from its portfolio.

The graph in Box 8 shows the impact of the Fed's open market sales on the price of government securities. The sales by the Fed *increase* the supply of securities available for the public to hold. The increase in supply, other things being equal, lowers the prices of government securities. This means the securities sell at a deeper discount than they did initially. In effect, this increases the yield on government securities. This makes them a more attractive asset for banks and the public to hold in their portfolios. Banks, securities dealers, and private investors are induced to buy the securities offered by the Fed because the price changes and yield changes caused by the increased supply serve to increase the quantity demanded. In Box 8 the supply curve for securities shifts outward and lowers the price of Treasury bonds, notes, and bills from P_1 on average to P_2 on average. The dollar value of quantity demanded increases accordingly from Q_1 to Q_2. The sales reduce the monetary base as banks and the public increase the quantity of securities they hold.

Similarly, open market purchases by the Fed reduce the supply of government securities available to banks and the public for their portfolios. The graph in Box 9 shows the impact of open market purchases. Once again the initial equilibrium price and quantity are P_1 and Q_1, respectively. After open market purchases, the supply of government securities available to banks and the public decreases. This increases the price of the securities, which means the effective yield at maturity will fall. Government securities are now a less attractive financial asset to banks and the general public. The quantity demanded therefore is willingly reduced by the amount of the Fed's purchases. As the price of securities goes up to P_3 in Box 9, the quantity demanded declines to Q_3. As banks and the public willingly sell their securities to

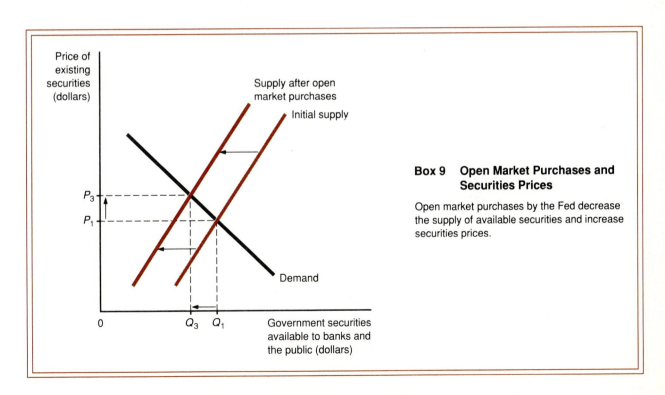

Box 9   Open Market Purchases and Securities Prices

Open market purchases by the Fed decrease the supply of available securities and increase securities prices.

the Fed, the monetary base increases. Bank excess reserves also increase, allowing a potential multiple expansion of checkable deposits.

This analysis points out an inevitable impact of the Fed's open market operations. As government securities are bought and sold, the equilibrium interest rates earned on these securities change. Because government securities are substitutes for loans and other financial assets held by banks and the public, a change in their interest rates will affect the demands for and supplies of all types of financial assets. In effect the Fed will influence the general level of interest rates in the economy when it conducts its open market operations. The Fed therefore influences the economy in two ways through open market operations:

1. It affects excess reserves and the monetary base available to banks and the public directly through open market sales and purchases.
2. If affects the equilibrium amounts of money holdings, spending, and investment through its impact on interest rates.

Money Supply, Money Demand, and Equilibrium Interest Rates

The stock of money available on any given day must be willingly held by the public. The quantity of money demanded depends on the interest rate, the price level, real GNP, and other variables. In general, the lower the market rate of interest, the greater the quantity of money demanded. The higher the level of real GNP or the price level, the greater the demand for money. The graph in Box 10 depicts the demand for money as a downward-sloping function of the interest rate.

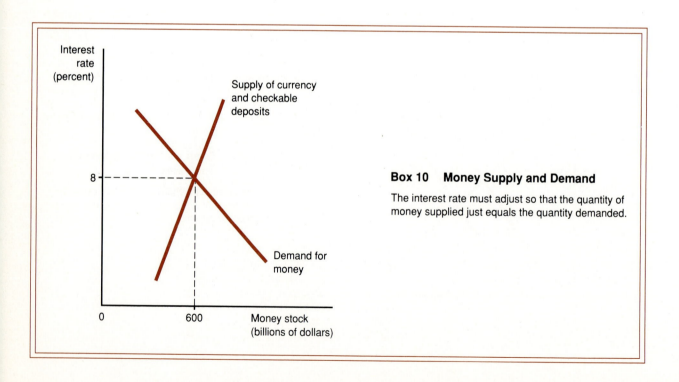

Box 10   Money Supply and Demand

The interest rate must adjust so that the quantity of money supplied just equals the quantity demanded.

CHAPTER 34 The Federal Reserve System and Its Influence on Money and Credit

International Operations of the Fed

In Chapter 4 we showed how the supply of and demand for the dollar in foreign exchange markets influence its price in terms of foreign currency. Changes in the price of the dollar affect the demand for U.S. exports and U.S. demand for imported goods, which in turn can influence real GNP and the price level.

Since the mid-1970s, when flexible foreign exchange rates became the norm, the Federal Reserve System has often intervened in foreign exchange markets to influence the price of the dollar. The Federal Open Market Committee of the Fed authorizes foreign currency purchases and sales, and a special manager for foreign operations is employed to supervise these operations. When the Fed buys and sells dollars and other foreign currencies on foreign exchange markets, it often does so in conjunction with similar operations by foreign central banks. In doing so it can affect the supply of and demand for dollars offered in foreign exchange so as to control the price of the dollar to achieve certain policy objectives.

Suppose the price of the dollar increases sharply in terms of a foreign currency such as the yen. This would increase the prices of U.S. exports in terms of foreign currency and thus would reduce the quantity of U.S. exports demanded. The higher price of the dollar could therefore serve to decrease aggregate demand for U.S. products. To avoid this the FOMC could instruct its manager for foreign operations to sell dollars on the foreign exchange markets. The increase in the supply of dollars in the foreign exchange market would put downward pressure on the dollar's price in terms of the yen. In this way the Fed can prevent the price of the dollar in terms of the yen from rising as much as it would otherwise.

Sometimes the Fed acts to prevent the price of the dollar from falling excessively. When the price of the dollar declines, this puts upward pressure on the prices of imported raw materials and imported final products, which contributes to inflation in the United States. When the Fed wants to avoid such declines in the price of the dollar, it buys dollars using its holdings of deposits denominated in foreign currencies. When the Fed buys dollars it increases the demand for U.S. currency, thus putting upward pressure on the price of the dollar in terms of foreign currency such as the yen. This prevents the price of the dollar from falling excessively.

By intervening in the foreign exchange markets in this way, the Fed acts to stabilize the price of the dollar. In the chapter on foreign exchange we'll investigate actions the Fed and other central banks have taken in recent years to influence the prices of the dollar and other currencies.

The **money supply** is a relationship between the quantity of money supplied in the form of currency and checkable deposits and the level of interest rates prevailing at a given point in time. An important influence on the money supply under the direct control of the Fed is the monetary base. Part of the monetary base, currency in circulation, is a component of the money stock. Bank reserves, the other component of the monetary base, are not part of the money stock. However, each dollar of bank reserves has the potential to support many times that amount of checkable deposits, depending on the willingness of banks to create checkable deposits by extending credit. Although the Fed has direct control over the monetary base, the banking system's willingness to lend out excess reserves is a major determinant of the quantity of checkable deposits supplied.

The willingness of the banking system to create checkable deposits out of its available reserves is influenced by the prevailing level of interest rates. As was pointed out in the preceding chapter, banks desire to hold more excess reserves at low interest rates than at high interest rates. It follows that for any given available amount of bank reserves supplied by the Fed, the amount of checkable deposits made available by the banking system tends to increase as interest rates increase. This is because the profitability of making loans and extending credit in general tends to increase as interest rates rise. The total quantity of money supplied therefore tends to increase as market interest rates go up. The graph in Box 10 shows an upward-sloping money supply curve. The money supply curve shows the relation-

Money supply:
A relationship between the quantity of money supplied in the form of currency and checkable deposits and the level of interest rates prevailing at a given point in time.

Securities Prices, Interest Rates, and the Monetary Base

ship between interest rates and the quantity of money supplied given the monetary base and all other influences on the willingness and ability of banks to extend credit.

In equilibrium, the interest rate must adjust so that the quantity of money demanded exactly equals the quantity supplied. The graph in Box 10 shows the demand for and supply of money balances. The equilibrium quantity of money balances is $600 billion at the equilibrium market interest rate (an average of all interest rates) of 8%. If the interest rate were higher than 8%, the quantity of money balances supplied would exceed the quantity demanded, and this would reduce interest rates. As interest rates fall, the quantity of money balances demanded would increase while the quantity supplied by the banking system would decline. Similarly, if the interest rate were below 8%, the quantity of money balances demanded would exceed the quantity supplied and the interest rate would increase to 8%.

How the Fed Influences the Supply Curve of Money and the Equilibrium Interest Rate

The *equilibrium* quantity of money balances and the equilibrium interest rate level depend on the demand for and supply of money. The Fed can shift the money supply curve by influencing bank excess reserves, but it has no direct influence over the demand for money. Whenever the Fed engages in operations that increase bank reserves or currency in circulation, it will shift the money supply curve to the right. As shown in **A** in Box 11, the increase in the money supply puts downward pressure on interest rates. Interest rates fall until the quantity of money demanded once again equals the quantity supplied. Similarly, open market operations by the Fed that decrease the monetary base tend to put upward pressure on interest rates (see **B**).

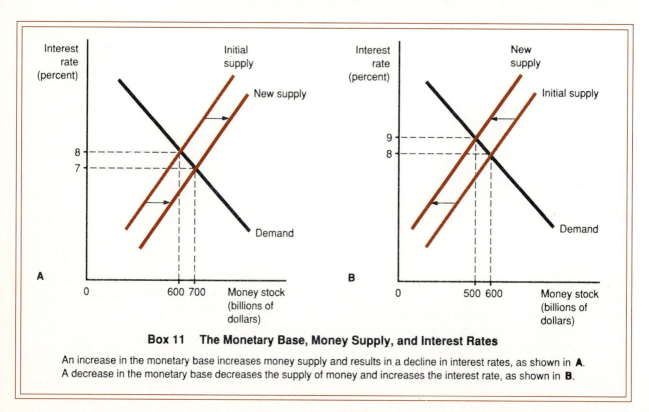

Box 11   The Monetary Base, Money Supply, and Interest Rates

An increase in the monetary base increases money supply and results in a decline in interest rates, as shown in **A**. A decrease in the monetary base decreases the supply of money and increases the interest rate, as shown in **B**.

1   The price of a $1,000 1-year Treasury bill is $950. Calculate the annual return on the bill assuming it is purchased and held for a full year.

2   How does the sale of government securities by the Fed affect their prices and yields?

3   Why does the quantity of money supplied by the banking system increase as market interest rates go up? How can the Fed shift the money supply curve?

The Power of the Fed

In this chapter we've emphasized the mechanics of how the Federal Reserve System can influence the monetary base and the money supply. Through open market operations, discount policy, and control of reserve requirements for depository institutions, the Fed can influence the monetary base for the economy. However, the equilibrium money stock is not directly under the Fed's control. This is because the money stock is composed mainly of checkable deposits. The volume of checkable deposits depends on the incentives banks have to extend credit to their customers. The quantity of checkable deposits supplied by banks tends to increase when the level of interest rates increases in the economy.

The Fed does have the ability to shift the money supply curve in the economy. By doing so it affects both the equilibrium interest rates in financial markets and the equilibrium stock of money. As equilibrium interest rates change, there are likely to be shifts in aggregate demand that affect the performance of the economy.

The Fed's policies can therefore affect both interest rates and the equilibrium money stock in ways that can influence real GNP and the price level in the economy. In the following chapter we analyze the impact of actions by the Fed that alter aggregate demand in the economy. To help you see how actions of the Fed affect the performance of the economy, we'll discuss the mechanism through which changes in interest rates and the equilibrium money stock affect aggregate demand curves.

Summary

1. The Federal Reserve System, called the Fed for short, is the central banking system for the United States. The Fed consists of the Board of Governors of the Federal Reserve System and 12 regional Federal Reserve Banks that perform central banking functions. The Federal Reserve Banks are the "bankers' banks" that hold reserve deposits, issue currency, and provide check-clearing services for commercial banks and thrift institutions.

2. The Federal Reserve System operates as an independent authority that is not under direct influence of the President or Congress. The Fed earns income on government securities it holds as assets and does not receive any funding from Congress. The Fed also loans funds to banks. About 85% of Federal Reserve Banks' assets are government securities. The major liability of the Federal Reserve Banks are Federal Reserve notes, which serve as the nation's currency.

3. The monetary base is the sum of currency in circulation and total bank reserves outstanding at any given time. The monetary base consists of liabilities of the

Federal Reserve System. The Fed can vary the monetary base by adjusting its liabilities and assets and by regulating banks to control reserve requirements.

4. By controlling required reserve ratios, the Fed can influence the maximum amount of checkable deposits that can be supported by any given amount of bank reserves. An increase in the required reserve ratio decreases excess reserves and can result in a chain reaction that will reduce the money supply. Similarly, a decrease in required reserve ratios increases excess reserves available from a given amount of reserves and can result in an expansion of the money supply.

5. The discount rate is the interest rate the Fed charges banks that borrow funds from the Federal Reserve Banks. As a lender of last resort the Fed can create bank reserves through discount loans for banks in danger of failing so as to maintain confidence in the bank and discourage bank runs. By making it easy to borrow to increase reserves, a decrease in the discount rate tends to be an expansionary influence on the money supply.

6. Open market operations by the Fed represent the major means of influencing bank reserves and the money supply. Open market operations consist of daily sales and purchases of government securities by Federal Reserve Banks. Sales of government securities by the Fed absorb bank excess reserves and decrease the potential of the banking system to create money. Fed purchases of government securities increase bank excess reserves and increase the potential of the banking system to create money.

7. When the Fed sells government securities, it puts downward pressure on securities prices by increasing the amount available for the public to hold. The lower prices of government securities mean that their yield to maturity increases. The public is induced to hold the larger supply of securities because their lower prices and higher yields make them more attractive as assets. Similarly, when the Fed buys government securities, it decreases the supply available to the public. This puts upward pressure on the prices of securities and lowers the yields to maturity. The public willingly holds a smaller quantity of securities in this case because their higher prices and lower yields make them less attractive as assets.

8. The money supply curve for the economy tends to be upward sloping. As the general level of interest rates increases, the quantity of money supplied by banks increases. This is because banks find it more profitable to make loans when interest rates rise. Higher interest rates therefore increase the quantity of checkable deposits created by the banking system.

9. The equilibrium quantity of money balances and the equilibrium level of interest rates adjust to equate the quantity of money demanded with the quantity supplied. The Fed can shift the money supply curve outward by increasing the monetary base, thereby putting downward pressure on interest rates. Similarly, a decrease in the monetary base shifts the money supply curve inward, putting upward pressure on interest rates. Although the Fed can influence money supply, it has no direct control over money demand. Actual money supply and interest rates depend on the interaction of the demand for and supply of money.

Key Terms and Concepts

Board of Governors of the Federal Reserve System
Regional Federal Reserve Banks
Federal Open Market Committee (FOMC)
Monetary base

Discount rate
Open market operations
Discount loans
Money supply

Problems and Applications

1. In what sense is the Federal Reserve System independent of Congress and the President of the United States? How can the President influence the Fed's policies despite the fact that the President has no direct control over the central bank?
2. The Fed increases its liabilities. Explain why this means that the monetary base will increase. How does the monetary base differ from the money stock?
3. Suppose the Fed wishes to increase the money stock by $100 billion over the next 3 months. What techniques can it use to accomplish its objective?
4. On a certain day the Fed buys $30 billion worth of government securities and sells $20 billion. Assuming all transactions that day are with banks and thrift institutions with accounts at the Fed, show the changes in the Fed's and the banking system's balance sheets. What effects will the Fed's operations have on securities prices and interest rates that day?
5. Suppose on another day the Fed sells $80 billion worth of government securities and buys $30 billion. Assuming all transactions are with depository institutions, show the changes in their balance sheets and the impact on securities prices and interest rates that day.
6. When the economy moves into a recession, bank demand for excess reserves increases. How can the Fed use open market operations to increase the money supply under such circumstances? Use supply and demand analysis to show the impact of the Fed's policies, assuming the demand for money is given.
7. The Fed decreases the monetary base. Show the impact of the Fed's action on the supply of money in the economy and the likely impact on the level of interest rates.
8. Under what circumstances will open market sales and purchases by the Fed have *no effect* on the level of interest rates in the economy?
9. Suppose the demand for money increases. How can the Fed act to prevent the market rate of interest from increasing?
10. Explain why Federal Reserve open market operations can increase bank reserves but do not necessarily guarantee an increase in the money supply.

Suggested Readings

Board of Governors of the Federal Reserve System, *The Federal Reserve System: Purposes and Functions,* 7th ed., Washington: Board of Governors of the Federal Reserve System, 1984. This is a statement of what the Fed is all about, prepared by the Fed itself.

Federal Reserve Bulletin. This is an official monthly publication of the Federal Reserve System that is loaded with data on money supply and financial markets. The bulletin periodically publishes a "Record of Policy Actions of the Federal Open Market Committee," which shows how the Fed attempted to affect interest rates and money supply during a certain period.

Frederick S. Mishkin, *The Economics of Money, Banking, and Financial Markets,* Boston: Little, Brown, 1986. Chapters 13, 16, 17, and 18 provide a detailed analysis of the operations of the Federal Reserve System.

A Forward Look

In the following chapter we show how monetary policies implemented by the Fed affect aggregate demand and macroeconomic equilibrium. We analyze the possible effects of changes in money supply on interest rates, equilibrium real GNP, and the price level in the economy over the short run and the long run.

Career Profile

PHIL GRAMM

Phil Gramm has guts. In 1983, when the Democratic Steering Committee voted to remove the Texas Representative from the House Budget Committee, Gramm resigned from his seat and won it back in a special election, this time as a Republican.

The falling out came over Gramm's support for the Gramm-Reagan-Stockman budget, which contained the heart of Reagan's economic proposals, including cuts in spending on federal programs of $131 billion. He got support for the bill from about 50 conservative Southern Democrats, enough to win the day for the Republicans and to infuriate his party's leadership.

Ideologically, Gramm is much better suited to the Republican party. A strong defender of free markets, he battles to reduce government spending and government involvement in the economy. Currently a Texas senator, Gramm is the only professional economist in a U.S. Senate that contains some 60 lawyers.

Gramm has been said to be the most unloved man in America for his assault on federal spending. But he has become a masterful politician, albeit of a new breed. He has few party ties, little respect for decorum, and uses the media to get his ideas directly to the public so as to pressure his fellow legislators, turning 30-second statements for the press into a form of art.

His personal declaration of war on the welfare state resulted in the Gramm-Rudman-Hollings Act, a bill that compels Congress and the President to quit deficit spending. It sets targets to eliminate the budget deficit and requires bills that raise federal spending or cut tax revenues to provide compensating tax increases or spending cuts.

Gramm may not have made friends among his fellow senators and congressmen, but no other single legislator has had as much impact on how Congress sets its priorities. His name is on two of the most important pieces of legislation of the Reagan era, and even his enemies admit he is a masterful tactician. Says one colleague, "Gramm is one of perhaps five congressmen who have changed the way government operates over the last 20 years." Not bad for an economics professor who's only been in politics for a little over a decade.

PART X

Stabilizing the Economy

Stabilization of the Economy Through Monetary Policy

Stabilization policies:
Policies undertaken by governing authorities for the purpose of maintaining full employment and a reasonably stable price level.

Remember that in earlier chapters we discussed the disruptive effects of cyclical unemployment and rampant inflation on the economy. Now that you understand some of the basic causes of unemployment and inflation, we can begin to examine policies that are designed to stabilize the economy. **Stabilization policies** are those undertaken by governing authorities for the purpose of maintaining full employment and a reasonably stable price level. The federal government often seeks to stabilize the economy by using its expenditure and taxing powers to influence macroeconomic equilibrium. Central banks also use their powers to stabilize the economy through their influence on money supply and the level of interest rates. In this chapter we concentrate on the way central banking authorities seek to stabilize the economy and the difficulties they encounter in doing so. We also discuss how the growth rate of the equilibrium money stock can affect real GNP and the price level over the long run and how central banks seek to avoid the specter of hyperinflation.

Monetary policy:
Actions taken by central banks to influence money supply or interest rates in an attempt to stabilize the economy.

Monetary policy consists of actions taken by central banks, like the Fed, to influence money supply or interest rates in an attempt to stabilize the economy. An effective monetary policy helps the economy avoid excessive cyclical unemployment and helps keep the price level reasonably stable. The major goal of this chapter is to explain how the Federal Reserve System's management of the money stock or interest rates through the means we discussed in the preceding chapter can affect aggregate demand and the performance of the economy.

Remember that there's a normal tendency for profit-motivated banks to increase loans during periods of economic expansion when interest rates are rising. The expansion of credit and the quantity of money supplied during periods of peak economic activity tend to increase aggregate demand just when it needs to be re-strained to prevent inflation from heating up. Similarly, during economic downturns there's a normal tendency for banks to cut back on making loans and increase their holdings of excess reserves as interest rates fall. As banks create fewer dollars of checkable deposits, the resulting reduction in the availability of credit and slowdown in the growth of the money stock could act to decrease aggregate demand and turn an economic contraction into a recession. By influencing the money supply the Fed often seeks to control interest rates on a day-to-day basis to stabilize aggregate de-mand in ways that smooth out the swings of the business cycle.

Monetary policymakers must also deal with the fact that a growing economy re-quires a growing money supply. Over time monetary policy must be set to ensure that the banking system has adequate growth in excess reserves so that the long-term upward trend in real GNP isn't held down by inadequate monetary growth. However, monetary policymakers must also take care to avoid excessive monetary growth that can cause high and continued rates of inflation.

By studying the macroeconomic effects of monetary policy, you can see how changes in financial markets caused by shifts in the money supply are transmitted to the rest of the economy. Daily shifts in the supply of money result in frequent changes in equilibrium interest rates. You'll now see that over longer periods, changes in market interest rates and the equilibrium quantity of money affect the willingness and ability of buyers to spend.

The shifts in aggregate demand that result from changes in monetary policy also affect the demand for money in ways that further influence financial market equilib-rium. In other words, there's a complex relationship between money, financial mar-kets, and product markets that we must understand to evaluate the ultimate impact of monetary policy.

Because this chapter brings together the analysis of product markets and macro-economic equilibrium with that of financial markets, you'll need to review the ma-terial in previous chapters. In this chapter we'll use the theories developed on ma-croeconomic equilibrium in earlier chapters. Be sure you understand the theories discussed in those chapters before beginning this chapter. You should also review the material on the demand for money in the chapter entitled "The Functions of Money."

After reading this chapter, you should be able to: *Concept Preview*

1 Discuss the mechanism through which monetary policy can affect interest rates.
2 Show how an expansionary monetary policy shifts the economy's aggregate demand curve and affects macroeconomic equilibrium.
3 Show how a contractionary monetary policy shifts the economy's aggregate demand curve and affects macroeconomic equilibrium.
4 Discuss the quantity theory of money and the possible long-term effects of monetary policy on the price level.
5 Discuss the basic ideas and implications of monetarism for monetary policy.
6 Evaluate some of the difficulties involved in choosing target goals for monetary policy.

Money and Short-Term Macroeconomic Equilibrium

Monetary policy affects the economy daily through its impact on investment spending, household spending, and international transactions. Economic stabilization is an art, not a science. No policymaker or economist has a flawless crystal ball that can foresee all the possible effects of a policy. Unexpected changes in an economy can frustrate the goals of the most carefully planned policies. The Federal Reserve System is one of two major forces acting to stabilize the U.S. economy. The other force is the federal government itself, whose spending and taxing policies affect aggregate demand and in some cases attempt to influence aggregate supply over the long run.

Fiscal policy, which is the use of government spending and taxes to stabilize the economy, is the subject of the following chapter. In many ways your understanding of the effect of fiscal policy on the economy will be enhanced by first mastering the impact of monetary policy on economic performance. Studying monetary policy will help you understand the role of money in the economy and will enable you to see how the goals of fiscal policy must be coordinated with those of monetary policy. You'll then be able to better understand some of the controversies you often read about in the newspapers regarding choice of appropriate policies to even out the swings of the business cycle.

Our first step in understanding how monetary policy affects the economy is to examine the mechanism through which changes in the monetary base (currency and bank reserves) by the Fed influence aggregate demand on a day-to-day basis.

Money Supply, Interest Rates, and Aggregate Demand: Short-Run Effects

In the preceding chapter we showed how increases in excess reserves available to banks increase the capacity of the banking system to make loans. As the Fed supplies the banking system with new excess reserves, an expansion of the money supply results as banks use the new reserves to extend credit and thereby create new checkable deposits. The increased supply of money puts downward pressure on interest rates and increases the quantity of credit demanded. The Fed also directly affects the level of interest rates through the impact of its open market operations on securities prices. As interest rates fall the opportunity cost of holding money falls, and the public willingly holds an expanded money stock created through new loans.

Expansionary monetary policy:
Action by the Federal Reserve System to increase the monetary base or its rate of growth.

Contractionary monetary policy:
Action by the Federal Reserve System to decrease the monetary base or its rate of growth.

The chart and graphs in Box 1 summarize the immediate effects on interest rates of a decision by the Fed to adjust the excess reserves available to depository institutions. As you can see, a decrease in the money supply raises interest rates while an increase in the money supply causes interest rates to fall.[1] When the Fed acts to increase the monetary base or its rate of growth by pumping excess reserves into the banking system, it is engaging in an **expansionary monetary policy.** Similarly, when the Fed acts to decrease the monetary base or its rate of growth by decreasing excess reserves available to depository institutions, it is said to be engaging in a **contractionary monetary policy.**

---

[1]Note that changes in money demand can also affect interest rates in the economy. An increase in money demand puts upward pressure on interest rates in much the same way as is done by a decrease in money supply. By the same token, a decrease in money demand will put downward pressure on interest rates.

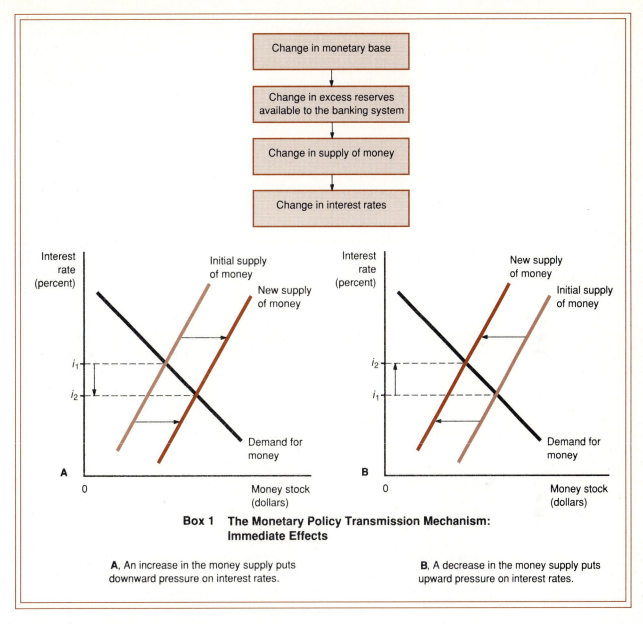

**Box 1   The Monetary Policy Transmission Mechanism:
Immediate Effects**

A, An increase in the money supply puts
downward pressure on interest rates.

B, A decrease in the money supply puts
upward pressure on interest rates.

Interest Rates and Aggregate Demand

In studying the effects of monetary policies we must investigate the relationship
between changes in financial markets and changes in product markets. Our next
step therefore is to show how the reduction in real interest rates caused by an
increase in money supply affects aggregate demand.[2]

The component of aggregate demand that is likely to be most responsive to
changes in market rates of interest is investment purchases. Lower real interest rates

---

[2]Interest rates referred to in this chapter are real interest rates. Recall that real interest rates are nominal
interest rates less the anticipated rate of inflation for the year. Similarly, the money stock and loanable
funds in this chapter are measured in base year dollars to adjust for the effects of changes in the price
level.

encourage increased planned investment purchases, while higher real interest rates cause business firms to scale back their planned investment expenditures. Of course, some consumer expenditures are also sensitive to changes in interest rates because such changes will affect the monthly payments associated with installment purchases. Here, to simplify the analysis, we will concentrate on the impact of changes in interest rates on investment purchases.

Graph **A** in Box 2 draws the demand curve for investment goods in the economy. When, through the transmission mechanism we just discussed, the Fed causes real interest rates to decline, the quantity of investment goods demanded increases. Other things being equal, the increase in investment purchases means the economy's aggregate purchases line will shift upward, as shown in graph **B.** Of course, an increase in aggregate purchases means the economy's aggregate demand curve will shift outward, as shown in graph **C.**

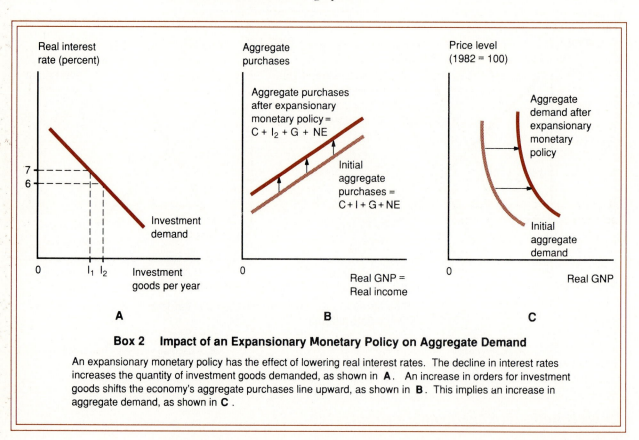

Box 2   Impact of an Expansionary Monetary Policy on Aggregate Demand

An expansionary monetary policy has the effect of lowering real interest rates. The decline in interest rates increases the quantity of investment goods demanded, as shown in **A**. An increase in orders for investment goods shifts the economy's aggregate purchases line upward, as shown in **B**. This implies an increase in aggregate demand, as shown in **C** .

We can now begin to see how an expansionary monetary policy can affect macroeconomic equilibrium through shifts in aggregate demand. A decrease in interest rates caused by an expansionary monetary policy affects the investment component of aggregate demand. As aggregate demand increases, other things being equal, it puts upward pressure on real GNP and the price level. You can test your understanding of how monetary policy works to influence aggregate demand by working out the implications of a contractionary monetary policy for the economy. An increase in real interest rates resulting from a decrease in the money supply will decrease planned investment purchases. This will shift the economy's aggregate purchases line downward.

A decrease in aggregate purchases at any given price level will shift the economy's aggregate demand curve inward, putting downward pressure on real GNP and the price level. The Fed can therefore act to restrain surging aggregate demand in periods of expansion by pursuing policies to increase the level of real interest rates in the economy. Now let's see how the Fed's use of an expansionary monetary policy can help pull the economy out of a contraction or a recession.

Using an Expansionary Monetary Policy to Eliminate a Recessionary GNP Gap: The Impact on Real GNP and the Price Level

When the economy is operating at an equilibrium level of real GNP that falls short of potential real GNP, a recessionary GNP gap will prevail. Under such circumstances there will be cyclical unemployment. Policies designed to stimulate aggregate demand can help restore full employment.

Assume the economy is initially in equilibrium at a real GNP level of $4,700 billion and a price level of 100. Potential real GNP, at which full employment would be achieved, is $5,000 billion. There is therefore a $300 billion recessionary GNP gap. The current level of aggregate demand is insufficient to result in an equilibrium real GNP equal to the economy's potential real GNP of $5,000 billion.

If you were Chairman of the Board of Governors of the Federal Reserve System, what would you do to eliminate the recessionary GNP gap and restore full employment? Well, if you followed the line of reasoning just given, you know that by engaging in an expansionary monetary policy the Fed can act to lower real interest rates. The decline in real interest rates will then increase planned investment purchases, which represent an important component of aggregate demand. As a result, the aggregate demand curve will shift outward.

The impact of just such a policy on macroeconomic equilibrium for the economy is illustrated in Box 3. After an expansionary monetary policy increases aggregate demand, equilibrium real GNP will increase from $4,700 billion to $5,000 billion, eliminating the recessionary GNP gap. You can now see how an expansionary monetary policy can be used to help pull the economy out of a recession. By acting to decrease real interest rates through its influence on bank excess reserves and the money supply, the Fed can stimulate aggregate demand and increase equilibrium real GNP to potential real GNP after a recession hits. But you can see that the Fed's policies also increase the price level. In the graph in Box 3 the price level goes up from 100 to 105 after the expansionary monetary policy shifts aggregate demand. There is therefore 5% inflation during the year as a result of the expansionary monetary policy. The Fed must take care not to decrease the level of interest rates too much so as to avoid initiating a process of inflation that can result from steady increases in aggregate demand. Too much growth in excess reserves for the banking system can result in shifts in money supply that can ultimately cause inflation to become a serious problem

Of course, the risk of inflation from increases in aggregate demand depends on how close the economy is to full employment. For example, if the economy were in a serious recession it would be operating with considerable excess capacity and high cyclical unemployment. Under such circumstances an expansionary monetary policy is likely to run little risk of starting an inflationary process. This is because the economy would be operating in the flat portion of its aggregate supply curve. Increases in aggregate demand would therefore have little effect on the price level

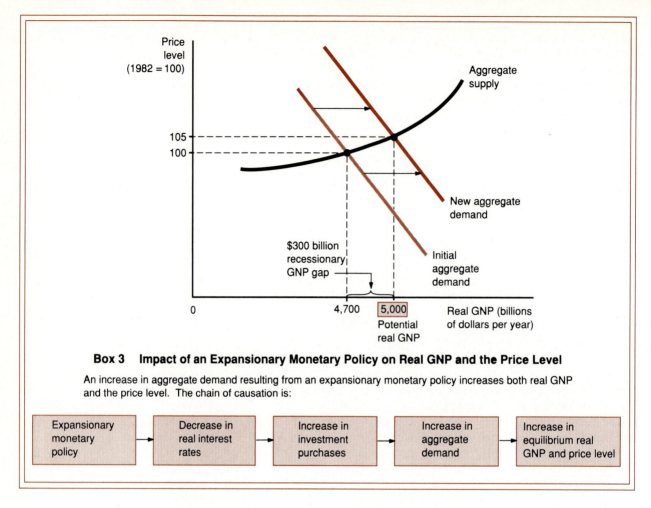

Box 3   Impact of an Expansionary Monetary Policy on Real GNP and the Price Level

An increase in aggregate demand resulting from an expansionary monetary policy increases both real GNP and the price level. The chain of causation is:

| Expansionary monetary policy | → | Decrease in real interest rates | → | Increase in investment purchases | → | Increase in aggregate demand | → | Increase in equilibrium real GNP and price level |

during a deep recession. The closer the economy is to full employment, however, the greater the risk that an expansionary policy designed to eliminate a recessionary GNP gap will start a process of demand-pull inflation.

How Effective Is Monetary Policy in Increasing Aggregate Demand?

Suppose you were a member of the Fed's Federal Open Market Committee. It would be nice to know exactly how much you would have to increase bank excess reserves so as to increase aggregate demand and eliminate a recessionary GNP gap. Unfortunately, monetary policy is not an exact science, and its effectiveness depends on how responsive both banks and investors are to changes in the monetary base and the level of real interest rates.

The effectiveness of an expansionary monetary policy in increasing aggregate demand depends on two basic factors:

1. The willingness of the banking system to create new checkable deposits by making loans using newly created excess reserves
2. The responsiveness of investment and other credit-sensitive purchases to declines in interest rates

Principles in Practice

Monetary Policy During the Great Depression: How the Fed Prevented the Banking System from Recovering and Allowed the Money Supply to Decline

Much of what you know about the Great Depression of the 1930s may come from reminiscences of older relatives. Whether or not they personally endured the severe hardships and poverty that afflicted large numbers of Americans, any adult who lived through those gloomy days can testify to the fear and pessimism engendered by the massive economic collapse.

How did the Federal Reserve System respond to this titanic challenge? To state the case tactfully, this was not the Fed's finest hour. Let's look at what happened during the Great Depression and what the Fed did—and didn't—do about it.

Between 1929 and 1933, one out of every four workers in the labor force was unemployed. Real GNP fell by one third over this period, and the price level declined by 25%. Investment purchases by business firms were reduced to virtually nothing. The great stock market crash of 1929 wiped out the accumulated wealth of many shareholders after the market plunged to an 80% decline in value.

Because of bank failures between 1929 and 1933, the public held a high proportion of money in the form of currency rather than bank deposits. Bank failures were common because banks lacked the reserves to meet the demand for withdrawals of deposits. The series of bank failures only served to increase the demand for currency, which in turn contributed to further bank runs and bank failures. Surviving banks naturally became very cautious in making loans because of their desire to hold liquid assets to meet depositor demands for currency. Banks held high proportions of their assets in excess reserves.

During this period the Fed allowed the money stock to decline. By not supplying the banking system with reserves to meet the demand for withdrawals, the Fed contributed to bank failures and to the unwillingness of bankers to extend loans. Ironically, during this time of acute economic distress, the Fed failed to fulfill its major function of ensuring the stability of the banking system. One of the major purposes of creating the Fed in 1913 had been to prevent bank failures. The Fed had the power to create bank reserves simply by making loans that would create bank deposits at the Fed. By allowing bank reserves to decline, the Fed contributed to the severity of the Depression and prolonged its duration.

The Fed also contributed to the stock market collapse by encouraging the expansion of credit in 1927. During that year the Fed had engaged in open market purchases that induced declines in interest rates and had encouraged borrowing to speculate on stock prices. When the Fed raised its discount rate in 1929 and started to put the brakes on money supply growth, banks began to call in loans. In the fall of 1929 the stock market collapsed, in part because of the panic selling of stocks to obtain funds to pay off loans.

The decline in the money supply during the Depression contributed to deflation in the price level, but this was insufficient to get the economy's self-correction mechanism to work. Aggregate production remained in equilibrium at a real GNP level well below the economy's potential.

The monetary policy pursued by the Fed during the early years of the Great Depression contributed to the severity of the economic decline. The Fed's unwillingness to supply the banking system with reserves undermined the system's integrity. As confidence in the banking system dissolved, the money stock contracted rapidly. This contributed to further declines in aggregate demand that aggravated the already miserable economic picture.*

The major lesson learned during the Depression is that measures must be taken to stimulate aggregate demand when economic forces contribute to its decline.

*For an excellent historical analysis of the Fed's policies, see Sidney Ratner, James H. Soltow, and Richard Sylla, *The Evolution of the American Economy,* New York: Basic Books, 1979, Chapter 22.

Suppose the banking system *does* respond to an increase in excess reserves by making more loans. As this occurs, banks will create more checkable deposits for their customers and the supply of money will increase, putting downward pressure on interest rates. The effectiveness of an expansionary monetary policy in increasing aggregate demand will then hinge on the responsiveness of investment purchases to the change in interest rates. The more responsive investors are to declines in real interest rates, the greater the increase in investment purchases from any given decrease in real interest rates.

In periods of deep recession it's possible that the short-term business outlook will be so gloomy that banks might prefer to hold on to their excess reserves rather than extend credit. Under such circumstances, because of the high risk of default on bank loans, bank managers prefer to hold liquid assets in the form of excess reserves. In this case the first factor listed earlier would render monetary policy ineffective. This is because the increase in excess reserves pumped into the banking system by the Fed would have little effect on money supply. If banks choose to hold excess reserves instead of using them to extend credit and thus create checkable deposits, there will be no increase in the equilibrium money stock. As a consequence, there would be little downward pressure on interest rates in the first place. If interest rates don't fall, investment purchases will not increase in response to the increase in the monetary base.

John Maynard Keynes was quite pessimistic about the effectiveness of monetary policy as a means of pulling an economy out of a deep recession. He argued that in a deep recession, banks would be unwilling to extend credit through loans or through purchase of bonds because of fear of default or fear of a fall in bond prices. Under such circumstances the Fed would have a hard time shifting the money supply curve to the right to lower interest rates.

Even if the Fed were effective in increasing the equilibrium money stock in a deep recession, Keynes argued that its effect on the market rate of interest might be negligible. This is because during a deep recession, money is likely to be a very attractive asset for households and businesses compared to stocks and bonds. After all, during a recession, inflation rates are low (or even negative as was the case during the Great Depression of the 1930s). This means there would be little risk of loss in purchasing power of the dollar during a recession. As people try to increase the quantity of money they hold during a recession, the Fed's attempt to lower interest rates is stifled. The increased money stock ends up being held as currency or checkable deposits. As a result, there is little increase in the supply of loanable funds. This means there will be little downward pressure on the level of interest rates.

Using a Contractionary Monetary Policy to Prevent the Economy from Overheating

Now let's turn the tables on you. Once again we'll put you in Alan Greenspan's shoes. As Chairman of the Federal Reserve Board, suppose you're more worried about inflation than about unemployment. Suppose the current rate of unemployment is only 5.5% and you have good reason to believe the economy is in danger of getting overheated. Recall that an overheated economy is one that is temporarily operating beyond its potential because of excessive aggregate demand. You know there is real danger of shifts in aggregate demand causing an inflationary process as the economy is approaching full employment. You also know that demand-pull inflation at full employment can start a wage-price spiral. That would mean that demand-pull inflation would be followed by cost-push inflation as workers negotiate wage increases to keep up with anticipated inflation. As Chairman of the Fed you want to avoid such an inflationary scenario. You're likely to recommend that a contractionary monetary policy be pursued to prevent an inflationary process from ever beginning.

The graph in Box 4 shows an economy that is initially in equilibrium at point *E*, at which real GNP is at its potential level of $5,000 billion per year and the price level is 100. If aggregate demand were to increase still further the economy would move to point *E'*, at which real GNP would increase to $5,500 billion and the price level would go up to 105. Because wages would tend to be fixed at least in the short-run period of about 1 year, the increase in the price level would not be matched by increased wages over the year. However, in the following year wages would start to increase as workers sought to keep up with inflation. The increase in wages would shift the aggregate supply curve inward. The economy would eventually move to point E'' on its long-run aggregate supply curve, at which point real GNP returns to potential real GNP and the price level increases to 110.

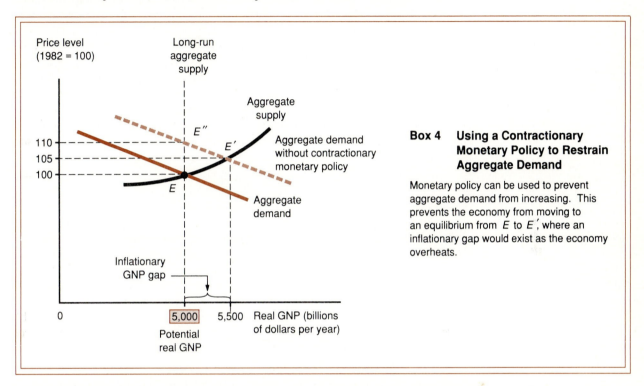

Box 4   Using a Contractionary Monetary Policy to Restrain Aggregate Demand

Monetary policy can be used to prevent aggregate demand from increasing. This prevents the economy from moving to an equilibrium from E to E', where an inflationary gap would exist as the economy overheats.

To prevent inflationary gaps from occurring, the Fed would have to engage in a contractionary monetary policy as the economy approaches full employment. To do so it would attempt to decrease the excess reserves available to depository institutions (or reduce their rate of growth) so as to put upward pressure on interest rates as the economy moves to full employment. In the graph in Box 4 monetary policy would be effective in preventing an inflationary gap if it could keep the aggregate demand curve from shifting outward. If monetary policy achieved this objective, the economy would never reach an equilibrium at point E' and would avoid the bout of stagflation that would eventually decrease aggregate supply and result in an equilibrium at E''. In this way the Fed can prevent a wage-price spiral from occurring.

Concept Check

1   A decline in aggregate demand is expected during the year as a result of a gloomy outlook for consumer spending. How can monetary policy be used to offset the adverse effects on the economy of the decline in aggregate demand?

2   What is the purpose of a contractionary monetary policy?

3   What influences the effectiveness of monetary policy in achieving its objectives?

Money, Real GNP, Prices, and Debates About Monetary Policy

Earlier in the chapter we pointed out that monetary policy is an art rather than a science. That might just be putting it mildly if we consider the fact that there's great controversy about how the economy is affected by changes in monetary policy and changes in the money stock. There's no disagreement among economists about the fact that monetary policy has the potential to influence aggregate demand. However, economists do disagree about the mechanism through which monetary policy affects aggregate demand and macroeconomic equilibrium. In this section we'll concentrate on the relationship between money and prices in the economy over the long run, when wages and prices are likely to be more flexible than they are over shorter periods.

The major impact of money supply on real GNP occurs mainly over a short period through the transmission mechanism we discussed earlier. Changes in money supply affect real interest rates, thereby affecting investment and other credit-sensitive purchases that in turn affect aggregate demand. The long-term impact on the economy of changes in the money supply depends on the relationship between growth in the money stock available, growth in potential real GNP, and shifts in the demand curve for money, which we now will study.

A long-term objective of monetary policy is to adjust the growth of the money stock to accommodate long-term growth in the transaction demand for money. Remember that as GNP grows, so does the transaction demand for money (see the chapter entitled "The Functions of Money"). By doing this central banks ensure an adequate stock of money and availability of credit to allow the economy to expand without excessive inflation or recession.

The Concept of Income Velocity of Circulation of Money

Before we examine the relationship between growth in the money stock and the macroeconomic equilibrium levels of real GNP and prices, we must first develop a new concept. Take out a dollar bill from your wallet or purse and look at it. Unless you've just gotten a nice crisp newly printed bill, the dollar is likely to be dirty and worn. It's seen a bit of action. In fact, each dollar of the money stock, in either checkable deposits or currency, is used several times each year to make purchases of final products. This means the dollar volume of final transactions that can be supported by a given quantity of money, on average per day over the year, is a multiple of the available money stock.

Income velocity of circulation of money:

The number of times per year on average a dollar of the money stock is spent on final purchases or paid out as income.

The **income velocity of circulation of money** is the number of times per year on average a dollar of the money stock is spent on final products. Because nominal GNP also equals aggregate income in the nation, income velocity also measures the number of times a year on average a dollar of the money stock is paid out as income. For example, in 1985 nominal GNP, representing the market value of final products at current prices that year, was $3,988 billion. The average daily stock of currency and checkable deposits that year (M1) was $626 billion. This means the $626 billion money stock supported nearly $4 trillion of aggregate income generated from the final production of goods and services that year. The income velocity of circulation, V, of money is computed from the following formula:

$$\text{Income velocity of circulation} = V = \text{Nominal GNP}/M1$$

where M1 is the average daily stock of currency and checkable deposits held over the year.

In 1985 the velocity of circulation of money was therefore

$$\$3,988 \text{ billion}/\$626 \text{ billion} = 6.37$$

If velocity is about 6 this year, the dirty old dollar in your wallet will be involved in 6 transactions during the year to purchase final products. This also means the dollar will be received as income 6 times during the year. You might use it to buy a gallon of gas, and the dollar will become part of the income of the gas station owner. He'll hold it awhile but will eventually spend it, say, on a cup of coffee at the local drugstore, when it will become income to the store owner. When a dollar of the money stock is not being used, someone is holding it either as a checkable deposit or as currency.

The Equation of Exchange

The **equation of exchange** is an identity that shows the relationship between nominal GNP, the money stock, and the income velocity of circulation of money. The equation of exchange is obtained directly from the definition of velocity. Velocity is

$$V = \text{Nominal GNP/M1}$$

Multiply both sides of the formula for velocity by M1. This gives the following result:

$$(M1)V = \text{Nominal GNP}$$

Nominal GNP can be expressed as the price level, P, multiplied by the quantity, Q, of final transactions, which is real GNP:

$$\text{Nominal GNP} = PQ = (\text{Price level})(\text{Real GNP})$$

If you just remember that money is measured by M1, the symbol M can be used for money to make the equation a little less cluttered. This gives:

$$MV = PQ$$

which is the equation of exchange. Note again that the relationship represented is an *identity*. The term MV represents total dollar expenditure on the nation's final products over the year. The term PQ represents total receipts from sale of final products over the year. Because receipts always equal expenditures, the equation is an identity.

Using the Equation of Exchange to Understand the Role of Money in the Economy

The preceding analysis of the impact of money on the economy emphasized how changes in money supply can affect interest rates and investment. These short-run effects of changes in the money supply shift aggregate demand, and they can increase or decrease real GNP when it diverges from its potential level in the short run.

Over longer periods, *provided velocity is more or less stable,* changes in the money supply will affect the price level. The **classical quantity theory of money** is a model of the long-run functioning of the economy that maintains that, over the long run, changes in the money stock result in proportional changes in the price level. We first discussed the ideas of the classical economists in the chapter on the forces of aggregate supply and demand. You'll recall that they believed flexibility of

Equation of exchange:
An identity that shows the relationship between nominal GNP, the money stock, and the income velocity of circulation of money.

Classical quantity theory of money:
A model of the long-run functioning of the economy that maintains that, over the long run, changes in the money stock result in proportional changes in the price level.

wages and prices would ensure that equilibrium real GNP would equal potential GNP. They believed that temporary deviations from potential real GNP would eventually be followed by shifts in aggregate supply that return the economy to equilibrium at full employment.

According to the classical quantity theory of money, the transmission mechanism through which changes in the money stock ultimately affect the economy differs from the mechanism previously discussed. In the short run, when wages and prices might be temporarily inflexible according to the classical economists, increases in money supply can affect interest rates, investment, and real GNP. However, in the long run, potential real GNP will be equilibrium real GNP and changes in the money stock can affect only the price level. To see this, you can think of Q in the equation of exchange as real GNP while P represents the price level. If money supply goes up while velocity is fixed then nominal GNP, which is represented by PQ, must increase. However, because in the long run an increase in M does not affect real GNP, any increase in nominal GNP will be fully accounted for by increases in the price level, provided V is constant. If V is constant, then increases in the growth rate of M will increase the rate of inflation whenever the growth rate of the money stock exceeds the growth rate of real GNP.

For example, suppose the federal government declares that each dollar in checking accounts and each dollar of currency is now worth 2 dollars. This will double the money stock. But if real GNP is equal to potential real GNP, the resulting increase in the dollar value of aggregate demand cannot result in more output. There might be a temporary overheating of the economy, but you know that real GNP cannot exceed its potential for long without causing decreases in aggregate supply. As you and your friends run out to spend your newly created dollars, prices are sure to rise if quantity supplied cannot increase. If velocity (V) is fixed and Q is also fixed at potential real GNP, the equation of exchange shows you that a doubling of the money stock will also double the price level in the economy!

In general, if the economy is already operating at its potential and V is constant, the price level will increase by the same proportion as the dollar amount of money in circulation increases. The increase in the price level increases the demand for money and therefore will induce people to hold the larger stock of money. This is because, given real GNP, an increase in the price level increases the transaction demand for money (see the chapter entitled "The Functions of Money"). If the price level didn't change, some other variable would have to change to induce people to willingly hold the available amount of money. Either a decrease in interest rates or an increase in real GNP would also induce people to willingly hold the larger money stock. The quantity theory of money, in its crudest form, does not consider changes in the interest rate. It also assumes that real GNP is in equilibrium at its full-employment level. Remember that the classical quantity theory of money was developed at a time when the classical economists believed the economy's self-correction mechanism would work to keep the economy operating at close to full employment. Therefore the price level must rise to induce the public to willingly hold the larger money stock.

The graph in Box 5 shows how the increase in aggregate demand caused by a doubling of the money stock will double the price level, assuming flexible prices and wages. The initial equilibrium is at point E along the vertical long-run aggregate supply curve (see the chapter on the forces of aggregate supply and demand for a discussion of this curve). A doubling of the money supply will increase aggregate demand. The new aggregate demand curve will intersect the long-run aggregate supply curve at point E'. At that point real GNP remains at its full-employment level, *but the price level has also doubled.*

CHAPTER 35 Stabilization of the Economy Through Monetary Policy

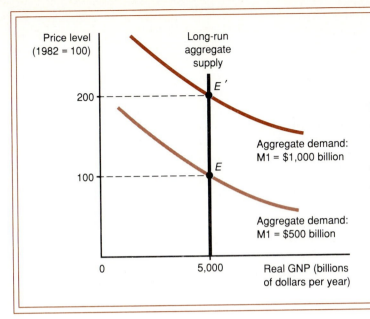

Box 5   Money Supply, Real GNP, and the Price Level: The Quantity Theory

In the long run, if all prices and wages are flexible, the price level is proportionate to the money stock. A doubling of the money supply will double the price level, as shown in the graph, by doubling the money value of aggregate demand.

Keep in mind that this conclusion is true only if nothing else changes as the money supply and price level change. This ensures a stable money demand and a fixed income velocity of circulation of money.

Monetary Policy: Implications of the Classical Quantity Theory

If the classical quantity theory is correct, it has some important implications for monetary policy. Suppose the income velocity of circulation is constant. Also assume that over the long run, wage and price flexibility would ensure that real GNP would not differ from potential real GNP for long. In a growing economy where the assumptions of the classical quantity theory held, stable prices could be maintained if the money stock were allowed to grow at the same rate as real GNP. For example, suppose potential real GNP were to grow at an annual rate of 3%. In this case, other things being equal, the right side of the equation of exchange, PQ, would also increase by 3% annually. Now if V were constant, how much can the money stock increase to prevent the price level from going up? The answer is 3%. What would happen if the money stock were allowed to increase more rapidly than 3%? For example, if the money stock were to grow at an annual rate of 10%, MV also would go up by 10% per year if V were constant. But this means the right side of the equation would also have to grow by 10% per year. Because the growth rate of real GNP is dependent on such factors as technological progress and growth in labor productivity, its rate of growth would be unaffected by the growth rate of the money stock. It follows that the growth rate of the price level would increase to make up the difference between the growth rate of the money stock and the growth rate of potential real GNP.

Assuming velocity is constant, the classical quantity theory of money implies that, over the long run, rapid inflation can be caused by growth of the money stock in excess of the long-term growth rate of real GNP. This implies that monetary policy can keep inflation under control over the long run by making sure the growth rate of the money stock does not exceed the growth rate of real GNP over the long run.

Is Velocity Fixed?

The classical quantity theory is based on the assumption that the income velocity of circulation of money is fixed on average over long periods of time. Is this hypothesis supported by the facts? The graph in Box 6 shows how the income velocity of circulation has varied over time. Velocity fell from 3.5 at the beginning of the Great Depression in 1929 to a low of slightly less than 2 in the mid-1940s. However, from 1945 it has almost steadily climbed, reaching its peak of over 7 between 1982 and 1983. Between 1983 and 1984 it declined. Then it rose again until 1985. From 1985 to 1987 it fell to 6, after which it started to increase again.

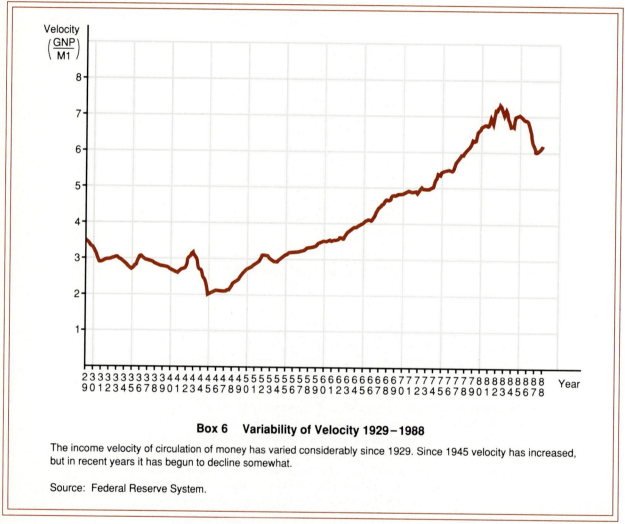

Box 6   Variability of Velocity 1929–1988

The income velocity of circulation of money has varied considerably since 1929. Since 1945 velocity has increased, but in recent years it has begun to decline somewhat.

Source: Federal Reserve System.

The variability of velocity casts doubt on the simplest version of the quantity theory, which is based on the assumption of fixed velocity. But why does velocity increase and decrease over time? The answer lies in shifts of the demand curve for money in the economy.

The higher the income velocity of circulation, the faster the turnover of dollars as income. Higher velocity means money is being used more frequently to purchase final products and is spending less time as idle cash balances. In other words, given nominal GNP and the level of interest rates over the year, an increase in velocity means the money demand curve has shifted inward. A decrease in money demand therefore is indicative of an increase in the velocity of circulation of money. You can readily see this from the formula for velocity. Given nominal GNP, an increase in V must mean the quantity of money held on average per day over the year has declined because V = Nominal GNP/M1. This implies that, other things being equal, the demand for money is less.

Velocity will vary as the demand for money varies. Any change in a nation's financial system that reduces the transaction costs of converting near money to money is likely to decrease the desired money stock demanded by the public. When this occurs, a smaller equilibrium money stock can support a given nominal GNP. This means velocity will increase. Technological change in the payment mechanism in an economy can increase velocity. For example, velocity will be increased by invention of a new computerized network that allows instantaneous transfer of funds in savings accounts to funds in checkable deposits.

There have been many financial innovations in the United States that explain the sharp increase in velocity from 1950 to 1980. One such innovation is widespread use of credit cards, which allow users to write one check in payment for several purchases made during a month. Many mutual fund accounts allow easy transfer of investment balances into money market funds that have check-writing privileges. These innovations have allowed the public to economize on the money they hold and thus have served to increase velocity.

More on Money, Prices, and Monetary Policy: Monetarism

You might think the variability of velocity over time has rendered the quantity theory of money useless. This is far from the truth, because many economists still believe the equation of exchange provides important insights into the way the economy functions and how monetary policy can affect the price level over time.

Monetarism is a theory of long-term macroeconomic equilibrium, based on the equation of exchange, that assumes that shifts in velocity are reasonably predictable. According to the monetarist approach, changes in money supply can affect aggregate demand in the short run in the ways discussed earlier in the chapter. Monetarists argue that changes in the money stock are the predominant influence on *nominal* GNP and nominal income in a nation. If predictions about changes in velocity are reasonably accurate, the monetarists maintain that monetary policy can be used in the long run to control the rate of inflation. After adjusting for the forecasted changes in the rate of increase (or decrease) in velocity, the monetarists argue that careful control of the equilibrium money stock is necessary to stabilize the economy. If the money stock is not allowed to grow rapidly enough to accommodate growth in real GNP after adjusting for any changes in V, monetary policy could cause a recession. This is because if monetary growth is not fast enough, nominal GNP (which is PQ in the equation of exchange) cannot increase. For example, suppose the money stock were to grow by less than the growth in real GNP. If after adjusting for changes in V the growth of MV is less than the growth of PQ (which is nominal GNP), growth in nominal GNP will be held back by inadequate availability of money. Typically, except in a severe recession, the price level *(P)* does not fall to allow Q, which is real GNP, to continue growing under such circumstances. This means businesses and households will not have adequate money to meet their daily requirements for transactions. As they increase their demand for money, the credit supplied to financial markets will shrink and real GNP growth will fall. Growth in real GNP

Monetarism:
A theory of long-term macroeconomic equilibrium, based on the equation of exchange, that assumes that shifts in velocity are reasonably predictable.

Economic Thinkers

MILTON FRIEDMAN

Milton Friedman, America's best-known monetarist and the apostle of libertarian economics, is a bold and outspoken defender of the free market system and advocate of a monetary rule. Because he is able to express complicated ideas in simple, often colorful language (such as using ice cream cone imagery in a letter to *The Wall Street*

Journal), Friedman is popular with the media and is a well-known public figure.

Friedman is a respected economist who has attacked the foundations of Keynesian economics. Friedman also believes wholeheartedly that free markets can do almost anything and that they work best without government interference. According to him, the key to a healthy, stable economy is for the money supply to expand at a constant rate in accordance with growth in the economy's capacity to produce. Business fluctuations are caused by short-run, erratic changes in the money supply, including such major downturns as the Great Depression, which Friedman says would not have developed if the Federal Reserve had increased the money supply after the stock market crash of 1929.

He is a firm believer in *laissez faire* capitalism and a diehard fan of Adam Smith. He has attempted to build on Smith's classic liberal philosophy and de-

fends it eloquently. For his work, he has received nearly every significant honor the field of economics has to offer, including the Nobel Prize in 1976. *A Monetary History of the United States, Capitalism and Freedom,* and *Free to Choose* are among his best-known works. He taught at the University of Chicago for 30 years, where he eventually led the strongly free-market economists associated with that university. He retired in 1977 and currently works out of the Hoover Institute at Stanford University.

In an attempt to replace government influence with market solutions, Friedman has advocated the elimination of licensing of physicians, public schools, agricultural price supports, and food stamps. He has made major contributions to economic theory in the areas of risk and insurance and by describing consumption patterns that are based on wealth, rather than current income alone.

---

may become negative, implying that an economic contraction or recession can be precipitated by inadequate monetary growth.

On the other hand, if monetary growth, after adjustment for changes in V, is much faster than real GNP growth, then nominal GNP will increase more rapidly than real GNP. This means the rate of inflation will increase. The major conclusion of the monetarists is that over the long run, the growth rate of the money stock is the major factor influencing the rate of inflation in the economy. Monetarists recommend concentrating on the long-term effects of monetary growth. They therefore focus on the impact of monetary growth on the price level. (See the Economic Thinkers box on Milton Friedman, America's preeminent monetarist.)

Suppose the long-term trend of about 3% annual growth in real GNP continues. At what annual rate must the money stock grow to prevent excessive inflation? According to the equation of exchange:

$$MV = (\text{Price level})(\text{Real GNP})$$

If real GNP goes up by 3% per year, then MV must also increase by no more than 3% per year to prevent inflation over the long run. If MV increases by less than 3% per year, then aggregate demand will grow less quickly than aggregate supply and there will be downward pressure on real GNP and the price level.

To prevent excessive inflation, a monetary growth management policy must also predict changes in V over the long term. For example, if velocity increases over time (as it did between 1950 and 1980), a 3% monetary growth rate will be inflationary. This is because both the increase in velocity and the increase in money supply will exert upward pressure on the price level over time. A strict monetary rule to increase money supply therefore could result in inflation if V changes unexpectedly.

On the other hand, if velocity declines, as it did between 1984 and 1987, then a 3% growth rate of the money stock will be deflationary. This means monetary growth would be inadequate to provide enough new money to accommodate economic growth. This could cause a recession because interest rates would rise unless the price level was flexible downward.

Monetarists believe that shifts in velocity are fairly predictable and therefore recommend a rule that would allow money supply to increase within the range of 3% to 5% per year, depending on predicted changes in velocity.

Concept Check

1   The money stock increases by 10% during the year. Assuming velocity is constant and real GNP is at its potential level, what is the long-run effect on the price level of the increase in the money stock?

2   Why would you expect interest rates to rise during a period of expansion in the economy, other things being equal?

3   How can an increase in the income velocity of circulation of money affect nominal GNP, assuming the money stock is fixed?

Can the Fed Control Both Interest Rates and Money Supply? The Policy Dilemma

The conflicting views of the short-run and long-run effects of monetary policy result in a dilemma for policymakers. Should they concentrate on managing aggregate demand over a short period of time by engaging in policies that affect interest rates? Or should they instead manage the long-term growth of the equilibrium money stock in a predictable way so as to maintain a stable price level over the long run? Unfortunately, it's impossible to achieve both of these goals simultaneously.

Shifts in Money Demand

The money demand curve is likely to shift periodically in response to changes in economic conditions. For example, in periods of economic expansion when real GNP or the price level increases, the demand curve for money will shift outward as the transaction demand for money increases. Similarly, during periods of economic contraction as real GNP or the price level declines, the transaction demand for money will also decline, shifting the money demand curve inward. Of course, the demand curve for money could shift for other reasons. Financial innovations that decrease the transaction cost of converting near money to money are likely to decrease the demand for money.

The shifts in the money demand curve that occur periodically make it difficult for the Fed to control both interest rates and the equilibrium quantity of money. The graph in Box 7 shows how an increase in the demand for money that occurs during an economic expansion will put upward pressure on interest rates. Initially the equilibrium interest rate is 7% and the equilibrium quantity of money is $600 billion. As

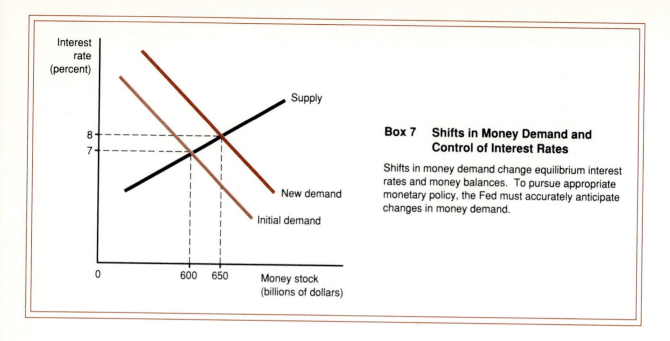

Box 7 Shifts in Money Demand and Control of Interest Rates

Shifts in money demand change equilibrium interest rates and money balances. To pursue appropriate monetary policy, the Fed must accurately anticipate changes in money demand.

the demand for money increases, the interest rate goes up to 8% and the equilibrium quantity of money increases to $650 billion.

The Fed could respond to the increased demand for money by increasing the monetary base. This would shift the money supply curve outward as excess reserves are pumped into the banking system and would put downward pressure on interest rates (see the preceding chapter). However, as the Fed acts to increase the money supply it increases the equilibrium quantity of money still further. This means that over the long run, particularly if the economy is close to full employment, aggregate demand is likely to increase and put upward pressure on the price level. This will cause a process of inflation over the long run if the growth rate of the money supply is excessive.

The problem the Fed has in controlling the money supply stems from the fact that other things are seldom constant as the money supply increases. Over time an increase in the money supply is likely to increase aggregate demand. In the long run a permanent increase in the money supply is likely to increase the price level. Either the increase in real GNP or the increase in the price level will increase the demand for money. If the growth rate of the money stock exceeds the long-term growth rate of real GNP after adjustment for changes in the rate of change of velocity, the monetary growth could start a process of inflation. As shown in Box 7, the increase in money demand will result in an increase in interest rates *and* an increase in the *equilibrium* quantity of money held.

Suppose the Fed tries to achieve an equilibrium level of M1 equal to $600 billion by increasing the monetary base. As you saw in Box 7, the increase in demand for money indirectly caused by the Fed's policy results in an equilibrium quantity of money equal to $650 billion.

This example shows that control of the equilibrium money stock is more of an art than a science! To control the equilibrium money stock, the Fed must accurately predict shifts in the demand for money that result from changes in its policy. Similarly, to predict the impact of its policies on the equilibrium money stock, the Fed must accurately predict shifts in the supply of checkable deposits that result from incentives of bankers to make loans.

Can the Fed Control Interest Rates?

The Fed has the ability to influence market interest rates through its open market operations and its control of the monetary base. As we just showed, the Fed cannot simultaneously control interest rates and the supply of money.

This analysis points out a dilemma for Fed policy. If the Fed chooses a target quantity of money to keep the price level within certain bounds over the long run and uses open market operations to maintain that equilibrium level of M1, it can expect substantial variability in the level of interest rates in the economy if money demand is unstable. This is illustrated in the graph in Box 8. Suppose the Fed acts to keep the equilibrium quantity of money fixed at $600 billion. Initially, when it begins this policy, the interest rate is 8%. If the demand for money increases, the Fed immediately takes action to decrease the monetary base so as to prevent the equilibrium money stock from going up. However, the resulting increase in money demand causes equilibrium interest rates to rise. To avoid clutter in the graph in Box 8, the money supply curves are not drawn. Each point labeled E with a subscript is a point of equilibrium through which a money supply curve could be drawn. The increase in the demand for money causes the interest rate to rise from 8% to 11% (moving from point E_1 to point E_2) when the equilibrium money stock is held fixed. Similarly, if the demand for money declines, the Fed would immediately increase the monetary base to once again obtain an equilibrium money stock of $600 billion at point E_3. However, the decrease in money demand causes the interest rate to decline. In Box 8 the interest rate falls to 5% after the decline in the demand for money.

By seeking to control the equilibrium money stock over the long run, the Fed gives up control of interest rates in the short run and could destabilize the economy.

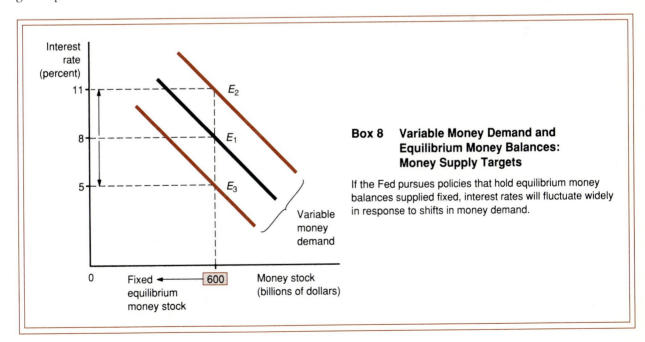

Box 8   Variable Money Demand and Equilibrium Money Balances: Money Supply Targets

If the Fed pursues policies that hold equilibrium money balances supplied fixed, interest rates will fluctuate widely in response to shifts in money demand.

On the other hand, if the Fed wants to keep equilibrium interest rates stable, it must vary bank reserves and money supply to achieve that goal. Shifts in money demand over the business cycle will have to be balanced by changes in monetary policy that cause shifts in the money supply. The resulting changes in the equilibrium money stock can cause inflation and recession.

For example, suppose the economy is expanding. As nominal GNP increases, so will the demand for money. Given the money supply curve, the increased demand for money causes the money demand curve to shift outward. This will tend to put upward pressure on interest rates. The graph in Box 9 shows that, given the initial equilibrium interest rate of 6% and the initial money supply curve, the increased demand for money resulting from expansion of the economy will cause the equilibrium interest rate to rise to 7%. The increase in interest rates would restrain aggregate demand. To keep the expansion on course, the Fed can take action to keep interest rates from rising. To do so it would increase bank reserves through open market purchases to shift the money supply curve outward, as shown in the graph in Box 9. As it does so, equilibrium interest rates remain at 6% but the equilibrium money stock increases from $500 billion to $600 billion.

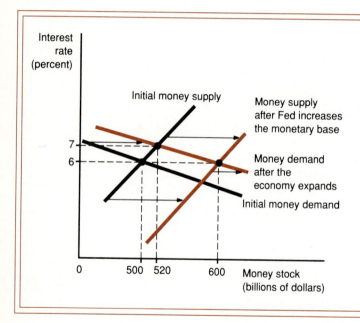

Box 9   How an Increase in Money Supply Can Keep Interest Rates from Rising During an Expansion

As the economy expands, the demand for money increases, putting upward pressure on interest rates. The Fed can keep interest rates from rising to 7% in the graph by expanding the monetary base. As the monetary base increases, so does money supply, putting downward pressure on interest rates. In the graph the Fed's policy keeps interest rates at 6% during the expansion but allows the money stock to grow from $500 billion to $600 billion.

The graph in Box 10 shows how the equilibrium money stock must vary to keep interest rates fixed as money demand shifts. If the Fed engages in policies that peg the interest rate at a fixed level of, say, 6%, then increases in money demand, as might occur when the economy expands, will increase the equilibrium money stock. In Box 10 the money stock is initially $600 billion. An increase in money demand increases the equilibrium money stock to $700 billion at point E_2. In response the Fed increases the monetary base to adjust money supply so as to prevent interest rates from going up. The increase in the monetary base shifts the money supply curve outward (this is not shown in the graph, but you can imagine an upward-sloping money supply curve going through each of the equilibrium points) and keeps interest rates from going up. This type of policy could result in inflation over

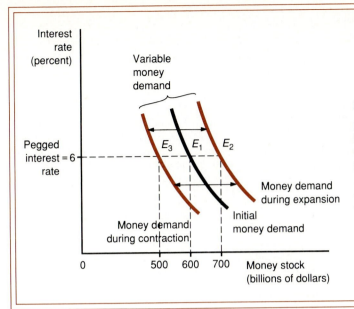

Box 10   Pegging the Interest Rate

If the Fed wishes to peg interest rates in the economy, it must pursue policies to allow the money stock to vary with changes in money demand. This means increasing the money supply during expansions when money demand increases and decreasing the money supply during contractions when money demand decreases.

the long run if the growth rate of the money supply exceeds the growth rate of real GNP after adjustment for changes in the growth rate of velocity.

Similarly, if the Fed decreases the monetary base when money demand is declining so as to prevent interest rates from falling, the equilibrium money stock will fall to $500 billion at point E_3. By pegging interest rates in periods of declining monetary demand, as is likely to be the case during contractions, the Fed can cause a recession. Fluctuation in the money stock that results when the Fed pegs interest rates can therefore contribute to inflation over the long run by allowing the money stock to grow but can cause recessions in the short run.

Monetary Policy Targets in the United States Since the End of World War II

If the Fed cannot simultaneously control interest rates and the equilibrium money stock, what does it do? During the period from 1942 to 1951 the Fed pursued policies to keep interest rates at low levels. At that time the federal government had accumulated a tremendous debt as a result of bonds issued to finance the country's participation in World War II. The Fed assisted the government in keeping its interest costs low by adjusting the money supply in response to shifts in money demand.

In 1951 the Treasury and the Fed reached a famous "accord" in which it was agreed that the Fed would have more discretion in influencing interest rates. During that period the Fed sought to keep interest rates within certain bounds and carefully watched bank excess reserves and discount loans as indicators of the availability of loanable funds. Unfortunately, the Fed's stabilization record during this period wasn't very good. It tended to engage in policies that decreased interest rates when the economy was booming. Similarly, when the economy was slack the Fed engaged in policies that tended to increase interest rates. Rather than stabilizing the economy, the Fed's policies throughout much of the 1950s and 1960s contributed to the severity of cyclical ups and downs of real GNP!

Principles in Practice

Monetary Policy, Real Interest Rates, and the International Value of the Dollar

By now you've learned enough about monetary policy to realize that in any given situation, there's no "ideal" policy that will fulfill every objective. In establishing any monetary policy, the leaders of the Federal Reserve System must balance the benefits of that policy with the negative consequences that may ensue.

This is a challenge the Fed confronts when it considers actions designed to raise or lower interest rates in the economy. In recent years, setting policy in this area has become a delicate balancing act.

Despite sharp declines in nominal interest rates, real interest rates remained quite high from 1981 to 1987. Real short-term interest rates, measured by the monthly average of the annual yield on 3-month Treasury bills less the annual rate of inflation, varied between 6% in 1981 and slightly over 3% by the end of 1986. The sharp rise in real interest rates in the early 1980s, when nominal rates jumped to double digits, contributed to the recession of 1982, which was one of the most severe recessions since the Great Depression of the 1930s. The monetary policy pursued since that time has brought inflation down considerably from the double-digit levels that prevailed in the early 1980s.

From 1984 to 1986, growth in real GNP was sluggish and unemployment remained at around 7% of the labor force. Although the Fed allowed nominal interest rates to fall considerably over this period, real interest rates remained quite high by historical standards. Throughout the 1960s real interest rates rarely rose above 2%. The 3% + real interest rates of the mid-1980s were viewed by many prominent economists as preventing the economy from achieving its potential.[*]

One reason the Fed has been reluctant to allow real interest rates to fall is its concern about rekindling inflation by overstimulating aggregate demand. However, the Fed has also been concerned about the impact of declining interest rates on the international value of the dollar. Our country's huge balance of trade deficits in the 1980s has placed dollars in the hands of many foreigners. To discourage these investors from selling their dollars in international currency markets, the Fed has sought to keep interest rates high. By using this technique to keep at a low level the supply of dollars available for sale, the Fed prevents the value of the dollar from plummeting in international currency markets.

Critics of the Fed's policies to keep interest rates and the international value of the dollar high argue that policymakers shouldn't worry about the exchange rate of the dollar if the cost of keeping its value high is preventing the economy from reaching its potential.[†] A lower-priced dollar eventually makes U.S. goods more attractive to buyers in foreign product markets by reducing the prices of such goods in terms of foreign currency. Also, a decline in the price of the dollar makes imports more expensive and encourages U.S. consumers to substitute domestic goods for foreign goods.

Many considerations go into the formulation of monetary policy. The Fed must be concerned about the impact of its actions that affect interest rates, because those actions also influence the price level, the stability of international currency markets, and the level of real GNP.

[*]For example, see James Tobin, "Advice for the Fed: Why Lower Interest Rates Wouldn't Hurt," *The New York Times,* September 14, 1986, p. F2.
[†]See Tobin.

In the 1970s the Fed began to choose monetary growth targets rather than interest rate targets. The Fed sought to control the growth rates of M1 and M2 while at the same time keeping short-term interest rates from fluctuating too widely. During this period, whenever an increase in real GNP or the price level caused an increase in money demand, there would be upward pressure on interest rates. The Fed would react by engaging in open market purchases of government securities. These purchases would increase securities prices, thereby decreasing interest rates. However, the open market purchases tended to increase the money supply, thus getting the Fed off its M1 target. The Fed would then react at the next Federal Open Market Committee meeting by decreasing the monetary base. Whenever the Fed missed its target on short-term interest rates, it would increase its rate of monetary growth. This made it hard to control the money stock, which by 1973 was growing at 8% per year and putting upward pressure on inflation and nominal interest rates. In

1974 the sharp increase in the price of oil along with high interest rates contributed to a recession.

Between 1974 and 1979 the money supply tended to grow along with the price level during that inflationary period. However, in 1979 the Fed began to engage in policies that sharply slowed the growth rate of M1. Because money demand continued to grow over that period, this resulted in upward pressure on nominal interest rates. By the end of 1980 nominal interest rates in the economy were in double digits.

In 1981 the prime rate rose to nearly 20%. Given the inflation rate of 9% prevailing at the time, this meant the real interest rate paid on loans in 1981 was at an unprecedented high level of 11%! The increase in interest rates decreased investment spending sharply and in 1982 contributed to the most severe recession the nation had experienced since the Great Depression of the 1930s. Apparently the Fed reduced the growth rate of M1 too sharply and caused a serious recession. The basic problem the Fed faced during this period was the familiar one of accurately predicting cyclical increases in money demand that put upward pressure on interest rates.

Since 1983 the Fed has worried less about inflation than previously. Inflation was sharply reduced after the 1982 recession. The Fed has allowed M1 to grow to accommodate increased demand for money in an expanding economy. In 1986 nominal interest rates fell sharply and inflation remained low. Throughout 1986 real interest rates remained quite high by historical standards. In 1986 the Fed engaged in policies that allowed real interest rates to fall. By 1987 fears of inflation increased as the economy approached full employment, and the Fed engaged in policies to increase real interest rates. The increase in interest rates, combined with the falling international value of the dollar, contributed to the stock market collapse in October 1987.

Concept Check

1 An increase in the demand for money occurs as the economy expands. Other things being equal, what will be the impact on the level of interest rates for the economy?

2 How will interest rates fluctuate over the business cycle if the Fed pursues policies to keep the money supply more or less fixed?

3 How can the Fed keep interest rates from fluctuating in a growing economy?

Monetary Policy: Goals and Obstacles

Stabilization of the economy through monetary policy operates mainly through the short-run impact on interest rates of changes in the monetary base. In the short run, declines in interest rates increase planned investment and other credit-sensitive purchases. This tends to increase aggregate demand and can increase real GNP. Conversely, increases in interest rates tend to decrease aggregate demand and decrease real GNP.

In the long run, the price level is more likely to be affected than real GNP when monetary growth exceeds the growth rate of real GNP and is not offset by declines in velocity. A basic difficulty with monetary policy is reconciling its short-term goals with its long-term goals.

Another problem encountered in actually administering monetary policy is predicting the effects of increases in money demand on interest rates and equilibrium money supply. As observed earlier, the Fed cannot simultaneously control the equilibrium money supply and equilibrium interest rates. As a result, the Fed has sometimes had to forgo its short-term goal of preventing recessions to pursue longer-term goals of reducing inflation.

One aspect of monetary policy that we haven't yet discussed is its impact on international trade. Changes in interest rates, money supply, and the price level can affect the ability of U.S. firms to compete with foreign suppliers. In view of our country's chronic excess of imports over exports in recent years, the Fed has had to temper its domestic policies with concern for international trade considerations. In the last part of the book you'll see how these considerations affect the Fed's policies.

Summary

1. Monetary policy consists of actions taken by central banks to influence interest rates and money supply in ways that affect aggregate demand.
2. An expansionary monetary policy consists of increases in the monetary base or its rate of growth, while a contractionary monetary policy consists of decreases in the monetary base or its rate of growth.
3. An expansionary monetary policy puts downward pressure on interest rates and encourages investment spending by business firms. The increase in aggregate purchases resulting from an expansionary monetary policy puts upward pressure on equilibrium real GNP. An expansionary monetary policy has the effect of shifting the economy's aggregate demand curve outward.
4. The effectiveness of an expansionary monetary policy in increasing aggregate demand depends on the willingness of the banking system to extend credit with newly supplied excess reserves and the responsiveness of investment spending to declines in interest rates.
5. A contractionary monetary policy can be used to prevent an economy from overheating. By increasing interest rates, such a policy puts downward pressure on aggregate demand and aggregate purchases.
6. The income velocity of circulation of money, which is nominal GNP divided by the money stock, measures the number of times each dollar of the money stock is received as income during a year.
7. The equation of exchange is an identity that shows the relationship between nominal GNP, the money stock, and the income velocity of circulation of money. The classical quantity theory of money argues that, over the long run, changes in the money stock will affect the price level rather than real GNP, provided the income velocity of circulation of money is stable. According to the classical theory, in the long run the price level in an economy is proportional to the supply of money. In this view, a doubling of the money supply will eventually double the price level.
8. The income velocity of circulation of money has varied considerably in the United States since 1929. Between 1960 and 1980 the income velocity of circulation of money increased as financial innovations reduced the demand for money. Behavior of income velocity has been very unstable in the 1980s.
9. Monetarism is a theory of long-term macroeconomic equilibrium, based on the equation of exchange, that assumes shifts in the income velocity of circulation of money are reasonably predictable. Monetarists argue that although monetary policy does influence aggregate demand, its use in the past has been subject to

errors that prevented its objectives from being achieved. To avoid destabilizing the economy through errors in monetary policy, monetarists advocate steady and predictable monetary growth each year.

10. Shifts in money demand affect interest rates. Money demand increases during periods of peak economy activity and declines as nominal GNP declines. Financial innovations that decrease the transaction cost of converting near money to money will also decrease the demand for money.

11. Shifts in money demand make it difficult for the Fed to control both interest rates and money supply simultaneously. This is because an increase in money supply induced by the Fed increases aggregate demand. The increase in aggregate demand will increase either real GNP or the price level, which in turn increases the demand for money. As the demand for money goes up, there is upward pressure on interest rates and an increase in the equilibrium quantity of money held. To control money supply requires accurate forecasts of shifts in money demand induced by shifts in aggregate demand.

12. When the Fed tries to keep interest rates stable, it must allow money supply to adjust to accommodate shifts in money demand. When the Fed keeps money supply fixed, shifts in aggregate demand that occur over the business cycle will result in fluctuations in interest rates.

Key Terms and Concepts

Stabilization policies
Monetary policy
Expansionary monetary policy
Contractionary monetary policy

Income velocity of circulation of money
Equation of exchange
Classical quantity theory of money
Monetarism

Problems and Applications

1. The current level of interest rates in the economy is about 8%. The Fed believes aggregate demand will decline during the year. How can the Fed counteract the expected decline in aggregate demand in a way that will prevent a recession?

2. Inflation is currently 4% per year. The Fed believes an increase in aggregate demand will put upward pressure on the price level during the year. What actions should the Fed engage in to counteract the inflationary pressures in the economy?

3. Show how an expansionary monetary policy influences the supply of money and the market rate of interest. How are the effects of an expansionary monetary policy transmitted to the economy at large in a way that affects real GNP and the price level? Use aggregate supply and demand analysis to predict the impact of an expansionary monetary policy.

4. Explain how a contractionary monetary policy will affect real interest rates and the quantity of investment goods demanded per year. Show how the contractionary monetary policy will affect macroeconomic equilibrium assuming that the aggregate supply curve is stable.

5. Suppose banks hold excess reserves made available through Federal Reserve open market purchases. Under such circumstances how effective will monetary policy be in stimulating the economy?

6. Suppose the demand curve for investment goods is a vertical line plotting investment purchases against the real rate of interest. Under such circumstances

how effective will monetary policy be in eliminating a recessionary GNP gap?

7. The economy is currently at full employment. During the year the money supply is increased by 25%. Assuming the income velocity of circulation of money is constant during the year, what will be the impact on the price level?

8. Suppose the Fed pursues a monetary policy that allows the money supply to grow at the same rate as the long-term growth rate of real GNP. During a 5-year period for which this policy is pursued, the income velocity of circulation of money doubles from 2 to 4. What will happen to the price level over the 5-year period?

9. Explain why the demand for money will increase as the economy begins to pull out of a recession. Why will interest rates tend to rise as the economy moves into this expansionary phase of the business cycle? How can the Fed prevent the rise in interest rates from dampening the recovery from the recession? Why does keeping interest rates from rising mean the money supply must grow?

10. Why are the long-term effects of monetary policy likely to differ from the short-term effects? Why can a policy designed to keep interest rates from fluctuating cause inflation in the long run?

Suggested Readings

Milton Friedman and Anna J. Schwartz, *A Monetary History of the United States 1868-1960,* Princeton, N.J.: Princeton University Press, 1963. This is a classic analysis of the role of money and monetary policy in influencing macroeconomic equilibrium in the United States.

Paul Meek, *U.S. Monetary Policy and Financial Markets,* Federal Reserve Bank of New York, 1982. This is a discussion of how monetary policy is carried out and how its effects are transmitted to the economy.

Henry C. Wallich, "Recent Techniques of Monetary Policy," Federal Reserve Bank of Kansas City, *Economic Review,* May 1984, pp. 21-30. This is a review of methods actually used in setting monetary policy in the United States.

A Forward Look

Fiscal policy is an alternative to monetary policy as a means of stabilizing the economy. In the following chapter we examine the impact of government purchases and net taxes on the operation of the economy and show how fiscal policy can be used to influence real GNP and the price level.

Stabilization of the Economy Through Fiscal Policy: Effects on Aggregate Demand and Aggregate Supply

You don't have to be an economist to understand that the federal government has a tremendous impact on the U.S. economy. If you have a job, you know that each pay period the federal government takes a considerable chunk of your paycheck in taxes. Through its tax policies the federal government can affect disposable income, which as you now know is a key influence on consumer purchases. The federal government is also a big spender. Its expenditures amount to more than $1 trillion annually, which is about one quarter of GNP. Retired workers rely on the federal government for their Social Security pensions, and defense contractors and their employees obtain much of their income from federal government purchases. Finally, federal tax and subsidy programs can also affect incentives to save, invest, and work.

Government spending and tax policies affect aggregate demand, and the impact of government policies on incentives can also affect aggregate supply over time. The federal government has legal responsibility under the Employment Act of 1946 and the Humphrey-Hawkins Act of 1978 to use its spending and taxing powers to help achieve full employment.

The President is required to submit an annual Economic Report to Congress describing the current status of the national economy. The *Council of Economic Advisers* assists the President in formulating the report and in recommending policies that maintain economic stability and pursue goals of full employment and low inflation. Congress has its own *Joint Economic Committee* that advises its members and studies economic problems.

In this chapter we'll examine the impact of the federal government budget on macroeconomic equilibrium. In the following chapter we'll zero in on the federal government budget deficit to analyze in depth its impact on you and on the economy. Before getting into the impact of the deficit on the economy, we must first understand how the federal government's annual budget affects the performance of the economy. The use of government spending and taxing for the specific purpose of stabilizing the economy is called **fiscal policy.** The short-term goals of fiscal policy are to prevent excessive unemployment and to control inflation. Over longer periods fiscal policy seeks to ensure adequate economic growth to permit improvements in the national standard of living. You've already seen how monetary policy seeks to influence aggregate demand to help control the cyclical ups and downs of the economy. Now you'll learn how fiscal policy can be used as a means of stabilizing the economy.

Fiscal policy:
The use of government spending and taxing for the specific purpose of stabilizing the economy.

Concept Preview

After reading this chapter, you should be able to:

1 Discuss the federal government budget and its impact on aggregate demand in the economy.
2 Explain how expansionary fiscal policies affect the economy and show how such policies can be used to eliminate recessionary GNP gaps.
3 Explain how contractionary fiscal policies affect the economy and show how such policies can help prevent inflation.
4 Show how built-in stabilizers automatically moderate shifts in aggregate demand.
5 Discuss means of gauging the impact of fiscal policy on the economy.
6 Explain how supply-side fiscal policies can affect the economy in the long run and assess the effectiveness of recent supply-side policies.

The Federal Budget and Its Impact on the Economy

When there's a presidential election, one of the biggest issues always is the state of the economy. In the United States we expect the President to pursue policies that reduce cyclical unemployment, keep inflation under control, and ensure adequate economic growth. The President is inevitably blamed for poor performance of the economy and is quick to claim the credit when the economy performs well. Inflation, unemployment, and the rate of economic growth are political issues. Pressure groups and ordinary citizens expect the federal government to take measures to achieve full employment and stable prices.

The spending and taxing activities of the federal government are influenced by many political considerations, not just those relating to stabilization. Our first step in understanding fiscal policy in the United States is to review the process through which federal government spending and taxes are approved annually.

The Federal Budget

The **government budget** represents a plan for spending funds and raising revenues through taxation, fees, and other means, and for borrowing funds if necessary. During the budgetary process politicians, citizens, and government officials propose, debate, and make decisions that affect government spending, taxing, and borrowing.

The federal government budgetary process is divided into four distinct stages established under the Congressional Budget and Impoundment Control Act of 1974:

Government budget:
A plan for spending funds and raising revenues through taxation, fees, and other means, and borrowing funds if necessary.

Stage 1: Submission. In early February the President submits to Congress the proposed budget, which contains the executive branch's recommendations for expenditures, taxes, and other financial considerations.

Stage 2: First Concurrent Resolution on the Budget. The President's proposals are debated in congressional budget committees. After the debate senators and representatives pass the First Concurrent Resolution on the Budget. This resolution, which is usually passed by March 15, represents a guide for a host of congressional committees as they consider legislation that determines government spending and financing. The resolution represents a broad consen..us on such issues as the target level of federal government spending and revenues and the budget deficit or surplus. The resolution also makes recommendations about government spending in 20 broad areas that represent distinct government functions, such as national defense.

Stage 3: Authorizations and Appropriations. Between May 15 and September 10, members of Congress debate and ultimately pass specific bills that authorize federal government agencies to spend funds on various programs and projects.

Stage 4: Second Concurrent Resolution on the Budget. This resolution, usually passed by September 15, sets a ceiling on federal expenditures. It also places a floor on federal revenues. Sometimes the limits set by the second concurrent resolution are inconsistent with the actual tax and spending bills enacted. When this is the case, additional reconciliation is necessary.

The budget sets the spending and revenue plan for the federal government's *fiscal year,* which runs from October 1 to September 30. When government revenues raised from taxation and means other than borrowing exactly cover government expenditures during the year, the budget is said to be *balanced.*

Government spending often exceeds actual government revenues raised. A *budget deficit* is the annual excess of government spending over revenues raised by taxes, fees, and charges. When the federal government budget is in deficit, the government must borrow funds by issuing such government securities as Treasury bills, notes, and bonds that are sold in credit markets. Also recall that a *budget surplus* prevails when government revenues exceed expenditures during the year. When the federal government runs a budget surplus, it can use the excess revenue to pay off some of its debt. The federal government budget in the United States has been in deficit consistently every year since 1970. As you undoubtedly know from watching the nightly news, the deficit is a hotly debated political and economic issue. As you'll see in the next chapter, chronic budget deficits have been blamed for high real interest rates and the negative balance of trade in recent years. In the following chapter we'll sort out the arguments for and against budget deficits. Our goal in this chapter is to examine the general effects of government spending and taxes on macroeconomic equilibrium so as to understand how the government budget can be used to stabilize the economy.

One recent innovation in the budgetary process stems from the *Gramm-Rudman-Hollings Act.* Starting in the 1987 fiscal year, this legislation has required that Congress and the President either cut expenditures or raise revenue each year to meet a specified limit on the deficit. If the President and Congress cannot agree on measures to meet the deficit ceiling, the new law requires mandatory reductions in both military and nonmilitary spending. However, Social Security, interest on the federal debt, and certain programs that assist the poor are exempt from these automatic cuts.

How the Federal Government Budget Affects Aggregate Demand: A Quick Review

As you know, government purchases represent a major component of aggregate demand. Nearly 1 out of every 10 dollars spent on the purchase of goods and services in the United States is spent by the federal government. The federal government also makes direct transfer payments to members of households and to state and local governments. These payments, which include welfare benefits, Social Security pensions, veterans' benefits, interest payments to holders of government securities, and grants to state and local governments, constitute sources of income to recipients. Government purchases and transfer payments, other things being equal, add to aggregate demand by increasing disposable income in the United States.

To finance its purchases of goods and services and the payments it makes to individuals and organizations each year, the federal government collects funds through taxation, which accounts for the bulk of federal government revenues. Taxes paid reduce the ability of households and business firms to purchase goods and services for their own private use and therefore tend to reduce aggregate demand.

The overall effect of the federal budget on aggregate demand depends on the expansionary effect of government purchases or other payments and the contractionary effect of taxes. When there is a budget deficit, the federal government adds more to aggregate demand than it takes away. This is because it will spend more on purchases and transfer payments than it raises from taxes. A budget deficit therefore indicates that the government is putting upward pressure on aggregate demand. The government can use this upward pressure to offset cyclical declines in investment or net export demand, thus employing fiscal policy to prevent the economy from falling into a recession.

The government can act to *decrease* aggregate demand by running a budget *surplus*. In this case the government collects more in taxes than it spends. Just as you save when you spend less than your income, so can the government save in this way by running a budget surplus. When it spends less than it collects in revenues, the federal government adds less to aggregate demand than it takes away. A budget surplus is therefore a contractionary influence on the economy that can be used to offset surges in consumption and investment demand that might cause inflation.

Government borrowing to finance a budget deficit can affect equilibrium in credit markets in ways that indirectly influence aggregate demand. This is because increased demand for credit by the government can put upward pressure on interest rates. The higher real interest rates can decrease investment purchases. Similarly, when the government runs a budget surplus, its decreased demand for credit can put downward pressure on interest rates. In the following chapter we'll examine the impact of the federal budget deficit on financial markets.

Concept Check

1 What is fiscal policy, and how does it influence aggregate demand in the economy?

2 Describe the process through which the federal budget is approved.

3 When does a budget deficit prevail?

Using Fiscal Policy to Influence Aggregate Demand

An **expansionary fiscal policy** is a policy under which the government acts to *increase* aggregate demand by adjusting its budget during the year. It can do this in any of the following ways:

1. By increasing its purchases of goods and services
2. By increasing transfer payments to individuals and organizations
3. By decreasing taxes

Of course, the government could choose to stimulate aggregate demand by both reducing taxes *and* increasing spending for either purchases or payments to individuals and organizations.

Expansionary fiscal policy can be used to increase equilibrium real GNP and reduce the cyclical unemployment that prevails when the economy is in a recession. This was the remedy proposed by Keynes for an economy in deep recession. In such an economy, banks are likely to be very cautious in making loans. Keynes also believed that in a deep recession investors would be quite unresponsive to reductions in interest rates that might result from an expansionary monetary policy. This is because in a recession the outlook for increased sales is gloomy. Keynes's solution was for the government to increase its spending when others would not. The government would allow its budget balance to shift to a deficit to eliminate a recessionary GNP gap. The resulting stimulus to aggregate demand could then increase aggregate purchases, and as aggregate production increased, unemployment would be reduced. Once the economy was on course again the government could reduce spending and let the budget return to balance.

To restrain aggregate demand, the government can engage in a **contractionary fiscal policy** that will either decrease government spending or increase taxes, or both. A contractionary fiscal policy can be used to put downward pressure on the price level, thereby combating inflation in periods when the economy is overheating. (See the Economic Thinkers box in this chapter for a profile of Paul Samuelson, one of the most prominent Keynesian economists today.)

Expansionary fiscal policy:
A policy under which the government acts to increase aggregate demand by increasing spending or decreasing taxes, or both.

Contractionary fiscal policy:
A policy under which the government acts to restrain aggregate demand by decreasing spending or increasing taxes, or both.

How an Increase in Government Purchases Can Help Pull an Economy Out of a Recession

Let's begin our analysis of fiscal policy by examining how an increase in government purchases can act to increase aggregate demand and eliminate a substantial reces-

Economic Thinkers

PAUL SAMUELSON

The first American to win the Nobel Prize in economics is also one of the few economists today to be widely respected by both professional economists and the general public. Paul Samuelson, an unofficial adviser to Presidents on the economy and a professor for more than 30 years at the Massachusetts Institute of Technology, was born in 1915 in Gary, Indiana, and received his Ph.D. in economics from Harvard in 1941.

His doctoral dissertation, *Foundations of Economic Analysis,* developed precise mathematical meanings for economic concepts. By introducing these techniques, he improved the level of scientific analysis of the profession as a whole, thereby earning himself a Nobel Prize in 1970. His dissertation is still considered a masterpiece today. Samuelson has explained basic economic principles to millions of students through an introductory textbook and has been published widely on topics ranging from international trade to welfare economics and monetary policy. He is one of the most prominent Keynesian economists writing today and supports government policies that call for fiscal and monetary measures to counter inflationary and re-cessionary cycles in the economy.

His comments frequently appear in *Newsweek* and *The New York Times.* His textbook is considered to be so much the mainstay of economic thought that radical thinkers put together *The Anti-Samuelson,* a chapter-by-chapter critique of his book and thereby a critique of modern U.S. economic thought. He has won every major award the economics profession has to offer, including the first John Bates Clark Medal for outstanding achievement by an economist under the age of 40.

Even though Samuelson has raised the technical precision of economic analysis, he is critical of those who believe economists can give definitive answers to questions that are often extremely complex. Generalizations can seldom be made, concludes this adviser to Presidents and educator of more than a generation of economists.

sionary GNP gap. In Box 1 the economy is currently in equilibrium at a level of real GNP equal to $4,000 billion. Potential real GNP is $5,000 billion. The economy is therefore experiencing a $1,000 billion recessionary GNP gap. It's also assumed that the economy is currently stagnating in a severe recession so that it's operating along the flat portion of its aggregate supply curve. This means the government can increase aggregate demand through the use of fiscal policy without heating up inflation during the year.

Remember from our analysis of the multiplier that less than $1 of autonomous spending, such as government purchases, is required to increase real GNP by $1. Suppose the marginal respending rate in the economy is 0.5. The marginal respending rate is less than 1 because a portion of increased annual income generated from an initial round of autonomous purchases is used to buy imported goods and to pay taxes, and some is saved. When the marginal respending rate is 0.5, the multiplier for any initial injection of new spending into the economy is:

$$\text{Multiplier} = 1/(1 - \text{Marginal respending rate})$$
$$= 1/(1 - 0.5) = 1/0.5$$
$$= 2$$

Each dollar of government purchases that is initiated at the beginning of the year will therefore ultimately increase real GNP and real income in the na-

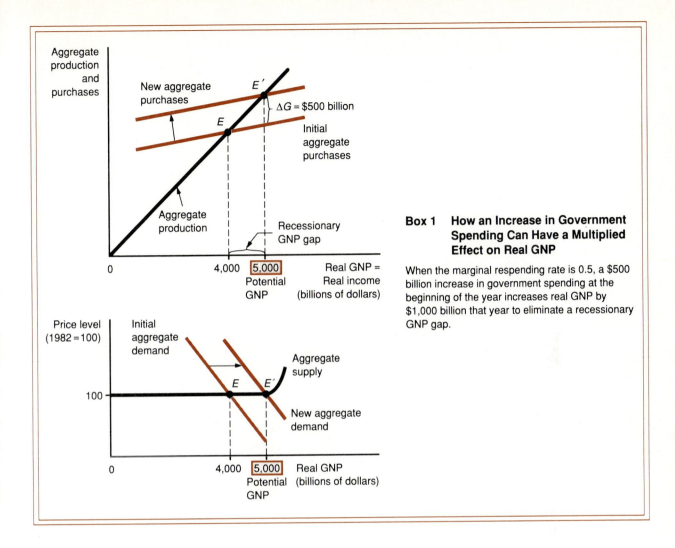

Box 1   How an Increase in Government Spending Can Have a Multiplied Effect on Real GNP

When the marginal respending rate is 0.5, a $500 billion increase in government spending at the beginning of the year increases real GNP by $1,000 billion that year to eliminate a recessionary GNP gap.

tion by $2 as it is spent and respent.

Assuming nothing else changes, an increase in government purchases that generates $500 billion in additional business receipts at the beginning of the year can eliminate the recessionary gap. This is because the total increase in spending resulting from the increase in government purchases, G, will be:

$$\text{Increase in real GNP} = (\text{Increase in } G) (\text{Multiplier})$$
$$= \$500 \text{ billion} (2)$$
$$= \$1,000 \text{ billion}$$

The graphs in Box 1 show how the expansionary fiscal policy will affect the macro-economic equilibrium for an economy in a recession. The economy is initially in equilibrium at point E, as shown in the upper graph where aggregate purchases just equal aggregate production at the current price level. Other things being equal, an injection of $500 billion of new government purchases shifts the aggregate purchases line upward and results in a new equilibrium at point E'. At that point real GNP increases to $5,000 billion as the recessionary GNP gap is closed.

The lower graph in Box 1 shows how the increase in government purchases shifts

---

Using Fiscal Policy to Influence Aggregate Demand   **805** the aggregate demand curve outward. The graph also shows that the expansionary policy has no impact on the price level when the economy is operating in the flat portion of its aggregate supply curve, as is likely to be the case in an economy experiencing a deep recession. The increases in aggregate demand that result from the expansionary fiscal policy are therefore unlikely to contribute to an inflationary process for an economy experiencing a fairly deep recession.

Using Tax Cuts or Government Transfers to Stimulate a Sluggish Economy

A sluggish economy can also be stimulated through a tax cut or an increase in government transfer payments. However, the impact of these measures on aggregate demand is not quite as direct as the impact of an increase in government purchases. Remember that *net taxes* represent the difference between government tax revenues and government transfers. Net taxes are reduced when government either lowers taxes or increases transfers. In effect, transfers can be viewed as negative taxes. To engage in an expansionary fiscal policy, the government reduces net taxes by either decreasing taxes or increasing transfers. In doing so the government acts to increase disposable income, which will result in increased consumer purchases.

Suppose instead of a $500 billion increase in government purchases the government reduces net taxes by that amount. You can think of the reduction in net taxes as either an increase in government transfers (such as Social Security or welfare payments) or a lump-sum refund of taxes distributed to all citizens. It's easy to show that the expansionary effect of the tax reduction is less than that of an equivalent dollar amount increase in government purchases. When the government makes purchases of $500 billion, it directly increases business receipts by that amount at the initial stage of the spending increase. However, when the government puts $500 billion directly in the pockets of individuals through a reduction in net taxes, purchases of U.S. final products will not go up by that full amount at the initial stage. This is because some of the increased disposable income that results from the cut in net taxes will be spent on imported goods and some will be saved.

For example, suppose the marginal propensity to save is 0.2 and the marginal propensity to import is 0.1. This means that 30% of the dollar value of the $500 billion tax cut, which is $150 billion, will not be directly spent on U.S. final products. The initial increase in purchases of U.S. final products that results from the tax cut will therefore be only $350 billion. The multiplier process thus begins with a $350 billion injection of new spending at the first round rather than $500 billion, as was the case when government purchases increased by $500 billion. The $350 billion initial increase in purchases will then be spent and respent as the multiplier process ensues. Some of the extra income generated in the respending process will be used to make purchases in the United States, but some will be saved, some used to purchase imported items, and some used to pay taxes on the newly generated income. Assuming a multiplier of 2 for the economy, this means the $500 billion tax cut will result in a $700 billion increase in real GNP ($350 billion × 2 = $700 billion).[1]

---

[1] We have to mention one more complication here. Tax cuts sometimes are a refund of taxes with no change in marginal tax rates, as is the case assumed in this example of a lump-sum tax refund. In other cases the marginal tax rate might be lowered when taxes are cut, as was the case under the Tax Reform Act of 1986. When the marginal tax rate is lowered, the multiplier itself is increased. Review the appendix to the chapter entitled "Aggregate Demand and Keynesian Analysis of Macroeconomic Equilibrium" to see how the multiplier is related to the marginal tax rate.

We can conclude that an increase in government purchases is more expansionary for the economy than a decrease in net taxes of an equal amount. Other things being equal, increasing transfer payments or reducing taxes is less stimulating to the economy than increasing government purchases.

The expansionary effect of a tax cut can also be less than that of an increase in government purchases because households might treat the extra income resulting from a reduction in net taxes differently from extra income earned. If the tax cut is viewed as only temporary, it's likely that a higher proportion of each dollar of the tax cut will be saved compared to a similar dollar of earnings. However, tax cuts have been used with some success in the past to help pull the economy out of recessions.

Tax cuts were proposed by the Kennedy Administration in the early 1960s to help pull the economy out of a serious recession. In 1964 Congress enacted the Kennedy tax cut proposal and reduced personal income taxes on average by 18%. These tax cuts were widely credited with spurring an increase in consumer purchases that lifted the economy out of the recession.

Similarly, President Ford persuaded Congress to reduce income taxes in 1975 to help increase aggregate demand during a recession. In this case much of the tax cut was apparently used to increase saving, and aggregate demand did not increase. In 1981 a tax cut designed to increase aggregate supply rather than aggregate demand was proposed by President Reagan and enacted by Congress. The actual effect of the Reagan tax cuts in the short run, however, was to increase the federal budget deficit. The resulting increase in aggregate demand helped pull the economy out of the recession of 1982.

Equal Increases of Government Purchases and Net Taxes Are Expansionary

The analysis of the previous two sections can be used to reach a surprising conclusion: An equal increase in government purchases and in net taxes has an expansionary effect on the economy. A $500 billion injection of government purchases would result in a $1,000 billion increase in real GNP, other things being equal, when the multiplier is 2 for an initial injection of new spending for the economy.

A $500 billion *increase* in net taxes to cover the increased government purchases would result in a multiplied *decrease* in private expenditures because it acts to decrease disposable income. But the initial reduction in private spending on U.S. goods and services resulting from a $500 billion increase in taxes would be less than $500 billion. This is because some of the $500 billion that is now collected in taxes would have been saved or used to purchase imported goods. Using the same marginal propensities to save and import as in the previous example, a $500 billion increase in net taxes will decrease purchases of U.S. goods by only $350 billion. The remaining $150 billion of the tax increase would have been spent on imports or saved anyway and would not have added to aggregate demand. The initial tax-induced reduction in spending on U.S.-produced goods and services of $350 billion will then result in a $700 billion reduction in real GNP, assuming a multiplier of 2. Notice that after the multiplier processes are played out, the reduction in real GNP attributable to the increase in net taxes is *less than* the increase in real GNP attributable to the increase in government purchases. As a result of the increase in government purchases that is fully covered by an increase in net taxes, there is upward pressure on aggregate demand. The impact on equilibrium real GNP is the multiplier effect of the purchases ($1,000 billion) less the multiplier effect of the taxes (− $700 billion), which results in a $300 billion increase.

Because the expansionary effect of each dollar of government purchases exceeds the contractionary effect of each dollar of taxes used to finance the purchases, the net effect on the economy of an equal increase in government purchases and net taxes is expansionary. An increase in government spending that is exactly covered by an increase in taxes will increase real GNP. It follows that increased spending adds to aggregate demand even when that spending doesn't contribute to increasing the government deficit! Beware, then, of politicians who say that increased spending won't add to inflationary pressures in an economy when that spending is fully financed by taxes. Fiscal policies that don't increase the deficit are nonetheless expansionary.

The Effects of Fiscal Policy on the Price Level

If the economy is not in a deep recession, its aggregate supply curve is likely to be upward sloping. This means that any expansionary influence on aggregate demand resulting from fiscal policy will increase both the price level and real GNP as the economy moves toward its potential real GNP. The increase in the price level will dampen private spending over the year, and the multiplier effect on the economy will be correspondingly less. Expansionary fiscal policy can also start an inflationary process when the economy is operating in the upward-sloping portion of its aggregate supply curve.

The graph in Box 2 shows how the price level effect chokes off some private purchases. The economy is initially in equilibrium at point *E*, at which real GNP is $4,500 billion and the price level is 100. The full-employment level of real GNP is $5,000 billion, implying that there is a $500 billion recessionary GNP gap. Fiscal policy is used to shift the aggregate demand curve outward. If the multiplier is 2, a $250 billion increase in government purchases would be sufficient to increase real

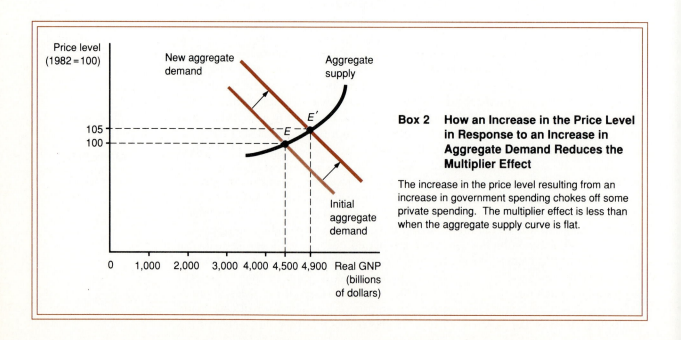

Box 2   How an Increase in the Price Level in Response to an Increase in Aggregate Demand Reduces the Multiplier Effect

The increase in the price level resulting from an increase in government spending chokes off some private spending. The multiplier effect is less than when the aggregate supply curve is flat.

GNP by $500 billion. If there were no increase in the price level, the resulting outward shift of the aggregate demand curve would be sufficient to eliminate the recessionary GNP gap. However, because the price level rises from 100 to 105 as a result of the increase in aggregate demand, the economy achieves a new equilibrium at point E'. At the new equilibrium, the price level is 105 and real GNP is only $4,900 billion. The higher prices choke off $100 billion in private purchases. In this case *more* than $250 billion in government purchases is required to increase real GNP by $500 billion.

The multiplier will be less than that implied by the formulas in previous chapters when the price level is responsive to changes in aggregate demand. In addition, there is more risk that fiscal policy can overheat the economy when it is already close to its potential real GNP. Fiscal policy must therefore be used with care to avoid starting an inflationary spiral when only a modest gap exists between potential and actual GNP.

Government spending and borrowing required for an expansionary fiscal policy can also affect the level of interest rates in the economy. In the next chapter we'll discuss this possibility and its consequences for private spending.

Contractionary Fiscal Policy

Contractionary fiscal policy seeks to restrain aggregate demand by either decreasing government purchases or increasing net taxes. By decreasing aggregate demand, a contractionary fiscal policy can help reduce inflation. Such a policy results in a re-duction of the federal budget deficit or a movement toward a budget surplus.

The graph in Box 3 shows how a contractionary fiscal policy can help eliminate an inflationary gap or prevent an economy from overheating in the first place. The economy is initially in equilibrium at point E, at which the price level is 100 and real GNP is at its potential level of $5,000 billion. An increase in aggregate demand could cause the economy to overheat. For example, if the aggregate demand curve

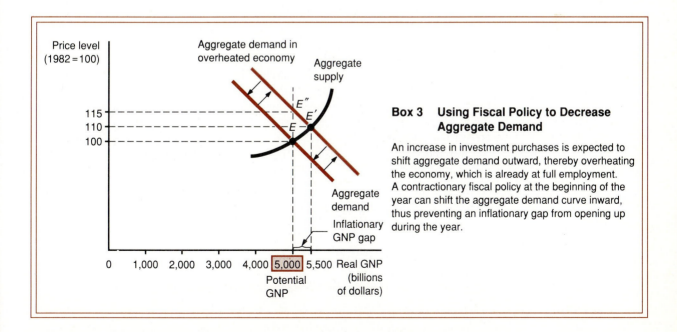

Box 3   Using Fiscal Policy to Decrease Aggregate Demand

An increase in investment purchases is expected to shift aggregate demand outward, thereby overheating the economy, which is already at full employment. A contractionary fiscal policy at the beginning of the year can shift the aggregate demand curve inward, thus preventing an inflationary gap from opening up during the year.

shifted outward due to a stock market boom that boosts household wealth, the economy could reach equilibrium at point E', at which real GNP would increase to $5,500 billion and the price level would go up to 110. If the economy is beginning to overheat in this way, a contractionary fiscal policy could serve to offset the increase in aggregate demand. For example, if the Council of Economic Advisers projects that investment will increase during the year, it might expect a $500 billion inflationary GNP gap like the one illlustrated in Box 3. A reduction in government purchases or an increase in net taxes could offset the expected increase in aggregate demand. Such a contractionary fiscal policy could keep the economy at point E and prevent it from moving to point E'. If nothing is done to prevent the economy from moving to E', the result could be an inflationary wage-price spiral that would eventually move the economy to point E'', at which GNP falls to $5,000 billion again and the price level rises to 115. In other words, fiscal policy can prevent a wage-price spiral from beginning.

Problems in Effectively Implementing Fiscal Policy

Contractionary fiscal policy often runs into political problems. During the budgetary process, elected representatives oppose cuts in government spending that are likely to reduce benefits to their constituents. Every senator and congressman wants budget cuts to reduce income in someone else's district! For this reason it's difficult to gain approval for cuts in government purchases and increases in net taxes. On the other hand, expansionary fiscal policies are quite popular. Increases in government purchases and reductions in net taxes provide direct benefits to politicians and their constituents.

The fact that the government budget has been almost consistently in deficit during both the ups and downs of the business cycle since 1970 appears to support the idea that there is an expansionary bias for fiscal policy. There is also a temptation for politicians in power to engage in expansionary fiscal policies just prior to major elections. The reasoning is that the party in power is more likely to be reelected during economic upturns than during downturns! In any event, it's clear that political considerations influence the federal budget. In many cases fiscal policy takes a backseat to political maneuvering.

Fiscal policy is based on forecasts of future shifts in aggregate demand. Unfortunately, such forecasts are often inaccurate. The thin line corresponding to potential real GNP is also difficult to see in practice. A tax cut or increase in government purchases designed to pull the economy out of a recession could easily overshoot the mark and actually overheat the economy! Stabilization policy is far from being an exact science.

Over the years, fiscal policy has had both its successes and its failures. The tax cut of 1964 increased aggregate demand at just the right time and encouraged economic growth. However, during the period 1965 to 1967 when government purchases were increasing for the Vietnam conflict, no tax increase was enacted. Despite a tax increase in 1968, the expansionary fiscal policy pursued by the Johnson Administration at that time contributed to a period of inflation as the economy overheated in the late 1960s and early 1970s.

Lags in Fiscal Policy Implementation and Effects on Real GNP

Wouldn't it be nice if fiscal policy could be used as a precision tool to keep the economy always at full employment with inflation under control? Unfortunately, any stabilization policy, monetary or fiscal, is difficult to implement flawlessly. There are often problems in timing. For example, as just pointed out, it's hard to determine exactly when an economy is slipping into a recession or beginning to overheat. As a result, there's often a *recognition lag* between the time the economy begins to move away from full employment and the realization by policymakers that such a movement is actually occurring. Remember from our analysis of leading indicators that economic forecasts are anything but infallible! Economists did a poor job of forecasting the major recessions in the 1970s and 1980s.

There's also an *administrative lag* in implementing a fiscal policy change. Sometimes it takes a year or longer for a major tax cut to be enacted. The tax cut of 1964 was actually 3 years in the making! Sometimes these lags are so long that the economy's own self-correction mechanism can begin to work before fiscal policy gets a chance to exert an impact.

Finally, there's an *operational lag* between the time a change is made in government purchases or net taxes and the time it takes for equilibrium real GNP to change. The multiplier process is not instantaneous. It takes awhile for increases or decreases in disposable income resulting from fiscal policy to have an effect on private spending.

Just as monetary policy has its critics (see the preceding chapter), so does fiscal policy. Many critics argue that the expansionary bias in fiscal policy and the lags in its implementation and operation are serious enough that it does the economy more harm than good.

Concept Check

1   Explain why a decrease in net taxes is less expansionary for the economy than an equal increase in government purchases.

2   Suppose the multiplier is 3. What will happen to equilibrium real GNP as the result of a $200 billion tax cut, assuming the marginal propensity to save is 0.2 and the marginal propensity to import is 0.1?

3   Why is the multiplier effect of fiscal policy reduced when the aggregate supply curve is upward sloping instead of a flat line?

Automatic Stabilizers and Cyclical Influences on the Budget Deficit

The ups and downs of the economy have an automatic effect on certain government expenditures and revenues. For example, when real GNP falls below its potential value, unemployment will increase. This increases government expenditures for unemployment insurance. Also, as real GNP declines, federal tax collections decline as well. Most taxes used by the federal government are collected from labor earnings and earnings from the use of capital or loanable funds. Naturally, as national income falls, so does tax revenue. Our earlier discussion concentrated on *discretionary* fiscal policy, which represents deliberate changes in government purchases and net taxes for the purpose of stabilizing the economy. We now turn our attention to the effects of *nondiscretionary* fiscal policy, which consists of changes in government spending and revenues that result automatically as the economy fluctuates.

The magnitude of the budget deficit or surplus is influenced by the inevitable fluctuations of the economy. Budget deficits or surpluses are not directly under the

Fiscal Policy in the 1980s and the Impact of the Tax Reform Act of 1986 on Macroeconomic Equilibrium

The road to economic stabilization, like the road to another well-known location, is paved with good intentions. As we'll see in this chapter, the government's fiscal policies aren't without flaw and in fact sometimes may have unintended effects on the U.S. economy. Let's take a closer look at the objectives and results of recent fiscal policies pursued by the federal government to see how close they've come to achieving their goals.

U.S. fiscal policy in the early 1980s was markedly expansionary. The cyclically adjusted high-employment budget deficit more than doubled from 1.9% of GNP in 1981 to nearly 5% of GNP in 1984. The growth of the deficit was mainly the result of political choices and the inauguration of tax cuts in the early years of the Reagan Administration. The Economic Recovery Tax Act of 1981 involved major reductions in net taxes and the marginal tax rate for many taxpayers. These tax reductions stimulated aggregate demand. At the same time government purchases increased as the result of a sharp increase in military spending. Although transfer programs were cut somewhat during this period, the overall effect of the government's fiscal policy was to shift the aggregate demand curve outward as the budget deficit ballooned to over $200 billion per year in the mid-1980s.

While the expansionary fiscal policy stimulated the economy in the early 1980s, an extremely tight monetary policy kept real interest rates at record high levels that increased from 3% in the early 1980s and peaked at nearly 10% in 1984. The monetary policy of the early 1980s, although it did eventually reduce the inflation rate considerably, resulted in a major recession that began in 1981 and lasted through 1982. Despite the expansionary fiscal policy, the high real interest rates caused by the contractionary monetary policy spurred the sharp decline in planned investment (especially construction of new structures) in 1982 that triggered the recession. As the tax reductions of the 1981 tax act started working at the end of 1982, investment recovered as businesses took advantage of new ac-

celerated depreciation rules that in effect subsidized investment. The lower tax rates for individuals also stimulated consumption, which helped the country recover from its most serious recession since the 1930s.

In 1986 real interest rates fell and a major new tax law was enacted. The Tax Reform Act of 1986 was a mixed bag of fiscal changes whose impact on aggregate demand was generally expected to be only slight. The law lowered marginal tax rates and eliminated many tax deductions for businesses and individuals. The lower marginal tax rates were expected to stimulate aggregate demand. However, the elimination of many personal deductions from income would reduce aggregate demand. In particular, during the transition year of 1987, taxes paid as a percentage of income were expected to increase for many taxpayers despite the mild reduction in marginal tax rates that year. In 1988, when the new lower marginal tax rates were fully in place, the effect would be more stimulative. The new tax law also eliminated provisions that subsidized saving of many taxpayers, and this too could encourage more consumption. However, because interest on consumer loans will no longer be deductible when the full effects of the new law are in place, the cost of borrowing money to finance consumer purchases will increase. This will act to decrease consumption.

The new tax law sharply reduced many of the subsidies to investment. The investment tax credit was eliminated, and depreciation rules were changed in a way that would decrease the subsidy to fixed investment. The new law is therefore likely to stimulate aggregate demand through a possible increase in consumption but to decrease aggregate demand through a decrease in investment as investors respond to the reduction in subsidies.

Predicting the effect of a new tax law is extremely difficult, and the responsiveness of both consumers and investors to the provisions of the Tax Reform Act remains to be seen.

control of policymakers, at least in the short run. Cyclical fluctuations in real GNP and the price level must therefore be accounted for if the government budget deficit is to be predicted accurately.

Automatic Stabilizers

Automatic stabilizers:
Features of the federal budget that automatically adjust net taxes to stabilize aggregate demand as the economy expands and contracts.

Automatic stabilizers are features of the federal budget that automatically adjust net taxes to stabilize aggregate demand as the economy expands and contracts. When the economy begins slipping into a contraction, these stabilizers act to increase transfer payments and reduce tax collections so as to automatically stimulate aggregate demand. When the economy begins to expand, the automatic stabilizers increase tax collections and reduce transfer payments so as to constrain growth in aggregate demand.

A key automatic stabilizer is the federal income tax. As the economy expands, income tax collections rise as income earned increases. Given government purchases, the increased tax collections prevent aggregate purchases from increasing in proportion to the increase in earnings. In a sense, the income tax acts as a damper on private spending as real GNP and real income increase. In that way it slows the growth of aggregate demand and controls upward pressure on the price level when the economy is expanding. This can help slow inflation if the funds are not spent by government but instead are used to reduce the government budget deficit.

Government tax receipts are also quite responsive to changes in business conditions. In part this is because the marginal federal income tax rates increase with income. The current tax structure has two marginal rates for most taxpayers: 15% and 28%. As national income increases, more people are pushed into the higher tax bracket. This causes taxes collected to increase more than in proportion to the increase in income.

Similarly, when a recession causes real GNP and national income to decline, taxes fall more than in proportion to the decline in real GNP. This is because more people are pushed into the lower tax bracket and their tax bills decline more than in proportion to their decline in income. Corporate profits taxes are particularly sensitive to shifts in the business cycle. During a recession, corporate profits typically plummet, as do receipts from the corporate income tax. The decline in tax collections during an economic contraction prevents aggregate demand from decreasing excessively.

Also included in the automatic stabilizers are programs that increase transfer payments to individuals when the economy contracts and decrease those payments when the economy expands. These changes in government payments don't require acts of Congress or changes in administration policies. This is because most transfers are part of *entitlement* programs that don't authorize a fixed dollar amount of expenditure but rather mandate government payments to individuals who meet certain eligibility standards. Because eligibility is based mainly on income and joblessness, government expenditures for these programs naturally increase during economic contractions when unemployment increases and income declines.

Government purchases of goods and services tend to be quite stable over the business cycle. The variation in government spending over the business cycle results from changes in transfer payments under entitlement programs. The major entitlement programs that serve as automatic stabilizers are:

1. *Unemployment insurance.* This is a program for which expenditures obviously increase during recessions when there are more unemployed workers and longer periods of unemployment. During expansions, as unemployment rates decline, unemployment insurance payments also decline.
2. *Cash assistance welfare programs.* When a recession hits, more people become eligible for programs of cash assistance like Aid to Families with Dependent Children and Supplemental Security Income. Although these programs are designed primarily for people outside the labor force, many eligible recipients manage to find at least part-time work when the economy is healthy. During contractions and recessions, more eligible recipients must rely on these welfare programs for their full support, so cash assistance to the poor increases. During expansions, more eligible recipients manage to find at least some work and payments decline.

3. *In-kind assistance.* These programs include food stamps, medical care, and housing assistance for people with annual incomes below certain threshold levels. As a contraction or recession hits, many workers lose their jobs or suffer reductions in earnings, thus becoming eligible for in-kind assistance. Government payments under these programs therefore increase during contractions, thus bolstering aggregate demand, while they decline during expansions, which puts a damper on aggregate demand.

4. *Social Security pension payments.* Social Security pension recipients below the age of 70 have typically had their pension payments reduced if they continued to work. The number of eligible recipients who have jobs declines during a contraction or recession, thus increasing government expenditures for pension payments. During an expansion more people eligible for Social Security pensions forgo part of their pensions to work and people are less likely to retire early, which reduces Social Security payments.

All of these transfer programs tend to maintain aggregate demand in periods when national income declines by automatically increasing payments as the number of eligible recipients increases. These payments increase the consumption component of real GNP that would otherwise decline as earnings fall. The programs increase net taxes by reducing transfers as the number of people entitled to benefits declines during an expansion.

Cyclical Effects on the Budget: Gauging the Impact of Fiscal Policy

The automatic stabilizers influence the size of the federal budget deficit. Obviously, when aggregate demand declines and the economy is in a downturn, tax receipts fall. However, because of the transfer programs discussed in the previous section, federal government expenditures tend to increase. Both the decrease in tax revenues and the increase in expenditures contribute to an increase in the budget deficit during recessions. Similarly, during boom periods, tax revenues increase and transfer payments decline, contributing to a decrease in the budget deficit or to a budget surplus.

High-employment deficit (or surplus):
The budget deficit (or surplus) that would prevail if the natural rate of unemployment were achieved.

To eliminate the cyclical effects of automatic stabilizers on the budget deficit, economists compute the cyclically adjusted **high-employment deficit (or surplus)**, which is the budget deficit (or surplus) that would prevail if the natural rate of unemployment were achieved. The high-employment deficit or surplus is calculated by estimating net taxes that the government would collect based on planned government purchases for the year and taxes and transfers based on potential real GNP.

The high-employment budget estimates the condition of the budget if the economy were achieving the natural rate of unemployment. Receipts and expenditures for the high-employment budget are typically based on an unemployment rate of 5% to 6%. The high-employment budget indicates the relationship between government spending and taxes for a given level of government purchases that would prevail if the economy achieved full employment. The high-employment budget is designed to show how much stimulus to aggregate demand the federal government is providing to the economy by setting net taxes equal to the amount that would be observed at full employment.

The graph in Box 4 shows how the federal budget deficit can vary with national income for the year. The line showing net taxes is upward sloping. As national income increases, so do net taxes. The slope of the curve increases as national income goes up because more people are pushed into tax brackets with higher marginal tax rates. Net taxes also rise with real GNP because government transfer payments are higher at lower levels of national income than they would be at higher levels. Remember that net taxes are taxes paid less transfers received. Government purchases are drawn as a horizontal line in the graph because they are authorized at the beginning of the year and are not subject to cyclical fluctuations, as are net taxes.

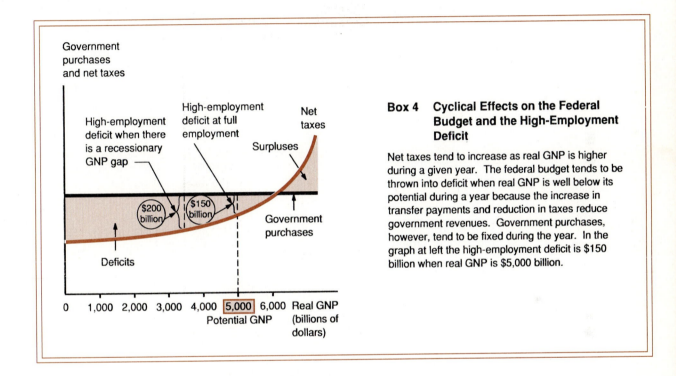

Box 4 Cyclical Effects on the Federal Budget and the High-Employment Deficit

Net taxes tend to increase as real GNP is higher during a given year. The federal budget tends to be thrown into deficit when real GNP is well below its potential during a year because the increase in transfer payments and reduction in taxes reduce government revenues. Government purchases, however, tend to be fixed during the year. In the graph at left the high-employment deficit is $150 billion when real GNP is $5,000 billion.

Whenever government expenditures exceed tax revenues for the year, a budget deficit prevails. When tax revenues exactly equal government expenditures, the budget is in balance. Finally, when revenues exceed expenditures, there will be a surplus. The graph in Box 4 shows that the lower the level of national income realized for the year, the higher the budget deficit. Conversely, the higher the level of national income, the lower the deficit. At some level of national income the budget would be in balance, and increases in national income beyond that would result in a surplus.

Suppose potential real GNP is $5,000 billion. At this high-employment level of national income, the deficit would be $150 billion. However, if national income during the year is less than $5,000 billion, the deficit would be greater because net tax collections would be less. The graph in Box 4 shows that if equilibrium national income were only $3,500 billion, the deficit would be $200 billion.

The actual high-employment deficit depends on government purchases and tax rates for the year. For example, if government purchases were less or tax rates were higher, the net taxes curve and the government purchases line might intersect at the point corresponding to potential real GNP. This implies that the budget would be in balance at the higher employment level. In gauging the impact of fiscal policy on the economy, it's important to use the cyclically adjusted high-employment budget. If policy makers want to expand the economy, they must choose a fiscal policy that increases the high-employment deficit. Such a policy will either shift the tax revenue line downward or shift the government purchases line upward. The actual budget deficit (or surplus) in a given year depends on both the high-employment deficit (or surplus) and the cyclical impact of the automatic stabilizers on the budget.

The high-employment budget has been in deficit almost continuously since 1960. This seems to indicate that expansionary fiscal policy has been more prevalent than contractionary policy. The high-employment budget deficit averaged close to 2% of GNP from 1960 to 1980 and was approaching 5% of GNP in the mid-1980s.

Projecting the actual budget deficit in any given year is riddled with pitfalls. For example, in 1982, which was a recession year, the Reagan Administration projected that outlays for fiscal year 1983 would be $757 billion while revenues would be $666 billion, resulting in a budget deficit of $91 billion. However, the President's economists did a poor job of forecasting the intensity of the recession. Unemployment turned out to be much higher than expected, and the growth rate of real GNP was −2.9% that year instead of the +3% projected by the President! This was complicated by the fact that in enacting the President's proposed budget, Congress cut expenditures less than the President wished. Congress also enacted a larger tax cut than the President requested. As a result, the actual federal budget deficit in 1983 turned out to be a whopping $195 billion, which was over $100 billion more than the amount projected by the President!

Concept Check

1   What are automatic stabilizers?

2   Explain why a budget approved by Congress will run a higher deficit during the year if a recession prevails than it would otherwise.

3   What is the purpose of calculating a cyclically adjusted high-employment budget deficit?

Supply-Side Fiscal Policies

Steady and predictable growth in aggregate demand gives business firms an economic environment that fosters confidence to make investment purchases. However, over the long run, economic growth depends on growth in aggregate supply. Policies that encourage saving, investment, and increased labor-force participation can act to increase the economic growth rate in a nation over the long run. Government policies can influence incentives to save, work, and invest by affecting the *net return* to these activities. For example, governments can directly subsidize these activities. Investment can be subsidized, as it has been in the United States, through credits that reduce tax bills to businesses investing in new structures and equipment. Government can also affect the net return to these activities through changes in marginal tax rates. Workers, savers, and investors respond to the *after-tax* return to engaging in productive activities. When marginal tax rates on labor, interest, or investment income decline, the after-tax return goes up, providing an incentive to undertake more of the activity.

Supply-side fiscal policies seek to influence long-run growth in real GNP through government subsidies and tax reductions. By increasing investment and work effort, these programs aim to shift the aggregate supply curve for the economy outward at a faster rate than would otherwise be the case. The effectiveness of these policies depends on the responsiveness of workers, savers, and investors to increases in the net returns to work, saving, and investment over the long run. Until recent years the impact of fiscal policy on aggregate demand had been emphasized. However, under the Reagan Administration the supply-side aspects of fiscal policy were in the limelight. The supply-side approach emphasizes the impact of tax cuts on aggregate supply over the long run. The supply-siders maintain that cuts in marginal tax rates—the tax rates on extra income—are likely to increase both work effort and investment in the long run. They contend that this will ultimately increase aggregate supply in the long run, thereby contributing to higher real GNP and lower price levels.

Supply-side fiscal policies: Policies that seek to influence long-run growth in real GNP through government subsidies and tax reductions.

How Supply-Side Fiscal Policies Can Influence Labor Markets

Let's first consider programs designed to increase work effort. The rationale for these programs is that when people decide whether or not to enter the labor force and how many hours to work, they look at the *net after-tax wages* they can earn. The higher the marginal tax rate, the lower the after-tax wage for additional work.

Suppose the marginal tax rate on labor income is currently 20%. The graph in Box 5 illustrates supply and demand in the labor market. Initially the market equilibrium wage is $10 per hour, and L hours of labor per year are supplied at that wage. The net after-tax marginal return to additional work is only $8. This is equal to the gross wage less the marginal tax of 20% on extra hourly earnings, or $2.

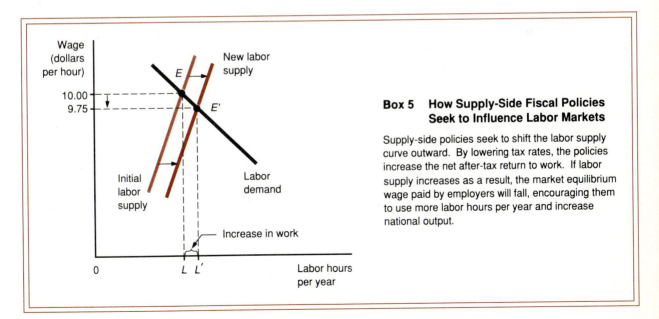

Box 5   How Supply-Side Fiscal Policies Seek to Influence Labor Markets

Supply-side policies seek to shift the labor supply curve outward. By lowering tax rates, the policies increase the net after-tax return to work. If labor supply increases as a result, the market equilibrium wage paid by employers will fall, encouraging them to use more labor hours per year and increase national output.

The labor supply curve can shift when tax rates are changed. Suppose the marginal tax rate applied to labor income is reduced to 15%. This means that at the current equilibrium wage the marginal net after-tax return to additional labor hours will go up to $8.50 (the $10 gross wage paid by employers less the $1.50 tax per hour of work resulting from the 15% marginal tax rate). The higher net marginal return to work resulting from the tax cut can attract more workers into the labor force and encourage existing workers to work more hours per year. As a result, the labor supply curve will shift outward and there will be downward pressure on wage rates. In Box 5, as a result of the tax-induced shift in labor supply, the market wage falls to $9.75 and the equilibrium number of hours worked increases to L'. The new equilibrium after-tax net wage will be 85% of the gross wage or $8.29.

Clearly the effectiveness of the tax cut depends on the increase in labor hours that it causes. If the policy results in more work per year, labor will become more abundant and labor costs will fall, thereby stimulating production in the economy and encouraging growth.

The responsiveness of labor supply to tax cuts can only be estimated. Workers could choose to pocket the increase in net wages as added income to be enjoyed and not work any extra hours at all. In fact, estimates suggest that for a large portion of the labor force, increases in wages in the past have had little effect on hours worked. Because tax cuts operate mainly through increases in net wages, this suggests that the response to modest tax cuts will be little if any increase in work effort. For that reason there is quite a bit of pessimism about the long-run impact of supply-side tax cuts.

However, this view is disputed by others who have argued that in the past the federal income tax has discouraged work effort. For example, one estimate by Jerry Hausman suggests that on average married males have worked 8% less because of income taxes than they would have otherwise. His results also suggest that a 10% increase in the net wage resulting from a cut in marginal tax rates would result in a 9% to 10% increase in hours worked per year for married women on average.[2] Again, these are only estimates based on past experience. No one knows what the actual response will be to reductions in marginal tax rates. Because the Tax Reform Act of 1986 did substantially decrease marginal tax rates for many Americans, there will soon be an opportunity to gauge the actual effects of a major tax cut on labor supply.

Supply-Side Incentives to Save and Their Impact in Credit Markets

A reduction in the marginal tax rate applying to interest income has the same effect in principle as that for labor income. Assuming that savers respond to the net after-tax marginal return to saving, a decrease in the marginal tax rate will increase the supply of saving. This will cause the curve for the supply of loanable funds for the economy to shift outward, as illustrated in Box 6.

Suppose the initial market rate of interest is 8%. This is the gross rate paid by debtors. If savers who supply loanable funds are subject to a 30% marginal tax rate, they will earn only 5.6% net interest after tax because their net return will be only 70% of the interest earned. The marginal tax rate on interest income typically is

---

[2]Jerry A. Hausman, "Labor Supply," in *How Taxes Affect Economic Behavior,* Henry J. Aaron and Joseph J. Pechman, eds., Washington, D.C.: The Brookings Institution, 1981.

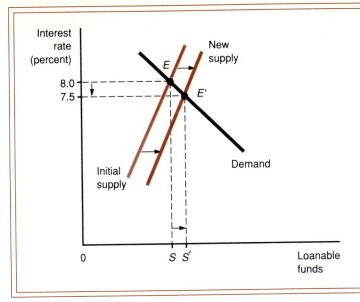

Box 6   How Supply-Side Policies Seek to Influence Credit Markets

Supply-side policies seek to increase the net after-tax return to saving. If this is successful in increasing the supply of saving, loanable funds will become more abundant, thereby putting downward pressure on interest rates and encouraging more investment.

higher on average than that on labor income because those who earn interest income are generally in higher tax brackets. If the marginal tax rate on interest income were reduced to 20%, the supply curve for loanable funds would shift outward. This is because the decrease in the marginal tax rate would raise the after-tax marginal net return to saving from 5.6% to 6.4%. The higher net return to saving provides an incentive to save more. As the supply of loanable funds curve shifts outward, the market rate of interest falls to 7.5%. After the new equilibrium is achieved, the quantity of annual savings supplied as loanable funds to financial markets increases from S to S' dollars per year and the net after-tax marginal return to saving is 80% of the gross interest rate of 7.5%, which is 6%. At the lower market equilibrium gross interest rate, investment will be encouraged, which will contribute to increased economic growth.

As is the case for reductions in the tax on labor income, the effectiveness of the tax cut in reducing market interest rates and increasing saving depends on the responsiveness of savers to changes in the after-tax interest they can earn on additional saving. Once again, no one knows how responsive savers will actually be to tax cuts. A number of empirical studies show that in the past saver response to changes in interest rates has been virtually nil in the United States.[3] Other studies estimate that saving is modestly responsive to changes in interest rates.

Under the Reagan Administration a number of supply-side policies sought to encourage personal saving. Two of these policies were:

1. *A reduction in the top marginal tax rate applied to income from saving.* The top marginal tax rate applied to nonlabor income has been reduced from 70% in 1980 to only 28% for most taxpayers in 1988. (Some taxpayers, however, will be subject to a marginal tax rate as high as 33%.)
2. *Special tax treatment of savings placed in individual retirement accounts.* Some taxpayers have been able to significantly reduce their taxes by placing

[3]Irwin Friend and Joel Hasbrouck, "Savings and After-Tax Rates of Return," *The Review of Economics and Statistics,* 65, November 1983, pp. 537-543.

some of their savings in special retirement accounts that allow them to defer taxes on the amounts saved provided they withdraw no income from the account until they retire. Critics of this tax break have argued that it merely results in a shuffling of saving from one account to another without increasing the actual amounts saved per year.

Tax Breaks that Subsidize Investment

A final type of supply-side policy involves tax breaks that directly subsidize business investment. These consist of investment tax credits for new equipment and structures and for research and development. Another technique that subsidizes investment is **accelerated depreciation allowances,** which are generous deductions from pretax business income that are allowed when firms acquire new equipment or new structures. These allowances permit firms to recover the cost of capital equipment on their tax accounts much more rapidly than the equipment actually wears out. The more rapid the depreciation allowed for tax purposes, the greater the immediate tax benefit from new investment.

Accelerated depreciation allowances:
Generous deductions from pretax business income that are allowed when firms acquire new equipment or new structures.

For example, suppose a firm buys a new drill press that costs $1 million and will last 10 years. If the firm is allowed to deduct one tenth of the cost of the machine each year ($100,000 per year) for 10 years and it is subject to a 50% marginal tax rate, the tax benefit of buying the machine will be $50,000 per year. However, if the firm is allowed to deduct one fifth of the cost of the machine ($200,000 per year) for 5 years, it will enjoy a tax saving of $100,000 per year for 5 years. The quicker depreciation enables the firm to get the tax benefit from the machine sooner. This provides more incentive to invest. Similarly, an investment tax credit of, say, 10% could be deducted from the firm's tax liability as an additional way of subsidizing investment.

The *marginal tax benefit* of investment is the annual reduction in taxes from each dollar of additional investment. The graph in Box 7 shows how investment demand can be affected by the marginal tax benefit of investment. Normally a firm invests each year up to the point at which the marginal return to the investment falls to

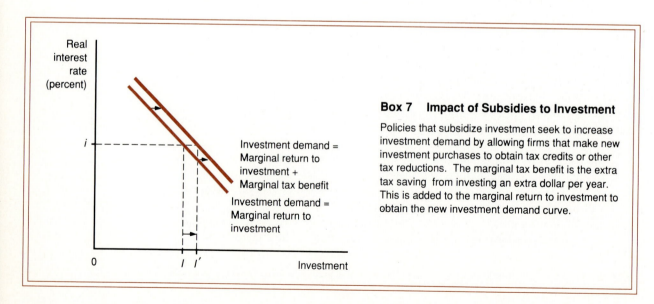

Box 7   Impact of Subsidies to Investment

Policies that subsidize investment seek to increase investment demand by allowing firms that make new investment purchases to obtain tax credits or other tax reductions. The marginal tax benefit is the extra tax saving from investing an extra dollar per year. This is added to the marginal return to investment to obtain the new investment demand curve.

equal the real rate of interest. In Box 7 the market rate of interest is i and business firms invest I dollars per year. When investment is subsidized through tax credits or accelerated depreciation, the marginal tax benefit of the investment must be added to its marginal return to obtain the full benefit to the firm. The full marginal return to the investment is now

Marginal return to the investment + Marginal tax benefit of the investment

where the marginal tax benefit is the reduction in tax due per year resulting from investing one extra dollar expressed as a percentage of that dollar. When the marginal tax benefit is added to the marginal return to investment, the investment demand curve shifts outward, as shown in Box 7. Given the market interest rate, i, this results in an increase in annual investment from I to I'.

As with all the previous supply-side policies we've discussed, the effectiveness of this policy in encouraging investment and therefore promoting economic growth depends on how responsive investment is to changes in the tax law. In a deep recession when the business outlook is gloomy, it's unlikely that added tax benefits for investment will have much effect. However, over the long run when the ups and downs of the business cycle average out, there's some evidence that subsidies to investment can increase the quantity of new investment goods demanded.[4]

Supply-Side Policies: Short-Run and Long-Run Impact

The idea behind supply-side tax cuts and subsidies is to shift the aggregate supply curve outward over time. However, it might be a considerable amount of time before the supply curve actually starts moving. Although increases in work effort could shift the aggregate supply curve outward immediately, it takes a number of years before any increased investment adds significantly to the existing capital stock. As a result, it takes awhile for supply-side policies to generate an increase in productive capacity for the economy. Meanwhile, unless the tax cuts are balanced with increases in other taxes or reductions in government spending, they will contribute to an increase in aggregate demand.

The graph in Box 8 shows the short-run impact of a supply-side tax cut similar to that enacted in 1981, which was not balanced by increases in other taxes or by a reduction in government spending. Because the effect of the Economic Recovery Tax Act of 1981 (ERTA) was to increase the federal deficit substantially, it shifted the aggregate demand curve outward. At the time this turned out to be a fine demand-side fiscal policy because the economy was in the depths of a severe recession! As a result, the tax cut contributed to an economic recovery toward the end of 1983 after its provisions became effective. However, the shift in aggregate supply even after a 5-year period appeared to be slight. ERTA didn't significantly contribute to an increase in saving and investment, and there was no marked increase in work effort.

This suggests that at least over a 5-year period the impact of a supply-side tax cut could be inflationary. The inflationary tendency was muted in the early 1980s because of the severe recession that prevailed in 1981 and 1982. The graph in Box 8 shows the impact of a supply-side tax cut that increases the budget deficit. The increase in the deficit shifts the aggregate demand curve outward. This contributes

---

[4]See William R. Hosek and Frank Zahn, "Real Rates of Return and Aggregate Investment," *Southern Economic Journal,* 51,1, July 1984, pp. 157-165.

Principles in Practice

Supply-Side Policies: An Assessment of Their Impact

The supply-side approach hit Washington like a storm with the election of Ronald Reagan in 1980. It moved quickly from a slogan to actual policy as President Reagan pushed through the Economic Recovery Tax Act of 1981 (ERTA). This new legislation featured a substantial tax reduction. However, unlike demand-side tax cuts, the provisions of ERTA were designed to increase aggregate supply. There was a 25% across-the-board reduction in income tax rates. The legislation concentrated on reducing *marginal* tax rates, which determine the *extra* taxes that taxpayers must pay on additional dollars of income earned during the year. The master stroke was a reduction in the top marginal tax rate applied to nonlabor income from 70% to 50%. Finally, there were various incentives designed to increase saving and investment. These included the development of individual retirement accounts (IRAs) that allowed savers to deduct from their taxable income a limited amount of their saving for retirement. Accelerated depreciation rules for business investment acted to reduce tax bills for firms investing in new machinery, vehicles, and structures.

The Reagan supply-side policies were dubbed "Reaganomics." In addition to securing passage of ERTA, the Reagan Administration also supported and obtained reductions in spending for Social Security and welfare payments for programs believed to have had adverse effects on work incentives. Federal spending was reallocated to finance a large increase in military expenditures.

Some supply-siders made extravagant claims for the impact of their policies on the economy. Among these claims were:

1. The ERTA tax cut would actually increase tax revenue rather than decrease it because it would encourage increased work and investment that would increase equilibrium real GNP.
2. The budget deficit would not increase substantially as a result of the tax cut. Even if there was a deficit, its inflationary effects would be offset by an increase in saving resulting in part from the tax cut.
3. The supply-side effect of increasing real GNP would put downward pressure on the price level and reduce inflation at the same time real GNP increased.

Many economists regarded these claims as excessive.* However, the economy managed to recover from a serious recession in 1982. Inflation was reduced sharply after 1982 and unemployment, although it remained at fairly high levels after the recession, seemed to be less of a problem. The Reagan Administration claimed credit for the recovery, and voters affirmed their confidence in the President and his economic policies with an overwhelming landslide reelection in 1984.

How much of the reduction in inflation and increase in real GNP can be attributed to the supply-side policies? First let's look at the results in the first half of the 1980s:

1. Economic growth between 1981 and 1985 was well below that projected by Reagan Administration economists. Actual growth in this 5-year period was 10.9%, well below the 19.1% predicted by Reagan economists.
2. The economy did recover from the recession of 1982, but many economists attribute this recovery to the increase in the money supply and other policies implemented by the Federal Reserve.
3. There did not appear to be any significant increase in work effort as a result of the reduction in marginal tax rates.
4. There was little appreciable increase in saving.
5. Federal tax revenues did not increase as a result of the ERTA tax cut. However, they did not decrease as much as many nonsupply-siders expected, indicating that the disincentive effects of high marginal tax rates are not negligible. However, reductions in tax revenues and increases in federal spending combined to increase the federal budget deficit to over $200 billion by 1986.

Critics of the supply-side policies of the early 1980s contend that they did little to shift the aggregate supply curve. The critics argue that the ERTA tax cut provided an increase in aggregate demand between 1982 and 1984 that pulled the economy out of the recession.† The new supply-side policies also coincided with other important changes in the economy, such as declining interest rates and declining oil prices, which acted to stimulate the economy. Prices of imported goods also fell during this period, which contributed to lower inflation.

The budget deficit did not fall, as many supply-siders hoped it would. Instead it steadily increased to record levels. Many economists argued that the large budget deficit kept interest rates at high levels throughout the early 1980s. High interest rates were blamed by many for reduced investment and increased imports in recent years.

In short, the report card on the supply-side policies of the early 1980s is mixed. There has been no significant increase in aggregate supply and its growth in the short run. However, many are hopeful that there will be favorable long-run effects on aggregate supply. The Tax Reform Act of 1986 has reduced many of the subsidies to investment that prevailed under ERTA, but the trend to lower marginal tax rates in the economy remains. Supply-siders still hope that over the long run, increases in work effort, saving, and investment will combine to increase the annual growth rate of real GNP.

*See Martin Feldstein, "Supply-Side Economics: Old Truths and New Claims," *American Economic Review,* 76, 2, May 1986, pp. 26-30.

†See Lawrence Chimerine and Richard M. Young, "Economic Surprises and Messages of the 1980s," *American Economic Review,* 76, 2, May 1986, pp. 31-36.

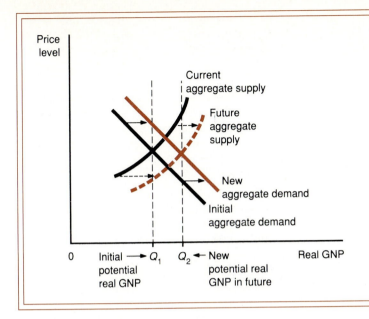

Price level

Current aggregate supply

Future aggregate supply

New aggregate demand

Initial aggregate demand

0   Initial → Q_1 Q_2 ← New   Real GNP
potential   potential real
real GNP   GNP in future

Box 8   Short-Run vs. Long-Run Impact of Supply-Side Policies

Supply-side policies take time to work. A supply-side tax cut immediately shifts the aggregate demand curve outward, putting upward pressure on real GNP and the price level. In the future if the policy is successful it will also shift the aggregate supply curve outward and increase the nation's annual potential to produce goods and services.

to a higher price level and a higher level of real GNP. Although the aggregate supply curve and potential real GNP can also shift outward, the magnitude of this shift is likely to be small over a 5-year period. As a result, the overall impact of the tax cut and resulting increase in the deficit is upward pressure on the price level and increases in real GNP. If the economy is close to full employment, the resulting increase in aggregate demand could result in an inflationary GNP gap that would overheat the economy and contribute to an inflationary spiral.

Over the long run, say, 10 years, further outward shifts in aggregate supply could exert downward pressure on the price level along with upward pressure on real GNP. However, it's unlikely that supply-side policies will result in a significant increase in potential real GNP in the short run. The notion that supply-side tax cuts can actually increase federal tax revenue is now discredited. The downward pressure of tax cuts on tax revenues doesn't appear likely to be offset by the upward pressure that increases in national income exert on tax collections.

Concept Check

1   The marginal tax rate on labor income is reduced from 20% to 10%. What effect will this have on the incentive to work?

2   How can policies that reduce the marginal tax rate on interest income serve to reduce the level of interest rates in the economy?

3   How can supply-side policies encourage investment?

Summary

1. Fiscal policy is the use of government spending and taxing for the specific purpose of stabilizing the economy and encouraging economic growth.
2. The federal government budget represents a plan for spending funds and raising

revenues through taxation, fees, and other means as well as plans for borrowing if necessary. The budgetary process consists of submission of the budget to Congress by the President and congressional review of budgetary proposals that culminates in actual appropriation of funds to government agencies and approval of ceilings on spending and a floor on revenue.

3. A budget deficit is the annual excess of government spending over revenues raised by taxes and other means. When a deficit prevails the federal government must borrow funds through issuance of Treasury bills, notes, and bonds to meet expenses not covered by tax revenues. A budget surplus prevails when government revenues exceed expenditures during the year.

4. The overall influence of the federal budget on aggregate demand depends on the expansionary effect of government purchases and other payments and the contractionary effect of taxes. When there is a budget deficit, the federal government adds more to aggregate demand than it takes away.

5. An expansionary fiscal policy is one for which the government acts to increase aggregate demand by adjusting its budget during the year. To increase aggregate demand the government increases spending or decreases taxes. A contractionary fiscal policy restrains aggregate demand through a decrease in government spending or an increase in taxes.

6. When an economy is in deep recession, increased aggregate demand will not put upward pressure on the price level. Under such circumstances an expansionary fiscal policy can be used to eliminate a recessionary GNP gap with little risk of inflation.

7. A sluggish economy can be stimulated by decreases in net taxes or increases in government spending. A dollar of government spending is more stimulating to the economy than a dollar cut in net taxes because a portion of the tax cut will be saved or spent on imports. Thus the economy can be stimulated without increasing the budget deficit when government spending increases are fully covered by increases in net taxes.

8. When the economy is experiencing only a mild recession, an increase in aggregate demand through an expansionary fiscal policy is likely to increase the price level. The increase in the price level will choke off some of the multiplier effect. Multipliers for fiscal policy are therefore lower when increases in aggregate demand cause the price level to increase.

9. A contractionary fiscal policy decreases aggregate demand and results in a multiplied decline in real GNP. Contractionary fiscal policies often meet political opposition as legislators seek to avoid cuts in government spending or increases in net taxes that would adversely affect their constituents. For this reason expansionary fiscal policies are more likely to be pursued than contractionary policies.

10. The cyclical ups and downs of the economy affect government tax collections and expenditures for transfers. Declines in real GNP reduce federal net tax collections as tax revenues go down and transfer payments go up. The opposite holds for the impact of increases in real GNP on the federal budget.

11. Automatic stabilizers are government revenue and expenditure programs that automatically adjust aggregate demand for changes in the level of real GNP.

12. Because of the impact of automatic stabilizers, the federal budget deficit tends to increase during recessions and economic downturns. The cyclically adjusted high-employment deficit gives the budget deficit (or surplus) at some selected level of high employment. The high-employment budget can be used to measure the impact of the federal budget on aggregate demand after adjusting for cyclical influences on the budget deficit.

13. The principles of fiscal policy are to run a high-employment deficit to stimulate a sluggish economy and to reduce the high-employment deficit or run a high-employment surplus to contract an overheated economy.

14. Fiscal policies that encourage saving, investment, and increased labor-force participation can increase a nation's rate of economic growth over the long run. Supply-side fiscal policies seek to influence long-run economic growth in real GNP through government subsidies and tax reductions. The effectiveness of supply-side policies depends on the responsiveness of workers, savers, and investors to increases in the net returns to work, saving, and investment.

15. Supply-side policies that lower taxes to encourage increased work in the long run could increase aggregate demand in the short run and thus put upward pressure on real GNP and the price level.

Key Terms and Concepts

Fiscal policy

Government budget

Expansionary fiscal policy

Contractionary fiscal policy

Automatic stabilizers

High-employment deficit (or surplus)

Supply-side fiscal policies

Accelerated depreciation allowances

Problems and Applications

1. Real GNP has declined during the past quarter, and the forecast is for a continued decline in real GNP because of a gloomy business outlook. Business investment is expected to plummet next year. As chairman of the President's Council of Economic Advisers, what fiscal policy would you recommend for the coming year?

2. Estimates indicate that of each $1 increase in national income 60¢ is spent on real GNP, 20¢ is used to pay taxes, 10¢ is spent on imported goods, and 10¢ is saved. The economy is currently in a deep recession with a $1,000 billion recessionary GNP gap and 15% unemployment. How much of an increase in government purchases for the year would be sufficient to pull the economy out of the recession and achieve full employment?

3. If the marginal respending rate is 0.6, calculate the impact on real GNP of a $1 billion reduction in net taxes. How much of a tax cut would get the economy out of the recession with the $1,000 billion recessionary GNP gap discussed in problem 2?

4. The economy is currently experiencing an $800 billion recessionary GNP gap. A proposal is made to increase transfer payments so as to stimulate aggregate demand. If the marginal respending rate on real GNP is 0.5, how much must transfers be increased to eliminate the recessionary GNP gap? Use a graph to show the impact on the economy assuming that the economy operates in the flat portion of its aggregate supply curve up to full employment.

5. Suppose the aggregate supply curve for an economy experiencing a $500 billion recessionary GNP gap is upward sloping. Use graphic analysis to show that, if the marginal respending rate is 0.5, elimination of the GNP gap requires that government purchases increase by more than $250 billion per year.

6. Suppose the price level is inflexible in the downward direction during the year. If the marginal respending rate is 0.5, calculate the tax increase or the decrease in government purchases necessary to eliminate a $1,500 billion inflationary GNP gap.

7. The President's advisers propose a budget that is designed to result in a deficit

of $60 billion for the year. In their estimates the advisers assume that the unemployment rate for the year will average 7%. Explain why their estimate will fall short of the actual deficit if the unemployment rate each month during the year averages 9% instead of 7%.

8. A law is passed requiring that the federal budget be in balance every year. Why would such a law prevent the automatic stabilizers from operating and thus be likely to destabilize the economy?

9. Suppose that taxes on interest income accruing to saving in all forms each year are abolished. Use graphic analysis to show the possible effects of this law on the supply of loanable funds in credit markets and the equilibrium market rate of interest. Show the impact of the tax elimination on investment.

10. The Tax Reform Act of 1986 eliminated the investment tax credit and reduced the tax benefit of accelerated depreciation allowances. Forecast the impact of these changes on investment demand and market interest rates.

Suggested Readings

Bruce Bartlett and Timothy P. Roth, eds., *The Supply-Side Solution,* Chatham, N.J.: Chatham House Publishers, 1983. This is a collection of essays on supply-side issues and policies designed to achieve supply-side objectives of increased economic growth and stabilization.

Barry P. Bosworth, *Tax Incentives and Economic Growth,* Washington, D.C.: The Brookings Institution, 1984. This book looks at the impact of taxes on saving, capital formation, investment demand, and labor supply.

David G. Davies, *United States Taxes and Tax Policy,* Cambridge: Cambridge University Press, 1986. This is an overview of the U.S. tax system and its impact on the economy up to 1985.

Rudiger Dornbusch and Stanley Fischer, *Macroeconomics,* 4th ed., New York: McGraw-Hill, 1987. Chapters 5 and 12 discuss issues in fiscal policy.

Charles R. Hulten and Isabel V. Sawhill, eds., *The Legacy of Reaganomics,* Washington, D.C.: The Urban Institute, 1984. This is a collection of essays analyzing the prospects for long-term economic growth in the United States and the impact of supply-side policies on growth during the Reagan Administration.

Joseph Pechman, *Federal Tax Policy,* 5th ed., Washington, D.C.: The Brookings Institution, 1987. This is a classic book on federal tax policy and its impact on the economy.

A Forward Look

The federal budget deficit is an important indicator of the impact of the federal government on aggregate demand. In the following chapter we examine issues relating to the status of the federal budget and examine the impact of the deficit on interest rates. We also consider issues relating to the impact of the national debt on the well-being of current and future generations.

The Federal Budget Deficit and the National Debt

You've read about it in the newspaper and heard about it on TV. Cartoonists depict it as a ghoulish monster. What is it? It's the federal government budget deficit. Why all the concern about the fact that the federal government hasn't been able to balance its budget in recent years? What effect do the deficit and the growth in the national debt have on you and your future well-being? We're now ready to begin an analysis of the impact of the deficit and the national debt on you and on the economy.

In fiscal year 1986 the federal budget deficit amounted to $220 billion. In that year the federal government borrowed that much money to help finance expenditures. The deficit in 1986 was equal to 22% of federal expenditures that year. This means that nearly 1 out of every 4 dollars spent by the federal government in 1986 was borrowed!

The federal budget has been in deficit consistently every year since 1970. Deficits also were the rule rather the exception throughout the 1960s when the federal budget was in deficit every year with the exception of 1960 and 1969. A consequence of chronic budget deficits is a growing national debt. In 1986 the debt of the federal government amounted to $2 trillion. Interest payments on the national debt represent nearly 15% of federal government expenditures annually.

In this chapter we examine how the federal deficit and the national debt affect the economy. As you'll see, by borrowing to finance its deficits the federal government can affect interest rates, future tax rates, the price level, and private investment. The deficit can also indirectly have adverse effects on the U.S. balance of trade with other nations. However, the effects of the deficit on the economy are quite complex and often misunderstood. Our goal in this chapter is to clarify the issues regarding the impact of the deficit and the national debt on economic performance and on our national well-being.

1 Discuss the advantages and disadvantages of an annually balanced federal budget.
2 Explain how the federal budget deficit's impact on interest rates can influence private investment, economic growth, and international trade.
3 Discuss the impact of the national debt on the well-being of current and future generations.
4 Discuss some of the problems involved in measuring the federal budget deficit and explain how the deficit has been reduced in recent years to comply with the Gramm-Rudman-Hollings Act.

The Federal Budget Balance Between Revenues and Expenditures

We explained the concepts of budget surplus and deficit in the preceding chapter. In each fiscal year since 1970, the federal government has consistently spent more than it has raised in revenue. For 8 years the Reagan Administration, which was ideologically opposed to the concept of a budget deficit, ran the largest deficits in history! The federal budget deficit grew from $73.8 billion in 1980 to $221.2 billion in 1986. Concern about the inability of the federal government to balance its budget led to passage of the Balanced Budget and Emergency Deficit Control Act of 1985. Commonly called the Gramm-Rudman-Hollings Act, this legislation (first discussed in the preceding chapter) placed limits on the federal budget deficit and stipulates annual reductions in the deficit with the goal of eliminating it by 1993. In 1987, mainly because of the new deficit reduction legislation, the deficit was trimmed to $150.4 billion. The table and graph in Box 1 show federal receipts, outlays, and the deficit or surplus for each year from 1950 to 1987.

As you've learned, a *federal budget deficit* prevails whenever government outlays in a given year exceed receipts (or revenues). A *federal budget surplus* prevails whenever outlays are less than receipts in a given year. For the 37-year period shown in the table, the budget has achieved a surplus in only 5 years.

As you saw from our analysis of fiscal policy in the preceding chapter, a federal budget deficit adds to aggregate demand and is an expansionary influence on the economy. Deficits are desirable during economic downturns to stabilize the economy. They are undesirable during inflationary periods because the boost they give to aggregate demand puts upward pressure on the price level.

Up until the 1930s it was viewed as prudent fiscal practice to balance the federal budget each year. However, a balanced budget rules out any chance for fiscal policy to stabilize the economy. If the budget were required to be in balance each year, the automatic stabilizers would be prevented from doing their job. This could destabilize the economy by decreasing aggregate demand when consumption, investment, and net exports are also declining. For example, if the economy experiences a recession, the federal government's net tax receipts will naturally fall. Transfers paid out will increase because payments for welfare, Social Security, and unemployment insurance benefits typically go up during a recession. The decline in income will also reduce income tax collections. If the budget is to be consistently in balance, this means government purchases would also have to decline during a recession to

Box 1 Federal Receipts, Outlays, and Budget Deficit or Surplus, 1950-1987 (billions of dollars)

Fiscal year or period	Total Receipts	Total Outlays	Surplus or deficit (−)	Fiscal year or period	Total Receipts	Total Outlays	Surplus or deficit (−)
1950	39.4	42.6	−3.1	1970	192.8	195.6	−2.8
1951	51.6	45.5	6.1	1971	187.1	210.2	−23.0
1952	66.2	67.7	−1.5	1972	207.3	230.7	−23.4
1953	69.6	76.1	−6.5	1973	230.8	245.7	−14.9
1954	69.7	70.9	−1.2	1974	263.2	269.4	−6.1
1955	65.5	68.4	−3.0	1975	279.1	332.3	−53.2
1956	74.6	70.6	3.9	1976	298.1	371.8	−73.7
1957	80.0	76.6	3.4	1977	355.6	409.2	−53.6
1958	79.6	82.4	−2.8	1978	399.6	458.7	−59.2
1959	79.2	92.1	−12.8	1979	463.3	503.5	−40.2
1960	92.5	92.2	.3	1980	517.1	590.9	−73.8
1961	94.4	97.7	−3.3	1981	599.3	678.2	−78.9
1962	99.7	106.8	−7.1	1982	617.8	745.7	−127.9
1963	106.6	111.3	−4.8	1983	600.6	808.3	−207.8
1964	112.6	118.5	−5.9	1984	666.5	851.8	−185.3
1965	116.8	118.2	−1.4	1985	734.1	946.3	−212.3
1966	130.8	134.5	−3.7	1986	769.1	990.3	−221.2
1967	148.8	157.5	−8.6	1987	854.1	1,004.6	−150.4
1968	153.0	178.1	−25.2				
1969	186.9	183.6	3.2				

Source: *Economic Report of the President*, 1988.

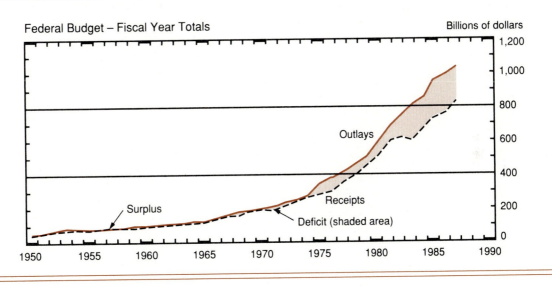

Federal Budget – Fiscal Year Totals

Billions of dollars

accommodate the decline in tax revenues and the increase in transfer payments. This would prevent the government from offsetting the decline in investment and consumption demand that normally occurs during a recession.

Similarly, an annually balanced budget prevents the federal government from constraining aggregate demand by running a surplus during periods when the economy is overheated. During boom periods, tax collections naturally rise and transfer payments decline. As a result, net taxes increase during a boom. If the government were to spend all of the increment in receipts, it would add to the already booming aggregate demand and thus aggravate the upward pressure on the price level.

An annually balanced budget therefore is likely to destabilize the economy. It contributes to declines in aggregate demand during downturns while increasing aggregate demand during upturns. Preventing the budget from ever being in deficit will clearly prolong recessions and might also contribute to the severity of recessions.

The recent concern about the federal budget imbalance is related to deficits rather than surpluses. On average over the past 25 years the federal budget has been an expansionary influence on the economy. The concern is that political pressures lead to the use of borrowing as a means of financing popular government programs. The borrowing of funds to finance current programs means that the taxes to pay for these programs are postponed to the future.

Financing Deficits: Money Creation vs. Borrowing from the Public

You know what happens when you want to spend more than you earn—you have to borrow the difference. The federal government also must borrow when it runs a deficit. The federal government deficit must be *financed*, which means that somehow the government must obtain the funds to meet its expenditures when receipts fall short of those expenditures. However, the federal government also has a little trick up its sleeve you don't have that represents an alternative to borrowing. The government can engage in policies that create new money to pay its bills! At the extreme the government has the power to simply *print* new currency to pay its bills.

The financing of a deficit by money creation is more expansionary than borrowing from the public. The resulting increase in the money supply is likely to increase the price level over the long run.

The federal government is unlikely to actually print new currency if it chooses to finance a deficit by money creation. This is because the federal government, just like most households and business firms, pays for most of its expenses by check. *Monetization of the federal deficit* occurs whenever the Federal Reserve takes action to expand the monetary base to finance the deficit. One way the Fed can do this is to simply loan the federal government the money to finance the deficit. The Fed does this by buying government securities. When the Fed does this it increases the monetary base in the same way it does when it engages in any open market purchase (see the chapters on the Federal Reserve System and monetary policy). Full monetization of the deficit occurs when the Fed purchases government securities in an amount equal to the deficit, thereby expanding the money supply while the federal government is running a deficit. Because such a policy increases bank excess reserves, it's also likely to result in a multiple expansion of checkable deposits.

When the federal deficit is monetized it carries a double punch for aggregate demand. First, the deficit contributes to an increase in aggregate demand because it allows an increase in government purchases without a corresponding increase in taxes. Second, monetization of the deficit contributes to an increase in the money supply, which results in downward pressure on the level of interest rates and upward pressure on the equilibrium money stock. The decrease in interest rates and consequent increase in private investment purchases then add further to aggregate demand. Monetizing the debt is therefore likely to result in upward pressure on the price level unless the economy is in a deep recession.

Because of the inflationary effects of financing the debt by money creation, the government more often chooses to borrow from the public. The government borrows by issuing Treasury bills, notes, and bonds, which as you know are government securities that are offered for sale in credit markets. When the government borrows from the public it must compete for available loanable funds in credit markets with households, business firms, and state or local governments. An increase in borrowing by the government to cover a deficit adds to the demand for loanable funds and puts upward pressure on interest rates. Under such circumstances the Federal Reserve does not intervene to increase its purchase of government securities and therefore does not increase the money supply to finance the deficit.

The effect of borrowing from the public is less expansionary than that of direct monetization of the deficit. When government securities are purchased by the public, a portion of loanable funds available from saving in the United States is allocated to make loans to the federal government. When the government borrows in this way there is no increase in bank reserves and no consequent expansion of the money supply. However, the impact on aggregate demand is more expansionary than would be the case if taxes instead of borrowing were used as a means of financing the deficit, because borrowing does not reduce disposable income while taxation does. In effect, borrowing to cover a federal budget deficit postpones the payment of taxes to the future. It also causes the federal government to incur a liability to pay interest on its debt to the people who acquire government securities.

The graph in Box 2 shows the impact on macroeconomic equilibrium of three possible means of financing government expenditures. Suppose federal government expenditures are $1,000 billion per year. If these expenditures are fully financed by tax revenues, the economy would be in equilibrium at point E_1, at which the price level is 100 and real GNP is $5,000 billion. If instead the government runs a $200 billion deficit and borrows that sum from the public, the aggregate demand curve would shift further outward and the economy would achieve equilibrium at a price level of 105 and real GNP of $5,500 billion. If the Fed monetized the $200 billion deficit, the aggregate demand curve would shift outward still further and the economy would be in equilibrium at a price level of 110 and real GNP of $6,000 billion

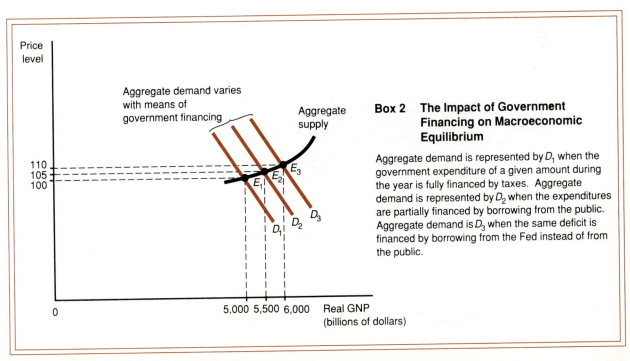

Box 2   The Impact of Government Financing on Macroeconomic Equilibrium

Aggregate demand is represented by D_1 when the government expenditure of a given amount during the year is fully financed by taxes. Aggregate demand is represented by D_2 when the expenditures are partially financed by borrowing from the public. Aggregate demand is D_3 when the same deficit is financed by borrowing from the Fed instead of from the public.

for the year. The conclusion is straightforward: Deficit financing is more expansionary than tax financing, but a monetized deficit is most expansionary of all!

How Borrowing by the Federal Government to Cover Deficits Affects Interest Rates: The Crowding-Out Effect

To understand the impact on interest rates of borrowing to cover the deficit, we must examine the impact of deficits on credit markets. The graph in Box 3 shows the credit market for the economy. The demand curve for loanable funds by private borrowers intersects the supply curve for loanable funds at an interest rate of 8%. At that interest rate the amount of loanable funds borrowed during the year to finance consumer durables and business investment would be $900 billion. In other words, if there were no borrowing by the federal government during the year, the market rate of interest would be 8% and the equilibrium volume of credit would be $900 billion.

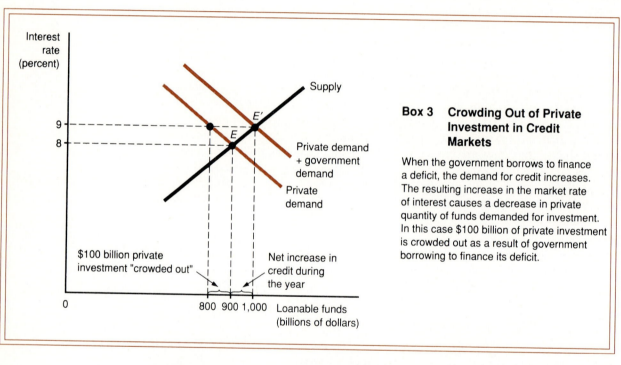

Box 3 Crowding Out of Private Investment in Credit Markets

When the government borrows to finance a deficit, the demand for credit increases. The resulting increase in the market rate of interest causes a decrease in private quantity of funds demanded for investment. In this case $100 billion of private investment is crowded out as a result of government borrowing to finance its deficit.

Now suppose the government must borrow $200 billion from the public to cover its deficit. This represents a substantial increase in the demand for loanable funds. As a result, the demand curve shifts outward and puts upward pressure on the level of interest rates in the economy. The new market equilibrium occurs at an interest rate level of 9% for the economy, and the equilibrium volume of credit extended at that interest rate is $1,000 billion. The government borrowing to finance the deficit has therefore resulted in an increase in the market rate of interest and a consequent increase in the quantity of loanable funds supplied. This analysis assumes that, as the government borrows, nothing else changes that might shift the demand or supply curves for loanable funds.

You should notice that the net increase in credit extended through the market is only $100 billion. However, the government borrows $200 billion. Where does the extra $100 billion in funds come from? To find out, go to the private demand for credit curve. At the new equilibrium interest rate of 9%, the quantity of loanable funds demanded for private investment falls from $900 billion to $800 billion for the year. In other words, the higher interest rate causes private investors to revise their plans and cut back their investment by $100 billion for the year. The **crowding-out effect** is the reduction in private investment purchases caused by higher interest rates that result from borrowing by the government to cover its budget deficit. In this case the crowding-out effect is a reduction in private spending of $100 billion per year.

Crowding-out effect:
The reduction in private investment purchases caused by higher interest rates that result from borrowing by the government to cover its budget deficit.

The extent of the crowding-out effect depends on the responsiveness of interest rates to the increased government demand for loanable funds and the reaction of private investors to the higher interest rates. If investment demand is unresponsive to a change in interest rates, the crowding-out effect will be quite small. For example, in a deep recession it's possible that investment demand will be quite unresponsive to changes in the interest rate. The crowding-out effect also depends on how responsive the quantity of loanable funds is to increases in the demand for credit. Once again, if the economy is in a deep recession there's likely to be a substantial amount of excess reserves available to the banking system. Under such circumstances the extra borrowing by the government might put little upward pressure on interest rates because the supply of loanable funds curve would be quite flat.

We can conclude that the crowding-out effect is less pronounced during a deep recession than it is when the economy is operating close to its potential. In fact, the increased government spending during a deep recession might improve the business outlook so as to encourage more investment!

The crowding-out effect dampens the expansionary impact of the federal budget deficit by reducing the private component of aggregate demand. The cutback in private spending then acts to reduce the multiplier effect of an increase in government spending. This implies that the upward pressure on the price level resulting from deficits in an economy close to full employment will be moderated as government spending displaces private investment.

The effect of deficits on interest rates has been a subject of empirical investigation by economists. Some studies have found little impact, which suggests that on average the crowding-out effect is small.[1] However, the crowding-out effect remains a matter of concern because even if it is small, a reduction in business investment can have serious long-term effects if it continues over a number of years. Less business investment means that U.S. workers will not have as much or as modern equipment with which to work. This will adversely affect their productivity. Thus if the crowding-out effect does cause a decline in investment, the result could be a decrease in the rate of improvement of living standards as worker productivity growth slows down the rate of increase in real GNP per person.

Deficits and the Balance of International Trade

Another possible detrimental effect of the deficit on the economy stems from the impact high interest rates have on the balance of trade. High real interest rates caused by the budget deficit increase the demand for U.S. dollars by foreigners who seek to acquire those dollars to purchase U.S. government securities and other U.S. financial assets. The increased demand for the dollar caused indirectly by the budget

---

[1]See Laurence H. Meyer, ed., *The Economic Consequences of Government Deficits,* Boston: Kluwer-Nijoff Publishing, 1983.

deficit can put upward pressure on the price of the dollar in terms of foreign currencies (see Principles in Practice, Chapter 4). As the price of the dollar goes up in terms of Japanese yen, German marks, and other foreign currencies, the prices of our exports in foreign markets increase as well. At the same time a high-priced dollar makes imports cheaper to Americans. The net effect of the higher price of the dollar is adverse to the balance of international trade in the United States because it discourages exports and encourages imports. A decline in net exports that results when the balance of trade is negative is a contractionary influence on the economy that hits certain industries harder than others.

There was concern in the early 1980s that high real interest rates in the United States also contributed to a higher international value of the dollar. Foreigners bid up the price of the dollar in terms of foreign currency at that time to make investments in the United States. As this occurred, the price of U.S. exports in terms of foreign currencies soared and the balance of trade, and therefore net exports, became negative. Despite a sharp reduction in the international value of the dollar in 1987, the balance of trade deficit remained negative. The federal government budget deficit can therefore indirectly prolong a balance of trade deficit if it keeps interest rates in the United States higher relative to interest rates in foreign nations.

Another way the budget deficit can adversely affect the balance of international trade is by contributing to an increase in disposable income in the United States. This occurs as a result of the deficit's expansionary effect on real GNP and because deficit financing allows lower tax rates. When the deficit results in higher disposable income than would normally be the case, it increases import purchases. This is because purchases of imports tend to vary with disposable income (see the chapters on the components of aggregate demand and on aggregate demand and Keynesian analysis of macroeconomic equilibrium). The greater level of import purchases made possible by deficit financing in turn contributes to a balance of trade deficit.

To the extent that there is crowding out of private investment, the deficit can also make U.S. industries less competitive in foreign markets. Government borrowing absorbs savings that could otherwise be channeled into new investments in technology and other cost-saving advances in U.S. industries. This means that unit costs of production in the United States will become higher relative to unit costs of foreign competitors who do make investments to keep up with advances in technology. Ultimately this indirect effect of the deficit is the most harmful to the international competitiveness of U.S. industries. Private investment is the key to advances in productivity, which in turn allow lower costs of production. When the budget deficit acts to curb the rate of private investment by keeping real interest rates high, it makes it harder to eliminate the trade deficit. Of course, if the deficit is used to finance government programs and investment (such as government research in new technologies), the negative impact of reduced private investment on productivity could be offset by the positive impact of federal programs.

Concept Check

1 How can the federal government deficit be monetized?

2 Why is the impact of the deficit less expansionary when the deficit is financed by borrowing from the public rather than borrowing from the Fed?

3 What is the crowding-out effect? How can the deficit serve to prolong the U.S. balance of trade deficit?

Economic Thinkers

ALICE RIVLIN

Alice Rivlin has long been interested in the interaction between economics and government policy making. She approached the topic academically first as a research fellow at the Brookings Institution, a famous center for social research.

She gained first-hand experience with the topic as a government consultant and as the first director of the Congressional Budget Office, which collects economic information for the legislature and analyzes the President's proposed budget, to include estimating the cost of proposed programs and anticipating tax receipts. Thanks to this office, lawmakers do not have to accept blindly the President's estimate of the economic impact of his budget.

Rivlin headed the office from its foundation in 1975 until 1983, when she returned to the Brookings Institution as the director of economic studies. She helpted establish a reputation of professionalism and accuracy for the budget office, enabling Congress to be better and more systematically informed. During her tenure, she did create controversy by predicting correctly, it turned out, that the President would be unable to keep his promise of a balanced budget by 1984. Republican congressmen were outraged, and many tried to plot her removal. However, when her predictions concurred with, or were more optimistic than those of the President, he was happy to quote her in televised addresses to the nation.

Born in Philadelphia in 1931, Rivlin earned her Ph.D. in economics from Radcliffe in 1958. She then went to the Brookings Institution, where she worked on a number of publications dealing with topics in economic policy. A lifelong Democrat, she has received high marks for objectivity from independent economists and praise from politicians in both parties.

The National Debt

You might not lose sleep over it yourself, but there are lots of politicians and other people in the United States who worry about the national debt. In this section we show how government deficits add to the national debt and examine the consequences of increased government debt for you and the economy.

The **national debt** is the dollar amount that the federal government owes to its creditors at a given point in time. Its creditors are the holders of the securities the government has issued in the past. The holders are entitled to interest payments and return of the face value of the securities upon maturity. The national debt is the cumulative legacy of previous government deficits. The national debt increases each year that the federal budget is in deficit. The debt can be reduced when the federal budget runs a surplus. When the budget is in surplus the federal government can reduce the size of the debt by not renewing government securities that mature. It can also use the surplus to pay off some debt before it matures. In this way the government reduces its demand for credit when a surplus prevails and puts downward pressure on interest rates.

As of December 1987 the national debt amounted to nearly $2.5 trillion. Of this total, $1.6 trillion was held by the public and the remainder was held by the Federal Reserve Banks and government agencies. The portion of the national debt held by the Fed and government agencies is debt the government owes indirectly to itself rather than to creditors. When interest is paid on this portion of the debt it usually returns to the Treasury, thereby increasing government revenues. Similarly, when

National debt:
The dollar amount that the federal government owes to its creditors at a given point in time.

Net federal debt:
The portion of the national debt owed to those other than the Federal Reserve and government agencies.

the debt held by the Fed and government agencies matures, the government itself obtains the funds. Only the portion of the national debt called the **net federal debt,** owed to those other than the Fed and government agencies, represents credit extended to the federal government.

The graph in Box 4 shows the national debt held by the public from 1950 to 1986. Notice how the volume of debt begins to skyrocket in 1975. Despite the increase in the dollar value of the debt since 1975, the national debt as a percentage of GNP has actually declined since 1950 when it amounted to 89% of GNP. The debt declined after 1950 as a percentage of GNP because much of the debt issued to finance government purchases during World War II was retired after that time. However, since 1980 the national debt has risen from 33% to over 45% of GNP.

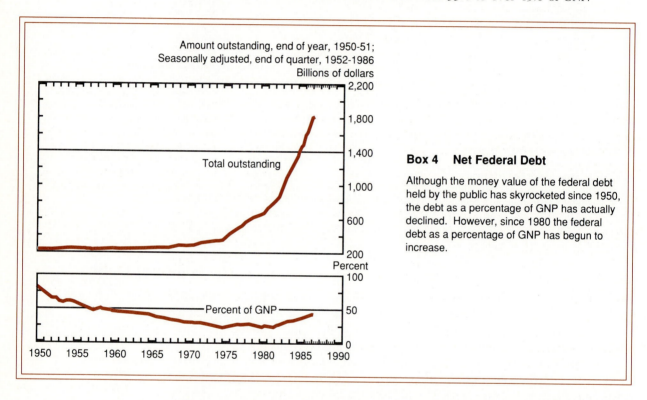

Amount outstanding, end of year, 1950-51;
Seasonally adjusted, end of quarter, 1952-1986
Billions of dollars

Total outstanding

Percent of GNP

Box 4   Net Federal Debt

Although the money value of the federal debt held by the public has skyrocketed since 1950, the debt as a percentage of GNP has actually declined. However, since 1980 the federal debt as a percentage of GNP has begun to increase.

The rise in the national debt as a percentage of GNP since 1980 reflects the sharp increase in the budget deficits since that time. During the Reagan Administration significant reductions in tax rates were enacted that were not accompanied by reductions in government spending. As a result, the deficit skyrocketed, contributing to the upward trend in the national debt as a percentage of GNP. (See the Economic Thinkers box in this chapter for a profile of former Congressional Budget Office director Alice Rivlin, who correctly predicted the fate of Reagan's promise to balance the federal budget by 1984.)

Who Are the Nation's Creditors?

The nation's creditors are the individuals and organizations that hold the net federal debt. These consist of all holders of U.S. government securities other than the Fed and government agencies. When taxes are used to pay off the debt, what really happens is that some people suffer a decrease in disposable income at that time while those who hold government bonds enjoy an increase in income. In other words, the retirement of and payment of interest on the debt transfer income among citizens. However, some of the debt is owned by foreigners. In 1986, for example, about 16% of the federal debt owned by the public was owed to foreigners. When interest payments are made to foreign holders, a portion of aggregate income earned in the United States must be used to pay the nation's foreign creditors. This could be a contractionary influence on the U.S. economy in the future if the foreign holders of U.S. debt don't use their interest earnings to purchase U.S. goods and services.

The bulk of the national debt is an **internal debt,** which is debt the nation owes to its own citizens. The **external debt** is the portion of the national debt that is owed to citizens of other nations. The internal debt is very different from private debt. Payment of interest and principal on the debt doesn't drain substantial income from the nation because much of it returns to U.S. citizens. As pointed out earlier, payment of interest on the debt redistributes income among U.S. citizens and therefore doesn't directly decrease aggregate demand. However, as the portion of the debt held by foreigners increases, the debt becomes more external. As more and more interest is paid out each year to foreign citizens, the repayment of the debt does exert some downward pressure on aggregate demand. This could contribute to future contraction of the economy.

We can also note that foreign saving in the United States prevents interest rates from rising as much as would be the case if the United States relied only on domestic savers to purchase federal government securities. Foreign saving in the United States therefore acts to offset some of the crowding-out effect that otherwise would result from the budget deficit.

The table in Box 5 shows the ownership pattern of the net federal debt in late 1986. As you can see, individuals, commercial banks, and state and local governments are the major creditors of the federal government. The portion of the debt held by foreigners depends on interest rates in the United States relative to those in

Internal debt:
The portion of the national debt owed to the nation's own citizens.

External debt:
The portion of the national debt owed to citizens of other nations.

Box 5 Net Public Debt of the U.S. Treasury by Holder, as of December 1986

Holder	Amount of debt (billions of dollars)	Percent of total
Commercial banks	230.1	14.4
Money market funds	28.6	1.8
Insurance companies	106.9	6.7
Other companies	68.8	4.3
State and local governments	273.1	17.0
Individuals	162.9	10.1
Foreign and international	251.6	15.7
Other investors	480.1	30.0
	1602.0	100

Source: *Economic Report of the President*, 1988.

foreign countries. In June of 1980, when interest rates in the United States were very high relative to those abroad, a whopping 22% of the net federal debt was held by foreigners.

Burden of the Debt

Will the federal government go bankrupt if it continues to run deficits? There's no need to worry about this because, as observed earlier, the federal government has tricks up its sleeve that a private debtor can't take advantage of. First of all, the federal government pays the interest on its debt from tax revenues. At the extreme, the government can print money to pay off its debt. The risk of default on the debt is therefore virtually nil. Of course, the government can always roll its debt over by issuing new securities to pay off the ones that mature. However, this will involve continued upward pressure on interest rates in credit markets.

The real question of the burden of the debt deals with what future citizens will have to give up to repay the debt. There are two major burdens resulting from a large debt:

1. *Future generations will have to pay more taxes to pay interest on the debt instead of receiving government goods and services in return for those taxes.* Interest on the national debt currently accounts for about 15% of federal government expenditures. This means that currently 15¢ of each dollar in taxes we pay is used to make interest payments to holders of the debt instead of to provide such services as roads, defense, and education. If there is no substantial decline in interest rates and the debt continues to grow because of additional deficits, then the portion of taxes allocated to interest instead of services will increase.
2. *If the crowding-out effect is substantial, a growing federal debt will decrease private investment and reduce the growth rate of the private capital stock.* This will have the effect of decreasing economic growth. As the growth rate of worker productivity declines because of a decrease in the growth rate of capital they have to work with, the growth in GNP per capita will also decline. This means that, because of the growing national debt, the standard of living of future generations will be lower than would otherwise be the case. The growth rate of potential real GNP can therefore be retarded by a growing federal debt.

The burden of the national debt can be offset, however, if some taxpayers are forward looking enough to increase saving so as to pay the higher taxes expected in the future as a result of the deficit. If taxpayers do save more in anticipation of the future burden of taxation, then the supply of loanable funds will increase. This will put downward pressure on interest rates and offset some of the crowding-out effect. Similarly, if the deficit actually serves to make real GNP higher than it would be otherwise by making cyclical downturns less likely, it will also contribute to higher savings on average.

Finally, the burden of the debt could be offset by increased benefits to future generations from government services. The nation might have fewer factories and machine tools, but this could be offset by more and better roads, better schools, and other government projects that increase worker productivity. This is particularly true if the federal government uses its borrowings to finance long-lasting projects such as roads, dams, and parks. The higher interest payments and decreased growth of the private capital stock in this case would be balanced by benefits from government investments enjoyed in the future.

1 How is the national debt related to the federal budget deficit?

2 What is the distinction between external and internal debt?

3 In what sense is the national debt a burden, and in what ways can that burden be offset?

Measuring and Reducing the Deficit

The size of the budget deficit provides information to citizens on both the state of federal government finances and the impact of the budget on aggregate demand. Interpreting the impact of the deficit on the economy is quite difficult because its magnitude is influenced by cyclical fluctuations in the economy and by some peculiarities in government accounting techniques. In this section we discuss some of the problems in interpreting the meaning of the deficit and in measuring its impact on the economy.

High Employment vs. the Actual Deficit

As was pointed out in the previous chapter, the actual budget deficit or surplus in any given year is influenced by the effects of the automatic stabilizers. When the economy is operating below its potential, the deficit naturally rises. To adjust for the cyclical effects of the automatic stabilizers, the high-employment budget deficit or surplus can be computed. The resulting figure can be used to show whether the federal budget would add to or detract from aggregate demand if the economy were operating at its potential.

For example, in 1982, which was a recession year, the actual budget deficit was $127.9 billion. In the same year the high-employment deficit was only $20 billion. The extra $107.9 billion in deficit spending for that year resulted from the cyclical effect of the automatic stabilizers on net taxes. The recession reduced tax collections and increased transfer payments above the level that would have prevailed if the economy had achieved a 6% unemployment rate.

Remember, when the economy is operating below its potential, a high-employment deficit provides a stimulus to boost aggregate demand to pull up real GNP.

Government Accounting Procedures, Borrowing, and the Deficit

The government accounting procedures used to measure the deficit are quite different from standard business practices. The federal budget doesn't distinguish between current and capital expenditures. Most businesses have a separate capital budget that limits borrowing for the purpose of acquiring capital assets. The federal budget doesn't link borrowing to the financing of capital assets, nor does it calculate depreciation on its assets as part of its expenses.

Part of the national debt is offset by tangible assets such as buildings, equipment, and roads that the government uses borrowed funds to finance. Borrowing allows the government to spread out payment for these assets in the same way that you would spread out payment for a car or a home over a period of years. In this sense it's normal and prudent for the government to finance some of its expenditures each year by borrowing. However, the government accounting techniques never make this clear because the deficit isn't linked with the financing of specific capital acquisitions.

Inflation and the Deficit

Inflation is great for debtors. When a borrower makes a loan at a given interest rate that isn't fully adjusted for future inflation, the borrower can pay off the loan in dollars that are worth less than those borrowed. Obviously, a debtor like the federal government that owes $2.5 trillion can gain substantially from inflation.

In periods of rising prices, some of the real value of the national debt is eroded. This effect is compounded by the fact that when market interest rates rise, the outstanding value of the national debt declines. This is because securities prices decline when interest rates rise. For example, in 1980, a period of high inflation, the effect of increasing interest rates and inflation was to reduce the real value of the net federal debt by $68.5 billion, according to calculations by Eisner and Pieper.[2] In that year the actual budget deficit was $61.2 billion based on NIPA figures. The gain to the government represented by the decrease in the real value of the debt can be thought of as an "inflation tax" on debt holders that reduces the burden of making payments on the debt. If the decrease in the value of the debt is viewed in this way, then when added to the actual deficit it results in a surplus of $7.3 billion in 1980! Of course, the process works in the opposite direction as well. In periods of declining interest rates and stable prices, the real value of the debt goes up. Therefore in the mid-1980s when interest rates fell rapidly and inflation cooled, the market value of the debt increased the face value of outstanding debt. This increase would have had to be subtracted from government revenues at that time. This means that the actual deficit *understates* the real deficit when interest rates are falling.

The federal government also owns assets that can be liquidated to pay off the national debt. Among these assets are gold, loans, structures, mineral rights, and revenue-producing enterprises such as power-generating facilities, railroads, and the Postal Service. In general, the value of government assets increases during periods of inflation and declines in periods of deflation. For example, in 1980 the market value of gold held by the federal government increased by $6 billion. The increased value of these assets can also be viewed as offsetting the budget deficit inasmuch as the value of the assets increases the net worth of the federal government. Eisner and Pieper estimated that, because of increases in the value of assets held by the federal government and decreases in the real value of outstanding government debt, the net liability of the federal government declined by $11.2 billion in 1980 when the actual budget deficit was $61.2 billion based on NIPA data.

Of course, if a similar calculation were done for 1986, the picture would be quite different. In 1986 the real value of the national debt outstanding was increasing because of declining interest rates over the year. Also in that year the price of gold was lower and the prices of many assets held by the government such as oil drilling rights plummeted because of declining oil prices.

Reducing the Deficit

The preceding discussion of accounting peculiarities for the federal budget is relevant to techniques that have actually been used to reduce the budget deficit in com-

---

[2]Robert Eisner and Paul J. Pieper, "A New View of the Federal Debt and Budget Deficits," *American Economic Review,* 74,1, March 1984, pp. 11-29.

Reducing the Deficit: Tax Increases, Spending Reductions, or Stopgap Measures?

It's the easiest thing in the world to run up a deficit, as many victims of the plastic plague of credit cards can testify. The hard part, for both individuals and governments, is how to decrease the level of deficits. How has the federal government been dealing with this weighty problem?

As we've seen in this chapter, there are two basic ways to reduce a budget deficit:

1. Raise more revenue through increases in taxation, through charges for government services, or from the sale of government assets.
2. Reduce government spending on both purchases and transfers.

The U.S. budget deficit skyrocketed in the first half of the 1980s because taxes were reduced while government spending increased. The Economic Recovery Tax Act of 1981 resulted in a sharp reduction in tax rates. Federal taxes amounted to 20.1% of GNP in 1981 but fell to 18.5% of GNP in 1986. At the same time government spending increased as a percentage of GNP. In 1978 federal spending was 21.1% of GNP, but by 1986 it had risen to 23.8% of GNP.

The major increase in federal spending over the period 1981 through 1986 occurred for government purchases that provide national defense. Defense spending rose from 4.8% of GNP in 1978 to 6.6% in 1986. However, defense spending wasn't the only culprit. Federal spending for Social Security benefits, medical care, and interest on the national debt also increased as a percentage of GNP over the same period. Attempts to reduce the deficit between 1981 and 1986 came mainly through cuts in nondefense spending other than Social Security, medical care, and net interest on the federal debt.

The Gramm-Rudman-Hollings Act required substantial reductions in the federal deficit beginning in fiscal year 1987. During that year the interim provisions of the Tax Reform Act of 1986 came into effect. These provisions were expected to increase tax revenue in 1987 to alleviate the deficit somewhat. However, there was little political support for cuts in Social Security benefits, which constitute a major portion of federal spending. In 1987 the administration was also strongly opposed to cuts in defense spending. Because Social Security and defense together amount to nearly three quarters of federal spending, this left little leeway for cuts!

Among the proposals suggested to alleviate the deficit in 1987 and later years are:

1. Reduction in price supports and other subsidies to farmers. In 1986 these programs required a record $25.8 billion in outlays.
2. Reduction in subsidies to mass transit and rural electrification.
3. Imposition of fees for users of such federal services as student and homeowner loans guaranteed by the federal government.
4. Sale of government assets to provide a one-time increase in revenues.

It remains to be seen whether these proposals for increasing revenue and reducing spending will be sufficient to meet the deficit reduction targets of the Gramm-Rudman-Hollings Act. Of course, Congress can always pass a new law that will allow modification in the deficit reduction targets.

---

pliance with the Gramm-Rudman-Hollings Act. In 1987, to meet budget deficit reduction targets, the Reagan Administration actually sold government assets to raise revenue! The process of selling government assets to private business interests is called **privatization.** For example, the government has negotiated the sale of such enterprises as the Conrail railroads and has sold government-held loans. As part of the 1988 budget, the Reagan Administration proposed the sale of Amtrak, the naval petroleum reserves, the Alaska Power Administration, and other real assets of the government. Privatization has been used heavily in the United Kingdom, where many industries in the past were acquired by the government as national enterprises. In recent years, the British Conservative government has sold billions of dollars worth of national enterprises to private interests.

Sale of government assets has been criticized as a mere stopgap measure to meet the budget deficit limits set by the Gramm-Rudman-Hollings Act. Asset sales provide the government with a one-time increase in revenue and can actually reduce future revenue if the assets sold generate income.

Reducing a budget deficit necessitates political decisions to increase taxes or reduce expenditures. The Reagan Administration sought to reduce the deficit through

Privatization:
The process of selling government assets to private business interests.

some spending cuts, increases in fees for certain federal programs, and sale of government assets. The administration was reluctant to raise taxes and to cut either Social Security and other transfer programs or national defense programs, which together account for over 70% of federal government expenditures. Because interest payments on the debt amount to another 15% of annual federal expenditures, this leaves only a scant 15% of expenditures on the block for cutting.

The political issues of reducing the deficit are quite complex. The gains from cutting the deficit and from reducing the national debt must be weighed carefully against the losses from either higher taxes or reduced government expenditures.

Concept Check

1 How do government accounting procedures differ from private accounting methods with respect to capital purchases?

2 How does inflation affect the deficit and the national debt?

3 What is privatization?

The Pros and Cons of Deficits and Debt

The federal budget has been in deficit almost consistently over the past 25 years. Between 1975 and 1985 the national debt as a percentage of GNP increased from 32% to 46%, while interest on the debt as a percentage of GNP went up from 1.3% to 3.2%. The national debt now amounts to nearly $8,000 per person in the United States, and over 15% of the debt is held by foreigners.

There are some real concerns about the effect of the deficit and the debt on the economy. The increased demand for credit by the government puts upward pressure on interest rates. If this effect is substantial, it can crowd out private investment. The crowding-out effect decreases the effectiveness of fiscal policy by causing a decrease in aggregate demand as investment declines. The long-term effects of a decline in private investment could be a decrease in the growth rate of worker productivity and living standards. This is because the capital stock available to businesses would grow less rapidly. The private capital stock is a key determinant of worker productivity.

Higher interest rates that might result from the deficit can also serve to keep the international value of the dollar high in terms of foreign currency, thereby decreasing net export demand. The deficit also keeps current taxes lower than would otherwise be the case given government expenditures. In this way the deficit allows disposable income to be higher than it would otherwise be and causes an increase in import purchases, which contributes to an international trade deficit.

The deficit can cause the price level to rise, just as any boost in aggregate demand does for an economy close to full employment. However, the deficit is most likely to be an inflationary influence on the economy when it is monetized by the Fed. Under those circumstances the deficit contributes to an increase in the money supply that is likely to be inflationary in the long run.

A growing national debt requires that larger percentages of federal expenditures

---

be allocated to paying interest on the debt. This means future generations will pay more taxes to transfer income to the government's creditors instead of receiving government goods and services. This is of particular concern if the nation's creditors live in foreign nations, because repayment of an external debt drains purchasing power from the nation and can therefore be a contractionary influence on aggregate demand.

The impact of the deficit and the national debt on the economy remains controversial. There's no doubt that the federal deficit and debt have unique characteristics. In making judgments about the pros and cons of deficits and debt, beware of simple analogies between the federal budget and private budgets!

Summary

1. A federal budget deficit prevails whenever government outlays in a given year exceed receipts. When the budget is consistently in deficit, the national debt increases. In 1986 the national debt amounted to $2 trillion, and interest payments on the debt were absorbing close to 15% of federal government expenditures.

2. The federal budget deficit can be financed by creation of new money or by borrowing from the public. Whenever the Federal Reserve increases the money supply to help the federal government cover a deficit, the deficit is said to be monetized. When a deficit is monetized in this way it adds to aggregate demand directly when the government spends the newly created funds and indirectly as the increase in bank reserves allows expansion of the money supply.

3. The federal budget deficit is usually financed by borrowing from the public rather than borrowing from the Federal Reserve Banks. Under such circumstances the increase in government purchases that are financed by the deficit is paid for by an allocation of saving to purchase government securities. There is no increase in bank reserves. However, borrowing is more expansionary than tax financing because disposable income is not reduced. In effect, borrowing to finance a federal budget deficit postpones the burden of taxation to the future.

4. When the government borrows in credit markets to finance a deficit, it puts upward pressure on interest rates by increasing the demand for loanable funds. The higher interest rates result in a crowding out of investment, and the quantity of loanable funds demanded declines in response to the higher interest rates. The government deficit therefore results in a crowding out of private investment as it causes the real interest rate to go up. The extent of the crowding-out effect depends on the responsiveness of investment demand to changes in interest rates.

5. Upward pressure on interest rates resulting from the deficit can also have adverse effects on the U.S. international balance of trade. High interest rates induce foreigners to hold dollars as saving in the United States rather than using them to purchase U.S. goods. This prevents the price of the dollar from falling in terms of foreign currency, thus making our exports more expensive to foreigners and making imports cheaper to U.S. buyers. In addition, the deficit contributes to higher disposable income, which also acts to increase imports.

6. The national debt is the dollar amount that the federal government owes to its creditors at a given point in time. The creditors are those who hold government securities and receive interest payments from the government.

7. The net federal debt is that portion of the national debt owed to those other than the Federal Reserve or government agencies.
8. The bulk of the national debt is an internal debt because it is owed to U.S. citizens. When interest is paid on the debt, income is redistributed from taxpayers to debt holders. However, a portion of the national debt is owed to foreigners who have purchased U.S. government securities. When interest is paid on this external debt, income is transferred from U.S. taxpayers to foreign citizens.
9. The burden of the national debt is the sacrifices U.S. citizens in the aggregate will have to make to repay the debt. Because the bulk of the debt is owed to U.S. citizens, repayment of the debt makes people who receive interest payments better off while making those who pay the taxes worse off.
10. Another burden of the national debt results from the sacrifices of government services in the future as more tax revenues are allocated to paying interest on the debt instead of providing government programs. In addition, if the crowding-out effect of deficit financing is strong, a growing national debt will cause the growth rate of private capital to decrease. This can make U.S. workers less productive and contribute to lower incomes and higher unit costs of production relative to foreign competitors.
11. The burden of the national debt can be offset if deficits result in higher saving each year than would otherwise be the case. Higher saving would put downward pressure on interest rates and offset the crowding-out effect. The burden of the debt can also be offset if the government invests in roads, schools, and other capital that increases the productivity of workers.
12. The federal budget deficit is influenced by the cyclical ups and downs of the economy.
13. Part of the federal deficit is used to finance tangible assets such as structures, buildings, and equipment that the government acquires.
14. Inflation erodes the real value of the national debt and allows the government to pay off its debt in dollars that have less purchasing power than those it borrowed. Increases in market interest rates decrease the value of the outstanding debt, while declines in market interest rates increase the value of the debt.
15. Privatization is the process of selling government assets. Privatization provides a one-time increase in funds to help reduce the deficit in a given year.
16. Federal deficits shift the aggregate demand curve outward, automatically compensating for declines in private spending during economic downturns. The deficit also transfers part of the burden for financing government capital projects to the future generations that will enjoy the benefits of those projects.

Key Terms and Concepts

Crowding-out effect   Internal debt
National debt   External debt
Net federal debt   Privatization

Problems and Applications

1. Suppose a new law is passed that requires the federal government to run a surplus each year until the national debt is paid off. Explain why such a policy would be likely to destabilize the economy and contribute to recessions when private components of aggregate demand decrease.

2. Suppose the federal government runs a chronic deficit of $200 billion per year and finances the deficit by selling new government securities directly to the Federal Reserve System. Show how, other things being equal, either currency in circulation or bank reserves will increase as a result of this means of financing the deficit. Why would the impact on the economy of this means of financing be the same as if the government merely printed money to pay its expenses? Why would the impact on the economy be inflationary in the long run?

3. Suppose the federal deficit is financed by borrowing funds from the general public. Track the impact of borrowing on interest rates, private saving, and private investment. Under what circumstances will government borrowing reduce private investment?

4. Suppose taxpayers increase the supply of saving as a direct result of the government deficit. Show how, if the increase in the supply of saving is large enough, the borrowing to finance the deficit will not affect interest rates and will not crowd out any private investment.

5. Why is financing government expenditures by borrowing more expansionary than tax financing?

6. Suppose that both the supply of saving and investment demand are completely unresponsive to changes in the market rate of interest. What will be the impact of a government deficit on consumption, investment, and aggregate demand? What impact will the deficit have on the price level and real GNP if the economy is in a deep recession so that the Keynesian aggregate supply curve holds?

7. How can a large deficit prolong a nation's international balance of trade deficit?

8. Over the years suppose that the portion of the net federal debt owned by foreigners increases from 5% to 30% of the amount outstanding. What is the implication of this change in the pattern of ownership of the debt for the burden of repaying it in the future?

9. Suppose all of the net federal debt is internal debt. In what sense does repayment of the debt involve a redistribution of income? Is there a burden of the debt on future generations in this case? In what ways can any burden of the debt on future generations be offset?

10. What is the impact of inflation and a higher real interest rate on the burden of repaying the debt and on taxpayers?

Suggested Readings

Council of Economic Advisers, *Economic Report of the President,* Washington, D.C.: U.S. Government Printing Office. The 1987 edition of the report discusses measures taken to reduce the deficit, including privatization.

David N. Hyman, *Public Finance: A Contemporary Application of Theory to Policy,* 2nd ed., Chicago: The Dryden Press, 1987. Chapter 13 contains a detailed analysis of the federal deficit and the national debt.

Laurence H. Meyer, ed., *The Economic Consequences of Government Deficits,* Boston: Kluwer-Nijhoff Publishing, 1983. This is a collection of articles that examine the economic effect of budget deficits.

A Forward Look

Economic policies often involve tradeoffs among goals. Among the goals of economic stabilization policies are avoidance of excessive unemployment, a reasonably stable price level, and adequate economic growth. In the following chapter we examine the tradeoffs and conflicts that arise in pursuit of these policy goals.

Tradeoffs Between Inflation and Unemployment and the Theory of Rational Expectations

By now you've had plenty of occasion to see the usefulness of the concept of opportunity cost, which we introduced in Chapter 1. Policymakers realize that the opportunity cost of pursuing policies to minimize cyclical unemployment can be increased inflation. It seems as though it's often difficult, at least in the short run, to simultaneously reduce inflation and reduce unemployment in modern economies. For example, in 1988 policymakers were worried that reduced unemployment rates would be accompanied by increased inflationary pressures for the economy. Over the long run policymakers must also consider the impact of stabilization policies on economic growth and aggregate supply. But policies such as subsidies and tax breaks that seek to increase the nation's productive potential over the long run can overheat the economy in the short run by increasing aggregate demand.

In recent years fiscal policy in the United States has been mainly expansionary and has not been used to reduce aggregate demand. On the other hand, the Fed has applied the monetary brakes on many occasions, and its contractionary policies of the early 1980s reduced inflationary pressures in the mid-1980s at the expense of precipitating a major recession in 1982.

In this chapter we consider the historical tradeoffs between inflation and unemployment. We also examine the effect of stabilization policies and expectations about inflation on the decisions of the participants in the economy. Remember that expectations of future prices and incomes are an important determinant of the demand for and supply of goods and services. Here we examine how such expectations are formed and consider the possible effects of changing expectations on nominal wages, aggregate supply, and macroeconomic equilibrium.

After reading this chapter, you should be able to:

1 Discuss the historical tradeoff between annual inflation and unemployment in modern economies through the use of the Phillips curve.
2 Show how shifts in aggregate supply can affect the tradeoff between the goals of reducing inflation and reducing unemployment.
3 Understand how rational expectations of changes in the price level can affect the behavior of workers and investors and influence macroeconomic equilibrium.
4 Understand some of the difficulties of implementing stabilization policies and explain how rational expectations about the effect of stabilization policies might frustrate achievement of their goals.

The Phillips Curve: Inflation vs. Unemployment

Throughout the world the 1970s was greeted as the "Age of Aquarius," as popularized in the musical *Hair*. When the 1980s rolled in, it appeared as though this decade would be characterized as the "age of inflation." Inflation in the United States in 1980 was running at an annual rate of 13.5%, and the nation was plagued by double-digit inflation from 1979 through 1981. Inflation was even worse in the nations of Western Europe. In the early 1980s both Italy and the United Kingdom had inflation galloping at 20% annual rates. Then in 1982 a recession hit as monetary authorities around the world engaged in policies to combat inflation. Inflation declined to 4% in the United States in 1982, and similar dramatic decreases in the rate of inflation were experienced in Western European nations. But unemployment rates soared to double digits in the United States, and the economies of Western Europe also suffered from recessions as inflation came down.

As you might expect from your familiarity with aggregate demand and aggregate supply analysis, declines in aggregate demand that cause recessions also serve to moderate inflation if aggregate supply is more or less stable. To see this, just shift an aggregate demand curve to the left (as we have done many times now), assuming a stable aggregate supply curve, and note how it results in downward pressure on prices but also decreases real GNP. We would expect that when inflation is primarily of the "demand-pull" type (see the chapter on the forces of aggregate supply and demand), reducing inflation by decreasing aggregate demand can also decrease equilibrium real GNP. The decrease in real GNP contributes to increased cyclical unemployment. In other words, reducing inflation by policies that cause aggregate demand to decline can also increase cyclical unemployment.

The tradeoff between inflation and unemployment implied by a model of demand-pull inflation has been well documented for certain historical periods. In the late 1950s A.W. Phillips, a British statistician, conducted research to examine the

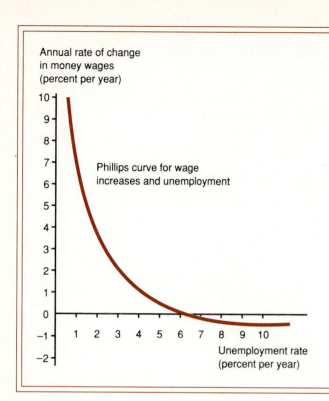

Annual rate of change
in money wages
(percent per year)

Phillips curve for wage
increases and unemployment

Unemployment rate
(percent per year)

**Box 1   Phillips Curve for the United
Kingdom, 1861-1957**

Phillips' original curve for the United Kingdom was
based on the data for annual changes in wage rates
and unemployment. The curve that was fitted through
points for data from 1861-1957 seemed to indicate
an inverse relationship between unemployment and
increases in wages.

historical relationship between unemployment and the rate of change in wages.[1] He
used data for the United Kingdom over the period 1861 to 1957. Phillips plotted the
annual rate of change in wages on the vertical axis of a graph and the annual unemployment rate on the horizontal axis. Phillips then made a remarkable discovery:
A curve sketched through the resulting scatter of points corresponding to the coordinates of the points seemed to fit the data very well. A curve similar to the one
sketched by Phillips is shown in Box 1. The curve traced out a negative relationship
between unemployment and the rate of change in wages. When unemployment increased, the rate of change in wages tended to decrease. However, as you can see,
the curve also showed that as unemployment fell below 5% or so, further decreases
in the rate of unemployment for the period studied then seemed to be associated
with faster increases in the rate of change in money wages. On the other hand, when
the unemployment rate was very high, say, over 6%, further increases in unemployment did not, for the period shown, tend to reduce the rate of change in wages very
much. In fact, in some years from 1861 through 1957, wages actually fell. In other
words, the rate of change in wages was negative over certain periods.

The relationship between annual changes in wages and the unemployment rate
is in accord with aggregate supply and demand analysis. When the unemployment
rate falls to 5%, the economy is likely to produce its potential level of real output.
Increases in aggregate demand at that point are likely to overheat the economy,
thereby causing rapid inflation and rapid increases in money wages over the year.
On the other hand, when there is slack in the economy and unemployment rates

[1]A.W. Phillips, "The Relationship Between the Unemployment Rate and the Rate of Change in Money Wage
Rates in the United Kingdom, 1861-1957," *Economics*, 25, November 1958, pp. 283-299.

are low, increases in aggregate demand result in more output and increased employment with little upward pressure on wages and prices. The Phillips curve is therefore consistent with a model of an economy in which aggregate demand fluctuates while the aggregate supply curve is fairly stable.

There was great interest in Phillips's work in the United States soon after he published his results. This is because it tended to support a widely held hypothesis among economists at that time that shifts in aggregate demand were mainly responsible for changes in equilibrium real GNP and the price level.

Economists were quick to adapt Phillips's work to U.S. data. However, they made one change: Instead of plotting the annual rate of change in money wages on the vertical axis, they plotted the annual rate of increase in the price level, which measures inflation. A curve drawn through the points corresponding to data for the United States for the 1960s seemed to fit very well. The graph shown in Box 2 appeared to confirm that there was indeed a negative historical relationship between inflation and unemployment in the United States. The curve showing the hypothesized inverse relationship between unemployment and inflation is called a **Phillips curve** in honor of A.W. Phillips.

Phillips curve:
A curve showing the hypothesized inverse relationship between annual unemployment and annual inflation in a nation.

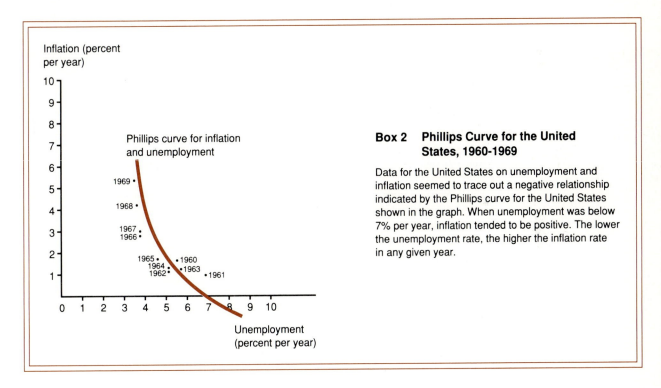

Box 2   Phillips Curve for the United States, 1960-1969

Data for the United States on unemployment and inflation seemed to trace out a negative relationship indicated by the Phillips curve for the United States shown in the graph. When unemployment was below 7% per year, inflation tended to be positive. The lower the unemployment rate, the higher the inflation rate in any given year.

Using the Phillips Curve

In the 1960s and early 1970s economists believed that the Phillips curve accurately represented the tradeoff between unemployment and inflation. It was taken for granted that unemployment could be reduced at the expense of higher inflation. Policymakers therefore believed that recessionary GNP gaps could easily be eliminated with expansionary fiscal or monetary policies. In the short run real GNP would quickly increase, and in the long run the price level would increase as the increase in aggregate demand resulted in an inflationary process.

In fact, these tradeoffs did seem to be confirmed by the data for the 1960s, as you can see by the good fit for these years in Box 2. However, when the turbulent 1970s approached, something seemed to go wrong with the standard Phillips curve that had held up so well as a policy tool in the 1960s.

Supply-Side Shocks and the Phillips Curve for the 1970s

Remember that the idea underlying the Phillips curve is that short-run fluctuations in aggregate demand are mainly responsible for changes in macroeconomic equilibrium. The theory behind the curve assumes that the short-run aggregate supply curve for the economy tends to shift outward at a regular and predictable pace. The theory also neglects the role played by inflationary expectations.

The 1970s were characterized by a series of supply-side shocks such as the unexpected increase in the price of petroleum products in 1973. There was also a series of crop failures in the early 1970s that pushed agricultural prices upward. These shocks sharply increased the price level and contributed to a period of stagflation.

In the 1970s, at least in the short run, the aggregate supply curve shifted *inward* more than the aggregate demand curve shifted *outward!* When this happens in a given year, you can expect the price level to rise and real GNP to fall. This scenario is shown in Box 3. Naturally, with a growing labor force, a fall in equilibrium real GNP means jobs become scarcer relative to the number of job seekers. This means unemployment increases while the price level also goes up! This is the case of stagflation that dominated the U.S. economy in the 1970s. Steady decreases in aggregate supply swamped the effects of increasing aggregate demand, and an increase in inflation was accompanied by *increased* rather than decreased unemployment.

Although this is exactly the opposite of what the Phillips curve suggests, it's just what happened during the 1970s! For example, between 1978 and 1980 the unem-

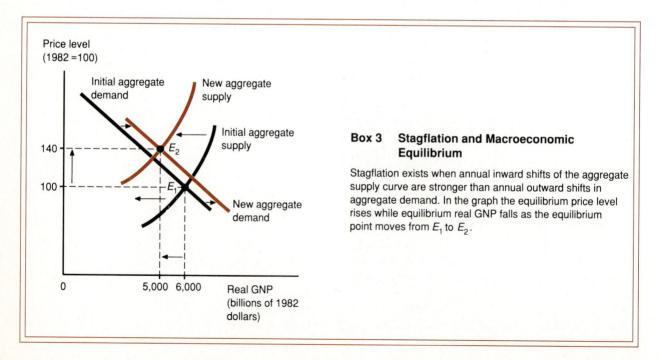

Box 3   Stagflation and Macroeconomic Equilibrium

Stagflation exists when annual inward shifts of the aggregate supply curve are stronger than annual outward shifts in aggregate demand. In the graph the equilibrium price level rises while equilibrium real GNP falls as the equilibrium point moves from E_1 to E_2.

ployment rate in the United States increased sharply from a bit less than 6% of the work force to over 7%. At the same time, the rate of inflation increased from slightly more than 8% per year to *over 13% per year.*

The graph in Box 4 plots points corresponding to U.S. annual inflation and annual unemployment from 1970 to 1980. Compare the pattern traced by the points in Box 4 with that shown in Box 2. The points don't trace out a clearly distinguishable pattern through which a neat Phillips curve can be drawn. Instead they are dispersed widely on the graph. For data after 1973 there are many cases of jumps in *both* inflation and unemployment in the same year. For example, both inflation and unemployment increased between 1973 and 1974. Although inflation declined between 1975 and 1976, there was only a slight decrease in unemployment that year. Then between 1979 and 1980 unemployment and inflation shot up together again.

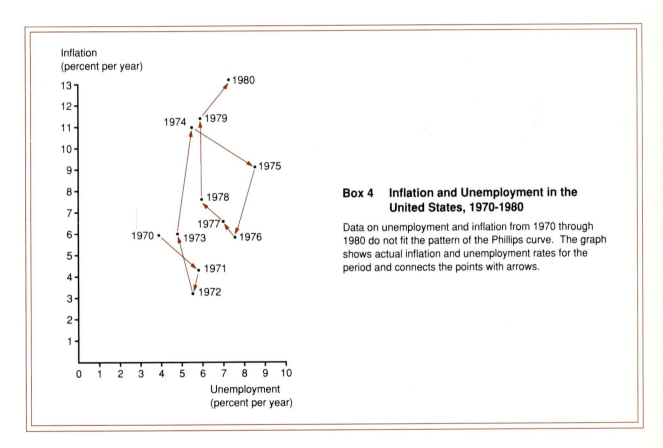

Box 4   Inflation and Unemployment in the United States, 1970-1980

Data on unemployment and inflation from 1970 through 1980 do not fit the pattern of the Phillips curve. The graph shows actual inflation and unemployment rates for the period and connects the points with arrows.

The Phillips Curve in the 1980s: Has the Tradeoff Between Unemployment and Inflation Returned?

Between 1980 and 1982 a familiar pattern reasserted itself as a recession hit. The unemployment rate started to increase but inflation dropped. In fact, there was a dramatic decline in the rate of inflation from 13.5% in 1980 to 6.1% in 1982, which was a recession year. However, the unemployment rate increased to about 10% in 1982 as a result of the contractionary monetary policy that raised interest rates. In the mid-1980s inflation remained fairly low at between 3% and 4% per year, but unemployment, which fell below 8% in 1983, remained between 7% and 8% per year. Then by the end of 1987 the unemployment rate fell below 6% but the rate of inflation inched up to the range of 4% per year.

Disinflation:

A sharp reduction in the annual rate of inflation.

The process of **disinflation** is one of a sharp reduction in the annual rate of inflation. When a process of disinflation occurs, the price level continues to rise but its rate of increase is sharply reduced. Disinflation was successfully achieved between 1980 and 1982 when the annual inflation rate fell from over 13% to a mere 4%. However, the policies that were successful in achieving disinflation also increased unemployment. Apparently the relatively high unemployment rate was one of the consequences of policies that achieved a relatively low inflation rate in the mid-1980s.

The graph in Box 5 shows the relationship between inflation and unemployment since 1980. Between 1980 and 1983 the familiar pattern of the original Phillips curve appears to be traced out as the process of disinflation increased unemployment substantially. From 1984 to 1986 inflation was reduced, but there was also a reduction in the unemployment rate.

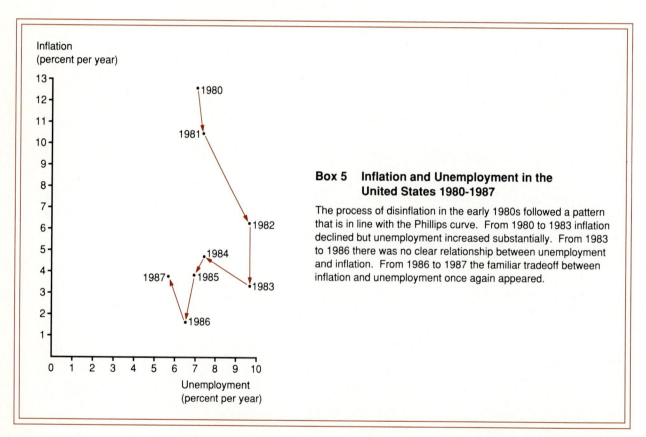

Box 5   Inflation and Unemployment in the United States 1980-1987

The process of disinflation in the early 1980s followed a pattern that is in line with the Phillips curve. From 1980 to 1983 inflation declined but unemployment increased substantially. From 1983 to 1986 there was no clear relationship between unemployment and inflation. From 1986 to 1987 the familiar tradeoff between inflation and unemployment once again appeared.

Between 1986 and 1987 the apparent tradeoff between unemployment and inflation reappeared. As the economy approached full employment in the late 1980s, inflation began to heat up as unemployment declined. This led many economists to believe that fluctuations in aggregate demand were once again dominating fluctuations in aggregate supply and that the Phillips curve tradeoff between unemployment and inflation once more would be a factor in the choice of stabilization policies.

1   What does the Phillips curve show?

2   What is the underlying macroeconomic theory that explains the shape of the Phillips curve?

3   Do the data for inflation and unemployment in the United States during the 1970s trace out the relationship implied by the Phillips curve?

The Theory of Rational Expectations and the Tradeoff Between Inflation and Unemployment

No one has a crystal ball that will accurately foresee the future. For this reason, many economic decisions must be made on the basis of some guess or expectation about what the future will hold. In considering macroeconomic equilibrium and the trade-off between inflation and unemployment, some economists have formulated theories that give heavy weight to the role of expectations in economic decisions. These theories are quite controversial, and many economists downplay the influence of expectations on decisions and macroeconomic equilibrium. In this section we examine how expectations about the future might be formed and the possible effects of changing expectations on aggregate supply and inflation. We also examine how shifts in expectations can cause shifts of the Phillips curve and therefore in the tradeoff between unemployment and inflation.

How Are Expectations Formed?

How are expectations formed about prices and future policies? In forming expectations, people use the information available to them along with some notion about the functioning of the sector of the economy in which they operate. This means they use past data on prices and also consider likely changes in the pattern of prices. One type of expectation formation is called *adaptive* expectations. When people form their expectations adaptively, they look at past values of the economic variable they are trying to forecast. On the basis of this past information they make educated guesses about the future behavior of the variable. If these guesses prove incorrect, people will learn from their mistakes and use the error to help make a better forecast next time. For example, suppose you want to forecast next year's price level. If you form your expectations adaptively, you will collect data on recent price levels and use these to make an educated guess. If you find that the current price level is lower than the one you expected, you might also lower your expectation of the future price level. If the price level is higher than you expected, you might raise your estimate of the future price level. Each time you might adjust your expectations according to the error of your previous forecast. Note, however, that because it takes time for you to recognize your mistakes, adaptive expectations imply a relatively sluggish adjustment of expectations when there is a change in the course of economic variables like the price level. It is quite likely that for a time you will systematically under- or overpredict the price level.

Some economists argue that the process by which expectations are formed is more complex than is suggested by the idea of adaptive expectations. These economists argue that it is rational for people to use *all* available information to help predict the future course of an economic variable—not just past behavior of that variable. Incorrect forecasts can prove costly, so it pays to minimize the size of possible error by utilizing any relevant economic models and data. Because it is "rational" for people making economic forecasts to use all relevant data available to them at costs they think reasonable, expectations formed in this manner are called *rational expectations*. More formally, **rational expectations** are the use by individuals of all available information, including any relevant economic models, in their forecasts of economic variables.

Rational expectations:
The use by individuals of all available information, including any relevant economic models, in their forecasts of economic variables.

To illustrate the difference between adaptive and rational expectations, suppose you are about to lend money to a friend for a year and you need to estimate next year's inflation rate so that you can charge an appropriate nominal rate of interest. If you form expectations adaptively, you will look at past rates of inflation, putting more emphasis on the recent past. For example, if the inflation rate has been 5% per year for the past 4 years, *adaptive expectations* will lead you to forecast an inflation rate of 5%. In contrast, if you form your expectations *rationally,* you will examine potential changes in Fed policy, the prospective federal budget deficit or surplus, the possibility of a supply-side shock, and any other relevant economic information. In addition, you will use all of this information in a simple model, like the type presented in previous chapters, to generate an inflation forecast. By using all of this information, you will quite likely generate a better forecast, that is, one that is subject to smaller error.

This is not to say that you must have a Ph.D. in economics or statistics to form rational expectations. It simply means you have enough experience to understand the factors influencing the prices of the goods or services you buy or sell. You may have had some contact with business managers or farmers who plan their activities by guessing what future prices will be. These people, although they may lack formal education, are often quite sophisticated in understanding the operation of the markets in which they sell their goods. They are often well aware of the fact that interest rates and government policies affecting interest rates will influence their profit opportunities.

Forecasting the future of the economy is a common activity of economists. However, the forecasts are not always correct. You might read *The Wall Street Journal* or *Time* magazine to follow economists' projections of the future. Every major daily newspaper has a business section in which information is published about possible changes in real GNP and prices. You sort out all the information available to you and form your own expectations.

Large corporations are more sophisticated in their information gathering. These firms may have their own economists and statisticians or may hire consultants to help them predict the future. They may use sophisticated economic forecasting models or simulation studies. Neither you nor the big corporation will necessarily make the correct forecast. The theory of rational expectations argues that expectations are based on some underlying notion, right or wrong, about the way the economy functions. The theory also assumes that people revise their expectations when new information becomes available.

The theory of rational expectations does not imply that people always perfectly anticipate the future. Sometimes their predictions about the levels of economic variables will prove correct, and sometimes the predictions will prove incorrect. But since rationally formed expectations exploit all available information and use all relevant economic models, forecasts of economic variables using such expectations will not be systematically high or low. Put another way, people's best guesses about the future course of important economic variables will vary from the actual path of such variables in a random manner.

How Changes in Rational Expectations Can Affect the Aggregate Supply Curve

Expectations of future inflation are important because they exert a strong influence on the nominal wage level at the beginning of the year. Changes in expectations can shift labor supply, and this in turn can affect equilibrium nominal wages in labor markets. For example, if workers expect inflation to rise, all other things being equal, labor supply will decrease, thereby increasing equilibrium nominal wages for the year. The resulting increase in unit labor costs will shift the economy's aggregate supply curve inward, putting upward pressure on the price level and downward pressure on real GNP. In this way changes in expectations can affect macroeconomic equilibrium.

We can easily show the implications of the theory of rational expectations for aggregate supply and macroeconomic equilibrium. Suppose the AFL-CIO wants to forecast next year's inflation rate so it can bargain for a new contract wage. Rationally formed expectations will not just look at past inflation rates. Rather they will be based on all available information and any relevant economic models. Suppose the AFL-CIO's staff economists project that a change in either fiscal or monetary policy will increase aggregate demand during the year. If labor unions anticipate that the increased aggregate demand will cause inflation to heat up, they will hold out for higher increases in nominal wages during the year to prevent their real wages from declining. When a policy to increase aggregate demand causes rational expectations to change in this way, the increase in aggregate demand is accompanied by a decrease in aggregate supply as nominal wages increase. This effect is illustrated in Box 6. As the aggregate demand curve shifts outward and rational expectation of

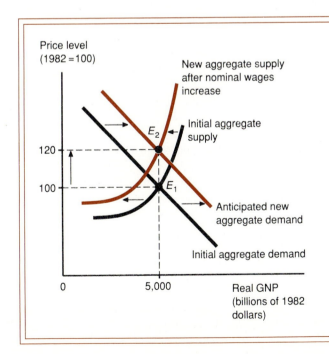

Box 6   Impact of Changes in Expectations on Macroeconomic Equilibrium

An anticipated increase in aggregate demand will decrease aggregate supply if it increases expectations of inflation. As expectations of inflation are revised, the labor supply shifts, resulting in an increase in nominal wages. The increase in nominal wages decreases aggregate supply. The theory of rational expectations hypothesizes that when changes in aggregate demand are anticipated, a change in aggregate demand will change the equilibrium price level but have no effect on equilibrium real GNP.

Economic Thinkers

ROBERT LUCAS

Although he was not the original author, Robert Lucas is generally credited with introducing the theory of rational expectations to macroeconomic thought. Another economist, John Muth, developed the concept in the early 1960s to analyze commodities markets. Lucas

took the idea and adapted it for use with the whole of macroeconomics, a revolutionary breakthrough that completely alters how economists model people's expectations of future events.

Lucas uses rational expectations to show that the proper role for government policy is not the active interventionism called for by Keynesians to counteract the business cycle. He shows that people can anticipate these actions, given their knowledge of policy, past experience, and expectations about the future. When people act on this anticipation, the effects of government policy are nullified. Lucas concludes that government policy should follow strict guidelines since discretionary policy has no effect.

Needless to say, these ideas raised controversy, and Lucas was initially considered to be on the fringe of economic thought. However, as more economists

have introduced rational expectations theory into their analysis, the method has become generally accepted, even if Lucas's conclusions have not.

Lucas earned his Ph.D. in economics in 1964 from the University of Chicago. There he received training in Keynesian analysis. By the late 1960s Keynesian economists were struggling to develop policies to reduce unemployment, and Lucas was disillusioned with their view of the economy. He wrote *Econometric Testing of the Natural Rate Hypothesis,* which was published in 1972 and is considered a landmark piece, and he has written numerous other articles using rational expectations analysis since that time. The work attracted many followers because of the high rates of inflation and unemployment that were occurring simultaneously at that time, for which Keynesian analysis offered no real solution.

inflation increases, the aggregate supply curve shifts inward because nominal wages and other input prices will rise in anticipation of the increased inflation. As a consequence, the increase in aggregate demand and resulting decrease in aggregate supply set up an inflationary process that causes the price level to rise, *but there is no change in equilibrium real GNP.* This is because it's necessary for product prices to rise more rapidly than input prices so that producers will have the incentive (which is increased profit) to produce more. When nominal wages and other input prices increase along with output prices, producers cannot profit by supplying more output.

The conclusion of the theory of rational expectations is that policies that shift the aggregate demand curve are unlikely to have much effect on real GNP and therefore on the unemployment rate if they also result in widespread changes in rational expectations of inflation. Instead policies that shift aggregate demand will also shift aggregate supply. As shown in Box 6, this implies that the price level will rise but that there will be no change in equilibrium real GNP.

Many economists believe that expectations of inflation are formed *adaptively* and as a result are quite sluggish and don't change rapidly when economic policies change. The critics of the theory of rational expectations argue that it assumes that workers and managers are much better informed than they actually are about changes in policy and the way the economy operates. Therefore many economists are skeptical of the controversial theory, which argues that stabilization policies are anticipated in a way that prevents them from changing real GNP.

The Top-Secret Work of the Bureau of Economic Analysis: How Quarterly GNP Growth Rate Data Influence Rational Expectations

Although the economists in the Bureau of Economic Analysis of the U.S. Department of Commerce don't carry badges or wear concealed firearms, the nature of their work requires that they be sworn to secrecy. These economists compile the data on quarterly estimates of GNP and related measures of economic performance that are issued as part of the National Income and Product Accounts. The data are important inputs into the formation of expectations regarding the future course of the economy and the establishment of policies designed to stabilize the economy. Advance knowledge of the report could allow a sophisticated investor to engage in a number of transactions that would guarantee immense profits almost overnight!

The preliminary GNP figures are usually made public 15 working days after the end of each calendar quarter. The estimates of GNP are arrived at by two independent teams of economists employed by the Bureau of Economic Analysis. These economists are literally locked up as a security precaution as they engage in the work necessary to produce the numbers. After the preliminary estimates have been made, they are delivered to the chairman of the President's Council of Economic Advisers and then to the President. The numbers are released to the press on the following day.*

The security precautions are designed to prevent leaks of the numbers before they are officially released to the public. In June of 1985, estimates were leaked to stock and commodity traders who were using the estimates to make decisions on trading. After an investigation, one Bureau staff member was fired for using the GNP data to make profits in stock and commodity trading.

The item of data that apparently is most useful to traders is the growth rate of GNP for the quarter. Growth is an important input into formation of rational expectations of inflation. When traders see stronger growth in real GNP than has been anticipated, they expect inflation to heat up. They then reason that the higher inflation will cause interest rates to rise, which will cause bond prices to fall. In this case knowledge of the official GNP estimates before they are officially announced would allow a sophisticated trader to sell bonds that he owns prior to the official release of the GNP growth rate for the quarter. The trader would then be able to buy the bonds back at a lower price the day the GNP statistics are released and the bond market dives as expectations of higher interest rates are newly formulated. The trader could also agree to sell bonds at a certain price on the day the statistics are released. The trader would then make a profit by buying the bonds at a low price on the day the statistics are issued and turning around to sell them at the agreed-upon higher price. Similarly, stock market prices tend to fall when interest rates are expected to rise. Investors with prior knowledge of GNP growth rates could make handsome profits by anticipating the plunge in stock prices after issuance of the GNP statistics.

As you can see, there are compelling reasons for the economists who develop quarterly GNP estimates to be locked up and sworn to secrecy!

Although the implications of the theory of rational expectations are very controversial and are the subject of much debate in professional economic circles, the ideas advanced by "rational expectations" economists have profoundly influenced both the research agenda of many economists and the public policy debate.

*See Timothy Tregarthen, "Leaks at the Bureau of Economic Analysis," *The Margin*, 2,1, January 1987, pp. 12-13.

One implication of the theory of rational expectations is that the economy has a very good self-correction mechanism that operates through shifts in aggregate supply generated by changes in rational expectations about inflation. This implies that once full employment is attained, any deviations from full employment will set up a process that will soon return the economy to equilibrium at potential real GNP. According to the theory of rational expectations, deviations from full employment will be random and temporary. For example, if there is an inflationary GNP gap, the theory holds that the resulting inflation will cause rational expectations to set up a process that will quickly decrease aggregate supply as nominal wages increase. This will result in downward pressure on real GNP and upward pressure on the price level until full employment is restored. Similarly, if there is a recessionary GNP gap, then there will be rapid downward pressure on the price level. This will result in downward revisions in rational expectations of inflation that will increase aggregate supply, which will swiftly move the economy back to full employment. The implications of the theory of rational expectations are exactly the same as those of the classical model of macroeconomic equilibrium we first discussed in the chapter on the forces of aggregate supply and demand. Hence adherents of the theory of rational expectations are often called *new classical economists.* University of Chicago economist Robert Lucas is generally credited with adapting the theory of rational expectations to macroeconomic thought (see Economic Thinkers box).

Inflationary Expectations and the Phillips Curve

The Phillips curve is based in part on the assumption that people don't formulate expectations about inflation that influence their behavior. But as we've just seen, inflationary expectations in certain cases can be an important influence on economic decisions and aggregate supply. If economic fluctuations are in fact attributable in part to shifts in aggregate supply caused by changes in rational expectations, then a change in inflationary expectations can shift the entire Phillips curve.

Suppose the Phillips curve would normally intersect the horizontal axis at the level of unemployment corresponding to the natural rate of unemployment when by and large no one expects inflation to be at a greater rate than it was in the previous year. If unemployment were less than its natural rate, the economy would be overheated, and as a result, there would be upward pressure on the price level that would cause inflation. If unemployment exceeded the natural rate, there would be downward pressure on the price level. In the graph in Box 7, the initial Phillips curve intersects the horizontal axis at a level of unemployment corresponding to 6%. This means there would be inflation if the economy achieved less than the natural rate of unemployment. However, there would be deflation, meaning a drop in the price level, if the actual unemployment rate exceeded the natural unemployment rate. A Phillips curve that intersects the horizontal axis at the natural rate of unemployment represents the curve for an economy in which inflationary expectations are stable and zero inflation is expected at full employment.

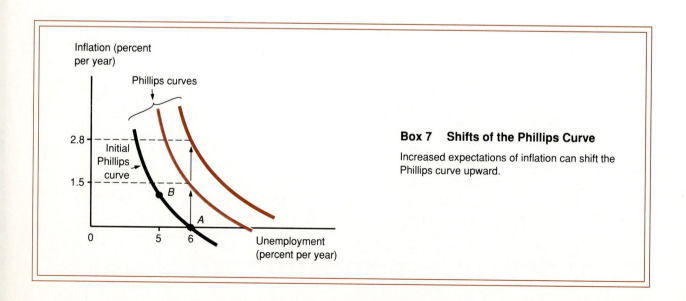

Box 7   Shifts of the Phillips Curve

Increased expectations of inflation can shift the
Phillips curve upward.

Now suppose that expectations of future inflation are revised upward and that as a result the aggregate supply curve for the economy shifts to the left. When this occurs, achievement of the natural rate of unemployment is unlikely to be associated with zero inflation. Even if the economy does achieve full employment, inflation will exist as a result of the precautions workers and other input suppliers take in negotiating contracts to increase wages and other input prices. As input prices rise, so do output prices! In effect, according to this theory of macroeconomic equilibrium and inflation, the *anticipation* of inflation actually *causes* inflation. As a result of increased inflationary expectations, the Phillips curve shifts upward, as shown in Box 7.

The idea of a shifting Phillips curve can explain how attempts to reduce the unemployment rate below the natural rate of unemployment can themselves initiate a process of cost-push inflation. The **accelerationist hypothesis** argues that attempts by policymakers to reduce unemployment below the natural rate can succeed only in the short run. The hypothesis maintains that aggregate demand policies that seek to reduce unemployment will have little effect on unemployment in the long run but will contribute to increased inflation. For example, suppose the natural rate of unemployment is 6% and policymakers mistakenly believe it is only 5%. As a result they pursue monetary or fiscal policies whose goal is to reduce the unemployment rate to 5%. In doing so they move along the Phillips curve that intersects the horizontal axis at 6% unemployment in Box 7 from point *A* to point *B*. If they do succeed in reducing unemployment to 5%, they will open up an inflationary gap as the economy overheats. Workers will find that inflation is greater than expected, and their real wages will decline. According to the accelerationist hypothesis, they subsequently will negotiate higher nominal wages in the following year. The consequent inward shifts in aggregate supply set up a process that results in inflation even if the economy attains full employment. The cost-push inflation induced by inward shifts of the aggregate supply curve moves the Phillips curve upward. Eventually the economy will eliminate the inflationary gap as real GNP declines and the price level rises, but the upward shift of the Phillips curve means that a higher rate of inflation will be associated with the full-employment level of real GNP.

It follows that when inflation is expected to increase, the Phillips curve will shift upward. A reduction in inflationary expectations shifts the curve downward. According to the theory of rational expectations, the culprit in shifting the Phillips curve is shifts in aggregate supply. As aggregate supply shifts and affects the price level, people revise their expectations of inflation and negotiate contracts for input services at the beginning of the year based in part on these revised expectations.

The implication of this analysis is that when inflationary expectations increase, the rate of inflation associated with any given rate of unemployment is higher. Policies that increase inflationary expectations can therefore aggravate the tradeoff between inflation and unemployment.

Accelerationist hypothesis: Argues that attempts by policymakers to reduce the unemployment rate below the natural rate can succeed only in the short run.

Concept Check

1   How are rational expectations formed, and why are they not always accurate?

2   How can expectations of inflation during the year by workers and other input suppliers shift the Phillips curve for the economy?

3   How can rational expectations of the effects of stabilization policies prevent those policies from achieving their goals?

Issues and Options in Stabilization Policy

Diagnosing the Causes of Cyclical Fluctuations in the Economy: Demand-Side Management

Perhaps the biggest problem faced by policymakers is to distinguish supply-side shocks from demand-side shocks. For example, suppose the natural rate of unemployment increases because of the influx of a large number of younger workers into the labor force. Because younger workers tend to quit jobs more often than older workers, this is likely to increase the natural rate of unemployment. Policymakers might confuse this with an increase in unemployment caused by a decline in aggregate demand. If they pursue expansionary policies to reduce unemployment, they will be shooting for an impossible goal. They might achieve temporary reductions in unemployment. However, in the long run the price level and inflationary expectations are likely to increase sharply as the economy eventually returns to the higher natural rate of unemployment. Also, with respect to demand-side shocks to the economy, it's clear that shifts in aggregate demand don't follow easily predicted patterns. The swings of the business cycle are difficult to forecast.

Among the factors that can cause a change in aggregate demand are:

1. *A change in the demand for investment goods.* Business optimism is fickle. The willingness of business managers to spend on new equipment and structures and to accumulate inventories depends on their forecasts of the future. If optimism about the future declines, investment demand falls. Other things being equal, the decline in investment demand decreases aggregate demand and can plunge the economy into a recession. Similarly, an upswing in business optimism increases business investment demand. This increases aggregate demand and serves to put upward pressure on the price level if the economy is at full employment.

2. *A change in consumer demand.* The willingness of consumers to spend affects aggregate demand. An increase in saving or in repayment of debt will decrease aggregate demand. This will tend to decrease real GNP and the price level in the short run. The opposite is true for a decrease in saving or an increase in borrowing to finance consumer expenditures, both of which will stimulate the economy.

3. *A change in the demand for money.* A shift in the desire to hold money balances will affect both spending and interest rates. For example, an innovation such as check writing on savings accounts is likely to decrease the demand for money and thus decrease interest rates. The lower interest rates will stimulate the economy. Similarly, an increase in the demand for money will be a contractionary influence on the economy. This is because an increase in money demand will tend to raise interest rates in the short run and thereby decrease spending.

Development of an active countercyclical stabilization policy requires predicting shifts in consumer demand, investment demand, and money demand. Government spending, tax reductions, or changes in the money supply can be used to offset the changes in private demand so as to minimize the amount of time for which equilibrium GNP differs from potential GNP. *The first problem of stabilization policy is therefore to predict shifts in aggregate demand.*

To deal with this problem, policymakers typically use economic indicators that show where the economy is headed. The U.S. Department of Commerce publishes an index of leading indicators that is used to gauge the future state of aggregate demand (see the Principles in Practice box in the chapter on the forces of aggregate supply and demand). Included in the index are the number of housing starts, the length of the workweek, stock prices, the money supply, changes in business inventories, new orders for goods, materials, and investment, and other variables. The theory is that these variables will begin to turn down before real GNP actually falls. However, the index is not perfect. It typically declines before a recession, but sometimes it declines and no recession follows. Economic forecasting remains an art rather than a science. Thus it's difficult to solve the first problem to formulate a countercyclical stabilization policy.

The second problem is to quickly implement policies that counteract the shift in private demand. This problem is particularly serious for implementation of fiscal policy. Government spending and taxes are political issues. Except for the automatic stabilizers, changes in government purchases and net taxes must come through the budgetary process. That process is a long one of presidential submission, congressional debate, and approval. It often takes bureaucrats time to actually spend money that has been appropriated. Appropriated funds for particular projects, such as military procurement, frequently are not spent until the next fiscal year. These lags often result in policies that accomplish too much too late.

There are also lags in monetary policy, even though monetary policy is generally more flexible than fiscal policy. It takes time to collect data and analyze its implications. When the Fed finally does decide on a countercyclical policy, it takes time for a change in the money supply to change the behavior of consumers and investors.

A third problem is to predict the impact of changes in money supply or the government deficit on real GNP and the price level. As you've seen in this chapter, changes in aggregate demand caused by economic policies may cause changes in rationally formed expectations of inflation. When this occurs, policies that affect aggregate demand through shifts in money supply, government purchases, or net taxes can also shift aggregate supply. This makes it more difficult to predict the ultimate effect of a change in economic policy on real GNP and the price level.

The reaction to stabilization policies is likely to differ depending on whether the policies are anticipated or unanticipated. The extent to which people plan for the future also influences the effectiveness of fiscal policy. For example, the expansionary effect of increases in budget deficits can be offset when people increase their saving to pay the higher future taxes implied by the deficit.

The Stabilization Policy Debate

Critics of stabilization policies argue that although the intentions of such policies are good, the policymakers often make mistakes that end up destabilizing the economy. Among the harshest critics of stabilization policies is Nobel Prize–winning economist Milton Friedman.[2]

Friedman argues that policy mistakes in the past have contributed to destabilizing the economy. For example, he points out that during the 1930s the Great Depression was made more severe than necessary by bad policies. In the early 1930s the Fed actually decreased the money supply. This contractionary policy contributed to

[2]Milton Friedman, *A Program for Monetary Stability,* New York: Fordham University Press, 1960.

lower prices and decreased aggregate demand at a time when the economy needed stimulation of aggregate demand. In the late 1930s the Fed increased reserve requirements for banks, which further contracted an economy that needed to expand (see Principles in Practice and Economic Thinkers boxes in the chapter on stabilizing the economy through monetary policy).

Friedman argues that the solution to imperfect stabilization policies is a preannounced government **policy rule** that will inform the public of future economic stabilization policies. For example, Friedman recommends that the money supply be increased at a steady rate of, say, 3% to 5% per year. Friedman's plan is based on his belief that much of the cyclical instability in the economy is caused by sharp swings in the money supply.

The goal of strict policy rules is to incorporate stable expectations of government responses to shocks in the economy into the choices of businesses, consumers, and investors.

An established policy rule for dealing with economic fluctuations would be incorporated in the underlying ideas about how the economy works that people use in formulating their expectations. Anticipated policies would therefore affect current decisions. Under strict policy rules the impact of government policy on private choices would be more predictable than under erratic policy decisions.

Proponents of flexible stabilization policies counter Friedman by arguing that discretion in adjusting policies, although admittedly not a perfect solution, has stabilized the economy. As evidence Friedman's opponents point out that, because of increased federal government activity to stabilize the economy, economic fluctuations in the Untied States have been much less severe since the end of World War II than during the prior period.

Incomes Policies and Wage-Price Guidelines and Controls

If there were a museum of stabilization policies, it would display some interesting artifacts. One probable item in the collection would be the "WIN" button. During the period of rapid inflation in the mid-1970s, President Gerald Ford proposed that Americans wear such a button, whose acronym stood for "Whip Inflation Now." The button didn't catch on, nor was inflation easily whipped at that time.

In addition to monetary and fiscal policy, a number of policies used in recent years have sought to deal with the problem of a wage-price spiral, in which the economy occasionally finds itself. Some of these policies, like President Ford's "WIN" idea, have appealed to patriotism or used psychological techniques to discourage business firms from raising prices. **Incomes policies** are policies that seek to curb inflation by directly influencing both prices and wages without reducing aggregate demand through the use of monetary or fiscal policy. Such policies were used in the United States in the 1960s and early 1970s but had fallen into disuse by the late 1970s.

One of the simplest types of incomes policies is called *jawboning*. This term in our museum was used by President Kennedy in the early 1960s and involves direct political pressure by the President on large corporations to keep prices from rising. In 1962 President Kennedy jawboned the steel industry into rescinding an already announced price increase. The underlying assumption of jawboning is that in the United States, prices are controlled by large corporations rather than influenced by broad forces of supply and demand. In many cases the political view is that price increases are not warranted as a result of increases in unit costs of production. In

Policy rule:
A preannounced government rule that will inform the public of future economic stabilization policies.

Incomes policies:
Policies that seek to curb inflation by directly influencing both prices and wages without reducing aggregate demand through the use of monetary or fiscal policy.

cases where jawboning prevents prices from rising when unit costs of production are in fact increasing, its effect will be to cause firms to fail and increase the rate of unemployment. Under such circumstances jawboning is likely to be ignored. The historical assessment of jawboning as a means of controlling inflation and reducing inflationary expectations is that over the long run it was probably ineffective.

A more sophisticated policy designed to deal with an economy locked into a wage-price spiral and with expectations of high and continued inflation is the use of government-established guidelines for wage and price increases. **Wage-price guidelines** are standards established by government authorities that seek to keep wage and price increases within certain bounds over a period. Wage-price guidelines were used by both the Kennedy and Johnson Administrations during periods when the U.S. economy was overheated. The guidelines sought to control inflation by limiting wage increases to the rate of increase of worker productivity plus an additional percentage. For example, if inflation was to be kept in the range of 3% annually and worker productivity increased by 2% during the year on average, the guidelines would sanction a 5% increase in wages for the year. The portion of the wage increase that accounted for the increase in productivity would not contribute to inflation because it would be balanced by an increase in the supply of goods. A 5% wage increase therefore would be believed to keep inflation within the range of 3%.

Wage-price guidelines: Standards established by government authorities that seek to keep wage and price increases within certain bounds over a period.

The guidelines were also applied to business firms and were intended to limit price increases to the percentage increase in labor costs. However, the wage-price guidelines as used in the United States had no mechanism for enforcement and were quite unpopular with unions and businesses that believed their well-being was adversely affected by the rules.

The most extreme form of an incomes policy is the use of wage-price controls and freezes. **Wage-price controls** are rules established by government authorities that result in control of prices, wages, and their rate of increase. Wage-price controls are like the price ceilings we discussed in Chapter 5. These rules substitute government controls for the laws of supply and demand. As you might expect, wage-price controls that are established below equilibrium levels will result in shortages in markets (see Chapter 5). For this reason such controls have been used rarely, mainly during periods of war. For example, wage-price controls were in effect in the United States during much of World War II and during the Korean War. In wartime these controls generally have been effective in keeping inflation down. However, as is the case with all effective price ceilings, they also result in shortages of goods and services in markets. The scarce items are usually rationed by various techniques.

Wage-price controls: Rules established by government authorities that result in control of prices, wages, and their rate of increase.

Wage-price controls were also used in the United States under the Nixon Administration during the period 1971-1974. The controls were introduced by President Nixon when the nation was in the throes of a wage-price spiral and period of stagflation in the early 1970s. Workers and businesses were believed to have high inflationary expectations during that time, and the controls were viewed as a way of combating such expectations and their effects on aggregate supply.

The Nixon Administration's use of the controls started with a wage-price *freeze* for a 3-month period beginning in August 1971. During that period most businesses were prevented by law from raising prices. Wages were also frozen over that period, as were rents that could be charged to tenants. Then, once the freeze was lifted, price and wage increases were kept in bound by rules and regulations limiting the rate at which they could increase. In cases where the controls were effective, shortages resulted.

There's little doubt that the wage-price controls reduced inflation during the period in which they were in effect. However, when they were removed in 1974, inflation heated up once again to double-digit levels as markets readjusted to eliminate shortages. At the same time the economy was battered by an unfavorable supply-side shock in the form of the OPEC oil embargo. As you can see, wage-price controls result in shortages and can also increase the variability of inflation. Remember from our analysis of inflation in the chapter entitled "Inflation and Its Consequences" that erratic inflation causes more distortion in the economy than does steady, predictable inflation. Because they result in shortages and contribute to erratic inflation, wage-price controls are used only rarely in peacetime in nations where inflation runs at moderate rates.

Summary

1. The Phillips curve shows a hypothesized inverse relationship between annual unemployment and annual inflation in a nation. The Phillips curve is based on the assumption that shifts in aggregate demand are mainly responsible for changes in equilibrium real GNP and the price level.
2. When the economy's aggregate supply curve shifts inward, the resulting stagflation causes both unemployment and inflation to increase during the year. The stagflation of the 1970s meant that the data on inflation and unemployment for those years poorly fit the relationship implied by the Phillips curve.
3. The process of disinflation in the United States in the early 1980s showed that the Phillips curve relationship remains relevant. During that period the rate of inflation was reduced at the expense of sharp increases in the rate of unemployment.
4. Expectations of future changes in the economy are important influences on the current decisions of business firms and households.
5. Adaptive expectations are those in which people look at the past performance of the economic variable to be forecast. Under adaptive expectations people who overestimate the rate of inflation in the current year will lower their estimate of the rate of inflation in the following year.
6. Rational expectations differ from adaptive expectations in that they are formed with more information and an idea about the process through which prices are determined in the economy. Although rational expectations are not always correct, they differ from actual magnitudes only by a random amount.
7. A change in rational expectations of future inflation can shift the Phillips curve because it results in a shift of the economy's aggregate supply curve. Expectations of increased inflation will result in decreases in labor supply that will put upward pressure on nominal wages. This will tend to increase the rate of inflation for each possible level of real GNP and unemployment during a given year.
8. Rational expectations of the effects of economic policies that seek to shift aggregate demand can frustrate the goals of those policies by causing simultaneous shifts in aggregate supply.
9. If they are to achieve their objectives, stabilization policies must be based on accurate forecasts of shifts in aggregate demand. Such policies must be quickly implemented to offset destabilizing shifts in aggregate demand.
10. Critics of stabilization policies argue that although the intentions of policymakers are good, they often make mistakes that actually end up destabilizing the economy.

11. A policy rule is a preannounced rule about stabilization actions conducted by the Fed and by the federal government that informs the public of future policies. Such policies would be fully anticipated by the public and could avoid destabilizing shifts in expectations that cause the aggregate supply curve to shift.

12. Incomes policies seek to control inflation by using government guidelines or controls to limit wage and price increases.

Key Terms and Concepts

Phillips curve

Disinflation

Rational expectations

Accelerationist hypothesis

Policy rule

Incomes policies

Wage-price guidelines

Wage-price controls

Problems and Applications

1. The economy is currently operating at 6% unemployment. An increase in aggregate demand is anticipated during the year while the economy's aggregate supply curve is anticipated to be stable. Why is the Phillips curve for such an economy likely to be downward sloping for the year?

2. Under what circumstances does the relationship implied by the Phillips curve suggest that the price level will fall while unemployment increases?

3. Suppose the annual rate of inflation is 15% and the unemployment rate is 4%. Monetary authorities decide to sharply cut back the growth rate of the money supply during the year and possibly even reduce the available money stock. Assuming that the policies of the monetary authorities are not anticipated by the public, show how the resulting process of disinflation will affect the economy. Draw the likely Phillips curve for the economy.

4. Show how an increase in expected inflation by workers who rationally expect a sharp increase in aggregate demand during the year can shift the aggregate supply curve. Explain why the theory of rational expectations implies a self-correction mechanism for the economy similar to that implied by the classical model of macroeconomic equilibrium.

5. How do expectations of future prices affect economic decisions? Think about how your expectations of future changes in the economy affect your own choices. After completing a course in economics, how will you form your own expectations of the future? How do rational expectations differ from adaptive expectations?

6. Why are rational expectations often different from actual outcomes?

7. During the year there are sharp increases in the prices of food and housing as a result of decreases in the supply of agricultural products and lumber. The price increases reduce the real wages of workers. Show how rational expectations of further inflation can shift the Phillips curve for the economy upward.

8. What can shift the Phillips curve for the economy downward?

9. Explain how a wage-price spiral could be started by increases in the money supply even though the economy is not at full employment.

10. Outline some of the difficulties involved in choosing and implementing a successful stabilization policy for the economy. Why do critics of stabilization policies favor a strict policy rule?

Suggested Readings

C.L.F. Attfield, D. Demery, and N.W. Duck, *Rational Expectations in Macroeconomics: An Introduction to Theory and Evidence,* Oxford: Basil Blackwell, 1985. This is an advanced discussion of the theory of rational expectations.

Rudiger Dornbusch and Stanley Fischer, *Macroeconomics,* 4th ed., New York: McGraw-Hill, 1987. Chapter 12 discusses some of the problems of implementing stabilization policies, while Chapter 14 discusses the tradeoff between inflation and unemployment along with expectations.

Robert J. Gordon, *Macroeconomics,* 4th ed., Boston: Little, Brown, 1987. Chapter 12 discusses the modern critique of stabilization policies.

A Forward Look

The growing importance of international trade in the U.S. economy has been emphasized throughout this book. In the following chapter we take an in-depth view of the process of international trade and the advantages and disadvantages of free trade for the economy and its participants.

Career Profile

GREGORY PALLONE

Four years after receiving his bachelor's degree in economics from the University of Michigan at Dearborn, Gregory Pallone is living in Zurich, Switzerland, working in international investment banking for the Swiss Bank Corporation. He's involved with structuring, marketing, and processing debt and equity for American and Canadian corporate and public borrowers who want to raise funds in the Swiss franc market.

Living abroad and working in international banking may sound like a dream job, but Pallone says he got where he is partly by accident and with a lot of hard work. After graduation he got a 2-year apprenticeship position with the Wall Street investment banking firm of Donaldson, Lufkin, and Jenrette. He worked as a corporate financial analyst, doing the financial analysis and computer modeling for offerings of debt and equity, mergers and acquisitions, and leveraged buyouts.

As his apprenticeship's end drew near, he applied to be a Fulbright Scholar at a German university. He planned eventually to attend graduate school in the United States, but he wanted more exposure to international finance and economics before entering an MBA program. Even though he didn't speak the language, he was accepted to four German universities. He was turned down for the Fulbright Scholarship but decided to go abroad anyway, investing some of his savings in an intensive German course to prepare for fall entrance into one of the universities.

The declining U.S. dollar enters the story here. The buying power of Pallone's savings was eroding fast. He decided he could solve his financial problems and get direct exposure to international finance with a position at a German or Swiss international bank. He was eligible for a special 18-month work permit as part of a Swiss-American exchange program and started in his current position in September 1987.

Pallone has always had advanced business study in mind, but when it came to picking an undergraduate major he wanted something with a broader background and more flexibility. He chose economics because he could combine his interest in business with a liberal education. When he returns to the United States in 1989, he will enter an MBA program.

International Economic Issues

International Trade, Productivity, and the Economics of Less Developed Countries

You know that the U.S. economy has become increasingly tied to the rest of the world through international trade in recent years. But if you read the newspapers and watch the nightly news, you also know that there are many pressure groups that seek to protect U.S. businesses from international competition. Who gains and who loses as a result of international trade, and do the gains outweigh the losses? As you read this chapter, you'll see why economists are usually strongly in agreement that there are net mutual gains from international trade. You'll also see how protectionism benefits some at the expense of others.

In this chapter we'll show how the international competitiveness of particular U.S. industries is related to the rate of change in productivity in those industries compared to productivity changes in competing foreign industries. Faster productivity growth in the United States relative to foreign nations can give U.S. firms a competitive edge in international markets by allowing producers to charge lower prices.

International trade contributes to our well-being by allowing an international division of labor and specialized production. International trade not only allows us to obtain products unavailable locally, but also allows net gains by permitting us to purchase some items at lower prices than would otherwise be possible.

Also related to the question of productivity and international trade are some of the unique problems of less developed countries. These nations suffer from low per capita incomes and are relatively less industrialized compared to more developed nations. In recent years the problem of world hunger, which is symptomatic of poverty in less developed nations of Africa, Asia, and other parts of the world, has received considerable attention. The possible cures for the problem of low standards of living in these nations are highlighted in this chapter.

After you understand the basis for and consequences of international trade, we can move on to examine the balance of international trade between the United States and the rest of the world and discuss the international monetary system. These topics, along with financial aspects of international trade, will be covered in the next chapter.

After reading this chapter, you should be able to:

1   Understand the underlying basis for international trade and the gains in well-being possible from free trade with foreign nations.
2   Discuss the principle of comparative advantage and show how productivity changes in specific industries can affect their comparative advantage in international trade.
3   Discuss controversies regarding free trade vs. protection of U.S. industries from foreign competition in light of the basic theory of international trade.
4   Analyze the impact on the economy of tariffs, import quotas, and other trade restrictions.
5   Discuss some of the unique economic problems of less developed countries and the causes of low per capita income and slow economic growth in those nations.

The Basis for International Trade

Nations differ in their endowments of natural resources. For example, the United States is well endowed with timber and coal. However, its climate is poorly suited for the production of coffee, bananas, and coconuts. A basis for trading with other nations exists for the purpose of obtaining goods that are unavailable or too costly to produce domestically. Another basis for international trade lies in the fact that human as well as natural resources vary among nations. For example, the Swiss are noted for their traditional skills in watch-making and producing fine chocolate candies. The Italians have long been known for the high quality of their leather goods.

Early in the book we discussed the advantages of specialization and the division of labor. **Specialization** means that workers in a nation do not produce all the goods and services desired by consumers in that nation. Instead labor and other resources in a nation are used to produce the goods and services for which these resources are best suited. Many Japanese workers specialize in the production of automobiles and electronic goods, while in the United States there are many factories whose employees excel in the production of aircraft. The larger output possible from specialization often results in economies of scale that lower production costs still further. The basis for international trade is firmly rooted in the gains that are possible from specialization as well as the gains that can be obtained from acquiring natural resources that are unavailable locally.

Specialization:
Use of labor and other resources in a nation to produce the goods and services for which those resources are best adapted.

When nations specialize in the production of certain items, output of those items in domestic markets exceeds the amounts demanded at current prices. The firms can then sell the surplus goods in foreign markets. The foreign currency obtained from these export sales can be used to buy the products of other nations. For example, Italy specializes in the production of wine. By doing so, it can gain foreign currency to purchase petroleum products, which it requires as an input in production but lacks in sufficient quantities as a domestically produced resource. Similarly, the United States can specialize in the production of wheat, which it can then export to Italy in exchange for Italian lire that can be used to purchase Italian wines. Firms can also gain foreign currency from offering services to foreigners, such as hotels and tourism. For example, China and the Soviet Union have recently sought to encourage tourism as a means of earning foreign currency to purchase goods offered for sale by Western nations.

We Americans are fortunate in that we live in a nation that is well endowed with both natural resources and a skilled labor force. Our country's vast and diverse productive capacity means we are less dependent on international trade than are other countries for such basic resources as fuel, food, and fiber. Other nations, like Japan and Israel, rely heavily on imports for basic natural resources. Such nations are under pressure to export goods and services to earn the foreign exchange necessary to finance their imports.

International trade is often opposed by groups that seek to insulate themselves from what they regard as unfair foreign competition. Many people argue that foreign competition is unfair because cheap foreign goods are produced with cheap labor and are heavily subsidized by foreign governments that are under pressure to earn dollars from international trade. Although there are long-run mutual gains from trade, in the short run it's clear that particular groups, such as workers with specialized skills or owners of specialized equipment, can be harmed by increased imports.

The Principle of Comparative Advantage

Mutual gains from international trade:
On average, citizens in all trading nations gain from exchanging goods in international markets.

There are **mutual gains from international trade,** which means that on average, citizens in all trading nations gain from exchanging goods in international markets. A simplified example can be used to illustrate the underlying basis for international trade. Suppose two nations both have the capability of producing bananas and wheat. Both nations have the same quantity of natural resources, labor, and capital. The table in Box 1 shows the production possibilities in the two nations when they devote all of their resources to producing either bananas or wheat.

Nation A has the opportunity to produce 20 tons of wheat *or* 20 tons of bananas per year if it specializes in one or the other. Nation B can produce 5 tons of wheat *or* 10 tons of bananas per year by specializing in production of one item or the other. Notice that with the same resources nation A can produce more wheat when it specializes in that good than can nation B when it specializes in wheat production. Similarly, nation A can produce more bananas when it specializes in production of that item than can nation B when it specializes in banana production. With the same resources nation A can therefore produce more than nation B no matter how it specializes.

Absolute advantage:
A nation has an absolute advantage over other nations in the production of an item if it can produce more of the item over a certain period with a given amount of resources than the other nations can.

A nation has an **absolute advantage** over other nations in the production of an item if it can produce more of the item over a certain period with a *given* amount of resources than the other nations can. You can see that nation A has an absolute advantage in the production of wheat over nation B in this example because with

Box 1 Production Possibilities for Two Nations

Nation A (annual output)		Nation B (annual output)	
20 tons of wheat and no bananas		5 tons of wheat and no bananas	
or		or	
20 tons of bananas and no wheat		10 tons of bananas and no wheat	

Opportunity cost	Nation A	Nation B
Each ton of wheat costs	1 ton of bananas	2 tons of bananas
Each ton of bananas costs	1 ton of wheat	0.5 ton of wheat

the same resources nation A can produce more wheat by specializing in wheat production than can nation B. In this example nation A *also* has the absolute advantage in the production of bananas because with the same resources as are available in nation B it can produce more bananas by specializing in banana production than can nation B.

Another way of interpreting nation A's absolute advantage over nation B in both wheat and banana production is to point out that in nation A each unit of either wheat or bananas can be produced with less input than it can be produced in nation B. For example, suppose for simplicity that the only inputs used to produce wheat are land and labor. Suppose both nations A and B have 2,000 labor hours available per year and the same amount of land. When nation A specializes in wheat production it can produce 20 tons per year with its 2,000 labor hours. The *labor cost* per ton will be

$$2{,}000 \text{ labor hours}/20 \text{ tons} = 100 \text{ labor hours per ton of wheat}$$

The labor cost per ton of wheat in nation B when nation B specializes in wheat production will be

$$2{,}000 \text{ labor hours}/5 \text{ tons} = 400 \text{ labor hours per ton of wheat}$$

Given the same quantity of land in both nations, wheat is four times as expensive in terms of labor required per ton in nation B as it is in nation A.

Similarly, just by looking at labor cost you can see that nation A's absolute advantage over nation B in banana production means it can produce bananas with fewer labor hours per ton than can nation B. The labor cost per ton of bananas in nation A would be:

$$2{,}000 \text{ labor hours}/20 \text{ tons} = 100 \text{ labor hours per ton of bananas}$$

In nation B the labor cost per ton of bananas is:

$$2{,}000 \text{ labor hours}/10 \text{ tons} = 200 \text{ labor hours per ton of bananas}$$

Bananas therefore cost twice as much in terms of labor input per ton in nation B compared to nation A.

Similarly, we can show that nation A's absolute advantage over nation B in both items would mean each ton requires less land in A than it does in B. *In general, when a nation has an absolute advantage in an item it can produce that item with fewer inputs per unit than foreign nations.*

Despite the fact that nation A has an absolute advantage over nation B, we can easily demonstrate that the citizens of nation A can gain by specializing in one of the goods and then trading with nation B to obtain the other. This remarkable conclusion stems from the fact that the gains possible from trade are determined by the opportunity cost of each unit of one good in terms of the other rather than by the input cost. To see this, begin by calculating the *opportunity cost per unit* of each of the commodities in each nation. To simplify the analysis, suppose that each ton of each commodity involves the sacrifice of a constant amount of the other commodity in each nation.

Because nation A can produce either 20 tons of wheat or 20 tons of bananas, it would give up the opportunity to produce 20 tons of bananas if it chose to specialize in the production of wheat. The *opportunity cost* of each ton of wheat is the sacrifice of bananas associated with each extra ton of wheat produced per year. Assuming constant costs per ton of wheat, the opportunity cost of each ton of wheat in nation A is 1 ton of bananas.

A similar calculation can be performed for nation B. Because nation B can produce either 5 tons of wheat or 10 tons of bananas, it follows that it gives up 2 tons of bananas for each extra ton of wheat, assuming constant costs. The opportunity cost of producing a ton of wheat is therefore 2 tons of bananas for nation B.

The opportunity cost of bananas for each of the two nations is calculated in the same way. The table in Box 1 shows that the opportunity cost of bananas is 1 ton of wheat in nation A and ½ ton of wheat in nation B, assuming constant costs.

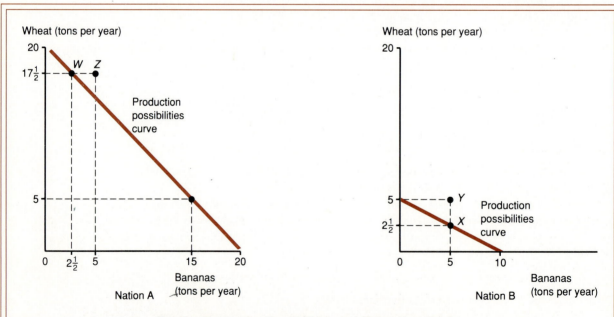

Box 2   Production Possibilities and Gains from Trade

Nation A enjoys a comparative advantage in wheat production while nation B has a comparative advantage in banana production. By trading, each nation can achieve points, such as *Z* for nation A and *Y* for nation B, that lie above their production possibilities curves.

Economic Thinkers

DAVID RICARDO

A cool head for business and astute judgment earned David Ricardo a fortune estimated at $2 million, an unbelievable sum for the early nineteenth century. Economics began for him as a hobby. He had little formal training, but when he retired from business in 1814 he began to pursue his interest in the invisible laws working behind the scenes in the market.

Instead of focusing on the details of the business world he knew so well, Ricardo created an abstraction of it, stripping it of everything unnecessary in order to study the mechanisms underlying its everyday life. Although perhaps his greatest contribution to the science of economics, this powerful analytical tool—modeling—was certainly not his only legacy. His 1817 book, *Principles of Political Economy and Taxation,* surveyed the field to that date and set the stage for economic debate for half a century.

In his exposition of the principle of comparative advantage as it relates to international trade, Ricardo used a clear-cut illustration involving the production of wine and cloth in Portugal and England (similar to the example of bananas and wheat used in this chapter).

Also set forth in his influential *Principles* is Ricardo's theory of economic growth, in which he posited that the economy ultimately would reach a "steady state" and cease to grow. At this point, Ricardo believed, the wage rate would decline to the subsistence level. Although drawing markedly different inferences, socialist philosopher Karl Marx was profoundly influenced by Ricardo's theory of economic growth.

Ricardo was born in England in 1772, the son of a Jewish immigrant. He went to work for his father at the age of 14 and started in business for himself at 22. He converted to Quakerism to marry the girl he loved, and when he retired he purchased a country estate and a seat in Parliament.

Ricardo earned his fortune mainly through securities and real estate investments. A strong supporter of freedom of speech and an opponent of government corruption and religious persecution, which were unpopular stances at the time, Ricardo nonetheless enjoyed tremendous popularity and was frequently called on to speak at the House of Commons.

The graphs in Box 2 show the production possibilities curves for these two goods in each of the two nations, A and B. The curves have been drawn under the assumption that there is a constant rate in each nation at which bananas are sacrificed for more wheat as resources are allocated from banana production to wheat production. This implies *constant opportunity costs per unit,* meaning that the opportunity cost of each unit of one of the goods in terms of the other is constant, as was assumed in the calculation in Box 1. The main point of the analysis also holds for the case of increasing costs, but the argument for that case is considerably more complicated. Note that the slope of each production possibilities curve represents the opportunity cost of bananas in terms of wheat multiplied by -1. The slope of the production possibilities curve for nation A is -1, which means each extra ton of bananas produced per year involves the sacrifice of 1 ton of wheat per year. The slope of the production possibilities curve for nation B is -0.5, which means each extra ton of bananas produced per year involves the sacrifice of ½ ton of wheat.

A nation has a **comparative advantage** over a trading partner in the production of an item if it produces that item at lower opportunity cost per unit than its partner does. The gains possible from international trade stem from the decrease in opportunity cost per unit of output that is possible when nations specialize in goods in whose production they enjoy a comparative advantage. By specializing, a nation uses its resources to do what it does at the lowest opportunity cost per unit relative to

Comparative advantage:
A nation has a comparative advantage over a trading partner in the production of an item if it produces that item at lower opportunity cost per unit than its partner does.

other nations. It then exports some of its annual output in exchange for other goods that can be obtained at lower opportunity cost per unit when they are produced by other nations. A theory of comparative advantage was one of the many contributions to economic thought of the eighteenth-century British economist David Ricardo (see Economic Thinkers box).

The graphs in Box 3 plot the opportunity cost of each ton of wheat in each of the nations in this example. It's clear that nation A has the comparative advantage in production of wheat over nation B because it can produce each ton of wheat at half the opportunity cost (in terms of bananas forgone) than is possible in nation B.

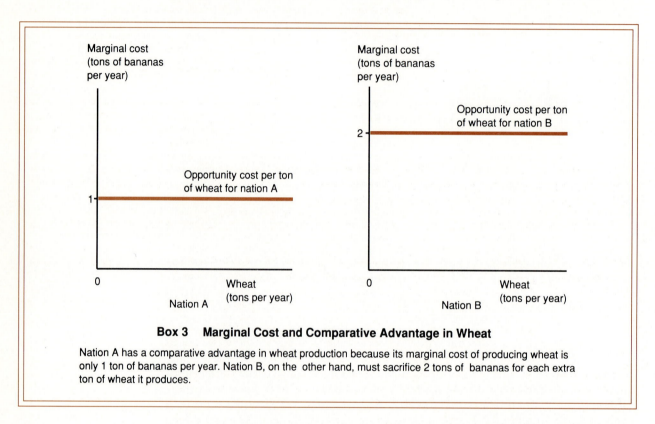

Box 3   Marginal Cost and Comparative Advantage in Wheat

Nation A has a comparative advantage in wheat production because its marginal cost of producing wheat is only 1 ton of bananas per year. Nation B, on the other hand, must sacrifice 2 tons of bananas for each extra ton of wheat it produces.

It's also easy to show that nation B has a comparative advantage in bananas, assuming its only possible trading partner is A. To see this, note that the opportunity cost of additional bananas for A is 1 ton of wheat. For each extra ton of bananas produced by A, the resources diverted from wheat production will result in a loss of 1 ton of wheat. In nation B, however, you can see by looking at the production possibilities curve in Box 2 that each ton of bananas produced involves the loss of only ½ ton of wheat. Thus if resources were reallocated in nation B to produce 2 more tons of bananas, the sacrifice would be only 1 ton of wheat.

The graphs in Box 4 show the opportunity cost of bananas in terms of wheat in each nation. Note that nation B has the comparative advantage in bananas. This is because it can produce the bananas at half the opportunity cost of A.

Despite its absolute advantage in both goods, nation A is *relatively more efficient in the production of wheat only compared to nation B.* Nation A gives up only 1 ton of bananas for each ton of wheat while nation B must give up 2 tons of bananas

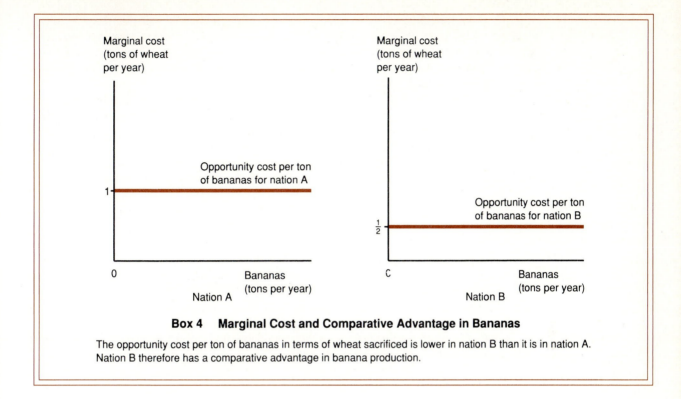

Box 4   Marginal Cost and Comparative Advantage in Bananas

The opportunity cost per ton of bananas in terms of wheat sacrificed is lower in nation B than it is in nation A. Nation B therefore has a comparative advantage in banana production.

for each ton of wheat. But nation A is *relatively less efficient in the production of bananas compared to nation B.* This is because it must give up a ton of wheat for each ton of bananas if it produces bananas, but nation B has to give up only ½ ton of wheat for each ton of bananas.

Gains from Specialization and Trade

It's easy to show how both nations can gain from specializing in the good for which they enjoy a comparative advantage and then trade to enjoy other goods. Suppose nation B uses all of its resources to produce bananas in a given year. By doing so it will produce 10 tons of bananas per year. Now suppose it offers 5 tons of its production to nation A. What is the maximum amount of wheat that nation A would trade for the 5 tons of bananas? It would cost nation A 5 tons of wheat to produce 5 tons of bananas. Therefore A would be no worse off if it traded 5 tons of wheat for the 5 tons of bananas. If the traders of nation B were skillful enough to extract a bargain like that, they would have 5 tons of bananas to enjoy and 5 tons of wheat. If nation B produced 5 tons of bananas and engaged in no trade, the best it could do, given its production possibilities curve, would be to enjoy 2½ tons of wheat. This would correspond to point *X* on its production possibilities curve in Box 2. By specializing in banana production and trading with nation A, the traders of nation B can enjoy as much as 5 tons of wheat! International trade therefore gives citizens of a nation the potential to achieve points like *Y* in Box 2 that lie above their production possibilities curve. Of course, citizens of nation B would be able to do this as long as they received anything more than 2½ tons of wheat for their 5 tons of bananas. If nation A were to trade anything less than 5 tons of wheat for the 5 tons of bananas offered by nation B, the citizens of nation A would also be able to achieve points above their production possibilities curve. *This means that international trade opens up the possibility of gains in world efficiency from resources by allowing additional mutual gains that would not be possible if each nation attempted to remain self-sufficient.*

It's easy to show how nation A can gain by specializing in wheat. Suppose nation A produced 17½ tons of wheat per year. The graph in Box 2 shows that at most, without trade, it could enjoy only 2½ tons of bananas per year. However, if nation A specialized in wheat production, it would be able to produce 20 tons per year. It could offer 2½ of these 20 tons to nation B in exchange for bananas. What is the maximum amount of bananas nation B would give up, without being made worse off, to obtain 2½ tons of wheat? Nation B would have to sacrifice as much as 5 tons of bananas to produce that much wheat by itself. This is the maximum amount of bananas it would be willing to exchange for 2½ tons of wheat. If it did give up 5 tons of bananas for 2½ tons of wheat, it would be no worse off. However, if traders for nation A could strike such a clever bargain, they would be able to consume 17½ tons of wheat per year and 5 tons of bananas. This would allow nation A to move *beyond* its own production possibilities curve from point W to point Z in Box 2. Of course, if nation B gave up anything less than 5 tons of bananas for the wheat, it would gain as well. As you can see, specialization according to comparative advantage allows mutual gains from trade that enable each trading nation to move beyond its own production possibilities curve.

Free international trade allows citizens in trading nations to enjoy consumption possibilities that extend beyond their own production possibilities. Although the simple example used to illustrate this point is quite abstract, it has great relevance to the world we live in. For example, Japan has a comparative advantage in 35mm cameras relative to the United States while the United States enjoys a comparative advantage in aircraft. U.S. workers can gain by specializing in the production of aircraft and other items in which the United States is likely to enjoy a comparative advantage. If aircraft are traded for cameras produced in Japan, the aggregate output of both these goods can increase. Americans can enjoy more cameras (because they will cost less when purchased from Japan) for any given output of aircraft than would be possible without international trade. At the same time, citizens of Japan can enjoy more aircraft (because they cost less when purchased from the United States) for any given output of cameras.

The Mercantilist Fallacy

The preceding analysis points out that international trade is not like warfare. What one nation gains in the aggregate from trade, its trading partner does not lose in the aggregate. International trade benefits all trading nations. This point was poorly understood by seventeenth- and eighteenth-century advocates of *mercantilism*. Mercantilism was a doctrine that argued that a nation could increase its power by encouraging exports and discouraging imports. In the eighteenth and early nineteenth centuries, gold and silver were used as international currency to settle foreign debts. A nation that consistently ran a balance of trade surplus would require nations with a balance of trade deficit to settle the difference in gold and silver. Nations that exported more than they imported thereby accumulated gold and silver in their national treasuries. The mercantilists mistakenly believed that nations that lost gold and silver were made worse off by international trade.

The well-being of a nation is not measured by gold, silver, or other commodities in storage. Instead its well-being depends on the goods and services its citizens can purchase with their available incomes. International trade allows citizens in the aggregate to expand their consumption possibilities beyond their domestic production possibilities. The gains from trade consist of the expansion of consumption possibilities. A nation that pursues policies that encourage exports but discourage imports so as to gain gold, silver, or other commodities to hold in storage simply gains purchasing power for the future that is not used currently. If imports are artificially restricted by such policies, citizens of the nation are deprived of the opportunity to enjoy imported goods that other nations can produce at lower opportunity costs.

Terms of Trade

The incentive to trade comes from the fact that consumers in each nation can gain by obtaining certain goods at lower opportunity cost than they can produce the goods domestically. To gain from trade, nation B would have to obtain wheat from nation A at any price *below* its opportunity cost of 2 tons of bananas for each ton of wheat. Similarly, to have incentive to trade, nation A would have to obtain bananas from nation B at a price that is *below* its opportunity cost of 1 ton of wheat per ton of bananas.

In actuality, prices for goods are determined by world demand and supply. The **real terms of trade** represent the actual market exchange rate of one good for another in international trade. For there to be incentive to trade, the terms of trade must be below the opportunity cost per unit of producing the good domestically. The greater the difference between the real terms of trade and a nation's opportunity cost of producing each extra unit of the good it wishes to import, the more the nation gains from trade. For example, nation B is better off if the terms of trade allow it to get each ton of wheat for 1½ tons of bananas than it is if it has to give up 2 tons of bananas for each ton of wheat. However, nation A is better off if the terms of trade are 2 tons instead of 1½ tons of bananas for a ton of wheat. *When the terms of trade for a pair of goods improve for one nation specializing in one good, they deteriorate for its trading partner specializing in the other good.* However, as long as the terms of trade are less than each nation's opportunity cost of producing each unit, *both nations still gain from engaging in specialization and trade*.

Suppose the agreed-upon real-world terms of trade are 1½ tons of bananas for each ton of wheat. It's now easy to show how each nation's *consumption possibilities* are extended beyond its *production possibilities* by international exchange of goods at the agreed-upon terms of trade. Note that the agreed-upon terms of trade can also be expressed as ⅔ ton of wheat for each ton of bananas.

For example, if nation A specialized in wheat production and traded its entire annual output of 20 tons for bananas, it would receive 30 tons of bananas in exchange by trading with nation B and other nations specializing in banana production. This means that by specializing, nation A can consume a maximum of 30 tons of bananas instead of 20 tons. A **consumption possibilities curve** shows combinations of two goods a nation can consume given its resources, technology, and international trade. The graph in Box 5 shows nation A's consumption possibilities curve when it can trade wheat at the rate of ⅔ ton for each ton of bananas. The consumption possibilities curve is not as steep as the production possibilities curve. This is because less wheat must be given up in trade than in production for each

Real terms of trade:
The actual market exchange rate of one good for another in international trade.

Consumption possibilities curve:
Shows combinations of two goods a nation can consume given its resources, technology, and international trade.

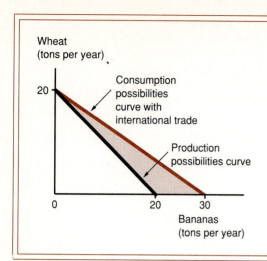

Box 5   Gains from Trade for Nation A

Given the agreed-upon terms of trade, nation A can enjoy points on its consumption possibilities curve that lie above its production possibilities curve. The combinations of wheat and bananas per year that can only be enjoyed through specialization and trade are represented by the shaded area in the graph.

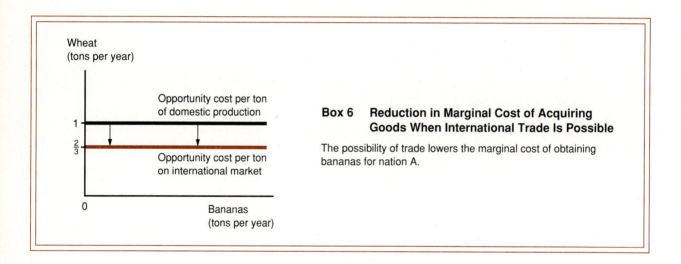

Box 6   Reduction in Marginal Cost of Acquiring Goods When International Trade Is Possible

The possibility of trade lowers the marginal cost of obtaining bananas for nation A.

ton of bananas. In fact, as shown in Box 6, at the agreed-upon terms of trade, the cost of a ton of bananas to residents of nation A has fallen from 1 ton of wheat to ⅔ ton of wheat. Naturally, bananas are a better buy as imports than they are when domestically produced.

The shaded area in the graph in Box 5 represents the combinations of wheat and bananas that can be enjoyed when trade is possible at the agreed-upon terms that could not be enjoyed if the nation tried to be self-sufficient in bananas and wheat. International trade therefore allows consumers the option to consume more of *both* wheat and bananas.

Similarly, the graph in Box 7 shows how trade shifts the consumption possibilities for nation B above its production possibilities. For example, by specializing in banana production and selling the entire annual crop of 10 tons on international markets, nation B could consume 6⅔ tons of wheat per year. If instead it allocated all of its own resources to wheat production, the most it could consume would be 5 tons of wheat. The slope of the consumption possibilities curve for nation B is steeper than the slope of its production possibilities curve. This reflects the fact that, as shown in Box 8, the possibility of international trade decreases the opportunity cost of enjoying a ton of wheat in the nation from 2 tons of bananas to only 1½ tons of bananas. The shaded area in the graph in Box 7 shows the combinations of wheat and bananas that are attainable through trade that would not be attainable if nation B attempted to be self-sufficient in wheat and bananas.

As a result of international trade, citizens in each nation now have the opportunity to enjoy points on their new consumption possibilities curves rather than their production possibilities curves. Because, given their resource availability, citizens in all trading nations will enjoy more goods and services when they trade, on average they will be better off. This is not to say that all citizens will be better off. As you'll see shortly, international trade can make some people worse off, especially in the short run. Some people oppose free international trade because they believe their incomes would be higher if trade were banned.

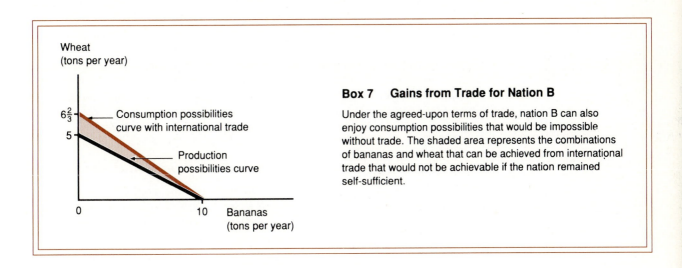

Box 7   Gains from Trade for Nation B

Under the agreed-upon terms of trade, nation B can also enjoy consumption possibilities that would be impossible without trade. The shaded area represents the combinations of bananas and wheat that can be achieved from international trade that would not be achievable if the nation remained self-sufficient.

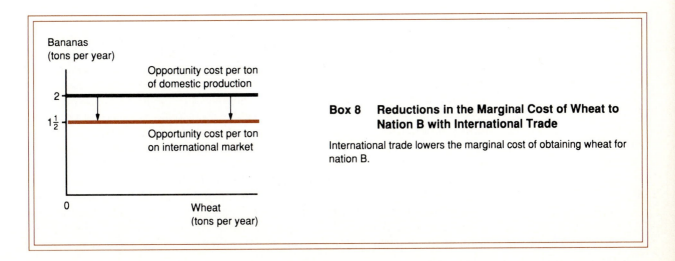

Box 8   Reductions in the Marginal Cost of Wheat to Nation B with International Trade

International trade lowers the marginal cost of obtaining wheat for nation B.

Under what circumstances does a nation enjoy a comparative advantage in the production of an item?

2 Explain how a nation can have an absolute advantage in the production of automobiles but fail to enjoy a comparative advantage in auto production.

3 How do the real terms of trade influence the gains possible from international trade?

Productivity and Trade

The comparative advantage enjoyed by producers of particular goods in a nation can be eroded over time when productivity growth lags behind that of competing foreign producers. For example, a U.S. comparative advantage in the production of steel relative to Japan can be eroded if Japanese producers gain in efficiency relative to U.S. producers. Throughout the 1970s, large U.S. steel firms operated in aging plants in which productivity growth lagged behind that of Japanese producers. As a result, many large U.S. steel producers have failed to compete successfully with Japanese firms in international and domestic markets.

If productivity in the Japanese steel industry increases faster than it does in the U.S. steel industry, the opportunity cost of each ton of U.S. steel will rise relative to the opportunity cost of Japanese steel. This will make U.S. steel less attractive in international markets because the Japanese will be able to sell steel at prices lower than U.S. producers while still covering their opportunity costs.

How to Lose Comparative Advantage in International Markets

To examine the trade process, it's useful to trace out the implications of lagging productivity growth in a U.S. industry such as steel. We can use the analysis of comparative advantage to show how lagging productivity could affect the competitiveness of the U.S. industry compared to the Japanese industry in international markets.

The graphs in Box 9 show hypothetical production possibilities curves between food and steel for the United States and Japan, assuming constant opportunity costs. The initial production possibilities curve for the United States has a slope of -1, indicating that the opportunity cost of each ton of steel is 1 ton of food. The initial Japanese production possibilities curve has a slope of -2. This means that the opportunity cost of a ton of steel is 2 tons of food. The graphs show the initial opportunity cost curves for steel in each of the two countries. Initially the United States enjoys a comparative advantage in steel production because its opportunity cost of each ton of steel is one half that in Japan when measured in terms of food forgone.

Now suppose that over time in both nations there is no productivity growth in food production but that productivity increases in the steel industry. Also assume that Japanese firms manage to achieve increases in steel productivity growth at a faster rate than do U.S. firms. Increases in productivity growth in the steel industry mean that the production possibilities curve will swivel outward and become flatter. The same resources will be capable of producing more output. In Box 9, productivity growth shifts the U.S. production possibilities curve until it intersects the horizontal axis at 12 tons per day. However, the productivity growth is much more pronounced in Japan, and its curve now intersects the horizontal axis at 10 tons per

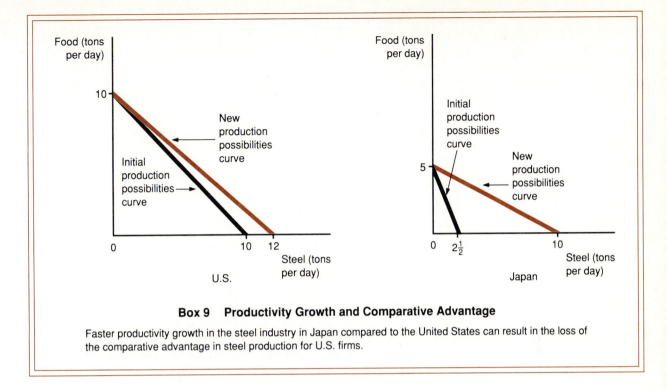

Box 9 Productivity Growth and Comparative Advantage

Faster productivity growth in the steel industry in Japan compared to the United States can result in the loss of the comparative advantage in steel production for U.S. firms.

day instead of 2½ tons. Notice that the Japanese production possibilities curve is now flatter than the U.S. production possibilities curve. *This means that the opportunity cost of a ton of steel in Japan has fallen below that in the United States.*

The graphs in Box 10 show that Japan's amazing growth in productivity has reduced the opportunity cost of a ton of steel in that country from 2 tons of food per

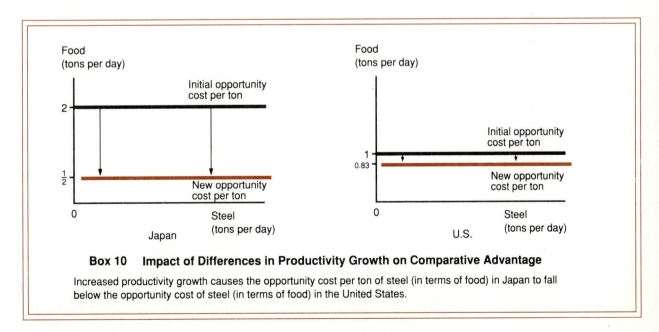

Box 10 Impact of Differences in Productivity Growth on Comparative Advantage

Increased productivity growth causes the opportunity cost per ton of steel (in terms of food) in Japan to fall below the opportunity cost of steel (in terms of food) in the United States.

day to only ½ ton. Meanwhile, in the United States the low growth of productivity in the steel industry has merely reduced the opportunity cost of a ton of steel from 1 ton of food per day to 0.83 ton. *As a result of lagging productivity growth, the United States, in this example, has lost its comparative advantage in steel production.* This is because Japan can now produce steel at a lower opportunity cost than the United States.

This example points out an important lesson: An industry that lags behind the times in technology or equipment will lose its comparative advantage in international markets.

Productivity Growth in the United States and Foreign Nations in the 1980s

In the early 1980s productivity growth on average in the United States lagged behind productivity growth in many foreign nations. The graph in Box 11 shows the average growth in national output per worker in 10 selected nations from 1981 to 1985. During this period, aggregate output per worker grew by only about 1% per year in the United States. In contrast, output per worker grew by 6% in Korea and nearly 3% in Japan. The lagging productivity growth in the United States relative to that in some foreign nations has contributed to a loss in comparative advantage for the United States in the world markets for some products. For example, Korea and Japan do in fact have a comparative advantage over the United States for many types of steel products.

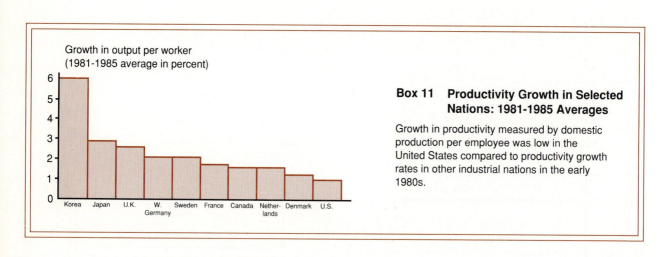

Growth in output per worker (1981-1985 average in percent)

Box 11 Productivity Growth in Selected Nations: 1981-1985 Averages

Growth in productivity measured by domestic production per employee was low in the United States compared to productivity growth rates in other industrial nations in the early 1980s.

The slow rate of productivity growth in the United States in the 1970s relative to that in foreign nations is often cited as the culprit for the decline of U.S. competitiveness in international markets. Since 1981, however, productivity growth in U.S. manufacturing has been impressive. From 1981 to 1987, output per labor hour in manufacturing increased at an average rate of 4.1% per year. Although employment in manufacturing has declined, manufacturing's share of GNP has remained constant.

The low average productivity rates for the United States shown in Box 11 in part reflect the shift to a service-oriented economy where productivity tends to grow more slowly than in manufacturing. The good news is that since 1985 U.S. manufacturers have begun to close obsolete plants and apply improved technology and management techniques that promise to result in future gains in productivity. Since 1985 productivity growth in U.S. manufacturing has begun to approach 3% per year. In addition, U.S. research in new technologies, such as superconductivity, might lead to the development of new products in which the nation will enjoy a comparative advantage.

Each nation enjoys a comparative advantage in some products relative to its trading partners. Although the lag in productivity growth in the United States in the 1980s has contributed to a loss of comparative advantage in some industries, the United States retains a comparative advantage in many other products and is gaining in still others as the pattern of productivity growth changes. Further, as time goes by the United States is likely to gain a comparative advantage in new products it develops.

Implications of Lagging Productivity Growth for U.S. Workers and Resource Owners

What are the implications for U.S. workers of loss of comparative advantage in particular export markets? Obviously, workers in industries such as steel and electronics, where comparative advantage has been eroded, will be harmed more than other workers. However, keep in mind that all nations enjoy a comparative advantage in some goods and services. For example, notice that in the example from the previous section, the United States will enjoy a comparative advantage in food production relative to Japan when it loses its comparative advantage in steel production. This is because when the opportunity cost of a ton of steel in terms of food in the United States rises above that in Japan, the opportunity cost of a ton of food in terms of steel must fall below that in Japan.

The impact of this adjustment process, however, is bitter medicine for U.S. workers in industries where comparative advantage is being eroded. As a result of lagging productivity gains, their wages will necessarily fall relative to wages enjoyed by workers in competing nations. For industries in which comparative advantage has been lost, some workers with specialized skills and other owners of specialized inputs will suffer permanent reductions in income. Some of these workers must find work in other industries because the demand for their services decreases along with the demand for exports of such goods. It's clear that in recent years the U.S. steel and electronics industries have undergone such disruptions. Similarly, disruptions have occurred in the textile industry, where lagging productivity growth has caused the United States to lose comparative advantage in international markets.

A key to keeping productivity growth high is adequate productive investment in new equipment and plants, and research and development of new products. Business investment in the United States has lagged in recent years, and many economists believe this is the chief cause of the nation's decline in productivity in manufacturing. During the 1970s, annual net investment in the United States averaged only about 6% of the value of domestic production. In Japan, annual net investment during the 1970s was nearly 20% of the value of domestic production. When investment doesn't grow quickly enough, workers have less capital equipment and less modern technology to work with. The reduction in capital per worker decreases productivity and contributes to declining wages. In addition to decreases in investment, increased government regulations to improve working conditions and environmental quality as well as rising energy prices are believed to have contributed to the U.S. productivity decline of the 1970s.

Protectionism vs. Free Trade

As noted earlier, declines in a nation's comparative advantage caused by declines in productivity growth inevitably disrupt particular industries. Workers with specialized skills lose their jobs, and owners of other specialized inputs also suffer reductions in income. These workers and input owners naturally would prefer to be protected from foreign competition because their incomes would be higher under such circumstances.

Arguments in Favor of Protecting Domestic Industries from Foreign Competition

The arguments in favor of free trade have already been covered in the analysis of comparative advantage. Free trade expands consumption possibilities in a nation beyond production possibilities. It allows higher standards of living by increasing real incomes from available resources. This implies lower prices for goods and services as well. In this section we look at the arguments *against* free trade and in favor of protecting domestic industries.

1. *National security.* Many people believe that self-sufficiency is necessary for reasons of national security. According to this argument, relatively inefficient domestic industries producing strategically important materials and commodities should not be allowed to go out of business because of foreign competition. A good domestic mix of industries, particularly for food, fiber, steel, and petroleum products, ensures that the United States will not be overly dependent on foreign sources of supply. Thus in the event of an international crisis, the United States will be assured of stable supplies of these basic goods. The inevitable cost of such protectionism is higher prices for American consumers.

2. *Reducing structural unemployment.* There are transaction costs associated with adjustment to a new industrial mix. For example, you might support protection of the U.S. automobile industry from competition with Japan because you think that in the long run the United States will be able to produce cars more cheaply than Japan. When the industry is protected in the short run, structural unemployment is reduced. In the long run consumers don't pay higher prices for cars when the fruits of a new investment program result in higher productivity gains and lower prices.

3. *Protecting infant industries.* Protection of a newly established or "infant" industry from foreign competition allows the new industry to expand to the point at which it can enjoy economies of scale. In this case consumers pay high prices as a result of protection in the short run but hope to enjoy lower prices in the future as the infant industry achieves gains in productivity in the long run. The problem with this argument is that it's difficult to identify an infant industry that will realize such gains. In addition, protected "infant" industries often fail to mature to the point where they can be competitive on their own, precisely because of the inimical effects of the absence of competition.

4. *Protecting U.S. industries against subsidized foreign producers.* Some governments subsidize exporting firms to allow them to sell their goods at lower prices

Principles in Practice

Protectionism in the United States: A Growing Trend?

Increased foreign competition has led to intense lobbying for protection by U.S. industries whose sales have been hurt as a result. The Reagan Administration, which was politically committed to free international trade, finally gave in to pressure to protect domestic industries from foreign competition. In the early 1980s the President negotiated "voluntary restraint agreements" with Japan and other nations to limit their exports of steel and automobiles to the United States. In addition, during the Reagan years, import quotas for textiles were tightened. Concern about the impact of increased foreign competition on employment opportunities in manufacturing has led to still more calls to protect U.S. industries from foreign competition.

Since 1947 the United States has used what is known as the "escape clause" of the International General Agreement on Tariffs and Trade (GATT) to provide temporary protection to domestic industries. Under the escape clause, industries that can prove to the U.S. International Trade Commission (ITC) that imports will threaten or otherwise cause serious economic injury can receive protection against those imports through import quotas or tariffs. Since 1947 more than 30 U.S. industries have applied for and received protection under the escape clause.[*]

Since 1962 the U.S. government also has provided trade adjustment assistance that cushions the impact of foreign competition on workers, businesses, and regions adversely affected by imports. These programs have very stringent eligibility requirements, and cash payments have been limited.

The issue of protection involves conflict between consumers and suppliers of specialized inputs, including labor, in industries whose profits and revenues are adversely affected by foreign competition. The political choice that must be made is between providing direct or indirect subsidies to these industries to keep them afloat or allowing them to go under if they can't compete. In the latter case the resources released from these industries would then have to find employment in other industries. Because the search for employment could take time, this implies increased structural unemployment and declines in national income until the transition has been made.

The conflict between avoiding economic dislocation from foreign trade and protecting consumers is clear from studies of the effects of previous protectionist measures:

1. An estimate of the impact of U.S. restrictions on imports of sugar, clothing, and automobiles in 1984 indicated that these measures cost low-income consumers twice as much as they cost upper-income consumers, suggesting that trade restrictions harm the poor more than the rich.[†]

2. Import quotas for Japanese cars from 1981 through 1983 increased the prices of those cars by an estimated $1,000 per vehicle and resulted in increased expenditure estimated at about $2 billion by consumers of Japanese cars. The quotas also contributed to a $370 per car price increase on average for U.S. cars over the same period. Although the quotas saved about 26,000 jobs in the United States, the cost per job saved was estimated at $160,000 per worker per year. This cost was paid by U.S. consumers of automobiles, who had to spend $4 billion more for cars per year as a result of the quotas when they were in effect![‡]

3. The Smoot-Hawley Tariff Act of 1930, which raised tariffs in the United States by about 60%, was widely credited with helping induce a worldwide depression by reducing equilibrium real GNP in foreign nations as U.S. demand for their exports plummeted.[§]

4. An estimate of the impact of seven recent escape-clause actions found that they raised prices to such a degree as to cost consumers $340,000 per job saved.[||]

Despite the costs, pressure for U.S. trade protection persists. Estimates indicate that the impact of trade protection on American consumers is increasing. The Institute of International Economics estimates that in 1985, U.S. consumers paid $65 billion more for purchases as a result of tariffs and quotas. For example, because of quotas on sugar imports, a box of candy that would otherwise cost $2 costs you $5! A leather handbag that would cost you $40 goes for $44 as the result of a tariff. Do you think we can afford protectionism?

[*]See Robert Z. Lawrence and Robert E. Litan, *Saving Free Trade,* Washington, D.C.: The Brookings Institution, 1986.
[†]Susan Hickok, "Consumer Cost of U.S. Trade Restraints," *Federal Reserve Bank of New York Quarterly Review,* 10, Summer 1985, p. 10.
[‡]Robert W. Crandall, "Import Quotas and the Automobile Industry: The Cost of Protectionism," *The Brookings Review,* 2, 4 (Summer 1984), pp. 8-16.
[§]See F.W. Taussig, *The Tariff History of the United States,* 8th ed., New York: E.P. Putnam, 1931, pp. 490-500.
[||]Gary Clyde Hufbauer, Diane T. Berliner, and Kimberly Ann Elliott, *Trade Protection in the United States: Thirty-one Case Studies,* Washington, D.C.: Institute for International Economics, 1986.

in foreign markets. These lower prices are not the result of more efficient production in the exporting country. Because some such subsidies could cause American industries to go out of business, they would give the foreign suppliers more control over market price in the long run. At that time the foreign government could reduce the subsidy, and prices of the imported goods would rise. Supporters of U.S. protection against such policies argue that there are gains from not letting the subsidized goods temporarily disrupt U.S. industries. The chief gain is the reduction in transaction costs associated wtih setting up and ceasing operations as foreign subsidies come and go. Another gain is a reduction in the risk that foreign suppliers will acquire monopoly power in the future.

The gains from protecting U.S. industries must always be weighed against the costs to American consumers in terms of higher prices and reduced real incomes. Remember that the gains from international trade are increased consumption possibilities and that those gains are mutually enjoyed by all trading partners. The purpose of international trade is not to maximize the difference between exports and imports! Even nations with huge balance of trade deficits, as has been the case for the United States during the 1980s, gain from international trade because such trade expands consumption possibilities. These gains of goods and services increase the standard of living of Americans in the aggregate. Most of the arguments against trade stem from the *redistribution* of income that results when some firms fail as a result of foreign competition. Because there is always a net gain as a result of international trade, ways have been found to compensate the losers (see Principles in Practice analysis).

The "Cheap Labor" Fallacy

One common argument in favor of protectionism is that American workers should be insulated against competition from "cheap foreign labor." For example, textile workers in the United States complain that products produced in the Far East using inexpensive labor are selling in the United States for very low prices, thereby reducing sales of domestic textiles. They contend that it's unfair for nations that use cheap labor to compete with them and cause them to lose their jobs. The strong implication of their argument is that the foreign firms exploit their workers unfairly by underpaying them.

There are a number of fallacies in this argument. Foreign workers, particularly in less developed nations, typically are less productive than American workers. This is because they often work with less capital equipment and less modern technology than American workers. These workers therefore are not necessarily "underpaid" or exploited in any sense. Their low wages are attributable to low productivity compared to U.S. workers.

Another fallacy in the argument is that it ignores the basis for gains from foreign trade. The gains from trade come from a nation's comparative advantage in producing an item. The source of the competitive advantage could be relatively abundant labor! The abundant labor supply with skills to produce certain goods, such as textiles, lowers the cost of producing textiles in terms of other goods. Naturally, an abundant labor supply means cheap labor. The cheap labor argument simply takes the reason for a nation's comparative advantage and tries to use it as an excuse not to benefit from the exporting nation's low marginal costs and prices! The cheap labor fallacy really sidesteps the main issues involved in the arguments for or against free foreign trade. The basis for gains from international trade is comparative advantage rather than absolute advantage.

Instruments of Protectionism: Tariffs

A **tariff** is a tax on imported goods. Those who favor protecting domestic industries against foreign competition often support tariffs as a means of making imported goods less attractive to domestic consumers. It's easy to show how a tariff works using simple supply and demand analysis.

Tariff:
A tax on imported goods.

   Assume that in the absence of any tariffs, imported cars would sell at an average price of $10,000 in the United States. At that price 3 million cars per year would be sold. The graph in Box 12 shows that the initial market equilibrium for foreign cars corresponds to point E_1, at which the demand and initial supply curves for foreign cars intersect. Now a tariff is placed on foreign cars sold in the United States, and the cost of selling foreign cars in the United States increases. Suppose the tariff is $1,000 per car. This means the marginal cost of selling a car increases from its initial level by $1,000. The supply curve shifts upward by $1,000, reflecting the increase in the cost of selling these cars in the U.S. market. The new market equilibrium corresponds to point E_2, at which the new supply curve just intersects the demand curve.

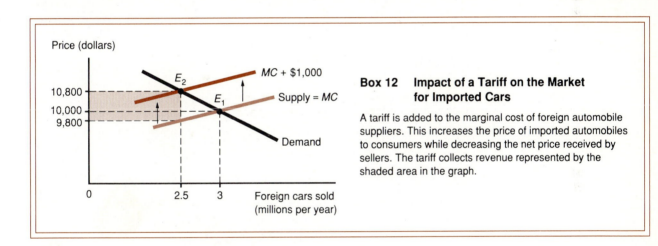

Box 12   Impact of a Tariff on the Market for Imported Cars

A tariff is added to the marginal cost of foreign automobile suppliers. This increases the price of imported automobiles to consumers while decreasing the net price received by sellers. The tariff collects revenue represented by the shaded area in the graph.

The tariff has the following effects in the market for foreign cars:

1. The price of foreign cars increases. In the graph in Box 12 the price goes up from $10,000 to $10,800. The extent of the price increase depends on the price elasticities of demand and supply for foreign cars. Other things being equal, the more inelastic the demand for foreign cars, the greater the increase in price.
2. The price *received* by foreign sellers of cars *declines* from its previous level. In Box 12 the price received by foreign sellers for each car sold is the $10,800 paid by buyers *less* the $1,000 tariff per car. The sellers' net price after payment of the tariff is only $9,800, which is $200 less per car than they enjoyed before the tariff was imposed. Foreign producers therefore don't benefit from the increase in the market price for their cars caused by the tariff. In fact, the profitability of selling cars in the U.S. market declines after the tariff is imposed. The impact of the price

decline on foreign sellers depends on the price elasticities of demand and supply for foreign cars. In general, both foreign manufacturers and their U.S. dealers suffer a reduction in income as a result of the tariff.

3. As a result of the increase in price, the annual quantity of foreign cars demanded decreases. In Box 12, as a result of the tariff, the annual quantity sold declines from 3 million to 2.5 million cars per year. The more elastic the demand for foreign cars, the greater the reduction in annual sales as a result of the tariff.

4. The tariff collects revenue that can be used to reduce reliance on other taxes, to increase government spending, or to reduce government budget deficits and debt. In this case the annual revenue collected from the tariff would be $1,000 multiplied by the 2.5 million cars sold, which is $2.5 billion. Note that the greater the reduction in sales of the foreign goods as a result of the tariff, the less revenue the tariff collects. In effect, tariffs that do a good job of protecting domestic producers from foreign competition are poor revenue producers because they cause sharp reductions in imports.

How does the tariff benefit domestic producers? The graph in Box 13 shows the demand for and supply of domestic cars. Assume that before the tariff is imposed the average price of domestic cars is also $10,000 and that domestic cars are perfect substitutes for foreign cars. Of course, this is a simplification because there are quality differences between domestic and foreign cars that often lead buyers to prefer cars of one producer, foreign or domestic, over those of other producers. Differences in quality allow prices for various models to differ. However, the basic point of the impact of a tariff on domestic producers can be brought out even though quality differences are ignored.

The increase in the price of foreign cars resulting from the tariff *increases the demand for domestic cars.* This is because domestic cars are a more attractive buy after the tariff is imposed on the substitute goods produced by foreign manufacturers. However, the increase in demand will increase the price of U.S. cars. In fact, if the two goods are *perfect* substitutes, the price of U.S. cars must go up to exactly $10,800. In Box 13 the effect of the tariff is to shift the market equilibrium for domestic cars from point E_1 to E_2. Annual sales increase from 5 million to 5.3 million cars. The impact of the tariff on the domestic market can be summarized as follows:

1. The price of domestic cars increases, and the annual quantity sold goes up. This makes consumers worse off. In fact, as a result of the general increase in the

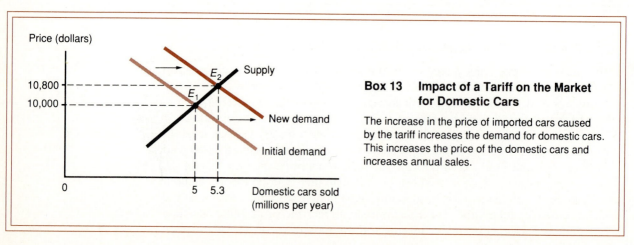

Price (dollars)

10,800

10,000

E_2 Supply

E_1

New demand

Initial demand

0

5 5.3

Domestic cars sold (millions per year)

Box 13   Impact of a Tariff on the Market for Domestic Cars

The increase in the price of imported cars caused by the tariff increases the demand for domestic cars. This increases the price of the domestic cars and increases annual sales.

price of cars caused by the tariff, the aggregate (foreign plus domestic) annual quantity sold will decline.

2. In the short run the profits of domestic automobile manufacturers will increase. Also, owners of specialized inputs and workers with specialized skills will benefit from the tariff as the prices received for specialized input services and wages increase in response to the increase in demand. In general, prices will remain higher than they would have been in the absence of a tariff.

In short, tariffs tend to increase the prices of both domestic and foreign goods. This redistributes income to domestic producers and owners of specialized inputs used in domestic production. Foreign producers suffer a decrease in sales, and domestic consumers suffer a decrease in real income. Government gains the revenue collected with the tariff.

Instruments of Protectionism: Import Quotas

An **import quota** is a limit on the quantity of foreign goods that can be sold in a nation's domestic markets. Import quotas can protect domestic industries just as tariffs do, but they don't generate any revenue that can be used to reduce government reliance on taxes. Import quotas were used from 1981 to 1984 to protect U.S. automobile producers. There are also import quotas on certain textiles, and special interests in a variety of industries continually seek to use their political influence to protect their interests with import quotas.

Import quota:
A limit on the quantity of foreign goods that can be sold in a nation's domestic markets.

Supply and demand analysis can be used to show the impact of import quotas. Suppose, as before, in the absence of any restrictions on international trade, the price of foreign cars would average $10,000 and 3 million foreign cars per year would be sold at that price. The initial equilibrium is at point E in the graph in Box 14.

Now suppose a strict import quota of 2.5 million foreign cars per year is imposed. This means that no matter what the price of foreign cars or the willingness of foreign producers to sell in domestic markets, no more than 2.5 million foreign cars will be permitted to enter U.S. markets each year. In effect, the quota truncates the foreign supply curve at point I, as shown in Box 14, which corresponds to 2.5 million cars per year. The quantity supplied cannot increase beyond the quota limit. The upward-sloping supply curve beyond point I is no longer relevant to the domestic market.

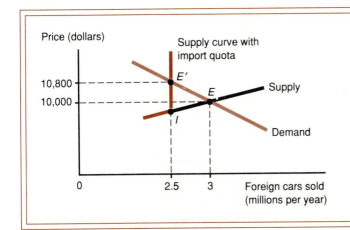

Box 14   Impact of an Import Quota on Foreign Car Sales

An import quota limits the number of new foreign cars that can be sold per year in the United States. This increases the market price of the cars. Sellers of foreign cars lose 500,000 sales per year, but this is offset by a gain in revenue from the higher price. This corresponds to point E', at which the demand curve intersects the vertical portion of the supply curve after the quota is imposed.

Instead the supply curve is the kinked dark curve, which is perfectly vertical at point *I*. The supply of foreign cars is therefore perfectly inelastic after 2.5 million cars per year are imported.

Given the new supply curve, the new market equilibrium corresponds to point *E'*. At that point the price of foreign cars increases to $10,800 per year. This corresponds to the point at which the demand curve intersects the vertical portion of the new supply curve. At that price the quantity demanded falls from 3 million to 2.5 million cars per year. *If the import quota is established at the same quantity that would result from the $1,000 tariff, the impact of the quota on the price of foreign cars is exactly the same as that which would result from the tariff.* The import quota can therefore protect domestic producers in the same way as the tariff. As a result of the import quota, the demand for domestic cars will increase, just as it did with the tariff as shown in Box 12. Domestic producers will gain, and owners of specialized inputs used in domestic production will also gain.

However, there are important differences between the tariff and the import quota:

1. The import quota does not raise any revenue for government authorities while the tariff does.
2. The import quota raises the market price paid by consumers of foreign cars but does not reduce the net price received by foreign sellers. Foreign sellers and their U.S. dealers will therefore gain revenue as a result of the quota because they will receive higher prices per car. However, this gain is offset by the reduction in revenue as sales volume declines by 500,000 cars per year as a result of the quota. The increase in revenue from the price increase could offset the decline in revenue from the sales decline when demand is very inelastic. *If demand for the foreign goods is very inelastic, then foreign sellers and their U.S. dealers might actually be better off with the quota than they would be under free trade!*

The Problem of Retaliation

Playing with tariffs is a bit like starting a war. The United States is both an exporter and an importer. Foreign governments whose citizens are harmed by tariffs or quotas might very well retaliate against the United States by placing tariffs or quotas on U.S. exports to their nations. They could also try to counter the effect of U.S. trade restrictions by subsidizing domestic producers. These subsidies would reduce the costs of selling in the United States and could be effective in increasing supply to counteract the effects of tariffs. However, this increase in supply will not have any effect if import quotas are used because the quotas limit the quantity that can be sold in the U.S. market.

The problem of retaliation must be considered by policymakers when tariffs and import quotas are used. The gains from tariffs and other trade restrictions in some industries could be offset by losses in others when foreign governments retaliate.

Concept Check

1 Suppose the domestic shoe industry finds that its sales decline because imported shoes are cheaper. What can the industry do to regain its sales?

2 How do tariffs and quotas protect domestic producers?

3 How do tariffs, quotas, and other instruments of protectionism affect domestic consumers?

International Economic Relations with Less Developed Countries

There is great disparity in levels of per capita income among nations in the world. **Real per capita output** is a measure of real output per person in a nation. It is calculated simply by dividing real GNP in a nation by the nation's population. Output per capita in the United States and other industrial nations generally ranges well over $10,000. However, in **less developed countries (LDCs)**, real GNP per capita is generally much less than $1,000 per year. In fact, in some very poor nations in Africa and Asia, output per capita is less than $200 per year! The incredible poverty and disparity in levels of average well-being among nations, measured by output per capita, is a source of great concern to many caring people. The problem is all the more serious because about 75% of the world population lives in LDCs. Unfortunately, there is no simple solution to raising living standards in less developed countries. The problems of these nations must be looked at within the context of international trade and economic relations.

Real per capita output: A measure of output per person in a nation; calculated by dividing real GNP by population.

Less developed country (LDC): A country whose real GNP per capita is generally much less than $1,000 a year.

Causes of Low Per Capita Output in Less Developed Countries

The problems of each particular nation with low income per capita are unique. In general, in LDCs, large portions of the population are engaged in agricultural pursuits and use older methods of farming. Despite the high input of labor in agriculture, many of these nations barely manage to produce enough food to feed their populations. Life expectancy is low, living conditions are often miserable, and people have a standard of material well-being that barely allows them to survive. However, in most LDCs, population growth is much higher than it is in industrialized nations.

A number of basic causes of relatively low per capita output can be identified:

1. *Low rates of saving and capital accumulation.* The key to economic growth is accumulation of capital such as roads, structures, bridges, equipment, and vehicles. To accumulate capital requires saving. Less developed countries are so poor that their saving is close to zero. To obtain capital these nations often must borrow from more industrialized nations. Per capita incomes are low in LDCs because workers have little capital equipment to work with. As a result, their productivity is low and therefore output per capita is low. This prevents them from saving. This is a vicious cycle that often requires assistance from other nations to break.

    Assistance can come from foreign governments, such as aid from the U.S. government, or from direct investment of private corporations. For example, if a U.S. tire manufacturer provides funds to build its own plant in an African nation, capital will flow into that nation and contribute to higher incomes.

2. *Poorly skilled and educated workers.* Human capital is as important as physical capital for the productivity of workers. In less developed countries, workers are often illiterate and have little training. Low productivity is caused by a lack of human capital as well as physical capital.

3. *Lagging technological know-how.* Production methods in less developed nations are often old-fashioned. The use of dated technology is related to the problem of lack of capital and a poorly informed and trained work force. The problem is particularly acute in agriculture where the use of more modern cultivation methods could result in enormous gains in productivity that would free labor

to be used in industrial activities and generate a surplus of food that could be exported.

4. *High population growth and unemployment.* Medical advances in many poor nations have reduced the death rate while the birth rate remains high. This contributes to population growth that often is as much as 10 times the rate in typical industrialized nations. The average age of the population tends to be low in poor nations, which contributes to a higher rate of natural unemployment. Much of the unemployment in less developed nations is disguised in the sense that many workers have marginal products close to zero. Customs and other traditions provide work with little social value to many people. For example, many government jobs could be dispensed with entirely and no one would be made worse off except the worker who loses a salary. Similarly, on many farms, four workers do what only one could do without any help. Spreading the work out over more workers than necessary disguises the fact that many workers have zero marginal products.

5. *Political instability and government policies that discourage production.* Many LDCs are in the throes of social upheaval. Political insurgence and guerrilla warfare are not uncommon in many nations of Africa, Asia, and Central and South America. Governments are sometimes corrupt, and international aid payments often enrich a few at the expense of many. Sometimes governments pursue policies that help in the short run at the expense of making long-run development slower.

Price control policies may keep food prices and prices of other basic goods low, but they inevitably destroy incentives for farmers to produce and innovate. Governments of LDCs often support their own currencies with price controls that overvalue the currency relative to its equilibrium value on international markets. This decreases demand for the nation's exports and makes imports appear to be cheap. This too discourages local businessmen and farmers from innovating to increase productivity.

International Trade and Less Developed Countries

Less developed nations are often dependent on trade with foreign nations to obtain capital and the technical know-how that is necessary for them to increase productivity and living standards. To pay for foreign capital in foreign currency is impossible unless the less developed nations export more. Increased exports of either agricultural or industrial products from these nations are likely to affect world prices and possibly make workers in industrialized nations worse off. Competition from less developed nations will increase if their economies begin to take off. At the same time, growing per capita incomes in these nations will provide broader markets for the products of the United States and other industrialized nations. There is great risk, however, that short-sighted protectionist policies in the advanced nations will prevent export growth in the poorer nations.

The United States, the Soviet Union, and other advanced nations often make gifts of direct aid and technical assistance to less developed nations. There are, of course, often political overtones to such gifts with hints of *quid pro quo*. The politicizing of foreign aid is a fact of life. The *World Bank*, an international organization of over 140 nations, also provides loans at reduced interest rates to help developing nations acquire capital. Such gifts and loans on favorable terms can help these nations acquire the capital necessary to enable them to increase per capita output.

1   What is a less developed country?

2   Why is per capita income so low in LDCs?

3   What types of goods and services do LDCs tend to import and export?

Summary

1. The basis for international trade stems from differences among nations in endowments of resources, skills, and technical know-how. International trade offers citizens in a nation the opportunity to specialize in the production of certain goods and exchange them for other goods produced in foreign nations.

2. There are mutual gains possible from international trade.

3. A nation has an absolute advantage over other nations in the production of an item if it can produce more of the item over a certain period with a given amount of resources.

4. A nation has a comparative advantage in the production of a particular good if its opportunity cost per unit is lower than that of its trading partners. Even nations that enjoy an absolute advantage in the production of all goods can gain from trade. A nation can gain from international trade by specializing in the production of goods in which it enjoys a comparative advantage and trading domestic surpluses of these goods for goods that other nations can produce at a comparative advantage.

5. Through international trade, citizens of a nation can obtain goods in which they do not enjoy a comparative advantage at prices that are below the opportunity costs per unit of producing those goods domestically. This allows consumption possibilities that would not be possible if the nation were self-sufficient in the production of all goods.

6. The real terms of trade represent the actual market exchange rate of one good for another in international trade. For there to be incentive to trade, the terms of trade for a good must be less than the opportunity cost per unit of producing that good domestically.

7. Changes in productivity growth between trading nations can alter the pattern of comparative advantage. When a nation's productivity growth lags behind that of its international competitors, its cost of production per unit will rise relative to that of its competitors. In the long run, this can cause it to lose its comparative advantage in the production of a good.

8. When lagging productivity growth causes a domestic industry to lose its comparative advantage in international markets, the income of input suppliers and workers in that industry will decline.

9. Loss of income in industries suffering from foreign competition often leads to demands for protection from foreign competition. Arguments in favor of protectionism include self-sufficiency in industries producing materials necessary for national defense, reduction in structural unemployment, protection of new industries just getting started, and protection of domestic sellers from unfair competition by subsidized foreign sellers.

10. The "cheap labor" fallacy turns the basis for gaining from trade into an argument

against trade. A nation with cheap labor might have low costs per unit, which gives it a comparative advantage in a good precisely because labor is cheap. Workers in foreign nations who are paid low wages often have lower productivity than U.S. workers.

11. A tariff is a tax on imported goods. Tariffs raise the price paid for the foreign goods on which they are levied and reduce the net price received by foreign sellers of those goods. As a result of the increase in the price paid by consumers, the quantity of foreign goods demanded tends to decline. A tariff raises government revenue and makes foreign goods more expensive relative to their domestically produced substitutes.

12. An import quota is a limit on the quantity of foreign goods that can be sold in a nation's domestic markets. Like tariffs, quotas seek to protect domestic producers from foreign competition. Quotas act to limit supply, thereby raising prices of goods produced by protected industries. However, quotas do not raise revenue for government authorities as do tariffs.

13. A less developed country is one for which real GNP per capita is generally much less than $1,000 per year. In such nations, large portions of the population typically are involved in agriculture and labor productivity is low. In addition, because of widespread poverty, saving and capital accumulation are low. High population growth often makes it difficult for increases in real GNP to outstrip annual increases in population so as to improve average living standards. Many less developed nations rely heavily on international trade to obtain capital equipment and technical know-how. These nations typically export raw materials or agricultural commodities.

Key Terms and Concepts

Specialization
Mutual gains from international trade
Absolute advantage
Comparative advantage
Real terms of trade

Consumption possibilities curve
Tariff
Import quota
Real per capita output
Less developed country (LDC)

Problems and Applications

1. Suppose two nations are capable of producing clothing and food. Nation A can produce 200 outfits per year or 10 tons of food. Nation B, which has an identical resource endowment, can produce 180 outfits per year or 5 tons of food. Assuming that constant costs prevail, plot the production possibilities curve for each of these nations. Which nation has the absolute advantage in the production of clothing? Which nation has the absolute advantage in the production of food?

2. Plot the opportunity cost per unit of clothing and the opportunity cost per unit of food for each of the two nations based on the data in problem 1. Which nation has the comparative advantage in food production? Which nation has the comparative advantage in clothing production?

3. Derive the consumption possibilities curve that would exist for each nation if the real terms of trade were 30 outfits of clothing for each ton of food.

4. Under what circumstances would changes in productivity result in no gains possible from international trade in the example in problem 3?

5. The decline in U.S. manufacturing jobs as a result of import competition has been particularly sharp since the mid-1970s in automobiles, steel, textiles, and shoes. Suppose you are asked to head a commission to improve the international competitiveness of these industries. What measures would you recommend to help these industries regain their comparative advantages?

6. How can shifting patterns in comparative advantage among nations cause structural unemployment? Explain why policies that increase aggregate demand cannot eliminate loss of jobs caused by competition from imports.

7. Why would an isolationist trade policy that banned international trade result in a sharp decline in the standard of living of U.S. citizens?

8. Firms in the domestic shoe industry argue in favor of shoe import quotas. They point out that a quota will not increase the costs of selling foreign-made shoes in the United States and therefore will not increase the prices of these shoes. Do you agree with their argument?

9. Suppose you are a Korean exporter of shoes. The U.S. Congress is considering the imposition of either a tariff or a quota on your shoes. Assuming that under the two proposals you will sell the same quantity in the United States, why would you prefer the quota to the tariff?

10. If you were an adviser to a less developed nation, what policies would you propose to raise per capita income in that nation?

Suggested Readings

Robert Z. Lawrence and Robert E. Litan, *Saving Free Trade,* Washington, D.C.: The Brookings Institution, 1986. This is an analysis of the costs and benefits of free international trade along with a discussion of protectionism and alternative ways to compensate the losers from free trade.

W. Arthur Lewis, *The Theory of Economic Growth,* Homewood, Ill.: Richard D. Irwin, Inc., 1955. This is a classic analysis of the development process and the problems of less developed nations.

Beth V. Yarbrough and Robert M. Yarbrough, *The World Economy: Trade and Finance,* Chicago: The Dryden Press, 1987. This is a comprehensive and up-to-date textbook on the theory and practice of international trade.

A Forward Look

In the following chapter we examine the balance of international trade between the United States and the rest of the world. We also discuss the international monetary system.

The Economics of Foreign Exchange and the Balance of International Trade

By now you're well aware of the growing importance of international trade in the U.S. economy. If you follow the news reports, you can't help being aware of the ups and downs of the price of the dollar in terms of foreign currencies. Between 1981 and 1985 the value of the dollar generally increased in terms of Japanese yen, West German marks, and other key currencies. However, in 1986 and 1987 the value of the dollar in terms of other key currencies began to plummet. The price of a unit of a nation's currency in terms of units of foreign money is an important determinant of the prices of its exports in foreign markets and of the prices you must pay for such imported products as Japanese cameras and German automobiles.

Our goal in this chapter is to provide you with a basis for understanding the causes and impact of fluctuations in foreign exchange rates on the performance of the U.S. economy. As you've already learned, when the United States imports more goods than it exports, the result is a balance of trade deficit. Such a deficit implies negative net exports, which, other things being equal, is a contractionary influence on the U.S. economy and spells trouble for those American industries that face foreign competition. The U.S. balance of trade deteriorated sharply in the 1980s. In 1981 the United States enjoyed an international trade surplus equal to 1% of real GNP. By 1986 the trade balance had moved to a deficit equivalent to over 4% of real GNP as imports outstripped exports! In this chapter we'll examine both the measurement and the consequences of balance of trade deficits and consider the financial aspects of international trade.

After reading this chapter, you should be able to:

1 Understand how international transactions between the United States and the rest of the world involve the exchange of dollars for units of foreign currency.

2 Use supply and demand analysis to show how exchange rates of one currency into another are established in foreign exchange markets.

3 Use aggregate supply and demand analysis to show the impact of changes in the real exchange rate of the dollar on macroeconomic equilibrium.

4 Explain the causes of currency appreciation and depreciation in foreign exchange markets and discuss the evolution of the current international monetary system.

5 Understand how a balance of trade deficit in the United States in a given year implies an increase in net foreign acquisition of U.S. financial and other assets in that year.

International Trade Transactions

If you've ever taken a trip to a foreign country, you know you must purchase foreign currency to pay your expenses while in the country. All your bills while you're in the country, even those you pay by credit card, will be in terms of that country's currency: French francs, Italian lire, Japanese yen. Credit card bills you receive when you return home will be converted to dollars based on the prevailing exchange rate at the time. You'll pay your bills in dollars, but the credit card company will have its bank pay the bills in the foreign currency.

In most cases when you visit a foreign country you go to a bank or other firm specializing in currency exchange to sell your dollars (or traveler's checks) for the local currency. The price of one nation's monetary unit in terms of the price of the monetary unit of another nation is called its **foreign exchange rate.** For example, the foreign exchange rate of the dollar for Japanese yen was 127 yen per dollar in mid-January 1988.

Foreign exchange rate:
The price of one nation's monetary unit in terms of the monetary unit of another nation.

The foreign exchange rate of the French franc in dollars is the number of dollars necessary to buy each French franc. For example, suppose the *foreign exchange rate of French francs* in dollars is 10¢ per franc. This means that if you exchange $100 you'll receive 1,000 French francs in return. You can then use your francs to purchase French goods and services while visiting the country.

Similarly, a French tourist visiting the United States will have to purchase dollars to meet her expenses while in this country. To do so, she'll go to an American bank or foreign exchange dealer where she'll sell her francs for dollars. The *foreign exchange rate of the dollar* for francs is the price of the dollar in francs. If it takes 10¢ to buy each franc, it follows that the foreign exchange rate for dollars is 10 francs per dollar. The foreign exchange rate of the dollar is the inverse of the foreign exchange rate of the franc:

Exchange rate of the dollar = 1/Exchange rate of the franc
10 francs per dollar = 1 franc/($0.10 per franc)

A U.S. tourist can figure out the equivalent number of dollars necessary to buy an item priced in francs by multiplying the price of the item in francs by the exchange rate:

$$\text{Dollar price} = (\text{Price in French francs})(\text{Exchange rate of francs})$$

For example, if your hotel room costs 1,500 French francs per night and the dollar exchange rate is 10¢ per franc, the price of the room in dollars is:

$$(\text{1,500 French francs})(\$0.10 \text{ per French franc}) = \$150$$

However, if the dollar exchange rate of the French franc were 18¢, as was the case in mid-January 1988, the cost of the room would be 1,500($0.18) = $270! When the dollar exchange rate of the French franc goes up, so do the dollar prices of items priced in francs.

Similarly, a French tourist would use the exchange rate of dollars expressed in francs to figure out the price of a hotel room in the United States in francs:

$$\text{Price in French francs} = (\text{Dollar price})(\text{Exchange rate of the dollar})$$

If her room costs $200 and the exchange rate is 10 French francs per dollar, the price of the room in francs will be:

$$(\$200)(10 \text{ francs per dollar}) = \text{2,000 French francs}$$

If instead the exchange rate of the dollar were only 5 francs per dollar, then the price of the hotel room would be only 1,000 French francs. Thus a decrease in the exchange rate of the dollar makes goods priced in dollars cheaper to people with French francs.

International Transfers of Bank Deposits Resulting from International Transactions

Foreign exchange market:
A market in which buyers and sellers of bank deposits denominated in the monetary units of many nations exchange their funds.

As is true for most transactions *within* the United States, most *international* transactions involve transfers of deposits among banks. However, in the case of international transactions the bank deposits are denominated in a variety of monetary units, such as dollars, francs, marks, pesos, and so on. The **foreign exchange market** is a market in which buyers and sellers of bank deposits denominated in the monetary units of many nations exchange their monies. Only a small fraction of daily transactions in foreign exchange markets actually involve trading of currency. When you buy francs in the form of paper currency or coins while visiting France, you engage in a retail transaction with a foreign exchange dealer, usually a bank. The retail price you pay for the francs in terms of dollars is naturally higher than the wholesale price representing the rate the bank must pay to exchange francs for dollars or dollars for francs. When banks and dealers trade currencies, each of the transactions is in the millions of dollars. The foreign exchange market is highly competitive. Hundreds of banks and other dealers maintain contact by telephone and electronics to exchange *bank deposits* denominated in one currency for those denominated in another currency.

How Foreign Trade Is Carried Out: An Export Transaction

Suppose an American grain dealer arranges to sell 10,000 bushels of grain to a French milling company. If the price of the grain is $4 per bushel, the total transaction involves $40,000. Naturally, the American grain dealer will want to be paid in dollars rather than francs, while the French miller will want to pay for the grain in francs.

Suppose the exchange rate is 10 francs to the dollar. To finance the transaction, the French miller will write a check for 400,000 French francs, which is the equivalent of $40,000 when the exchange rate is 10 francs to the dollar. The miller will then send the check directly to the U.S. grain dealer, who will present it to his bank for conversion to dollars, or the miller will use his check to purchase a bank draft (a check drawn on his bank) made out to the grain dealer in U.S. dollars. The latter option is more commonly used than the former. The French miller will pay the bank a small fee for the draft.

In effect the French bank, in assisting the miller in his international trade transaction, loses deposits of 400,000 francs. Where do these francs go? They go to a U.S. bank or other foreign exchange dealer who obtains the 400,000 francs in exchange for $40,000. Assume the francs are sold to a U.S. bank. This bank then holds the francs as a deposit in a French bank, called a *correspondent bank*, in which it has an account, or in its French branch (if it has one) for future use or sale. As long as the French francs are held in a French bank after the sale of the grain, there is no reduction in the French money stock. U.S. banks acquire deposits in French banks denominated in francs that can be invested in French assets or used to buy French goods and services. Of course, the banks buy and sell foreign currencies to make a profit. By holding the francs, they can either invest in French assets or sell the francs to another company that wishes to use them to purchase French goods. Each time the bank engages in an exchange of currencies it earns a fee. The grain exporter in turn has his deposits increased by $40,000 at his bank when he deposits the draft from the French bank. The $40,000 draft will be written against the French bank's account in a U.S. correspondent bank. As a result of the export transaction, U.S. banks obtain assets of 400,000 francs, which are held in foreign banks, and new liabilities of $40,000.

The table in Box 1 summarizes the immediate financial implications of the grain export transaction for accounts in French and U.S. banks.

Box 1 Changes in Assets and Liabilities of U.S. and French
Banks as a Result of Export of U.S. Grain to France

French banks

Assets	Liabilities
No change	−400,000 French francs deposited in account of grain importer
	+400,000 French francs deposited in U.S. banks

U.S. banks

Assets	Liabilities
+400,000 French francs deposited in French banks	+$40,000 deposited in grain exporter's account

---

How Foreign Trade Is Carried Out: An Import Transaction

Suppose a U.S. distributing company imports 20,000 video cassette recorders from a producer in Japan. The wholesale price of the VCRs is 12,500 Japanese yen per unit. If the exchange rate of the yen is $0.008 per yen, the dollar price of a VCR is:

$$\text{Dollar price} = (12{,}500 \text{ yen})(\$0.008 \text{ per yen}) = \$100$$

The total cost of the 20,000 VCRs in dollars is $2 million, which is equivalent to 250 million Japanese yen at the current exchange rate of $0.008 per yen. Note that at this exchange rate it will take 125 yen to purchase each dollar. The exchange rate of the dollar in this example is therefore 125 yen per dollar.

The mechanics of the transaction are similar to those we discussed for the export of grain from the United States to France. However, in this case the U.S. distributor goes to his local bank to arrange the exchange of dollars into yen to pay for his purchase of imported goods. He writes a check for $2 million (plus a small fee to the bank) in exchange for a bank draft made out to the Japanese exporter for 250 million yen. The U.S. importer's account is debited by $2 million as a result of his purchase. The $2 million ends up in the hands of a Japanese bank or other foreign exchange dealer who purchases the dollars in exchange for 250 million yen. For example, the yen could be supplied by any U.S. bank holding deposits denominated in yen at a Japanese bank. The Japanese exporter ends up with 250 million yen more in his account. As long as the Japanese bank or other dealer purchasing the dollars for yen keeps these dollars on deposit at an American correspondent bank, there is no reduction in the U.S. money stock. The dollars held in these accounts can be used to purchase U.S. financial assets, such as corporate bonds or government securities, or held to finance future import transactions in which dollars will be sold for foreign currency.

The table in Box 2 summarizes the immediate impact of the import transaction on assets and liabilities in U.S. and Japanese banks.

Box 2 Changes in Assets and Liabilities of U.S. and Japanese Banks as a Result of a U.S. Import Transaction

Japanese banks

Assets	Liabilities
+$2 million deposited in U.S. banks	+250 million Japanese yen deposit of VCR exporter

U.S. banks

Assets	Liabilities
No change	−$2 million deposit of U.S. importer
	+$2 million deposit of Japanese banks

---

1 It takes 1,200 Italian lire to purchase a U.S. dollar. How much U.S. money is necessary to purchase a bottle of Italian wine that sells for 8,000 lire?

2 Explain why an export of corn to Italy will result in U.S. banks gaining deposits of lire in Italian banks.

3 Why will Italian banks gain deposits of dollars in U.S. banks when U.S. firms import wine from Italy?

Foreign Exchange Markets

Whenever a foreign firm or individual purchases U.S. goods or services, a supply of foreign currency to be exchanged for dollars is created. Similarly, when U.S. firms and citizens wish to purchase foreign goods and services, a demand for foreign currency is created. Because of the many banks and dealers buying and selling bank deposits and other funds denominated in various currencies, the market for foreign exchange of any money is quite competitive. **Foreign exchange** is the money of one nation held by citizens of another nation either as currency or as deposits in banks.

Foreign exchange:
The money of one nation held by citizens of another nation either as currency or as deposits in banks.

Keep in mind that foreign exchange must be willingly held either as currency in the account of a bank or as assets denominated in foreign monetary units. For example, foreigners holding dollars must either keep them as idle balances in their U.S. correspondent banks or lend them out to U.S. firms or governments. They make such loans by purchasing the debt instruments of governments, banks, or households. Of course, the foreign holders of dollars can also use them to make direct investments in the United States by purchasing U.S. assets such as real estate or corporate stocks. The demand for U.S. dollars as foreign exchange depends on foreign demand for U.S. goods and services and the willingness of foreigners to hold their dollars as deposits (or cash) for future use or to invest the dollars in U.S. real and financial assets.

The supply of dollars to foreigners depends on the willingness of U.S. households, firms, and governments to exchange their dollars for foreign currency. This in turn depends on U.S. demand for foreign goods and services as well as the willingness of U.S. citizens and governments to use dollars to acquire financial and real assets denominated in foreign monetary units.

There are really many foreign exchange markets—one for each possible pair of currencies. Of course, the market of dollars for francs is the same as the market of francs for dollars. This is because once the equilibrium exchange rate of dollars for francs is established, so is the equilibrium exchange rate of francs for dollars.

For example, suppose the equilibrium dollar price of West German marks is 50¢ per mark. The equilibrium exchange rate of marks for dollars must therefore be 2 marks per dollar. If this were not the case, what would happen? For example, suppose a dollar cost only 1 mark while the mark cost 50¢. Under such circumstances you could make some quick profits as a foreign exchange dealer. When the mark is priced at 50¢, you can buy 2 marks for $1. If the price of the dollar were 1 mark at the same time, you could then turn around and sell each of those marks for $1, thus making a quick $1 profit on your initial $1 purchase! Profit opportunities like this would exist whenever there were discrepancies in the exchange rate of dollars into one currency and that currency into dollars. Because firms specializing in foreign exchange transactions will be quick to seize opportunities to earn profit when such exchange rate discrepancies do occasionally crop up, the discrepancies are usually quickly eliminated. In the preceding example, the demand for marks would increase, pushing up the price of the mark in terms of dollars, and the supply of dollars offered in exchange for marks would increase, putting downward pressure on the price of the dollar in terms of marks. The exchange rates of the mark and of the dollar would adjust until it was no longer possible to make profits by buying marks and then quickly selling them for dollars.

Equilibrium Exchange Rates

Just like any good or service, the price (exchange rate) of a nation's currency in terms of any foreign currency depends on the market demand for and supply of the nation's currency. The graph in Box 3 shows the demand and supply curves for dollars based on the exchange rate of marks for dollars, which represents the price of a dollar in terms of marks.

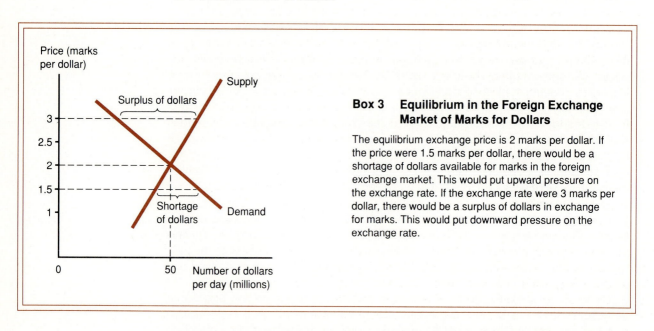

Box 3   Equilibrium in the Foreign Exchange Market of Marks for Dollars

The equilibrium exchange price is 2 marks per dollar. If the price were 1.5 marks per dollar, there would be a shortage of dollars available for marks in the foreign exchange market. This would put upward pressure on the exchange rate. If the exchange rate were 3 marks per dollar, there would be a surplus of dollars in exchange for marks. This would put downward pressure on the exchange rate.

The demand for dollars by those who hold marks depends on the desires of those people and businesses to use dollars to purchase U.S. goods and services and to invest in U.S. financial and physical assets. The lower the price of a dollar in terms of marks, the greater the West German demand for dollars to use for those purposes. Other things being equal, the lower the price of a dollar in terms of marks, the lower the cost of purchasing U.S. items for those who hold marks. To see this, suppose the current price of a personal computer manufactured in the United States is $2,000. If the current exchange rate is 2 marks per dollar, that computer will cost a West German citizen 4,000 marks. However, if the exchange rate were only 1 mark per dollar, the same computer would cost a West German only 2,000 marks. Naturally, the lower the price of the dollar in foreign currency, the lower the price of U.S. goods, services, and assets (denominated in dollars) in terms of the foreign money and the greater the demand for these items by foreigners. The increase in demand increases the quantity of dollars demanded by holders of the foreign currency. The demand curve for dollars is therefore downward sloping.

The supply of dollars offered in exchange for foreign currency, such as the West German mark, depends on the willingness of holders of dollars to purchase marks. The supply of dollars for marks depends on the desires of U.S. citizens to purchase West German goods and services and to invest in West German assets. Other things being equal, an increase in the exchange rate of dollars in terms of marks is likely to increase the quantity of dollars supplied in exchange for marks. To see why this is so, suppose the price of a new BMW available as a U.S. import is 50,000 marks. If the exchange rate is 2 marks per dollar, the dollar equivalent of the marks necessary to purchase the car is $25,000. Now suppose the exchange rate increases to 2.5 marks per dollar. How much will the car now cost someone paying in dollars? To find out, simply multiply the 50,000 marks by the 1/2.5 dollars necessary to buy each mark. The price in dollars is now only $20,000. Naturally, the BMW, as well as other West German goods, is now more attractive to holders of dollars because its price in terms of dollars is lower. A higher exchange rate increases the quantity of dollars supplied to foreign exchange markets because it increases U.S. demand for imports. The supply curve of dollars for a foreign currency therefore slopes upward.

In Box 3 the equilibrium price of the dollar is 2 marks per dollar. At that price the number of dollars demanded per day by holders of marks exactly equals the number of dollars supplied per day by holders of dollars in exchange for marks. If instead the equilibrium price were 3 marks per dollar, the quantity of dollars supplied for marks would exceed the quantity demanded. The resulting surplus of dollars offered for marks would put downward pressure on the exchange rate of marks for dollars. If the price of dollars were 1.5 marks, the quantity of dollars demanded by holders of marks would exceed the quantity of dollars supplied for marks by holders of dollars. The resulting shortage of dollars would put upward pressure on the exchange rate of marks per dollar.

Actual equilibrium exchange rates change in response to shifts in the demand for and supply of dollars for foreign currencies. In fact, foreign exchange rates are quite volatile. They move up and down almost daily. The fluctuations of foreign exchange rates make international transactions a bit risky. For example, suppose a U.S. automobile dealer contracts to import 20 BMWs at a price of 40,000 West German marks apiece. If the current exchange rate is 2 marks per dollar, he expects the cars to cost $20,000 each for a total outlay of $400,000 for the order. He will pay for the cars on delivery, expected in about 3 months. If over the 3 months the exchange rate falls to 1.5 marks per dollar, each BMW will cost the dealer $26,666 and his total outlay for the 20 cars will be $533,333! Of course, if the price of the dollar in terms of the mark were to rise, his cost in terms of dollars would fall. For example, if 4 marks were necessary to purchase each dollar, the price per BMW would only be $10,000. As you can see, fluctuating exchange rates add some risk to international transactions.[1]

The table in Box 4 shows exchange rates of various foreign currencies per dollar existing in mid-July 1986 and in mid-January 1988. The table also shows exchange rates of dollars for foreign currencies: the number of dollars necessary to purchase

---

[1]Some of this risk can be controlled for by engaging in forward transactions in foreign exchange markets. To do so, traders purchase marks at a fixed price for delivery 1 to 3 months in the future.

Box 4 Foreign Exchange

Country	U.S. dollars per unit of foreign currency	Foreign currency per U.S. dollar
July 11, 1986		
Britain	1.5015 U.S. dollars per British pound	0.666 British pound per U.S. dollar
Canada	0.7257 U.S. dollar per Canadian dollar	1.378 Canadian dollars per U.S. dollar
France	0.1420 U.S. dollar per French franc	7.0445 French francs per U.S. dollar
Italy	0.000665 U.S. dollar per Italian lira	1,500 Italian lire per U.S. dollar
Japan	0.006186 U.S. dollar per Japanese yen	161.65 Japanese yen per U.S. dollar
W.Germany	0.4554 U.S. dollar per German mark	2.196 German marks per U.S. dollar
January 13, 1988		
Britain	1.822 U.S. dollars per British pound	0.5488 British pound per U.S. dollar
Canada	0.77 U.S. dollar per Canadian dollar	1.2868 Canadian dollars per U.S. dollar
France	0.1804 U.S. dollar per French franc	5.285 French francs per U.S. dollar
Italy	0.000813 U.S. dollar per Italian lira	1,203.00 Italian lire per U.S. dollar
Japan	0.007855 U.S. dollar per Japanese yen	127.30 Japanese yen per U.S. dollar
W.Germany	0.6101 U.S. dollar per German mark	1.6390 German marks per U.S. dollar

a unit of foreign currency. It's a good idea to compare these exchange rates with those prevailing today. To do so, open a copy of any major newspaper and turn to the financial section, where exchange rates for the dollar are reported daily.

The Determinants of Foreign Exchange Rates

Remember that the demand for dollars by foreigners is generated by the desire and ability of foreigners to buy U.S. goods and services and to acquire real and financial assets denominated in dollars. These are the factors that determine the supply of dollars in foreign exchange markets.

The foreign exchange rate of the dollar is likely to change in response to change in a variety of economic conditions that cause the demand for or supply of dollars in foreign exchange markets to change. The major influences on the demand for and supply of dollars include:

1. *Foreign demand for U.S. exports.* For example, if British importers sharply increase their demand for U.S. grain while not decreasing their demand for other U.S. products, British demand for U.S. dollars will go up. The entire demand curve for dollars by British citizens will shift outward. Other things being equal, an increase in British demand for U.S. exports tends to put upward pressure on the

exchange rate of the dollar, which is its price in terms of British pounds.

An increase in foreign demand for U.S. exports could result from increases in real income in foreign nations. Remember that income is a major determinant of import demand (see the chapter on the components of aggregate demand). As income increases in a foreign nation, the annual dollar volume of imports from the United States tends to increase. An increase in real income in foreign nations will therefore tend to put upward pressure on the exchange rate of the dollar. A decrease in income in foreign nations that are customers for U.S. exports will tend to decrease the demand for U.S. dollars and put downward pressure on the price of the dollar.

From 1985 to 1988, lagging income and high unemployment rates in many foreign nations were responsible for slack demand for U.S. dollars, which put downward pressure on the price of the dollar in terms of foreign currency.

Similarly, changes in tastes can affect the demand for U.S. goods by foreigners. If U.S. products become more fashionable, the demand for U.S. dollars by foreigners will increase, putting upward pressure on the price of the dollar.

The graph in Box 5 shows how an increase in the demand for dollars by West German citizens resulting from an increase in West German demand for U.S. exports will cause an increase in the exchange rate of the dollar. If the growth rate of real income in West Germany exceeds that in the United States, the result is likely to be upward pressure on the exchange rate of the dollar, as shown in Box 5.

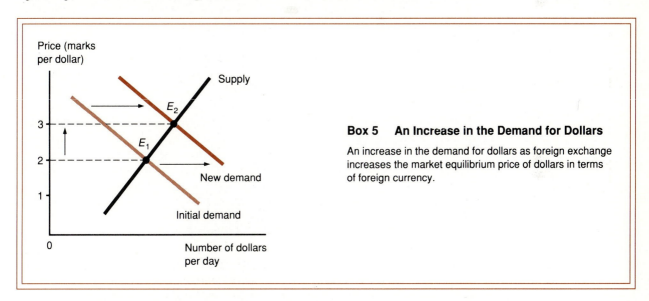

Box 5   An Increase in the Demand for Dollars

An increase in the demand for dollars as foreign exchange increases the market equilibrium price of dollars in terms of foreign currency.

2. *U.S. demand for imports.* An increase in U.S. demand for imports will increase the supply of dollars offered in foreign exchange markets. For example, if U.S. demand for BMWs and Mercedes-Benzes increases along with the demand for other German products, the result will be an increase in the supply of dollars on the foreign exchange market. This will decrease the exchange rate of the dollar. The graph in Box 6 shows how an increase in the supply of dollars reduces the price of the dollar in terms of marks.

A major factor influencing U.S. demand for imports is real income in the United States. An increase in aggregate real income tends to increase the U.S. demand for imports. As this occurs, the supply of dollars offered in foreign exchange markets

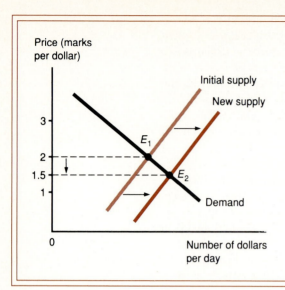

Price (marks per dollar)

Initial supply

New supply

3

E_1

2

1.5 E_2

1

Demand

0

Number of dollars per day

Box 6   An Increase in the Supply of Dollars

An increase in the supply of dollars as foreign exchange decreases the market equilibrium price of dollars in terms of foreign currency.

increases, putting downward pressure on the price of the dollar. Similarly, a decrease in aggregate real income in the United States will decrease U.S. demand for imports, and as the supply of dollars declines, there will be upward pressure on exchange rates.

3. Real interest rates in the United States relative to those in foreign nations. The willingness of foreigners to hold dollar assets in the United States depends on the interest rates that can be earned on assets denominated in dollars. The higher U.S. real interest rates are relative to real interest rates in foreign nations, the greater the demand by foreigners to hold dollar financial assets and, other things being equal, the higher the exchange rate of the dollar.

High real interest rates in the United States in the early 1980s contributed to strong demand by foreigners for dollars and caused the exchange rate of the dollar to soar. As U.S. interest rates fell relative to those in foreign nations in 1985 and 1986, the exchange rate of the dollar against such key currencies as the mark and the yen began to plummet. Note that these changes in the demand for dollars can be caused either by a change in U.S. real interest rates or by changes in foreign real interest rates.

Similarly, higher real interest rates in the United States relative to those in foreign nations will decrease the supply of dollars offered on foreign exchange markets. This is because U.S. investors will be less interested in selling dollars to make loans and buy securities of foreign governments and businesses. This will also tend to put upward pressure on the exchange rate as the supply curve of dollars shifts to the left.

4. Profitability of direct investment in U.S. businesses and real estate relative to profitability of similar investments in foreign nations. Foreigners also demand dollars to purchase U.S. corporate stock, real estate, and other assets. As the profitability of U.S. assets rises relative to that of assets in foreign nations, the demand for dollars to make such investments increases, putting upward pressure on exchange rates. Similarly, the supply of dollars to make direct investments in foreign nations decreases, and this too puts upward pressure on the exchange rate of the dollar.

5. *Expectations of an increase in the price of the dollar in terms of foreign currency.* The demand for and supply of a given currency also depend on the expectations of future changes in exchange rates. This is because a profit can be made by buying a currency at a low price and selling it at a higher price. Expectations of a higher future price of the U.S. dollar will increase the demand for dollars, putting upward pressure on the exchange rate. Similarly, expectations of a decrease in the price of the dollar in terms of foreign currency will decrease the demand for dollars and put downward pressure on the exchange rate.

If the exchange rate of the dollar is expected to rise, the supply of dollars will tend to decrease as U.S. importers decide to wait until the exchange rate increases to make purchases from foreign nations. This is because an increase in the price of the dollar in terms of foreign currency causes a decrease in the price of foreign currency in terms of the dollar. This means that imports will become cheaper as the exchange rate of the dollar rises. The decrease in the supply of dollars then puts upward pressure on the exchange rate.

6. *The price level in the United States relative to the price levels in foreign nations.* If the prices of U.S. goods go up by 10% relative to prices of competing goods supplied by foreign producers and the exchange rate is unchanged, it follows that the effective price of U.S. goods in foreign currency will also be 10% higher. This will decrease the quantity of U.S. goods demanded by foreign buyers. This in turn will decrease the demand for dollars, which will tend to reduce the exchange rate. Further, an increase in the U.S. price level relative to that in foreign nations will make foreign goods cheaper relative to U.S. goods, other things being equal. This will increase the demand for imported goods. The increase in import demand will increase the supply of dollars offered on foreign exchange markets. This will put still further downward pressure on the exchange rate of the dollar. Similarly, a fall in U.S. prices relative to foreign prices will increase the demand for U.S. exports and thus increase the price of the dollar in terms of foreign currency.

Appreciation and Depreciation of Currencies

As was just pointed out, exchange rates change frequently under the current system of international exchange. **Currency appreciation** occurs when there is an increase in the number of units of one nation's currency that must be given up to purchase each unit of another nation's currency. For example, the dollar appreciates relative to the West German mark if the equilibrium price (the exchange rate) of a dollar increases in terms of the mark. If the equilibrium price of a dollar goes up from 2 marks to 3 marks, the dollar has appreciated relative to the mark.

Similarly, **currency depreciation** occurs when there is a decrease in the number of units of one nation's currency that must be given up to purchase each unit of another nation's currency. You can see from the data in Box 4 that the dollar depreciated against the mark between 1986 and 1988 when its exchange rate fell from 2.196 marks per dollar in July 1986 to only 1.639 marks per dollar in January 1988.

When the dollar appreciates in terms of the mark, it follows that the mark depreciates in terms of the dollar. When it takes more marks to purchase a dollar, it's clear that fewer dollars are needed to purchase a mark. Similarly, if the dollar depreciates in terms of the mark, it follows that the mark appreciates in terms of the dollar. You can see this in Box 4 because between July 1986 and January 1988 the mark appreciated from 0.4554 to 0.6101 mark per dollar.

Note that when the U.S. dollar appreciates, other things being unchanged, goods

Currency appreciation:
Occurs when there is an increase in the number of units of one nation's currency that must be given up to purchase each unit of another nation's currency.

Currency depreciation:
Occurs when there is a decrease in the number of units of one nation's currency that must be given up to purchase each unit of another nation's currency.

and services produced in the United States become more expensive in terms of foreign currencies. This decreases the foreign demand for U.S. goods and services and tends to decrease U.S. net exports and real GNP. Similarly, because foreign currencies depreciate when the U.S. dollar appreciates, foreign goods become cheaper in terms of U.S. currency. This induces U.S. citizens to spend more dollars on foreign goods and services, which also decreases aggregate demand for U.S. goods.

Currency appreciation or depreciation in a free market results from shifts in either the demand for or supply of the currency. To forecast changes in foreign exchange rates thus requires an understanding of the forces underlying the demand for dollars and assets denominated in dollars held by foreigners. It also requires an understanding of the forces influencing the supply of dollars offered in exchange for foreign currencies.

The Principle of Purchasing Power Parity

Purchasing power parity:
A principle that states that the exchange rate between any two currencies tends to adjust to reflect changes in the price levels in the two nations.

The principle of **purchasing power parity** of one nation's money for another's states that the exchange rate between any two currencies tends to adjust to reflect changes in the price levels in the two nations. The logic behind purchasing power parity is that similar goods produced in different countries should sell for the same price when exchange rates and transaction costs are taken into consideration. Using this logic, a rise in the U.S. price level tends to cause the dollar to depreciate in terms of foreign currency. Similarly, a decline in the U.S. price level relative to foreign price levels tends to result in an appreciation of the dollar in terms of foreign currency. If the principle held precisely, then whenever the U.S. price level rose 10% relative to, say, the West German price level, the price of the dollar in terms of the mark would fall by *exactly* 10%.

The principle of purchasing power parity applies only if markets for foreign exchange are free. As you'll soon see, central banks and other governing authorities often intervene in foreign exchange markets. For example, the Fed might buy dollars on the international market, thereby increasing demand and preventing the price of the dollar from falling in terms of foreign currencies. Similarly, governments often control exchange rates to keep the prices of imports low to their citizens.

Even when foreign exchange markets are free, there is often a lag between changes in the price levels and changes in foreign exchange rates between two nations.

Impact of Changes in Foreign Exchange Rates on Macroeconomic Equilibrium

Nominal exchange rate:
The price of a unit of one nation's currency in terms of a unit of a foreign currency.

Real exchange rate
(of a nation's currency): The sacrifice of goods and services that foreign buyers must make when they use their own currency to purchase goods of the first nation worth one unit of that nation's currency.

Why worry about changes in foreign exchange rates? The reason for the concern is that changes in foreign exchange rates can affect macroeconomic equilibrium. To understand how fluctuations in foreign exchange rates can affect aggregate demand and aggregate supply in a nation, we must first examine the distinction between changes in *nominal* exchange rates and changes in *real* exchange rates.

Nominal and Real Exchange Rates

The **nominal exchange rate** of a currency is the price of a unit of that currency in terms of a unit of a foreign currency. The **real exchange rate** of a nation's

Principles in Practice

When the Dollar Depreciates, the Yen Appreciates: The Impact of a High Yen on the Japanese Economy

While we usually think of high prices as generating high profits, it's not necessarily so when it comes to the value of a nation's currency.

For example, in 1986 and 1987 the value of the dollar depreciated sharply against the yen. The price of the dollar plunged from 240 yen in 1985 to 120 yen in early 1988. The flip side of the coin is that the yen appreciated sharply against the dollar. Whenever it takes fewer yen to buy a dollar, it also takes more dollars to buy each yen. The high yen thus makes Japanese goods more expensive in terms of dollars.

While some Japanese producers decided to bite the bullet and settle for less profit per unit of exports, the toll of a high yen, which the Japanese call *endakka*, will eventually be reduced international demand for Japanese goods. For example, 1986 profits in Japan's electronics industries fell 80% from the previous year. The Toyota Motor Corporation suffered a 17% drop in profits in 1986. This was a bitter pill to swallow for the Japanese, who exported $174 billion worth of goods in 1985, amounting to 13% of their GNP. Export shipments of color televisions plummeted in 1987, and by mid-1988 Japanese auto exporters were bracing for a sharp decline in sales of their products in the United States. The high yen came at a time when Japan already was facing increased competition from producers in South Korea, Taiwan, and Brazil.

As a result of the appreciation of the yen, prices of Japanese goods in terms of dollars would have increased by 50% between 1985 and mid-1987, assuming that sellers were unwilling to accept fewer yen for exported goods. The higher yen forced Japanese exporters to choose between accepting lower profits for their exports or allowing prices to rise in terms of foreign currency, which in turn would mean a decrease in quantity demanded. The impact on Japan was enormous. The major steel producers reduced their work forces by the thousands from 1985 to 1987. Huge steel furnaces were idle, and coal mines were closed. A major shipbuilding firm laid off nearly 40% of its workers in 1986 and cut the salaries of those workers who were fortunate enough to retain their jobs. Japanese manufacturing in 1986 was characterized by layoffs, plant closings, production cutbacks, and falling profits.

The export industries that fuel the Japanese economy also took a beating as a result of the appreciating yen. In a nation for which net exports are such a substantial portion of GNP, it's inevitable that overall growth will be adversely affected. The only good news for Japan as a result of the volatile exchange rates is that the appreciation of the yen decreased the prices Japan pays for key imports such as petroleum. The lower prices of such key imports contributed to lower costs of production, which in turn allowed Japanese sellers to hold the line on prices without decreasing profits as much as would otherwise be necessary.

The decline in exports is likely to have a reverberating effect on the Japanese economy for years to come. Business firms in 1986 and 1987 cut back on plans for new investment in plant and equipment. The decline in income caused a reduction in housing starts. Corporate profits fell, and wage increases for Japanese workers became difficult to obtain, which acted to reduce consumer demand. Increased unemployment in Japan also was expected to put a crimp in the spending plans of many Japanese consumers. The appreciation of the yen undoubtedly will put downward pressure on real GNP and the price level in Japan throughout the remainder of the 1980s.

---

currency is the sacrifice of goods and services that foreign buyers must make when they use their own currency to purchase goods of the first nation worth one unit of that nation's currency. For example, an increase in the real exchange rate of the dollar in terms of the yen occurs when the price of the dollar in terms of the yen increases after adjustment for differences in the rates of inflation in both countries. When the real exchange rate of the dollar increases, foreigners must give up more purchasing power for each dollar's worth of U.S. goods they buy. The real exchange rate of the dollar rose markedly between 1981 and 1985. As this occurred, U.S. goods became more expensive to foreigners.

The other side of the coin is that an increase in the real exchange rate of the dollar means U.S. buyers will sacrifice fewer goods and services for any given purchase of foreign goods denominated in foreign currency. For example, the purchase of 400,000 yen worth of Japanese goods involves less of a sacrifice for U.S. buyers when the real exchange rate of the dollar rises in terms of yen. Remember: When

---

the exchange rate of the dollar appreciates in terms of the yen, the exchange rate of the yen in terms of dollars must fall.

Changes in real exchange rates therefore affect the attractiveness of U.S. exports in foreign markets and also affect U.S. demand for imports by changing the prices of imports and exports after adjustment for inflation.

Real Exchange Rates and the Relative Prices of Imports in the United States from 1977 to 1986

The graph in Box 7 shows an index of the real exchange rate of the dollar against foreign currencies, adjusted for changes in the price levels in the United States and abroad since 1977. As you can see, the real exchange rate increased sharply from 1980 to 1985 before beginning to fall. Also plotted on the graph are the relative prices of U.S. imports. You can see that the price of imports fell on average over the period 1980 to 1985 compared to the average of all other goods. Despite the decline in the value of the dollar since 1985, the relative prices of imports (other than petroleum products) have not increased substantially. *Empirical evidence suggests that import prices respond with a lag of up to 2 years to changes in exchange rates.* Evidence indicates that the profit per unit of output increased for foreign suppliers to U.S. markets between 1980 and 1984 when the dollar appreciated. When the dollar began to depreciate, many foreign sellers apparently chose to get along with less profit per unit rather than raise prices significantly.[2] In addition, many foreign currencies are tied to the dollar, and the dollar has not depreciated substantially against them. Over the period during which the dollar depreciated against the yen

[2]See *Economic Report of the President, 1987,* Washington, D.C.: U.S. Government Printing Office, 1987, p. 116.

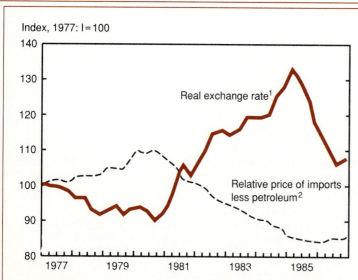

Index, 1977: I = 100

Real exchange rate[1]

Relative price of imports less petroleum[2]

Box 7   Real Exchange Rate and Relative Price of Imports

Despite the fall in the real exchange rate since 1985, the relative price of imports has not increased substantially. There is usually a lag between changes in exchange rates and changes in import prices.

[1]Trade-weighted value of the dollar adjusted by relative wholesale prices.
[2]Ratio of implicit price deflator for imports less petroleum to GNP implicit price deflator.
Source: *Economic Report of the President,* 1987.

and the mark in the 1980s, it actually appreciated against the Korean won, thereby making Korean goods less expensive to U.S. buyers!

Why did the dollar appreciate so much in the early 1980s, and why did it finally begin to decline in 1985 and 1986? Like most prices, the price of the dollar responds to changes in influences on its demand and supply. A key factor that has influenced the price of the dollar in recent years has been real interest rates in the United States relative to those in foreign nations. The high real interest rates that prevailed in the United States from 1981 to 1985 increased the demand for the dollar so that it could be used by foreigners to make investments in U.S. real and financial assets. The large budget deficit and Federal Reserve policies to reduce the rate of inflation in the early 1980s contributed to high real interest rates. Not surprisingly, policies in 1985 and 1986 that sharply lowered real interest rates resulted in marked depreciation of the dollar on international markets.

Impact of a Higher Dollar on Aggregate Demand

When the real exchange rate of the dollar increases, you now know that our exports will become more expensive to foreigners while imported goods will become less expensive to U.S. buyers (although there's sometimes a lag in the change in the prices of imports). Other things being equal, we would expect increases in the real exchange rate of the dollar against a broad group of currencies to increase demand for imports in the United States while decreasing the demand for U.S. exports abroad. This means that a high dollar can contribute to lower net exports. As net exports decline, there will be a reduction in employment in export industries and in industries facing strong competition from foreign suppliers. This is exactly the scenario that the U.S. economy found itself in from 1980 to 1985.

An increase in real exchange rates therefore decreases aggregate demand, with the extent of the decrease depending on the size of the economy's export sector and the extent to which domestic industries must compete with foreign sellers at home. A decrease in aggregate demand caused by an increase in the real exchange rate of the dollar is illustrated in the graph in Box 8. As you can see, the result of

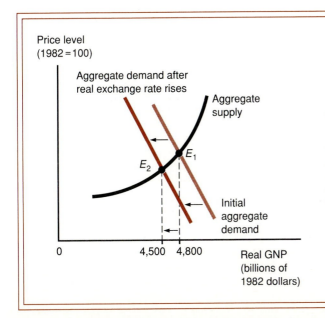

Box 8   Impact of an Increase in the Real Exchange Rate of the Dollar on Aggregate Demand

An increase in the real exchange rate of the dollar decreases aggregate demand. This puts downward pressure on real GNP and on the price level. A decrease in the real exchange rate of the dollar would increase aggregate demand, which would be an expansionary influence on the economy.

the decrease in aggregate demand is downward pressure on both real GNP and the price level. The unemployment resulting from the decline in real GNP will be concentrated in both export industries and industries facing strong foreign competition. For example, from 1981 to 1985 the U.S. automobile and textile industries were particularly hard hit by the high price of the dollar. U.S. agriculture, which relies heavily on export sales, was also adversely affected.

You can now see why there is concern when the value of the dollar is high. An increase in the real exchange rate of the dollar can be a contractionary influence on the economy that hits certain major industries particularly hard.

Similarly, a decrease in the real exchange rate of the dollar can increase aggregate demand by increasing U.S. export demand while decreasing U.S. demand for imports. This acts to increase employment in export industries and, after a lag, in industries that compete with imports. The decline in the real exchange rate of the dollar after 1985 resulted in a boom in U.S. export industries in 1987 and 1988. However, because of the delayed effect of the decline on import prices, import demand was slow to respond, which dampened the expansionary effect.

Remember: When the price of the dollar in terms of foreign currency goes down, the price of the foreign currency in terms of the dollar must go up. The decline in the real exchange rate of the dollar beginning in 1985 caused an increase in the real exchange rate of yen in terms of dollars. As shown in the Principles in Practice box, this was a contractionary influence on the Japanese economy.

Impact of Changes in Real Exchange Rates on Aggregate Supply

Changes in real exchange rates can also affect macroeconomic equilibrium through effects on aggregate supply. Remember that aggregate supply will shift when input prices change. The United States and many other nations import substantial amounts of raw materials and machinery. An increase in the real exchange rate of the dollar means that the prices of imported inputs, after adjustment for inflation, will decline.

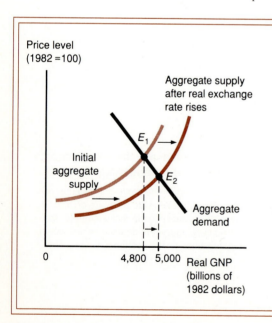

Box 9   Impact of an Increase in the Real Exchange Rate of the Dollar on Aggregate Supply

An increase in the value of the dollar makes imported raw materials and machinery cheaper. The resulting decline in input prices increases aggregate supply, putting upward pressure on real GNP and downward pressure on the price level given aggregate demand. A decrease in the real exchange rate of the dollar can decrease aggregate supply, causing inflation to heat up while real GNP declines.

A high-priced dollar can therefore contribute to lower input prices and cause the aggregate supply curve to shift outward, as shown in the graph in Box 9.

The increase in aggregate supply that results from a higher real exchange rate of the dollar puts upward pressure on real GNP but downward pressure on the price level. A higher-valued dollar can therefore contribute to both increased employment and lower inflation through its impact on aggregate supply.

On the other hand, a decline in the real exchange rate of the dollar will contribute to a decrease in aggregate supply by raising the prices of imported inputs. The decrease in aggregate supply will be a contractionary influence on the economy and will put upward pressure on the price level.

Of course, the magnitude of the supply-side effects will depend on the importance of imported inputs in production.

Conclusion: Impact of Changes in Foreign Exchange Rates on Macroeconomic Equilibrium

As you can see from the preceding analysis, changes in real exchange rates have a complex impact on macroeconomic equilibrium in the economy. A higher-priced dollar, through its effect on aggregate demand, is a contractionary influence on the economy. But through its effects on aggregate supply, the higher-priced dollar is an expansionary influence on the economy because it lowers the prices of imported inputs. Depending on whether the demand-side or supply-side effects are stronger, a higher-priced dollar can either increase or decrease real GNP.

However, there's little doubt that a higher-priced dollar will moderate inflationary pressures in the U.S. economy. The reason for this is that both the demand-side and supply-side effects of the increase in the real exchange rate put downward pressure on the price level.

There's one other complication in the analysis that we must consider and that we'll investigate later in greater detail. You'll recall from our analysis of the circular flow of income and expenditure in the chapter on the GNP that whenever net exports are negative, foreign saving in the United States must increase. An increase in the real exchange rate of the dollar that contributes to a further deterioration of the U.S. balance of trade therefore increases the supply of foreign saving in the United States, as you'll see in detail soon. This puts downward pressure on U.S. real interest rates by increasing the supply of loanable funds in U.S. credit markets. The lower real interest rates can increase the quantity of investment goods demanded by U.S. businesses, which will serve to increase aggregate demand in the United States. This interest rate effect will moderate the contractionary influence of the negative net exports on U.S. real GNP.

The graph in Box 10 shows a case where the higher real exchange rate acts to decrease equilibrium real GNP. As you can see, the aggregate demand curve shifts inward in response to lower net export demand by a greater amount than the aggregate supply curve shifts outward in response to lower input prices. As real GNP declines, there will be an increase in the unemployment rate in the economy.

We can analyze the impact of a decrease in the real exchange of the dollar in a similar fashion. You know that, other things being equal, a lower dollar will increase demand for U.S. exports and decrease U.S. demand for imports. This will tend to increase aggregate demand, putting upward pressure on U.S. real GNP and the price level. Similarly, a lower-priced dollar will contribute to higher input prices as a result of increases in the prices of imported raw materials and machinery. As this

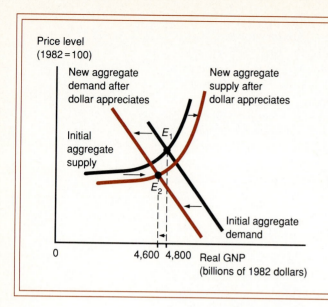

Price level (1982 = 100)

New aggregate demand after dollar appreciates

New aggregate supply after dollar appreciates

Initial aggregate supply

E_1

E_2

Initial aggregate demand

0   4,600 4,800   Real GNP (billions of 1982 dollars)

Box 10   How a Higher Dollar Can Decrease Equilibrium Real GNP

When the aggregate demand curve shifts further to the left than the aggregate supply curve shifts to the right when the dollar appreciates on international foreign exchange markets, equilibrium real GNP will fall.

occurs, aggregate supply will decrease, which in turn will put downward pressure on real GNP and upward pressure on the price level. We can conclude that a decrease in the real exchange rate of the dollar will contribute to inflationary pressures in the United States and will either increase or decrease real GNP depending on whether the demand-side or supply-side effects are stronger. As the real exchange rate of the dollar declined in 1987 and 1988, the demand for U.S. exports boomed. The demand-side effects were quite strong at that time and real GNP increased, as did inflationary pressures in the economy. The graph in Box 11 shows how a decline in the real exchange rate of the dollar can result in an increase in equilibrium real GNP.

Finally, we might also point out that a lower-priced dollar means that foreign saving in the United States will decline as the U.S. balance of trade improves. As this

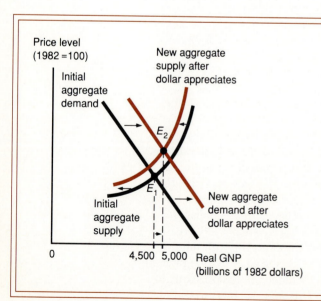

Price level (1982 = 100)

Initial aggregate demand

New aggregate supply after dollar appreciates

E_2

E_1

Initial aggregate supply

New aggregate demand after dollar appreciates

0   4,500 5,000   Real GNP (billions of 1982 dollars)

Box 11   How a Lower Dollar Can Increase Equilibrium Real GNP

When the impact of the lower dollar on aggregate demand is stronger than its effect on aggregate supply, real GNP will increase. In 1987 and 1988 the strong increase in aggregate demand resulting from increased exports dominated the U.S. economy and acted to increase equilibrium real GNP, as shown in the graph, while at the same time putting upward pressure on the price level.

occurs, there will be upward pressure on real interest rates in the United States in response to a decrease in the foreign supply of loanable funds in credit markets.

Concept Check

1   What could cause the foreign exchange rate of the dollar to increase?

2   In early 1987 the price of the dollar in terms of yen plummeted. What could have caused the decline in the yen price of dollars?

3   How can an increase in the real exchange rate of the dollar against foreign currencies influence macroeconomic equilibrium in the United States?

International Payments and the International Monetary System

You've just seen how fluctuations in foreign exchange rates can affect the economy. The current international monetary system allows exchange rates to be influenced by market forces. However, governments and central banks influence exchange rates as they intervene in foreign exchange markets in an attempt to control the macroeconomic effects of exchange rate fluctuations on their economies.

We're now ready to discuss the evolution of the current international monetary system. As you'll see, flexible foreign exchange rates have been the exception rather than the rule throughout much of history. This section gives you a quick tour of the way the international monetary system has changed since 1900. We begin with an analysis of the gold standard, which, prior to the Great Depression of the 1930s, was a system that kept fluctuations in foreign exchange rates within narrow bounds.

1. *The gold standard.* For much of the time prior to the 1930s, the international payments system was based on a **gold standard**, under which currencies were required to be convertible into gold at fixed prices. For example, the dollar was worth $1/20$ ounce of gold during one period under the gold standard. Similarly, the British pound was worth $1/4$ ounce of gold until the beginning of World War I. This meant that it took $5 to buy a British pound because $5 was necessary to buy $5/20 = 1/4$ ounce of gold. The gold convertibility established fixed exchange rates as long as nations kept the value of their currency constant in terms of units of gold.

It's easy to see how the system worked. Suppose the price of a case of Scotch whiskey was 100 British pounds. It would take $500 to purchase the case at the fixed exchange rate. Suppose, however, the British pound appreciated so that it took $6 to buy each British pound. Under the gold standard, no one would buy pounds for dollars at any exchange rate significantly higher than $5. This is because they could just as easily arrange to buy $1/4$ ounce of gold for each pound. This would cost only $5 plus a modest fee for transferring gold to British ownership. Under the gold standard, currencies could fluctuate only in narrow bands that depended on the costs of transferring ownership of gold between nations.

There were some important consequences of international movements of gold ownership. Each nation used gold as an international reserve that constituted its monetary base. When a nation lost gold, its money supply usually decreased because of the decline in bank reserves. This tended to reduce the price level in that nation in the long run. Similarly, when a nation gained gold, its money supply increased. This tended to increase its price level in the long run. *Under the gold standard,*

Gold standard:
An international monetary system that required that currencies be convertible into gold at a fixed price.

changes in relative price levels among nations caused by gold flows tended to keep currencies from appreciating or depreciating in the long run.

Under the gold standard, few nations played the game strictly according to the rules. To avoid changes in their price levels, nations commonly changed the official quantity of gold that could be exchanged for their currency. By devaluing their currency in terms of gold, the nations allowed their currency to officially depreciate. For example, if the pound were devalued to be worth ⅛ ounce of gold, it would take only $2.50 to purchase each pound. Such a devaluation would stimulate demand for British exports without the need for the price level to fall through an outflow of gold. Nations hesitated to let their price levels fall for fear that reductions in the money supply would cause short-run unemployment and recessions because of inflexible wages.

2. *The Bretton Woods system.* In 1944, representatives of the United States and other industrial nations met at Bretton Woods, New Hampshire, to develop a new international monetary system. This system was also based on fixed exchange rates. *However, the* **Bretton Woods system** *tied the value of foreign currencies not to gold but to the U.S. dollar!* This is because the United States had accumulated a great deal of foreign exchange and gold during the war and was in a strong financial position compared to most European nations, many of which were shattered as a result of the war. The dollar was directly convertible into gold by foreign governments and central banks at the fixed price of $35 per ounce. Central banks agreed to intervene in foreign exchange markets to buy or sell currencies whenever these currencies appreciated or depreciated. Few of these nations had any gold and instead held dollars as their international reserves. Of course, such purchases and sales of currencies would alter the money supplies within those nations just as gold flows did under the old gold standard. The United States, on the other hand, had the responsibility to buy and sell gold under the system to keep the price at $35 per ounce.

The Bretton Woods agreement also established the **International Monetary Fund (IMF)**, which set rules for the international monetary system to make loans to nations that lacked international reserves of dollars. The system allowed countries to *devalue* (officially depreciate) or *revalue* (officially appreciate) their currency in terms of dollars. Nations would devalue or revalue their currency on occasion to affect net exports in ways designed to stabilize their economies.

Dissatisfaction with the Bretton Woods system developed in the 1960s because nations whose currencies were undervalued relative to the equilibrium exchange rate in terms of dollars were unwilling to allow the international price of their currency to rise. A rise in the price of these nations' currencies in terms of dollars would have made their exports more expensive and increased the price of their imports. The resulting decline in net exports would have decreased aggregate demand in those nations. Another problem was that, under the Bretton Woods rules, the United States could not devalue its currency to stimulate net exports. In 1971 the United States suspended convertibility of the dollar into gold, and by 1973 the United States and other nations in the Bretton Woods system abandoned fixed exchange rates in favor of a system of flexible or *floating* rates determined in part by market forces.

3. *The current system.* The current international monetary system allows free-market determination of exchange rates but also allows central banks to buy and sell currencies to stabilize exchange rates. In effect the current system is a **managed float** in which central banks affect the supply of and demand for currencies in ways that influence equilibrium in foreign exchange markets. Under the system, central

Bretton Woods system:
An international monetary system developed in 1944 and based on fixed exchange rates, with the value of foreign currencies tied to the U.S. dollar.

International Monetary Fund (IMF):
Established under the Bretton Woods agreement; set rules for the international monetary system to make loans to nations that lacked international reserves of dollars.

Managed float:
Describes the current international monetary system, under which central banks affect supply of and demand for currencies in ways that influence equilibrium in foreign exchange markets.

banks frequently buy their own nation's currency on international foreign exchange markets to keep it from depreciating. They often resist currency depreciation because it would make imported goods, such as those from the United States, more expensive for their citizens. However, when central banks buy their own currency they lose reserves of foreign currency such as dollars. The dollar remains a strong reserve currency, and holders of dollars use them to invest in the United States. The loss of reserves by debtor nations, such as Mexico, is a matter for concern because of fears that these nations will have trouble obtaining the dollars they require to repay international debts in the future. When these nations lose their dollar reserves of foreign exchange, the only way they can acquire more dollars is by running a balance of trade surplus with the United States in the future. A loss in dollar reserves combined with a decline in net exports from these nations means they run the risk of defaulting on their international loans. This would reduce the profitability of U.S. banks that hold those loans as assets.

The current system also has a paper substitute for gold called a **special drawing right (SDR),** which is created by the International Monetary Fund and distributed to member nations to use as international reserves. International reserves are stocks of foreign currencies or other assets that nations can use to make international payments. SDRs are substitutes for foreign currency that fulfill the role previously played by gold in settling international debts when a nation lacked the foreign exchange to do so. Gold is now completely demonetized because no major currency is convertible to gold. Gold now can be bought and sold on the free market like any good or service.

Special drawing right (SDR):
A paper substitute for gold that is created by the International Monetary Fund and distributed to member nations to use as international reserves.

The International Balance of Payments and Balance of Trade and Foreign Saving in the United States

In the chapter on the GNP we showed that when the United States runs a balance of trade deficit, foreign saving in the United States must increase. We can now examine the financial relations between the United States and the rest of the world to show how the balance of trade deficit is equal to the increase in foreign saving in the United States over any given period.

A nation's international **balance of payments** is a statement showing the net exchange of that nation's currency for foreign currencies from *all transactions* between that nation and foreign nations in a given year. For example, the U.S. balance of payments statement shows the number of dollars supplied for *all* foreign transactions and the number of dollars demanded by *all* foreign nations. *The actual number of dollars purchased by foreigners must always equal the actual number sold over the year.*

The international transactions reported in the balance of payments accounts include exports and imports of goods, transactions for foreign services (including expenditures of dollars abroad by U.S. travelers), purchase of foreign shipping and insurance services, and transactions involving the exchange of financial and other assets.

Balance of payments:
A statement showing the net exchange of a nation's currency for foreign currencies from all transactions between that nation and foreign nations in a given year.

The Current Account

The table in Box 12 shows the U.S. balance of payments accounts with the rest of the world in 1985. The *current account* summarizes the transactions involving in-

---

The International Balance of Payments and Balance of Trade and Foreign Saving in the U.S.

917

Box 12   U.S. International Balance of Payments, 1985
(billions of dollars)

Current Account	Amount
1. Merchandise exports	+$214.4
2. Merchandise imports	−338.9
3. Balance of trade = Merchandise exports − Merchandise imports	−124.4
4. Net investment income	+25.2
5. Net military transactions	−2.9
6. Net travel and transportation receipts	−11.1
7. Other services	+10.6
8. Balance on goods and services	−102.7
9. Remittances, pensions, and other transfers	−15.0
10. Balance on current account [a]	−117.8
Capital Account	
11. Foreign assets in U.S.	+127.1
12. U.S. government assets abroad	−2.8
13. U.S. private assets abroad	−25.7
14. U.S. official reserve assets [b]	−3.8
15. Statistical discrepancy	+23.0
16. Capital account balance	+117.8

[a] Excludes military.
[b] Consists of gold, SDRs, convertible currencies, and
U.S. reserve position in IMF.

Source: *Economic Report of the President,* 1987.

ternational exchange of goods and services purchased during the year and other miscellaneous transactions, including unilateral transfers and military transactions. A plus sign indicates that the transaction earned U.S. sellers the equivalent amount of dollars in foreign exchange. A minus sign indicates a transaction in which the dollar equivalent in foreign exchange was supplied by U.S. buyers to foreigners. Lines 1 and 2 of the table show the dollar value of transactions involving exports and imports of merchandise in 1985. Line 3 shows the **balance of trade,** which is the difference between the dollar value of *merchandise* exported by American firms and U.S. imports of foreign-produced goods.

The balance of trade gets the most attention in the press because of its impact on industrial employment in the United States. In 1985 the dollar value of U.S. imports exceeded the dollar value of U.S. exports, resulting in a balance of trade deficit of $124.4 billion. This means that exports of merchandise by U.S. firms didn't earn enough foreign money to balance the imports of foreign goods by Americans. When the dollar value of U.S. exports exceeds the dollar value of U.S. imports, a balance of trade surplus prevails. For example, in 1975 the United States had a balance of trade surplus of nearly $9 billion.

Because international trade transactions also involve receipt and payment of interest and investment income during the year and the exchange of services, the balance of trade provides an incomplete picture of the U.S. net inflow and outflow of current payments. For example, as shown on line 4 of the table, net investment

Balance of trade:
The difference between the value of merchandise exported by a nation's firms and the nation's imports of foreign-produced goods.

Principles in Practice

The Group of Five Attacks the Dollar: How Central Bank Action Influences Exchange Rates Under the Managed Float

The "Group of Five" may sound like the title of a forties thriller, but it's the name given to the group of nations composed of the United States, Japan, West Germany, France, and the United Kingdom. In September 1985, after months of negotiation, these nations agreed on a plan to cause the international value of the dollar to depreciate in an effort to improve the U.S. balance of trade and head off political attempts in the U.S. Congress to increase protectionism. The Group of Five's action started a trend in foreign exchange markets that eventually resulted in the dollar plummeting in 1986 and 1987. The implementation of the group's plan shows how central bank intervention in foreign exchange markets can affect exchange rates under what is called the "managed float."

The Group of Five plan involved central bank sales of dollars on open markets to increase the supply, thereby putting downward pressure on the price of the dollar. For example, when the Federal Reserve sells dollars, it creates deposits for U.S. banks and uses those dollars to pay for purchases of deposits denominated in foreign money that the banks hold at their correspondent banks abroad. Thus one consequence of the plan was an increase in bank reserves that put upward pressure on

money supply and downward pressure on real interest rates in the United States. By selling dollars, foreign central banks decrease bank reserves in their nations because banks that buy the dollars will pay for them with deposits at their central banks. By affecting bank reserves, the Group of Five plan put upward pressure on interest rates in foreign nations while putting downward pressure on interest rates in the United States. This too helped shift private demand and supply in the foreign exchange markets to decrease the price of the dollar.

The plan was successful in reducing the price of the dollar substantially within a short period. The attack on the price of the dollar was launched at 6:00 a.m. on the seventh-floor trading room of the Federal Reserve Bank of New York. That day the staff purchased 675 million West German marks for about $250 million, thus substantially increasing the supply of dollars offered for sale against marks. That transaction and sales of dollars against other currencies by other central banks significantly lowered the price of the dollar.*

As you can see, the managed float allows central banks to manipulate supply and demand and adjust foreign exchange rates so as to achieve political objectives.

*See "The Dollar: Diary of an Attack," *The Margin,* 1, 3, November 1985, p. 18, for an account of the happenings in foreign exchange markets that week.

---

income in 1985 from international transactions was $25.2 billion. This is the amount by which receipts from U.S. investments abroad exceeded payments to foreign investors in the United States in that year. Lines 5, 6, and 7 of the table show other service transactions, including those for travel and transportation. The *balance of goods and services* on line 8 shows that when international transactions for services are added to those for merchandise, Americans supplied $102.7 billion more to foreigners than foreigners supplied in the dollar equivalent of foreign currency to the United States in 1985.

The category of transactions with foreign nations shown on line 9 is unilateral transfers. These are payments for pensions, remittances, and other transfers of funds, such as gifts and foreign aid. Net international transfer payments in 1985 amounted to $15 billion.

When all current international transactions are considered, the total earnings and outlays of dollars in foreign exchange can be calculated to get a picture of net exports, which is the difference between the value of all exports and the value of all imports in the current year. The **balance on current account of the balance of payments** shown on line 10 in Box 12 is roughly equal to U.S. net exports as measured by the National Income and Product Accounts.[3]

Balance on current account of the balance of payments: Measures U.S. net exports for the year, including transactions involving services, investment income, and transfers.

[3]Because of slightly different accounting techniques, the balance on current account is not exactly equal to net exports.

The International Balance of Payments and Balance of Trade and Foreign Saving in the U.S.

919

In 1985, however, the United States had a deficit on current account of over $117 billion. This means Americans supplied foreigners with that many more dollars than foreigners supplied to the United States in foreign exchange for American goods and services and interest and investment income that year.

In 1981 the United States had a surplus on current account of $6.3 billion. The graph in Box 13 shows the U.S. merchandise trade balance (balance of trade) and the current account balance from 1950 to 1986. The balance of trade has been in deficit every year since 1975. Except for a short period in the late 1970s and early 1980s, the current account has also been consistently in deficit since 1975.

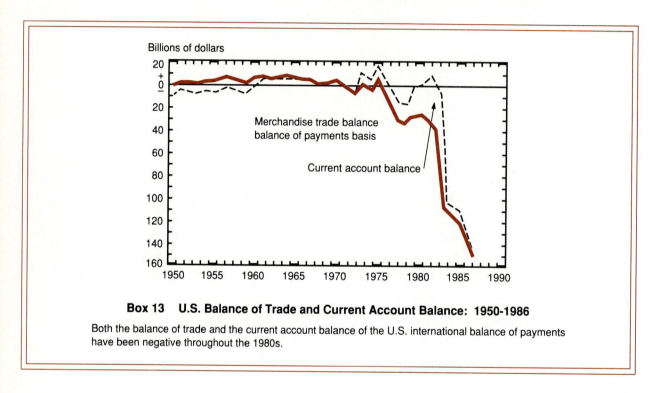

Box 13   U.S. Balance of Trade and Current Account Balance: 1950-1986

Both the balance of trade and the current account balance of the U.S. international balance of payments have been negative throughout the 1980s.

The Capital Account

The balance on current account represents the relationship between current earnings of dollars from international trade and current payments of U.S. dollars to acquire foreign exchange to settle payments to foreigners. When the current account is in deficit as it was in 1985, this means the United States has to pay more dollars out in international transactions than it earned from international transactions during the year.

In 1985 the United States had to borrow and sell assets to finance the deficit on current account. The increase in foreign assets in the United States on line 1 of the capital account in Box 12 represents borrowing from foreigners to balance the current account deficit. This represents *foreign saving in the United States.* Lines 12 through 14 represent sales of assets by individuals, the U.S. government, and the Federal Reserve System to offset the current account deficit.

In 1985 foreigners increased their holdings of assets in the United States by $127.1 billion, as shown on line 11 of the table in Box 12. This is called a capital inflow. In the same year U.S. government holdings of assets abroad fell by $2.8

billion and U.S. private assets abroad declined by $25.7 billion, as shown on lines 12 and 13. The reduction of these assets represents a way to obtain dollars to finance the current account deficit.

The reduction in U.S. official reserve assets of $3.8 billion shown on line 14 reflects the net change in U.S. official reserve assets abroad in the form of gold, SDRs, convertible currencies, and reserves at the IMF that are necessary to make the accounts balance. Decreases in official reserve assets abroad can be thought of as *exports* of foreign exchange, gold, and other international reserve assets held by the Federal Reserve and the U.S. government. When the United States draws down its official reserve assets as it did in 1985, in effect it purchases U.S. dollars from foreign holders using official reserves to settle the balance of payments accounts. Decreases in official U.S. reserves therefore represent a way to acquire U.S. dollars to offset the current account deficit.

When the data gathered for the capital account don't exactly match, the difference is called a statistical discrepancy. The statistical discrepancy in 1985 was $23 billion. This sum represents foreign payments of dollars in the United States that the data gatherers estimate existed but cannot track down by source. For example, a portion of the $23 billion obtained in this way could result from smuggling and other illegal transactions involving exports of U.S. goods and services.

The last line of the table in Box 12 shows the capital account balance, which is + $117.8 billion. *The capital account balance is a surplus that is exactly equal to the deficit on the balance on current account.* Whenever the current account is in deficit, there must be a net increase in real and financial assets held by foreigners. You learned this earlier in the circular flow analysis in the chapter on the GNP. *Whenever net exports are negative, foreign saving in the United States increases by an amount equal to the excess of imports over exports.* Similarly, if net exports were positive, the balance on the current account would be a surplus, which would be offset by a net increase in U.S. saving abroad that would be reflected in a capital account deficit. As was pointed out earlier in this chapter, foreign saving in the United States increases the supply of loanable funds in U.S. credit markets, thereby putting downward pressure on real interest rates in the United States.

The way the capital account is related to the current account points out an important long-term implication of chronic deficits on the current account. A deficit on the current account implies that the United States must borrow from foreigners or sell foreign assets. As this occurs, the United States in the aggregate becomes more indebted to foreigners or reduces its holdings of foreign assets. The deficits on the current account since 1975 have resulted in a sharp increase in foreign ownership of U.S. assets while U.S. ownership of foreign assets has declined. In the future this means that foreigners will earn more U.S. interest and investment income each year, which in turn will mean that the United States will have to export more or import less to avoid a deficit on the current account. Similarly, by reducing its holdings of assets abroad the United States will have less income from abroad to offset import purchases of U.S. citizens.

The long-term implication of chronic balance of trade deficits for the United States is therefore that more of the real income from capital in the United States will be paid out to foreigners in the future and less of that income will go to U.S. citizens.

Causes of the Balance of Trade Deficit

Earlier in the chapter we showed how changes in real interest rates can affect the balance of trade and net exports for the United States. In reality the causes of the

The International Balance of Payments and Balance of Trade and Foreign Saving in the U.S.

921

trade deficit are quite complex and cannot be attributed to any single factor, such as an upward movement in the real exchange rate of the dollar. In the preceding chapter we suggested that one possible reason for decreased U.S. exports and increased import demand has been lagging productivity growth in certain manufacturing industries. However, there are other factors that have contributed to growing trade imbalances between the United States and the rest of the world in the 1980s.

Since 1980 economic growth in the United States has been higher than that in other nations. Many less developed nations have been plagued by decreased demand and lower prices for raw materials, which has reduced income growth in those nations and has also reduced demand for imports from the United States. The table in Box 14 shows growth rates of real GNP and real domestic demand from 1982 to 1985 for the United States and some of its key trading partners. As you can see, growth in demand and real GNP in the United States was stronger than in the other nations. Growth of real GNP for less developed nations in the Western Hemisphere, Africa, and the Middle East averaged less than 1% per year from 1980 through 1986. The slow growth in these nations dampened their demand for U.S. exports.

Box 14 **Growth in Real Domestic Demand and Real GNP**
United States and Key Trading Countries: 1982-1985
(average annual percentage change)

Country	Growth in real GNP	Growth in real domestic demand [a]
United States	4.2	5.6
Canada	4.2	4.2
Japan	4.3	3.1
France	1.2	0.8
Germany	2.4	1.9
Italy	1.7	1.5
United Kingdom	3.1	3.1

[a] Real domestic demand is the sum of personal consumption, gross private domestic investment, and government purchases of goods and services.

Source: *Economic Report of the President,* 1987.

In addition, high real interest rates and increased profitability of U.S. businesses from 1982 to 1985 contributed to increased demand for dollars by foreigners to invest in the United States. The competition for dollars for investment purposes put upward pressure on the price of the dollar in terms of foreign currencies. This higher real exchange rate of the dollar made U.S. goods more expensive abroad, which further decreased foreign demand for U.S. exports. Because of the appreciation of the dollar during the early 1980s, foreign currencies depreciated relative to the dollar, which caused imports to become cheaper. The appreciation of the dollar encouraged imports, thereby further increasing the balance of trade deficit.

The U.S. trade balance has worsened against its major trading partners. For example, the U.S. balance of trade deficit with Japan increased from $19 billion in 1982 to over $55 billion in 1986. The U.S. trade balance with Western Europe went from a surplus of $5 billion in 1982 to a deficit of over $30 billion in 1986. The U.S. trade balance with nations of the Far East and Latin America also worsened over the same period.

Concept Check

1 How did the gold standard work as an international monetary system?

2 The balance on the current account of the U.S. balance of payments is − $140 billion. What is the balance on the capital account?

3 How will foreign saving in the United States be affected if the United States runs a balance of trade surplus? What effect will the balance of trade surplus have on real interest rates in the United States?

Summary

1. A nation's foreign exchange rate is the price of its monetary unit in terms of the monetary unit of another nation. Buyers and sellers of bank deposits denominated in the monetary units of many nations exchange monies in the foreign exchange market.

2. An export transaction for a U.S. seller requires that the foreign buyer purchase dollars by writing a check on his own bank account denominated in his nation's currency. When paid, the exporter gains dollars and U.S. banks gain deposits in foreign banks denominated in foreign currency. An import transaction by a U.S. buyer results in payments in foreign currency to foreign suppliers and acquisition of dollar deposits in the United States by foreign banks as dollars are used to purchase foreign currency from foreign banks.

3. Foreign exchange is the money of one nation held by citizens of another nation either as currency or as deposits in banks.

4. The number of dollars demanded as foreign exchange tends to increase as the price of a dollar declines in terms of foreign currency. This is because as the price of the dollar declines, U.S. goods become cheaper in terms of foreign currency.

5. The demand for dollars as foreign exchange will increase in response to an increase in foreign demand for U.S. exports, an increase in real interest rates in the United States relative to those in foreign nations, expectations of a future increase in the price of dollars in terms of foreign currency, or a decrease in the price level in the United States relative to the price levels in foreign nations.

6. The number of dollars supplied in exchange for foreign currency depends on the demand of U.S. citizens for foreign goods, services, and assets. An increase in the price of the dollar in terms of foreign currency increases the number of dollars supplied to foreigners because it makes foreign goods cheaper to U.S. buyers.

7. The supply curve of dollars offered in exchange for foreign currency can shift in response to any change that increases the demand by holders of dollars for U.S. goods and services or assets.

8. Currency appreciation occurs when there is an increase in the number of units of one nation's currency that must be given up to purchase one unit of another nation's currency. Currency depreciation occurs when there is a decrease in the number of units of one nation's currency that must be given up to purchase one unit of another nation's currency.

9. The principle of purchasing power parity of one nation's currency for another's states that the exchange rate between any two currencies tends to adjust to reflect changes in the price levels in the two countries.

10. The real exchange rate of a nation's currency is a measure of the sacrifice of goods and services that foreign buyers must make when they use their own currency to purchase goods of the first nation worth one unit of that nation's currency.

11. A change in the real exchange rate of the dollar can shift both aggregate supply and aggregate demand. An increase in the real exchange rate of the dollar will decrease inflationary pressures in the U.S. economy. The effect of the higher dollar on equilibrium real GNP depends on both the demand-side and supply-side effects. A higher dollar decreases aggregate demand by reducing net exports, but it also increases aggregate supply by reducing the prices of imported inputs.

12. The gold standard was an international monetary system that required that currencies be convertible into gold at a fixed price. The gold standard limited the range of variation in exchange rates because it was cheaper to pay in gold than in foreign currency when the exchange rate rose above certain limits. Under the gold standard, nations tied their money supply to gold inflow and outflow. As a result, price levels eventually went up and down as nations gained or lost gold.

13. The Bretton Woods system tied the value of foreign currencies to the U.S. dollar, which was convertible into gold at the rate of $35 per ounce. The Bretton Woods system collapsed in 1973 when a system of flexible exchange rates was agreed upon. Currently exchange rates are influenced by the forces of supply and demand, but central banks frequently intervene in the market to affect supply and demand.

14. An international balance of payments is a statement showing the net exchange of a nation's currency for foreign currencies for all international transactions in a given year.

15. The balance of trade shows the difference between the value of merchandise exports and imports. A balance of trade deficit exists when merchandise imports exceed merchandise exports for the year, while a balance of trade surplus exists when merchandise exports exceed imports for the year.

16. The balance on current account of the balance of payments measures U.S. net exports for the year, including transactions involving services, investment income, and transfers. A deficit on current account puts downward pressure on aggregate demand.

17. The capital account of the international balance of payments shows transactions involving physical and financial assets for the year. A deficit on the current account must always be offset by an equal surplus on the capital account.

Key Terms and Concepts

Foreign exchange rate	Foreign exchange
Foreign exchange market	Currency appreciation

Currency depreciation
Purchasing power parity
Nominal exchange rate
Real exchange rate
Gold standard
Bretton Woods System

International Monetary Fund (IMF)
Managed float
Special drawing right (SDR)
Balance of payments
Balance of trade
Balance on current account of the balance of payments

Problems and Applications

1. Suppose you export lumber to Italy. The current exchange rate is 1,500 lire to the dollar. If you sell $300,000 of lumber to an Italian builder, show the effect of your transaction on the balance sheets of U.S. and Italian banks.

2. As a U.S. auto dealer, you import 200 BMWs from West Germany during the year. The total dollar volume of your import transaction is $3 million. The current exchange rate is 2 West German marks per U.S. dollar. Show the impact of your import transaction on the balance sheets of U.S. and West German banks.

3. Suppose the dollar depreciates on international markets so that it is only worth 1.5 marks. Each BMW that cost 30,000 marks last year still costs the same in terms of marks this year. Calculate last year's and this year's cost of a BMW in terms of dollars. Assuming that as an auto dealer you pay an average of 30,000 marks per BMW and still import 200 cars this year, calculate the cost of your annual order using the new exchange rate.

4. The U.S. dollar can be purchased for 1.40 Canadian dollars. How many U.S. dollars are necessary to purchase a Canadian dollar?

5. The current price of the dollar in terms of Japanese yen is 140 yen per dollar. Suppose real interest rates increase in Japan but fall in the United States. Use supply and demand analysis to show how the change in relative interest rates is likely to affect the exchange rate of the dollar in terms of yen.

6. Suppose the price level increases in Japan relative to that in the United States. What impact is the Japanese inflation likely to have on the exchange rate of the dollar in terms of yen?

7. Suppose U.S. firms mount a successful advertising campaign that increases Japanese demand for U.S. goods. Assuming that nothing else changes, predict the effect on the price of the dollar in terms of the yen.

8. The current account balance for the U.S. international balance of payments is −$150 billion. What effect have international transactions had on aggregate demand in the United States during the year? What is the balance on the capital account of the U.S. international balance of payments for that year?

9. Explain why a U.S. surplus on the current account of the international balance of payments implies that U.S. ownership of assets abroad must increase. Why does a deficit on the current account imply that foreign ownership of U.S. assets must increase?

10. In 1987 the real exchange rate of the dollar depreciated sharply against the Japanese yen and the West German mark. However, there was little improvement in the U.S. international balance of trade. Explain why the fall of the dollar in 1987 had little short-run impact on the balance of trade deficit. Why will the long-run impact of a permanent depreciation of the dollar be more likely to reduce the balance of trade deficit? Why is it difficult to predict the impact of changes in real exchange rates of the dollar on equilibrium real GNP?

Suggested Readings

Economic Report of the President, 1987, Washington, D.C.: U.S. Government Printing Office, 1987. Chapters 3 and 4 discuss the U.S. trade deficit and how it has been influenced by exchange rates and economic policies.

Franklin R. Root, *International Trade and Investment,* 5th ed., Cincinnati: South-Western Publishing Co., 1984. This textbook on international trade presents a good discussion of financial aspects of international trade.

A Forward Look

In the final chapter we look at issues of ideology and economics. We discuss alternative economic systems, especially that of the Soviet Union, and compare these systems with the mixed economy of the United States.

Economics and Ideology: Socialism vs. Capitalism

Thanks to Mikhail Gorbachev's policy of *glasnost* (openness), you probably know that the Soviet Union is undergoing a period of change and economic reform. However, even if the Soviet economy is restructured according to Gorbachev's plan, it will remain fundamentally different from the U.S. economy. As observed early in the book, nations differ greatly in the rules and institutions that they use to organize economic activity and to distribute goods and services among individuals and alternative uses.

An **economic system** is an accepted way of organizing production, establishing rights to ownership and use of productive resources, and governing economic transactions in a society. The evaluation of alternative economic systems is often closely tied to political and moral views and preferences about what is right and wrong. The *ideology,* or opinions, regarding human rights often influences our ideas about the desirability of one economic system compared to another. We discuss ideological issues only briefly in this chapter. Instead our emphasis is on understanding the way modern socialist economies, particularly that of the Soviet Union, have operated and how the operation of these economies might change in the future.

The two basic alternative economic systems are capitalism and socialism. As you learned in Chapter 6, *capitalism* is generally associated with private ownership of economic resources, free enterprise, and exchange of goods and services in markets. **Socialism,** on the other hand, usually is associated with government ownership of productive resources and central planning, as opposed to decentralized market exchange, to determine prices and resource use. Modern economies are quite complex and varied. At least some free enterprise and market exchange exist in many economies that define themselves as socialist systems. At the same time many so-called capitalist systems, including those of the United States and Canada, have extensive government sectors that provide goods and services such as pensions, run

Economic system:
An accepted way of organizing production, establishing rights to ownership and use of productive resources, and governing economic transactions in a society.

Socialism:
An economic system that is usually associated with government ownership of resources and central planning to determine prices and resource use.

railroads and other enterprises, account for over a third of GNP, and employ over a fifth of the labor force!

Before you begin this chapter you should understand that the basic economic problems confronting human beings in all nations are similar irrespective of the economic system under which they must conduct their daily affairs. The problem of scarcity is universal. People can be expected to respond to incentives no matter how they are governed. This means we can always obtain insights into human behavior in any economic system by analyzing the benefits and costs of alternative actions within the framework of the rules people must obey. Neither socialism nor capitalism as economic systems can wave wands to make scarcity go away and erase the laws of supply and demand.

Concept Preview

After reading this chapter, you should be able to:

1 Discuss the ideas of Karl Marx and the ideological underpinnings of socialism.
2 Discuss modern socialist economies, particularly that of the Soviet Union.
3 Explain central planning as a means of allocating resources in a command economy.
4 Discuss issues involved in evaluating economic performance in modern economies.

Ideological Issues: Workers vs. Capitalists—The Ideas of Karl Marx

Modern socialism has much of its roots in the ideas of Karl Marx (1818-1883), whose classic work *Das Kapital*, first published in 1867, emphasized the conflict between economic classes. (See Economic Thinkers box.) Marx believed that workers would be exploited by capitalists. Marx and other economists of his era were convinced that the capitalist system of the nineteenth century would generate labor market forces that would keep factory wages at the subsistence level; that is, workers would be paid wages that barely allowed them to survive. In the early days of industrialization, Marx's theory would have been confirmed. Working conditions in factories were abominable, and wages were extremely low. The "iron law of wages" formulated by the nineteenth-century classical economist David Ricardo argued that if wages were to increase above the subsistence level, forces would be set up to push wages down. Ricardo hypothesized that population would increase because of improved health of the working class as wages rose above the subsistence level. The increase in population would then increase the supply of labor, which in turn would put downward pressure on wages until they returned to equilibrium at the subsistence level.

Labor theory of value:
Maintains that only labor can produce something worth paying for.

Much of Marx's work was based on the **labor theory of value,** which maintained that only labor could produce something worth paying for. Capitalists treated labor like any other commodity and paid wages that just allowed that labor to survive. However, because workers did in fact produce more than the value of the resources necessary for their survival (the subsistence wage), the capitalist was able

Economic Thinkers

KARL MARX

During his lifetime Karl Marx alienated as many people with his stubbornness and intolerance as he attracted with his brilliance and dynamic personality. His lifelong friend was Friedrich Engels, a fellow revolutionary who was his collaborator, compatriate, and benefactor.

In works like the *Communist Manifesto* and *Das Kapital,* Marx advocated defending the oppressed and forged a concept of class conflict that became the center of his theories of economic and political development. He emphasized the importance of economic conflict as the source of class conflict and social change. According to his theories, the division of society's wealth among economic classes inevitably causes conflict between those classes. Capitalism will destroy itself because of conflict between workers and capitalists over the division of wealth and income.

He worked with revolutionary groups until the end of his life, preparing for the day when capitalism would collapse. Marx was the epitome of the German scholar: meticulous, deep thinking, and a painstaking perfectionist.

Despite financial assistance from Engels, who led a double life of capitalist and communist revolutionary, Marx and his family lived in extreme poverty in London, where they fled after being expelled from Germany, France, and Belgium. Marx worked on *Das Kapital* day after day at the British Museum and occasionally wrote articles for the New York *Tribune.*

Even though he was never financially rewarded, this driven economist, sociologist, historian, and philosopher changed the history of the world with his views of economic conflict. His ideas spurred social progress in early capitalistic economies and ultimately resulted in drastic changes in the social systems under which much of the world's population lives.

to lay claim to a surplus value from the labor used in production. **Surplus value** was defined by Marx as the difference between a worker's subsistence wage and the value of the worker's production over a period. The surplus value was the source of the capitalist's profit, which in Marx's view was obtained merely by exploiting workers. In Marx's opinion the capitalist was completely unproductive. The capital equipment with which he provided his workers merely represented the value created by other workers, who in turn were exploited by other capitalists. In Marx's analysis, surplus value represented the sum of earnings paid out in the form of interest, rent, and profit that actually were generated by the productivity of labor.

Marx argued that the capitalist system he observed in his lifetime would not survive. He believed that increases in demand for goods associated with population growth would encourage capital accumulation but that competition among capitalists would keep profits from increasing. Despite capitalists' attempts to continually exploit workers, Marx believed that profit would decline in the long run. This would be attributable in part to the fact that as more capital was used in place of labor, the reduction in labor use would reduce profits. Remember that Marx believed that all profits were derived from the exploitation of workers. Less employment meant less profits.

Capitalists, who owned the factories and other capital equipment, were viewed as a separate and distinct class from workers, who owned virtually nothing. The capitalist survived as a parasite in Marx's view, exploiting the worker by paying him less than the value of his production.

Surplus value:
Defined by Karl Marx as the difference between a worker's subsistence wage and the value of the worker's production over a period.

Ideological Issues: Workers vs. Capitalists—The Ideas of Karl Marx

929

The capitalist was seen as attempting to increase profits by accumulating more capital and by investing in better technology and equipment. Marx believed that workers would not gain from capital accumulation because their wages would remain close to the subsistence level. In fact, many would lose their jobs as capital was substituted for labor in production and a vast "reserve army of the unemployed" was expected to spring into existence, aggravating the labor supply problem and putting still further downward pressure on wages. Eventually there would be a deficiency in aggregate demand as a result of unemployment, and Marx expected this to cause the collapse of capitalism. As the size of the work force declined because of increased use of capital, profits would decline, thus contributing to the collapse of the system. Eventually the working class would revolt and establish a socialist system.

The basic notion of conflict between capitalist and worker is accepted by many people, and today about one third of the world's population lives under some form of communism based directly or indirectly on Marxian ideas. In other nations, such as Italy and France, the government is not under communist control but there are strong communist parties.

Why Did Marx's Prediction Fall Short of Reality for Modern Nonsocialist Economies in the Twentieth Century?

For the vast majority of workers, wages clearly have risen above the subsistence level in most so-called capitalist nations. In a nutshell, Marx's predictions about wages proved to be wrong because labor market conditions in most capitalist nations did not develop as he expected. Although competition among firms does tend to push economic profits *in a given industry* down to zero in the long run, new profit opportunities always arise with changes in demand and technology. Entrepreneurs who seize the opportunity to respond to changes in supply and demand can earn profits by creating new products and processes. There may still be conflict between workers and capitalists, as can be seen by occasional labor disputes between unions and employers. However, there is no doubt that *both* workers and their employers have gained from the tremendous growth in productivity associated with capital accumulation.

Simple analysis of labor market changes over time will show you why wages have risen well above the subsistence level in most nations. Suppose that at the beginning of the industrial revolution, wages were close to subsistence. Over time population growth can be expected to increase the supply of workers, which puts downward pressure on wages. However, increased capital accumulation increases the productivity of workers. When productivity increases, employers are willing to pay higher wages because each worker produces more and adds more to employer revenue. A firm that doesn't raise wages when productivity increases is likely to lose workers to competing firms that can pay higher wages and still increase profits by hiring away the first firm's most productive workers. Competition among firms for labor services tends to bid up wages because additional profits can be made by hiring more workers when their productivity increases. The resulting increase in demand for workers puts upward pressure on wages.

Over time it's apparent that on average the increase in demand for labor outstripped the increase in supply. Population growth in industrial nations turned out to be much slower than many nineteenth-century economists predicted. The rate of increase in worker productivity was also greater. As shown in the graphs in Box 1,

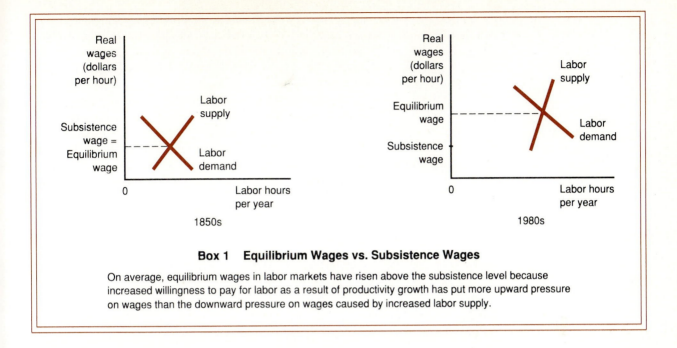

Box 1   Equilibrium Wages vs. Subsistence Wages

On average, equilibrium wages in labor markets have risen above the subsistence level because increased willingness to pay for labor as a result of productivity growth has put more upward pressure on wages than the downward pressure on wages caused by increased labor supply.

shifts in the demand for and supply of labor have pushed wages well above subsistence for the average factory worker since the 1850s.

Marx's prediction of a huge reserve army of the unemployed simply didn't materialize. Technological advances increased the incomes of workers in modern capitalist economies and helped provide the markets for the goods produced by the huge capitalist system. Although the business cycle still exists and there are inevitable ups and downs in the economy, the lot of the worker on average has improved vastly since the turn of the century. Of course, labor unions have helped provide a voice for workers and have contributed to higher wages in capitalist systems. But less than a fifth of the labor force in the United States currently belongs to unions. The main factors keeping wages high are competition among employers for workers and technological change and investment that contribute to increased labor productivity.

Finally, advances in social policy as evidenced by increased government transfer programs and social insurance have helped alleviate poverty and improve working conditions. Much of the growth of government in the United States, particularly in the 1970s, can be attributed to policies designed to ensure retired workers minimum standards of living through more generous Social Security pensions. Welfare programs provide support for the nonworking poor. Government intervention in the marketplace to pursue social goals and provide services that profit-motivated firms lack the incentive to make available has served to prevent the social unrest that Marx expected to lead to revolution.

All this is not to suggest that the modern mixed economy works perfectly. Poverty and low wages for unskilled workers remain as social problems in the United States and other nonsocialist economies. In spite of this country's many advantages, a distressingly large percentage of the U.S. population is still classified as living in poverty. There is also concern about the monopoly power exercised by firms in certain sectors of the economy. However, the widespread misery and the vast gap between the well-being of the entire class of workers and a small minority of capitalists that were envisioned by Marx have failed to materialize in modern industrialized economies. Extensive social programs administered by governments and improved productivity of workers have served to lift average living standards well above the subsistence level for the vast majority of workers.

Concept Check

1 What are the basic differences between capitalism and socialism?

2 What is the labor theory of value?

3 In what sense did Marx argue that workers would be exploited by capitalists?

Socialism and the Soviet Economic System

Marx's ideas spawned revolutionary activity throughout Europe in the late nineteenth century. The threat of revolution and social unrest induced politicians to support social reform in many nations. In Germany during the late 1800s the first system of social insurance was enacted with the support of Chancellor Bismarck. Other nations passed similar legislation to use government power to improve working conditions and alleviate poverty.

The Union of Soviet Socialist Republics came into existence as the first socialist state with the Bolshevik revolution of 1917. Although Czarist Russia was relatively less industrialized compared to nations such as Great Britain, industrialization had already begun in Russia at the time of the revolution. The gap between per capita income in Czarist Russia and the relatively prosperous states of Western Europe at the time was nowhere near as great as the gap today between less developed countries and the developed nations. One estimate puts per capita income in Russia in 1914 at 22% to 40% that of the richest nations in Western Europe.[1]

The socialist system of the Soviet Union over the years has adapted to deal with the unique economic and political problems faced by its people. The communist leadership of the Soviet Union has implemented a system of centrally planned socialism that has industrialized the nation and vastly improved living standards. Although per capita GNP in the Soviet Union remains about half of that in the United States, the accomplishments of the system cannot be ignored. The system has managed to function largely without the profit motive and without private ownership of capital and land. Under the socialist system, the Soviet Union was transformed into a major industrial power in the relatively short time between 1917 and 1937. Economic growth in the Soviet Union was very high during this period. Despite the incredible destruction of human and physical resources it incurred during World War II, the Soviet Union recovered substantially to become the second largest economic power after the United States in the postwar era.

Most recently, under the leadership of Mikhail Gorbachev as General Secretary of its Communist Party, the Soviet Union has begun a major new program, called *perestroika,* to restructure its economy. The new plan seeks to rely less on central government direction of the economic system by the year 1991.

[1]Paul R. Gregory and Robert C. Stuart, *Soviet Economic Structure and Performance,* 2nd ed., New York: Harper & Row, 1981, pp. 33-34.

The Command Economy

Although the Soviet economy is changing, over most of its existence it has been characterized as a **command economy** because resource allocation decisions have been determined largely by the central planning authorities who set production goals. A command economy differs from a market economy in two important ways:

1. *In a command economy the state owns productive resources, including natural resources, land, factories, financial institutions, retail stores, and the bulk of the housing stock.* Thus in the Soviet Union government enterprise and ownership of resources are the rule rather than the exception. The government and its many enterprises naturally pay wages to their employees, but freedom of choice in jobs and occupations is not as extensive as in the United States and other democratic nations. Much of the farmland is state owned. However, in many cases large farms are cooperatives in which individual farmers have extensive rights in using land and may choose to set aside land for personal use. Citizens of the Soviet Union do have the right to own personal property such as cars, furniture, clothing, and tools. Private ownership of homes is permitted, but the majority of the population lives in government-provided housing.

2. *In the command economy, authoritarian methods are used to determine resource use and prices.* The Soviet Union is a **centrally planned economy,** which means that politically appointed committees plan production by setting target outputs for factory and enterprise managers, and generally manage the economy to achieve political objectives. **Gosplan** is the central planning board for the Soviet Union. This agency drafts a 5-year economic plan detailing production targets, methods of production, labor use, and investment in new plants and other capital projects for the literally thousands of enterprises run by the government. Each year separate enterprises receive detailed instructions on how to meet short-run production objectives. The planning authorities of Gosplan, in conjunction with other government agencies, in the past have set prices to achieve their targeted objectives.

The Communist Party of the Soviet Union exercises considerable control over the planning process and the economy. A state planning committee reports directly to the *Politburo,* the major policymaking agency in the Soviet Union, whose members are appointed by the Central Committee of the Communist Party. The Communist Party exercises control over the ministries and other agencies of the government and controls appointments of government bureaucrats and managers of enterprises. *Nomenklatura* is a comprehensive list maintained by the party of jobs in government, industry, agriculture, the army, and the party itself. This list is used to control appointments and limit them to loyal party members. In the Soviet Union only about 10% of the population are members of the Communist Party, but almost all managers and planners are party members! Political control of the economic system is guaranteed by this system of controlling appointments to managerial-level jobs.

Restructuring the Soviet Command Economy: Perestroika

If General Secretary Gorbachev's plan for restructuring the Soviet economy is successful, there will be less reliance on planning in the Soviet Union in the 1990s than there has been in the past. Beginning on January 1, 1988, about 60% of Soviet enterprises were put on a self-financing basis. Managers of these enterprises under the reform will decide what to produce and how to produce it. Wages will be tied to profitability. Enterprises that fail to earn a profit (yes, profit!) will be forced to cease

Command economy:
An economy in which resource allocation decisions are determined largely by the central planning authorities who set production goals.

Centrally planned economy:
An economy in which politically appointed committees plan production and manage the economy to achieve political goals.

Gosplan:
The central planning board for the Soviet Union.

operations. This means that some Soviet workers could face the grim prospect of unemployment if their managers cannot operate at a profit. The new system has only begun in the Soviet Union, and because there is considerable opposition among Communist Party members, it remains to be seen whether political forces will actually allow the new system to work.

The restructuring will sharply reduce the role of Gosplan in the Soviet economy. The new system will allow competition among government-run enterprises, and many prices will be set in markets rather than through the central plan. Among the first workers to face unemployment under *perestroika* are likely to be thousands of Gosplan employees who will be forced to learn new skills!

Under the restructuring, the central plan will simply set guidelines on production goals. Individual factories will have to compete to meet the goals.

Pricing and Resource Allocation in the Centrally Planned Soviet Economy

Prices in a command economy are not set by the forces of supply and demand. Instead planners determine the quantity of goods and services to be produced in accordance with their political goals. In the Soviet Union the State Committee for Prices (Goskomtsen) in the past has set prices annually for over 200,000 wholesale and retail items. Price in a command economy does not serve as a signal that influences profits and therefore incentives of private enterprise to produce, as is the case in the capitalist system. This is obviously because there is little private enterprise in the Soviet Union, and prior to restructuring the state enterprises were in business to satisfy the planners instead of earning maximum profits! There is one sector in the Soviet Union in which the forces of supply and demand were allowed to work more or less unfettered even prior to *perestroika*. Agricultural output from farmers' private plots is generally sold in free markets. Under restructuring, more sectors of the Soviet economy will have prices determined by the forces of supply and demand.

Planning authorities also set wages in a command economy. The planners do understand the function of wages as a means of providing incentives to work. Work that requires more skill is generally compensated with higher wages, and this encourages workers to undergo the training necessary to acquire additional skills. Wages also vary by region to encourage labor to migrate to growing areas where climatic conditions are not exactly ideal. A worker with given skills can earn more by agreeing to work in Siberia than he can by staying in Moscow. Positive wage differentials are also paid for hazardous jobs. Finally, there are bonus and incentive payments designed to encourage workers to meet or exceed production targets and to reward more productive workers. Supply and demand are therefore considered in setting wages in the Soviet Union, and planners appear to have a solid understanding of labor markets.

Under the *perestroika* reforms, the prices of many products are likely to rise, bringing the prospect of inflation to the Soviet Union. The average monthly earnings of Soviet citizens are about $300. In the past it has been a Soviet policy to subsidize the costs of food and other consumer products. For example, in recent years planners set the price of meat at half the cost of producing it. The low prices resulted in shortages. In 1987, despite the efforts of planners, production of many popular consumer items fell and shortages of meat, butter, and other food staples were common. Under the new system, prices will rise to equate quantities demanded with quantities supplied. Unless wages rise as well, many Soviet citizens will find their real incomes declining. This could lead to social unrest in the Soviet Union and give rise to a political backlash to eliminate the reforms.

Materials Balance in the Centrally Planned Economy

Planning the operation of a complex economy is a monumental task. Planners must keep track of supplies of inputs and balance available resources with output goals. Outputs of one factory often end up being inputs in another factory. Bottlenecks and shortages of produced goods and services can stall the plan and create chaos. Planners must constantly keep track of raw materials and inventories of produced goods to make sure they end up at the right place at the right time. For example, if the plan is changed to require more electric turbines, given the scarcity of resources the output targets of other goods must be adjusted to free resources so they can be used to produce the inputs required for the additional turbines.

You can imagine the difficulty of tracking all the cement, steel, machinery, building materials, and fuel through the economy to make sure everything is available to meet the plan's production targets. Planning technicians must review the plan to make sure that the planned supplies of each basic commodity exactly equal the demand. Keep in mind that in a planned economy, price is rarely used to equate quantity demanded with quantity supplied. Instead this task must be *administratively* accomplished through directives to individual managers and their subordinates. A **materials balance** exists when the supply of each intermediate product equals its demand as an input in some other productive process.

Materials balance:
Exists when the supply of each intermediate product equals its demand as an input in some other productive process.

When a shortage of a key commodity, like cement, arises because of some unforeseen circumstance, the plan must be revised. Planners must set priorities for allocating cement away from some uses or allocating other inputs away from other uses so as to increase cement production. Unforeseen scarcity of materials means that planners must reduce the quantities of some outputs to maintain targeted levels of production of other items. Alternatively, the planners can import the material that is in short supply.

The Soviet Union's economic plan is so complex that even a slight hitch creates a major logjam. Traditionally, when there has been a problem with the plan, Soviet planners have reallocated inputs away from the production of consumer goods so that military and heavy industry production goals could be met. Thus if there's a shortage of steel, the annual output of washing machines and other appliances will be the most likely candidates for cuts in output!

Satisfying Consumer Demand in the Soviet Union

In a market system, as you have seen through much of the book, prices provide incentives for business firms to produce the most profitable goods and services. Resource use in a decentralized market system is not planned by any single authority. Instead the economy is a mass of interrelated markets in which prices act as signals. An increase in consumer demand sets in motion an elaborate process of signaling that gives firms an incentive to produce more of the desired goods. The responsiveness of the market economy to changes in consumer demand is sometimes called **consumer sovereignty.**

Consumer sovereignty:
The responsiveness of the market economy to changes in consumer demand.

In a strict command economy, an increase in consumer demand for phonograph records is unlikely to induce planners to produce more. Production goals are set with political rather than consumer objectives in mind. The supply of a given consumer good like automobiles is fixed by the plan and is completely unresponsive to changes in demand or price in the short run. Of course, political considerations could dictate changes in production targets to increase the supplies of consumer goods. However, once the supply is fixed and a price is set, changes in demand will generate no response from government enterprises.

The graph in Box 2 uses supply and demand analysis to illustrate how shortages of consumer goods can develop in a centrally planned economy. Suppose planners have set annual production of private passenger automobiles at 2 million units per year in a 5-year plan. Soviet citizens are no different from other consumers in the sense that they have downward-sloping demand curves for cars and other consumer goods, as illustrated in Box 2. The price of cars is set by planners to ensure that the annual quantity demanded just equals the fixed annual quantity supplied. Suppose the price is set at 15,000 rubles, corresponding to point A in the graph.

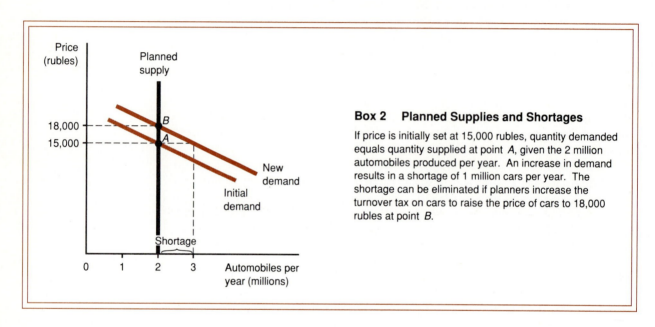

Box 2   Planned Supplies and Shortages

If price is initially set at 15,000 rubles, quantity demanded equals quantity supplied at point A, given the 2 million automobiles produced per year. An increase in demand results in a shortage of 1 million cars per year. The shortage can be eliminated if planners increase the turnover tax on cars to raise the price of cars to 18,000 rubles at point B.

Now suppose the demand for cars increases next year. The increase in demand would raise the price of cars if prices were determined in markets. However, here the planners determine the price. Assuming that Gosplan chooses not to revise the plan to increase the price or production of cars, the result will be a shortage of cars. At the price set by planners, the quantity demanded will be 3 million cars per year while the quantity supplied will be only 2 million. The 1 million–car shortage will be rationed by long waiting lists, which are typical in the Soviet Union and other planned economies. Of course, the planners could eliminate the shortage by revising the plan to increase the price of cars.

Turnover tax:

A sales tax used to raise revenue for the government; often used in planned economies to eliminate shortages in consumer markets.

Planners in the Soviet Union often eliminate shortages in consumer markets by using the **turnover tax,** which is a sales tax used to raise revenue for the government. This tax is included in the prices of goods and services sold in the Soviet Union but is not separately itemized as are sales taxes in the United States. The turnover tax is often set at an amount that increases the wholesale price of the scarce item to a level that clears the market. For example, to clear the market for cars, the price in Box 2 would have to increase to 18,000 rubles. A turnover tax of 3,000 rubles per car thus would reduce quantity demanded sufficiently to equal the fixed quantity supplied of 2 million cars per year. In the Soviet Union, Gosplan in the past has not placed a high priority on satisfying desires for consumer goods and has tolerated shortages of such items. Cuts in output of consumer goods, as pointed out earlier, are commonly implemented to solve materials balance problems.

Labor Allocation and Occupational Choice in the Soviet Economy

Planners in the Soviet Union actively influence the supply of labor through a variety of policies designed to develop the human capital necessary to fulfill the goals of Gosplan. The availability of education is closely linked to the goals of the planners. Consequently, Soviet students often enjoy less freedom of choice in education compared to American students. However, Soviet authorities are well aware of the benefits of education in terms of productivity gains, and education expenditures as a percentage of GNP are quite high and comparable to those in the United States.

Workers with given skills are placed in jobs by authorities to achieve the goals of the plan. Workers are not required to accept the jobs they are offered, but their range of alternatives is usually much narrower than is the case in a nonsocialist economy. Graduates of specialized schools and universities are required to work for 3 years in a job in which they are placed by authorities. Workers do change jobs regularly in the Soviet Union, where the annual turnover rate is about 20%. However, special bonuses and privileges associated with longevity on a job act as incentives to reduce worker turnover.

One advantage of a planned economy is that planners directly control investment and influence most spending by consumers to avoid the fluctuations in aggregate demand that characterize market economies. The planners seek to coordinate the plan so that all those willing to work at the established wages can find jobs. This might lead you to believe that unemployment is not a serious problem in the Soviet Union. The Soviet authorities don't publish unemployment data, so it's impossible to determine whether the Soviet economy is ever plagued by high unemployment. However, it's clear that planning is not an exact science, and occasional mistakes are likely to result in labor shortages and surpluses. There is also likely to be frictional and structural unemployment in the Soviet system as a result of job switching and changes in output structure caused by revisions in the plans. As a result of *perestroika*, unemployment may rise considerably in the Soviet Union in years to come.

Incentives Under Central Planning

Put yourself in the place of a typical plant manager in the Soviet Union whose operations are managed by Gosplan and are not self-financing. Your prime objective, and the criterion on which you'll be evaluated for bonuses, advancement, and other rewards, is to meet the goals of the plan. This means you are required to meet the output targets that are assigned to you. Notice that your objectives don't necessarily include cost minimization and manufacturing quality products that satisfy your customers. There are no rewards for producing goods of better quality than those called for by the planners or for varying the product mix in ways that might enhance customer satisfaction. As a manager, you'll also be cautious about exceeding your output targets. Your output target might increase in the future if you're too zealous in cranking out goods this year, and a higher output target could mean a lower bonus for you.

Prior to *perestroika*, output rather than profits was the goal in the Soviet economy. Because the output mix favored by planners was heavy industry rather than consumer goods, planners maximized output of steel, coal, and energy, which are used as inputs in new investment or in military goods.

The planning goals affect incentives in unusual ways. For example, geologists in the Soviet Union who drill for oil have been rewarded with bonuses after they drill a minimum number of meters into the ground each month. However, workers and managers know that the drills work more slowly as they go deeper into the ground. To make sure they get their bonuses, the drillers drill lots of shallow holes! The incentive is therefore to drill to maximize the meters per month rather than maximize oil discoveries![2] In other words, managers are often evaluated on their inputs rather than their output.

A goal of the restructuring programs is to force managers to pursue profits and avoid distortions like this that waste economic resources.

Investment in the Soviet Union

All investment in the Soviet Union is done by the state. The planners control the future as well as the present by determining how funds are allocated to expand productive capacity. Not surprisingly, there are no stock markets in a society that has no capitalists. Financing of new ventures is under the centralized control of Gosplan. Funding for independent new ventures by small-scale innovators is hard to come by.

The annual growth rate of real GNP in the Soviet Union fell from over 6% in the early 1950s to less than 3% in the late 1970s. In the early 1980s the growth of real GNP in the Soviet Union was estimated to be 2% annually. One estimate of combined input productivity growth indicates that total productivity growth was negative throughout the 1970s.[3] The falling GNP growth rate in the Soviet Union could be attributed to the stifling effect of centralized financing of new projects and the planners' apparent bias toward large-scale investment.

There is a great deal of ideological conflict in the Soviet Union regarding investment. The Marxian ideology maintains that capital is unproductive. Following this reasoning, loanable funds that are used to finance capital should not be subject to interest charges because investments do not generate any marginal return to pay those charges. Conflict over use of the interest rate as a price to compare the marginal return to an investment with its marginal cost makes it difficult for Soviet planners to achieve efficiency in investment decisions. The ideological conflict has turned capital investment into a purely administrative task based on national priorities as determined by the planners.

Private Enterprise in the Soviet Union

Although there is some private enterprise in the Soviet Union, owners of enterprises cannot legally hire employees for the purpose of making a profit, nor can they act as intermediaries in the trading of goods. Most of the private enterprises that exist in the Soviet Union are in professional and personal services and in farming. A

---

[2]See Marshall I. Goldman, *USSR in Crisis: Failure of an Economic System,* New York: W.W. Norton & Co., 1983, pp. 38-39.
[3]*Technology and Soviet Energy Availability,* Washington Office of Technology Assessment, 1981, p. 250.

reform that went into effect in 1987 legalized private businesses in 29 areas, thus encouraging private enterprise in crafts and services.

Most of the people engaged in private enterprise in the Soviet Union also have another job in a state enterprise. Physicians, repair people, and free-lance construction workers can trade privately with consumers. However, the taxes these professionals and craftsmen must pay on their private earnings are so high that many choose to provide their services without reporting the income to the authorities. As mentioned earlier, farmers who have their own plots of land can farm those plots as they choose and sell the produce in free markets. Private farming accounts for close to 25% of agricultural output in the Soviet Union, and it's generally agreed that the private farms are much more productive than those owned by the state.

There is a vast underground economy in the Soviet Union characterized by black market sales of consumer goods. These activities are generally illegal. Exact figures on the size of this sector are hard to come by, but it could be a substantial portion of GNP. In many cases goods sold on the black market are stolen or are made using materials and equipment owned by Soviet enterprises. In some cases people with connections profiteer by selling goods they control as managers. Managers might take high-quality merchandise produced in their plant and reserve it for sale to the highest bidder in the black market. Highly pressured managers might even purchase scarce materials on the black market to meet their production targets!

Those who own private automobiles are tempted to transport black market goods, and there's a thriving black market in gasoline. It's likely that substantial amounts of the harvest on collective farms are diverted to the black market for profit. Penalties for underground profit making are severe, even including the death penalty, but there are many Soviet citizens willing to take the risk.

Economic Performance and Problems in the Soviet Economy

As you would expect in a socialist state, Soviet citizens do enjoy some advantages that are not available in the United States. Medical care is provided at no cost, and rents in government housing are often well below the costs of providing that housing. Most higher education is tuition free, and public transportation is generally of high quality and available at low cost.

A serious problem in the Soviet Union is its agricultural sector, which employs about 20% of the labor force. In the United States less than 3% of the labor force is engaged in agriculture. Productivity in Soviet agriculture is only a fraction of the corresponding level in the United States. Of course, the Soviet Union is not well endowed with fertile soils, and its growing season is much shorter than that in the United States. Climatic conditions are not favorable, and there are often sharp swings in agricultural output because of droughts and other problems.

However, the low productivity in Soviet agriculture appears to be caused mainly by poor incentives and inefficient operations of large collectivized farms. Collective farms were first organized in the late 1920s in an attempt to achieve economies of scale in agriculture and increase planning control over the agricultural sector. Russian peasants resisted collectivization, and it was forced on the agricultural sector by the government.[4] Prior to collectivization, the peasants were given ownership rights to their land by Lenin in return for their support of the revolution. At the time of

---

[4]Millions of peasants were imprisoned or killed during the period of forced collectivization in the late 1920s and 1930s. See Gregory and Stuart, pp. 103-105.

the revolution, peasants constituted 80% of the population. Stalin, dissatisfied with the agricultural surplus generated by the peasants, decided to collectivize farms in the late 1920s. The resulting struggle and bloodbath represent a grim period in Soviet history that probably still has an impact on agricultural incentives.

Despite its problems, the Soviet Union's economy is a formidable apparatus that has achieved significant economic growth in a relatively short period. During World War II some 20 million Soviet citizens were killed, and the nation lost nearly 10% of its prewar population. From a historical perspective, therefore, Soviet economic performance has been admirable.

Concept Check

1 Why is the Soviet Union characterized as a command economy? How will *perestroika* change the way the Soviet economy functions?

2 How are prices set in a centrally planned economy?

3 What is meant by materials balance in a centrally planned economy?

Other Socialist Systems

There is great diversity among socialist economic systems in different nations, just as there is among capitalist systems. Socialist economies have varying degrees of political control over resource allocation and income distribution, and there also are varying degrees of government enterprise, subsidies, and production. In particular, socialist nations differ considerably in the extent to which they allow production for private profit and market exchange of goods and services.

Socialism in Yugoslavia, for example, varies markedly from that in the Soviet Union. Although most enterprises in Yugoslavia are state owned, managers are selected by workers and are encouraged to operate so as to earn a profit. Enterprises in Yugoslavia have more discretion than Soviet enterprises in determining productive methods and output levels. Most goods and services are sold in markets, and both prices and output levels are determined by the interaction of supply and demand. Central planning is not relied on in Yugoslavia as it is in the Soviet Union. Each enterprise in Yugoslavia uses its profits either to invest in additional productive capacity or to distribute to workers. Workers thus have an incentive to keep costs low because they can increase their income by sharing in their enterprise's profits.

In Hungary, much farming is privately run for profit, and agricultural commodities are sold in markets. There is also limited private enterprise for other industries. The "New Economic Mechanism" introduced in Hungary in 1968 decreased reliance on planning and allowed managers greater leeway in choosing product mixes. Small businesses were encouraged. By the mid-1980s, the private sector accounted for about 5% of Hungary's work force. Despite its small percentage of the work force, estimates indicate that the private sector in Hungary produced as much as 20% of GNP.

Indicative planning:
A system in which government encourages voluntary compliance by industrial and labor interests to coordinate economic decisions so as to achieve politically determined objectives.

Government ownership of or financial interest in large industrial enterprises is common in the United Kingdom, France, Italy, and other European nations. France uses a system called **indicative planning** in which voluntary compliance by industrial and labor interests is encouraged to coordinate economic decisions so as to achieve politically determined objectives. Although the Japanese government does

Principles in Practice

Economic Well-Being in the Soviet Union

If you were a Soviet citizen, there would be much you could be proud of. You could boast that your nation is a world leader in the production of satellites and submarines. You might also brag that the Soviet Union is at the forefront in developing new technologies for oil drilling and that it efficiently manages a system of natural gas delivery that is without a doubt the largest in the world.

But despite the *perestroika* reforms, you'd have to admit that the Soviet Union remains almost backward in the production of such consumer electronic items as personal computers, stereo systems, and VCRs that we take for granted. You might also lament the fact that in the past 20 years the quality of consumer goods that are available seems to have deteriorated. Finally, you might also point out that there has been a growing malaise among workers and that hard work has become the exception rather than the rule.

The typical Soviet citizen lacks the opportunity to consume many of the material goods and services that Americans in all walks of life take for granted.* Except for a privileged few in the nation, obtaining basic goods and services, particularly food products, is often an ordeal that hardened Soviet citizens accept as a fact of life. Because of the priorities that planners have given in the past to heavy industry and defense, there are periodic shortages of such items as toothbrushes, bathroom tissue, and soap. Soviet citizens complain about the poor quality of many domestic consumer goods, such as clothing. The problem is often one of retail distribution rather than production. The ministries in charge of distributing consumer goods apparently lack the incentives to get the right goods to the right place. Searching for goods seems to be a well-known Soviet sport. Long lines and empty store shelves are commonplace.

The problems of Soviet agriculture and the unwillingness of planners to import many of the foodstuffs desired by consumers result in food shortages. Government stores perennially run short of fruits, vegetables, and meats, and in many cities people must stand in line to buy these scarce items.

Prices of basic consumer goods are often well within the means of ordinary Soviet citizens. The problem isn't ability or willingness to pay but unavailability. This is manifested in thriving black market transactions and high savings rates. Soviet citizens tend to save their earnings because they have little opportunity to spend their income on the items they desire. When such opportunities, legal or illegal, do crop up, typical Soviet citizens readily empty their wallets or purses. In free agricultural markets in the Soviet Union where food can be obtained at prices that equate quantity supplied with quantity demanded, prices inevitably are quite high, reflecting the scarcity of foodstuffs. Some goods regarded as luxuries by planners are priced very high. For example, a compact car in the Soviet Union costs nearly $13,000, which puts it out of the reach of the average citizen, who earns only about $300 per month. Televisions, priced at $1,000 in 1987, were also very expensive for Soviet citizens.

Despite heavily subsidized rents, housing is still a problem for many Soviet citizens. Housing is in short supply, and it's common for more than one family to share the same apartment! The typical citizen pays less than 10% of household income in rent. However, the low rents often provide the housing ministries with little funding to maintain state-supplied housing. Poor maintenance induces many Soviet citizens to use their savings to buy cooperative apartments, which sold for the equivalent of $15,000 to $20,000 in the early 1980s. However, these apartments are also in short supply, and there are waiting lists to purchase them.

Automobiles are very scarce relative to demand for them, and the typical waiting period for a consumer to purchase one is 3 to 4 years. There are special stores where luxury goods and some scarce items are available. However, these stores are open only to privileged Communist Party members, who account for less than 5% of the population. This elite group consists of factory managers and people with high positions in government ministries, and they enjoy access to chauffeured cars and preferential treatment in obtaining housing. The distribution of real income in the Soviet Union is apparently far from the socialist ideal of perfect equality. There is a vast gap, not only in income, but also in privileges, between the elite and the working class.

The Gorbachev program for reform recognizes the problems of the Soviet economy as it seeks to move to a policy of *uskorenie,* which means acceleration. The goal is to accelerate social and economic progress in the Soviet Union so as to improve the well-being of the average Soviet citizen. It remains to be seen whether *perestroika* and *uskorenie* will accomplish their objectives. The program faces a rough road because it will inevitably involve tradeoffs. Soviet citizens might balk at giving up job security and some of their social programs, including subsidized prices, in exchange for the greater freedom of choice and efficiency promised by the reforms.

*See Marshall I. Goldman, *USSR in Crisis: The Failure of an Economic System,* New York: W.W. Norton & Co., 1983, Chapter 4, for an excellent account of the plight of the Soviet citizen. Although Goldman's account applies to the Soviet Union of the early 1980s, little has changed since then with regard to availability of consumer goods. Shortages and bare shelves remain a problem in the Soviet Union as it moves into the 1990s.

no formal economic planning, the Ministry of International Trade and Industry has actively encouraged the growth of particular export industries. The ministry has been instrumental in promoting government policies that protect and subsidize certain industries.

Most Western European nations have more elaborate systems of social security than those offered in the United States. In Sweden, for example, all citizens enjoy a tax-financed comprehensive health insurance program, and the government provides nursery and day-care services as well as subsidizing families with children. Government ownership of industries, provision of health services, and provision of income maintenance for the aged and the poor exist in all mixed economies to some degree.

The People's Republic of China, which was established as a communist state in 1949, in the past functioned under one of the strictest forms of the command economy. China's 5-year plans emphasized heavy industry, defense, and self-sufficiency. Wage differentials were frowned on as a way to motivate and allocate labor. Although planning was never as centralized in China as it was in the Soviet Union, production goals were often set at unrealistically high levels that were seldom attained.

In the 1970s China opened its doors to international trade, foreign investment, and communication with the West as it had not done since 1949. At that time China began to rely less on planning and more on markets. Worker incentives have been improved through a system of bonuses, and private enterprise, particularly in agriculture and consumer goods, has been encouraged as a way to increase production.

Socialism vs. Capitalism

It's fitting to close this book with observations on the differences between socialism and capitalism as they relate to the major issues of our time. After reading this chapter and this book, you undoubtedly realize that basic economic problems and challenges respect no cultural, geographic, or political boundaries. The principles of economics you have studied are relevant to all societies that must cope with the problems of producing goods and services to satisfy the often conflicting desires of their members.

By now you also understand that differences among economic systems often boil down to differences in the degree to which economic decisions are made politically or individually. Economic rights are intertwined with human rights. This means that the differences between ideology and economics are often difficult to separate. Political control of economic affairs at the extreme means collective ownership of economic resources and a command economy where resources are allocated according to political goals.

However, the command economy must come to grips with the fact that human beings respond positively to incentives that allow them to enjoy increases in net benefits. A pure command economy is unlikely to have a productive labor force. Most socialist politicians understand this and realize they must deal with the issue of incentives. Ideological commitment is often a poor substitute for material rewards in motivating the average worker. Productivity growth and innovation, while they may come from ideologically committed people, tend to increase when material rewards are possible. The fundamental view of human beings as maximizing the net benefits of their actions given the constraints under which they must operate is no less relevant to people working in socialist systems than it is to those working in capitalist systems.

With these observations in mind, it's possible to outline some of the main distinctions between capitalism and socialism as two opposing economic systems. Keep in mind throughout our discussion that pure socialism and pure capitalism are rarely found in practice and that most economic systems are actually a mix of socialism and capitalism. However, political conflict between the two systems rages, particularly in less developed countries, where it often threatens revolution, insurgency, and wider conflict. The two systems are studied and often supported by opposing politicians as they seek the best way to deal with economic and social problems in their particular countries. Among the important issues to consider in looking at the pros and cons of the two systems are:

1. *The extent to which pursuit of self-interest and market exchange of goods and services produce results that coincide with a general political consensus regarding national goals.* It can be argued that narrow self-interest will result in the failure of an economic system to provide many goods and services that are essential for the survival of a society. This means there are public goods, such as national defense, that cannot be provided in markets. This shortcoming requires the intervention of government authorities to ensure provision of basic public goods. At the extreme, the command economy is based on distrust of the profit motive and other pursuit of self-interest. As a result, the command economy resorts to central planning and full government control of productive resources to achieve national objectives.

2. *The way an economic system distributes well-being among members of a society.* The distribution of material well-being is a prime consideration for many people in evaluating alternative economic systems. Socialism is, after all, founded on the Marxist notion of class conflict and exploitation of workers by capitalists. In a socialist economy, profit in effect is earned by the state and redistributed to workers in the form of government services or wages and subsidies. In modern mixed economies, the issue of distribution of well-being is addressed through government transfer programs that use tax revenues to increase the incomes of the poor. In some nations with mixed economies (Norway, Sweden, and New Zealand are good examples), transfer programs and government provision of health and other services result in less income inequality than is observed in centrally planned socialist economies.

3. *The achievement of technological efficiency.* Technological efficiency is achieved when output is produced at minimum possible cost. The equity-efficiency tradeoff, which you have encountered many times in this book, also holds for economic systems. While private enterprise in markets is not perfect in achieving technological efficiency, competitive markets provide incentives for producers to keep their costs as low as possible. Changes in prices of inputs and in technology evoke a quick response in a competitive system. In a command economy, such changes often require a complete revision of the plan that can be very costly and time consuming. Also, the strict objectives of a plan frequently put pressures on managers in a planned economy and provide little reward for innovation. Critics of the market system, however, argue that monopoly power often stifles incentives to achieve cost reductions necessary for technological efficiency.

4. *Freedom of choice and responsiveness to consumer demands.* In a market sys-

tem, prices and supply respond to changes in consumers' willingness and ability to pay for goods and services. In a centrally planned economy, individual freedom of choice is subordinated to the political goals of the planners. In such a system, little effort is devoted to matching supplies of consumer goods with demand, nor are market prices used as a signal to produce more or less of particular items.

5. *Economic growth and fluctuations.* In much of this book we've been concerned with the causes and costs of economic fluctuations in nonplanned economies. The wastes associated with unemployment are considerable. In addition, inflation creates serious problems in resource allocation and income distribution. A command economy can control both aggregate demand and aggregate supply to achieve greater economic stability. However, even in the command economy, control is not perfect. Inflation and unemployment are less of a problem in planned economies, but they can still occur. However, both inflation and unemployment are most likely to be the result of supply-side rather than demand-side shocks in planned economies where aggregate demand is strictly controlled.

Both the Soviet Union and the United States over time have shown the ability to achieve remarkable growth in real GNP per capita. However, in recent years productivity gains and economic growth have lagged in both nations. The challenge of the twenty-first century will be to maintain economic growth and encourage improvements in all nations. Ultimately the material well-being of the world's population depends on the benefits that can be squeezed from the limited resources available on this earth.

Summary

1. An economic system is an accepted way of organizing production, establishing rights to ownership and use of productive resources, and governing economic transactions in a society.
2. An ideology is an opinion regarding human rights that influences a person's perception about the desirability of one economic system compared to another.
3. Capitalism is an economic system associated with private ownership of economic resources, free enterprise, and exchange of goods and services in markets. Socialism is associated with government ownership of productive resources.
4. Karl Marx was a nineteenth-century economist and philosopher whose ideas emphasized conflict between economic classes and the notion that workers are exploited by capitalists. Much of his argument was based on the labor theory of value, which maintains that only labor can produce something worth paying for.
5. Marx believed that capitalists would pay workers only a subsistence wage. He defined surplus value as the difference between wages paid to workers and the value of what workers produced. According to Marx, surplus value was the source of the capitalist's profit and was derived from the exploitation of workers.
6. Marx's theory predicted the eventual collapse of the capitalist system because of substitution of capital for labor, increased unemployment, and declining profits.
7. Marx did not take into account the possibility that increased productivity of workers would increase the wages that employers willingly pay above the subsistence level. He also neglected to consider the fact that profit opportunities arise in new enterprises as profit levels fall to zero in existing industries.

8. The Soviet economic system has been one of centrally planned socialism that can be characterized as a command economy. In the Soviet Union the state owns most productive resources and uses authoritarian methods to determine resource use. Recent reforms in the Soviet Union are designed to decrease reliance on rigid planning and encourage government enterprises to compete in satisfying production goals. Prices under the new system will be allowed to respond to conditions of supply and demand.

9. A basic objective of central planning in the Soviet Union is to obtain a materials balance, which requires that the supply of inputs equal their demand in each planned use.

10. Imbalances between the quantities of consumer goods demanded at prices set by planners and the quantities supplied have been common in the Soviet Union. Soviet planners often use a turnover tax to reduce quantities demanded for goods in short supply.

11. Socialist systems in Yugoslavia and Hungary rely less on central planning than has the system of the Soviet Union in the past. The People's Republic of China is another socialist economy that in recent years has sought to rely less on planning. Many nations in Western Europe are characterized by extensive social welfare systems and government ownership of enterprises. Although central planning is rare in these nations, the extensive role of government in the economy gives the economies of these nations a distinct socialist character.

12. At bottom all economies are a mix of socialist and capitalist systems and face similar economic problems.

Key Terms and Concepts

Economic system
Socialism
Labor theory of value
Surplus value
Command economy
Centrally planned economy

Gosplan
Materials balance
Consumer sovereignty
Turnover tax
Indicative planning

Problems and Applications

1. Why does the labor theory of value imply that profit can be obtained only by exploiting workers?

2. Why did Karl Marx's theory of economic development in capitalist economies imply that profit would fall as capital was substituted for labor? In your answer be sure to explain how Marx thought profit was related to the concept of surplus value.

3. Explain why wages on average in modern nonsocialist economies have risen above subsistence levels. Why have profits not fallen to zero permanently?

4. What is a command economy?

5. How does Gosplan set wages in the Soviet Union to allocate labor to various uses? Do the wages set reflect the forces of supply and demand?

6. The 1986 Chernobyl nuclear disaster in the Soviet Union required the use of a considerable amount of concrete to seal the damaged nuclear reactor. How do you think the unplanned demand for materials to produce concrete affected the materials balance in the Soviet Union in 1986 and 1987?

7. Suppose that in their current 5-year plan, planners in the Soviet Union decide

to produce 10 million pairs of blue jeans each year and set the price at 40 rubles per pair. Use supply and demand analysis to show how an annual shortage of blue jeans can result and how a turnover tax can eliminate the shortage.

8. Suppose planners in the Soviet Union set the price of men's suits at 50 rubles and specify the production of 20 million suits per year. Show how a surplus can result if planners fail to consider consumer demand for the suits.

9. Suppose you're a production manager in a ball-bearing factory in the Soviet Union that is not self-financing. Your annual goal is to produce 50 million ball bearings. Explain why you might lack the incentive to exceed the quota even though you have the skills and resources to do so. What incentives do you have to carefully control the quality of your product?

10. Why are interest rates not used in the Soviet Union to measure the opportunity cost of funds allocated to capital construction projects?

Suggested Readings

Marshall I. Goldman, *USSR in Crisis: Failure of an Economic System,* New York: W.W. Norton & Co., 1983. This is a critical account of economic performance and incentives in the Soviet Union prior to the Gorbachev era.

Paul R. Gregory and Robert C. Stuart, *Soviet Economic Structure and Performance,* 2nd ed., New York: Harper & Row, 1981. This is a comprehensive and highly readable text on the economy of the Soviet Union.

Ed A. Hewett, *Reforming the Soviet Economy: Equality Versus Efficiency,* Washington, D.C.: The Brookings Institution, 1988. This book shows how the Soviet economy works now and how the proposed *perestroika* reforms will change the way it functions.

Glossary

Absolute advantage
A nation has an absolute advantage over other nations in the production of an item if it can produce more of the item over a certain period with a given amount of resources than the other nations can.

Accelerated depreciation allowances
Generous deductions from pretax business income that are allowed when firms acquire new equipment or new structures.

Accelerationist hypothesis
Argues that attempts by policymakers to reduce the unemployment rate below the natural rate can succeed only in the short run.

Accounting cost
Measures the explicit costs of operating a business—those that result from purchases of inputs.

Acreage control program
Provides cash payments to farmers who agree to take some of their land out of production for certain crops.

Aggregate demand curve
Shows how the amount of aggregate domestic production demanded, measured by real GNP, will vary with the price level.

Aggregate expenditure
The sum of consumption expenditures, investment expenditures, government purchases, and net exports during the year. Equivalent to real GNP.

Aggregate household debt
The purchasing power of the sums of money outstanding that households have borrowed and are currently obligated to repay.

Aggregate household wealth
The purchasing power of all assets owned by households.

Aggregate purchases
The market value of final goods and services that will be purchased at any given level of income.

Aggregate quantity demanded
The amount of real GNP that buyers are willing and able to purchase at each possible price level.

Aggregate quantity supplied
The quantity of real GNP supplied by producers that is associated with a given price level.

Aggregate real income
The nominal (money) income of a nation, adjusted for inflation. Equivalent to real GNP.

Aggregate supply curve
Shows the aggregate output of final products, as measured by real GNP, that will be produced at each possible price level over a given period.

Aggregates
Broad totals of economic variables such as production or unemployment.

Allocative efficiency
Attained when all possible mutual gains from exchange are enjoyed.

Antitrust statutes
Seek to prevent "unfair" business practices that give rise to monopoly power.

Automatic stabilizers
Features of the federal budget that automatically adjust net taxes to stabilize aggregate demand as the economy expands and contracts.

Autonomous consumption
The portion of annual consumer purchases that is independent of current disposable income.

Autonomous purchases
Purchases such as investment or autonomous consumption that cause the economy's aggregate purchases line to shift.

Average cost
Total cost divided by the number of units of output produced over a given period. Also called *average total cost* or *unit cost*.

Average fixed cost
Fixed cost divided by the number of units of output produced over a given period.

Average input cost
The price of an input.

Average product (of an input)
The total output produced over a given period divided by the number of units of that input used.

Average revenue
Total revenue per unit of a good sold.

Average tax rate
The amount of taxes paid divided by the dollar value of the item taxed.

Average variable cost
Variable cost divided by the number of units of output produced over a given period.

Backward-bending labor supply curve
Implies that the substitution effect on a worker's labor services outweighs the income effect only at relatively low wages.

Balance of payments
A statement showing the net exchange of a nation's currency for foreign currencies from all transactions between that nation and foreign nations in a given year.

Balance of trade
The difference between the value of merchandise exported by a nation's firms and the nation's imports of foreign-produced goods.

Balance of trade deficit
Prevails when a nation's expenditures on imported products over the year exceed receipts by domestic firms from sales of exports.

Balance on current account of the balance of payments
Measures U.S. net exports for the year, including transactions involving services, investment income, and transfers.

Bank
A commercial bank or thrift institution that offers checkable deposits.

Bar graph
A graph that shows the value of a Y variable as the height of a bar for each corresponding value of the X variable.

Barrier to entry
A constraint that prevents additional sellers from entering a monopoly firm's market.

Barter
The process of exchanging goods (or services) for goods (or services).

Behavioral assumption
Establishes the motivation of persons for the purpose of understanding cause-and-effect relationships among economic variables.

Bilateral monopoly
Exists when only one buyer and one seller trade input (or output) services in a market.

Black market
A market in which sellers sell goods to buyers for more than the legal prices.

Board of Governors of the Federal Reserve System
Supervises the operation of the nation's banking system and acts as an authority to regulate the money supply. The Board consists of 7 governors, each appointed by the President to serve a 14-year term.

Bonds
Securities issued by corporations and governments representing the promise to make periodic payments of interest and repay a debt of borrowed funds at a certain time.

Bretton Woods system
An international monetary system developed in 1944 and based on fixed exchange rates, with the value of foreign currencies tied to the U.S. dollar.

Budget constraint
As defined by a consumer's income and its purchasing power, indicates that income must equal expenditure.

Budget deficit
The amount by which government expenditures exceed government revenues in a given year.

Budget line
Shows an individual's opportunities to purchase two goods if he spends all of his monthly income on these two goods at their current prices.

Budget surplus
An excess of government revenues over government expenditures in a given year.

Business cycle
The term used to describe the fluctuations in aggregate production as measured by the ups and downs of real GNP.

Business firm
An organization under one management set up for the purpose of earning profits for its owners by making one or more items available for sale in markets.

Capital
The equipment, tools, structures, machinery, vehicles, materials, and skills created to help produce goods and services.

Capitalism
Characterized by private ownership of economic resources and freedom of enterprise in which owners of factories and other capital hire workers to produce goods and services.

Cartel
A group of firms acting together to coordinate output decisions and control prices as if they were a single monopoly.

Centrally planned economy
An economy in which politically appointed committees plan production and manage the economy to achieve political goals.

Ceteris paribus
A Latin phrase meaning "other things being equal." Used to acknowledge that other influences aside from the one whose effect is being analyzed must be controlled for in testing a hypothesis.

Change in aggregate demand
A shift of the economy's aggregate demand curve that causes the economy to move to a new macroeconomic equilibrium.

Change in aggregate supply
A shift of the economy's aggregate supply curve as the relationship is altered between the price level and real GNP supplied.

Change in demand
A change in the relationship between the price of a good and the quantity demanded caused by a change in a demand determinant other than the price of the good.

Change in input demand
A shift of an entire input demand curve caused by a change in one of the determinants of input demand other than price.

Change in money demand
A change in the relationship between the level of interest rates and the stock of money demanded in the economy caused by a change in economic conditions.

Change in quantity demanded
A change in the amount of a good buyers are willing and able to buy in response to a change in the price of the good.

Change in quantity supplied
A change in the amount of a good sellers are willing to sell in response to a change in the price of the good.

Change in relative price
An increase or decrease in the price of a good relative to the average change in the prices of all goods.

Change in supply
A change in the relationship between the price of a good and the quantity supplied in response to a change in a supply determinant other than the price of the good.

Check clearing
The process of transferring Federal Reserve deposits among banks as checks are paid.

Checkable deposits
Represent money deposited in bank accounts that can be used to write checks that are accepted to pay debts, or that can easily be converted to currency.

Classical model of macroeconomic equilibrium
Implied that excessive unemployment of workers and unused productive capacity would set up forces that would eventually result in increases in real GNP and eliminate the unemployment of workers.

Classical quantity theory of money
A model of the long-run functioning of the economy that maintains that over the long run, changes in the money stock result in proportional changes in the price level.

Closed shop
A union arrangement with an employer that permits hiring only of union members.

Collateral
An asset a borrower pledges to a lender in case of default.

Collective bargaining
The process of negotiating for wages and improvements in working conditions between a labor union and employers.

Command economy
An economy in which resource allocation decisions are determined largely by the central planning authorities who set production goals.

Commercial banks
Firms that acquire funds by accepting checkable deposits and savings deposits of households and business firms and use these funds to make loans to businesses and individuals.

Commodity money
An item that serves the functions of money but also has value in uses other than as the medium of exchange.

Common property resource
A resource (such as the ocean) whose use is not priced because property rights for payment of services have not been established.

Comparative advantage
A nation has a comparative advantage over a trading partner in the production of an item if it produces that item at lower opportunity cost per unit than its partner does.

Compensating wage differential
A difference in money wages necessary to make total compensation for similar jobs equal when nonpecuniary wages are not equal to zero.

Competitive firm
One that sells its product in a perfectly competitive market in which it is a price taker.

Competitive input market
A market in which neither individual buyers nor individual sellers can influence the prices of input services.

Complements
Goods whose use together enhances the satisfaction a consumer obtains from each.

Conglomerate
A firm operating plants that produce many different kinds of goods and services.

Conglomerate merger
A merger of firms selling goods in unrelated markets.

Constant returns to scale
Prevail when economies of scale no longer exist and when average costs do not increase as a result of diseconomies of scale in the long run.

Constant-costs industry
One for which input prices are unaffected by the quantity produced or the number of firms in the industry.

Consumer equilibrium
Attained when a consumer purchases goods over a period until the marginal utility per dollar is the same for all goods consumed.

Consumer price index (CPI)
The price index most commonly used to measure the impact of changes in prices on households. The index is based on a standard market basket of goods and services purchased by a typical urban family.

Consumer sovereignty
The responsiveness of the market economy to changes in consumer demand.

Consumer surplus
The difference between the total benefit of a given quantity purchased by a consumer and the expenditure necessary to purchase that quantity.

Consumption function
A relationship between aggregate consumer purchases and disposable income in a certain year given all other determinants of consumption.

Consumption possibilities curve
A curve showing combinations of two goods a nation can consume given its resources, technology, and international trade.

Contestable market
A market in which entry of sellers is easy and exit is not very costly.

Continuous variable
A variable that can realistically and meaningfully take on minute fractions of values

Contraction
A downturn from peak economic activity in the business cycle during which real GNP declines from its previous value.

Contractionary fiscal policy
A policy under which the government acts to restrain aggregate demand by decreasing spending or increasing taxes, or both.

Contractionary monetary policy
Action taken by the Federal Reserve System to decrease the monetary base or its rate of growth.

Coordinates
A pair of numbers that corresponds to a pair of values for variables X and Y when plotted on a set of axes.

Corporate profits taxes
Those amounts corporations pay as taxes to governments out of their annual receipts from the sale of goods and services.

Corporation
A business that is legally established under state laws that grant it an identity separate from its owners.

Corrective subsidy
An amount paid to consumers or producers of a good equal to the marginal external benefit of the good.

Corrective tax
A tax levied on polluters to simulate a charge equal to the marginal external cost of their actions.

Cost-push inflation
Inflation caused by continual decreases in aggregate supply.

Craft union
An organization of workers in a particular skilled job, such as plumbers, electricians, carpenters, or musicians.

Credit
The use of loanable funds supplied by lenders to borrowers who agree to pay

back the borrowed funds according to an agreed-upon schedule.

Credit unions
Depository institutions whose depositors are called "members" and belong to a particular organization such as a business firm or government. Credit unions make loans only to their members for the purpose of financing homes or personal goods and services (such as cars).

Cross-elasticity of demand
A number used to measure the sensitivity of consumer purchases of one good to each 1% change in the prices of related goods.

Crowding-out effect
The reduction in private investment purchases caused by higher interest rates that result from borrowing by the government to cover its budget deficit.

Currency appreciation
Occurs when there is an increase in the number of units of one nation's currency that must be given up to purchase each unit of another nation's currency.

Currency depreciation
Occurs when there is a decrease in the number of units of one nation's currency that must be given up to purchase each unit of another nation's currency.

Curve
A straight or curved line drawn to connect points plotted on a set of axes.

Cyclical unemployment
The amount of unemployment resulting from declines in real GNP during periods of contraction or recession or in any period when the economy fails to operate at its potential.

Default
Nonrepayment of the principal and interest on a loan.

Deflation
The rate of downward movement in the price level for an aggregate of goods and services.

Demand
A relationship between the price of an item and the quantity demanded.

Demand curve
A graph that shows how quantity demanded varies with the price of a good.

Demand for money
The relationship between the sums of money people willingly hold and the level of interest rates in the economy given all other influences on the desirability of holding money instead of other assets.

Demand-pull inflation
Inflation caused by increases in aggregate demand.

Demand schedule
A table that shows how the quantity demanded of a good would vary with price, given all other demand determinants.

Depletable resource
A resource for which there is a given amount of known reserves available at any point in time.

Depository institutions
Institutions that make loans and offer checkable deposit and time deposit accounts for use by households and business firms.

Depreciation
An estimate of the value of capital goods that wear out or become obsolete over the year. Also called the *capital consumption allowance*.

Derived demand
The demand for an input that is derived from the demand for the product that the input is used to produce.

Diminishing marginal rates of substitution
The marginal rates of substitution between any two goods X and Y will tend to decline as more X is substituted for Y along any consumer's indifference curve.

Discount loans
Bank borrowings from the Federal Reserve System; also called *advances*.

Discount rate
The interest rate Federal Reserve Banks charge member banks for loans.

Discounted present value
The current value of funds to be received in future periods.

Discouraged worker
A worker who leaves the labor force (stops actively seeking a job) after unsuccessfully searching for a job for a certain period.

Discrete variable
A variable that cannot vary by fractions of units.

Discrimination in labor markets
Occurs when minority-group workers with skills, experience, and training comparable to those of workers in other groups are paid lower wages and have less opportunity for employment and advancement.

Diseconomies of scale
Increases in average costs of operation resulting from problems in managing large-scale enterprises. Also called *decreasing returns to scale*.

Disinflation
A sharp reduction in the annual rate of inflation.

Disposable income
The amount of income available for households to spend after receipt of government transfer payments and payment of taxes. Also called *disposable personal income*.

Dividend
The portion of a corporation's profit paid to its stockholders.

Division of labor
The specialization of workers in particular tasks that are part of a larger undertaking to accomplish a given objective.

Economic cost
The monetary value of all inputs used in a particular activity or enterprise over a given period.

Economic growth
The expansion in production possibilities that results from increased availability and increased productivity of economic resources.

Economic model
A simplified way of expressing how some sector of the economy functions. Consists of assumptions that establish relationships among economic variables.

Economic profit
Profit in excess of the normal profit; the difference between total revenue and the opportunity cost of all inputs used by a firm over a given period.

Economic rents
Earnings that exceed the opportunity cost of an activity.

Economic resources
The inputs used in the process of production.

Economic system
An accepted way of organizing production, establishing rights to ownership and use of productive resources, and governing economic transactions in a society.

Economics
The study of the use of limited productive resources in a society to satisfy the unlimited desires of its members.

Economies of scale
Reductions in unit costs resulting from increased size of operations. Also called *increasing returns to scale* or *economies of mass production*.

Economy
The mechanism through which the use of labor, land, structures, vehicles, equipment, and natural resources is organized to satisfy the desires of those who live in a society.

Elastic demand
Prevails if the price elasticity of demand for a good is a number that exceeds 1, ignoring the minus sign.

Elastic supply
Prevails when the price elasticity of supply is greater than 1.

Emissions charges
Prices established for the right to emit each unit of a pollutant.

Emissions standards
Limits established by government on the annual amounts and kinds of pollutants that can be emitted into the air or water by producers or users of certain products.

Entrepreneurship
The talent to develop products and processes and to organize production of goods and services.

Equation of exchange
An identity that shows the relationship between nominal GNP, the money stock, and the income velocity of circulation of money.

Equilibrium
Prevails when economic forces balance so that economic variables neither increase nor decrease.

Equimarginal principle
States that to maximize utility, a consumer must equalize the marginal utility per dollar spent on each good.

Excess burden
The loss in net benefits from resource use caused by the distortion in choices resulting from taxation.

Excess capacity
The difference between the output corresponding to minimum possible average cost and that produced by the monopolistically competitive firm in the long run.

Excess reserves
The difference between total reserves and required reserves of a bank held against deposits.

Expansion
An upturn of economic activity between a trough and a peak during which real GNP increases.

Expansion path
Shows how the use of inputs by a producer will vary as the firm expands output.

Expansionary fiscal policy
A policy under which the government acts to increase aggregate demand by increasing spending or decreasing taxes, or both.

Expansionary monetary policy
Action taken by the Federal Reserve System to increase the monetary base or its rate of growth.

External debt
The portion of the national debt owed to citizens of other nations.

Externalities
Costs or benefits of market transactions that are not reflected in the prices buyers and sellers use to make their decisions.

Federal Open Market Committee
An arm of the Federal Reserve System. Affects the amount of excess reserves available to banks by instructing the Federal Reserve Bank of New York to buy or sell government securities on the open market.

Federal system of government
Numerous levels of government, each with its own powers, exist to provide services and regulate private affairs.

Fiat money
Money that is accepted as a medium of exchange because of government decree rather than because of its intrinsic value as a commodity.

Financial intermediaries
Firms that specialize in borrowing funds from savers and lending those funds to investors and others.

Fiscal policy
The use of government spending and taxing for the specific purpose of stabilizing the economy.

Fixed costs
Costs that do not vary as a firm varies its output. Also called *overhead costs*.

Fixed input
An input whose quantity cannot be changed over the short run.

Foreign exchange
The money of one nation held by citizens of another nation either as currency or as deposits in banks.

Foreign exchange market
A market in which buyers and sellers of bank deposits denominated in the monetary units of many nations exchange their funds.

Foreign exchange rate
The price of one nation's monetary unit in terms of the monetary unit of another nation.

Fractional reserve banking
A process by which a banking system creates checkable deposits by making loans in some multiple of the reserves it actually has on hand to pay withdrawals.

Fractional reserve ratio
The ratio of a bank's actual reserves to total receipts for deposits.

Free rider
A person who seeks to enjoy the benefits of a public good without contributing to its costs.

Frictional unemployment
Represents the usual amount of unemployment resulting from people who have left jobs that did not work out and are searching for new employment, or people who are either entering or reentering the labor force to search for a job.

Full employment
Occurs when the actual rate of unemployment is no more than the natural rate of unemployment.

GNP gap
The difference between potential and actual GNP.

Gold standard
An international monetary system that required that currencies be convertible into gold at a fixed price.

Gosplan
The central planning board for the Soviet Union.

Government budget
A plan for spending funds and raising revenues through taxation, fees, and other means, and borrowing funds if necessary.

Government failure
Exists when voters approve programs for which marginal benefits exceed marginal costs.

Government purchases of goods and services
Expenditure on final products of business firms and all input costs, including labor costs, incurred by all levels of government in the United States.

Government securities
Interest-bearing debts of the federal government in the form of Treasury bills, Treasury notes, and Treasury bonds.

Government transfers
Payments made directly to certain citizens or organizations for which no good or service is received in return at that time. Transfers usually are financed by taxes.

Gross national product (GNP)
The market value of an economy's final goods and services produced over a period of 1 year.

Gross private domestic investment
Investment purchases by business firms: expenditure on new machinery and equipment (producer durables), the value of new residential and nonresidential construction, and the change in business inventories during the year.

High-employment deficit (or surplus)
The budget deficit (or surplus) that would prevail if the natural rate of unemployment were achieved.

Horizontal merger
Occurs when competing sellers in the same market merge into a single firm.

Human capital
Represents the skills and qualifications of workers that stem from education and training.

Hypothesis
Statement of a relationship between two or more variables.

Imperfect competition
Exists when more than one seller competes for sales with other sellers of competitive products, each of whom has some control over price.

Implicit costs
The costs of nonpurchased inputs, to which a cash value must be imputed because the inputs are not purchased in a market transaction.

Implicit GNP deflator
An implicit index for all final products, derived as the ratio of nominal GNP to real GNP (multiplied by 100); an index of the average of the prices used to deflate nominal GNP.

Import quota
A limit on the quantity of foreign goods that can be sold in a nation's domestic markets.

Income effect
A change in the consumption of a good *only* as a result of the variation in the purchasing power of money income caused by a price change.

Income effect of a wage change
The change in hours worked resulting from the change in income caused by the wage change.

Income elasticity of demand
A number that measures the sensitivity of consumer purchases to each 1% change in income.

Income velocity of circulation of money
The number of times per year on average a dollar of the money stock is spent on final purchases or paid out as income.

Incomes policies
Policies that seek to curb inflation by directly influencing both prices and wages without reducing aggregate demand through the use of monetary or fiscal policy.

Increasing-costs industry
One for which the prices of at least some of the inputs used increase as a direct result of the expansion of the industry.

Indicative planning
A system in which government encourages voluntary compliance by industrial and labor interests to coordinate economic decisions so as to achieve politically determined objectives.

Indifference curve
A graph of various market baskets that provide a consumer with equal utility.

Indifference curve analysis
A technique for explaining how choices between two alternatives are made.

Indifference map
A way of drawing indifference curves to describe a consumer's preferences.

Indirect business taxes
Taxes levied on business firms that increase their costs and are therefore reflected in the market value of goods and services sold.

Induced consumption
The portion of annual consumer purchases in a given year that responds to changes in current disposable income.

Industrial union
A union that represents all workers in a particular industry, regardless of their craft or skill.

Industry
A group of firms selling a similar product in a market.

Inelastic demand
Prevails if the price elasticity of demand for a good is a number equal to or greater than zero but less than 1, ignoring the minus sign.

Inelastic supply
Prevails when the price elasticity of supply is equal to or greater than zero but less than 1.

Inferior goods
Goods that have negative income elasticity of demand.

Inflation
The rate of upward movement in the price level for an aggregate of goods and services.

Inflationary GNP gap
The difference between equilibrium real GNP and potential real GNP when the economy is overheated.

Injection (of spending)
A purchase made by business firms, governments, or foreign buyers that increases the flow of income in a nation.

Input market
A market used to trade the services of productive resources for income payments.

Inputs
The labor, capital, land, natural resources, and entrepreneurship that are combined to produce products and services.

Interest
The price for the use of funds, expressed as a percentage per dollar of funds borrowed.

Intermediate products
Products produced by business firms for resale by other firms or for use as materials or services that will be included in the value of resold goods.

Internal debt
The portion of the national debt owed to the nation's own citizens.

Internal labor market
Exists within a firm when it fills positions by hiring its own employees, rather than new employees, to fill all but the lowest-level jobs.

Internalization of an externality
Occurs when the marginal cost or marginal benefit of a good has been adjusted so that market sale of the item results in the efficient output.

International Monetary Fund (IMF)
Established under the Bretton Woods agreement; set rules for the international monetary system to make loans to nations that lack international reserves of dollars.

Intersection

The point at which two curves drawn on the same set of axes cross.

Investment

The process of replenishing or adding to capital stock.

Isocost line

Gives all combinations of labor and capital that are of equal total cost.

Isoquant

A curve showing all combinations of variable inputs that can be used to produce a given quantity of output.

Isoquant map

Shows the combinations of labor and capital that can be used to produce several possible output levels.

Job finding

Occurs when an unemployed worker accepts an offer of a new job.

Job search

The process of looking for suitable work either by those just entering the labor force or by those having just experienced a job separation.

Job separation

Occurs when a worker leaves a job for any reason: quitting, being fired, or being laid off.

Keynesian model of macroeconomic equilibrium

Assumes that because of rigid nominal wages the economy can be in equilibrium at less than full employment.

Labor

The physical and mental efforts of human beings in the production of goods and services.

Labor force

The total number of persons over age 16 with jobs and workers who are actively seeking a job but currently do not have one.

Labor supply curve

Shows a relationship between a worker's hourly wages and labor hours supplied for work over a given period.

Labor theory of value

Maintains that only labor can produce something worth paying for.

Labor union

An organization formed to represent the interests of workers in bargaining with employers for contracts concerning wages, fringe benefits, and working conditions.

Law of demand

States that in general, other things being equal, the lower the price of a good, the greater the quantity of that good buyers are willing and able to purchase over a given period.

Law of diminishing marginal returns

States that the extra production obtained from increases in a variable input will eventually decline as more of the variable input is used together with the fixed inputs.

Law of diminishing marginal utility

States that the marginal utility of any item tends to decline as more is consumed over any given period.

Law of increasing costs

States that the opportunity cost of each additional unit of output of a good over a period increases as more of that good is produced.

Law of supply

States that in general, other things being equal, the higher the price of a good, the greater the quantity of that good sellers are willing and able to make available over a given period.

Layoff

The temporary suspension of employment without pay for a period of 7 consecutive days or more.

Leakage (of spending)

A portion of income that is not used to purchase domestically produced goods during the year.

Less developed country (LDC)

A country whose real GNP per capita is generally much less than $1,000 a year.

Limited liability

A legal provision that protects the owners of a corporation (its stockholders) by putting a ceiling equal to the purchase price of their stock on their liability for debts of the corporation.

Long run

A period of production long enough that producers have adequate time to vary *all* the inputs used to produce a good.

Long-run aggregate supply curve

Shows the relationship between the aggregate quantity supplied and the price level that would be observed if nominal wages and other money prices were flexible enough to allow the classical self-correction mechanism to work.

Long-run competitive equilibrium

Exists in an industry when there is no tendency for firms to enter or leave the industry or to expand or contract the scale of their operations.

Long-run cost

The minimum cost of producing any given output when all inputs are variable.

Long-run industry supply curve

A relationship between price and quantity supplied for points where the industry is in long-run competitive equilibrium.

Lorenz curve

A plotting of data showing the percentage of income enjoyed by each percentage of households ranked according to their incomes.

M1

The stock of money measured by the sum of currency, traveler's checks, and checkable deposits held by the public on a particular day of the year in the United States.

M2

The sum of M1 and certain near monies; a measure of liquid assets held by the public.

M3

The sum of M2 and large-denomination ($100,000 and more) certificates of deposit.

Macroeconomic equilibrium
Occurs when the quantity of real GNP demanded equals the quantity of real GNP supplied.

Macroeconomics
A branch of economic analysis that considers the overall performance of the economy with respect to total national production, consumption, average prices, and employment levels.

Managed float
Describes the current international monetary system, under which central banks affect the supply of and demand for currencies in ways that influence equilibrium in foreign exchange markets.

Manager
A person who coordinates decisions within a firm.

Marginal analysis
A method economists use to study decision making; involves a systematic comparison of benefits and costs of actions.

Marginal benefit
The dollar value placed on the satisfaction obtained from another unit of an item.

Marginal benefit of work
The extra income received from extra work, including any nonmonetary satisfaction obtained from a job.

Marginal cost
The sacrifice made to obtain an additional unit of an item.

Marginal cost of work
The value of extra leisure time given up to work.

Marginal external benefit
The extra benefit that accrues to third parties when a positive externality is present.

Marginal external cost
The extra cost imposed on third parties when a negative externality is present.

Marginal input cost
The change in total input cost associated with a change in input services hired.

Marginal product (of an input)
The increase in output from one more unit of an input when the quantity of all other inputs is unchanged.

Marginal profit
The change in profit from selling an additional unit of a good, representing the difference between the marginal revenue from that unit and its marginal cost.

Marginal propensity to consume
The fraction of each additional dollar of annual disposable income that is allocated to consumer purchases.

Marginal propensity to import
The fraction of each extra dollar of income used to purchase imported products.

Marginal propensity to save
The fraction of each additional dollar of annual disposable income that is saved.

Marginal rate of substitution
The quantity of one good a consumer would give up to obtain one more unit of another good while being made neither better off nor worse off by the trade.

Marginal rate of technical substitution of labor for capital
A measure of the amount of capital each unit of labor can replace without increasing or decreasing production.

Marginal respending rate
The extra purchases that result from each extra dollar of income.

Marginal return on investment
The percentage rate of return on investment of additional sums used to purchase more capital.

Marginal revenue
The extra revenue obtained from selling an additional unit of a good.

Marginal revenue product (of an input)
The change in total revenue that results when one more unit of that input is hired.

Marginal tax rate
The extra tax paid on extra income or the extra dollar value of any other taxed item.

Marginal utility
The extra satisfaction received over a given period by consuming one extra unit of a good.

Market
An arrangement through which buyers and sellers meet or communicate for the purpose of trading goods or services.

Market basket
A combination of goods and services.

Market demand curve
Shows the relationship between the price of a product and the total quantity demanded by *all* consumers willing and able to purchase the product at each price, other things being equal.

Market demand for an input
The sum of the quantities demanded by all industries and other employers using that input at any given price.

Market equilibrium
Attained when the price of a good adjusts so that the quantity buyers are willing and able to buy at that price is just equal to the quantity sellers are willing and able to supply.

Market failure
Occurs when the price system fails to allocate resources so as to achieve allocative efficiency.

Market supply curve
Gives the sum of the quantities supplied by all firms producing a product at each possible price over a given period.

Market supply of an input
A relationship between the price of the input and the quantity supplied for employment in all industries and other uses.

Materials balance
Exists when the supply of each intermediate product equals its demand as an input in some other productive process.

Maximin strategy
The strategy that maximizes the minimum (or worst) outcomes of all possible strategies.

Means test
Establishes the fact that people in the groups eligible for welfare payments have incomes and property below the amounts that are minimally acceptable.

Median voter
Given an odd number of voters, the voter whose most-preferred outcome is the median of all the most-preferred outcomes.

Median voter rule
States that when the marginal benefit of a pure public good declines for each voter as more of the good is made available, the political equilibrium under majority rule always corresponds to the median most-preferred outcome when there is an odd number of voters.

Microeconomics
A branch of economic analysis that concentrates on the choices made by individual participants in an economy. Also called *price theory*.

Mixed economy
An economy in which governments as well as business firms provide goods and services.

Monetarism
A theory of long-term macroeconomic equilibrium, based on the equation of exchange, that assumes that shifts in velocity are reasonably predictable.

Monetary base
The sum of currency in circulation and total bank reserves outstanding at any given time.

Monetary policy
Actions taken by central banks to influence money supply or interest rates in an attempt to stabilize the economy.

Money
Anything that is generally accepted as payment for goods or services. Money also serves as a standard of value, a standard of deferred payment, and a store of value.

Money demand curve
Shows a relationship between the level of interest rates in the economy and the stock of money demanded at a given point in time.

Money supply
A relationship between the quantity of money supplied in the form of currency and checkable deposits and the level of interest rates prevailing at a given point in time.

Monopolistic competition
Exists when many sellers compete to sell a differentiated product in a market in which entry of new sellers is possible.

Monopoly power
The ability of a firm to influence the price of its product by making more or less of it available to buyers.

Monopsony
A single buyer with no rivals in an input market.

Monopsony power
The ability of a single buyer to influence the price of an input service it purchases.

Most-preferred political outcome
That alternative for which the marginal benefit just equals the tax a voter would pay if he were able to purchase the good or service in a market at a price equal to his assigned tax per unit.

Multiplier
A number that can be used to multiply a change in purchases that results in a shift of the aggregate purchases line to obtain the change in equilibrium real GNP that results from those purchases.

Multiproduct firm
A firm that produces several different items for sale in markets.

Mutual gains from international trade
On average, citizens in all trading nations gain from exchanging goods in international markets.

Mutual savings banks
Depository institutions operating in some states that are similar to savings and loan associations in that they primarily attract savings deposits and in the past have specialized in making mortgage loans. Mutual savings banks are owned by their depositors.

National debt
The dollar amount that the federal government owes to its creditors at a given point in time.

National income (NI)
Net national product less indirect business taxes.

National Income and Product Accounts (NIPA)
The official system of accounting to measure the flows of income and expenditures in the United States.

Natural monopoly
A firm that emerges as a single seller in the market because of cost or technological advantages contributing to lower average costs of production.

Natural rate of unemployment
The percentage of the labor force that can normally be expected to be unemployed for reasons other than cyclical fluctuations in real GNP.

Natural resources
Acreage and the physical terrain used to locate structures, ports, and other facilities; also, natural materials that are used in crude form in production.

Near monies
Assets that are easily converted to money because they can be liquidated at low cost and little risk of loss.

Negative externality
A cost associated with the use of resources that is not reflected in prices. Also called *external cost*.

Negative income tax
Provides for government payments to people whose income falls below certain levels.

Negative (inverse) relationship
Depicted by a downward-sloping curve on a set of axes; indicates that variable Y decreases whenever variable X increases.

Net benefit
The total benefit of the quantity of a good purchased less the dollar sacrifice necessary to purchase that quantity.

Net exports
Any excess of expenditure on exports over imports.

Net federal debt
The portion of the national debt owed to those other than the Federal Reserve and government agencies.

Net national product (NNP)
Gross national product less capital consumption allowances (depreciation).

Net private domestic investment
Gross private domestic investment less depreciation.

Net taxes
The difference between taxes and transfer payments.

Nominal exchange rate
The price of a unit of one nation's currency in terms of a unit of a foreign currency.

Nominal GNP
The market value of a nation's aggregate production of final output based on current prices for the goods and services produced during the year.

Nominal income
The actual number of dollars of income received over a year.

Nominal interest rate
The annual percentage amount of money that is earned on a sum that is loaned or deposited in a bank.

Nominal wages
Hourly payments to workers in current dollars.

Nonpecuniary wages
The nonmonetary aspects of a job that must be added to or subtracted from money wages to obtain total compensation per hour of work.

Nonprice rationing
A device that distributes available amounts of goods and services on a basis other than willingness to pay.

Nonscarce (or free) good
A good for which the quantity demanded does not exceed the quantity supplied at zero price.

Nonwage money income
Includes pensions, welfare payments and subsidies, interest, dividends, allowances, and any other type of income that is available independent of work.

Normal goods
Goods that have positive income elasticity of demand.

Normal profit
That portion of a firm's cost that is not included in accounting cost. A measure of the implicit costs of owner-supplied resources in a firm over a given period.

Normative analysis
Evaluates the desirability of alternative outcomes according to underlying value judgments about what is good or bad.

Okun's Law
States that each 1% increase in the unemployment rate is associated with a 2.5% reduction in real GNP.

Oligopoly
A market structure in which a few sellers dominate the sales of a product and where entry of new sellers is difficult or impossible.

Open market operations
The Federal Reserve System's purchases and sales of government securities, conducted by the Federal Open Market Committee.

Opportunity cost
The cost of choosing to use resources for one purpose measured by the sacrifice of the next best alternative for using those resources.

Origin
On a set of axes, the point designated by 0, at which variables X and Y both take on values of zero.

Paradox of value
People are willing to give up zero or very small amounts of money to obtain certain items that provide them great total benefit.

Parity
The idea that the prices of agricultural commodities must rise as fast as the prices of goods and services on which farmers spend their income.

Parity price ratio
The ratio of an average of prices of goods sold by farmers to an average of prices of goods on which farmers spend their income.

Partnership
A business owned by two or more persons, each of whom receives a portion of any profits.

Payoff matrix
Shows the gain or loss from each possible strategy for each possible reaction by the rival players of a game.

Perfectly competitive market
Exists when (1) there are many sellers in the market; (2) the products sold in the market are homogeneous; (3) each firm has a very small market share of total sales; (4) no seller regards competing sellers as a threat to its market share; (5) information is freely available on prices; (6) there is freedom of entry and exit by sellers.

Personal consumption expenditures
Household and individual purchases of both durable and nondurable goods and services.

Personal income
National income plus government transfer payments and income received from sources other than sale of productive services, less Social Security payroll taxes, corporate profits taxes, and undistributed corporate profits.

Personal saving
Disposable personal income less all spending by individuals and all interest payments.

Personnel management
The process by which managers monitor worker performance and provide rewards for workers who perform efficiently.

Phillips curve
A curve showing the hypothesized inverse relationship between annual unemployment and annual inflation in a nation.

Planned investment purchases
Purchases of new or replacement residential and nonresidential structures, producer durable equipment, and additions to inventories that business firms intentionally make during the year.

Plant
A physical structure in which a firm's owners or employees conduct business.

Point of diminishing returns
Corresponds to the level of usage of a variable input at which its marginal product begins to decline.

Policy rule
A preannounced government rule that will inform the public of future economic stabilization policies.

Political equilibrium
An agreement on the quantity of a public good to supply through government, given the rule for making the public choice and given the taxes per unit of the public good for each voter.

Pollution
Waste that has been disposed of in the air, in water, or on land that reduces the value of those resources in alternative uses.

Pollution right
A government-issued certificate allowing a firm to emit a specified quantity of polluting waste.

Positive analysis
Seeks to forecast the impact of changes in economic policies or conditions on observable items like production, sales, prices, and personal incomes, then tries to determine who gains and who loses as a result of the changes.

Positive (direct) relationship
Depicted by an upward-sloping curve on a set of axes; indicates that variable Y increases whenever variable X increases.

Positive externality
A benefit associated with the use of resources that is not reflected in prices. Also called *external benefit*.

Potential real GNP
The level of GNP that would prevail if the economy achieved the natural rate of unemployment over a period.

Poverty income threshold
The income level below which a person or family is classified as being poor.

Preferences
Individual likes and dislikes.

Price ceiling
Establishes a maximum price that can legally be charged for a good or service.

Price discrimination
The practice of selling a certain product of given quality and cost per unit at different prices to different buyers.

Price elasticity of demand
A number representing the percentage change in quantity demanded of a good resulting from each 1% change in the price of the good.

Price elasticity of supply
A number that indicates the percentage change in quantity supplied resulting from each 1% change in the price of a good, other things being equal.

Price floor
A minimum price established by law.

Price index
A number used to measure the price level. The value of the index is set at 100 in the base year.

Price leader
One dominant firm in an industry that sets its price to maximize its own profits, after which other firms follow its lead by setting exactly the same price.

Price level
An indicator of how high or low prices are in a given year compared to prices in a certain *base year*.

Price system
A mechanism by which resource use in an economy is guided by prices.

Price war
A bout of continual price cutting by rival firms in a market; one of many possible consequences of oligopolistic rivalry.

Prime rate
The interest rate a bank charges its most creditworthy customers for short-term loans of less than 1 year.

Private goods
Goods whose benefits are rival in consumption and for which exclusion of those who refuse to pay is relatively easy.

Privatization
The process of selling government assets to private business interests.

Producer price index
Measures movements in the prices of a broad aggregate of products purchased by producers rather than consumers.

Product group
Represents several closely related, but not identical, items that serve the same general purpose for consumers.

Production
The process of using the services of labor and capital together with other inputs, such as land, materials, and fuels, to make goods and services available.

Production function
Describes the relationship between any combination of input services and the maximum attainable output from that combination.

Production possibilities curve
Shows the maximum possible output of one good that can be produced with available resources given the output of an alternative good over a period.

Productive efficiency
Attained when the maximum possible output of any one good is produced given the output of other goods. At this point it is not possible to reallocate economic resources to increase the output of any single good or service without decreasing the output of some other good or service.

Productivity
A measure of output per unit of input.

Profit
The difference between the revenue a firm takes in over any given period and the costs incurred in operating the firm over the same period.

Progressive tax
A tax for which the fraction of income used to pay it increases as income increases.

Property rights
Privileges to use or own goods, services, and economic resources.

Proportional tax
A tax for which the percentage of income paid in taxes is the same no matter what the taxpayer's income.

Public choices
Choices made by voting.

Public goods
Goods that are consumed equally by everyone whether they pay or not.

Purchasing power of a dollar
A measure of how much a dollar can buy.

Purchasing power parity
A principle that states that the exchange rate between any two currencies tends to adjust to reflect changes in the price levels in the two nations.

Pure inflation
Occurs when the prices of all goods rise by the same percentage over the year.

Pure monopoly
Exists when there is a single seller of a product that has no close substitutes.

Pure monopsony
Exists when a single firm buys the entire market supply of an input that has few if any alternative employment opportunities.

Pure public good
A good that provides benefits to all members of a community as soon as it is made available to any one person.

Quantity demanded
The amount of an item that buyers are willing and able to purchase over a period at a certain price, given all other influences on their decision to buy.

Quantity supplied
The quantity of a good sellers are willing and able to make available in the market over a given period at a certain price, other things being equal.

Rational behavior
Seeking to gain by choosing to undertake actions for which the extra benefit exceeds the associated extra cost.

Rational expectations
The use by individuals of all available information, including any relevant economic models, in their forecasts of economic variables.

Real exchange rate (of a nation's currency)
The sacrifice of goods and services that foreign buyers must make when they use their own currency to purchase goods of the first nation worth one unit of that nation's currency.

Real GNP
A measure of the value of a nation's aggregate output of final products obtained by using market prices prevailing for products during a certain base or reference year.

Real income
The purchasing power of nominal income.

Real interest rate
The actual annual percentage change in the purchasing power of interest income earned on a sum of money that is loaned out.

Real marginal return to investment
An estimate of the percentage of each dollar invested that will be returned to a firm as additional revenue per year (adjusted for the effects of changes in the price level).

Real per capita output
A measure of output per person in a nation; calculated by dividing real GNP by population.

Real terms of trade
The actual market exchange rate of one good for another in international trade.

Real wages
Nominal wages deflated to adjust for changes in the purchasing power of the dollar since a certain base year.

Recession
Exists when the decline in real GNP measured at an annual rate occurs for two consecutive 3-month reporting periods.

Recessionary GNP gap
The difference between the equilibrium level of real GNP and potential real GNP when the economy is operating at less than full employment.

Recovery
The term used to describe an expansion in economic activity after a trough if the expansion follows a period of contraction severe enough to be classified as a recession.

Regional Federal Reserve Banks
Perform central banking functions for banks within each of 12 Federal Reserve districts.

Regressive tax
A tax for which the fraction of income used to pay it decreases as income increases.

Renewable resource
A natural resource that can be restocked in time, such as fish, timber, and wildlife.

Rent
The price that is paid for the use of land.

Rent seeking
The process by which people compete to obtain government favors that increase the economic rents they can earn.

Required reserve ratio
The minimum percentage of deposits that a bank must hold in reserves to comply with regulatory requirements.

Required reserves
The dollar value of currency and deposits in Federal Reserve Banks that a bank must hold to meet current regulations.

Reserve multiplier
The maximum amount of new money stock that can be created from each dollar increase in excess reserves available to the banking system.

Reserves
Balances (of a modern U.S. bank) kept on deposit with the Federal Reserve Bank in the bank's district or as currency in its vault.

Retained earnings
The portion of corporate profits not paid out as dividends.

Risk
Measures the variation of actual outcomes from expected outcomes.

Risk averse
Describes an investor who, if given equal expected returns, would choose an investment with lower risk.

Rule of reason
Holds that acts beyond normal business practice that unduly restrain competition for the purpose of excluding rivals can be used to infer intent to monopolize an industry.

Saving
The amount of income not consumed in a given year.

Savings and loan associations
Depository institutions that acquire funds chiefly through attracting savings deposits and have in the past specialized in making mortgage loans.

Scarcity
The imbalance between the desires of those in a society and the means of satisfying those desires.

Screening
A process in which an employer limits the number of applicants for a job to those it believes are most likely to succeed in the company.

Secondary reserves
Government securities held by banks.

Selling costs
All costs incurred by a firm to influence the sales of its product.

Shirking
Behavior by workers that prevents a firm from achieving the maximum possible marginal product of labor over a given period.

Short run
A period of production during which some inputs cannot be varied.

Shortage
Exists if the quantity demanded exceeds the quantity supplied of a good over a given period.

Short-run supply curve
The portion of a competitive firm's marginal cost curve above the minimum point of its average variable cost curve.

Shutdown point
The point a firm reaches when price has fallen to a level below that which just allows the firm to cover its minimum possible average variable cost.

Signals
Indicators displayed by job applicants and used by prospective employers to predict the future satisfaction and productivity of an applicant.

Simple majority rule
A means for reaching public choices that enacts a proposal if it obtains affirmative votes from more than half the voters casting ballots in an election.

Single-product firm
A firm that produces only one type of item for sale in markets.

Slope
On a curve, measures the rate at which the Y variable, on the vertical axis, rises or falls as the X variable, on the horizontal axis, increases in magnitude.

Social cost of monopoly
A measure of the loss in potential net benefits from the reduced availability of a good stemming from monopoly control of price and supply.

Social regulation
The use of government power to intervene in markets so as to reduce the risk of accidents and disease and to achieve other social goals such as equality of opportunity for all persons.

Socialism
An economic system that is usually associated with government ownership of resources and central planning to determine prices and resource use.

Sole proprietorship
A business owned by one person.

Special drawing right (SDR)
A paper substitute for gold that is created by the International Monetary Fund and distributed to member nations to use as international reserves.

Special-interest group
An organization that seeks to increase government expenditures or induce government to take other actions that benefit particular people.

Specialization
Use of labor and other resources in a nation to produce the goods and services for which those resources are best adapted.

Stabilization policies
Policies undertaken by governing authorities for the purpose of maintaining full employment and a reasonably stable price level.

Staffing
The process of recruiting and hiring workers to perform the various tasks required to produce goods and services.

Stagflation
Term coined to describe an economy in which real GNP stagnates at a given level or actually declines from one period to the next while inflation ensues at relatively high rates.

Structural unemployment
Unemployment resulting from shifts in the pattern of demand for goods and services or changes in technology in the economy that affect the profitability of hiring workers in specific industries.

Substitutes
Goods that serve a purpose similar to that of a given item.

Substitution effect
The change in consumption of a good only as a result of a change in its price relative to the prices of other goods.

Substitution effect of a wage change
The change in hours worked resulting only from a change in the opportunity cost of an hour of leisure.

Supply
A relationship between the price of an item and the quantity supplied by sellers.

Supply and demand analysis
Explains how prices are established in markets through competition among buyers and sellers, and how those prices affect quantities traded.

Supply curve
A graph that shows how quantity supplied varies with the price of a good.

Supply schedule
A table that shows how the quantity supplied of a good is related to the price.

Supply-side fiscal policies
Policies that seek to influence long-run growth in real GNP through government subsidies and tax reductions.

Supply-side shock
A sudden and unexpected shift of the aggregate supply curve.

Surplus
Exists if the quantity supplied exceeds the quantity demanded of a good over a given period.

Surplus value
Defined by Karl Marx as the difference between a worker's subsistence wage and the value of the worker's production over a period.

Tangency
A point at which two curves just touch each other but do not intersect.

Target price
Guarantees sellers of agricultural commodities a minimum price per unit of output.

Tariff
A tax on imported goods.

Tax credit
A reduction in the tax liability for a person or corporation making certain purchases or engaging in certain activities.

Tax expenditures
The losses in revenue to the federal government as a result of tax breaks granted to individuals and corporations.

Tax preference
An exemption, deduction, or exclusion from income or other taxable items in computing tax liability.

Tax shifting
Occurs when a tax levied on sellers of a good causes the market price of the good to increase.

Taxes
Compulsory payments associated with income, consumption, or holding of property that persons and corporations are required to make each year to governments.

Technology
The knowledge of how to produce goods and services.

Theory
Establishes relationships between cause and effect; a simplification of actual relationships.

Theory of games
Analyzes the behavior of individuals or organizations with conflicting interests.

Time deposits
Interest-bearing accounts at commercial banks and thrift institutions for which the bank can legally request a 30-day notice before paying out the funds.

Time series data
Data that show the fluctuations in a variable over time.

Total benefit
The maximum sum of money a consumer would give up to obtain a certain quantity of a good.

Total cost
The sum of the value of *all* inputs used to produce goods over any given period; the sum of fixed costs and variable costs.

Total expenditure
Over any given period, the number of units of a product purchased over that period multiplied by the price of the product *(PQ)* equals the total revenue of sellers.

Total product curve
Describes how output varies in the short run as more of any one input is used together with fixed amounts of other inputs under current technology.

Total product of a variable input
The amount of output produced over any given period when that input is used along with other fixed inputs.

Total revenue
The dollars earned by sellers of a product; the amount sold over a period multiplied by the price *(PQ)*.

Total utility
The total satisfaction enjoyed from consuming any given quantity of a good.

Total value added in a nation
The difference between the market value of *all* products of business firms and the market value of all intermediate products.

Transaction costs
Costs incurred in enforcing property rights to traded goods, locating trading partners, and actually carrying out the transaction.

Transaction demand for money
The sum of money people wish to hold per day as a convenience in paying their bills.

Transfer payments
Payments for which no good or service is currently received in return and that therefore do not represent expenditures for the purchase of final products.

Turnover tax
A sales tax used to raise revenue for the government; often used in planned economies to eliminate shortages in consumer markets.

Unemployed person
A person over age 16 who is available for work and has actively sought employment during the previous 4 weeks.

Unemployment rate
Measures the ratio of the number of people classified as unemployed to the total labor force.

Unit elastic demand
Prevails if the number that measures the price elasticity of demand for a good is exactly equal to 1, ignoring the minus sign.

Unit elastic supply
Prevails when elasticity of supply is just equal to 1.

Utility
The satisfaction consumers receive from items they acquire, activities they engage in, or services they use.

Variable
A quantity or dollar amount that can have more than one value.

Variable costs
Costs that change with output. Variable costs are the costs of variable inputs.

Variable input
An input whose quantity can be changed.

Vertical integration
A term used to describe a firm that owns plants used in various stages of its production.

Vertical merger
A merger of a firm with its suppliers.

Wage-price controls
Rules established by government authorities that result in control of prices, wages, and their rate of increase.

Wage-price guidelines
Standards established by government authorities that seek to keep wage and price increases within certain bounds over a period.

Wage-price spiral
Exists when higher product prices result in higher wages, which in turn increase prices still further through a decrease in aggregate supply.

Wages
The prices paid for labor services.

Wealth
The sum of the current values of all assets a person owns.

Welfare programs
Government programs to assist the poor in the United States who are unable to work.

Index

Each boldfaced term in the index indicates a key term that is defined in the text. The boldfaced page number shows where the key term is first explained and highlighted in a marginal definition.

Q

Quality differences in labor services, 444-445
Quantity, market equilibrium price and, 58-66
Quantity demanded, 47
  change in, 49-50
Quantity supplied, 54
  change in, 55-56
Quotas
  agricultural production, 377
  cartel pricing and, 301

R

Rational behavior, 16-21
  marginal analysis of, 19-20
  using graph to analyze, 21
Rational expectations, 854
  aggregate supply curve and, 855-858
  theory of, 846-866; *see also* Inflation and
      unemployment
Real exchange rate, 908-910
  of dollar
    and aggregate demand, 911-912
    and aggregate supply, 912-913
  relative prices of imports and, 910-911
Real gross national product, 530-533; *see
      also* Gross national product, real
Real income, 589-591
Real interest rate, 594-596
  investment demand and, 642-644
  monetary policy and, 794
Real interest rate effect, 607
Real marginal return to investment, 643
Real per capita output, 891
Real terms of trade, 877
Real wages, 591-592
Real wealth effect, 607
Recession, 557-558
  consumer spending and, 663-664
  government purchases and, 803-806
  Keynesian aggregate supply curve and, 664-
      666
  Keynesian analysis of, 661-666
  supply-side–induced, 690-691
Recessionary GNP gap, 614
  exports and, 675-678
  marginal propensity to import and, 675-678
Recognition lag, 811
Recovery, 558-**559**
Redistribution of income
  foreign competition and, 886
  inflation and, 593
  price instability and, 599
  and wealth from creditors to debtors, 593
Reduction of federal budget deficit, 840-842
Regional Federal Reserve Banks, 748-751
Regressive tax, 398
Regulation
  government; *see* Government regulation
  market, 320-330
    market entry by competing sellers and,
        324-327
    pros and cons of government regulation
        in, 327
    regulation of pricing in, 320-327
  of pollution, 355-357

Regulation—cont'd
  of pricing, 320-324
    and market entry by competing sellers,
        324-327
    social, 343-345
Regulatory commissions, 324-325
Relative prices
  changes in price level vs. changes in, 584-585
  of imports and real exchange rates, 910-911
Relevant market, 314-315
Renewable resources, 363-364
Rent, 477
  economic, 426-428
  interest, profit, and, 477-499; *see also*
      Interest, rents, and profits
  land, 491-496
Rent control, 82-84
Rent seeking, 370
Rental income, gross national product and, 542
Required reserve ratio, 729
  control of, 755-756
Required reserves, 729, 756
Reserve banking, fractional, 726
Reserve multiplier, 734-736, **735**
Reserve ratios, required, 729
  control of, 755-756
Reserves, 727
  bank, 727
  excess, 729
    bank demand for, 737-739
  government securities and, 757-761
  required, 729
    depository institutions and, 756
  secondary, 741
  total, 732
Resources
  allocation of
    government, market failure and, 331-348;
        see also Market failure
    land rents, profit, and, 491-496
    Soviet economy, 934-935
  demand for, input markets and, 412-435; *see
      also* Input markets and demand for
      resources
  exhaustible, 361-364
  monopoly ownership of entire supply of,
      264-265
  technology, production possibilities, and, 25-
      31
  underutilization of, 32
Respending process, 668-669
Retained earnings, 173-174
Retirees, Social Security system and, 403
Revenues
  government, 395-397
    federal budget deficit and, 828-834
  maximizing, 129
Ricardo, David, 873
Right to work laws, 458
Risk, 489
Risk averse, 489
Rival in consumption, 340
Rivlin, Alice, 835
Rivalry, conscious, 299-300

Robinson-Patman Act, 313
Rule of reason, 314

S

Salaries
  for economists, P5-P7
  male and female, 430-431
Sales tax, 396
  monopoly and, 278-279
Samuelson, Paul, 804
Saving, 480
  and consumption, 640
  credit markets and, 818-820
  economic growth and, 698-700
  and income and consumption function, 635-
      637
  and investment
    and capital stock, 478-480
    and inflationary distortions, 598
    and macroeconomic equilibrium, 660
  marginal propensity to, 637-638
  market supply of, 487
  personal, 25A3
  supply-side incentives for, 818-820
  U.S., foreigners and, 546-547, 917-923
Savings and loan association, 709
Savings-investment balance, 30A6-30A7
Scarcity, 2
  prices, marketing prospects, and, 72-75
  and tradeoffs, 40
Screening, 449
Secondary reserves, 741
Securities
  government, 741
    bank reserves and, 757-761
  prices of, 763-769
Self-equilibrating markets, 60
Sellers and subsidy, 383
Selling costs, 295
Seniority, unions and, 462
Sherman Antitrust Act of 1890, 312, 458
Shirking, 449-450
Short run, 188
  for competitive firm, 213-219
  decision to shut down in, 227-229
  profit, price, and output in, 213-219
Shortage, 58
Short-run cost curves for single-product firm,
      194-204
Short-run equilibrium of firm under
      monopolistic competition, 290-291
Short-run impact of license fees and fixed
      annual subsidies, 232-234
Short-run supply, theory of, 219-231
Short-run supply curve, 229
Short-run total cost curve, 199
Short-term macroeconomic equilibrium, money
      and, 774-781
Shut down in short run, 227-229
Shutdown point, 228-229
Signals, 449
Silver coins, 707, 708
Simple majority rule, 401
Single-product firm, 179
  short-run cost curves for, 194-204

DISCOVER WHAT "MAKING THE GRADE" IS ALL ABOUT

Study Guide to Accompany
ECONOMICS
DAVID N. HYMAN

DONALD P. MAXWELL

Study Guide for ECONOMICS
By Don Maxwell

Each study guide chapter contains:
- chapter objectives;
- key term vocabulary exercises;
- a chapter summary that is also a fill-in exercise;
- a series of topic-centered modules that have activities designed to reinforce key concepts; activities include work with graphs, fill-in charts and tables, completion exercises, and other interactive tasks.

Selected chapters contain exercises based on actual news articles, emphasizing the application of economics skills in business environments.

The mini-exam is a self-test that includes both multiple choice (15-20) and discussion questions with answers to all questions.

MAKE THE GRADE with the Study Guide for ECONOMICS by Don Maxwell.

Contact your bookstore manager for availability, or to order call 800-323-4560. Ask for Maxwell Study Guide (0-256-07505-0). Macro Version (0-256-07489-5). Micro Version (0-256-07491-7).